HOUGHTON ★ MIFFLIN ★

HISTORY PROGRAM

★ ★ ★

man's unfinished

Houghton Mifflin Company · Boston

New York · Atlanta · Geneva, Illinois · Dallas · Palo Alto

journey

A World History

Marvin Perry

Contributing Area Specialists

Theodore H. Von Laue

Howard R. Anderson:
Consulting Editor

Jean Herskovits

Donald M. Lowe

Lana D. Goldberg:
Classroom Coordinator

Donald Warren, Jr.

Joel H. Wiener

About the Authors and Editor

Marvin Perry, senior author and general editor, is a member of the history department of the Bernard M. Baruch College of the City University of New York. He has also taught at Walton and Washington Irving High Schools in New York and at the City College of the City University of New York. Mr. Perry is coauthor of *Panorama of the Past: Readings in World History.* He is responsible for all chapters except those contributed by area specialists.

Theodore H. Von Laue, an authority on Russian history, is the Jacob and Frances Hiatt Professor of History at Clark University. A former member of the history faculty at Swarthmore, Bryn Mawr, the University of California (Riverside), and Washington University, Dr. Von Laue is the author of *Sergei Witte and the Industrialization of Russia; Why Lenin? Why Stalin?;* and *The Global City.* He contributed Chapters 28 and 31, and portions of Chapters 17 and 32, on Russia, Eastern Europe, and the postwar period.

Jean Herskovits, a specialist on African history and culture, is Associate Professor of History at the State University of New York, College at Purchase, and has also taught at Brown University and Swarthmore College. Dr. Herskovits has done research in Nigeria and the Ivory Coast and is the author of *A Preface to Modern Nigeria: The "Sierra Leonians" in Yoruba, 1830–1890.* She contributed Chapters 10, 11, 25, and 35 on Africa.

Donald M. Lowe, an authority on Chinese history, is Associate Professor of History at San Francisco State College. He has also taught at Duquesne University, the University of California (Riverside), the Center for Chinese Studies at Berkeley, and the City College of the City University of New York. Dr. Lowe has traveled throughout Asia and is the author of *The Function of "China" in Marx, Lenin, and Mao.* He contributed Chapters 9, 26, and 33 on Asia.

Donald Warren, Jr., a specialist in Latin American affairs and Brazilian history, is Professor of History at Long Island University. Dr. Warren has also taught at Columbia University and the State University of New York and is the author of *The Red Kingdom of Saxony.* He contributed Chapters 16 and 36 on Latin America.

Joel H. Wiener, a specialist in British history, is Assistant Professor of History at the City College of the City University of New York. Dr. Wiener's publications include *A Descriptive Finding List of Unstamped British Periodicals, 1830–1836* and *The War of the Unstamped: A History of the Movement to Repeal the British Newspaper Tax, 1830–1836.* He contributed portions of Chapters 23 and 32 on Britain and postwar Western Europe.

Howard R. Anderson, consulting editor and former President of the National Council for the Social Studies, has taught history in the secondary schools of Michigan, Iowa, and New York. Dr. Anderson also taught at the University of Iowa and Cornell University, and was Provost of the University of Rochester.

Lana D. Goldberg, classroom coordinator, has taught history in the secondary schools of New York City. She tested the contents of this book in the classroom, assisted with research, and prepared study materials for the text and the Instructor's Manual.

Consultants

For valuable assistance in reviewing portions of the manuscript, the authors wish to express their appreciation to fellow historians teaching at branches of the City University of New York: Joan Gadol, for reading the Ancient World, Middle Ages, and Transition to Modern Times; Andrew Whiteside, modern European history; Howard Adelson, Ancient World and Middle Ages; Herbert Strauss, Fascist Dictatorships and World War II; Emil Polak, Ancient World and Middle Ages; Emanuel Chill, the French Revolution and Napoleon; and George Bock, the Scientific Revolution.

Library of Congress Catalog Card Number: 75-125123   ISBN: 0-395-03366-7

Contents

Unit Five   Revolution and the Rise of Nationalism   427

List of Maps

The past is not dead history; it is the living material out of which man makes himself and builds the future. —René Dubos

The Emergence of Western Civilization

Unit One ————————

1

The bronze ceremonial chariot below reflects the importance of the wheel to early man. Though lacking the wheel, Stone Age man in England transported and shaped stones averaging four tons each to build Stonehenge (left). This awe-inspiring religious site may have been used to calculate the seasons.

The Dawn of Man

CHAPTER FOCUS

Origins of the Universe and Man's Development
The Life of Early Man

Earth is the home of man, but man did not always live here. There was a time when Earth contained plants and animals but no human life. And at an earlier period in time there was no life at all on Earth. No plants grew, no animals stirred, nothing breathed. There was no birth and no death. Further back in time there was a universe of stars, galaxies, and space but no planet Earth. How did they come into being —this universe that stretches to the edge of eternity, this Earth that has followed the same path about the sun for billions of years?

This question is among the most profound that man will ever ask; it excites the imagination and challenges the mind. Scientists are not certain that they will ever know the full answers to this question. But in recent years they have made extraordinary progress in their investigations. Let us examine present-day thinking about this fundamental question.

The big bang theory may explain how the universe was formed. Earth, the other eight planets in our solar system, and most of the stars that we see—including our sun, the nearest star—belong to our huge disc-shaped *galaxy* called the Milky Way. The Milky Way contains some 100 billion stars and has a diameter of 600,000 trillion miles or 100,000 light years. (An object traveling at the speed of light—186,300 miles per second—will cover about 5.8 trillion miles in an earth year.) About 4.4 light years—25 trillion miles—separate the sun from the nearest other star in the Milky Way. A spaceship traveling at the speed of light would take 100,000 years to fly across our galaxy. Traveling at the same speed, it would take one million years to cover the ocean of empty space that separates the Milky Way from the nearest other galaxy. And beyond this neighboring galaxy are billions more "islands" of galaxies separated by billions more oceans of space. Clearly Earth is an insignificant speck in this incredibly vast universe. It takes up far less space and is far less noticeable than a tiny cork floating on the Pacific Ocean.

How did the many galaxies come into being? The explanation which is currently favored by most scientists is the *big bang theory.* Ac-

cording to this theory, some ten billion years ago there existed in the universe only a gigantic ball of matter, very tightly packed together. This ball contained the only matter and the only radiation existing in the universe. Gradually pressure within this hot, dense ball of matter increased, and finally there occurred an enormous explosion of unimaginable force. Pieces of matter flew outward in all directions, eventually forming the galaxies. These galaxies today, ten billion years later, are still rushing away from each other at fantastic speeds. Scientists believe that within the first half hour after the big bang, protons and neutrons fused together into nuclei to form the elements.

The solar system develops. Our solar system—the sun and the nine planets that orbit it—occupies a very small space within the Milky Way. Scientists are uncertain as to how the solar system came into being. The most widely accepted theory is that the solar system was born some 4.5 billion years ago when a cloud of dust particles and gas began to condense in space. Gravity drew the cloud into a smaller and denser mass that began to spin. As it did so, the mass flattened, and part of the cloud formed whirling eddies around a central mass, circling it in much the same way that our planets today revolve around the sun. As the central mass contracted, its temperature rose. The temperature continued to increase until it reached twenty million degrees, causing thermonuclear reactions that released enormous amounts of energy. This nuclear burning marked the birth of our sun. The eddies that circled the newly born sun became increasingly more compact as the force of gravity acted on them. From this condensation of gas clouds our planets and their satellites were formed. Because the gas clouds that became planets were far too small to generate the high temperature needed to produce their own nuclear energy,

Before he learned to use metals, man made tools and weapons of stone. His skill in working stone is evident in this flint hand ax. Beautifully cut and shaped, it is both a tool and a work of art.

they fell short of becoming suns and became planets instead.

Scientific theories may have a wide impact.
Scientific theories often raise questions outside the world of science. This has been the case with the theories suggested by scientists to account for the origins of the universe, origins of the solar system, and particularly the evolution of man (discussed below). These theories have caused a stir amongst some men of religion who fear that the Biblical account of creation is being challenged.

Some men of religion reject the scientific theories of creation, insisting that they are based upon insufficient evidence. Most clergymen, however, do not see a conflict between the theories of science and the account in the Bible. They say that it was God who created the original fireball that eventually became the universe. They say further that it was God's laws of nature that caused the fireball to explode into a universe and the dust clouds to form into our solar system. These clergymen also see the hand of God guiding the process of evolution. It was God, they say, who first created life. And it was the mysterious hand of God that directed the course of evolution. It was not accident but God's design that led to the emergence of man. That billions of years may have passed before man walked on Earth, these clergymen do not consider a contradiction with the Biblical six days. For who knows how long one of God's days is? Each Biblical day could be equivalent to a billion years or more.

For these reasons, few clergymen today quarrel with scientists. Rather, they have come to regard every increase in man's knowledge of nature as shedding light on God's handiwork.

Darwin suggests how life may have evolved.
In the nineteenth century English naturalist Charles Darwin developed the *theory of evolution* (the theory that forms of life gradually evolve, or change, and that new forms result from older ones). The theory of evolution, say scientists, helps to explain how living forms,

Millions of old stars cluster in the center of the Spiral Galaxy in Pegasus (above); in the arms are young blue stars, interstellar dust, and gas.

including man, developed from early forms of life that appeared on earth billions of years ago. Darwin's theory can be summarized briefly:

1. Struggle for existence. Because all living organisms (including man) tend to reproduce faster than the food supply, there never is enough food available to keep all alive. Because animals must compete for the limited food available, there takes place within nature a continuous *struggle for existence.*

5

2. Survival of the fittest. In this battle for life—which includes obtaining food, defeating or avoiding enemies, and finding mates in order to reproduce—not all infant organisms grow to become adults. Nor do all adults survive long enough to reproduce or to live a long life. There is not enough food or living space to enable all living organisms to survive. If a pair of elephants, for example, sired six offspring, all of which survived, and each of the female offspring had six young that also survived, and so on—in just 750 years the descendants of the original pair would number nineteen million! What determines which giraffes, camels, or elephants will survive and which will perish? Obviously the advantage is with those members of the species that are stronger, faster, better camouflaged against their enemies, or in other ways better fitted for the struggle for survival than are other members of the species. Thus there also operates within nature the law of *survival of the fittest.*

3. Natural selection. Darwin noted that within a species there are wide variations. In the distant past, for example, some giraffes were born with longer necks than their brothers and sisters. The longer-necked giraffe found it easier to reach into the trees for his food and to peer over the bushes and spot enemies. Thus favored by nature, this giraffe survived and passed on his advantage to his offspring. Over hundreds of thousands of years the short-necked giraffes died out because they were unable to compete successfully with long-necked giraffes. This principle of *natural selection* explains why some members of a species (those that are favored by nature) survive and reproduce and why those less fit to compete in the struggle for survival perish.

4. New species. Over long centuries of evolution new species have emerged from earlier forms of life. Members of a species inherited variations that distinguished them from other members of the species. After millions of years the former became so different that they could not breed with the others. Thus a new species

had been created. According to Darwin's theory, man himself was a product of evolution and natural selection, evolving from earlier, lower, nonhuman forms of life.

Scientists search for early man. The discoveries of Raymond A. Dart and Louis B. Leakey, two anthropologists, have shed light on one of the great adventure stories of our time—the search for early man. Their studies indicate that in South and East Africa, about two million years ago, there existed a creature called *Australopithecus* (os-tray-loh-pih-*thee′*-kus), which made his home and found his food on the ground. *Australopithecus* was also on his way to walking erect. He made and used very simple tools and hunted small animals.

More advanced than *Australopithecus* was *Homo erectus,* which appeared some 500,000 years ago. He could run better (because he stood fully erect), used fire, made weapons that enabled him to hunt large animals, and probably had an early form of speech. His appearance was more humanlike and his brain much larger than that of *Australopithecus.*

Both *Australopithecus* and *Homo erectus* represented stages in the evolution of man. It would take hundreds of thousands more years for man as we know him today (*Homo sapiens, say′*pih-enz) to make his appearance on the earth.

CHECK-UP

1. What explanation is given for the formation of the galaxies? Of the solar system?

2. What did Darwin mean by the term "survival of the fittest?" How does the principle of natural selection work? How may natural selection result in a new species?

3. What were the characteristics of *Australopithecus?* In what ways did *Homo erectus* differ from *Australopithecus?*

Anthropologists and archaeologists give us insight into man's past. Before discussing the ways of life developed by early man, let us consider how knowledge of man's distant past has been acquired. Much of what we know about our ancestors comes from the research of anthropologists and archaeologists. Anthropologists study virtually everything about man. Some anthropologists specialize in studying man's physical traits. They examine skeletal remains (bones, teeth, skulls) of man and other primates. These preserved remains of once living organisms are called *fossils*. By analyzing skeletal remains and fossils, anthropologists seek to understand man's physical appearance at various stages of his development. Other anthropologists study early man's culture—his art, religion, government, family patterns, sexual customs, food habits, and so on. They try to reconstruct the life of early man.

There are also cultural anthropologists who study the ways of modern-day primitive societies such as those of Congo pygmies, Arctic Eskimos, and Australian aborigines. It is likely that present-day primitive people live much the way our ancestors lived 10,000 or even 20,000 years ago. Some modern-day primitives do not grow food, but are hunters and food gatherers, as was early man. They too use only the simplest of weapons and tools. By studying the habits of these primitives, we may get a look back in time at the ways of life followed by our distant ancestors.

Archaeology is a branch of anthropology. Detectives on the trail of early man, archaeologists locate and analyze the material remains left behind by our ancestors. These remains, called *artifacts,* include pottery, ornaments, tools, weapons, and the like. Artifacts may be found in caves, on the site of settlements, or in graves. By studying these artifacts, archaeologists try to reconstruct early man's life.

Anthropologists and archaeologists excavate, date, and interpret remains. A major task for anthropologists and archaeologists is to determine the age of the fossils and artifacts they discover. They know that objects found several feet below ground are likely to be older than objects found close to the surface. Determination of the age of artifacts took a giant step forward with the discovery by Willard F. Libby that the age of objects containing carbon could be measured by tests of radioactivity. Carbon is the basic ingredient of all living matter, and all organisms contain a certain amount of radioactive carbon (carbon 14) as long as they are alive. Once they die, the amount of carbon 14 decreases at a fixed rate. By finding out the amount of carbon 14 in a fossil or artifact, it is possible to determine its age. Radioactive potassium-argon is used in a similar way to determine the age of fossils.

How do archaeologists and anthropologists know where to start looking for remains that are likely to be buried under the sand or the vegetation of centuries? Sometimes construction workers stumble upon ancient remains. Sometimes archaeologists note irregularities in the surface of the ground, such as slight depressions or mounds. Heavy rainfall or an earthquake may expose fossils and artifacts. A recent promising development is the use of the cesium magnetometer (*see'*zih-um mag-neh-*tom'*eh-ter), a device which indicates variations in the earth's magnetic field. When the magnetometer is used in exploring a site, it indicates underground disturbances (such as graves or foundations) which may have been caused by man.

Once the archaeologist has found a promising site, his work has only begun. He must start digging to find graves and the remains of ancient buildings. Sometimes buildings are reconstructed to provide a better idea of how they

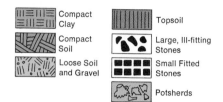

	Compact Clay		Topsoil
	Compact Soil		Large, Ill-fitting Stones
	Loose Soil and Gravel		Small Fitted Stones
			Potsherds

Patience and painstaking detail characterize the work of archaeologists. After being surveyed and mapped, a site is divided into sections. Each section is carefully excavated (left, above) and any artifacts found are put in baskets for sorting, cleaning, and identifying. Because they are often clues to a culture, potsherds can be among the most important finds in a "dig." In the simplified section drawing above, note the different layers of soil and the reuse of earlier construction by later occupants. Very early remains such as dinosaur bones are often fossilized (left) and must be cut free of the rock in which they are found. They are then covered with a preservative, coded as to their location, measured, and carefully studied to determine their origin and age.

appeared when in use. Every "find" must be photographed where it is found, labelled, cleaned, and later identified and classified. Objects which contained carbon are carefully packed and shipped off for carbon-14 testing.

Pollen is microscopically examined. Long hours are spent piecing together human and animal bones, broken pottery, and the fragments of other artifacts. More time is spent comparing artifacts with findings from other sites so that some careful guesses can be made as to their age.

The archaeologist's work is slow and painstaking, writes Walter Shepherd:

It may take weeks, months, or even years, for almost every stone over an acre or more, to a depth of several feet, may have to be picked up, looked at, and put in its proper pile. . . . At every stage of the work detailed records are written up, photographs are taken, drawings are made, and catalogues of the finds prepared. And when all is over, everything except the objects removed for study and exhibition is put back exactly as it was before the dig—even to relaying the turf on top.

For weeks and even months after a site has been excavated the archaeologist works to interpret his findings as scientifically as possible. Years later a new discovery may force him to revise theories he has formulated.

PALEOLITHIC MAN

The period in which the earliest man lived is known as the Old Stone Age, or *Paleolithic* (pay-lee-oh-*lith'*ik) period. The Old Stone Age began some two million years ago with the manlike creatures whose remains were uncovered by Dr. Leakey. It ended some 13,000 to 12,000 years ago. What was life like in Paleolithic times?

In the Old Stone Age man is a hunter. Paleolithic man lived near streams from which he could obtain fish and water and hunt game that came to drink. Sometimes he built tent-like structures of branches; sometimes he lived in caves. He obtained food by fishing, hunting, and gathering roots, nuts, and fruit. Searching for food was a full-time job. Because man in the Old Stone Age had not learned how to farm, he never established permanent villages. When his food supply ran short, he had to look for a new place to live.

During the long centuries of the Paleolithic Age, man's progress was very slow. Conditions of life changed very little for tens of thousands of years. Yet important developments did occur in the Old Stone Age that had an enormous effect upon man's future. What were the accomplishments of man in the Old Stone Age?

During the Paleolithic Age man's mental powers developed and he became considerably more intelligent than any animal. Man developed spoken languages, which enabled him to share his knowledge, his experiences, and his feelings with others. Family life, hunting bands, and later tribal patterns emerged, though there was no organized system of government. Perhaps the ablest of the hunters was accepted as the headman or chieftain of the tribe.

Paleolithic man develops tools and discovers fire. Old Stone Age man took his first long step forward when he learned how to make simple but useful tools out of wood, bone, and stone. These crude tools are the first indication we have of man acquiring skills that gave him some control over his environment. They were not merely objects that man picked up from the ground, but instruments that he pictured in his mind and shaped with his hands. Thus the shaping of the first crude tools and weapons is evidence of thoughtful behavior.

Some tools were used to dig up roots, peel the bark off wood, and remove the skins from animals. Others were used as weapons to kill animals. Paleolithic man invented the spear, the needle, and fishhooks. He learned how to snare and trap animals. The invention of tools was man's first great stride forward. It meant that man, unlike the animals, was learning how to think.

Man's second great stride forward was his discovery of how to control fire. This was a remarkable achievement. Fire gave man warmth and protection and enabled him to cook his meat. Originally man, like the animals, was afraid of fire. But once he learned to control it, he used fire to great advantage. Concludes British science writer Ritchie Calder:

"To take fire and tame it—to confront nature in its most terrifying form of lightning and to see its fire not as a threat but as a promise—that was primitive man's first epic victory over nature."

As a hunter man develops certain characteristics. The Old Stone Age lasted two million years—more than 99 per cent of human history. During this period man lived as a hunter. Success in hunting depended upon speed, strength, and mental ability. The hunter had to study and analyze the habits of his prey. He had to judge weather conditions, to recall the location of caves and watering places, and to build better tools and weapons. The Old Stone Age hunter, says a present-day anthropologist,

must have eyes like a lynx, ears like a cat, and a nose like a wolf: he must know the tracks of animals in the grass, the habits of the deer at sunrise and at midday, the watering places, the rhythms of nature. And the hunter does not go through the same seasonal round year after year. He can never be sure that the same situation will repeat itself, can never be certain that wolves and bears will react as he expects. He needs a cool head, steady nerves, and a swift and unerring eye.

Those whose inferior intelligence prevented them from tracking animals and coping with new problems did not survive the struggle for life. Evolution favored those hunters who had sufficient brain capacity to learn and to remember. As a result, says science writer and anthropologist John E. Pfeiffer, "the size of the brain in early man nearly doubled during the rise of hunting. . . . Hunting reshaped the brain by enriching experience and putting an extra premium on the capacity for learning. . . . Events ruthlessly weeded out those with an inferior capacity for learning and remembering."

Man's emotions were also shaped by the two-million-year experience of hunting. Man came to enjoy the excitement of finding, chasing, and killing his prey. He came to look upon the animals he hunted as enemies, and thus developed aggressive feelings toward them. The most successful hunters relished the admiration

they received from their companions. Some students of human behavior feel that man has never broken with his hunting past. These thinkers regard warfare as a crueler and more elaborate form of hunting. In their eyes man the hunter and killer of animals became the hunter and killer of his fellow man. Like hunting, warfare called forth aggressive feelings, and the excitement of battle brought man pleasure. Heroism in combat increased his prestige within the community. This relationship between hunting and warfare is discussed by British science writer Nigel Calder:

In truth we evolved as hunters and we remain the most efficient predatory animals of all, shrewd of brain, infinitely adaptable of body, and with hands to make and wield weapons. . . . In sport and in war . . . we recapture something of the excitement of the chase, which was the everyday occupation of the first of our species. . . .

Men, the hunters, . . . have put such intellectual and physical resources into hunting their fellow men that we can now conceivably achieve . . . our own total extinction. . . . We know it perfectly well, yet we do not shrink from the preparations, because warfare continues to fascinate us. In nations, as in individuals, readiness to fight is still regarded as the mainstay of honor. . . .

. . . the soldier to this day represents that missing hunter in each of us. . . . I do not believe that we shall ever eradicate [eliminate] war, even with the fear of nuclear annihilation [total destruction], until we have properly diagnosed and treated this ultimate source of war's fascination.

In the Old Stone Age man develops art and religious beliefs. Old Stone Age man displayed an extraordinary talent for art. One student of prehistory maintains that "prehistoric man began to create works of art which can rival anything that has been achieved in the last 10,000 years." On the walls of caves in various parts of southern France and Spain are preserved some of prehistoric man's finest artistic achievements. These drawings include human beings, human hands, various animals, and hunting scenes. Like our modern artists, prehistoric

Animals were a part of man's life from early times. Using simple colors, Neolithic man captured their spirit surprisingly well in cave paintings (above). Later, much of man's art appeared on pottery. Neolithic potters gradually learned to combine straight and curved lines into pleasing forms and to decorate their work (left).

painters tried to express their innermost thoughts and feelings. Their art, writes a modern art historian, "may represent man's first attempt to express his vision of the world and the relationship of one living creature with another."

At a very early period prehistoric man began to develop religious beliefs. The sun that brought warmth or caused drought, the life-giving rains which might bring disastrous floods, the wind which cooled him in summer and froze him in winter, the thunder and lightning of storms—very likely all of these seemed magic powers to Paleolithic man. Because he feared the forces of nature and wished them to be helpful rather than destructive, Paleolithic man made offerings to them. When a prehistoric artist drew an animal with a spear in its side, he may have hoped that this would bring him luck in the hunt. He began to bury his dead, sometimes including beautifully made weapons and tools in the graves. This generous act suggests that he believed in some form of life after death.

Making bomboo arrow tip

Small groups of people scattered throughout the
tropical areas of the world still follow a Neolithic
way of life. Along the Orinoco River in southernmost Venezuela live the Yanomamö, a group of about
10,000 Amerinds (American Indians) who had practically no contact with the outside world before 1958.
Their scattered villages, protected by high walls of upright poles, contain large shelters of poles and
thatch, open on three sides and ringing a clearing.
Outside lies the garden of fruits and vegetables. The
Yanomamö also fish the rivers and hunt the wild
animals of the rain forest. Each village specializes
in certain goods and must obtain what it lacks by
trading with other villages.

Yanomamö society is extremely male-oriented. Since
unwanted female babies are killed, some villages
have as many as 30 per cent more men than women.
To be respected, a man must be aggressive and brave.
At feasts between allied tribes male visitors and
hosts strive to impress each other. Their bodies
decorated with paint, armbands of brilliant parrot
feathers, and headdresses of buzzard down, they
parade and dance across the clearing. Night-long
trading follows their feast. Visitors chant their
requests for goods and hosts reply in a similar
fashion. The next morning the actual trade quickly
takes place. Visitors receive bows and arrows, cotton yarn, baskets, machetes, hammocks, dogs, and—
most important—women. Later, they will throw a
feast to supply the needs of their hosts.

Yanomamö life has changed little for centuries. But
other modern-day Neolithic societies are being
changed as contact with the outside world increases.
Modern technology which changes the environment,
settlers who drive Neolithic peoples from their
traditional lands by treachery or outright murder,
and diseases to which the people have no immunity
are rapidly destroying Neolithic populations and
their culture. Many anthropologists feel that the
present generation of Neolithic Amerinds may well
be the last.

*Visitors
entering village*

Headman trading

Homo sapiens *appears.* Some 75,000 to 100,-000 years ago, when ice sheets covered large parts of the earth, Neanderthal (nee-*an'*der-tahl) Man appeared. He lived in caves, warmed himself with fire, and skillfully hunted game. Although short, squat, and heavily muscled, with a massive receding jaw, Neanderthal Man was an advanced human being. Because of his brain size, he is classified as a sub-species of *Homo sapiens,* the species to which modern man belongs. Some 30,000 years ago the sub-species of Neanderthal Man died out. But our direct ancestors survived the Ice Age to enter the Neolithic (nee-oh-*lith'* ik) period, or New Stone Age, which began some 10,000 to 12,000 years ago.

NEOLITHIC MAN

The New Stone Age was marked by several developments: (1) farming and domesticating animals, (2) permanent settlements, (3) improved crafts and specialization of work, (4) making of pottery, and (5) trade. So important were these achievements that they are referred to as the Neolithic Revolution.

Man begins to live a settled life. Instead of hunting and gathering wild plants and roots, man learned to live on crops he had planted, cultivated, and harvested, and on animals he had tamed. This was a tremendously important step forward. It enabled man to overcome the uncertainty of obtaining food by hunting or gathering, and to form communities. Farming revolutionized man's life, writes Miles Burkitt:

For the first time villages sprang up and a simple form of community [village] life emerged. Not everyone would have to spend his whole time in collecting food in order to live. Specialization became possible—some tilled the soil, others looked after the animals, others made the various necessary tools, others protected the community. . . . But with the rise of community life man [had] . . . to learn to live in close contact with his fellows. Customs necessary for the very existence of any human [community], however primitive, [had] to

be evolved, for no group can long survive whose members freely lie, steal, murder, and so on. As the communities increased in size and importance, the problem arose of how to enforce these customs in days when no centralized police force had been thought of. . . . The small Neolithic communities were doubtless very primitive and simple, but the germ of our own civilization was there.

Man also learned to tame or domesticate such hitherto wild animals as sheep, goats, and cattle. They gave him a steady supply not only of meat but also of hides, wool, and milk. Domesticated dogs helped man hunt game and protect his herds from wild animals.

Life for the Neolithic farmer differed in important ways from the life of the Paleolithic hunter. Although he hunted occasionally, the farmer was not free to wander where he pleased but had to remain close to his crops. His life as a tiller of the soil was less adventurous than that of the hunter. It was an effort for man to adjust to the routine of this new life. "It was man's first sacrifice of liberty for the sake of security," writes archaeologist Jacquetta Hawkes.

Neolithic man lived in communities located near his fields. He built houses of sun-dried brick, stone, or logs and in some instances plastered or painted the walls. Villages were sometimes protected by ditches and wooden fences. In some large villages temples were built where Neolithic man worshiped his gods.

Man learns to specialize and to exchange goods. Important advances in crafts took place in Neolithic times. Neolithic man (and woman) learned to spin and weave cloth and to make baskets. He learned to make earthenware jars and dishes in various sizes and shapes, and used them for many different purposes. As life became less of a struggle, man was able to spend more time shaping articles that were decorative as well as useful. Village life made it possible for Neolithic man to specialize. Instead of trying to supply all his own needs, a man might be a potter, miner, farmer, weaver, or arrow-maker. He came to depend on specialists to supply many of the things he needed. The result was barter—exchange of one good or service for another—within the village and gradually the development of trade with neighboring communities.

Archaeologists conclude that Neolithic men generally lived at peace with one another. In some Neolithic villages that have been uncovered there were no ditches or fences to protect the community from attack by hostile neighbors. In places where ditches and fences were built, says archaeologist Jacquetta Hawkes, they were "usually on a scale more appropriate to protection against marauding [prowling] animals than against human enemies." Miss Hawkes also points to the absence of weapons in graves as another indication that Neolithic man was not very warlike. In late Neolithic times, however, things changed. In the graves for this period battle axes, daggers, and other weapons have been found. Perhaps an abundance of good land accounted for the peacefulness of early Neolithic society. In late Neolithic times a rising population may have resulted in competition for good land, which led to warfare.

In late Neolithic times, between 5000 and 6000 years ago, man made great advances. Transportation improved enormously with the invention of the wheel and the sail. The former enabled man to transport larger loads of goods by land. The sail encouraged the use of rivers and bodies of water in carrying on trade with more distant communities. With the development of the plow more efficient tilling of the soil became possible. Early farmers had relied upon digging sticks and hoes to break up the soil for planting. The plow made this slow and difficult task easier. In time man developed a way of yoking oxen to the plow. With oxen pulling the primitive plow, the farmer could till much more land. "By harnessing the ox," writes Professor of Archaeology V. Gordon Childe, "man began to control and use a motive power other than that furnished by his own muscular energy. The ox was the first step to the steam engine and [gasoline] motor." Another important invention

was the potter's wheel, which enabled man to fashion pottery more quickly and precisely.

The late Neolithic period also marks the beginning of the use of metals by men in some advanced societies. Copper, which was easily fashioned into tools and weapons, was the first metal to be used. Tools and weapons made from copper lasted longer than those made of stone and flint, since they could be recast and reshaped if broken. In time men discovered how to make bronze by combining copper and tin in the proper ratio. Bronze was an improvement over copper because it was harder and made possible a sharper cutting edge. Soon it was used not only for tools and weapons but also for jars and figurines. Because of the widespread use of bronze, the late Neolithic period is called the Bronze Age.

What are the characteristics of a civilized society? Man made great strides forward during the Neolithic Age. But it was still the period of prehistory, for man had not yet learned to write. In some parts of the world about 5000 years ago man invented writing. It is this discovery of writing which marks the end of prehistory. Once man began to keep written records, the historical period began. What we think of as civilization also developed about this time. What is meant by civilization? How did a civilized society differ from the earlier societies of Neolithic man?

Historians use the term *civilization* to distinguish between prehistoric societies and the considerably more advanced societies that developed later. Civilized societies had certain features that prehistoric societies lacked. (1) Civilized societies developed writing and built cities. (2) States with definite boundaries emerged, with an organized system of government. (3) Increasingly, men worked at specialized jobs. They were farmers or craftsmen, merchants, priests, or government officials. The city dweller obtained food from the farmer in the countryside. The farmer, in return, received pottery and other goods manufactured in the city. Specialization encouraged trade, regional

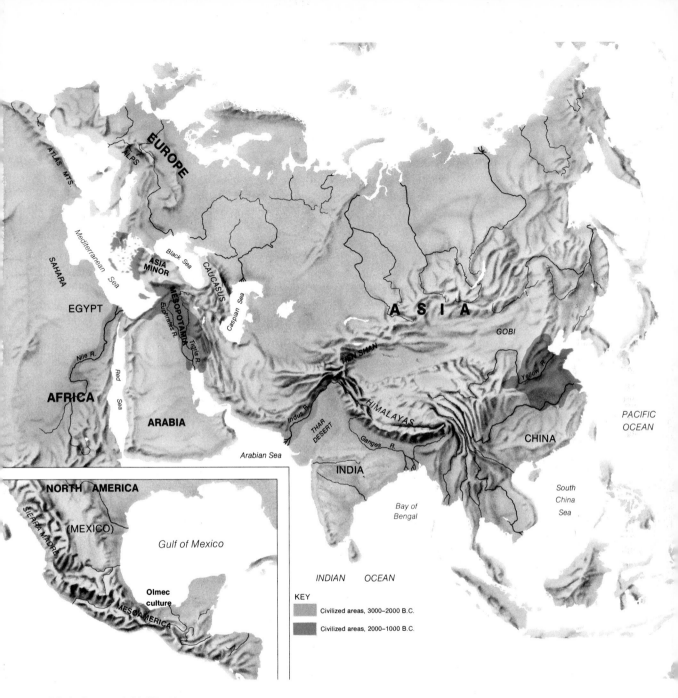

KEY

Civilized areas, 3000–2000 B.C.

Civilized areas, 2000–1000 B.C.

Birthplaces of Civilization

as well as local. Men had more leisure and devoted more attention to the life of the mind and to the development of the arts. (4) As political life became more organized, so did religion. A priesthood developed and beliefs were formed into a set of moral codes. (5) A more complex life called for the construction of temples, palaces, monuments, roads, and docks.

Man's first civilizations rose in the Near East, in the lands of Egypt and Mesopotamia. While these civilizations built upon the achievements of Neolithic man, the rise of civilization did not result automatically from Neolithic advances. Only a handful of prehistoric societies that had reached the Neolithic stage succeeded, by themselves, in making the great leap into civilization. Most prehistoric societies that had learned how to farm were not able to advance to civilization by themselves. They either acquired civilization from the handful that did advance beyond the Neolithic stage or remained uncivilized. The rise of civilization in the Near East was therefore not just a step forward from prehistory but one of the major breakthroughs in man's history. In the following chapter we shall discuss the conditions that made possible the rise of civilization in Egypt and Mesopotamia.

CHECK-UP

1. Describe the work of anthropologists and archaeologists. How are they able to reconstruct what life was like long ago? Where do they search for ancient remains?

2. How did man get his food supply during the Old Stone Age? Why did he not establish permanent villages?

3. What were the accomplishments of Paleolithic man? How did his life as a hunter influence human development?

4. How did the development of tools and the discovery of fire change ways of living during Paleolithic times?

5. What developments characterize the Neolithic Revolution? How did farming drastically change life for man? How did village life bring about specialization?

6. How did the wheel, the sail, and the plow revolutionize life in Neolithic times? Why is the late Neolithic period sometimes called the Bronze Age?

7. What is the meaning of the term civilization? What are the characteristics of a civilized society?

Summing Up

Tremendous amounts of energy were involved in the formation of the universe and of the solar system of which Earth is a part. Located in the galaxy called the Milky Way, the solar system is part of a universe so immense that distances are measured in light years. Earth became the planet we know over millions of years. Darwin's theory of evolution sheds light on how the varied and complex forms of plant and animal life found on earth today arose. Most clergymen see no conflict between scientific theories and the Biblical description of creation. Indeed, they feel each increase in man's knowledge of nature provides added information on God's handiwork.

Man is unique among living creatures because he can use complex tools, think in abstract terms, has awareness of the past, and is concerned for the future. Hundreds of thousands of years passed before the early ancestors of man evolved into *Homo sapiens.*

The studies of archaeologists and anthropologists afford insights into man's distant past. Most of man's time on earth has been spent in the Old Stone Age. Paleolithic man was a hunter who learned to make simple tools and control fire. He also displayed talent for art and developed religious beliefs.

In the New Stone Age, man lived in settled communities, learned to domesticate animals, and to plant and harvest crops. Specialization made possible improved craftsmanship and led to the exchange of goods. Some 5000 years ago the invention of the wheel and the sail revolutionized transportation. Advanced societies began to work copper and use this metal in tools and weapons. Man invented writing and began to keep written records. Civilized societies emerged in Egypt and Mesopotamia. They were characterized by the rise of urban centers, organized government, states with fixed boundaries, increased specialization of labor, expanded trade, and religious beliefs organized into moral codes.

Chapter Highlights

Can you explain? ────────────────────────────────

artifacts   light year   theory of evolution   natural selection
civilization   galaxy   prehistory   big bang theory
fossils

Can you identify? ────────────────────────────────

anthropologist   Milky Way   *Australopithecus*   Paleolithic period
solar system   Darwin   Neolithic Revolution   Neolithic period
archaeologist   *Homo sapiens*   *Homo erectus*   Bronze Age

What do you think? ───────────────────────────────

1. Why are scientists interested in prehistory? What are the sources of their information? How accurate are they?

2. What are likely next steps in the exploration of space? Is such exploration worth what it costs? Why?

3. Does the fact that race horses can be bred for speed or hardy high-yield cereal grains can be developed shed any light on Darwin's theory of evolution? Why?

4. What can be learned from studying present-day primitive societies? How can such islands of primitive life still exist in the twentieth century? Are they likely to change? Why?

5. How did man's development as a hunter influence his mental development? How did increasing mental development help early man to survive?

6. Why did early man develop art and religion?

7. How did Neolithic man bring stability and security into his life? What sacrifices did this new way of life require?

8. How does a civilized society differ from Neolithic society?

The Assyrians, among the great warriors of the ancient Near East, were also noted for superb relief carvings. This one (left) shows one of their rulers hunting. Through careful attention to details, Assyrian sculptors overcame the rigidity of stone to produce a carving full of life and feeling. The glazed tile portrait of a man from Palestine (above) depends for its impact on the use of rich color and elaborate dress.

The Ancient Near East

CHAPTER FOCUS

The People of Egypt
The Peoples of Mesopotamia
Contributions of Other Near Eastern Nations
Two Empire Builders
The Legacy of the Ancient Near East

In the lands of Egypt and Mesopotamia some 5000 years ago men first built cities, developed systems of writing, constructed large-scale temples and monuments, and worked at specialized tasks such as farming, handicrafts, trading, priesthood, and administration. These are all considered signs of civilized life.

Why civilization arose first in the lands of the Near East is one of the great unanswered questions of history. Most experts believe that it was no coincidence that Egypt and Mesopotamia developed along the banks of rivers—the Nile in Egypt and the Tigris and Euphrates in Mesopotamia. Rivers gave man water for himself and his crops. They were also excellent avenues for trade, "moving roads" on which goods could be transported easily and quickly.

Because rainfall in these regions was seasonal, it was necessary to store the life-giving water of the rivers. Irrigation works—dams and canals—were therefore developed. To build and maintain these works, men had to learn how to cooperate, how to work together. Cooperation is an essential ingredient of civilized life. The farmers in these river valleys, writes anthropologist Richard Carrington, "had to consult together and decide how the layout of the irrigation works could best be designed to meet their common needs. They then had to carry out the actual labor of construction [together], and later to agree on the proportion of water to be allotted to each family. . . . This principle of cooperative effort for the good of the whole community instead of [for] certain privileged individuals is fundamental to civilized society, and irrigation is one of its earliest manifestations." If the people had been able to satisfy all their needs without much effort—that is, if they were able to obtain all the food they wanted merely by picking it off trees—it is unlikely that civilization would have arisen there. In an environment where man has few challenges, he is not forced to be inventive and creative or to cooperate with his fellow men. Similarly, had these regions presented too great a challenge to man, it is unlikely that civilization would have arisen there. An environment where the climate was too cold or too hot, the soil poor, or the rivers too wild for man to control would have discouraged man from trying to develop further. In Egypt and in Mesopotamia the environment was neither too hostile to man nor too lush. The soil could be worked, the river waters could be stored. But to build irrigation works required great effort and intelligence. This was the challenge faced by the early inhabitants of Egypt and Mesopotamia. In overcoming this challenge they put themselves on the path of civilization.

The People of Egypt

The Nile gives life to Egypt. Egyptian civilization developed in the fertile valley of the Nile River. For good reason Egypt has been called "the gift of the Nile." Without this mighty river which flows for more than 4000 miles, all Egypt would be desert. Water from the river was used to irrigate crops. When the Nile overflowed its banks, the floodwaters left behind a layer of rich black earth on the land. This fertile soil was excellent for crops. The Egyptians worshiped their life-giving river:

Hail to thee, O Nile, that issues from the earth and comes to keep Egypt alive! . . .
[Thou art] the Bringer of Food, rich in provisions, creator of all good. . . .
. . . O Nile, . . . thou who makest man and cattle to live!*

* Selections from *Ancient Near Eastern Texts Relating to the Old Testament* ed. by James B. Pritchard (3rd edn., with Supplement, copyright © 1969 by Princeton University Press). Reprinted by permission.

But the waters of the Nile did not always bring life. If the river's overflow was less than usual, there was hunger; if the floods were too great, they washed away soil and homes.

The Egyptians learn how to control the Nile. The Egyptians met the challenge of the Nile by learning how to control the river. They were fortunate that the Nile's overflow was regular and predictable. Early in their history the Egyptians learned how to store the floodwaters of the Nile. Then they dug canals so that the water would reach fields that were being farmed. When the flood was over and the river lower, they used buckets at the end of long poles to lift water from the river. In working out problems of irrigation the Egyptians had to develop geometry and engineering. They had to learn how to map out the land. They also had to organize and direct large groups of workers and to keep written records of the yearly floods, the irrigation of fields, and the crops that were

Forerunners of Western Civilization	Approximate date	Other Civilizations
Mesopotamian city-states	**3200–2500** B.C.	Harappan culture (India)
Egypt united; pyramids begun		
Sumerian civilization	**2500–2000** B.C.	
Code of Hammurabi	**2000–1500** B.C.	Aryan invasions of India begin
		Yellow River civilization (China)
Hittites	**1500–1000** B.C.	Rise of Olmec civilization (Mexico)
Tutankhamen rules Egypt		
Exodus of Hebrews from Egypt		
Height of Assyrian Empire	**1000–500** B.C.	Chavín de Huantar unites northern Peru
Phoenicians		
Greek city-states develop		Birth of Buddha (India)
Lydians		Birth of Confucius (China)
Persian Empire; Zoroastrianism		

planted. By learning how to control the Nile and to organize workers, and by keeping written records, the Egyptians took a giant step forward in the development of civilization.

Geography favors Egypt. The Nile gave Egypt more than life. It gave the country unity. The river made it easy to go from one village to another. In time all the villages were united into a large kingdom.

Geography favored Egypt in still another way. The huge deserts to the east and west of the Nile protected Egypt from attack. For long periods of time the country remained prosperous and peaceful. This enabled Egypt to develop one of the most advanced civilizations of the ancient world.

The ruler of Egypt is also a god. The ruler of Egypt was called *pharaoh* (fair'oh). To the people of Egypt the pharaoh was more than a king. He was also a god. The Egyptians prayed to many gods, and among them was their god-king. In his honor they built giant temples and

Egyptian Empire About 1450 B.C.

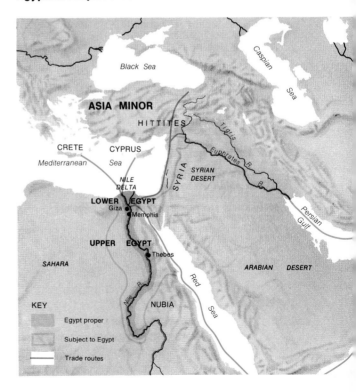

The Nile has changed little over the centuries. The barren desert still broods over the green croplands on its banks; boats like those used in the time of the pharaohs still carry produce up and down the great waterway (top). Agriculture, too, has changed little. The harvest scene above, which decorated an ancient tomb, might still be seen today.

tombs called pyramids. They sang the praises of their pharaoh: "What is the king of Upper and Lower Egypt? He is a god by whose dealings one lives, the father and mother of all men, alone by himself, without an equal."

The pharaoh was all-powerful. His word was not to be questioned. He had great wealth, for his subjects mined gold and copper, and his ships traded with other countries. In time strong pharaohs built an *empire:* they conquered nearby lands and ruled over other peoples. Conquered nations had to pay the pharaoh taxes in food and goods. They also supplied Egypt with slaves.

Today we do not believe our rulers are gods, nor do we want or need all-powerful rulers. We say that all the people should have a voice in the government. This was not the feeling of the ancient Egyptians. They were honored to be ruled by one who knew the secrets of heaven and earth:

What is there that thou dost not know? Who is there that is as wise as thou? What place is there which thou hast not seen? There is no land which thou hast not trodden. . . . Authority is in thy mouth and perception [insight] is in thy heart. . . . All is done according to thy will, and whatever thou sayest is obeyed.

The Egyptians believed that their god-king could help them gain life after death. In this life he was their protector and their helper who caused the Nile to overflow. The pharaoh tried to be a good ruler. He kept the irrigation works in order and told officials to treat the people fairly. One pharaoh gave the following instructions to his son: "Do right so long as thou abidest on the earth. Calm the weeper, oppress no widow, expel no man from the possessions of his father. . . . Take heed lest thou punish wrongfully. . . . Slay not a man whose good qualities thou knowest." In all ancient Egypt's long history, it was very rare for the common people to take up arms against their god-king.

Nobles, priests, and scribes enjoy privileges.
The pharaoh had many officials to help him govern Egypt. They collected taxes, checked on the irrigation works, and carried out the pharaoh's laws. These high officials belonged to a privileged class of nobles. Also privileged were the priests, who took care of religious activities. Nobles and priests lived in fine houses with beautiful gardens and had many servants.

Next in importance to nobles and priests were *scribes*—educated men who kept records and wrote letters. Theirs was an honored profession, for scribes were very much in demand. One Egyptian father advised his son: "Learn to write, for this will be of greater advantage to you than all the other trades I have [listed for] you. . . . School is useful for you, and the work done there will [last forever], like mountains." Beneath the nobles, priests, and scribes in Egyptian society was a small middle class made up of merchants and craftsmen. Below them were masses of the poor.

Most people in Egypt are peasants or slaves.
The peasants lived in small huts and worked on the land from dawn to sunset. A large part of their crops went for rent and taxes. Often they were required to help build temples and tombs for the pharaohs.

At the bottom of society were the slaves, acquired when Egypt conquered other lands. In the ancient world it was common practice to enslave prisoners of war. In Egypt slaves became the household servants of nobles and priests. Slaves of outstanding ability might be appointed to important positions in the government. Many slaves, however, were forced to work in the pharaoh's gold and copper mines. Chained, often whipped, unable to rest, denied adequate food, and always suffering from the heat, such slaves usually lived short and miserable lives. No one mourned them, for the life of a slave was cheap.

The Egyptians believe in life after death. In time the Egyptians came to believe that the good were rewarded with eternal life (immortality). The dead were supposed to travel to another world, where they returned to life. The Egyptians saw the "Other World" as a pleasant place where the dead person would enjoy the company of his friends. Servants made him comfortable and took care of all his wants. Under clear skies he paddled a canoe, fished, hunted, or picnicked with his family. On holidays musicians and dancing girls provided entertainment.

Upper-class Egyptians made careful preparations for the journey to the Other World. Embalmers used salts to keep the dead body from decaying. It was then carefully wrapped in fine linen. To make the *mummy* appear lifelike, the lips and cheeks were painted, and artificial eyes provided. Egyptian embalmers were very skillful and painstaking, working for months in preparing a single mummy. Archaeologists have found mummies which still had hair, skin, and teeth after thousands of years.

After being painted, wrapped, and adorned with jewelry, the mummy was ready for the great adventure. A long funeral procession, headed by priests chanting prayers, marched to the place of burial. At the door of the tomb, the funeral party often did a religious dance. Buried with the mummy was the *Book of the Dead,* a scroll which listed examples of good behavior as well as prayers for the dead and songs of praise to the gods. It was believed that those who had lived evil lives were turned over to a wild beast called the Devourer of Souls.

The type of tomb depends on the dead man's wealth.
The poor had no tombs and simple funerals. Only some handfuls of food and a few kitchen utensils were buried with them. The burial of a pharaoh, however, was a grand occasion. His resting place was a tomb filled with everything the pharaoh might need in the Other World. The people of Egypt believed that their pharaoh would live forever:

... he dies not: this king lives forever. He has escaped his day of death. . . . Men fall, and their names cease to be: therefore [the gods] take hold of this king by his arm, and lead him to the sky, that he may not die upon earth among men. This king flies away from you, you mortals. He is not of the earth, he is of the sky. . . . He goes up to heaven like the hawks, and his feathers are like those of the wild geese; he rushes at heaven like a crane, he kisses heaven like the falcon, he leaps to heaven like the locust. He ascends to the sky! He ascends to the sky on the wind, on the wind! The stairs of the sky are let down for him that he may ascend . . . to heaven.

The tomb of Tutankhamen is a fabulous find.
In 1922 British archaeologist Howard Carter discovered the unplundered tomb of the pharaoh Tutankhamen (toot-ahnk-*ah'*men). His hands shaking, Carter made a hole in the sealed door of the tomb, inserted a candle, and peered in. As his eyes grew used to the light, he saw "strange animals, statues, and gold—everywhere the glint of gold." By the first light that had pierced the darkness of the chamber for three thousand years, Carter and his companions saw*

a roomful—a whole museumful it seemed—of objects, some familiar, but some the like of which we had never seen, piled one upon another in seemingly endless [number]. . . . Right opposite to us . . . were three great gilt couches, their sides carved in the form of monstrous animals. . . . Next, on the right, two statues caught and held our attention; two life-sized figures of a king in black, facing each other like [guards], gold kilted, gold sandalled, armed with [club] and staff, the protective sacred cobra upon their foreheads.

These were the . . . objects that caught the eye at first. Between them, around them, piled on top of them, there were countless others—exquisitely painted and inlaid caskets; alabaster vases; . . . strange black shrines, from the open door of one a great gilt snake peeping out; bouquets of flowers or leaves; beds; chairs beautifully carved; a golden inlaid throne; a heap of curious white . . . boxes; staves of all shapes and designs; beneath our eyes, on the very threshold of the chamber, a beautiful . . . cup of [clear] alabaster; on the left a confused pile of overturned chariots, glistening with gold and inlay; and peeping from behind them another portrait of a king. . . .

Presently it dawned upon our bewildered brains that in all this medley of objects before us there was no coffin or trace of mummy. . . . We reexamined the scene before us, and noticed for the first time that between the two black sentinel

* From *The Tomb of Tut-Ankh-Amen* by Howard Carter and A. C. Mace (London: Cassell and Co. Ltd., 1930). Reprinted by permission of Curtis Brown Ltd.

A symbol of awe to ancient Egyptians, as it is today, the Great Pyramid of Khufu towers over lesser tombs in the barren desert around Giza. The grandeur surrounding the burial of a pharaoh is typified by the gold mask of Tutankhamen, an outstanding example of Egyptian skill in working with metals and semi-precious stones. Many of the paintings on the walls of tombs depicted the judging of the soul. Below, Anubis weighs the heart of the princess Entiu-ny against the figure of the Goddess of Truth.

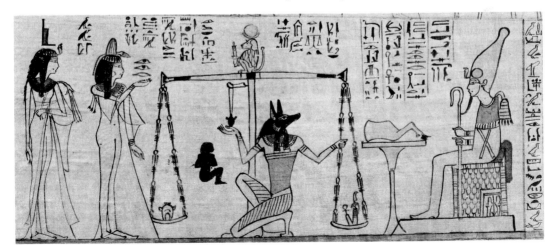

statues on the right there was another sealed doorway. The explanation gradually dawned upon us. We were but on the threshold of our discovery. What we saw was merely [an entryway].

They found the mummy of the king lying in a coffin of solid gold! His face was covered with a gold mask, his hands crossed over his chest. On his forehead was a tiny wreath of flowers, perhaps, thought Carter, "the last farewell offering of the widowed girl queen to her husband. . . . There was nothing so beautiful as those few withered flowers, still [keeping] their tinge of color. They told us what a short period three thousand three hundred years really was."

The Egyptian pharaohs have pyramids built.
Sometimes the final resting place of the pharaoh was a giant pyramid. The Great Pyramid built by the Pharaoh Khufu (*koo′*foo) stood 481 feet high. It contained some two million stone blocks. The base of the pyramid was almost a perfect square, each side measuring about 755 feet. It took some twenty years to build this royal tomb. Without modern equipment, using logs as rollers and levers, teams of Egyptian workmen dragged two- and three-ton stones up ramps and into place! Only skillful architects and engineers could have built such a monument. A people which devoted so much energy and time to building tombs and pyramids must have been greatly concerned with the afterlife.

The royal tombs are an invitation to thieves.
Even before the civilization of ancient Egypt declined, some royal tombs were plundered. Indeed, the tomb of Tutankhamen is the only undisturbed royal tomb ever found. Some three thousand years ago, for example, an Egyptian tomb robber told a court:

We went to rob the tombs in accordance with our regular habit. . . . We took our copper tools and forced a way into the pyramid of this king. . . . We found its underground chambers, and we took lighted candles in our hands and went down . . . and we found the burial place of [the king and queen]. . . . We opened their . . . coffins. . . . The noble mummy of this king was completely [covered] with gold, and his coffins were adorned with gold and silver inside and out and inlaid with all kinds of precious stones. We collected the gold we found, . . . together with his jewels, . . . furniture . . . consisting of . . . gold, silver, and bronze, and divided them amongst ourselves.

The Egyptians used a different type of hieroglyphs on records meant to endure (left) from those used in less permanent records such as the legal document (center). The cuneiform script of the Mesopotamians (right) was written on clay tablets.

The Egyptians seek to enjoy life on earth. The Egyptians did not live just to prepare for the afterlife. They also tried to enjoy life on earth. They liked good food, games, hunting, and romance. Indeed, in the Other World they expected to do all the things that pleased them on earth. They did not consider the Other World an escape from a dreadful life upon the earth. Had not the gods given them the fertile black soil, the life-giving waters of the Nile, the warm African sun, and the desert to keep out invaders? Were they not ruled wisely and justly by the pharaoh, child of the sun-god?

The Egyptians develop a system of picture-writing. For some 3000 years the Egyptians carved the picture symbols of their system of writing (*hieroglyphics*) on stone walls and temples. Hieroglyphs were painted on scrolls and on coffins and the inner walls of pyramids. With the end of Egyptian civilization, the meaning of the hieroglyphs was lost. No one could read what the ancient Egyptians had written. Then, in 1822, a young French expert in languages discovered how to read the hieroglyphs, and increased our knowledge of ancient Egypt.

The Egyptians wrote stories, poems, and history. Many of their poems were hymns to the gods. Others dealt with love, as in the following poem.*

Seven days . . . I have not seen [my loved one]
And a sickness has invaded me.
My body has become heavy. . . .
If the chief of physicians come to me,
My heart is not content with their remedies. . . .

To say to me: "Here she is!" is what will revive
    me;
Her name is what will lift me up. . . .
If she opens her eye, my body is young again;
If she speaks, then I am strong again;
When I embrace her, she drives evil away from
    me.

* Selections from *Ancient Near Eastern Texts Relating to the Old Testament* ed. by James B. Pritchard (3rd edn., with Supplement, copyright © 1969 by Princeton University Press). Reprinted by permission.

The Egyptians practice medicine, use mathematics, and develop a calendar. Egyptian doctors combined magic with medicine. They believed that disease was caused by the gods. To remove evil spirits from the body, doctors used strong drugs and spoke mysterious words. Yet they were the first real doctors in the world's history. They knew something about the workings of the body, how to heal wounds, set broken bones, and make use of healing drugs. Kings from other lands used Egyptian doctors.

The Egyptians made use of geometry in surveying the land and building pyramids. The priests also developed a solar (sun) calendar based on a year of 365 days, the best calendar introduced in ancient times.

For many centuries life in Egypt changed very little. Today we believe in change. We search for new and better ways of doing things. We develop new ideas. The ancient Egyptians did not have this attitude. They looked to the past. They believed that the gods wanted them to retain the religion, art, and ways of life of their ancestors. The Egyptians were certain that their way of life was best. They would not change it. To live as did their fathers was what they wanted out of life.

CHECK-UP

1. What is meant by the term civilization? What factors led to the rise of civilization in the ancient Near East?

2. Why is Egypt called "the gift of the Nile"? How did the Nile unify the country?

3. What powers were exercised by the pharaoh of Egypt? What responsibilities did he have? How did the Egyptian people view their pharaoh?

4. What was life like for the privileged classes in Egypt? For the peasants and slaves?

5. What can be found inside a royal tomb? What do the contents of a royal tomb tell us about the Egyptian religion?

6. What contributions did the Egyptians make to civilization?

To the east of Egypt, in the land of Mesopotamia (mes-oh-poh-*tey*′mih-uh), another great civilization developed. *Mesopotamia* is the Greek word for "land between the rivers." Two rivers, the Tigris (*tie*′gris) and the Euphrates (yoo-*frey*′teez), flow through Mesopotamia and empty into the Persian Gulf. In the valleys of these rivers, men farmed the fertile land, built cities, and developed a high level of civilization at an early period.

Despite the fertility of the soil, life in Mesopotamia is never easy. It was hard to control the waters of the Tigris and Euphrates. Sometimes they broke through the man-made dikes and flooded the land, ruining crops and destroying villages. At other times the river did not provide enough water. Then crops failed and people died. At times great windstorms that had blown across desert lands left the countryside covered with a layer of sand. At other times heavy thunderstorms turned the fields into a sea of mud, making travel almost impossible. Unlike Egypt, which was protected by deserts, Mesopotamia had no natural barriers to invasion. Floods, drought, blistering heat, swamps, sandstorms, and invading armies made life difficult and unsafe.

Mesopotamian civilization rests upon the achievements of the Sumerians. The first people to develop an advanced civilization in Mesopotamia were the Sumerians (soo-*meer*′ih-unz). Although Mesopotamia was invaded and conquered by different peoples, the achievements of Sumerian civilization survived and endured. The Sumerians made tools and weapons of gold, silver, and bronze. Their pottery, formed on a potter's wheel, was glazed and baked in ovens. This made it both durable and waterproof. Elaborate houses, palaces, and temples were built of bricks that had been dried in the sun or baked in ovens. The Sumerians

engaged in trade and made advances in flood control and irrigation. Like the Egyptians, the Sumerians developed a system of writing to represent their ideas. Instead of hieroglyphics, however, they used cuneiform or wedge-shaped symbols. Using a stylus or stick, they drew these symbols on tablets of wet clay which they then baked in the sun to harden.

Man's first cities arise in Mesopotamia. Sumer's (*soo*′merz) profitable trade and food surpluses made possible by irrigation helped bring about the development of man's first cities. Eventually these cities became centers around which small states developed. There were a dozen or so of these city-states, each consisting of a city and the countryside surrounding it. Each city-state was devoted to a specific god. The chief priest of the city exercised wide powers, and was, in effect, both priest and king. It was his duty to rule the city according to the wishes of its god, to bring the city glory by making war on neighboring city-states. Weakened by these frequent wars, the city-states of Sumer eventually were conquered by foreign invaders. But Sumerian civilization was not destroyed. The patterns of civilization first developed by the Sumerians were adopted and added to by later peoples in Mesopotamia. The result was a distinctly Mesopotamian civilization.

The Code of Hammurabi tells us much about Mesopotamian society. One of the conquerors of Sumer was a Babylonian (bab-ih-*loh*′nih-un) king named Hammurabi (hahm-oo-*rah*′bee). During his reign old Sumerian laws were brought together in a single code of laws which applied to all people. The Code of Hammurabi was carved on stone pillars eight feet high. At the opening of the twentieth century, French archaeologists discovered and translated a copy of this code.

Through its laws we learn that nobles and priests were favored over common people, and freemen over slaves. Punishments were very severe, but the laws sought to establish justice, and all classes were bound by them. The laws dealt with everything that seemed to affect the community: marriage, family relations, irrigation, military service, religion, crime, business dealings, and ownership of property. This code of laws remained the basis for the Mesopotamian legal system for 1500 years. Following are some of the provisions of Hammurabi's code.*

If a seignior [free man] accused another seignior and brought a charge of murder against him, but has not proved it, his accuser shall be put to death. . . .

If a seignior stole either an ox or a sheep or an ass or a pig or a boat, if it belonged to the church or if it belonged to the state, he shall make thirtyfold restitution [repayment]. If it belonged to a private citizen, he shall make good tenfold. If the thief does not have sufficient to make restitution, he shall be put to death. . . .

If a seignior has harbored in his house either a fugitive male or female slave belonging to the state or to a private citizen and has not brought him forth at the summons of the police, that householder shall be put to death.

If a robber has not been caught, the robbed seignior shall set forth the particulars regarding his lost property in the presence of god, and the city and governor, in whose territory and district the robbery was committed, shall make good to him his lost property. . . .

If a seignior was too lazy to make the dike of his field strong . . . and a break has opened up in his dike and he has accordingly let the water ravage the farmland, the seignior in whose dike the break was opened shall make good the grain that he let get destroyed. . . .

*Selections from *Ancient Near Eastern Texts Relating to the Old Testament* ed. by James B. Pritchard (3rd edn., with Supplement, copyright © 1969 by Princeton University Press). Reprinted by permission.

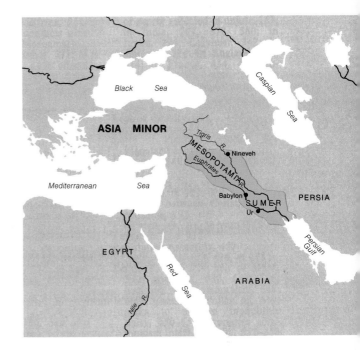

Hammurabi's Empire About 1700 B.C.

If a seignior wishes to divorce his wife who did not bear him children, he shall give her money to the full amount of her marriage-price and he shall also make good to her the dowry which she brought from her father's house and then he may divorce her. . . .

If a son has struck his father, they shall cut off his hand.

If a seignior has destroyed the eye of a member of the aristocracy, they shall destroy his eye. . . .

If a seignior has knocked out a tooth of a seignior of his own rank, they shall knock out his tooth.

Babylon is renowned throughout the ancient Near East. Next to the Euphrates River was Babylon (*bab'*ih-lon), the greatest city of Hammurabi's empire. "That great city, . . . that mighty city," it was called in the Bible. "In magnificence there is no other city that approaches it," wrote a Greek historian of the fifth century B.C. A double row of walls guarded the city from attack. Canals protected it from the floodwaters of the Euphrates. The streets were wide but unpaved. Though most of the one-story houses had gardens, there were no sewers. Babylon was a center of business activity. The development of carts and, later, four-wheel wagons pulled by oxen or donkeys furthered trade with other regions. From Babylonian harbors ships sailed up and down the Euphrates. Along the waterfront were booths where merchants sold their goods.

The Ancient Near East

Religion plays an important role in Mesopotamia. The people of Mesopotamia believed in many gods (*polytheism*); and in addition to the gods common to all, each city had its own particular god. He was the central figure of the city's life: the real owner of the land, the real ruler of the city. Temples were built in his honor. In ancient Babylon, we are told, there were over a thousand temples built for the gods. Special care was given to the greatest of all temples, the one built for the god Marduk (*mahr′dook*). In this temple, said an ancient

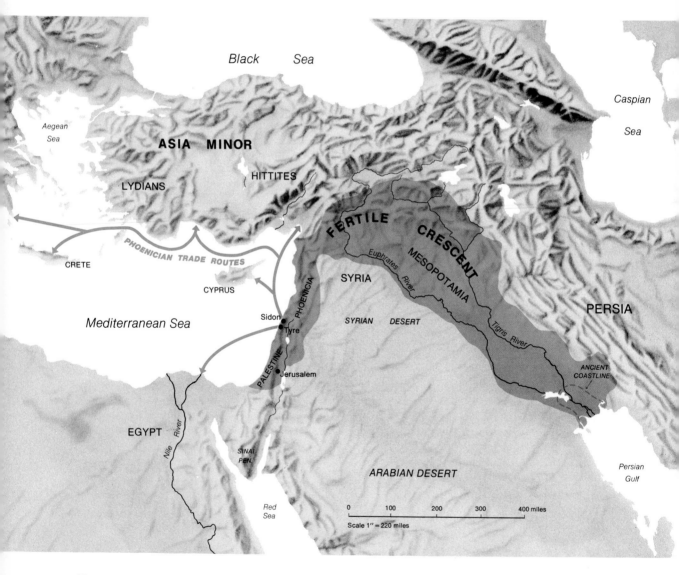

historian, was "a great golden image of [Marduk] sitting at a great golden table, and the footstool and chair are also of gold. . . . Outside the temple is a golden altar. There is another altar, whereon are sacrificed the full-grown of the flocks." In honor of Marduk one Babylonian king brought to the temple "silver, gold, costly precious stones, bronze, . . . everything that is expensive, . . . the products of the mountains, the treasures of the seas."

Unlike the Egyptian pharaoh, the kings of Mesopotamia did not look upon themselves as gods. They believed that they were great men whom the gods had chosen to rule the people. No important decision was made by kings or priests without first consulting the gods. To find out what the gods wanted, the priests sacrificed an animal. Then they examined the liver, intestines, or other parts of the dead animal to find out the answer. Sometimes they found their answer in the stars or in dreams.

Mesopotamian man sees gods and demons everywhere. The Mesopotamians believed there was a god in the fire and another in the river. They looked on evil demons as the cause of sandstorms, disease, and nightmares. To protect himself from these demons, Mesopotamian man wore charms and begged his gods for help. He prayed to Gira, the fire-god:

Scorching Fire, warlike son of Heaven,
Thou, the fiercest of thy brethren, . . .
Judge thou my case. . . .
Burn the man and woman who bewitched me;
Burn, O Fire, the man and woman who bewitched me;
Scorch, O Fire, the man and woman who bewitched me;
Burn them, O Fire;
Scorch them, O Fire;
Take hold of them, O Fire;
Consume them, O Fire;
Destroy them, O Fire.*

* From "Mesopotamia: The Cosmos as a State" by Thorkild Jacobsen in *The Intellectual Adventure of Ancient Man,* Henri Frankfort (University of Chicago Press, 1966). Reprinted by permission.

Though both the Egyptians and the Mesopotamians believed in many gods, their attitude toward the gods differed greatly. Whereas the Egyptians thought that the gods were friendly and protected them, the Mesopotamians believed that the gods and demons who surrounded man made his life miserable. The Mesopotamians' life was, in fact, harsher and more insecure than that of the Egyptians. Hence they saw floods and drought which destroyed crops, or enemy soldiers who killed their families, as punishments or expressions of divine ill-will. Thus Mesopotamian man lived always in fear of his gods.

The peoples of Mesopotamia develop an advanced civilization. The Mesopotamians had cities, written laws, a merchant class, and a system of banking. Craftsmen made fine bowls and plates out of bronze and copper. Engineers designed dikes, dams, reservoirs, and canals to control and store the waters of the Tigris and Euphrates Rivers. Architects built temples to honor the gods. Mesopotamian priests and scribes wrote poems and kept records of treaties, laws, battles, and business dealings. Astronomers knew the difference between planets and stars and invented a twelve-month lunar (moon) calendar with a seven-day week.

Religion and magic dominate Mesopotamian medicine. In Mesopotamia, as in Egypt, medicine was tied to religion and superstition. To cure a patient, doctors and priests often tried magic. In one case a priest tore the heart out of a kid goat. Reciting magic words, he handed the still-beating heart to the sick person. Another superstition held by Mesopotamian man was: "If a snake falls on the sick man's head, that sick man will get well."

Mesopotamian doctors did not know much about the workings of the human body. Believing that illness was caused by demons and evil spells, doctors had little desire to study the body. But sometimes doctors were more scientific. They described the patient's illness and used drugs to effect a cure. Some successful operations were also performed. Surgeons had to be very careful when operating on a noble. The Code of Hammurabi stated: "If a physician has treated a man of rank . . . for a severe wound and caused the nobleman to die, or has removed a cataract from the eye of a nobleman . . . and caused the loss of the eye—let his hands be cut off."

The Mesopotamians find life harsh and expect nothing better after death. The scorching sun, the heavy rains, the sandstorms which turned the soil into whirling dust, the destructive floodwaters of the Tigris and Euphrates Rivers, and frequent invasions made life in Mesopotamia difficult and unsafe. Whereas the Egyptians faced life with confidence, the Mesopotamians felt helpless and afraid. Unlike the Egyptians, they did not look forward to a pleasant afterlife. Mesopotamian man was certain that happiness after death was only for the gods, not for lowly man. He also believed that when men died they went to the lower world, or Netherworld. Just as the dry and apparently dead seeds of a plant are buried in the earth and then come to life again, so man enters the realm beneath the earth when he dies. This place of human rebirth, the Netherworld, was described

by the Mesopotamians as a huge dark cave "where they sit in darkness, where dust is their food and clay their meat; they are clothed like birds with wings for garments; over bolt and door lie dust and silence."

The Egyptians felt that man could do great things in his lifetime, that his pyramids and temples would last forever. The Mesopotamians thought man was unimportant, no more than a slave of the gods. He counted for nothing. Whatever man did was like the wind; it could not last. Mesopotamian man thought little of himself, found life full of pain, and had nothing to look forward to after death.

CHECK-UP

1. Why was life difficult for the people of Mesopotamia?
2. What were the achievements of Sumerian civilization?
3. What does the Code of Hammurabi tell us about Mesopotamian society?
4. Why did Mesopotamian man fear his gods? In what ways did religion dominate Mesopotamian medicine?
5. What were the achievements of the peoples of Mesopotamia?

Contributions of Other Near Eastern Nations

HITTITES AND LYDIANS

In Asia Minor, in what today is Turkey, lived two peoples in ancient times who made important contributions to civilization. The Hittites (*hit'*ites) were probably the first people to work iron ore into iron. This knowledge spread to other peoples in Asia, North Africa, and Southern Europe. Iron tools and weapons became commonplace all over the ancient world. The Lydians (*lid'*ih-unz) were probably the first people to make use of coins. The practice of stamping a small piece of gold and silver

with its value and using it as money spread to other lands. The invention of coinage was a great aid to international trade because coins came to be accepted as payment for goods and services throughout the Mediterranean world and beyond.

PHOENICIANS

On the eastern coast of the Mediterranean, between Egypt and Mesopotamia, was the land of Phoenicia (fih-*nish'*uh). Because they lived near the sea, the Phoenicians were shipbuilders,

To rulers in the ancient Near East the cedars of Lebanon were valued for use in the finest buildings. So great was the demand that the trees nearly became extinct. From Phoenician ports they were carried throughout the Near East in ships like those shown above, which were protected by the "eye of god" at their bow, the earliest example of a figurehead. Trade between lands was facilitated after the Lydians introduced the use of coins such as those shown here.

sailors, and merchants. They were adventurous seamen who carried the culture and products of the ancient Near East to regions as distant as England. They also established colonies in North Africa, southern Spain, and the islands of the Mediterranean Sea.

Because they carried ideas as well as products from one port to another in the Mediterranean world, the Phoenicians are known as *carriers of civilization*. But the Phoenicians made an important contribution of their own to civilization by devising the first alphabetic written language. Our system of writing is based on the alphabet which the Phoenicians developed and which the Greeks improved by adding vowels.

HEBREWS

The Hebrews came originally from Mesopotamia. At one time they were slaves in Egypt. After being led out of Egypt by Moses, they settled in Palestine, present-day Israel. The Hebrews regarded Palestine as a holy land promised to them by God. During the course

On the island of Crete in the Aegean Sea, about 2500 B.C., Minoan civilization developed. A seafaring people like the Phoenicians, the people of Crete traded with the lands around the Mediterranean. Minoan craftsmen made fine pottery, daggers, and intricately carved stone seals. Their palaces such as that at Phaistos (left) were built on several levels linked by wide stone stairs. Besides rooms set aside for religious ceremonies or as living quarters, Minoan palaces contained paved courtyards, pillared halls, and a theater. On the walls were paintings of graceful women with elaborate hairstyles and of athletes. Boxing, wrestling, and racing were popular with the Minoans. A unique sport was bull-dancing, in which young men and women showed their bravery by making daring somersaults over wild bulls (below).

When Minoan civilization declined, cultural leadership of the Aegean area passed to Mycenae on the mainland of Greece. Traders like the Minoans and skilled goldsmiths, the Mycenaeans were eventually overcome by internal problems and invaders from the north. But in the same area would arise Greek civilization, the greatest civilization of the ancient Mediterranean world (see Chapter 3).

Mediterranean Sea

MT. LEUKA
Knossos
MT. IDA
Phaistos

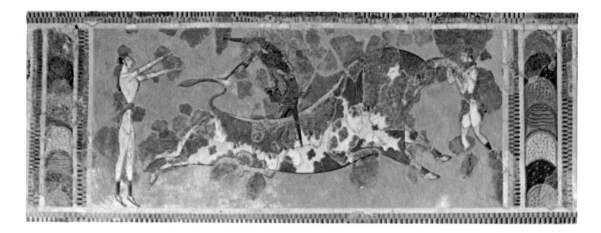

of their history many Hebrews were driven out of Palestine by powerful invaders, but they never forgot their homeland. The Hebrews made extraordinary contributions to the history of civilization.

1. Belief in one God. The Hebrews gave to the world the idea of *monotheism,* or belief in one God. To them there was no power greater than their God, Yahweh. He was the Creator and Ruler of Heaven and Earth.

In the beginning God created the heaven and the earth . . .

And God said, "Let there be light." And there was light. . . .

And God said, "Let the earth bring forth grass." . . . And it was so.

And God said, "Let the earth bring forth the living creature after its kind." . . . And it was so.

At first the Hebrews looked upon God as the God of Judaism alone. Later, He was regarded as the God of all peoples. The Hebrew idea of one God was passed on to Christianity and Islam.

2. Rules of right and wrong. The Hebrews set up rules of conduct—the Ten Commandments—that are followed today by Christians and Muslims as well as Jews. The Hebrews believed that the Ten Commandments were given to man by God. They were the foundations of the law. God's law commanded man not to murder, steal, commit adultery, or tell lies about his neighbors. He wanted men to honor their parents, love their neighbors, care for the needy, and protect the weak. If man broke God's commandments, God would punish him.

3. The Old Testament. The Hebrews gave us sacred writings. Over the centuries the ancient Hebrews wrote down their thoughts, prayers, and history. These writings make up the Old Testament, the first part of the Bible. The Old Testament includes poetry, wise sayings, love songs, and accounts of important events. It has one main religious purpose—to teach man about God. Both Jews and Christians regard the Old Testament as sacred.

4. Social justice and a better world. Among the Hebrews were high-minded men who considered themselves messengers of the Lord. They were called *prophets.* The Hebrew prophets cared nothing for money or possessions. They wanted only to remind the Hebrews to act according to the teachings of the Lord. It was not enough, said the prophets, to pray to God or to celebrate religious holidays. God demanded that man be just, merciful, and righteous at all times. Man must avoid evil, said the prophets. Only then would he gain God's favor. The prophets criticized the rich and strong for mistreating the poor and weak. There is no justice, said the prophet Amos, when the rich "lie upon beds of ivory, . . . eat the lambs out of the flock, . . . devise for themselves instruments of music, . . . drink wine in bowls,"* while all the time the poor are made to suffer. A man who harmed or cheated his fellow man, said the prophets, could never serve God. With ringing words they cried out for justice:

> Cease to do evil,
> Learn to do well,
> Seek justice, relieve the oppressed,
> Judge the fatherless, plead for the widow.

"What doth the Lord require of thee: Only to do justly, and to love mercy, and to walk humbly with thy God."*

The Hebrew prophets impressed upon civilization man's duty to fight evil, injustice, and poverty. They taught that there could be no knowledge of God without love of man. They dreamed of a new and better world in which peace would come to all men:

And many peoples shall go and say: come ye and let us go up to the house of . . . God . . . and He will teach us of His ways. . . . And they shall beat their swords into plowshares and their spears into pruning-hooks. Nation shall not lift up sword against nation. Neither shall they learn war any more.*

The prophets were among the world's great teachers of morality. Their words, 2000 years old, still have meaning today. Mankind still strives to realize the prophets' dream for world peace; it is still moved by the prophets' plea to care for the poor, the needy, and the oppressed.

The Hebrews showed little talent for art. Their temples, built by Phoenician architects,

---

* From *The Holy Scriptures According to the Masoretic Text* (Philadelphia: The Jewish Publication Society of America, 1957). Reprinted by permission.

did not compare with the pyramids and temples of Egypt. Science did not interest them. They believed that the secrets of the universe were known only to God. To the ancient Hebrews nothing was more important than to serve God. This was their message to the world, their contribution to civilization. It still inspires people today.

CHECK-UP

1. What did the Hittites, Lydians, and Phoenicians each contribute to the development of civilization?
2. What major contributions did the Hebrews make to civilization?

Two Empire Builders

ASSYRIA

In the highlands north of Mesopotamia lived a people known as the Assyrians (uh-*sihr′*ih-unz). About 670 B.C. the Assyrians conquered the entire Fertile Crescent (see map). Equipped with iron weapons and superbly organized, the Assyrian army slaughtered its enemies and terrorized the ancient Near East. Assyrian kings boasted of their bloody deeds:

Like the Thunderer (the storm-god Adad) I crushed the corpses of their warriors in . . . battle.

Assyrian Empire About 670 B.C.

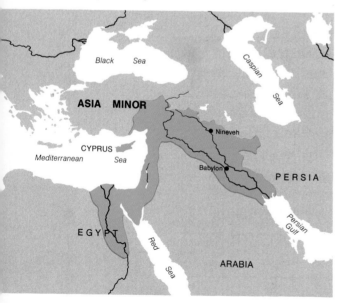

. . . I made their blood to flow over all the ravines and high places of mountains. I cut off their heads and piled them up at the walls of their cities like heaps of grain. I carried off . . . their goods and their property beyond reckoning. . . . Their troops who had fled before my weapons and had thrown themselves at my feet, I took away as prisoners and added to the people of my country.

To control their empire, the Assyrians developed roads and an efficient postal system. But after their enemies united and destroyed the Assyrian capital in 612 B.C., the empire collapsed.

PERSIA

The Persians rule a large, organized empire. The greatest empire of the ancient Near East was established by the Persians. By 500 B.C. the Persians ruled the lands from Egypt to India. They united all the peoples—Egyptians, Babylonians, Assyrians, Hebrews, Phoenicians, Hittites, and Lydians—under one rule. Persian kings were wise rulers. They built roads to tie their empire together and started a postal system. They established an effective administrative system for governing a large empire. The emperor appointed governors to supervise the twenty provinces that made up the empire. The emperor kept track of these governors through his "Eyes and Ears of the King," inspectors who served as a check on local officials. The conquered peoples in the provinces were generally treated fairly. They were

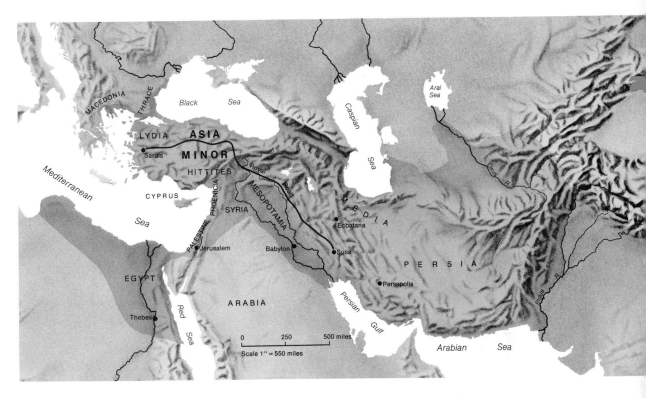

Persian Empire About 500 B.C.

allowed to keep their local customs and traditions. As long as they paid their taxes, provided recruits for the emperor's army, and refrained from rebellion, they had little to fear from the Persian emperor.

The Persian religion teaches men to be good to each other. In their religion, called *Zoroastrianism* (zoh-roh-*as*′trih-un-iz'm), the Persians came to believe in two divine powers—the Wise Lord Ahura-Mazda (*ah*′huh-ruh *maz*′duh) who was in constant struggle with the Evil Spirit, Ahriman (*ah*′rih-mun). The Wise Lord created man but gave him the choice of doing good or evil. The Persians believed that all men who served Ahura-Mazda, God of Truth, Goodness, and Light, spoke the truth and were good to others. After death, the good joined the Wise Lord in a realm of light and goodness called Paradise (which is a Persian word). Evildoers,

on the other hand, were cast into hell, a realm of darkness and torment.

The Persian Empire brings unity to the ancient Near East. The different peoples of the Near East were united in a single empire by the Persians. The Persian Empire represented a fusing of the different civilizations of the ancient Near East. Writes historian Milton Covensky, "In architecture, for example, the Persians fused Near Eastern styles and practices. Persian palaces were built on terraces in the Babylonian fashion; the winged bulls at the palace gates were taken from the Assyrians; the vast colonnades of their halls derived from Egypt." The Persians were tolerant of the different religions and cultures of the peoples who made up their empire. They permitted cultural variety under their rule and from other cultures borrowed that which appealed to them.

Ancient Persian sculpture, more static than Assyrian, gives a feeling of dignity and ceremony. This relief from the capital of Persepolis portrays the royal guard.

CHECK-UP

1. What Assyrian policies undermined their rule of the Near East?

2. How did the rule of Persian kings reveal wisdom? What sort of unity did the Persians bring to the ancient Near East?

The Legacy of the Ancient Near East

To students, the civilizations of the ancient Near East may seem part of a distant past of little importance to today's world. Yet these ancient civilizations are worth studying. Their discoveries, ideas, and ideals represent part of mankind's cultural achievements. And many of the cultural products of these civilizations were passed on to other peoples. They have become part of our heritage.

1. The men and women of the ancient Near East were not entirely different from us. They were parents, farmers, artists, craftsmen, writers, statesmen, merchants, and doctors. They too had cities, governments, schools, armies, and laws, and followed religious teachings. They also fought wars, worked for a living, worried about their children, and educated them in their customs and beliefs.

2. The peoples in the ancient Near East made advances in science, mathematics, architecture, writing, law, and medicine. From the Hebrews who lived in the Near East, western civilization obtained the belief in one God and standards of right and wrong. The Bible, one of the most important books in the history of western civilization, and writing itself are products of the ancient Near East.

3. These civilizations show us that men learn from each other. The peoples of the ancient Near East did not keep entirely to themselves. They exchanged goods, ideas, and ways of doing things and thus enriched their lives.

4. Perhaps most important of all, by studying about these early civilizations, we learn how painful and difficult it was for man to develop a high level of civilization. It took tens of thousands of years before man learned to farm the land rather than hunt for his food. Then many centuries passed before he learned to build great cities and develop a system of writing. The peoples of the ancient Near East built the base on which much of modern civilization rests. Without their achievements, our world would probably be much different today.

Chapter Highlights

Can you explain?

empry   hieroglyphics   monotheism   polytheism

scribes   prophets   immortality   pharaoh

mummy

Can you explain?

empire   hieroglyphics   monotheism   polytheism

scribes   prophets   immortality   pharaoh

mummy

Can you identify?

Asia Minor   Babylon   Zoroastrianism   Code of Hammurabi

Mesopotamia   Nile River   carriers of civilization   *Book of the Dead*

Fertile Crescent

What do you think?

1. What skills did the Egyptians develop as a result of the Nile's flooding?

2. Compare our attitude toward our rulers and government with the Egyptian's view of his ruler and government.

3. How did the Egyptian concept of death compare with Mesopotamian beliefs?

4. What was the "good life" for the Egyptians? For the Hebrews? What similarities and differences can you see in these two approaches?

5. Why do you think civilization first rose in the Near East?

6. How did the physical hardships of life in Mesopotamia affect its people's spirit and outlook?

7. How did the position of the pharaoh of Egypt compare with that of the king in Mesopotamia?

8. Why are the ideas of the Hebrew prophets still meaningful today?

9. The Assyrians and the Persians provide two examples of empire-building. Can either approach be justified? Why?

10. The peoples of the ancient Near East built the base on which much of modern civilization rests. Give evidence supporting this statement.

On the rocky heights above Athens stood the Parthenon (left), a masterpiece of architecture. A temple devoted to Athena, Goddess of Wisdom, the Parthenon was decorated with superb relief sculpture (top). The Iliad, an account of the Trojan War by the poet Homer, was a favorite subject of Greek artists, who often depicted scenes from the war on vases (below). In modern times archaeologists used Homer's writings to locate Troy, long believed to be only a legendary city.

Greek Civilization

CHAPTER FOCUS

The City-States of Greece
The Greeks at War
The Achievements of Greek Civilization

Of the different peoples who lived in the ancient Mediterranean world two stand out—the Hebrews and the Greeks. They are the main founders of *western civilization*—the civilization of Europe and America. The ancient Hebrews gave western civilization its belief in one God and many of its rules of conduct. The ancient Greeks made great contributions to art, mathematics, literature, and government; they are also the founders of philosophy and many of our sciences. To no other people do we owe so much. Almost everything interested the Greeks, and they did almost everything well. Never in history has one people shown such universal talent. Even today we are amazed and inspired by their achievements. Who were these ancient Greeks? How did they live? What did they accomplish?

Geography helps shape the Greek way of life.
Greece had little land suited for agriculture. The soil was poor, and there were many hills and narrow valleys. Unsuccessful with grain crops, Greek farmers, particularly in mountain regions, turned to cultivation of grapes and olives. Peasants worked long and hard, and lived under the constant threat of hunger. Because there was not enough good land, many Greeks left their homeland and established Greek settlements in other parts of the Mediterranean world.

Because the mountainous land gave Greece a jagged coastline with many good harbors, early in their history the Greeks became a seafaring people. Greek ships sailed the Mediterranean and Black Seas, founding colonies and visiting ports in Europe, North Africa, and the Near East. A wide variety of goods from the ancient world was sold in the Greek markets:

grain from Egypt and Italy, fruit from Phoenicia and Sicily, fish from the Black Sea, copper from the island of Cyprus (*sigh'prus*), tin from England, glass from Egypt, dyes from Phoenicia, ivory from Africa, perfumes and ointments from Arabia. In exchange for these goods the Greeks exported wood, marble, pottery, wine, and olive oil.

The Greeks live in city-states. Greece's many mountains, bays, and islands tended to divide the people. Whereas Egypt became a united country under one ruler, the Greeks lived in small communities called *city-states*. The Nile united Egypt, but the mountains and the sea separated the Greek city-states. Moreover, the Greeks did not wish to live in a large country with one ruler. They wanted to be close to the government of their own city and its problems. To them the small city-state was the best possible way of life, the only way they wished to live.

Greek and Phoenician Colonies (About 550 B.C.)

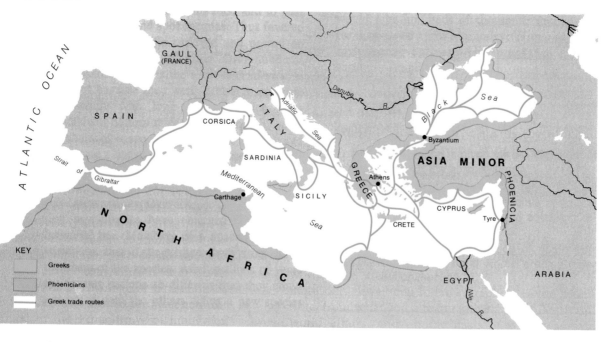

SPARTA

Sparta trains its youth for warfare. In southern Greece was the city-state of Sparta. The Spartans produced no great artists, writers, or philosophers. Culture and learning did not interest them. The Spartans were great warriors, still remembered for their courage in battle.

The Spartans became a nation of heroes. Only by excelling in battle did a Spartan gain the respect and admiration of his fellow citizens. To the Spartan, the war hero was the greatest of men: "He who . . . loses . . . life in winning glory for his city and his fellow citizens, . . . the whole city mourns for him; . . . and his tomb and his children are honored among men; . . . never is his name and fair fame destroyed; . . . though he lies beneath the earth he becomes immortal."

Why did the Spartans put so much stress on courage and war? Early in their history they had conquered a large number of people. These people became state slaves, *helots,* who were assigned to individual Spartans to labor on their farms. Since the Spartans were greatly outnumbered by the helots, the Spartans lived in constant fear of a helot revolt. Only if the slaves were held down by force could the Spartans feel safe. To protect themselves against a slave uprising and to defend Sparta from outside attack, the Spartans turned their land into a military camp. While the helots did all the work, their Spartan masters trained themselves for battle. The Spartan's only purpose in life was to fight for his homeland. Boys who appeared too weak to become soldiers were left to die.

After boys reached seven years of age, they were sent to military camps. Here they lived, learning the art of war, until they were thirty. They toughened their bodies and learned to act bravely at all times and to endure pain. To develop resourcefulness, they were taught to steal. If they returned empty-handed, they were severely punished; if caught in the act, they would also be punished. The Spartan boys thus learned to think and act quickly and to endure

Ancient Greece

c. 2600 B.C.	Beginnings of Minoan civilization on Crete
c. 1600 B.C.	Mycenaean culture develops in Greece
c. 900–c. 600 B.C.	Greek city-states develop
c. 760 B.C.	Greeks begin colonization of Mediterranean
490–479 B.C.	Persian Wars
479–429 B.C.	Golden Age of Greece
431–404 B.C.	Peloponnesian Wars
338 B.C.	Philip of Macedon conquers Greek city-states
336–323 B.C.	Alexander the Great rules

pain. Wrote one Greek biographer: "So seriously did the Spartan children go about their stealing that a youth, having stolen a young fox and hidden it under his coat, let the animal bite and claw him to death rather than let the fox be seen. . . . I myself have seen several youths quietly endure whipping to death."

The Spartans fail to achieve true excellence. The Spartans set out to develop a certain kind of man—a fearless warrior. They succeeded. In all of Greece there were no braver warriors than the Spartans. Other Greeks admired the Spartans for their courage and obedience to authority. But they also criticized the Spartans because their education was too one-sided. It was not enough just to be good in battle. The really excellent man, said the Greeks, did not neglect his mind or ignore art and literature. Thus it is not in Sparta, but farther to the north —in Athens—that we find the best of the Greeks.

ATHENS

Athens is the first democracy. Athens was the leading city-state of ancient Greece. It was also the first state to become a *democracy.* In fact, the word "democracy" comes from the Greek word meaning rule by the people. In other lands the common people had no say in the government. They were ruled by pharaohs,

The ever present sea encouraged the Greeks to become skilled fishermen and traders. Inland, rugged
mountains such as those at Delphi (bottom, left)
hampered agriculture. In the scene at Ios (top) we
can see the division of land into small plots and
the terracing which permits maximum usage of
land. The people winnowing wheat (right) are
using an ancient procedure; their pitchforks and
the paving of their threshing floor have changed
little over the centuries. On the steep slopes
where crops cannot be grown, sheep and goats
have grazed since ancient times, their herders
using the long quiet hours to spin wool (below, right).

kings, or powerful nobles. The citizens of Athens, however, governed themselves. The government of Athens, said the great Athenian (uh-*thee'*nih-un) statesman Pericles (*per'*ih-kleez), "is in the hands of the many and not of the few." Every week the adult male citizens of Athens gathered in a large open area on the side of a hill. Their meeting was the *Assembly,* the lawmaking body of Athens. In the United States we elect senators and congressmen to make laws for us. They are our *representatives.* The number of Athenians was small enough so that representatives were not needed. The citizens themselves sat in the Assembly, debated, and voted. They themselves made the laws for the city, decided whether to sign a treaty, go to war, or make peace. They determined how the city's money would be spent.

The Athenians give mankind a lesson in citizenship. Athenian government officials took care of the public buildings, kept the waterfront safe for ships, watched over the city's food supply, and so on. These officials were *chosen by lot* (a process similar to having your name picked out of a hat). They held office for one year and could not hold the same position again. This gave every male citizen a chance to become a government official. Athenians also served their city by acting as jurors in court cases. The Athenian felt very close to his city. A man who would not attend the Assembly, hold government offices, or serve on juries was looked down upon. He was called a "useless" person. Few people in history have shown such pride in and devotion to their city as did the Athenians.

Athens is a city of free citizens. The Athenians cherished freedom of speech and thought. Citizens could criticize leading generals and statesmen without being punished. In the Assembly everyone was free to say what he thought. The poorest shoemaker had the same right to speak and vote as did the richest landowner. The learned Greek thinker Plato (*pley'*toh) said that Athens "is full of liberty and free speech.

. . . Each man can plan his own life as he pleases." When the Athenians felt that a citizen threatened their freedom, he was exiled from the city. Although Athenian democracy was truly a great achievement, it did have a number of shortcomings. Slaves, foreigners, and women—the majority of the population—had no say in the government.[1]

The Athenians make great contributions to civilization. The Athenians were proud of their democracy and their freedom. They were equally proud of their artists, poets, playwrights, scientists, and philosophers. The Athenians wanted to learn about man and nature and to develop their minds. They believed that a man's life was empty if he did not use his reason. They loved to question and to learn from wise men. They also loved to surround themselves with beauty. Even average citizens could enjoy good plays, good music, and fine art. Today we criticize our city and state governments for putting up public buildings and housing projects that are ugly and drab. The Athenians insisted that all their public buildings be works of art. Perhaps no other people in the history of the world cared so much for the arts and the fine things of life as did the Athenians. Certainly no other people contributed more to civilization. A present-day historian says of ancient Athens: "the contribution made to European culture by this one city is quite astonishing. . . . Athens . . . was clearly the most civilized society that has yet existed."

The Athenians boasted of their superior civilization. They said that they were the teachers of all Greece. But their achievement was greater than that. Today we can say that the Athenians became the teachers of much of mankind. What Pericles told his fellow Athenians some 2400 years ago still holds true today: "Future ages will wonder at us as the present age wonders at us now."

[1] It is estimated that the total population of Athens was over 300,000. This included about 40,000 male citizens, 50,000 slaves, 19,000–24,000 foreigners, and some 200,000 women and children.

What are some important aspects of daily life in Athens? All of life is not just art and thought. What was daily life like in ancient Athens?

1. Home and outdoors. While the Greeks surrounded themselves with beautiful public buildings, the streets of their cities were narrow, muddy, and dirty, their homes small and unattractive. The inside of a Greek house, however, was more appealing than the outside. In homes of the wealthy, there were graceful furniture and beautiful vases and other works of art.

Greece's warm climate led people to spend much of their time outdoors. They gathered with their friends in the marketplace to discuss the news of the day. They also exercised and watched young athletes perform on the athletic fields.

2. Position of women. In ancient Greece women took care of the home and children. They did not participate in public affairs, could not own property, and did not go to school. They were expected to spend their time at home. One Greek writer said that women "must be carefully trained to see and hear as little as possible and to ask the fewest questions." In the main, the Greeks agreed with the thinker Aristotle (*ar'*ihs-tot'l), who said, "the male is by nature superior, and the female inferior, and . . . the one rules and the other is ruled." A playwright wrote: "It is proper for women who are wise to let men act for them in everything." Yet there was much tenderness in marriage. On a Greek gravestone a mourning husband wrote these words: "What profit hath a man whose wife is gone, and who is left alone on earth?" There are also many scenes in Greek literature which show that husband and wife had a deep

In a timeless scene (above) wives in ancient Greece care for the home and spin wool just as women do today. Before settlements grew large, game was still plentiful and hunting (center) was a common occupation. As Greeks colonized other lands, trade increased and merchants became important, as indicated in the detail of a vase (left). They dealt in luxuries and staples such as grains, which could not be raised in sufficient quantity in Greece.

love for each other. In one such scene a worried wife tells her husband as he goes off to war: "It were better for me to go down to the grave if I lose thee."

3. Athletics. The Greeks cherished learning, but they also knew the importance of a healthy and strong body. They admired a beautiful form, graceful movements, and a handsome face. An Athenian drinking song went: "For a man health is the first and best possession, second best [is] to be born with shapely beauty."

To make the body strong and graceful, the Greeks encouraged athletics. The complete man, they said, must participate in sports. Every four years athletic games were held at Olympia. (Our present-day Olympics are a continuation of this ancient Greek celebration.) The best athletes from all Greece competed in races, jumping, throwing the discus and javelin, wrestling, boxing, and other contests. Winners of these events were greatly honored, and poets sang of their deeds. In a dignified ceremony a wreath was placed on the head of the victorious athlete. It was a proud moment.

4. Slavery. Like other peoples in the ancient world, the Greeks had slaves. Today we consider slavery a great evil, but in the ancient world slavery was accepted as part of life. Few disagreed with Aristotle, who held that "some should rule and others be ruled." In Greece, as in other parts of the ancient world, slavery had nothing to do with race or color. Greek slaves were mostly prisoners captured in war. Slaves who worked in the mines of Greece had a short hard life, but household slaves were often regarded as trusted members of the family. Sometimes they were given their freedom and some property.

5. Religion. The Greeks believed in many gods and built temples and held celebrations to honor them. But Greek religion was unlike most other religions. There were no holy books or commandments telling people how to behave; there were no unchanging beliefs that people had to accept. No one was forced to pray in a certain way. Unlike the Hebrews, the Greeks did not draw their attitude toward life from

Throwing the discus is still part of the Olympic Games. Though the technique has changed, required as always are the graceful movement and strength exemplified by this sculpture.

their religion. In time the Greeks began to pay less attention to their old religious beliefs. Some Greek thinkers developed a concept of one God.

CHECK-UP

1. How did geography affect Greek life?

2. Why did the Spartans stress preparation for war? What training did male Spartans undergo from childhood?

3. How did the democratic process work in the city-state of Athens? What privileges and rights did each citizen have? What were the weaknesses of Athenian democracy?

4. What was daily life in Athens like for women? For slaves? Why were athletics important to the Greeks?

The Greek city-states do not achieve unity. The Greeks of the different city-states had many things in common. They spoke the same language, believed in the same gods, participated in the same athletic contests, and considered themselves different and better than non-Greeks, whom they called barbarians. Yet the Greeks were not politically united. Each Greek was loyal to his own city-state. And the many city-states were often at war with one another.

When the mighty Persian Empire threatened to conquer all Greece, the Greeks put aside their own quarrels and united. This was a crucial period for the history of civilization. Had the Greeks been defeated, they might not have developed as rich and lasting a civilization as they did. This would have been a great loss for all mankind.

Persia invades Greece. For years little Athens had been a thorn in the side of the Persian Empire. She had helped the Greek city-states in Asia Minor that revolted against Persia. Athens had even defeated a Persian army sent to punish her. Xerxes (*zerk'*seez), King of Persia, was the most powerful ruler of his time. He decided to use his power to crush the proud Athenians and to conquer all Greece. On foot, on horseback, and by ship, the army of Xerxes —several hundred thousand men and some 500–600 ships—moved towards Greece.

The Persian army reached the Hellespont (*hel'*es-pont), the strait which is part of the waterway connecting the Black Sea and the Mediterranean. Ships were positioned close together with planks laid from one to the next to serve as bridges to carry the huge army across the strait. But when this work was completed, a violent storm smashed everything. Xerxes was furious. He was used to having his own way. According to Herodotus (he-*rod'*oh-tus), an ancient Greek historian, Xerxes "gave orders that the men responsible for building the bridges should have their heads cut off," and that the sea should be whipped three hundred times. As the Persians swung their whips, they shouted: "You salt and bitter stream, your master lays this punishment upon you for injuring him, who never injured you. But Xerxes the King will cross you, with or without your permission."

The Spartans show their courage. Finally the Persians crossed the Hellespont and made their way into Greece. They approached the mountain pass of Thermopylae (ther-*mop'*ih-lee), which was defended by some 7000 Greeks led by 300 Spartans. For two days the Persians attacked, but the Greeks, although badly outnumbered, heroically defended the pass. The Persians could not break through. Then a Greek traitor showed the Persians how they could attack the Greeks from the rear. Realizing their danger, most of the Greeks retreated to safety. Only the 300 Spartans and a handful of other soldiers refused to retreat. Death was certain, but for the Spartans there could be no other way. Retreat was dishonorable. Wrote Herodotus: "Here they resisted to the last, with their swords if they had them, and, if not, with their hands and teeth, until the Persians, coming on from the front over the ruins of the wall and closing in from behind, finally overwhelmed them."

Persia's navy is destroyed. The Persians advanced into Greece, destroying and burning. The Athenians had to flee from their city. The only hope for the Greeks was to destroy the Persian fleet. Without a navy, communication with Persia would be threatened. The Persians would have to retreat. In the waters of the Bay of Salamis (*sal'*uh-mis) the two navies met in a life-and-death struggle. The Greeks were fighting for their homeland and their freedom. Aeschylus (*es'*kih-lus), a writer of plays, described their fighting spirit:

Ancient Greek World

Forward, you sons of Hellas! Set your country free! Set free your sons, your wives, tombs of your ancestors, and temples of your gods. All is at stake: now fight!*

The battle lasted all day. The Persian navy greatly outnumbered the Greek fleet. But this

* From Aeschylus, *The Persians,* in *Prometheus and Other Plays,* translated by Philip Vellacott (Harmondsworth, Middlesex, England: Penguin Books Ltd., 1961). Reprinted by permission.

was no advantage. The Persian ships were crowded together in the narrow strait between Salamis and Attica (*at'*ih-kuh). Attacked by the swifter Greek ships, the Persian fleet soon was in a state of confusion. Some Persian ships were sunk, others collided with each other. Many were captured; the rest fled. The sea was filled with wreckage. The bodies of Persian

MACEDONIA

THRACE

EPIRUS

Aegean

Sea

Hellespont

PERSIAN EMPIRE

✗ Thermopylae

Delphi ●

Plataea ✗   ✗ Marathon

Salamis ✗   ★ Athens

ATTICA

SAMOS

Olympia ●

DELOS

PELOPONNESUS

★ Sparta

RHODES

Mediterranean   Sea

KEY

▨ Athenian Empire

✗ Battles in Persian Wars

CRETE

Athenian Empire About 450 B.C.

sailors and soldiers were washed up on the shore.

The depth of horror Xerxes saw; close to the sea
On a high hill he sat, where he could clearly watch
His whole force both by sea and land. He wailed aloud,
And tore his clothes, weeping.*

In 479 B.C., a year after their great victory at Salamis, the Greeks also defeated the Persians on land.

Against tremendous odds, the Greeks had fought the Persians and won. Never did the Greeks have greater pride in being Greek. There is no people like us, they said. The victory over the Persians helped bring on a

---

* From Aeschylus, *The Persians,* in *Prometheus and Other Plays,* translated by Philip Vellacott (Harmondsworth, Middlesex, England: Penguin Books Ltd., 1961). Reprinted by permission.

golden age of Greek culture when Greek art and drama reached their height.

Athens dominates an alliance of city-states. Because they feared still another attack from Persia, many of the Greek city-states remained united to protect themselves. They called their *alliance* the Delian (*dee'lih-un*) League, an association of independent city-states which agreed to aid each other in the event of war with Persia. Athens soon came to dominate this league. The other city-states realized that they were losing their independence not to Persia but to Athens, which had set out upon the path of empire.

The Peloponnesian War causes great suffering. Sparta decided that Athenian power must be checked before it was too late. Once again the Greeks were at war—this time with each other. The war between Athens and Sparta, called the Peloponnesian War,[2] lasted 27 years. Many other Greek city-states became involved in the fighting between Athens and Sparta. There was great suffering and destruction throughout Greece. The war, finally won by Sparta, revealed a major weakness of the Greeks. They were unable to live peacefully with each other. War, which seemed the normal way of life for the city-states, helped bring about their downfall.

The Greeks are conquered. By the middle of the fourth century B.C. the weakened Greek city-states were threatened by another powerful enemy. To the north of Greece was the land of Macedonia (mas-eh-*doh'*nih-uh). Led by King Philip, the Macedonians developed a well-trained army. When Macedonia threatened Greece, the city-states united too late and with too little. Consequently, they were unable to hold off the Macedonians. By 338 B.C. the

---

[2] Peloponnesian (pel-oh-pah-*nee'*zhun) is derived from the term used for the southern peninsula of Greece, the Peloponnesus, where Sparta was located.

Greek city-states had lost what they loved most —their independence and their freedom.

After Philip was murdered, his son Alexander, then 20 years old, came to power. Alexander was a remarkable person. Before becoming a king and commander, he had studied science, mathematics, and philosophy with the great Athenian philosopher Aristotle, and he loved to read poetry. Proud, ambitious, and with a will of iron, Alexander was determined to conquer the huge Persian Empire which had united the ancient Near East. He succeeded: his troops conquered Egypt and other lands of the ancient Near East, advancing all the way to India without losing a battle. Alexander also proved himself to be a wise ruler. He built cities and encouraged trade and the spread of Greek civilization. He tried to unite Greeks and the peoples of the Persian Empire under one government in which the two peoples would live together as brothers.

When Alexander died at the age of 33, his empire was divided among his generals. In the years following Alexander's death contacts between Greeks and the peoples of the ancient Near East increased. Each learned from the other. But the kingdoms established after the breakup of Alexander's empire did not retain their independence. By the first century B.C. they, along with other countries in the Mediterranean world, had fallen to the Romans, the greatest conquerors of the ancient world.

CHECK-UP

1. Why was Persia determined to defeat Athens? How were the Greeks able to defeat Persia?

2. What were the causes of the Peloponnesian War? Why was the war a tragedy?

3. What kind of man was Alexander? What kind of ruler was he?

Alexander's Empire in 323 B.C.

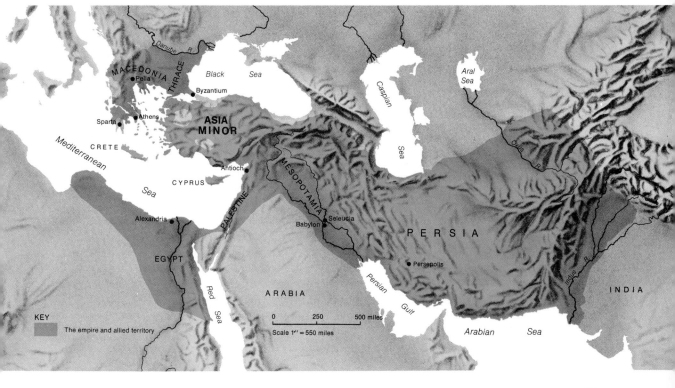

KEY
The empire and allied territory

0   250   500 miles
Scale 1" = 550 miles

Although the Greeks were conquered, Greek civilization never died. It spread throughout the Mediterranean world and lives on today in the civilizations of Europe and America. What were some of the achievements of Greek civilization?

DEMOCRACY

The Greeks made important advances in government and politics. They developed the concepts of democracy and active citizenship. The government in most of the ancient Greek city-states, especially in Athens, was run by the people. There was freedom to think as one wished and to express one's opinions. There were elections, jury trials, written constitutions, and debates. The Greeks stressed the importance of good citizenship and rule by law. Their concept of the citizen has served as a lasting example through the ages. From the ancient Greeks later peoples learned much about how to govern themselves.

PHILOSOPHY

Greek philosophers raised basic questions about life. Our word *philosophy* (fih-*los'*oh-fee) is derived from a Greek word meaning "love of wisdom." Philosophers ask and try to answer vital questions about man and nature. The first true philosophers in the western world were Greek. Many of the questions that mankind has been struggling to answer for centuries were first asked by the Greeks: What is beauty? What is the best form of government? What is good? What is the purpose of education? What is justice? What is the purpose of life? How did the world begin? Of what is it made?

Socrates urges man to understand and develop himself. Socrates (*sok'*ruh-teez) was a simple Athenian stonecutter. He never wrote anything. Yet he is regarded as a great teacher-philoso-

pher, perhaps the greatest in history. Socrates went around asking people questions. Always polite and never raising his voice in anger, the wise Socrates urged his fellow Athenians to think about how they lived their lives. "No greater good can happen to a man than to discuss human excellence every day," he said. Socrates left a strong impression on his audience. Said one of his admirers:

When I heard Pericles and other good orators, I thought them fine speakers, but I felt . . . no confusion in my soul or regret for my slavish condition; but . . . [Socrates] has . . . very often . . . [caused me to think that] the life I lead was not worth living. . . . For he compels me to admit that I am very [wrong] in going on neglecting my own self. . . . I am ashamed before him and before no one else.

What was Socrates trying to accomplish? Why, after 2400 years, is he still considered so important?

1. Acquiring knowledge. Socrates wanted people to see how little they really knew. Once man recognized his own ignorance, he would wish to acquire knowledge.

2. Character training. Socrates wanted men to be concerned about their character and their own souls. Man struggles to get money and power, said Socrates, yet he neglects what is most important—making himself as good a person as possible. To his fellow Athenians, Socrates would say: "My good sir, you are an Athenian, a citizen of the city which is . . . noted for its wisdom and power; are you not then ashamed to be worrying about your money and how to increase it, . . . instead of worrying about the knowledge of good and truth and how to improve your soul?" Socrates urged men to do good and to avoid evil. He believed that the purpose of education was to mold character, to make of man something that was beautiful and good. This, he felt, was the highest aim in life.

3. Mastery of self. To achieve a good character, said Socrates, man must learn to master himself, to control his emotions, and to develop his mind. Behavior must be dictated by the mind and not by the heart. Without self-control and clear thinking, a man cannot achieve excellence of character.

Socrates' questioning arouses opposition. In the marketplace, surrounded by a crowd, Socrates asked his questions. When Socrates showed the Athenians how little they really knew, they were embarrassed. He made enemies among the leading men of Athens. They accused him of harming the youth of Athens by asking disturbing questions. For a good part of his life Socrates had questioned the practices of the day and discussed philosophy with all who would listen. No harm had come to him, for Athenians had the right of free speech and free thought. But after the war with Sparta, Athens felt the letdown and uncertainty of defeat. During these troubled times, Socrates was brought to trial. Had he agreed to give up teaching, had he begged forgiveness, he would have received only minor punishment. But Socrates refused because to do so would be going against his conscience. Even when death threatened, the old philosopher remained true to himself. A man of worth, said Socrates, does not think about "the chances of life and death when he acts." He cares only about "acting justly or unjustly." Socrates told the jury that he would not appeal to them "with weeping and wailing, or say and do many other things which . . . are unworthy of me. . . . I would very much rather defend myself as I did, and die, than as you would have had me do, and live. I think that it is a much harder thing to escape from wickedness than from death."

Socrates was convicted and ordered to drink poison. To the Greeks the supreme test of a man's character was how he met death. Socrates, to the very last, remained noble, dignified, and wise. His death, like his life, reflected credit on a great Athenian.

Although his friends urged him to delay drinking the poison until the last possible moment, Socrates refused. "I think that I should gain nothing by drinking the poison a little later but my own contempt for so greedily saving up a life which is already spent." He then "drank the poison quite calmly and cheerfully" and gently rebuked his friends when they wept over their misfortune at losing him. Within a short time Socrates, whom his student Plato called "of all the men of our time the best, the wisest, and the most just," was dead.

Plato finds fault with democracy. Plato was Socrates' most famous follower. Like his beloved teacher, Plato also stressed the importance of knowledge and good character. Plato lived in difficult times. Athens had not recovered from the Peloponnesian War; the wise Socrates had been executed. The citizens of Athens seemed less devoted to their city; their leaders were criticized for being selfish and dishonest. Plato blamed democracy for the troubles of Athens. Whereas most Athenians believed in their democratic way of life, Plato attacked it. What were Plato's criticisms of democracy?

1. Mob rule. In a democracy all the people help to run the government. Plato did not believe that most people had the knowledge or the experience to help make decisions about spending government money, declaring war, or making new laws or an alliance with another city-state. Such decisions required sound judgment and clear thinking. But, said Plato, the average person cannot be trusted to think clearly. He is easily confused, and jumps to conclusions without thinking. His decisions are influenced by his prejudices. Yet in a democracy we allow such people to sit in the Assembly and vote. For Plato, democracy meant mob rule.

2. Poor leaders. Moreover, said Plato, democracy fails to produce good leaders. The democratic leader is more concerned with staying in power than with doing what is right. He tends to do what will make him popular with the people. If the people shout for war, the democratic leader will not try hard to keep peace.

The people will be properly governed, continued Plato, only when the wisest men, the philosophers, are given power.

... there will be no end to the troubles of states, or indeed, ... of humanity itself, till philosophers become kings in this world, or till those we now call kings and rulers really and truly become philosophers. ... There is no other road to happiness, either for society or the individual.

Philosopher-kings would not be interested in money or power. They would not act out of ignorance or prejudice. Nor would they be pushed by the excitable common people into making bad decisions. These philosophers would spend many years getting the education and experience needed to become rulers. They would be the wisest and best of men, the only ones fit to govern. Under Plato's system, the common people would lose their right to take part in the government, but, said Plato, they would be sure of having just and able rulers.

For over 2000 years men have discussed and debated the ideas of Plato. His message, says French philosopher Alexandre Koyré, "reaches out to us across the centuries." From reading Plato, says Koyré, we can learn much:

Watch out, [Plato] warns us. See to the education of the city, of its future citizens, of its future governors. Do not restrict yourselves to training them for a specific job, trade, or function: moral education, respect of truth, devotion to the city [are] what make good citizens. Never forget that friendship and the spirit of helpful cooperation form the link that holds the city together. ... Never allow discord, fear, and hatred to take root in the State.

Watch out: do not allow distrust of law to gain a foothold ... in your city. Distrust for law is the poison that causes the complete dissolution of the State. ...

Be on guard: choose carefully those who are to hold the reins of public power.

Aristotle is both a philosopher and a scientist. Aristotle had studied at the academy established by Plato. He wrote on many topics—government, drama, art, biology, physics. Like other Greek philosophers, Aristotle wondered about good character, the good life, and the meaning of happiness. He, too, insisted that a man who never develops his mind can never be truly happy. "Educated men are as much superior to uneducated men," said Aristotle, "as the living are to the dead."

Aristotle was one of the first great scientists. He wanted to learn everything about nature. He studied plants, animals, and the heavens. He kept careful records of his observations. Like a good scientist, Aristotle believed that a theory should be accepted only if it "agrees with the observed facts." For centuries people used the writings of Aristotle as we would an encyclopedia.

SCIENCE AND MEDICINE

The Greeks make many contributions to science. The Greeks were as interested in science and mathematics as in philosophy. They had what all scientists need—curiosity. Greek scientists believed that man had the intelligence to understand nature. The Hebrews regarded the universe as God's creation. They believed that man had been placed on earth not to study nature but to carry out the teachings of the Lord. The Greeks, on the other hand, were curious about nature. They wanted to make sense out of it. They wanted to know how the universe began, of what it was made, and how it worked. They were the first to suggest that it was regulated by laws of nature. They tried to discover these laws through reason. One Greek thinker, with the insight of a modern scientist, said that all things were made of tiny indestructible atoms. Because the Egyptians and Mesopotamians saw gods and demons as the causes of changes in nature, they could never become true scientists. The Greeks, on the other hand, rejected magic. They sought a rational (naturalistic and logical) explanation for why things happened. By removing the gods from storms, rivers, and trees, the Greeks enabled man to examine and analyze nature.

Greek science reaches its height in the period after the death of Alexander the Great. In the period after the death of Alexander the Great, Greek science made great strides forward. Astronomers (those who study the planets and stars) said that the earth was round. They calculated the distance from earth to the moon and to the sun, and figured out the number of days in a year. This was all done without a telescope. While most Greek astronomers believed that earth was the center of the universe, Aristarchus (ar-is-*tar'*kus) correctly maintained that earth and the other planets moved about the sun. But this was too startling an idea to be accepted by many people of his time. The mathematician Euclid (*yoo'*klid) developed the geometry that serves as the basis for the geometry now studied in our schools.

The greatest scientist of this period was Archimedes (ahr-kih-*mee'*deez). He made many inventions and discovered laws of chemistry, physics, and mathematics. When the Romans attacked the city where Archimedes lived, machines developed by him and other scientists were used to beat back the attackers. An ancient writer described the scene:

Archimedes . . . shot against the [enemy on] land . . . all sorts of missile weapons, and immense masses of stone that came down with incredible noise and violence, against which no man could stand. . . . In the meantime huge poles thrust out from the walls . . . sunk some [of the ships] by [letting fall] . . . great weights . . . upon them; [other ships were] lifted up into the air by an iron hand or beak. . . .

. . . arrows and darts . . . inflicted a great slaughter among [the Romans], and their ships were driven one against another; while they themselves were not able to [strike back] in any way. . . .

. . . the Romans [were so terrified] that, if they did but see a little rope or a piece of wood from the wall, [they] instantly [cried] out that there it was again, Archimedes was about to let fly some

engines at them; [and] they turned their backs and fled.

The Greeks develop medical science. The foremost medical school of the ancient world was located on the Greek island of Cos. It reached the height of its fame under the leadership of Hippocrates (hih-*pok'*ruh-teez). The doctors at the school of Hippocrates were true scientists. They studied diseases, took notes on the appearance and behavior of sick people, and kept a careful record of medicines and methods used to treat patients. They were kind to their patients. "Sometimes give your services for nothing," said one of these doctors, "for where there is love of man there is also love of the art [of medicine]." Unlike other doctors, the medical men trained by Hippocrates questioned the common belief that diseases were caused by the gods. They believed that men who said the gods cause an illness were hiding behind their own ignorance. Doctors today take an oath that was first used in the school of Hippocrates: "I swear . . . that, according to my ability, . . . I will follow that system of [treatment] which . . . I consider for the benefit of my patients. . . . With purity and with holiness, I will pass my life and practice my art [of medicine]."

THE ARTS AND HISTORY

The Homeric hero seeks honor. The Greek storyteller Homer was one of the first poets of the western world. So magnificent was Homer's verse that even today some consider him the greatest poet in the history of western civilization. Homer wrote about an early period in Greek history. He described the deeds of noble warriors who proved their worth in battle. To the Homeric hero what counted most was his honor and reputation. He hoped to win "a glorious name" in battle, and thus be remembered forever. But the true Homeric hero was more than just a brave warrior. In addition to being courageous, he was also a man of intelligence and character. He was, said Homer, "both a speaker of words and a doer of deeds."

In the following passage from the *Iliad* (*ihl'-ih-ad*), Andromache (an-*drom'*uh-kee) begs her husband Hector not to fight. Hector answers in the spirit of a Homeric hero:

"Hector," she said, "you are possessed. This bravery of yours will be your end. You do not think of your little boy or your unhappy wife, whom you will make a widow soon. . . . And when I lose you I might as well be dead. There will be no comfort left, when you have met your doom—nothing but grief."

"All that, my dear," said the great Hector, . . . "is surely my concern. But if I hid myself like a coward and refused to fight, I could never face [my people]. . . . Besides, it would go against [my nature], for I have trained myself always, like a good soldier, to take my place in the front line and win glory."

Homer helped shape the attitudes of the ancient Greeks. Young students grew up reciting his poems. From Homer the Greeks learned to respect courage, honor, and loyalty. They sought to imitate the Homeric heroes who combined "nobility of action with nobility of mind."

The entire populace attends the theater in Greece. The Greeks were the first, and perhaps best, writers of plays. These were presented in outdoor theaters built into the side of a hill. The theater in Athens, for example, held 18,000–20,000 people. Once a year a series of plays was put on. The opening day was eagerly awaited by Athenians and foreign visitors. It was a public holiday. Prisoners were released from jail so that they could watch the performances. Money was given to the poor so that they too could buy

At theaters such as the one shown below, Greek drama and comedy were performed in settings of natural beauty. The themes of these ancient Greek plays still are relevant and many of the plays are produced today. Dressed in the traditional robes and wearing the masks which were an integral part of Greek plays, modern actors perform Sophocles' masterpiece, Oedipus Rex.

seats. Women wore their finest clothes and jewelry. Many people brought lunches to the theater, for the performances lasted from sunrise to sunset. A day at the theater could be very exciting. A nineteenth-century British historian says of the Athenian audience that they expressed

their feelings in the most unmistakable manner. The noise and uproar produced by an excited crowd of 20,000 persons must have been . . . deafening. . . . The ordinary [ways] of signifying pleasure or disgust were much the same in ancient as in modern times. . . . [They] consisted of hisses and groans on the one hand, and shouts and clapping of hands on the other. The Athenians had also a peculiar way of marking their disapproval of a performance by kicking with the heels of their sandals against the front of the stone benches on which they were sitting. Stones were occasionally thrown by an irate audience.

There are two types of Greek plays—tragedy and comedy. Tragedies described the sufferings, triumphs, and weaknesses in the lives of great men. Because they dealt with the great questions of life, the themes of Greek tragedies have remained modern through the centuries. Euripides' (yoo-*rip'*ih-deez) protest against the destruction caused by war was written for all time and all peoples:*

I mourn for my dead world, my burning town,
My sons, my husband, gone, all gone! . . .

Come, you widowed brides of Trojan fighting-men,
Weeping mothers, trembling daughters,
Come weep with me while the smoke goes up from Troy![3]

Tragedies also expressed the Greek view of life —that men who are too proud will suffer misfortune. If men let success go to their heads, if

---

* From Euripides, *The Women of Troy,* in *Prometheus and Other Plays,* translated by Philip Vellacott (Harmondsworth, Middlesex, England: Penguin Books Ltd., 1961). Reprinted by permission.

[3] Troy: city in northwest Asia Minor, destroyed by the Greeks after a ten-year war.

they think themselves as powerful as the gods, if they achieve success unjustly, they eventually will be punished. As an example, the Greeks pointed to the fate of the Persian Emperor Xerxes, whose dreams of conquest were too ambitious. Instead of conquering Greece, the mighty Xerxes saw his forces destroyed.

Greek playwrights could also be lighthearted. In their comedies they ridiculed politicians, generals, philosophers, and other well-known figures. Aristophanes, the greatest of the Athenian comic poets, used his sharp wit to plea for an end to the destructive war with Sparta and to attack what he considered a decaying educational system. Some of his lines are among the most hilarious in world literature.

The Greeks are lovers of beauty. No other people in the ancient world, perhaps in all of history, loved beauty as much as did the Greeks. In their temples, public buildings, theaters, and statues—even in their vases and coins—the Greeks sought to produce works of art that might be admired forever.

Beauty of style . . . and grace and good rhythm depend on simplicity. (PLATO)

We are lovers of the beautiful, yet simple in our tastes. (PERICLES)

Beautiful but simple. This is a good description of Greek art. The Greeks sought beauty in forms that were true to nature. They tried to build temples and statues that were as simple, graceful, and well-balanced as nature's finest creations. Art to them was a challenge. Their artists tried to build or carve forms such as nature intended, without the flaws and imperfections caused by accident or chance. A Greek statue showed man at his best, without a flaw, without a weakness—an athlete with a perfect body in motion, a woman with a perfect form.

The Greeks seek to learn the lessons of history. The Greeks were greatly interested in history. By studying the past, they hoped to learn how men have acted and thought in difficult times. They believed that the history of the past provided lessons for the present, for human nature does not change. The two greatest Greek historians were Herodotus, who wrote about the Persian Wars, and Thucydides (thoo-*sid'*ih-deez), who described the war between Athens and Sparta.

Thucydides was greatly concerned with accuracy. He believed that history must not be written by the ignorant or the prejudiced. The historian should always search for the truth. He must check all his facts; his conclusions must be based on evidence. Thucydides made a special effort to provide an accurate report of events.

VIEW OF LIFE

Over the centuries, men have been inspired by the Greek attitude toward life. Perhaps the most significant contribution made by the Greeks was their conception of the good life. They believed that a man should give careful thought to how he leads his life. "The unexamined life," said Socrates, "is not worth living." For the Hebrews, the good life meant obeying the laws of their God. What did the Greeks mean by the good life?

1. Moderation. The good life, said the Greeks, was one of moderation. The moderate man does not give in to all his desires. He does not eat, drink, or even sleep too much. He has other interests than games, clothes, and money. He has a healthy body and a sound mind. Above all, he has self-control. His emotions never get the best of him but are always ruled by his reason. He is never boastful or excessively proud. Greek leaders were careful to behave moderately. Many rulers of other lands, however, acted differently. They had monuments built to reflect their power and expected their subjects to treat them as gods. The gods rule in heaven, said such rulers, and the king is their representative on earth. All men must humble themselves before him, for, being chosen by the gods to rule, he becomes godlike.

Greek leaders were utterly different. They never lost sight of the fact that they were human beings. They deliberately tried not to overstep the bounds of moderation. As British historian Gilbert Murray says, "There must be . . . no triumph, no boasting, no maltreatment of the enemy dead, no killing of prisoners of war." When Alexander the Great demanded that his subjects treat him as a god, his Greek soldiers lost much of their respect for him. They regarded this lack of moderation as a weakness in character that prevented a man from living the good life. "Moderation," said an ancient Greek playwright, is "the noblest gift of Heaven."

2. Versatility. To lead a good life, a man must be versatile—capable of doing many things. He should be able to understand mathematics, discuss philosophy, appreciate art, take part in the affairs of his city, and keep in good physical condition. The versatile man would never find life boring. Because he had many and varied interests, people would not be bored with him.

3. Intelligence. Few peoples have admired intelligence as much as did the Greeks. The Greeks insisted that ignorance prevents a man from living a good life.

The Hebrews believed that in the Old Testament God had revealed to man how to live the good life. To live properly, man had only to carry out God's commandments. For the Hebrews "the fear of the Lord is the beginning of wisdom." The Greeks, on the other hand, felt that man, by using his mind, could reason out his own rules of behavior. The Hebrews wanted only to live by the word of God and cared nothing about uncovering the secrets of nature. They felt that man needed no further explanation of how the world began than that given in the Old Testament. The Greeks had a tremendous desire to learn everything about the world around them. They were never afraid to ask questions, or to use their minds to find answers. The Hebrews are noted for their prophets, messengers of God who were deeply concerned with man's sufferings and who foretold what would happen if God's laws were violated. The Greeks

Much of our knowledge of Greek art comes from Roman copies. In the mosaic (top) a Roman artist copied a Greek painting of Alexander's (far left) victory over Darius (center), the King of Persia. Greek art also influenced India. In the Buddhist relief above, the faces and postures are Asian, but the draperies are of Greek origin. In the masterful Nike (Winged Victory) of Samothrace (right), the Greek sculptor captured the impression of rushing wind.

are best represented by their philosophers, men of thought to whom the acquiring of knowledge gave meaning to life. Through the Greeks, western man learned that the highest aim of life is not to gain power or pleasure but to seek knowledge.

4. Freedom and participation. The Greeks believed that freedom was essential for the good life. Only by allowing citizens to participate in government could a city prosper. Only in such a free society could a man fully develop his artistic and intellectual talents and become a complete man.

5. Humanism and excellence. Like the Mesopotamians, the Greeks knew that life was often cruel. For one thing, it ends too quickly. We never fulfill all our dreams. Moreover, life is often filled with hardship and grief. "The lot of man [is] to suffer and die," wrote Homer. But whereas the Mesopotamians had a low opinion of man and felt life to be meaningless, the Greeks believed that man was capable of doing great things. They agreed with the playwright Sophocles (*sof'*oh-kleez), who wrote: "Wonders are many on earth, and the greatest of these is man." Placing a great value on man and his abilities is called *humanism.* The Greeks, the first true humanists, concentrated on getting the most out of life in this world. They believed that man's true greatness lay in the full development of his talents, in developing the best that was within him. "Always be the best, always be above all others," a Homeric father instructed his son. By striving for excellence in everything they did, the Greeks found meaning in life. The man who could create great works of art, or write beautiful poetry, or achieve victory in an athletic contest, or do his duty as a loyal citizen, or understand the secrets of nature—such a man achieved true excellence. He was fit to walk with the gods.

A people with such a view of life deserve to be remembered forever. For centuries men have admired the Greeks for their wisdom, their talents, their love of freedom, their appreciation of beauty, and the rich and full lives they lived. We have much to learn from them today.

CHECK-UP

1. What democratic principles did the Greeks develop? What were Plato's criticisms of democracy?

2. What is philosophy? What was Socrates trying to accomplish? Why did he make enemies?

3. Why is Aristotle considered a many-sided genius?

4. What contributions did the Greeks make in science and medicine?

5. What view of life is reflected in Greek tragedies? Why does Greek drama still move us today?

6. What did the Greeks mean by the good life? What qualities must man develop to lead one?

Summing Up

Geographic conditions fostered the rise of city-states in Greece and encouraged sea-borne commerce. Two city-states stood out—Sparta for its warriors, and Athens for its artists, writers, and philosophers. Democracy first evolved in Athens. The Athenians built beautiful public buildings, served their city in peace and war, and held physical fitness as well as learning in high esteem.

Although the city-states fought among themselves, they united to turn back the invasion of the huge Persian Empire. After that conflict some city-states remained united in the Delian League, dominated by Athens. This led to a long and destructive war between Athens and Sparta. In the fourth century B.C. the weakened city-states were taken over by Philip of Macedon, and his son Alexander extended his conquests from Egypt to India. But when he died at 33 this empire was divided among his generals.

Among the achievements of Greek civilization are contributions to democratic government and politics, to philosophy, to science and medicine, and to the arts and history. The Greek view of the good life stressed moderation, versatility, intelligence, freedom, the worth of man, and excellence.

Chapter Highlights

Can you explain? _____

city-state	representatives	moderation	philosophy
helot	alliance	versatility	humanism
democracy			

Can you identify? _____

western civilization	Euclid	Aristotle	Alexander
Sparta	Assembly	Xerxes	Plato
Athens	Hellespont	Socrates	Salamis
Peloponnesian War	Herodotus	Homer	Macedonia
Hippocrates	Euripides	Delian League	
Pericles	Archimedes	King Philip	

What do you think? _____

1. In what ways was Athens a more balanced society than Sparta?

2. What aspects of Greek civilization do you find most impressive? Why?

3. How does American democracy differ from democracy as practiced by the Greeks? Is there any place for the direct democracy of the Greeks in the present-day United States? Why?

4. Contrast Greek religion and the religion of the Hebrews and the Egyptians.

5. How do you think a citizen of Athens would react to the way an American citizen meets his civic responsibilities?

6. By what method did Socrates hope to lead man to the truth? What did he mean by the truth?

7. Describe a day at the Greek theater. How did Greek plays reflect Greek life?

8. What can we learn about Greek ideals from studying a Greek temple, statue, or vase?

9. How did the Greek view of the good life differ from the Hebrew view? From the Mesopotamian view? What does present-day man consider to be the good life?

10. To learn about the Hebrews we study the works of their prophets; to learn about the Greeks we study the works of their philosophers. Give evidence supporting this statement.

11. Plato had a basic mistrust of the average man's ability to think and act with reason and intelligence. Do you think he was justified? Why or why not?

12. According to the Greeks, man is the greatest of creations. How did they express this belief? Is man as highly regarded in the twentieth century? Why?

The Roman Republic

Defenders of Rome and conquerors of far-flung lands, Roman soldiers were a frequent subject of artists. The Latin warriors (left) typify the sturdy farmer who replaced his tools with weapons when the need arose. Through triumphal arches victorious generals paraded captives and booty. The Arch of Constantine (left and above) is noteworthy for its battle scenes, most of which were taken from earlier pieces of sculpture.

CHAPTER FOCUS

The Struggle for Political Equality in Rome
The Expansion of Rome
Internal Strife Plagues the Roman Republic
The Dictatorship of Julius Caesar

In the beginning of the fifth century B.C., when the Greeks were defending their way of life against the invading forces of the mighty Persian Empire, Rome was just a small town in Italy. In the centuries that followed, Rome conquered and ruled an empire greater than Persia's, greater than Alexander's. It was the largest and best-organized empire of the ancient world, perhaps in all history.

The genius of the Greeks lay in their creativity and their intelligence. They were superb sculptors, architects, philosophers, dramatists, and scientists. The Romans, on the other hand, were distinguished as soldiers, lawgivers, and rulers. They knew how to conquer nations and govern men. When the Roman Empire was at its height, the Mediterranean world knew the blessings of peace and law and order. Millions of men from distant lands and different backgrounds were proud to say that they were citizens of Rome.

The Struggle for Political Equality in Rome

It took Rome centuries to grow from a small town to the capital of a great and efficiently governed empire. In the process Rome was threatened by class warfare, foreign enemies, and civil war. At times it seemed that Rome might not survive these dangers. The story of how Rome struggled to solve her problems can tell us much about the nature of politics and politicians, the problems of government, and the behavior of men under trying conditions. Learning about the Romans and their problems can help us to understand many of the political and social problems of our own times.

Strategically located, the Italian Peninsula is influenced by Greeks and Etruscans. The story of Rome begins in the Italian Peninsula, a land with fertile plains and few good harbors. Italy's geographical position, jutting out into the Mediterranean, aided Roman expansion. Once Rome conquered the Italian Peninsula, her armies could march north and west into Gaul (France) and Spain. Her ships could sail to Illyria (ih-*leer*'ih-uh, in modern Yugoslavia), Macedonia, Greece, Asia Minor, Egypt, North Africa, and Spain.

The Italian Peninsula was inhabited early in history and was influenced by two peoples— Greeks and Etruscans. Greek colonists, who settled in Sicily and southern Italy, brought Greek ideas, arts, and system of writing to the peninsula. Western and northern Italy were settled by the Etruscans, who perhaps came originally from Asia Minor. The Etruscans built cities that contained sewage systems and temples. Both the Greeks and the Etruscans helped to civilize Rome.

Rome becomes a republic headed by two elected consuls. About 509 B.C. an Italian tribe, the Latins or Romans, drove out their Etruscan king and established a *republic*—a government without a king. Under the republic, power was held by wealthy landowners called *patricians* (puh-*trish*'unz). These nobles dominated the government and were determined to keep power out of the hands of the common people or *plebeians* (pleh-*bee*'yunz).

Though the early Romans desired strong leadership, they did not want to be ruled by a king. They replaced the king with two *consuls* from the patrician class. The consuls gave direction to the daily affairs of government, supervised the work of lesser officials, and served as judges. In time of war they commanded the army. The fact that consuls were elected for a one-year period prevented any one of them from gaining too much power. A further safeguard was that the government could not act unless both consuls agreed. In times of emergency, however, the consuls might nominate a *dictator,* one who could exercise full power for a maximum period of six months. In this early period of the Republic only patricians attained the high office of consul.

The Senate has broad powers. In the Republic's early history the senators were drawn only from among the patricians. They held office for life and served as advisors to the consuls and other officials. They also had the power to approve or reject laws passed by the assembly. In time the Senate became the most important part of the government. It controlled the spending of money, determined relations with other lands, and exercised considerable influence over not only the consuls but also the army. The Senate jealously guarded patrician interests and privileges. But it also provided Rome with experienced, capable, and devoted leaders.

Patricians also dominate the assembly. There was also an assembly of soldier-citizens called the *comitia centuriata* (koh-*mit*'ih-uh ken-too-rih-*ah'*tuh). It voted on laws proposed by the government officials, elected the chief government officials (including the consuls), and had the power to make war and peace. While both plebeians and patricians came to serve in the *comitia centuriata,* it was dominated by the nobles. Thus the patricians held a tight grip over the three principal organs of the Roman government—consuls, Senate, and *comitia centuriata.*

Plebeian dissatisfactions lead to concessions by the Senate. The plebeians had many complaints against patrician rule. Interest rates on loans were very high and penalties for nonpayment were merciless. Plebeians who could not pay back their loans lost their land and might be sold into slavery. The patricians controlled the courts as well as the lawmaking bodies. In order to preserve their power, the patricians forbade any intermarriage with the plebeians.

Denied an effective voice in the government and living under difficult economic conditions, the plebeians decided to do something to improve their inferior position. They waged a struggle (called the Conflict of the Orders) with the patricians. In this class struggle, which lasted over 200 years, the common people had one advantage. They were needed as soldiers in wars against Rome's enemies. To put pressure on the patricians, the plebeians threatened not to serve in the army. Recognizing that their services were essential to Rome, the Senators gave in to some plebeian demands.

The patricians did not favor democracy, and they were less than eager to increase the participation of the common people in the government. However, even though they believed themselves best qualified to govern Rome, they were not blindly selfish. Being practical men, they realized that they would have to give the plebeians some rights if Rome were to endure.

What rights do the plebeians win? In the early stages of the class struggle the plebeians won

The Roman Republic

c. **509** B.C.	Roman Republic founded
494–287 B.C.	Conflict of the Orders
c. **270** B.C.	Rome controls Italian Peninsula
264–146 B.C.	Punic Wars (264–241, 218–201, 149–146)
148 B.C.	Rome conquers Macedonia (Greece)
133, 123 B.C.	Gracchi attempt reforms
60 B.C.	First Triumvirate established
c. **47–44** B.C.	Caesar controls Rome
27 B.C.	End of Roman Republic

Ancient Italy

Etruscan history dates back to the early seventh century B.C. Like other Mediterranean peoples, the Etruscans were seafarers who traded with and raided North African cities and Greek colonies in Italy. They also farmed the fertile river valleys of western and northern Italy. Etruscan civilization had considerable impact on Roman customs and art. Although the Romans overthrew the Etruscan king, for two centuries the Etruscans were permitted to retain their language and cultural traditions. Etruscan homes were decorated with scenes of daily life. In the ceremony pictured above, musicians play the reed pipes and lute, instruments in common use throughout the Mediterranean world. The sympathetic portrait of a married couple (right) is a profound expression of tenderness and love.

the right to form their own assembly, the *concilium plebis* (kohn-*kil*'ih-um *pleh*'bis). This Plebeian Assembly had two important powers: (1) It could elect *tribunes*—officials who would protect all plebeians asking their help. (2) It also could pass laws that affected the common people. At first some acts passed by the Plebeian Assembly had to have the approval of the patri-cian Senate. But in 287 B.C. the Senate lost its right to veto acts of the Plebeian Assembly.[1]

[1] By the middle of the fourth century B.C. there were three lawmaking assemblies in Rome: *comitia centuriata, concilium plebis* (Plebeian Assembly), and *comitia tributa* (trih-*boo*'tuh, Assembly of the Tribes). The two Assemblies became virtually fused and may for practical purposes be considered as one.

A major complaint of the plebeians was that Rome had no written code of laws but only customs and traditions handed down from the past. This absence of written laws, the plebeians believed, made possible unfair arrests and harsh punishments. About 449 B.C., because of the pressure exerted by the plebeians, the customary laws were put down in writing. The new Roman law code, called the Twelve Tables, gave the plebeians some protection against unfair and cruel patrician officials.

In their struggle for equality, the plebeians won other victories. Soon after the Twelve Tables were drawn up, the plebeians gained the right to intermarry with patricians. In less than a century higher positions in government, including that of consul, were opened to plebeians. Interest rates on loans were reduced, and it became much more difficult to enslave a man who had failed to repay a loan.

Class lines are less sharp but Rome is not a democracy. After two centuries of struggle, the plebeians were considered equal by law to patricians. They were able to hold the most important positions in the state, to enter the Senate, and to have a voice in lawmaking. These revolutionary changes in the Roman government were generally accomplished peacefully, a tribute to the political wisdom of the early Roman Republic.

Nevertheless, Rome was not a true democracy. Political power still was largely in the hands of an upper class made up of patricians and wealthier plebeians. In general only rich plebeians held the office of tribune. Though the tribunes were supposed to aid the common people, they tended to side with the patricians. Sometimes patricians arranged for their daughters to marry politically powerful plebeians. Such marriages strengthened the alliance between patricians and wealthy plebeians. To maintain their position as the upper class, patricians bribed members of the Assembly. And although some plebeians were members of the Senate, this powerful body remained under patrician control.

It was in the Senate that the most influential citizens of Rome debated the vital issues of the day. The Senate gave a sense of direction to the Roman Republic, particularly during the early period of Rome's great expansion (264–133 B.C.). The patricians tended to identify their own interests with those of Rome. Yet for centuries the patricians served Rome well and provided able leadership.

CHECK-UP

1. What powers did the Roman consuls have? What safeguards prevented them from becoming too powerful?

2. Why was the Senate the most important body in the Roman government? What powers did the Assembly have?

3. What were the complaints of the plebeians? How did they force the patricians to make concessions? What rights were won?

The Expansion of Rome

Rome began as a little town on the Tiber (*tie'-ber*) River. By 133 B.C. the Romans had not only unified Italy, but fought victorious land and sea wars which made their country the foremost power in the Mediterranean world.

The first stage in Roman expansion is gaining control of the Italian Peninsula. Uniting Italy was no easy matter. Roman expansion was resisted by Etruscans and Italian tribes and by the Greek city-states in the southern part of the peninsula. The mountains that run north and south in the peninsula interfered with troop movements. By the middle of the third century, however, Rome had emerged as the unchallenged ruler of the Italian Peninsula. In the process of conquering Italy, the Romans demonstrated a devotion to their city, a toughness of character and a genius for warfare. They knew how to wage war successfully, how to gain allies, and how to treat a defeated enemy. These are the basic skills of empire builders. Let us analyze them.

Roman farmers make brave soldiers. The Italian Peninsula was largely conquered by armies made up of Roman citizens. Each male citizen was a soldier. When soldiers were needed, the Roman farmer put down his farm implements and took up his weapons. Each citizen-soldier provided his own weapons. The wealthier citizens served in the cavalry, those of medium wealth in the heavy infantry, and the poor formed lightly armed troops.

The sturdy Roman farmer made an excellent soldier. Strong of body, loyal to his city, and experienced in battle, the Roman soldier was capable of marching over thirty miles a day despite the fact that armor, weapons, and other equipment might weigh as much as eighty pounds.

The Roman is a well-disciplined soldier. Soldiers who deserted their post, lost their weapons, or fled from battle were disgraced. "They may not return to their own country nor would anyone . . . receive such a person into his house," wrote an ancient historian.

. . . those soldiers who have once fallen into misfortune are utterly ruined. . . . Consequently it sometimes happens that men confront certain death at their stations, because, from their fear of the punishment awaiting them at home, they refuse to quit their posts; while others, who have lost shield or spear on the field of battle, throw themselves upon the foe, in hopes of recovering what they have lost, or of escaping by death from certain disgrace.*

* Polybius, *The Histories,* translated from the text of F. Hultsch by Evelyn S. Shuckburgh (London: Macmillan and Company Ltd., 1889). Reprinted by permission.

Not only the fear of punishment but also the promise of glory and prizes caused the Roman soldier to fight hard. Soldiers who had distinguished themselves in battle were praised by their commanders in front of the other soldiers and were rewarded with gifts:

In the capture of a town those who are first to mount the walls are presented with a gold crown. The recipients of such rewards not only enjoy great glory among their comrades in the army and an immediate [fame] at home, but after their return home they are marked men in all solemn festivals. They alone, who have been singled out by the consuls for bravery, are allowed to wear robes of honor on those occasions, and moreover they place their awards in the most conspicuous places in their houses, as visible tokens and proofs of their valor. No wonder that a people whose rewards and punishments are allotted with such care should be brilliantly successful in war.*

The Romans develop superior battle formations. The Romans did not use better weapons than their enemies. All peoples had virtually the same weapons—swords, spears, daggers, bows and arrows, and stones. Roman advantage lay in superior discipline and organization. The Romans adopted and improved upon battle formations first used by the Greeks. While opponents often fought in the manner of an unorganized mob, the Romans formed three lines 250 feet apart. When the enemy approached within twenty or thirty yards, the front line hurled javelins (light spears) to inflict casualties and spread confusion in the enemy ranks. Then this first line charged with swords extended like bayonets. This procedure was repeated by the second line. The third line, consisting of hardened veterans, was held in reserve. It was rarely needed. This formation, refined and improved over the years, gave courage and confidence to the Roman soldier. He knew that he could count on his disciplined comrades to do the task assigned them.

* Polybius, *Ibid.*

Rome shows wisdom in dealing with friend and foe. In the conquest of Italy, Rome did not always fight alone. When there was a common foe, Rome formed alliances with Italian states. Furthermore, Rome was skillful in turning former enemies into friends. Some defeated foes were granted Roman citizenship; others were permitted to retain their local self-government. All the Italian states welcomed security from foreign attacks and an end to internal warfare. Mindful of these and other benefits of Roman rule, the peoples of the Italian Peninsula came to accept Rome as the head of a military and diplomatic alliance.

The conquest of the peninsula made Rome a great power. It also started her on the road to empire. Roman expansion into lands bordering the Mediterranean was not part of a deliberate plan. Indeed, some Roman leaders opposed involvement in foreign adventures. They did not want Rome to extend her power beyond the borders of Italy. But it seems as though it is almost impossible for a great nation not to use its power to further its interests, not to get involved in the quarrels of other states, and not to acquire outlying territory. Almost unwillingly, Rome built an empire.

Carthaginian expansion threatens Rome's allies. On the coast of North Africa, at the point where Africa is nearest Italy, was located the ancient city of Carthage (*kahr′*thihj). Founded in the ninth century B.C. by the Phoenicians, Carthage had gained her independence and become a prosperous and powerful city. In time she controlled a large part of the North African coast, parts of Spain, and the Mediterranean islands of Corsica, Sardinia, and Sicily. Carthaginian merchants carried on a rich trade with these lands and with Africa south of the Sahara. The Carthaginian presence in the islands off the coast of Italy was interpreted by some Romans as a threat to Rome as well as to the south Italian cities that were allies of Rome. When Carthage moved to gain control of the narrow waterway separating Sicily from

the Italian mainland, Rome feared that the Carthaginians next would launch an attack against Rome's south Italian allies. Although not eager for war, Rome claimed she had an obligation to protect her Italian allies. Thus in 264 B.C. Rome became involved in a long and destructive struggle with Carthage.

Rome builds a navy to challenge Carthage. Without a large navy, Rome had no chance of defeating Carthage. Rising to the challenge, Rome built fleets and engaged Carthage in war at sea. The Romans soon found a way of using their disciplined soldiers to advantage in naval warfare. When the Romans pulled close to an enemy ship, they lowered a gangplank to its deck. Across it raced Roman soldiers, and in the hand-to-hand fighting which followed, the Romans almost always won. But Rome also met with setbacks. Hundreds of ships and over a hundred thousand men were lost in storms. Probably in no other naval war in all history have so many men died by drowning.

Despite these disasters, Rome never considered making anything but a victor's peace with Carthage. Carthage, exhausted by the long struggle and aware that her hired soldiers had lost their fighting spirit, made peace in 241 B.C. Rome received Sicily in the peace settlement, and three years later took the islands of Sardinia and Corsica.

In 218 B.C. Carthage and Rome again go to war. Carthaginian attempts to expand in Spain led to a second war with Rome. Carthage was led by Hannibal, one of the most remarkable generals in history. Hannibal planned to invade Italy and capture the city of Rome. Instead of attacking by sea, he decided to cross the Alps and invade the Italian Peninsula from the north. With a veteran army of 40,000 foot soldiers and cavalry, as well as war elephants, Hannibal advanced from Spain across southern Gaul into Italy. Across the steep and icy mountain passes of the Alps struggled the Carthaginians. Sometimes man and beast lost their

At one time Carthaginian coins were widely used in the Mediterranean world. This coin, minted about 221 B.C., shows the secret weapon with which Hannibal hoped to conquer Rome.

footing and plunged to their deaths. But Hannibal and his men never lost heart. Some 26,000 fighting men finally descended into Italy, ready to do battle with Rome.

For almost fifteen years Hannibal wages a victorious war in Italy. In 216 B.C. at Cannae (*kan'ee*), a battle which still is studied in military schools, Hannibal showed his genius as a commander. He deliberately pulled back the center of his army, thus drawing the Romans into a pocket. Meanwhile the Carthaginian cavalry swung around to the rear of the tightly packed Roman soldiers. The Romans were thus trapped between Hannibal's infantry and cavalry. With a force of some 45,000 men (including barbarian tribesmen from Gaul), Hannibal defeated a Roman army of 60,000 men. Twenty-five thousand Romans were killed and 15,000 captured. It was one of the worst disasters in Roman history.

The Roman historian Livy described the battlefield:

All over the field Roman soldiers lay dead in their thousands. . . . Here and there wounded men, covered with blood . . . were dispatched by a quick blow as they struggled to rise from amongst the corpses; others were found still alive with the sinews in their thighs and behind their knees sliced through, baring their throats and necks and begging who would to spill what little blood they had left. Some had their heads buried in the ground, having apparently dug themselves holes

and by smothering their faces with earth choked themselves to death.

Rome was shocked when it learned of the defeat. "The streets were loud with the wailing and weeping of women," wrote Livy. All Rome feared that Hannibal would now march on the capital. To prevent panic, the Senate ordered women and children to stay at home. Desperate for manpower, Rome armed 8000 slaves. Adding to Rome's difficulties was the defection of some Italian allies to Hannibal. But the Romans remained firm. They did not, says Livy, breathe a word about peace.

Hannibal fails to deal Rome a knockout blow. After the victory at Cannae, Hannibal hoped that all the Italian allies would rise against Rome. But he was mistaken. Most remained loyal to Rome, proving the wisdom of Rome's generous policy towards the conquered Italian states. Finally, Rome was strong enough to threaten Carthage, and Hannibal had to withdraw from Italy. Returning to North Africa, he was defeated in 202 B.C. As a result, Carthage lost all her territory except that bordering the capital, paid Rome a large indemnity (sum of money), and surrendered all war elephants and all but ten warships to her Roman conquerors.

In the second war with Carthage Rome, despite terrible defeats, was victorious in the end. The Romans had never lost heart. Misfortune served only to increase their determination. The Romans sometimes lost battles, but not wars. This firmness of character helps to explain why Rome was able to build a great empire.

Some Romans demand the destruction of Carthage. Although Carthage was too weak to be a threat, many Romans hated and feared the city. Because of these feelings, Rome burned Carthage to the ground after a brief third war. The destruction of the city was witnessed by the Roman historian Appian (*ap'ih-un*) who also recorded the thoughts of the Roman general in command:

Scipio looked over the city which had flourished for over 700 years since its foundation. . . . [It] had ruled over such extensive territories, islands, and seas, and been as rich in arms, fleets, elephants, and money as the greatest empires, but . . . had surpassed them in daring and high courage. . . . Though deprived of all its arms and ships, it had yet withstood a great siege and famine for three years, and was now coming to an end in total destruction; and he is said to have wept and openly lamented the fate of his enemy. After meditating a long time on the fact that not only individuals but cities, nations, and empires must all inevitably come to an end, . . . he quoted the words of Hector from Homer—"The day shall come when sacred Troy shall fall, and King Priam[2] and all his warrior people with him." And when Polybius, who was with him, asked him what he meant, [Scipio] turned and took him by the hand, saying: "This is a glorious moment, Polybius; and yet I am seized with fear and foreboding that some day the same fate will befall my own country."

[2] Priam (*pry'*um): ruler of the Asia Minor city of Troy when it fell to the Greeks.

Rome expands eastward. Victory over Carthage made Rome supreme in the western Mediterranean. During the long period of wars with Carthage Rome had also expanded in the eastern Mediterranean, into lands that had belonged to Alexander's empire. By 133 B.C. Rome had conquered Greece, Macedonia, and part of Asia Minor, and Egypt had become her ally. And this was still not the end of Roman expansion.

Rome allows conquered peoples considerable self-government. The eastern part of the empire was tied to Rome by alliances, and local rulers remained in power as long as they obeyed Rome. Western lands were organized as provinces under governors appointed by the Roman Senate. Rome allowed her provincial subjects a large measure of self-government and did not interfere with the religions and local customs of these subjects. British historian R. H. Barrow sums up Rome's attitude towards the conquered lands.

Growth of Roman Power (264–202 B.C.)

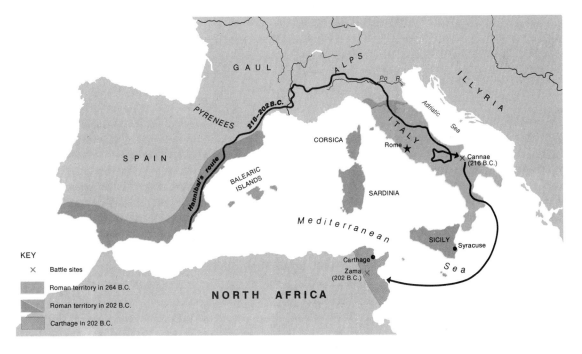

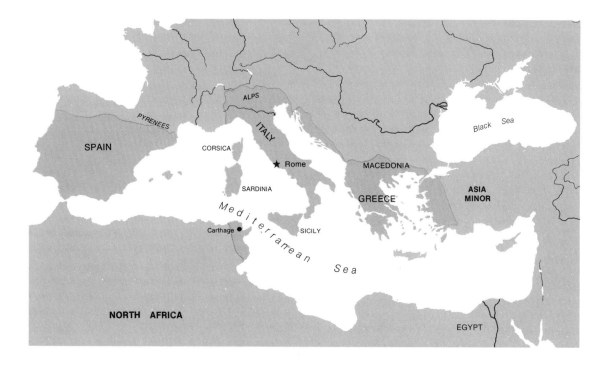

Growth of Roman Power (133 B.C.)

Rome never fought to impose a political idea or a religious creed; with unique generosity she left local institutions and manners of thought and life untouched. She fought to "impose the ways of peace," and by peace she meant the positive blessings of settled order and security of life and property with all that those blessings imply.

The new provinces present problems for Rome. Rome treated the people in these conquered provinces differently from the way she had treated the Latin and Italian allies. Whereas the latter were drafted into the Roman army, the provincials served only in an emergency. Rome was sure neither of the loyalty of the people in the provinces outside the peninsula nor of their readiness to meet Roman standards of discipline.

Roman primacy in Italy had aroused little opposition. The same could not be said of Roman rule in the provinces, which had to pay taxes to Rome. Roman governors, tax collectors, and businessmen found the provinces a source of quick wealth. They "swooped down . . . like crows on the bloody battlefield after the battle," writes a twentieth-century historian. Whereas provincials welcomed the peace and security provided by Roman rule, they complained about being unfairly used for Rome's profit. From time to time Senators concerned about misgovernment in the provinces protested, and minor reforms were instituted. But in general the exploitation continued.

Rome uses brutal but effective measures to crush rebellion. When tribesmen in the province of Spain took to robbery, revolts, and breaking agreements with Rome, the Roman commander dealt with them severely:

[He said to the rebelling tribesmen]: . . . Of course, . . . poorness of soil and [poverty] forced you to do these things. If you wish to be friendly, I will give you a good land for your poor people and settle them in three divisions, in a fertile country.

[Tricked] by these promises, they . . . came together at the place where [the commander] directed. He divided them into three parts, and showing to each division a certain plain, he commanded them to remain in this open country until he should assign them their places. Then he came to the first division and told them as friends to lay down their arms. When they had done so, he . . . sent in soldiers with swords who slew them all, they, meanwhile, crying aloud and invoking the names and faith of the gods. In like manner he hastened to the second and third divisions and destroyed them while they were still ignorant of the fate of the first.

CHECK-UP

1. What qualities did a good Roman soldier possess? Compare him with the Spartan soldier. Why were the Romans usually victorious in battle?
2. Why was Hannibal considered a military genius? Why did he fail to defeat Rome?
3. How did the Romans meet the Carthaginian challenge? Why did they destroy Carthage?
4. What were Rome's policies toward conquered peoples both in Italy and in foreign lands?

Internal Strife Plagues the Roman Republic

From 509 B.C. to 133 B.C. two major movements dominated the history of the Roman Republic. One was the Conflict of the Orders—the struggle of the plebeians to win more nearly equal rights with the patricians. A second was the growth of Rome from a small city-state into a great empire.

From 133 B.C. to 27 B.C. two developments were noteworthy: (1) the struggle of the poor to improve their standard of living; and (2) the rise of *demagogues* (*dem'*uh-gogs), ambitious army commanders who wished to take over control of the Roman government.

Rome experiences a crisis in agriculture. In the second century B.C. the small farmer, the sturdy and loyal Roman citizen who served his nation well in war, was losing his land. During the war with Hannibal much of the land in Italy was ruined. Farmhouses and farm equipment were destroyed; farm animals were slaughtered. Since the small farmer lacked the money to restore things to normal, wealthy landowners were able to buy farms at a low price. While the small farmer was being squeezed out, prisoners of war in large numbers were brought to Italy to work as slaves on large plantations called *latifundia* (lat-ih-*fun'*-dih-uh). Small farmers who formerly had in-creased their income by working part time for wages on neighboring large estates no longer were needed. Sinking ever deeper into poverty and debt, they gave up their land and went to look for work in the cities of Italy, particularly Rome.

Landless and idle poor and exploited slaves endanger Rome. Some Romans were disturbed by the growth of large estates in the countryside and the plight of the poor. They realized that the thousands of landless peasants who came to Rome had little chance of employment. Unhappy and restless, these former peasants had become an impoverished laboring class. They were a source of danger to the Republic. Moreover, the large number of slaves also posed a threat to Rome. When slaves in Sicily revolted against their masters, Roman armies had to fight for three years before they could crush a slave army of some 60,000. Greatly concerned by these conditions, Tiberius Gracchus (*grak'*us), who came from one of Rome's most honored families, made himself the spokesman for land reform:

The wild beasts that roam Italy have their dens and lairs to shelter them, but the men who fight and die for Italy have nothing but air and light. Homeless . . . they wander about with their wives and children. . . . It is for the wealth and luxury of others that they fight and die. They are called masters of the world, [but] they have no clod of earth to call their own.

Should the state provide land for the landless?

Tiberius Gracchus offered a simple solution for the problem of the landless peasant. The state should limit the size of large estates and give the peasant land even if it meant taking land from some of the wealthy. Tiberius Gracchus was elected tribune in 133 B.C. In trying to introduce reforms, he made enemies in the Senate. Men of wealth thought him dangerous, a threat to their property and to the power of the Senate. They wanted to maintain conditions as they were, with wealth and power concentrated in the hands of a few leading families. When Tiberius Gracchus sought re-election as tribune—at that time a violation of Roman tradition—Senators killed him and perhaps 300 of his followers. Their bodies were dumped into the Tiber.

The Senate eliminates a second Gracchus reformer.

The cause of land reform next was taken up by Gaius Gracchus, a younger brother of Tiberius Gracchus. An emotional and gifted speaker, Gaius Gracchus won the support of the common people and was elected tribune in 123 B.C. He went even further than his brother in demanding reform. And being more clever, he tried to win the support not only of the poor but of other groups within the state. In one law pushed through by Gaius Gracchus businessmen were given government contracts to collect taxes in the eastern part of the empire. Gaius Gracchus also promised citizenship to more Italians. By another law the city poor were given grain by the state at less than half the market price. Gaius Gracchus also reintroduced his brother's plan for distributing land to the poor. Like his brother, Gaius Gracchus aroused the anger of the wealthy nobles in the Senate. A brief civil war raged in Rome, during which Gaius Gracchus (who may have committed suicide) and 3000 of his followers per-

ished. The Gracchi had failed, and most of their reforms were set aside.

The Senate had won in its struggle against the Gracchi, but Rome had lost. For as long as there were land-hungry peasants and hundreds of thousands of city poor, there was danger of civil war. Discouraged and angry with their lot, the city poor lost faith in Rome. They gave their support to clever politicians who provided food at low cost and free admission to games. Had Rome been able to provide work for the unemployed, perhaps the Republic would have survived.

By killing the Gracchi, the Senate had substituted violence for reason in dealing with basic issues. The test of good government is its ability to solve internal problems peacefully. The attacks on the Gracchi and their followers introduced murder as a means of coping with a troublesome opposition. Rome had entered a period of violent political conflicts in which each side sought to destroy its opponents.

Loyalty and patriotism grow weaker.

Rome in the first century B.C. was very different from the Rome that had defeated Hannibal, destroyed Carthage, and conquered Macedonia and Greece. Fear of Carthage had kept the Romans united and loyal to their country. Capable of magnificent cooperation in fighting foreign wars, the Romans were often bitterly divided over domestic issues. Increasingly the upper classes became more concerned with their personal comforts and interests than with the welfare of Rome. Nobles craved luxury and power. The poor, denied lands and employment, demanded cheap food and free entertainment. They were ready to back whoever made the most glittering promises. The devotion and heroism that characterized the Romans in the early days of the Republic seemed to have disappeared. The Republic had passed the peak of its greatness.

Promises lure the poor to volunteer for army service.

A shrewd commander named Marius (*mair'*ih-us), to bring his army up to strength,

Besides triumphal arches, Roman sculptors excelled in making statues in stone and bronze. The best are so lifelike that they seem capable of speech and movement. In the bust of Caesar (right) the sculptor has captured the great Roman leader's dignity and strength of character. The above painting of a young couple shows how the Romans adopted the Etruscan practice of wall painting.

recruited the poor of Rome to serve a long enlistment. This was a necessary move, since there was a shortage of fully qualified manpower. But it was also dangerous. Before this, the army was made up of draftees who owned property. These soldiers had a stake in Rome and were loyal citizens. The city poor, on the other hand, had long since become disillusioned. They volunteered for service because Marius had promised them money, the spoils of war, and pensions. These soldiers gave their loyalty to Marius rather than to Rome. And they remained loyal to their commander only as long as he made good on his promises.

Marius had set an example that other ambitious commanders would follow. A popular general who wins the loyalty of the city poor can build a powerful army with which to seize supreme power. In time Rome would be torn by civil war as generals used their troops to further their own ambitions.

The Gracchi brothers had been sincere reformers who sought the support of the poor in order to help them. Later, the men who appealed to the city poor were chiefly interested in personal power. They promised the poor cheap grain and free land and recruited them into their armies for selfish reasons.

Demagogues come into conflict with leading senatorial families. The Senate felt that Rome must be governed by a small group of her best citizens. Earlier these families had used force to prevent the Gracchi from weakening the authority of the Senate. They were equally opposed to later leaders who sought to establish one-man rule in Rome.

Conflict between the Senate and the Assembly further undermined the Republic. When threats to Roman rule broke out in Asia Minor, both claimed the right to name the commander to lead Rome's legions. The Assembly favored Marius; the Senate, Sulla. In the brief civil war that followed, Sulla captured Rome and thus won the right to the command in Asia Minor. But while Sulla was away, Marius seized power in Rome. When Marius died shortly after, his place was taken by his adopted son. Sulla's return to Rome after a successful campaign led to bloody riots. Having defeated Marius the Younger, Sulla became dictator of Rome. Though he had absolute power, his chief interest was in the welfare of Rome. He believed that the best way to protect Rome from future demagogues was to strengthen the power of the Senate. Sulla therefore restored the Senate's right of veto and limited the powers of the tribunes. Having put through these reforms, he retired.

Although Sulla's motives were good, his actions had hurt Rome. Like Marius, he had resorted to violence. In a "good cause" Sulla had displayed frightening cold-blooded cruelty. Without any legal sanction, his chief opponents had been marked for death, their property confiscated (seized by the public treasury), and their children and grandchildren declared ineligible for public office.

CHECK-UP

1. What was the predicament of the Roman farmer? What solutions were offered by the Gracchi? What was the outcome?

2. Why did the poor follow Marius? Why did this create a dangerous situation for Rome?

3. How did Sulla come to power? What changes did he make in Roman government? Were his policies good for Rome? Why?

The Dictatorship of Julius Caesar

The Senate proved incapable of exercising the power and leadership that had been restored to it by Sulla. Soon other leaders eager for power fought each other for supremacy in Rome. In 60 B.C. two army leaders—Pompey and Julius Caesar—and a wealthy banker named Crassus agreed to take over Rome. For the next ten years this group, called the Triumvirate (try-*um'*vih-reyt), ruled Rome. They eventually fought with each other and Caesar, the ablest of these men, emerged as the unchallenged leader of Rome. Who was Caesar? What is his place in history?

Julius Caesar displays great ability and a driving ambition. Named consul in 59 B.C., Caesar realized the importance of a military command in the struggle for power. He therefore got himself appointed commander of the legions in Gaul. The following year he began the conquest of that part of Gaul outside Roman control. His campaigns in Gaul and his invasion of Britain showed Caesar to be a brilliant military commander, greatly admired by his loyal troops. His victories alarmed the Senate, which feared that Caesar aimed to become the ruler of Rome. With the support of Pompey, who was jealous of Caesar's success, the Senate ordered Caesar to give up command of his army. Giving up his command would leave Caesar defenseless. For Caesar there was no choice. With his loyal troops he marched on the city of Rome.

Once again civil war raged in the peninsula and in the provinces. Pompey's army proved no match for Caesar's troops and gradually opposition was put down throughout the provinces. Seeing that Caesar was certain to be victorious, the Senate had him appointed dictator in 46 B.C. As undisputed master of the state

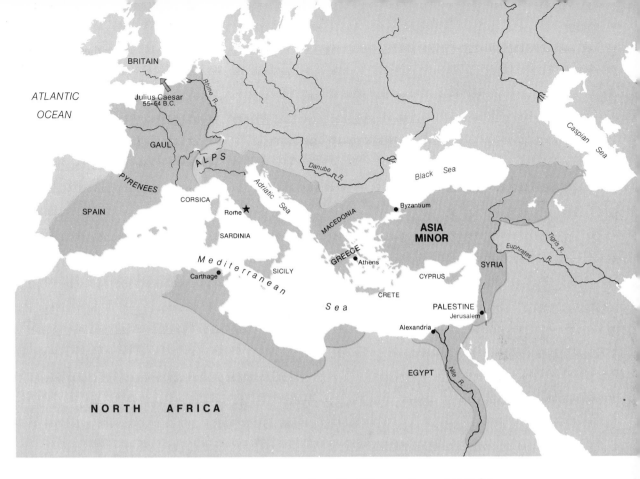

ATLANTIC
OCEAN

BRITAIN

Julius Caesar
55–54 B.C.

Rhine R.

GAUL

ALPS

PYRENEES

Danube R.

Black Sea

Caspian Sea

SPAIN

CORSICA

Adriatic Sea

Rome ★

SARDINIA

MACEDONIA

Byzantium

ASIA
MINOR

GREECE

Athens

Euphrates R.

Tigris R.

SYRIA

Mediterranean

SICILY

CYPRUS

Carthage

CRETE

Sea

PALESTINE
Jerusalem

Alexandria

EGYPT

Nile R.

NORTH   AFRICA

Caesar was free to use his best judgment in governing the Roman world.

Caesar introduces reforms and provides efficient government. Caesar realized that under the Republic Rome had suffered too often from unrest and violence. Her leaders seemed chiefly concerned with increasing their own wealth and power. The people were no longer devoted to Rome. Caesar knew that only strong leadership could keep Rome from collapse. For nearly two years, 46–44 B.C., Caesar ruled Rome with absolute power. But he realized that he must win the support of the provinces and of the common people if he wished to stay in power. He therefore reformed the system of collecting taxes in the provinces, eliminating much of the stealing and corruption that had become common. He made it easier for people in the provinces to become citizens and even

Growth of Roman Power (44 B.C.)

made it possible for provincials to be elected senators. He settled 100,000 of Rome's poor in the provinces, giving them land.

Caesar had the energy, intelligence, and qualities of leadership needed by a great statesman. Many historians have paid tribute to his many talents. Writes American historian Charles Alexander Robinson, Jr.:

With the possible exception of Alexander the Great and Hannibal, Caesar was the most brilliant military genius the world had thus far produced. He was, too, a master of simple prose, an orator of great clearness and force, and [a tireless] builder of public works. His . . . personality [was] so warm that it won the passionate devotion of his followers. He was mild to the conquered; and when political enemies laid down their arms, they found him a friend and benefactor. Beginning as

77

an unscrupulous politician, Caesar grew into a great statesman. He righted the most grievous wrongs; . . . he held out to the inhabitants of the whole empire a picture of a happier, more stable, and more prosperous life.

Caesar's vanity and love of power arouse opposition. Roman nobles, jealous of his success and afraid of his ambition, grew to hate Caesar. They feared that, in his quest for absolute power, he would destroy the Senate and end Roman self-government forever. The Republic which had existed for over four and a half centuries would be destroyed. To prevent this from happening, a group of nobles assassinated Caesar on March 15, 44 B.C. Cicero, a distinguished Roman statesman, orator, and man of letters, summed up the mood of the assassins. "Our tyrant deserves his death," said Cicero, for his "was the blackest crime of all. . . . [He was] a man who was ambitious to be king of the Roman people and master of the whole world. . . . The man who maintains that such an ambition is morally right is a madman, for he justifies the destruction of law and liberty."*

Caesar's death does not restore the Republic. The assassination of Julius Caesar led to renewed civil war as rival leaders once again competed for power. Octavian (ahk-*tey'*-vih-un), Caesar's adopted son, ultimately defeated all rivals and become the unchallenged leader of Rome. Like Caesar, Octavian was determined to put an end to the violence and civil wars that were destroying Rome. Like Caesar, he believed that Rome must have strong leadership. By becoming absolute ruler of Rome, Octavian succeeded in restoring order. His rise to power marks a dividing line in Roman History.

From 509 B.C. until Octavian became master of Rome in 27 B.C. Rome had been a self-governing Republic. With Octavian one sees

*From *Roman Civilization, Sourcebook I: The Republic,* edited by Naphtali Lewis and Meyer Reinhold (New York: Columbia University Press, 1955), p. 294. Reprinted by permission.

the beginnings of imperial rule in the Roman Empire. For the next 500 years Rome would be ruled by emperors. In the next chapter we shall analyze the achievements of Octavian and examine highlights of imperial Rome.

CHECK-UP

1. What qualities made Julius Caesar great? Why were the Senate and Pompey opposed to Caesar?

2. What reforms did Caesar introduce to win the support of the common people and of the provinces? Why did opposition develop to his rule?

Summing Up

Rome gradually expanded from a town to a state with far-flung boundaries. Her soldiers demonstrated loyalty to the state, bravery, and skill in battle. The Roman capacity for turning former enemies into friends, sense of justice, and efficient government contributed to Rome's power in the Italian Peninsula. Rome built an empire by defeating Carthage and the states of the eastern Mediterranean. Gradually she pushed her European borders northward.

Long-standing tensions between upper and lower classes became serious during the second century B.C. when a growing number of patricians established latifundia which squeezed out small farmers. The idle and landless poor flocked to the city of Rome, where they posed a threat to law and order. Many of them were lured into the army by commanders who promised them plunder and pensions. Instead of the traditional loyalty to the state, these men were loyal to their generals. This enabled army leaders to gain control of Rome. Julius Caesar, the ablest of these men, was named dictator by the Senate. He introduced long-needed reforms and restored efficient government. But his growing power led to his assassination in 44 B.C.

Chapter Highlights

Can you explain?

consul	alliance	patrician	plebeian
republic	demagogue	dictator	provincials
legion	tribune	latifundia	land reform

Can you identify?

Cannae	Carthage	Julius Caesar	Plebeian Assembly
Sulla	Senate	Pompey	Hannibal
Gaul	Triumvirate	Twelve Tables	Tiberius and Gaius Gracchus
Marius	Etruscans	Conflict of the Orders	

What do you think?

1. What problems plagued the Roman Republic? Does the United States today have any similar problems?

2. What talents did the Romans display in building their empire? Compare their policies for governing an empire with those of the Persians.

3. What might your life be like if you were living in a Roman province? What were the advantages and disadvantages of Roman rule?

4. How did the Gracchi appeal to the poor? Was this approach better than that used by Marius? Why?

5. What caused poverty in ancient Rome? What causes poverty in the United States today?

6. Why are reformers such as the Gracchi brothers often regarded as dangerous by their government?

7. Why did patriotism and loyalty to Rome decline?

8. Did Sulla's ideals ignore realities of the situation in Rome? Explain.

9. What qualities did Alexander, Hannibal, and Caesar have in common?

Left: Temple, Baalbek (Lebanon)
Below: Aqueduct, Nîmes (France)
Right: Theater, Leptis Magna (Libya)

The Roman Empire

CHAPTER FOCUS

Imperial Rule in the Roman Empire and
the Roman Peace

Society and Culture

The Rise of Christianity

The Decline and Fall of Rome

The Legacy of Rome

Excellent engineers, Roman architects adapted Greek architecture to their own needs. Constructions designed for practical use (left) contrasted sharply with those devoted to ceremonies (top). The lower half of the aqueduct, still used as a roadway, reflects the durability of Roman architecture.

Once the enemies of Caesar had been defeated, the struggle for mastery of Rome became a contest between Mark Antony, a friend of Caesar, and Octavian, Caesar's adopted son. Each considered himself the rightful heir of Caesar. Antony allied himself with Cleopatra, Queen of Egypt, who had gained her throne with Caesar's support. In 31 B.C., the forces of Octavian won a decisive naval battle. Shortly afterwards, Antony and Cleopatra committed suicide. At the age of 33 Octavian had become the unchallenged ruler of the Roman world.

Octavian restores order. Octavian's triumph marked the end of almost a century of civil war and political murder. The struggle for power had taken a heavy toll among Romans and Italians, as well as among peoples in the provinces. Greece, Macedonia, and Asia Minor were on the verge of ruin because of property destruction and looting. Dishonest and greedy governors and businessmen had bled the provinces in order to build personal fortunes. The whole empire longed for peace and orderly government. People regarded with awe the man who at long last had brought an end to conflict.

Like Caesar before him, Octavian believed that only a powerful ruler could prevent Rome from collapsing under the weight of its many problems. When Caesar had tried to introduce one-man rule, he had been assassinated by senators who sought to preserve the centuries-old tradition of senatorial leadership. By the time of Octavian, however, the leading families of Rome had come to realize that Rome needed strong rule in order to prevent future disorders. The Roman upper class gave Octavian their willing support. Moreover, Octavian sought to win the confidence of the senators. Instead of trying to take away all the Senate's power, he encouraged the Senate to give him advice, permitted it to administer certain provinces in the Empire, and let it have its own treasury. By allowing the Senate to retain its dignity and some of its power, Octavian won the support of the senators. It was a shrewd move by a man who knew both how to gain and to hold power.

Octavian acquires extensive powers. One of the chief causes of disorder in the Republic had been the growth of professional armies loyal to their commanders rather than to Rome. The Senate had been unable to control these commanders. Determined to prevent ambitious generals from again disrupting Rome's government, Octavian tried to keep an iron grip on the army. He had himself declared its supreme commander. He also received the power to propose and veto laws.

Besides these powers, the Senate gave Octavian various titles which indicated the high regard the Romans had for him. Octavian normally used the title of *Augustus,* which was one also used for the gods and suggested that the bearer held a very high position.

Augustus was regarded as the First Citizen of Rome. This implied that the Republic still existed. Augustus himself claimed that his goal was not to set up one-man rule but to correct the worst abuses of the Republic. Actually, however, Augustus had absolute power. Later emperors eventually abandoned the pretense that the Republic still lived. The rise of Augustus to power thus marks the death of the Roman Republic and the birth of the Roman Empire.

Augustus introduces important reforms. To prevent corruption, Augustus had the activities of governors in all provinces carefully supervised. Moreover, he allowed the provinces a large measure of self-government. Those provinces that were peaceful he placed under the supervision of the Senate. Provinces that were potentially troublesome were placed directly under his own control. As a rule, the Romans did not interfere with the customs or religious beliefs of the provincials. Provincials who served in the Roman army were granted Roman citizenship. This gave them and their families many benefits, and made the provincials feel that Augustus was interested in their welfare. By fighting corruption, ending ruinous wars, and extending citizenship to more people, Augustus helped restore prosperity in the provinces.

Augustus also tried to restore those qualities that had made the Romans a great people—devotion to the state, close family ties, hard work, discipline, simple living. Laws were passed encouraging people to marry and raise families. Some of the poor in Rome found work in the construction of public buildings. But Augustus never managed to solve the problems of unemployment and poverty in Rome, and the city's poor continued to live on the free or cheap grain provided by the state.

Augustus is a very able ruler. Although he had seized power by illegal means and could be merciless with his enemies, the government established by Augustus was highly efficient. While his introduction of absolute rule put Rome on the path of military dictatorship from which the state was never to retreat, Augustus gave Rome peace and a large measure of prosperity. Augustus' greatest mistake was in not working out a plan for determining his successor. Because there was no legal procedure for choosing Rome's ruler, ambitious leaders often resorted to violence in order to become emperor.

The reign of Augustus marks the beginning of Rome's greatest age. For 200 years the vast Roman Empire enjoyed the blessings of *Pax Romana* (*paks'* roh-*mah'*nuh)—the Roman Peace. During this period Rome gave the Mediterranean world peace, law, and good government. The ancient world had never before experienced such a long period of peace and order. The elaborate and efficient system of administration the Romans developed to govern their vast Empire revealed a great talent for organization. Roman officials generally performed their tasks with a sense of duty and with skill. Provincial governors tried not to interfere with the customs of the people in the provinces.

But in two areas of the Empire, Egypt and Judea (joo-*dee'*uh), there was dissatisfaction with Roman rule. Rich in grain, Egypt was forced to provide food for the city of Rome,

Roman Empire

31 B.C.	Roman Empire established
31 B.C.–**180** A.D.	*Pax Romana*
66–70 A.D.	Revolt in Judea
161–180 A.D.	Marcus Aurelius rules
212 A.D.	Citizenship granted to all freemen in Empire
284–337 A.D.	Totalitarian rule of Diocletian and Constantine
376 A.D.	Visigoths cross Danube
378 A.D.	Battle of Adrianople
476 A.D.	Roman Empire in the West falls

Armor decorated with carvings of Roman gods and goddesses and an imposing stance depict Augustus' grandeur.

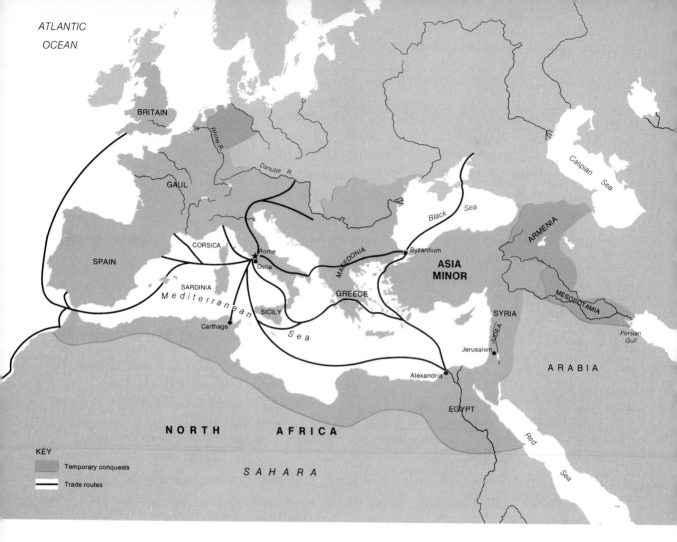

ATLANTIC
OCEAN

BRITAIN

Rhine R.

GAUL

Danube R.

SPAIN

CORSICA

Rome
Ostia

SARDINIA

M e d i t e r r a n e a n

SICILY

Carthage

S e a

GREECE

MACEDONIA

Black   Sea

Byzantium

ASIA
MINOR

Caspian Sea

ARMENIA

MESOPOTAMIA

SYRIA

JUDEA

Jerusalem

Alexandria

EGYPT

Persian
Gulf

A R A B I A

N O R T H   A F R I C A

Red

Sea

KEY

Temporary conquests

Trade routes

S A H A R A

Roman Empire in 117 A.D.

and Roman emperors drained Egypt of its wealth. But it was Judea, the land of the Hebrews, that gave Rome the most trouble. While the Romans generally did not interfere with Jewish religious practices, the Jews still hoped to become independent of Roman rule. As anti-Roman feeling spread, Roman policies became more severe. In 66 A.D. the Jews revolted. After four years of battles, famine, and plagues, Jerusalem fell to the Romans.

The Empire continues to prosper. The emperors following Augustus extended the borders of the Empire in Asia Minor, pushed their conquests in Europe to the Rhine and Danube Rivers, and conquered much of England. In many parts of the Empire the Romans cleared forests, drained swamps, irrigated deserts, and cultivated undeveloped lands. They built roads across mountains and deserts and improved harbors. Hundreds of new cities sprang up, particularly in southern France, and old cities grew larger and wealthier. These cities enjoyed a large measure of freedom and self-government in local matters. From England to the Arabian desert and from the Danube River to the sands of the Sahara some 70 million people, speaking different languages and having different customs, were united under Roman rule. Spaniards and Syrians, Gauls and Britons spoke Latin, the tongue of Rome, traveled on Roman roads, used a Roman system of weights and measures, obeyed Roman laws, swore an oath of allegiance to Roman emperors, and were defended by Roman legions. Almost all were proud and pleased to be called citizens of Rome.

Over the network of roads made safe by Roman soldiers, and across the Mediterranean Sea swept clear of pirates, large quantities of goods were transported. A brisk trade by sea and over land grew up, both with the provinces and with Arabia, Africa, and Asia. Goods from all over the known world flowed into Rome: gold, silver, copper, tin, fruit, and salt from Spain; wool, cheese, ham, and glass products from Gaul; iron, hides, and tin from Britain; wine, honey, and marble from Greece and Macedonia; textiles, olive oil, carpets, and jewels from Asia Minor; leather goods, perfume, drugs, and timber from Syria, Judea, and Arabia; grain from Egypt. From Persia, China, and India, lands beyond the borders of the Empire, Rome received silk, spices, pearls, cotton, jewels, perfumes, and drugs. From African lands south of the Sahara came gold, ivory, wild animals, and black slaves.

The borders of the Empire were defended by the mighty Roman legions. Greek and Roman culture was carried to far-off lands in the Empire. During the 200 years of *Pax Romana,* Rome was ruled by good emperors and wicked ones, by intelligent emperors and by incompetents, by those devoted to Rome and by men who sought only pleasure. Nevertheless, the peace and prosperity endured. The period of *Pax Romana* was one of the finest periods in world civilization. In the words of a Roman writing in the second century, it was

a world every day better known, better cultivated and more civilized than before. Everywhere roads are traced, every district is known, every country open to commerce. Smiling fields have invaded the forests; flocks and herds have [driven out] the wild beasts; the very sands are sown; the rocks are planted; the marshes drained. There are now as many cities as there were once solitary cottages. Reefs and shoals have lost their terrors. Whereever there is a trace of life there are houses and human habitations, well-ordered governments, and civilized life.*

CHECK-UP

1. How did Octavian win the support of the Senate? How did he strengthen his power?

2. What reforms did Augustus introduce?

3. Describe life in the Roman Empire during *Pax Romana.*

Society and Culture

The genius of the Greeks provided the basis of Roman culture. Roman philosophy, literature, science, architecture, law, and Latin, the language of Rome, owed an immeasurable debt to the Greeks. Concludes British classicist Gilbert Murray: "Roman civilization, as it became more perfect, became more Hellenic [Greek] and as it decayed tried to grasp tightly the bits of Hellenism that it still could hold."

ROMAN SOCIETY

Roman society becomes divided into classes.
The structure of Roman society had changed considerably since the days of the early Republic. Under the Republic all citizens, regardless of wealth, were considered equals before the law. By the second century of the Empire, the law divided Roman citizens into two classes. The upper class consisted of senators, successful businessmen, army veterans, and government officials. At the head of this upper class

* Tertullian, *Concerning the Soul,* reprinted from Solomon Katz: *The Decline of Rome and the Rise of Mediaeval Europe.* Copyright 1955 by Cornell University Press. Used by permission of Cornell University Press.

was a small group of wealthy landowners, the senatorial families. The lower class consisted of peasants, artisans, small tradesmen, and the city poor. At the bottom of society were the slaves. If an upper-class Roman broke the law he would probably be punished lightly; a lower-class Roman, on the other hand, might receive much sterner punishment for the same crime. The lower-class wrongdoer might be sentenced to death by crucifixion or to a slower death working in the mines.

There are wide differences in ways of living. Wealthy Romans lived in elegant homes. Their mansions had marble columns, inner courtyards with gardens and fountains, and furniture made of bronze and rare woods inlaid with ivory. The common people, however, lived in three- or four-story apartment houses built over stores. Crowded together in small apartments, the poor faced the usual problems of slum dwellers—crime, fire, and filth.

The upper-class Roman woman took charge of household tasks and household slaves. She enjoyed more freedom than did the women of Greece. She could testify in court and could own property. Upper-class Romans often had high regard for their wives, and consulted them regarding business matters. They expected their wives to charm guests with witty conversation.

As the Empire grew richer, wealthy Romans came to cherish the luxuries of the East and of Africa. Spices and precious stones played a large part in the trade with India, and Chinese silk was particularly prized. Other luxuries came from Africa. Caravans carrying gold, ivory, ostrich plumes, wild animals, and some black slaves crossed the desert from tropical Africa to Roman ports on the Mediterranean coast.

Many upper-class Romans pursue a life of pleasure. Wealthy Romans dressed in fine silks, wore gold ornaments and jewels, and took a lively interest in literature and art. Especially noteworthy were costly banquets in which the wealthy tried to outdo each other in offering elaborate and unusual dishes. Reclining on couches, waited upon by slaves, and entertained by dancers, acrobats, and musicians, Roman nobles dined far into the night on such unusual dishes as boiled ostrich with sweet sauce, roast parrot, flamingo boiled with dates, and sow's udder stuffed with salted sea urchins.

ENTERTAINMENT

Although the Romans adopted Greek drama, their major forms of entertainment were chariot races and gladiatorial contests. The Roman historian Tacitus (*tas′*ih-tus) noted that youths talked of little else: "Really I think that the . . . passion for gladiators and horses [is] all but conceived in the mother's womb. . . . Few indeed are to be found who talk of any other subjects in their homes, and whenever we enter a classroom, what else is the conversation of the youths?"

The Roman audience craves brutality. Roman citizens crowded into amphitheaters such as the Colosseum to watch highly skilled gladiators engage in life-and-death struggles with each other or with wild animals. Perfumed water poured from fountains and music entertained the audience between contests. The holiday crowds expected brutal spectacles, and were seldom disappointed. Often the crowd demanded death for the defeated gladiator. The shedding of blood aroused the spectators to a frenzy. "Kill him," they screamed, "beat him, burn him! Why does he meet the sword so timidly? Why didn't he fight more bravely? Why does he die so unwillingly?" While the gladiators fought for their lives, the spectators gambled on the outcome.

To satisfy the Romans' craving for brutality, hundreds of tigers might be set against elephants and bulls. Wild bulls tore apart men clothed in animal skins; dwarfs or cripples engaged each other in combat. During the reign of the Emperor Titus (*tie′*tus), for example, 5000 beasts were slaughtered in one day. Much of the African trade, in fact, was devoted to supplying the animals for these contests.

In 79 A.D. a sudden eruption of Mount Vesuvius buried the city of Pompeii and most of its inhabitants under molten lava and volcanic ash. Since excavated by archaeologists, Pompeii (above) serves as a grim reminder of what can happen to a city located at the foot of a volcano. Mt. Vesuvius (in the background) has erupted many times since, but never so destructively. Most of the inhabitants of Pompeii had no chance to escape. Their bodies have been found petrified in positions of excruciating agony throughout the ruins of the city (center). Like homes throughout Rome, the homes of Pompeii had walls decorated with frescoes of simple scenes of everyday life, such as the bakery shown at left. A bakery similar to this one was found in the ruins of the city, just as it looked when business was interrupted by the eruption of Vesuvius. The burial by Vesuvius destroyed, but it also preserved. Today, centuries after the Roman Empire fell, the ruins of Pompeii record, in detail far more revealing than any historical document, how the Romans lived and worked.

The Romans also have less sensational forms of amusement. Hunting was always popular, as was boating. Because they lived in a world at peace, Romans were encouraged to travel widely. Simpler forms of amusement were games of chance, especially with dice.

Another less sensational source of pleasure was the public bath. Located in different parts of the city and open to all classes of Romans, the public bath was a social meeting-place. Here, before dinner, the Romans bathed, swam, conversed, read, and relaxed. They could also lift weights, do calisthenics, and have their bodies oiled and massaged.

SLAVERY

The Romans depend heavily on slave labor. Slavery was accepted as an essential part of life in the ancient world. Only a handful of philosophers condemned it. Neither the Hebrews nor the early Christians called for its end.

In the early days of the Republic most slaves were poor farmers who had lost their freedom for nonpayment of loans. Once Rome began to conquer other lands, the number of slaves increased enormously. In the first war with Carthage (page 69), Rome enslaved 75,000 prisoners of war. The conquest of Gaul by Caesar probably brought hundreds of thousands of captives into the Roman slave markets. It is estimated that at the time of Augustus slaves accounted for a quarter of the population of Italy.

Slaves are generally regarded as less than human. During the days of the early Republic, slaves were often treated as if they were not men. Beaten for minor offenses or at the whim of their masters, they were forced to work until they dropped in their tracks. Slaves who displeased their masters might be branded on the forehead, mutilated, thrown to wild beasts in the arena, crucified, or burned alive. Worst treated were the slaves who worked in the mines or rowed the galleys which carried Romans and their goods across the Mediter-

ranean. Slaves also worked on the large plantations. Many were trained to fight as gladiators. More fortunate and more talented slaves became household servants, or even teachers or artists, tradesmen, or artisans.

The lot of slaves improves under the Empire. Because Rome fought few major wars during the period of *Pax Romana,* the number of prisoners of war that could be enslaved decreased sharply. Moreover, many slave owners provided in their wills for the freeing of their slaves. Many who remained enslaved were permitted to develop a trade or to set up small businesses. Some philosophers urged more humane treatment and some emperors passed laws protecting slaves from excessively cruel masters.

PHILOSOPHY

The Romans learn philosophy from the Greeks. Two schools of philosophy dominated the Roman world. One was Epicureanism (ep-ih-kyoo-*ree'*an-is'm), the other Stoicism (*stoh'*-ih-siz'm), and both originated in Greece. The founder of Epicureanism was Epicurus, a Greek philosopher who taught in Athens. Like most Greek thinkers, Epicurus was concerned with the question of human happiness. Man can achieve happiness, said Epicurus, when his body is "free from pain" and his mind "released from worry and fear." He told his followers that happiness could be found in thought and by enjoying simple pleasures such as conversation with good friends or reclining "on the soft grass by a running stream under the branches of a tall tree." There could be no happiness, said Epicurus, when one worries about death.

While some Romans followed Epicurus' teachings, others, especially among the upper class, interpreted his freedom from "worry and fear" to mean the right to do anything that would give pleasure. With a motto of "eat, drink, and be merry," these Romans surrounded themselves with luxury, indulged in enormous banquets and drinking bouts, called for increasingly exotic entertainment, and led immoral lives. Epicurus would have been horrified at the way his philosophy came to be interpreted.

More widely accepted than Epicureanism is Stoicism. Stoicism had more appeal for Romans than did Epicureanism. Stoic philosophers stressed the idea of the brotherhood of man. All men, freeman and slave, Greek and barbarian, are brothers. They should treat each other with decency, kindness, and respect. To be able to live in accordance with moral law was the Stoic's highest ideal. Stoic philosophers believed in the dignity of man. Every human being is precious. No one has the right to abuse, mistreat, or humiliate another human being. The Roman philosopher Seneca (*sen'*ih-kuh) stated: "We are members of one great body. Nature has made us relatives. . . . She planted in us mutual love, and fitted us for a social life. . . . You must live for your neighbor if you would live for yourself."

Seneca also expressed the high-mindedness of the Stoics when he denounced the vicious gladiatorial contests and demanded that slaves be treated humanely. "Kindly remember that he whom you call your slave sprang from the same [human] stock, is smiled upon by the same skies, and on equal terms with yourself, breathes, lives, and dies."

The Stoics urged men to live without luxury, to control their emotions, to be self-sufficient, and to live virtuously regardless of their lot in life. Most famous of the Roman Stoics was the Emperor Marcus Aurelius (*mahr'*kus oh-*ree'*-lih-us), who expressed his beliefs in the following manner:

In the morning when thou risest unwillingly, let this thought be present—I am rising to [do] the work of a human being. Why then am I dissatisfied if I am going to do the things . . . for which I was brought into the world? Or have I been made for this, to lie in the bedclothes and keep myself warm? But this is more pleasant. Doest thou exist then to take thy pleasure, and not at all for action

or exertion? Dost thou not see the little plants, the little birds, the ants, the spiders, the bees working together to put in order their several parts of the universe? And art thou unwilling to do the work of a human being, and dost thou not make haste to do that which is according to thy nature? But it is necessary to take rest also. . . . However, nature has fixed bounds to this, too. She has fixed bounds both to eating and drinking, and yet thou goest beyond these bounds, beyond what is sufficient.

SCIENCE, ENGINEERING, ARCHITECTURE

The Romans care little about scientific theory. The Greeks wanted to understand how the world began and of what it was made. They enjoyed inquiring into the secrets of nature. Such speculation did not interest the Romans. They were concerned with practical science—science that could be used to build roads, bridges, tunnels, and reservoirs. Roman engineers planned roads that were unsurpassed for centuries. They developed an efficient sewage system, and some of the aqueducts they constructed to carry water to the cities of the Empire are still in use. Their practicality was also revealed in medicine. They built hospitals, developed a public health service, and made advances in sanitation, though they had little interest in medical theory.

The Romans are great builders. Roman architecture was greatly influenced by Greek models. However, whereas the Greeks identified beauty with simplicity, Roman buildings were larger and more ornate. In many parts of the Empire the Romans built public buildings, theaters, amphitheaters, public baths, and temples. Architecture, like engineering, revealed the skill of Roman engineers. Instead of requiring a large proportion of interior space for roof support, Roman arches and vaults permitted large open spaces inside buildings. The Romans built things to last. The ruins of Roman buildings can be seen throughout the area occupied by the Empire, and there are even some examples of Roman architecture that are still in use.

LAW

Roman law is one of Rome's greatest contributions to civilization. During the course of its long history from Republic to Empire, Rome developed legal principles and practices that still survive. The law codes of Italy, Spain, France, and Latin America, particularly those provisions dealing with the family, private property, and business contracts, are based on Roman law. Roman law protected the property and person of Roman citizens. Saint Luke wrote in the New Testament: "It is not the Roman custom to condemn any man before the accused meets his accusers face to face and has an opportunity to defend himself against the charge." The law, said the famous Roman writer and orator Cicero, "cannot be bent by influence or broken by power or spoiled by money." Cicero knew that obedience to law is one of the requirements of civilized life. "We are servants of the law in order that we may be free," he said.

Many principles of Roman law still have meaning today. The timelessness of legal principles that evolved in Rome can be seen in the following statements from Roman jurists (lawyers) and legal codes.

According to natural law, all men are equal.

Ignorance of the law does not excuse.

The principles of law are these: to live uprightly, not to injure another man, to give every man his due.*

No one is compelled to defend a cause against his will.

Liberty is a possession on which no evaluation can be placed.

* This statement and those which follow are from *Roman Civilization, Sourcebook II: The Empire,* edited by Naphtali Lewis and Meyer Reinhold (New York: Columbia University Press, 1955), pp. 535, 539, 540, 547–548, 550, 551. Reprinted by permission.

No one suffers a penalty for what he thinks.

. . . every individual is subjected to treatment in accordance with his own action and no one . . . [inherits] the guilt of another.

In inflicting penalties, the age and inexperience of the guilty party must be taken into account.

The burden of proof is upon the party [accusing], not on the party denying.

The credibility of witnesses should be carefully weighed [in judging their testimony]. . . . [One should take into account] whether [a witness'] life is honorable and blameless or on the contrary he is a man branded with public disgrace, . . . whether he is hostile to the party against whom he bears testimony or friendly to the party for whom he gives his testimony.

A father is not a competent witness for a son, nor a son for a father.

If some of the witnesses contradict the others, even though they are a minority [they may] be believed, . . . for it is not to numbers that one must look, but to the sincere credibility of the witnesses and to the testimony in which the light of truth most probably resides.

LITERATURE

The greatest of all Roman poets is Virgil. Virgil did for Roman literature what Homer had done for Greek. In some of the finest poetry written in Latin, the *Aeneid* (eh-*nee'*id), he glorified his beloved Rome. The *Aeneid* is the epic of Aeneas, a Trojan hero whose descendants supposedly founded Rome. Virgil was certain that Rome's destiny was to rule the world. The Greeks might be better sculptors, orators, or thinkers, said Virgil, but only the Romans knew how to govern an empire.

Others . . . shall hammer forth more delicately a breathing likeness out of bronze, coax living faces from the marble, plead causes with more skill, plot with their gauge the movements in the sky, and tell the rising of the constellations. But you, Roman, must remember that this is to be your skill, . . . [to impose the habit of peace], to show mercy to the conquered, and to wage war until the haughty are brought low.

The poet Horace has a deep understanding of human nature. Horace enjoyed both the luxury of the banquet table and the simple pleasures of country life. His poetry touched upon many themes—the pleasures of good wine, the beauty of nature, the benefit of moderation, the molding of character, and the beauty of love and friendship.

Horace urged his fellow Romans to think about how they lived their lives and warned them of the wastefulness of luxury. "Why do we strive so hard in our brief lives for great possessions?" he asked:

The more a man denies himself, so much the more will he receive from the gods. . . . My stream of pure water, my woodland of few acres, and sure trust in my crop of corn bring me more blessing than the lot of the dazzling lord of fertile Africa, though he know it not.*

He instructed the Romans to "reap the harvest of today, putting as little trust as may be in the morrow!" He reminded them of the dangers of civil war and class conflict:

What plain is not enriched with Latin blood, to bear witness with its graves to our unholy strife. . . . What pool or stream has failed to taste the dismal war! What sea has Italian slaughter not discolored! What coast knows not our blood!

Horace could also be lighthearted, as when he wrote about the magic powers of wine:

. . . thou unlockest the thoughts of the wise; . . . thou restorest hope to hearts distressed, and addest power and courage to the poor man, who after thee trembles not at the crowns of angry kings or soldiers' weapons.

* The quotations by Horace are from *The Odes and Epodes of Horace,* translated by C. E. Bennett for The Loeb Classical Library (Cambridge, Mass.: Harvard University Press, 1914). Reprinted by permission.

Ovid writes of love. Ovid's poetry did not approach Virgil's patriotic fervor or Horace's high morality. He preferred to write of wealth, fashion, romance, and the enjoyment of life, and is best known for his advice to lovers. To the man who wants to capture a woman's love Ovid advised:

Just play whatever part she'd have you play:
Like what she likes, decry what she decries,
Say what she says, deny what she denies.
Laugh when she laughs. She weeps? Be sure you
    weep.
Let her dictate the rules your face must keep.*

Ovid had other helpful hints for the lover:†

Don't judge a woman by candlelight, it's deceptive. If you really want to know what she's like, look at her by daylight, and when you're sober. . . .

Tell her how you are pining for her; do everything you know to win her over. She will believe you fast enough. Every woman thinks herself attractive; even the plainest is satisfied with the charms she deems that she possesses. . . .

Tears, too, are a mighty useful resource in the matter of love. They would melt a diamond. Make a point, therefore, of letting your mistress see your face all wet with tears. Howbeit, if you cannot manage to squeeze out any tears—and they won't always flow just when you want them to—put your finger in your eyes.

To the woman out to capture a man, Ovid offered these suggestions:†

If you want to retain your good looks, you must restrain your temper. . . . Rage puffs out the face [and] gorges the veins with blood. . . . If any of you women looked at yourselves in the glass when

* Abridged from *Ovid Recalled* by L. P. Wilkinson (Cambridge, England: Cambridge University Press, 1955). Reprinted by permission.

† Reprinted from *The Art of Love and Other Love Books of Ovid.* Copyright © 1959 by Grosset & Dunlap, Inc. Published by Grosset & Dunlap, Inc. Reprinted by permission.

you were in a raging temper, you wouldn't know yourselves, not one of you! Another thing, just as unbecoming, is pride. You must have a soft, appealing expression if you want to attract a lover. . . .

Your first preoccupation, my dears, should be your manners. When a woman's manners are good, she never fails to attract. Manners indeed are more than half the battle. Time will lay waste your beauty, and your pretty face will be lined with wrinkles. The day will come when you will be sorry you looked at yourself in the mirror, and regret for your vanished beauty will bring you still more wrinkles. But a good disposition is a virtue in itself, and it is lasting; the burden of the years cannot depress it, and love that is founded on it endures to the end.

Juvenal is critical of his fellow men. The Roman poet Juvenal was an angry man who saw evil and vice everywhere. In biting words Juvenal expressed his disgust for the wealthy of Rome. In court "a man's word is believed just to the extent of [his] wealth. . . . Though he swear on all the altars, . . . a poor man isn't believed." When a poor man suffers from a fire, "although he's stripped of all and begging a snack, no one will give him a paltry handout, no one a bed, or even offer him shelter, a roof above his head." But let the great house of a rich man burn, and everyone rushes to his aid. Everyone praises honesty, but few practice it, for crime brings the criminal "huge mansions, gardens with trees, fine tables, and old silver cups."

Juvenal hated the noise and traffic of the city. The streets are too crowded to walk, and dangerous besides:*

> Though
> we hurry, we merely crawl;
> We're blocked by a surging mass ahead,
> a pushing wall

* The quotes by Juvenal are from *The Satires of Juvenal,* translated by Hubert Creekmore. Copyright © 1963 by Hubert Creekmore. Reprinted by arrangement with The New American Library, Inc., New York.

Of people behind. A man jabs me,
> elbowing through, one socks
A chair pole against me, one cracks
> my skull with a beam, one knocks
A wine cask against my ear. My legs
> are caked with splashing
Mud, from all sides the weight of
> enormous feet comes smashing
On mine, and a soldier stamps his
> hobnails through to my sole. . . .

> a piece of pot
Falls down on my head, how often a
> broken vessel is shot
From the upper windows, with what a
> force it strikes and dints
The cobblestones! . . . as many sure
> deaths are lying in wait
In the night as the open windows you
> pass beneath on the street.

While Rome made important contributions to civilization in literature, architecture, engineering, and especially government and law, the most important development to take place in the Roman Empire was the rise of a new religion, Christianity.

CHECK-UP

1. Describe the class system under the Roman Empire.

2. What unusual forms of entertainment interested the Romans?

3. Where did the Romans get their slaves? How were slaves treated in the Roman Republic? How did their lot change during *Pax Romana?*

4. What contributions did the Romans make in the fields of philosophy, engineering, and architecture? What advances did the Romans make in law?

5. How does Horace's poetry show his understanding of human nature? Why can Ovid's poems still be called modern?

6. Why is Juvenal considered a critic of the times?

In the reign of Augustus' successor, the Emperor Tiberius, a Palestinian Jew named Jesus was executed by the Roman authorities. At the time few people paid much attention to this incident. Almost no one understood that what had taken place was one of the most important events in the history of the world.

Not much is known about Jesus' childhood. Like other Jewish youths, Jesus most likely attended the Jewish place of worship, the synagogue, where the rabbis taught him ancient Hebrew law. As he grew into manhood, Jesus felt called by God to aid the sick and unfortunate and to spread a message of love among his fellow Jews. Like the Hebrew prophets of old, Jesus denounced the wicked and the rich and urged men to love their neighbors and their God:

Ye have heard that it hath been said, Thou shalt love thy neighbor, and hate thine enemy.

But I say unto you, Love your enemies, bless them that curse you, do good to them that hate you, and pray for them which despitefully use you, and persecute you.

Jesus attracts some followers amongst his fellow Jews. Why did some Jews become followers of Jesus?

1. Jesus the prophet. Jesus reminded some Hebrews of their ancient prophets. From the depths of his heart he called out for love of God, love of man, and justice for the poor and the oppressed. With burning anger he expressed his hatred of wickedness and warned his fellow Jews that the Kingdom of God was at hand. To some Palestinian Jews, Jesus was a prophet, a holy man inspired by God.

2. The personality of Jesus. Some Jews were also attracted by Jesus' religious nature. They were impressed by stories that he performed miracles and by his teachings, which were directed toward the lowly and the poor.

3. Belief in heaven. At the time of Jesus several ideas were receiving wide attention among the Jewish people. They were not new ideas, but they had not received much attention in the past. One of these ideas was a belief in an afterlife. In the early history of the Hebrews almost nothing had been said about life after death. The Hebrews believed that the wicked were punished and the righteous rewarded during life on earth. But it was obvious to all that this did not always happen. Often the wicked prospered and the righteous suffered. Over the centuries a large number of Jews came to believe that God would reward the righteous with a place in heaven. Jesus spoke often of an afterlife. When he talked of heaven, some Jews understood him, believed him, and followed him.

4. Concept of the Messiah. A second idea widespread at the time was the hope of a *Messiah*. There were different interpretations of this concept among the Hebrews. Essentially, however, it meant that in the days of the Messiah the Jews would be freed of foreign control and those Jews who had been driven into exile would return to Palestine, their Promised Land. The land would prosper and the people, under the protecting eye of God, would be righteous and happy. Most Jewish thinkers thought of the Messiah in terms of a period in history—a *Messianic* (mes-ih-*an*'ik) *Age* which would bring the Jews prosperity, unity, peace, and freedom from sin. A small group of Jewish thinkers believed that the Messiah would be a *person*—a great leader, a descendant of mighty King David—who would liberate the Jews from Roman rule, gather into Palestine the Jews who lived in other lands, and build a great nation in Palestine. Many Jews eagerly awaited the coming of this great age. Many of Jesus' early followers, convinced that he had been sent by God to redeem the Jewish people, regarded him as the Messiah.

Rise of Christianity

c. **4** B.C.–c. **30** A.D.	Jesus of Nazareth
c. **35** A.D.–c. **65** A.D.	Paul's missionary activities
64 A.D.	Start of persecution of Christians
313 A.D.	Christianity granted religious tolerance
395 A.D.	Christianity becomes official religion in Rome

The ties between early Christianity and Judaism are very strong. Christianity began among the Jews. Mary, the mother of Jesus, her husband Joseph, Jesus himself, and all his early followers were Jews. From Judaism, Christianity obtained many of its basic beliefs —the idea of one God, the demands of the prophets that man do good, avoid evil, and care for the weak, the poor, and the oppressed, the insistence that man must obey God's commands, the concept of a Messiah, the belief in the Old Testament as sacred writing.

Most Jews do not accept the teachings of Jesus. Most Jews doubted that Jesus was the Messiah. They did not believe that Jesus would lead the Jews in a holy war against their Roman conquerors. Hebrew priests felt that Jesus claimed too much power, that he acted as if he himself could forgive a man for his sins. Only God, said the priests, can forgive sins. They felt that the humble carpenter from Galilee was being arrogant when he said that he would sit at the right hand of God. They took this to mean that Jesus was claiming that he above all other men was favored by God.

Jewish leaders felt that Jesus was trying to undermine the authority of ancient Hebrew laws. Jesus preached that the spirit of the law was more important than its letter, that right living and a pure, loving heart counted more than obedience to laws and rules. Jewish leaders feared that Jesus sought to change ceremonies and rules that were centuries old. To the Jewish leaders Jesus was a troublemaker, a subversive who was trying to change the ancient Hebrew faith.

The Roman authorities resent Jesus. The Romans feared that this popular preacher would arouse the Jews to revolt against Roman rule. Discontent with Rome was already high in Palestine. The Romans wanted no additional troubles. When Jesus' Jewish enemies turned him over to the Roman authorities, the Roman governor of Judea, Pontius (*pon'*shus) Pilate, thought his death would be to the advantage of Rome. He therefore ordered his soldiers to execute Jesus by crucifying him, a common form of execution for criminals among the Romans.

A movement that seemed a failure becomes a leading religion. To anyone living at the time, it must have appeared that Jesus had been a failure. Executed like a common criminal, he had left behind only a handful of followers. It seemed doubtful that the small Jewish-Christian band that embraced Jesus as the Messiah (Christ) would survive. Yet within four centuries millions of men throughout the Mediterranean world had declared themselves to be *Christians* (followers of Christ), and Christianity had become the official religion of the Roman Empire. How do historians account for the triumph of Christianity in the Roman Empire?

1. The inspiration of Jesus. Many people were attracted to Jesus because of his personality, life, and death. Many who heard about the life of Jesus were inspired by his sense of mission, his love of man, and his concern for the suffering and the poor. They did not doubt that he had performed miracles. They grieved when told how Jesus suffered execution on the cross, and believed that he had risen from the

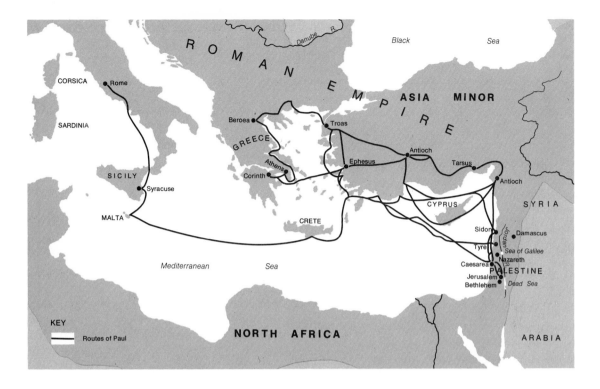

The Journeys of Paul

dead and ascended to heaven. They were certain that Jesus was more than just a holy man, that he was indeed the Son of God. They would heed his words as they would those of God Himself.

2. The influence of Paul. An educated Greek-speaking Jew named Saul—who would be known to the world as St. Paul—changed Christianity from a Jewish sect into a world religion. At first he had ridiculed the early Jewish-Christians who considered Jesus the Messiah. While on a mission to persecute the Christians, Paul had a vision in which he believed that Jesus spoke to him. Completely transformed by this experience, Paul felt that he had been selected by God to spread Jesus' teachings. Paul aided the growth of Christianity in three important ways.

(a) At the time of Jesus' death, Christianity was not a new religion. It was just a sect within Judaism. Jesus had preached only to his fellow Jews. He had almost no contact with the gen-

tiles or non-Jews. It was Paul who carried Jesus' message to the gentiles. He insisted that anyone, gentile as well as Jew, could become a Christian. By encouraging gentiles to follow Jesus, Paul turned Jesus' teachings into a new religion.

(b) Paul was a missionary, perhaps the greatest in history. He traveled to many parts of the Roman Empire—the Near East, Asia Minor, Greece, Italy—converting people to Christianity and establishing churches where the followers of Jesus could meet and pray. By keeping in close touch with these churches, Paul helped them to survive.

(c) Paul gave to Christianity a set of doctrines that became the basis of the new religion. Paul taught that: (1) all men, Jew and gentile, were deep in sin; (2) Jesus had been sent by God to save mankind from sin; (3) by dying on

The early Christians often portrayed Jesus as a Good Shepherd caring for his flock. In this fresco (top, left) he is dressed in Roman style. Being clean-shaven themselves, the Romans did not picture him with a beard as later artists would do. Early Christian churches had Greek columns and Roman arches and a simple interior (above). Mosaics depicting the apostles and early saints and martyrs decorated the walls. A fine example of these mosaics is that of the Apostle Andrew. In Christian tradition Andrew, the brother of the Apostle Peter, was executed by crucifixion.

the cross, Jesus had atoned for men's sins, making it possible for them to rise with him to eternal life-after-death in heaven; (4) by faith, by believing in Christ, his teachings, and his mission, man could gain this salvation.

The message of Jesus was soon written down in the New Testament, the second part of the Bible. Besides relating the life of Jesus and his teachings, the New Testament contains the letters written by Paul and other early Christians to various Christian churches throughout the Roman Empire. Its purpose was to inspire men to believe in Jesus and to lead a Christian life.

3. The appeal of heaven. The idea of a heavenly life after death appealed to many people. To most men death is terrifying. Christianity offered not only a life after death, but a place in heaven to all who would follow Christ. The promise of eternal life led many people to become Christians.

4. Appeal to the oppressed. To the poor, the oppressed, and the slave, Christianity stretched out a hand of love. Jesus had a special place in his heart for the sufferer:

Blessed are the poor in spirit: for theirs is the kingdom of heaven,
Blessed are they that mourn: for they shall be comforted.
Blessed are the meek: for they shall inherit the earth.
Blessed are they which do hunger and thirst after righteousness: for they shall be filled.
Blessed are the merciful: for they shall obtain mercy.
Blessed are the pure in heart: for they shall see God. . . .
Blessed are they which are persecuted for righteousness' sake: for theirs is the kingdom of heaven.

Men burdened with misfortune found new hope in Christ's words. Life on earth might be misery, but it was bearable if they could look forward to an afterlife when they would be comforted by God in the kingdom of heaven.

5. Ease of conversion. It was relatively easy to become a Christian. The convert had only to be baptized. He did not have to go through any painful initiation ceremonies. Moreover, Christianity, unlike some of the pagan religions, welcomed women converts.

6. Communal love and organization. Contributing to the success of Christianity was the fact that early in its history it built a strong organization, the church. At first the church was simply communities of the faithful that united believers in a locality. The local church provided social services for the poor. It was a place in which one could find brotherhood and comfort when times were hard. The church spread the message of Christ and won converts for the new religion.

7. Similarity to Greek philosophy. Christianity won supporters among some educated people who had accepted Greek philosophy. The teachings of Christianity were similar to some of the ideas taught by Greek philosophers. Like the Stoics, St. Paul had said that all men were brothers and that men should strive for goodness, pursuing neither wealth nor excessive pleasure. The school of Greek philosophy based on Plato's teachings (see pages 53–54) taught that there is a higher world than earth and that the soul should try to reach it. This was somewhat similar to the Christian idea of heaven. Thus the teachings of Christianity were not completely strange to those people in the Roman world who had studied Greek philosophy. This fact made it easier for educated people to embrace Christianity.

8. Similarity to mystery religions. In the eastern part of the Roman Empire several pagan religions were popular. Because their practices were secret and known only to a small group, they are called "mystery religions." These mystery religions had many beliefs and ceremonies similar to those of Christianity. Several of them told of a god who had come to earth, died, and then risen. Thus the central idea of Christianity—the mission, death, and resurrection of Jesus—was not an entirely new or unfamiliar notion. It was a belief that paralleled the teachings of the mystery religions. This made it easier for the followers of these religions to convert to Christianity. Adding to the appeal of Christianity was the fact that, unlike the gods of the mystery cults, Jesus had actually lived. Because Jesus had been a historical figure, people found it easier to believe in him than in the mythical gods of the mystery religions.

9. Benefits of Roman rule. Christianity benefited in many ways from its association with the Roman Empire. Christian missionaries traveled throughout the Empire over the excellent and safe Roman roads and across the Mediterranean Sea made secure from pirates. Moreover, Rome did not at first interfere with the Christians, since they were few in number and posed little threat to authority.

Christianity arouses the hostility of Rome. As the number of Christians increased, Roman officials became hostile to the new religion. To the Romans, the Christians were queer people who would not accept the Roman gods, would not engage in pagan festivals, stayed away from the gladiatorial contests, condemned war, and, at times, refused to serve in the army. Christian refusal to worship the emperor as a god was interpreted as an act of disloyalty to Rome. Roman officials blamed Christians for plagues, famine, and other disasters. Ignorant common people accused the Christians of cannibalism[1] and immorality.

In an effort to keep Christianity from spreading, some emperors launched cruel persecutions against the followers of Christ. Christians were imprisoned, beaten, starved, and taken to the Colosseum to be burned alive, torn apart by wild beasts, or crucified to amuse the Roman mob. The Roman historian Tacitus describes how one Emperor, Nero, persecuted Christians: "Dressed in wild animals' skins, [the Christians] were torn to pieces by dogs or crucified, or made into torches to be ignited after dark as substitutes for daylight."

Persecutions contribute to the triumph of Christianity. Rather than discouraging Christianity, these persecutions strengthened the determination of the Christians to continue to practice their faith. In fact, the persecutions won new converts for Christianity. "The victims of persecution going to their deaths with fanatical [devoted and unreasoning] and heroic enthusiasm for the new faith became martyrs. . . . After each persecution, the Church . . . drew into her fold men dumbfounded by the courageous loyalty of those who had been put to death."*

Christianity continued to expand. Finally, in 313 A.D. the Roman Emperor Constantine allowed the Christians to practice their religion freely. Later Constantine himself converted to Christianity, becoming the first Christian Emperor of Rome. During the reign of Theodosius I (thee-oh-*doh'*shus, 379–395) Christianity became the official religion of the Roman Empire, and worship of the old gods was declared illegal. Christianity had triumphed.

CHECK-UP

1. Why did some Jews follow Jesus? Why did others reject his teachings? How did the Roman authorities view Jesus?

2. What reasons explain the triumph of Christianity?

3. Why did Christianity arouse the opposition of Roman officials? Why was it later accepted as the state religion?

---

[1] The ignorant thought that the Christian Sacrament of Communion involved the actual consumption of human flesh.

* Selections from *An Introduction to Medieval Europe, 300–1500* by James Westfall Thompson & Edgar Nathaniel Johnson are reprinted with the permission of the publisher, W. W. Norton & Company, Inc., New York, N.Y. Copyright © 1937 by W. W. Norton & Company, Inc. Copyright renewed 1965 by Edgar Nathaniel Johnson. Reprinted also by permission of George Allen & Unwin Ltd.

The Decline and Fall of Rome

During the 200-year period of *Pax Romana,* Rome was at the height of her power. But we might recall the words of the Roman commander who had Carthage burned to the ground: "This is a glorious moment, . . . yet I am seized with fear and foreboding that some day the same fate will befall my own country."

Third-century Rome suffers from anarchy. In the third century a series of crises weakened the Roman Empire. A principal cause for the turmoil was the problem of succession to the throne. Since Rome never arrived at a legal formula for choosing the emperor, in the third century there was a continual struggle for power. Ambitious generals, supported by their soldiers, murdered emperors and each other in their struggle to gain power. In the 50-year period following 235 A.D. Rome had 26 emperors, and 25 of them died violently. Under the rule of incompetent military men economic conditions in Rome went from bad to worse. In order to reward soldiers and pay the costs of war, emperors raised taxes, enormously increasing the distress of the people. Many productive citizens of the Empire were reduced to poverty by the greed of the army, which seized food and clothing from townspeople and peasants.

Signs of decay were everywhere. Plagues reduced the size of the population. Piracy and thievery went unchecked. Roman coins declined in value as their silver content was reduced and more copper was added. Because people no longer trusted Roman coinage, prices increased, and barter (the exchange of goods for other goods rather than money) became widespread. Deteriorating roads slowed travel and transportation. Industry and trade declined sharply. During this period of total disorder, or *anarchy,* the provinces were swept with revolt and Germanic barbarians plundered the border regions and destroyed towns. In both the cities and countryside, life had become unbearable for millions of people. To the citizens of Rome it seemed that nothing could go right.

Two strong emperors try to cope with the many problems threatening the Empire. In the last part of the third century and the beginning of the fourth century, Diocletian (dye-oh-*klee'*-shun) and Constantine introduced desperate measures to deal with the worsening crisis. In doing so they turned the Roman Empire into an early type of *totalitarian* state. The state became all powerful and controlled men's every action. Cities that had traditionally enjoyed a large amount of freedom and local self-government were now ruled by the emperor's officials. Taxes were oppressive and in order to collect them the state froze unskilled workers, small businessmen, and artisans into their jobs. They were closely watched by the state. They had no hope of improving their condition. They were forced to hold their jobs for life and to pass them on to their children. Small farmers and farm workers were not allowed to leave the land. Government agents hunted down farmers who fled from the land to escape the crushing taxes, and forced them to return. Farmers became virtual *serfs*—peasants who are bound to the land. Townspeople were forced to become government tax collectors, a policy which helped to ruin the once prosperous class who had governed the towns. It was a thankless job, for the tax collector himself had to furnish the difference in money between what the state demanded and the actual amount that he was able to collect. The government made it very difficult for a tax collector to give up his job, and it was passed on to his son. The office of Roman tax collector, once a high honor, had become a nightmare.

Diocletian and Constantine had brought some order out of confusion, rescuing Rome from warring generals and keeping the Empire from collapsing. But the price was heavy. In trying to save Rome they had turned the Empire into "a vast prison for scores of millions of men." The civilization and prosperity of the Roman Empire had rested upon a network of self-governing cities. By overburdening city dwellers with taxes and regulations, Diocletian and Constantine had shattered the vitality of city life throughout the Empire. In both the cities and the countryside, millions of people had lost confidence in Rome. The prosperity and order of the days of *Pax Romana* could not be restored by Diocletian and Constantine. The Roman Empire would continue to decline until it was finally overrun by Germanic invaders.

Historians discuss reasons for Rome's decline. The fate of Rome has long intrigued historians. They recognize the fact that there were many reasons for Rome's collapse, though some historians find certain explanations more important than others. Before describing how the Empire fell under the onslaught of Germanic tribesmen, let us examine some of the underlying reasons leading historians give for Rome's decline and fall.

1. Manpower shortage. Professor A. E. R. Boak of the University of Michigan believes that a manpower shortage was one of the major causes for the decline of the Empire. As a result of a declining population there was a "decrease in the manpower available for agriculture, industry, and public services." The shrinking population caused a decline in production and also made it difficult to get soldiers for the army.

2. Ambitious generals. British historian Max Cary believes that the weakening of Rome's frontier defenses played a major part in Rome's collapse. The attempts of third-century generals to seize the throne caused a breakdown in army discipline, seriously endangering the frontiers. The failure of the frontier defense forces "is partly to be sought in the replacement of Italian recruits . . . by provincials from the less Romanized districts, who lacked the . . . discipline" of the Italian soldiers.

3. Upper-class indifference. To Russian-born American historian Michael Rostovtzeff (ruh-stohf't'sef), Rome declined because the attitudes of the upper classes had changed. No longer dedicated to Rome, they became interested only "in pleasure, the pursuit of gain, and the attainment for themselves and their families of the material advantages of civilization." The best people in Rome "grew dissatisfied with life" and became indifferent to the political, military, and economic problems of Rome.

4. Oppressive government. Still another cause for the collapse of Roman power was oppressive government. British historian Donald Dudley concludes:

From the time of Diocletian on, [the Empire] had degenerated into a totalitarian state, controlling and directing all activities in its own interests. . . . Frozen into their hereditary occupations, struggling under the twin burdens of taxes and inflation [decreasing value of money coupled with rising prices], further harassed by incessant demands for loans, gifts, and labor, exposed to the greed of an army of corrupt officials, the citizens of the late Empire had neither the means nor the motive to better their lot. . . . The citizen was reduced to a helpless individual, to whom the state and its agents were . . . [enemies]. And the barbarians must often have seemed preferable to [the Roman state and its agents]. The excessive demands of the state were, without doubt, the chief cause of the final downfall of the [Empire in the] West.

5. Unhealthy economy. Another British historian, F. W. Wallbank, finds the major cause of the Empire's decline in Rome's failure to improve methods of producing goods. This was a basic weakness of an economy based on slavery. Since the slave derived no benefits from his labor, he had no incentive to find new and better ways of doing things. Moreover, the slave owner considered it degrading to work with his hands. Because he had no interest in improving ways of producing things, no advances were made in agriculture. There were no new industries springing up to provide jobs and opportunities for a higher standard of living among the masses. Hence, Rome never

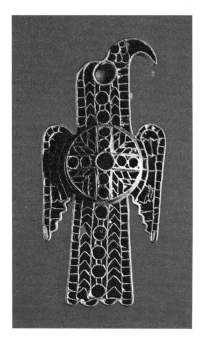

The Germanic barbarians brought a new quality—less polished but often powerful—to European art. The crude relief above is combined with a sophisticated abstract design characteristic of Northern European art. The finest barbarian work was devoted to personal ornaments (left).

had an economy which could be called healthy. Her wealth, which benefited only a few, was based not on increased production but on looting the provinces.

Furthermore, in order to defend the borders of the Empire, it became necessary to increase greatly the size of the army. To feed, clothe, arm, and transport the expanded army, says British historian A. H. M. Jones, "taxation had to be enormously increased. . . . The heavy burden of taxation was probably the root cause of the economic decline of the Empire." Heavily taxed to pay for the army, to provide free food for residents of Rome, and to support the clergy, many peasants became poverty-stricken

and deserted their farms. The peasant population "slowly dwindled in numbers" and farms became wastelands.

6. Unwieldy size. Many historians suggest that Rome's empire was too vast to be governed effectively. It was impossible for officials in Rome to keep close watch over conditions in the provinces. Nor could they be assured that provincial officials in regions distant from Rome would carry out their commands. Diocletian had tried to meet this problem by splitting the Empire into two parts, East and West, each with its own emperor. Rome continued as the center of power for the Empire in the West. The capital of the Eastern Roman Empire was

Constantinople, which had avoided some of the crises that were destroying the Empire in the West. In fact, A. H. M. Jones believes that dividing the Empire contributed to its decline. "Formerly the emperors had been able to draw freely on the wealth of the East to finance the defense of the West. From the time of Diocletian the relatively poor western parts had to make do on their own resources with occasional aid from the East."

7. *Barbarian invasions.* French historian H. A. Piganiol (pee-gah-*nyol'*) blames "all the ills from which the Empire suffered . . . [on] the continuous war conducted by the unorganized bands of those Germans who had succeeded in living for centuries at the frontiers of the Empire without being civilized." Rome did not die because her society was in decay. She was "destroyed by a brutal blow." Who were these barbarians? How were they able to conquer Rome?

The deathblow to Rome is dealt by invading Germanic barbarians. East of the Rhine River and north of the Danube, the northern frontier of the Roman Empire, lived several Germanic peoples. Not yet civilized and organized in tribes rather than in states, they were regarded by the Romans as barbarians. These barbarians originated in the forests and marshlands of northern Europe. The harsh climate of their native region, the uncleared forest lands which made farming difficult, and a growing population caused them to migrate slowly southward. By the fourth century these warlike tribesmen were massed along Rome's Rhine-Danube frontier. Only the Roman troops at the border kept the barbarians from crossing into the Empire. The Roman historian Tacitus described the customs of these Germanic tribesmen:

The Germans have no taste for peace. . . .

When not engaged in warfare, they spend some little time in hunting, but more in idling, abandoned to sleep and gluttony. All the heroes and grim warriors dawdle their time away, while the care of house, hearth, and fields is left to the women, old men, and weaklings of the family. . . .

No nation abandons itself more completely to banqueting and entertainment than the German. It is accounted a sin to turn any man away from your door. The host welcomes his guest with the best meal that his means allow. . . .

Drinking bouts, lasting a day and night, are not considered in any way disgraceful. Such quarrels as inevitably arise . . . are [often] settled . . . by blows and wounds. Nonetheless, they often make banquets an occasion for discussing such serious affairs as the reconciliation of enemies, the forming of marriage alliances, the adoption of new chiefs, and even the choice of peace or war. . . .

. . . they go in for dicing . . . in all seriousness . . . and are so recklessly keen about winning or losing that, when everything else is gone, they stake their personal liberty on the last decisive throw. The loser goes into slavery without complaint.

Barbarians desire to cross into Rome. Attracted by the warm climate, riches, and advanced civilization of Rome, the Germans had for years been penetrating the Empire. At first Rome kept close watch at the border to prevent the barbarians from slipping across. However, when it became difficult to recruit enough soldiers to serve in the Roman army, Rome began to hire barbarians. Some Germans rose to high positions in the army. Other barbarians were allowed to settle inside the frontier where there was surplus agricultural land. Rome felt that this would help increase her food supply. She also hoped that settled tribes would become sufficiently Romanized to help fight off further invasions.

The peaceful penetration turns into a dangerous invasion. The Germanic invasion of Rome in the last part of the fourth century was triggered by the coming of the Huns, a savage people from Central Asia who spread terror wherever they went. Ammianus Marcellinus (am-ih-*ey'*nus mahr-seh-*lye'*nus), a Roman historian, said of these terrible Huns: "A race of men, hitherto unknown, had suddenly descended like a whirlwind from the lofty mountains, as if they had risen from some secret recess of the earth. . . . They were . . . destroying everything in their way."

Even the warlike Germans were terrified by the Huns. One Germanic tribe fleeing from the Huns, the Visigoths, sought refuge within the Roman Empire. In 376 A.D. the Roman emperor reluctantly permitted the Visigoths to cross the Danube. Two years later, Rome was at war with her unwelcome guests.

At the Battle of Adrianople the Visigoths defeat a Roman army. In 378 the Visigoths defeated the Romans at the Battle of Adrianople (ey-drih-an-*oh*′p'l). This defeat was a disaster for Rome. It showed that the once unbeatable Roman legions could be defeated. This meant that Rome could no longer defend her borders. Germans and Huns began pouring into the Em-

The Divided Empire (About 400 A.D.)

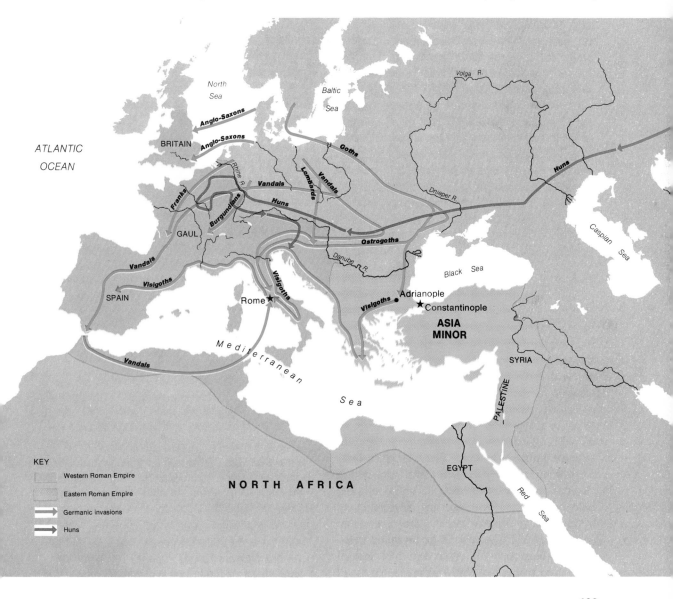

pire. The collapse of the Western Roman Empire was only a matter of time. In 410 the city of Rome was plundered by the Visigoths. In the middle of the fifth century the Huns under the cruel Attila (*at'*ih-luh) threatened Italy. Aided by Germanic tribes, the Romans held off the attacking Huns, and Attila's death ended their threat to the Empire. Some Huns settled in Hungary, and others returned to Asia. But Rome's collapse continued. One province after another fell to invading barbarians. In 455 Rome was sacked by another barbarian tribe, the Vandals. Kingdoms ruled by Germanic chieftains were carved out of the once-mighty Roman Empire. Germanic soldiers in the pay of Rome gained control of the government and dictated who the emperor should be. In 476 A.D. these German officers overthrew the Roman Emperor Romulus Augustulus and placed a fellow German, Odoacer (oh-doh-*ey'*ser), on the throne. The Roman Empire in the West had fallen.

Several barbarian kingdoms replace the Roman Empire in the West. The barbarians, attracted by the superior civilization of the Romans, had sought to conquer Rome, not to destroy Roman civilization. Even before the Empire had fallen, many barbarians had accepted Christianity. After the collapse of the Empire, the barbarian kingdoms continued to make use of Roman law, Roman art forms, Roman administrative procedures, and Latin, the language of Rome. Nevertheless, these scattered survivals of Roman culture could not restore the Empire in the West.

While the Roman Empire in the West had fallen to different Germanic tribes, the Eastern Roman Empire or Byzantine Empire remained strong. Led by capable emperors, possessing a strong army and loyal troops, and using the wealth of the East to buy off attackers, the Byzantine Empire survived the barbarian invasions. We shall discuss its place in history in Chapter 6.

CHECK-UP

1. What signs of decay could be seen in the Roman Empire in the third century?

2. How did Diocletian and Constantine try to deal with the crisis?

3. How do historians account for the decline of the Roman Empire?

4. Why was the Battle of Adrianople significant?

The Legacy of Rome

The Roman Empire in the West had fallen, but Rome left the world a heritage that endured for centuries.

1. The idea of a world empire united by law and good government never died. In the centuries following the collapse of Rome, men continued to be attracted to the idea of a unified world state. They still dreamed of bringing together the different peoples of the world. Writes British historian Christopher Dawson: "Through all the chaos of the dark ages that were to follow [the collapse of Rome], men cherished the memory of the universal peace and order of the Roman Empire, with its common religion, its common law, and its common culture."

2. While Rome declined in the West, the Byzantine Empire endured for another thousand years. The Eastern line of Roman emperors continued virtually unbroken until the capital, Constantinople, was conquered by the Turks in 1453. While art, learning, and city life declined in Western Europe after the barbarian invasions, the Byzantine Empire kept alive the culture and urban civilization of the ancient world.

3. The Romans founded many cities throughout the Mediterranean world, and also in Germany and Britain, which continue to exist today. In many of these cities one can still see the remains of Roman roads, bridges, aqueducts, and public buildings. These cities became

the political, economic, and cultural centers of the civilization which was to emerge centuries later during the Middle Ages.

4. Roman law remained a vital force in Western Europe long after Rome declined. It influenced Church law and formed the basis for the law codes of many European nations. It has been said, writes present-day historian Charles Sherman, that "Rome conquered the world three times: first by her armies, second by her religion [Christianity], third by her law. This third conquest, most pacific [peaceful] of all, is perhaps the most surpassing [outstanding] of all."

5. Latin, the language of ancient Rome, lived on long after Rome had perished.

It was in Latin that the Western Church Fathers wrote: it was into Latin that St. Jerome translated the Bible; it was in Latin that for centuries poets, historians, and theologians [who study man's relationship to God] wrote their works. The Church in the West used Latin for its ritual and for its official documents. . . . As the language of literature, learning, and law during the Middle Ages, Latin was in effect an international language which recognized no frontiers in the West. In contrast, therefore, to all the centrifugal forces of the period, Latin served as a bond of unity.

For a thousand years after the disintegration of the Empire, Latin survived as the leading, and for much of that time the only, language of literature. For learning and law it was supreme until the seventeenth and eighteenth centuries.*

From Latin came Italian, Spanish, Portuguese, French, Romanian, and Romansh (spoken in part of Switzerland). Many words in English are derived from Latin, and the literature of ancient Rome is still studied today.

6. Rome kept alive the philosophy, literature, science, and arts of ancient Greece. By way of Rome Greek culture spread to Western Europe. By preserving, spreading, and adding to the culture of Greece, Rome made an incalculable contribution to western civilization.

7. Christianity was born within the Roman Empire and was greatly influenced by Roman law and Roman organization. Its adoption as the official religion of Rome encouraged its growth. Christianity became a key element in the civilization that emerged in Western Europe during the Middle Ages.

* Reprinted from Solomon Katz: *The Decline of Rome and the Rise of Mediaeval Europe.* Copyright 1955 by Cornell University Press. Used by permission of Cornell University Press.

Chapter Highlights

Can you explain?

barbarians	gentiles	gladiator	public bath
totalitarian	serfs	Messiah	mystery religion
missionary	synagogue	subversive	self-government

Can you identify?

Adrianople	Horace	Augustus	Christianity
Virgil	Attila	Paul	Epicureanism
Jesus	Judea	Diocletian	Marcus Aurelius
Aeneid	Ovid	Constantine	*Pax Romana*
Seneca	Juvenal	Stoicism	New Testament

1. Why did the Senate accept one-man rule by Octavian but not by Caesar?

2. What methods did the Romans use to unite 70 million people from different lands into one empire?

3. Compare the life of an upper-class Roman woman with her counterpart in Greece.

4. What are the basic principles of Epicureanism and Stoicism?

5. Why is law considered one of Rome's greatest contributions to civilization? Discuss three legal principles developed in Rome that are accepted today.

6. What aspects of Roman life would you criticize? What aspects do you consider praiseworthy?

7. What parallels can be drawn between Virgil and Homer?

8. Why is Paul credited with turning Jesus' teachings into a new religion?

9. What is the concept of the Messiah? How did the different interpretations of the Messiah lead some to follow Jesus and others to reject him?

10. How did Roman persecution of the Christians strengthen the new religion? Is persecution always self-defeating? Explain.

11. What were the economic, political, and social reasons for the decline of Rome? Do you think any of these are found in present-day American society? Discuss.

12. What benefits from Roman rule survived after the overthrow of the Empire in the West? Why was the Latin language important to the new states that evolved in Western Europe?

13. Why were the Romans able to establish an empire that endured for centuries?

The Middle Ages

Unit Two ———

Byzantine and Islamic Civilizations

Medieval Europe: Feudal Lord and
Catholic Church

Awakening of Western Europe

Byzantine and Islamic Civilizations

The period following the collapse of the Roman Empire in the West is known as the Middle Ages. In the Early Middle Ages a new civilization, blending Graeco-Roman survivals, Christianity, and the traditions and experiences of the Germanic invaders, was taking shape in Western Europe. While Western Europe was forging a new society, what was happening to the rest of the old Roman Empire—North Africa, Spain, and the lands of the eastern Mediterranean?

When the Roman Empire in the West finally collapsed in 476, the eastern provinces continued to prosper for another thousand years. In the Eastern Roman Empire, Byzantine civilization was taking form. Like the civilization emerging in Western Europe during the Early

The Hagia Sophia (left) reflects two civilizations. A Byzantine church, it became a Muslim mosque after Constantinople fell to the Turks. Today it is a museum where Byzantine mosaics appear next to passages from the Koran. In the fresco from a Yugoslav church (above) a Byzantine artist depicted Christ's descent into limbo, where abide the souls of those barred from heaven but not condemned to hell.

Middle Ages, Byzantine civilization was a mixture of the old and the new. To its heritage from ancient Greece and Rome were added many features that made Byzantine civilization distinct from other cultures.

While Western Europe was struggling through the disorders of the Early Middle Ages and the Byzantine Empire endured, a new religion was born in Arabia. Islam expanded rapidly and by the middle of the eighth century its followers had built a vast empire. Islamic civilization reached a level which rivaled that of the Byzantine Empire. Eventually both Byzantine and Islamic civilizations were dealt staggering blows by invading tribesmen from Central Asia. The story of how these two civilizations developed and declined is discussed in the following pages.

Byzantine Civilization

About 600 B.C. the Greek colony of Byzantium (bih-*zan*′shum) was founded on the shores of the Hellespont where Asia meets Europe. This site was chosen by the Roman Emperor Constantine for a second capital city of the Roman Empire in 330 A.D. The second Roman capital, Constantinople, was established to make it easier to govern the eastern provinces of the Empire. The peoples of these eastern lands were mainly Greek-speaking and were heirs to the learning of ancient Greece.

Byzantine Civilization

330 A.D.	Constantinople becomes capital of Roman Empire in the East
527–565 A.D.	Eastern Roman Empire expands
863 A.D.	Conversion of Slavs begins
c. **975**–c. **1025**	Cultural height of Byzantine Empire
1054	Orthodox Church breaks with Rome
1204–1261	Crusaders capture Constantinople, set up Latin Empire of the East
1453	Constantinople falls to Ottoman Turks

Rome's eastern provinces suffer less from the barbarian invasions than do the western. In the troubled fourth and fifth centuries A.D., the eastern provinces were more fortunate than those in the West. Whereas the western lands of the Roman Empire suffered a decline in agriculture and trade, the eastern lands remained relatively prosperous. Moreover, the major onslaughts of the Huns and the Germanic tribes were directed against the Roman Empire in the West. Though frequently attacked, the eastern provinces had sufficient wealth and military strength to withstand the barbarian attacks. Thus in the Early Middle Ages, while the towns of Western Europe lay nearly deserted or in ruins and most people lived in small villages, Constantinople remained a magnificent city with a population of over 500,000 people. Great walls and towers guarded the city from attack. On one of the gates was written: "Christ our God, guard thy city from all disturbances and wars. Break victoriously the force of the enemy." For centuries invading armies tried to break through the walls but could not.

Trade flourishes in Constantinople. Behind these walls was a wondrous city of palaces and open squares, of churches and schools. Though trade in Western Europe during the Early Middle Ages was nearly at a standstill, Constantinople was a busy commercial center. From

Mediterranean lands and parts of Asia merchants came to Constantinople to do business. They bought Byzantine silk goods, woolen fabrics, salt, weapons and armor, and gold and silver bowls. Goods from many parts of the world were sold in Constantinople: carpets from Persia, silk from China, pepper and copper from India, spices from Southeast Asia, jewels from Ceylon, ivory from sub-Saharan Africa, honey, slaves, furs, and fish from Russia. After silkworms were smuggled out of China, which had a monopoly on the silk trade, Constantinople developed a flourishing silk industry.

Greek learning is cherished in Constantinople. Whereas learning in the West had declined, Constantinople was noted for its libraries and schools, for its artists, doctors, and scientists. Children from noble and middle-class families attended school. The works of ancient Greek philosophers and scientists continued to be read and studied. Wrote one twelfth-century traveler:

The Greek inhabitants are very rich in gold and precious stones and they go clothed in garments of silk with gold embroidery, and they ride horses, and look like princes. Indeed, the land is very rich in all cloth stuffs, and in bread, meat, and wine. Wealth like that of Constantinople is not to be found in the whole world. Here also are men learned in all the books of the Greeks.

The Byzantine emperor is all powerful. The Byzantines believed that their emperor derived his authority from God. Therefore he had to be obeyed. The emperor made laws, appointed government officials, conducted relations with other nations, and commanded the army and navy. Not only was he the head of the state, he also had the power to choose the head of the church. "I am priest and king," said one Byzantine emperor. The emperor also supervised trade and industry. Generally he chose the man who would succeed him to the throne. Nevertheless, despite the immense powers he wielded,

Spread of Christianity (About 1000 A.D.)

the emperor's position was often insecure. Attempts to overthrow him were common. In the more than 1000-year history of the Byzantine Empire, 65 emperors were removed by force, 41 of them dying violently. Rebels who overthrew the king claimed that they were carrying out God's will. The emperor, they insisted, was no longer favored by God and had to be replaced.

Despite the changes that had taken place in Western Europe with the collapse of the Roman Empire in the West and the establishment of Germanic kingdoms, the early Byzantine emperors insisted that the Roman Empire was still one. These early emperors claimed they were successors to Augustus, ruling the West as well as the East. But attempts to regain the lost western provinces were successful only for a time. After the sixth century the Byzantine emperors found they had enough problems at home without taking on the responsibilities of distant provinces.

The Byzantines establish their own Christian church. Like the people in Western Europe the Byzantines were Christians. Over the centuries, however, many differences of belief and practice had developed between Eastern and Western Christianity. The dispute worsened when an eighth-century emperor ordered that all images and paintings be removed from the Byzantine churches. This aroused the anger of the Roman Church, and contributed to a growing disunity between Eastern and Western Christianity. Disputes over church ceremonies, the rights of the clergy, and Church holidays worsened the relations between the two churches. The Byzantines would not accept the Pope of Rome as head of all Christians. Eventually the Christian church was split in two: in the West, the Roman Catholic Church, headed by the Pope; and in the East, the Eastern (Greek) Orthodox Church, whose spiritual leader was the Patriarch (*pey'-trih-ahrk*) of Constantinople. The final break came in 1054.

Foreign invaders threaten the Byzantine Empire. The most pressing problem faced by the Byzantine Empire was the constant threat of foreign invasion. From the east came the Persians, who considered themselves heirs to the great Persian Empire of the ancient world (pages 36–37). Later came Arabs from the south, fired with the zeal of a new religion. To the north, the Byzantine Empire was threatened by Slavic tribes from Eastern Europe. Since the time the barbarians had begun to make inroads into the Roman Empire of the West, the Byzantine Empire had faced nearly continuous attack.

The Byzantines have a powerful army and navy. The backbone of the Byzantine army was its heavy cavalry. Wearing steel helmets and suits of armor and armed with sword, dagger, bow and lance, Byzantine horsemen performed superbly in battle. Byzantine ships attacked

Byzantine Empire at its Height (6th Century)

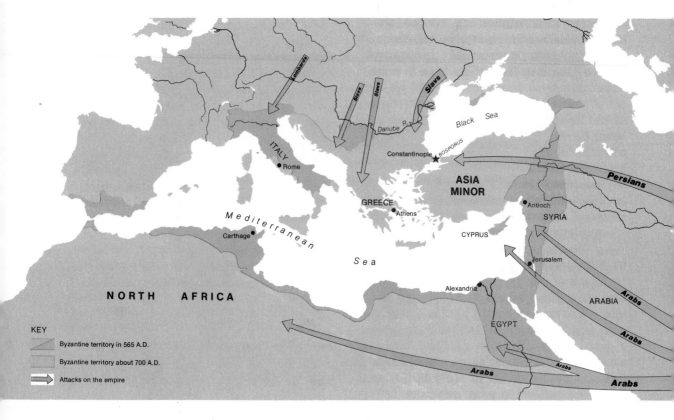

KEY

Byzantine territory in 565 A.D.

Byzantine territory about 700 A.D.

Attacks on the empire

their opponents with battering rams. Their major weapon against enemy ships, however, was "Greek fire"—a chemical substance that was either thrown like a hand grenade or shot through the air in pots by a catapult. Greek fire burned fiercely upon hitting an enemy ship.

Byzantine emperors used diplomacy to solve their problems. They encouraged would-be enemies to expand at the expense of neighboring nations rather than to attack Byzantine provinces. Byzantine diplomats tried to get other nations to fight their battles for them or at least to side with them. They gave expensive gifts to friends and large bribes to enemies. All these tactics plus the experienced Byzantine military enabled the empire to survive despite the enemies that nibbled at her borders.

The empire survives attack by the Seljuk Turks. Toward the end of the eleventh century the Seljuk (sel-*jook'*) Turks, who came originally from Central Asia, invaded and overran most of Asia Minor. This rich area had provided soldiers and grain for the Byzantine Empire. At the same time the Byzantine Empire lost its provinces in southern Italy to Norman adventurers from France. Only the waters of the Bosporus separated Constantinople from the Turks, and other enemies threatened the Byzantine Empire to the north and the south (see map). Yet once again the empire withstood the threat, regained some lands to the north, and restored its profitable trade.

Western Christians attack Constantinople. The Byzantine Empire also suffered at the hands of the Latin Christians from Europe. In 1204 Constantinople was captured and plundered by Western European armies on the way to fight the Muslims in the Holy Land. While the westerners failed to take over the entire Byzantine Empire, they ruled Constantinople and the surrounding regions until a Byzantine emperor regained control in 1261. The conquest of Constantinople by the westerners greatly weakened the Byzantine Empire. Fur-

ther weakened by crushing taxation, a declining agriculture and trade, civil and foreign war, and a mercenary (hired) army whose loyalty to the state was uncertain, the empire began to totter. Fourteenth-century Byzantine emperors and writers sadly compared their unhappy present with their glorious past:

There is no more money anywhere. Reserves are exhausted, the imperial jewels have been sold, and taxes bring in nothing, as the country is ruined.

The bygone splendor and prosperity of Byzantium [are] . . . gone.

The Ottomans deal a deathblow to the tottering empire. Originally from Central Asia, the Ottoman Turks had moved westward, adopted the religion of Islam, and seized outlying parts of Byzantine territory. In 1453 they laid siege to Constantinople itself. Outnumbered nearly 16 to 1, the Byzantine forces had no hope of withstanding the Turks. Constantinople fell. The Turks killed the emperor, slaughtered thousands of men, women, and children, and looted churches, palaces, and monasteries. After a thousand years the Byzantine Empire had come to an end.

Its conquest by the Turks aroused considerable fears throughout Europe. Wrote one Italian cardinal:

. . . the splendor and glory of the East, the school of the best arts, the refuge of all good things has been captured, despoiled, ravaged, and completely sacked by the most inhuman barbarians and the most savage enemies of the Christian Faith. . . . Much danger threatens Italy, not to mention other lands, if the violent assaults of the most ferocious barbarians are not checked.

The cardinal's fears were not misplaced. In the centuries to come, the Ottoman Turks, rulers of a large empire, would threaten many other European lands.

The Byzantine Empire makes significant contributions to civilization. During its thousand years the Byzantine Empire preserved the science, mathematics, literature, and philosophy

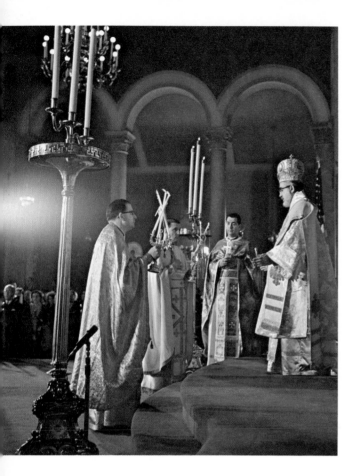

The most enduring feature of Byzantine civilization has been its religion. The ceremony at the Eastern Orthodox Church in New York (left) has changed little from those once held in Constantinople. The magnificence of the Eastern Orthodox Church is reflected in the Russian ikon (holy picture) above. Note the Cyrillic lettering identifying the figures. The addition of gold, precious stones, and pearls has transformed a simple painting into a priceless treasure.

of the ancient Greeks and Romans. Its men of culture were familiar with the riches of Greek learning. When the Byzantine Empire began to decline in the fourteenth century, many of its scholars and artists moved to Italy. This helped to acquaint the western world with the learning of Greece and Rome. "The Byzantines carried the torch of civilization unextinguished at a time when the barbarous Germanic and Slav tribes had reduced much of Europe to near chaos; and they maintained this high degree of civilization until Western Europe gradually emerged and began to take form," concludes American historian Speros Vryonis.

Byzantine architects designed some of the world's most beautiful churches. Particularly noteworthy is the Church of St. Sophia, which always impressed visitors. When a group of Russians in the late tenth century observed a ceremony in St. Sophia, they wrote: "We know not whether we were in heaven or on earth; for on earth there is no such splendor or beauty."

The Byzantine Empire has fine artists and skilled craftsmen. Byzantine artists made pictures from tiny pieces of stone or glass arranged in detailed patterns. These *mosaics* revealed a superb feeling for color. Religious paintings were done in rich tones of blue, green, and red highlighted with gold and ivory. The skills of Byzantine craftsmen were known throughout the Mediterranean world. Wealthy residents of Constantinople owned silver plates engraved with religious scenes, golden cups, jewelry in elaborate settings, and delicately carved ivory jewel boxes. Byzantine artisans also made finely worked bronze doors, candleholders, and altar fronts for Italian churches and monasteries.

The Byzantines have commercial and cultural ties with Eastern Europe. Many of the Slavic peoples of Eastern Europe were converted to Christianity by Byzantine missionaries. "To the nations that Byzantium converted," writes French historian Charles Diehl, "it introduced the concept of government, the principles of law, a more civilized way of life, and an intellectual and artistic culture." Particularly important was the conversion of the prince of Kiev (*kee′*yehf) in southern Russia. Kiev was one of the trading posts established by Swedish Vikings in the ninth century. It became the most important trading center along the route connecting Constantinople with Northern Europe. From Kiev the Eastern Orthodox Church spread to other towns in Russia. Byzantine architects and engineers built churches and towns in Russia, and missionaries gave the Russians and the Slavic peoples of Eastern Europe an alphabet based on Greek. This enabled them to develop a literature of their own. In addition to these contributions, the Byzantine Empire held off repeated Muslim attacks and prevented Islam from penetrating very deeply into Central and Eastern Europe. The culture of Constantinople thus served as the basis for the civilizations which developed in Russia and elsewhere in Eastern Europe.

CHECK-UP

1. Why did the Roman Empire in the East survive while that in the West declined?

2. What powers did the Byzantine emperor have? Why was his position insecure?

3. Why did the Eastern Orthodox Church break away from the Roman Catholic Church?

4. What factors led to the decline and fall of the Byzantine Empire?

5. What important contributions did the Byzantine Empire make to civilization?

The Rise and Expansion of Islam

After the fall of the Roman Empire in the West, three civilizations came to the fore in the lands that had once been united by Roman rule. The Western part of the Empire was to develop as Latin Christendom. In the Eastern part of the Empire, which survived the barbarian invasions, the Byzantine Empire flourished. But these two Christian civilizations were confronted by a powerful new rival which overran lands that once belonged to the Roman Empire and united many different peoples under the banner of a vital new religion—Islam.

Islam developed about 600 A.D. in the Arabian Peninsula. Arabia is largely desert, and in those times most Arabs were *bedouins* (*bed′*-oo-inz), herdsmen who wandered across the desert in search of water and pastureland for their herds of sheep, goats, and camels. Warfare was common in the desert, for the different tribes fought to control waterholes and grazing lands. Moreover, since a tribe's wealth was measured by the size of its herds, there were frequent raids between tribes. With tents as their shelter and swift racing camels and fine horses on which to make raids, the bedouins lived a life of freedom and independence.

But not all Arabs were nomads living in the desert. Some dwelt in towns established in the fertile region around natural wells. Others lived in the trading towns that dotted the coasts of the Arabian Peninsula. These coastal towns were connected to the few towns in the interior by caravan routes.

Mohammed is inspired to bring the word of God to the Arabs. A leading inland trading center in Arabia was the town of Mecca. Here, in about 570, the founder of a new religion was born. His name was Mohammed. Orphaned by the age of six, Mohammed grew up in the home of relatives. As a young man, he took part in the caravan trade, the lifeblood of Mecca. When Mohammed married a rich widow, he achieved worldly success and respect.

Possessed of a sensitive nature, Mohammed often took long walks in the desert, pondering the nature of God and the hereafter. He spent many hours at prayer, especially during the night. About the time of his fortieth year, Mohammed believed that he was visited by an angel who ordered him, "Recite! in the name of thy Lord!" Transformed by this vision, Mohammed was convinced that God had chosen him to serve as His messenger. Mohammed had found his life's mission—to bring the revealed word of God to the people of Arabia. The religion he founded was called *Islam,* which means surrendering oneself to God, or Allah. The followers of Islam were *Muslims,* "those who submit to God's will."

Until Mohammed began to spread his message of the one God, most Arabs had been pagans. They believed in spirits of good and evil, as well as in many gods. Mecca was the holy city for most of these pagan worshipers. The old beliefs were beginning to decline, however. In their place some Arabs, particularly in the southern part of the peninsula, had turned to Judaism, the first religion to teach the idea of one God.

The Islamic community is founded in Medina. The people of Mecca refused to accept Mohammed as a prophet. Mohammed the business-

Islamic Civilization

c. **570–632**	Mohammed
622	The Hejira
632–738	Expansion of Islam
661–750	Umayyad Caliphate
732	Battle of Tours
750–1055	Abbasid Caliphate

man they respected, but they had little use for Mohammed the Prophet. What would happen to their profitable business which stemmed from Mecca's fame as a holy city for the worship of pagan gods if people began to follow Mohammed's teachings?

Faced with constant persecution, Mohammed and his small band of followers slipped secretly out of Mecca. On September 20, 622, they reached Medina, a town about 200 miles north of Mecca. The flight to Medina is known as the *Hejira* (heh-*jie'*ruh) or "breaking of former ties." It is one of the most important events in Muslim history and is commemorated today by yearly pilgrimages.

The date of the Hejira is the year 1 of the Muslim calendar, for from that date Mohammed began to gain followers rapidly. Their ranks swelled by bedouin tribes, the Muslims raised an army. In 630 Mohammed returned to Mecca in triumph. When he died two years later, he left behind a growing religion. What were the teachings of the religion of Islam?

The message of Islam is found in the Koran. To Muslims, their holy book, the Koran (koh-*ran'*), is not the teachings of Mohammed but the word of God as it was revealed to Mohammed. Being the word of God, the Koran may not be changed or questioned. Muslims believe that the Koran contains the rules God has set for man:

1. The Koran teaches that there is only one God, *Allah.* Its message is strictly monotheistic,

stating that only God should be worshiped. Islam considers the Hebrew prophets and Jesus as messengers of God. Mohammed, the last of these messengers, is also the greatest. Whereas Christians worship Jesus as being divine, Muslims view Mohammed not as divine but as the greatest of the prophets. They respect and love Mohammed, but they worship only Allah. Nor are Muslims allowed to make or worship idols or images. Allah is the Creator and Ruler of Heaven and Earth; He gives life and takes it away. Allah is all powerful, merciful to those who believe in Him and lead good lives. He should be worshiped in fear, for He is the Judge of men's deeds. On the Day of Judgment the dead will rise from their graves and stand before Him to be judged. For the unbeliever and the wicked, Allah will have no pity. In chains they will be dragged into hell, a fearful place of "scorching winds and seething water in the shade of pitch-black smoke, neither cool nor refreshing. . . . [There] . . . sinners . . . shall eat [bitter] fruit . . . [and] drink boiling water . . . as the thirsty camel drinks."

But Allah is also just. He punishes only the wicked and the unbeliever. Those who believe in Him and lead upright lives shall enter a garden of pleasure called Paradise. For the Arabs, who were surrounded by the hot, dry desert, Paradise was a place of delight, "a kingdom blissful and glorious:"

[Allah] will reward [the believers] . . . with robes of silk and the delights of Paradise. Reclining there upon soft couches, they shall feel neither the scorching heat nor the biting cold. Trees will spread their shade around them, and fruits will hang in clusters over them.

They shall be served with silver dishes, . . . silver goblets, . . . and cups brim-full with ginger-flavored water.

2. A Muslim is required to perform five religious duties.

(a) A person becomes a believer, or a Muslim, by repeating and believing the statement of faith: "There is no God but Allah, and Mohammed is His Prophet."

(b) Five times a day the believer faces the holy city of Mecca and prays from certain standard postures of reverence.

(c) He has a religious duty to give alms (money) to the poor.

(d) During the holy month of *Ramadan* (ram-uh-*dahn'*) the Muslim is forbidden to eat or drink from sunrise to sunset.

(e) If he can afford it, he is expected to make at least one pilgrimage to Mecca.

3. Allah demanded that Muslims do good and avoid evil. The faithful Muslim respects his parents and is true to his word. He is honest in business and does not charge interest on loans. A lover of peace, the true Muslim regards all Muslims as brothers: "Know ye that every Muslim is a brother to every other Muslim. . . . It is not [right] for any one of you therefore, to take unto himself anything that belongs to his brother unless it is willingly given him by that brother."

4. The Koran also regulated daily living. It forbade Muslims to drink wine, eat the flesh of pigs, or gamble. Although the Koran urged that women be treated with kindness, it said that God made man superior to woman. A Muslim was allowed to have as many as four wives at the same time, provided he could support them and would treat them alike. While it was fairly easy for a Muslim to divorce his wife, it was difficult for an unhappy wife to leave her husband. The Koran also permitted a husband to beat his wife. However, a divorced wife could keep at least part of her dowry and was not forbidden to remarry.

There are similarities and differences between Christianity and Islam. Both Christianity and Islam are based on belief in one God. Both regard the Old Testament of the Hebrews as sacred, and look upon the Hebrew prophets and Jesus as messengers of God. Both stress kindness and fairness in dealing with one's neighbor. For Muslims as well as Christians, good behavior is rewarded and sin is punished.

There are also differences between the two religions. Islam has no priests, no sacraments, and no religious images such as statues or paintings of Mohammed. Muslims consider Mohammed a *man* chosen by God as the Prophet; Christians regard Christ as *divine,* God's son who came to earth to show man the way to heaven. Muslims expect to find in heaven all the pleasures that they desired or lacked on earth—plenty of water, trees, fruit, and the company of beautiful women. The Bible, of course, speaks of heaven in different terms.

Islam expands to the east and west. After Mohammed's death in 632, the leadership of Islam passed to Abu Bakr (uh-boo-*bak*'er) a close friend of the Prophet. Abu Bakr became the first *Caliph* (*kay*'lihf) or successor to Mohammed. He and the caliphs who succeeded him advocated the *jihad* (jih-*hahd'*), or holy war to convert nonbelievers to Islam. Under the first four caliphs the soldiers of Islam burst out of the arid Arabian Peninsula and in less than twenty years conquered vast areas of the Persian and Byzantine Empires. In little more than a century after the Prophet's death the empire of Islam had spread to include most of Spain, North Africa, the Middle East, and part of India. The forces of Islam also exercised control over most of the Mediterranean. How was Islam able to expand so rapidly?

1. Inspired by the message of Mohammed, Muslim warriors carried both a sword and an unswerving faith into battle. Believing that they were fighting for a holy cause, the Muslims fought hard and well. Did not the Koran state that those who died on the *jihad* would gain a place in Paradise?

2. This faith was reinforced by the Arabs' desire to escape from the barren Arabian Peninsula where they faced a constant struggle to get enough food and water. For centuries small groups of Arabs had pushed their way into the fertile lands of Palestine, Syria, and the Persian Gulf. Islam gave the many tribes a single cause. United under its banner, the Arabs penetrated the rich Byzantine and Persian Empires.

3. The Byzantine and Persian Empires had been engaged in destructive wars with each other for many years. Neither was strong enough to withstand the Muslim forces.

The Umayyads rule the caliphate for nearly a century. In 661 a member of the Umayyads (oo-*my*'yadz), an influential family in Arabia, became caliph. For nearly a century the Umayyads controlled the expanding Muslim empire. The Umayyad caliphs introduced sound government and efficient administration that included an extensive postal system. They generally pursued sensible policies towards conquered peoples, requiring them only to provide food for the army and pay taxes. They did not force conquered peoples to become Muslims, although many did. Because they, too, were believers in one God, Christians and Jews were generally treated well. Many even obtained prominent positions in the army and the government.

The Abbasids change the outlook of the empire. In 750 the Umayyads were overthrown by Abbas (ah-*bahs'*), descended from an uncle of Mohammed. Abbasid (*ab*'uh-sid) rule changed the character of the empire. Under the Umayyads the chief positions in the government had been held by Arabs. This was resented by Persian, Syrian, Egyptian, and other non-Arab converts to Islam. Though the Abbasids themselves were originally Arab, they were more interested in taking the best from peoples they ruled. Government officials were drawn from the different peoples that made up the empire, with Persian influence being particularly strong. Many Persian customs were adopted as well as many elements of Persian culture. Like Persian kings, the Abbasid caliphs held absolute power. A person holding an audience with the caliph was required to stretch himself out and kiss the floor. This kind of behavior was unknown to the independent Arabs of Arabia. The Abbasids moved the capital from Damascus in Syria to Baghdad in Iraq. Baghdad became the commercial and cultural center of the Muslim world.

The power of the Abbasids declines. The Abbasid caliphs soon found that their empire was too large to be governed effectively from one center of power. Often the men they appointed to govern outlying parts of the empire revolted and set up rival Muslim states. Seeking to strengthen their position, the Abbasids brought Turks from Central Asia to Baghdad as palace guards. Intrigue and treachery even-

tually made these guards, regarded as slaves, the true power behind the throne. Religious dissent also played a part in weakening Abbasid power. Though the Muslims did not change their faith, different interpretations of the Koran and disputes over the right of succession to the caliphate divided the empire internally. The followers of different Islamic sects were often bitterly at odds with one another. In North Africa and Spain rival caliphates sprang up. Instead of one caliph, there were soon

Expansion of Islam

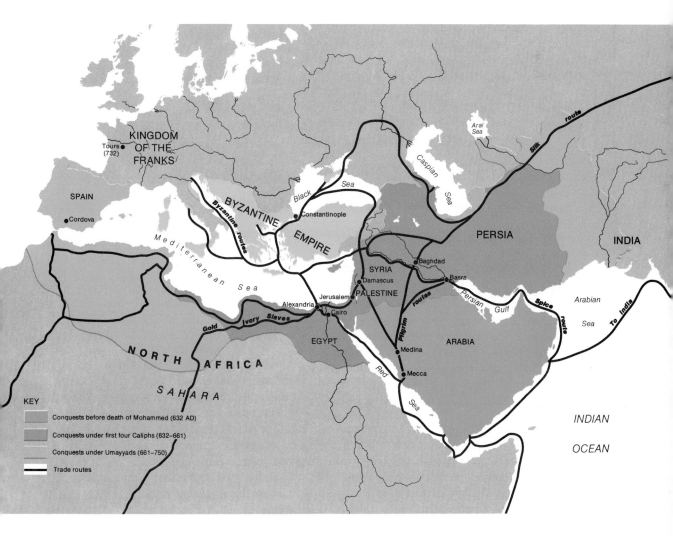

KEY

Conquests before death of Mohammed (632 AD)

Conquests under first four Caliphs (632–661)

Conquests under Umayyads (661–750)

Trade routes

three. By the tenth century the empire had broken into some twelve rival states and lay open to foreign invasion. In the eleventh century the Seljuk Turks, who had converted to Islam, extended their control over much of the Muslim empire in Persia and Asia Minor. Abbasid caliphs remained on the throne but exercised virtually no authority.

At the very end of the eleventh century Muslim lands were invaded by Western Europeans seeking to win the Holy Land for Christianity (see pages 152–157). The long period of warfare, known as the Crusades, weakened the Muslim empire still further.

(see pages 152–157)

CHECK-UP

1. How did Mohammed come to establish a new religion? Why did many Arabs at first reject his message?

2. What are the basic teachings of Islam? How does the Koran regulate daily life?

3. Name some similarities and differences between Christianity and Islam.

4. Why did Islam spread so rapidly?

5. Why were the Umayyads successful? Why did the Muslim world lose its unity under the Abbasids?

Society and Culture of the Muslim World

A Muslim civilization takes shape. Despite invasions and wars, the cultural unity of the Muslim world endured. Millions of Muslims from three continents continued to share a common language and culture. The golden age of Muslim culture occurred during the early part of Abbasid rule. When the Arab Muslims had begun their conquests, they had little in the way of culture except their language and their religion. The peoples they conquered in the Byzantine and Persian Empires were culturally far more advanced. To Islam they contributed a rich heritage in literature, philosophy, science, and art. A distinctly Muslim civilization took form and endured long after the empire broke up into separate states.

During the Early Middle Ages, when learning and town life had declined in Western Europe, the Muslim world had a rich and varied civilization. Its cities were renowned for their magnificent palaces and *mosques,* the Muslim place of worship, and for their schools, libraries, and bustling marketplaces.

The wealth of the Muslim world depends upon commerce. The Muslims gained possession of North African and Middle Eastern trading centers, thereby taking over the commercial activity of the old Roman Empire. Muslim merchants were highly respected and did business with most parts of the known world. Their ships visited the East African coast as well as the ports of India, Southeast Asia, and China; their caravans crisscrossed Central Asia and crossed the Sahara into black Africa. The extent of Muslim trade is shown in the following description by a medieval traveler:

[To Baghdad] . . . came all the products of the world in constant stream. Spices of all kinds, . . . sandalwood, . . . teak for shipbuilding, ebony for artistic work, jewels, metals, dyes, and minerals of all kinds from India and [Southeast Asia]; porcelains and . . . musk [used in perfume] from China; pearls and white-skinned slaves from the lands of the Turk and the Russian; ivory and Negro slaves from East Africa—all were brought here by traders and nagivators after long and arduous journeys by land and sea. At the same time the city merchants carried on a profitable trade with China in the products of the Caliphate: dates, sugar, glassware, cotton, and iron. Even more brisk was the internal trade between the various provinces of the empire, all of which trade flowed through Baghdad. Egypt's rice, grain, linen, and paper; Syria's glass and metalware; Arabia's spices, pearls, and weapons; Persia's silks, perfumes, and garden produce—all found their way here.

Through the Golden Horn, the harbor of Istanbul (left), pour the products and peoples of East and West, as they have since the days of Byzantine glory. Across the land, caravans (above) still carry Muslim pilgrims to Medina and Mecca. While modern transportation is replacing camels, the wastes of the desert (top) have changed little since Mohammed's day.

The constant trade encouraged Muslims to travel. Since Arabic was used or known in all the regions where Muslims traded, there were few language barriers. One famous Muslim traveler, Ibn Batuta (*ib″n bah-too′tah*) of Morocco, covered more than 75,000 miles in caravans or on board trading ships. Trade and travel led to an interest in geography. In many cases works by Arab geographers served for centuries as the only guide to Asian and particularly African lands and peoples.

Industry and agriculture also contribute to the prosperity of the Islamic world. Muslim textiles of cotton, silk, muslin, and damask were in high demand, and carpet weaving became a fine art.

Leatherworking of many kinds was of high quality, as was metalworking. Muslim artisans demonstrated unusual skill in setting enamel and precious stones into gold and silver, in making glazed tiles of many colors, in painting and enameling glass, and in carving stone in intricate designs.

Muslim agriculture in many ways was as advanced as Muslim industry. Extensive use of irrigation made many dry regions productive. This increased the food supplies available and made possible city life on a large scale. More types of food became available, especially fruits. Oranges, lemons, apricots, and melons were introduced into Europe by the Muslims.

Muslim society is flexible. Muslim society was divided into an aristocracy and the common people. To the first class belonged the caliph and his family, officials in the government, and prominent military men. Among the common people there were three groups: (1) the educated—literary men, scholars, artists, merchants, and professional men; (2) the country population of farmers and herdsmen; and (3) slaves. Since men of talent could rise to high positions in the government, the division between nobility and common people was not rigid.

Slavery is common in the Muslim world. Long before Mohammed, slavery had existed in Arabia. The Prophet considered it part of the natural order of things and did not try to abolish it. Slaves had no rights and could own no property. The slaveowner was allowed to sell, give away, or rent his slaves. Since free Muslims were not allowed to be sold into slavery, it was necessary to obtain slaves from distant lands. Muslim slave traders did a good business in both black and white slaves. However, the Koran did urge humane treatment of slaves and considered it praiseworthy for a master to free a slave. Household slaves were often treated as though they were members of the family, and some slaves rose to high positions in government.

Learning flourishes in the Muslim world. The Muslims were greatly interested in books and learning. Universities were established in leading Muslim cities—Baghdad, Damascus, Jerusalem, Alexandria, Cairo, Cordova. The book business flourished. In universities, palaces, and the homes of wealthy merchants could be found large libraries. American historian F. B. Artz discusses libraries in the Muslim world during the Middle Ages:*

We hear of a private library in Baghdad, as early as the ninth century, that required 120 camels to move it from one place to another. Another scholar of Baghdad refused to accept a position elsewhere because it would take 400 camels to transport his books; the catalogue of this private library filled ten volumes. This is the more astonishing when it is realized that the library of the King of France in 1300 had only about 400 titles. In the thirteenth century before the [Mongols] sacked the city [1258], Baghdad had 36 public libraries and over a hundred bookdealers. . . . The larger libraries were staffed with educated librarians, copyists, and binders. . . . The . . . public library . . . in Cairo, . . . called the House of Wisdom, . . . by the eleventh century claimed to have over a million volumes on its shelves. By 1250 the most valuable material in the Islamic libraries had become available to European scholars in translation. This transference came just in time, for, shortly after the middle of the thirteenth century, the Mongols in the East and the Christians in Spain began to destroy Islamic books in a wholesale manner. . . . Fortunately, a large number of Islamic books survived in Egypt, Persia, and India, from whence most of our knowledge of Muslim civilization has come.

Muslims make advances in mathematics, astronomy, physics, and chemistry. Muslim scholars collected the works of ancient Greek scientists and translated them into Arabic. Besides this preservation of the Greek heritage, Muslim scholars made known discoveries of

* From *The Mind of the Middle Ages* by Frederick B. Artz (New York: Alfred A. Knopf, Inc., 1954). Reprinted by permission.

Indian scientists and mathematicians and made contributions of their own to man's knowledge. They improved upon the mathematics and geometry of the Greeks, adopted and passed on to the West the concept of the zero and "arabic" numerals from India, and probably did the first work in algebra. Using the work of the second-century Greek astronomer Ptolemy (*tuhl′*eh-mih) as a basis, Muslim astronomers made significant contributions to man's knowledge of the heavens; many of the stars still bear the Arabic names given them by these astronomers. The Persian Omar Kháyyám (kie-*yahm′*) who was also a poet, devised a calendar more accurate than the one we now use. In physics and chemistry great contributions were made. An important work on optics was done by the Persian Alhazen (al-hah-*zen′*). He showed that sight occurs when rays passing from objects are received by the eye. Chemists developed several methods which are basic to chemical research and devised some of the laboratory equipment which is used today. They also discovered several important chemical compounds. Like the Greeks, the Muslims were deeply interested in the world about them.

Muslim health care is advanced for that age. Muslim medicine was based chiefly on knowledge inherited from the Greeks. The writings of Hippocrates and Galen (*gay′*len) served for centuries as the Muslims' guides to medicine. Since the Koran forbade the dissecting of the body, there was little investigation into the structure of the body and its functions. But Muslim surgeons were generally far ahead of their Western contemporaries. In Western Europe operations were generally performed by barbers. Muslim surgeons, on the other hand, received special training and were required to pass examinations. Among the operations they performed were amputations, the removal of cancerous tissue, and the peeling of cataracts on the eye.

The painting at left, from a Persian manuscript, illustrates a pharmacist mixing cough syrup, the recipe for which is in the text. On the astrolabe (right), used to observe the position of the heavenly bodies, Arabic numerals mark off 360 degrees.

Muslim medical men also made advances in the use of drugs to heal the sick and sometimes used anesthetics in performing operations. Prescriptions could be filled in the leading cities of the empire. To prevent fraud and health hazards, government inspectors periodically checked druggists' supplies.

Muslim hospitals were efficient; the best had separate wards for fevers, surgical cases, eye disease, and dysentery. Well ahead of their time were those Muslim doctors who recommended humane treatment for the insane. The Persian al-Razi (al-*ray'*zee, Rhazes), one of the leading physicians of the Muslim world, wrote about smallpox, measles, kidney stones, poisons, skin diseases, and ways of maintaining one's health. His most important contribution was his careful diagnosis of illnesses:

The eruption of the smallpox is preceded by a continued fever, pain in the back, itching in the nose, and terrors in sleep. These are the more peculiar symptoms of its approach; . . . then also a pricking which the patient feels all over his body; a fullness of the face, which . . . goes and comes; an inflamed color, and vehement redness in both . . . cheeks; a redness of both the eyes; a heaviness of the whole body; great uneasiness, the symptoms of which are stretching and yawning; a pain in the throat and chest, with a slight difficulty in breathing, and cough; a dryness of the mouth, thick spittle, and hoarseness of the voice; pain and heaviness of the head; inquietude, distress of mind, nausea, and anxiety; . . . heat of the whole body, an inflamed color, and shining redness, and especially an intense redness of the gums.

The Muslim world contributes great scholars. Many of the great Muslim physicians were also philosophers. Al-Razi, Ibn er-Rushd (er-*roosht'*, Averroës), and Ibn Sina (*see'*nuh, Avicenna) wrote many philosophical as well as medical works. The early Muslim philosophers were concerned mainly with religious matters. Later philosophers, showing a strong Greek influence, stressed the importance of intelligence and of reason. The works of Ibn er-Rushd and Ibn Sina were studied in Western universities that flourished late in the Middle Ages.

The Muslims wrote histories of Muslim lands and peoples. The leading Muslim historian, Ibn Khaldun (kal-*doon'*), is also considered by many to be the father of sociology. He discussed how cultures differed, the development of their institutions, and their arts and sciences. Ibn Khaldun, concludes one student of Muslim history, "did not merely document the events of the past . . . but gave history a new dimension by trying to find rational laws to explain it and the human behavior that shaped it. . . . [He was aware of] the many factors that influence human events—the relentless physical facts of climate, geography, and economy, as well as the moral and spiritual forces that guide man's destiny."

Muslim art and architecture set high standards. Art forms borrowed from other peoples were developed into an original style which is distinctly Islamic. Muslim art was strongly influenced by religious beliefs. Because the Koran prohibited the faithful from copying human figures, Muslim artists turned all their talents into developing intricate and graceful geometric designs. The pages of manuscripts, especially the Koran, copper and brass utensils, the walls of buildings, and the small rugs used in prayer revealed a wide range of designs. Written Arabic was especially adaptable, since it could be written in an elaborate or simple style and combined well with other designs.

In Persia, where there was a long tradition of art, the restrictions on depicting the human form were to some extent ignored. Delicate miniatures of hunters, warriors, and court scenes were painted on ivory, bone, and wood.

In the mosque, art and architecture were combined to make graceful structures. The solid rounded arch of the Romans was transformed into a delicate "horseshoe" arch supported by slender columns. Mosaics of light and dark stone and of glazed tiles made graceful patterns on the walls. Domes were often used in mosques, each of which had a *minaret* —a slender tower from which a *muezzin* (moo-*ez'*in) summoned the faithful to prayer.

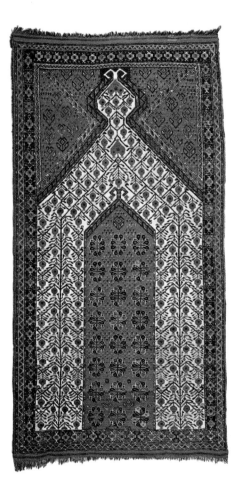

When Muslims pray, they kneel on a prayer rug with the design pointing toward Mecca. The Turkoman rug (left) and the Alhambra in Spain (above) suggest the extent of the Muslim empire. The use of floral design and script reveals the skill of Muslim artists.

The Arabic language helps unify the Muslim world. Perhaps the most important contribution of Muslim civilization was one which came originally from Arabia—the Arabic language. Arabic was not only the language of the Koran. It was also the language of trade and foreign relations throughout the Muslim world. Moreover, non-Muslim businessmen who had dealings with Muslim merchants often learned Arabic. This helped to make Arabic an international language.

The Muslims develop a varied literature. A very adaptable language, Arabic is rich in expressions that please the ear and excite the imagination. The foremost work in Arabic is, of course, the Koran, which set the style for the later literature of the Islamic world. Because religion was an inseparable part of Islamic culture, much Muslim literature dealt with interpretation of the Koran, religious philosophy, and Islamic traditions. But there were also many popular tales and legends. The Persian contribution to this literature was great; much of the best writing was done by Persians, and many of the traditional tales had a Persian origin. Men of education throughout the Muslim world wrote poetry and a variety of prose. Poets—women as well as men—were highly regarded in Muslim society and had the support of the caliphs, many of whom were themselves skilled at writing verse.

CHECK-UP

1. How did commerce influence life in the Muslim world?
2. What were the achievements of the Muslims in industry? Agriculture? Science? Medicine?
3. How did Islam influence Muslim art? What influence did it have on literature?

Decline of Muslim Civilization

In the thirteenth century a new wave of invaders, the Mongols, burst out of Central Asia. For centuries nomadic tribes had wandered the highlands and plains of Mongolia, seeking pasture for their herds. Warfare between the tribes was common. In the beginning of the thirteenth century, however, the tribes were united by a remarkable man, Chinggis (*ching'*gihz, or Genghis) Khan, one of the greatest conquerors of history. The new Mongol Emperor molded the nomadic horsemen into a well-disciplined, fast-moving, and loyal fighting force.

The Mongols disrupt the Muslim world. Ruler of a unified and strong kingdom and eager for plunder and glory, Chinggis Khan turned to the rich civilization of China. He demonstrated an extraordinary skill as a military strategist and leader of men. In four years his armies destroyed the capital of North China and gained enormous wealth—articles of gold and silver, silk fabrics, horses and cattle, and slaves. From China, Chinggis turned westward to the Muslim lands. The superb Mongol archers, mounted on fast-moving ponies, poured across Asia into Persia, plundering the land and devastating cities. Deliberately killing and burning to terrorize the lands they invaded, the Mongols destroyed schools, libraries, mosques, and palaces and slaughtered tens of thousands of Muslims. By 1227, when Chinggis Khan died, the eastern part of the Muslim world had fallen under the iron heel of the Mongols.

The death of Chinggis Khan fails to end the Mongol threat. In 1237 some 150,000 Mongol horsemen invaded Europe. The terrifying horde swept across Russia and through Poland and Hungary. Panic spread throughout Europe. "A terrible dread of this barbarian people took possession of even the most remote countries, not only France, but also Burgundy [in France] and Spain, where the names of the [Mongols] had hitherto been unknown," wrote a French knight. Western Europe was saved only by the death of the Great Khan, one of Chinggis' sons, in 1241. Upon hearing of their emperor's death, the Mongol generals returned to Mongolia to elect a new ruler.

Though Western Europe had been spared, the Muslim world was less fortunate. One after the other, the Muslim states fell and in 1258 the Mongols stormed Baghdad, the cultural capital of the Muslim world, leaving it in ruins. Among the thousands of corpses littering the streets of Baghdad was that of the last Abbasid caliph.

The Ottomans become the dominant power in the Middle East. Following the decline of Mongol power, the Muslim world entered a period of disunity and anarchy. At this time other Turkish nomads from Central Asia, the Ottomans, were on the march. Early in the thirteenth century they established themselves in Asia Minor. During the next century these vigorous warriors, who had converted to Islam, extended their conquests into the Balkans. By the middle of the 1400's they threatened the remnants of the Byzantine Empire. In 1453 Constantinople, which had withstood hundreds of attacks since its founding, fell to Ottoman forces. Soon most of the Middle East and North Africa, and much of Eastern Europe, were under Ottoman control. The Ottoman Turks developed an extremely efficient fighting force and a system of administration which held most of their empire together for nearly 500 years.

Once again there was a unified, and for a time powerful, Islamic empire in the Middle

Mongol and Turkish Invasions

c. **1055**	Seljuk Turks invade Byzantine lands and take over Persia
1162–1227	Chinggis Khan
1258	Mongols sack Baghdad
1290–1326	Beginning of Ottoman expansion
1326–1918	Ottoman Empire
1453	Ottoman Turks take Constantinople

Mongol Empire (1294)

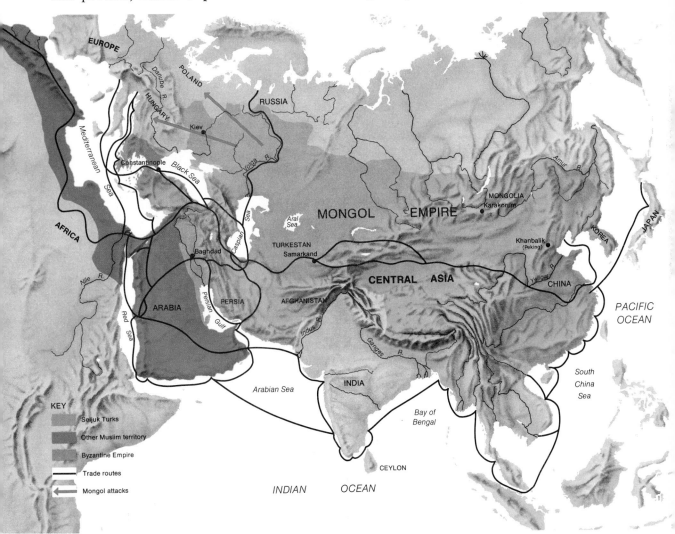

KEY

Seljuk Turks

Other Muslim territory

Byzantine Empire

—— Trade routes

⟵ Mongol attacks

KEY

In 1350
In 1481
In 1683

Growth of Ottman Empire

East. But under the Ottomans the Muslim world failed to regain the cultural greatness that it had achieved during the Middle Ages. For much of the Middle Ages the Muslim world had been far more advanced than Western Europe. Eventually, however, scientific, economic, and cultural superiority passed to the West. In comparison the Muslim world lacked vitality and originality. The decline of Muslim civilization was due to (1) the destruction of Muslim cultural centers and the weakening of the Muslim world by invading armies of Mongols and Turks, (2) a rigid interpretation of the Koran that blocked change and reform, and (3) the despotic rule of Ottoman sultans opposed to new ideas and new ways.

The Turks conquered both the Byzantine Empire and most of the Muslim world. In the following chapter we shall turn to the third civilization that emerged on the ruins of the Roman Empire: Latin Christendom or Western Europe.

CHECK-UP

1. How did invasions by Mongols and Ottoman Turks affect the Muslim world?

2. What was noteworthy about the Ottoman Empire?

Summing Up

The Byzantine Empire survived the overthrow of the Roman Empire in the West by nearly a thousand years. During this period Constantinople was not only the imperial capital but the seat of the Eastern Orthodox Church and the center of trade between Asia and the Mediterranean lands. The learning of the Graeco-Roman world was preserved in the Byzantine

Empire and in time transmitted to Western Europe and to Russia.

For many centuries the great rivals of the Byzantine Empire were the Muslims. The religion of Islam, founded by Mohammed about 600 A.D. in the Arabian Peninsula, attracted many followers. Mohammed's successors launched holy wars to convert nonbelievers to Islam. In little more than a century Islam had spread westward across North Africa and into Spain and eastward into India. The Arabic language helped to unify this vast Muslim world. In general Muslim rulers provided efficient government and dealt generously with conquered peoples.

The wealth of the Muslim world depended upon commerce by land and sea with Asia, the Middle East, Africa, and Spain. Not only did the Muslims cherish and preserve Graeco-Roman learning, they also made important contributions in mathematics, the sciences, and medicine.

Both the Byzantine Empire and most of the Muslim lands of the Middle East fell under the control of the Ottoman Turks. Although the Ottomans, who had converted to Islam, gave unity to the Muslim world, they could not restore the cultural and economic greatness which had been enjoyed by Islamic lands during much of the Middle Ages.

Chapter Highlights

Can you explain?

bedouins	caliph	jihad	muezzin
mosaics	mosques	minaret	

Can you identify?

Abbasids	Muslims	Hejira	Ottoman Turks
Umayyads	Mohammed	Constantinople	Byzantine Empire
Koran	Seljuk Turks	Mecca	Patriarch of Constantinople
Ramadan	Kiev	Allah	Chinggis Khan
Baghdad	Mongols	Islam	Eastern Orthodox Church

What do you think?

1. In what way did the Byzantine Empire contribute to the cultural awakening of Western Europe? To Eastern Europe?

2. Why was Constantinople considered a "second Rome"?

3. What did the teachings of Jesus and Mohammed have in common? Why did they make so lasting an impression on the world?

4. Why did the Muslim empire flourish under the Umayyads? Begin to break up under the Abbasids?

5. It has been said that the Muslims transmitted culture by the sword and the caravan. What does this mean?

6. Compare the cultural outlook of the Muslims and the ancient Greeks.

7. What can we learn about Muslim civilization from studying its literature?

8. What do you think were the most significant achievements of Muslim civilization? Why?

9. How did the Arabic language contribute to the unity of the Muslim world?

7

Medieval Europe: Feudal Lord and Catholic Church

CHAPTER FOCUS

The Rise of Feudalism
Life of the Feudal Lord
Life of the Serf
Decline of Feudalism and Serfdom
Growth of the Medieval Church

Worldly life in the Early Middle Ages centered around the manor and the simple but strongly built manor house (above). The culmination of medieval architecture was the Gothic cathedral. The French cathedral shown at left is a Gothic masterpiece which reflects man's aspiration to build an inspiring place of worship. Through stained-glass windows (inset) light pours in jeweled hues across the interior. Guilds often donated money for windows which, like this one showing carpenters, represented their craft.

With the passing of the Roman Empire in the West, Western Europe entered the *Middle Ages,* or *medieval period.* In the Early Middle Ages (500–1050) it became clear that a new civilization was taking shape in Western Europe. This new civilization, which developed slowly over the centuries, was a mixture of Graeco-Roman, Christian, and Germanic elements.

Thus in the Middle Ages three new civilizations emerged in the lands once ruled by Rome. In the last chapter we discussed two of these civilizations, Byzantine and Islamic. In this and the following chapter we shall discuss the distinctive civilization that arose in Latin Christendom (*Kris'*n-dum, Western and Central Europe). This chapter will concentrate upon the foundations of medieval Europe—the feudal lord and the Catholic Church.

131

When the Western Roman Empire collapsed, it broke into different parts. Separate kingdoms under Germanic leaders were set up in Gaul (France), Italy, Spain, and England—lands formerly ruled by Rome. While the German invaders did preserve some of the law, administrative procedures, and culture of the Roman world, there was no strong central government to protect life and property. The system of law and order developed by the Romans broke down. Bands of armed men roamed the countryside killing and stealing. The Early Middle Ages were so filled with violence, confusion, and disorder that they are sometimes called the *Dark Ages.*

Charlemagne's Empire

Charlemagne rules a great empire. In the last third of the eighth century, however, Charlemagne (*shahr'*leh-main), a Frankish ruler, built a large empire in Western and Central Europe. Charlemagne's administration provided a considerable amount of order throughout his lands. This political unity helped to spread Christianity in Western Europe. Charlemagne also advanced education and culture. On Christmas day in the year 800 he was even crowned Emperor of the Romans by the Pope. This ceremony signified that the Roman ideal of a unified empire had not died. Doubtless there were some who believed that Charlemagne was reviving the Roman Empire in the West. But Charlemagne's empire, which held together much of present-day France, Germany, and Italy, did not survive his death in 814. Europe returned to political disunity.

Cities, trade, and learning decline in the West. In the days of Rome's glory, there had been great cities in which merchants, craftsmen, and government officials lived. There were libraries, theaters, stadiums, and schools. In the markets were spices, slaves, and luxury items from distant lands. Many upper-class Romans were well educated. They read the works of Latin and Greek authors and enjoyed going to the theater. But in the last years of the Empire, trade, town life, and cultural development declined. This was caused by ineffective government, civil wars, invasions, a dwindling city population, and shortage of money. This decline continued into the Early Middle Ages, especially after control of the Mediterranean Sea and its trade passed into Muslim hands. Many cities were almost deserted. Seeking security, many people moved to large estates, or *manors,* where they could be protected by powerful noblemen. Most people lived like pioneers. Few could read or write. They worried chiefly about staying alive and had little interest in book learning.

ATLANTIC

OCEAN

NORTHMEN

CELTS

CELTS

CELTS

ANGLO-SAXONS

London

North Sea

SAXONS

Baltic Sea

Novgorod

SLAVS

LETTS

Dnieper R.

POLES

Kiev

English Channel

CELTS

NORMANS

Paris · Seine R.

Rhine R.

FRANKS

CZECHS

BAVARIANS

Bay of Biscay

BURGUNDIANS

SLOVENES

MAGYARS

Danube R.

Black Sea

BASQUES

IBERIANS

CORSICA

ITALIANS

Rome

SERBS

BULGARIANS

Constantinople

SARDINIA

MUSLIMS (MOORS)

Mediterranean

SICILY

GREEKS

MUSLIMS (MOORS)

MUSLIMS (SARACENS)

Sea

**As the power of kings declines, that of feudal
lords increases.** During the declining years of
the Roman Empire and the centuries of the
Early Middle Ages kings had little power. The
lack of strong rulers led to a new system of
government and landholding. It was called
feudalism. Under feudalism power passed into
the hands of powerful men called lords, who
seized or owned large estates. These lords were
all-powerful in their own regions. They had
their own armies and administered the laws for
the people on their estates. Often lords went to
war with each other. There was no central government strong enough to keep the peace.

Peoples of Europe, 800–1000

Middle Ages (1)

500–1050	Early Middle Ages
529	Monte Cassino founded
768–814	Charlemagne
787–900	Viking expansion and con-quests
1050–1270	High Middle Ages

Both sturdy and swift, the Viking ship carried warriors (top) who spread terror throughout Northern and Western Europe and braved the Atlantic to reach the shores of America.

While the roots of feudalism reach back into the days of the late Roman Empire, feudalism became the dominant form of government after the disintegration of Charlemagne's empire in the ninth century. The kings who inherited Charlemagne's broken empire were unable to maintain effective control over their territories. Moreover, during this period Western Europe suffered from frequent raids. Northmen from Scandinavia threatened coastal regions from England to Spain; Magyars from Central Asia followed the paths of other Asian invaders of Central and Eastern Europe. Italy and the nearby Mediterranean islands were frequently attacked by Muslims using North African ports as naval bases. The authority of weak kings was further diminished by such raids. As power came to be exercised by feudal lords, Western Europe entered an age of feudalism.

The lord and his vassals have mutual obligations. Because he lived in a period of warfare, the medieval lord needed allies. To obtain them, he granted another lord, called a *vassal,* some land, called a *fief* (*feef*). Both lords and their vassals were members of the upper class (nobility). In granting the vassal a fief, the lord promised to protect him in case of attack. In return, the vassal agreed to perform certain duties for the lord. It was a two-sided bargain: the lord promised protection and land to his vassals; the vassals agreed to render certain services to their lord.

1. Military service. The most important duty of a vassal was to help his lord in battle. When his lord went to war or when an enemy attacked the lord's land, the faithful vassal rushed to help. Usually the vassal had to give service for forty days each year, but sometimes he did so for longer periods.

2. Feudal payments. The vassal also had to make certain payments to his lord. If a lord were captured by an enemy, it was the vassal's duty to help pay the ransom. When a lord gave his eldest daughter in marriage or when his son was knighted, he demanded and expected a contribution from his vassals.

3. Court service. In feudal days each lord had his own law court. Vassals had to serve in the lord's court. Sometimes a lord quarreled with his vassals. At other times disputes arose between vassals of the same lord. Such questions were brought to the lord's court. All the lord's vassals met to decide who was guilty. Every lord had the right to trial by his fellow lords. Usually a lord would not punish one of his vassals unless he had the approval of the court.

CHECK-UP

1. What conditions led to the rise of the feudal system? Why?

2. What services did a vassal owe his lord? What did he get in return? Who do you think benefited more from this arrangement? Why?

3. Why did the empire established by Charlemagne fail to survive his death? What factors enabled some feudal lords to become more powerful than kings?

Life of the Feudal Lord

The lord, above all else, was a warrior. He enjoyed the excitement of battle, and welcomed a chance to prove his courage and to seize his enemy's possessions. Lords lived by the sword and were often captured, wounded, or killed in combat.

A lord's son was trained to be a knight. He learned how to wear armor, ride a war horse, and fight with sword and lance. When the youth had proved his ability and courage, he was knighted. It was an impressive ceremony. While other knights looked on, the youth knelt before a lord and received a light tap on the shoulders with a sword. With his entrance into knighthood he became a man who, by inheritance, marriage, or his courage, might become a powerful lord.

Knights are expected to behave like Christian gentlemen. In time a code of behavior called *chivalry* evolved. True knights were supposed to be Christian gentlemen: generous with their wealth, honorable in their dealings with fellow knights, courteous to women, and loyal to their lords. To break one's word, to attack an unarmed man, or to mistreat a captured opponent was considered dishonorable. In one castle some captured knights were kept in chains. Their bodies were unwashed, their clothes torn. When a lord saw how the knightly prisoners were treated, he said: "If we are knights, we ought to pity knights. Free them from [their] chains, bathe them and cut their hair, give them new clothes, and let them sit with me at the table." The code of chivalry, however, applied only to the upper class. Common people and non-Christians were often mistreated by knights and lords.

It was also the duty of knights to defend the Church against her enemies and to protect women, the helpless, and the orphan. "Most Holy Lord," prayed a knight, "cause thy servant here before thee . . . never to use this sword . . . to injure anyone unjustly but let him use it always to defend the Just and the Right."

Knights lived for glory and risked their lives in combat to win the respect of fellow lords. They wanted troubadours to sing of their heroic deeds. For a knight there could be no happiness without honor and glory.

The medieval castle is planned to withstand attack. Standing alone, high on a rocky hill or by the bend of a river, was the lord's castle. There were no buildings near it, and nearby trees and bushes had been cut down. An approaching enemy could easily be seen, for there was no place to hide. The castle was surrounded by a stream or a *moat*—a wide ditch filled with water. When an enemy force approached, the drawbridge across the moat was raised. Troops took their position high on the castle walls to defend the fortress.

There are several ways to storm the castle. Attacking forces laid careful plans to capture a castle. First, they would try to fill part of the moat with logs and dirt so that it could be crossed. Once they had a road across the moat, they would try to go under, over, or through the castle walls. As the attackers raised ladders against the castle walls, its defenders hurled boiling water, hot oil, melted lead, and huge stones at the climbing soldiers. While attempts were made to scale the castle walls, other attackers tried to break down part of the wall. Huge battering rams pushed by soldiers would hammer away at the wall, or machines called catapults would hurl big stones at it until it crumbled.

Sometimes the attackers used a movable tower, the top of which was as high as the castle wall. This tower was built of heavy timber and moved on wheels or rollers. When it came close to the wall, a drawbridge was lowered to the castle wall. The soldiers in the tower, and others who moved into it, would then rush across the wall and attack the enemy.

Other times the attackers might try to dig a tunnel under the castle's walls. Often alert defenders heard the digging and would build a tunnel of their own to join it. Then a savage underground battle would be fought between attackers and defenders.

The castle is also the lord's home. In the castle lived the lord and his lady, members of the family, guests, men-at-arms, ladies who attended the lord's wife, and servants. The most important room in the castle was the great hall. Here the lord ate his meals, gave orders to his servants, and entertained his guests. At night when the lord retired to his bedroom, household servants placed rough straw mats on the floor of the great hall and went to sleep. On the walls hung shields, lances, deer antlers, and bear heads. Great logs burned in the huge fireplace. At one end of the room stood a long oaken table at which the lord, his family, and his guests ate their meals. Castles were drafty, cold, dark, and dirty. Smoke from the fireplace blackened the walls. Dogs, cats, and rats competed for scraps of food that the lord and his guests threw on the floor.

The lady of the castle is a housekeeper. The following lines from medieval literature suggest the role of the lady of the castle:

Woman, go within and eat and drink with your maids. Busy yourself dying silks. Such is *your* business. *Mine* it is to strike with the sword of steel.

The lady of the castle made certain that all household duties were carried out properly. She looked after the servants and taught young girls how to sew, spin, and weave. When guests came for dinner, she was a charming hostess. To please her husband, she practiced singing, dancing, and horseback riding.

The wife of a feudal lord was at the mercy of her husband. If she annoyed him, she could expect a beating. To protect her, the Church limited the size of the stick with which she

Despite medieval man's concern with religion, he also delighted in depicting scenes of everyday life. In elaborate tapestries, master weavers portrayed ladies at various household tasks (left), lords fighting, banquets, and hunting scenes. In contrast to the serenity of this scene in a fanciful garden is the manuscript illumination (below) capturing the excitement of the tournament. Mounted on galloping "great horses," knights with lances extended met head on in contests only slightly less deadly than warfare.

could be hit. In one scene from a medieval poem a great lord is angered at a remark made by his wife. "He shows his anger in his face, and strikes her in the nose so hard that he draws four drops of blood, at which the lady meekly says, 'Many thanks, when it pleases you, you may do it again.'" Even though the lord mistreated his wife, he left her in charge of the castle when he was away.

Chivalry improves the lot of noble ladies. As chivalry evolved, noblewomen were held in greater respect. Wandering minstrels called *troubadours* sang love songs to their favorite ladies and praised their beauty and charm. Knights were taught to honor ladies. They tried to win a lady's love with kindness, gentleness, and consideration. They dressed neatly, played soft music, and sang love songs: "The great beauty, the good manners, the shining worth, the high reputation, the courteous speech, and the fresh complexion which you possess, good lady of worth, inspire me with the desire and the ability to sing." The warrior was becoming a gentleman. It was felt that no man could be a true knight unless he admired and adored a lady.

The medieval lord has several forms of amusement. In times of peace, medieval lords became bored. For excitement they held *tournaments* —contests in which knights engaged each other in combat to prove their skill. These tournaments could be almost as dangerous as real battle.

The medieval lord also amused himself by hunting. Surrounded by a yelping pack of hunting dogs, or using trained falcons, he searched the forests for wolves, bears, and boars.

After dinner, which was often a great feast, the lord called for his minstrels. These talented musicians played harps, guitars, or flutes and sang about the deeds of brave knights. Clowns, called *jesters,* amused the lord with clever remarks and foolish actions. The lord also enjoyed the performances of jugglers, acrobats, magicians, and animal trainers, all of whom wandered from castle to castle in search of an audience. They knew that a good performance would bring them food, a place to sleep, and also some coins.

Life for the lord is not all play or warfare. The manorial lord also had to keep track of the needs of the manor and to see that these needs were met. He decided what crops should be planted on his own land and when, and what buildings needed repair. He kept his men-at-arms ready for battle. His officials settled disputes between peasants on the manor and watched over supplies; his law court judged quarrels between vassals.

CHECK-UP

1. What did chivalry involve? What group lived by this code? Which groups were outside it?

2. How would an enemy attack a castle? Why was this a difficult task?

3. Would you consider the castle a comfortable home? Why? What were the responsibilities of the lady of the castle?

4. The life of the lord included both recreation and responsibilities. Describe them.

Life of the Serf

Most peasants become serfs. In the last years of the Roman Empire in the West, many peasants had given their land to lords in return for protection from thieves and warrior bands. Others had lost their land because of debt. In the Early Middle Ages there were few farmers who owned the land they worked. Most peasants lived in farming villages on *manors*— estates held by a lord and containing his manor house. These peasants, called *serfs,* received from the lord a hut in which to live and land to farm. In return, they farmed the lord's land and did various jobs for him. Their whole life was spent on the manor. It was their world and they seldom left it.

Whereas the lords tried to fill their days with excitement, life for the common people was dull and hard. They lived and worked on the manor. From the labor of the common people the lord drew his wealth.

The manor is largely self-sufficient. Almost everything needed for daily life was found on the manor. The peasants grew grain and raised cattle, sheep, goats, and hogs. Blacksmiths, carpenters, and stonemasons did the building and repairing. Women made clothing. In the forests were wild animals that the lord would hunt; in the pastures cattle grazed. The lord's war horses were given special care. The lord's oven baked the peasants' bread and his mill ground their corn. A priest cared for the religious needs of the people. When a manor was attacked by another lord, the peasants found protection inside the walls of the manor house. (In the eleventh century wealthy lords began to build great castles to take the place of the less strong manor houses.) The manor house and the huts of the peasants built along the road leading to the manor formed a small village. The manor was almost self-sufficient—able to produce everything it needed. Some goods, however, such as salt and iron, had to be obtained from the outside.

The common people rarely left the manorial village. Dense forests separated one manor from another. Poor roads and few bridges made travel difficult; thieves and warring knights made it dangerous. Peasants lived, worked, and died on the lord's estate and were buried in the village churchyard. They knew almost nothing of the outside world.

What are the obligations of the serfs? Most peasants who lived on the manor were not freemen. As serfs they had many duties to perform for their lord and there were many things that they could not do without the lord's consent. And if a lord lost his manor to another lord, the peasants remained on the manor, bound to their duties although their lord had been replaced. In many ways, then, the serf's freedom was restricted.

1. Bound to the manor. The serf could not leave the manor, even to travel to the next village, unless the lord gave him permission.

2. Marriage restrictions. Before a serf could marry, he had to pay a fee to the lord. Sometimes the lord would not allow the serf to marry the woman of his choice. Moreover, the lord could select a wife for his serf and force him to marry her. If the serf objected to the lord's choice, he could pay a fine instead.

3. Use of the lord's equipment. The serf had to use the lord's equipment and buy goods from the lord. He had to bake his bread in the lord's oven, grind his wheat in the lord's mill, and press his grapes in the lord's winepress. The serf paid for these services in kind—that is, with part of his produce.

At certain times of the year the serf had to buy wine from his lord even if he had no use for it. On one manor, if the serf failed to buy the two gallons required by the lord, "then the lord shall pour a four-gallon measure over the man's roof; if the wine runs down, the [serf] must pay for it; if it runs upwards, he shall pay nothing."*

4. Food for the lord. A serf had to turn over to the lord a portion of the grain and vegetables harvested on his own plot of land. Often the lord also demanded chickens, eggs, and pigs.

5. Labor for the lord. The lord kept for himself the best land on the manor. The serf had to work his allotted land and give a portion of his crops to the lord. And he had to work his lord's land and turn over all its crops to the lord. In addition, the serf had many other tasks. He had to help dig ditches, gather firewood, build fences, and repair roads and bridges. His wife helped to make clothing for the lord's family and household servants. The serf probably worked about three days a week for his lord.

Although the serf was not free, neither was he a slave. His children could not be taken from him and sold. As long as the serf carried out his duties to his lord, he had a right to live in his cottage and to farm his strip of land. Unlike the modern factory worker, the serf never had to worry about unemployment. Moreover, the

* Selections from *An Introduction to Medieval Europe, 300–1500* by James Westfall Thompson & Edgar Nathaniel Johnson are reprinted with the permission of the publisher, W. W. Norton & Company, Inc., New York, N.Y. Copyright © 1937 by W. W. Norton & Company, Inc. Copyright renewed 1965 by Edgar Nathaniel Johnson. Reprinted also by permission of George Allen & Unwin Ltd.

Often lavishly decorated, the Book of Hours contained the prayers and religious instruction for hours of the day set aside by the Church for devotional purposes. In this page for March, serfs labor in the fields outside the walls of the castle. At the top is a section of the zodiacal band.

lord gave him protection from bandits and attacks by other lords.

Sensible lords did not overtax or mistreat their serfs. They knew that unhappy serfs might become dangerous. Such lords took to heart the following warning by the Church: "The great must make themselves loved by the small. They must be careful not to [arouse] hate. . . . If [peasants] can aid us, they can also do us harm.

You know that many serfs have killed their masters or have burned their houses."*

Farming is inefficient in many ways. How was farming carried out on the manor?

1. Three-field system. Medieval farmers understood that the soil loses its fertility if the same crops are planted year after year. Since they did not as a rule use fertilizers, they developed a *three-field system.* Each year two fields would be planted, while the third field was allowed to lie *fallow,* or idle. Because nothing was planted in this field, the land regained its fertility and was ready for use the following year.

2. Strip farming. Each field was divided into strips. Many of these strips were the lord's, but some were set aside for his serfs. The serf did not have one plot of land to farm. Instead, he had strips in each of several fields. The strip system was an attempt to be fair, for all the fields were not equally fertile. By having land in each field, the serf would farm both good and poor soil. No serf would have all good land while another had only poor.

3. Cooperative farming. No single peasant could plow or harvest without help. Even if the serf owned a plow, he would not have enough oxen to pull it. Since the plow was heavy, the oxen small, and the harness poor, a team of eight oxen might be needed to plow the land. (By the twelfth century, probably because of an improved harness, four oxen were needed.) The peasants thus *worked together* on all the strips in the fields. Each peasant received the produce from his own strips, but all the plowing and harvesting was done cooperatively, with all the serfs on the manor helping each other.

4. Primitive methods. Medieval farmers used primitive tools. Their plows were clumsy and hard to pull. Because there was little iron, they

* Selections from *An Introduction to Medieval Europe, 300–1500* by James Westfall Thompson & Edgar Nathaniel Johnson are reprinted with the permission of the publisher, W. W. Norton & Company, Inc., New York, N.Y. Copyright © 1937 by W. W. Norton & Company, Inc. Copyright renewed 1965 by Edgar Nathaniel Johnson. Reprinted also by permission of George Allen & Unwin Ltd.

used wooden farm tools. Handicapped by poor equipment and largely ignorant of fertilizers, medieval farmers did not make good use of the soil. Today, with scientific farming and improved seed, a farmer can get a yield of 32 bushels of wheat per acre; with the primitive methods and poor seed of the Middle Ages, he could get only six to eight bushels.

The serf lives poorly. Huddled together along the side of the village road were the peasants' huts. On a small manor there might be only fifteen huts, on a large manor as many as sixty. These cottages were small, crude, and uncomfortable. They had thatched roofs, floors and walls of mud-plastered logs, and open windows that were stuffed with straw in the winter. There was only one room. In the center burned a small fire, the smoke escaping through a hole in the roof. The bed was often a pile of straw. The peasant shared his home with his chickens and pigs who wandered about loose.

Unlike the lord, the serf almost never sat down to a feast. His daily food consisted of vegetables from his garden, brown bread, cereal, cheese, and soup. Fresh meat, milk, and butter were luxuries. There were many wild animals in the forests, but the serfs were forbidden to hunt them. At times of bad harvests, many peasants died of starvation. When asked about his life, a medieval plowman replied:

I work very hard. I go out at dawn driving oxen afield and yoke them to the plow. For fear of my lord I dare not stay at home even when the winter is very cold. Every day I must plow a full acre or more. . . .

What else do you do?

I have to get the hay for the oxen, water them, and clean out the sheds.

Great is your labor!

Verily, it is because I am not free.

Nobody could mistake the medieval serf. His coat was made of rough material. "His hood," said a medieval writer, "was full of holes and his hair stuck out of it." As the serf worked in the field, "his toes peered out of his worn shoes with their thick soles," and he was covered with mud up to his ankles. "He had two mittens . . . with worn out fingers." Walking alongside him was his wife, who looked old beyond her years. "She went barefoot on the ice so that the blood flowed." In a worn cradle lying on the ground "a little child covered with rags" lay crying.

At best, the serf has a hard lot. The serf worked in the fields from sunrise to sunset. This back-breaking labor left him exhausted. By the time he was 35, he looked like an old man. Disease crippled and killed many of his children. When lords engaged in feudal warfare, the serf suffered. Sometimes his home was destroyed, his animals stolen, and his crops ruined. The serf's misery was passed on to his children. They, too, were born into a life of serfdom, although some escaped the system by becoming priests.

If a serf had a cruel lord, his life was made even more miserable. Such lords had little love for their serfs and sometimes mistreated them. They regarded peasants as ugly and dirty creatures. Peasants were often insulted by medieval writers.

Peasants are those who can be called cattle. They have such hard heads and stupid brains that nothing can penetrate them.
They have one squint eye and the other is blind.
They have one good foot and the other twisted.
The devil did not want the peasants in hell because they smelled too badly.*

The peasant's pleasures are simple. Although the peasant's life was hard and dull, he did enjoy some pleasures. He saw the performances put on by wandering minstrels, acrobats, bear

* Selections from *An Introduction to Medieval Europe, 300–1500* by James Westfall Thompson & Edgar Nathaniel Johnson are reprinted with the permission of the publisher, W. W. Norton & Company, Inc., New York, N.Y. Copyright © 1937 by W. W. Norton & Company, Inc. Copyright renewed 1965 by Edgar Nathaniel Johnson. Reprinted also by permission of George Allen & Unwin Ltd.

trainers, and actors. On holidays serfs gathered in front of the church to sing, dance, and wrestle. Peasants had their own amusements, too. For example, there might be a contest in which three or four blindfolded men, each swinging a heavy stick, would try to kill a pig or goose let loose in a fenced-in area. When they stumbled or hit each other, the audience roared with laughter. These were the pleasures of simple, illiterate people.

CHECK-UP

1. How did peasants become serfs? How did serfs contribute to the welfare of the lord of the manor?
2. In what ways was a serf's freedom limited? What advantages did he enjoy?
3. What methods of farming were used on the manor? Why was agricultural yield limited?
4. Why was the serf's life a constant struggle?

Decline of Feudalism and Serfdom

Changing times lead to the decline of feudalism. Feudalism developed in a period when kings were weak. The real rulers were lords who owned large amounts of land. Lords did not want kings to grow stronger. They feared that a strong monarch would reduce their power and take away their land. Late in the Middle Ages kings did just that. In France, Spain, and England powerful monarchs established strong central governments. In some cases these kings had been great lords who had taken power and land away from other lords. Now, instead of many lords, each having control over his own region, one king ruled a nation. Instead of the people being loyal to a lord, they became subjects of a king. The lords still existed, but they had lost much of their power to strong kings. How were kings able to defeat or win over feudal lords and replace feudalism with monarchies—states led by kings?

Townspeople side with the king against feudal lords. In the eleventh and twelfth centuries there was a revival of town life in Western Europe. In their struggles with feudal lords, kings were aided by townspeople who themselves found fault with these lords. For one thing merchants wanted good roads for the transportation of goods. But most roads passed through lands belonging to feudal lords little interested in keeping them in repair. Moreover, feudal warfare made travel unsafe. Townsmen also complained about tolls that they might have to pay when crossing the lands of a feudal lord. Only a king who ruled a large territory could improve these conditions. Moreover, a strong monarch would establish one law for the entire land. This was much better than having to obey the many different and conflicting laws decreed by feudal lords. The king could also issue coins which would have the same value throughout the land. For all these reasons the townsmen helped the monarch in his struggle against the feudal lords. They often loaned or gave the king money with which he could hire officials to administer his laws and soldiers to enforce them, particularly against feudal lords.

Gunpowder destroys the military superiority of armed knights. The introduction of gunpowder also worked to the advantage of kings. The heavily armored knight on horseback fighting with sword or battle ax was no match for the king's soldiers armed with muskets. Nor could the walls of the lord's castle withstand the pounding of the iron balls fired from cannon.

Actually, even before gunpowder was introduced, armored knights had not fared well in fighting against determined commoners armed with longbows or crossbows. If his warhorse was wounded or killed, the dismounted knight was an awkward and not very dangerous foe.

Serfdom also declines. The revival of town life also contributed to the decline of serfdom. Some serfs fled to the new towns where, after a year and a day, they were considered freemen who could work for pay. Serfs who remained on the lord's land began to earn some money by selling food to townsmen. This enabled them to buy their freedom from the lord, who needed ready cash to pay for goods bought from merchants. As lords increasingly needed money, they began to accept cash payments from serfs in place of work or foodstuffs. Serfs who began meeting their obligations by making cash payments to lords gradually became rent-paying tenants. In time they no longer were bound to the lord's land.

Still another condition contributing to the decline of serfdom was the expansion of farm lands. Lords owned vast tracts of forest and swamp lands. If these lands could be cleared, drained, and farmed, the lord would increase his income. But serfs were unwilling to move from their holdings to do the hard labor needed to make the land suitable for farming. To encourage serfs to make such a change, lords promised them freedom from most or all obligations. In many cases the settlers fulfilled their obligations to the lord by paying a tax, rather than by performing services or providing food. They had become freemen.

CHECK-UP
1. Why did feudalism decline? What role did townsmen play?
2. What led to the decline of serfdom?

Growth of the Medieval Church

The Middle Ages is an Age of Faith. During the late Roman Empire and the Early Middle Ages, the Christian Church grew in importance and power. In many ways it took the place of the Roman Empire in the West. People had once been citizens of one Roman Empire; now most people in the lands once united by Rome were members of one Catholic Church. There was no longer an emperor in Rome, but there was the Pope, head of the Catholic Church.

To the people of the Middle Ages, religion was all important. This period is thus known as an Age of Faith. Medieval man believed that the Church was God's agent on earth. Its rules were God's rules; its teachings were God's teachings. Medieval man believed that God had created Earth, sun, moon, and all other heavenly bodies. He looked upon man as God's most important creation. Although man was often wicked and unworthy, he was still the child of God. Man's main concern was to follow God's commands. He saw life as a great drama with man the actor and God the critic. If man played his role well, he could look forward to a life in heaven. There, in the company of God and the angels, saints, and martyrs (those who had died for their religious beliefs), he would enjoy eternal life. On the other hand, wicked behavior on earth meant endless tortures in the fiery pits of hell.

The Church teaches that Jesus had sacrificed himself for mankind. The Church taught that Jesus had come down to earth to redeem man from sin and enable him to rise to heaven. He had died on the cross so that sinful man might be saved. Now, the Church taught, man must believe in Christ. "Let your hearts be in heaven, your thoughts in the skies," wrote a medieval poet. What Christ demanded of man can be seen in the following statement by a medieval churchman:*

> In the first place, to love
> the Lord God with all one's
> heart, all one's soul, and
> all one's strength.
> Then, [to love] one's neighbor as oneself.
> Then not to kill.
> Not to steal. . . .
> To honor all men.
> Not to do to another what one
> would not have done to oneself.
> Not to seek soft living.
> To relieve the poor.
> To love one's enemies.
> Not to be proud.
> To visit the sick.
> To bury the dead. . . .
> To console the sorrowing.
> To prefer nothing [above] the
> love of Christ.
> Not to yield to anger. . . .
> Not to forsake charity.
> Not to swear. . . .
> To utter truth from heart
> and mouth.
> To do no wrong to anyone,
> and to bear patiently
> wrongs done to oneself.
> To put one's hope in God.

The Church grows rich and powerful. The Church owned a great deal of land, received many gifts, and collected taxes from the people. During most of the Middle Ages the Church also controlled education, for clergymen (churchmen) were virtually the only ones who could read and write and pursue higher education. The Church also had many privileges. Clergymen were tried only in Church courts. They did not have to serve in feudal armies. Moreover, despite its large landholdings, the Church insisted that it did not have to pay

* From *The Rule of St. Benedict,* translated by Abbot Justin McCann (Westminster, Maryland: The Newman Press, 1952). Reprinted by permission.

A **Sacrament** is both a sign of and a means to God's grace. According to the Roman Catholic Church, the seven Sacraments were founded by Christ and are carried on by the Church.

1. **Baptism** initiates one into the Church and unites one to Christ.

2. **Penance** reunites man to Christ after man has sinned.

3. The **Eucharist, or Holy Communion,** is the Body and Blood of Christ. The priest changes bread and wine into Christ's Body and Blood as Christ did at the Last Supper.

4. **Confirmation** strengthens the baptized Christian, allowing him to live a mature Christian life.

5. **Matrimony** unites a man and woman in marriage.

6. In **Holy Orders** a man enters the priesthood.

7. **Extreme Unction** is an anointing and a blessing given to a seriously ill person to restore his spiritual and possibly his physical health.

---

taxes to kings or feudal lords. Its wealth, its control over learning, its efficient organization, and the widely accepted belief that its Sacraments (see box) and teachings were necessary for salvation gave the medieval Church enormous power and influence.

Clergymen have different ranks. Many clergymen served the Church. In almost every manorial village there was a *priest.* Supervising the religious activities of priests in a given district was a *bishop,* generally a man of noble birth. At the head of the Roman Church (the Church in the West) was the Pope, who came to be elected to his position by high-ranking clergymen called *cardinals.*

The Pope is regarded as God's representative on earth. The Pope exercised great powers and had very important responsibilities. He felt himself responsible for the souls of all Christians. It was his duty to lead Christian Europe on the path marked out by God's commandments. To carry out this holy duty, medieval Popes demanded complete obedience from all Christians. Wrote one Pope: "When Christ [rose] into heaven, he left one vicar [deputy] on earth and hence it was necessary that all who wished to be Christians were to be subjected to the [rule] of the vicar." No churchman, king, lord, merchant, or serf was supposed to challenge or question the Pope.[1]

Powerful kings come into conflict with the Pope. When feudal lords lost much of their power to strong kings late in the Middle Ages, the Pope demanded that these kings obey him and respect the rights of the Church. Innocent III, the most powerful of medieval Popes, said that the Pope was "less than God but more than man, . . . [he] shall judge all and be judged by no one." The true Christian had to serve the Church and defend it from its enemies. Catholics were taught that to resist the Pope was to turn against God. Medieval Popes even claimed the right to remove disobedient kings from their thrones. When Popes tried to put these powers into practice, they often met with bitter resistance from rulers. Kings argued that taxes should be paid on Church property in their country. The Church would not accept this demand. Nor did kings want the Pope to tell them how to rule their people. Clashes between kings and the Pope eventually weakened the Church.

[1] The belief that the Bishop of Rome (the Pope) acts as Christ's earthly agent is derived from a passage in the Gospel of Matthew, in which Christ said to the Apostle Peter: "Thou art Peter, and upon this rock [the Greek word for rock is Petrus] I will build my Church." These words were taken to mean that Christ intended Peter to head the Church. Peter's appointment as first Bishop of Rome was interpreted by the Church to mean that Peter and his successors had authority over all other churchmen and over matters of faith and morals.

Orders of monks render dedicated service to the Church. Since the early days of the Church, there had been men who believed they could best serve Christ by withdrawing from this world. These men became *monks*. Seeking nothing for themselves and wanting only to love and serve the Lord, monks withdrew to a *monastery* far away from the cares and pleasures of everyday life. To the people of the Middle Ages the monk was the finest example of the Christian life.

St. Benedict founds one of the earliest monasteries. The son of an Italian nobleman, Benedict was sent to Rome in the late fifth century for an education. Disturbed by the sinful life he saw in Rome, young Benedict fled the city. For several years he lived in a lonely cave on top of a cliff where he thought about God and how best to serve Him.

In time Benedict came to believe that there was a better way to serve God than by living as a hermit. Joining with other holy men, Benedict established a monastery at Monte Cassino in south-central Italy. In this house the monks lived in a communal fashion and served God together.

The rules Benedict drew up for the monastery called for poverty, obedience, study, and labor. Monks were required to work hard, talk little, joke not at all, and pray often. They could not own property, "absolutely nothing, neither a book, nor [writing paper], nor pen." Everything belonged to the monastery. At all times monks had to obey the *abbot*, the head of the monastery. The faithful monk would always "keep the fear of God before his eyes. . . . Let him ever remember all the commandments of God."

Monks contribute to civilization. The monks performed useful tasks. Some made furniture or clothing; others worked in the fields or prepared food in the kitchen. Still others copied old Greek and Roman manuscripts. Copying books was hard work. Their pens moving slowly and carefully, monks spent many hours in this labor of love. "He who does not know how to write," wrote one monk, "imagines that it is no labor, but though only three fingers hold the pen, the whole body grows weary." And another monk wrote: "I pray you, good readers who may use this book, do not forget him who copied it. It was a poor brother, named Louis, who, while he copied the volume . . . endured the cold, and was obliged to finish in the night what he could not write by day."* Monks who copied Greek and Roman manuscripts made an important contribution to civilization. During the Early Middle Ages, they kept learning from dying out.

Monks carried out various other important tasks. They gave food and shelter to the homeless, converted the Germanic tribes to Christianity, taught peasants better ways of farming, and organized schools.

The people of the Middle Ages believed that monks set an example of the Christian way of life. A young nobleman described the holy spirit that existed in the monastery:*

I watch the monks at their daily services, and at their nightly [prayers] from midnight to the dawn; and as I hear them singing so holily, . . . they seem to me more like angels than men. Some of them have been bishops or rulers, or else have been famous for their rank and knowledge; now all are equal, and no one is higher or lower than any other. I see them in the gardens with the hoe, in the meadows with fork and rake, in the forests with the ax. When I remember what they have been, and consider their present condition and work, their poor and ill-made clothes, my heart tells me that they are not the dull and speechless beings they seem, but that their life is . . . with Christ in the heavens.

Farewell! God willing, . . . I too shall [become] . . . a monk!

St. Francis embodies the Christian ideal. In the beginning of the thirteenth century, a handsome

* From *The Story of Europe* by Samuel Bannister Harding. Copyright 1912, renewed 1940 by Scott, Foresman and Company. Reprinted by permission.

Italian youth was seated in church. He heard the priest read these words of Christ:

> And as ye go, preach, saying,
> The kingdom of heaven is at hand.
> Heal the sick, cleanse the lepers,
> raise the dead, cast out devils:
> freely ye have received, freely give.

The young man was named Francis. He came from the town of Assisi (uh-*see'*zee). Deeply moved, he felt that Christ had spoken these words directly to him. Francis had found his life's mission. He would live as Christ had lived 1200 years earlier. He would give up all his possessions, comfort the sick, help the poor, and everywhere preach the message of the Lord. Soon Francis gathered a group of followers. Dressed in rags, usually penniless, and often barefoot, they wandered from town to town preaching love of God and love of man.

Many tales have been told about how St. Francis cared for those who suffered. One day when traveling on the road he came across a leper, horribly disfigured. St. Francis felt pity for the poor man who was a victim of this dreadful disease. Dismounting from his horse, he gave money to the leper and kissed his head. After that he often visited lepers, bringing them money and kindness.

St. Francis denied himself the pleasures of this world, devoting his life to prayer and helping the poor. He wanted only to serve Christ. The life of St. Francis shows how important religion was to the people of the Middle Ages.

Friars try to set an example of Christian living. Some holy men felt that withdrawal from the world was not the best way to serve God. Some, like St. Francis, wandered from place to place, aiding the poor and needy and teaching the ways of God. They tried to show people by example how a good Christian should live. These men, called *friars* rather than monks, were likely to be Franciscans or Dominicans. The former religious order was founded by St. Francis; the latter by St. Dominic, the prior of a monastery in Spain.

Medieval monks spent hours copying manuscripts and illustrating them with religious scenes and decorative borders (right). To illustrate man's faith in God, the famous Italian artist Giotto painted St. Francis (kneeling, above) driving out demons by the power of prayer.

The Church fights heresy. The greatest crime in the Middle Ages was *heresy*—holding beliefs which the Church considered wrong. The medieval Church believed there was only one way to reach Heaven, and that was to obey God's rules as taught by the Church. Heretics were regarded as evil men because they rejected the authority of the Church and might influence others to do likewise. In setting themselves above the teachings of the Church, heretics separated themselves from the Church. If heresy became widespread, the Church would ask kings and feudal lords to defeat it with the sword.

The Church excommunicates heretics. Those who disobeyed the Church could be excommunicated. *Excommunication* meant that a person would be expelled from the Church and denied the Sacraments. Anyone who helped such a person would himself be excommunicated. Medieval man believed that an excommunicated person would be denied admission to heaven. On earth he would live without the fellowship of friends; he would die without the comfort of a priest. To a Christian there could be no punishment more horrible than excommunication. Often the threat of excommunication was enough to convince a would-be heretic to mend his ways. Rather than be separated from the Church, he would confess his error and seek forgiveness.

The Inquisition tries heretics. In the thirteenth century the Church strengthened the *Inquisition,* a Church court which tried heretics. A person accused of heresy was brought before clergymen who acted as judges in the court. The Church urged the accused to confess his error and to ask forgiveness. Often torture was used to make the accused admit his wrongdoing. If he confessed and asked forgiveness, the Church welcomed him back. If the accused would not confess, he was excommunicated and turned over to the state for punishment, which occasionally was death by burning at the stake.

Why would men of God approve of torturing and executing persons whose beliefs were different from their own? Clergymen who punished heretics were certain that they were doing right. They firmly believed that only the Church could lead men on the road to salvation. Heretics and those who followed their teaching were destined for Hell unless they turned back to the Church. The death of a heretic made it easier to save the souls of the living.

What are some of the achievements of the Church? The medieval Church was an important and powerful organization. It greatly influenced the behavior and thoughts of Western Europeans. The Church cared for the needy, the sick, and the traveler. It tried to check violence and bloodshed. To reduce warfare among feudal lords, the Church proclaimed the Truce of God, which prohibited fighting on certain days of the week and on holy days.

The Church was a great civilizing force in the Middle Ages. It kept alive some of the learning of ancient Greece and Rome. During the Early Middle Ages, when learning had sunk to its lowest point, churchmen continued to read and write and to teach others to do so. Monks preserved and copied ancient Greek and Roman manuscripts. During the High Middle Ages, cathedral schools developed into universities. It was the Church, then, that sponsored higher education and learning.

The medieval Church gave unity to the people of Western Europe. This unity was furthered by missionaries who converted the heathen to Christianity. No longer citizens of one Roman Empire, almost all Europeans were members of one Church and worshiped one God.

CHECK-UP

1. What were the powers and privileges of the medieval Church? What services were rendered by priests? Monks? Friars?

2. What were the powers and responsibilities of the Pope?

3. Why was St. Benedict considered a pillar of the Church? Why is the life of St. Francis still admired?

4. Why was excommunication considered a dreadful punishment?

5. What social and cultural role did the Church play in the Middle Ages?

Summing Up

With the passing of the Roman Empire in the West, Western Europe entered the Middle Ages. The Early Middle Ages were characterized by (1) a decline in trade, town life, and learning, (2) the weakening of central authority and the growing power of lords, (3) the rise of serfdom and manorialism, and (4) the growing power of the Church.

In return for military and other services, feudal lords gave land to other nobles. Among the feudal lords a code of chivalry grew up. The sons of lords were educated in knightly warfare, and much of their adult life was concerned with combat.

Peasants sought security by living as serfs on a manor. Each serf was assigned land for his own use and in return helped to work his lord's land. While not slaves, the serf and his family could not leave the manor. They had to give a portion of their produce to the lord and to obey his regulations.

With the revival of trade and the growth of towns, feudalism and serfdom declined. Backed by the townspeople, strong kings took power away from feudal lords. Serfs gained their freedom by escaping to the towns or becoming tenants who paid cash rents instead of performing services and fulfilling obligations for lords.

The medieval Church was a powerful organization, and religion was of immense importance to the people of the Middle Ages. Through the Sacraments, the Church cared for the welfare of men's souls; it taught them to lead Christian lives. To strengthen the faith, it excommunicated heretics. The Church also tried to reduce feudal warfare. Monks and friars cared for the sick and the poor and helped preserve the learning of the Graeco-Roman world.

Chapter Highlights

Can you explain?

bishop	strip system	feudal lord	monastery
vassals	clergy	Pope	excommunication
cardinal	serfs	feudalism	heresy
tournament	fief	monk	three-field system
chivalry	priest	friars	manor

Can you identify?

Charlemagne	St. Benedict	medieval period	St. Francis
Truce of God	Dark Ages	Inquisition	

What do you think?

1. How did the disintegration of Charlemagne's empire help bring about the feudal system?

2. What elements of chivalry would you like to see preserved today? Of which do you not approve?

3. Among the feudal nobility, what was the attitude toward women? Compare it with the attitude of the ancient Greeks and Romans.

4. Why was the lot of a serf better than that of a slave?

5. Why would it have been difficult to make great advances in farming on a manor?

6. Why was religion so very important to most people in Western Europe during the Middle Ages? What effect did this have on the power of the Pope? Is religion as important today?

7. Why was heresy considered a dangerous crime against both Church and state? Do you think the Inquisition served a useful purpose? Why?

8. Why can the Church be called one of the greatest unifying forces in the medieval world?

9. In what ways was the medieval Church a political, social, and economic institution as well as a religious one?

prince telles choses proufitables selon le langaige du pais pour
instruire toute les assistens. Donc cestes choses ainsi tractees du
regime de maison en passent soubz silence auscunes choses part
culieres dignes de narracion. Nous faisons fin de ce second liure
ou quel nous auons bute art du regime domestique selon nre
science par laide de celui dont toute science et bonte vient.

Icy fine le second liure du regime des princes ou quel est tracte
du gouuernement de maison. Et comance le tiers liure le quel tracte
du regime de cite et communite. Dont le premier chapitre declaire
que la comunite de cite est auscunement principale et est constitue
pour cause de bien.

Awakening of Western Europe

With a rise in prosperity, markets in medieval towns (left) bustled with business. One could have new clothes made, visit the barber, buy food for a meal or a banquet, and obtain remedies for various ills. The smell of different foods, spices, leather, and woodsmoke stimulated the nose, and exotic goods captured the eye. Here people met to discuss local events, trade the latest gossip along with their goods, and enjoy the performances of musicians, troubadours, and jugglers (above).

In the Early Middle Ages (500–1050 A.D.) Western Europe was a pioneer society struggling to overcome invasion, disorder, and weak government. Trade, town life, and learning declined. Nevertheless, during these centuries of confusion, the foundations of a new civilization were taking shape. It took centuries for medieval civilization to mature, and in the twelfth century it entered its golden age. In the last three sections of this chapter we shall examine the achievements of this civilization—its philosophy, literature, science, technology, and architecture.

151

The cultural awakening of the twelfth century was enormously aided by a revival of trade and the rebirth of town life. In the second section we shall discuss the medieval town—its origins, its conditions of life and work, and its impact upon medieval civilization.

The chapter opens with an account of the Crusades—the prolonged conflict between Christendom and Islam. The Crusades, we shall see, were one indication that Western Europe had grown stronger and was bursting with vitality. Like the revival of trade, the growth of towns, and the flowering of culture, the Crusades were a sign that the Early Middle Ages had ended and that Western Europe was ready for new experiences and new achievements.

The Crusades: Christianity and Islam in Conflict

In 1095 Pope Urban II made one of the most dramatic speeches in history. Speaking to a gathering of French lords and clergy, Urban called for a war against the Muslim Turks, whose empire included Palestine, the land where Christ was born. He told the French lords that the Turks were "an accursed race, a race utterly [separated] from God," which had killed Christians and destroyed churches in the Holy Land. It was the duty of the Franks (Frenchmen), he said, to destroy these enemies of Christ. God has granted you, said Urban, "remarkable glory in arms, great courage, . . . and strength" to crush your enemies. He commanded the Franks to regain Palestine.

Stirred by his words, the lords cried out: "It is the will of God! It is the will of God!" Urban took up their cry: "Let this then be your war cry in combat, because this word is given to you by God. When an armed attack is made upon the enemy, let this one cry be raised by all the soldiers of God: It is the will of God! It is the will of God!" Kneeling before the Pope, the lords begged to be sent to the Holy Land.

After this speech thousands of Christian Europeans said their prayers, left their homes, and set out for Palestine. The Crusades had begun. (*Crusade* comes from an old French word meaning "to mark with a cross.") Latin Christendom (*kris"*n-dum)—as Western and Central Europeans had come to call their civilization—was engaged in a holy war with the Muslims that would last for almost 200 years.

Why does Pope Urban call for a crusade? There were several reasons for the Pope's action.

1. The Pope wanted Jerusalem, where Jesus was crucified, to be in Christian hands. The early Muslim rulers were fairly tolerant of other religions. With the coming of the Seljuk Turks, this policy was drastically changed. The Turks persecuted non-Muslims and prevented Christian pilgrims from visiting holy places in Palestine.

2. By urging thousands of feudal lords into combat, Urban would strengthen papal (the Pope's) power. The great lords would be using their swords in behalf of the Church. They would look to the Pope for leadership.

3. The Church hoped to reduce feudal warfare in Europe by sending war-hungry and land-hungry knights to fight in the Holy Land.

4. In 1054 the Eastern Orthodox Church, centered at Constantinople, had broken away from the Catholic Church in Rome (see page 112). Urban hoped that the Crusades might reunite the two churches.

Why are feudal lords eager to wage war against Islam? The feudal lords also had reasons for taking up arms against the Muslims.

1. They hoped to gain land and wealth from the Muslims.

2. They saw the Crusades as a chance to participate in a glorious adventure in which they could earn everlasting fame.

3. They felt it to be their religious duty to win Palestine from the Muslims, whom they called "infidels" (nonbelievers) and "God-hating dogs."

Excitement spread through Western Europe. Lords and knights began to organize crusading armies.

Common people are also gripped by the crusading spirit. Preachers wandered through the villages urging peasants to take part in the holy war. One of these preachers was a remarkable old man called Peter the Hermit. Small and thin, with a long grey beard, Peter dressed in dirty clothes, lived on fish and wine, and went barefoot through the countryside. He set out across northern France and Germany, arousing the peasants with fiery speeches. Loading their possessions on carts, thousands of peasants, with their wives and children, joined Peter's march to Jerusalem. Though poor, ignorant, and without adequate supplies, they were filled with religious enthusiasm. Many felt sure that Peter was leading them straight to heaven.

The undisciplined peasant crusaders turn into a mob. The commoners, numbering many thousands, began their holy war by slaughtering thousands of French and German Jews. As they crossed into Christian Hungary, they looted and murdered. In a quarrel over the sale of a pair of shoes, for example, some 4000 Hungarians were killed. By August, 1096, the peasant mob had reached Constantinople. To the daughter of the Byzantine emperor, the peasant crusaders appeared to be "a countless throng of ordinary people with their wives and children, all with the red cross [symbol of the Crusades] on their shoulders. They outnumbered the grains of sand on the seashore and the stars in the sky."* The cultured Byzantines feared this ignorant mob of peasants—and with good reason. The crusaders burned houses and

* Reprinted by permission of G. P. Putnam's Sons from *The Crusades* by Regine Pernoud. Copyright © 1962 by Martin Secker and Warburg Ltd.

Middle Ages (2)

1050–1270	Height of medieval civilization
1066	Normans conquer England
1095	Start of the Crusades
1209	Founding of Cambridge University, England
1215	Magna Carta
1267–1273	Aquinas writes *Summa Theologica*
c. **1300–1400**	Struggles with kings weaken medieval Church
c. **1321**	Dante completes the *Divine Comedy*
1348–1350	Peak of the Black Death
c. **1387**	Chaucer starts *Canterbury Tales*

stole everything they could, even the lead from the roofs of churches. The emperor got them out of Constantinople as quickly as he could.

Few peasant crusaders ever reached Jerusalem. Some had died of sickness and exhaustion on the journey across Europe. After leaving Constantinople, most of the remainder were massacred by the Turks. Their bones lay scattered in the fields and along the shores of Asia Minor. The Peasant Crusade was a disaster, proving that faith alone could not win Jerusalem.

An army of feudal lords is more successful. While the Peasant Crusade was meeting disaster, an army of feudal lords was being organized. It included some of the most famous warriors in Europe. On the long journey to Jerusalem the crusaders faced many hardships:*

[In the desert] hunger and thirst [attacked] us everywhere and we had hardly anything left to eat

* Reprinted by permission of G. P. Putnam's Sons from *The Crusades* by Regine Pernoud. Copyright © 1962 by Martin Secker and Warburg Ltd.

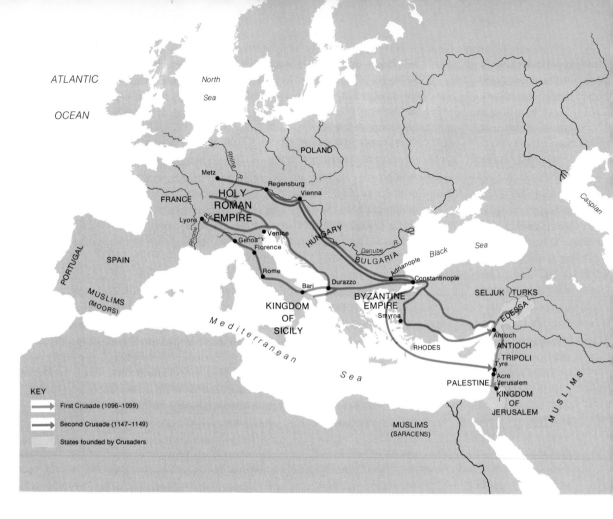

KEY
First Crusade (1096–1099)
Second Crusade (1147–1149)
States founded by Crusaders

First and Second Crusades

except thorns, which we pulled up and rubbed in our hands: such was the food on which we wretchedly lived. Most of our horses died there, so that many of our knights had to go on foot; because of our lack of mounts we used . . . goats, sheep, and dogs to carry our baggage. . . .

We penetrated into the . . . mountain that was . . . lofty and narrow. . . . The horses fell headlong into the ravines, and each pack animal dragged another down. On every side the knights gave way to despair and beat their breasts for sorrow and sadness.*

Finally, in June, 1099, the crusaders, "mad with joy," reached the walls of Jerusalem. Five weeks later they fought their way into the city

and without mercy slaughtered the Muslim and Jewish inhabitants. The scene, recorded by a Christian knight, was an example of religious *fanaticism*—extreme dedication to a belief, expressed by excessive and unreasoning zeal in its support. Killing for Christ and conquering for Christianity had come to be regarded as noble acts.*

Once in the town, our pilgrims pursued the Saracens [Muslims], massacring them as they went, right up to the Temple of Solomon, where they [gathered] their forces and fought a most furious battle with our people throughout the whole day, so that the whole Temple ran with their blood.

* Reprinted by permission of G. P. Putnam's Sons from *The Crusades* by Regine Pernoud. Copyright © 1962 by Martin Secker and Warburg Ltd.

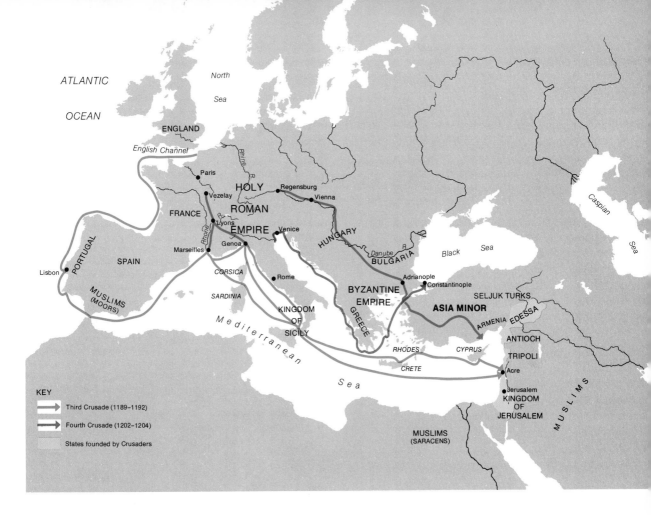

Map

ATLANTIC OCEAN

North Sea

ENGLAND

English Channel

Paris

Vezelay

FRANCE

Lyons

Marseilles

Genoa

SPAIN

Lisbon

PORTUGAL

MUSLIMS (MOORS)

CORSICA

SARDINIA

Rome

HOLY ROMAN EMPIRE

Regensburg

Vienna

Venice

HUNGARY

Danube R.

BULGARIA

Black Sea

Adrianople

Constantinople

BYZANTINE EMPIRE

GREECE

KINGDOM OF SICILY

Mediterranean Sea

RHODES

CRETE

CYPRUS

ASIA MINOR

SELJUK TURKS

ARMENIA EDESSA

ANTIOCH

TRIPOLI

Acre

Jerusalem

KINGDOM OF JERUSALEM

MUSLIMS

Caspian Sea

Rhine

Rhône

MUSLIMS (SARACENS)

KEY

Third Crusade (1189–1192)

Fourth Crusade (1202–1204)

States founded by Crusaders

After our men had at last routed the [nonbelievers], they seized the Temple and a great number of men and women, whom they killed or left alive as they thought fit. On the roof of the Temple of Solomon a large group of [nonbelievers] of both sexes had taken refuge. . . . Soon the crusaders were running all over the town, carrying off gold, silver, horses and mules, and . . . plundering the houses, which were crammed with riches.

Then, full of happiness and weeping for joy, our people went to worship the Sepulcher [tomb] of our Savior Jesus and to discharge their debt to Him. The next morning, they climbed up to the roof of the Temple, attacked the Saracens, both men and women, and drawing their swords, cut off their heads. . . .

. . . the whole town was almost entirely filled with corpses.

Third and Fourth Crusades

For the time being, the crusaders had won. A Christian ruled the Kingdom of Jerusalem. Three other Christian states were set up on lands taken from the Muslims. But the Muslims were determined to regain the land seized by the Christian invaders and to avenge the slaughter of their kinsmen. To them, the Franks were uncivilized murderers. When the Muslims attacked the Christian kingdoms, the call for another crusade was raised in Western Europe.

Later Crusades fail. Some of the greatest kings of Europe took part in the Second (1147–1149) and Third Crusades (1189–1192). But both Crusades failed. The Muslims continued

During the Crusades, mounted Christian knights and foot soldiers stormed Muslim strongholds in the Middle East. To protect what they had won, crusaders built castles such as the Krak des Chevaliers ("Castle of the Knights") in Syria (top).

to regain lands lost earlier to the Christians. On the Fourth Crusade (1202–1204), the crusaders never even reached the Holy Land. Instead, they captured and looted Constantinople (see page 113).

There was even a Children's Crusade. A twelve-year-old French shepherd boy named Stephen believed that God had commanded him to lead children to the Holy Land. With the help of God, the children would conquer

Jerusalem. Some 30,000 French youths, both rich and poor, followed Stephen. "The very children put us to shame," declared Pope Innocent III. The children got as far as Marseilles (mar-*sey'*), a port in southern France. There they expected the Lord to cause the waters of the sea to part, just as the waters of the Red Sea had parted for Moses, so that the children could walk across. Actually, most of the children were lost at sea or kidnapped by Christian merchants and sent to North Africa, where they were sold into slavery.

In 1291, almost two hundred years after Pope Urban's speech, the last Christian outposts in the Holy Land fell to the Muslims.

What are the results of the Crusades? Although the Crusades had failed to win the Holy Land for Christendom, they had an important impact upon Western Europe.

1. At first the Crusades strengthened the power of the papacy. It was the Pope who had inspired and given direction to the crusading armies. The Church increased its tax income to support the Crusades. After a while, however, Popes began to call for crusades against all enemies of the Church, including Christian heretics and German emperors. To many it seemed that the Pope was arousing religious enthusiasm among Christians merely to increase the political power of the Church. People criticized the Pope and questioned the wide political powers claimed by the Church.

2. Western Europeans who went on the Crusades came to know and value the products of the East—sugar, rice, fruits, spices, silks, pistachio nuts, cotton, cosmetics, mirrors, dyes, and many others. The increased demand for these luxury goods in Europe led to greater trade between Western Europe and Constantinople, and in time with Muslim lands.

3. The Crusades enabled some of the Italian city-states to increase their wealth and commercial power. Italians sold supplies to the crusaders. The crusaders sailed across the Mediterranean on Italian ships. Italian banking houses provided funds for the expansion of commerce. The growing trade between East and West was carried on largely by Italian merchants and seamen.

4. During the Crusades thousands of Western Europeans settled for longer or shorter periods of time in the parts of Palestine controlled by the Christians. Muslims and Christians came to know and even to respect each other. Christians used Muslim doctors, who were famous for their skills. Followers of the two religions permitted one another to pray in peace. They hunted together, discussed the differences between their religions, and even intermarried. The old hatreds were disappearing. Wrote one Christian: "It is certain, even if our beliefs are different, that we have the same Creator and Father, and that we must be brothers. . . . Let us then remember our common Father and feed our brothers."

5. The Crusades weakened the power of feudal lords, contributing to the decline of feudalism. Many lords died in the fighting. Others spent most of their income and savings in meeting the costs of transporting themselves, their men-at-arms, and horses to the Holy Land. Many serfs were able to buy their freedom from lords who were desperate for funds.

CHECK-UP

1. Why did Pope Urban call for a crusade? Why were many lords eager to take part? How did the crusading spirit affect the common people and even the children of Europe?

2. Describe the hardships that confronted the crusaders.

3. To what extent were the Crusades successful? A failure?

4. What were the results of the Crusades in terms of (a) papal power, (b) knowledge of new products, (c) trade, (d) the future of feudalism?

In Roman times there had been many cities in Western Europe, particularly in Italy and southern France. Some of these cities began as Greek colonies; others were built by the Romans. In the late Roman Empire, as trade declined and taxation increased, the number of middle-class townspeople decreased and cities sank into decay. By the Early Middle Ages most people lived in small villages on manors. For the most part, town life had come to an end. By the twelfth century, however, Western Europe again had many busy towns. What led to the rebirth and growth of towns?

The main reason for the growth of towns is the revival of trade. During the disorder of the Early Middle Ages trade was reduced to a trickle. But by the end of the 1100's commerce had greatly increased in Western Europe. European ships again sailed the Mediterranean and the eastern Atlantic. Merchants transported goods from ports to inland towns and exchanged goods at great fairs. The items sold in European markets came from many countries —spices, jewels, perfumes, and silks from the East, ivory from Africa, furs from Russia, timber, honey, and hunting hawks from Scandinavia, wool from England, cloth from Belgium, and wine from France.

Many trade routes followed rivers or crossed the sea from one good harbor to another. At harbors and where trade routes met, merchants gathered to buy and sell. Towns arose at these crossroads of trade, near fortified castles, by monasteries, and on the sites of old Roman cities. Into the new towns came craftsmen and serfs seeking freedom and fortune. The following medieval account shows how a town developed around a castle.

After this castle was built, certain traders began to flock to the place in front of the gate . . . of the castle; that is, merchants [and] tavern keepers. Then other outsiders drifted in for sake of food and shelter. . . . Houses and inns were erected for their accommodations. . . . These [buildings] increased so rapidly that soon a large [town] came into being.

Townsmen demand freedom from feudal restrictions. When towns rose on lands held by feudal lords, some of the lords tried to treat the townspeople as they did serfs. The townsmen objected. They expected to marry whom they pleased and to do as they wished with their property. They wanted to make their own laws and to settle disputes in their own law courts. To do these things, the townsmen had to be independent of the feudal lords. Sometimes by fighting, but more often by money payments, the townspeople gained their freedom. Lords were forced to grant *charters* to the townsmen. These charters gave the townsmen certain rights, or *privileges*. Townsmen gained the rights to govern themselves, set up their own system of taxes, and establish their own law courts. Towns became self-governing city-states, the first since Graeco-Roman days. Because of the greater freedom and opportunities in the towns, many serfs fled from the manors to the growing towns. Serfs who had bought their freedom also moved into towns in large numbers.

Medieval towns are small, crowded, and dirty. Because medieval townsmen feared attacks their towns were protected by thick high walls. Outside the walls was a deep moat like that surrounding a castle. Travelers entering the town had to cross a drawbridge and pass through a gate. At night the drawbridge would be raised and the gates closed. A gallows for hanging criminals was often erected near the main gate. The bodies of executed criminals were often left hanging on the gallows to serve as a grim warning to would-be lawbreakers.

The streets within the walls of the town were narrow, crooked, and dirty. Rats, pigs, and dogs competed for the garbage that people threw from their doors and windows. Unpleasant odors from slaughterhouses, stables, and rotting garbage were always in the air. Because of dirt and overcrowding, disease spread rapidly. Housing conditions were poor. It was common for twelve or more people to live in three small rooms. Built of wood, several stories high, and almost on top of each other, medieval houses were firetraps.

At night the streets were dark and dangerous. There was no real police force. The few elderly watchmen who made their rounds from street to street were no match for thieves and hoodlums. Honest folk who had to be out after dark always carried arms and never set out alone.

Medieval towns are centers of business activity. Merchants bought and sold goods that had come from as far away as India and China. Shoemakers, carpenters, weavers, silversmiths, and other craftsmen opened up shops to prac-

Trade Routes in Medieval Europe

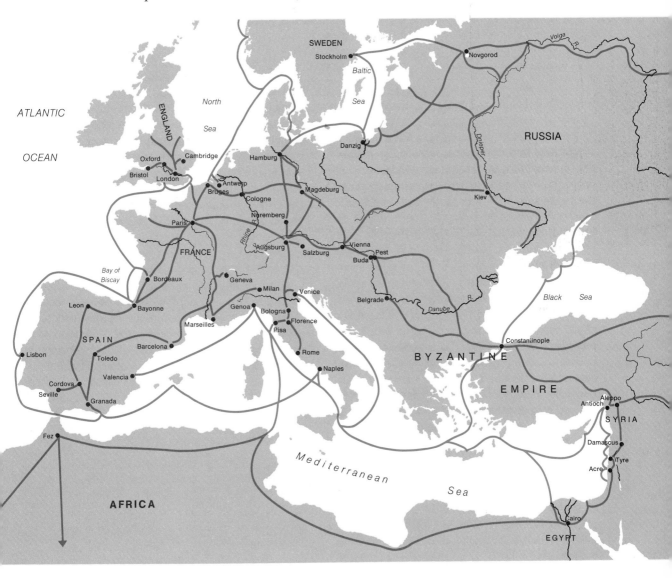

tice their trade. A visitor to Paris, wrote a twelfth-century Frenchman, sees:

many fine people at the changers of gold and silver and moneys; . . . he sees . . . the streets completely filled with good workmen who are practicing their different trades. This man is making helmets, this one mailed coats [armor]; another makes saddles, and another shields. One man manufactures bridles, another spurs. Some polish sword blades . . . and some are dyers. . . . And these here are melting gold and silver. They make rich and lovely pieces: cups, drinking vessels, and eating bowls; . . . jewels worked in with enamels; also rings, belts, and pins. One could certainly believe that . . . there was a fair every day, [the town] was so full of wealth. It was filled with wax, pepper, . . . dye, . . . [fine furs], and with every kind of merchandise.

How different this was from the Early Middle Ages!

Merchants and craftsmen form guilds. Merchants within the town banded together in an organization called a *merchant guild*. Townsmen practicing the same trade united in a *craft guild*. The guilds played an important role in the governing of the towns but their main purpose was to protect their members from the competition of merchants and craftsmen who did not live in the town. The merchant guild prevented outsiders from doing much business in the town. Before craftsmen new in the town could practice their trade, they had to be admitted to the craft guild. If a shoemaker settled in a town and opened a shop without being accepted by the guild, he would not be in business long. The guildsmen would close his shop, burn his goods, and lock him in the town pillory. A wooden device which was locked around a prisoner's head and hands, the pillory caused as much disgrace as discomfort. In this way the guilds were able to control the business life of the town.

The guilds discourage competition among their members. To make money, attract customers, and increase sales and profits, a present-day businessman might keep his store open late and cut prices. In the Middle Ages, however, the guilds discouraged competition. They set strict rules to prevent any member from making significantly more money than his brother guildsmen. All members of the shoemakers' guild, for example, had to keep their shops open the same number of hours, pay their employees the same wage, produce shoes of equal quality, and charge customers a so-called "just price." These rules were strictly enforced. Violators could be fined, thrown out of the guild, or even beaten. An English herring merchant tells us that when he "sold his merchandise at a [lower] price than other merchants of the town, . . . they [attacked] him, beat him and ill-treated him, and left him there for dead."*

The guilds maintained high standards of workmanship. They checked on members to make sure that regulations were followed and standards of quality met. Their way of enforcing these rules was effective. When a merchant sold spoiled fish, for example, the guild locked him in the pillory and burned the fish under his nose. A merchant who sold sour wine was forced to drink "a quart of his own wine and to have the rest poured over him."

The guild is also a social club. Guild members held meetings in the guild hall, celebrated holidays together, and marched as a group in parades. The guild also cared for members who were sick or poor and widows and children of deceased members, as is indicated by the following merchant guild rules for the town of Southampton, England:

And if a guildsman is ill and is in the city, wine shall be sent to him, two loaves of bread and a gallon of wine and a dish from the kitchen; and

* Selections from *An Introduction to Medieval Europe, 300–1500* by James Westfall Thompson & Edgar Nathaniel Johnson are reprinted with the permission of the publisher, W. W. Norton & Company, Inc., New York, N.Y. Copyright © 1937 by W. W. Norton & Company, Inc. Copyright renewed 1965 by Edgar Nathaniel Johnson. Reprinted also by permission of George Allen & Unwin Ltd.

two . . . men of the guild shall go to visit him and look after his condition.

And when a guildsman dies, all those who are of the guild and are in the city shall attend the service of the dead. . . .

If any guildsman falls into poverty and has not the wherewithal to live and is not able to work or to provide for himself, he shall [receive aid] from the guild.

It is difficult for a young man to become a guildsman. For a young man to become a member of a craft guild, he first had to serve as an *apprentice* to a *master* craftsman. For a period lasting from two to seven years, the young apprentice lived in his master's house, ate at his table, helped him in his shop, and learned his trade. During this time he received little or no pay.

After completing his apprenticeship, the youth became a *journeyman*—a day laborer who worked for a master for a daily wage. To become a master, the journeyman had to prove his skill to the guild. This meant presenting a piece of work, his *masterpiece,* to the guild's governors. For example, a journeyman wishing to become a master baker might present the guild with a cake he had baked. If it was judged to be worthy, the "new master" was admitted to the guild and was free to open his own shop. To gain the necessary funds, it was not unusual for the new master to marry the daughter of a wealthy master.

International fairs are held. As trade increased, great *fairs* were held in places on the main trade routes. Merchants from many countries traveled great distances to attend these fairs. There they set up booths to exhibit their wares. Visitors to the fair could buy swords, leather saddles, oriental rugs, shoes, silks, furs, furniture of fine woods, and other goods.

Medieval fairs were exciting events. Townspeople and peasants from the countryside were eager to attend. They stared at goods from faraway places and heard merchants speak strange languages. They enjoyed shows put on by acrobats, actors, performing bears, and roosters trained to fight. The following account by an Englishman shows that the fair was not just a place of business:

On the eve of . . . the first day of the fair in the year 1305, the traders and pleasure seekers, the friars and the jesters, . . . [acrobats], walkers upon stilts, hurried across the grass . . . from the [grounds] on which the fair was being held, to the Gallows under the Elms, where officers of state . . . [waited]. Trade in the fair was forgotten while [a prisoner] was hanged. . . . Then, all being over, the stilt-walkers strode back across the field, the woman again balanced herself head downwards on the points of swords; there was [laughter] again round the guitar.

Increased trade leads to advances in business techniques. Because of their strategic position in the Mediterranean, Italian towns acted as the middlemen between the trade centers of the eastern Mediterranean and those of Western Europe. From Byzantines in Constantinople, from Muslims in Egypt and Syria, and from their fellow Italians located in trading colonies along the Black Sea, Italian merchants acquired spices, silks, sugar, dyes, and other luxury goods, many of them from as far away as India and China. On Italian ships these goods were transported to Italy and then carried to parts of Germany and France. From the resale of these goods, Italians made a handsome profit.

In the fourteenth century the Italians extended their trade and increased their profits by sailing westward into the Atlantic Ocean to the markets of the Netherlands (Holland and Belgium) and England. On the return voyage, the Italians brought back wool and unfinished cloth which stimulated the Italian textile industry. This increase in trade led to advances in business techniques in several ways. (1) Merchants seeking to raise more money entered into business organizations such as partnerships. This enabled businessmen to expand their business and increase profits. (2) The increase in business activity gave rise to systematic bookkeeping. Without careful records no large-scale

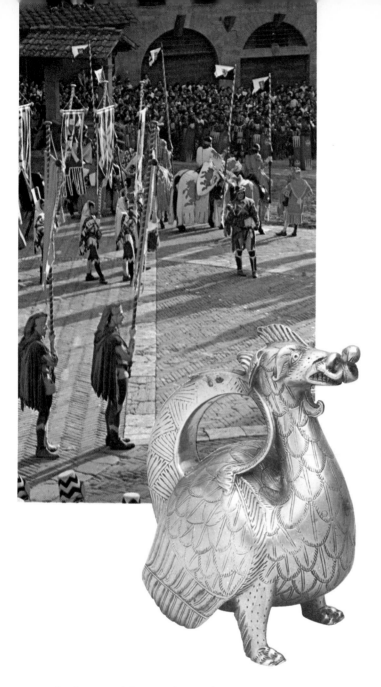

A council of masters in a craft judged the work of medieval craftsmen (above). Often this work was done for a religious institution. The finely made bronze dragon swallowing a man held water which priests used to cleanse their hands. In parts of Europe medieval guild ceremonies have been incorporated into modern pageants (left, top).

business activity can be conducted on a continuous basis. (3) To make it easier for merchants of different lands to do business with each other, banking and credit facilities were developed and expanded. This made it unnecessary for merchants to carry large amounts of cash. It also made borrowing easier.

Townsmen enjoy many amusements. Townsmen wrestled, bowled, ice-skated, danced, and practiced using sword and shield and bow and arrow. Tennis was popular in England and France, while the Irish enjoyed hockey. Soccer became so violent that for a while it was banned in England. The rich played chess, using beautifully carved and expensive pieces. On holidays guildsmen carrying colorful banners paraded through the streets and troubadours played while the townspeople danced. Sometimes traveling actors, troubadours, and circus performers visited the town. Brutal contests between trained animals were also popular. The medieval townsmen also enjoyed gambling and drinking.

What is the significance of the medieval town?
Many of today's great European cities began as small medieval towns. Some of the streets and houses built in the Middle Ages still stand. The growth of towns had a great impact upon Western Europe.

1. Rise of the middle class. The growth of towns led to the rise of a new class of people called the *middle class*—merchants and craftsmen who lived in the towns. Middle-class ways of living differed greatly from those of clergymen, feudal lords, and serfs. The clergy prepared men for heaven; feudal lords lived only for warfare and hunting. Serfs lived on an isolated manor and had little chance to get ahead. The townsman was a new man. He had freedom and he had money. He was busy with business and town affairs. His world was the market rather than the Church or the manor. He was competitive, critical, and progressive. In the centuries to come, the middle class would play a vital role in the history of Western Europe.

2. Decline of feudalism. The rise of a middle class contributed to the decline of feudalism. Merchants had many complaints against feudal lords. When merchants settled on a lord's territory, the lord demanded a tax. When they crossed a lord's bridge, he demanded a toll. Warring lords and bandits made travel unsafe. Merchants wanted a strong king to restrain feudal lords from interfering with business. They made loans to a king and paid him taxes so that the king could hire soldiers to put feudal lords in their place and could pay officials to administer royal law.

3. Decline of serfdom. The growth of towns also contributed to the decline of serfdom. Seek-ing freedom and fortune, serfs fled to the new towns. After remaining in the town for a year and a day, a serf became a freeman. The lord could not compel him to return to the manor. "City air makes a man free," went a medieval proverb. Moreover, serfs who remained on the manor were able to sell surplus produce to the townsmen. In this way many raised enough money to buy their freedom.

4. Advances in business practices. Increased trade and the growth of towns led to many advances in business. Money, which had almost disappeared after the fall of Rome, again jingled in the pockets of merchants. A system of banking was developed, making it easier to borrow money and to carry on large-scale trade. The note of a banker promising to pay a given amount on demand came to be accepted as a substitute for gold or silver.

The Crusades and the growth of towns were evidence that a new Western Europe was taking shape. Much of the confusion of the Early Middle Ages had come to an end. Western ships sailed across the Mediterranean seeking trade and conquest. Towns grew in number, size, and wealth. Kings began to establish strong central governments. While all this was taking place, there were also advances in learning and the arts.

CHECK-UP

1. How did the revival of trade help bring about the rebirth of towns?

2. Describe a typical medieval town. In what ways was it similar to a small town of today? Different?

3. Why did the Italian cities profit most from the increase in trade?

4. What were the two types of guilds? How did each serve the interests of members? Control the business life of towns?

5. What advances in business techniques were made during the Middle Ages?

6. What were important results of the growth of towns?

During the Early Middle Ages fighting and lawlessness made life in Western Europe difficult and unsafe. There was little time or opportunity for schooling, and most of the great books of ancient Greece and Rome had all but been forgotten. Except for the clergy, few men in Western Europe could read or write. In Byzantine and Muslim lands, on the other hand, learning was held in high regard. Works of the ancient Greeks and Romans were preserved, and new books were written. Learned professors taught in Muslim and Byzantine universities.

Western Europe experiences a cultural awakening. Gradually conditions in many parts of Western Europe improved. In the High Middle Ages (1050–1270), Western Europe experienced a cultural awakening. Magnificent churches, richly decorated with stained-glass windows and sculpture, were built in many Western European towns. At newly established universities brilliant professors lectured to eager students. Some of the greatest works of western literature were written, and men's interest in science increased. What led to this cultural explosion?

1. The increased power of kings put an end to much of the disorder and violence that had existed for centuries. Travel was made safer for merchants, students, and teachers. There was a surplus of food so that more people could live in towns and make a living by occupations other than farming. Because of improved conditions, goods, ideas, and learning spread rapidly to many parts of Western Europe.

2. As the population in towns increased, there was a growing need for businessmen, bankers, lawyers, doctors, and government officials. Schools and universities were established to prepare young men for careers in law, medicine, teaching, government, and the Church.

3. The revival of trade and the Crusades increased contacts with the advanced civilizations of the Muslim world and the Byzantine Empire. From these peoples Western Europe learned about the writings of ancient Greek and Roman philosophers and scientists. This awakened interest in learning.

4. Although neglected during the Early Middle Ages, learning never completely died out. In Church schools and monasteries some writings of the ancient Greeks and Romans were still read. Some men outside the Church also recognized the value of education. One of them was the Emperor Charlemagne (r. 771–814). Some of the ablest men of Europe taught in his palace school. During the centuries of disorder following the decline of Rome, men such as these had kept alive an interest in books and ideas. They helped prepare the way for the cultural awakening that began in the 1000's and continued into the next three centuries.

Universities arise in leading European cities. Many of Western Europe's great universities were founded during the twelfth and thirteenth centuries. In France and England the universities were controlled by teachers, but the Italian University of Bologna (buh-*loh′*nyah) was called a "Students' University." Students hired and paid professors. To get their money's worth, the students set down strict rules for their teachers. Professors were dismissed for being absent, for giving boring lectures, and for not dealing adequately with their subject. If a teacher wanted to take a trip, he had to leave behind a sum of money to guarantee his return.

What subjects are studied? Before going to the universities, medieval students were taught the seven liberal arts: grammar, rhetoric (speech), dialectics (logic), arithmetic, geometry, astronomy, and music. At the university they could specialize in law, medicine, the liberal arts (including philosophy), or theology (religion). Many teachers were priests or monks, especially

The physical surroundings have changed, but university classes today differ little from those in medieval times (above). Usually written in Latin, medieval manuscripts (above, left) were laboriously copied by hand.

those who taught philosophy and theology. They spent much time reading and discussing the Bible and the writings of churchmen. They tried to understand and organize in logical fashion the beliefs and rules of the Church. Among typical questions that interested both students and professors were: How can we prove that God exists? How does God want man to live his life? What is heaven like? How can man avoid falling into the hands of the devil? What powers do angels have? What powers do kings have? What is the best type of government? What is a fair price for the goods sold by a merchant?

Students put in a long, hard day. Students rose before 5 o'clock in the morning, went to church between 5 and 6, and attended class until 10 A.M. After a meal of beef and soup mixed with oatmeal, they returned to class until 5 in the evening. After dinner, they sat in rickety chairs

or on benches and by candlelight studied their notes until bedtime.

Often students learned under difficult conditions. In many classrooms, they sat on straw scattered over the floor. During the winter the rooms were cold and damp. Because the printing press had not yet been invented, books were copied by hand and hard to get. The professor read slowly to the class while students took notes. Later the students memorized their notes in order to pass examinations.

Medieval students have problems familiar to university students today. Students in medieval universities received letters from home urging them to play less and study more. One angry father wrote to his son: "I have learned . . . that you do not study in your room or act in the schools as a good student should, but play and wander about, disobedient to your master and [engaging] in sport." Another father complained that he had sent his son to college to study but the youth preferred "play to work and strumming a guitar while the others are at their studies." Sometimes parents received good news from their sons: "Sing unto the Lord a new song, praise Him with stringed instruments and organs, rejoice upon the high-sounding cymbals, for your son has . . . answered all questions without a mistake."

Students were always in need of money, and they knew whom to ask:

Well-beloved father, I have not a penny, nor can I get any [except] through you, for all things at the University are so [expensive]; nor can I study in my [lawbooks], for they are all tattered. Moreover I owe ten crowns in dues to the Provost [head of school], and can find no man to lend them to me; I send you word of greetings and of money.

The Student hath need of many things if he will profit here; his father and his kin must . . . supply him freely, that he be not [forced] to pawn his books, but have ready money in his purse, with . . . decent clothing, or he will be . . . [called] a beggar; wherefore, that men may not take me for a beast, I send you word of greetings and of money. . . .

Well-beloved father, to ease my debts . . . at the tavern, at the baker's, with the doctor, . . . and to pay . . . the laundress and the barber, I send you word of greetings and of money.

At times medieval students turned to drinking, gambling, and fighting instead of studying. In Oxford University, students "went through the streets with swords and bows and arrows . . . and assaulted all who passed by."* Some-

times students got so out of hand that nervous townspeople hid behind locked doors. One worried observer described the behavior of rowdy students:

They are so quarrelsome that there is no peace with them. . . . Many of them go about the streets armed, attacking the citizens, breaking into houses. . . . They quarrel among themselves over dogs, women, or what not, slashing off one another's fingers with their swords, or with only knives in their hands and nothing to protect their [bodies] rush into conflicts from which armed knights would hold back.*

There are many brilliant teachers in the Middle Ages. Students came from all parts of Europe to study with well-known teachers in universities. Two of the most famous medieval scholars were Peter Abelard and St. Thomas Aquinas (ah-*kwy'*nus).

Handsome, intelligent, of noble blood, and with a gift for song and humor, Peter Abelard became the most popular teacher of his time. Students flocked to Paris to hear his lectures. One admirer wrote Abelard:

Neither distance nor mountains nor valleys nor roads [crowded] with [bandits] prevented the youth of the world from coming to you. Young Englishmen crowded to your classes across a dangerous sea; all quarters of Spain, Flanders [part of modern Belgium], Germany sent you pupils; and they were never tired of praising the power of your mind. I say nothing of all the inhabitants of Paris and the most distant parts of France, [who] were also thirsty for your teaching, almost as if no science existed which could not be learned from you.

Abelard's romance with the beautiful Heloise (ey-loh-*eez'*) has for centuries inspired poets and lovers. When Heloise was 16, Abe-

* Selections from *An Introduction to Medieval Europe, 300–1500* by James Westfall Thompson & Edgar Nathaniel Johnson are reprinted with the permission of the publisher, W. W. Norton & Company, Inc., New York, N.Y. Copyright © 1937 by W. W. Norton & Company, Inc. Copyright renewed 1965 by Edgar Nathaniel Johnson. Reprinted also by permission of George Allen & Unwin Ltd.

* Selections from *An Introduction to Medieval Europe, 300–1500* by James Westfall Thompson & Edgar Nathaniel Johnson are reprinted with the permission of the publisher, W. W. Norton & Company, Inc., New York, N.Y. Copyright © 1937 by W. W. Norton & Company, Inc. Copyright renewed 1965 by Edgar Nathaniel Johnson. Reprinted also by permission of George Allen & Unwin Ltd.

lard, who was already famous, became her private tutor. Instead of study, wrote Abelard, "we spent our hours in the happiness of love. . . . Our speech was more of love than of the books which lay open before us; our kisses far out-numbered our reasoned words; . . . love drew our eyes together far more than the lesson drew them to the pages of our text." Their romance, however, had an unhappy ending. Heloise became a nun and Abelard devoted his life to learning and teaching.

Abelard urges his students to trust human reason. Abelard taught that the beliefs of the Church were a matter of reason as well as of faith. These beliefs could be understood and explained by man. "The first key to wisdom," said Abelard, is "frequent questioning." By questioning "we arrive at the truth." Though he sought to apply reason to religion, Abelard did not seek to challenge the beliefs of the Church. "I [would] never be a philosopher . . . if this were to separate me from Christ," he said. Abelard sought only to make Christian beliefs more intelligible to man.

Abelard's teachings aroused the opposition of leading churchmen. They criticized him for placing too much trust in reason. The beliefs of the Church, they said, could not be understood or explained by man's mind. They were mysteries of God that had to be accepted on faith. These opponents of Abelard feared that encouraging reason and searching for explanations of Christian beliefs would lead to heresy (pages 147–148). The way to God was through faith, not through reason, they said. They were afraid that Abelard was a dangerous teacher who could lead youth away from the beliefs of the Church. These churchmen forced him to give up teaching and spend his remaining years in a monastery. But Abelard's influence could not be erased. Scholars continued to honor reason.

Aquinas is a great thinker. A modest and devout churchman, St. Thomas Aquinas is considered the outstanding scholar of the medieval period. His writings fill many volumes and cover many topics. Like Abelard, he encouraged man to use his mind. Aquinas felt that, whenever possible, man should use reason to explain the teachings of the Church. He did not believe that reason would lead people away from faith. Rather, he maintained that the more a man used his mind, the stronger would become his faith. Aquinas was greatly influenced by the ancient Greek philosopher Aristotle and tried to prove God's existence by using Aristotelian methods of reasoning. He said that every action must have a cause. If there were no God, how then could we explain the beginning of the universe? Clearly God was the First Cause that set the universe in motion and gave it its superb organization. Like Abelard, Aquinas was attacked by churchmen who feared reason and believed that it was enough for man to have deep faith in Christ.

Aquinas also writes about the nature and powers of government. Aquinas said that government existed for three main reasons: (1) to keep peace within the society and to guard its subjects from foreign attack; (2) to encourage people to live moral and good lives; (3) to ensure "a sufficient supply of the necessities for a good life" to its subjects. Aquinas said that a king should rule for the benefit of his people. Tyrants who pass unjust laws and do nothing for the common good have abused their power. They are not fit to rule. The people have the right to disobey, resist, and depose such tyrant kings.

CHECK-UP

1. What led to the cultural explosion in the High Middle Ages?

2. Describe the life of a medieval student. What did he study?

3. What was the basic point of view of Abelard and of Aquinas? What contributions to learning did each make?

Advances in Science and Technology

The Middle Ages is not an age of science. Medieval churchmen, who controlled education, were more interested in the world to come than in investigating the world of nature. With some exceptions, few medieval thinkers felt a need to make discoveries and to search for new knowledge. They devoted their lives to studying religion, pleasing God, and preparing themselves for heaven. They believed that "He is a miserable man who knows all things and does not know God; and he is happy who knows God even though he knows nothing else." The best minds of the Middle Ages studied the Bible and the writings of important churchmen. They had neither the time nor the interest to investigate nature.

Professor M. Postan of Cambridge University, England, offers this explanation for the relative poverty of medieval science:

The purpose of scientific inquiry is to build up piecemeal a unified theory of the universe, of its origin and its working. But in the Middle Ages was that process really necessary? Did not medieval man already possess in God [and] the story of Creation . . . a complete explanation of how the world came about and of how, by what means, and to what purpose, it was being conducted?

Byzantines and Muslims share their knowledge with Western Europe. In the High Middle Ages, however, increased contacts with the Muslim world and the Byzantine Empire aroused interest in science and medicine. For centuries Muslims and Orthodox Christians of the Byzantine Empire had studied the scientific writings of the ancient Greeks and had done scientific research of their own. These books had not been available in Western Europe during the Early Middle Ages. However, in the 1100's and 1200's, from Constantinople and from Muslim centers of learning in the Mediterranean area, scientific writings began to enter Western Europe. They were often translated from Arabic into Latin by learned Jews and Arabs as well as Christians. The ancient Greek manuscripts on science and the investigations of the Muslims presented new and exciting concepts to Western Europeans. This awakened an interest in science. Some historians feel that the scientific work of the High Middle Ages was an important chapter in the rise of modern science.

Roger Bacon is interested in science. An English churchman, Roger Bacon wanted to learn all he could about nature. He criticized professors for neglecting science. Bacon felt sure that science would benefit man. He predicted that one day man would build ships "without rowers, . . . cars . . . without animals. Also flying machines can be constructed so that a man sits in the midst of the machine [turning] some engine by which artificial wings are made to beat the air like a flying bird. . . . Also machines can be made for walking in the sea and rivers, even to the bottom without danger."

Progress is made in medicine during the High Middle Ages. In the Early Middle Ages, Western Europeans knew much less about medicine than did the ancient Greeks. They often tried to cure sick people by means of magic and superstition.

For warts, take . . . a mouse's blood, . . . smear the warts therewith; they will soon depart away. . . .

For heartache, if he have within a strong pain in the heart, . . . work him a stone bath, and in it let him eat southern radish with salt; by that may the wound be healed.

Barbers usually acted as surgeons. Since instruments were not sterilized and no anesthetics were used, these operations were always dangerous for the patient.

In the High Middle Ages, European doctors learned to identify some diseases and to describe their effects upon patients, although they still did not know how to cure them. People who suffered from a contagious disease were segregated to keep others from catching it. This was an important advance. Hospitals were established in most larger towns. In Italian schools, students read the medical writings of ancient Greeks and Romans and of medieval Muslim and Jewish doctors. Professors taught their students about the workings of the body by *dissecting* (taking apart) animals and human corpses, even though the Church opposed the latter practice. Some medieval doctors performed successful operations.

Important advances are made in technology.

New inventions enabled man to accomplish his daily tasks with greater ease and also permitted him to have more leisure time. Some of these medieval "inventions" had been in use outside of Europe for some time. But once Western Europeans acquired them, they so improved these new tools and made such strides in their use that western technology eventually outstripped that of all other areas.

Agriculture profited considerably by new technology. A heavier plow replaced the old plow, which was light and could not cut very deeply into the soil. The new plow enabled the farmer to do his work more effectively and quickly and increased the amount of land that could be cultivated. Heavy, moist soils, which were fertile but offered too much resistance to the light plow, could now be put to use. Summarizing the importance of the heavy plow, Professor Lynn White, Jr., writes that the benefits of the heavy plow and "the saving of peasant labor . . . combined to expand production and make possible that accumulation of surplus food which is [necessary for] population growth, specialization, . . . urbanization, and the growth of leisure."

Another important aid to agriculture was the invention of the collar harness. The old yoke harness was used to good advantage with oxen, but it tended to choke horses. Because the horse moves faster than the ox, it is more valuable for agricultural work. But its value was not realized until the invention of the collar, which prevented the harness from choking the animal.

Other technological developments had far-reaching results. The introduction of arabic numerals (page 123) and of paper had a tremendous impact on science and education. Gunpowder, long used in China, changed the nature of warfare in Europe. The armored knight stood little chance against cannon and foot soldiers armed with muskets, and the fortified castle fared little better. The windmill made use of a free resource, flowing air, to provide power. And the mechanical saw not only did the work of several men but also could cut and trim logs far more quickly. Perhaps even more important were advances in navigation. The development of a rudder permitted ships to be steered more easily and precisely. The compass gave sailors an accurate idea of their position. Ships thus could make longer voyages with far less risk.

In later centuries, we shall see, western nations acquired empires and exercised power over vast areas of the world. The power of Western Europe over long-established civilizations lay largely in her technological skills. Technological superiority enabled Western Europe to dominate many peoples and nations of the world. And it was during the Middle Ages that Western Europeans began to outstrip other peoples in the development of technology. Professor White explains the importance of the Middle Ages to the history of technology:

By A.D. 1000 at the latest . . . the West began to apply water power to industrial processes other than milling grain. This was followed in the late twelfth century by the harnessing of wind power. From simple beginnings . . . the West rapidly expanded its skills in the development of power machinery, labor-saving devices, and automation. . . . Not in craftsmanship but in basic technological capacity the Latin West of the later Middle Ages far outstripped its elaborate, sophisticated, and aesthetically [artistically] magnificent sister cultures, Byzantium and Islam. . . .

By the end of the fifteenth century the technological superiority of Europe was such that its small nations would spill out over all the rest of the world, conquering, looting, and colonizing. The symbol of this technological superiority is the fact that Portugal, one of the weaker states of [Europe], was able to become and to remain for a century, mistress of the East Indies.

Medieval churches honor God. Architecture tells us much about the people of past ages. When we look at an ancient Greek temple we see the work of a talented people who believed in the greatness of man. The Greeks believed that man could create works of art which were more beautiful than the wonders of nature. A medieval church tells us a different story. It was built not to glorify man, but to praise God. It was the house of the Lord, where humble man prayed to his Creator. Here medieval man forgot the pains of hunger, disease, and war and turned his thoughts to God. Medieval man considered his church his finest creation and prayer his noblest moment.

It took fifty or more years to build some cathedrals. Building a church was an act of faith in which the whole town took part. People gave their money and their labor to make the church beautiful. Usually located in the center of town, the church was also used as a school, library, and theater.

In the twelfth century, tall graceful churches that seemed to reach into the heavens began to appear in France. Called *Gothic cathedrals,* these churches soon were built in many cities of Europe. Worshipers who entered a Gothic cathedral thought they were in the presence of God. The windows of stained glass contained religious scenes. When the sun shone through these brilliantly colored windows, the inside of the church lit up like a jewel. Lighted candles atop gold candlesticks, religious paintings, beautifully carved altars and statues of Christ, the Virgin, and the saints added to the beauty and religious mood of the Gothic cathedral. Kneeling in prayer, men felt "here is the Court of God and the gate of heaven."

CHECK-UP

1. Why was knowledge of science less advanced in Western Europe during the Early Middle Ages than among the Byzantines and Muslims?

2. In the High Middle Ages, what advances did Western Europeans make in medicine? In technology and science? What long-range impact did these advances in Western Europe have upon the world?

3. What can be learned about the beliefs and values of medieval man from viewing a Gothic cathedral?

Medieval Folk Songs and Literature

The people of the Middle Ages were not interested just in religion. While priests preached about the joys of heaven, wandering poets, called *troubadours,* expressed great love of life. They sang of the pleasures of wine, youth, the open road, spring, knights, and romance. Many troubadours were young university students. In taverns, surrounded by their friends, they sang loudly and cheerfully: "Let us drink deeply, then drink once more."

The troubadours are the folk singers of the Middle Ages. Like folk singers today, troubadours composed poems and wandered from castle to castle, singing to all who would listen. They were always welcome and were often rewarded with clothes, money, jewels, arms, and horses. Their songs dealt with all aspects of medieval life, but the troubadours were especially fascinated with love. They praised beautiful and gentle ladies and described the joys and sorrows of young love. They expressed the pains of love:

I would tell her I loved her, did I know but the
    way.
Could my lips but discover what a lover should
    say.
Though I swear to adore her every morning I rise,
Yet, when once I'm before her, all my eloquence
    flies.
Oh, ye gods, did ye ever such a simpleton know?
I'm in love and yet never have the heart to say so!

They even gave advice to lovers:

> It is good to be merry and wise;
>   It is good to be honest and true
> It is good to be off with the old love—
>   Before we be on with the new.

Sometimes the troubadours laughed at ladies who tried to hide their age behind a mask of makeup; sometimes they poked fun at romance:

> You say the moon is all aglow,
>   The nightingale a-singing—
> I'd rather watch the red wine flow,
>   And hear the [glasses] ringing.
>
> You say 'tis sweet to hear the gale
>   Creep sighing through the willows—
> I'd rather hear a merry tale,
>   'Mid a group of jolly fellows!
>
> You say 'tis sweet the stars to view
>   Upon the waters gleaming—
> I'd rather see, 'twixt me and you
>   And the post, my supper steaming.

Romantic love is a favorite theme. Much of the literature of the later Middle Ages dealt with romantic love. Troubadour poets glorified women and love. Noblemen and their ladies developed a code of proper behavior for lovers. Writers dealt with questions such as, What is love? What is the effect of love? What persons are fit for love?

One French writer even listed some rules of love. Do they apply today?

It is well known that love is always increasing or decreasing. . . .

No one should be deprived of love without the very best of reasons. . . .

It is not proper to love any woman whom one would be ashamed to seek to marry.

A true lover does not desire to embrace in love anyone except his beloved.

When made public, love rarely endures.

The easy attainment of love makes it of little value; difficulty of attainment makes it prized. . . .

When a lover suddenly catches sight of his beloved, his heart palpitates.

A new love puts to flight an old one.

Good character alone makes any man worthy of love. . . .

Real jealousy always increases the feeling of love. . . .

He whom the thought of love vexes [annoys] eats and sleeps very little. . . .

A true love considers nothing good except what he thinks will please his beloved.

Legends are put in writing. While learned men discussed religion and philosophy and the troubadours sang of love, the common people enjoyed marvelous tales about great heroes and frightening monsters. These stories were eventually put in writing, and even today make exciting reading. One of the earliest tales, the epic of *Beowulf,* originated in Northern Europe.

Grendel, a monster "from hell began a series of savage crimes." He raided a great hall and slew thirty warriors, "dragging the dead men home to his den." No man in the kingdom was safe. "Like a dark death shadow the . . . demon" attacked and killed. "The tales of the terrible deeds of Grendel" reached the great warrior Beowulf. "Of living strong men he was the strongest, fearless and gallant and great of heart." Beowulf prepared to do battle with Grendel.

One day the savage monster decided "to feast his fill on the flesh of men." Creeping silently up to the king's "high-roof house," Grendel,

Music, most of it religious in nature, played an important part in medieval life. Manuscripts of religious music (above) were as ornately decorated as books. Popular music on the themes of love and beauty, composed and sung by troubadours and minnesingers, was improvised, often by small orchestras (right).

"with fiendish strength" broke through the door, "though fastened of iron, . . . and rushed in rage o'er the shining floor." Inside the great hall the demon "quickly clutched a sleeping [warrior], . . . tore him in pieces, bit through the bones, gulped the blood, and gobbled the flesh." Then Grendel "sprang on [Beowulf] lying outstretched, clasping him close with his monstrous claw." But Beowulf fought fiercely back. Grendel "soon found that never before had he felt . . . in all the earth a mightier hand-grip." The monster struggled to free himself. "His courage fled; but he found no escape." Grendel, "the foe of God, [howled] his hideous hymn of

pain." He could not escape from "the man who was greatest of . . . men in the strength of his might, who would never rest while the wretch was living." Finally Beowulf ripped off Grendel's arm. The wounded monster fled to his den knowing "in his heart that his hours were numbered, his days at end." The monster died but Beowulf faced a new challenge. "The mother of Grendel, a monstrous hag, . . . [swore] a dreadful revenge for the death of her son!" Thus continued the adventures of Beowulf.

Beowulf is probably the most famous of the many exciting tales told and retold by the common people. In other tales heroes battled fire-breathing dragons, rescued ladies, defended their king, drove out the Muslims, and showed their courage in tournaments.

Dante is considered the greatest of medieval poets.

Dante Alighieri (ah-lee-ghee-*air′*ee) was one of the earliest serious writers to use the *vernacular* or native language—Italian—rather than Latin to express his thoughts. Later writers followed his example, which influenced the development of national languages. In honor of his beloved Beatrice, Dante wrote some of the finest love poetry of all literature:

My lady carries love within her eyes;
All that she looks on is made pleasanter;
Upon her path men turn to gaze at her;
He whom she greeteth feels his heart to rise
And droops his troubled visage,[1] full of sighs. . . .
The look she hath when she a little smiles—
'Tis such a new and gracious miracle.*

The *Divine Comedy,* Dante's most important work, is an outstanding expression of the religious beliefs and attitudes of the Middle Ages and a masterpiece of world literature. It has led many to consider Dante the greatest medieval poet. The *Divine Comedy* describes the poet's journey through Hell, Purgatory,[2] and Paradise. The people of the Middle Ages believed that those who were not Christians, and Christians who disobeyed God, were condemned to hell after they died. They saw hell as a place of bottomless pits, burning sand, violent storms, ice, darkness, and fearful monsters. They agreed with Dante's expression of the words written at the entrance of Hell: "through me is the way among the lost people. . . . Leave [all] hope, ye who enter [here]!"

For medieval man, hell was as real and terrible as Dante's description:

[1] Visage: face.
* From *Dante: Poet and Apostle* by Ernest H. Wilkins (Chicago: University of Chicago Press, 1921). Reprinted by permission of Robert H. Wilkins and Eleanor W. Turner.
[2] Purgatory: in the *Divine Comedy,* region between Heaven and Hell where sinners perform acts which will purify them and permit them eventually to enter Heaven.

[There was] a cruel and strange beast with three throats, . . . red eyes, a greasy and black beard, and a big belly, and paws armed with nails. [This monster clawed and bit the sinners, tearing them apart. There were also] horned demons with great whips who were beating [the sinners] cruelly from behind. [A snake bit one sinner in the neck; the bitten spirit] took fire and burned and [became] all ashes as he fell. . . . [After] he was thus destroyed, . . . the dust drew together . . . [and became] that same [sinner again]. [The process was then repeated.]

Hell was ruled by Lucifer (the Devil), who has three faces, each a different color, and two great bat-like wings. "With six eyes he was weeping, and over three chins were trickling the tears. . . . At each mouth he was crushing a sinner with his teeth."

Chaucer is the first great English writer.

Whereas Dante had described an imaginary world, the world of Geoffrey Chaucer was a real and lively one. In *The Canterbury Tales* he preserved for all time a picture of life in England late in the Middle Ages. *The Canterbury Tales* describe 29 Englishmen and women who were making a pilgrimage to a shrine at Canterbury. They were a colorful group.*

There was a Knight, a most distinguished man,
Who from the day on which he first began
To ride abroad had followed chivalry,
Truth, honor, generousness, and courtesy.
He had done nobly in his [lord's] war. . . .

With the knight was his son:

Singing he was, or fluting all the day;
He was as fresh as is the month of May.
Short was his gown, the sleeves were long and
    wide;
He knew the way to sit a horse and ride,
He could make songs and poems and recite,
Knew how to joust [3] and dance, to draw and write.

* The quotations from Chaucer are taken from *The Canterbury Tales,* rendered modern by Nevill Coghill (Harmondsworth, Middlesex, England: Penguin Books Ltd., 1952). Reprinted by permission.
[3] Joust (*just*): to fight in a tournament.

There was a monk who preferred the excitement of the hunt to studying "until his head went round":

A Monk there was, one of the finest sort
Who rode the country; hunting was his sport. . . .
This Monk was therefore a good man to horse;
Greyhounds he had, as swift as birds, to
    course. . . .

His head was bald and shone like looking-glass;
So did his face, as if it had been greased.
He was a fat and [well-conditioned] priest.

In contrast to the monk there was a "holy-minded" Parson on the journey. Although poor

Yet he was rich in holy thought and work.
He also was a learned man, a clerk,[4]
Who truly knew Christ's gospel and would preach
    it. . . .
I think there never was a better priest.

A simple plowman was also there:

He was an honest worker, good and true,
Living in peace and perfect charity.
And, as the Gospel bade him, so did he,
Loving God best with all his heart and mind . . .
For steadily about his work he went
To thresh his corn, to dig or to manure
Or make a ditch; and he would help the poor
For love of Christ and never take a penny
If he could help it. . . .

A "worthy woman" from the city of Bath had lived an exciting life:

Her kerchiefs were of finely woven ground;[5]
I dared have sworn they weighed a good ten pound,
The ones she wore on Sunday, on her head.
Her hose were of the finest scarlet red
And gartered tight; her shoes were soft and new.
Bold was her face, handsome, and red in hue,
A worthy woman all her life, what's more
She'd had five husbands, all at the church door. . . .
And she had thrice been to Jerusalem,
Seen many strange rivers and passed over
    them. . . .
In company she liked to laugh and chat. . . .

[4] Clerk: a student of Church history.
[5] Ground: cloth

Chaucer won lasting fame for *The Canterbury Tales*. Few writers have provided a better picture of their times.

CHECK-UP

1. What were favorite subjects of medieval songs and legends?
2. What do songs and literature tell us about medieval standards of behavior?
3. What can *The Canterbury Tales* tell us about life in fourteenth-century England?

The Legacy of the Middle Ages

The medieval period was an Age of Faith. Man lived primarily for the promise of heaven. His thoughts dealt largely with religion. Medieval man accepted sickness, disease, hunger, and violence as part of life. He felt there was little that man could do about these things. "For the medieval man," writes Professor Crane Brinton, "much of his life was out of his own hands, in the hands of God working through society. . . . Medieval man was more nearly than we resigned to a world he could not greatly change." How different this seems from our modern world of rapid change, a world of science and invention! Yet we owe much to the Middle Ages. What contributions did the Middle Ages make to civilization? This summary will suggest how deep in the past are the roots of the present.

1. Rise of universities. The Middle Ages saw the rise of universities. Among the present-day universities that were founded in the Middle Ages are those of Cambridge and Oxford (Britain), Vienna (Austria), Bologna (Italy), Prague (Czechoslovakia), Paris (France), Salamanca (Spain), and Cologne (koh-*lohn'*, Germany). In these universities were introduced many practices still carried on today—lectures, examinations, the wearing of cap and gown, the granting of degrees.

2. Growth of cities. Many great modern cities began as little towns during the Middle

Ages. In many European cities one can still see churches, houses, and city walls that were built in the Middle Ages.

3. Building of Gothic cathedrals. Gothic architecture was an original creation of the Middle Ages. We still build some churches and university buildings in the Gothic style.

4. Development of modern languages. Our modern languages took form during the Middle Ages. French, Spanish, Italian, Romanian, and Portuguese developed from the Latin of Rome. Dutch, German, Norwegian, Swedish, and Danish grew out of the speech of the German barbarians. English evolved from Anglo-Saxon —a Scandinavian language which developed from German—modified by Norman French.

5. Formation of states. States began to take shape in the later Middle Ages. In England, France, and eventually in Spain kings overcame feudal lords, united the country, and created strong states. Both Italy and Germany, however, remained divided into separate and independent regions until the middle of the nineteenth century.

6. Ideals and manners. From the Middle Ages we have inherited the ideals of chivalry— loyalty, bravery, generosity, courtesy, good manners, and respect for womanhood. Our idea of a gentleman is still based largely on the medieval code of chivalry.

7. Stress on reasoning. Some medieval thinkers began to stress reasoning. They said that in many cases man can understand the ways of God. Indeed, God wants man not only to follow His teachings, but also to understand them. Some, like St. Thomas Aquinas, tried to show that the theories of ancient Greek philosophers agreed with the teachings of the Church. In the Middle Ages reason was applied mainly to religion. Few thinkers searched for new knowledge. While this was not an age of science, men did revive some of the rational ideas of the Greeks, and they received training in analyzing and explaining complicated ideas. The mind of Western Europe was sharpened. This training in thinking prepared men for the future when the theories of science would be-

come more important to man than the study of religion.

8. Technology. During the Middle Ages Europe started to take the lead over the rest of the world in the development of technology. In the centuries following the Middle Ages, Europeans used their superior technological skills to extend their power over much of the world.

9. Contributions to liberty. In a number of ways the Middle Ages contributed to the growth of liberty. The view that the power of government should be limited is in part an outgrowth of the Middle Ages. Medieval thinkers such as Aquinas insisted that kings must obey the teachings of God and care for the needs of the people. They felt that citizens should be protected from cruel and oppressive government.

Feudal lords also resisted absolute rule by kings. English lords in particular insisted that they had certain rights that no king could take away. They maintained that laws had to be approved by both king and lords.

Some political thinkers went even further. They said that the king obtained his power only with the consent of the people. If the king behaved like a tyrant, the people had the right of rebellion. "To kill a tyrant is . . . fair and just," said one English schoolman.

In still another way liberty was advanced during the Middle Ages. There developed the tradition that a lord accused of a crime should be judged by his fellow lords. He had the right of trial by jury. In the modern world this right to a trial was extended to all men regardless of class.[6]

[6] In England all freemen accused of a crime were entitled to trial by a jury of other freemen. The famous Magna Carta, a landmark in the growth of liberty, stated:

No freeman shall be seized, or imprisoned, or dispossessed, or outlawed, or in any way destroyed; nor will we condemn him, nor will we commit him to prison, excepting by the judgment of his peers [social equals], or by the law of the land.

To none will we sell, to none will we deny, to none will we delay right or justice.

175

The Middle Ages, therefore, advanced the cause of liberty in four ways: (1) by urging limitations on the powers of the king; (2) by developing the idea that government rests upon the consent of the governed; (3) by asserting that the people have the right to resist rulers who act like tyrants; and (4) by establishing the principle of the right of trial by jury.

Chapter Highlights

Can you explain?

apprentice	charter	fairs	master craftsman
troubadours	middle class	journeyman	Crusades
masterpiece	craft guild	Gothic architecture	merchant guild

Can you identify?

Beowulf	Peasant Crusade	Franks	Children's Crusade
Aquinas	Abelard	Chaucer	Jerusalem
Roger Bacon	Dante	Holy Land	*Divine Comedy*
Pope Urban			*The Canterbury Tales*

What do you think?

1. How did the Muslims view the Crusades?

2. How did the Crusades contribute to the growth of trade in Western Europe?

3. Why did medieval towns develop where they did? What were the advantages of town life? The disadvantages?

4. What were the advantages of being a guildsman? What restrictions did the guild impose? Why?

5. Why did many serfs run away to live in towns?

6. How did the increased trade and the use of money affect social classes?

7. Why were fairs important in the Middle Ages?

8. Had you lived in the Middle Ages, to what class (feudal nobility, middle-class townspeople, clergy, serfs) would you have wished to belong? Why?

9. How did the attitude toward learning differ in (a) the Early Middle Ages, (b) the Muslim and Byzantine empires, (c) the High Middle Ages?

10. Can student demands and pressures on the medieval university be compared to the campus unrest of today? Why?

11. Why were Byzantine and Muslim science and technology more advanced about 1100 A.D. than were science and technology in Western Europe?

12. What can be learned from medieval folksongs? How do *Beowulf* and *The Divine Comedy* reflect medieval man's tastes in literature? What great gift did Chaucer display in *The Canterbury Tales*?

13. What contributions to civilization were made during the Middle Ages?

The Foundations of Western Civilization

A Short Survey of Ancient and Medieval Life

CHAPTER FOCUS

The Ancient World

The Ancient Near East
Ancient Greece
Rome
Rise of Christianity

The Middle Ages

Byzantine and Islamic Civilizations
Latin Christendom
Awakening of Western Europe

The Ancient World

The Ancient Near East

Some 5000 years ago man's first civilizations arose in the Near Eastern lands of Egypt and Mesopotamia. Here men first built cities, developed systems of writing, constructed large-scale temples and monuments, and worked at specialized tasks such as farming, handicrafts, trading, priesthood, and administration. These are all considered signs of civilized life.

EGYPTIAN CIVILIZATION

Egyptian civilization developed in the fertile valley of the Nile River. Without this mighty river, all Egypt would be desert. Water from the Nile was used to irrigate crops. When the Nile overflowed its banks, the floodwaters left behind a layer of rich black earth which was excellent for crops. The Nile also served as a "moving road" on which merchants carried goods. (See map, page 21.)

The ruler of Egypt was a god-king called pharaoh (*fair'*oh). Pharaoh was all-powerful, and his word was not to be questioned. He had great wealth, for his subjects mined gold and copper and his ships traded with other lands. In time strong pharaohs conquered nearby lands and ruled over other peoples. The Egyptian people did not object to having an all-powerful ruler. They believed that their god-king could help them gain life after death. Moreover, the pharaoh tried to be a good ruler. He kept the irrigation works in order and told officials to treat the people fairly.

A major feature of ancient Egyptian civilization was belief in life after death. Egyptians believed that the dead journeyed to an "Other World" where they would enjoy all the pleasures of life. Because of this belief, the dead body of an upper-class Egyptian was carefully embalmed. Pharaohs were laid to rest in giant tombs filled with everything they might need in the Other World.

The Egyptians did not live just to prepare for the afterlife. They also tried to enjoy life on earth. They liked good food, games, hunting, and romance.

The Egyptians developed a high level of civilization. Hymns to the gods, songs praising the pharaoh, and business transactions were recorded by a system of picture writing called *hieroglyphics.* Egyptian astronomers devised an accurate calendar. Although Egyptian doctors combined medicine with magic, they did know how to heal wounds and set broken bones. Engineers demonstrated great skill in building irrigation works and pyramids.

For many centuries life in Egypt changed very little. Today we believe in change, in finding new and better ways of doing things. We develop new ideas. The ancient Egyptians, however, looked to the past. They believed that the gods wanted them to retain the religion, art, and ways of life of their ancestors.

LIFE IN MESOPOTAMIA

To the east of Egypt, in the valley between the Tigris (*tie*′gris) and Euphrates (yoo-*frey*′teez) Rivers, was the land of Mesopotamia (mes-oh-poh-*tey*′mih-uh, map, page 29). The people of Mesopotamia had cities, written laws, a merchant class, and a system of banking. Craftsmen made fine bowls and plates out of bronze and copper. Engineers designed dikes, dams, reservoirs, and canals to control and store the waters of the Tigris and Euphrates Rivers. Architects built temples to honor the gods. Mesopotamian priests and scribes wrote poems and kept records of treaties, laws, battles, and business dealings. Astronomers knew the difference between planets and stars and invented a twelve-month lunar (moon) calendar with a seven-day week.

The scorching sun, the heavy rains, the sandstorms which turned the soil into whirling dust, the destructive floodwaters of the Tigris and Euphrates Rivers, and frequent invasions made life in Mesopotamia difficult and insecure.

Whereas the Egyptians faced life with confidence, the Mesopotamians felt helpless and afraid. Unlike the Egyptians, they did not look forward to a pleasant afterlife. Mesopotamian man was certain that happiness after death was only for the gods, not for lowly man. He believed that when men died they went to the Netherworld, a huge dark cave "where they sit in darkness, where dust is their food and clay their meat."

The Egyptians felt that man could do great things in his lifetime, that his pyramids and temples would last forever. The Mesopotamians thought man was unimportant, no more than a slave of the gods. He counted for nothing. Whatever man did was like the wind; it could not last. Mesopotamian man thought little of himself, found life full of pain, and had nothing to look forward to after death.

HEBREW CONTRIBUTIONS

The Hebrews, of Mesopotamian origin, eventually settled in Palestine. Though few in numbers, the Hebrews made extraordinary contributions to western civilization.

1. Belief in one God. The Hebrews gave to the world the idea of *monotheism,* or belief in one God. To them there was no power greater than their God, Yahweh. He was the Creator and Ruler of Heaven and Earth. At first the Hebrews looked upon God as their very own. Later, He was regarded as the God of all peoples. The idea of one God was passed on to Christianity and Islam.

2. Rules of right and wrong. The Hebrews set up rules of conduct—the Ten Commandments—that are followed today by Christians and Muslims as well as Jews. The Hebrews believed that the Ten Commandments were given to man by God. They were the foundations of the law. God's law commanded man not to murder, steal, commit adultery, or tell lies about his neighbors. He wanted men to honor their parents, love their neighbors, care for the needy, and protect the weak. If man broke God's commandments, God would punish him.

3. The Old Testament. Over the centuries the ancient Hebrews wrote down their thoughts, prayers, and history. These writings make up the Old Testament, the first part of the Bible. The Old Testament includes poetry, wise sayings, love songs, and accounts of important events. It has one main religious purpose—to teach man about God. Both Jews and Christians regard the Old Testament as sacred.

4. Social justice and a better world. Among the Hebrews were high-minded men who considered themselves messengers of the Lord, or *prophets.* The Hebrew prophets cared nothing for money or possessions. They wanted only to remind the Hebrews to act according to the teachings of the Lord. It was not enough, said the prophets, to pray to God or to celebrate religious holidays. God demanded that man be just, merciful, and righteous at all times. Man must avoid evil. Only then would he gain God's favor. The prophets criticized the rich and powerful for mistreating the poor and weak. A man who harmed or cheated his fellow man, said the prophets, could never serve God.

The Hebrew prophets impressed upon civilization man's duty to fight evil, injustice, and poverty. They taught that there could be no knowledge of God without love of man. They dreamed of a new and better world in which peace would come to all men.

THE PERSIAN EMPIRE

The greatest empire of the ancient Near East was established by the Persians. By 500 B.C. the Persians ruled the lands from Egypt to India (map, page 37). They united all the peoples—Egyptians, Babylonians, Assyrians, Hebrews, Phoenicians, Hittites, and Lydians— under one rule. Persian kings were wise rulers. They built roads to tie their empire together, started a postal system, and established an effective administration system for governing a large empire.

The civilization of the Persian Empire represented a fusing of the different civilizations of the ancient Near East. Conquered peoples in the provinces were generally treated fairly. They were allowed to keep their local customs and traditions. As long as they paid their taxes, provided recruits for the emperor's army, and refrained from rebellion, they had little to fear from the Persian emperor.

Ancient Greece

Of the different peoples who lived in the ancient Mediterranean world, two stand out—the Hebrews and the Greeks. They are the founders of *western civilization*—the civilization of Europe and America. The Hebrews gave western civilization its belief in one God and many of its rules of conduct. The ancient Greeks made great contributions to art, mathematics, literature, and government; they are also the founders of philosophy and many of our sciences. To no other people do we owe so much. Almost everything interested the Greeks, and they did almost everything well. Never in history has one people shown such universal talent. Even today we are amazed and inspired by their achievements.

ACHIEVEMENTS OF GREEK CIVILIZATION

Greece's many mountains, bays, and islands tended to divide the people. Whereas Egypt became a united country under one ruler, the Greeks lived in small *city-states* (map, page 49). They did not wish to live in a large country with one ruler, but to be close to the government of their own city and its problems.

Athens was the leading city-state of ancient Greece. It was also the first state to become a *democracy.* In fact, the word "democracy" comes from the Greek word meaning rule by the people. In other lands the common people had no say in the government. They were ruled by pharaohs, kings, or powerful nobles. The citizens of Athens, however, governed themselves. Adult male citizens met weekly to make laws, determine how the city's money would be spent, or decide whether to go to war or make peace. They served the same function as United States senators and congressmen. A man who would not attend the Assembly, hold government offices, or serve on juries was called a "useless" person.

The Athenians cherished freedom of speech and thought. Citizens could criticize leading generals and statesmen without fear of being punished. The poorest shoemaker had the same right to speak and vote as did the richest landowner. Although Athenian democracy was truly a great achievement, it did have a number of shortcomings. Slaves, foreigners, and women—the majority of the population—had no say in the government.

The Athenians were proud of their democracy and their freedom. They were equally proud of their artists, poets, playwrights, scientists, and philosophers. Even average citizens could enjoy good plays, good music, and fine art. Today we criticize our city and state governments for putting up public buildings and housing projects that are ugly and drab. The Athenians insisted that all their public buildings be works of art. Perhaps no other people in the history of the world cared so much for the arts and the fine things of life as did the Athenians. Certainly no other people contributed more to civilization. A present-day historian says of ancient Athens: "the contribution made to European culture by this one city is quite astonishing. . . . Athens . . . was clearly the most civilized society that has yet existed."

The Greeks of the different city-states had many things in common. They spoke the same language, believed in the same gods, participated in the same athletic contests, and considered themselves different and better than non-Greeks, whom they called barbarians. Yet the Greeks were not politically united. Each Greek was loyal to his own city-state. And the many city-states were often at war with one another. These wars weakened the city-states,

preparing the way for foreign invaders. By 338 B.C. the Greek city-states were conquered by the land of Macedonia, located to the north of Greece. Alexander the Great, ruler of Macedonia and Greece, also conquered the huge Persian Empire. His troops conquered Egypt and other lands of the ancient Near East, advancing all the way to India without losing a battle (map, page 51).

Although the Greeks were conquered, Greek civilization never died. It spread throughout the Mediterranean world and lives on today in the civilizations of Europe and America. What were some of the achievements of Greek civilization?

The Greeks made important advances in government and politics. They had elections, jury trials, written constitutions, and debates in the Assembly. The concepts of democracy and active citizenship developed by the Greeks have served as lasting examples through the ages.

The first true philosophers in the western world were Greek. Many of the questions that mankind has been struggling to answer for centuries were first asked by the Greeks: What is beauty? What is the best form of government? What is good? What is the purpose of education? What is justice? What is the purpose of life? How did the world begin? Of what is it made?

The greatest Greek philosopher, Socrates (sok'ruh-teez), was a simple Athenian stonecutter who never wrote anything. Yet he is regarded as one of the greatest teacher-philosophers in history.

Socrates wanted men to be concerned about their character and their own souls. Man struggles to get money and power, said Socrates, yet he neglects what is most important—making himself as good a person as possible. To achieve a good character, said Socrates, man must learn to master himself, to control his emotions, and to develop his mind. Behavior must be dictated by the mind and not by the heart. Without self-control and clear thinking, a man cannot achieve excellence of character. Socrates believed that the purpose of education was to mold character, to make of man something that is beautiful and good. This, he felt, was man's highest aim in life.

Socrates' most famous follower, Plato (*pley'-toh*), also stressed the importance of knowledge and good character. Plato was critical of democracy. For Plato, democracy meant mob rule. He did not believe that most people had the knowledge or the experience to help make decisions about spending government money, declaring war, or making new laws or an alliance with another city-state. Such decisions, said Plato, required sound judgment and clear thinking, characteristics not possessed by the average person, who was easily confused by his emotions and his prejudices.

Plato believed that the people would be properly governed only when the wisest men, the philosophers, were given power. Because philosophers would spend many years getting the education and experience needed to become rulers, they would not act out of ignorance or prejudice. Philosopher-kings would not be interested in money or power. Nor would they be pushed by the excitable common people into making bad decisions. They would be the wisest and best of men. Though the common people would lose their right to take part in the government, they would be sure of having just and able rulers.

Aristotle (*ar'*ihs-tot'l) was both a philosopher and a scientist. Aristotle had studied at the academy established by Plato. He wrote on many topics—government, drama, art, biology, physics. Like other Greek philosophers, Aristotle wondered about good character, the good life, and the meaning of happiness. He, too, insisted that a man who never develops his mind can never be truly happy. "Educated men are as much superior to uneducated men," said Aristotle, "as the living are to the dead."

Aristotle was one of the first great scientists. He wanted to learn everything about nature. He studied plants, animals, and the heavens and kept careful records of his observations. Like a good scientist, Aristotle believed that a theory should be accepted only if it "agrees with the observed facts." For centuries people used the writings of Aristotle as we would an encyclopedia.

The Greeks were as interested in science and mathematics as in philosophy. The Hebrews regarded the universe as God's creation. They believed that man had been placed on earth not to study nature but to carry out the teachings of the Lord. The Greeks, on the other hand, were curious about nature. They wanted to know how the universe began, of what it was made, and how it worked. They were the first to suggest that it was regulated by laws of nature, and they tried to discover these laws through reason. Because the Egyptians and Mesopotamians saw gods and demons as the causes of changes in nature, they could never become true scientists. By seeking a rational (naturalistic and logical) explanation for why things happened, by removing the gods from storms, rivers, and trees, the Greeks enabled man to examine and analyze nature.

The Greeks were also greatly interested in history. By studying the past they hoped to learn how men have acted and thought in difficult times. They believed that the history of the past provided lessons for the present, for human nature does not change.

The Greek storyteller Homer was one of the first poets of the western world. So magnificent was Homer's verse that even today some consider him the greatest poet in the history of western civilization. Homer helped shape the attitudes of ancient Greece. Young students grew up reciting his poems. From Homer the Greeks learned to respect courage, honor, and loyalty.

The Greeks were the first, and perhaps the best, writers of plays. Tragedies expressed the Greek view of life—that men who are too proud will suffer misfortune. If men let success go to their heads, if they achieve success unjustly, they eventually will be punished. Greek tragedies described the sufferings, triumphs, and weaknesses in men's lives. Because they dealt with the great questions of life, the themes of Greek tragedies have remained modern through the centuries. The Greeks also wrote comedies which ridiculed politicians, generals, philosophers, and other well-known figures.

No other people in the ancient world, perhaps in all of history, loved beauty as much as did the Greeks. In their temples, public buildings, theaters, and statues—even in their vases and coins—the Greeks sought to produce works of art that were as simple, graceful, and well balanced as nature's finest creations.

THE GREEK VIEW OF LIFE

Over the centuries, men have been inspired by the Greek attitude toward life. Perhaps the most significant contribution made by the Greeks was their conception of the good life. They believed that a man should give careful thought to how he leads his life. "The unexamined life," said Socrates, "is not worth living." For the Hebrews, the good life meant obeying the laws of their God. What did the Greeks mean by the good life?

1. Moderation. The good life, said the Greeks, was one of moderation. The moderate man does not give in to all his desires. He does not eat, drink, or even sleep too much. He has other interests than games, clothes, and money. He has a healthy body and a sound mind. Above all, he has self-control. His emotions never get the best of him but are always ruled by his reason.

2. Versatility. To lead a good life, a man must be versatile—capable of doing many things. He should be able to understand mathematics, discuss philosophy, appreciate art, take part in the affairs of his city, and keep in good physical condition. Because he had many interests, the versatile man would never find life boring nor would others be bored with him.

3. Intelligence. Few peoples have admired intelligence as much as did the Greeks. They insisted that ignorance prevents a man from living a good life. Because they had a tremendous desire to learn everything about the world around them, the Greeks were never afraid to ask questions, or to use their minds to find answers. From the Greeks, western man derived the view that the highest aim of life is not to gain power or pleasure but to seek knowledge.

4. Freedom and participation. The Greeks believed that freedom was essential for the good life. Only by allowing citizens to participate in government could a city prosper. Only in such a free society could a man fully develop his artistic and intellectual talents and become a complete man.

5. Humanism and excellence. The Greeks believed that man was capable of doing great things. They agreed with the playwright Sophocles (*sof'*oh-kleez), who wrote: "Wonders are many on earth, and the greatest of these is man." Placing a great value on man and his abilities is called *humanism.* The Greeks, the first true humanists, concentrated on getting the most out of life in this world. They believed that man's true greatness lay in the full development of his talents, in developing the best that was within him. The man who could create great works of art, or write beautiful poetry, or achieve victory in an athletic contest, or do his duty as a loyal citizen, or understand the secrets of nature—such a man achieved true excellence.

Rome

The genius of the Greeks lay in their creativity and their intelligence. They were superb sculptors, architects, philosophers, dramatists, and scientists. The Romans, on the other hand, were distinguished as soldiers, lawgivers, and rulers. They knew how to conquer nations and govern men. When the Roman Empire was at its height, the Mediterranean world knew the blessings of peace and law and order. Millions of men from distant lands and different backgrounds were proud to say that they were citizens of Rome. It was the largest and best organized empire of the ancient world, perhaps in all history.

THE EXPANSION OF ROME

Rome began as a little town on the Tiber (*tie'*-ber) River. By 133 B.C. the Romans not only had unified Italy, but had fought victorious land and sea wars which made their country the foremost power in the Mediterranean world. (See maps, pages 65, 71, and 72.) In the process of conquering Italy, the Romans demonstrated a devotion to their city, a toughness of character, and a genius for warfare. They knew how to wage war successfully, how to gain allies, and how to treat a defeated enemy.

The Italian Peninsula was largely conquered by armies made up of Roman citizens. Each male citizen was a soldier. When soldiers were needed, the Roman farmer put down his farm implements and took up his weapons. The sturdy Roman farmer made an excellent soldier. Strong of body, loyal to his city, and experienced in battle, the Roman soldier was capable of marching over thirty miles a day despite the fact that armor, weapons, and other equipment might weigh as much as eighty pounds.

The Romans did not use better weapons than their enemies. All peoples had virtually the same weapons—swords, spears, daggers, bows and arrows, and stones. Rome's advantage lay in superior discipline and organization. Soldiers who deserted their post, lost their weapons, or fled from battle were disgraced. Those who fought well, on the other hand, achieved lasting fame and rich rewards. The Romans also adopted and improved upon battle formations first used by the Greeks.

The conquest of the Italian Peninsula made Rome a great power and started her on the road to empire. Roman expansion into lands bordering the Mediterranean was not part of a deliberate plan. Indeed, some Roman leaders opposed involvement in foreign adventures. But it seems as though it is almost impossible for a great nation not to use its power to further its interests, not to get involved in the quarrels of other states, and not to acquire outlying territory. Almost unwillingly, Rome built an empire.

Victory over the North African state of Carthage (*kahr'*thij) made Rome supreme in the western Mediterranean. During the long period of wars with Carthage, Rome had also expanded in the eastern Mediterranean. By 133 B.C. Rome had conquered Greece, Macedonia, and part of Asia Minor, and Egypt had become her ally. And this was still not the end of Roman expansion.

THE ROMAN PEACE

For about 500 years—from 509 B.C. to 27 B.C. Rome was a republic governed by a senate and assemblies rather than by a king. Decades of civil war caused by army leaders ambitious for power, agricultural crises causing farmers to move to the cities, food shortages, decreased patriotism, and a widening gulf between rich and poor led to the downfall of the Roman Republic. Between 46 and 44 B.C. Julius Caesar, commander of the legions in Gaul, gained power in Rome. Caesar tried to solve the problems besetting the Republic but was assassinated because of his dictatorial rule. In 27 B.C. a strong leader, Octavian (ahk-*tey'*vih-un), became the unchallenged ruler of Rome. Octavian—or Augustus, as he came to be known—was the first Roman emperor. Augustus put an end to civil wars and gave Rome peace, security, and prosperity.

The reign of Augustus marked the beginning of Rome's greatest age. For 200 years the vast Roman Empire enjoyed the blessings of *Pax Romana* (*pahks'* roh-*mah'*nuh)—the Roman Peace. During this period Rome gave the Mediterranean world peace, law, and good government. The ancient world had never before experienced such a long period of peace and order. The elaborate and efficient system of administration the Romans developed to govern their vast Empire revealed a great talent for organization. Roman officials generally performed their tasks with skill and a sense of duty. Provincial governors tried not to interfere with the customs of the people.

The emperors following Augustus extended the borders of the Empire in Asia Minor, pushed their conquests in Europe to the Rhine and Danube Rivers, and conquered much of England. (See maps, pages 77 and 84.) In many parts of the Empire the Romans cleared forests, drained swamps, irrigated deserts, and cultivated undeveloped lands. They built roads across mountains and deserts and improved harbors. Hundreds of new cities sprang up, and old cities grew larger and wealthier. These cities enjoyed a large measure of freedom and self-government in local matters. From England to the Arabian desert and from the Danube River to the sands of the Sahara some 70 million people, speaking different languages and having different customs, were united under Roman rule. Spaniards and Syrians, Gauls and Britons spoke Latin, the tongue of Rome, traveled on Roman roads, used a Roman system of weights and measures, obeyed Roman laws, swore an oath of allegiance to Roman emperors, and were defended by Roman legions. Almost all were proud to be called citizens of Rome.

Over the network of roads made safe by Roman soldiers, and across the Mediterranean Sea swept clear of pirates, large quantities of goods were transported. A brisk trade by sea and over land grew up, both with the provinces and with Arabia and distant parts of Africa and Asia. Goods from all over the known world flowed into Rome.

The borders of the Empire were defended by the mighty Roman legions. Greek and Roman culture was carried to far-off lands in the Empire. During the 200 years of *Pax Romana,* Rome was ruled by good emperors and wicked ones, by intelligent emperors and by incompetents, by those devoted to Rome and by men who sought only pleasure. Nevertheless, the peace and prosperity endured. The period of *Pax Romana* was one of the finest periods in world civilization. In the words of a Roman writing in the second century, it was

a world every day better, better cultivated and more civilized than before. Everywhere roads are traced, every district is known, every country open to commerce. Smiling fields have invaded the forests; flocks and herds have [driven out] the wild beasts; the very sands are sown; the rocks are planted; the marshes drained. There are now as many cities as there were once solitary cottages. Reefs and shoals have lost their terrors; wherever there is a trace of life there are houses and human habitations, well-ordered governments, and civilized life.

THE DECLINE AND FALL OF ROME

In the third century a series of crises weakened the Roman Empire. A principal cause for the turmoil was the problem of succession to the throne. Since Rome never arrived at a legal formula for choosing the emperor, in the third century there was a continual struggle for power. Ambitious generals, supported by their soldiers, murdered emperors and each other in their struggle to gain power. In the 50-year period following 235 A.D., Rome had 26 emperors, and 25 of them died violently. Under the rule of incompetent military men economic conditions in Rome went from bad to worse. In order to reward soldiers and pay the costs of war, emperors raised taxes enormously, increasing the distress of the people. Many productive citizens of the Empire were reduced to poverty by the greed of the army, which seized food and clothing from townspeople and peasants.

Signs of decay were everywhere. Plagues reduced the size of the population. Piracy and thievery went unchecked. Roman coins declined in value as their silver content was reduced and more copper was added. Because people no longer trusted Roman coinage, prices increased, and barter became widespread. Deteriorating roads slowed travel and transportation. Industry and trade declined sharply. During this period of total disorder, or anarchy, the provinces were swept with revolt and Germanic barbarians plundered the border regions and destroyed towns. In both the cities and the countryside life had become unbearable for millions of people. To the citizens of Rome it seemed that nothing could go right.

Some emperors tried desperately to end the chaos and restore prosperity and order. One emperor even split the Empire into two parts, East and West, hoping that this move would make it easier to administer the vast Roman lands. But the Roman Empire in the West continued to decline. Historians have suggested a number of explanations to account for the decline and fall of the Roman Empire. (1) The attempts of generals to seize power weakened the army and the frontier defenses. (2) Declining agriculture, debased coins, high taxes, and slave labor weakened the Roman economy. (3) Oppressive government and the indifference of the upper class resulted in attitudes of discouragement and despair. (4) The very size of the Empire hindered the development of effective government.

Finally the weakened Empire in the West was overrun by Germanic barbarians (map, page 103). By the end of the fifth century A.D. the once-great Roman Empire in the West had been broken up into a number of Germanic kingdoms. The barbarian kingdoms continued to make use of Roman law, Roman art forms, Roman administrative procedures, and Latin, the language of Rome. But since these institutions were only scattered survivals of Roman culture, their use could not restore the Empire in the West.

THE LEGACY OF ROME

The Roman Empire in the West had fallen, but Rome left the world a heritage that endured for centuries.

1. The idea of a world empire united by law and good government never died. Men continued to dream of bringing together the different peoples of the world under one law and government.

2. While the Roman Empire in the West fell apart, the Eastern Roman (Byzantine) Empire endured for another thousand years. The line of Eastern emperors continued virtually unbroken until the capital, Constantinople, fell to the Turks in 1453. While art, learning, and city life declined in Western Europe after the barbarian invasions, the Byzantine Empire kept alive the culture and urban civilization of the ancient world.

3. The Romans founded many cities throughout the Mediterranean world, western Germany, France, and Britain which exist today. In many of them one can still see the remains of Roman roads, bridges, aqueducts, and public buildings. These cities, which played a vital role in the ancient world, would become the political, economic, and cultural centers of the civilization which was to emerge in Western Europe centuries after the fall of Rome.

4. Roman law remained a vital force in Western Europe long after the fall of the Empire. It influenced Church law and formed the basis for the law codes of many European nations. It has been said, writes twentieth-century historian Charles Sherman, that "Rome conquered the world three times: first by her armies, second by her religion [Christianity], third by her law. This third conquest, most [peaceful] of all, is perhaps the most [outstanding] of all."

5. Latin, the language of ancient Rome, lived on. From it came Italian, Spanish, Portuguese, French, Romanian, and Romansh (spoken in part of Switzerland). Many words in English are derived from Latin, and the literature of ancient Rome is still studied today.

6. Rome kept alive the philosophy, literature, science, and arts of ancient Greece. By way of Rome, Greek culture spread to Western Europe. By preserving, spreading, and adding to the culture of Greece, Rome made an incalculable contribution to western civilization.

7. Christianity, born within the Roman Empire, was greatly influenced by Roman law and Roman organization. Its adoption as the official religion of Rome encouraged its growth. Christianity became a key element in the civilization that emerged in Western Europe during the Middle Ages.

In the reign of Augustus' successor, the Emperor Tiberius, a Palestinian Jew named Jesus was executed by the Roman authorities. At the time few people paid much attention to this incident. Almost no one understood that what had taken place was one of the most important events in the history of the world.

Not much is known about Jesus' childhood. Like other Jewish youths, Jesus most likely attended the Jewish place of worship, the synagogue, where the rabbis taught him ancient Hebrew law. As he grew into manhood, Jesus felt called by God to aid the sick and unfortunate and to spread a message of love among his fellow Jews. Like the Hebrew prophets of old, Jesus denounced the wicked and the rich and urged men to love their neighbors and their God. Those who heeded God's word, Jesus told the people, would enter heaven.

The ties between early Christianity and Judaism were very strong. Christianity began among the Jews. Mary, the mother of Jesus, her husband Joseph, Jesus himself, and all his early followers were Jews. From Judaism, Christianity obtained many of its basic beliefs —the idea of one God, the demands of the prophets that man do good, avoid evil, and care for the weak, the poor, and the oppressed, the insistence that man must obey God's commands, the concept of a Messiah, the belief in the Old Testament as sacred writing.

While some Jews became followers of Jesus, most did not. Most Jews doubted that Jesus was the Messiah who would lead the Jews in a holy war against their Roman conquerors. Jewish leaders felt that Jesus was trying to undermine the authority of ancient Hebrew laws. They feared that Jesus sought to change ceremonies and rules that were centuries old. To the Jewish leaders Jesus was a troublemaker, a subversive who was trying to change the ancient Hebrew faith.

Roman authorities feared that this popular preacher would arouse the Jews to revolt against Roman rule. Discontent with Rome was already high in Palestine, and the Romans wanted no additional troubles. When Jewish enemies of Jesus turned him over to the Roman authorities, the Roman governor, Pontius (*pon'*shus) Pilate, thought his death would be to Rome's advantage. He therefore ordered his soldiers to execute Jesus by crucifying him, among the Romans a common form of execution for criminals.

To anyone living at the time, it must have appeared that Jesus had been a failure. Executed like a common criminal, he had left behind only a handful of followers. It seemed doubtful that the small Jewish-Christian band that embraced Jesus as the Messiah (Christ) would survive. Yet within four centuries millions of men throughout the Mediterranean world had declared themselves to be *Christians,* and Christianity had become the official religion of the Roman Empire.

A number of reasons help to explain the triumph of Christianity in the Roman Empire. Many people were attracted to Jesus' religious nature and his love of his fellow man. They grieved that he had suffered on the cross. They were certain that Jesus was more than just a holy man, that he was indeed the Son of God. Converts to Christianity were also attracted by its stress on the afterlife and its concern for the poor and humble.

An educated Greek-speaking Jew named Saul—who would be known to the world as St. Paul—changed Christianity from a Jewish sect into a world religion. Jesus had had almost no contact with the gentiles, or non-Jews. Paul, however, insisted that anyone, gentile as well as Jew, could become a Christian. By encouraging gentiles to follow Jesus, Paul turned Jesus' teachings into a new religion. He traveled to many parts of the Roman Empire and established churches where the followers of Jesus could meet and pray (map, page 95).

The Christian refusal to accept many Roman customs and to acknowledge the Roman gods made many Romans hostile to the new religion.

Christians were blamed for natural disasters such as famines, and their refusal to worship the emperor as a god was regarded as an act of disloyalty to Rome. In an effort to keep Christianity from spreading, some emperors launched cruel persecutions against the followers of Christ. Christians were imprisoned, beaten, starved, burned alive, torn apart by wild beasts, or crucified to amuse the Roman mob.

Rather than discouraging the Christians, these persecutions strengthened their determination and faith. Moreover, non-Christians, impressed by the courage of the persecuted Christians, became converts to the new religion. Christianity continued to expand. By the last part of the fourth century, Christianity had become the official religion of the Roman Empire and worship of the old gods was declared illegal.

The Middle Ages

Byzantine and Islamic Civilizations

The period following the decline of the Roman Empire in the West is known as the Middle Ages or medieval period. In the Early Middle Ages three new civilizations came to the fore in the lands that had once been united by Roman rule. The western part of the Empire was to develop as Latin Christendom. In the Eastern part of the Empire, Byzantine civilization flourished. These two Christian civilizations were confronted by a powerful new rival —Islamic civilization—which overran lands that once belonged to the Roman Empire and united many different peoples under the banner of a vital new religion.

BYZANTINE CIVILIZATION

Though the Roman Empire in the West collapsed in 476 A.D., the Eastern Roman (Byzantine) Empire continued to survive and prosper. (See map, page 112.) Like the civilization emerging in Western Europe, Byzantine civilization was a mixture of the old and the new. The Byzantine Empire preserved the science, mathematics, literature, and philosophy of the ancient Greeks and Romans. This learning was passed on to the lands of Western Europe.

Constantinople, the capital, was a crossroads of trade. Through it flowed goods and ideas from the Mediterranean world, the Near East, Africa, and Asia. The skills of Byzantine craftsmen were known throughout the Mediterranean world. Byzantine architects designed some of the world's most beautiful churches. These reflected a strong Asian influence. Byzantine religious paintings and mosaics revealed a superb feeling for color.

The Byzantine Empire had commercial and cultural ties with Eastern Europe. To Eastern Europe it brought Christianity (map, page 111), an alphabet, and the Byzantine style of art and architecture. In addition to these contributions, the Byzantine Empire held off repeated Muslim attacks and prevented Islam from penetrating very deeply into Central and Eastern Europe. Byzantine culture thus served as a protector of Christianity and as an important influence upon the civilizations that developed in Russia and elsewhere in Eastern Europe.

ISLAMIC CIVILIZATION

About 570 A.D. an Arab named Mohammed founded a new monotheistic religion called Islam. Islam spread very rapidly, and by the middle of the eighth century its followers, the Muslims, had built a vast empire stretching from Spain to India (map, page 119). Islamic civilization reached a level which rivaled that of the Byzantine Empire. Muslim merchants were highly respected and did business with most parts of the known world. Their ships visited the East African coast as well as the ports of India, Southeast Asia, and China; their caravans crisscrossed Central Asia and crossed the Sahara into black Africa. The constant trade and travel led to an interest in geography. In many cases works by Arab geographers served for centuries as the only guide to Asian and particularly African lands and peoples.

The Muslims were greatly interested in books and learning. Universities were established in leading Muslim cities, and the book business flourished. In universities, palaces, and the homes of wealthy merchants could be found large libraries. Muslim scholars preserved the works of ancient Greek scientists and translated them into Arabic. They improved upon the mathematics and geometry of the Greeks, adopted and passed on to the West the concept of the zero and "arabic" numerals from India, and probably did the first work in algebra. Muslim astronomers devised an accurate cal-endar and made significant contributions to man's knowledge of the heavens; many of the stars still bear Arabic names. Chemists developed several methods which are basic to chemical research and also discovered several important chemical compounds. Like the Greeks, the Muslims had wide-ranging interests.

Muslim health care was advanced for that age, and Muslim surgeons were generally far ahead of their western contemporaries. Among the operations they performed were amputations, the removal of cancerous tissue, and the peeling of cataracts on the eye. Muslim medical men also made advances in the use of drugs to heal the sick and sometimes used anesthetics in performing operations. Many of the great Muslim physicians were also philosophers.

Eventually both Byzantine and Islamic civilizations were dealt staggering blows by invading Mongolian and Turkish tribesmen from Central Asia. (See maps, pages 127 and 128.)

Latin Christendom

While Byzantines and Muslims were preserving the learning of Greece and Rome and making new contributions to civilization, Western Europe entered the Middle Ages. Separate kingdoms under Germanic leaders evolved in Gaul (France), Italy, Spain, and England—lands formerly ruled by Rome. A new civilization blending Graeco-Roman, Christian, and Germanic elements was taking shape in Latin Christendom.

While the German invaders preserved elements of the law, administrative procedures, and culture of the Roman world, they established no strong central government to protect life and property. Law and order broke down, and bands of armed men roamed the countryside, killing and stealing. The Early Middle Ages (500–1050 A.D.) were characterized by so much violence, confusion, and disorder that they are sometimes called the Dark Ages.

In the last third of the eighth century, however, a Frankish ruler, Charlemagne (shahr'-leh-main), put together a large empire in Western and Central Europe (map, page 132). Charlemagne's administration provided a considerable amount of order and thus aided the spread of Christianity in Western Europe. Charlemagne also encouraged education and culture. But Charlemagne's empire did not survive his death in 814. Western Europe returned to political disunity, and cultural development nearly ceased.

In the days of Rome's glory, there had been great cities in which merchants, craftsmen, and government officials lived. There were schools, libraries, theaters, and stadiums. Spices, slaves, and luxury items from as far away as India and China were traded in city markets. But in the last years of the Empire trade, town life, and cultural development began a decline which continued into the Early Middle Ages. Many cities were almost deserted. Seeking security, poor people moved to large estates, where they would be protected by powerful noblemen. Few people could read or write, or indeed had any interest in book learning. Their chief concern was to stay alive.

RISE OF FEUDALISM

During the latter years of the Roman Empire in the West and the centuries of the Early Middle Ages, kings had little power. This situation, particularly after the decline of Charlemagne's Empire, led to a new system of government and landholding, called *feudalism*. Under feudalism power passed into the hands of lords, who held large estates. Each lord was all powerful in his own region. He had his own army and administered the laws on his estate. Feudal lords often went to war with each other, for there was no central government strong enough to keep the peace. Moreover, during this period Western Europe suffered from frequent invasions (map, page 133). Northmen from Scandinavia plundered coastal regions from England to Spain; Magyars from Central Asia followed the routes taken by earlier Asian invaders into Eastern and Central Europe. Italy and the nearby Mediterranean islands were frequently attacked by Muslims from North African ports. Ineffective kings, further weakened by these raids, found themselves dependent on feudal lords and unable to assert authority over them.

Because he lived in a period of warfare, the medieval lord needed allies. To obtain them, he granted another lord, called a *vassal,* some land, called a *fief* (*feef*). Both lords and vassals were members of the upper class (nobility). The granting of a fief was a two-sided bargain: the lord promised his vassals protection and land; the vassals agreed to render certain services, particularly military, to their lord.

MANORIALISM

During the latter years of the Roman Empire in the West, many peasants had turned over land to nearby lords to gain protection from thieves and roving warrior bands. Others had lost their land because of debt. Consequently, in the Early Middle Ages few farmers owned the land they worked. Most peasants lived in farming villages on *manors*—estates held by a lord and containing his manor house. These peasants, called *serfs,* received from the lord a hut in which to live and some land to farm. In return, they performed various services for the lord, including the farming of his land.

Almost everything needed for daily life was found on the manor. The peasants grew grain and raised cattle, sheep, goats, and hogs. Blacksmiths, carpenters, and stonemasons did the building and repairing. Women made clothing. In the forests were wild animals that the lord would hunt; in the pastures cattle grazed. A priest cared for the religious needs of the people. When a manor was attacked by another lord, the peasants found protection inside the walls of the manor house. The manor house stood at some distance from the huts of the peasants, which formed a small village. The manor was almost self-sufficient—able to produce everything it needed. Some goods, however, such as salt and iron, had to be obtained from the outside.

The common people rarely left the manor. Dense forests separated one manor from another. Poor roads and few bridges made travel difficult; thieves and warring knights made it dangerous. Peasants lived, worked, and died on the lord's estate and were buried in the village churchyard. They knew almost nothing of the outside world.

In many ways the serf's freedom was restricted. He could not leave the manor without the lord's permission. Before a serf could marry, he had to pay a fee to the lord. Sometimes the lord would not allow the serf to marry the woman of his choice. Moreover, the lord could select a wife for his serf and force him to marry her or to pay a fine instead. The serf had to use the lord's equipment. He had to bake his bread in the lord's oven, grind his wheat in the lord's mill, and press his grapes in the lord's winepress. The serf paid for these services in kind—that is, with part of the grain and vegetables harvested on his own plot of land. Often the lord also demanded chickens, eggs, and pigs.

The lord kept for himself the best land on the manor. The serf had to work his allotted land and give a portion of his crops to the lord. And he had to work his lord's land and turn over all its crops to the lord. In addition, the serf had to help dig ditches, gather firewood, build fences, and repair roads and bridges. His wife helped to make clothing for the lord's family and household servants.

Although the serf was not free, neither was he a slave. His children could not be taken from him and sold. As long as the serf carried out his duties to his lord, he had a right to live in his cottage and to farm his strips of land. Unlike the modern factory worker, the serf never had to worry about unemployment. Moreover, the lord gave him protection from bandits and attacks by other lords.

DECLINE OF FEUDALISM AND SERFDOM

Feudalism developed in a period when kings were weak. Feudal lords wished to keep things that way. They realized that a strong monarch might take over their land and reduce their power. Late in the Middle Ages kings did just that. In France, Spain, and England powerful monarchs established strong central governments. In some cases these kings were great lords who had taken power and land away from other lords. In time, instead of many lords, each having control over his own region, one king ruled a nation. Instead of the people being loyal to a lord, they became subjects of a king. The lords still existed, but they had lost much of their power to strong kings. How did this come about?

In the eleventh and twelfth centuries there was a revival of town life in Western Europe. In their struggles with feudal lords, kings were aided by townspeople who had grievances against the lords. Merchants needed good roads for the transportation of goods, but most roads passed through lands of feudal lords little interested in keeping them in repair. Moreover, feudal warfare made travel unsafe. Townsmen also complained about tolls that they often had to pay in crossing the lands of a feudal lord. Only a king ruling a large territory could improve these conditions. Moreover, a strong monarch would establish uniform law in his realm. This would be much better than having to obey the many different and conflicting laws decreed by feudal lords. A king could also issue coins which would have the same value throughout the land. For all these reasons the townsmen helped the monarch in his struggle against feudal lords. They often loaned or gave him money with which he could hire officials to administer his laws and soldiers to enforce them.

The introduction of gunpowder also worked to the advantage of kings. Knights on horseback, clad in heavy armor and wielding a sword or battle ax, were no match for the king's soldiers armed with muskets. Nor could the walls of the lord's castle withstand the pounding of heavy iron balls fired from cannon.

Actually, even before gunpowder was introduced, armored knights had not fared too well in fighting determined commoners armed with longbows or crossbows. If his warhorse was wounded or killed, the dismounted knight was an awkward and not very dangerous foe.

The revival of town life also contributed to the decline of serfdom. Some serfs ran away to the new towns where, after a year and a day, they were considered freemen who could work for pay. Serfs who remained on the land began to earn some money by selling food to townsmen. In time some serfs were able to buy their freedom, for a lord needed ready cash to pay for goods bought from merchants. As the lords' need for money increased, lords began to accept cash payments from serfs in place of work or foodstuffs. Serfs who began meeting their obligations with cash payments gradually became rent-paying tenants, no longer bound to the lord's land.

Still another factor contributing to the decline of serfdom was the expansion of farm lands. Many feudal lords owned vast tracts of forest and swamp lands. By having these lands cleared, drained, and farmed, the lord could increase his income. But most serfs were unwilling to move from their holdings to do the hard labor needed to prepare these lands for farming. To induce serfs to make such a change, lords promised them freedom from most or all obligations. Many former serfs, resettled on cleared land, fulfilled their obligations to the lord by paying a tax, rather than by performing services. They had become freemen.

THE AGE OF FAITH

During the late Roman Empire and Early Middle Ages, the Catholic Church grew in importance and power. In many ways it took the place of the Roman Empire in the West. People had been citizens of one Roman Empire; now most people in the lands once united by Rome were members of one Catholic Church. There no longer was an emperor in Rome, but there was the Pope, head of the Catholic Church.

To the people of the Middle Ages, religion was all important. For this reason the medieval period has been called an Age of Faith. Medieval man believed that the Church was God's agent on earth. Its rules were God's rules; its teachings were God's teachings. Medieval man believed that God had created Earth, sun, moon, and all other heavenly bodies. He looked upon man as God's most important creation. Although man was often wicked and unworthy, he was still the child of God. Medieval man's main concern was to follow God's commands. He saw life as a great drama with man the actor and God the critic. If man played his role well, he could look forward to a life in heaven. There he would enjoy the company of God and the angels, saints, and martyrs. On the other hand, wicked behavior on earth meant endless tortures in the fiery pits of hell.

The medieval Church was powerful. It owned vast tracts of land, received many gifts, and collected taxes from the people. During most of the Middle Ages the Church also controlled education, for clergymen (churchmen) were virtually the only ones who could read and write. The Church also had many privileges. Clergymen were tried only in Church courts. They did not have to serve in feudal armies. Moreover, despite its large landholdings, the Church insisted that it did not have to pay taxes to kings or feudal lords. Its wealth, its control over learning, its efficient organization, and the widely accepted belief that its teachings and its Sacraments (such as Baptism, Communion, and Extreme Unction) were necessary for salvation gave the medieval Church enormous power and influence.

Many clergymen served the Church. In almost every manorial village there was a priest. Supervising the religious activities of priests in a given district was a bishop, generally a man of noble birth. At the head of the Church was the Pope, who was elected to his position by high-ranking clergymen called cardinals. The Pope exercised great powers and had very important responsibilities. He felt himself responsible for the souls of all Christians. It was his duty to lead Christian Europe on the path marked out by God's commandments. To carry out this holy duty, medieval Popes demanded complete and unquestioning obedience from all Christians—churchmen, kings, lords, merchants, and serfs alike. Catholics were taught that to resist the Pope was to turn against God. Medieval Popes even claimed the right to remove disobedient kings from their thrones. When Popes tried to put these claims into practice, they were likely to encounter resistance from rulers. Kings, in turn, argued that taxes should be paid on Church property, but the Church would not accept this demand. Finally, kings did not want the Pope to tell them how to rule their people. Clashes between kings and the Pope eventually weakened the Church.

Since the early days of the Church, there had been men who believed they could best serve Christ by withdrawing from this world.

These men became *monks*. Seeking nothing for themselves and wanting only to love and serve the Lord, monks withdrew to a monastery far removed from the cares and pleasures of everyday life. All monks in the monastery had some task. Some made furniture or clothing; others worked in the fields or prepared food in the kitchen. Still others copied old Greek and Roman manuscripts. Monks also served as teachers, converted peoples worshiping pagan gods to Christianity, taught peasants better ways of farming, organized schools, and gave food and shelter to the needy. To the people of the Middle Ages the monk was the finest example of the Christian life.

Some holy men felt that withdrawal from the world was not the best way to serve God. Some, called *friars,* wandered from place to place, aiding the poor and needy and teaching the ways of God. They tried to show people by example how a good Christian should live.

Holding beliefs which the Church considered wrong, or rejecting the authority of the Church, was known as *heresy.* The medieval Church believed there was only one road to heaven— obedience to God's rules as taught by the Church. Heretics were evil because they not only set themselves above the teachings of the Church but might influence others to do like-wise. Whenever heresy threatened to become widespread, the Church would ask kings and feudal lords to use force to crush it.

Those who disobeyed the Church could be *excommunicated*—expelled from the Church and denied the Sacraments. Anyone who helped such a person would himself be excommuni-cated. Medieval man believed that an excom-municated person would be denied admission to heaven. On earth he would live without the fellowship of friends; he would die without the comfort of a priest. To a Christian there could be no punishment more horrible than excom-munication. Often the threat of excommuni-cation was enough to convince a would-be heretic to mend his ways. Rather than be sepa-rated from the Church, he would confess his error and seek forgiveness.

In the thirteenth century the Church strength-ened the Inquisition, a Church court which tried heretics. Persons accused of heresy were brought before clergymen who acted as judges in the court. The Church urged the accused to confess his error and to ask forgiveness. Often torture was used to make the accused admit wrongdoing. If he confessed and asked forgive-ness, the Church welcomed him back. If the ac-cused would not confess, he was excommuni-cated and turned over to the state for punish-ment, which might be burning to death at the stake.

Why would men of God approve of torturing and executing persons whose beliefs were dif-ferent from their own? Clergymen who pun-ished heretics were certain that they were doing right. They firmly believed that only the Church could lead men on the road to salvation. Here-tics and those who followed their teaching were destined for hell. The death of a heretic made it easier to save the souls of the living.

The medieval Church, a very important and powerful institution, greatly influenced the be-havior and thoughts of Western Europeans. The Church cared for the needy, the sick, and the traveler. It tried to check violence and blood-shed. To reduce warfare among feudal lords, the Church proclaimed the Truce of God, which prohibited fighting on certain days of the week and on holy days.

The Church was a great civilizing force in the Middle Ages. During the Early Middle Ages when learning in Western Europe had sunk to its lowest point, churchmen continued to read and write and to teach others to do so. Monks preserved and copied ancient Greek and Roman manuscripts. During the High Middle Ages, cathedral schools developed into universities. It was the Church, then, that sponsored higher education and learning.

The medieval Church gave unity to the peo-ple of Western Europe. This unity was furthered by missionaries who converted the heathen to Christianity. No longer citizens of one Roman Empire, almost all Europeans were members of one Church and worshiped one God.

In the Early Middle Ages (500–1050 A.D.) Western Europe was a pioneer society struggling to overcome invasion, disorder, and weak government. Trade, town life, and learning declined. Nevertheless, during these centuries of confusion, the foundations of a new civilization were taking shape. Three major developments indicated that the Early Middle Ages had ended and that Western Europe was awakening to new experiences and new achievements. These developments were: (1) the Crusades, (2) the revival of commerce and the growth of towns, and (3) the cultural awakening of the twelfth century, the high point of medieval civilization.

THE CRUSADES

In 1095 Pope Urban II made one of the most dramatic speeches in history. Speaking to a gathering of French lords and clergy, Urban called for a war against the Muslim Turks, whose empire included Palestine, the land where Christ was born. He told the French lords that the Turks were "an accursed race, a race utterly [separated] from God," which had killed Christians and destroyed churches in the Holy Land. It was the duty of the Franks (Frenchmen), he said, to destroy these enemies of Christ and regain Palestine.

Aroused by this speech, thousands of Christian Europeans said their prayers, left their homes, and set out for Palestine. The Crusades had begun. (*Crusade* comes from an old French word meaning "to mark with a cross.") Latin Christendom—as Western and Central Europeans had come to call their civilization—was engaged in a holy war that would last for almost 200 years.

There were several reasons for the Pope's action.

1. The Pope wanted Jerusalem, the birthplace of Jesus, to be in Christian hands. The religious tolerance of the early Muslim rulers was drastically changed with the coming of the Seljuk Turks. The Turks persecuted non-Muslims and prevented Christian pilgrims from visiting holy places in Palestine.

2. By urging thousands of feudal lords into combat, Urban would strengthen papal (the Pope's) power. The great lords would be using their swords in behalf of the Church. They would look to the Pope for guidance.

3. The Church hoped to reduce feudal warfare in Europe by sending war-hungry and land-hungry knights to fight in the Holy Land.

4. Urban hoped that the Crusades might reunite the Eastern Orthodox Church in Constantinople and the Catholic Church in Rome.

The feudal lords had reasons of their own for taking up arms against the Muslims.

1. They hoped to gain land and wealth from the Muslims.

2. They saw the Crusades as a chance to participate in a glorious adventure in which they could earn everlasting fame.

3. They felt it to be their religious duty to win Palestine from the Muslims, whom they called "infidels" (nonbelievers) and "God-hating dogs."

At first the Christian forces succeeded in conquering the Holy Land and other Muslim lands. But the Muslims soon won back most of the lands lost. (See maps, pages 154 and 155.) Finally, in 1291, the last Christian outpost in the Holy Land fell to Muslim forces. Although the Crusades had failed to win the Holy Land for Christendom, they had far-reaching results which greatly influenced life in Western Europe.

1. At first the Crusades strengthened the power of the papacy and the Church. It was the Pope who had inspired and given direction to the crusading armies. However, when Popes began to call for crusades against all enemies of the Church, including Christian heretics and German emperors, it seemed to many that the Pope was merely trying to increase the Church's authority. People began to question the wide political powers claimed by the Church.

2. Western Europeans who went on the Crusades came to know and value the products

of the East—sugar, rice, fruits, pistachio nuts, cotton, silks, spices, cosmetics, mirrors, dyes, and many others. The increased demand in Europe for these luxury goods led to greater trade between Western Europe and Constantinople, and in time with Muslim lands.

3. The Crusades enabled some of the Italian city-states to increase their wealth and commercial power. Italians sold supplies to the crusaders, who sailed across the Mediterranean on Italian ships. The growing trade between East and West was carried on largely by Italian merchants and seamen and backed by Italian banking houses.

4. The Crusades contributed to the decline of feudalism by weakening the power of feudal lords. Many lords died in the fighting. Others spent most of their income and savings in meeting the costs of transporting themselves, their men-at-arms, and horses to the Holy Land. Many serfs were able to buy their freedom from lords who were desperate for funds.

GROWTH OF TOWNS AND TRADE

During the disorder of the Early Middle Ages, trade had been reduced to a trickle. But by 1100 commerce had increased in Western Europe. European ships again sailed the Mediterranean and the eastern Atlantic (map, page 159). The goods sold in European markets came from many countries—spices, jewels, perfumes, and silks from the East, ivory from Africa, furs from Russia, timber, honey, and hunting hawks from Scandinavia, wool from England, cloth from Belgium, and wine from France.

Many trade routes followed rivers or crossed the sea from one good harbor to another. At harbors and where trade routes met, merchants gathered to buy and sell. Towns arose at these crossroads of trade, near fortified castles, by monasteries, and on the sites of old Roman cities. Into the new towns came craftsmen and serfs seeking freedom and fortune.

When towns rose on lands held by feudal lords, some of the lords tried to treat the townspeople as they did serfs. The townsmen objected. Townsmen expected to marry whom they pleased and to do as they wished with their property. They wanted to make their own laws and to settle disputes in their own law courts. To do these things, the townsmen had to be independent of the feudal lords. Sometimes by fighting, but more often by money payments, the townspeople gained their freedom. Lords granted charters to the townsmen, giving them certain privileges. Thus townsmen gained the right to govern themselves, set up their own system of taxes, and establish their own law courts. Because of greater freedom and opportunities in the towns, many serfs ran away from the manors to the growing towns. Serfs who had bought their freedom also moved into towns in large numbers.

Because medieval townsmen feared attacks, their towns were protected by thick high walls and heavy gates that were closed each night. The streets within the town were narrow, crooked, and dirty. Rats, pigs, and dogs competed for the garbage that people threw from their doors and windows. Unpleasant odors from slaughterhouses, stables, and rotting garbage were always in the air. Because of dirt and overcrowding, disease spread rapidly. Housing conditions were poor. It was common for twelve or more people to live in three small rooms. Built of wood, several stories high, and almost on top of each other, medieval houses were firetraps.

At night the streets were dark and dangerous. There was no real police force. The few elderly watchmen who made their rounds from street to street were no match for thieves and hoodlums. Honest folk who had to be out after dark were careful to carry arms and never set out alone.

The growth of towns led to the rise of a new class of people called the *middle class*—merchants and craftsmen who lived in the towns. Middle-class ways of living differed greatly from those of clergymen, feudal lords, and serfs. The clergy prepared men for heaven; feudal lords lived only for warfare and hunting. Serfs lived on an isolated manor and had little chance to get ahead. The townsman was a new man. He had freedom and he had money. He was busy with business and town affairs. His world was the market rather than the Church or the manor. He was competitive, critical, and progressive. In the centuries to come, the middle class would play a vital role in the history of Western Europe.

Medieval towns were centers of business activity. Merchants bought and sold goods that had come from as far away as India and China. Shoemakers, carpenters, weavers, silversmiths, and other craftsmen opened up shops to practice their trade. A visitor to Paris, wrote a twelfth-century Frenchman, sees:

. . . the streets completely filled with good workmen who are practicing their different trades. This man is making helmets, this one mailed coats [armor]; another makes saddles, and another shields. One man manufactures bridles, another spurs. Some polish sword blades . . . and some are dyers. . . . And these here are melting gold and silver . . . [to] make . . . eating bowls, . . . jewels worked in with enamels, also rings, belts, and pins.

Because of their strategic position in the Mediterranean, Italian towns acted as the middlemen between the trade centers of the eastern Mediterranean and those of Western Europe. From Byzantines in Constantinople, from Muslims in Egypt and Syria, and from their fellow Italians located in trading colonies along the Black Sea, Italian merchants acquired luxury goods, many of them from as far away as India and China. On Italian ships these goods were transported to Western Europe and resold, earning handsome profits for the Italians.

In the fourteenth century the Italians extended their trade and increased their profits by sailing westward into the Atlantic Ocean to markets in the Netherlands (Holland and Belgium) and England. On the return voyage, the Italians brought back wool and unfinished cloth which stimulated the Italian textile industry. This increase in trade led to advances in business techniques. Merchants seeking to raise more capital entered into business organizations such as partnerships. This enabled them to ex-

pand their business and increase profits. The increase in business activity gave rise to systematic bookkeeping, without which no large-scale business activity can be conducted on a continuous basis. To make it easier for merchants of different lands to do business with each other, banking and credit facilities were developed and expanded. This made it unnecessary for merchants to carry large amounts of cash, and it also made borrowing easier.

CULTURAL AWAKENING OF WESTERN EUROPE

During the Early Middle Ages fighting and lawlessness made life in Western Europe difficult and unsafe. There was little time or opportunity for schooling, and most of the great books of ancient Greece and Rome had all but been forgotten. Except for the clergy, few men in Western Europe could read or write.

In the High Middle Ages (1050–1270) Western Europe experienced a cultural awakening. Magnificent churches were built in many towns. At newly established universities brilliant professors lectured to eager students. Some of the great works of western literature were written, and men's interest in science increased. What led to this cultural explosion?

1. The increased power of kings put an end to much of the disorder and violence that had existed for centuries. Travel was made safer for merchants, students, and teachers. There was a surplus of food so that more people could live in towns. Because of improved conditions, goods, ideas, and learning spread rapidly to many parts of Western Europe.

2. As the population in towns increased, there was a growing need for businessmen, bankers, lawyers, doctors, and government officials. Schools and universities were established to prepare young men for careers in law, medicine, teaching, government, and the Church.

3. The revival of trade and the Crusades increased contacts with the advanced civilizations of the Muslim world and the Byzantine Empire.

4. Although neglected during the Early Middle Ages, learning never completely died out.

In Church schools and monasteries some writings of the ancient Greeks and Romans were still read, and some men outside the Church also recognized the value of education. Western Europeans also learned about the writings of the ancient Greeks and Romans from the Byzantines and Muslims.

IMPORTANCE OF MIDDLE AGES

The medieval period was an Age of Faith. Man lived primarily for the promise of heaven, and his thoughts dealt largely with religion. How different this seems from our modern world of rapid change, of science and invention! Yet we owe much to the Middle Ages.

1. The Middle Ages saw the rise of universities. Among the present-day universities that were founded in the Middle Ages are those of Cambridge and Oxford (Britain), Vienna (Austria), Prague (Czechoslovakia), Paris (France), Bologna (Italy), Cologne (Germany), and Salamanca (Spain). In these universities were introduced many practices still carried on today—lectures, examinations, the wearing of cap and gown, the granting of degrees.

2. Many great modern cities began as little towns during the Middle Ages. In many European cities one can still see buildings and walls that were built in the Middle Ages.

3. Our modern languages took form during the Middle Ages. French, Spanish, Italian, Romanian, and Portuguese developed from the Latin of Rome. Dutch, German, Norwegian, Swedish, and Danish grew out of the speech of the German barbarians. English evolved from Anglo-Saxon—a Scandinavian language which developed from German—modified by Norman French.

4. In England, France, and eventually Spain, kings overcame feudal lords, united the country, and created strong states.

5. From the Middle Ages we have inherited the ideals of chivalry—loyalty, bravery, generosity, courtesy, good manners, and respect for womanhood. Our idea of a gentleman is based largely on the medieval code of chivalry.

6. Important advances were made in technology. These included the heavy plow, the collar harness, gunpowder, the windmill, the mechanical saw, and the compass. In the centuries after the Middle Ages, we shall see, western nations acquired empires and exercised power over vast areas of the world. The power of Western Europe over long-established civilizations lay largely in her technological skills. And it was during the Middle Ages that Western Europeans began to outstrip other peoples in the development of technology.

7. Some medieval thinkers began to stress the importance of reasoning. They said God wants man not only to follow His teachings, but also to understand them. Some tried to show that the theories of ancient Greek philosophers agreed with the teachings of the Church. While this was not an age of science, men did revive some of the rational ideas of the Greeks and they received training in analyzing and explaining complicated ideas. The mind of Western Europe was sharpened. This training in thinking prepared men for the future when the theories of science would become more important to man than the study of religion.

8. The Middle Ages advanced the cause of liberty. The view that the power of government should be limited is in part an outgrowth of the Middle Ages. Medieval thinkers insisted that kings must obey the teachings of God and care for the needs of all the people. Many feudal lords resisted absolute rule by kings, insisting that they had certain rights no king could take away. They maintained that laws had to be approved by both king and lords. Some political thinkers went even further. They said that the king obtained his power only with the consent of the people. If the king behaved like a tyrant, the people had the right of rebellion.

In still another way liberty was advanced during the Middle Ages. There developed the tradition that a lord accused of a crime should be judged by his fellow lords. He had the right of trial by jury. In the modern world this right to a jury trial has been extended to all men regardless of class.

The Shaping of Civilizations in Asia, Africa, and the Americas

Unit Three———

Asia in Ancient and Pre-Modern Times

CHAPTER FOCUS

India
China
Japan

Buddha and his teachings have long been a major subject of Asian art. The sculpture of the Buddha (far left) from the late Gupta period of India reveals the dignity and serenity of one far removed from the cares of the world. Knowing all, he is still at peace. In time, more approachable figures appeared in Buddhist art. One of these was Kuan-yin, China's Goddess of Mercy, shown here as an ornately painted wooden statue carved in the thirteenth century. In contrast is the contemporary Zen Buddhist shrine from Kyoto, Japan. It reflects the simplicity and love of nature characteristic of the Japanese.

Since early historical times Asia has lured the West with its luxury goods—silk, porcelain, tea, precious stones, and spices. Early travelers and merchants thought of it as an exotic continent, with rich and wonderful civilizations. Three major societies emerged in Asia—Indian, Chinese, and Japanese. Despite some contact and cultural exchange, each society developed its own unique civilization. Thus each must be looked at sympathetically from within.

The Indian subcontinent is a very large peninsula that extends southward into the Indian Ocean. This peninsula is surrounded along the north by the Himalayas and by other mountains in the northwest. Within the subcontinent there is a great variety of landscape—mountains, forests, and great plains. It is a land where the annual climate can more or less be divided into three seasons: a mild winter from October to February, an extremely hot and dry summer lasting till June, relieved by a rainy season from July to September. Man is very much at the mercy of the forces of nature in the subcontinent. Yet, wherever there is enough water, whether rainfall or river water used for irrigation, cultivation of crops can be very fruitful. It is within this geographic and climatic environment that an early civilization arose. From along the Indus River, settled ways of life extended next to the Ganges (*gan'*jeez) River valley, and eventually to the rest of the peninsula.

Although the Himalaya range contains the world's highest mountains, averaging 20,000 feet in height, India is not sealed off from the rest of the world. Far from it. Along the northwest frontier there are several passes through the mountains which have, over the centuries, permitted peoples from Central and Western Asia to enter the subcontinent with ease. The growth of Indian civilization is the story of successive migrations and invasions of people from Western Asia (present-day Afghanistan and Iran). These movements added layer upon layer to the original Indian culture. Though different peoples influenced each other, each group nevertheless remained distinct, preserving some of its customs and ways of life. Out of this interaction of different cultures evolved a rich and varied civilization.

The Harappan culture develops in the Indus River valley. Our knowledge of early India is very scanty and based almost entirely on archaeological evidence. By about 3000 B.C. a fairly advanced civilization had already developed in the valley of the Indus River. This Indus Valley, or *Harappan,* culture forms the oldest layer of Indian civilization. From archaeological findings we know that its people were of medium height, dark-skinned, long-headed, narrow-nosed, and slender. They were farmers who grew wheat, barley, peas, and sesame, and domesticated various animals, including cattle. For tools and weapons they used bronze and copper as well as stone. Jewelry, seals, and pottery uncovered by archaeologists indicate that the people of the Indus Valley were skilled craftsmen. Because their agriculture produced surplus food, they were able to support towns. Excavations on the sites of these towns suggest that the inhabitants were prosperous and carried on some trade with the rest of Asia and the Near East. These people had a written language, which we are just beginning to decipher. There is evidence that the Harappans worshiped a Mother Goddess and a fertility god. We do not have sufficient evidence to know the details of their beliefs. But it is generally assumed that their religious worship provided the basis for the multitude of gods in Hinduism, which was to become the dominant religion in India.

Indo-Aryans overcome the Harappans. Between about 2000–1000 B.C., small groups of peoples from Central Asia began to filter into the Indian subcontinent. Speaking an Indo-Aryan language, these newcomers were tall and fair-skinned, pastoral herders rather than settled farmers. Because their livelihood depended upon the herding of cattle and horses, the Indo-Aryans had not developed towns. Like many nomadic peoples, they were organized into tribes. Each tribe, led by a chieftain, had its priests, warriors, and followers. The priests played an important role in Indo-Aryan life.

Although the Indo-Aryans had no written language, they had many myths and legends. These were preserved from generation to generation by the priests, who committed the religious hymns to memory. The Indo-Aryans worshiped and made sacrifices to various gods representing the forces of nature—the sun, rain, fire, and so on. Although they were less culturally developed than the Harappans, the Indo-Aryans tended to look down upon the earlier settlers of the Indus valley. Their armies, though small in number, proved to be superior to the Harappan forces. The Indo-Aryans were thus able to dominate the Harappans.

Gradually a new society, the Hindu society, emerged from the Indo-Aryan and Harappan cultures. Hindu civilization, which developed well before the birth of Christ, has persisted until modern times in spite of subsequent migrations and invasions by other peoples. Let us therefore look at this society in some detail.

Hindu society is agricultural. It has been estimated that 85 to 90 per cent of the population were peasants who farmed the land and raised livestock. Hindu society was therefore predominantly agricultural, with the people living in small villages. On the outskirts of these villages of small huts were the fields and pastureland. Besides the farmers working in the fields, there were artisans and merchants in each village. The peasant's way of life was hard, for he was very much at the mercy of nature. Water was a constant problem, though irrigation systems were developed at an early period to water the fields. But periodically the water supply would fail, and there would be famine and starvation.

The patriarchal family is the basis of society. Life in the Hindu village community was not completely bleak, however. Close family ties gave the people a deep sense of security. Hindu society placed great importance upon the *patriarchal* family (a family in which the male head has the dominant role). The Hindu family usually included the father and his wife, their chil-

Ancient and Traditional India

c. **3000**–c. **2000** B.C.	Harappan culture
c. **2000**–c. **1000** B.C.	Aryans invade India
c. **1000**–c. **300** B.C.	Development of Hinduism
c. **563**–c. **483** B.C.	Buddha
327–325 B.C.	Invasion of Alexander the Great
c. **321**–c. **184** B.C.	Maurya dynasty; humanist rule of Asoka
320 A.D.–c. **535** A.D.	Gupta dynasty; advances in art, science, medicine
712–743 A.D.	Early Muslim penetration
1526–1858	Mughal Empire

dren, the wives of married sons, and grandchildren, plus others who were directly related to the father. They all lived together either in one house or in two or more houses located near each other. Within the patriarchal family, the father's authority was absolute. From an early age children were taught to respect the elder members of the family group. All members shared in the ups and downs of that family's fortune. Land, household property, and earnings did not belong to individuals but to the family group in common. Persons unable to work were supported by working members of the family. For its members, the Hindu family insured food, shelter, security, and a sense of belonging.

The patriarchal family still exists in India today, particularly in the countryside. It differs markedly from western families. In the latter, children are urged to compete, to excel, to succeed, and to strike out on their own when they become adults. Western youths are expected to demonstrate personal independence, achievement, and initiative. The traditional Hindu family stresses obedience to elders, labor for the good of the family, and the preservation of ancient customs. Some observers believe that, because it discourages initiative, the Hindu

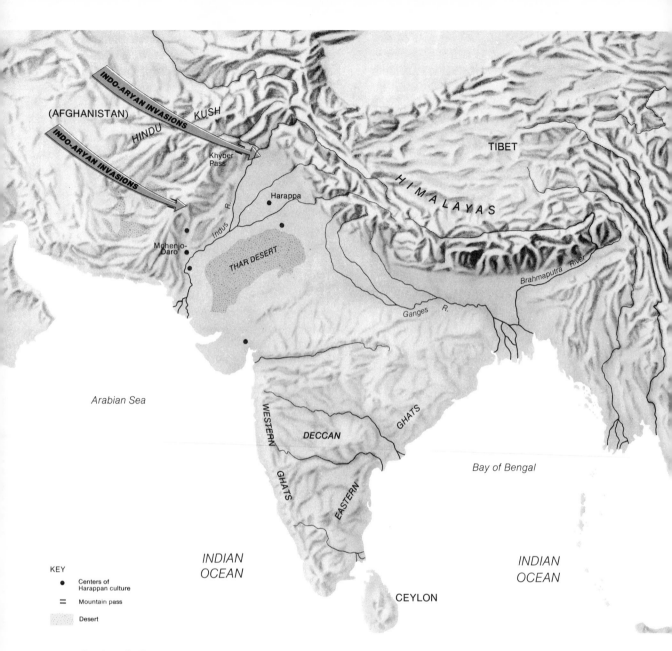

KEY
- • Centers of Harappan culture
- = Mountain pass
-   Desert

Ancient India

family is out of place in the modern world. Others would still like to preserve the values of the traditional family.

Hindu women had a subordinate position in the family. From childhood they learned household tasks and respect for their fathers and brothers. A woman's husband was usually chosen for her, and after marriage she was expected to devote herself to her husband's well-being. Though she could own some property and might be respected for her advice, a woman was expected to keep well behind the scenes: "She should do nothing independently even in her own house. In childhood subject to her father, in youth to her husband, and when her husband is dead to her sons, she should never enjoy independence." Upper-class women were especially restricted. When they appeared in public, they were expected to be veiled and accompanied by servants.

The caste system imposes a rigid social grouping. Religion was most important in the Hindu way of life. There were many gods, and different groups of people worshiped them in different ways. From these many different religious practices a rigid social grouping, the *caste* system, emerged. Members of a caste all worshiped in the same way, followed the same occupation, and had the same customs and dietary restrictions. Each caste lived in a separate section of a village or town. In effect, each caste was a self-contained community, preserving its own ways by having as little to do with other castes as possible. A person literally was born, lived, worked, married, and died all within his caste. He could not marry outside it or change from one caste to another. If he broke any of the caste laws, he would be excluded from the caste, and even his family would have nothing to do with him.

To complicate the social system, a caste could include many sub-castes. For example, within the caste of potters there might be many sub-castes based on place of birth, type of pottery made, religious practices, and family relationships. It has been estimated that there were between two and three thousand different castes and sub-castes in Hindu India. If the basic unit of Hindu society was the patriarchal family, then the caste was the framework within which were carried on all social and economic activities.

All of these castes were grouped under four class divisions. At the top were the priests, the *Brahmins*. Second in importance were the rulers and warriors. These two groups, supposedly representing the social virtues of wisdom and valor, made up the Hindu upper classes. Below them were the merchants, whose virtue was to be industrious. At the bottom of the society was the serving class, the *Sudras* (*soo'*druhs), whose duty it was to serve the other three classes. Sudras included farmers, servants, and other lowly castes.

The Brahmins were highly privileged. They alone were permitted to teach religion, recite the sacred hymns, and perform the ritual ceremonies of Hinduism. They also set the religious and social standards for the other three classes. All three upper classes could study the hymns, but the Sudras were not even allowed to hear some of them.

Below these four classes, and not considered as being a part of them, were the outcastes, also known as *untouchables*. These casteless, classless persons were regarded as the lowest of all human beings and were considered by all Hindu classes to be unclean or polluted. Anyone coming into contact with them would be considered to have been contaminated. Hence no caste members of Hindu society would have any dealings with the untouchables, who led a very segregated life. It was their lot to do menial tasks which caste members would not perform, such as the cremation of corpses and the execution of criminals.

Religion is the basis for Indian society. The Hindu religion developed from the religious beliefs and practices of the Harappans and the Indo-Aryans. Hinduism involves a multitude of religious rites and thousands of gods. But underlying the wide differences in practice is a common outlook: life in this world is only illusion, a dream. The only reality is the World Soul, the inexplicable whole of which all forms of life are a part. Man's life is a continual struggle to become worthy enough to return to the World Soul. But the world into which man is born is one of desire, action, and suffering. Desire drives man to action, but action never satisfies him; it only increases his appetite. This leads to further desire, frustration, and therefore suffering. The longer a man lives and the more he becomes involved in the things of this world, the more suffering he will experience.

In his pursuit of possessions, pleasure, and power, man commits sins for which he must pay. But atonement for sins does not occur during a man's lifetime. When the body dies, the soul is reborn again into another body. This rebirth of the immortal and indestructible soul is called *reincarnation*. The soul of a man who has sinned is reborn into a lower caste or a lower form of animal. Thus death offers man no escape from the misery of life. This cycle of birth and reincarnation from one painful life to another is called the *Wheel of Life*.

The ultimate goal of the soul is to escape the misery of earthly life and return to the World Soul. To achieve this liberation from the Wheel of Life, the Hindu must deny himself worldly pleasures and selfish actions. He must live simply and righteously, engaging in soul-searching contemplation to gain knowledge of the World Soul. The Hindu who follows this way is gentle, fearless, nonviolent, modest, and compassionate. One of the sacred hymns of Hinduism, the *Bhagavad-gita* (*bug'*uh-vud-*gee'*tah), describes the proper life:

When one renounces all the desires which have arisen in the mind, and when he himself is content within his own self, then is he called a man of steadfast wisdom.

He whose mind is unperturbed in the midst of sorrows and who entertains no desires or pleasures; he from whom passion, fear, and anger have fled away—he is called a sage of steadfast intellect.

He who feels no attachment toward anything; who, having encountered the various good or evil things, neither rejoices nor loathes—his wisdom is steadfast.

After death, the soul of such a man will reappear in a member of a higher caste. If each succeeding life is righteous, eventually the soul will appear in the body of a Brahmin, the only caste which may attain freedom from rebirth. Even the Brahmin does not automatically rejoin the World Soul after death. He, too, must lead an upright life to free himself from the Wheel of Life. For the vast majority in Hindu society, then, the Wheel of Life must continue.

Buddhism rejects the rigid and exclusive Hindu standard. About the fifth century B.C. a new religion developed within Hindu society as a reaction against this rigid, exclusive religious standard. Known as Buddhism, it promised the path of salvation to all, not just the Brahmins.

Buddhism was founded by Siddhartha Gautama (sid-*dahr'*tuh *gah'*uh-tuh-muh), who became known as the Buddha, "the Enlightened One." We know very little of Gautama's actual life. According to tradition, Gautama was a high-born prince, brought up in the sheltered life of the court. Shielded from any knowledge of sorrow or the suffering of the poor, he had everything a prince could wish. But inwardly he was unhappy. One day Gautama met a dying old man, then a sick man in great pain, next a corpse, and finally a religious ascetic (one who practices strict self-denial). These encounters were a tremendous shock to the prince who had known nothing but luxury and comfort. Gautama was so horrified by the suffering and poverty he had seen that he began to seriously question the beliefs he had been taught. Why was there such sorrow in the world? Was there no hope for the poor? He renounced his life of ease and pleasure and set out as an ascetic to find the answers to his questions. For many years Gautama followed the Hindu way of self-denial and contemplation, but he was still unhappy and troubled. Finally, at the age of thirty-five, he sat down under a sacred fig tree and took a vow never to leave the spot until he found religious enlightenment. He spent 49 days in meditation. At first the various Hindu gods and goddesses protected him. Then came the evil spirit of the world, who used both terrifying demons and seductive maidens to sway him from his purpose. But Gautama resisted all temptation. On the forty-ninth day, there was revealed to him the reason for life's sufferings and what man must do to overcome them. He had become the Buddha, the Enlightened One, and had the knowledge to free himself from the Wheel of Life.

For the rest of his life, the Buddha preached his message of salvation. The essence of this

Hinduism is an inseparable part of Indian life.
Since ancient times Indian art has illustrated the
great Hindu legends such as the love story of Radha
and the god Krishna (below). Skilled performers such
as the Kathakali dancers (right) keep these classic
tales alive. Pilgrims still bathe in the Ganges
(above), believing that its waters purify. In the
background are the temples of Benares, a holy
city to both Hindus and Buddhists.

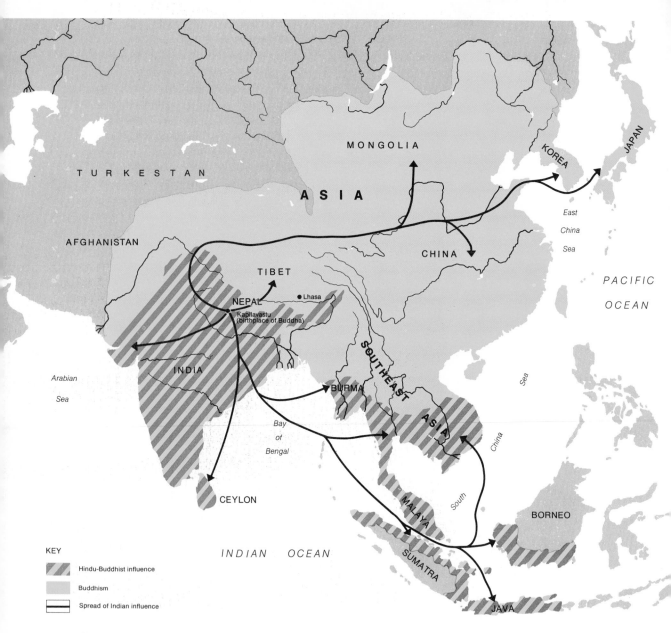

KEY

▨ Hindu-Buddhist influence

▨ Buddhism

☐ Spread of Indian influence

Spread of Hinduism and Buddhism

message is found in the Four Noble Truths:

1. Suffering is the major part of our life. "Birth is sorrow, age is sorrow, disease is sorrow, death is sorrow, contact with the unpleasant is sorrow, separation from the pleasant is sorrow, every wish unfulfilled is sorrow."

2. Suffering is caused by desire. "The thirst for power, the thirst for pleasure, the thirst for existence— . . . there is the origin of suffering." Desire can never be satisfied; it only leads to unfulfillment and further desire. This is why life itself is suffering.

3. Man must overcome desire. Only by overcoming his desires can man free himself from suffering. "Drive away desire. Forego desire. Free yourselves of desire. Be ignorant of desire."

4. The Middle Way leads to enlightenment. By avoiding extremes, by refraining both from excessive self-indulgence and from excessive self-denial, man achieves enlightenment. The Middle Way is reached by leading a good life and following the Noble Eightfold Path: Right Views, Right Resolve, Right Speech, Right Conduct, Right Livelihood, Right Effort, Right Recollection, and Right Contemplation.

The message of the Buddha was at once exalted, compassionate, and simple. Buddhism stresses gentleness, kindness, and love:

May every living being, weak or strong, large or small, seen or unseen, near or far, born or yet unborn—may every living thing be full of joy.

May none deceive another, or think ill of him in any way whatever, or in anger or ill-will desire evil for another.

Just as a mother, as long as she lives, cares for her only child, so should a man feel all-embracing love to all living beings.

He should feel boundless love for all the world, above, below, and across, unrestrained, without enmity. Standing, walking, sitting, or lying down, he should be firm in the mindfulness of love. For this is what men call the sublime mood.

Originally the teachings of the Buddha involved no worship of any deity. When the Buddha died, his followers believed that he had entered *Nirvana,* a state of absolute, spiritual oneness with the World Soul, which lies beyond our worldly understanding or imagination. Eventually, as Buddhism became increasingly complex, the Buddha was worshiped as a deity.

Buddhism spreads to other parts of Asia. For a few centuries following the death of the Buddha, Buddhism spread throughout India. It had special appeal to the Sudras. But the universal approach of Buddhism, where salvation is open to all, could not fit into the rigid structure of Hindu society. By the ninth century A.D. Hin-duism had re-emerged as the dominant religion in India.

While Buddhism declined in the land of its birth, it became extremely popular in other lands. In a modified form known as Mahayana (mah-*hah'yah'*nuh) Buddhism, it spread to other parts of Asia. Mahayana Buddhism stressed the belief in a multitude of Bodhisattvas (boh-dih-*sat'*was), those destined to become buddhas. Because they had compassion for all living creatures, instead of entering Nirvana for themselves, Bodhisattvas would remain in this world, helping man to achieve salvation.

I take upon myself . . . the deeds of all beings. . . . I have vowed to save all things living, to bring them safe through the forest of birth, age, disease, death, and rebirth. I think not of my own salvation, but strive to bestow on all beings the royalty of supreme wisdom.

Mahayana Buddhism thus introduced the possibility of obtaining salvation through the mercy and grace of the Bodhisattvas. This humanized Buddhism even further, for it assured salvation to anyone who had faith in and love for the Buddha.

Politically, India is characterized by disunity. While the Indian social system remained rigid until the modern period, there was constant political change. The subcontinent was never unified under one rule. Instead, kingdom succeeded kingdom as the rulers of small states waged war against each other. Adding to this domestic disunity were periodic invasions from Central and Western Asia.

Following in the footsteps of the Persians who had invaded India four centuries earlier, Alexander the Great invaded the Indus River valley in 327 B.C. He made no attempt to take over the subcontinent. But his invasion paved the way for the Maurya (*mah'*oor-yuh) Empire. Under Asoka (uh-*soh'*kuh), the greatest king of ancient India and one of the noblest rulers in all history, the Maurya Empire covered all of India but the south. Asoka was a humanist as well as a capable ruler. He promoted reform and the codification of law, and encouraged the teachings of Buddhism. As a devout Buddhist, Asoka stressed the virtues of gentleness, love, and nonviolence. He was concerned with the welfare of all his subjects. "I have had . . . trees planted to give shade to man and beast. . . . I have caused wells to be dug; resthouses have been erected, and numerous watering places have been provided . . . for the enjoyment of man and beast."

Beginning in the second century B.C., northern India for some 500 years was plagued by a series of invasions. Descendants of settlers left behind in Persia and Afghanistan by India's earlier invaders followed the traditional route into the subcontinent. From Central Asia came other invaders who soon established caravan routes linking India with their homelands and with China. Along these caravan routes went Indian products and Buddhist missionaries. Gradually Buddhism came to be an Asian, rather than merely an Indian, religion.

Asoka's Empire

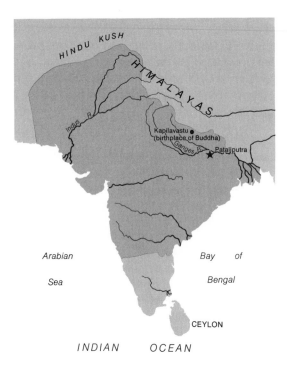

Southern India prospers economically. While northern India was involved in constant warfare, southern India (from the Deccan south) underwent a development marked by a great expansion of trade. From western lands came a heavy demand for Asian products—precious stones, ivory, textiles, rare birds, animals, and spices. Arab and Persian merchants carried these products from India to the West. To obtain the spices desired by the West, Indian merchants developed a steady trade with the East Indies and Southeast Asia. The spice trade had important cultural results. Many Indian merchants settled throughout Southeast Asia, bringing with them the customs and beliefs of Hinduism and Buddhism. The two religions flourished in the new area and left lasting traces in Southeast Asian culture. Ruins of ancient cities, temples, and palaces reflect the impact of Hindu-Buddhist thought, art, and architecture on Southeast Asia.

Culture flourishes under Gupta rule. By the fourth century A.D. northern India, under the Gupta rulers, entered a period of great cultural development. Mathematics made great advances as so-called "arabic" numerals, the zero, and the idea of infinity were developed. Indian surgery was far ahead of that practiced in the rest of the world; surgeons not only set broken bones but performed plastic surgery. In medicine a wide range of drugs came into use. To the literary traditions of Hinduism was added the work of many poets and dramatists. Art and architecture, both heavily influenced by Hinduism and Buddhism, flourished. Hinduism re-emerged as the dominant Indian religion.

Muslim invasions have a lasting impact on India. In the 700's the first of a new wave of invaders swept into India, heralding a conquest which was to have a lasting impact on the subcontinent. The first of these invaders were Afghans, and they were followers of Islam, a religion born only the century before in Arabia (see Chapter 6). In the centuries which followed, successive waves of invaders advocating

Islam succeeded in gaining control of most of the Indian subcontinent. Islam rapidly spread eastward from India. In many parts of Southeast Asia it replaced Hinduism and Buddhism as the dominant religion.

Islam came into immediate conflict with Buddhism and especially Hinduism. Unlike Hinduism, in which there is worship of many gods, Islam is monotheistic. A simple religion, Islam proclaims the brotherhood and equality of all men before the one God, Allah. This view obviously conflicted with the rigid Hindu caste system. Furthermore, the Islamic prohibition against the portrayal of Allah or any human form in either painting or sculpture conflicted sharply with the Hindu representation of many gods in all forms. In addition, the Hindus and the Muslims had different restrictions with respect to foods that were forbidden. Because the Hindus believed that all life was part of the World Soul, they prohibited the

To honor the memory of his wife, Shah Jahan had the Taj Mahal built. On its completion, he reportedly ordered its builders blinded to prevent the duplication of their work. A superb blending of Islamic and Hindu art, the Taj is both an architectural masterpiece and an enduring monument to love.

killing of animals and the eating of meat; except for pork and wine, the Muslims had no dietary restrictions. Hindu and Muslim social, religious, and cultural life were thus worlds apart.

Despite the conflict between Muslims and Hindus, early Muslim rule of India was fairly tolerant. Hindu princes who agreed to support their Muslim overlords were permitted to continue to rule their own kingdoms. Muslim power reached its height during the sixteenth century with the founding of the Mughal (*moo'*gahl) Empire by Turkish-Mongol invaders.

The first Mughal emperor, Akbar, was also the greatest. An exceptional administrator, he

Mughal Empire

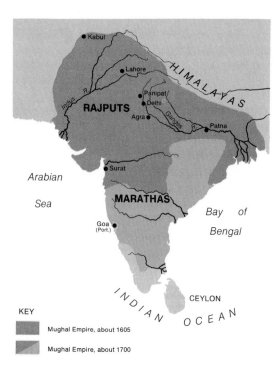

KEY

■ Mughal Empire, about 1605

▨ Mughal Empire, about 1700

conquerors was superimposed on the vast Hindu majority. Mughal administration thus lacked support at the base of society. Aurangzeb's policies and growing corruption in his government further weakened Mughal administration and the empire began to break apart.

The Muslims continued to control areas in India until the eighteenth century, but most of their power was gone. Nevertheless, Muslim rule had a lasting effect on India. Many Hindu areas remained under the control of Muslim princes. Muslim culture added another layer to the diversity and variety of Indian society. Far more important was the social-religious impact, for basic differences in religion and customs continued to separate Muslim rulers from the Hindu populace. For the Hindu masses at the bottom of society, the pattern of life was little changed by Muslim rule. Their caste system, patriarchal family, and religious practices continued as before.

was noted for tolerance in an age when bitter religious conflict was the rule. Besides eliminating the traditional Muslim tax on non-Muslims, he allowed Hindus to occupy high offices in his government and encouraged intermarriage between Hindus and Muslims. The Mughal Empire was characterized by the splendor of its court and the beauty of its art and architecture. Its blend of Muslim and Hindu themes and styles reflected cultural exchange, as did the development of the Urdu language (spoken today in Pakistan) from Hindi and Persian.

In the mid-seventeenth century, however, the "World Shaker," Aurangzeb (*oh'*rungzeb), ascended the Mughal throne. He completely reversed Akbar's policies, antagonizing Muslim allies and persecuting Hindus. Even at the height of its power the Mughal Empire had never succeeded in unifying the entire subcontinent. The political authority of the Muslim

CHECK-UP

1. How did geography and climate influence the development of Indian civilization?

2. What kind of society was developed by the Harappans? The Indo-Aryans?

3. What were the characteristics of Hindu society?

4. What is the caste system? What are its four major divisions? What are the rights and duties of each caste? How did the caste system impose a rigid social grouping?

5. Why is it so difficult, according to Hinduism, to escape from the misery of life? What is reincarnation? How can the faithful Hindu free himself from the Wheel of Life?

6. Who was Siddhartha Gautama? What message did he preach? Why did Buddhism spread to other parts of Asia?

7. Why did India lack political unity? What were the cultural achievements of Gupta India?

8. Why did Islam conflict with Hinduism? How did Akbar seek to blend the life styles of Hindus and Muslims? What policies did Aurangzeb follow?

China

Too often westerners, not familiar with Asia, lump different Asian societies together. Actually, Chinese civilization is very different from Indian civilization. The two developed quite separately from each other. The lasting achievement of Indian civilization has been a deep concern with religion, with things of the spirit. The achievement of the Chinese, on the other hand, has been their concern for the relationship between morality and politics, a practical concern with government and society. It is this which will provide the theme for our survey of Chinese civilization before modern times.

The civilizations of the eastern Mediterranean and of India had close contact with one another and with other geographic areas. Chinese civilization, however, developed in the relatively distant region of East Asia, far from other major cultural centers. This does not mean that the Chinese were, either racially or culturally, untouched by foreign influence. Over the centuries immigrants, merchants, and invaders from Central and Western Asia carried foreign influences into China. But, because the Chinese were remote from the other major centers of civilization, they were able to absorb outside influences slowly, while developing their own pattern of culture.

Chinese civilization develops in the Yellow River basin. Chinese civilization originated in the Yellow River basin of North China. Over the centuries it gradually extended southward to the Yangtze (*yahng'dzuh'*) River of Central China and later to the Hsi (*shee,* West) River of South China. China, of course, is a vast country, and its range of climate reflects this size. Winters in the north can be severely cold, whereas the southern summers are almost tropical. Drought is common in the north while the south is humid and well watered. The area from the basin of the Yellow River to the Hsi River is known as *China Proper* and is the source of much of the country's food. Bordering China Proper are the broad fertile plains of Manchuria, the arid plains and deserts of Mongolia, the vast expanse of Sinkiang (*shin'jih-ahng'*), and the towering mountains and barren plateaus of Tibet.

The Yellow River basin had a rich topsoil which encouraged successful agriculture. Here the first Chinese farming communities developed before 2000 B.C. Archaeological remains and written records suggest that by 1000 B.C. there was already a fairly advanced civilization in the Yellow River valley. Here the ancient Chinese established settled, fortified communities, surrounded by fields of rice and millet. They also domesticated animals and raised silkworms. Excellent bronze artifacts and utensils from this period, with highly sophisticated designs, testify to the technical advance of these people.

Ancient and Traditional China

c. **2000**–c. **1000** B.C.	Yellow River civilization
c. **551**–c. **479** B.C.	Confucius, stress on ethics
c. **500**–c. **400** B.C.	Taoism develops
221–206 B.C.	Ch'in dynasty; language standardized
c. **206** B.C.–c. **220** A.D.	Han dynasty; advances in science and technology
c. **25** A.D.	Buddhism reaches China
618–907 A.D.	T'ang dynasty; mandarin system develops; arts flourish
960–1279	Sung dynasty
1279–1368	Mongol (Yuan) dynasty
1368–1644	Ming dynasty

211

For centuries rice has been China's most important crop. Intensive cultivation permits farmers to make maximum use of the land. Rice is also important in ceremonies. The bronze vessel from the Yellow River civilization was used for ritual offerings of food.

The Chinese written language had also developed by this period. Unlike other written languages, the Chinese language has no alphabet. Instead, there are characters representing words. Originally each character represented a pictograph or an idea. This resulted in literally tens of thousands of individual characters, and made Chinese a most difficult language to master. But mastery of the language guaranteed the educated person a privileged position in Chinese society. Over the centuries, the Chinese language has changed very little, and only slowly. In spite of the geographical ex- panse of the country, comparable in size to the entire European continent, there has been greater cultural unity in China than in Europe. To a considerable extent, this cultural unity arose from the stability of the Chinese language and literature.

The Chinese believe there is interaction between heaven and earth. Ancient Chinese society was divided quite strictly into three classes. At the top were the warriors and rulers. Then came the largest group, common people who were peasants, artisans, and merchants. At the bottom were domestic slaves, quite often prisoners captured in wars.

The Chinese believed that there was constant interaction between heaven and earth. There was an order in heaven and an order on earth, and these two separate orders tended to affect each other. The human link between earth and heaven was the ruler, known as the "Son of Heaven." Unlike the Egyptian pharaoh, the Son of Heaven was not regarded as divine. It was his duty to make offerings and sacrifices to heaven, so as to reinforce the earthly order. Thus, the Chinese ruler was not only head of the state but also had a religious function. This was quite different from Hindu society, which called for a sharp distinction between ruler and priest.

Chinese society becomes less rigid. Over the centuries, as ancient Chinese society developed, the rigidity of the old class divisions loosened somewhat. Population increased, as did trade and commerce. This meant increased wealth, especially among artisans and merchants. From Western and Central Asia were introduced iron weapons and horseback-riding. Superior weapons and greater mobility made possible the rise of powerful regional rulers who not only competed among themselves but at times challenged the authority of the Son of Heaven.

Under these changed conditions, the old belief in an order on earth reinforced by the order in heaven came to be questioned by an increasing number of people. Consequently, about 550 B.C. philosophers and thinkers began to give thought to the problem of social and political order. This was the period that brought forth the teachings of Confucius, the Legalists, and Taoism.

Confucius stresses the development of character. The most famous thinker of this period was K'ung Fu-tzu (*koong' foo'dzuh'*), known to the world as Confucius. Disturbed by the political unrest which caused social disorder

and suffering among the people, Confucius urged a reinterpretation of the ancient belief in heavenly and earthly order. In addition to the emphasis on ritual and sacrifice, he stressed *ethics*—the development of an ideal character. Confucius' ideal gentleman would cultivate proper conduct in his relations with others. An early Chinese text states:

Behave when away from home as though you were in the presence of an important guest. Deal with the common people as though you were officiating at an important sacrifice. Do not do to others what you would not want others to do to you. Then there will be no dissatisfaction either in the state or at home.

To be able to practice five virtues everywhere in the world constitutes humanity. . . . [These five virtues are] courtesy, magnanimity [unselfishness], good faith, diligence [application to a goal], and kindness. He who is courteous is not humiliated, he who is magnanimous wins the multitude, he who is of good faith is trusted by the people, he who is diligent attains his objective, and he who is kind can get service from the people.

The gentleman has neither anxiety nor fear. . . . When he looks into himself and finds no cause for self-reproach, what has he to be anxious about; what has he to fear?

All of the sayings of Confucius emphasize proper personal conduct. In this sense, Confucius was very idealistic about human nature. He believed that if people were to conduct themselves properly, all social and political problems would somehow disappear. His teaching therefore emphasized the correct relations between a ruler and his subjects, between a father and his son, between a husband and his wife, between an elder brother and his younger brother, and between friends. Except for the relations between friends, the other four relationships were between superiors and inferiors. This involved benevolence or kindness on the part of superiors, and devotion to duty or obedience on the part of inferiors. In teaching his students Confucius sought to improve their character. He wanted to train wise and moral men for positions of leadership in the government.

The Legalists are cynical about human nature.

In sharp contrast to Confucius' emphasis on ethics, the philosophy of Legalism placed no reliance upon human conduct. The Legalists were cynical about human nature—man cannot be trusted to conduct himself properly. And the people really cannot know what is good for them. Therefore, the restoration of order in society would have to depend upon the enactment of strict laws and their enforcement under threat of harsh punishment. The Legalists believed that it is the duty of the ruler to rule, and the duty of the people to obey. Unlike the Confucian emphasis on character, Legalism is a philosophy of authoritarian government by law.

Taoism distrusts both Confucian ethics and Legalist politics.

Taoism (*dow'iz'm*), the teaching of a legendary figure called Lao-tzu (*lou'-dzuh'*), was a philosophy of protest. It distrusted both Confucian ethics and Legalist politics, advocating instead a return to nature. While Confucianism stressed man's place in society, Taoism concentrated on the liberation of man from social obligations. Society and politics, according to the Taoist, were artificial restraints placed upon man. Only by being his own natural self and seeking to fit into nature can man discover the true Way (the *Tao*). Tao is noninvolvement in the activities of this world. Rejecting the world of convention and knowledge, Taoism urges man to live simply and in close contact with nature. Since Tao is so far apart from the ways of this world, it cannot even be described in our worldly language. Instead, it becomes a mystical communion with nature.

Confucianism, Legalism, and Taoism were three of the more important philosophies which arose during the fifth and fourth centuries B.C., when Chinese society was in turmoil and thinkers speculated about society and government. These philosophies represented three entirely different approaches to the problem of restoring order, and over the centuries they would influence Chinese civilization profoundly.

But these philosophies were not able to alter the course of warfare among regional rulers. While Confucianism eventually became most important in China, the immediate impact of Confucius' teaching was negligible. North China, centered along the Yellow River basin, remained divided among various warring states.

The Ch'in establish a centralized state.

By 221 B.C. one ruling house finally succeeded in eliminating its rivals in North China and establishing the first unified Chinese empire, the Ch'in.[1] Although it lasted only fifteen years, the Ch'in dynasty was significant both in its accomplishments and failures. With respect to accomplishments, the Ch'in consolidated the 14,000-mile-long Great Wall as a defense against the nomads from the North. It standardized weights and measures as well as coinage, and the written language was made uniform throughout the empire.

One of the leading officials of the Ch'in was a Legalist, and the dynasty proceeded to establish a centralized state on Legalist principles. China was divided into equal administrative units, and all authority stemmed from the emperor. Here was where the Ch'in failed. The empire collapsed soon after the death of its capable first emperor. This dramatic failure indicated the impossibility of one-man rule over so extensive an area as China, unless the ruler was assured of adequate regional support. Later dynasties learned this lesson and gradually, through long trial and error, a stable political arrangement was developed.

China expands and prospers under the Han.

The next dynasty, the Han, ruled China for nearly four centuries. One of the most powerful and successful dynasties in Chinese history, the Han extended the political boundary of the empire into southern China. In addition, the

---

[1] From the Ch'in we get our name for China. To the Chinese, it is *Chung-kuo* (*joong'gwoh'*), the Middle Kingdom, center of the universe.

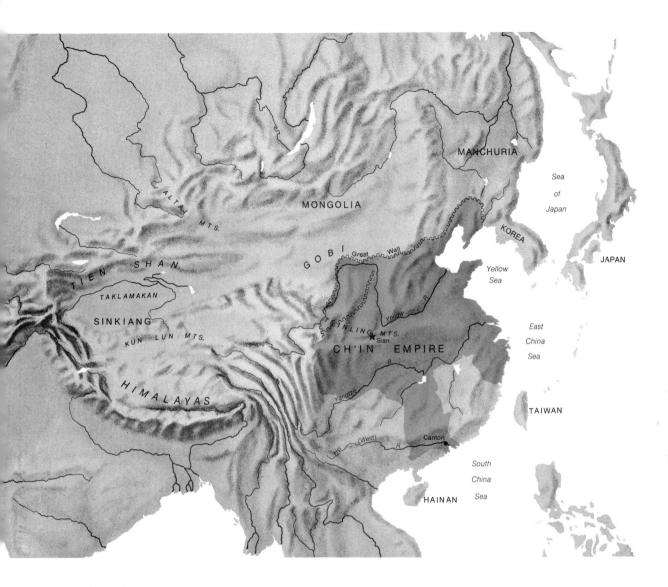

China: Ch'in Empire (221–206 B.C.)

government sent military expeditions far into Central Asia. Trade was greatly expanded, paper was introduced, and the manufacture of porcelain begun. Porcelain and silk were exported over Central Asian trade routes to India and even the Roman Empire. Internally, the Chinese made advances in science, agriculture, and manufacturing techniques.

The most significant development under the Han was the setting up of civilian government and the dynasty's support of Confucian teachings. Legalist in its approach, the Han government nevertheless recognized the need to balance the power of the regional rulers. Steps were taken to create a civil service, based on Confucian education, to carry on the various functions of government. Such officials would be more dependent on, and therefore more loyal to, the dynasty than were the regional rulers. Ch'in Legalism had had little local support. The Han government, by creating a partnership with Confucian officials, sought to con-

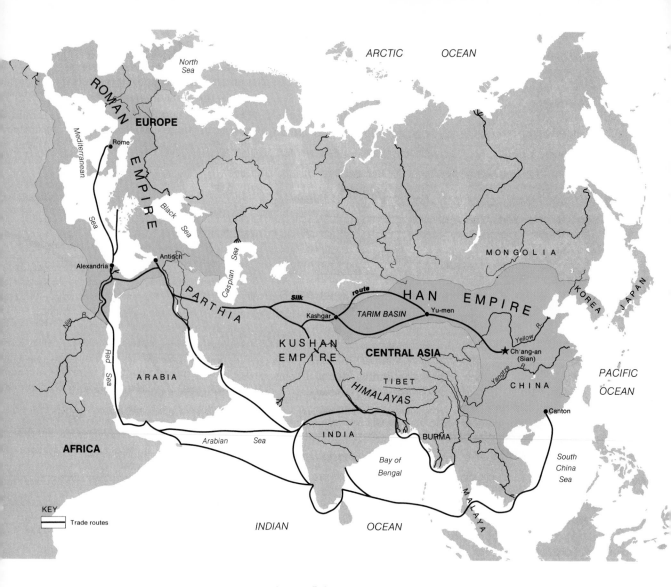

China: The Han Empire and Eurasia (100 A.D.)

tain the regional rulers and won considerable popular support. A start was made in setting up an examination system for selection of future officials. Candidates were examined on their knowledge of ancient writings and their grasp of Confucian teachings. From the successful candidates, government officials were chosen. The primary goal of education became one of preparing for the examinations. This was the beginning of a trend which was to dominate

Chinese government and society until well into modern times.

However, by the third century A.D. the Han dynasty was overthrown. It had been weakened by corruption within the government administration, lack of money, a deterioration of frontier defenses against warlike nomads, an increase in the power of the regional rulers, and rebellion by discontented peasants. With the overthrow of the Han dynasty, China reverted to various regional dynasties for nearly four centuries.

The T'ang dynasty ushers in a period of cultural and economic development. On the surface, the period from the third century to the sixth century may appear to be one of political disunity and internal collapse. There was a decline in the influence of the Confucian ideal. The uncertainty of the times led to increased interest in the otherworldly teaching of Taoism. On the other hand, closer relationships with the nomadic invaders exposed the Chinese to new influences and ideas from Central Asia. Missionaries and merchants brought the teachings of Mahayana Buddhism (page 207) to China, and it soon became very popular. Buddhist monasteries were established and became places of refuge and safety in a time of trouble.

By the end of the sixth century China was once more reunited, and in 618 the T'ang dynasty was established. The T'ang, in power until 907, was one of the most important dynasties in China, comparable to that of the Han. T'ang China was a leading military power, with her borders extending into South China and Central Asia. The unity of so large an area brought order and encouraged trade and the exchange of ideas. From India came advances in astronomy, mathematics, and medicine. Chinese culture became a model for other societies, especially those of Japan and Korea. Foreign merchants and missionaries came to the T'ang capital, and many resided there. Within China literacy increased with the development of book printing. Outstanding lyric poetry was written at this time, reflecting both the Taoist appreciation of nature and emotion and the Confucian desire for an orderly and virtuous society. In the arts, Chinese sculptures showed the influence of Indian Buddhism, while painters depicted the beauties of the Chinese landscape. Buddhist influence underwent a decline, and Confucianism reappeared as the basis of government.

Even more important than these cultural advances were the significant economic and political developments under the T'ang and the subsequent Sung (*soong,* 960–1279) dynasties. By this time, China's population had increased greatly. During the Sung it may have reached 100 million. The city of Hangchow (*hahng'joh'*) in central China, for instance, by the mid-thirteenth century had a population of over a million.

There were changes in the countryside, too. Instead of an aristocracy owning large estates, there came to be many more holdings of medium size. Most of the new landowners, called *gentry,* were educated in Confucian philosophy and held positions in the government. For the peasant, however, the period of prosperity meant little. The population rise in China's cities and towns meant that the peasants had to produce more food and continue to pay the major burden of taxes.

The increase in population was paralleled by tremendous growth in manufacturing and trade, both domestic and foreign. Coal and iron mining increased to meet the needs of the growing population. The invention of the compass made sea voyages far safer and was a great encouragement to trade. Instead of long and hazardous journeys overland through Central Asia, trade became a sea venture. Paper money came into wide use, further encouraging trade. To Korea and Japan went fine silks, books, art objects, and Chinese copper currency. Chinese porcelain was in high demand not only in Korea and Japan but also in Southeast Asia, India, the Near East, and even East Africa. China imported mainly cotton textiles, but horses from Central Asia and fine woods, precious stones, spices, and ivory from the tropics were also imported.

An enduring pattern of relations between state and society develops. The T'ang and Sung improved upon the Han government and developed a pattern of political relations between state and society which endured up to modern times. It is this pattern which largely explains the apparent stability of traditional China.

At the head of the traditional Chinese state was the emperor, the Son of Heaven. The emperor still maintained his ancient function of making ritual sacrifices to heaven for the wel-

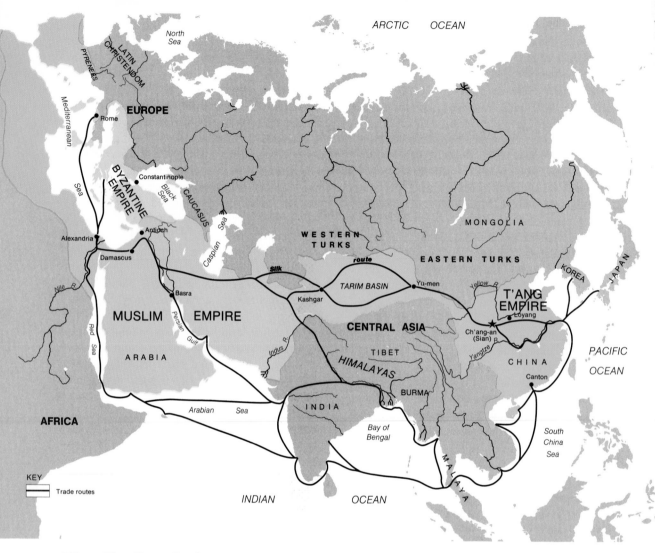

China: The T'ang Empire and Eurasia (750 A.D.)

fare of his subjects. He represented the paternal authority of the entire society and, in theory, this authority was unlimited. Much depended upon the individual emperor. A good emperor could accomplish much good; a poor one might do great harm.

In actual practice, however, the Chinese emperor was not an absolute ruler. No matter how powerful an individual he might be, the vastness of his empire meant that he could not rule

without delegating some authority to loyal subordinate officials. Through trial and error, it became clear that military men were less trustworthy than civilian officials. Military commanders had a tendency to build up their own power, which could lead to the overthrow of central imperial authority. Therefore, by T'ang times the emperor had come to rely upon civilian officials, known as *mandarins,* to fill government positions. The mandarins were selected for their Confucian learning and virtues by means of a sophisticated examination system. The teachings of Confucius and his students, preserved in the Classics, served as the basis for the exams. It took many years of study to prepare for the preliminary tests. Successful candidates took further tests—each increasingly difficult—at higher levels, and only a few ever passed the final set of exams, held at the capital under the personal supervision of the emperor.

Mandarins selected under the examination system provided a government that was in fact both economical and efficient. It gave China officials who were intelligent, well educated, and trained to respect order. But in time the mandarins developed interests of their own which conflicted with those of the emperor. Although the emperor could always remove a few really ineffective officials, he could not abolish the entire mandarin system. China's traditional government, consequently, reflected a compromise between the emperor and the mandarins. This partnership was further complicated by a third group, made up of members of the emperor's private household. These men had easy access to his confidence, and sometimes were able to sway the emperor's decisions. The emperor, in turn, could play upon the rivalry between mandarins and members of the imperial household in order to preserve his own authority.

It was truly remarkable that emperors might come and go, and dynasties follow one another, yet the partnership of the Confucian mandarins in the exercise of imperial authority remained. The foundation for the mandarins' political influence stemmed from their hold over land-ownership and from their mastery of Confucian learning.

Several factors contribute to a stable Chinese society. In a mainly agricultural society such as traditional China's, landownership represents the most stable and honored form of wealth. Landowning made possible not only wealth, but also leisure for the gentry. Both time and money were needed by anyone who wished to be educated in the prolonged, arduous task of Con-

fucian learning. The gentry landowners were generally the only ones able to afford a Confucian education for their sons. And Confucian learning was essential for anyone who hoped to pass the examination that would qualify him for appointment as a mandarin official. Thus gentry landowning, Confucian education, and mandarin politics were closely tied together to provide the foundation for a stable partnership with imperial authority.

Yet traditional China, unlike Hindu India, did not have a society of rigid social groups. There was no impassable caste barrier separating the landowning Confucian mandarins from the vast majority of Chinese, who were poor and illiterate peasants. A talented son from a poor peasant family, if he could somehow find the time and money necessary for an education and could pass the examinations, would automatically be accepted as one of them by the Confucian mandarins. There was no social discrimination; rags-to-riches success stories were possible even if unlikely. However, for the vast majority of poor peasants, their fate remained unchanged from generation to generation. And sometimes, when conditions became really bad, peasant rebellions broke out.

The family is the basis of traditional Chinese society. The world of mandarin politics was far removed from the day-to-day life of the typical Chinese peasant. But for both the rich and poor, high and low, life centered around the family, which since ancient times had been the most important unit of Chinese society. The traditional Chinese family was a little self-contained world, so tightly knit that political changes had little effect on it. It ideally included not only uncles, aunts, nephews, and nieces, but also distant in-laws and second and third cousins. Within the family, authority stemmed from the grandparents or father. The older generation was superior to the younger, and usually man was superior to woman, although an older woman was also respected. Children were brought up to respect their elders. Primary emphasis was placed upon obedience rather than self-reliance. The ideal son showed *filial piety,* respect toward his father, at all times. Only within this stable, self-contained world of the family could a person find meaning and comfort.

Confucius taught that a son should follow and respect the ways of his father, even three years after the latter's death. The traditional family thus extended not only horizontally to include all living relatives, but also backward in time to include the deceased ancestors of earlier generations. The family had great respect for the spirits of dead ancestors, made offerings to them, and told them of important family events. This ancestor worship gave members of the family a tremendous sense of continuity from one generation to another.

American historian K. S. Latourette describes the important role played by the family in Chinese society:

Most men and women felt their primary loyalty to be to their family. If a man defrauded the state to benefit his family, his dishonesty was popularly condoned [overlooked]. . . . The family had functions which in the modern West are commonly assumed by the state. It educated its youth, cared for its unemployed, disciplined its erring members, and supported its aged. In turn the state held the family accountable for the misdeeds of its members. . . .

The individual was of far less importance than the family. The individual member was to make his earnings available to his less fortunate relatives. By that same token, he knew that he himself, if overtaken by ill fortune, could always be sure of a bowl of rice in his family village. . . .

Since descent was by the male line, boys were more highly valued than girls. . . . Women were in an inferior position . . . [but] they were not without honor. A mother was revered by her sons, and a mother-in-law and a grandmother, particularly if she were a widow, had much influence in the home. Moreover, if she had force of character a woman could dominate her husband.

Confucianism underlies the Chinese way of life. The world of public affairs and that of the private family were tied together by the ethical

Chinese artists have always appreciated the beauty of their land. The lyric poet Li Po, writing in the T'ang dynasty, and Wu Wei, painting during the Ming dynasty, shared this love of nature. Perhaps Wu Wei's Scholar Seated Under a Tree *(above) is meditating on Li Po's* Question and answer among the mountains:

You ask me why I dwell in the green mountain;
I smile and make no reply for my heart is free of
  care.
As the peach-blossom flows down stream and is gone
  into the unknown,
I have a world apart that is not among men.*

* From The Penguin Book of Chinese Verse, *translated by Robert Kotewell and Norman K. Smith, A. R. Davis, editor (Harmondsworth, Middlesex, England: Penguin Books Ltd., 1962). Reprinted by permission.*

teachings of Confucius. These teachings emphasized the proper relations between superiors and inferiors in the family and in everyday life, as well as in government. Over the centuries these teachings came to be accepted by most members of society and provided a basis not only for family relationships but also for relationships in the world of politics. This widely accepted ethical outlook came to be known as *Confucianism*.

Confucianism was not a religion. It did not teach about life after death but concerned itself primarily with the ethics of this world. Nor did Confucianism advocate a program of social change or reform. Instead, it held that if everyone were to cultivate virtue and conduct himself properly, social problems would disappear. At its best, Confucianism emphasized the importance of the ethical man as the foundation for both family and society in general. Yet, by ignoring the possible need for social reform, it tended to foster the acceptance of things as they were. It encouraged people to cling to traditional attitudes and ways of doing things. Thus Confucianism contributed to social stability. Because Confucianism looked to the past, it tended to hinder the development of new attitudes which might be more appropriate to changing times.

The stable partnership between emperor and mandarins, the togetherness and continuity within the family, the Confucian emphasis upon proper personal conduct and lack of emphasis upon social change are the elements which largely account for the apparent stability of traditional China for a period of more than a thousand years.

The Mongols conquer China. In the thirteenth century China was invaded and conquered by nomads from Central Asia, the Mongols. The Mongols set up the Yuan (you-*ahn'*) dynasty (1279–1368), and made China part of an empire which stretched from Korea to Russia. Because they brought the Central Asian trade routes under one control, international commerce prospered. The Chinese economy shared in this prosperity. There came to China not only foreign merchants such as Marco Polo, but also the first Christian missionaries. But the Yuan dynasty, by refusing to rule in partnership with the Confucian mandarins, brought about its own downfall. In place of the mandarins it resorted to non-Chinese officials. As a result, the dynasty lacked regional and local support, and lasted less than a century. As foreign intruders in Chinese government, the Mongols left little impression upon China's political system.

Traditional ways of living are restored under the Ming. The Ming dynasty (1368–1644), which succeeded the fall of the Mongols, was a Chinese restoration of the traditional partnership between emperor and mandarins. In areas such as art and scholarship the dynasty continued the development which was interrupted by the Mongol interlude. Ming gentry had both the income and the leisure to enable them to become art collectors, poets, and painters. They went to the theater and read such outstanding novels as *All Men Are Brothers, Golden Lotus,* and *Monkey*. A remarkable feature of the early Ming dynasty was a short-lived period of maritime exploration, when Chinese junks sailed as far as India and East Africa in search of exotic goods and tribute (see pages 362–363).

CHECK-UP

1. Why did the Chinese develop a civilization which was largely free from foreign influence? In what important respects did the civilization of China differ from that of India?

2. What have archaeological remains revealed about the culture which developed in the Yellow River valley?

3. What were the responsibilities of the Chinese ruler? How did his role differ from that of the Egyptian pharaoh?

4. Who was Confucius? What was his philosophy? What was his view of human nature?

5. What are the major ideas of the Legalists and

the Taoists? How did Legalism and Taoism differ from Confucianism?

6. What were the achievements of the Ch'in dynasty? What lesson did future rulers learn from its failure?

7. Why did China thrive under the Han dynasty? What important cultural, economic, and political developments took place under the T'ang?

8. Who were the mandarins? What role did they play in Chinese government? How were they selected?

9. What position did the family occupy in Chinese society? What guidelines did Confucianism provide for family life? How did it contribute to social stability?

10. Why was Mongol rule of short duration?

Japan

The islands of Japan have a favorable, temperate climate with plentiful rainfall. Though the land is mountainous, the soil is fertile and most suitable for rice cultivation. Because Japan is located off the Asian mainland, the country is easily defended against outside attack, yet is close enough to the Asian continent to receive successive waves of influence. However, although Japan adopted many features of Chinese culture and of Buddhism, its isolation allowed it to develop in a distinct way. Our brief survey will focus on how Japanese society absorbed foreign influences and adapted them into a unique pattern of its own.

Present knowledge of prehistoric Japan still has many gaps. Archaeological discoveries indicate a series of early cultures, spanning a long period. They range from cultures using stone implements to those with fairly advanced use of pottery. The most recent of these prehistoric cultures was that of a group of warriors who migrated to Japan from Northern Asia about the third century B.C. From Asia they brought iron weapons and bronze tools and a knowledge of farming. Gradually they mixed with the earlier settlers of the islands to develop the present-day Japanese.

Early Japanese society is organized into clans. In Japan each clan, or *uji* (*oo-jee*) was composed of families who claimed a common ancestor, and who worshiped the same deity. Over the generations, members of each clan came to believe that they were descended from the particular deity that they worshiped. Each uji

had its own chieftain, its own military force, and its own customs and laws. The clan, in effect, was socially and economically self-sufficient. A person owed his primary allegiance to the clan. Well into modern times the clan, rather than the individual or the family, was the basic unit of Japanese society. In this important sense Japanese society differed from the Chinese, where the family was the basic unit.

Warfare among clans was common. Eventually, by the third century A.D., the Yamato (*yah-mah-toh*) clan emerged as the most powerful. The Yamato claimed direct descent from the Sun Goddess, the greatest of all Japanese deities. Though the Yamato never conquered all the other clans, it was so powerful that all paid allegiance to it. Thus the Yamato clan chief in time became the ruler of Japan, and his power was passed on to his son. Other clan chiefs became the leading hereditary officials in Japan.

Ancient and Traditional Japan

c. **200** A.D.	Yamato gain ascendancy over other clans
552–604	Buddhism reaches Japan
592–622	Rule of Prince Shokotu
653–669	Taika Reforms
794–1185	Heian period; cultural development
1185–1568	Feudal period; rise of samurai

Shinto encourages the development of a sensitivity to beauty. The early Japanese practiced a simple religion known as *Shinto.* They worshiped various deities as superior spirits or forces. In addition, they also worshiped anything beautiful or awe-inspiring in the world of nature. To them, beauty revealed the work of the gods. Shinto emphasizes ritual purity and has no doctrine or system of ethics. Only after cleansing away pollution can a man undertake worship. From this uncomplicated religion the Japanese derived a tremendous sensitivity for natural beauty and artistically pleasing design. Priests led ritual observances at various shrines dedicated to a deity or an aspect of nature, and the Yamato clan chief acted as the head priest. When the office of leading clan chief became that of the Japanese emperor, he retained the position of head priest.

Japan borrows freely from Chinese culture. Ever since the second century B.C. the Japanese had had contacts with China. From the latter, the Japanese learned how to make and use bronze tools and iron weapons. In addition, it was from the Chinese that Japan derived her writing system, even though the spoken languages were entirely different. Because it was not easy to use Chinese characters to express Japanese words, the Japanese began to develop a writing system of their own in the ninth century. Since educated Japanese knew how to read and write Chinese, they were familiar with Chinese literature and thought, especially the teachings of Confucius.

From the seventh to the ninth century, the period of the T'ang dynasty in China, the borrowing from China was encouraged by the Japanese imperial court. During this period the imperial clan was seeking to consolidate, centralize its control of Japan, and weaken the power of other clans. This was especially true during the rule of Prince Shotoku (592–622). Interested in reforming and strengthening the Japanese government along the lines of the Chinese model, Prince Shotoku hoped that Confucian teachings would counteract clan

Japan

loyalty. He initiated the policy of sending embassy missions to China, a practice which continued up to the ninth century. With the ambassadors went merchants and students, who brought back Chinese merchandise as well as knowledge.

Prince Shotoku's policy was continued in the *Taika (tie-kah) Reforms* of the mid-seventh century. These reforms modeled the imperial government of Japan on the central government of T'ang China. To counteract the power of the clans, the imperial government tried to abolish private ownership of land, turn over cultivated lands to the peasantry, appoint trusted officials to govern outlying provinces, and introduce a new tax system. If these measures could have been fully carried out, they would have greatly strengthened imperial authority. A splendid capital was built at Nara, with broad streets and perpendicular blocks in imitation of the T'ang capital, and Chinese dress and customs became fashionable. The eighth century marked the height of Japanese borrowing from China, when anything Chinese seemed to be accepted as good.

Buddhism becomes popular in Japan. One further element of great importance was borrowed from China. This was the Buddhist religion, which represented a more sophisticated form of religion than Shinto. The Buddhist beliefs in salvation through the mediation of Bodhisattvas (page 207) had great appeal for the Japanese. Buddhist devotees pledged land and money to temples and monasteries so that prayers could be said on their behalf. Gradually these Buddhist temples became very wealthy and powerful, and often even interfered in political affairs. Buddhism was also a vehicle for the transmission of Chinese artistic influence. Temple architecture and sculpture reveal the Japanese sensitivity to beauty while also reflecting Chinese influence. Both Nara and the subsequent capital, Kyoto (*kyoh-toh*), are famous for their Chinese-style temples.

Regionalism undercuts the power of the imperial government. By the end of the eighth century, in order to get away from the political interference of the powerful Buddhist temples, the imperial court was moved to Kyoto. This period of Japanese history, lasting from 794 to 1185, is known as the *Heian* (*hay-ahn*) period. But the government did not succeed in extending its authority throughout Japan. The various clans were too powerful in the different regions to permit Japan to be unified under one government. Moreover, the imperial government never succeeded in developing a Confucian mandarin system to provide officials loyal to the emperor. The clans continued to control their own large estates. And the imperial government, plagued by intrigue and by groups who did not accept government policies, continued to appoint officials whose offices had ceased to have much power. Soon powerful families took over control of the government, though the court aristocracy remained nominally in office.

By the eleventh and twelfth centuries, some regional clan leaders controlled huge estates. On the large income from rice grown on these estates these leaders were able to build private armies. Regional clan leaders had their own administration and law. They also held the actual power in Japan. Nevertheless, because of the Japanese respect for form and tradition, the symbolic authority of the emperor and his court aristocracy was maintained, without interruption, up to modern times.

Feudal relationships develop between lord and samurai. Between the twelfth to the sixteenth century all hopes of imperial centralization ended as conflict developed among various regional leaders. An aristocratic class of military retainers, the *samurai* (*sam-oo-rie*), emerged. In return for a grant of rice income from the landed estates, these retainers would pledge

Japan's history is reflected in her art. The masterly Burning of the Sanjo Palace *(above)* captures the chaos of the feudal period. In sharp contrast was the serenity of family life, reflected in the woodblock print below. Japanese humor is manifested in the netsuke *(right)* of a pilgrim mending his sandal.

loyalty and military service to a regional lord. The relation between lord and samurai was hereditary, passing from one generation to another. Since this practice in many ways resembled the feudalism of the Middle Ages in Europe, it came to be known as Japanese feudalism.

Gradually there developed within the military aristocracy a cult of behavior known as *Bushido* (*boo-shee-doh*). This cult of the samurai emphasized the virtues of loyalty, bravery, and honor. Many tales sprang up which celebrated these samurai virtues. The military aristocracy was very different from the court aristocracy— the former lived a vigorous and unsophisticated life, whereas the life of court aristocrats was over-refined and unproductive.

Culture flourishes at the Heian court. Politically impotent and cut off from the regional centers of power, the court aristocracy dedicated itself to a highly sophisticated and luxurious style of life. In a sense the Heian court can be compared to the court of Louis (*l'wee*) XIV in France (see page 407). The Heian aristocracy developed arts partly influenced by China and partly expressing the sensitivity of the Japanese. The world's first novel, *The Tale of Genji,* portrays life at the Heian court.

The refinement of court life, and also the Japanese respect for tradition, eventually came to be embodied in the tea ceremony, flower arrangement, and Noh drama. In the tea ceremony each object to be used was carried separately to a special room and arranged accordingly to unbreakable rules. The tea was made in a special way, with each movement set by tradition. It took years of study to master this art as well as that of selecting and arranging flowers to give the most satisfying sense of beauty without violating any traditions. Noh drama, which evolved from symbolic dances, was chanted by actors and a chorus. Its themes were taken from Shinto and Buddhist traditions, and the movement of its elaborately dressed and masked performers were highly stylized and governed by long tradition.

Changes appear in feudal Japan. Beneath the aristocracy in feudal Japan were the peasants, who supported lords and samurai by cultivating crops such as rice. These peasants led a very poor and precarious existence. They lived in straw-thatched huts and often were at the mercy of the natural elements. Socially, they were looked down upon by all elements of society. Japanese laws and customs discriminated against them. However, because of the constant feudal warfare, it was possible for some peasants to join the samurai and gradually ascend socially. Feudal Japan, therefore, by no means had a closed society.

Feudal conflict and instability actually encouraged the economic development of Japan. A rising demand for goods led to increased trade and commerce. The economy shifted from a barter basis to money. The population increased, and towns and cities grew up at major trade routes and coastal ports. Commercial rather than political centers, these towns often possessed considerable self-government.

CHECK-UP

1. What was the uji? How was it self-sufficient? What were the results for Japanese society?

2. How did the Shinto religion reflect Japanese sensitivity to beauty?

3. Name some ideas and practices the Japanese borrowed from the Chinese.

4. What were the Taika Reforms?

5. How did Japanese feudalism develop? How did it affect the power of the emperor?

6. Who were the samurai? What was Bushido?

7. How did feudal conflict contribute to economic growth?

Summing Up

In our brief survey of the civilizations of India, China, and Japan, we have seen that there is no single prototype of Asian society and culture. Each of these societies possessed its own unique characteristics. Indian society was typified by a closed caste system in which religious values were emphasized. Chinese society, with roots deep in Confucian ethics, was dominated by a partnership between the imperial dynasty and the gentry-mandarins. Lastly, Japanese society might be described as a dynamic tension of powers. The recognized imperial form of authority, which had little power, was confronted by the actual feudal power of regional leaders. The power of each regional leader, in turn, was constantly threatened by other regional leaders.

Chapter Highlights

Can you explain?

reincarnation	ethics	Wheel of Life	patriarchal family
subcontinent	mandarins	caste system	

Can you identify?

Asoka	Nirvana	samurai	Four Noble Truths
uji	Bushido	Ganges River	Indo-Aryans
Harappans	Yellow River	Confucius	Sudras
Akbar	Buddha	Taika Reforms	Indus River
untouchables	Hinduism	Taoism	Brahmins
Buddhism	Shinto	Legalism	

What do you think?

1. How does a Hindu family differ from a western family in attitudes and outlook? What can each learn from the other?

2. Was life more depressing for the untouchables of India than for a minority group in the United States? Why?

3. What is the difference between a class system and a caste system? Which prevails in the United States?

4. Does the philosophy of the Wheel of Life appeal to you? Why?

5. How did Buddhist philosophy differ from Hindu philosophy? Which do you prefer?

6. What social and religious factors have contributed to the hostility between Hindus and Muslims?

7. Why did China, a larger country than India, achieve greater cultural and political unity?

8. What do you think of the qualities Confucius said should characterize a gentleman? What would you add or subtract?

9. Would you have preferred to live in Hindu India, Confucian China, or feudal Japan? Why?

10. How did the role of emperor differ in China and Japan?

11. How did Japanese feudalism differ from feudalism in Western Europe?

12. What factors helped make Chinese society stable?

13. Why did Japan do a great deal of cultural borrowing from China?

10

Sub-Saharan Africa to the Mid-1800's

CHAPTER FOCUS

African Geography
States and Empires of the Western Sudan
States of the Forest and Guinea Coast
The Peoples of West-Central Africa
Southern Africa
Central and East Africa
Africa in 1800

Artists in Benin worked under royal protection, creating works for religious ceremonies and for royal pleasure. Ivory was one of the main decorative materials used. The elephant tusk (far left), was carved with countless tiny figures, each one different. Probably from Ife the Benin artists learned to use wax to mold bronze into plaques (above) which decorated the pillars of the oba's (king's) palace. These plaques narrate the history of the Benin kingdom from its early days to the arrival of the Europeans who were to conquer it. The gathering of tribal chiefs of Chad (left) shows the coexistence of the old and new in present-day Africa. Clad in traditional robes and bearing swords, the chiefs ride their horses along a paved highway. Some of these chiefs serve as agents of the national government, helping their peoples to develop a sense of national unity.

To Europeans and Americans, Africa was until recent times the "Dark Continent." But the darkness was in the eye of the beholder. Africa, we now know, was no more without history, culture, and civilization than was Europe during the so-called "Dark Ages" following the overthrow of the Roman Empire in the West.

It is wrong to look upon Africa as isolated, and it is wrong to see it as unchanging, or changed only by influences from the outside. For far too long most of the outside world would not believe that anything important, or beautiful, or original, or complex could have come from Africa. Indeed, not until the 1950's would most scholars concede that man himself may have originated in Africa (see page 6). Being outsiders themselves, those who wrote about Africa saw an outside origin for everything. If, as in West Africa, there was an empire with a divine ruler, that *had* to be because of the influence of Egypt. If there was magnificent art, as in Nigeria or the Congo, it *had* to reflect Portuguese influence. If there were impressive ruins, as in southern Africa, they *had* to show the presence long ago of wandering Phoenicians. If there was a belief in a Supreme Being, a Creator, it *had* to stem from early Hebrew, Christian, or Islamic contacts.

Archaeology and history have now shown us that these ways of looking at Africa are false. Where there were contacts, there were exchanges of ideas as well as goods. But how can we know who took and who gave? Today we know that all peoples are creative. We also know that cultural influences do not move only in one direction, and this knowledge challenges assumptions of outside influence in Africa.

During much of the first millennium B.C. ways of living in North-Western Europe and in the western Sudan were similar in important ways. Peoples in both areas practiced agriculture and knew the use of iron; in neither were there cities or trade over vast areas. Between 300 B.C. and 200 A.D. groups of people called the *Bantu* (a collective name because they speak related languages) migrated into regions south of the Sudan and east of the Guinea (*gin'*ih) Coast. Their descendants live there today. Though less dramatic because more prolonged, this expansion was similar in many ways to the penetration of Western and Southern Europe by waves of migrating tribes of Goths, Vandals, Huns, Franks, Angles, Saxons, and others.

African Geography

In Africa, as everywhere, geography has affected history. Africa is a huge land mass—the area south of the Sahara, sub-Saharan Africa, is more than twice the size of the United States. In it are hundreds of diverse peoples. These groups of people are sometimes called *tribes* or tribal societies. But "tribe" is a word often misunderstood, and has sometimes been used to suggest "primitive" groups. When the word is used properly, it refers to any group of people claiming a common ancestor, bearing a common name, having traditional economic rights in the land they occupy, and sharing a way of life. Members of the tribe must see themselves and be seen as separate from their neighbors, and be bound to act together when their well-being is threatened. Today, for example, in the Congo alone—itself one-third the size of the United States—there are some 600 such tribes, each speaking its own traditional language and retaining many of its traditional customs.

Much of sub-Saharan Africa is savanna. Only about a fifth of sub-Saharan Africa is tropical rain forest—the "jungle" so often shown in films. Except for a few stretches where there is temperate climate and except for mountainous country in the Cameroons and in a few parts of South and East Africa, sub-Saharan Africa is *savanna*—grassland with scattered trees and, now and then, a river. Some of this land was suitable for agriculture; some for raising cattle and gathering the food that grew wild. Except in the rain forest, people could move fairly easily from one place to another. This fact contributed to two trends in the history of Africa: migration and conquest.

The Sahara and Africa's rivers prevent easy access to the interior. Other geographical features affected contact with the outside world. Most important was the Sahara in the north. Although it was possible to cross this desert, especially after the introduction of the camel in the first century A.D., the desert did cut off *easy* access to and from the Mediterranean world. Moreover, sub-Saharan Africa is a plateau which rises sharply from the coast. This abrupt rise causes rivers to fall sharply. The resulting rapids and falls make it very hard to penetrate the interior. The pattern of the winds and the ocean currents also discouraged contact with the outside world. On the west coast Africans used large canoes for trade along the coast and up and down the great Niger (*nie'*jer) River. But because of prevailing winds and ocean currents, they could not move north of the Sahara coast. Nor did Europeans, before fifteenth-century improvements in navigation (page 362), sail far southward for fear they would be unable to return. In contrast, off the east coast the *monsoons*—winds which are northeasterly half the year and southwesterly the other half—enabled ships to sail as far south as Madagascar, and to return when the monsoons shifted. Hence, at an early period the ports of East Africa became part of a growing Indian Ocean trade. West Africa, on the other hand, had no contact by sea with the rest of the world for centuries.

CHECK-UP

1. Why was Africa once called the Dark Continent? What is wrong with this view?

2. How does the tropical rain forest differ from the savanna? Why was access to the interior of Africa difficult?

Sub-Saharan Africa to the Mid-1800's

c. **300** B.C.	Use of iron tools begins in Sudan
c. **200** B.C.	Nok culture at height
c. **1** A.D.–c. **1600** A.D.	Bantu migrate south
c. **500** A.D.–c. **1100** A.D.	Empire of Ghana
c. **1000**–c. **1810**	Hausa States
c. **1230**–c. **1400**	Mali Empire
c. **1400**–c. **1690**	Kingdom of Kongo
c. **1400**–c. **1800**	Luba-Lunda empire
c. **1400**–c. **1900**	Benin
c. **1464–1591**	Empire of Songhay
1472	Portuguese reach Bight of Benin
c. **1600–1837**	Oyo Empire
c. **1600**–c. **1900**	Kingdoms of Dahomey and Ashanti
1652	Dutch settle at Cape of Good Hope
c. **1725**–c. **1850**	Atlantic slave trade at height
c. **1800**–c. **1840**	Zulu expansion
c. **1810**–c. **1900**	Fulani Empire
1814	Britain takes over Cape Colony
c. **1830**–c. **1880**	Refugees from Zulu expansion move north
1835–1837	Boers make Great Trek

States and Empires of the Western Sudan

States develop in the western Sudan. The belt of savanna between the Sahara and the coastal forest of West Africa is called the western Sudan; the Arabs who knew of it gave it the name Bilad-as-Sudan (bih-*lad'* as-soo-*dan'*), "Land of the Blacks." The earliest sub-Saharan states of which we know arose here. One reason for their development was the knowledge of iron-working. In Africa, as in Europe, iron tools led to a technological revolution. They increased agricultural production on lands already in use and made it possible to use new lands which were less easy to cultivate. More food meant a larger population, which encouraged expansion. Iron working also brought into use new and better weapons, and—as an Arab writer of the twelfth century put it—the ability to dominate "stone- and bone- and wood-using neighbors." Those who had iron could conquer lands and organize centralized government.

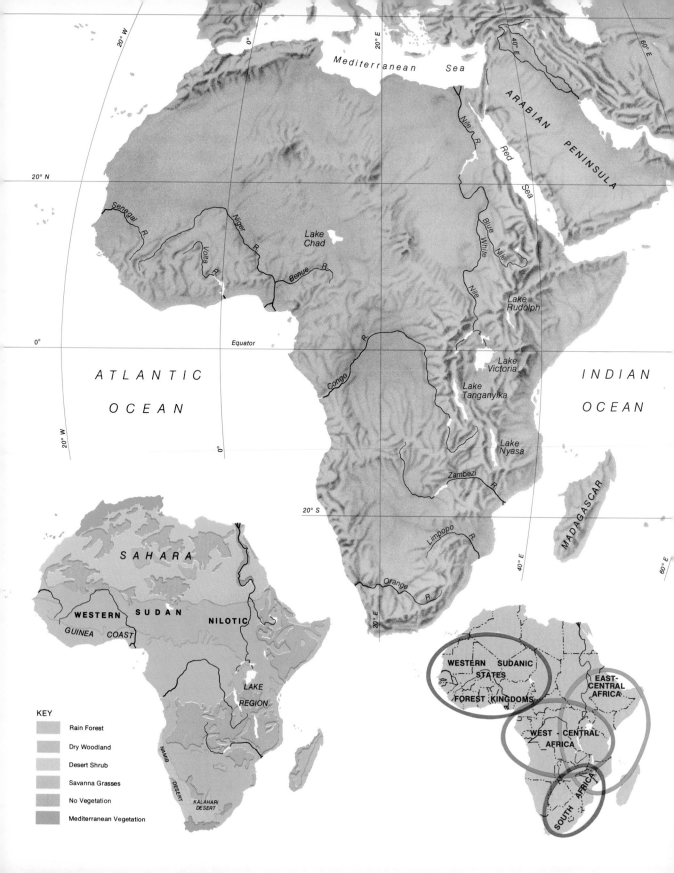

Mediterranean Sea

ARABIAN PENINSULA

20° N

Senegal R.

Niger R.

Volta R.

Lake Chad

Benue R.

Nile R.

Red Sea

Blue Nile

White Nile

Nile R.

Lake Rudolph

0°   Equator

ATLANTIC OCEAN

Congo R.

Lake Victoria

Lake Tanganyika

INDIAN OCEAN

Lake Nyasa

Zambezi R.

MADAGASCAR

20° S

Limpopo R.

Orange R.

SAHARA

WESTERN

SUDAN

NILOTIC

GUINEA COAST

LAKE REGION

NAMIB DESERT

KALAHARI DESERT

KEY

Rain Forest

Dry Woodland

Desert Shrub

Savanna Grasses

No Vegetation

Mediterranean Vegetation

WESTERN SUDANIC STATES

EAST-CENTRAL AFRICA

FOREST KINGDOMS

WEST - CENTRAL AFRICA

SOUTH AFRICA

A second essential reason for the growth of these states was trade. The arrival of the camel in North Africa made it possible to cross the Sahara. A complex network of trade routes developed, linking the southern shores of the Mediterranean with the western Sudan. Traders from the fringes of the desert, from North Africa, Egypt, and even the Middle East wanted to exchange their salt, their beads and bracelets, their copper and cloth, and later their manuscripts in Arabic for gold, slaves, and ivory from the forest regions south of the Sudan. Unable to conquer the forest peoples, the peoples of the savanna became "middlemen." Groups of them came to dominate the territory through which the trade passed. Thus they acquired wealth, which enabled them to increase their power.

Ghana grows wealthy through trade and tribute. The earliest of these sub-Saharan states, called Ghana, probably was in existence by 500 A.D. At the height of its power in the middle of the eleventh century, Ghana was an empire which included large parts of the modern states of Mauritania, Senegal, and Mali. North Africans marvelled at its wealth and power. A tenth-century Arab described the ruler as "the wealthiest of all kings on the face of the earth on account of the riches he owns and the hoards of gold acquired by him and inherited from his predecessors since ancient times."

What made Ghana and its kings so wealthy and powerful? Their wealth came from trade and tribute. Like the states that came after her, Ghana sought to control the sources of gold in the south and of salt in the north, as well as the caravan routes in between. Her rulers succeeded in the case of the gold and the trade routes, and they taxed the salt and such other goods as

African Geography

This feature is intended to illustrate the interaction of geographical features and human history in Africa. Each cultural region (right) will be treated in detail in the appropriate section of the chapter.

copper that were brought in from the north and then exported to the forest region. Also important was the trade in slaves. The king's subjects were at times summoned from their fishing and farming to go on slave raids into the edge of the forest beyond their southern frontier. They sold their captives to North African traders, who took them across the desert for resale to Mediterranean buyers.

We have no sources that tell us how the common people of Ghana lived. But we do know from Arabic accounts how the kingdom was governed. Al-Bakri (al-bak-*ree'*), a North African scholar, wrote:

When [the king] gives audience to his people, to listen to their complaints and set them to rights, he sits in a pavilion around which stand ten pages holding shields and gold-mounted swords: and on his right hand are the sons of the princes [or subordinate kings] of his empire, splendidly clad and with gold plaited into their hair.*

Justice for serious offenses was the responsibility of the king. In appeals, final guilt was determined, as in medieval Europe, through trial by ordeal. Such a test is described by Al-Bakri:

When a man is accused, . . . a headman takes a thin piece of wood, . . . sour and bitter, . . . and pours upon it some water which he then gives to the defendant to drink. If the man vomits, his innocence is recognized and he is congratulated. If he does not, . . . the accusation is accepted as justified.

Ghana had, then, a strong monarch, a council of ministers, a system of administering justice, a steady source of revenue, and a bureaucracy (government officials).

Muslim forces conquer Ghana. In 1067, a year after William of Normandy had conquered England, Al-Bakri wrote from Cordova in southern Spain,* "The king of Ghana can put 200,000 warriors in the field, more than 40,000 of them

* From *The African Past* by Basil Davidson (London: Longmans, Green & Co., 1964; copyright 1964 by Basil Davidson). Reprinted by permission of the Longman Group Ltd. and of Little, Brown, Inc.

being armed with bow and arrow." It is not surprising that the army of Almoravids from North Africa needed 22 years—from 1054 to 1076—to conquer the kingdom.

The Almoravids attacked Ghana for two reasons. Being devout Muslims, they waged a *jihad* (page 118) to convert nonbelievers. Equally important, they sought the wealth of the "infidels" (nonbelievers). Having already seized the Saharan deposits of salt, they now wanted the fabled gold. In the fourteenth century the Arab historian Ibn Khaldun wrote of the disaster that overtook Ghana: "[The Almoravids] . . . spread their dominion over the negroes [of Ghana], devastated their territory, and plundered their property. Having submitted them to a poll [head] tax, they imposed on them a tribute, and compelled a great number of them to become Muslims.

Although the North Africans could not themselves retain control, by the thirteenth century there was little left of the ancient unified kingdom of Ghana.

Mali combines Muslim and traditional African characteristics. Other states arose in the western Sudan during the time of Ghana's glory as well as after its fall. They too thrived on trade and tribute and established centralized rule. Attacks from across the desert, though always destructive, were rare; the periods of peaceful trading were much longer. In the savanna belt as far eastward as Lake Chad and even beyond, as one historian has put it:

. . . one strong power and ruling people, or federation of peoples, would rival or succeed or co-exist with another, sometimes overlapping in time and place, sometimes continuing its life under different names and dynasties [ruling families]. . . . But any picture of one empire simply ousting another in mechanical succession would be false: the development of the whole region was rather a continuous growth of governing institutions interrupted by dynastic rivalries, foreign invasion, and the individual changes and chances of history.

In this sense the Mali Empire of the Mande people followed Ghana. Located to the east of Ghana, by the tenth century it had made a modest start. By the middle of the eleventh century its rulers had been converted to Islam. In Ghana some of the people had become Muslims, but its rulers had not. But beginning with Mali, Islam's agents concentrated on the conversion of the rulers. Not until the nineteenth century did the great Muslim reformer, Uthman dan Fodio, change this pattern and place the emphasis on bringing the masses into the fold of Islam. Although in Mali, as in Ghana, most of the people retained their traditional beliefs, Mali was an Islamic state with Muslim rulers. That was the major difference between it and Ghana.

Islam brought a unity among African Muslims that cut across tribal loyalties, though rivalries among Muslim groups often limited that unity. It also brought Islamic law and literacy to a small group of African scholars, teachers, and officials. All these changes furthered administrative control over an expanding area.

As in the case of Ghana, the location of Mali enabled it to exploit the caravan trade. Ghana had controlled the sources of gold but not of salt. The invading Almoravids had controlled the sources of salt but never of gold. At its height in the mid-fourteenth century, Mali controlled both. In the more fertile lands east of Ghana, Mali's people tilled the soil as well as traded. Its rulers encouraged the growth of new crops such as cotton. In the cities craftsmen wove cloth and worked with wood, metals, and animal skins.

The Muslim world saw for itself the wealth of Mali when its most famous ruler, *Mansa* (emperor) Musa, made a pilgrimage to the holy city of Mecca in 1324. He took with him vast amounts of gold and hundreds of people to wait on him. Five hundred slaves served as the "traveler's checks" of that day, for they could easily be sold to pay the expenses of the journey. Each of the men sent ahead of the main party carried, as a symbol of the might of the emperor, a gold staff weighing four pounds. According to one account of this astonishing pilgrimage, 60,000 men accompanied the emperor, and in the caravan of oxen, camels, and mules, forty mules carried his gold. One Arab writer learned in Cairo a decade later of Mansa Musa's visit: he had "left no emir [Muslim title of ruler] nor holder of a royal office without a gift of a load of gold. He and his company gave out so much gold that they depressed its value in Egypt and caused its price to fall."

During the reign of Mansa Musa, Mali reached a size comparable to that of the great states of its day. It was recognized as a world power, and sent ambassadors to such other countries as Morocco. The city of Timbuktu became a center of learning, as well as of trade and religion, and was known as such throughout the Muslim world for over two centuries.

By 1400, however, Mali had shrunk to the tiny state it had been five centuries earlier. What caused this collapse? Some of Mali's problems were similar to those of other large empires. It was too large to be controlled effectively from a central point. It had grown by conquest, and the conquered peoples were waiting for a chance to break away. In the second half of the fourteenth century, some of its rulers were too ambitious, and others were incompetent. Rivalry for power led to civil war. Armies invaded the country from the north, south, and east. But in contrast to Rome, one of these attacking forces came from a state able to replace Mali as a center of power. This new state was called Songhay (*sohng'*high).

Songhay builds the largest kingdom in the western Sudan.

From a start not much later than Mali's, Songhay took over the dominant role in the western Sudan. Like its predecessor, Songhay became a wealthy, centralized empire because it controlled the north-south trade routes. As in Mali, there was agriculture as well as trade, and some of the people raised cattle. Since about 1000 A.D. scholars in Songhay had been literate in Arabic. At its capital, Gao, and at Timbuktu, which it came to control, Songhay continued the learned tradition of Mali. Leo Africanus, a North African traveler, described

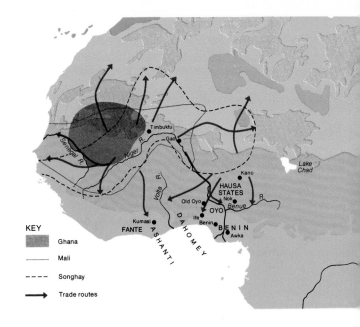

West Africa

Timbuktu in the early sixteenth century: "Here are great store of doctors, judges, priests, and other learned men, that are bountifully maintained at the king's cost and charges, and hither are brought divers [various] manuscripts or written books out of Barbary [North Africa], which are sold for more money than any other merchandise."*

Extending its boundaries by conquest, Songhay at its height in the early sixteenth century was larger even than Mali. One reason for this expansion was the country's cavalry. Wrote Leo Africanus, ". . . [the king] hath always 3000 horsemen, and a number of footmen that shoot poisoned arrows, attending upon him. They often have skirmishes with those that refuse to pay tribute, and so many as they take [prisoner], they sell unto the merchants of Timbuktu."*

* "The Kano Chronicle." From *Sudanese Memoirs,* by H. R. Palmer (Lagos, 1928), Vol. III, pp. 104–106. Reprinted from Roland Oliver and Caroline Oliver, *Africa in the Days of Exploration,* © 1965, Prentice-Hall, Inc., Englewood Cliffs, N.J. Reprinted by permission.

But the Songhay Empire, too, was destroyed. The causes were weakness and a devastating Moroccan invasion in 1591. The Moroccans, armed with muskets, easily defeated the cavalry and infantry of Songhay, who were armed only with bows and arrows, spears, and swords.

By the end of the seventeenth century the era of great empires in the western Sudan was at an end. Important states and kingdoms continued to exist to the east, but in the lands Songhay had ruled there was continual warfare and further fragmentation. Trade within the savanna and across the Sahara was disrupted. And the trade in gold, ivory, and slaves now flowed in a new direction. As the Moroccans invaded Songhay, the Dutch and English were joining the Portuguese in establishing trading posts along the coast. With its trade dwindling, the Sudan became isolated from the Mediterranean as it had never been during earlier centuries.

Islamic reform affects the states of the western Sudan. Some—but not all—rulers of Songhay had been devout Muslims; others had rejected Islam. But with the end of empire, Islamic influence declined. Many Africans gave up Islam and returned to the traditional tribal religions which most of the Sudanic peoples had never abandoned. Not until the eighteenth century was Islam again to gain converts and power.

A movement for religious reform that spread through the Muslim world in the eighteenth century was to affect West Africa too, and its impact would be political as well as religious. Many of the leaders of this reform in the western Sudan came from the Fulani, or Fulbe (*fuhl′bey*), people. Originally from what is today Senegal, they had spread through much of the Sudan by the 1700's. Some were pastoral, moving in small groups with their cattle from place to place. Some settled in the cities, where

At the height of the Songhay Empire, Timbuktu was a leading economic and cultural center. The view below of the modern town shows the Mosque of Sankoré from which evolved a university which attracted scholars from all over the Islamic world. Although the empire fell, the university continues to be renowned, and the town, a blend of African and Islamic buildings, is being rediscovered by travelers.

they were traders or Muslim clerics or teachers.

Picking up late seventeenth-century reforming impulses, Fulbe in modern Guinea led a revolt and after decades of fighting set up a "purified" Muslim theocratic state. Towards the end of the century other Fulbe leaders accomplished the same end in Senegal. These successes and the general wave of Islamic reform were to influence an important *jihad* (or war in the way of Islam) in northern Nigeria in the years after 1800, and that in turn would spur others to the religious and political changes that brought new massive empires to the region. Islamic states, by the 1860's they encompassed most of the western Sudan.

CHECK-UP

1. Why did the earliest sub-Saharan states develop in the western Sudan? How did trade affect the growth of these states?

2. How did Ghana become wealthy and powerful? How was the kingdom of Ghana governed? Why did the Almoravids conquer it?

3. Why did Mali become a wealthy and powerful state? What led to its collapse?

4. Why did Songhay grow powerful? Collapse?

5. How did the Islamic reform movement affect the western Sudan? Why did the western Sudan decline in importance at the end of the seventeenth century?

States of the Forest and Guinea Coast

In the forest south of the savanna other groups of Africans built different kinds of states. They, too, used iron and grew powerful through trade and conquest. The empires of the Sudan never conquered these peoples for two reasons—geography, and the fact that Ghana, Mali, and Songhay looked northward. The only interest the savanna states had in the forest lands was economic. They sought the gold, forest products, and people to enslave. The tropical rain forest could be penetrated, but waging war there was very different from fighting in the grasslands. Cavalry was useless, for horses could not survive in the rain forests because of the tsetse fly, which carried sleeping sickness.

Four of the largest and most influential forest kingdoms arose between the Ivory Coast and the Niger River, extending inland at times 500 and more miles. As with the Sudanic kingdoms, their founders in each case were from a single tribe. In three of these kingdoms (Ashanti, Dahomey, Oyo)—but less clearly in the most easterly (Benin)—the founding tribes moved into long-settled areas as conquerors. These forest states grew to be kingdoms—

Benin in about the fifteenth century; the three others from about the seventeenth. All of them —especially Ashanti and Dahomey—profited from the slave trade with Europeans on the coast. From the seventeenth century to the nineteenth, that trade moved the economic—and therefore political—center of gravity in West Africa from north to south. Benin, however, was a highly organized and prosperous state when the Portuguese first made contact with its rulers in the 1470's.

Slave trading makes Benin wealthy and powerful. Benin (beh-*neen'*), the first of the forest states known to Europeans, was also the oldest. Encompassing a large region just west of the Niger River, Benin was unusual in several ways. Among the states of the Guinea Coast, it was the only kingdom; among the great kingdoms, it was the only one on the coast.

The king of Benin had nearly absolute power. He worked through associations whose members he himself appointed. All commoners, these were key men in running the government and the army. The king gave them titles which could not be inherited. He had the power to create new titles, and to give them to any free-born men in the kingdom. In this way the king countered the restrictions palace officials placed on his power.

Before the appearance of the first Europeans, the Portuguese, in the late fifteenth century, Benin's economy rested on agriculture and coastal trade. But it was the Atlantic slave trade that was to give Benin great wealth, and with it, greater power. The kingdom reached its height earlier than the other forest states, that is, in the fifteenth and sixteenth centuries. The first Portuguese, soon to create a demand for ivory, pepper, and slaves, arrived at the port of Benin in the 1470's. Within a few decades the trade was almost entirely in slaves. There, as elsewhere in Africa, the profitable trade in men drove out almost all other commerce.

The Portuguese realized the importance of Benin and, unlike Europeans of later centuries, dealt with their counterparts there as equals. The king of Benin sent an ambassador to Portugal; the Portuguese sent missionaries and traders with presents for the king of Benin. The king ordered several of his subjects and relatives to become Christians, and the missionaries found many who wished to learn to read and taught them to do so.

But the Portuguese themselves did not remain long. The fatal fevers of the Guinea Coast —not understood until the late nineteenth century—killed many Europeans and frightened away more. By 1520 direct trade with Benin was declining; the Portuguese had found other outlets elsewhere. The earlier importance of the kingdom gradually diminished. By the seventeenth century Benin's economy was overshadowed by the activities of other states on the coast and in the forest. But Benin, still an effective state ruled by its original dynasty, was "re-discovered" by the English in the late nineteenth century.

Powerful Oyo excels in art. The Oyo Empire, the second of the forest states to emerge after Benin, grew to be the largest of the forest states. Tradition says its founders moved south into the forest to found the city of Ife (*ee'*fay). The Yoruba (*yoh'*ruh-buh, the collective name for the descendants of the many peoples ruled by Oyo) regard Ife as their spiritual home. In the late fourteenth or early fifteenth century, the Oyo state began to expand. Oyo's capital, Old Oyo, was inland, but being north of the forest, it was free from the tsetse fly. Consequently, unlike all other forest and coastal states, the Oyo had cavalry. This made their army a formidable threat to their southern and western neighbors. In the 1730's and 1740's, when Oyo fought Dahomey, a European traveler wrote:

. . . being all horsed, and a warlike nation, in a short time [Oyo] mastered half the King of Ardrah's [Dahomey's] territories, and made such a slaughter amongst his subjects that the number of the dead was commonly expressed by saying they were like the grains of corn in the field. . . . This nation strikes such a terror into all the [neighboring] Negroes, that they can scarce hear [Oyo] mentioned without trembling.

Having extended their borders, the Oyo rulers, like the leaders of the savanna kingdoms, collected tribute in goods and slaves from the conquered people. In return the Oyo, like the Romans, gave subject peoples a measure of internal stability and defended the frontiers.

Ife, the Yoruba spiritual center, was also a center of Yoruba art. Terra-cotta (baked clay) sculptures dating as far back as 900 B.C. have been found in the grasslands to the north. Perhaps their makers influenced the ancestors of the Yoruba, who also produced outstanding terra-cotta sculpture. From Ife we have the finest examples of the "lost-wax process" of metalcasting, the method of metal sculpture also found in Benin and other parts of West Africa. By this process Ife's sculptors fashioned magnificent larger-than-life-sized portraits of their ancestral rulers and priests, known today as the Ife bronzes.

The economy of Oyo was based largely on agriculture and trade. From its beginnings, trade was mostly to the north. For horses and other goods Oyo exchanged slaves, kola nuts—a stimulant highly valued in the Sudan and in North Africa—and the wares of its craftsmen.

The king of Oyo exercises limited powers. The Oyo king (or *Alafin,* ah-*lah'*fin) was chosen from eligible candidates who came from the different branches of the royal family. A group of seven hereditary chiefs made the final choice. Once installed, the king ruled with the advice of a council made up of the same seven important chiefs. A nineteenth-century Yoruba described them as "the voice of the nation; on them devolved the chief duty of protecting the interests of the kingdom." The king needed their consent to declare war, and they evaluated his performance as ruler. The council might give the king parrot eggs and tell him that because of his misdeeds or lack of wisdom, "the gods reject you, the people reject you, the earth rejects you." He then had to commit suicide. To prevent abuse of the council's power, one member had to die with the Alafin. There were other groups, such as men's societies and trading societies, which had direct or indirect political power. As in Rome, the power of the Alafin and his government was most effective near the capital. Farther away, the rulers of lesser kingdoms, restricted by similar checks, followed their own interests, which tested the strength of central control. An Ashanti proverb, appropriate beyond their borders, says, "The antelope's hide splits where it is thinnest."

The Oyo Empire never developed a unified administration. Although most of the peoples within it had a not dissimilar way of life, each group cherished its own identity as part of a smaller kingdom. Only under special circumstances, such as when threatened with attack, did it have a feeling of being part of the larger empire.

Dissensions were to grow, and when they coincided with other assaults on the empire, Oyo fell apart. Very damaging was the eighteenth-century shift of trade from north to

This realistic portrait of a ruler is one of the famous bronzes from Ife, the probable source for the metalworking techniques used by Benin artists. The lines on the face are tribal marks.

south. Disorder in the Sudan and in Oyo's northern provinces disrupted the trans-Saharan trade at the very time European demand for slaves was growing on the coast. Since Oyo was never able to dominate the peoples of the coast, her economy suffered greatly from this shift in trade. Towards the end of the century Oyo's army was weakened, and outlying parts of the empire were able to break away. With its northern provinces gone, Oyo's army became less effective; no longer could the cavalry get horses.

A Fulani jihad destroys the Hausa states. A weakened Oyo then had to meet external threats as well, especially from the north. To the east of Songhay, in the north of modern Nigeria, there had grown up seven states of the Hausa (*how'*sah) peoples. Until the fourteenth century, there was no trade between these states and North Africa, nor had Islam penetrated them. But by the early sixteenth century, four

239

of them had grown into kingdoms and were able to revolt against Songhay. By the eighteenth century all seven Hausa states had grown in size and influence, with centers of trade, education, and culture. At least one of their cities had a population of 100,000.

Between 1800 and 1830, however, they were in one sweep replaced by a single empire—that of the Fulani (or Fulbe), people—which lasted until the British occupation of the 1890's. Originally a nomadic pastoral people, since the twelfth century the Fulani had moved gradually east and south from the far western Sudan. They worked their way through Ghana, Mali, and Songhay, and by the sixteenth century had reached the Hausa states and even beyond. Many of the Muslim Fulani were teachers and scholars, and a growing number were civil servants and diplomats for the Hausa kings. In the late eighteenth century one of them, Uthman dan Fodio, gained fame as a reformer. Influenced by currents of reform from the Muslim world, he wanted to cleanse the practice of Islam, which he believed had been corrupted since its earliest days, and condemned everything, religious and nonreligious, that was not pure Islamic orthodoxy as he understood it. He also wanted to wipe out all non-Islamic religious practices. He gathered more and more followers who were dedicated to his cause. In 1804 he proclaimed revolt and a jihad against the Hausa rulers. His armies went from victory to victory. Not only did they conquer the Hausa states and set up their own empire there, but they also attacked Oyo.

The Fulani take over Oyo. The weakened Oyo Empire offered little resistance. Richard and John Lander, the famed "discoverers" of the true course of the Niger, visited the capital in 1830 and reported the following state of affairs:

All seems quiet and peaceable in this large dull city, and one cannot help feeling rather melancholy, in wandering through streets almost deserted and over a vast extent of fertile land on which there is no human habitation and scarcely a living thing to animate or cheer the prevailing solemnity. The walls of the town have been suffered to fall into decay, and are now no better than a heap of dust and ruins, and such unconcern and apathy pervade the minds of the monarch and his ministry that the wandering and ambitious Fellata [Fulani] has penetrated into the very heart of the country, made himself master of two of its most important and flourishing towns, with little, if any, opposition, and is gradually, but very perceptibly . . . sapping the foundations of the throne of Yarriba [Yoruba].

In 1837 the Fulani destroyed the Oyo capital, and talked of "dipping the Koran into the sea." The Alafin and those close to him moved a hundred miles south into the forest. There, Oyo's successor states fought off Fulani attacks in later years. Some Yoruba remained in the conquered areas. Others, refugees from the Muslim holy war and from the Yoruba wars among states of the former empire, moved south and founded new cities of thousands of people. For over fifty years these successors to the Oyo Empire fought each other to dominate what might have become a new Yoruba empire. Only gradually did they learn that the next empire to control them would be British.

Ashanti and Dahomey prosper as middlemen in the slave trade. The presence of Europeans along the coast challenged Ashanti (uh-*shahn'*-tee) and Dahomey (dah-hoh-*may'*) in two ways. First, neither of these states originally reached the coast. They knew of the trade with the Europeans, especially after the mid-seventeenth century when it became vast and profitable because the owners of sugar plantations in the Americas were clamoring for more and more slaves. But the coastal peoples controlled direct access to the slave trade and tried to deny it to their northern neighbors. Like the Sudanic peoples, Ashanti and Dahomey wanted to be the profiting middlemen. Second, the Europeans brought guns and gunpowder. Both Ashanti and Dahomey, then, had an added reason to make their way to the coast. If they did not maintain their supply of modern weapons, they might perish.

Ashanti is usually described as a "confederacy" and Dahomey as a "kingdom." These, of course, are Western terms, but they do point to important differences in the way the two states were governed. Ashanti was made up of divisions, each of which had its own ruler, the *hene* (*hey′*neh). The ruler of the capital was called the *Asantehene* (king of the Asante or Ashanti). He was looked upon as sacred, but his power was far from absolute. He himself had to deal with the lesser kings (later called "chiefs") and needed their consent to declare war. In theory, he owned all the gold in the kingdom—the Europeans called this area the Gold Coast—but in fact most of the wealth he gained during his reign was passed on to his successor. The power of the Asantehene and the division chiefs was further limited by councils. Each division had a council of state, made up of the heads of kinship groups. Though they could not themselves become kings, they had the power to remove an oppressive or unlucky king. Each regional *hene* also had to consider the wishes of

the assemblies of "young men," commoners who represented the military manpower of the kingdom.

The king of Dahomey, on the other hand, was an absolute ruler. He took care that no one in the kingdom grew strong enough to challenge him. Close checks on his ministers kept them from opposing him, though a king would not act directly contrary to their advice. The king also chose his successor, although this choice was often disputed after his death. Once he had become king, a ruler was all-powerful. In theory, the king of Dahomey owned *everything* —and every person—in the kingdom. Though he never claimed this right, the king did in fact acquire considerable wealth for himself, the royal family, and his kingdom. The chief sources of this wealth were taxes and tributes of all kinds, the produce raised on the royal estates which were worked by slaves, and the sale of war captives into slavery. Dahomey was the only African state known to have had a system of plantation slavery.

Dahomey had a large standing army, with all men required to do military service. Famous

West African artists were skilled metalworkers. The figures at the top are Ashanti weights used to weigh gold on a two-sided scale. Human figures such as these are rare; usually animals or geometric designs were produced. The skill of the craftsmen made these practical objects works of art. The Dahomean brass sculpture (left) convincingly captures the drama of an encounter between hunter and springing leopard.

and feared by both Europeans and Africans were units in the Dahomean army of "Amazons"—specially picked women "devoted to the person of the king and valorous in war." A nineteenth-century English traveler described them thus:

They wear a blue and white striped cotton [coat] . . . of stout native manufacture, without sleeves, leaving freedom for the arms. The skirt or tunic reaches as low as the kilt of the [Scottish] Highlanders. A pair of short trousers is worn underneath, reaching two inches below the knee. The [cartridge-box] . . . forms a girdle, and keeps their dresses snug and close. . . . Upon the whole, these women certainly make a very imposing appearance, and are very active. From their constant exercise of body (for the women in all cases do the principal part of both domestic and agricultural labors here as well as at other places), they are capable of enduring much fatigue.

Ashanti and Dahomey were major powers on the Guinea Coast through the nineteenth century. Though both had their capitals inland, both had their sights on the coast and its trade. Dahomey never absorbed the coastal peoples, but did control them and profited from the slave trade. Ashanti, however, had to deal with the coastal Fante states, which were not only well organized, but also received aid from Europeans—first from their forts along the coast, later from the British colony called the Gold Coast. The English were, however, impressed with Ashanti from the start. In 1817 a group interested in exploration and trade visited Kumasi (kuh-*mah'*see), the Ashanti capital, and wrote:

Our [earlier) observations . . . had taught us to conceive a spectacle far exceeding our original expectations; but they had not prepared us for the extent and display of the scene which here burst upon us. An area of nearly a mile in circumference was crowded with magnificence and novelty. The king, his tributaries, and captains were resplendent in the distance, surrounded by attendants of every description, fronted by a mass of warriors which seemed to make our approach [impossible]. The

sun was reflected, with a glare scarcely more supportable than the heat, from the massy [sic] gold ornaments, which glistened in every direction. More than a hundred bands burst [out] at once on our arrival, with the peculiar airs of their several chiefs. The horns flourished their defiances, with the beating of innumerable drums and metal instruments, and then yielded for a while to the soft breathings of their long flutes. . . . At least a hundred large umbrellas or canopies, which could shelter thirty persons, were sprung up and down by the bearers with brilliant effect, being made of scarlet, yellow, and the most showy cloths and silks, and crowned on the top with crescents, pelicans, elephants, barrels, and arms and swords of gold.

The Europeans were, in fact, crucial in affecting the fate of Ashanti and Dahomey. Dahomey remained a powerful state until the French conquered it in the 1890's. For a century it had not suffered a major attack from Africans (as Oyo had) or from Europeans (as Ashanti had). Dahomey was spared partly because of its internal strength and vitality. Smaller than Ashanti—no more than 100 miles from north to south and 50 from east to west—Dahomey was governed efficiently and tightly. Partly it was spared for reasons found in other people's history—in other words, luck.

Slavery in Africa differs from slavery in America. The idea of slavery was not new to Africa. Like Europeans and Asians of ancient and medieval times, Africans had long known systems where people were bound to other people or to the land. But the type of slavery that was to grow up in the New World was beyond their imagination. Though there were some variations most groups in Africa had what is called "domestic slavery."

"Domestic slaves," usually war captives or hostages, but also debtors or those convicted of crimes, were certainly regarded as inferiors in society. But they had certain rights. Usually what they lost was their freedom of movement. They could move within the tribal lands (if only on their master's behalf), but could not leave them. Many of these slaves rose to high positions. In some centralized states, they were sent to govern provinces; in others, they became local administrators. Thus they sometimes could rise to power over free men. Generally, however, their services were at the command of their owners.

An Ibo (*ee'*boh) described the way his people regarded their domestic slaves at the end of the eighteenth century:

Those prisoners [of war] which were not sold or redeemed we kept as slaves: but how different was their condition from that of slaves in the West Indies! With us they do no more work than other members of the community, even their master. Their food, clothing, and lodging were nearly the same as ours, except that they were not permitted to eat with those who were freeborn; and there were scarce any other differences between them than a superior degree of importance which the head of the family exercises over every part of his household. Some of these slaves even have slaves under them, as their property and for their own use.

The trade in slaves had been going on for centuries in Africa. The North Africans had traded for slaves, and in East Africa slaves had been key commodities in the Indian Ocean trade. But in the Mediterranean the African slaves were not slaves because of their race, which became a feature of the system in the Americas. In Europe, where traces of slavery continued through the Middle Ages and, in some places, even later, it was mainly based on religious differences. Christians enslaved Muslims and others who were not Christians; Muslims enslaved Christians and "pagans." But because these differences often coincided with differences in race, they came to feed European ideas of racial superiority.

Europeans in the western hemisphere thought Africans could survive the tropical climate better than other peoples. They were right, but they did not understand that the Africans survived because they were used to such an en-

vironment, not because of their race. Their mistaken idea caused Europeans and Americans to draw general conclusions about Africans and their descendants, conclusions which were often wrong and usually served to justify their dominance over the enslaved.

Four methods are used to get slaves for export to America. How did the Europeans obtain African slaves? In West Africa the trade was entirely in African hands. Europeans were not allowed into the interior by the Africans who were in power on the coast. Slaves almost always came from the hinterland, for only in cases of punishment for crimes or debt did coastal or other chiefs and traders sell their own people. The majority of slaves were collected in four other ways. (1) A large proportion were prisoners of war—captives taken in wars between tribes or states. These wars often were started for political reasons that had nothing to do with the slave trade. (2) Slaves were sent to rulers by weaker tribes over which they had some control; these slaves could be sold in turn to Europeans. (3) They were captured in slave raids carried out by coastal Africans. One victim, later freed, described his capture:

On the morning of that unhappy day . . . about the year 1825, . . . I left home about eight o'clock for the farm, about three miles distance from home. . . . No sooner had I got to the farm and just cut sufficient corn for my load, than the repeated reports of muskets at the town gate acquainted me of my dangerous situation. All my endeavor to escape . . . utterly proved a failure, as I was surrounded by a number of men, who were very eager as to whose lot my capture should fall.

(4) Some Africans sold some of their domestic slaves when ceremonial or political or social demands made it necessary.

All these men, women, and children were brought to the coast, where European ships were anchored offshore. The price for slaves was paid in guns and cloth, bars of iron and of copper, rum and gin, beads, tobacco, and gunpowder. One seventeenth-century European, himself a trader on the coast of West Africa, wrote:*

As the slaves come down to Fida [in modern Dahomey] from the inland country, they are put into a booth, or prison, built for that purpose near the beach, all of them together; and when the Europeans are to receive them, they are brought out into a large plain, where the surgeons examine every part of them, to the smallest member, men and women being all stark naked. Such as are [found] good and sound are set on one side, and the others by themselves. . . . Each of [those] which have passed as good is marked on the breast with a red-hot iron, imprinting the mark of the French, English, or Dutch companies, so that each nation may distinguish [its] own and prevent their being changed by the natives for worse, as they are apt enough to do. . . .

The branded slaves, after this, are returned to their former booth, where the [agent] is to feed them at his own charge, which amounts to about two pence a day for each of them, with bread and water, which is all their allowance. There they continue sometimes ten or fifteen days, till the sea is still enough to send them abroad. . . . Before they . . . come out of their booth, their former black masters strip them of every rag they have, without distinction of men or women.

We can only guess how many million Africans were exported as slaves. Estimates have ranged to fifteen million and even higher; the most reliable one, calculated with great care and after extensive research, puts the figure at about 9½ million imported into the Americas and therefore probably some eleven to 11½ million exported from Africa. Leaving aside the deeper questions of moral outrage, this massive loss of vital, productive people was the most important consequence to Africa.

The slave trade has serious consequences for West Africa. What were the other effects of the slave trade? The economic impact on Africa is

* From *History of the Slave Trade to America*, edited by Elizabeth Donnan, Vol. I (Washington, D.C.: Carnegie Institution of Washington, 1930). Reprinted by permission.

the most obvious. It was not the slave trade alone that caused the rise of the forest kingdoms, for they were powerful long before it became important. But the slave trade combined with events to the north to increase the wealth and importance of the forest kingdoms. Even in these states, however, the trade in no way helped their economies to grow. It did not spur the raising of crops, or produce more goods for export. Instead of stimulating economic growth, the imports from Europe made the African states more dependent on others.

The political effects of the slave trade were not the same everywhere. Some states became more powerful as a result, some were weakened, some destroyed. Ashanti, for a time Benin, and most of all Dahomey, grew in strength with the trade. Oyo, which gained briefly in power, was undermined when slave raids and wars worsened already existing conflicts among her lesser kingdoms. Kongo-Angola, some 1200 miles down the western coast, was ultimately ruined by the trade.

To the east of Benin, in the Niger Delta, were city-states tightly organized specifically to control the slave trade. They thrived on selling peoples who lived north of them. These people to the north, the Ibo, were organized into village communities governed by village elders. They obeyed the religious code of the ancestors and of their gods. Secret societies, some connected with ancestral worship and some with oracles (spirits who divined), played important political roles. But there was no centralized state to wield political power over the entire region in which they lived.

The presence of the Europeans and the slave trade affected warfare. Africans, the same as people everywhere, needed no outsiders to make them fight among themselves. But the economic incentives of the slave trade made their wars, with their prospects of captives for sale, more frequent, especially in coastal regions. And, because they were fought with firearms, wars became steadily bloodier. No one would question the words of one recent

In Zanzibar (above) Arab slave dealers bought and sold Africans acquired from the East African mainland. Most African slaves were put to work in the clove plantations on the island; some were shipped to slave markets in Arabia.

African historian, that the slave trade "brutalized all the people who took part in it, black as well as white." The other effects are important, but they cannot overshadow this fact, or the tragedies of the Africans who were its victims.

CHECK-UP

1. Why were the kingdoms of the forest never conquered by the states of the Sudan?

2. What were Benin's sources of wealth? Why did Benin decline?

3. Why did Oyo become powerful? What was Yoruba art? How did the king of Oyo differ from the king of Benin? What eighteenth-century development hurt the Oyo economy?

4. Who was Uthman dan Fodio? Why did he call for a jihad against the Hausa rulers? What were the results?

5. Why did Ashanti and Dahomey prosper? How did the government of the two states differ? Why was Dahomey able to resist outside invasion?

6. How did slavery in Africa differ from the type of slavery that developed in America? How did racial prejudice become a part of slavery?

7. How were African slaves obtained? What effect did the slave trade have on West Africa economically? Politically?

In the vast equatorial forests of the Congo, forests in some places dense enough to be called jungle, live small tribes. Like most of the peoples south of the equator in Africa, they belong to a group called the Bantu. As was pointed out earlier, the Bantu are not part of the same "tribe." The term "Bantu" means that the languages of all Bantu groups are related, even if the peoples cannot in most instances understand each other.

The Bantu-speaking groups of the rain forest were never able to unite into states. What we know now about their history concerns movements and migrations of small numbers of people. South of the forest, however, a broad band of savanna stretches from the west coast to the lakes in East Africa. Here, where men could move much more easily, chieftaincies and kingdoms have flourished for hundreds of years.

West-Central Africa

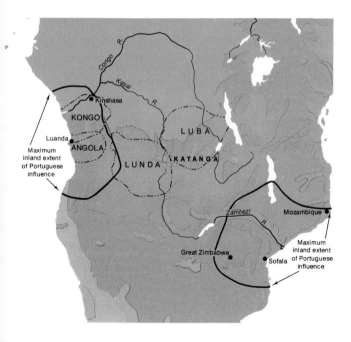

The centuries from 1400 to 1800 (and in some parts of Africa almost to 1900) were ones of movement of peoples, of conquest and consolidation, and of growth and decline of kingdoms and empires. In spite of many differences, West-Central Africa had a pattern not unlike that in the western Sudan. Looming large are the stories of the coastal kingdoms of Kongo and Angola, and of the Luba and Lunda empires, far into the interior. As one historian has said, for the five centuries before 1900 the history of the southern savanna "is the story of the development of a Luba-Lunda culture in the east and of a Kongo and colonial Portuguese culture in the west."

These African states faced some familiar challenges. Foremost was that of how to incorporate peoples. In the case of the Luba and Lunda empires, there was the problem of how to dominate the sources of trade in the interior. The people of the Kongo and Angola shared a problem with the West African forest kingdoms: how to deal with the Portuguese who, as in the case of Benin, began to arrive in the fifteenth century.

African and Portuguese interests conflict in the Kongo. Founded in the fourteenth century some one hundred miles inland from the mouth of the Congo River, by the time the Portuguese first landed the Kongo had grown to resemble other African states. The king was the figure of greatest political and administrative importance. Like the king of Dahomey, he could appoint and dismiss officials and the strength of the state depended on how well the king ruled. In contrast to Dahomey, however, there were no clear rules of succession. There was no royal family from whom a new king had to be chosen. Candidates worked for years to gain support; and when the king died there were usually two strong, rival factions.

The importance of the king's personality, as well as opposing factions which could be played off against each other, gave the Portuguese the chance to dominate Kongo. Though they did not necessarily set out to undermine the kingdom, their domination had that effect. At first, as in Benin, the Portuguese looked upon the king as a person to be respected and treated as an equal. For his part, the King of Kongo was genuinely interested in what the Portuguese at first offered: as well as trade they brought priests who taught both Christianity and reading, and craftsmen who taught European techniques such as bricklaying. A few Kongolese were offered the chance to go to Portugal for formal education.

The King of Kongo, baptized as Affonso in 1480 before his reign began, was a converted Christian. But he never lost sight of the best interests of his people. What he wanted from the Portuguese was a partnership that would let Africans choose what they thought best of what Europe offered and keep what they valued of their own ways. This was the first expression of what came to be the continent-wide African attitude towards Europe.

But this conflicted with Portuguese desires. They looked upon the Kongo first as a source of trade, and second as a Christian kingdom that they could control. Because of these aims, the Portuguese sought to impose their way of life upon the Kongolese. This soon led the Portuguese to seek to dominate them, especially since Portugal's economic interest turned exclusively to the slave trade.

The slave trade and invasions weaken Kongo.

Because the Portuguese had managed to get a foothold in the kingdom itself, slave trading in Kongo differed from that on the Guinea Coast. In the Kongo, and later in Angola, they were able to move into the interior themselves. More often, they sent their special agents to stir up wars and to take the captives to the coast where they were sold. These agents, called *pombeiros* (pohm-*bey*'rohs) were part-African and part-

Portuguese, and later, Africans. Affonso I, who had become king with Portuguese help in 1506, was outraged. In 1526 he wrote to the king of Portugal:*

. . . we cannot reckon how great the damage is, since the mentioned merchants are taking every day our natives, sons of the land, and the sons of our noblemen and vassals and our relatives, because the thieves and men of bad conscience seize them, wishing to have the things and wares of this Kingdom which they are ambitious of; they seize them and get them to be sold; and so great, Sir, is the corruption and licentiousness that our country is being completely depopulated, and Your Highness should not agree with this nor accept it as in your service. And to avoid it we need from . . . [your] Kingdoms no more than some priests and a few people to teach in schools, and no other goods except wine and flour for the holy sacrament. . . . We beg of Your Highness to help . . . us in this matter, commanding your . . . [traders] that they should not send here either merchants or wares, because it is *our will that in these Kingdoms there should not be any trade of slaves nor outlet for them.*

His request was in vain. It was not till long afterwards that the Portuguese tried to seize political control of the kingdom, or to enforce their will with arms. But they continued to increase their slave trading. The close connection between missionaries and slave traders (indeed, some missionaries themselves traded in slaves) undermined the contributions Affonso had wanted from the Portuguese.

The strength of the Kongo kingdom, sapped by the slave trade, was further weakened by frequent invasions from the east. Until the late 1600's the pattern continued the same: Portuguese slave trading, combined with searches for gold and silver mines, with scarcely more than formal gestures at mass conversion, and less and less interest in education for the Kongolese.

* From *The African Past* by Basil Davidson (London: Longmans, Green & Co., 1964; copyright 1964 by Basil Davidson). Reprinted by permission of the Longman Group Ltd. and of Little, Brown, Inc.

Portuguese domination does little for Angola.
Starting in the 1570's, Portuguese interest in Angola, the kingdom to the south, became greater than that in Kongo. When the first Portuguese traders, looking for slaves, met the king of Angola early in the sixteenth century, they found that he was just a minor ruler. But the demand for slaves gave him an opportunity to expand his realm. The guns brought him by the traders made possible successful wars and raids on his neighbors. By the middle of the century the King of Angola had become an important figure. When the Portuguese decided to impose a strong Christian government on Angola, war broke out and lasted, on and off, for decades. When they were not fighting, the Angolans and Portuguese were uneasily trading—slaves for alcohol, cloth, and tobacco. The Portuguese "conquest" of Angola did not bring the hoped-for results, for the "puppet-kingdom" never became the effective partner in trade that Portugal needed. The relationship—as unproductive as any in Africa—continued into the nineteenth century. On the Portuguese side, slave trading was the major concern; political and cultural stagnation characterized Angola.

Centralized states develop in the interior. The peoples in the interior also were affected by the coastal trade. States just out of reach of the Portuguese troops competed for control of the trade routes and slave-buying centers. Well into the interior of Africa two empires, in existence before the 1600's, entered the picture in the eighteenth century. The first, belonging to the Luba, grew to include most of what is now called Katanga. Its ideas of kingship and how to run a centralized state spread to its neighbors to the west, the Lunda.

During the seventeenth century the Lunda built an empire which included most of the southwestern part of the present-day Congo (Kinshasa) and reached into Angola to the west and Southern Rhodesia to the east. By 1700 the whole savanna was covered with Luba-Lunda states. Trade routes ran from Luanda in Angola to the heart of the Lunda Empire in Katanga, where there was salt and copper. Other routes extended to the north. And there was an important route to the east from Katanga to Mozambique (moh-zam-beek').

Until the nineteenth century, the Lunda dominated the trade and politics of the interior. Through small middleman states they carried on trade in three directions: to the west with the Portuguese; to the northwest with the English, French, and Dutch on the coast north of the Congo River; to the east with Arab and other Muslim traders of the Indian Ocean.

In Central Africa, as elsewhere, kingdoms tended to follow a familiar path. The stresses brought by the slave trade affected ways of ruling. Held together when their kings were effectively in power, these kingdoms tended to fall apart in times of weakened control. In summary, "The interaction between the growing slave trade and the normal evolution of the political system explains most of the history of the kingdoms in Central Africa from 1500 to 1900."

CHECK-UP

1. What problems of the West-Central African states were similar to those of the states of the western Sudan?

2. Contrast the role of the king of Kongo with that of the ruler of Dahomey. Why was it easy for the Portuguese to dominate Kongo?

3. What relationships did the king of Kongo want with the Portuguese? What were the expectations of the Portuguese? What factors weakened Kongo?

4. How was Angola affected by Portuguese domination?

5. What enabled the Luba and Lunda kingdoms to become strong?

Southern Africa—the lands below the Limpopo River on the east and modern Angola on the west—has since the sixth century A.D., or even earlier, been inhabited by two distinct peoples. The first, the earlier inhabitants, included two groups called the Hottentots and Bushmen. They were gradually pushed to the southwest by the migrations and growth of the second group, the southern Bantu. Related in languages to the Bantu of Central Africa, these groups were relatively recent arrivals in the south. But both scholars and spokesmen for the South African government have tended to exaggerate the lateness of their arrival. After the twelfth century A.D., significant numbers of southern Bantu were south of the Limpopo. But their expansion was gradual. The growing populations of the southern Bantu moved slowly across the land, absorbing some Bushmen and Hottentots and pushing the rest into smaller and smaller areas to the west and south. By the end of the eighteenth century the Bantu were still moving into unsettled lands along the southeast coast. They had by then been living in the northern and eastern parts of southern Africa for some 500 years.

The Bushmen and Hottentots are hunters and gatherers. The ways of life of the Bushmen and Hottentots were very different from those of the Bantu peoples. The Bushmen, whose cave paintings have brought them worldwide fame, were part of a group who once peopled the southern half of the African continent. For centuries they were pursued and persecuted by waves of intruders who pushed them south and west—first the Hottentots, then the Bantu, and finally the Europeans. Their way of life was similar to that of Paleolithic (Old Stone Age) man (see pages 9–13). Bushmen hunted, gathered food, and used stone tools. A Zulu (the Zulu are one of the Bantu groups in southern Africa), described them in the mid-nineteenth century:

[They] . . . are very much smaller people than all small people; they go under the grass, and sleep in anthills; they go in the mist; they live in the up country in the rocks. . . . Their village is where they kill game; they consume the whole of it, and go away. . . . They are dreaded by men, . . . for men do not see the man with whom they are going to fight. . . . Their strength is like that of the fleas, which have the mastery of the night. . . . They see them for their part, but they are not seen.

The Hottentots were cattle herders who lived in camps and moved over the countryside to find water and grazing land for their animals. Like the Bushmen, they did not grow food, but gathered what grew wild. They shared with the Bushmen religious beliefs in a creator god and in the power of the moon, sun, and stars as forces, represented by gods, that could affect their lives. There were Hottentot myths about these forces and rituals for worshiping them. Both Bushmen and Hottentots had a far simpler political structure than other African peoples we have discussed. Among the Bushmen, the elders "ruled." The Hottentots had a somewhat more complex system centered around clans. But neither people had chiefs or courts.

Bantu-speaking peoples migrate southward. Much more important than Bushmen and Hottentots to the later history of southern Africa were the Bantu-speaking peoples. When the Bantu arrived and how far they had spread in southern Africa before the arrival of Europeans are very important questions. They are important not only for historians, but because they must be raised in any discussion of the racial policies of the Republic of South Africa. In the Republic the white minority controls absolutely the lot of the black majority, a policy which the government justifies in part by saying that (except for the Bushmen and Hottentots, of whom almost none now remain), the country had no African population until the eighteenth century. According to that government, the Europeans found much of southern Africa uninhabited, and therefore it belongs as much to them as to any Africans.

Today we know that by 1593—more than fifty years before any European settlers arrived —the Xhosa (*koh'*sah) had reached as far south as the Umtata River. The vanguard of the Bantu-speakers moving down the coast, by the eighteenth century the Xhosa had crossed the Great Fish River without meeting anyone who challenged their claim to the land, except for bands of Hottentots. Inland, other Bantu-speaking groups settled as far south as the Orange River with no one to interfere with their movement. From about the thirteenth through the seventeenth centuries they spread southward and eastward over the plateau.

Cattle are the basis of the southern Bantu way of life. How did the style of life of these Bantu-speakers differ from that of various West African groups? While there were differences among the dozens of tribes who spoke the related Bantu languages, there were also patterns they all shared. Probably the most important single feature was the role of cattle in their way of life. Cattle were the basis of the economy; their milk was a source of food, and their skins, of clothing. But they were much more than an economic factor. A man's status in his community depended on the number of cattle he owned. Cattle had to be sacrificed in the most important religious ceremonies. Only cattle could be used to pay the dowry, or "bride-wealth," given by the future husband to the family of the girl to make a marriage binding. The center of every village, the *kraal,* was the place where the cattle were kept, and it was also where the men came together to talk over matters of policy or of law and to share their main meal at night. Men tended the cattle; women had another role to play in the economy. For the Bantu were agriculturalists as well as herders, and the women grew the crops, mostly millet and maize (corn).

The Bantu form states on a tribal basis. The Bantu-speakers did not form large states. Rather, in the words of one historian, their "political organization was of a form natural to a people . . . actively colonizing new ter-

Centuries ago the Bushmen occupied half the African continent. Short of stature and living a simple life, they were pushed towards the south and west by the expanding Bantu. Finally they reached the Kalahari Desert where they live today almost as men did in Paleolithic times. The Bushman's life has changed little over the centuries; he uses stone tools and continues to support himself by hunting. Many centuries ago the Bushmen began to paint pictures of the animals they hunted; the cave paintings which survive have told us much about life in the Old Stone Age. Though simple in style, these paintings have great vitality. They are an early testimony to man's desire to express in a visual form what he sees and feels.

ritory." Each tribe had only a few thousand members. As with all African groups, kinship (see pages 267–268) was very important, but the state reached beyond blood ties.

Each tribe among the southern Bantu claimed its own territory, even though boundaries were rather vague and changed from time to time. The chief controlled the right to use the land, and there was no permanent individual ownership. However, unless it committed a serious crime, a family could continue to use land it had started cultivating. A chief could permit people from outside the tribe to use tribal lands if they gave him customary gifts and thus acknowledged his authority. But such privileges were never permanent. Nor did they mean that *ownership* of the land had changed hands. The ownership of the land remained always with the tribe, and newcomers could not prevent people of the owning tribe from also using the land. These concepts of land ownership and use are extremely important in the later history of southern and eastern Africa.

Warfare was common among the expanding Bantu groups. Major causes were arguments over succession and disputes stemming from the fairly frequent splitting of tribes as the population increased. There were also "frontier" problems between neighboring tribes. Though frequent, fighting did little permanent damage. It consisted mainly of seizing cattle and grazing lands on a disputed border. Few soldiers were killed, and civilians were rarely attacked. Almost never did the victors try to crush the enemy, and captives were ransomed for cattle. Throughout the eighteenth century, no southern Bantu group had a standing army.

The Dutch settle in southern Africa. The early European explorers seeking a water route to India, first Portuguese and later Dutch, quickly recognized the importance of the Cape of Good Hope. First and foremost, it was the halfway point on the way to India and the East Indies. The climate was temperate, and it was free of the fever and diseases that threatened men and animals elsewhere in Africa. The Dutch were the first to realize the Cape's possibilities as a permanent way-station. In 1652 Jan van Riebeeck (*yahn′ van ree′beck*) founded what one historian has called a "cabbage patch" for the ships of the Dutch East India Company. No one then thought that settlers might spread inland from the Cape. No one dreamed that it would become the largest and most controversial white settlement in Africa. All the Dutch wanted was meat, vegetables, and wine for their ships. Gradually, however, the growing population extended the colony's area of settlement. Mostly Dutch and a few French Huguenots (*hyoo′geh-nots*, Protestants who had fled religious persecution in France), they were called *Boers* (the Dutch word for farmers). Instead of trying to raise crops for sale, they developed a subsistence economy similar to that of the Hottentot cattle raisers, and later the Bantu, with their cattle and crops. The Boers bartered cattle with the Hottentots they did not kill, grazed their own cattle, and hunted. They moved as their economy demanded, and some of them were soon beyond the reach of the Dutch company's authority. By 1702 they already had clashed with the Xhosa, the Bantu-speakers who had penetrated farthest to the south and east. By that time individual Boers were used to regarding tracts of land of 6000 to 10,000 acres as their own, for they needed the grazing land to raise cattle.

Clashes between Bantu and Boers are frequent. In 1779 the Boers and the Xhosa fought the first of their many frontier wars. The basic problem was not that the two peoples were so different but that their economic interests were so similar. Both had growing populations. Both raised cattle and placed a high value on them, even if not in the same way. Both needed more and more land for their growing herds. Both guarded their land and their cattle jealously, and for both boundaries were vague. In a word, Boers and Bantu (for this was to be true of the groups north of the Xhosa, too) were competing; both realized that the gains of one were the loss of the other. And because they com-

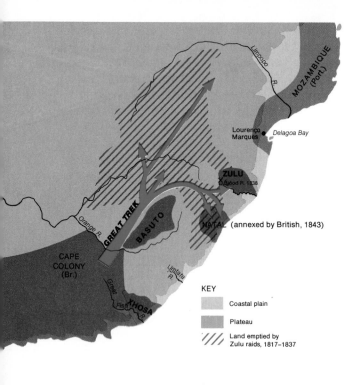

KEY

Coastal plain

Plateau

Land emptied by
Zulu raids, 1817–1837

Southern Africa

peted for the things which were of the greatest importance to their lives, their fighting was bitter and continuous.

There was constant misunderstanding. The Boers did not try to understand the Africans; the Africans had little opportunity to understand anything about the Boers but the superiority of their weapons, which usually, but not always, brought Boers victory in conflicts. Each side made the mistake of assuming that the other was acting as it would itself. The Boers thought that when they "conquered" land it became theirs. They, and the British later, believed that if payment was made to an African chief, they then *owned* the land and could exclude others from it. The Africans thought that they had simply extended to the Europeans the right to *use* the land, just as they would to any other tribe which made payments to acknowledge the chief's ultimate authority. The Africans did not see the European use as permanent, nor

did they see it as preventing them from also using the land.

It is hardly surprising, then, that fighting on the "frontiers" was frequent. Most often the cause of any given "war" was cattle raiding. Seizing cattle and grazing lands was the traditional Bantu way of fighting. The Boers, in return, raided the Bantu herds, sometimes believing that the cattle had been stolen from them earlier, often just to increase their own herds.

What these encounters meant was that both the Bantu groups and the Boers and later Europeans had a constant frontier problem. Quite apart from the continual disturbances, Africans and Boers stood in the way of each other's expansion. The government at the Cape was utterly confused about its jurisdiction. Most serious of all, the Bantu-speaking groups in the south were driven back upon other Africans to the north and east, creating intertribal tension, pressure, and war. These wars brought results that were further to confuse the Europeans who later came to Natal (nuh-*tal'*), the region on the northeast coast.

The Zulu establish a powerful nation. These tensions were compounded by the rise of that most remarkable of southern Bantu peoples, the Zulu. There were two reasons for their rise to prominence: one, a set of circumstances, the other, an individual. The circumstances were that by the end of the eighteenth century the lands along the northeast coast—Zululand and Natal—were overcrowded. Population was continuing to grow, and as Bantu groups competed for land, warfare became more frequent and intense. Earlier states were small in size and tended to break into even smaller political units whose members moved out into vacant land adequate for an expanding people. Now conditions were suddenly reversed. Lack of space forced people to consolidate, and rivalry over control of scarce resources created the need for well-organized and disciplined armies.

The man who revolutionized the military structure, fighting methods, and aims of the

Zulu was Shaka (sometimes written Chaka), their king from about 1816 to 1828. In 1824 a British expedition sent to discover the source of the gold and ivory that were reaching Delagoa Bay, encountered Shaka's *kraal*:

The whole country, so far as our sight could reach, was covered with numbers of people and droves of cattle. The king came up to us and told us not to be afraid of his people, who were coming on-ward. The cattle had been assorted according to their color, each drove being thus distinguished from others near it. A distinction had also been made from the shape of the horns. These had been twisted by some art or skill into various forms.*

After counting 5654 cattle, the visitors found the conversation turning to other things:

Chaka went on to speak of the gifts of nature. He said that the forefathers of the Europeans had be-stowed on us many gifts, by giving us all the knowledge of arts and manufactures, yet they had kept from us the greatest of gifts, a good black skin: for this did not necessitate the wearing of clothes to hide the white skin, which was not pleasant to the eye. He well knew that for a black skin we would give all we were worth, our arts and manufactures.*

At this time Shaka's power was at its height. How had he become powerful, and what did his power mean for the Zulu and their neighbors? At the end of the eighteenth century, the Zulu had been one of many small tribes of Bantu-speakers whose languages (and therefore they themselves) are called collectively Nguni (un-goo′nih). They lived in the corridor between the southeastern coast and the mountains that mark the inland plateau some 100 miles to the west. The Nguni are one of the two main branches into which the southern Bantu are divided; the other, the Sotho, live on the plateau to the west of the mountains.

* Henry Fynn, in *Annals of Natal,* by J. Bird. From *South African Explorers* by Eric Axelson (Oxford, 1954), pp. 170–178. Reprinted from Roland Oliver and Caroline Oliver, *Africa in the Days of Explora-tion,* © 1965, Prentice-Hall, Inc., Englewood Cliffs, N.J. Reprinted by permission.

The Nguni military system breeds loyalty to the "central" government. In the mid-eighteenth century the Nguni were feeling the pressures for consolidation. Dingiswayo, the leader of one small group, recognized the need to reform the traditional military practices of these groups. The change was major: from then on the army was to be organized into "age-regiments." Young men of about the same age were brought together into a regiment with a name of its own. The regiments were attached to one of the households of the royal family. By this system, then, men of about the same age from all the different groups came together. They thus de-veloped a new loyalty which had nothing to do with their families or tribes, a loyalty, in a sense, to the "central" government.

This system was not only new for the Nguni, it was different from the organization of fighting forces in most other parts of Africa. Usually when new groups were conquered by a given state, the men were "drafted" into that state's army. But they were allowed to fight as a separate unit. This method brought instability for the conquerors and tended to perpetuate old loyalties. Might not the soldiers of conquered groups bide their time until they saw a chance to revolt against the conqueror?

But the new Nguni system tended to break up old allegiances, to foster a new loyalty, and to bring stability even though the regiments only came together occasionally. Shaka made further changes in this system once he had con-solidated his power. He created an efficient standing army completely loyal to him by keep-ing the age-regiments on active service, some-times for many years. He appointed and could dismiss their officers. The men were forbidden to marry while on active service, and they lived in special military settlements. Their military training and discipline was rather like that in ancient Sparta (see page 43).

As ruler of the Zulu, Shaka himself provided the cattle and other supplies that sustained the regiments. But the royal resources, large as they were, could not meet the army's demands for food unless there were continual seizures of more cattle. Shaka thus not only kept his soldiers' loyalty, he gave them a compelling reason to fight and win. Since his army was so intensely loyal, the king could ignore traditional political procedures. He no longer needed to consult the tribal council. He might ask the advice of the military leaders in order to keep their loyalty, but since he alone could appoint and dismiss them, this was hardly a check on his powers.

Shaka had the reputation of being a military genius; he has often been called the "Black Napoleon." But he was a harsh ruler. His wars scattered the peoples that he did not conquer and kept groups along his borders in constant terror. A few of the groups he tried to incorporate moved to the north. Others themselves consolidated in self-defense.

The repercussions of Shaka's wars were felt far and wide—north into modern Tanzania (tan-zah-*nee'*uh), and to the south among tribes who, like the Xhosa, were caught from the other side by the expanding Boers. Although it took them a long time to realize it, the Europeans, too, were to feel the impact of this great African leader and his successors.

The Great Trek brings the Boers to the Zulu frontier. It was not until after Shaka's assassination in 1828 that the Boers created a serious problem for the Zulu. In 1814 the British had officially taken over control of the colony at the Cape. Starting in 1836 some Boers began what is called the *Great Trek*. They were outraged by restrictions imposed by British authority, an authority they disliked even more than that of the Dutch company. They were confused and distressed by a frontier policy that was constantly changing as various British administrators tried to handle the difficult problem of cattle raids and border skirmishes. Particularly offensive to the Boers was Britain's abolition of slavery in all British colonies. Even though the Boer economy was not dependent on slave labor, the unchanging seventeenth-century Protestant beliefs of the Boers insisted on the

distinctiveness and inferiority of the Africans. The sister of one of the leaders of the Great Trek provides the following straightforward explanation of this view:

. . . it is not so much [the freedom from slavery granted to Africans by the British] that drove us to such lengths [as trekking] as their being placed on an equal footing with Christians, contrary to the laws of God and the natural distinction of race and religion, so that it was intolerable for any decent Christian to bow down beneath such a yoke; wherefore we rather withdrew in order thus to preserve our doctrines in purity.*

And so these Boers continued their search for new 6000-acre parcels of land. Crossing the mountains in the northeast of Cape province, they moved into what would be called Natal, just south of the Zulu strongholds. The new lands they found appeared to be uninhabited. Shaka's wars had driven off some peoples and killed others. To no European did it seem that those who remained would need to "own" all that vacant land. The Boers also had their eyes on land to the north, in Zululand. Their leaders, showing their firearms, tried to pry concessions from the Zulu, who played for time. By surprise attack and ambush, the Zulu even scored a few victories. But their defeat in 1838, at a battle called Blood River, taught the Zulu that, whatever their fighting skills, their spears could not match guns.

British annexation of Natal leads to war with the Zulu. Determined not to permit an independent Boer state, the British annexed Natal in 1843. The Zulu continued to be a threat to white settlers. Their raids contributed to squabbles between British and Boers, but for a time neither group was eager to meet the expense of seeking a military solution to the problem.

Finally—partly to soothe the Boers—the British decided to humble the Zulu. Early in

* Henry Fynn, in *Annals of Natal*, by J. Bird. From *South African Explorers* by Eric Axelson (Oxford, 1954), pp. 170–178. Reprinted from Roland Oliver and Caroline Oliver, *Africa in the Days of Exploration*, © 1965, Prentice-Hall, Inc., Englewood Cliffs, N.J. Reprinted by permission.

1879 their troops moved into Zululand. To the utter astonishment of the British, the Zulu forces wiped out an entire regiment. The British defeated the Zulu six months later, but not before the British generals had learned to respect Zulu tactics and fighting ability. Nevertheless, the defeat brought to an end Zulu independence.

1. What was life like for the Bushmen? The Hottentots?

2. Who were the southern Bantu? How far had they penetrated into southern Africa before the Europeans arrived? Why is the answer to this question important?

3. What important role did cattle play in Bantu life?

4. Why did the Cape of Good Hope attract European settlers? Who were the Boers? Why did they clash with the Bantu?

5. How did the Zulu become powerful? Why was the Nguni military system important in building a central government?

6. Why was Shaka able to wield great political power?

7. What caused the Great Trek? What was the result?

Central and East Africa

Far to the north of Zululand, Africans felt the shockwaves of the military might of Shaka and his successors. As the Zulu conquered and absorbed some tribes, others fled—to the west, the northwest, and the north. Some moved across the Limpopo River, some crossed the Zambezi, some moved around the southern lakes into modern Tanzania. Everywhere these fleeing peoples brought disruption. The problems of politics, land, and cattle that had concerned them farther south were carried with them.

The Shona are middlemen who dominate trade. The setting for these nineteenth-century events was the region which includes present-day Zambia, Malawi (mah-*lah'*wee), Southern Rhodesia, and Mozambique. Here, as everywhere in Africa, there were many groups of people, and there was political variety. As elsewhere, large states had developed through centuries of migration and conquest. Their wealth and strength came from the richness of the soil, and from the trade in ivory, gold, and copper, and later, slaves. The most famous state, Mutapa, at its height extended from the Zambezi River to the Limpopo. The world came to marvel and puzzle at the ruins of its walled capital city, Great Zimbabwe (zeem-*bah'*-bway). Nineteenth-century European travelers and those who followed them would not believe that such impressive and elaborate stone buildings could have been erected by Africans. They said that the Portuguese had built the city, or perhaps the Phoenicians long before, or the Arabs, or even the Chinese. They were wrong. The Portuguese themselves had written in the early sixteenth century: "Fifteen or twenty days' journey inland [from Sofala, *soh'*fah-luh] there is a great town called Zimbabwe, in which there are many houses of wood and of straw. It pertains to the heathen and the king of Monomotapa often stays there." These "heathen"—that is, non-Christians—were Bantu-speakers called Shona, who began building in stone sometime between the late eleventh and thirteenth centuries. They were probably one of many groups who, from about 1000 A.D., migrated in waves from the Congo basin through Katanga and then south into what became Southern Rhodesia.

Since late in the first millennium A.D. Arabs who came from the coast to the north had been trading for ivory at Sofala. Even before the Shona arrived, the Iron Age people of Rhodesia and the lands south of the Limpopo were mining the plentiful gold and copper. In Central Africa, as all over the continent, Africans had long known and worked the mineral wealth that the world was later to "discover" and value so highly. As the Shona built their states, they increased trade with the coast. Soon their rulers controlled both the coastal trade and the sources of wealth. But like the rulers of ancient Ghana, they never mined the gold themselves, nor did they manage to seize its sources. Early in the sixteenth century a Portuguese traveler and trader told how the Africans mined gold:

They dig out the earth and make a kind of tunnel, through which they go under the ground a long stone's throw, and keep taking out [ore] from the veins, with the ground mixed with the gold, and when collected they put it in a pot and cook it much in fire; and after cooking they take it out and put it to cool, and when cold the earth remains and the gold all fine gold.

Here, as in the kingdoms of West Africa and elsewhere in Central Africa, rulers maintained their power through their control of trade and the collection of tribute. Economic and political control was made possible by the religious authority of the ruler. One Portuguese observer wrote that the common people "believe their kings go to heaven, and when they are there, . . . ask them for whatever they require."

Zulu wars and foreign traders have a considerable impact on East-Central Africa. For the Shona kingdoms and their counterparts north of the Zambezi (the best known was called Malawi), three outside pressures were important before the late nineteenth century. (1) Most disruptive was the last—the invasions set off by the Zulu in the 1830's. The movement and warfare of these invaders, of which the most important were the Ndebele and Ngoni,[1] destroyed kingdoms that had been in existence for centuries. The other two influences came earlier. (2) Indian Ocean traders, sailing into coastal ports, wanted not only the gold and ivory of the interior, they wanted slaves. (3)

[1] The Ngoni (un-*goh*'nih) should not be confused with the Nguni, one of the two main branches of the southern Bantu. The Ngoni were one of the many small Nguni-speaking tribes who fled northward in the confusion and violence of the Zulu expansion.

The Portuguese, who arrived on the coast in the early sixteenth century, were especially interested in gold. Only in the eighteenth century did they and other Europeans become seriously interested in the East African slave trade.

Control of the long trade routes into the interior strengthened the Mwene Mutapa's (muh-*way*'nee muh-*tah*'puhz) empire and its successor kingdoms south of the Zambezi, and also the Malawi kingdom to the north of it. Because they prized gold more highly than ivory, the Portuguese became far more involved in trade with the lands to the south of the Zambezi. As in Kongo and Angola, they meddled in the internal affairs of Mutapa and aggravated an already unstable political situation. Another Shona dynasty had already taken over the old capital, Zimbabwe. Portuguese involvement in succession disputes and other problems speeded the Mutapa decline.

Cities on the East African coast engage in the Indian Ocean trade. Along the East African coast south of Cape Guardafui (gwar-dah-*fwee*') were port cities. They seem from their earliest days to have been city-states independent of one another. For some 2000 years they engaged in the Indian Ocean trade, maintaining contact with the interior for the products they exported.

The population of the coast varied through the centuries. It is probable that the earliest people were "Bushmanoid." During the centuries when the Mediterranean world traded with the coast, newcomers, possibly from the Arabian Peninsula or from Abyssinia (Ethiopia) or Somalia, had probably moved in and absorbed the original coastal inhabitants as far south as Zanzibar. From the fourth to the tenth centuries, little is known of the history of the East African coast. This seems to be the period during which Bantu peoples moved north to become the main group of people both along the coast and inland. When Muslim geographers take up the story, they write of the "Land of Zanj," and the "Zanjis" are consistently described as blacks.

We now know that credit is no more likely to go to outsiders for establishing these settlements and their thriving trade than for building Zimbabwe. Historians had long thought that Islamic influence created these towns and that Arab Muslims controlled them. The few known Greek and Roman sources suggest that East African coastal centers were important long before Mohammed's birth. Later chronicles reveal that, despite growing Muslim influence, especially from the thirteenth century on, there was much that was African about the towns.

What was the trade on which these towns depended? Towards the end of the last millennium B.C., when the East African coast came into the commercial system of Asia, the "outside" world sought there ivory, slaves, and gold. There were also minor interests in aromatic gums, tortoiseshell, rhinoceros horn, leopard skins, and even in hides, cotton, copper, and iron. In exchange for these products Arab and later Persian merchants, and even some from India, brought spears, knives, axes, some cloth, and as time went on, beads and porcelain. Some of the porcelain came from as far away as China. Although the Chinese did not themselves trade with East Africa, they knew of its existence by the ninth century A.D.

Trade in slaves is a vital part of the Indian Ocean trade. The trade in slaves, often closely related to that in ivory, was probably as old as Indian Ocean commerce itself. The connection between slaves and ivory grew from the problem of transportation. Where draft animals could not survive because of the tsetse fly, goods had to be carried by men. If more men were needed to carry ivory to the coast than to bring back goods obtained in exchange, some of the porters were sold as slaves and reached the Asian mainland in numbers. The first revolt of black warrior slaves in Mesopotamia came in 696; less than two centuries later, it took fifteen years to suppress a slave revolt in southern Iraq. East African slaves were found in India in the centuries that followed, and Chinese manuscripts refer to black slaves.

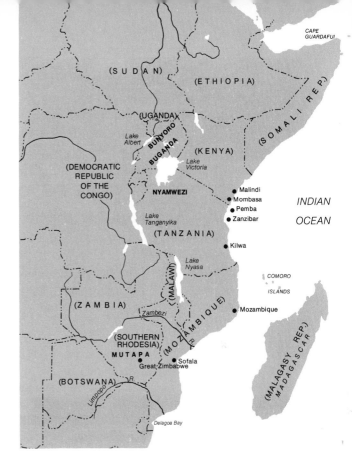

East-Central Africa

The tale of a Persian Gulf sea captain in the tenth century makes clear that, as in West Africa, slaves for overseas sale were sometimes acquired through raids and that they might come from any social rank. He tells of being on a ship driven by a storm towards the East African coast. Expecting certain death on landing, the sailors were agreeably surprised to find the "king" hospitable and willing to trade. After business was concluded, the king came on board the ship with seven companions:

When I saw them there, I [the sailor] said to myself: In the Oman market this young king would certainly fetch thirty dinars, and his seven companions sixty dinars. Their clothes alone are not worth less than twenty. . . . Reflecting thus, I gave the crew their orders. They raised the sails and weighed anchor. . . .

257

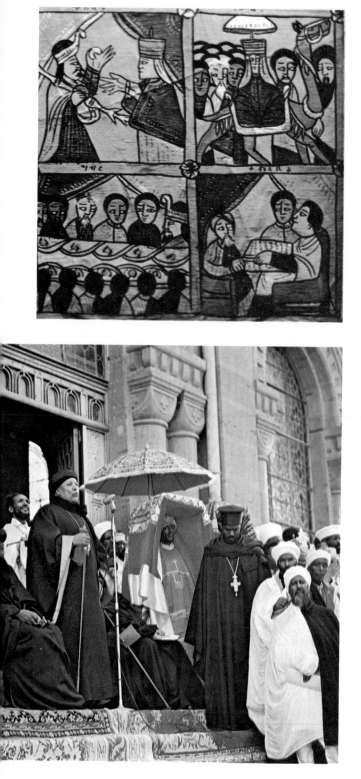

Ethiopia combines elements of African, Arabian, Hebrew, and Byzantine cultures. By the Christian era it was a leading power in the Red Sea, trading with Greece, Egypt, Arabia, and India. The royal family claims descent from King Solomon and the Queen of Sheba, whose visit to the king noted for his wisdom is recorded in an early manuscript (top, left). Ethiopia has a long Christian tradition. Its Coptic Church, while related to the Eastern Orthodox Church, has its own religious language and ceremonies. When Jerusalem was retaken by the Muslims, the king of Ethiopia planned a new Christian holy city to be built in the mountains of his land. Named for the king, Lalibela consisted of ten churches and chapels, all carved out of solid rock and entered by trenches (above). Religion continues to be of importance in present-day Ethiopia, where the Coptic Church is a large landholder and acts as a conservative force in politics. Present-day rituals (left) show a strong influence of the past.

When the day came, the king and his companions were put with the other slaves, whose number reached about 200 head. He was not treated differently from his companions in captivity. The king said not a word. . . . He behaved as if we were unknown to him. . . . When he got to Oman, the slaves were sold, and the king with them.

The nature of the East African trade changed little over the centuries, although its volume rose and fell, as did the prosperity of the coastal towns. An important increase in trade came in the thirteenth century, when Islam was expanding all along the shores of the Indian Ocean—into India, Malaya, and Indonesia. This expansion brought about what has been called "the first real incorporation of the [East African] coastal region within the world of Islam." During that century Muslims came to control the Indian Ocean trade. To East Africa they brought mosques and other aspects of Islamic culture that the coastal peoples made their own. It was probably in these years that the culture and language called Swahili (swah-*hee'*lee) began to take shape among the Islamized Bantu and coastal settlers.

The height of prosperity for the Indian Ocean traders came between the late fourteenth and the late fifteenth centuries. With the increase in wealth came a change in the way of life in the coastal towns. This was when the stone cities later described by the Portuguese were built. For the rich, town living was elegant: in Mombasa, for example, there were semidetached houses with flat roofs, courtyards, quarters for women, and elaborate arrangements for sanitation. There were many costly beads for ornaments, and Chinese porcelain was commonly used.

The fifteenth and sixteenth centuries brought the Portuguese, with trade their major aim, to the East African coast. Having made their way around the Cape, they sought to take over the long-established trade of the Indian Ocean. Portuguese merchants sailed into the Persian Gulf and to India and the East Indies. In East Africa, along their route, they made their first settlements at Sofala and Kilwa. North of the Zambezi their bases were virtually all offshore islands, such as Mozambique, Zanzibar, Pemba, and Mombasa.

A Portuguese sailor described the conquest of Mombasa:

The king of the city refused to obey the commands of the King our Lord, and through this arrogance he lost it, and our Portuguese took it from him by force. He fled away, and they slew many of his people and also took captive many, both men and women, in such sort that it was left ruined and plundered and burnt. Of gold and silver great booty was taken here, bangles, bracelets, earrings, and gold beads, also great store of copper with other rich wares in great quantity, and the town was left in ruins.

Except for interfering in the gold-controlling region south of the Zambezi, the Portuguese stayed away from mainland ventures. Even their impact on the coast north of Sofala was not lasting. By the early eighteenth century Portuguese influence in the Indian Ocean had been broken by the Omani of the Arabian Peninsula. Trade then resumed the pattern of 200 years earlier, even though the gold reaching Sofala was still in Portuguese hands. The Swahili city-states revived under the rule of Arabs whose allegiance, at least in name, was to the rulers of Oman.

Inland East Africa is affected by Zulu invasions and the activities of Arab traders. Since the mid-1400's there have been large-scale population movements in the interior of East Africa —Uganda (you-*gan'*duh), Rwanda (ruh-*wahn'*duh), Burundi (boo-*run'*dee), and inland Tanzania and Kenya. The migrating peoples usually were absorbed by those who already lived there and most came to speak local Bantu languages. Like the invaders of fourth- and fifth-century Rome, the newcomers took over existing states and adopted some of the customs they found. But they established new dynasties; the important Bantu-speaking kingdoms of Bunyoro (bun-*nyor'*oh) and later Buganda were among their heirs. Similar kinds of movement—though of different peoples—

with some similar results took place into Kenya and eastern Tanganyika.

Central and southern Tanganyika were not disturbed by outside pressures before the early nineteenth century. There, many Bantu-speaking groups lived without combining into a single political or economic system. In at least one case, however, that of a people called the Nyamwezi (nigh-um-*we'*zee), the rulers built an organization large and powerful enough to bring about trade between the coast and the interior, and to control that trade.

After 1800 three forces brought about upheaval in East Africa: (1) the Ngoni invasions from the south; (2) the domination of the coast by Arabs from Oman; and (3) Arab penetration into the interior, leading to an enormous increase in the slave trading.

(1) The Ngoni, moving up from the south, crossed the Zambezi River in 1835, and by 1840 had moved into southwestern Tanganyika (now part of Tanzania). Their advance had three main effects. First, the Ngoni absorbed small, disorganized tribal groups into the new states they themselves founded. Second, their invasion let loose raiders and refugees who created turmoil on the fringes of Ngoni settlement. Third, they provided a reason for peoples to unite in order to resist the Ngoni.

(2) The Arabs, not the Europeans, were the chief outside influence on East Africa in the first 80 years of the nineteenth century. In theory the ruling family of Oman, a state on the coast of southeastern Arabia, had had the allegiance of the coastal rulers and their "Arabized" Swahili-speaking peoples since 1700. Actually Omani rule was not effective on the East African coast until the Seyyid Said (*sey'*yid sah-*yeed'*) seized power in Muscat, the capital of Oman, where he reigned from 1806 to 1856. Said built a navy and forced the coastal African towns to pay tribute and customs duties. Having made Zanzibar his East African base, he began growing cloves on a large scale there. By the end of his rule the island was producing three-quarters of the world's supply!

Zanzibar soon became the busiest port on the East African coast, the center for foreign ships looking for slaves and ivory in exchange for goods from three continents: Europe, Asia, and America. In 1840 Said moved his capital to Zanzibar and gathered wealthy Arabs around him to carry on trade and to own and run plantations.

(3) Said encouraged other Arabs to make their fortunes by trading in the interior. With the credit obtained from Indian "merchant-financiers" these Arabs stocked trading caravans and moved into interior Africa for months, or even years, at a time. They displaced the Nyamwezi, the pioneers of trade in the hinterland, for besides cloth and beads the Arabs could offer guns and ammunition.

The East African slave trade remained closely tied to the trade in ivory. In the nineteenth century it reached huge proportions. Some African slaves were exported to far-away China, but the greatest number went to India's Malabar Coast. By the time of Seyyid Said, vast numbers of slaves were also used on Zanzibar's plantations.

CHECK-UP

1. What was Great Zimbabwe? Why were the Shona wealthy?

2. How were the Shona kingdoms affected by the Zulu wars? By foreign traders?

3. Why was trade in ivory often closely related to trade in slaves?

4. What effect did Muslim control of the Indian Ocean trade have on East Africa? What was the effect of the arrival of the Portuguese?

5. What forces caused upheaval in inland East Africa? What were the results?

6. Why did Arab influence in East Africa increase? How did this affect the slave trade?

Africa in 1800

What was Africa like in 1800, at the start of the century when Europeans would "discover" that continent's interior? For all their diversity, the many parts of black Africa shared certain characteristics. (1) Most important, they had their own histories. This obvious fact escaped nineteenth-century Europeans who, for their own reasons, thought that they were "opening up" the continent and bringing "civilization" to peoples seen as "savages," even if *noble savages*." (2) Sub-Saharan Africa had recently been deeply affected by massive movements of people. On both the western and eastern coasts slave trading brought about a devastating loss of manpower. It also shifted economic strength and political power to coastal peoples and their rulers. In the eastern and central interior the continuing movement of Bantu-speakers that had been going on for centuries was still bringing about changes. (3) Large-scale warfare was being used to bring about political consolidation in the forest states of West Africa, in Zululand in the southeast; and, backed by crusading Islam, in the western Sudan. The direct or indirect effects of these conflicts were to touch large parts of the continent.

Chapter Highlights

Can you explain?

middlemen	pagans	terra-cotta	pastoral
tribe	savanna	bride-wealth	domestic slavery

Can you identify?

Ashanti	Bantu	Natal	Fulani
Zulu	Hottentots	Sudan	Songhay
Benin	Dahomey	Mali	Great Trek
Shaka	Nguni	Hausa states	Kongo
Boers	Bushmen	Mansa Musa	Uthman dan Fodio
Yoruba art	kraal	Ghana	Great Zimbabwe

What do you think?

1. What are some commonly held misconceptions about Africa? Why have they been accepted?

2. How did skill in iron-working make possible the growth of powerful states?

3. What conclusions can you draw from the pilgrimage of Mansa Musa?

4. What was the effect of the Muslim penetration of the states of the western Sudan? Of the forest?

5. How could the slave trade make African states wealthy?

6. How did racial theories develop from the enslavement of Africans? On what incorrect conclusions were they based?

7. The slave trade "brutalized all the people who took part in it, black as well as white." Do you agree? Why?

8. How would you characterize Portuguese influence in Africa?

9. Why is it said that the life style of the southern Bantu was based on cattle?

10. Why did the Boers and Bantu clash?

11. What were the direct and indirect results of the Nguni reform of their military system?

11

African Cultures

CHAPTER FOCUS

Daily Life and Beliefs
The Oral Tradition
Music in Sub-Saharan Africa
The Art of Sub-Saharan Africa

The tasks which women perform daily are often in-corporated in ceremonies. To the accompaniment of drums and song, women at a Hausa wedding (left) pound a yam-like vegetable in a mortar which differs from the everyday utensil only in size. Initiation ceremonies involve music and dance and the use of masks. The Mende mask (above) is used to drive out evil spirits before initiation into a women's society in Sierra Leone.

Africa is a vast continent, varied in climate and natural resources, and peopled by many groups, each with its own identity and language and a history of its own. Clearly there can be no single "African way of life." Nor was there one in the past.

We know little about how people lived in sub-Saharan Africa long ago. The findings of archaeologists give us some information about early settlements: the tools used, fragments of pottery that suggest contact between peoples, and food resources. Objects found as part of burials suggest some form of a cult of ancestors.

263

But these remains can tell us nothing about what the people who once lived at a site held sacred. The earth carries no record of the songs they sang, the stories they told, their rivalries, their fears and hopes. Furthermore, in much of Africa south of the Sahara archaeological explorations are just beginning, if they have been started at all. Then, too, remains of past eras are better preserved in some places than in others.

Before European contact, North Africans visited parts of Africa below the desert and recorded their impressions or those of traders who had been there. Written mainly in Arabic, these early records are invaluable even though they deal with only a relatively small part of the continent. After the fifteenth century, descriptions of sub-Saharan Africa came from Euro-peans—traders (usually in slaves), explorers, missionaries, and administrators. Some of the accounts contain close observation of daily life and religious ceremonies. Others describe trading practices or customs which to the writers appeared strange or impressive or "inhuman." All reflected, as did North African accounts, an outsider's point of view. If carefully read, however, all can tell us much that is valuable, even if the information is incomplete.

From these sources and especially from the more recent reports of trained scholars (a growing number of whom are themselves Africans), we gain insights into the African ways of life. Despite the great variety of cultures, important underlying similarities do exist, brought about by the movement of peoples and the contacts among them.

Daily Life and Beliefs

FORMS OF GOVERNMENT

Ways of living of the many different peoples in sub-Saharan Africa varied from region to region. Often even those living near each other had different ways of organizing their families. Their languages were different, and the gods they worshiped had their own local identities. Each tribal group had its own traditions about ancestors who had founded the families that made up the tribe.

Governments also differed. Some tribes were not organized into states at all; for them the unifying ties were religion and kinship (family). But many, especially in West Africa, did have states with definite boundaries, a ruling class of kings or chiefs, nobles, elders, priests, heads of secret societies, and military leaders. The rulers were responsible for stability and order within their lands, and for defense against invasion. They were the links to the ancestors who looked out for the fortunes of the tribe.

Many parts of eastern and southern Africa did not have large states. Each tribe had a major—indeed, a royal—lineage. As in other parts of Africa, the chief was the actual and symbolic head of his people. He always came from the royal lineage, and his close relatives held other high offices or were members of his council. As in West Africa, the chief (through his ancestors) was the link between the tribe and its ancestors; his role was thus central to important religious beliefs.

Although he was absolute in theory, the chief only rarely acted as an autocrat. In many groups, he not only was advised by a small council, but also submitted policies to general discussion among the men, who could even criticize the chief during the debate. But there were no votes, and at the end the chief proclaimed the "sense of the meeting." This practice gave him literally the last word, though if a disagreement were serious enough, his followers could take strong measures. Some chiefs were assassinated, and sometimes civil war broke out. At other times a part of the group broke away.

WORK PATTERNS

All over Africa the land was very important. In the traditions of each tribe the early ancestors had laid claim to the land with the approval of the gods of the earth, and thus gave their descendants inalienable rights over the land and its use. The head of a "family" was the guardian of that part of the tribal land assigned to it. This land was not only for the use of the living generation but was held "in trust" for generations yet to come. The land was sacred because it connected the living to their ancestors, gave them food, and determined their way of life.

Agriculture dominates African life. Seasonal changes —the rains, the dry seasons—dictate the rhythm of work and of ceremonial life, and formerly of warfare. Both farming and pastoral peoples have a calendar for these seasonal changes. That is to say, there is a right time for planting each crop and harvesting it, or for finding the best pasture for the herd in any given season.

Africans are skilled farmers. In areas of intensive farming, their knowledge of the type of soil best suited for each crop has impressed professional agriculturalists. Not all regions are equally fortunate. Where there is only one harvest, poor soil, and drought, there is scarcity of food. Many folk tales have the "season of hunger" as their theme. But where soil conditions and rainfall are favorable, as on the Guinea Coast, the yield is high, and food surpluses are large.

In farming areas both men and women till the soil. But among pastoral groups, women grow the food, while the men tend the cattle and work at their crafts. Everywhere the clearing of fields and usually the initial hoeing—which prepares the ground for planting, as does plowing in western societies—are done by men only. Planting and weeding, tending the growing crops, and harvesting are in most regions women's work. Men hunt and fish, dig wells, fell trees, build houses, walls, and fences, and harvest tree crops such as the nuts from the oil palm.

Specialization takes many forms. Where there are food surpluses, there is specialization. Craftsmen such as blacksmiths (and for the wealthy, silversmiths, goldsmiths, and brassworkers), weavers, leatherworkers, woodcarvers—all work in family groups or are organized into guilds. Blacksmiths, who in the Sudan do not marry outside their own groups, are regarded throughout the continent as having special supernatural powers, which come from the guardian spirits of their craft.

There are hunters, priests, and diviners (see page 273). Officials serve rulers by overseeing the collection of tribute and the supplying of manpower for communal labor and for war. Prosperous and expanding communities have groups of professional musicians and entertainers.

The crafts are chiefly in the hands of men, but women also have their specialized places in the economy. They spin cotton (a task for old women), dye cloth, make pots, and process food. They brew beer and prepare palm oil and cooked foods for sale in the market. In much of West Africa and the Congo they are traders as well. And some women are diviners, with recognized skills in doctoring.

Mungo Park, a Scottish explorer, wrote in 1799 of Segou (say-*goo'*) on the Niger River, deep in the Sudan (now Mali), a city in a region of specialization and flourishing trade:

From the best inquiries I could make I have reason to believe that Sego [Segou] contains altogether about 30,000 inhabitants. . . . The view of the extensive city, the numerous canoes upon the river, the crowded populations, and the cultivated state of the surrounding country, formed altogether a prospect of civilization and magnificence which I little expected to find in the bosom of Africa.

SOCIAL INSTITUTIONS

The social class system ranges from simple to complex. Where there is specialization, there are local and regional markets and trade is carried on over great distances. There also are

265

wealthy men, who are influential. And there are social classes.

Class distinctions start from simple divisions within some groups or tribes of family heads and elders—the men who have the authority to make social, economic, and religious decisions for their group. But complex and varied forms exist, too. An outstanding example is the system of the Wolof people living in Senegal and the Gambia, who have six "classes:"

(1) Those of freeborn descent
(2) Descendants of slaves of the freeborn
(3) Blacksmiths and leatherworkers, who can intermarry
(4) Descendants of slaves of blacksmiths and leatherworkers
(5) Minstrels
(6) Descendants of minstrel slaves

Membership in each "class" is inherited through the father, and marriage between members of different groups is not permitted.

The Reverend Samuel Johnson, a Yoruba historian writing in the late nineteenth century, tells about the customs of his countrymen, who have far fewer class distinctions: "Promiscuous marriages were not allowed: freeborn must be married to freeborn, slaves to slaves, and foreigners to foreigners." He adds, however, "Kings and nobles . . . were at liberty to . . . [take] wives from any tribe, and those wives might be of any condition of life."

The Abbé Kagamé (ab-*bay′* kah-gah-*may′*) from Rwanda tells of another type of social division, one which shows the importance of cattle in the pastoral economy of eastern and southern Africa (page 250):

Rwanda society was based on three elements, . . . of social and political order as well as religious, . . . which determined the life of the country: first, *The King;* second, *The Warrior,* the right arm of the king . . . ; third; *The Cow,* wealth of and by itself, instrument of domination by the king over his subjects, determinant of social position of the various members . . . of the country.

Plural marriage has an economic basis. All African groups sanction the marriage of a man to more than one woman. Actually, however,

it is a privilege enjoyed mainly by men of wealth and position. Since plural marriage is expensive, any man with a number of wives, except in ruling families, is likely to be well along in years. The main reason for plural marriage is to have more children. Children were—and are —an economic asset to their families. No man could hold a position of political power without the support of a large family. Having many sons and daughters produced the resources which made possible generous hospitality, essential in establishing one's social position and for attracting followers.

A senior wife welcomed co-wives because they would share domestic chores. It was not unusual for a wife to contribute her savings to help her husband meet the cost of another marriage. But as with other human institutions, there also were tensions. Jealousy and quarreling existed among co-wives, often expressed indirectly through songs as household tasks were performed. The rhythmic pounding of grain, for example, made a fine accompaniment to such quarrels.

The payment of bride-wealth is an important obligation. Africans see marriage as a union between two families as well as between two individuals. Both families have obligations. Before a family can give its consent to a marriage, they must consult the ancestors. In each society, tradition determines the ritual and the economic obligations of the bridegroom to the parents of his future wife. The most important of these obligations is the payment of what is called *bride-wealth.*

Bride-wealth is not buying a wife, as it has mistakenly been called so often. A Dahomean reaction to the idea of wife-buying is relevant: "Does the French father who gives his daughter a dowry buy a husband for her?" An example taken from southern and eastern Africa, where the payment of bride-wealth is made in cattle, will make clear how wrong it is to think that a man "buys" his wife. In the first place a wide group of relatives, friends, and contemporaries contributes to the payment. Then the cattle

KEY

	Negroid
	Caucasoid
	Mongoloid
	Bushman
	Pygmy

Africa's Peoples

received by the girl's family are distributed by her father to those who earlier had given cattle to make up *his* son's bride-wealth. This double transfer of cattle may involve fifty or more head, for it is a matter of prestige for both families that the number be large.

The family is the basis for social relationships. For all groups the family was the most important unit. It was believed that these families were descended from common ancestors. Families made up extended families, clans, and finally tribes. African families are organized on the principle that there are two separate and significant lines of descent. One is descent through the father's family, and the other is through the mother's family. Africans generally trace what we call "legal descent" on one side of the family only. A child, male or female, whose descent is traced through the father belongs to a *patrilineal* (pat-rih-*lin'*eh-ul) family. If he traces his descent through the mother, he belongs to a *matrilineal* family. The family heads in both kinds of descent groups are men. For the patrilineal family, it is the most senior elder; in the matrilineal family, it is the mother's brother or her sister's son. The importance of "legal" descent is that succession to office, the use of family land for farming, and the rights over the family herds stem from belonging to a descent group.

In both types of family there are generally three divisions. First comes the *immediate family,* which is made up of a man, his wife or wives, and their children. Next in size and often of greatest importance is the *extended family.* In patrilineal systems it is made up of the families of brothers and their sons who farm and live near each other; in matrilineal systems it includes the mother's brothers, her sons and daughters, and her sister's sons and daughters. Members of the extended family cooperate in economic, social, and religious activities. The third division, the *clan,* contains many extended families living within a wide area. The clan head is the representative of the ancestors. Clan members share traditions of origin, the ancestral moral code (including regulations governing marriage), and ritual obligations.

Households live in compounds. Where descent is traced through the father, the immediate family lives in a *compound,* a number of separate houses usually enclosed by a wall or fence. A large compound may be subdivided into several enclosed courtyards. The family head lives in what is called the "big house." This usually is a one-room house, similar to the other dwellings in the compound, but larger. Another house is set aside for the unmarried sons of the compound head and also his younger brothers (by the same mother) who have chosen to

join his household. This is a men's house which is given various names such as a bachelor's house or barracks. In pastoral areas the barracks is the house which guards the entrance to the *kraal* against cattle raiders. Each wife also has a house, in which she lives with her young children. The young boys who no longer sleep in their mother's house will have their own house, often one which they themselves have built. Less common is the practice of having the young unmarried girls sleep in a house where they are chaperoned by an older woman. The compound also includes storage houses and granaries, as well as a shrine for the ancestors.

The houses of a compound usually are grouped around a large clearing where dances and other communal activities are held. Often an entrance house, used for social meetings, leads into the compound. Not all compounds are large; some may have only five or six houses, or even fewer, with no more than ten people living in them.

A woman's duties include taking care of house and children, seeing to the supply of water for the household, collecting firewood for cooking, and growing and preparing food. She spends hours in preparing the main meal of the day. First she pounds grain in a mortar to make the starchy meal generally described as "stiff porridge." With this staple goes the very important sauce, or stew, or soup that has many names and usually contains vegetables. To these vegetables are added palm or other oil, or peanuts, and, where the standard of living allows, fresh or smoked fish, dried shrimp, game, or meat. In West Africa, the Sudan, and the Congo, where people like a "hot" diet, red peppers are a major ingredient of this "stew." Pastoral peoples use milk products with their starchy staple, as well as vegetables and, when possible, game. Many African groups drink a lightly fermented beer which is rich in vitamins. Palm wine and kola nuts, wherever these are available, are greatly enjoyed. Beer, wine, and kola nuts also have important ceremonial uses.

Men, both married and unmarried, eat together in large groups. In many societies the adolescent and even pre-adolescent boys are included. The head of the household eats alone, or shares his meal with a visitor of equal rank. Young children of both sexes, and daughters until they marry, eat in their mother's or grandmother's house.

Age-grades determine the individual's role in society. Most societies in Africa have some form of division by age and some form of initiation to mark attainment of manhood. The age-grade has special meaning for the western world. The Boy Scouts, an organization which began in England, are an adaptation of the Bantu age-grades. R.S.S. Baden-Powell, founder of the Boy Scouts, spent some years in southern Africa as a British army officer. He thought that the Bantu system could be adapted to build character and educate boys for citizenship in England. From this inspiration came the Boy Scouts.

Initiation into the age-grades varies from group to group and region to region. Length of time also varies—for some groups in Kenya initiation lasts several years. The severity of tests of courage, strength, and obedience covers a wide range. These initiations always have an educational side. Boys learn the traditions of the group (its "history"), its moral code, and its nature lore. Some groups are trained in arts and crafts. Each age-grade performs communal tasks, and promotion is automatic for all members when a new group is initiated. There are also initiations for girls, designed chiefly to prepare them for marriage. Close friendships, cooperative work-groups, mutual aid and recreational clubs—all grow out of the bonds of the age-grade.

When boys enter manhood, they join men's societies which enforce traditional behavior, especially by keeping watch over the conduct of the younger generation and of women. In some places there are parallel women's societies. Some societies also play political roles, limiting the power of the rulers and hereditary counselors.

Children learn to respect and obey their elders. Children learn early that there is a hierarchy based on age. They must defer not only to elders or members of the mother's or father's generation. Even a brother or sister only a few years older will exact obedience from younger brothers and sisters. Many Africans believe that an orderly way of life depends on such respect. Thus a proverb criticizing western ways states, "In 'civilization' there is no senior"—that is, age is not respected in the West. However, grandparents are known to be more permissive than parents, and children often prefer to live with them. It is said that young children are taught to respect their parents by their grandparents, though children say, "Grandparents scold with the mouth; parents with a stick."

From his parents and grandparents, from other adult members of the household, and from his age-mates and playmates the child learns good manners, the proper forms of address and greetings for those who form his world, and the correct use of language. A scholar has said that a four or five year old child in western Congo has a command of his language, *Kikongo,* equal to a European child's command of his language at twelve.

Growing up involves learning the tasks of adults. The child learns work habits and skills by imitating in play the members of his household. On moonlit nights there may be dancing in which the children join. There are games and songs that go with stories the mother or grandmother tells while the stew is on the fire. Children also swap stories and riddles among themselves.

Between father and son, especially a young father, there is growing intimacy. Among the Dogon in present-day Mali, "on the errands on which he accompanies his father," writes Denise Pauleme, "the little boy learns quickly to recognize the limits of the fields, the beginning of the village, the names of plants and animals." A proud father will lead his little boy "by the hand to the public meeting place of the men. . . .

Children learn many tribal traditions and legends from the stories their grandmothers tell (right). At an early age they start learning the tasks of adulthood. This Masai boy (top, right) is one of the children entrusted with the important job of herding cattle in the rolling grasslands of Tanzania. With manhood, the boy becomes a warrior. Raiding, once an important part of Masai life, no longer is permitted though the Masai warrior (above) continues to carry his spear.

Some [children] from the age of four or five seem to follow the conversation with interest."

From the age of five or six children learn to share the work of their parents. At that age, the little Dogon boy carries the midday meal to the older boys guarding sheep and goats. He is sent to cut fodder for the animals and to water the onion beds for his father. Soon he himself leads the animals to pasture. At dawn he goes to the fields with the older boys to drive away the monkeys and birds who feed on the growing crops. The boys play toy drums and flutes, throw stones, and use slingshots to frighten them. At nine a boy knows most of the insects, birds, and rodents, and can trap the edible ones.

In Dahomey a little girl of five goes with her mother to market, does small tasks about the house, and pulls up weeds in the field. By the time she is ten or eleven, she can cook all the staple foods and looks after the younger children when her mother is away for days at a distant market. Under the guidance of a relative, she has learned to sell products at the market. She goes about the village or through the local market offering her stock of chewing sticks for cleaning teeth, lumps of sugar, and small portions of salt, or cooked food provided by her mother. What the girl earns belongs to her.

Craftsmen's sons watch their elders at work and play at their father's craft. For example, on the day sacred to the Dahomean god of iron and war, blacksmiths may not work. On that day the children take over the forge. Boys of eight or nine, who normally only work the bellows for their fathers or older brothers, handle the red-hot iron with the tongs, and hammer the metal on an anvil. Meanwhile a three or four year old boy works the bellows.

Boys and girls of nine and younger help with the planting in Dahomey, and by the time a boy is eleven or twelve he has mastered the essentials of farming. At fifteen or sixteen, with the help of his friends, a boy will have built a small house in his father's compound. Mornings and early afternoons, he works in his father's fields, but in his free time he also cultivates his own field, the "evening field." This is similar to the practice domestic slaves once followed. The boy sells the produce from his field and uses what he earns to pay dues to the social club he and his age-mates have formed. Later he saves money for the expenses incurred in courtship.

In pastoral communities young boys begin to herd small stock at an early age. From about ten they help tend the cattle, gradually learning all the tasks of the pastoralists. The Zulu herdboys, we are told by A. T. Bryant,

out on the veld [open grazing area] . . . were studying the nature of plant and tree, the habits of insects, the peculiarities of rocks, and learned to interpret the meaning of the winds and clouds and mists, could give the names of grasses and medicinal uses of many trees and herbs, could describe the quality of the different kinds of wood. . . .

They also learned another lesson, as related by the famous South African novelist, Thomas Mofolo:

Herding in Basutoland was long ago bad and painful. . . . The cattle of the principal herdboy would feed . . . in the largest pasture where there was much grass. . . . At the drinking place his cattle were first to drink when the water was still clean. Above all, he would bully the others. The boys had to share everything with him. . . . If they did not, there was the stick.

RELIGION

In all of Africa the relationship between man and the powers of the universe affects all aspects of life. Man, therefore, praises, prays to, and makes offerings to those powers he believes can help him. He seeks to appease unfriendly or mischievous powers.

Beliefs about the Creator vary greatly. To explain these powers, Africans turn back to the beginning of time. Westerners call these explanations myths, but to the Africans they are spoken "scriptures." Each group or tribe traces the origin of the world to a Supreme Being, the Creator. As the parent of man, the Creator is his guardian and protector. He is also man's judge, who inflicts severe punishment for serious violations of the moral code.

There are great variations in the views held of the Creator. Some groups see him as remote, too preoccupied with the larger universe to play an active role in the lives of men. Yet, because of man's great need for security and reassurance, a special partiality towards mankind is also attributed to the Creator. The Nuer of East Africa, for example, say that God is everywhere, "like wind" and "like air," that he walks among men. All the tribes share beliefs, as did the ancient Egyptians and Mesopotamians and the Greeks and Romans, in many forces that rule the lives of men. They all have ways to call on the gods to give insight into the future, to learn how to win friendships or how to turn away the anger of supernatural forces.

Nature deities represent forces of nature. The Creator is believed to delegate certain powers to natural forces—the earth, thunder and rain, the waters of the sea and rivers, the great forests. These natural forces are represented by nature deities. Also important everywhere are the "little people" of the forest who give medicine and magic cures to man. Many societies also include twins among those given supernatural powers by the forest spirits.

In the elaborate ritual worship of the Yoruba and Dahomeans in particular, the Great Gods are organized into families, each with undisputed rule over a "domain" or "kingdom." Each family of gods, in turn, assigns tasks to its offspring. Hence there are many deities. In addition to their principal gods, many African groups have local deities adopted from earlier peoples or from neighboring tribes. In Dahomey the divine families include the gods of the sky, the earth, thunder, and the sea. Each has its own priesthood, men and women who spend a long period of seclusion to prepare themselves to "receive their gods." The gods are believed to descend during rituals "into their heads"; in a trance known as "possession," the priests or

priestesses take on the personalities of the gods. These are revealed most clearly in their dances.

The ancestors are very important in African religions. In the supernatural world, as in the world of men, age carries responsibility for the well-being of the group. Thus ancestors are the intermediaries between their living descendants and the powers of the universe. If properly served with ceremonial offerings as tradition requires, the ancestors will help to protect the living and bring them prosperity.

Among the southern Bantu (specifically the Ngoni of modern Malawi), where rank is very important, the ancestors are felt to be the main link with the Creator. Writes Margaret Reed:

It was taken for granted that when the Paramounts [the highest ranking chiefs] died they would continue to be powerful . . . and that their position in the spirit world would enable them to influence the Great Spirit—the Creator of all things, the ultimate source of power, particularly of sending rain, success in war, . . . [and] deliverance from pestilence [fatal epidemic].

The souls of men are an expression of individuality. In large societies and small, belief in the powers of the ancestors affirms the essential oneness of the group. But man is not only a member of a family. He is also an individual with his own destiny, his own personality, his own wish to achieve satisfactions in life and an honored place among his ancestors after death.

The Creator, who gives a destiny to each human being, also gives him one or more souls. These souls define what we may call the total personality of the man. For the Ashanti (and the Akan of Ghana and the Ivory Coast), a son (or daughter) gets his soul from his father. The people call this soul his "luck." He must take care that he never seriously angers his father by his conduct. For even though the father would not consciously wish misfortune to overtake his son, his anger would weaken the soul given his son. This would lessen its power to bring "luck." In addition to this soul of "luck," there is a personal soul which determines the temperament of the individual. Sometimes there is also a third soul. Among the Dahomeans an ancestral soul and a personal soul are joined by the soul given to every man and woman, a soul which is "part of the Creator."

Even societies in which belief is less formalized have ideas about the multiple soul and reincarnation (rebirth). Offerings made to the soul are most often given by the individual *to his own head*—the seat of knowledge, judgment, and decision. There are few places in the world where the relation between knowledge and power receives greater emphasis than in the religious systems of West Africa.

Divination is an approach to dealing with the supernatural. Supernatural forces that influence the fortunes of men are thought to share human traits. Man can win favor with these forces through prayer, praise, and offerings. However, if he neglects or angers them, they will thwart and punish him. To find out which deity or ancestor to appeal to or appease one consults a specialist—a *diviner*. Divination, therefore, is everywhere an indispensable approach to dealing with the supernatural.

Divining practices vary greatly and often are very complex. In East Africa seers or prophets receive their revelations in dreams or from communication with spirits. During trances the Akan diviners in modern Ghana are possessed by gods or the "little people" of the forest, and sometimes by powerful ancestors, who give them the information they seek. The most complex divination is that practiced by the Yoruba and called "Ifa." This system of divination has spread to many neighboring groups in Africa and can also be found in Cuba, Brazil, and elsewhere in the New World. The Ifa diviner spends years in training, for he must master many verses and myths to interpret the patterns made by his throws of palm kernels. Other forms of divination are throwing cowrie shells or kola nuts, and reading omens.

Ancestral figures are made of many different materials and may be elaborate or quite simple. This expressive carving comes from the Kuba people of the Congo region.

Worship involves both simple and complex rituals. What of worship in these many religious systems? A Yoruba authority writes of his people's practices:

The rituals follow set, fixed, and traditional patterns. "The way it is done" is the guiding principle whether worship is public or private. . . . Prayers are offered not only at worship, but at any time and in any place as the worshiper feels and the occasion demands. . . . Usually women are the more religious. [They stop] . . . by wayside shrines, sacred trees, sacred brooks, at crossroads, asking for a blessing on their journey, their work, their wares, their family.

273

In the great African kingdoms the pageantry of the public rituals in the worship of gods and ancestors was impressive. It combined the artistry of dance, song, and musical accompaniment with a great display of wealth. The skill of carvers, metalworkers, and weavers was reflected in the emblems of political power, the masks of dancers, and all objects that surrounded the gods. The simpler and more humble rituals often had more emotional meaning, perhaps because they were less spectacular, and children had more of a chance to observe closely. Nevertheless, the great spectacles, which still can be seen, stir the imagination and give dramatic texture to life.

The family gods and guardian spirits and the ancestors receive traditional ritual attention almost daily through simple offerings and invocations. In Yorubaland the family diviner regularly calls on the family and throws the palm kernels to find out if all is well. Before he drinks, the Ashanti-Fante man will pour some drops from his glass on the ground for the earth spirits and the ancestors. Everywhere before a great tree is cut down, an offering will be placed at its base. Offerings are given to the "little people" when medicinal herbs are gathered in the bush. Offerings are also made when crops are planted and when they are harvested.

The Africans, then, are a deeply religious people. But it is wrong to conclude, as some observers have on the basis of shallow impressions, that Africans are obsessed by fears of the supernatural powers that surround them. An African authority on the religion of the Yoruba concludes that it "permeates their lives so much that . . . it forms the theme of songs . . . , finds vehicles in myths, folktales [some of which we know as Uncle Remus stories], proverbs, and sayings." All this, as well as psychological security in a world of complex forces, is what his religion offers an African.

CHECK-UP

1. What have been our sources of information on sub-Saharan Africa? What allowances must be made in using them?

2. What was the role of a tribal chief? His responsibilities?

3. Why was the land important? What was the concept of land use and ownership?

4. How was work divided between men and women?

5. Why was plural marriage approved? What is bride-wealth? What is a patrilineal family? A matrilineal family? Why is "legal" descent important?

6. Explain the difference between the immediate family, the extended family, and the clan. What is the role of each?

7. What are age-grades? Why are they important? What values and tasks do children learn?

8. What are African views of the Creator? What are nature deities? The "little people" of the forest?

9. What part do ancestors play in African religions? How do Africans view the soul?

10. What is the role of a diviner? In what different ways do Africans worship?

The Oral Tradition

No attempt to understand any culture can be complete without an informed look at its arts. Such a look is especially important for sub-Saharan Africa, which is richly endowed in many art forms. It has an extensive oral literature. Its music, dance, and woodcarving have had worldwide influence since the end of World War I. Its peoples have excelled in the production of brass, bronze, and fired-clay sculpture, in ivory carving, weaving, and decorative leatherwork and beadwork, since long before their earliest contact with the West.

In a book of this nature it is impossible to discuss the special characteristics of each outstanding art-producing group, much less to show the variation in style within groups. Only a few examples can be given to suggest the vitality of all the African arts and to show that the arts cannot be separated from African life.

Africa has a rich heritage of tales and legends.

There is no group, no matter how small, isolated, or poor in economic resources, that lacks a lively oral literary tradition. Everywhere the family elders could recount the adventures of gods and men in ancient times and especially the adventures of the important ancestors of the group, beginning with its founder. The prosperous kingdoms and the ruling regional chiefs had professional performing groups to keep a record of ancestral deeds in song and to entertain at court.

The accounts—myths, legends, chronicles —known throughout Africa as "histories" were told by elders. More immediate (and more entertaining) were the tales told nightly around a mother's or grandmother's fire while the evening meal was cooking, in the men's houses of the compound or kraal, among groups of adolescents, and in the initiation camps.

A famous Dahomean storyteller explained, "We in Dahomey say that tales tell of things which never happened and are made up by people. History is the true story, and the life of Dahomey is based on history. But one learns from the tale what one can."

Ashanti legend tells that stories were originally the property of the sky-god and bore his name. But by performing a series of seemingly impossible feats, the trickster Anansi (Spider) bought from the sky-god the right to have the stories renamed Anansi Stories. (In the New World there are many stories called by his name in Surinam, Guyana, Jamaica, and elsewhere in the Caribbean area.)

Dahomean diviners say that, "Everything that happens on earth has happened in the sky before." And the diviners call on the repertory (stock) of oral tales and legends in reading a person's fortune.

Tales usually have an opening formula which is a dialogue between the storyteller and his audience. In the Ivory Coast there is this opening formula:

Teller:	I'll tell a tale.
Listeners:	Let's hear it.
Teller:	It isn't altogether true.
Listeners:	Let's hear it.
Teller:	But neither is all a lie.

This opening sets the stage for an interchange between storyteller and audience, and thus begins a dramatized performance in which the audience joins in song and in exclamations of approval. (Africans interacted with their audiences long before American theater companies introduced the technique.)

There is a wide variety of stories.

Of the various types of African tales recorded, the animal tales are the best known. This is not only because the animal tales are many and told widely, but because the Br'er Rabbit stories which were published by Joel Chandler Harris in the last quarter of the nineteenth century became fixed in the minds of collectors of tales as the "pure" African stories, whereas other types were not "truly" African.

The fact is that in any group, in any part of the continent, many kinds of tales are told besides tales of animal-tricksters. In Dahomey, for example, there are animal-trickster tales centering about Tortoise and Rabbit, tales about the adventures of orphans, twins, hunters, precocious (unusually advanced) children; tales of kings and commoners, of men and women. They are dramatic or comic stories on themes that apply to human experience everywhere: gratitude and ingratitude, loyalty and betrayal, fidelity and infidelity, jealousy between co-wives, rivalry between brothers.

The animal-trickster tales show the least variation in plot in their distribution over the African continent. The trickster is a small animal, intelligent, cunning, and without scruples. He victimizes a series of his fellow creatures, but there is usually at least one animal who is his special bait. This victim is larger and stronger than the trickster, and not very bright, and the trickster often makes a fool of him. However, the trickster is not always a winner. In one tale told in Ghana, Anansi gathers up all the wisdom of the world in a calabash (gourd) and decides to keep it all for himself by hiding it in a treetop. He puts the calabash against his chest and begins to climb a tree, but can make no progress. His young son watching him tells him to put the calabash on his back. In anger that his son should have the wisdom which he lacked, Anansi dashes the calabash to the ground, and wisdom spreads throughout the world.

The stories about hunters and twins—and twins are often hunters—are long dramatic tales of adventures in distant forests inhabited by the great animals and supernatural beings. The hunter is the culture hero; he explores new lands, finds new settlements for his family, and gains knowledge of magic and magic cures from the "little people." If he is a twin, he enjoys the powers given him by the spirit-guardian of twins.

Orphan stories deal with what we might call the "Cinderella" theme; the successful outcome for the orphan is, however, brought about by the dead mother instead of the fairy-godmother. The precocious children, who derive special powers from their ancestors, pit their strength, skill, and trickery against giants and ogres. These are the tall tales, full of extravagant fantasy.

Stories of everyday life are popular. It is in the stories of the everyday world, of the experiences of ordinary men and women that the gifted storyteller shows his ability. He enlarges on traditional incidents, introduces comic asides, and makes his audience part of the story. In the excellence of his imitation, the aptness of the songs he introduces or may even improvise (make up) to refer to some current event, he makes of these tales, whether dramatic or comic, theater of the first order.

A much favored type of story is based on a theme that involves three possible choices, or three incidents to test an issue. At the end of the story the listeners enter into a lively discussion about the choice made by the hero or whether the tests proved the point. The comments may be witty, serious, or comic.

A story from Dahomey has a theme of "testing loyalties":

There was a hunter who hunted. Good. This man was also a good farmer. So his best friend came and asked him to work in his field. He named the day. The diviner came and asked him to come and work in his field. He named the same day. And his father-in-law came and asked him to come to his field. And he, too, named the same day.

On the appointed day, the hunter took his gun and went hunting. He shot at an animal but did not stop to see whether he had killed it. He left at once for his father-in-law's field, and once there explained that since his best friend and his diviner had also named the same day for work in their fields, he went hunting to bring back a deer for his father-in-law's feast that evening. "But when I shot, I killed a man." The father-in-law ordered him to leave at once. "You killed a man belonging to the king, and now you come here to hide!"

The hunter next went to his diviner with the same story. The diviner exclaimed: "You gave me money and I gave you your destiny. You killed a man belonging to the king, and now you come here to hide. . . . You cannot hide in my house!"

The hunter then went to his friend and told him the sad tale. The friend asked him if he had told anyone that he had killed a man. "No, I told no one." So his friend took his hoe and said, "Come, let us go bury him." And the ending is: "In the life Mawu (the Creator) gave me, I wanted to know whom one could follow until death—friend, diviner, or father-in-law. . . . It is the friend who is first."

Proverbs serve many purposes. No group in sub-Saharan Africa is without proverbs. The fine Nigerian novelist, Chinua Achebe, tells us that for the Ibo the proverb is the palm oil with which words are eaten. In the African literary tradition the proverb adds savor to argument and topical comment. It is used to instruct, to admonish, to present a case in court, to start or parry a verbal attack, to soothe, to caution. Many tales, particularly those told to and by children, have moral endings which make use of proverbs.

The Dahomean proverb—*Humor governs the world well*—expresses an attitude toward life. It is also a direct reference to the traditional role of satire in tales. Humor, biting or comic, is an inseparable part of storytelling, whether used by professional storytellers or in the family compounds on any night, or dramatized in song by trained performing societies.

The second proverb, from the Ashanti of Ghana, has been widely reported in varied phrasing from the entire continent: *The Creator says, "I have sent sickness into the world, but I have also sent cures."* This reflects another attitude toward life, an attitude which recognizes the trials that beset man but refuses to be passive to fate. For if the Creator has provided "cures," then it is up to man to seek them out —to strive, to hope, to overcome.

A third proverb expresses a theme which recurs with many variations in tales and song: *All showing of teeth is not a laugh.* Here is the clearly sounded note of caution, of not being taken in easily.

Here are some random proverbs, again of wide distribution throughout Africa:

When you place your tongue in pawn, you cannot redeem it.

The poor man does not choose his sleeping place.

Shame hurts more than a wound.

If gold dust had no value, it would be called sand.

War lies in wait on a narrow path.

Praise-songs are found throughout sub-Saharan Africa. The term "praise-song" for the poetry of sub-Saharan Africa is known from the Wolof (page 266) in the northwest to the Xhosa (page 250) in the south, from the peoples of the Guinea Forest belt to those of East Africa, where long epic poems that intone praises of the great cattle herds and great warriors have been recorded.

The Wolof, as we have seen, list the professional praise-singers—men and women—among their social classes. Praise-singers are not only entertainers, they are the custodians of traditional history as well. Though their social position may be low, many praise-singers may have considerable influence. For while their songs "praise," they can also "scandalize" a name. They have the right to mock, and even insult, without being punished.

A scene from the novelette *Karim*, published in 1934 by Ousmane Socé, Senegalese writer and diplomat, tells us about the role of these entertainers in everyday social life. Karim is wooing a popular young lady. He has a rival in her cousin. The two suitors, escorted by singers, friends, and guitarists, appear before the girl. There follows a traditional battle in song between the rival singing groups. Victory goes to the side most acclaimed by the audience.

A Xhosa professor of literature describes his own peoples' praise-songs and the social role of praise-singers: "the bard who is composer and public reciter was versed in tribal history and lore, as well as being witty. He had a position of honor in the community." He also explains, "the African traditional praise-poem is not, as most whites believe, just a song of praise. . . . The praises are primarily the happenings in and around the tribe during the reign of a given chief, praising the worthy, decrying what is unworthy." In other words, these praises are histories in verse; they serve as social commentary. They can be epics of the trials and struggles of a people, as when they tell of the pressures of the whites to take the land, end the people's freedom, and change their ways of life.

A passage from the novel *Chaka* shows a less formal use of the praise-song among the Zulu. The young Chaka (or Shaka, pages 253–254), a despised and tormented herdboy, kills a lion unaided. "The affair of the lion caused a good deal of jealousy in the village; the young men and warriors felt ashamed when everyone pointed to Chaka." And the girls composed a song of admiration. In an aside the author tells us, "there is nothing more galling for a person than to be sung at by women in mockery and contempt, just as there is nothing so pleasant as when they sing one's praises."

Yet another type of praise-song was found among the Bemba of Zambia: "Old men, usually blind, sang songs [in] praise of their chief. . . . Dreams would come to them in the night, and in the morning they would wake and say, 'I have dreamed good things' . . . and they would walk round and round the village singing so that the chief's heart would be lightened, and he would give them great rewards."

The Dahomeans say frankly that the imagery of praise is designed to flatter. "Not only chiefs and important people like flattery, but the gods, too, like praise." They distinguish the praise-singers who have a good memory and merely repeat traditional phrasing from those who have a "heart that understands much." These last are the creative poets. In the modern idiom, it would be said that they had "soul."

There are other forms of poetry. Not all songs are praise-songs. A Dahomean lament comments obliquely on the fate of Dahomey under foreign rule, while singing about a succession of deaths in the family:

Sadness came to us and you laughed,
   Your day will come;
Sadness came to the trees and the vines laughed,
   The day of the vines will come;
The water had grief and the fish laughed,
   The day of the fish will come.*

A nonreligious song ends with a well-known proverb:*

When I am on the river
I whisper and say,
"Flow softly,"
And for that my two feet
Know the earth of the farther bank;
One who is in a boat at sea,
Does not quarrel with the boatman.

There are also ritual songs which are sung to nature deities. An example is this one the Gabon (guh-*bohn'*) Pygmies sing to their Rainbow God after a thunderstorm:*

Rainbow, O Rainbow!
You who shine all high, so high,
Above the great forest,
Amid the black clouds,
Dividing the dark sky.

You have thrown,
Winner in the contest,
The Thunder that growled,
Growled so loud, irritated,
Was his anger against us?

Amid the black clouds,
Dividing the dark sky,
Like a knife slicing an overripe fruit,
Rainbow, Rainbow!

And he has taken flight,
Thunder, the killer of men,
Like the antelope before the panther,
And he has taken flight,
Rainbow, Rainbow!

Mighty bow of the Hunter on high,
Of the Hunter who pursues the herd of clouds
Like a herd of frightened elephant;
Rainbow, tell him our thanks.

Tell him: "Be not angry!"
Tell him: "Be not vexed!"
Tell him: "Do not kill us!"
For fear has seized us.
Rainbow, tell him.

* From *Dahomean Narrative: A Cross-Cultural Analysis* by Melville J. and Frances S. Herskovits (Evanston, Ill.: Northwestern University Press, 1958). Reprinted by permission.

* Translated by Frances and Jean Herskovits from *Les Pygmées de la Forêt Equatoriale* by R. P. Trilles (Paris: Bloud and Gay, 1931). Reprinted by permission.

And the Dahomeans address the Sun God thus:

Softly, softly, Lisa-o,
Softly, O Sun-God,
Do not ravish the world.
Ram pawing the earth with hooves of flame,
Ram pounding the earth with horns of fire,
Do not ravish the world,
Do not destroy us.*

CHECK-UP

1. What types of literature are likely to be included in the oral tradition of a tribe?

2. What are some of the best-known types of African tales? What are some typical themes and subjects?

3. How do storytellers make the telling of a tale a theatrical experience?

4. What purposes are served by proverbs? Explain one of the proverbs given in the text. What attitude toward life does it reflect? What lesson does it teach?

5. What is a praise-song? What purposes do praise-songs serve? What other types of song are there?

Music in Sub-Saharan Africa

Music is important in African life. "The African is born, named, initiated into manhood [and womanhood], armed, warriored, housed, betrothed, wedded, and buried to music." This statement, written in 1932 about East Africa, reflects the importance of music to life throughout Africa. Musical performances are held in the village square, the street, the courtyard, and for many groups in Africa, the marketplace.

In broad terms we can group the characteristics of African music within three major areas:

1. *West Coast.* The music of the coastal peoples from the Gambia to northern Angola, as described by a specialist, places a strong emphasis on percussion instruments, and uses a "hot" rhythm. Drums are essential in most types of music played.

2. *East Coast.* Music of the East African area from the Horn of the continent to eastern South Africa and including Mozambique, with its remarkable Chopi musicians (see page 282), differs from West Coast music in the types of musical instruments used, the restricted role of drums, and the "absence of 'hot' rhythms."

3. *Central Africa.* The music of Central Africa, in the heart of the continent, differs from that of the West Coast, says one authority,

* From a translation by Frances Herskovits in *Poetry Magazine* (Vol. XLV). Reprinted by permission.

"in terms of degree rather than kind." More intensive study may show closer relationships.

Music may reflect cultural exchange. Music, literary resources, and art styles are excellent transmitters of culture. They appeal to deep-seated impulses, and because they are adopted by a people and not imposed by outsiders, they are not resisted. Modified usually by the techniques, needs, and values of those who adopt them, borrowed art forms achieve identities of their own. Thus there are regional, local, and even individual styles of related forms. It is important to stress such individual styles because so much thinking about Africa assumes collective activity in all aspects of life. This view is too often overemphasized. In the final analysis, in Africa, as elsewhere, an individual is a master drummer, a famous composer, a dance leader who excels at creating new dances. The Dahomeans, as we noted, call these creative individuals those whose "heart understands much," those who, each in his own way, bring something new, emotionally stirring, and pleasurable to their creations.

Music may blend a traditional style with influences from outside. Historically, the principal outside influences have been Islam and the Christian missions. Both continue to be factors in the African scene. A more recent influence is that of music from the western hemisphere. American jazz and more recently rock and roll, the Caribbean calypso, the Cuban rumba, and the Brazilian samba have been incorporated into such new musical forms as the highlife (a sort of reverse lend-lease, for we know that these New World forms are themselves African-influenced). This influence from the outside is shaping the musical styles of dance music throughout the African continent. And both intra-African and external influences today penetrate even remote villages by means of the transistor radio. In the cities television, films, and records increase the musical interchange.

Music in Ghana reflects the richness of the musical heritage. To illustrate briefly just one set of musical activities and resources of West Africa, let us look at Ghana. The distinguished Ghanaian musicologist, Professor Nketia (un-kay-*ty'*ah), singles out two types of music: (1) the traditional music of the "organized" or ritual event, (2) the "spontaneous" music of what might be called the recreational event.

"Spontaneous combinations," he tells us, "enjoy the greatest freedom of expression. [They draw freely] on the musical repertory of the society, or better still, improvise." For musical events that are "organized" there is set traditional music. Musical types for girls' puberty festivals and worship of the gods are "narrowly restricted," though there is some latitude for the dirges sung by women. Professor Nketia adds an important observation which holds for all of sub-Saharan Africa:

One finds everywhere that festivals are protracted [drawn out]. . . . Simple ceremonies which can be performed in a few minutes take a whole morning, a whole afternoon, or the best part of the night in order to allow for the enjoyment of the music and dancing. . . . The music of worship is not cultivated merely out of dread of the gods but because it is emotionally satisfying.

The principal instrument of Ghanaian music is the drum. It comes in a variety of shapes and sizes. There is the important battery of drums made out of hollowed-out tree trunks; there are calabash (gourd) drums and pressure drums shaped like hourglasses. Some are played with one stick, or two; some by hand or stick-and-hand technique; and the pressure drum, by armpit control and a stick.

Other instruments include flutes and trumpets of varied types, rattles, gongs, bells, percussion sticks, bamboo or gourd stamping tubes, hand pianos, xylophones, and stringed instruments.

While there are instrumental ensembles, particularly ensembles of drums—the famous "talking drums"—or sometimes horns which play texts of oral literature (proverbs chiefly), the more usual combinations are instruments and voices. The player of a stringed instrument is often the vocalist, and he may sing solo or be joined by a chorus. Stringed bands were, in fact, important traditionally among the Akan peoples and are important in modern music. Nevertheless, the most common accompaniment to song is drumming, often joined by handclapping of singers and audience.

Song types in Ghana include children's songs used in games, stories, and children's rituals; men's songs for communal labor, warfare, and hunting; women's songs such as dirges, grinding and other domestic songs, and songs used in women's rites and recreation. There are also musical types for chiefs (and songs for modern politics), and religious songs. Professor Nketia writes:

The interplay of leader and performers results in the alternation of solo and chorus, or . . . call and response in songs; in drumming, the contrasting parts of the master drummer and one or more secondary drummers; in flute ensembles, alternating or sometimes intertwining parts of leading flute and the response flutes. . . . This arrangement gives the leading singer or player a free hand in improvisation. . . . The . . . arrangement of pieces may also be determined by consideration of the dance routine . . . in which dancers and master musicians collaborate in the unfolding of the dance drama.

These drum-dancers from Lesotho reveal the exuberance and total involvement which characterize African dance at its best. The farmers (top) illustrate another instance of the interweaving of ritual and everyday life. As they hoe the ground to prepare it for seed, they chant in unison.

281

The Chopi are outstanding musicians. Among the Chopi of Mozambique xylophone orchestras are the major type of musical expression. The Chopi are artists of such musical sophistication and accomplishment as to astound even Africans who can speak with pride of their own particular traditional musical resources.

Xylophone orchestras have been used in dance performances for centuries. In the 1560's a Portuguese priest reported, "Their dance represents all the actions of warfare, [such] as surrounding the enemy, being surrounded, open warfare, conquering, being conquered, taking wood and water by force, and everything else which can occur in war, all very appropriately expressed."

Orchestras are found in every large village of the Chopi country. A western musician tells us: "To hear an orchestra of twenty or more players performing with absolute assurance, improvising upon the theme or coming together in perfect unison . . . is a grand musical experience." Important chiefs have their own orchestras of *Ngodo* (un-*goh'*doh) performers. A student of this music tells us that a *Ngodo* is an orchestral dance in nine to eleven movements. "Each movement is distinctive and separate. . . . The whole performance lasts about 45 minutes." A new Ngodo is composed every two years. The lyrics to the songs are composed before the music. These may be gay, sad, or topical. They are not songs for war dances. They satirize overbearing authorities and take sly digs at the pretentious, protest against injustice, and mock intrigue. Writes western musicologist Hugh Tracey, "What better sanction could be brought to bear upon those who outrage the ethics of the community than to know that the poets will have you [shamed or ridiculed] in their next composition?"

To the Western observer commenting on "the apparent [contradiction] that even the saddest songs are sung to gay music," the Chopi explanation was, "We must dance our sorrow."

When the Chopi composer has the verses fixed in his mind, he sits down at his xylophone and works out the melody; once his right hand has mastered the tune, he begins to fill in the harmonies with his left. The "score" completed, he is ready for the dance leader. Together they work out the dance routine. Songs as well as dances are then taught to the dancers. Singing is in unison, with occasional harmonic passages performed by the leader. "It is against this highly developed pattern of melody, contramelody, and action that Chopi poetry is heard," says Tracey.

To become a skilled xylophone player takes many years. Learning begins early. Tracey notes: "A father will take his seven or eight year old boy and sit him between his knees while he plays. The boy will hold the two beaters . . . while his father clasps his hands over his son's and continues to play the usual way. . . . The boy soon got to know the feel of the instrument and after a few months would be able to strike any note he wanted." Children also make their own practice xylophones. A lad of twelve who was allowed to play with a Ngodo orchestra was considered a prodigy. He was related to the leader of the Ngodo and came from a family of generations of famous Ngodo leaders. As in any culture, musical genius is rare, but the ideal is to become a leader of a Ngodo orchestra. Such a position makes one a composer of lyrics and music for all the movements of the orchestral dance performance.

CHECK-UP

1. How is music closely linked to every stage of African life?

2. How does African music reflect cultural exchange? Individuality?

3. What is the difference between traditional music and spontaneous music? How is music used in ceremonies? What are some different types of song?

4. Who are the Ngodo performers? What role do they play in Chopi society?

After the First World War, the West "discovered" African art. Exhibits in Paris, in Munich, in London, and in Brussels, and the comments of artists, art critics, and art historians reflected a steadily growing interest in the arts of Africa. European enthusiasm for American jazz (Europeans never doubted the influence of Africa on jazz), the publication in France and Germany of collections of African legends and tales, many of the Uncle Remus type; African-influenced dances, such as the Charleston, all created audiences for things African. In the United States in the 1920's a surge of interest in African achievement, centered in New York City, crystallized in what was called "the Negro Renaissance."

Actually the "discovery" came some twenty years earlier. In 1897 the city of Benin, capital of the once great Benin kingdom (pages 237–238), was sacked by the British in reprisal for the murders of an official mission. The booty the soldiers brought back to England consisted of several thousand pieces—principally bronze and ivory carvings. They quickly found their way into important collections (some private) in England and especially Germany. Indeed, so eager were the Germans to acquire a massive collection of Benin art for the Berlin museum that their agents were at the Liverpool docks waiting for the soldiers' return. In the United States the Field Museum of Natural History in Chicago acquired the first Benin pieces in 1899.

But the great African influence on the art of the early twentieth century—an influence that has since become part of the mainstream of contemporary art—was not the Benin bronzes or ivory carvings. It was African woodcarving —sculpture in wood.

At the turn of the century a group of young artists living in Paris were in rebellion against what might be called the Arts' Establishment. The mood to experiment, to create new forms, was strong. The response of these "rebels" to African woodcarving was immediate and enthusiastic. African carvings began to be sought not as curiosities, but as works of art. The fame of African art spread. The earliest art objects to win acclaim were understandably from the French African colonies—the western Sudan and the Ivory Coast, and later French Equatorial Africa and the Belgian Congo.

AFRICAN SCULPTURE

There are major art-producing areas in Africa. The peoples who have produced the outstanding works of African art inhabit the Atlantic coast from Senegal to northwestern Angola, and the inland area watered by the Niger and Congo Rivers and their tributaries, including the Cameroon highland area, and small regions in the area extending to the African great lakes. In general terms this is also the area of peoples whose music is characterized by "hot" rhythms. Not all peoples of this vast area are producers of art objects, and not all groups who produce art achieve overall excellence. What is impressive is that there are so many groups with the tradition of master-carvers who have originated or taught the art forms for which each group is deservedly famous.

Many peoples excel in woodcarving. Sculpture in wood was developed by sedentary (settled) farming peoples whose lives centered in village communities, and who held to a traditional way of life despite pressures of conquest. Two important ritual cycles celebrated this way of life. One related to the human life cycle, with special ceremonial emphasis on the attainment of manhood and womanhood, and on the funeral and commemorative rites that dramatized the end of life on earth and its beginnings in the world of the ancestral generations. The other cycle, related to the first, was of rituals concerned with the fertility of the fields and the yield of forest and stream. These rituals were performed for nature deities and all those forces that protected communal and individual well-being and thwarted enemy designs.

It is probable that both the range and variety of styles of woodcarving are due in no small measure to the fact that it is the most democratic of African arts. In nearly all of this vast area wood is plentiful and anyone can easily obtain it. This has encouraged the carving of a vast and varied number of human and animal figures. Especially important are masks—initiation masks, ancestral masks, secret-society masks, masks with political functions, masks used in entertainment to disguise the identity of social critics.

Masks have many functions. What is the role of this most democratic of African arts—woodcarving—in everyday living? A detailed study made of the masks of the Dan, who live in the Liberian forests and the savanna country of the Ivory Coast, sheds light on this question.

The Dan are famous for their masks, which are made in different styles to conform to distinct traditional functions. There are initiation masks, peacemaking masks, masks to inspire respect, and amusing masks. At the initiation camp, the "school of art and custom," boys carve masks with elaborate headdresses. These masks are carved to look beautiful so that people will associate good luck and happiness with the initiation.

The large peacemaking mask, with its animal-like features, is impressive. Its function is to impose peace, not only within the village, but also in wars between different towns or chiefdoms. The mask comes and sits down on the battlefield, raising its hand to command peace. "Nobody would dare to brandish his sword after that." The leopard-society mask both complements and supercedes the peacemaking mask. Bearing the function of lawgiver, the leopard-society mask ranks above all the others. It is the court of highest appeal which passes the sentence of death.

284

Most people think of masks as covering only the head. This photograph of a Makishi dancer from Barotse province in Zambia shows that the mask is actually the entire costume. Accompanied by ritual music and song, the mask is art in motion.

The masks whose function it is to entertain, though less important, are more numerous, and their public appearances are more frequent. They are divided into dancing masks and fault-finding masks. The dancing masks sing the praise of chiefs and warriors, bring good news, and in dances imitate animals and townsmen. The fault-finding masks "play rough."

Though the functions of the various masks differ, masks are as one if some offense is committed against any of them. Disrespect to one is the affair of all. In serious cases, the punishment comes from the leopard-society mask.

The blacksmith is closely tied into ideas about masks. As the one who made the tools which carve the masks, he is regarded as their father, and has complete immunity against action by the masks.

There is a wide range of carved objects. The range of objects ornamented with carvings is wide—musical instruments such as drums and trumpets; chieftain's stools, whose symbolic carvings have traditional ritual and political importance; doors and locks to granaries and shrines; house posts, ceremonial food bowls and food ladles, cups, goblets, combs, headrests, and containers for cosmetics. To this list may be added twin figures, fertility dolls, staffs used during dances, images on altars and in outdoor shrines, carvings used in divination, and emblems of political office.

While there were professional carvers, many a youth learned to carve during his retreat in the initiation camp. Apprentices came to renowned master-carvers from great distances, and carvers were known to travel outside their own group on invitation from an important patron. It is interesting to note that all accounts report that these professional carvers did not earn a living from their art, but had to supplement it through farming or other gainful tasks.

Africa has a long tradition of metal sculpture. Metals—in contrast to wood—were costly, scarce, and usually available only to rulers, ruling families, and men of substance. Copper, brass, and bronze bars were brought from across the Sahara and later by European traders in exchange for slaves (or gold). Some copper is believed to have reached West Africa from the Katanga and Zambia mines in Central Africa in the days of pre-European contact. Gold, scarce and precious, was not much used for sculptured art objects until modern times. Only in modern Ghana did local mining make possible lavish use of gold for political emblems for rulers and their retainers, and even generally for personal adornment.

The most famous metal sculpture is thus of brass or bronze. Both historically and artistically the most productive centers of this art are found in present-day Nigeria. A Dutch visitor, in describing the splendor of Benin in 1668, mentioned a royal palace the size of the city of Haarlem in Holland, its many columns decorated with bronze plaques. These plaques, which have been much studied since their introduction to the western world, represent scenes in the lives of kings and retainers, the costumes and ornaments indicating the rank of each. They also show Portuguese officials and soldiers who visited Benin in the fifteenth and sixteenth centuries. There were also bronze sculptures, a large number of which had ritual use and a place on the altars of the royal ancestors. Large bronze leopards served as royal emblems and stood at the entrance to the king's audience chamber. The ruler and his retinue and favorites wore brass pendants and other sculptured objects.

Tradition tells that in 1280 the Benin ruler invited an Ife (ee'fay) brass-caster to come to Benin. At that time sculpture in brass or bronze was a flourishing art in Ife. The superb Ife heads are of such astonishing perfection of modeling and detail as to rank with the classical sculpture of the Graeco-Roman tradition. The figures are believed to be commemorative heads of important political and religious persons. These naturalistic portrait heads and figures were cast some 200 years before Columbus reached America. One can only speculate about the complexity and affluence of the culture that produced the artists who created these masterpieces in bronze. Their creators could not have achieved such mastery of bronze without a tradition of metal sculpture.

Recent archaeological discoveries have brought to light examples of bronze objects that scientific dating shows to be earlier than those from Ife. These have come from excavations near Awka, east of the Niger River. Archaeology may uncover additional sculpture in western Nigeria and provide an answer to the puzzle of why no later work to equal the Ife bronzes has been found.

Many interesting art objects in metal are found from Dakar in Senegal to the Congo. From Ghana comes an unusual form of metal sculpture—the Ashanti gold weights. Used for weighing gold dust, the gold weights are miniature in size, naturalistic or stylized. They include geometric designs and representations of insects, animals, birds, and humans. Some are symbols of proverbs, and many are modeled with fantasy and humor.

In Dahomey brass-casting was carried on by a family group of metalworkers (as it is today), whose production was mainly by royal command. Small figures of animals and humans were often arranged in group compositions with a realistic central figure or figures and stylized accompanying ones. These brass sculptures were chiefly prestige items, used for display and as gifts of royalty to visiting embassies and court favorites.

The Bamum of the Cameroons specialized in brass sculptures—large masks, elephant heads, small pendant masks, figurines, and bowls of pipes. The Bakota of Gabon nailed thin hammered sheets of brass or copper, or sometimes both, to religious and ancestral figures of wood.

Ivory and stone carving reveal great variety.
The most famous ivory carvings are identified with Benin, the most numerous with the Congo, though small numbers of ivory objects have been found in much of Africa.

In Benin there was a guild of master-carvers in ivory. Working in a special quarter of the capital under the patronage of the king, they produced elaborately carved tusks to place on the altars of the royal ancestors, ivory trumpets, statuettes, masks of differing sizes, goblets, gongs, carvings used by diviners, and objects of personal adornment.

The centers of ivory carving in the Congo were in the north and east. Carved tusks were treated with red palm oil. Generations of use added new dimensions to the play of light and shade on the patterns cut into the ivory. Outstanding among the Congo ivory carvings are delicate miniature pendant masks and statuettes which show strong and imaginative mastery of the medium. Their uncluttered surfaces are in marked contrast to the elaborate Benin traceries.

Of historic as well as artistic interest are the stone carvings found scattered by the hundreds in fields in Guinea and Sierra Leone (sih-*ehr'*uh lih-*ohn'*), those discovered in a grove north of Ife in Nigeria, and in a deserted cemetery in Angola, in what had been part of the Bakongo kingdom. They are, with only two known exceptions, of sandstone, a soft, easily worked stone. Not only is the date when they were carved unknown, but—except for those most recently found in Angola—the peoples among whom they originated are unknown.

Stone carvings in Guinea and Sierra Leone, all representations of humans, range in size from less than four inches to seven or eight. Their facial features leave no doubt as to their sub-Saharan origin. The Kissi of Guinea have incorporated them into their ritual cycle. In every village there is an "image of the dead," as they are called. Those that have been revealed through dreams or through divination as representing an ancient family ancestor are placed on the family altar. The many others remain anonymous, but are nevertheless regarded as ancestors of earlier inhabitants or their guardian spirits. In Sierra Leone the Mende make offerings for good harvests to the stone carvings discovered on their land.

The Nigerian stone carvings average close to two feet in height and consist of groups of seated figures with facial markings which recall those of the Ife bronzes. The varied facial expressions suggest that they are portrait figures, and the differing quality of the figures indicates the work of many craftsmen. They may represent ancestral figures from the north, brought to the Yoruba grove for safety from threatened destruction by invading Muslim Fulani in the early nineteenth century.

Stone carvings of the Cross River area in eastern Nigeria differ from any reported from sub-Saharan Africa. Cylindrical in shape, they stand upright on the graves of clan heads. The head only is treated with partial realism, and the features appear engraved rather than carved. These carvings are reported to have been executed over several centuries and as late as 1900.

Terra-cotta figurines are the oldest African sculpture known. The oldest known African sculptures are terra-cotta (fired clay) human and animal figurines found in a tin mine in northern Nigeria in 1943. These pieces, said to belong to an ancient Nok culture, are dated between 500 B.C. and 200 A.D.

Within recent years archaeologists have found human representations in terra-cotta in Mali, southwestern Ivory Coast, and the Lake Chad area. Everywhere the terra-cottas were found on graves or associated with burials. They are probably several centuries old, though in the Ivory Coast and Ghana clay and pottery images are still fashioned at time of burial or as commemorative images on graves or in shrines.

What is significant is that there is similarity in style between the Nigerian figures and those as far apart as Mali, the Ivory Coast, and Chad. This resemblance permits speculation about closer unity among the cultures of West Africa in pre-Islamic times.

Definitely in contact with each other were the regions that produced the Nok terra-cotta figurines and the Ife terra-cotta and bronze figures. There are similarities in their stylistic naturalism and in much specific detail.

The technique of working in terra-cotta, probably developed by the Nok culture, was adopted and refined in Ife (above).

GRAPHIC AND OTHER EXPRESSIVE ART FORMS

In the earlier discussion of the oral literary tradition impressive unities emerged for all of sub-Saharan Africa. All peoples told stories, used proverbs, and made up words to songs. Musical art forms and the dance, whether ritual or recreational, also existed in all societies, large or small, agricultural, pastoral, or nomadic. The combination of song, accompanying instruments, and the dance produced musical drama in densely populated areas, and what might be called "musical skits" in small communities.

In the production of the visual arts of whatever materials, and by whatever techniques,

African dress reveals as much sensitivity to beauty as do sculpture and music. From material woven in narrow strips of rich colors (above) comes the justly renowned kente cloth (top, right). In other areas designs play as important a role as color, as illustrated by this picture of Fulani women (below). The Zulu warrior (below right) has made the most of contrast; the bright colors of his dress glow richly against his dark skin.

there is no such overall distribution of these art forms. But outside the areas of outstanding art production people found pleasure in decoration, itself artistic expression.

Many peoples express art through personal adornment. Among the pastoral peoples, and in South and East Africa, decoration appeared mainly as personal adornment. The warriors had decorated shields and finely wrought spears; other people lavished attention on elaborate hair styles, body painting, the decorative use of animal skins, feathers, beads, metal ornaments, and costumes for ritual and festive social occasions. Many of the ornaments worn answered a twofold need: they gave pleasure as objects of beauty, and, having been treated by medicine men, afforded protection against human or supernatural ill-will.

The emphasis on the decorative and a superlative degree of artistry in personal adornment among the largely Muslim peoples of the western Sudan, northern Nigeria, and neighboring areas can be explained in religious terms. The Koran's prohibition on representing human and animal figures has limited artistic forms to geometric decorations, often, however, enhanced by use of colors. Abstract geometric designs decorate walls, leather work, mats, woven cloth, jewelry, basketry, metalwork, and pottery.

In the area of outstanding art production south of the Islamic regions the decorative arts are also present in many varieties. For example, titleholders in southern Iboland paint their compound walls in geometric designs; the carving on the little tables they use is also in geometric patterns.

Woven cloth is another form of art. Some important decorative art forms suggest unities in traditional values that go beyond regional differences. One is woven cloth. The silk *kente* cloths woven by the Ashanti are deservedly famous—and expensive. Weaving is done on narrow looms, and the long strips are sewn together to form great coverings worn much as the Romans wore their togas. The geometric patterns, no two of which are alike because each unit of design is a proverb, combine the red of the earth, the gold of the sun, the green of the forest, some blue, and some black in harmonious blends which are brilliant against the dark oiled skins of the wearers. Cloths of cotton may be as beautiful in different ways.

Other fine examples of artistic weaving are found throughout West Africa, and the Congo (Kinshasa) rafia cloths, with their geometric designs, are famous. The Dahomeans have expressed their artistry in their appliquéd cloths. Using European trade cloth of white, black, or gold as background, a special guild of cloth sewers formed symbolic compositions. Working under the patronage of the king, they sewed the great state umbrellas which sheltered the king and his attendants and the smaller ones for men of rank. They also sewed the ritual costumes of cult initiates and cloth hangings. (As with paintings and tapestries in western culture, these appliquéd cloths served as art objects, giving pleasure and showing status.)

Rock paintings are the oldest expression of African art. No discussion of African art would be complete without reference to the earliest African art known—the art of the Bushmen (see page 249). This art, found in North, South, and East Africa, consists of multi-colored rock paintings which depict scenes in the lives of the people. Hunters and the animals hunted, encounters with enemies, cattle raids—all are painted with such liveliness and feeling as to make them the outstanding graphic art produced in Africa, even though some paintings are given a date of 6000–5000 B.C. Although they disappeared from North Africa long ago, in southern Africa the Bushmen painted these rock paintings until the close of the last century. "The presence of this art in a way of life otherwise so meager offers striking comment on attempts to evaluate total ways of life as 'higher' or 'lower'," observes an Africanist scholar.

CHECK-UP

1. When was African art "discovered" by the West? What was the response?

2. What are some different types of African sculpture? For what purposes are sculptured objects used?

3. Why is woodcarving considered a democratic type of art? What different functions are served by masks?

4. What type of ivory carving was produced in Benin? The Congo? What is unique about the stone carvings found in Guinea and Sierra Leone?

5. What types of work were done in clay?

6. How is personal adornment a form of artistic expression? How has Islam influenced artistic expression?

7. Why can the handwoven cloth of the Ashanti and of Dahomey be considered a form of art?

8. What evidence is there of the artistic creativity of the Bushmen?

Summing Up

The discoveries of the twentieth century have brought remarkable examples of African art to world attention. Equally important, they have revealed the existence of African cultures that must be taken into account in revisions of the record of world civilization.

The sub-Saharan African cultures, for all their individual differences, share one very important feature: in all of them all aspects of life are closely linked. Family life (in widest terms), a group's economy, its political roles, its religion, art, music, performing skills, and also its food habits, its codes of behavior within the group and with outsiders—in short, all that is permitted, all that is forbidden, all that is approved or disapproved form a unified whole.

In its broadest outlines this unity is not uniquely African. Throughout history most human groups have seen a unity in the way they lived, in their past and present, and in their hopes for the future. This was true of western culture until the changing scientific outlook and the massive technological changes characteristic of the period since the Industrial Revolution brought about an increasing secularization of life. In modern western culture economic systems, family structure, politics, law, religion, art, music, literature—each falls into a separate category and constitutes a separate part of people's lives. But most of the world's peoples, throughout time, have not made such separations; for them, and specifically for Africans, life could not be so divided.

Recognizing this African way of ordering life, observers have come to a conclusion (until recently seldom challenged) that change in one aspect of life must disrupt, even destroy, all others. Thus, it has often been argued that the introduction of Christianity (or Islam), western education, western technology—all these were bound to destroy African traditions. But this view is based on three incorrect assumptions: (1) that in the face of a challenge from outside (a challenge clearly believed overpowering by those with open or less conscious racial biases), African culture will crumble. (2) That, given a choice, Africans will select what is western, modern, external. (3) That traditional cultures and especially African cultures are static, and therefore lack the flexibility to change according to choice and chance.

The fact is that Africans, like many other peoples, are bending their energies to meet the challenges of the twentieth century. But, since the three assumptions are wrong, Africans are intent on finding ways to "modernize" on their own terms. For accepting innovation is not new for Africa, and Africans have throughout their history met challenges. Africa's peoples have retained many aspects of centuries' old traditions, and in some cases have retained them with a total world view intact despite great pressures. It may not be the same view of life and the world that their ancestors had, but it is not necessarily less African because, as with our own way of life, it has changed through time.

Chapter Highlights

Can you explain?

compound	kinship	initiation	plural marriage
lineage	specialization	age-grade	bride-wealth
"histories"	communal labor	intensive farming	extended family
clan	matrilineal	patrilineal	immediate family

Can you identify?

kraal	Ife	Ngodo	praise-song
Chopi	Benin	spontaneous music	kente cloth
diviner	proverbs	nature deities	terra-cotta

What do you think?

1. What part did democracy play in African tribal life?

2. Why was storytelling an integral part of African life?

3. How does African family life differ from that in the United States? Consider the roles of the different members.

4. Would plural marriage be as advantageous in the United States as in Africa? Why?

5. Does the African child mature earlier than the American child? Why?

6. What purposes are served by the payment of bride-wealth? How does it differ from the western custom of a dowry?

7. Why is African literature closely linked to African life? Is this equally true in the United States? Why?

8. Are older people more respected in Africa than in the United States? Why?

9. Why are ancestors more important in African life than they are in American life?

10. Why has African sculpture impressed westerners?

11. How are all aspects of African life linked together? How does this differ from life in modern western countries?

12. Can change in one aspect of life disrupt all others? Why?

13. How did Africans adopt foreign cultural influences and modify them to suit an African identity?

Ancient American Civilizations

CHAPTER FOCUS

North America: From Hunters to Villagers
Mesoamerica: From Villages to Great States
South America: From Regionalism to Empire

Throughout the ages the serpent has been important to many religions. In the Americas, the Great Serpent Mound of the Mound Builders coils near a creek in Ohio. To the southwest, the Hopi still perform the snake dance as a climax to a nine-day ceremony. In this rare photograph (left) dancers emerge from the kivas bearing live snakes, which they look upon as messengers to the gods responsible for rain. Perhaps the most complex use of the serpent as a symbol was that which evolved in Mesoamerica around Quetzalcóatl, the Feathered Serpent God. In the sculpture above, an Aztec artist has successfully captured the fluid motion of the uncoiling serpent and the otherworldly expression of the god.

Some time between 40,000 and 20,000 B.C., long before the last Ice Age ended, bands of hunters began to drift into America over a land bridge which once connected Alaska with Siberia in northeastern Asia. Though these migrations from Asia were probably of small size, by 7000 B.C. man had spread all the way to Cape Horn in South America—a distance of some 11,000 miles. Although the northern regions were mostly ice-covered, large areas that today are desert or semi-desert were then fertile grasslands on which roamed mammoths, mastodons, and giant sloths as well as smaller animals and rodents. The hunters killed whatever they could, usually small animals, to satisfy their hunger. To add to their diet, they gathered roots, berries, and wild grains, among them the ancestor of modern corn. They did not think of storing food for times when game was scarce.

As the ice retreated, the climate became warmer and drier and much of the grassland became semi-desert or desert. The big game disappeared, and hunters became more dependent on food gathering. By 3500 B.C. squash, corn, and beans—which made up the basic diet of nearly all the American peoples—had begun to be cultivated. Since there was less need to travel long distances to find food, people began to band together in small villages. They continued to spend part of their time on hunting trips.

Eventually they discovered that clay could be shaped into pots and dishes and hardened by drying in the sun. Though more fragile than stoneware, this pottery took far less time and effort to make. By 1500 B.C. these elements—the cultivation of plants, the development of semi-permament villages, and the making of pottery—had resulted in sedentary (settled) agriculture in many parts of ancient America.

North America: From Hunters to Villagers

North America includes Mexico, but because Mexico has such a variety of civilizations, we shall discuss it as part of Mesoamerica in the next section. The peoples who settled America were misnamed Indians by Columbus, and the name stuck. To distinguish between them and the people of India, Americans are often called Amerinds.

Except for the Eskimos and Aleuts, Amerinds have a common, though unknown, origin. Because they had such a variety of cultures, it is impossible to discuss them in general terms. The variety of landscape in North America is reflected in the cultural differences that developed there before the Europeans arrived. We can classify these cultures under eight very broad headings: (1) Eskimo and the related but dissimilar Aleut, (2) Fishermen of the Northwest Coast, (3) the California peoples, (4) the Forest Peoples of Canada, (5) Peoples of the Eastern Woodlands, (6) the Mound Builders of the Southeast, (7) the Hunters of the Great Plains and the Southwest, and (8) the Villagers of the Southwest.

The Eskimos make maximum use of their environment. The Eskimos are not Amerinds, nor do they speak a language related to any Amerindian language. They probably appeared on the northern coast of North America about 2000 years ago. Their origin is a puzzle, for there do not appear to be any Eskimo traces in Asia.

The Eskimos are a prime example of a people who have made the most of what they have. To the highest degree they reflect a concept basic to many of the Amerinds—the need to be at harmony, rather than in conflict, with one's natural surroundings. Along the coast walrus, whales, fish, and seals were hunted; Eskimos living inland also hunted caribou. From the bone and ivory of sea animals they made harpoons, fishhooks, knives, needles, sleds, and goggles to limit the glare of sun on snow and ice; from the skins of seals and arctic animals they made warm weatherproof clothing and tents for summer use. Seal oil was used in lamps which gave both light and warmth. In their leisure time the people made carvings of bone and especially ivory and decorated them with scenes of their daily life. They even made use of their forbidding surroundings by using their natural deepfreeze to store meat, and some of them built houses of snow and ice.

The Eskimos did not develop agriculture, for it was impossible in the frozen wastes. Nor did they have any kind of central government. Because they depended upon hunting for their living, only a few people could be supported by the fish and game in any given area. The Eskimos thus lived in family groups, in houses of driftwood, whalebone, sod, and stone.

The Eskimos lived just one step away from famine. When times were particularly hard, old people or the very young were sometimes abandoned and left to freeze to death. This was a way of ensuring the strong and healthy with enough food to enable them to keep hunting. The old and very young could not contribute to the needs of the family, and were thus a serious drain on meager food supplies during times of famine. Generally, however, the family was closely knit, with each member doing his share to ensure survival.

Aleut culture is little developed. Related to the Eskimos but still a separate people are the Aleuts (*al'*ee-oots), who have posed considerable problems to archaeologists. Although they lived along the islands on the path of the migration from Asia, the earliest remains of Aleut origin come from the eastern part of the Arctic. Like the Eskimos, the Aleuts lived on the products of the sea. Their culture, however, was far less developed. Though the Aleuts made fine baskets and masks of driftwood, their weapons, clothing, and housing reflected a very simple level of culture.

The Northwest Coast Amerinds develop a complex economy without agriculture. From southern Alaska to what is today the state of Washington lived Amerinds who lacked pottery and agriculture but still developed villages and a high level of culture. The people of the Northwest Coast—the Haida (*hie'*dah), Kwakiutl (kwah-key-*oo*'t'l), Tlingit, and Tsimshian— apparently developed their complex culture without the influence of any other Amerinds, for their basic cultural traits are unique in America. Primarily fishermen, especially of salmon, they also hunted the wild animals of the forest and gathered seeds and berries. Since their main source of food came from one area, they were able to live in villages. Their houses, built of wooden planks, could hold as many as 50 people. Prominently displayed by each house, or even a part of it, was the family *totem pole.* These wooden poles were elaborately carved with figures representing the family *totem*—an animal spirit such as the bear or

Ancient American Civilizations

c. **1200**–c. **100** B.C.	Olmec civilization in Mexico
c. **1000**–c. **500** B.C.	Chavín de Huantar dominates northern Peru
c. **100** B.C.–c. **1000** A.D.	Nazca and Mochica cultures, Peru
c. **200** A.D.–c. **900** A.D.	Mesoamerican urban centers
c. **300**–c. **1000** A.D.	Height of Mayan civilization in Mesoamerica
c. **600**–c. **1000** A.D.	Tiahuanaco unites Andean cultures
c. **1000**	Toltecs invade Mayan region
c. **1325**	Tenochtitlán founded by Aztecs
c. **1427–1521**	Aztec state dominates Mesoamerica
c. **1438–1532**	Empire of the Incas unites Andean region

whale—and the history of an ancestor who had a special relationship with this spirit. The totem pole indicated who a family was; a stranger of the Bear people, for example, could expect to find hospitality in any house with the bear totem. Besides totem poles, the peoples of the Northwest Coast carved stone, bone, and masks of wood used in elaborate ceremonies and dances. For fishing they made sixty-foot dugout canoes. Their clothing, particularly blankets, was also decorated, as were baskets and boxes made out of one board which was steamed and bent into shape.

Like other Amerinds the Northwest peoples believed that one should live in harmony with nature. For example, if the salmon catch was more than was needed, they believed that the salmon spirits would punish them. Among the spirits in which they believed was a Raven, both a creator and a trickster, who delighted in making fools of people.

SIBERIA

ARCTIC OCEAN

Bering Strait

ESKIMO

ESKIMO

ALEUT

ESKIMO

PACIFIC OCEAN

TLINGIT

HAIDA

TSIMSHIAN

KWAKIUTL

Hudson Bay

NASCOPIE

CREE

ALGONQUIAN TRIBES

SHOSHONE

BLACKFOOT

OJIBWAY

SIOUX

Great Lakes

HURON
IROQUOIS

WYANDOT

DELAWARE

LENAPE

PAIUTE

CHUMASH

NAVAHO

PAWNEE

ATLANTIC OCEAN

HOPI
ZUNI
APACHE

HOHOKAM

COMANCHE

CHEROKEE

Mississippi R.

CREEK
NATCHEZ

Rio   Grande

Gulf of Mexico

Caribbean   Sea

SIBERIA

ARCTIC OCEAN

Bering Sea

ALASKA

Arctic   Circle

Maximum Extent of Glaciation

NORTH AMERICA

ATLANTIC OCEAN

GREAT PLAINS

MIDDLE

AMERICA

SOUTH AMERICA

PACIFIC OCEAN

CAPE HORN

KEY

	Eskimo and Aleut
	Northwest Coast
	California
	Forest
	Eastern Woodlands
	Southeast
	Great Plains—Southwest Hunters
	Southwest Villagers

KEY

Maximum extent of glaciation

→ Migration routes

Though the peoples of the Northwest Coast did not have a central government, they had three definite social classes: (1) a wealthy nobility, (2) commoners, and (3) slaves. They acquired slaves by raiding neighboring peoples. These raids were an important part of Northwest life. Also important was the *potlatch* ceremony, a gigantic giveaway celebration. A means of gaining prestige, the potlatch was also a form of trade. Huge amounts of food, blankets, slaves, tokens of great value called coppers, carvings, and canoes would be given away or destroyed by one noble to impress another. To keep his prestige, the receiver would then have to hold an even more impressive and costly potlatch.

The peoples of California are food gatherers. Many different peoples lived in the California area, in small tribes which had little interchange of ideas. Their way of life was simple, devoted almost entirely to gathering and fishing. Unlike their showy and well dressed neighbors, the California peoples wore little more than rags and lived on the edge of starvation. Agriculture was of the simplest type; there was practically no pottery and only a few small sculptures in stone. Despite this simple level, however, the Californians made baskets of outstanding quality, using every technique known to modern basketmakers. Especially noteworthy were "gift" baskets covered with brightly colored feathers woven in simple designs and further ornamented by pendants of shell.

The Forest Peoples are hunters. In the great northern forest which stretched across Canada south of the treeless plain of the tundra to the Great Lakes lived Ojibway (oh-*jib′*way, or Chippewa), Algonquian, Cree, and Nascopie (*nas′*kuh-pee). The forest influenced their lives

North American Peoples

The inset shows the migration routes that probably were followed into the Americas.

as the tundra did the lives of the Eskimos. Hunters of deer and beaver, the Forest Peoples lived and often hunted in family groups. From the hunt came the skins for their tents and clothing, from the forest the wood for bows and arrows and the bark for birchbark canoes and utensils. The Forest Peoples held beliefs similar to those of other hunters. There were spirits of the hunt, ancestral spirits, and a trickster who liked to play pranks. Two or three times a year there would be huge festivals which thousands of people might attend. At these feasts there were dances to the spirits of the hunt as well as races, wrestling matches, and other tests of skill.

The peoples of the Eastern Woodlands make an attempt to unite. South of the Forest Peoples lived Amerinds who combined hunting and fishing with farming. The warmer climate made possible a greater variety of foods and a less arduous life than in the great northern forest, though life was never easy. One authority on Amerindian cultures writes:

Even in a country teeming, as the saying goes, with game, the chase is bound to be a shaky provider, there being nothing stable about a supply of wild meat. But through fat times and lean, snows and spring, meat had to be brought in. Inevitably there were strings of empty-handed days. Then starving times . . . moved in to creep among the lodges. Especially at the end of the long winters there were weeks when the woods seemed to grow magically still and all game vanished, and the world sank into the semblance of death that preceded the first stirrings of spring. Famished people ate broth made of smoke, snow, and buckskin, and the rash of pellagra appeared like tattooed flowers on their emaciated bodies.

At some point the cultivation of corn was introduced. This led to the development of villages of bark wigwams or long houses capable of holding a hundred people. High walls of timber protected them from frequent attacks by enemy tribes. War was common, a means of showing bravery and gaining slaves. Sometimes captives were adopted into the tribe, but often prisoners were not only expected to endure agonizing torture without showing pain but also to sing bravely throughout.

Besides the spirits of nature and ancestral spirits, the peoples of the Eastern Woodlands believed in the Great Manitou, Master of Breath. To them, life was a conflict between good and misfortune, dark and light. When they died the people went to the Land of the Dead; brave warriors inhabited the sky.

In time, to decrease warfare, five of the tribes formed a confederation. The code of the confederacy was:

I, Deganawida, and the Confederated Chiefs, now uproot the tallest pine tree, and into the cavity thereby made we cast all weapons of war. Into the depths of the earth, deep down into the under-earth currents of water flowing to unknown regions, we cast all weapons of strife. We bury them from sight and we plant again the tree. Thus shall the Great Peace be established.

The Five Nations—Delaware, Huron, Iroquois (*ihr'*oh-kwoi), Lenape (*len'*uh-pee), and Wyandot—had a rather complex organization. From each nation certain women appointed councilors from specific families. From these tribal rulers, fifty councilors were chosen to represent the tribes in the Five Nations. Also having a say in the confederation's affairs were the Solitary Pine Trees, wise men who had usually earned their position by bravery in war. In theory, the five tribes acted together in matters concerning them all; actually, rivalry among the members of the Five Nations continued to be strong. Feared and hated by their neighbors, by the time Europeans arrived the Five Nations controlled the eastern part of what is now the United States from Lake Michigan to the coast and from Tennessee to Canada.

Despite their political organization, their development of farming, and extensive trade, the people of the Eastern Woodlands developed little art. Porcupine quills were used to decorate clothing. Special masks, carved from a living tree so that they would have the power of life, represented spirits of nature in False Face ceremonies. The people did, however, have a sort of literature besides oral tradition. Belts of beads or shells, called *wampum,* served not only as money but as records. By studying these belts, Keepers of the Wampum were reminded of specific events and thus were able to pass on tribal traditions.

The Mound Builders develop a complex society. In the Southeast a high level of culture flourished some 2000 years ago. Advanced cultivation of corn, trade routes reaching from the Rocky Mountains to the Atlantic Ocean and from the Great Lakes to the Gulf of Mexico, and crafts which included metalworking may indicate contact with the peoples of Mesoamerica to the south. The outstanding characteristic of this culture was mounds built of earth. Early mounds seem to have served for burial and as religious symbols. Later, mounds were made in the form of pyramids and were topped by wooden temples, which also may indicate contact with Mesoamerica. The Mound Builders also created distinctive artforms—mica silhouettes of human figures or animals, carvings on bone and shell, and finely carved stone pipes.

In some parts of the Southeast villages evolved into city-states. Warfare was waged to gain male victims for sacrifice and women to do menial tasks, though captives might be adopted into the nation—a practice common among many Amerindian tribes.

Peoples of the Plains and the Southwest develop an advanced culture based on hunting. Today many people are apt to think of the brave in feathered warbonnet, brandishing spear and bow, and mounted on a swift horse, as typical of the Amerind. Because the warriors of the Plains and the Southwest—Comanche, Pawnee, Sioux (*soo*), Navaho, and Apache—put up such determined resistance to the white men who colonized the West, they remain to many "the Redskins." But before the coming of white men, these people lived quite different lives. Some were hunters of the huge herds of buffalo, some were farmers, and all gathered roots, seeds, and berries. Raids on neighboring tribes were common, and Plains warriors took scalps to show their bravery. They lived in semi-permanent houses of earth or timber, generally in small groups, worshiped the Buffalo Spirit and gods of the sky, and had secret societies.

To become a member of one of the special tribal societies, a boy of eleven or twelve would set out alone to seek his spirit guide. For days he would pray and fast and in time an animal or nature spirit, such as the thunder spirit, would appear to him in a vision. On his return to the tribe, he would be introduced into a secret society to learn its chants and rituals. Tribal traditions of the Plains were contained in medicine bundles, which held objects which symbolized great events. In the Southwest shamans ("medicine men") made prophecies, cured sickness, and recited spells to protect crops. The complexity of myths, some of which show a strong relationship to Mesoamerican legends, indicate that centuries earlier these people had had a more settled way of life, probably before the land became too arid for profitable farming.

The coming of the Spaniards had a tremendous impact on these cultures, for with the white men came horses and sheep. The Amerinds of the Great Plains and the Southwest became herders and fast-moving hunters and raiders feared by all their neighbors. Clothing, housing, and handicrafts soon reflected this new mode of life.

The Villagers of the Southwest stress moderation and harmony with nature. In the same area inhabited by the Navaho and Apache there were three of the oldest and most advanced cultures of North America. Since ways of living in these cultures were generally similar and all depended on village life, their people can be grouped together as Villagers. Archaeologists have found traces of these people going back thousands of years. By 500 A.D. they had developed an advanced form of agriculture based on corn and made possible by extensive irrigation systems. Their houses, each accommodating many families, were solidly built of adobe or stone. Where raids by neighboring tribes forced them to live in easily defended sites, they built their villages into cliffs.

Among the earliest of the Villagers were the Hohokam, "Those Who Have Gone," who occupied the mesas (small plateaus) from 300 B.C. to 1400 A.D. Master farmers, they developed an extensive system of irrigation canals. On finely made pottery realistic figures of animals were painted. They played a ball game similar to one played all over Mesoamerica. Eventually other tribes moved in peacefully with the Hohokam and a general Villager culture developed, reaching its height between 1050 and 1300 A.D. Finely woven baskets with geometric designs, blankets woven by the men, and superb pottery, beautifully decorated both with animal figures and geometric designs, revealed a highly developed culture.

In *kivas* (underground chambers) secret societies met and carried on tribal traditions. A council of elders advised clan chiefs, who had to agree unanimously before action could be taken. Women were highly respected, with descent determined through the mother. The people worked together growing crops and gathering seeds and berries, and each family was careful to build up a reserve stock of food for times of drought.

The religious beliefs of the Villagers reflect the complexity of their society. They believed that the good life consisted in living in harmony with nature and various supernatural forces: "Man depended on the blessings of the gods; the gods depended on the prayers and magical ceremonies of the people." Their religion stressed no extremes such as self-torture or dread of the natural processes of life. Man should live in moderation, with reverence for life. He should have respect for others and for the traditions of the past. And the peoples of the mesas practiced their beliefs. War, waged only when necessary to survival, was so rare that when a warrior returned to his village he had to undergo a long ceremony to purify him of his "insanity."

Figures of the gods, known as *kachinas,* were made by the Hopi ("Peaceful Ones"), as they are to this day. Magic ceremonies and dances became increasingly complex; myths revealed that the people had thought long and deeply about life, as shown in the following fragments from the beginning of a Zuñi (*zoo′*nyee) creation legend.

Before creation began there was only the "one who contains everything," Awonawilona; otherwise there was blackness and nothingness. Awonawilona created life within himself; the mists of increasing and the streams of growing flowed from him. He assumed a form and was the maker of light, the sun. When the sun appeared the mists gathered together and fell as water, becoming the sea in which the world floats. (From within himself Awonawilona formed seed and impregnated the waters.) Then, in the warmth of the sun, green scum formed over the great waters and became solid and strong. It was divided and became Earth Mother of the Four Directions and Sky Father who covers everything. . . .

When men first reached [the] outer world it was dark. They were strange creatures, black and scaly, with short tails, owls' eyes, huge ears, and webbed feet. They were adapted only for the underworld and were hardly able to stand upright. . . . The first sunrise was terrible with the howling and terror of the newly emerged human race.

At the end of the 1200's drought came to the Southwest. Hunters from the north, whose food supply diminished with the long dry spell, made increasingly frequent raids on the villages, forcing their inhabitants southward. Some migrated to northern Mexico; others remained in the Southwest, their culture continuing in a modified form to the present.

CHECK-UP

1. Where did the Amerinds probably originate? What led to their development of sedentary agriculture? Why was it significant?

2. How did the Eskimos adapt to their environment?

3. What enabled the Northwest Coast peoples to develop villages although they did not have sedentary agriculture? What was the significance of the totem pole? Of the potlatch ceremony?

4. What type of life did the California peoples lead? The Forest Peoples?

5. What were the religious beliefs of the peoples of the Eastern Woodlands? Describe the confederation of the Five Nations. In what ways was it successful? A failure?

6. What were the characteristics of the Mound Builders? How did their culture reflect possible contact with Mesoamerica?

7. What was life like for the Hunters of the Plains and the Southwest? How was this changed by the coming of the Spaniards? How did a boy become a member of a special tribal society?

8. What were the agricultural achievements of the Southwestern Villagers? How did they view life?

Mesoamerica: From Villages to Great States

Mesoamerica—Mexico, Guatemala, El Salvador, and Honduras—had the most highly developed cultures and probably the largest population of ancient America. It now appears to have been the source of the first cultivated corn, the food upon which all its cultures depended. Archaeologists have devoted years of study to its cultures. They have disagreed with each other—sometimes violently—about places of origin, influence, dating of cultures, and relative importance of civilizations. In the light of new discoveries theories that have been care-

With delight in the humorous and graceful, the potters of Colima captured the people and animals about them in clay (above). The typical scenes of everyday life (right) done by Nayarit potters tell us much about village life in Western Mexico.

fully developed over a number of years have proved false, and theories once thought absurd have turned out to be accurate. Any statements about Mesoamerican civilization should therefore be viewed with caution.

Village cultures develop in Mesoamerica. Between 1500 and 200 B.C. sedentary agriculture developed in Mesoamerica. Farmers lived in villages in houses of branches woven together with vines and daubed with mud. The farming land was owned by the village as a whole, and the people worked together to supply their needs. Corn, beans, squash, and chile were the main crops, supplemented by fruits and nuts which grew wild and by game and fish.

In the wet lowlands covered by dense rain forest, fields were cleared by cutting down and burning the trees. On the cleared land, made fertile by a rich layer of wood ash, farmers harvested two or three crops a year. But the fertility decreased rapidly, and after one or two years of intensive use the land would be aban-

doned for several years, while new fields were prepared and used. A village thus had to have available a large amount of land to grow enough crops each year.

These early farmers also made a great variety of pottery for practical, everyday use as well as special pottery for burial with the dead. Typical of all the Mesoamerican cultures of this period were rather crudely made but charming figurines of women. Decorated with little lumps of clay to indicate headdresses, necklaces, and earrings, sometimes adorned with red or white paint, with elaborate and varied hairstyles, these figurines revealed an astonishing variety on a basic theme.

The Western Mexican cultures advanced little beyond this village way of life and its arts. At the same time that a high level of cultural achievement was reached in other areas of Mesoamerica, the Western Mexicans continued to live in villages and to make pottery which reflected a simple way of life and a delight in the world which surrounded them.

The Olmec are master stoneworkers whose influence is far reaching. At the same time the village communities were developing, the *Olmec* —one of Mesoamerica's great civilizations— flourished on the coast of the Gulf of Mexico. Miguel Covarrubias (mee-*gehl′* koh-bah-*roo′*-byahs), one of the first archaeologists to recognize the importance of the Olmec, writes: "Alongside these [village] cultures, of a clearly peasant spirit, looms the obscure and mysterious great 'Olmec' culture, decidedly urban in character."

The Olmec culture has probably given archaeologists more headaches than any other Mesoamerican culture. The Olmecs appeared in the hot swampy lowlands of the Gulf Coast of Mexico with a fully developed, advanced culture about 1200 B.C. They probably practiced the same sort of agriculture as the village communities, but politically they had a well-organized society. Their way of life centered around the cult of the werejaguar—a jaguar with a human face, or a human body with a jaguar face. The snarling face of the werejaguar appeared everywhere—on monuments, as figurines, or in mosaic floors—in the Olmec region. Writes Covarrubias:

It is easy to understand this jaguar obsession in the mystic solitude of the jungle, which is like a tall, green cathedral, where every noise, every rustle of leaves, every distant crackling of broken twigs brings to mind the presence of the dreaded maneater. To the ancient Indians the jaguar was a symbol of supernatural forces—not a simple animal, but an ancestor and a god.

It is believed that this werejaguar represented the rain god, a deity of immense importance to an agricultural people.

There were three other characteristics of Olmec art: colossal stone heads, baby-faced sculpture, and exquisitely worked jade. The basalt for the colossal heads, which weighed an average of eighteen tons each, probably came from mountains some 60 miles away from the main Olmec centers. Transportation of such immense sculptures through the swamps and across the many rivers of the Gulf Coast would have been practically impossible. Archaeologists therefore tend to think that the stone was carried on rafts along the Gulf and then up rivers into the interior. Clearly a large population was necessary to supply the labor needed to transport these tons of stone. And a highly organized society would have been necessary to enable the Olmecs to plan and supervise the labor.

The finest expression of Olmec art was superb jades which rank among the world's finest jade carvings. To the Olmec, as to all the peoples of Mesoamerica, jade was the most precious substance. Carved with masterly skill and beautifully polished, Olmec jades were part of offer-

Eloquent testimony to Olmec skill is the jade figure above. Note the similarity of his features to those of the werejaguar he is holding.

302

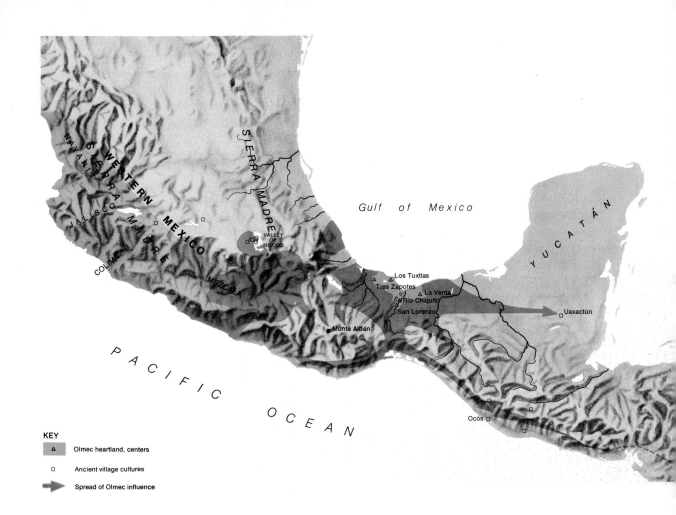

Gulf of Mexico

Los Tuxtlas
Papaloapan
Tres Zapotes
La Venta
Río Chiquito
San Lorenzo
Monte Albán

Uaxactún

SIERRA MADRE

NAYARIT

WESTERN MEXICO

JALISCO

SIERRA MADRE

COLIMA

MEZCALA

VALLEY OF MEXICO

YUCATÁN

PACIFIC OCEAN

Ocós

KEY

△ Olmec heartland, centers

□ Ancient village cultures

➜ Spread of Olmec influence

Olmec Civilization

ings and burials throughout the Olmec area as well as in regions remote from the Olmec centers. Olmec sculpture, whether of colossal heads or fine jades, was expressive and powerful and revealed a profound knowledge of the techniques of stoneworking. Yet all this work was done without metal tools.

Olmec ceremonial centers were laid out on a careful plan, with buildings facing a set direction. Temples were raised on manmade earthen mounds. These practices were to become common throughout Mesoamerica.

Urban planners and master stoneworkers, the Olmecs were also great travelers. Whether they went to distant regions to colonize or only to trade is not known. Since jade was not present in the Olmec area, it must have been obtained from other regions by trade. Olmec jades, paintings, sculpture, and carving on stone appear with the remains of other cultures in the Valley of Mexico, in mountainous Western Mexico, in the area thought of as Mayan, and as far south as El Salvador.

The Olmecs also developed a calendar and hieroglyphic writing. Whether these achievements were brought into the Olmec area from another culture, or whether the Olmecs were their originators, we may never know. The calendar later used in much of Mesoamerica differed from the Olmec, but the idea of measuring time existed in the Olmec period. Olmec art influenced the art of other peoples, and the Olmec practice of building pyramids and ceremonial centers was followed throughout Mesoamerica. The game played at Olmec ballcourts with a hard rubber ball later became quite elaborate and acquired considerable religious significance. Clearly the civilizations of Mesoamerica owe a great debt to these early settlers of the Gulf Coast.

Olmec civilization flourished for several centuries, but by the beginning of the Christian era its ceremonial centers had been abandoned, their sculptures deliberately broken and buried, and the secrets of the master stonecarvers lost.

Great urban centers develop in Mesoamerica.
Between 300 and 1000 A.D. there was a cultural explosion in Mesoamerica. While agriculture remained the mainstay of the economy, an urban culture developed and trade became increasingly widespread. This was the age of magnificent achievements in sculpture, ceramics, mural paintings, and architecture. Splendid ceremonial centers were constructed from careful plans. Great interest in astronomy developed, and a complex calendar system came into being. Hieroglyphs were used in sculpture and in books made from cured skins or the bark of trees. A definite social system developed with an aristocracy of priests, rulers, and warriors.

Religion served as the unifying force for the Mesoamerican cultures. At the head of society were ruler-priests who may have been regarded as personifications of the gods. To the all-important rain god of the earlier period was added the corn god, and the cult of the culture-bringer Quetzalcóatl (ket-sahl-*koh'*ah-t'l) began to develop. Mesoamerican society of this period had two centers: (1) the village attuned to the cycle of agriculture, and (2) the ceremonial center where priests studied the heavens, prophesied, directed the activities of society, and prayed to the gods. Except in a few cases village and ceremonial center remained separate. Eventually some ceremonial centers also became true cities where merchants, artisans, and peasants as well as priests lived.

Great cultural centers emerged at Teotihuacán (tey-oh-tee-wah-*kahn'*) in the Valley of Mexico, at Monte Albán to the south, and in the Mayan area (see maps, pages 306 and 309). Archaeologists disagree as to whether Teotihuacán or Monte Albán developed the first urban center. Because Teotihuacán's influence was so extensive, let us look at it first.

Teotihuacán becomes a dominant society based on religion.
In a valley a few miles northeast of present-day Mexico City one of America's first cities was founded.

> And they called it Teotihuacán
> because it was the place
> where the lords were buried.

The area around Teotihuacán ("place of the gods") had been settled since the times of early farming. By 300 A.D. the civilization known as Teotihuacán dominated the Mesoamerican scene. Its people were renowned as "wise men, knowers of occult things, possessors of the traditions."

Most imposing of Teotihuacán's many buildings were the Pyramids of the Moon and of the Sun. The former stood at the end of a broad, mile-long avenue of temples and palaces; its location indicates that it was of great importance. On the outskirts of the ceremonial center merchants and artisans lived in what was apparently the Teotihuacán idea of apartment houses—groups of rooms built around courtyards.

Priests dominated Teotihuacán, and religion determined the cycle of life. In the city and in nearby ceremonial centers were many temples, their walls decorated with paintings of the gods, especially Tláloc (*tlahl'*ok), the god of rain. In one painting this all-important god, wearing an elaborate headdress and a jade mask, stood with arms outstretched, rain pouring from his open hands. Below him, people frolicked in his paradise, the place of water and mists [where] "things are always blossoming and growing green. . . . Never is any hunger there, nor illness, nor poverty." Singing jaguars and coyotes paraded across the wall of another temple. Everywhere the themes of water and growth were present.

Besides paintings of the gods, Teotihuacán was noted for masks carved of various stones. Perhaps used to cover the faces of dead priests and nobles, these masks had a serene, godlike expression. There was also a great variety of very high-quality pottery. Figurines with triangular-shaped heads—the hallmark of Teotihuacán—echoed the serenity of the stone masks. They were at once simple and sophisticated, as was the painted and carved pottery used for burial with the dead.

The refined style of Teotihuacán pottery spread over much of Mesoamerica. But we do not know if Teotihuacan governed other areas or just traded with them. We do know that between 300 and 600 A.D. Teotihuacán pottery reached both coasts, the Mayan area, and especially Monte Albán. Architectural ideas from Teotihuacán doubtless accompanied this trade. Trade, of course, was not one way. Teotihuacán also was influenced by other Mesoamerican cultures. But the influence of Teotihuacán on other cultures was far greater than their influence on Teotihuacán.

About the middle of the seventh century nomadic tribes from the north descended on Teotihuacán, just as the barbarians had descended on Rome. The city was burned and abandoned and its inhabitants fled. But so great an impression had been made by its civilization that, nearly a thousand years later, the Aztecs would speak of Teotihuacán with awe.

At Monte Albán a calendar is developed and burials become elaborate. Between 1000 and 500 B.C. an unknown people began to level the top of Monte Albán (*mohn'*tey al-*bahn'*), a mountain near modern Oaxaca (wah-*hah'*kah) City in southern Mexico. On it they erected a large ceremonial center. Isolated from the Valley of Mexico and the Gulf Coast by lofty mountains and deep canyons, Monte Albán developed a distinctly local culture. At the same time, definite Olmec influences reached it early in its history and later it was strongly influenced by Teotihuacán. Monte Albán, like the Olmec centers, developed the characteristics of civilization surprisingly early. By 300 B.C. it had a class system, hieroglyphic writing, and the beginnings of the numeral system that became the base for the calendar used throughout Mesoamerica. Indeed, increasing support is given to the theory that the people of Monte Albán were the inventors of this calendar.

About 100 A.D. a people known as the Zapotec (*sah'*poh-tek), whose descendants live today in the valley below, became the rulers of Monte Albán and began rebuilding the ceremonial center. In the clear light of the morning sun the lines of the massive buildings and wide stairs were sharp and clear, a "symphony of stairways," as one photographer has called it. The buildings of Monte Albán, unadorned with sculpture, were built of carefully fitted stones covered by smooth stucco. Monte Albán was a magnificent architectural achievement. Writes American archaeologist John Paddock:*

With a technology in which the wheel was not used for transport, there were no draft animals, and no metals were used, how could Monte Albán be built at all? Was there some totalitarian system for mobilizing the entire population to labor on those gigantic temples? To carry the water? To work for weeks grinding a jade pebble . . . by invisible degrees into a work of art? To bring offerings over the mountains, on foot, from the two oceans? Was it a slave state that collapsed when the victims revolted? . . .

* Adapted by permission from John Paddock, "Oaxaca in Ancient Mesoamerica," in Paddock, ed., *Ancient Oaxaca* (Stanford, Calif.: Stanford University Press, 1966), pp. 152–153. Reprinted by permission.

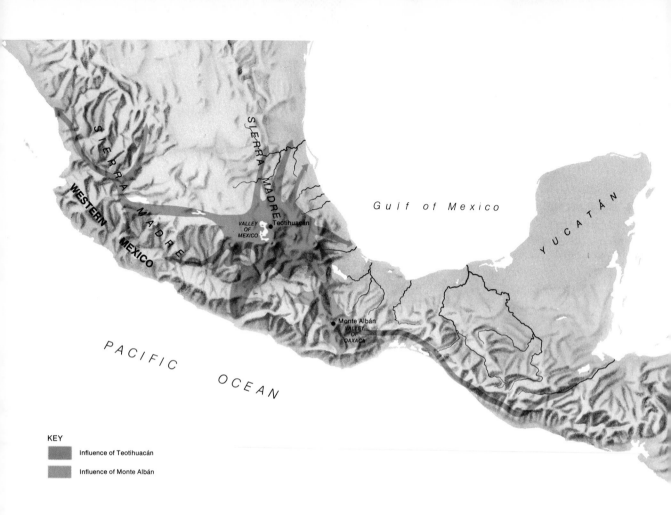

KEY

■ Influence of Teotihuacán

■ Influence of Monte Albán

Mesoamerican Urban Centers

For all the magical beauty of Teotihuacán's city plan and integration into its landscape, the Zapotec architects of the same period matched—or perhaps anticipated—the accomplishment in their own way. They left for us at Monte Albán a city of unrivaled majesty in a setting that would have overwhelmed lesser men before they began. . . .

The men and women who toiled up that long hill with some offering for the gods—food for their priests, wood or water for their temples—may have felt in their tired bodies that a valley location would be more "practical." But these people were participating in the life of a metropolis; they could see that they were making it possible. They could stand dazzled before those mighty temples, stroll

half an hour to circle the immense open plaza, watch the stunning pageantry of the ceremonies, stare as fascinated as we [do today] at the valley spread mile after mile below. They knew that no other such center existed for hundreds of miles— and even then their city had only rivals, not superiors. . . . With their own humble hands, or those of their remembered ancestors, the common people had made the buildings.

No whip-cracking slave driver was needed. The satisfaction of helping to create something simultaneously imposing, reassuring, and beautiful is enough to mobilize endless amounts of human effort.

The Zapotecs were greatly concerned with death. At Monte Albán they built elaborate

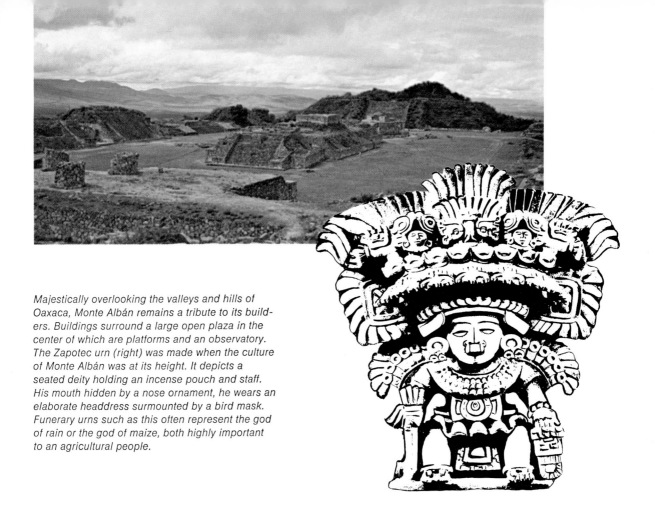

Majestically overlooking the valleys and hills of Oaxaca, Monte Albán remains a tribute to its builders. Buildings surround a large open plaza in the center of which are platforms and an observatory. The Zapotec urn (right) was made when the culture of Monte Albán was at its height. It depicts a seated deity holding an incense pouch and staff. His mouth hidden by a nose ornament, he wears an elaborate headdress surmounted by a bird mask. Funerary urns such as this often represent the god of rain or the god of maize, both highly important to an agricultural people.

tombs of slabs of stone. The inner walls were covered with paintings and contained ornate clay statues of the gods who kept watch over the tomb's occupant. With the dead person were buried standing figures of pottery or elaborate hollow urns. This concern with death, with elaborate burial places, and rich offerings reflected the Mesoamerican belief in an afterlife. Though each Mesoamerican culture had a different concept of the afterlife, all believed that death was not the absolute end of existence. Food, tools, and weapons were buried with the dead person to aid him in his journey to the place of the fleshless or to paradise.

Zapotec civilization at Monte Albán reached its height by 300 A.D. Then a gradual decline

set in. No longer did potters model figurines by hand; the same mold was used over and over and art lost its individuality. At the same time, symbols that had served earlier as mere decoration were so lavishly used that the form of pottery and sculpture became completely buried under a wealth of detail. About 900, for reasons which shall probably never be known, the Zapotecs abandoned Monte Albán. The tombs continued to be used until the sixteenth century, but the buildings "fell stone by stone over the silent years for lack of repairs."

The Maya build a great civilization based on religion. The Maya (*my'*ah) reached the highest level of civilization in ancient America. Probably originating in the highlands of Guatemala and southernmost Mexico,[1] by 300 A.D. they occupied the Petén (pey-*ten'*) lowland in northern Guatemala and the nearby river valleys of southeastern Mexico. There were also Mayan outposts as far away as Honduras. This region is one of dense tropical rain forest, of huge trees tangled with thick vines where the orchid grows wild, where rainfall may average 150 inches a year. A region of huge rivers with powerful currents, of poisonous insects, deadly reptiles, and fierce animals, it would hardly seem a likely area for a thriving civilization. Yet, despite its dangers, the rain forest also offers dozens of edible plants and a host of game. The hot humid climate encourages rapid plant growth and the rivers provide "roads" through the rain forest.

Here the Maya built ceremonial centers and cities of extraordinary beauty. On lofty mounds built up of earth they raised temples covered with stucco painted in bright colors and ornamented with sculpture. The temples were reached by gracefully proportioned stairs, perhaps decorated with hieroglyphs or sculpture at the side. Along the outer walls of the temples and on the slanting roof combs which topped them marched sculptures of priests and rulers. Simply dressed in cape and loincloth or kilt, they bore enormous and elaborate headdresses which contained masks, jade, flowers, and the long flowing plumes of tropical birds. Inside, the temples were small and dark, though the walls often were covered by beautiful carvings. The total impression these temples gave was one of stateliness, tranquillity, and grace. Even the hieroglyphs, elsewhere in Mesoamerica fairly simple, became works of art, with numerals and symbols so interwoven that each glyph formed a separate picture. Perhaps only the Chinese combined writing so effectively with art.

The Maya occupied and controlled a large part of Mesoamerica and traded extensively with other areas, but there are no indications

[1] Some archaeologists believe the Maya are the descendants of the Olmec.

The Island of Jaina has yielded hundreds of Mayan sculptures in clay. Less formal than most Mayan art, they serve as an encyclopedia of Mayan life.

that they had an empire under a central government. Even after the middle of the eighth century, when warriors became an increasingly important class, there was little political unity. Mayan civilization continued to be made up of large and small ceremonial centers loosely united by similar religious beliefs and practices and by dependence on one calendar and system of writing.

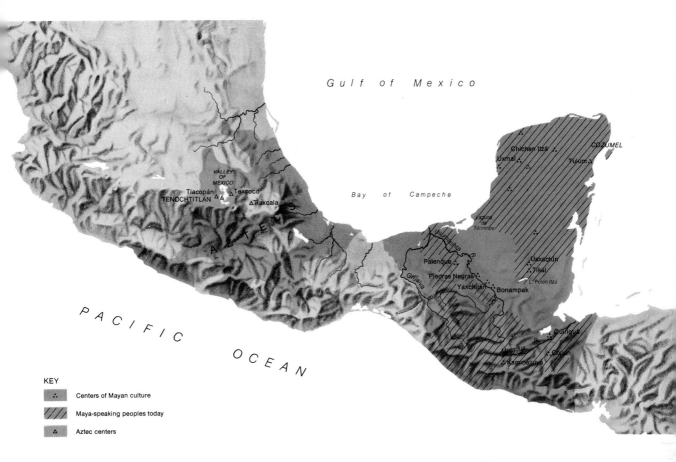

KEY

.⋅.	Centers of Mayan culture
/////	Maya-speaking peoples today
△	Aztec centers

Mayan and Aztec Civilizations

Religion dominated Mayan culture. The common people worshiped natural forces—the sun, rain, earth, storms, and animal spirits. The nobles worshiped the gods of growth, fertility, death, and later, war. The priests, who dominated Mayan society, had much more complex beliefs. By piecing together the legends that have survived, the concepts revealed in the few remaining books, and the art of the ceremonial centers, it appears that the priests had a sophisticated and abstract view of man's place in the universe and of space and time. Of primary importance was the cycle of life, death, and rebirth in an afterlife, which a priest expressed in the following words:

All moons, all years, all days, all winds, reach their completion and pass away. So does all blood reach its place of quiet, as it reaches its power and its throne. . . . Measured was the time in which [the people] could know the Sun's benevolence. Measured was the time in which the grid of the stars would look down upon them; and through it, keeping watch over their safety, the gods trapped within the stars would contemplate them.

The measurement of time, not only in days and years, but in periods of 20, 400, 8000 years or more, became an obsession with the priests. It made astronomy a dominant science. Mayan astronomical achievements rivaled those made in the ancient Near East, for the Mayan priests accurately calculated eclipses and the positions of stars and planets. The Mayan calendar was so accurate that it surpassed that used in Europe until the end of the sixteenth century. Eventually Mayan life as a whole became subservient to the priests' obsession with time. No seeds could be planted, no crops harvested unless the day and month were favorable; the priests foretold a man's future and determined when a couple should be married or a new temple built.

Mayan astronomical achievements are even more surprising when we see how very simple the Mayan number system was. Based on a unit of 20, it consisted of a dot (1), a bar (5), and zero—which the Maya were using centuries before it was developed in India. Using this system, the Maya were able to make complex calculations into the millions.

The common people live simply. The dominant role of the priesthood to a large extent explains why we know so little about Mayan life. Whereas the art of Western Mexico depicted every aspect of life, the Maya devoted practically all their art to religion. Elaborate ceremonies, religious symbols, acts of worship, priests—these are the subjects of Mayan art. This art imparts a sense of magnificence and awe; the best of it has a naturalism and beauty which unquestionably rank it among the world's masterpieces. Nevertheless, it tells us little about the people who toiled in the fields and provided the labor that built the ceremonial centers. Without their labor, of course, the great achievements would have been impossible. Our knowledge of the common people comes mainly from Spanish commentators who reached Mesoamerica long after the great Mayan civilization had come to an end, and from the present-day descendants of the ancient Maya. "In fact," writes archaeologist Michael Coe, "the old village-farming way of life [throughout Mesoamerica] has never . . . been altered in any way until today."

The people lived in simple houses with steep thatched roofs which overhung the walls to give protection from the hot sun and heavy rain. They dressed simply, wore earplugs and pendants, painted and sometimes tattooed their bodies, and wore their hair long. The heads of babies were flattened and elongated and their eyes were crossed, for these were considered marks of beauty. All the healthy members of a village worked together growing crops for the priests and nobles as well as for their own use. Those who were unable to work were cared for by other members of the village.

The great Mayan centers are abandoned. Between the mid-800's and 900's the Mayan centers in southeastern Mexico and the Petén were abandoned. Many theories have been proposed to explain this catastrophe—overpopulation, decreasing soil fertility, natural disasters, famine, plague, civil wars, invasion. Perhaps a combination of events led to the fall of this great civilization. A Mayan priest writing several centuries later might have been describing just such a series of calamities:

When our eyes were suddenly opened to the snatching of "alms"; when the common people began to suffer from the taking of "gifts" by the collectors; when the soldiers took property in the manner of warriors, it was as if a mountain had descended upon our shoulders. . . .

The vegetation was fast disappearing, owing to so much cropping. Too many mouths in our houses; too many mouths for the number of calabashes [squash].

The strength of many great warriors ebbs away. . . . There is no one left on whom to lean. . . .

There is no one left with sufficient understanding to set in order the days [calendar]. . . . And so there will be no great abundance of water.

[There came enemies from the north and west.] In great distress we were scattered among the forests and in the mountains. . . .

We mourn the scattering abroad of the books of hieroglyphic writing. . . . For months there was discord among the [chiefs], and all true men suffered deeply. . . .

The lords bind up their faces in pain because true men swelter in toil, and hunger is their burden, and because of their bad conscience about protecting the people. . . .

One by one the stars fall.

In the jungles of southeastern Mexico, on a plateau overlooking the plains which lead to the sea, is Palenque, an outstanding example of Mayan architecture. Once brightly colored, today its temples gleam white against the dense greens of the surrounding jungle. The remains of sculptured stucco figures still grace the outside walls, the roof, and the lofty roof comb of the Temple of the Sun (above). In the background is the Temple of the Inscriptions, its carved hieroglyphs still a mystery. Within this temple is the tomb of a great lord or priest, his bones, adorned with a treasure in jade, guarded in a stone sarcophagus. The lid of the sarcophagus (shown in the stone rubbing, right) is one of the masterpieces of Mayan art. Many archaeologists believe that this carving represents the Mayan belief in death and rebirth. On the earth monster reclines the figure of a young man with his hands raised in blessing. Above him serpents coil about a stylized corn plant, the Mayan tree of life, on top of which a mythical bird perches. Encircling the central carving is a band of astronomical designs.

311

The Toltec-Mayan culture foreshadows Aztec culture. Though the great centers were abandoned, Mayan civilization did not die out entirely. In the peninsula of Yucatan, which had ceremonial centers dating to the period of early Mayan history, there was a rebirth of Mayan culture. But the new culture was not entirely Mayan. At the end of the ninth century invaders from central Mexico, the Toltec, conquered the Mayan centers in a series of bloody battles. The culture that developed was a combination of Toltec and Mayan. Mayan-style pyramids were decorated with Toltec sculpture, especially the feathered serpent which represented Quetzalcóatl (ket-sahl-*koh'*ah-t'l), a major Toltec god.

The Feathered Serpent God is found throughout Mesoamerica under various names. Quetzalcóatl (the Toltec name) was believed to be also god of wind and of the morning star.[2] He it was who brought the people the gifts of civilization—corn, the calendar, arts and crafts, laws, and a moral code that stressed peace, humility, and concern for one's fellow men. Wherever he appeared, Quetzalcóatl was a kindly and loving god. His followers made him offerings of flowers and corn as symbols of sacrifice. In Mesoamerican myth he was opposed by the dark god Tezcatlipoca, the god of the Toltec warriors. The struggle between the two gods supposedly split the Toltec state and led to its downfall.

The Toltec warriors who appeared in the Yucatan had changed the worship of Quetzalcóatl considerably. Instead of flowers or butterflies, his priests demanded human blood and hearts. The art of Toltec-Mayan civilization thus showed overwhelming concern with warfare and sacrifice. Sculptures of eagles and jaguars eating hearts, altars covered with carvings of skulls, paintings of battles, and statues of warriors abounded. These same themes would be carried to an extreme by the last great civilization in Mesoamerica—the people known today as Aztecs.

The Aztecs build a mighty state. The Aztecs are probably the best-known of the ancient American peoples. Their origin is shrouded in legend, but it is generally agreed that they were hunter-warriors who came from arid northern Mexico. About 1325 they founded the city of Tenochtitlán (tey-noch-tee-*tlan'*, modern Mexico City) on an island in a lake. Rather than developers of a civilization, the Aztecs were *synthesizers*—they adopted and adapted many aspects of other cultures. The style of their architecture and sculpture, the calendar they used, and many of their arts and crafts had been developed by earlier cultures. What made the Aztecs noteworthy was the fact that they set up a political rather than a religious state.

Originally hired warriors of stronger states, by the early 1400's the Aztecs had the strongest state in the Valley of Mexico. Their Eagle and Jaguar Knights had defeated many other states and made them vassals of Tenochtitlán. But the Aztecs did not rule directly over these vassal states. Instead, they demanded tribute in the form of food and clothing, precious stones, gold, and silver. They also demanded prisoners, who were sacrificed to renew the sun.

The Aztecs traded with peoples throughout Mesoamerica. Because they had contact with so many different peoples, they found it necessary to keep extensive written records of taxes due, tribute paid by vassal states, and goods sold. They named and described the natural features of the land and hundreds of plants and animals. This enabled them to make many advances in medicine and to improve agricultural production.

The records of Tenochtitlán and the history of the Aztecs were painted on long strips of paper which were folded to make a book. These books tell us much about Aztec society. It was clearly dominated by warriors, the Eagle and Jaguar Knights, though priests continued to

[2] The study of the gods of Mesoamerica is incredibly complex and confusing. Each Mesoamerican god appears in several forms and sometimes contradictory gods bear the same name. The Black Tezcatlipoca (tehs-kah-tle-*poh'*kah) was a god of night; as the Blue Tezcatlipoca he was god of day.

play an important role. Besides conducting sacrifices, they predicted events, supervised the calendar, and advised the emperor.

Merchants were equally important in Aztec society, and poets were held in high regard. Virtually every educated Aztec tried his hand at writing poetry. These poets show us that warfare and sacrifice did not completely dominate Aztec life. A love of beauty and a feeling of sadness at the shortness of life were common themes:*

> Like a precious necklace,
> like ointment,
> like emeralds,
> like gold,
> like a beautiful flute,
> I value our songs,
> they are flowers to the god.

> Is life really lived in the form world?
> We are not always on earth—
> only a little while here.
> Though it be jade, it is shattered.
> Though it be gold, it is broken.
> Quetzal feather is torn.
> We are not always on earth—
> only a little while here.

Sculpture and architecture, in which they excelled, reflected the Aztec personality. Massive in size and severe in line, Aztec sculpture seems cold and overpowering. The Aztec's gods inspired awe rather than love; the emphasis on war and the dominant role of the military accustomed him to strife and hardship. Yet much of the smaller Aztec sculpture had a realism and a simplicity that were most appealing.

The Aztec ruler was surrounded by luxury. Jade pendants, bracelets, and earplugs adorned his body. He wore a cape of thousands of tiny feathers and a headdress of magnificent plumes. On his table were gold plates, goblets carved of rock crystal, and the delicacies of a commercial

* Reprinted by permission of Faber and Faber Limited from *Firefly in the Night* by Irene Nicholson.

empire that covered a climate ranging from temperate to tropical. In the courtyards were exotic plants, birds, and animals. The word of the Aztec ruler was supreme in Tenochtitlán; even his mightiest nobles and priests fell at his feet when he appeared. As for the common people, they provided the labor force that sustained the Aztec economy. Those who failed to pay tribute or fell deeply into debt might be enslaved until they had paid off what they owed.

But Aztec rule was less absolute than it might appear. Outside Tenochtitlán were vassal states that frequently revolted in protest to demands for more tribute and men for sacrifice. And Tlacopán (tlah-koh-*pahn'*) and Texcoco (tehs-*koh'*koh), the allies of Tenochtitlán, were uneasy that the alliance might be broken at any time by the far more powerful Aztec state.

CHECK-UP

1. What area is included in Mesoamerica? What kind of culture developed there between 1500 and 200 B.C.?

2. What were the major characteristics of Olmec culture? In what areas did the Olmec excel? Why is their culture considered a mother culture?

3. Describe the great urban centers of Mesoamerica. How did they differ from ceremonial centers?

4. Why was Teotihuacán a major center of civilization? What were the achievements of the builders of Monte Albán?

5. How did the Zapotecs view death? What insight does this give us into Mesoamerican religious beliefs?

6. Why was the Mayan region an unlikely one for a thriving civilization? How did the Maya use their environment to advantage?

7. What was noteworthy about Mayan art? Religion? What advances did the Maya make in astronomy? In mathematics?

8. Why is it difficult to learn about Mayan life? What have Spanish accounts told us about daily life?

9. What may have brought about the destruction of the great Mayan centers? What happened to Mayan civilization in the Yucatan?

10. Why have the Aztecs been called synthesizers? What is original about their society?

11. What kinds of written records did the Aztecs keep? What were their religious beliefs? How did they regard poets and merchants?

12. What kind of life did the Aztec ruler lead? How much power did he have?

South America: From Regionalism to Empire

The pre-Inca cultures make advances in agriculture. With the important exception of the Incas, knowledge of the ancient cultures of South America is very slight. There are no written records, and archaeologists have only begun to scratch the surface of what appears to be a rich field. We have only a vague, though intriguing, picture of the pre-Inca cultures of South America outside the Central Andean region—the Peruvian coast and the Andes of Peru and Bolivia. However, pottery, architectural remains, and burial sites indicate that many distinct cultures existed.

In tropical regions of Brazil, Venezuela, and Bolivia there were peoples who apparently followed a way of life similar to that of the village cultures of Mesoamerica. Farther to the north and west there were peoples who developed knowledge of metalworking well before this skill appeared in Mesoamerica. Indeed, it is likely that metalworking was carried to Mesoamerica from the lands to the south. In Costa Rica, the Isthmus of Panama, and northern South America several cultures were noted for exceptionally fine objects made of gold. What is surprising is that these peoples made use of every technique possible in working with gold and also copper and silver.

Ancient South American civilization reached its peak in the Central Andean region. About 400 B.C. the village-type culture of Chavín de Huantar (chah-*been'* dey wahn-*tahr'*) appeared. As in Mesoamerica at this period of history, religion dominated society and art. The feline deities of Chavín are found on the pottery and textiles throughout the north-central highlands. Chavín thus gave religious unity to the area. But Chavín was unable to provide political unity; by the first century A.D. several local centers of culture had appeared. These regional centers apparently had little contact or exchange of ideas with each other. Nevertheless, important advances were made in agriculture. Terracing came into wide use in the highlands, while irrigation was practiced along the arid coast. These formed the foundations on which the great Andean cultures would be built.

The Nazca and Mochica develop outstanding cultures. About 600 A.D. the regional differences crystallized into two outstanding coastal cultures—the Nazca and the Mochica (moh-*chee'*kah). The Nazca adapted the intricate geometric designs woven into their textiles for decorating exceptionally fine pottery. The Mochica used geometric designs mainly for weaving. Their pottery consisted of delightfully modeled human and animal figures. The Mochica were probably more organized politically than were the Nazca. They had skillfully constructed ceremonial centers and a definite class structure.

Tiahuanaco briefly unifies the Central Andes. Regionalism led to frequent conflict among the various cultures of the Central Andes. Finally, about 1000 A.D., the Tiahuanaco (tyah-wah-*nah'*koh) culture succeeded in imposing its religion and its style of architecture upon nearly the entire Central Andean area. Its buildings, decorated with geometric designs, were constructed of carefully fitted, massive stones (some slabs weigh over 100 tons).

But like Chavín, Tiahuanaco was unable to wipe out all the regional traits which had characterized the Central Andean cultures for centuries. By 1200 local cultures had reappeared. These new cultures, however, were organized on a political rather than a religious base and had well-planned urban centers. The fifteenth century saw the emergence of a vital new state in what is now Peru. This Peruvian state is often referred to by the name of its ruler, the *Inca*.

The Incas build the greatest empire in ancient America. Like the Aztecs, the Incas were originally an insignificant tribe. But between 1438 and 1527 they built the largest empire in ancient America. It stretched from southern Colombia to central Chile and from the Pacific Ocean to Bolivia.

In the Peruvian state life revolved around worship of the sun and of the Inca as its direct descendant. The Inca had absolute power. Since he was regarded as divine, to question the Inca's decrees would have been to defy the sun. From the capital at Cuzco (*koos'koh*) his commands set daily life throughout the empire in a rigid pattern.

Peruvian methods of conquest bear some similarity to those employed by some modern states. First the Incas tried to convince unconquered peoples that the Inca way of life was best for everyone. Persuasion was followed by threats. Only when these methods failed did the Incas resort to war. After a new area was conquered, it was carefully drawn into the network of Inca society. If its people had shown strong resistance to rule from Cuzco, entire villages and tribes would be moved to new areas in the empire. By interspersing loyal subjects and unwilling vassals, the Incas reduced the danger of revolt and war.

Most of the cultural accomplishments of the Incas were products of pre-Inca cultures. Inca

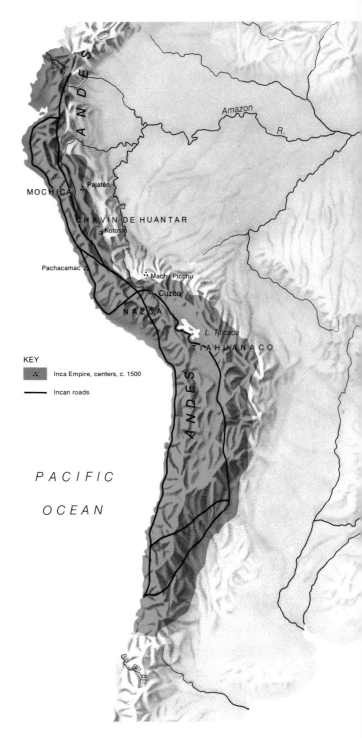

KEY

Inca Empire, centers, c. 1500

Incan roads

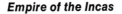

Empire of the Incas

315

Before they developed pottery, the Andean peoples were skilled weavers. The basis for later Nazca designs were the textiles of Paracas (below), whose colors have remained bright over the centuries. In contrast to this stylization is the realistic portrait vase (right) made by a Mochica artist. The silver llama and alpaca above reveal the skill of Incan metalworkers.

artists adopted Nazca symbolism, Mochica realism, and Tiahuanaco-style architecture. Farmers used agricultural methods developed in ancient times. Like the Aztecs, the Incas were synthesizers. Their great achievement was a complex, highly efficient system of government. For all levels of society there was a carefully planned administration. Each village had a leader who was under the supervision of provincial officials. These provincial officials kept population records and lists of agricultural produce, looked after the welfare of the people, and enforced the laws. Punishment for crimes was severe, usually death.

Gold, representative of the sun, was the most precious substance in Peru. Gold was worn as an ornament by the Incas and the nobility; the walls of the Temple of the Sun in Cuzco were covered in gold, and the Inca even had gardens in which trees, flowers, birds, and animals all were made of gold and of silver.

The Incas devoted considerable attention to astronomy. They used geometry and geography in surveying and mapping the land and arithmetic for keeping records. The Incas developed a unique system of bookkeeping. All mathematical records and calculations were kept by means of *quipus* (*kee'*poos), different colored cords of varying lengths, knotted at intervals to indicate specific sums. An early book on the Incas states, "Every year, an inventory of all the Inca's possessions was made. Nor was there a single birth or death, a single departure or return of a soldier, in all the Empire, that was not noted on the *quipus*."

The Peruvians built an excellent system of roads, over which the Inca's messengers raced to all parts of the empire. They paved the main roads, spanned canyons with swinging bridges of woven reeds, and sometimes dug tunnels through mountains.

The Incas have a rigid class system. In the empire of the Incas a person was born into a certain class and could move out of it only under exceptional circumstances. The Incas and the nobility lived in luxury, while the common people faced hardships daily. They dressed simply, ate plain foods, and were expected to obey instantly the commands of their superiors. Of the crops they planted in the village-owned fields, a portion was always set aside for the Inca's personal use and for the needy. Large granaries and warehouses held surplus grain, potatoes, and wool from the herds of llama and alpaca. These supplies were doled out to the needy. This provided a considerable amount of security for the common people. The state's detailed provincial records and strict administration of laws, on the other hand, deprived the people of privacy and individual achieve-

ments. And to some of the people in the empire, personal liberty was more important than security. They resented the government supervision and the forced adoption of sun worship and of Quechua (kay-*choo'*ah), the Incas' language. Though unsuccessful, revolts against rule from Cuzco were not uncommon.

CHECK-UP

1. What advances were made by the pre-Incan cultures? Why was the culture of Chavín de Huantar important?

2. What is regionalism? How did it affect cultural development in the Central Andes?

3. What were the achievements of the Nazca? The Mochica? What role did Tiahuanaco play in Central Andean development?

4. Who was the Inca? What were his methods of conquest? Describe his rule.

5. What were the social classes in the Incan state?

6. What were the strengths of the Incan state? The weaknesses?

Summing Up

The cultures of ancient America existed on several levels. It is impossible to call these cultures either simple or complex; within a culture a simple way of life might be accompanied by advanced artistic ability. Only the Mesoamericans developed a system of writing, but the lack of written records did not prevent the development of sophisticated social and political systems in other parts of America. Metal was used mainly for ornamentation, yet the peoples of the Americas erected architectural masterpieces and showed a mastery of stone carving that has seldom been equalled. Despite the lack of draft animals (the llama and alpaca of Peru were used only as pack animals) and the wheel (used only on toys), extensive trade routes were established and highways that were feats of engineering skill were built. Even cultures without advanced agricultural techniques had highly skilled craftsmen and artisans; some of their techniques cannot be bettered today. Many of the peoples of the ancient Americas developed complex mythologies and religious beliefs; some showed amazing skill in astronomy despite their lack of technical development in other fields.

While there was great variety and individuality among the peoples of ancient America, they generally all sought to live in harmony with nature. There was little security in their ways of life, yet until the rise of the great states the Amerind revealed a deep inner tranquillity. His self-possessed outlook was expressed in the art, the dances, the legends, and the ritual which were an inseparable part of his life. A bowl, a basket, a blanket was decorated not because it was destined for ritual use, but because it was more pleasing to the eye. The Amerind saw no reason why practical objects could not also be artistically attractive and thus managed, even on the simplest level of culture, to surround himself with beauty.

Chapter Highlights

Can you explain?

kiva	quipu	regionalism	tundra
pyramid	tribute	wampum	synthesizers
mesas	potlatch	sedentary	totem pole
hieroglyphs	kachinas	werejaguar	

Can you identify?

Aleut	Inca	Olmec	Monte Albán
Zapotec	Cuzco	Maya	Great Manitou
Amerinds	Nazca	Tiahuanaco	Mound Builders
Yucatan	Five Nations	Mesoamerica	Teotihuacán
Ice Age	Aztecs	Chavín de Huantar	Quetzalcóatl
Toltec	Mochica	Tenochtitlán	Solitary Pine Trees

What do you think?

1. Did what you read suggest that the Amerind adapted effectively to his environment? Why?

2. How can one account for the fact that comparatively few people spread over such great distances in so short a span of time?

3. In what ways were Amerindian civilizations similar to Egyptian civilization? Different?

4. Can the Amerindian view towards man's environment be reconciled with modern technology? Why?

5. What were some of the forms of artistic expression used by Amerinds?

6. The Mesoamericans knew about the wheel yet did not put this knowledge to practical use. Why?

7. Why did Amerinds possess a deep inner tranquillity?

8. What are the major achievements of the Mesoamerican cultures in the fields of diet, religion, science, and art?

9. Why was religion so much a part of Amerindian culture?

Transition to Modern Times

Unit Four——————

The Renaissance

The Reformation

The Scientific Revolution

Exploration, Colonization, and Commercial Expansion

The Rise of Nation-States

The Renaissance

Renaissance artists strove for realism, especially in the portrayal of human subjects. The works of Italy's three greatest artists show how well they achieved this goal. Da Vinci's notebook sketches (far left) capture a variety of facial expressions. In his painting of the doomed soul who is being dragged into hell (left), Michelangelo vividly portrayed despair. In contrast is the serenity of Raphael's Madonna of the Chair (above), a work unified by its curved forms.

CHAPTER FOCUS

The Spirit of Humanism
The Literature of the Renaissance
Renaissance Artists

The Middle Ages contributed much to western civilization. It gave us universities, great works of literature, graceful Gothic cathedrals, and our modern languages. Yet medieval civilization differed considerably from the civilization of the modern world.

Society during the Middle Ages was centered on the Church and the manor and rested upon an agricultural economy. Land was the source of wealth for both Church and feudal lord. For the medieval serf, agriculture and the crafts related to it were the only means of survival. Gradually this way of life began to change as trade increased and towns grew up during the High Middle Ages. A new class of people—the townsman—arose. Neither churchman, lord, nor serf, the townsman stood outside the traditional pattern of medieval society. His life centered not around the Church or the manor, but around the town, and his place in society was determined not by birth but by wealth and achievement.

The townsman was a force for change, a dynamic element that weakened the power and influence of lord and clergy and provided a new way of life for those serfs who had gained their freedom. He led a busy life based on commerce and was interested in learning and the arts as well. This concern with the goods, pleasures, and activities of this world gave him a *secular* rather than a religious attitude. Eventually the middle-class townsman helped to bring about a new era that served as a bridge to modern times.

During this new era, the major feature of the medieval world—the unity of Christianity under the Catholic Church—ended (see Chapter 14). Extraordinary advances were made in science (Chapter 15). Europeans discovered, explored, conquered, and settled vast new lands (Chapter 16). Lords lost much of their power to kings, who succeeded in creating strong nation-states (Chapter 17). The new era was ushered in by the period called the *Renaissance* (ren-eh-*sahns'*), which we shall study in this chapter.

The Renaissance marked a rebirth of interest in learning, culture, and worldly affairs. To people of the time this seemed to be an echo of the Graeco-Roman attitude toward life. The origins of the Renaissance are summarized by Canadian historian Wallace K. Ferguson:

The Renaissance grew out of the Middle Ages and was a period of gradual transition. But its most typical culture was that of the cities and their people. From this point of view it may be said that the Renaissance began when the new urban and secular elements in European culture began to weigh down the balance against the feudal and ecclesiastical [Church] elements which had dominated the civilization of the Middle Ages.

Renaissance man thought of himself as living in a new age. He had new ideas and a new attitude toward life. What was this new view of life and man which arose during the Renaissance? How was this outlook different from that of the Middle Ages?

The Spirit of Humanism

Man is . . . worthy of all admiration. . . . Man is rightly . . . believed to be a great miracle, . . . a being to be admired.

> (*Pico della Mirandola*)

What a piece of work is man! . . . how noble in reason.

> (*Shakespeare*)

Renaissance man has a humanist outlook. These words of Renaissance writers capture the mood of the times. During the Middle Ages man praised the greatness of God. People of the Renaissance admired the intelligence and remarkable talents of man. Medieval man saw preparation for heaven as the most important reason for life. To Renaissance man the challenge and pleasure of living seemed more important than the promise of heaven. But Renaissance man, though paying less attention to religion than did medieval man, was neither a nonbeliever nor a heretic. He continued to believe in the teachings of the Church. But to his religious beliefs he added many new, worldly interests.

Medieval man admired the monk's way of life. He found it superior to an active life in society. Medieval man often thought that wealth and pleasure were sinful. These were not the views of Renaissance man. "Do not imagine . . . that one can seek perfection by fleeing from the crowd, shunning the sight of everything beautiful, and locking oneself up in a monastery," wrote a Renaissance figure. Renaissance man wanted to live an active and full life. He wanted to be involved in the affairs of this world, to experience its joys and sorrows. Believing that "man is born in order to be useful to other men," Renaissance man took a keen interest in the activities of his city. Like the ancient Greeks, he came to view life as essentially social. The good life was to be found in the bustling city, not in the seclusion of the monastery. He thought it good to be rich and to have fine possessions. Renaissance man looked for intellectual and artistic excitement and adventure. He wanted to express himself, to develop his talents. He would show the world that he was a gifted individual and an unusual person. "I wish to work miracles," said the great Leonardo da Vinci.

This stress on man and his talents is called *humanism.* Humanists wanted to learn all they could about the beauty of the body, the powers of the mind, and the feelings of the heart. They had confidence in man's ability. Of one humanist it was written:

He was taught from his boyhood everything that [was suitable for] a man of good family. . . . He was able to handle with skill weapons, horses, and musical instruments; and he was also an enthusiastic student of arts and letters. . . . He made himself master of everything for which he might be praised. . . . When a youth, he shone at weapon-practice; with his feet together he could spring over the shoulders of a standing man; he had hardly an equal at jumping with the spear. . . . He threw up a silver coin with such force that those who were with him in the cathedral heard it strike against the roof. . . . He taught himself music, and his work gained the approval of skilled musicians; . . . he loved to play the organ, and was considered one of those most highly skilled in that art. . . . He took up papal and civil law for some years, but with such dilligence, and so many late nights, that he made himself ill through too much study. . . . But since he could not live without study, at the age of twenty-four he turned to physics and mathematics.

The Renaissance

1469–1492	Lorenzo de Medici rules Florence
1495	Leonardo da Vinci begins painting *Last Supper*
1508–1512	Michelangelo paints ceiling of Sistine Chapel
1509	Erasmus' *Praise of Folly* published
1514	Raphael appointed chief architect of St. Peter's in Rome
1532	Machiavelli's *The Prince* and Rabelais' *Pantagruel* published
1594–1595	Shakespeare writes *Romeo and Juliet*
1605	First part of Cervantes' *Don Quixote* published

It is no wonder that the Renaissance has been described as "the discovery by man of himself and of the world."

Humanists admire Graeco-Roman culture. Humanists were fascinated with the culture of ancient Greece and Rome. To them the writings of the ancients were as precious as crown jewels. Machiavelli, a Renaissance scholar and statesman, tells us that in the evening he would enter his study, put on silken robes, and as he studied his favorite authors he would imagine that he was in an ancient palace conversing with the Romans of old. "And for the space of four hours I forget the world [of today and] . . . pass indeed into their world."

Why this enthusiasm for the ancient world? From the literature of Greece and Rome, Renaissance man learned how to explore and to enjoy life in this world. To the Greeks and Romans living well was an art. They did not view life as merely a preparation for heaven. They sought a life that combined thought and action. They admired a good mind in a healthy body. The humanists wanted to recapture this

Much of Renaissance art has meaning beyond that of the subject presented. Michelangelo's design for the tomb of Giuliano de Medici includes figures representing Day (left) and Night. The unfinished features of Day's face, in contrast with the realism of the body, heighten the symbolism of the figure. Botticelli's Primavera (above) recalls the newness of life each spring.

love of life. Moreover, they found the literature of the ancients exciting to read and beautiful to recite. They wanted to imitate its style.

While interest in Graeco-Roman literature had increased toward the end of the Middle Ages, only a handful of these ancient writings were known. Many Greek and Roman works lay neglected, their whereabouts unknown, their words unread. With the Renaissance, however, man's desire to learn about the great works of the past knew no bounds. Renaissance humanists sought to read, print, and restore to circulation every scrap of ancient literature that could still be found.

Medieval scholars, influenced by their religious faith, had shown little interest in the Graeco-Roman way of life. Feeling that they had sufficient guide for living in the teachings of Christianity, they tried to fit the ideas of ancient writers into a Christian framework. They used Greek ideas to explain Christian teachings. Renaissance humanists, on the other hand, believed that the writers of the ancient world could teach mankind much about life, art, and society. In the pages of these ancient books Renaissance humanists found brilliant discussions on the nature of man, the conduct of statesmen, and the meaning of beauty.

Italy takes the lead in developing Renaissance culture. Italy was the homeland of the Renaissance. Italian city-states such as Florence, Venice, and Milan had grown rich from the revival of trade in the Middle Ages. In such cities wealthy merchants and bankers became interested in art and literature. It became fashionable to collect Greek and Roman books and to beautify the home with art objects.

The greatest city-state of the Renaissance was Florence. Some of the finest artists and writers of Italy either came from Florence or moved there. Rich Florentine bankers and merchants owned beautiful homes which they decorated with masterpieces of art. The work of Florentine craftsmen, particularly the goldsmiths, was known and admired throughout Europe. Florentine citizens were proud of their city. They spent large sums of money on the arts and crafts to make it beautiful. Soon Florence was as much a center of culture as Athens had been. It was looked upon as the cultural capital of Europe. "This is an age of gold, which has brought back to life . . . poetry, eloquence, painting, and architecture, sculpture, music. And all this at Florence," wrote a Renaissance humanist.

Men of wealth subsidize the arts. Artists and writers were helped and encouraged by men of wealth who had the leisure to enjoy art and literature. Some of the leading *patrons* or supporters of culture were Popes. They collected many Greek and Roman manuscripts and hired artists to build and decorate churches. Kings, merchants, bankers, and princes competed with each other to attract men of talent to their courts. Lorenzo de Medici (*mey'*dee-chee), ruler of Florence from 1469 to 1492, was one of the most famous patrons of culture. Lorenzo loved all the arts. He sent humanists to Greece to search for ancient books. He expanded the university at Florence to give the youth of the city an opportunity to study the learning of the past. Writers and artists were frequent guests at his home. Painters and sculptors who produced works of art for Lorenzo were well paid. Under the lead of Lorenzo, says a present-day historian, "Florence became the mother of the arts and the cultural capital of Italy, imitated but unsurpassed by rival states. He set the pace, and other princes were compelled to compete, but he was the highest bidder for the services of scholars and artists and carried off all the prizes for the glory of Florence and the greater glory of the Medici."

CHECK-UP

1. What role did the townsman play in medieval society?

2. What attitudes were characteristic of Renaissance man? How did these outlooks differ from those of medieval man?

3. What is humanism? What interests did a humanist have?

4. What factors made Italy the center of the Renaissance?

5. What contribution did Lorenzo de Medici make to the development of culture during the Renaissance?

Petrarch is the father of humanism. Francesco Petrarch (*pee'*trark), born in Arezzo (ah-*reyt'*-tsoh), Italy, was the first great humanist of the Renaissance. He collected ancient Latin and Greek manuscripts. He wrote Latin poetry in an attempt to imitate the style of great Roman writers. Petrarch enjoyed reading about the deeds of Roman heroes. He regarded books as "welcome . . . companions . . . [that] encourage you, comfort you, advise you, . . . take care of you, . . . [and] teach you the world's secrets."

Petrarch wanted to explore the inner life of man. He sought to discover and to portray his own deepest feelings. He felt that while observing nature, while reading the literature of Greece and Rome, while writing poetry, while alone engaged in thought, man finds out more about himself—"whence [he] comes, where he goes, and why he is born."

In 1341 the University of Paris hailed Petrarch as the finest poet of the Christian world. Princes considered it an honor if this prince of poets visited their courts.

Petrarch appreciated the beauty of nature. He described the blue waters of lakes, the snowy peaks of mountains, and the songs of birds. But he is most remembered for the tender poems written to his beloved Laura.

If this should not be Love, O God, what shakes
    me?
If Love it is, what strange, what rich delight?

Petrarch loved to write so much that he often worked at his desk throughout the night. When a worried friend urged him to relax and not to work so hard, he replied, "nothing weighs less than a pen, and nothing gives more pleasure; it is useful not only to the writer but to others far away, perhaps even to those who will be born a thousand years from now." On July 19, 1374, Petrarch, the father of humanism, was found dead in his library, his head resting on an open book, his pen fallen from his hand.

Erasmus and Rabelais encourage humanist learning outside Italy. Perhaps the most famous and respected Renaissance humanist was Desiderius Erasmus, a gentle Dutchman. Erasmus encouraged the new humanist learning in the Low Countries (Holland and Belgium), the German states, and England. His desire for knowledge led him to study Greek when he was 34, though he was often sick and short of money.

Erasmus was deeply interested in man's behavior. He hated ignorance, superstition, and greed. He wanted man to be kind and reasonable. In his greatest work, *Praise of Folly,* Erasmus attacked the stupidity and wrongdoing of churchmen, kings, and philosophers. Although often critical of the Church, throughout his life Erasmus remained a faithful Catholic.

The humanist spirit in France was expressed by François Rabelais (frahn-*swah'* rah-*b'leh'*). Rabelais was a monk who rebelled against the monastic way of life and left the monastery to practice medicine. A man who wrote "Let nothing in the world be unknown to you" could not be happy in a monastery. Rabelais imagined a new type of "monastery," one devoted to the humanist way of life. Instead of the humble and disciplined life of medieval monks, Rabelais' "Renaissance monks" would do exciting things. They would ride, hunt, handle weapons, "read, write, sing, play upon several instruments, speak five or six . . . languages." Above all they would not be tied down by strict rules. Only one regulation would they obey: "Do what you want." How different this was from the monastery of St. Benedict!

Cervantes' classic, Don Quixote, **reflects a humanist assessment of chivalry.** In the sixteenth century tales of chivalry were still enormously popular in Spain. A poor Spaniard named Miguel de Cervantes Saavedra (me-*gel'* day sair-*bahn'*tehs sah-*bay'*drah), who had

Birthplace of the Renaissance, Florence combines medieval and Renaissance architecture, as this modern view of the city's main square (top, left) shows. The ornate gold, pearl, and enamel cup (left), created by the renowned Florentine goldsmith Benvenuto Cellini, reflects the splendor of Renaissance Florence. When Venice erected the statue of General Colleoni (above), it started a tradition of honoring great generals by equestrian statues.

written many undistinguished poems and plays, began to wonder what would happen to a knight if he actually were to appear in sixteenth-century Spain. The result was *Don Quixote* (*dohn' kee-hoh'tey*), one of the greatest and best-loved books in the world. Cervantes' knight was an elderly poor gentleman, healthy but lean, who

spent whole nights from sundown to sunup and his days from dawn to dusk in poring over his books, until finally, from so little sleeping and so much reading, his brain dried up and he went completely out of his mind. . . . At last, when his wits were gone beyond repair, he [thought of] the strangest idea that ever occurred to any madman in this world. [He decided], . . . in order to win a greater amount of honor for himself and serve his country at the same time, to become a [roving knight] and roam the world on horseback in a suit of armor; he would . . . [put] into practice all that he had read in his books.*

He took the name Don Quixote de la Mancha. For his noble lady, he chose "a very good-looking farm girl who lived near by" and called her Dulcinea (*dool-see-nay'ah*) del Toboso.

One morning, without telling anyone, Don Quixote mounted his horse, which was as much skin and bones as he was, put on his badly fitting armor, and went looking for adventure.

He came across a group of merchants, whom, in his madness, he took for knights. Don Quixote no sooner imagined a thing to be true than it became real to him:

. . . with bold and knightly bearing, he settled himself firmly in the stirrups, [lowered] his lance, covered himself with his shield, and took up a position in the middle of the road. . . . When they were near enough to see and hear plainly, Don Quixote raised his voice and made a haughty gesture. "Let everyone," he cried, "stand where he is, unless everyone will confess that there is not in all

---

* This and the following quotations are adapted from *The Ingenious Gentleman Don Quixote de la Mancha* by Miguel de Cervantes Saavedra, translated by Samuel Putnam. Copyright 1949 by The Viking Press, Inc. Reprinted by permission of The Viking Press, Inc.

the world a more [beautiful lady] than the Empress of La Mancha, the peerless Dulcinea del Toboso."

The merchants stopped short, struck as much by Don Quixote's appearance as by his words. They realized right away "that they had to deal with a madman." Out of curiosity they began to talk with Don Quixote, asking to see a picture of his lady. He refused, saying "The important thing is for you—without seeing her —to believe and confess" that she is the most beautiful woman in the world. "Otherwise, monstrous . . . creatures that you are, you shall do battle with me."

When the merchants started to tease him, Don Quixote lost his temper. Lowering his lance, he charged "with such wrath and fury" that his horse stumbled and fell. The hapless knight "went rolling over the plain for some little distance, and when he tried to get to his feet, found that he was unable to do so, being too [loaded down] with his lance, shield, spurs, helmet, and the weight of [his] . . . armor." This was only the first of many adventures caused by Don Quixote's wild imaginings.

Although Cervantes had originally intended just to make fun of books of chivalry, *Don Quixote* has come to have greater significance. By contrasting its hero's world of fantasy with real life, it shows how man's hopes and fantasies shape his view of reality. *Don Quixote* expressed the rational, humanist spirit, mocking the "artificial" medieval ideals of chivalry and portraying all of the natural emotions of man, his hopes and fears, his triumphs and failures. Because it gives the reader both wisdom and enjoyment, its appeal is worldwide.

Machiavelli presents a new theory of the ideal political leader. During the Middle Ages, it was believed that a ruler should act as a good Christian. He should always remember that his first duty was to God. He should set an example for his subjects by leading a good life. However, one Renaissance writer, Niccolò Machiavelli (*neek-koh-loh' mah-kyah-vel'lee*), separated

The Renaissance emphasis on the individual led artists to develop a new creativity in portraiture. They tried to capture the personality as well as the physical appearance of their subjects. Two contrasting subjects were Cesare Borgia (above), on whose career Machiavelli based The Prince, and the humanist Erasmus (left).

religion from political theory. He looked at the behavior of rulers of men as Cervantes looked at chivalry—in the cold light of reason. In *The Prince* Machiavelli describes how rulers actually gain and keep power. The successful ruler, says Machiavelli, thinks not about God and the teachings of the Church but about power and the survival of the state. If it will help the state, the ruler lies, breaks treaties, and attacks his enemies. If the prince tries to act like a good Christian, his country will probably be destroyed by those states whose rulers are more crafty. Only a foolish ruler will trust another ruler. Machiavelli concluded that most men are selfish, cowardly, cruel, and evil. Therefore, the successful prince must follow the law of the jungle, not the teachings of Christ. Only in this way, said Machiavelli, does a state triumph over its enemies. Some political scientists believe that *The Prince* accurately describes how leaders of state have always behaved and always will behave.

CHECK-UP

1. Why is Petrarch considered the father of humanism? How did the work of Erasmus and Rabelais help to spread the spirit of humanism?
2. What is the significance of *Don Quixote*?
3. What lessons was Machiavelli trying to teach to politicians of his time in *The Prince*?

Renaissance art expresses the humanist outlook. The artists of the Renaissance expressed as deep an interest in man as did Renaissance writers. Medieval paintings were mostly religious. Medieval artists and sculptors decorated churches, painted religious scenes, carved statues of Christ, the Virgin, the saints, and angels. Human figures were usually draped and rigid, and until the fourteenth century faces showed little expression. Renaissance artists, however, painted and sculptured every subject, nonreligious as well as religious, that interested them. Even in their religious paintings, they tried to capture a subject's feelings. In Renaissance portraits, the body seems ready to move; the face is alive with expression. It is said that when a great Renaissance sculptor saw how lifelike was the statue he had created, he shouted: "Speak, then! Why will you not speak!"

Leonardo da Vinci is an example of Renaissance versatility. Leonardo da Vinci (lay-oh-nahr'doh dah *veen'*chee) was the most extraordinary man of the Renaissance. His talents were endless. As a boy he was known for his fine singing voice. When Leonardo was about fourteen, he studied painting with a great artist. Soon young Leonardo outshone his teacher. He became an expert painter, and an engineer, scientist, and inventor as well. He was versatile —he did many things well. He had unlimited curiosity and tireless energy. Never has the world seen so many-sided a genius. As a scientist and inventor, Leonardo was far ahead of his time. He designed flying machines, submarines, and machine guns. He drew accurate maps and studied the geological history of the earth. To find out more about the human body, he dissected (took apart) human corpses and made careful drawings of what he saw.

Some artists of Leonardo's time learned art by copying the great masters. Leonardo was

different. He did not want to imitate other artists. He wanted to discover beauty for himself. He tried to show nature as he saw it with his own eyes, and urged painters to study the beauty of nature and the movements of people. Artists, said Leonardo, "should be on the watch in the streets and squares and fields and then make sketches." In this way their painting would be true to life.

Raphael's madonnas reflect the Renaissance spirit. Raffaello Santi (Raphael) grew up in a world of color and design. His father was a painter whose patron was an Italian nobleman. From the time he began painting till he was seventeen, Raphael served as an apprentice to experienced artists. Under the skillful guidance of his teachers, Raphael's talent developed.

Raphael was especially noted for his paintings of madonnas—portraits of the Virgin and Christ Child. Raphael's madonnas are real people. They clearly reflect the humanism of the Renaissance. The Virgin appears warm and gentle, the Christ Child soft and tender. So moved were people by the beauty of Raphael's madonnas, that they believed they could work miracles. Popes and princes paid for Raphael's services. "I have such love of perfection," wrote one high churchman, "that I too have decided to have my portrait painted by Raphael." Though he died at the age of 37, the master painter left the world many great paintings.

Michelangelo excels both as a sculptor and a painter. Many regard Michelangelo Buonarotti (me-kehl-*ahn'*jay-loh bwoh-nah-*roh'*tee) as the greatest painter and sculptor of the Renaissance. After his mother passed away, young Michelangelo was placed in the care of a marble cutter. There the youth learned the art of sculpturing. Though he later served as an apprentice to a painter, his true interest remained sculpture. He called sculpture "the first of arts [be-

One of Michelangelo's most difficult assignments was the painting of the ceiling of the Sistine Chapel. The fresco above captures the impact of the moment of the creation of the sun, one of the Old Testament themes Michelangelo illustrated.

cause] . . . each act, each limb, each bone [is] given life and, lo, man's body is raised breathing, alive, in wax or clay or stone."

Michelangelo's sculpture is huge, powerful, and realistic. His marble statue of the Biblical David is giant size—about seventeen feet high.

It shows Michelangelo's excellent knowledge of the human body. His statue of Moses shows the power and strength of a prophet who spoke with God.

When Michelangelo was 33, Pope Julius II called him to Rome to paint the ceiling of the

Sistine (sis-*teen'*) Chapel. Michelangelo decided to tell the story of the Bible from the creation of the world to the great Flood of Noah's time. For six years Michelangelo worked stretched out on his back atop a high platform, the sun's heat beating down on him from the roof of the chapel and paint dripping into his eyes. When darkness came, he worked by candlelight. Many nights he slept on the platform. Many days he ate only stale bread. He suffered from painful cramps in the legs; his eyesight began to fail. He rarely took time to visit anyone. "I have no friend of any kind and I do not need any," he wrote. All his energies went into his work. "I have been here a thousand years," wrote Michelangelo to his father; "I am more exhausted than man ever was." His health was permanently ruined, but Michelangelo had created some of the greatest painting of all time.

When Michelangelo was 63 years old, Pope Paul III ordered him to do more work in the Sistine Chapel. The result of five and a half years' labor and suffering was *The Last Judgment*. This painting shows Christ sitting in judgment on his throne in heaven. With him are the Virgin and his apostles. His arm raised high, Christ judges the souls of men. At the bottom of the picture are the doomed souls, who have been condemned to hell.

The development of a theory of perspective was one of the major advances of Renaissance painting. Renaissance art marks a sharp break with the flat, two-dimensional style of medieval art (page 147). Instrumental in developing the theory of perspective was Leonardo da Vinci, whose notebooks of sketches such as the one for the Adoration of the Magi *(above) reveal the care with which he plotted his works. By the technique of converging lines aimed at an imaginary vanishing point, da Vinci gave his paintings distance and depth.*

CHECK-UP

1. Why can Leonardo da Vinci be called a many-sided genius? How did he try to capture real life in his art?

2. How did Raphael's work reflect the spirit of the Renaissance?

3. What was noteworthy about Michelangelo's sculptures? What is so remarkable about the ceiling of the Sistine Chapel?

Summing Up

Historians view the Renaissance as beginning a new age in history. The men of the Renaissance also felt that their age was different from the Middle Ages. They felt that they lived in a remarkable period. They were proud of the many writers and talented artists of the time.

One Renaissance writer thanked God that he had been "born in this new age, so full of hope and promise, which [has more] nobly gifted souls than the world has seen in the thousand years that [came before] it." By stressing living well in this world, by encouraging man to develop his reason and his talents, by seeking to understand and to enjoy the beauty of nature, the Renaissance helped to create the secular attitudes of the modern world.

Chapter Highlights

Can you explain?

humanism	madonnas	secular
versatile	Renaissance	patrons

Can you identify?

Cervantes	*The Prince*	Machiavelli	Lorenzo de Medici
Venice	Erasmus	da Vinci	Michelangelo
Florence	Raphael	Graeco-Roman culture	Rabelais
Petrarch	*Don Quixote*	Sistine Chapel	

What do you think?

1. Do you believe that culture rises and falls? If so, what periods you have studied thus far might be considered cultural high points? What do you think is the level of present-day culture?

2. Why can the middle-class townsman be called a force for change?

3. Compare medieval man's outlook on life with Renaissance man's outlook. What was the purpose of life according to each?

4. Why were Renaissance humanists so fascinated with the Graeco-Roman world? How did they hope to keep its riches alive?

5. Why can Petrarch, Erasmus, and Rabelais be called modern men? Do you think their views would be accepted in today's world?

6. What lesson was Cervantes trying to teach the world through his knight Don Quixote? What qualities does this story have that make it a classic?

7. Some political scientists believe that *The Prince* accurately describes how rulers have always behaved and will always behave. What is your opinion?

8. What new developments took place in artistic expression during the Renaissance? How did these developments bring art closer to that of the modern world?

9. What is so exciting about the age of the Renaissance? Would you like to have lived during this era? Why?

14

The Reformation

During the Middle Ages the Catholic Church helped to unify the peoples of Europe. The teachings of the Church were accepted as truth. People who refused to accept what the Church taught were called heretics (page 147). The Church felt that heretics would lead men away from God, and in the eyes of the Church there could be no greater crime. Therefore the Church believed it had a duty to prevent heretics from spreading their dangerous ideas. At times the Church exterminated heresy by fire and sword. Those who killed heretics were looked upon as warriors of God.

Early in the sixteenth century Martin Luther, a German monk, protested against some of the beliefs and practices of the Catholic Church. The Church declared Luther a heretic, and tried unsuccessfully to stop him from spreading his ideas. Luther's actions led to a great split in Christian Europe. Many Christians broke away from the Catholic Church and became *Protestants* (because they *protested* against the Church). The thousand-year-old religious unity of Western Europe came to an end. This breakup of the Church is called the *Protestant Reformation* or *Protestant Revolt*. Why and how was Luther able to start the Reformation?

Revelation (the Apocalypse), the last book in the Bible, foretells the last judgment. In a woodcut (left) German artist Albert Dürer showed The Four Horsemen of the Apocalypse *responsible for the end of the world: Death on a skeletal horse, Want carrying an empty scale, Sickness holding a sword, and War shooting an arrow. A close friend of Luther, Lucas Cranach painted several portraits of the Protestant reformer. The painting* Martin Luther *above, in the Nationalmuseum of Stockholm, was done in 1526.*

Criticism of the Catholic Church increases. By the sixteenth century many people in Europe, especially the Germans, found fault with the Church. They resented the fact that the center of Church power was Rome. They complained because income flowed to Rome. They felt that many churchmen were less interested in religion than in luxurious living and power. Monks were criticized for being rude and ignorant. Most bishops came from the nobility and used the income from Church-owned lands to live like great lords. It was common for the papacy at Rome to expect bishops to pay a large sum of money when they were appointed to office. Sometimes a young nobleman was named to a high Church position because his family was related to or had influence with men high in the Church. The Pope was criticized for acting more like a great lord than the head of the Church. He ruled over a large area in Italy and had his own army. He fought wars with other rulers and used his religious authority to bring about their defeat.

In the German states, concern for religion was greater than in the Italian states. The Italians were more affected by the worldly spirit of the Renaissance than were their neighbors to the north. Angered by conditions in the Church, many Germans called for reform. They wanted to return to the days of early Christianity when churchmen were poor but deeply religious, when the Church was chiefly concerned with preparing souls for heaven and not with acquiring land and collecting taxes.

In the Middle Ages the Church more than once had been criticized by clergy and laymen. These criticisms sometimes led to reforms. This time, however, attacks against the Church led to open revolt. The leader of this revolt against the Church was Martin Luther.

Luther finds the teachings of the Church inadequate. Luther was a troubled man. More than anything he wanted to please God and reach heaven. He hoped to come closer to God by leading the strict life of a monk. He prayed and fasted more than was required of him. He visited holy places.

But Luther did not find the peace of mind for which he sought. He still felt like a sinner. He worried about how he who was just "dust and ashes, . . . full of sin" could ever satisfy Almighty God, the Creator and Lord of Heaven and Earth. Luther, filled with terror, feared that he could never enter heaven, that his soul would be damned.

Luther discussed his problems with other monks, but his fears did not lessen. He went through a terrible emotional struggle daily, asking himself over and over again, "How can I please God?"

Finally, Luther thought that he had found a way for lowly man to please God. Man could be saved, said Luther, by *faith*. He believed that if man had in his heart a deep and boundless love for God, he would be saved. This faith, said Luther, could be obtained only by reading and taking to heart God's words as written in the Bible. Having reached these conclusions, Luther stated: "Thereupon I felt as if I had been born again and had entered Paradise through wide-open gates. Immediately the whole of Scripture [the Bible] took on a new meaning for me."

Luther became more and more dissatisfied with the teachings of the Church. First, he insisted that man could reach God *by faith alone*. The Church, however, held that faith alone was not enough, that it was not sufficient just to love God and feel the meaning of Christ's words in one's heart. Faith must be combined with *good works* such as participation in the Sacraments (see box, page 144), church attendance, pilgrimages, aid to the poor, and donations to the Church. The Church stated that one could not be a true Christian without performing these good works. According to Luther, good works did not bring a person closer to God. The doors of heaven would be opened only to those who had deep faith.

Luther disagreed with other Church teachings. The Church held that only the clergy had the knowledge to explain the meaning of the Bible. Luther insisted that a person did not need a priest to explain the Bible to him. Each man,

The Reformation and Counter Reformation

1483–1546	Luther
1509–1564	Calvin
1517	*Ninety-Five Theses* of Luther
1519–1556	Charles V Holy Roman Emperor
1534	English Church breaks with Rome
1540	Society of Jesus gains approval by Pope
1545–1563	Council of Trent

Europe About 1520

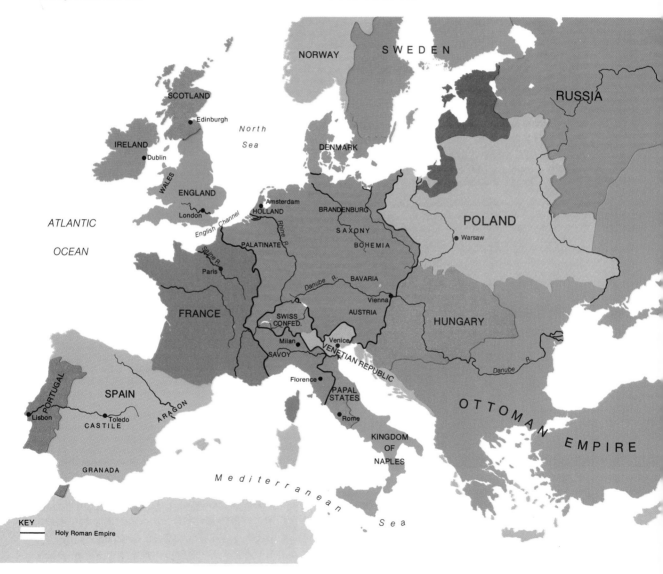

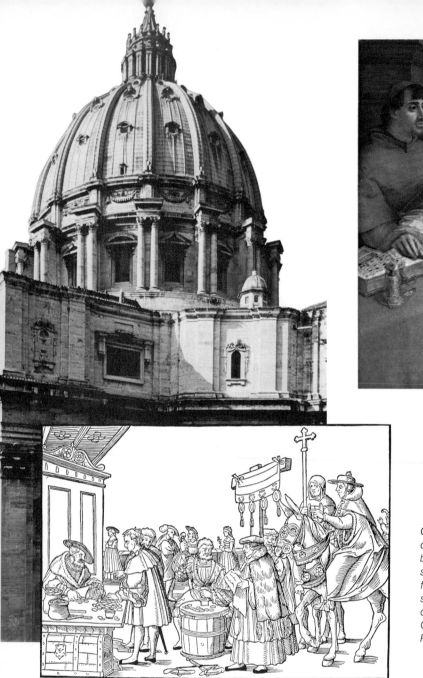

German artists depicted the widespread discontent with the Church, symbolized by St. Peter's in Rome (above, left). They showed agents selling indulgences (left) for prices determined by the buyer's social status rather than his spiritual condition. Particularly resented by the Germans was the luxury that surrounded Pope Leo X (above).

by reading the Bible in good faith, could discover its meaning for himself. Moreover, the Church held that the clergy were closer to God than laymen (non-clergymen), and that laymen could reach God only with the aid of the clergy. Luther disagreed. In his eyes, there was no difference between a clergyman and a layman. Every Christian was a priest who could communicate directly with God. Finally, Luther refused to accept the Pope as the highest and final authority on matters of Christian faith. To him the Pope was a man like any other Christian— no wiser, no better, no holier.

Luther attacks the system of indulgences. Soon Luther and the Church were engaged in a bitter quarrel. It began over the question of how a man should receive pardon for his sins. The Church taught that forgiveness of sins depends upon (1) confessing one's sin to a priest, (2) expressing sincere regret and desire not to sin again, (3) paying for one's sins by doing *penance* such as fasting or prayer. In time there developed the practice of gaining pardon for one's sins by buying an *indulgence*—that is, by making a donation of money to the Church. Indulgences had originally been granted for good works such as making a pilgrimage or going on a crusade. But in the 1300's the Pope began to grant indulgences to those who, as part of their penance, gave money to the Church. The Church still taught that a sinner should confess his sins, express regret, and show his sorrow by prayer and fasting. But many people found it convenient to believe that the buying of an indulgence made further penance unnecessary. Some clergymen, eager to increase sales, from which they received a percentage, failed to make clear what the indulgences could and could not do. Although this was not what the Church taught, people came to believe that an indulgence was a ticket to heaven.

Luther was greatly angered by the buying and selling of indulgences. He was shocked that the Church should foster the idea that men could buy their way into heaven.

The Church excommunicates Luther. On October 31, 1517, Luther posted on a church door his *Ninety-Five Theses,* arguments in which he denounced the whole system of indulgences. Soon Luther attacked other beliefs of the Church. On June 15, 1520, the Pope gave Luther sixty days to renounce his beliefs. Otherwise, he would formally be declared a heretic and be dealt with accordingly. Before a crowd of cheering students, professors, and townspeople, Luther burned the Pope's order. In the following January the Pope excommunicated Luther. This order was published in Germany on May 6, 1521.

Meanwhile, Holy Roman Emperor Charles V (see page 401) had arrived in Germany to hold his first parliament. The members of this legislative group included princes, high clergymen, and wealthy *burghers* (middle-class townspeople). They asked Luther once again to give up his beliefs. He answered that to change his views would be going against his conscience. This he would not do. "On this I take my stand. I can do no other. God help me. Amen." Luther was then declared an excommunicated heretic by the Church and was outlawed by the state. Friends of Luther feared for his life. A powerful German prince protected him, and for almost a year Luther stayed in hiding. During this time he translated the New Testament into German.

Protestantism spreads in Europe. Luther had gained many supporters throughout Germany. Wrote one churchman to the Pope: "Nine tenths of the people are shouting 'Luther!' and the other tenth shouts 'Down with Rome!' " The Church and the emperor tried to stop the rebellion from spreading but were unsuccessful. Lutheranism and other forms of Protestantism spread from Germany to Denmark, Sweden, Norway, Holland, England, Switzerland, and other parts of Europe. Why did Luther gain the support of many Germans? Why did Protestantism spread to regions outside Germany?

1. Humanist influence. The humanists of the Renaissance helped prepare the way for the Reformation. They criticized churchmen for not acting like good Christians. They said that rituals, ceremonies, pilgrimages, and other merely "external" acts (or works) were not the best way of reaching God. They began an independent study of the Bible in order to examine the origins and true meaning of Christianity.

This early print illustrates the process of printing a book using movable type, a development which greatly facilitated the spread of ideas. The first book for which this process was used was probably the Bible.

2. *Discontent with the Church.* Conditions in the Church had angered many people, particularly the Germans. They felt that it was too late to reform the abuses of the Catholic Church. Because they favored a complete break with Rome, Luther became their hero. They considered him a holy man who would lead them closer to God.

3. *Opposition to Church taxes.* Religion was not the only reason why Germans supported Luther. Many Germans were angry about the taxes that they had to pay the Church. This money was taken out of the German states and sent to Rome. Many Germans believed that

most of it was spent for the luxurious living of the Pope and the higher clergy in Rome. Wrote one angry supporter of Luther:

We see that there is no gold and almost no silver in our German land. What little may perhaps be left is drawn away daily by the new schemes invented by the [Pope and his officials]. . . . What is thus squeezed out of us is put to the most shameful uses. Would you know, dear Germans, what employment I have myself seen that they make at Rome of our money? It does not lie idle! Leo the Tenth gives a part to nephews and relatives. . . . A portion is consumed by so many most reverend cardinals (of which the holy father created no less than one and thirty in a single day), as well as

Protestant and Catholic Churches in Europe (About 1600)

to support innumerable . . . officials . . . of the great head Church. These in turn draw after them, at untold expense, copyists, [minor church officials], messengers, servants, . . . mule drivers, grooms. . . . They construct houses all of marble. They have precious stones, are clothed in purple and fine linen, and dine sumptuously. . . . In short, a vast number of the worst of men are supported in Rome in idle [luxury] by means of our money.

Instead of money flowing to Rome, the townspeople wanted it to be spent to further trade and industry. Many rulers of German states felt that money paid to the Church decreased the amount of money that they could collect in taxes.

4. Anti-Italian sentiment. Not only were leading churchmen wealthy and corrupt. They were also Italian. Germans felt that they were being taken advantage of by these Italians who controlled the most important offices of the Church. Those Germans who embraced Lutheranism and denounced Catholicism believed that they were striking a blow which would free German Catholics from Roman or Italian domination.

5. Desire to reduce Church influence. At this time Germany, unlike England and France, was not a single united country. Rather, it was divided into hundreds of states, most of them ruled by princes. Many princes and lords backed Luther because they saw a chance of taking over the valuable Church property in their states. Kings in other countries became Protestants because they, too, wished to reduce the influence of the Church in their lands. They wanted to do away with Church courts, Church taxes, and Church officials who interfered with the king's power.

Calvinism develops in Switzerland. The Reformation spread to other lands. In Geneva a young Frenchman named John Calvin became the leader of the Swiss Protestants. Calvin agreed with Luther that good works would not gain a man entry into heaven. But instead of saying that all those who had deep faith would enter heaven, Calvin taught that only a few people would reach heaven. These chosen few had already been picked by God at their birth. They were *predestined* to enter heaven. Those whom God had not chosen in advance could never enter heaven no matter how religious or good they might be. But how could a man know if he was predestined to enter heaven? Calvin said that there was no sure way of knowing. But most likely the man who lived simply and religiously, and who avoided sin, was favored by God. Calvinists believed that a man who sought pleasure was destined for hell. Calvin tried to turn Geneva into a holy city. There were laws punishing those who gambled, made noise in church, drank at certain hours, sang "outrageous songs," and did not know their prayers. Calvinism spread to parts of Germany, Holland, England, and America. The Puritans who came to Massachusetts from England were followers of Calvin.

CHECK-UP

1. What is meant by the term Protestant Reformation?

2. What faults did many people find in the Catholic Church? How did they plan to correct these faults?

3. What kind of man was Martin Luther? Why was he dissatisfied with the teachings of the Church?

4. What is an indulgence? How did the sale of indulgences set off the quarrel between Luther and the Church?

5. What were the *Ninety-Five Theses?* How did they lead to Luther's excommunication?

6. Why did so many Germans follow Luther? Why did Protestantism spread to other countries in Europe?

7. What did John Calvin mean by "predestination"? How did he try to change Geneva to meet his religious beliefs?

The Counter Reformation

The Church seeks to check Protestantism. The spread of Protestantism alarmed the Catholic Church. It seemed as if the Church which had existed for some 1500 years was going to break up into many parts. The Church therefore fought back. This effort to combat Protestantism is called the *Counter Reformation,* or the *Catholic Reformation.* How did the Church try to check the spread of Protestantism?

The Council of Trent recommends reforms. Leading churchmen gathered at a council which met in the city of Trent in Italy (1545– 1563) to deal with the dangers facing the Church. The Council of Trent *did not change* any of the teachings of the Church. Catholics were to continue to accept the Church teachings (1) that only the clergy could explain the Bible, (2) that the clergy possessed spiritual powers not held by laymen, (3) that both *faith and good works* were necessary in order to be saved, and (4) that the Pope was the highest and final authority in the Church.

The Council of Trent recommended important reforms. It drastically reduced the buying and selling of Church offices and indulgences.

It insisted that only worthy people should enter the clergy, and established seminaries to train clergymen. It promoted monastic reforms.

The Society of Jesus fights against Protestantism. A young Spanish nobleman named Ignatius Loyola (ig-*nay'*shus loy-*oh'*lah) founded the Society of Jesus (the Jesuits, *jez'*oo-its). This religious order took as its main objective service to the Pope. The aims of the Jesuits were: (1) to keep Catholics from turning Protestant, (2) to win back to Catholicism those who had become Protestants, and (3) to spread Catholicism to other parts of the world. Without the missionary and educational work of the Jesuits, it seems likely that more lands might have become Protestant.

The Index and the Inquisition are attempts to prevent the spread of dangerous ideas. To prevent the spread of heretical ideas, Catholics were not allowed to own, read, or sell certain books which the Church considered dangerous to right thinking and right living. This list of books which Catholics were forbidden to read was called the *Index*.

To meet the challenge of Protestantism, the Church brought back the Inquisition, the Church court used in the Middle Ages to try heretics. In Italy and Spain the Inquisition turned over thousands of heretics to the state for execution.

The papacy supports Catholic rulers. The papacy allied itself with Catholic rulers in Europe in an effort to suppress Protestantism. Religious warfare kept Europe in turmoil for over a hundred years.

In many respects, the Counter Reformation was successful. It corrected many abuses within the Church that disturbed religious people during the time of Luther. It restored Catholicism to some states such as Bohemia (in modern Czechoslovakia) which were strongly Protestant, and it kept Protestantism from spreading to still more countries in Europe. The Church

Founded to strengthen Catholicism in Europe, the Society of Jesus also encouraged the conversion of non-Christians. Here two Portuguese Jesuits discuss religion with the Mughal Emperor Akbar (page 209) and his court. While Christian missionaries were influential elsewhere, in Asia their impact was slight.

remained strong. But it failed to win back millions of people who had left the Church forever to become Protestants. There were now Protestant states in Europe as well as Catholic ones, and in Protestant lands the Catholic Church had no authority whatsoever.

1. How did the Church try to stop the spread of Protestantism?

2. What basic Church doctrines did the Council of Trent reaffirm? What important reforms did it recommend?

3. How successful was the Counter Reformation?

Results of the Reformation

The early leaders of the Reformation were men of religion. They wanted to save men's souls. They tried to restore the same deep faith and love for God that had characterized the first followers of Christ. To Luther nothing was more important than reaching heaven. He had little interest in improving life on earth for the common people. He had no use for the art and literature of the Renaissance. Because the Reformation was more concerned with salvation than with things of this world, it was closer in some ways to the thinking of the Middle Ages than to the Renaissance. But despite the fact that the Reformation was concerned mainly with religion, it had far-reaching effects upon modern history and upon all phases of men's lives. What were the results of the Reformation?

1. Religious unity destroyed. The Reformation destroyed the religious unity of Europe. No longer was there one Church to which all Christian Europeans belonged as they had in the Middle Ages. Christians were now divided into Catholics and Protestants. Protestants themselves were divided into different religious groups. In general the people of Northern Europe became Protestant while those in Southern Europe remained Catholic.

2. Power of kings strengthened. By weakening the Church, the Reformation strengthened the power of kings. In the countries that became Protestant, kings assumed Church powers and seized its wealth. In Catholic countries, the Church had to yield many of its privileges to the kings in order to keep their allegiance. In general, by 1648 people looked for leadership to their king, rather than to the Pope.

3. Business encouraged. Some historians feel that the Reformation aided the growth of business. They hold that the Catholic Church did not approve of the businessman's way of life. The Church felt that businessmen were too concerned with the things of this world. Many Protestants, on the other hand, favored the thrift and industry of businessmen. Calvinists in particular felt that they were doing God's work when they were successful in business.

4. Religious freedom advanced. Despite the fact that Lutherans, Calvinists, and Catholics persecuted those who disagreed with their religious beliefs, in the long run the Reformation contributed to greater religious freedom. In time it became clear that the only way people could live peacefully together was to allow each person to practice the religious views in which he believed.

5. Individual liberty advanced. Neither Luther nor Calvin believed in the democratic freedoms—freedom of speech and the right of all men to participate in the government. Luther was not a political revolutionary. He did not seek to undermine the power of the German princes. He did not preach disobedience to established government. It is not proper, said Luther, "for anyone who would be a Christian to set himself up against his government, whether it act justly or unjustly."

Calvin desired a government in which the clergy would exercise considerable power. He insisted that the main duty of government was the enforcement of Calvinist teachings. In practice this led to annoying rules that interfered with the private life of a citizen.

Nevertheless, some historians feel that the Reformation did advance the cause of individual liberty. Luther had challenged the authority of the Church. Protestants could henceforth read the Bible and seek to understand it for themselves. Calvinist thinkers urged rebellion against kings who interfered with Calvinist religious beliefs and practices. Because the Protestants opposed the long-established authority of the Church and in some instances felt a religious duty to resist absolute kings, some historians believe that the Reformation contributed to the growth of political as well as religious liberty.

CHECK-UP

1. How did the Reformation destroy religious unity? Strengthen the power of rulers? Encourage business? Advance religious freedom?
2. What was the effect of the Reformation on democratic freedoms?

Chapter Highlights

Can you explain?

burghers	seminaries	laymen	Protestants
predestined	good works	penance	indulgences
faith	papacy		

Can you identify?

Calvin	Jesuits	Loyola	Counter Reformation
Puritans	Luther	Council of Trent	Protestant Reformation
Index	Inquisition	*Ninety-Five Theses*	

What do you think?

1. How did Luther and the Catholic Church differ on the questions of (a) salvation, (b) interpreting the Bible, (c) the clergy, and (d) the position of the Pope?

2. What was Luther's moral objection to the sale of indulgences?

3. How did the Renaissance help bring about the spirit of the Reformation?

4. Do you think Luther's original goal was reform or revolt? Why?

5. Why did kings and princes see the Protestant Reformation as a great opportunity for them?

6. What would your life be like if you lived in Calvin's Geneva?

7. How did each of the following help check the spread of Protestantism: (a) the Jesuits, (b) the Index, (c) the Inquisition?

8. Would you consider Luther a "Renaissance man"? Why?

9. Do you think Calvin believed in democracy? Support your point of view with specific examples.

10. How was the Protestant Reformation influenced by other movements of the age?

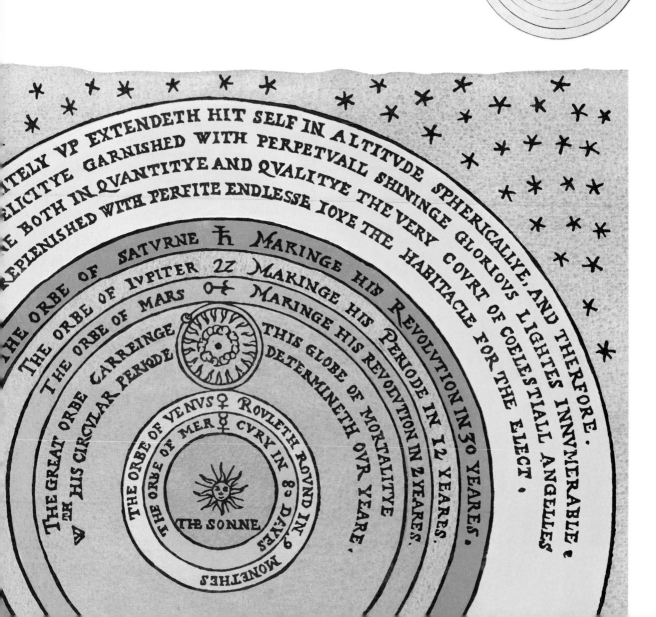

...ITELY VP EXTENDETH HIT SELF IN ALTITVDE SPHERICALLYE, AND THERFORE.

...ELICITYE GARNISHED WITH PERPETVALL SHININGE GLORIOVS LIGHTES INNVMERABLE.

...E BOTH IN QVANTITYE AND QVALITYE THE VERY COVRT OF COELESTIALL ANGELLES

...REPLENISHED WITH PERFITE ENDLESSE IOYE THE HABITACLE FOR THE ELECT.

THE ORBE OF SATVRNE ♄ MAKINGE HIS REVOLVTION IN 30 YEARES.

THE ORBE OF IVPITER ♃ MAKINGE HIS PERIODE IN 12 YEARES.

THE ORBE OF MARS ♂ MAKINGE HIS REVOLVTION IN 2 YEARES.

THE GREAT ORBE CARREINGE THIS GLOBE OF MORTALITYE

☿ ♄ HIS CIRCVLAR PERIODE DETERMINETH OVR YEARE.

THE ORBE OF VENVS ♀ ROVLETH ROVND IN

THE ORBE OF MERCVRY IN 8⁰ DAYES

9 MONETHES

THE SONNE

The Scientific Revolution

CHAPTER FOCUS

Advances in Astronomy and Physics
Advances in Medicine and Biological Sciences
Achievements of the Scientific Revolution

Medieval man accepted the Ptolemaic view that Earth was the center of the universe. Botticelli's illustrations for the Divine Comedy *(page 173) reflect this view. Dante and Beatrice (above) ascend to the starry region beyond the planets revolving about Earth (above, left). This view of the universe was shattered by Copernicus and Galileo. The diagram (left) reflects the Copernican concept that the planets revolve in circular orbits about the sun. The work of Kepler showed these orbits to be elliptical, which is our present concept of the solar system.*

All the movements discussed in this unit helped upset medieval ways and attitudes. The Renaissance encouraged man to think more of this world than of the afterlife. The Reformation split Europe into Protestant and Catholic countries, ending the religious unity of the Middle Ages. The Age of Exploration and the Commercial Revolution (Chapter 16) led to economic expansion and to the conquest and colonization of many parts of the world. Europe had advanced well beyond the limited world of the medieval manor and the confining economy of the medieval guilds. The growing power of kings weakened feudal lords and Church—the two foundations of medieval society—and led to the rise of nation-states (see Chapter 17). But, more than anything else, it was the Scientific Revolution that brought an end to the medieval outlook on life. The Scientific Revolution produced new methods of thinking and increased man's knowledge of nature.

Religion influences medieval thought about the universe. During the Middle Ages science and religion were closely related. Because of this, medieval man looked at the universe very differently from the way we do today. How did medieval man view the universe?

1. In the Middle Ages it was believed that God had created the world especially for man. The Lord had placed Earth in the center of the universe. While Earth remained motionless, the sun, the planets, and the stars circled about it. Being in the center of the universe made man feel that he was important in the eyes of God. It was comforting to know that God had given man the light of the moon, the warmth of the sun, and rain from the clouds. Man never doubted that he was the child of God, and that the Lord loved him and looked after him.

2. Medieval man was certain that the universe was small and closed in like a walled town. Heaven lay just beyond the stars. There God, the King of Kings, looked down upon man and judged his behavior. Man felt good to know that heaven was close by. He looked forward to being with God after death.

3. Medieval thinkers believed that the universe was not everywhere the same. Because the moon, stars, sun, and other heavenly bodies decorated God's courtyard, they were superior to anything on Earth. They were made of a shining substance too fine to be found on Earth. It was as if Earth were the cellar of a giant castle and heaven the tower. In climbing the staircase one would notice a continuous improvement in the surroundings. In the Middle Ages heavenly objects such as the moon were regarded as clean, pure, clear, and unchanging —objects of beauty, perfection, and holiness. Today we know that the moon is just ordinary rock, that deep holes and rugged hills scar its surface. We do not say the moon is "better" or "holier" than Earth. In describing the universe we do not look for a "spiritual" quality. Rather, we talk about carbon, nitrogen, hydrogen, and oxygen content.

4. For the most part, medieval man did not search for new knowledge. He accepted unquestioningly what the Church told him. When he wanted an answer to a question, he did not seek it through experimentation. Instead, he turned to the Bible, to the traditions of the Church, and to the writings of ancient scholars, particularly the great Greek thinker Aristotle (page 54). What the "authorities" had written, medieval man accepted as the truth.

This is how medieval man looked at the universe. Today we have a different picture of the universe. How did this change in outlook come about?

Copernicus corrects man's view of the universe. The medieval view of the universe was shattered by the Scientific Revolution. One of the first great thinkers of the Scientific Revolution was Nicolaus Copernicus (nik-oh-*lay'*us koh-*pur'*nih-kus), a Polish churchman, doctor, and astronomer. Modern astronomy begins with his *Concerning the Revolution of the Celestial Spheres,* published in 1543, the year of his death. Copernicus did not believe that Earth was the center of the universe, although the view had been taught by the highly regarded ancient Greek astronomer Ptolemy (*tuhl'*eh-mih) and was accepted by the Church authorities. Copernicus thought that the planets, including Earth, moved around the sun. "The sun sits . . . upon a royal throne ruling . . . the planets which circle around him," he wrote. This shift from an earth-centered universe to a sun-centered universe has caused a great change in men's thinking over the centuries.

With Earth no longer the center of the universe but just another planet, man seems less important. Today we know that Earth is merely a tiny speck in a giant, endless universe. Our sun is only one of millions of suns. Our planet might be one of billions of other planets. We wonder if life exists elsewhere in the universe. Could this huge universe have been created just for man as medieval man believed? In a universe where we measure distances in thousands of billions of miles, how important are man's problems, hopes, successes, and failures? What does a man's lifetime mean in a universe billions of years old? In the Middle Ages man was certain that he was the child of God and that the universe had been created just for him. This gave medieval man a feeling of security. Modern man, finding himself in an endless ocean of floating stars and whirling suns, feels lost, alone, and insignificant. We understand the feelings of the seventeenth-century French philosopher who said: "the silence of infinite [endless] space frightens me."

Copernicus' theory that Earth moves around the sun was not accepted by most thinkers of his time. Most churchmen rejected the Copernican theory because it seemed to conflict with the Bible. Professors attacked it because it contradicted the theories of ancient scientists.

Critics of the Copernican theory asked: How could a body as heavy as Earth move at such speed through space? If Earth spins on its axis, why does a stone dropped from a height fall directly below instead of to a point behind where it was dropped? Why do objects not fly off the Earth as it spins? What keeps the moon moving about the spinning Earth instead of getting lost in space?

Galileo urges use of experimentation. Some seventy years after the publication of Copernicus' theory, a brilliant Italian scientist-mathematician named Galileo Galilei (gah-leh-*lay*'oh gah-leh-*lay*'ee) gave evidence that Copernicus was right. This got Galileo into much trouble with the Church and the Inquisition.

Even as a young boy Galileo showed remarkable talent. He was a good musician and his paintings received praise. Most of all, young

The Scientific Revolution

1543	Copernicus' work on heliocentric theory published
	Vesalius' final work on anatomy published
1609, 1619	Kepler announces laws of planetary motion
1610	Galileo's discovery of Jupiter's satellites supports heliocentric theory
1620	Francis Bacon's work stressing importance of scientific method published
1628	Harvey's work describing circulation of the blood published
1632	Galileo tried by Inquisition
1632–1723	Leeuwenhoek
1638	Galileo's work dealing with motion, acceleration, and gravity published
1687	Newton announces the laws of motion

Galileo loved to make and play with mechanical toys.

Galileo is considered the father of experimental science. Before Galileo, few scientists made any attempt to discover the laws of physical motion by applying the experimental method. They were satisfied to draw conclusions based upon the teachings of ancient thinkers and upon what they could see with the naked eye. They did not test these conclusions by setting up proper experiments. Galileo insisted that man could not increase his knowledge of nature without performing "sensible experiments and necessary demonstrations." This insistence on the experimental method is the foundation of modern science.

The discoveries of Galileo helped to destroy the medieval view of the universe—that view which combined the teachings of Aristotle's physics and Ptolemy's astronomy with Church doctrines. In Ptolemy's astronomical picture of the universe Earth occupied a central position,

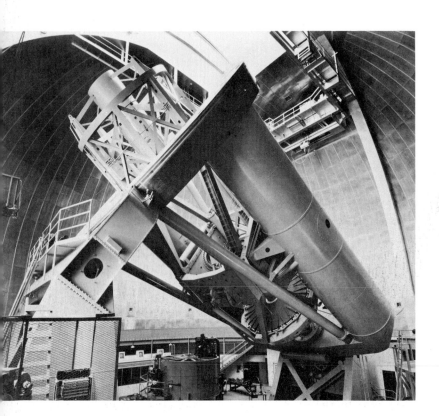

The advances made in astronomy since Galileo's time are reflected in the model of his telescope (above) compared with the 200-inch Hale Telescope (left), the largest in the world. Many modern telescopes are designed for cameras and radio rather than the eye. Using them, astronomers can photograph and listen to the universe.

with the planets and sun revolving about it. This seemed to agree with the Church's notion that the universe was designed especially for man, God's most important creation.

Aristotle's physics claimed that the universe was divided into two parts. Below the moon everything was made of the four elements—water, earth, fire, and air. In the region of the moon and beyond, where the stars and planets shone, everything was made of ether (*ee'*ther), a "higher" substance not found on Earth. While objects on the dark and motionless Earth changed and deteriorated, the heavenly bodies moving in perfect circles about Earth were pure and unchangeable. The medieval mind found it easy to accept the idea that the heavens were

made of a superior substance. Dante and Aquinas, two of the greatest minds of the Middle Ages, believed that when God created the universe He set the planets and stars in motion. God's angels and spirits continued to guide these heavenly objects.

Medieval ideas of motion are based on the teachings of Aristotle. Medieval man's view of motion was based largely on the teachings of Aristotle. Aristotle said that objects made of the heavy elements (earth and water) fell downwards to Earth. Objects made of the lighter elements (air and fire) flew upwards into space. Each object, almost as if it had a will of its own, tried to find its proper place in the universe. A flame, for example, will fly upward because the sky is its proper home. A stone falls to the ground, for it is only fitting and natural that heavy objects move downwards.

Two things were wrong with this medieval explanation of motion. (1) Medieval thinkers did not understand that objects do not move because angels push them or because these objects are trying to find their rightful place in the universe, but because the objects obey a basic law of nature. (2) Medieval thinkers did not understand that the *same* laws of nature operate both in the heavens and on Earth. Thinking that heavenly objects and earthly objects were made of different substances, they believed that heavenly objects could not possibly follow the same laws of motion as did earthly objects.

Most thinkers cling to the old views. Copernicus had raised questions about the earth-centered universe, but the views of Aristotle and Ptolemy continued to have the support of leading churchmen and philosophers. To challenge these eminent men, to question ideas held for centuries, to doubt a view of the universe endorsed by the Church was no small matter. Galileo knew this, but it did not stop him from revealing his discoveries.

Searching the heavens with a telescope he had built, Galileo gave evidence that Copernicus was right: the sun is the center of our system of planets and Earth and the other planets move about it. With his telescope he also saw spots on the sun and craters on the moon. Heavenly objects, said Galileo, were not any purer or more perfect than those found on Earth. Nature was the same throughout the universe. Nor were the heavens unchangeable, as Aristotle had said. When Galileo discovered that new stars were being formed, he proved that change occurs in the heavens as well as on Earth. The *same* physical laws must hold for Earth and the other planets.

Galileo's views come under heavy attack. By challenging Aristotle and supporting Copernicus, Galileo made enemies. "To the [displeasure] of all the philosophers," wrote one of his friends, "very many conclusions of Aristotle were by [Galileo] proved false through experiments and solid demonstrations. . . . Many philosophers . . . were aroused against him." Galileo's enemies would not accept his views. Some opponents even refused to look through Galileo's telescope. The enemies of Galileo put their trust in Aristotle and the Bible. Did not the Bible say that once Earth was formed it could not be moved?

When Galileo discovered that Jupiter had satellites revolving about it in the same manner that the moon revolves about Earth, he was criticized by his fellow scientists. They agreed with the ancient view that there were seven planets moving about Earth—Mercury, Venus, Mars, Jupiter, Saturn, the moon, and the sun. According to this way of thinking, Jupiter's satellites would also have to be regarded as planets. This would mean an increase in the number of planets. Many thinkers found this upsetting. One Italian astronomer attacked Galileo in the following words:

There are seven windows given to animals . . . through which the air is admitted to the . . . body: . . . two nostrils, two eyes, two ears, and a mouth. . . . From this and many other similarities in nature, such as the seven metals, . . . we gather that the number of planets is necessarily seven. Moreover, these satellites of Jupiter are invisible to the naked eye, and therefore can exercise no influence on the earth, and therefore would be useless, and therefore do not exist. . . . Now, if we increase the number of planets, this whole and beautiful system falls to the ground.

Galileo's views also brought him into conflict with the Church. Put on trial before a Church court, Galileo was accused as follows:

. . . you, Galileo, . . . aged seventy years, were in the year 1615 denounced to this Holy Office for holding as true the false doctrine . . . that the Sun is the center of the world and immovable and that the Earth moves, . . . and for following the position of Copernicus, which is contrary to . . . Holy Scripture.

Kepler began his study of the heavens as an apprentice of Tycho Brahe. Using the naked eye to observe the heavens, Brahe concluded that Earth and the moon orbit the sun, while the other planets revolve around Earth. The picture above shows Brahe making astronomical calculations in his observatory.

Fearful of being punished, the elderly scientist promised not to teach the Copernican theory.

Galileo's work started men thinking in new directions. He urged the use of mathematics and experimentation and saw natural law as uniform throughout the universe. These are the foundations upon which modern science rests. An essential principle of modern science is that nature is uniform—that the laws of nature that operate on Earth are also in operation in the rest of the universe. A second premise of science is that these laws of nature can be reduced to mathematical equations—that mathematics is the key to an understanding of the physical laws of the universe. A third basic principle of modern science is the reliance upon the experimental method. The genius of Galileo started man thinking in these directions.

Kepler develops laws on the motion of planets.

Galileo's acceptance of the Copernican theory was not an isolated case. Among his contemporaries was Johannes Kepler (yoh-*hahn'*ehs *kep'*ler) of Germany, one of the greatest astronomers of all time. Kepler gave further evidence to support the Copernican theory. He studied the orbits (paths) of the planets and devised mathematical formulas which expressed the speed at which the planets moved in relation to their distance from the sun. These formulas are called the Laws of Planetary Motion. Kepler's laws made sense only if one first accepted the Copernican view that planets move in orbits about the sun. In one important way, however, Kepler differed from Copernicus. Copernicus had accepted the ancient Greek belief that planets move in circular orbits. He could not break away from the notion that circular motion was a sign of perfection and therefore natural for heavenly objects. Kepler's first law demonstrated that the path of a planet is oval-like—an ellipse rather than a circle. This cleared up many questions about the movement of planets that had puzzled astronomers for centuries.

In his second law Kepler showed that planets moving in their elliptical orbits pick up speed when they approach the sun. In his third law he derived a formula expressing the mathematical relationship between the time it takes a planet to orbit the sun and its distance from the sun. Using Kepler's laws, an astronomer could figure out the location of each planet at a particular time.

While Kepler had discovered the true path of a planet (an ellipse) and had derived mathematical formulas for the movement of the planets, one crucial question remained unanswered: Why do planets stay in their orbits around the sun instead of flying off into space? The answer was not long in coming.

Newton ties together the ideas of earlier scientists. Copernicus, Galileo, and Kepler had introduced revolutionary ideas about the nature of the universe. What was needed now was someone who could *synthesize* or tie together these views by showing that there were certain basic and unchangeable laws of nature that caused the entire universe to operate as it did. This was accomplished by Sir Isaac Newton, an English mathematician and scientist. Newton asked himself, what makes the planets move about the sun? Why don't they race away from the sun or crash into it? Why do apples fall to the ground instead of flying into the sky? Is it possible that the same law of nature accounts for the movement of planets and the falling of apples?

Newton could not accept the medieval notion that there were different kinds of movement for objects on Earth and in the sky. Before Newton, Galileo had made important contributions to the study of motion. He had insisted that there was no place in the study of motion for religious beliefs or fanciful and unproven philosophical ideas. To think sensibly about motion, said Galileo, one must make use of experiments and mathematics. By showing that falling bodies obeyed mathematical laws, Galileo helped prepare the way for Newton.

Newton holds that natural laws operate everywhere. Newton proved that planets move about the sun for the same reason that apples fall to the ground rather than fly upwards. They are obeying the *law of gravity*. Newton showed that the entire universe was like a machine. All parts of the machine—sun, stars, moon, earth, and all the other planets—obeyed the same law of gravity.

Newton also formulated laws which dealt with *rectilinear motion*—movement in a straight line. (For the discussion that follows it is helpful to imagine an object moving through the air in a horizontal straight line.) Earlier thinkers had also dealt with the same subject. Aristotle believed that an object was kept in motion by a rush of air pushing it from behind; some medieval thinkers suggested that the energy or *impetus* which put an object in motion also kept it moving until the energy was burned up. Though the impetus theory was a step towards the truth, neither it nor Aristotle's "air engine" was a correct explanation of rectilinear motion.

Expanding upon conclusions reached by Galileo, Newton formulated the *law of inertia*. This law states that (1) a body at rest will stay at rest unless a force acts upon it causing it to move, and (2) a body in motion will continue to move in a straight line as long as no force interferes with it.

According to the law of inertia, an arrow could move endlessly in a straight line. But since it meets resistance from the air and experiences the downward force of gravity, it will fall to the ground. Similarly, an object rolling along a completely smooth surface continues to roll in the same direction forever. Since few surfaces are perfectly smooth, friction resulting from the contact of the rolling object with the surface and from air resistance halts its motion. (Imagine the Pacific Ocean as a perfectly smooth, frictionless sheet of ice. If someone in California pushed a hockey puck onto the ice and there were no air resistance, the puck would travel in a straight line across the ice sheet until it hit the coast of Asia—in other words, until contact with the Asian continent prevented further inertial motion.)

The importance of the law of inertia is that it makes motion as natural a condition as rest. People rarely ask why a body at rest continues to remain at rest. A body in motion should be viewed in the same way. The inertia theory does away with Aristotle's air engine and the impetus theory. According to the law of inertia, a body in motion needs neither an outside agent nor fuel to keep it moving. What causes it to halt or change its direction is the resistance provided by another force. Newton's laws showed that planets would move in a straight line endlessly into space were they not held in orbit by the gravitational pull of the sun.

The universe of Newton differed considerably from the small geocentric (earth-centered) universe enclosed by a circle of stars—the view held by Aristotle, Ptolemy, and medieval thinkers. For Newton the universe was *infinite,* or endless, having no limits and no center.

Newton showed that the universe was like a giant clock, all of whose parts worked together in perfect harmony. By using mathematics, a scientist could figure how fast the planets moved and the distances they covered. Newton had proved that it was a law of nature, not anything else, that explains why planets move and why apples fall to the ground. The universe was *uniform,* each part of it subject to the same physical laws. A religious man, Newton considered God to be the great Creator of the universe, the Clockmaker Who set the universe in motion.

Newton revolutionizes man's understanding of the universe. The discoveries of Newton convinced many thinkers that there were no longer secrets or mysteries to the working of nature. The laws of motion and of gravity are at work throughout—in the heavens as well as on Earth. Everything follows laws of nature that are rational and can be understood by man.

Newton's work was a magnificent achievement. He had stretched his powers of concentration and thought to the limit. A twentieth-century biographer of Newton says admiringly of the great scientist: "I believe that Newton . . . could sit for hours with the whole powers of his mind fixed on whatever difficulty he was concerned with. I imagine him . . . in the orchard on a summer afternoon or in the kitchen on a winter's evening, completely ignorant of what was going on around him, pondering the motions of the heavenly bodies." Newton's contemporaries regarded him as the greatest mind of his age. "Does he eat, drink, and sleep like other men?" asked an admirer.

CHECK-UP

1. What was medieval man's view of the universe? Why did this view give him a feeling of security?

2. How did Copernicus help change this medieval view? How was his theory received?

3. Why is Galileo considered the father of experimental science? How did his work help to destroy the medieval view of the universe? Why was he so bitterly attacked?

4. What great scientific contribution did Kepler make?

5. Why was Newton's synthesis of the work of those that came before him so vital? How did his law of gravity completely shatter the medieval view of motion?

6. What is Newton's law of inertia? What is its significance?

7. Why was Newton's universe compared to a giant clock? Why is his work considered so outstanding an achievement?

Advances in Medicine and Biological Sciences

Vesalius is the father of modern anatomy. In 1543 Copernicus published his heliocentric theory which was to revolutionize man's view of the universe. That same year a Belgian named Andreas Vesalius (*an'*dreh-uhs veh-*say'*lih-uhs) published a work which would revolutionize man's view of himself. While still a schoolboy, Vesalius wanted to learn all he could about the human body. He turned to the writings of ancient thinkers, but was disappointed. The great minds of the past knew little about *anatomy*—the structure of the body. To learn about anatomy, young Andreas dissected bodies of mice, rats, dogs, and cats.

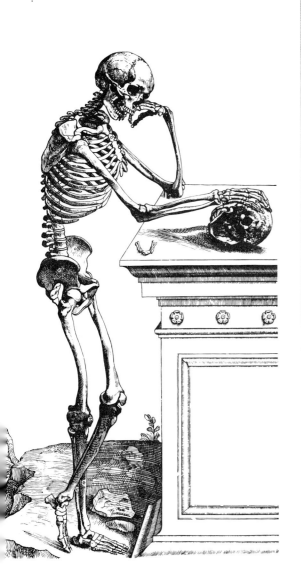

The Renaissance interest in realism led to a new interest in anatomy. By reviving the Hellenistic method of studying the body system by system, Vesalius laid the foundation for modern biology. At left is one of his drawings for a text on the body. Increased knowledge of biology made possible advances in medicine. Doctors learned to prescribe medicines that were prepared in pharmacies like the one shown above.

While a university student, Vesalius studied with some of the best doctors of his time. But he was not satisfied with his professors. Almost everything they taught they had learned from the writings of Galen (*gay'*len), an ancient Greek doctor. Moreover, these professors showed little or no interest in dissection to find out how the body functioned. To satisfy his curiosity about the human body, Vesalius searched cemeteries for skeletons to examine. Once he climbed the gallows in the middle of the night to remove a decaying corpse for study.

During his lifetime Vesalius performed many dissections. He came to know more about anatomy than any other doctor in Europe. He urged his students not to rely on Galen but to investigate for themselves. "How many things have been accepted on the word of Galen . . . and often contrary to reason? . . . Indeed, I myself am wholly astonished at my [former] stupidity and too great trust in the writings of Galen and other anatomists." Because Vesalius urged the scientific study of the human body, he is called the father of modern anatomy.

Harvey sheds light on the circulation of the blood. William Harvey, an English doctor, was another pioneer in the history of science. Harvey did not try to understand the workings of the heart by reading the writings of others. Instead, he experimented with living animals. "I found the task so . . . full of difficulties," he wrote, "that I was almost tempted to think . . . that the motion of the heart was only to be [understood] by God." However, Harvey's experiments soon bore results. He discovered that blood flows from the heart, is pumped through the body, and then returns to the heart. This is called the *circulation* of the blood. Harvey's discovery was another triumph for the experimental method.

Leeuwenhoek discovers the world of micro-organisms. An uneducated Dutch store-keeper, Anton van Leeuwenhoek (*an'*tohn vahn *ley'*vehn-hook), had an unusual hobby. He spent many hours grinding glass lenses. In time this patient craftsman was making the finest lenses in the world. Under his simple but effective microscope, objects appeared hundreds of times larger than they really were. Leeuwenhoek wanted to examine everything with this magnifying lens. He studied the eye of an ox, the brain of a fly, the wool of sheep, and the seeds of plants. He watched the blood racing through a tadpole's body.

One day Leeuwenhoek put some water under his microscope and made a remarkable discovery. He saw "living creatures, . . . little animals," swimming and dashing about. Soon he was looking with "wonder [at] 1000 living creatures in one drop of water." Leeuwenhoek had uncovered a mysterious new world—the world of *microorganisms,* living things too small to be seen with the naked eye. Both Newton and Leeuwenhoek had opened up new worlds for men to explore: Leeuwenhoek had discovered the world of the infinitely small, Newton had pondered the infinite reaches of the universe.

Bacon views science as the servant of man. Sir Francis Bacon, an English writer and philosopher, was not a prominent scientist, but he did play an important role in the Scientific Revolution. Bacon wanted science to serve man, to help him to live a more comfortable life, to give him more insight into the world around him. Like Galileo, Bacon urged scientists to investigate nature, to challenge the old authorities, and to acquire new knowledge through experimentation. He wanted scientists to free themselves from the cobwebs of the past, from ignorance and prejudice, and to strike out on new paths of discovery. Bacon's insistence on scientific attitudes foretold the direction modern science would take.

CHECK-UP

1. How did Vesalius learn so much about the structure of the body? Why is he called the father of modern anatomy?

2. How did Harvey and Leeuwenhoek open new worlds for medicine and biology?

3. Why is Francis Bacon credited with contributing much to the Scientific Revolution?

Achievements of the Scientific Revolution

The Scientific Revolution increased our knowledge of nature and destroyed the medieval view of the universe. It also gave man a new way of looking at nature—the scientific way. Today scientists question and experiment. They search for new knowledge and better ways of doing things. They do not accept something as true merely because Aristotle said it or because it is written in the Bible. They demand proof supported by experiment. They rely upon mathematical calculations. The scientific attitude was expressed by Leeuwenhoek, the Dutch lensmaker: "My investigations are made only with the object of discovering the truth as much as is in my power. . . . [I want] to put the truth before the eyes of all, and with the little talent that I have to remove [ignorance] from the world."

The Scientific Revolution has never ended. Today science continues to make great advances. Wonder drugs fight disease. Rocket ships race through space. Factories are run by automation. And, most of all, our understanding of the physical universe is still expanding, still revealing new wonders of the workings of nature. All this would never have happened without the achievements of the great scientists who began the Scientific Revolution.

Chapter Highlights

Can you explain?

anatomy	microorganisms	impetus	orbit
satellites	ellipse	rectilinear motion	experimental method
circulation	synthesize	law of gravity	law of inertia

Can you identify?

Francis Bacon	Galileo	Leeuwenhoek	Scientific Revolution
Newton	Ptolemy	Kepler	Laws of Planetary Motion
Copernicus	Harvey	Vesalius	

What do you think?

1. How is man affected by the knowledge that Earth is just a tiny part of a gigantic universe? What problems does this create for him?

2. Why were many clergymen and thinkers opposed to the theories of Copernicus and Galileo?

3. What role did Aristotle play in shaping medieval science? What errors did he make?

4. How did Galileo help pave the way for Newton?

5. How did the universe of Newton differ from the universe visualized by medieval thinkers? Why was Newton's work so significant?

6. How did Vesalius, Harvey, and Leeuwenhoek advance the field of medicine?

7. In what ways did Francis Bacon foreshadow the direction of modern science?

8. The Scientific Revolution had far-reaching effects on fields other than science. Do you agree or disagree with this statement? Why?

9. Newton had a different view of the universe than did Aristotle, and the views of present-day scientists differ from those of Newton. Why have these changes in outlook come about?

Exploration, Colonization, and Commercial Expansion

CHAPTER FOCUS

Factors Leading to the Age of Exploration
Portuguese Expansion in Africa and India
Spain's Empire in the New World
Colonization of the New World
Empires of the North Atlantic Powers
Commercial Revolution
The Legacy of Exploration and Commercial Expansion

The Age of Exploration extended man's knowledge of both hemispheres. The map of Brazil (left) shows how the unfamiliar peoples, plants, and animals of America impressed a Portuguese cartographer. The arrival of western ships in Asia led eastern peoples to record their impressions of Europeans. The Persian carpet above incorporated European ships in its design, a departure from the floral and geometric patterns usual in Muslim art.

At the same time that Europe was being transformed by the forces of the Renaissance and the Reformation, daring seafarers were making discoveries that stirred the imagination. During the great Age of Exploration (1415–1620) European sea captains found a way to reach India by sailing around Africa, discovered a new world across the Atlantic, and sailed around the globe for the first time. European nations began to conquer and colonize lands thousands of miles away. The Age of Exploration marks the beginning of the imperial expansion that by 1900 enabled Europeans to control much of the globe. The Age of Exploration exposed most of the world to European ways, an influence that persists to this day.

359

Factors Leading to the Age of Exploration

Why did European expansion occur during the Renaissance era and not earlier? Travel was not new to Europeans. Merchants had long been familiar with the caravan routes to Asia, and the Vikings probably reached North America as early as the eleventh century. Still, these travels had no significant effect upon European society. No conquests or colonization followed. Of all the medieval movements of expansion, only the Crusades had far-reaching effects. But all the Christian conquests in Palestine had been regained by the Muslims by the end of the thirteenth century, and Europeans once again withdrew to their own lands.

After Columbus accidentally discovered the Americas at the end of the fifteenth century, however, Europe set out to conquer and colonize vast areas of the world. Between the Middle Ages and the Renaissance what had changed so much in Europe? Why did Columbus' voyage lead to many others? What attitudes of mind and conditions of society led Europeans to venture overseas? Why was it Europeans and not Asians who expanded so aggressively? The causes of the Age of Exploration are to be found in (1) a desire for economic gain, (2) a desire to spread Christianity, (3) improvements in navigation and shipbuilding, and (4) a search for glory and adventure.

Desire for economic gain encourages voyages of exploration. The Portuguese took the lead in voyages of exploration. More than anything else the desire for wealth pushed the Portuguese and other European nations to make long sea voyages. As the Portuguese ships sailed farther and farther south along the west coast of Africa in the fifteenth century, they traded in fish, ivory, and gold. They were looking for a larger prize, for they knew that a fortune could be made from trade with Asia. Since cattle in Europe were slaughtered in the fall, Asian spices were needed to preserve the meat and keep it edible until spring. Unless meat were cured with peppercorns or clovebuds obtained from the East, it would spoil.

At the time, Muslims controlled commerce in the huge area between Egypt and China, and from Timbuktu in Africa to the Volga River in southern Russia. On the European end, the Italian city-state of Venice had a virtual *monopoly* (exclusive control) on trade with the Muslims. Oriental goods flowed through Venetian hands to the rest of Europe; scarce European gold poured into the pockets of Venetian middlemen and Muslim traders. Portuguese merchants hoped to crack this Venetian-Arab monopoly by finding a sea route to the Indian Ocean. Some believed that the Indies could be reached by sailing southeast around Africa; a few believed that the Orient could be reached directly by sailing westward across the Atlantic;

Exploration and Commercial Expansion

c. **1418–1460**	Prince Henry of Portugal promotes exploration
1488	Dias enters Indian Ocean
1492	Columbus reaches America
1498	Da Gama reaches India
1500	Cabral chances upon Brazil
1513	Balboa sights the Pacific Ocean
1519–1521	Cortés conquers Mexico
1519–1522	Magellan's fleet circumnavigates globe
1531–1532	Spanish conquest of Peru
1600	English East India Company founded
1604	Dutch East India Company formed
1638–1667	Dutch establish monopoly of East Indian trade
1664	French East India Company founded

a handful even proposed sailing northeast through the Arctic Ocean. Eager for spices, gold, dyes, and other Asian goods, European kings and merchants alike threw their support behind overseas expeditions.

Merchants support voyages of exploration. The Age of Exploration was made possible by the rise of a hard-working merchant class. These merchants organized expeditions that roved the seas in search of markets and profits. Like feudal lords, they were quite capable of using force to protect their interests. They became so powerful in Renaissance times that before they would consent to pay taxes, they demanded that kings grant them certain privileges. And in Flemish and English towns, merchants' sons and daughters married into the aristocracy.

This medieval painting captures the flavor of Venice in 1271, when ships flying the lion of St. Mark dominated the eastern Mediterranean. Among the ships are those which carried Marco Polo on the first stage of the journey to China. There Marco became a trusted representative of Kublai Khan. The wonders he described on his return to Venice inspired Europeans to expand their trade with Asia.

In Lisbon (Portugal), Florence (Italy), or Bristol (England), merchants came to look at themselves not as servants of their rulers but as rich partners of poor kings.

Christian zeal encourages exploration. The desire to spread Christianity also pushed Europeans into the Atlantic on voyages of discovery. Catholic Spain and Portugal in particular felt that they had a God-given duty to convert "heathen" Africans and Asians to the religion of Christ. The arrival of the Spaniards and Portuguese in the Americas opened up a huge new field for conversion.

Christian zeal also spurred a search for Prester John, a legendary Christian ruler said to live somewhere in "the Indies." The Portuguese hoped to enlist his aid in religious wars against the Muslims.

Improvements in technology and navigation make longer voyages practical. The Age of Exploration was made possible by improvements in shipbuilding and gunnery and by increased knowledge of navigation. Ships and naval weapons had changed little since Roman times. Then, in the fifteenth century, the galley oarsman was replaced by the sail, and the battering ram by the cannon. Neither sails nor gunpowder were new. In the Mediterranean Sea and Indian Ocean merchant vessels had always relied on the winds. And during the Renaissance guns shooting iron balls were commonly used in land warfare. For sea battles, however, maritime powers used galleys, long ships propelled by oarsmen. Their commanders tried to ram an enemy craft and sink it, or to board it and fight the enemy hand to hand.

With the introduction of sails and cannon ships could, for the first time, sail far out at sea, heavily armed, but lightly manned. These innovations, quickly adopted by the Portuguese, were extremely important. Soon Portuguese shipyards were turning out ships that were unusually seaworthy, capable of surviving the fierce gales of the South Atlantic. These ships also could maneuver better than enemy craft, and their greater size enabled them to withstand the recoil from cannon.

To these technological advances were added improvements in navigation. Seamen learned how to find their latitude by observing the position of stars, in particular the Pole Star. Later, they plotted their position by noting the sun's zenith (highest point) north or south of the equator at noon. And they kept improving the accuracy of the mariner's compass.

The Renaissance spirit of adventure encourages exploration. The restless spirit of the Renaissance helped launch the Age of Exploration. The Renaissance was an age of individualism, when unusual men craved adventure and excitement. Sea captains who ventured into uncharted oceans, explorers who penetrated unknown lands, soldiers who conquered vast territories—such men were driven by curiosity, the desire for glory, and the hope of fame. This spirit of adventure, which distinguished Europe from China in the fifteenth century, encouraged exploration.

China lacks the incentive to make voyages of discovery. China had greater wealth than fifteenth-century Europe and was as far advanced in navigational and technical skills. By 1400 the Chinese were supreme on the seas from Japan to East Africa. An ambitious emperor sent well-armed junks (sailing vessels) on diplomatic missions to lands bordering the Indian Ocean. They first appeared at Calicut in India in 1407, and later visited the Middle Eastern ports of Hormuz and Aden, and even Malindi in East Africa. These voyages proved that the Chinese were able sailors and navigators. Why, then, did they not round the Cape of Good Hope to reach the West African coast? The principal reason appears to be that the Chinese emperor was seeking neither markets nor converts. He was searching for tribute and rare products. His merchants traded for such luxuries as ostrich feathers, giraffes, zebras, and the like. For this reason the junks were called "jewel ships." Their exotic cargo was not for sale. It made delightful "toys" for the chosen few at the imperial court.

This type of trade had no effect on either commerce or ways of living in the rural villages. In China there was no popular demand for foreign wares. Moreover, China's landowners and mandarin officials (see page 218) regarded merchants as little better than peasants. Consequently Chinese merchants had no incentive to venture into unknown seas for trade. The Chinese economy remained stable and self-sufficient.

Later Chinese emperors even lost interest in voyages to the Indian Ocean. They ruled a huge land empire, and were not eager for maritime expansion. Moreover, the Chinese emperors felt no religious obligation to spread their faith. When China returned to its landlocked isolation, the Chinese surrendered control of the Indian Ocean to Arab (and before long Portuguese) traders.

CHECK-UP

1. What economic factors encouraged voyages of exploration? What role did religion play? The spirit of the Renaissance?
2. What improvements took place in technology and navigation? How did this affect exploration?
3. Why did the Chinese not play a leading role in the great voyages of discovery?

Portuguese Expansion in Africa and India

Prince Henry of Portugal encourages voyages of exploration. "Gold, Glory, and God" sum up the great Age of Exploration, 1415–1620. It began in 1415 with Portugal's capture of the North African city of Ceuta (say-*oo'*tah) and reached its climax in the finding of sea routes to both the West and East Indies. It did not end until Europeans settled down to the economic development of their new colonies in Africa, Asia, and the Americas.

Prince Henry of Portugal is a decisive figure in the Age of Exploration. No sailor himself, nevertheless he was the person who opened the great age of daring deeds and commercial enterprise. His maritime policy began both the economic and religious expansion of Europe overseas.

In the capture of the Muslim city of Ceuta, Henry's men liberated over a thousand Christian slaves. Henry vowed to devote his life to conquering all Muslim regions of Africa for Catholic Portugal.

In Ceuta, too, Prince Henry learned the source of African gold. Previously, Europeans had believed that Arab traders brought gold from India by ship. In Ceuta, however, the Portuguese learned that camel caravans brought gold dust across the Sahara from Timbuktu. Since gold and silver were in short supply in fifteenth-century Europe, the Portuguese were understandably eager to reach the true source of African gold. Gold lured Prince Henry's sea captains farther and farther south along the West African coast.

The Portuguese also wanted to break the Muslim-Venetian control over the overland route to the spices of Asia. Economic desire led to the search for an all-water route to the Orient.

Prince Henry helps advance maritime knowledge. At the time, Portugal enjoyed greater internal stability then any other nation in Europe. On the southwestern tip of Portugal, Prince Henry founded a naval station at Sagres (*sah'*-greysh). For 40 years he directed the gathering of geographical information. To Sagres came Italian pilots, Jewish astronomers from the Mediterranean, Basque seamen who knew Atlantic waters. From Arab scholars and Portu-

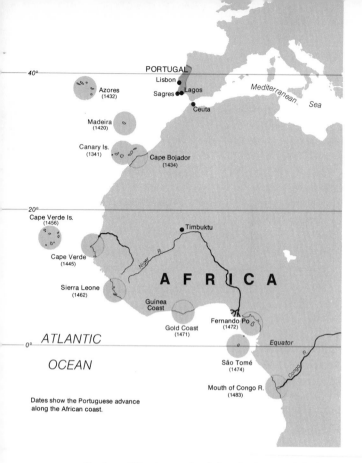

Portugal Explores the Atlantic Coast of Africa

Dates show the Portuguese advance along the African coast.

guese sailors Prince Henry collected information about the stars and tides, winds and currents. His mapmakers used this information to draw secret maps of African coastal waters. These maps and charts permitted Portuguese sailors to sail with confidence out of sight of land. Prince Henry himself sailed on no voyages, but his success in advancing maritime knowledge caused the sea-conscious English to call him "the Navigator." His interest in maritime research helped his small kingdom to move ahead of wealthier European states in the search for a sea route to India—and the lucrative spice trade.

THE PORTUGUESE AND AFRICA

Prince Henry also gave Portugal an economic advantage over other European states by stressing two very profitable installations—the forti-

fied trading post and the plantation. These two institutions provided the economic base for Portugal's maritime empire. With some variations, both were introduced in Africa, Asia, and the Americas by European colonial powers that followed in the Portuguese wake.

The fortified trading post and the plantation lay the base for empire. In each region where a considerable number of Africans lived, the Portuguese built a trading post and protected it with arms. This fortified trading post provided safe storage for African merchandise awaiting shipment to Portugal. At the trading post goods were also sold or bartered to Africans, and from them the Portuguese obtained products typical of the region: palm oil, ivory, slaves, and especially gold.

Usually a ship's cannon were enough to "persuade" an African chief (and later Asian princes) to grant Europeans a trade monopoly. In return, armed forces stationed at the fortified trading post protected cooperative African chiefs from attack by tribal enemies. The fortified trading post in West Africa set the European colonial pattern for centuries to come. It ensured a steady, cheap supply of regional products for export. A handful of men manned it, got rich, and returned to Europe for a life of leisure. Hudson Bay, Macao off the coast of China, and Nagasaki, Japan, are well-known later examples of the fortified trading post, an institution developed by the Portuguese.

Sugar cane had long been cultivated in subtropical Asia by slave labor. In the Near East, Christian crusaders found sugar so much to their liking that it soon was sold in Europe for medicinal purposes. To meet the growing demand, the Portuguese developed a *plantation* system that greatly increased the supply of sugar. This plantation system was to have profound economic and social effects throughout the world. On the uninhabited islands of Madeira (1420), off Morocco and São Tomé (*soun'* too-*may'*, 1490) off the West African coast, the Portuguese leveled broad fields, planted acres and acres of cane, built a sugar mill, and raised oxen to turn the mill. Cutting sugar cane is backbreaking toil, and within twenty-four hours of the cutting the juice has to be pressed out of the stalks and boiled. For such a rapid operation the planter needed hundreds of strong workers. These laborers had to be brought to the plantation, fed and clothed, and persuaded to stay there. Like the trading post, the plantation called for a considerable outlay of cash. Because profits from the sale of sugar in Western Europe kept rising, plantations were established in Brazil (1520) and on the Caribbean islands (1650). Only a shortage of labor limited the expansion of the colonial plantation. This problem was largely solved by the introduction of slave labor.

Slavery changes in nature. The growth of slavery after 1443 had a great impact on commerce. In 1441 a Portuguese captain returned to the Portuguese port of Lagos (*lah'*goosh) with ten African slaves. Prince Henry sent them to Rome as a gift to the Pope. Two years later Prince Henry presided over the auction of 235 black slaves. They were baptized, given some education, and in time probably were absorbed into Portuguese life.

The Portuguese seizure of these Africans and their sale in Europe as slaves marks a turning point in the history of slavery. Slavery had existed in Africa and Asia for centuries. Since slavery itself was not new, why was the date 1443 so important?

1. The nature of slave labor changed. In medieval Europe local serfs usually had done the heavy work in the fields. African slaves were too scarce for their skills to be wasted on rude labor. As servants, barbers, or musicians they did light work in the household. After 1443, however, African slaves were increasingly drafted to work on the sugar-cane plantations as field hands.

2. The volume of slave traffic rose sharply. Plantation agriculture spread from the Mediterranean to the tropics in Africa, Asia, and the Americas. Negro labor was used in increasing amounts to cultivate not only sugar, but also cacao, cotton, tobacco, and coffee. Black slaves also were used in mining gold and diamonds. For four centuries after that first slave auction in 1443, the demand for slaves kept growing. By 1850 perhaps ten million Africans had been torn from their homelands and sent overseas in chains.

3. The social status of the slave changed for the worse. Until 1443 a free person might become a slave because of religious wars or economic misfortune. Christians and Muslims had viewed slavery as a legal condition subject to change by ransom or the granting or purchase of freedom. The slave had not necessarily differed in physical appearance from his captor. But whatever his race, he probably had differed in the gods he worshiped. The slave was generally a prize of war waged in the name of religion. Neither the Bible nor the Koran questioned the rightness of slavery. The Church, in fact, later became a large-scale slaveowner in the New World. But after 1443 Europeans gradually came to associate slavery not just with religious beliefs they considered wrong but with African birth. The notion grew that the black African was born to be a slave. Medieval religious intolerance had begun to blend into modern racial prejudice.

4. The pattern of European slaving became increasingly destructive. After 1443 Europeans traded arms for slaves and encouraged warfare among African tribes. For example, in 1455 the Pope authorized the Portuguese to "attack, subject, and reduce to perpetual slavery the Saracens [Muslims], pagans, and other enemies of Christ on all the coast of Guinea." The Pope further granted Portugal a monopoly to trade there in gold, ivory, and slaves. The slave trade became an important source of income to coastal African tribes. Slave wars and slave trading stripped interior villages of their young men.

Missionary efforts are only partially successful. The Portuguese had less success in founding religious missions in Africa than in establishing trading posts and plantations. While

By the 1600's the Portuguese trading post at Macao (above) reflected both European contact and Asian customs. The modern picture of the Portuguese-held island shows that these influences continue.

THE PORTUGUESE AND INDIA

1488: *Dias sails into the Indian Ocean.* The Portuguese spent 68 years sailing the coast of West Africa before they found the passage to India. In 1488 a South Atlantic gale blew the expedition of Bartholomeu Dias (bar-too-loo-*may'*oo *dee'*ash) around the tip of the African continent. Only days later, when the exhausted crew at last saw land again—but with the sun rising to their right rather than to their left— did they realize that they had entered the Indian Ocean and were sailing north along the east coast of Africa. Dias called the tip of Africa "Stormy Cape." His king, jubilant at the news Dias brought, gave the Cape its present name, the Cape of Good Hope.

1498: *Vasco da Gama reaches India.* Dias' discovery of the Cape of Good Hope encouraged Portugal to send Vasco da Gama on a diplomatic mission to the Indies. Da Gama's fleet was actually an armed commercial squadron. Three ships were armed with a total of twenty small cannon; one carried provisions. Estimates of the number of men aboard range from 170 to 320. Da Gama's voyage from the Cape Verde (*vair'*dey) Islands to South Africa was by far the greatest navigational feat of the century. It described a great arc of 3800 miles across the South Atlantic Ocean. (Making a similar bold sweep in 1500, Pedro Cabral's fleet blundered upon the coast of Brazil.)

Da Gama was out of sight of land for fourteen weeks. In November, 1497, his fleet cast anchor with uncanny accuracy only 100 miles north of the Cape of Good Hope. Rounding the Cape, da Gama sailed east, then north. Soon he began to see the minarets and white plaster houses of Mozambique. His fleet had entered the high culture area of East Africa (pages 256–257). Although Arab traders considered the Portuguese trading wares of little value, the townspeople were friendly until they realized that their visitors were Christians.

Da Gama had the good fortune to obtain the services of Ibn Majid, the outstanding Arab pilot of the day. Ibn Majid guided the Portu-

tropical diseases took a heavy toll of white friars sent to convert the "heathen," the greed of European traders for "black ivory" (slaves) probably doomed missionary efforts anyway. For the slave traffic caused Africans to fear and hate the white Europeans.

guese fleet across the Indian Ocean to Calicut, the city on India's Malabar Coast that the Portuguese had been hoping to reach since 1420. Here da Gama uttered what is probably the best-known sentence of the Age of Exploration: "We come in search of Christians and spices."

As ambassador from the King of Portugal, da Gama

got ready the following things to be sent to the King [of Calicut]: twelve pieces of striped cloth, four scarlet hoods, six hats, four strings of coral, a case containing six washstand basins, a case of sugar, two casks of oil, and two of honey.

When the Arabs present saw these gifts, they laughed in contempt, saying that nothing but gold was acceptable to the king. Obviously there was no great demand for European wares. Yet da Gama returned home from this great pioneer voyage to Calicut with goods valued at sixty times the cost of the expedition.

Since Europe offered little that Indian princes wanted (including, of course, Christianity), how did the Portuguese acquire the spices, drugs, and dyes they took back to Europe? As did later Europeans, they resorted to ruthless methods, backed up by the ship's cannon, to force the Indians to provide them with trade goods. One of the Portuguese crewmen tells us that da Gama

ordered the boats to go and plunder the small [Indian] vessels, . . . and the two ships in which they found rice and many jars of butter, and many bales of stuffs. . . . Then [da Gama] commanded them to cut off the hands and noses of all the crews and put all that into one of the small vessels, into which he ordered them to put the friar [an Indian envoy on board under safe conduct], also without ears or nose or hands, which he had ordered to be strung up around his neck. . . . When all the Indians had thus been executed, he ordered their feet to be tied together; . . . they were . . . put on board, heaped up on top of each other, mixed up with the blood that streamed from them, and he ordered . . . the sails to be set for the shore, and the vessel set on fire. . . . And the small vessel with the friar, with all the hands and ears, was also sent on shore under sail without being fired.

By using terror and violence, da Gama set the pattern for later European expeditions to the Orient. Europeans did not shrink from capturing unarmed vessels, setting fire to them, and using other forms of terror to "persuade" minor princes to grant exclusive trading rights. A legally-minded Portuguese found a way to justify Portugal's "right" to the goods of the East:

It is true that there does exist a common right to all to navigate the seas and in Europe we recognize the rights which others hold against us; but the right does not exist beyond Europe and therefore the Portuguese as Lords of the Sea are justified in confiscating the goods of all those who navigate the seas without their permission.

Europeans take over the Asian trade. One result of da Gama's voyage was a drop in spice prices in Western Europe's markets. Goods transported from Calicut to Europe by water cost the Portuguese only a fifth of what they cost when transported by the Arab-Venetian land-and-water route. By eliminating the Muslim middlemen and ending the Venetian monopoly, the Portuguese brought Oriental goods within the reach of many more European consumers. After 1498 commercial activity increased in both Asian and European cities.

In the Indian Ocean the Europeans were dealing with long-established states. How did they manage to gain control of the Asian trade?

1. Military power. Because their ships were armed with cannon, the Portuguese could sail at will in Eastern waters. The Chinese war-junk could not compete with a Portuguese man-of-war, writes Italian historian Carlo Cipolla:

The Chinese junk could compare honorably with western sailing vessels for mercantile endeavors or voyages of discovery. . . . The problem, however, was that the junk never developed into a man-of-war. . . . [It] remained essentially a vessel suited for ramming and boarding.

European vessels had an overwhelming superiority in weapons. Bombardment by the ship's cannon would terrify coastal Asian cities. Then well-armed soldiers would land and quickly overcome opposition. In that way Europeans gained control of strategic Asian ports and of the sea routes over which moved the goods acquired by European traders. Administration of densely populated inland areas was left to local rulers who respected European power. Fearful of "deadly fevers," Europeans had little desire to settle in Asia.

2. Commercial enterprise. Portuguese merchants could not rely entirely on force to do business. Except for expensive cannon and clocks and cheap kettles and mirrors, Europe produced few wares that Oriental princes wanted to buy. Therefore, to make money, the Portuguese took advantage of their ships and their knowledge of far-away markets. Soon they became the middlemen in the old inter-Asian commerce that flourished from the East Indian Ocean to the South China Sea.

Sometimes sailing Chinese junks, Portuguese merchant captains traded Indonesian sandalwood and spices for cargoes of Chinese silk and porcelain. These luxury goods brought high prices in the bazaars of India's Malabar Coast and even higher ones in the markets of Western Europe. Profits from the Oriental carrying trade were double those from goods shipped to Europe. Carrying pepper, cinnamon, ivory, cloves, and nutmeg, Portuguese fleets plied the Indian and Atlantic Oceans in the long (six to nine months) and dangerous voyage to Portugal. To pay for the expensive Asian goods, Europeans used bullion (gold and silver) and gems from the New World.

3. Superiority complex. In Asia the Portuguese sought to establish Christianity along with trade. But the Christian mission met with little success. Because Asian converts to Christianity were regarded as outcasts, few Asians braved the social and political disgrace that went with religious conversion. The religious-racial superiority complex of the Europeans also contributed to the failure of Christianity in Asia. A Portuguese had no doubt that Christianity was the only true faith. He believed that God empowered the Pope to distribute among Christians all lands not already in Christian hands. Since the souls of the non-Christians were doomed to hellfire, the living heathen had no real right to the lands on which they lived. At their first meetings, a Portuguese could not help admiring some Asians, whom he took to be Christians. Then he came to despise Asians because they were not Christians. Later, since Asians tend to have darker skins than Europeans, the Portuguese came to associate dark skin with heathenism. Portugal was but the first of the European nations to regard dark skin as socially undesirable.

Naval superiority and commercial ruthlessness, combined with the conviction that Christianity was the one true faith, gave the Portuguese a psychological advantage over Asians. "Gold, Glory, and God" aroused them to a singleness of purpose stronger than the will of Asian peoples to resist. A British expert on the West in the Orient concludes:

There seems to be no doubt that a policy of expansion cannot succeed unless it is executed with full and confident determination. These were the qualities which enabled three of the smallest and least powerful European states [Portugal, Netherlands, England] in the sixteenth century to carry out undertakings which reason would say were beyond their strength.

CHECK-UP

1. Why was Prince Henry of Portugal an important figure in the Age of Exploration? What conditions within Portugal enabled her to take the lead in exploration?

2. How did fortified trading posts and the plantation system lay the base for empire?

3. Why is 1443 a turning point in the history of slavery? How did the nature of slave labor change after that date? The social status of slaves?

4. Why were the voyages of Dias and da Gama important?

5. What great attraction did India hold for the Portuguese? How were the Portuguese able to gain control of the Asian trade?

SPANISH VOYAGES OF EXPLORATION

1492: Columbus reaches America. Between 1483 and 1484 King John of Portugal turned down the proposal of an Italian seaman, Christopher Columbus, to sail westward to India. Columbus had estimated that the voyage would cover only 2500 miles (which it did—but not to India!). The king's nautical advisers were better informed. They probably had a close idea of the actual distance westward to Asia—10,000 miles.

Spain, which had just conquered the last Moorish stronghold on her soil, was interested in Columbus' proposal. Queen Isabella provided the restless Genoese mariner with a small fleet to try the westward passage to India. Leaving the Canary Islands on September 6, 1492, Columbus sailed west along the tradewind zone, familiar to him from voyages to Africa. After a month of good weather and fast sailing, signs of land appeared. On the early morning watch of October 12 the lookout on the *Pinta* saw a cliff of white sand gleaming in the moonlight and shouted, *"Tierra, tierra!"* Watling's Island is the present name for this strip of coral, thirteen miles long and six across. From the friendly copper-colored islanders Columbus learned of a rich country to the south (probably Cuba). There he expected to meet the Grand Khan of China, for whom he had a letter from Queen Isabella.

The non-Christian world is divided between Spain and Portugal. To prove to the queen that he had reached India, Columbus brought back some of the Oriental-looking people who had greeted him. Naturally he called them Indians. The queeen promptly condemned their enslavement, but expressed joy that her "Admiral of the Ocean Sea" had found the all-water route to India. When the rulers of Spain sent the news to Pope Alexander VI, he quickly granted them all lands already discovered and to be discovered "in the direction of India." King John of Portugal threatened Spain with war; he feared that the Pope had granted Spain too great an advantage over Portugal.

At Tordesillas (tor-dey-*see'*yahs) in 1494 diplomats agreed to a line of demarcation west of the Azores (see map, page 370). The Treaty of Tordesillas presumed to divide the non-Christian world into Spanish and Portuguese spheres of influence.

Westerners judge Columbus' first transatlantic voyage as the most important voyage ever made. It opened to European trade and influence the unknown hemisphere soon to be called the New World.

1519–1522: Magellan's fleet circumnavigates the globe. After Columbus, other explorers sailed west under the flag of Spain. One expedition, commanded by Portuguese seaman Ferdinand Magellan, sailed around the world. Magellan's famous voyage was far more difficult and no less significant than those of Columbus and da Gama. Magellan entertained the same vain dream as several other mariners: that a certain bay or river on the east coast of the New World would prove to be the western passage to India.

In September, 1519, Magellan's five ships set sail from Seville, Spain, with several hundred men on board. After exploring the Plate River estuary between present-day Argentina and Uruguay, Magellan pressed on until faced with mutiny from a crew cold and weary from South Atlantic gales. His waterlogged fleet wintered at latitude 50° south, about 200 miles from the tip of South America. There they met tall Amerinds (Indians of the Americas), whom the Europeans called Patagonians ("big feet"). When spring at last came, three of Magellan's

PACIFIC OCEAN

160°E

40°S

AUSTRALIA
(Undiscovered)

120°E

Tordesillas Line

PHILIPPINE
ISLANDS

Magellan

Tropic of Cancer

40°N

160°W

JAPAN

South
China
Sea

Canton • • Macao

CHINA

EAST
INDIES

• Malacca

SOUTHEAST
ASIA

ASIA

CEYLON

Arctic Circle

ARCTIC
OCEAN

80°N

INDIA

Goa • • Calicut

0°

80°E

INDIAN
OCEAN

MUSCOVY
(RUSSIA)

40°N

Hormuz •
PERSIA

CAPE GUARDAFUI

ARABIA

0°
120°W

NORTH
AMERICA

Hudson
Bay

Hudson

Hudson

NEWFOUNDLAND

Amsterdam
ENGLAND NETHERLANDS
London EUROPE
Bristol Paris • Venice
Plymouth • Brest • Genoa
FRANCE
Cartier SPAIN

Red Sea

Mediterranean Sea

Magellan (El Cano)

Tenochtitlán •
Cortés
Gulf of
Mexico Veracruz

J. Cabot

Madrid
PORTUGAL
Lisbon •• Seville

AFRICA

Malindi •
Mombasa •
Kilwa •
Mozambique •
Sofala •

MADAGASCAR

WATLING IS.
CUBA

Balboa

Caribbean
Sea

AZORES

MADEIRA IS.

CANARY
IS.

Columbus

Vespucci

Equator

40°S

Tropic of Capricorn

Equator

CAPE
VERDE
IS.

Vespucci

GUINEA
COAST

Pizarro

Lima •
• Cuzco

SOUTH
AMERICA

BRAZIL

Dias

40°S

Rio de Janeiro •

Da Gama

CAPE OF GOOD HOPE

Buenos Aires •
Vespucci

Cabral

OCEAN

PATAGONIA

Strait of
Magellan

SOUTH

ATLANTIC

TIERRA DEL
FUEGO

Tordesillas Line

40°E

80°E

80°S

120°E

120°W

80°W

40°W

0°

KEY

Spanish
Portuguese
English
Dutch
French

Return routes not shown

ships continued southward, reaching a point where the nights lasted but three hours. With enormous skill and luck they navigated the raging tides and the tortuous passages of the strait that now bears Magellan's name. Emerging into the "Great South Sea," Magellan found it so calm that he called it *mar pacífico* (pah-*see′*fee-koh). At latitude 32° south he turned northwest and headed for the "Isles of the Moluccas where the cloves grow." He believed that some islands there lay on the Spanish side of the Tordesillas Treaty line. Pigafetta, an Italian on the voyage, describes the horrors of the Pacific crossing:*

We were three months and twenty days without getting any kind of fresh food. We ate biscuit, which was no longer biscuit, but powder of biscuits swarming with worms, for they had eaten the good. It stank strongly of the urine of rats. We drank yellow water that had been putrid for many days. We also ate some ox hides that covered the top of the mainyard. . . . We left them in the sea for four or five days, and then placed them for a few moments on top of the embers, and so ate them; and often weak sawdust from boards! Rats were sold for one-half ducado apiece, and even then we could not get them. But above all other misfortunes the following was the worst. The gums of both the lower and upper teeth of some of our men swelled, so that they could not eat under any circumstances and therefore died. . . . However, I, by the grace of God, suffered no sickness. We sailed about four thousand *leguas* [10,000 miles] during those three months and twenty days through an open stretch in that Pacific Sea. In truth it is very pacific, for during that time we did not suffer any storm. . . . Had not God and His blessed mother given us so good weather we would have all died of hunger in that exceeding vast sea. Of a verity I believe no such voyage will ever be made [again].

* From Antonio Pigafetta, in *The European Reconnaisance,* edited by J. H. Parry (New York: Harper & Row, Publishers, Inc., 1968). Reprinted by permission.

Two ships and their now-small crews at last reached land, the Philippines, situated in Spanish waters. Magellan—like Columbus and da Gama before him—proved less able as a diplomat than as a sea captain. He perished in a needless skirmish with the Filipinos. Because the prevailing easterly winds made return through Spanish Pacific waters impossible, the two ships kept sailing eastward through Portuguese waters. The *Victoria* eluded capture, rounded the Cape of Good Hope, and wobbled back to Spain with a rich cargo of cloves. Of the hundreds of men who had left Seville three years before only eighteen emaciated sailors completed the circumnavigation of the globe.

Magellan's voyage showed that the "Great South Sea," first sighted by Balboa in 1513, was far more vast than suspected. His circumnavigation of the globe proved that (1) all the oceans on the earth are connected; (2) Eurasia and the Americas are separated by water; and (3) the world is indeed round. Even though Magellan's voyage also shattered the theory that the Indies discovered by Christopher Columbus lay off the coast of Asia, the Spaniards continued to use the name "West Indies."

SPANISH CONQUESTS IN AMERICA

At the time of the Columbian discovery, perhaps 15 or even 25 million Amerinds inhabited the land that stretched from Hudson Bay to Tierra del Fuego (*tyey′*rah del foo-*ay′*goh). They had no general name for themselves, no awareness of common descent. Culturally, Amerinds varied from the most primitive Patagonians in Argentina to the Inca's polished noblemen in Peru. Indeed, in language and technology Amerinds differed from one group to another far more than did the peoples in the European nations at the time. Like the sub-Saharan Africans and the Polynesians, the Amerinds were cut off from European and Asian technology. They knew neither the potter's wheel nor the wagon wheel; they had no metal tools or draft animals. A leading historian concludes:

Generally speaking, the level of mastery over the environment attained in Mexico and Peru by 1500 seems very similar to what the ancient Mesopotamians and Egyptians had achieved by about 2500 B.C. A four-thousand-year lag was far too great for the Amerindians to make up when the Spanish conquistadors [conquerors] burst in upon their seclusion.

Tenochtitlán turns religion into horror. By 1500, Tenochtitlán (tey-noch-tee-*tlahn'*), the capital of the Aztec state in Mexico (see pages 312–313), drew tribute from many vassal states. Its trade routes extended east to the Gulf of Mexico and as far south as present-day Nicaragua. The great market in Tenochtitlán, wrote one of the first Europeans to see it, equalled the finest European markets:

[There were] . . . dealers in gold, silver, and precious stones, feathers, cloth, and embroidered goods, and other merchandise in the form of men and women to be sold as slaves. . . . Then there were merchants who sold homespun clothing, . . . and others who sold cacao, . . . henequen cloth, . . . rope, and shoes. . . . In another section they had skins of tigers, lions, deer, and other animals. . . .

[Also there were] . . . those who sold beans and other vegetables, . . . those who sold fowls, turkeys, rabbits, deer, ducks, young dogs, and other things of that sort, . . . [as well as] sellers of fruit and . . . those who sold cooked food, and all the kinds of pottery. . . . And there were those who sold . . . sweets, . . . and sellers of lumber, and sellers of firewood. . . .

I must [also] mention the paper, . . . [and] I forgot to tell about the salt and the people who made stone knives, cutting them right out of the stone itself. Then there were the fishwives, and those who sold little loaves made from a kind of seaweed they took from the lake, which hardens and tastes something like cheese. And they sold hatchets made of brass, copper, and tin, and gourd cups, and decorated wooden pitchers.

Aztec traders had come to have a special position in the state. They not only sought out new markets but acted as spies, informing their rulers in Tenochtitlán of the weaknesses and strengths of neighboring states. Where the trader went, the warrior followed. Aztec warriors, believing that they fought and died for the glory of the gods, were seldom defeated.

Religion dominated Aztec life. The Aztecs believed that the sun and the rain gave them life, and that these elements were personified by gods. They believed that the gods could be worshiped and kept alive only by the greatest of gifts—human hearts and blood. Brave young Aztec nobles felt it an honor to be one of the few chosen as the yearly sacrifice to the gods. But human sacrifice soon ceased to represent a high and holy honor. The Valley of Mexico suffered a series of famines, and the Aztecs became convinced that the more victims sacrificed, the more glory the gods would give the state. They instituted the Sacred War to collect sacrificial victims from their increasingly unwilling allies and enemies. By the early 1500's thousands of prisoners of war were being sacrificed each year, and Tlacopán (tlah-koh-*pahn'*) and Texcoco (tehs-*koh'*koh)—the allies of Tenochtitlán—sought in vain for a way to end the slaughter.

The Inca state in Peru is regimented. By 1500 the state ruled by the Incas (see pages 315–317), controlled the largest empire in the Americas. With its capital in Cuzco, Peru, its borders extended from southernmost Colombia to central Chile. Specially trained messengers running in relays could cover 150 miles a day carrying the Inca's commands over an excellent system of roads. Merchants and administrators followed the same routes, and inns were provided for their comfort. Government officials provided the Inca with accurate information about his subjects and their needs. From the tribute he exacted, the Inca doled out food and clothing to the needy.

Because many peoples under the Inca's rule had no desire to be so ruled, all subjects were kept under constant supervision. Every aspect of their lives was strictly regulated, and peoples who revolted were moved to new lands far from their homes. All were required to accept the

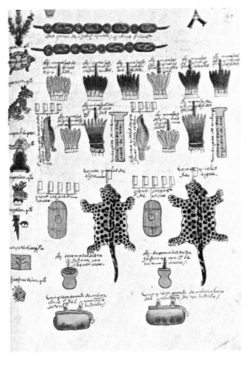

On a ridge in the Andes the Incas built Machu Picchu (above) of huge blocks of granite carefully worked to fit together without mortar. Terraces and aqueducts supplied the people with food and water. The Aztecs kept track of vassal states by means of tribute rolls (left), which listed products such as cacao (often used as money), jade, and ocelot skins. The abstract figure (above, left) is from Colombia, source of some of the finest American goldwork, little of which escaped the greed of the conquistadores.

state religion of sun worship and to speak only Quechua (kay-*choo'*ah), the language of their conquerors. Moreover, there was a strict class system. The Incas, their relatives, and former rulers of conquered provinces made up the nobility which governed the state. Everyone else performed manual labor, wore a specific style of dress, was rarely permitted to travel, and had to marry as directed. None dared criticize the Inca or his policies.

The conquistadores are few but mighty. In 1519 strange white men appeared on the Gulf coast of Mexico. In a few years they had penetrated deep into South America. Their passage brought ruin to great civilizations. Although a mere handful of Spaniards, they managed to overturn empires that appeared to be strong and stable. First welcomed as gods, they were soon recognized as *conquistadores* (kon-kee-stah-*doh′*rehs, conquerors). But by the time the Aztecs and Incas realized this, it was too late. Tribes that had long been oppressed by the great Amerindian states willingly joined the conquistadores. As it turned out, of course, both the oppressors and the oppressed fell under the yoke of the Spaniards.

Some of the conquistadores wanted gold and adventure. Some were determined to crush the worship of idols, and some sought a new and easier life. Many were exceptionally daring. Garcilaso de la Vega, son of a conquistador and an Inca princess, paid them this tribute:

Nothing discouraged them, nothing repelled them, nothing exhausted them. Neither hunger nor danger, nor wounds, nor sickness, nor bad days and even worse nights, could keep them from pushing constantly forward, over land and sea, in search of the unheard-of feats that, for all time, have left a halo of glory around their names.

Cortés reaches Mexico and meets Aztec messengers. Hernán Cortés (air-*nahn′* kor-*tehs′*) was a typical Spanish conquistador—courageous, courteous, impulsive, generous, charming, and ruthless. Sailing from Cuba to mainland America in 1519, his fleet of eleven vessels carried 508 soldiers, two priests, sixteen horses, and small cannon. On the Gulf shore of Mexico he found a safe harbor. There, on Good Friday, he founded a town he aptly named Villa Rica de la Vera Cruz (*bee′*yah *ree′*kah dey lah *bey′*rah *kroohs′*), "Rich City of the True Cross." Here ambassadors from Moctezuma (mok-tey-*soo′*mah), the ruler of Tenochtitlán, met him, bearing gifts to one they believed a messenger of the legendary Quetzalcóatl (ket-sahl-*koh′*ah-t'l, see page 312).

From the start Moctezuma followed a faint-hearted policy toward the Spaniards. Instead of attacking their outnumbered forces and driving them into the sea, he sent them gifts of gold and intricate featherwork, hoping to bribe the intruders to leave Mexico. He could not know of the truth in Cortés' jest that "The Spaniards were troubled with a disease of the heart, for which gold was a specific remedy." Moctezuma's gifts of gold, of course, only spurred the Spaniards to seek its source.

Aided by Malinche, Cortés gains allies. To prevent the fearful from sailing back to Cuba for reinforcements, Cortés had his ships sunk. Then the Spaniards had to march inland. To penetrate a land bristling with spies and soldiers, Cortés followed a policy of dividing in order to conquer. He took care that, no matter how exhausted, his soldiers should appear calm and alert in the presence of Amerinds. Slain men and horses were secretly buried at night. Fighting fierce battles against overwhelming numbers and yet offering honorable terms in victory, Cortés won over the proud Tlaxcalans (tlahs-*kah′*lahns), who hated Aztec rule. He persuaded them that the Spaniards would help overthrow the Aztecs. The beautiful slave girl Malinche (mah-*leen′*chay) aided Cortés in this diplomatic master stroke. Cortés exploited her talents as interpreter (she spoke the Indian languages of Maya and Nahuatl (*nah′*-wah-t'l), and before long Spanish), as diplomat (she had been born into the Aztec nobility), and as spy and informant (on the friends and foes of Moctezuma).

Tenochtitlán falls to the Spaniards. When the Spaniards and their allies at last reached the lake-city of Tenochtitlán, Moctezuma offered no resistance. Not long after, one of Cortés' lieutenants invited the Aztec nobles to a feast and massacred them. The Aztecs then rose in arms against the Spaniards, and soon after Moctezuma was killed. In one of the fiercest battles of the Conquest, the Spaniards had to fight their way out of Tenochtitlán, leaving behind more than half their number wounded and slain. Most of the Aztec treasure they tried to carry away was sunk in the lake.

Instead of being discouraged by this staggering defeat, Cortés became more determined than ever to seize control of Mexico. Gathering recruits from vassal states restless under Aztec rule, Cortés began a three-month siege of Tenochtitlán. Moctezuma's successor, Cuauhtémoc (koo-ah-oo-*tay*'mok), did his utmost to repel the invaders. With a small loyal army Cuauhtémoc resisted until most of his warriors had been killed or captured by the Spaniards and their Amerindian allies. The end came with the capture of the last Aztec emperor in 1521.

Divided by civil war, the empire of the Incas falls to Pizarro's forces. The conquest of the empire of the Incas (1531–1532) was as dramatic as the fall of Tenochtitlán. The empire had been weakened by a civil war over which of two brothers was to be Inca. When the Spanish commander, Francisco Pizarro, ordered his few men to seize the Inca Atahualpa (ah-tah-*wahl*'pah), the empire fell apart. The Inca's loyal foot soldiers, armed with spears, warclubs, and bows and arrows, were no match for Spanish cannon, Toledo steel, and mounted conquistadores. Not one Spaniard was killed in the bloodbath which took hundreds of Peruvian lives high in the Andes in 1531.

Pizarro treacherously promised to set Atahualpa free once ransom had been paid— a room filled with gold (worth perhaps $150 million today!). Once the gold was collected, Pizarro had Atahualpa strangled. Less the fifth that went to the ruler of Spain, Atahualpa's ransom was divided among some 150 Spanish soldiers. Then the original conquistadores began to kill each other in their greed for more gold. This kept Peru in an uproar until the first Spanish viceroy made his stately way into Lima (*lee*'mah) in 1551.

The Araucanians defy conquest. In sharp contrast to the sudden collapse of the empire of the Incas stands the resistance of the Arau-

canians in Chile. Inca forces had invaded but failed to subdue Chile; now it was the turn of the Spaniards. Unlike the Incas, the Araucanians lived in simple agricultural villages. They did without roads, granaries, taxes, officials, and records. Their leader, Caupolican (kow-poh-*lee*'kahn), had attained the chieftainship by carrying a heavy beam on his shoulder longer than did any rival. A British historian describes the prolonged conflict between Spaniard and Araucanian:

In the course of the skirmishing, . . . Garcia [Spanish governor of Chile] cut off both hands of a captive and sent him away with a message that he would treat in the same way all who resisted, but that those who submitted might have peace. The Indians, so far from being intimidated by this example, were roused to fury. In November, 1557, they . . . attacked the Spanish army as it advanced southwards, the unfortunate man holding out before his comrades his mutilated limbs and urging them to avert a like fate by valor in fight. Their valor was vain against horses, crossbows, muskets, and cannon more powerful than any yet seen in these wars: seven hundred prisoners were taken and ten captive chiefs were hanged. . . . The resistance of the natives, although never completely quenched for nearly three centuries, died down, partly owing to the ravages of smallpox.

Like many an Amerindian tribe in North America, the Araucanians were not subdued until the nineteenth century. As a rule, the less complex their political state, the more capable were Amerinds to resist—but not defeat— the well-armed Europeans. Often those who refused to submit to Spanish rule withdrew into remote regions.

CHECK-UP

1. Why do westerners consider Columbus' first transatlantic voyage to be the most important voyage ever made? What hardships did Magellan and his crew endure on their voyage? What was its significance?

2. Where was the Aztec state? What was the role of religion in Aztec life? Why were Aztec allies dissatisfied?

3. Where was the Inca empire? What territory did it include? Why were many subject peoples dissatisfied with Inca rule?

4. Who were the conquistadores? What were their goals? How did Moctezuma react to news of the Spaniards' arrival?

5. How was Cortés able to defeat the Aztecs? What enabled Pizarro to overthrow the Inca empire so easily?

6. How did the Araucanian way of life differ from that of the Inca's subjects? Why were the Araucanians long able to resist foreign conquest?

Colonization of the New World

Spanish and Portuguese settle in the New World. The Spaniards were the first Europeans to settle in the New World. On his second voyage, in 1493, Columbus brought 1500 settlers to America and laid the basis for present-day Latin American culture. If the conquistadores had introduced the horse, the use of the wheel, and firearms to the Americas, just what did the first settlers bring?

The settlers brought their languages, Spanish and Portuguese, and imposed their Catholic faith upon the Amerinds. The replacing of hundreds of Amerindian languages and beliefs by just two languages and one religion ensured a degree of cultural unity. To the Americas, the Spanish and Portuguese also brought the metal fishhook, the potter's wheel, the plow, new techniques of weaving, and European methods of agriculture. Grains, some root vegetables, and fruits—apples, pears, plums, peaches, lemons, limes, and oranges—were added to the American diet. The introduction of cattle, sheep, goats, pigs, mules, donkeys, and poultry affected both diet and transportation. The European settlers introduced their legal codes, their concept of private property, and their style of architecture. These European products and ways took root in Spanish and Portuguese lands from Florida to southern Chile.

Great problems face the European colonizers. In implanting their own way of life in the New World, European settlers faced several problems. One was the vast size and diversity of the New World: wide rivers and broad plains, deep forests and endless deserts, lofty mountains and trackless swamps. Reports on the amazing variety of the American climates, wildlife, and vegetation grew fabulous in the telling in the Old World. In fact, natural obstacles made communication between one region and another hazardous and slow.

A greater problem was the cultural differences of the American peoples. They worshiped many gods and spoke many tongues. Spaniards and Englishmen might detest one another, but their Christian European heritage enabled them to understand each other. Few Europeans were able to understand Amerindian ways. At first dazzled by Amerinidian cultures, most Europeans soon came to look down on Amerinds as "savages." Few Europeans doubted that the New World religions must give way to Christianity.

The greatest problem in the New World was scarcity of labor. European diseases such as smallpox drastically cut down the supply of Amerindian labor. So did massacres and slave raids. The population of the Americas before the Conquest, roughly estimated at 15 to 25,000,000, dropped within a century to 1 to 4,000,000. This drastic decline may well be the greatest population disaster in history. It explains why labor scarcity was the leading colonial problem. Who was going to till the fields, mine the precious metals, and build the cities and missions? The various ways different European nations solved these problems account for many of the cultural differences that exist in the Americas today.

Spanish colonists expect Amerinds to do manual labor. Spaniards soon settled in regions once inhabited only by Amerinds. Because the Spanish Crown had granted conquistadores and early colonists huge tracts of land, before long there was hardly any free land to attract more farmers from Spain. In the populous highlands of North and South America the Spanish colonists, like the former Aztec and Inca governors and priests, lived off slave and servile labor. The Amerindian peasant or *peon* humbly continued to supply food, shelter, and services; only his masters had changed. His labor erected the elaborate cathedrals, universities, and palaces of Lima (in Peru), Mexico City, and San Salvador (in Central America), where Spanish viceroys and archbishops ruled. For the Spanish and Portuguese settlers, forced Indian labor had much the same effect as had gold treasure for the conquistadores. It made them rich and hence idle. Spanish and Portuguese continued to migrate to the New World, hoping to gain wealth through discovering and mining precious metals and gems. Manual labor, of course, was left to the peons. Forced labor, particularly in the silver mines of Bolivia and Mexico, cost the lives of thousands of Amerinds.

In Spanish colonies the Amerind is mistreated and humiliated. At first the Spaniards enslaved the Amerinds and forced them to work on plantations and in mines. But Queen Isabella soon declared that, because the Amerinds had been converted to Christianity, they could not be enslaved. Thus the Amerind was not a slave in *name*. Like the colonist, he was a subject of the Crown. The colonist could use Amerindian labor only after the Spanish Crown had licensed him to do so. Amerinds were settled in villages which were self-contained legal units. Each village had its church and its own system of law (which had to conform to royal decrees). A certain amount of land was allotted to each village and was owned by the community as a whole. The village, rather than the individual Amerind, was also responsible for tribute payments. The fact that the Amerind could not be bought or sold meant little, since he could be assigned to a colonist and forced to labor for him. The ex-soldiers and their descendants, called *creoles,* looked upon the Amerinds as fit only for labor. Creoles therefore resisted the royal policy of protecting the Amerinds by isolating them in their own villages. The Crown might command, but the Crown was in Europe.

Because the Crown continued to insist that the Amerind pay tribute in money, he had to work. He labored long hours for minimum pay. Working conditions on cacao plantations, in textile factories, and in silver mines were bad. More often than not the Amerind was ill, exhausted, poorly fed, beaten, and in rags. Even the Church, which did much to protect the Amerinds, came to profit from their exploitation by creoles. Colonists who made fortunes in the New World gave large gifts to the Church. On neither its land nor its other wealth did the Church pay taxes. Church-owned plantations and investment in industry brought increased income and made the Church the leading moneylender in the Americas.

The Church tries to protect the Amerinds. Like the Crown, the Catholic Church tried to protect the Amerinds from the creoles' greed. But it had little success. In their villages the Amerinds learned Christian ways from Catholic friars. The most famous of these was Bartolomé de las Casas (bar-toh-loh-*may'* dey lahs *kah'*sahs), who denounced the cruelty of the Spaniards toward the Amerinds. Las Casas often exaggerated accounts of Spanish cruelty. But his campaign to end exploitation of the Amerinds gained the support of the Spanish king, who appointed Las Casas the "Protector of the Indians."

Las Casas' views were shared by most of the other friars the Crown sent to preach to the Amerinds. Backed by the Crown, the Church prevented the colonists from working all Amerinds to death and helped to create a sense of spiritual togetherness in the Spanish and Portuguese colonies. By allowing the Amerinds to perform their ritual dances during Christian holy days, it lessened the shock of cultural change. The Catholic Church gave Amerinds the feeling that their old ways had some spiritual value. Thus, despite their conversion to Christianity, the Amerinds retained a little self-respect and some of their own culture.

In Paraguay the Jesuits established mission villages where the Amerinds might learn European crafts and agriculture. These missions were plagued by slave raids from Brazil and later came under attack from Spanish colonists deprived of what they considered their rightful source of labor. The Crown permitted the Jesuits to arm the Amerinds—a practice strictly forbidden elsewhere in the Americas. Speaking Guaraní (gwah-rah-*nee'*), the Amerindian language in Paraguay, the Jesuits taught their Amerindian charges how to plant and harvest, to pray and sing, and to dress and marry in the European way. The economic success of the Jesuit missions aroused the antagonism of the creoles, and eventually even the Crown felt threatened. In the mid-eighteenth century the Society of Jesus was expelled from Spanish and Portuguese territory in America. With its going, the Paraguayan missions collapsed.

The hot climate led the Mediterranean peoples to erect buildings with thick walls painted white to reflect the sun, small deepset windows, and interior courtyards. This Spanish church in Pisac, Peru (left), reflects this style of architecture. The coming of the Spaniards radically changed ways of life in the Great Plains and the Southwest (page 299). The painting by the Sioux Chief Pretty Hawk below shows the readiness with which the Amerinds adopted the horse.

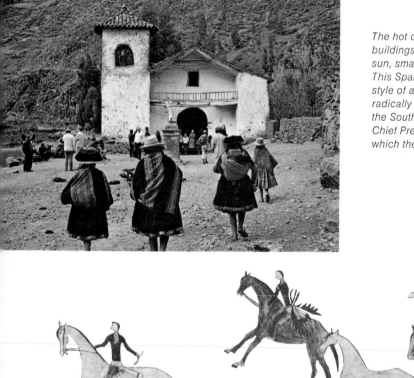

The Amerind withdraws from colonial society. Although the Amerind was hardly free to move about, the village system did save him from outright enslavement and possible extermination. The Amerind became a Christian but not a European; outside his village he had no place in the new colonial society. Even the Church, which championed his cause, regarded the Amerind as a child not responsible for his actions. The Amerind therefore shunned creole ways except for Catholicism. He became fatalistic, an attitude that to this day reflects his acceptance of his fate and his indifference to the world beyond his village.

African slaves labor on tropical plantations. In the islands of the Caribbean Sea, Amerinds were quickly killed off by disease, overwork, and the Spanish cruelty denounced by Las Casas. Present-day medical knowledge suggests that Old World diseases by themselves were deadly enough to kill off the Caribbean Amerinds. The Crown naturally became alarmed at the drop in the free labor force and the resultant loss of tribute from the Amerinds. Therefore it licensed the importation of black slaves from Africa (and a handful of white slaves). It gave two reasons for this action. (1) Since the blacks had already been enslaved in Africa, conversion to Christianity could not change their legal status. (2) Since Africans were supposed to be accustomed to heavy field labor in a tropical climate, they could endure this work better than Amerinds unused to such toil.

In any case, the African soon did most of the work in *tierra caliente* (*tyey'*rah kah-*lyehn'*-tey, hot land). Tierra caliente comprises the long semi-tropical and tropical arc along the Atlantic and Caribbean coasts from south Brazil to Delaware Bay in North America. Portuguese slavers bought slaves on the Guinea Coast of Africa and shipped them directly to the tierra caliente. Slave ownership was even a condition for the receipt of a grant of land from the king in Portuguese America.

A complex economic system draws on three continents. Slaves from Africa were used in America to produce tropical goods for consumption in Europe. In Brazil, African slaves were often purchased with the very sugar and tobacco produced on plantations by earlier arrivals from Africa. About 1650 Dutch and later English and French capitalists took over uninhabited Caribbean islands and established sugar plantations. Sugar was called "white gold." To make maximum use of land, only this one cash crop was planted. Food was imported from Europe or North America to feed white master and black slave. By 1700 plantation colonies were the most prized colonial possessions. They yielded far greater profits than colonies in temperate zones (Chile, Canada, or Connecticut).

The planter rarely took good care of his field hands. As high-priced as slaves were, the planter still found it cheaper to work them hard and to buy replacements than to try to keep them healthy. As a result, in most plantation regions there were more African-born than American-born slaves, more male than female slaves. All slaves were supposed to be baptized and given Christian names. But only relatively few—those who became domestics or overseers —absorbed much European culture.

CHECK-UP

1. What new animals, plants, tools, and institutions did Europeans bring to America? What problems faced Europeans who settled in the New World? How did the shortage of labor lead to conflict with the Amerinds? What solution was imposed?

2. What was the relationship of the Amerinds to the Crown? How did the colonists treat the Amerinds? What was the reaction of the Church? How did the Church help Amerinds preserve their self-respect?

3. Why were African slaves imported to work on the plantations? How were they treated?

The Dutch are more successful in Asia than in the New World. In the last years of the sixteenth century the Dutch, long a seafaring people, began to seek another route to the spices of Asia than that controlled by Portugal. Dutch seamen sailed north of Scandinavia and then along the coast of Russia. When this approach proved a failure, they set out across the Atlantic, hoping to find a northwest passage to Asia. Henry Hudson, an Englishman employed by the Dutch, sailed up the Hudson River as far as Albany in the vain search for an outlet to the Pacific. On the basis of Hudson's voyage the Dutch claimed the land along the Hudson River and soon established settlements there. These Dutch holdings in the Hudson Valley, including what is now New York City, were soon seized by Britain. In South America the Dutch took Surinam, some Caribbean islands, and the rich parts of Brazil. Brazil was soon lost to the Portuguese, but Surinam and the Dutch Antilles remain under Dutch sway to this day.

Dutch naval action in the East, however, brought far greater rewards. Holland, when it lay under Spanish control, had profited enormously from Iberian trade, but Protestant Holland's struggle for independence closed Spanish ports to the Dutch in 1568. In 1580 when the king of Spain became the ruler of Portugal as well, he closed Lisbon to Dutch ships. Undaunted, the Dutch decided to trade directly with India and the East Indies held by the Portuguese. Involvement in a long series of European wars forced Spain to concentrate her sea power and that of Portugal in the Atlantic to protect the routes to the New World. This enabled Dutch fleets to sail around Africa and into the Indian Ocean without meeting much opposition. Soon the Dutch controlled the East Indies and its rich spice trade.

Unlike the Spanish and Portuguese, the Dutch devoted almost no effort to spreading Christianity. Their interests lay almost exclusively in trade and profit. Dutch merchants monopolized the spice trade of the East Indies, shared in the trade with India, and outdid all other Europeans as slave traders. The following comment by a Chinese observer is a wry tribute to their skill and success as businessmen:

[These "Red Barbarians"] are greedy and cunning, are very knowledgeable concerning valuable merchandise, and are very clever in the pursuit of gain. They will risk their lives in search of profit, and no place is too remote for them to frequent. . . . These people are also very resourceful and inventive. They make sails like spiders' webs, which can be set at any angle to catch the wind. If one falls in with them at sea, one is certain to be robbed by them.

French control is short, but French influence endures. Because of her involvements in the religious and political struggles of sixteenth-century Europe, France had little energy left for exploration and colonization. Consequently, France lagged behind Portugal and Spain in the race for overseas possessions. French sea captains, searching for a northwest passage to Asia, explored the coast of Newfoundland, Labrador, and Canada, but attempts to establish settlements failed.

At the end of the sixteenth century, after Henry IV had put an end to the religious wars that had weakened and divided the nation, France became more aggressive in overseas expansion. In the early 1600's Samuel de Champlain explored the region of the St. Lawrence River and the Great Lakes and founded the city of Quebec. Champlain's efforts to develop Canada met with little success, for the land

The Mercantilist Foundation of Colonialism

KEY

English

French

Dutch

Portuguese

Spanish

Swedish

NORTH AMERICA

LOUISIANA

NEW SPAIN (MEXICO)

NEW FRANCE

NEW ENGLAND

VIRGINIA

FLORIDA

Great Lakes

Mississippi R.

Quebec

Montreal

Plymouth

Jamestown

Mexico City

Gulf of Mexico

CUBA

Caribbean Sea

ATLANTIC OCEAN

PACIFIC OCEAN

GREENLAND (Denmark)

ICELAND (Denmark)

SWEDEN

DENMARK

ENGLAND

NETHERLANDS

FRANCE

SPAIN

PORTUGAL

NEWFOUNDLAND

Hudson Bay

Equator

NEW GRANADA (COL.)

NEW ANDALUSIA (VEN.)

GUIANA

NEW CASTILE (PERU)

Lima

SOUTH AMERICA

Amazon R.

BRAZIL

NEW ESTREMADURA (CHILE)

LA PLATA

ATLANTIC OCEAN

NORTH AMERICA

NEW NETHERLAND

NEW SWEDEN

Fort Orange (Albany)

New Amsterdam (New York)

Fort Christina (Wilmington)

ATLANTIC OCEAN

lacked gold and silver to attract settlers. Some Frenchmen, however, did make substantial profits from the fur trade. Missionaries and traders continued to explore the region of the Great Lakes and the Mississippi valley. In 1718 a French colony was established at New Orleans.

France also acquired islands in the West Indies. On these islands wealthy Europeans built large plantations and imported thousands of African slaves for the labor force. In Africa, France established trading posts in Senegal and acquired wealth from trading in slaves, ivory, ostrich feathers, and gold dust. The sugar colony of St. Domingue (*san' doh-mang'*)in the Caribbean earned France more profits than any other colony.

British sea power and the greater population in the Thirteen Colonies led to the loss of France's North American empire. The hope of building an empire was shattered during the Seven Years' War (1756–1763). As a result of this war France lost both Canada and India to Britain. But French influence in Canada has endured. Today millions of Canadians speak French and cherish French cultural traditions.

England establishes colonies in America and Asia. Searching for a northwest passage to Asia, John Cabot, an Italian in the pay of England, explored the Atlantic coast of what is now the United States. England laid claim to this coast and at the beginning of the seventeenth century established permanent settlement there. English colonists crossed the Atlantic in search of land, greater economic opportunities, and freedom of religion.

To the New World they brought a tradition of liberty that had developed in England over the centuries. In America, English settlers established representative assemblies modeled after the British Parliament, drew up bills of rights to protect liberties to which they had grown accustomed in England, and adopted English legal procedures.

Britain also acquired islands in the West Indies. Plantations on these islands, cultivated largely by slave labor, provided England with sugar and tobacco. Slaves were transported from Africa, where trading posts flourished on the west coast.

Like the Dutch, the English took advantage of Spain's involvement in Europe and in the Atlantic to establish direct trade with Asia. By 1600 England had already established a foothold in India, and during the Seven Years' War she gained supremacy there (see Chapter 26).

English and French settlers drive the Amerind from his land. The English and French settlers encountered comparatively few Amerinds in North America, and geographic conditions in the temperate zones favored neither plantation agriculture nor large-scale mining. The Protestant settlers from England did not want the Amerind's labor nor did they see any compelling need to save his soul. Many of these settlers had obtained passage to America by agreeing to serve a master for five to seven years. Once their term of service ended, they, like other North European colonists, wanted virgin land to farm themselves. White men, therefore, simply drove the red men away, cleared the land, and settled down with their families. They did their own work on *freeholds* (land that they owned outright) and produced little for export to Europe. This type of small landholding in the region north of Delaware Bay was new and unique. It is the only one that the Portuguese did not first pioneer in the Old World.

In New France, however, the *seigneurs* (seh-*nyur'*) felt much the same way about labor as did the Spanish *señores* (sey-*nyoh'*-rehs). The seigneurs had received large land grants and tried to establish in the New World the same noble-peasant relationship that prevailed in France. Beaver pelts and other furs were to the French what silver was to Spain. As settlement and the growing demand for furs reduced the beaver population and the supply of game, the Amerinds drew back into the interior. French trappers and fur traders also moved inland. A mutual tolerance developed between the two races. Catholic missionaries, such as Marquette, lived with the Amerinds and converted many to Christianity. Thus, while Dutch and English colonists clung to the coast, the French explored the heartland of North America during the seventeenth century. While Dutch and English Protestants lived apart from the Amerind and drove him away, French Catholics attempted to learn his ways and to teach him some European ways.

CHECK-UP

1. What success did the Dutch have in the New World? In Asia?

2. Where in America and Asia were French colonies established? English colonies? How successful were they?

3. Contrast English and French landholding in America. How did their policy toward the Amerinds differ?

Commercial Revolution

So great was the economic growth of Europe during the Age of Exploration that historians refer to the period 1450–1700 as the *Commercial Revolution.* Writes American historian L. B. Packard of this period:

. . . changes in methods of conducting business, in trading centers, in shipping, in the financial aspects of commerce, and in . . . [economic] theories . . . were so numerous, so pronounced and so rapid that the total effect seems to have been revolutionary. . . . Commerce, like most other phases of civilization, passed between the fifteenth and eighteenth centuries from medieval to modern form and manner.

The Commercial Revolution encourages the growth of capitalism. A basic feature of the Commercial Revolution was the rapid growth of *capitalism.* The capitalist-type economy eventually spread throughout Europe and affected the entire globe. What are the basic characteristics of capitalism?

1. Under capitalism *the means of production are privately owned.* Businessmen, not the government, own the mines, factories, trading firms, and banks.

2. Capitalist businessmen seek *unlimited profits,* not just an adequate living for themselves and their families.

3. In order to acquire profits, capitalists *compete* with other businessmen.

4. To make and increase profits, capitalists run their businesses with maximum *efficiency.*

5. Capitalists view *business success as a great good,* a worthy goal for which to strive. They regard a man successful in business as worthy of admiration and respect, a leader in society.

The origins of modern capitalism can be found in the increased economic activity of the late Middle Ages. Growing trade between the Italian city-states and Muslim centers of population, Constantinople, Northern Europe, and Asia stimulated the growth of capitalism in Italy in a number of ways.

1. Profits from trade enabled Italian merchants to accumulate large amounts of capital. This capital was reinvested, or plowed back into the business, or was invested in other business enterprises.

2. Merchants entered into business agreements such as partnerships. By pooling their capital, businessmen were able to expand their business and increase their profits.

3. The increase in business activity called for systematic bookkeeping, without which no large-scale business activity can be conducted efficiently.

The art produced during the period of the Commercial Revolution reflected the affluence and growing importance of the merchant class. Jan Vermeer's The Piano Lesson (above) depicts a room in the house of a Dutch family. Its rich furnishings suggest that a man who helped build the Dutch commercial empire became wealthy. One of the first great European capitalists was Jacob Fugger, shown at right in his office. His bookkeeper, who painted the picture, stands at a chest of drawers bearing the names of cities in which Fugger had branch offices. Fugger was a powerful man who extended loans to Emperor Charles V (page 401).

4. To meet the demands of trade, banking and credit facilities were developed and expanded, thus making it unnecessary for merchants to carry large amounts of cash. The availability of banks and credit also made borrowing easier.

The Age of Exploration greatly speeded up the growth of capitalism. The volume of trade soared as European ships crossed the oceans carrying spices, silk, tea, carpets, coffee, and precious gems from the East; furs, corn, sugar, cacao, and fish from the Americas; and slaves and ivory from Africa. Silver and gold from the mines of the New World vastly increased the supply of money available for investment in new business ventures.

Joint-stock companies emerge. The tremendous increase in business activity created problems. It took large amounts of capital to build, buy, or rent ships, fill their holds with a profitable cargo, recruit officers and crew, and provide sufficient provisions for the long voyage to Asia. Moreover, while profits were great, so too were risks. Many ships never completed the long and dangerous ocean voyage. Few individual businessmen or partnerships had sufficient capital to pay the high costs of an Asian voyage or to absorb the loss of a disaster at sea. To overcome this difficulty, there emerged a new type of business arrangement, the *joint-stock company*. The joint-stock company operated in much the same manner as a present-day corporation. A number of investors, large and small, purchased shares of stock which gave them part ownership in the business. This arrangement attracted large amounts of capital and at the same time reduced the risk to investors. A man could afford to invest a moderate sum in a joint-stock company, for if the company failed, he would lose only the money he invested.

Two of the most successful joint-stock companies were the English East India Company and the Dutch East India Company. Both were formed early in the seventeenth century. In one extremely profitable voyage the English Company returned 220 per cent to its investors; for centuries the Dutch East India Company paid its stockholders annual dividends averaging 18 per cent.

The influx of precious metals leads to a sharp rise in prices. Bars of gold and silver began to move from Mexico to Spain in 1522. From Spain they usually moved on to the money markets of Antwerp in Belgium and Milan in Italy. The sudden increase in the supply of gold and silver without a comparable increase in the production of goods led to a rapid rise in prices throughout Europe. By 1650 the cost of most goods had nearly quadrupled; wheat and hay sold in the Paris market for fifteen times their price in 1500. Lords who received fixed money payments from peasants found their income increasingly insufficient. Because of the rapidly rising cost of living, the worker found his wages bought less and less. The merchant's pocketbook, on the other hand, was usually full because he owned goods whose money value kept rising.

Mercantilist policies strengthen royal power in Europe. During the Age of Exploration and the Commercial Revolution, European kings increased their power enormously. This combination of great economic growth and expanding royal power gave rise to *mercantilism*. Mercantilists sought to increase national power; they wanted their state to compete favorably with other states. They hoped to achieve this by regulating and directing national economic activity. The manor-centered economy of the Early Middle Ages had given way to a town-centered economy in the High Middle Ages. This, in turn, gave way to the nation-centered mercantilist economy. What practices were characteristic of mercantilist states?

European rulers sought to increase their power. In the 1600's a king's power was judged by the luxury of his court and the size of his armed forces. A king short of cash could not afford to build a large navy or to recruit a large army. Until the French Revolution (see Chapter 19) he had no authority to draft his subjects into military service. Most armies were made up of mercenaries (hired soldiers). In mercantilist Europe, then, to be powerful a king needed bullion (gold and silver). To increase the country's supply of bullion, the king encouraged exports, for the sale abroad of domestic goods meant that money was flowing into the country. To stop precious metals from leaving the country, the king would try to reduce imports. The accumulation of wealth in the form of bullion was the first principle of mercantilism. To increase the wealth of the state, mercantilist kings encouraged the formation of joint-stock companies, which generally made their money from trade. Mercantilist kings granted these joint-stock companies certain privileges; in return they received a fixed share of the companies' profits.

Colonies played a vital role in mercantilist thinking. Mercantilists expected a colony to be a profitable enterprise for the mother country. They regarded it as a mammoth mine (Peru) or a giant plantation (Brazil). Mercantilists saw the world beyond Europe as an extended trading post: Africa producing slaves, ivory, and gold; Asia turning out spices, dyes, and textiles; the Americas, silver, sugar, and furs. To the mother country the colony had to bring in wealth either directly in the form of silver or indirectly in the form of spices from the East Indies or slaves from Africa. Mercantilists naturally insisted that colonies should buy their goods from the mother country, not from other lands.

Iberian mercantilism is resented by other nations. Global mercantilism really began with the division of world trade between the Catholic powers—Spain and Portugal—in 1494. For nearly a century thereafter the Portuguese grew rich by monopolizing the trade in African slaves and Asian spices, and the Spanish Crown prospered from its share (the royal fifth) of American treasure. The Crown restricted each colony to trade with the mother country. Thus, for Mexican chocolate to reach Peru, it first had to be shipped to Seville in Spain. This regulation understandably annoyed the colonists. Since they couldn't trade with each other legally, they resorted to smuggling, a practice which was to have disastrous results for the economies of Spain and Portugal.

Mercantilist monarchs in other European nations realized that the way to weaken the power of the Spanish king (who also ruled Portugal after 1580) was to cut off the flow of bullion from America and of precious cargoes from Asia. The lure of easy wealth brought pirates and buccaneers to the Caribbean to prey on Spanish ships. Merchant privateers smuggled goods into Spanish colonies, plundered towns along the Caribbean coast, and captured treasure ships. Finally, joint-stock companies with royal support waged naval war against Spain. These pried open the closed mercantilist system in the Atlantic and divided among themselves many of the Portuguese holdings in the Indian Ocean.

Spain's monopoly began to crack in 1562 when a daring English merchant, John Hawkins, brought European goods and African slaves to the Spanish settlements in the Caribbean. The colonists welcomed him, and he sold his contraband at a good profit. In 1577–1580 his cousin, Francis Drake, entered the Pacific, captured Spanish ships, and in Panama seized a year's output of Peruvian silver. Unwilling to run the risk of capture by returning to the Atlantic, Drake sailed westward across the Pacific, completing the second circumnavigation of the globe. Such exploits indicated that England could do more than "singe the King of Spain's beard." English seamen showed that Spanish naval power was far from invincible. Before long, the French and the Dutch also began to prey on Spanish shipping.

Dutch mercantilism flourishes in the West and East Indies. The Dutch found attacks on Portuguese commerce highly profitable. This led to the formation of Dutch joint-stock companies whose sole business was to commit "acts of hostility against the ships and property of the King of Spain and his subjects" in the Indies. The Dutch West India Company was chartered in 1621. Only seven years later Piet Heyn (*peet hine*) captured a Spanish silver-fleet in the Caribbean.

For the first and last time this operation, so often attempted before and since by Dutch, English, and French sailors and freebooters, was crowned with complete success. By a combination of good luck, good seamanship, and good leadership, Piet Heyn cornered the silver fleet from Mexico . . . and captured it intact without firing more than a shot or two. This fleet was worthy of its legendary name and fame. One hundred and seventy-seven thousand pounds of silver worth eight million guilders formed the principal part of the booty which flowed into the West India Company's coffers. . . . Nor could the rest of the booty be classified as chicken feed. Only 66 pounds of gold are recorded in the official inventory; but a thousand pearls, nearly two million hides, and substantial quantities of silk, musk, amber, . . . "and many other rarities" figure in the same list. [These last items probably came from the Philippine Islands.] No wonder the United Provinces [of the Netherlands] went wild with joy and that Piet Heyn became the most popular man in the country.

While the Dutch were a major force in the Americas for a relatively brief period, their control of the East Indies endured for nearly three centuries. Following a mercantilist policy, the Dutch East India Company concentrated on Indonesia and control of the seas in the East Indies. The forts and fleets of the Dutch East India Company enforced and protected its monopoly in pepper and spices. Later cotton, silk, tea, and coffee made up the bulk of its trade.

European states pursued mercantilist policies from 1500 until well into the 1700's. According to mercantilist theory, a country's power depended upon its wealth in metals. In order to increase their supply of gold and silver, kings (1) sought to increase exports and decrease imports, (2) tried to prevent colonies from trading with anyone but the mother country, and (3) encouraged the growth of home industries and joint-stock companies because they increased domestic production and colonial trade.

CHECK-UP

1. What are the characteristics of capitalism? How did a joint-stock company operate? What was the effect of the flow of precious metals to Europe?

2. What is mercantilism? How did mercantilist policies strengthen royal power in Europe?

3. How did Spain and Portugal seek to monopolize trade with America and Asia? How did other nations react? How did the American colonies react to trade restrictions? How was this monopoly weakened?

4. What success did the Dutch have in the New World? In Asia?

The Legacy of Exploration and Commercial Expansion

1. Commercial expansion. Europe experienced an enormous expansion of business activity. The supply of money increased, trade expanded, and large-scale business enterprises (joint-stock companies) were formed. All of these developments stimulated the growth of capitalism. This business expansion rested in part upon the exploitation and mistreatment of Africans, Americans, and Asians. Writes French historian Henri Sée (on-*ree' say'*):

The slave trade, despicable though it was, must be recognized as bringing in enormous profits. Therefore it was one of the important sources of capitalism. . . . Very justly does [nineteenth-century economist] Sombart say: "We have become rich because whole races, whole peoples have died for us; for us continents have been depopulated." Innumerable bits of evidence show that the colonial commerce and the exploitation of the native populations added enormously to the flood of wealth which poured into Europe.

2. Shifts in business centers. As a result of the new trade routes opened up during the Age of Exploration, the Italian city-states lost their position as the leading commercial centers of Europe. The European states on the Atlantic coast grew prosperous as the Italian states declined in commercial importance. The early beneficiaries of the new trade routes were Portugal and Spain. Portugal lost out in the East Indies when Spain proved unable to stop Holland from taking over the Asian trade. At first enriched by treasure from her American lands, Spain's home industries lost their prosperity. More and more articles manufactured outside Spain were smuggled into her American ports by enterprising Dutch and English merchants. In exchange Holland and England got the lion's share of the American bullion. Whereas Spanish wealth rested on conquest, plunder, and mining in the Americas, English and Dutch prosperity rested upon trade in slaves and spices, smuggling, and banking. Despite the decline of Spanish power, the Spanish overseas empire held together against the determined assaults of other European powers. Portuguese Brazil also stayed intact. Not until the nineteenth century did the Spanish and Portuguese empires in America disintegrate.

3. Worldwide circulation of food products. A wide variety of food products flowed from one part of the world to another. From the tropical East and West Indies there flowed to Europe ever increasing quantities of colonial goods: sugar, rice, tea, cacao, and tobacco. From the Americas the rest of the world received four very important vegetable staples— potatoes, corn, sweet potatoes, and manioc (a plant with a large starchy root from which tapioca is produced). The potato and corn thrived in Europe, manioc in Africa, and the sweet potato in Asia. Their transplantation greatly increased the food supply on all three continents of the Old World. American manioc did so well in Africa, for example, that it may have allowed the population to increase despite the millions of slaves shipped to the Americas. In America the Asian orange and banana flourished. So did the sheep, chickens, pigs, horses, and cattle brought to the Americas by Europeans.

4. Population changes. The balance of world population began to shift. Up to 1420 continents had little contact with one another. Once Europeans started mingling with Africans, Amerinds, and Asians, epidemics began to rage in all parts of the world. No one at the time understood their cause. Contagious diseases doubtless were carried from one part of the world to another by European carriers. Between 1493 and 1650 disease wiped out millions.

Epidemics killed off more people in the New World than elsewhere. While European, African, and Asian peoples had gradually built up some immunity to each other's bacteria, Amerinds had remained completely isolated from the bacteria of all three continents of the Old World. To the New World came malaria and yellow fever as well as smallpox, measles, and chicken pox. The resulting drop in the Amerindian population made mass revolts against European colonization impossible.

In tropical Africa the Portuguese quickly learned that one out of two white men died in their first year of residence, probably from malaria. Consequently Europeans avoided living in the "white man's grave" and visited Africa only to acquire slaves. About ten per cent of the slaves shackled and stifling below deck perished in the sea voyage from Africa to the Americas. (The death rate among European crewmen was even higher.)

In tropical America, however, the conditions were better for Europeans. Only one out of six would die in the first year. White planters in Brazil regarded seven to ten years as the productive life of an African slave. Since slaves did not reproduce their numbers here, the continued transportation of African males was essential to the "South Atlantic System" which linked Europe, Africa, and the Americas in a triangular trade.

Despite plagues in London and other European cities, the population of Europe after 1500 was probably growing at a greater rate than that of the rest of the world. The percentage of the white men on earth kept rising because of (a) an increased supply of food in Europe, to a very large extent the result of the cultivation of corn and potatoes transplanted from America, (b) the high death rate of Amerinds because of disease and forced labor, (c) the short life span of millions of African slaves in the New World.

5. Emergence of a world economy. With the Commercial Revolution we have the beginnings of a world economy. Europeans ate American sugar and paid for Asian spices and silk with American silver. In this global economy, Europe was banker and profit-taker. Whatever happened in the financial and business centers of Europe came to affect, for good or ill, more and

The Colonial System, 1763

AUSTRALIA
(NEW HOLLAND)

NEW GUINEA

MOLUCCAS

CELEBES

PHILIPPINES (Sp.)

BORNEO

JAVA

EAST
INDIES

SUMATRA

PACIFIC OCEAN

Macao

ASIA

SIBERIA

BENGAL

Madras
Pondicherry

INDIAN OCEAN

Bombay   Goa   MALABAR
COAST

North Pole

RUSSIA

CLAIMED BY RUSSIA,
SPAIN, AND ENGLAND

GREENLAND
(Denmark)

CANADA

NORTH
AMERICA

NEW SPAIN

LOUISIANA

ICELAND
(Denmark)

DENMARK

BRITISH
ISLES

DUTCH
REP.

FRANCE   EUROPE

New Orleans (Fr.)

THIRTEEN
COLONIES

MIQUELON
ST. PIERRE

PORTUGAL   SPAIN

GIBRALTAR (Br.)

FLORIDA

WEST

INDIES

ST. DOMINGUE
SANTO DOMINGO

AZORES

MADEIRA IS.

CANARY IS.

AFRICA

MOZAMBIQUE

NEW
GRANADA

GUADELOUPE

MARTINIQUE

CAPE VERDE IS.

SENEGAL
(Fr.)

PERU

GUIANA
SURINAM

ANGOLA

CAPE COLONY
(Dutch)

SOUTH
AMERICA

BRAZIL

ATLANTIC
OCEAN

LA
PLATA

KEY

Spain

Portugal

England

France

Dutch Republic

Flow of trade

more people on earth. For example, once European capitalists began to cut Brazilian dyewood, to mine Bolivian silver, or to sell the hides of Venezuelan cattle, the life of Amerinds was changed in untold ways. And in Africa the modern slave traffic—the richest of all mercantile trading—seems to have led to continuous warfare between tribes. In European commercial cities fortunes were made or lost because of fluctuations in the price of pepper or sugar. European merchants would buy some regional article such as Guinea ivory, Zanzibar cloves, or Japanese lacquer and offer it for sale on the world cash market. As a result there were probably regional upheavals in age-old relationships between landowner and peasant, king and merchant, and even clergyman and layman.

Local handicrafts, textiles, and other goods also circulated around the globe. As they got rich from world trade, Europeans took to hanging Chinese wallpaper, collecting jade and ivory carvings, and wearing the long Muslim garment called (in Hindi) pyjamas. The demand for "india" ink and calico and for Chinese porcelain ("china") was so great that industries were set up in Europe to produce similar goods for the ever growing market.

6. *Increased knowledge of the earth.* The Age of Exploration increased man's knowledge of his planet. American historian Boies Penrose concludes:

. . . the discoveries . . . did lead to a growth of knowledge on an unparalleled scale. Not only did men gain a vast comprehension of the earth itself, but such fields as botany, zoology, geology, chemistry, and medicine . . . were vastly extended by the knowledge of the new-found plants, animals, and other natural products. By all this, the narrow concept of history and geography . . . gave way to a widespread and genuine interest in civilization as whole, . . . to a boundless appreciation of the ever expanding world horizon.

7. *Colonization of the New World.* The Americas felt the impact of European ways far more than did Africa or Asia. The Stone Age all but disappeared under the weight of Iron Age implements such as the metal fishhook, the musket, the wheel, and the printing press. Even more important in the long run than European technology was the bringing of the western outlook on life to the Americas. North and South Americans still regard private property, representative government, the Christian church, and the liberal arts as stable institutions. The Spaniards and the Portuguese were the most influential of the European colonizers, for they planted their language, religion, and style of living among a large and mixed population descended from three continents. And in Latin America, Amerindian cultures, instead of being almost totally wiped out (as they were in Canada and the United States), persisted or blended with Spanish and Portuguese culture.

Therefore, the most significant consequence of the Age of Exploration was the settlement of the western hemisphere by white and black peoples. All the way from Argentina to Canada new nations with multiracial societies emerged. The imposition of African slavery in the New World resulted in the short-term enrichment of Europe, but it also planted the seeds of later racial conflicts. The violence in recent United States history is but one grim reminder of the prolonged and widespread influence of the Age of Exploration and the Commercial Revolution.

CHECK-UP

1. Why did the center of European commerce move to the North Atlantic?

2. What new food products were exchanged among Europe, Asia, Africa, and America?

3. What effect did the Age of Exploration and the Commercial Revolution have on the world population?

4. Why did the Commercial Revolution mark the beginning of a world economy? Why was the impact of European ways greater in America than in Asia or Africa?

Chapter Highlights

Can you explain?

bullion	freehold	middleman	mercantilism
tribute	creoles	conquistador	fortified trading post
capitalism	monopoly	circumnavigate	joint-stock company
peon	plantation	northwest passage	

Can you identify?

Atahualpa	Incas	West Indies	Jesuit missions
Tenochtitlán	Ceuta	Cortés	Prince Henry
Araucanians	Aztecs	Drake	East Indies
Hudson	Las Casas	Moctezuma	Treaty of Tordesillas
Sagres	Magellan	Age of Exploration	Cape of Good Hope
da Gama	Pizarro	Dias	Columbus

What do you think?

1. Contrast European attitudes toward exploration and trade with those of the Chinese. Was this fortunate for Europe? Why?

2. Why did the introduction of plantation agriculture increase the use of slave labor?

3. How did the African slave trade lead to increased racial prejudice?

4. Why can the motivation behind the Age of Exploration be summed up with the words "Gold, Glory, and God"?

5. Had Cuauhtémoc been the Aztec ruler in 1519, could he have successfully defended his country?

6. In the cultural exchange between Spaniards and Amerinds, who gained more? Why?

7. Why did the Spanish Crown demand tribute from the Amerinds?

8. Why did the Dutch, French, and English make no determined effort to take over Spain's New World empire?

9. Why was Spain unable to maintain her monopoly on trade with America? Why did Portugal lose her monopoly on trade with Asia?

10. How did the Spanish and the Portuguese influence the economic, political, and cultural life of Latin America?

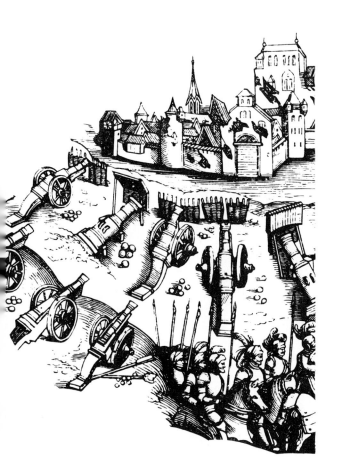

17

The Rise of Nation-States

In the modern world the nation-state is the basic form of political organization. The nation-state consists of millions of people who speak the same language, have similar traditions, live in a defined geographical area, and obey the same laws. The national state was born in the Middle Ages when kings, aided by money from townsmen, hired troops, and improved weapons, succeeded in curbing the power of feudal lords. The states they established grew more powerful in early modern times as kings continued to wrest power from both nobles and Church and to strengthen their hold over the country. National states did not develop everywhere in Europe at the same time. They were formed in England, France, and to a lesser extent in Spain during the Middle Ages. The foundations of the Russian nation-state were laid late in the fifteenth century. Not until they became united in the latter part of the nineteenth century did Germany and Italy become national states. In this chapter we shall outline the growth of European states from their medieval beginnings until the eighteenth century.

Warfare played an important role in the formation of nation-states. Kings, aided by townsmen and using improved weapons, attacked the holdings of feudal lords (above and left). Equally important was the development of centralized government. In some nations the trend was toward absolutism. In England, Parliament (top, left) came to play an increasingly powerful role. This painting of Edward I's Parliament shows the judges sitting on woolsacks symbolizing England's wealth from trade.

FRANCE: A TENDENCY TOWARD ABSOLUTISM

In the Middle Ages, France was broken up into several regions, each ruled by a feudal lord who had his own army and was responsible for the administration of justice in his territory. There was a king of France but he had little control over the feudal lords. His power was largely confined to his own lands, which were small in comparison to those of some of the great lords. The feudal system thus prevented unity. Perhaps the major obstacle to unity was the fact that by the middle of the twelfth century the king of England ruled over half of France.

French kings expand their holdings. By the early 1200's, however, the French king, Philip Augustus (r. 1180–1223), had succeeded in stripping the English king of most of his territory in France. By acquiring these lands,

The Rise of Nation-States: France

1180–1223	Reign of Philip Augustus; English rule in northern France ends
1337–1453	Hundred Years' War
1562–1598	Religious wars in France
1589–1610	Reign of Henry IV
1598	Edict of Nantes
1624–1642	Richelieu serves as Louis XIII's chief minister
1635–1648	France involved in Thirty Years' War
1642–1661	Mazarin serves as chief minister to Louis XIII and Louis XIV
1643–1715	Louis XIV
1685	Repeal of Edict of Nantes
1701	War of the Spanish Succession

Philip became more powerful than any French feudal lord.

During the next two centuries, the power of the French monarchy continued to grow as the king's rule was extended over more territory. His officials collected taxes; many cases previously tried in the feudal courts of nobles were transferred to royal courts; and the right of nobles to engage in private warfare was restricted. The French king in the early 1300's was far from the absolute ruler he would become in the late seventeenth century. Nor had the French people acquired a feeling of oneness. But the seeds of both royal absolutism and French unity had been planted. France was moving in the direction of a unified state in which the king claimed unlimited power.

The Hundred Years' War stimulates French unity. Late in the Middle Ages the first of several bitter conflicts broke out between France and England. Known as the Hundred Years' War, the struggle between the two nations lasted from 1337 to 1453. The war profoundly affected both countries. At first the war went badly for France, as English foot soldiers armed with the new and powerful longbow won decisive victories. By 1415 most of northern France, including the city of Paris, had fallen into English hands. At this critical point appeared a young peasant girl, Joan of Arc. Believing that she had been commanded by God to drive the English out of France, she rallied the demoralized French army, inspired the French people to fight for their land, and gave courage to a weak king. Although Joan later was captured by the English, condemned as a heretic (page 147) by the Church court, and executed, she had inspired the French people with a new sense of devotion to their country. The English were driven from all of France except the port city of Calais (kah-*leh*'). The Hundred Years' War was important because it

had aroused in the French people a sense of unity. French patriotism had made a great stride forward.

A powerful national state emerges. By the end of the fifteenth century French kings had created a national state and strengthened the monarchy. They had accomplished this by (1) taking over territories of lords either through war or marriage, (2) driving the English out of France, (3) appointing royal officers to administer justice and collect taxes over wide areas of the country, and (4) arousing in the French people a sense of loyalty to the king.

ENGLAND: A TENDENCY TOWARD LIMITED MONARCHY

When Roman legions withdrew from England in the fifth century A.D., the country was invaded by Germanic tribesmen, the Angles and Saxons, who established several small kingdoms. In 1066, Normans from northwestern France invaded and conquered Anglo-Saxon England. Descendants of the tough Scandinavian Northmen who had first raided and then settled in France, the Normans had adopted the French language and been converted to Christianity.

William the Conqueror establishes strong royal power in England. William of Normandy, the Conqueror of England, was determined to establish effective control over his new kingdom.

Woven in France, the Bayeux Tapestry is a detailed record of the Norman conquest of England. Done in brilliant colors, the tapestry is 231 feet long and 20 feet wide. In this detail, English spearmen defend a hill against the mounted and better armed invaders from Normandy.

Keeping about a sixth of the land for himself, he distributed the remainder among Norman nobles. These Norman barons swore an oath of loyalty to William and promised to provide him with soldiers when he needed military help. No feudal baron had enough soldiers to threaten William's power. In still another way William strengthened royal power. To determine the value of his possessions, he sent officials out into the English countryside. They made a careful inventory of each manorial estate, listing the number of tenants, cattle, sheep, pigs, and farm equipment. These facts, recorded in a document called the *Domesday* (*doomz'*day) *Book,* enabled William to determine how much tax money he could demand.

In these ways William firmly established royal power. Because he conquered all of England, future English kings did not have to travel the long and painful road to national unity followed by the French kings. The foundations were quickly laid for a unified national state in England.

The kings who followed William sought to increase royal power and national unity. Although some rulers were weak, in general the power of the monarch continued to grow. Royal

Europe in 1490

Map labels:
SHETLAND IS.
ORKNEY IS.
NORWAY
SWEDEN
(FINLAND)
Christiania
Stockholm
Novgorod
MUSCOVY
Moscow
(RUSSIA)
KHANATE OF KAZAN
SCOTLAND
Edinburgh
North Sea
Riga
TEUTONIC ORDER
IRELAND
Dublin
Copenhagen
DENMARK
Baltic Sea
Danzig
LITHUANIA
ENGLAND
London
ATLANTIC OCEAN
HANSEATIC LEAGUE
BRANDENBURG
Warsaw
Kiev
KHANATE OF THE CRIMEA
KHANATE OF ASTRAKHAN
(from England, 1491)
NETHERLANDS
Antwerp
SAXONY
BOHEMIA
POLAND
NORMANDY
Paris
LUXEMBOURG
Prague
BRITTANY
FRANCHE COMTE
BAVARIA
Vienna
Buda
MOLDAVIA
SWISS CONFED.
AUSTRIA
HUNGARY
FRANCE
SAVOY
MILAN
VENICE
Black Sea
Avignon
GENOA
Adriatic Sea
PORTUGAL
NAVARRE
FLORENCE
PAPAL STATES
Constantinople
Lisbon
SPAIN
ARAGON
CORSICA
Rome
OTTOMAN
Madrid
Toledo
NAPLES
(United, 1469)
CASTILE
SARDINIA
EMPIRE
GRANADA (to Spain, 1492)
BALEARIC IS.
Mediterranean
SICILY
CYPRUS (to Venice)
KEY
CRETE (to Venice)
Sea
Boundary of Holy Roman Empire

officials collected taxes, administered the king's justice, and kept careful records of government affairs.

The king's courts create a common law. The achievements of Henry II are particularly worth noting. During the reign of Henry I royal judges began to travel to different parts of the kingdom to try cases. This system, expanded under Henry II, is noteworthy for three reasons. (1) Throughout England, cases came to be tried in the king's court rather than in the court of the local noble. Thus the power of the king was strengthened and that of the barons weakened. (2) The decisions of royal judges were recorded and used as guides for future decisions. Eventually, the decisions of these judges became the

common law for all Englishmen, replacing the laws of the feudal barons and the older Anglo-Saxon law. The common law helped to unite the people, provided a fairer system of justice, and became the foundation of the English legal system. (3) From the practice of sending judges to various parts of the realm there developed a jury system which brought to the attention of the judge cases which it felt should be heard in court. From this system there eventually emerged the practice of trial by jury, a fundamental right that in time was guaranteed to all Englishmen.

The Magna Carta limits the powers of the king. In the thirteenth century, during the reign of the son of Henry II, King John (1199–1216), English royal power suffered a setback. This had important consequences for the future.

When John tried to collect dues illegally from the barons and to punish them without a proper trial, they resisted. Too weak to overcome them, John was forced to set his seal to the *Magna Carta* (Great Charter) in 1215. Historians regard this agreement between feudal barons and King John as an important part of the foundation on which English and American liberties rest. In the Magna Carta were stated certain principles that came to be applied more widely than was the original intention.

1. The Magna Carta stated that no unusual taxes "shall be imposed in our kingdom except by the common council of our kingdom." Over the centuries this provision came to mean that the king could not levy taxes without the consent of Parliament and that Englishmen could not be taxed except by their own representatives in Parliament.

2. The Magna Carta provided that "no freeman [can] be taken or imprisoned or dispossessed or banished or in any way destroyed . . . except by the lawful judgment of his peers or by the law of the land." In time this was expanded into the principle that the accused had a right to a jury trial and could not be imprisoned unless tried and convicted.

3. Implied in the Magna Carta was the notion that the king cannot rule his subjects any way he wishes but must govern according to the law. Centuries later, when Englishmen sought to limit the king's power, they would call attention to this idea in the Magna Carta.

Parliament grows in power. A second development that had even more to do with the rise of a limited monarchy in England was the growing strength of Parliament. The roots of the English Parliament extend to Anglo-Saxon days. Before the Norman conquest the tradition had already been established that the king was expected to take into consideration the advice of the leading men in his realm. William the Conqueror continued this tradition by seeking the advice of important churchmen and nobles. These advisors to the king assembled in a body called the Great Council. Gradually the point of

The Rise of Nation-States: England

1066	Norman conquest of England
1215	Magna Carta
1337–1453	Hundred Years' War
1485–1603	Tudors rule England
1534	English Church breaks with Rome
1603	Stuart family comes to throne
1628	Petition of Right
1640–1660	Long Parliament (suppressed by Cromwell, 1653–1660)
1642–1646	English Civil War
1649	Charles I executed; Cromwell comes to power
1653–1658	Cromwell rules as Lord Protector
1688–1689	Glorious Revolution
1689	Bill of Rights

view emerged that the king should not decide major issues without consulting the Great Council. This was the "common council" to which the barons referred in the Magna Carta. Later, lesser landowners (knights) and townsmen (burghers) were also summoned to meet with the king. Thus there emerged two branches of the Great Council—the House of Lords that included bishops and nobles, and the House of Commons composed of knights and burghers. These two branches were the basis for the English Parliament.

The main reason the power of Parliament grew over the years was its control over money matters. Frequently in need of money, yet unable to levy new taxes without the approval of Parliament, the king had to turn to Parliament for help. On such occasions Parliament was in a position to obtain additional powers from the king.

Thus there emerged in England during the Middle Ages a strong king, a centralized government, and a unified state. But the rights of the people were protected by certain principles implicit in the common law, the Magna Carta, and the rise of Parliament: (1) Englishmen had certain liberties, (2) the king could not violate these liberties, and (3) the power to govern rested not with the king alone but with king and Parliament together.

SPAIN: A TENDENCY TOWARD INTOLERANCE

Spain, like France and England, had been a Roman province. When the Empire in the West collapsed, Spain was overrun by Germanic tribesmen who dominated the country until early in the eighth century. At that time Muslims from North Africa invaded Spain.

Spain prospers under Muslim rule. Under the rule of the Muslims, Spain entered a period of prosperity and creativity unmatched anywhere else in Europe. While Christian Europe was emerging from the hardships of the Early Middle Ages, Muslim Spain was basking in a golden age. Improved irrigation techniques aided agriculture. The Muslims introduced into Spain oranges, grapefruit, dates, strawberries, rice, sugar cane, cotton, and numerous other new crops. Wine production became a major industry. Other successful enterprises included various handicrafts and the mining of gold, silver, iron, copper, and rubies. Spanish harbors were crowded with ships from North African and Asian lands.

The Muslim interest in learning was reflected in libraries and universities. Poets, philosophers, and musicians were held in high regard. French and Italian scholars visited Spanish centers of learning, where they came into contact with great Muslim scholars and rediscovered the writings of ancient Greece and Rome. These contacts stimulated the great cultural awakening that took place in twelfth-century Europe.

Under Muslim rule, Christians and Jews enjoyed the right to practice their own religion. Many Christians admired Muslim culture and adopted Muslim ways. Jews shared in the intellectual life of Muslim Spain and often rose to high positions in the government. However, there were tensions between Muslims and Christians because the former never succeeded in

The Rise of Nation-States: Spain

711	Muslims invade Spain
1009–1492	Reconquest of Spain from Muslims
1479	Aragon and Castille united
1492	Fall of Granada; Columbus reaches America
1516–1556	Charles I rules Spain
1556–1598	Philip II rules Spain
1588	Defeat of Spanish Armada
1700	Bourbon dynasty established

conquering all of Spain. In the north there were small Christian kingdoms dedicated to the *Reconquista* (rey-kohn-*key'*stah)—the drive to reconquer Spain for Christianity. It would take 500 years to achieve this goal. At the same time as the Crusades were waged in the Holy Land, Christian knights in Spain were fighting a holy war against Islam. By the middle of the thirteenth century Granada, a small area in the south, was all that remained of the Muslim domains in Spain. The rest of Spain was divided into four Christian kingdoms: Castile (kas-*teel'*), Aragon, Navarre (nuh-*vahr'*), and Portugal.

The fall of Granada completes the Reconquest. In 1469 Ferdinand, heir to the throne of Aragon, married Isabella, heir to the throne of Castile. This was a decisive step in the unification of Spain. Under Ferdinand and Isabella the Muslim kingdom of Granada was conquered by 1492. Soon after, the French were ejected from the Spanish region of Navarre in the north. Except for Portugal, the entire Iberian Peninsula was under Spanish rule. The long and bitter struggle against Islam had important consequences for Spain. Spanish Catholicism became rigid and intolerant. The proud Spanish people mistrusted and resented foreigners. These attitudes were reflected in persecution of Muslims, Jews, and Christians accused of heresy.

Spanish rulers seek to unify their country. In their efforts to unite Spain under one rule,

Ferdinand and Isabella first found it necessary to bring under their control the nobles who had achieved great power during the Reconquest. They also had to find a way to work with the powerful Church organizations. After achieving political control, the Catholic monarchs set about the spiritual reconquest of Spain. Determined to unite the nation by enforcing acceptance of Catholicism, their policies reflected the intolerant spirit of the Reconquista. In 1492 they expelled the Jews from Spain. Later the Muslims were forced to choose between conversion to Christianity or expulsion. For the Jews and Muslims who had lived in Spain for centuries and had contributed greatly to Spanish cultural life, this was a terrible tragedy. But Spain also suffered. Both Jews and Muslims had been active in commerce and industry, and the Muslims had also made great contributions to agriculture. Because it was the hated "foreigners" who had succeeded in these activities, the Spaniards came to regard commercial life and farming with scorn. Writes British historian J. H. Elliot: "The year 1492 saw the disappearance from Spain of a dynamic community, whose capital and skill had helped enrich Castile. The gap left by the Jews was not easily filled. . . . The effect of the expulsion was thus to weaken the economic foundations of the Spanish monarchy."

GERMANY AND ITALY: PROLONGED DISUNITY

By the close of the fifteenth century French, English, and Spanish kings had succeeded in developing unified states. Italy and Germany, however, did not achieve unification until some 400 years later.

Several obstacles block German unity. In 962 a German king was crowned Holy Roman Emperor. The territories of the Holy Roman Empire at its height consisted roughly of modern Belgium, Holland, Germany, Austria, Czechoslovakia, and part of France and Italy. This Holy Roman Empire lasted until 1806, but it was hardly even a shadow of the ancient Roman Empire in the West, nor did its emperor wield the power of a Roman emperor or of Charlemagne. Indeed, he failed to weld even the German-speaking lands into a German nation. What obstacles stood in the way of German unity?

1. Holy Roman Emperors sought to extend their power in Italy, thus squandering wealth and energy that could have been put to better use in their German lands.

2. Attempts to expand the Holy Roman Emperor's power into Italy led to bitter conflicts with the Church. The Pope ruled the Papal States in central Italy and opposed efforts by the Holy Roman Emperors to increase their power.

The Pope also quarreled with the Holy Roman Emperors over the appointment of bishops. Determined to liberate the Church from any control by emperors, kings, and lords, Pope Gregory VII insisted that only the Church had the power to appoint clergymen. This ruling was strongly resisted by Holy Roman Emperor Henry IV. For the emperor depended heavily upon the income and services (including fighting men) that he obtained from bishops whom he appointed and granted fiefs (page 134). If the emperor lost control over the appointment of bishops, his power would suffer. In the course of the dispute Pope Gregory also claimed that the Pope could depose emperors. This worsened the conflict.

The struggle between Henry IV and Pope Gregory VII had important consequences for Germany. When Pope Gregory excommunicated (page 147) Henry IV, German nobles, eager to weaken the power of the emperor, rebelled. During the fighting that followed, German feudal lords increased their power at the expense of their ruler. In the ensuing years the struggle between Pope and Holy Roman Emperor was renewed. Its long-range consequence was the weakening of the emperor's power. In effect, the German lords became princes ruling their own regions (principalities) over which the emperor had little or no authority. This weakening of central authority held back German unification.

3. The fact that the Holy Roman Emperor was an elected ruler further hampered attempts to build a unified state. The emperor was chosen by electors representing various German states. Besides principalities, there were bishoprics ruled by bishops and under Church law. Important trading centers and some bishoprics eventually became free cities independent of any government but that of their citizens. The Holy Roman Emperor had virtually no authority over these different types of states.

Italy fails to achieve unity. Like Germany, Italy achieved unity only in modern times. Northern Italy included the commercially powerful city-state of Venice and lands that were part of the Holy Roman Empire. Central Italy was ruled by the Pope, who opposed the creation of a unified Italy; southern Italy came under the domination of foreign rulers. The division of Italy into separate principalities and city-states, the lack of a strong ruler who could unite all of Italy, and the lack of a sense of nationality prevented Italian unification for centuries.

PATTERNS OF NATION-BUILDING

Various patterns of state-building developed during the Middle Ages. France, Britain, and Spain emerged as national states under strong kings, while Italy and Germany remained disunited. The differences in nation-building reveal some significant points.

1. The patterns of unification differed in France and England. In France the king's rule expanded slowly as a result of wars and marriage arrangements. In England, on the other hand, unity was achieved in a relatively short period as a result of the Norman Conquest.

2. There also was a difference in the type of national state that evolved in the two countries. In England, even though the king was a strong ruler he was bound to respect rights listed in the Magna Carta and established by the common law. Moreover, Parliament had become an established part of the English government (although at this time it had considerably less power than it came to have centuries later). It

was, therefore, during the Middle Ages that the foundations of limited monarchy were being laid in England. The French kings had no comparable restrictions placed on them by a law-making body. France tended toward absolute monarchy.

3. Spain moved toward unity during the centuries that Christian states struggled to drive out the Muslims. The decisive step towards unity was the marriage of Ferdinand of Aragon and Isabella of Castile. The centuries of conflict with the Muslims made Catholic Spain intolerant of non-Christians. However, the persecution and expulsion of Muslims and Jews was an economic loss to the country.

4. Italy and Germany failed to become unified states during the Middle Ages. The Holy Roman Empire was a loose association of largely independent regions. The emperor had little control over the many German princes. His power was further weakened by conflicts with the Pope. Italian unity was hampered by the fact that the Pope and foreign kings held large areas of the peninsula.

CHECK-UP

1. What is a nation-state? What contributed to the development of nation-states?

2. How was the power of the French monarch increased by Philip Augustus? How did the Hundred Years' War contribute to French unity?

3. How did William the Conqueror establish strong royal power in England? What advances in the legal system did Henry II introduce?

4. What is the significance of the Magna Carta? Why? How was the power of Parliament increased?

5. Why did Spain prosper under Muslim rule? What was the Reconquista? What measures did Ferdinand and Isabella use to unify Spain? With what results?

6. What were the obstacles to German unity? What factors prevented Italian unification?

7. How did the nation-states that evolved in France and England differ?

As the Middle Ages drew to a close the power of feudal lords and Catholic Church declined. States led by kings recognizing no higher authority came to dominate the political life of Europe. The competition among these states for wealth and power caused the outbreak of many wars during the sixteenth and seventeenth centuries. The principal causes of these wars were the ambition of one power to dominate Europe and the religious hatreds which arose as a result of the Reformation and Counter Reformation.

SPAIN: GREATNESS AND DECLINE

The Hapsburgs create a great empire. The marriage of Ferdinand of Aragon and Isabella of Castile had brought about Spanish unity. Later Spanish monarchs continued this policy of political marriages. One daughter of Ferdinand and Isabella was married to a Hapsburg prince who was the son of the Holy Roman Emperor. The offspring of this marriage, who became Charles I of Spain, inherited both Spanish and Hapsburg lands. In addition to Spain, Austria, and the Netherlands, he ruled the lands Spain had conquered in America (pages 371–375). Then, in 1519, he was elected Holy Roman Emperor. As Charles V of the Holy Roman Empire he ruled the greatest empire in Europe since the days of Charlemagne. The size of Charles V's empire made transportation and communication difficult, and differences in languages, customs, and religions of the people in his empire prevented the development of a sense of unity. As ruler of Spanish America as well as of much of Europe, Charles V had immense power and wealth. But he soon found his power challenged by political and religious disputes.

1. France felt threatened because lands ruled by Charles V encircled her and prevented French expansion in Italy. While Charles V won important battles, he was not able to subdue France. By the middle of the sixteenth century the struggle between France and the Hapsburgs had reached a stalemate. Nevertheless, French resistance to Charles V was important; it blocked the domination of Europe by one power, a problem which was to become increasingly acute in European history.

2. As Holy Roman Emperor, Charles V sought unsuccessfully to bring greater unity to his lands. His attempts to create a strong central power in Germany were resisted by the German princes and the free cities. A further obstacle to German unity was the Protestant Reformation (see Chapter 14). As the Catholic Holy Roman Emperor, Charles sought to crush Protestantism by waging war against those German princes who supported the views of Martin Luther. Unable to stamp out Lutheranism, Charles was forced to compromise and to permit German princes to choose either Lutheranism or Catholicism as the religion of their realm. All subjects in a given state had to conform to its official religion.

3. In the 1520's and 1530's Charles had been unable to deal vigorously with the Lutheran princes because the Hapsburg lands were threatened by the Ottoman Turks. Having conquered Constantinople and put an end to the Byzantine Empire, the Muslim Turks moved northward into Hungary and became a major sea power in the Mediterranean. The struggle between the Hapsburgs and the Ottomans continued for centuries; as late as 1683 the Turks besieged Vienna, the capital of Austria.

Exhausted by years of conflict and problems that he could not solve, in 1556 Charles gave up his throne and retired to a monastery in Spain. He gave his Spanish lands, the Netherlands, and lands in Italy to his son, Philip II. His brother Ferdinand became ruler of the Hapsburg possessions in Austria and was elected King of Bohemia and Hungary and also Holy Roman Emperor. The two branches of the Hapsburg family usually were united in matters of European policy. But Spain was a great sea power with vast lands in the New World, and her problems did not directly concern the Austrian Hapsburgs.

Philip II enforces religious conformity in Spain.

Philip II believed that he was chosen by God to rule, and he was determined to be a just king who governed in accordance with God's law. Like his father, Philip had a deep love for Catholicism. Like other sixteenth-century rulers, Philip II believed that a state would be weakened or even destroyed if it tolerated more than one religion. Philip ordered his domains searched for Protestant heretics. Tried before the Inquisition, heretics were urged to renounce their beliefs. Those who refused were imprisoned; some were tortured and executed. Since Protestantism had not taken deep roots, it was relatively easy to eliminate it from Spanish soil.

Philip also lashed out at the descendants of the Muslims. Those who had not fled earlier persecutions had adopted some outward forms of Catholicism in order to escape persecution. These "converted" Muslims, the Moriscos (moh-*rees'*kohs), retained many of their ancient traditions, including the Arabic language, and many continued to practice Islam in secret. When Philip imposed new restrictions, including a ban on Arabic, the Moriscos of Granada rose in rebellion. After a struggle marked by cruelty on both sides, the Moriscos were subdued and sent to other parts of Spain. Their children were to be raised in Christian homes.

Philip II becomes involved in disastrous wars.

In foreign affairs Philip sought not only to promote Catholicism but also to increase Spanish power. The following major developments occurred during his reign:

1. The Protestant Dutch in the Netherlands, aided by Protestant England, sought to break away from Catholic Spain and eventually gained their independence.

2. England supported the Dutch, and English pirates carried out many successful raids on Spanish ships and colonies in the New World. To punish England, Philip sent a huge fleet, the Spanish Armada, to invade England. Poor planning and storms prevented the Spanish fleet from picking up an invasion force in the Netherlands. As the Armada approached the coast, it was harassed by English ships. The Armada continued north, rounding Scotland in an effort to return to Spain. Many ships and men were lost; Spanish prestige suffered a heavy blow. Philip's crusades against Holland and England, both Protestant lands, had ended in failure.

3. During the second half of the sixteenth century France was torn by civil war which grew out of the rivalry between powerful nobles, some Catholics and others Protestants (or *Huguenots, hyoo'*geh-nots). Each side wished to dominate the weak French kings. As a militant Catholic and hoping to dominate France, Philip II of Spain naturally assisted the French Catholics. His hopes of dominating France collapsed when Spanish troops were forced to withdraw from French soil. The leader of the Huguenots, Henry of Navarre, became King Henry IV of France. Once again a strong Hapsburg power had been prevented from becoming the unchallenged master of Europe.

4. After the death of the King of Portugal, Philip was next in line for the Portuguese throne. Because Portuguese patriots had no wish for a Spanish king, Philip II sent troops into Portugal. They easily overcame Portuguese resistance. Portugal was united with Spain, and Philip acquired Portugal's vast overseas empire. Because the interests of Spain were always placed first, this union was unfortunate for Portugal.

5. For years, from ports in North Africa, the Turks had raided and threatened Christian lands in the Mediterranean Sea. The continued threat to commerce finally roused Spain and Venice to action. In 1571 their combined fleets —some 300 ships—confronted a Turkish naval force of about the same size. Never before had so many ships taken part in a single battle. The victory of the Christian forces at the Battle of Lepanto showed that the Turks could be de-

ATLANTIC

OCEAN

Europe About 1560

KEY

Spanish Hapsburgs

Austrian Hapsburgs

Route of the Spanish Armada, 1588

Boundary of the Holy Roman Empire

feated. But having heavy commitments in other parts of the world, a few years after Lepanto, Spain agreed to a truce with the Turks.

Unwise economic policies undermine Spain's strength. In the middle of the sixteenth century Spain was regarded as the foremost power in Europe. The Spanish soldier—disciplined, tough, and proud—had no equal. Wealth from the New World poured into Spain's treasury. Yet a century later Spain had become little more than a second-rate power. What caused her decline? (1) The wars fought by Charles V and Philip II had proved a terrible drain on Spanish resources. (2) Unlike other Western European states, Spain lacked a hard-working enterprising middle class. Spanish society placed a low value on commerce and handicrafts. This caused young men to become soldiers or to

enter the clergy or government service—all occupations which contributed little to agricultural and industrial production or to the expansion of trade. (3) Spain lost many ambitious young men to the promises of the New World. (4) Much of Spain's wealth was temporary, for most of it came from the looting of Aztec and Inca treasure and from Spain's control of American products. The Spanish kings did not realize that a country's true wealth lies in the productiveness of its economy. Moreover, the successful raids of English and Dutch pirates and smuggling in the Americas lessened Spain's income from her colonies. In addition, the amount of silver mined in the New World gradually decreased. By the middle of the seventeenth

Pieter Breughel's Triumph of the Dead *(above), inspired by the futile resistance of the Flemish to their Spanish conquerors, has a timeless message. When the battle is over, Death is the only victor. Rich and poor, of whatever nation, Death carries all away.*

fought Lutherans. The conflict which developed into the Thirty Years' War broke out in the Kingdom of Bohemia (in modern Czechoslovakia) in 1618 when a Catholic Hapsburg prince was selected to succeed to the throne. Protestants, fearful of Catholic rule, started a civil war which led to the election of a Protestant ruler for Bohemia. Meanwhile, the Hapsburg candidate had been elected Holy Roman Emperor. Allied with Hapsburg Spain and supported by German Catholic princes, he had little difficulty in bringing Bohemia back into the Catholic fold.

The war was then extended to other German Protestant states. The possibility that the Hapsburgs might use the pretext of a religious war to unify the Holy Roman Empire and extend their power over Germany alarmed neighboring states anxious to maintain a balance of power. Protestant Denmark's intervention met with defeat. The increased danger brought Protestant Sweden into the conflict. Catholic France, fearing Hapsburg expansion, became an ally of Sweden. Led by the Swedish king, Gustavus Adolphus (gus-*tay*′vus uh-*dahl*′fus), and able generals, the Swedes rolled back the Hapsburg advance. As the war dragged on, France became increasingly involved. Thus what began as a religious war developed into a long struggle to prevent the Hapsburgs from dominating Europe. Like the wars of France against Charles V and Philip II, the Thirty Years' War was, to a large extent, a struggle to maintain the balance of power in Europe.

The Thirty Years' War has a lasting impact. The Thirty Years' War had important results for the future of Europe.

1. The Hapsburgs failed to gain control over the German states. Germany would remain disunited for over 200 years.

2. The Thirty Years' War made it clear that Europe was likely to remain divided into independent states, each determined to maintain its sovereignty. The medieval dream that Europe might be united under the Holy Roman

century it had become impossible for Spain to continue its high level of spending for armaments and war. To add to the economic decline, rising inflation made life increasingly difficult for the poor.

THIRTY YEARS' WAR: DECLINE OF HAPSBURG POWER

Germany becomes a battleground. In the German states of the Holy Roman Empire the Reformation contributed to disunity as Catholics

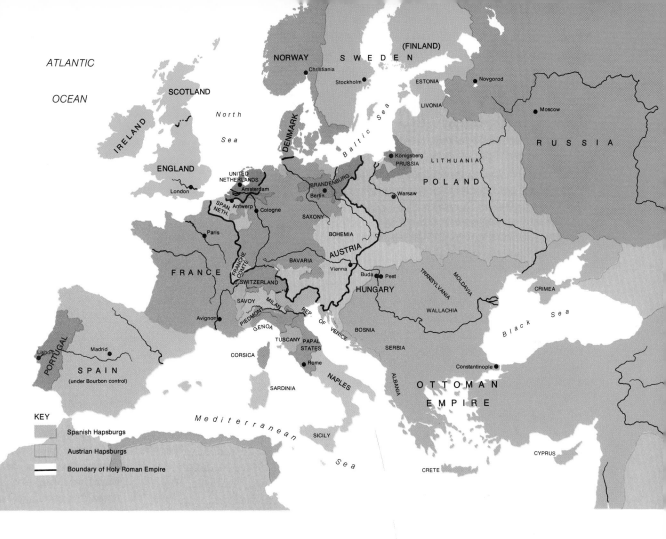

ATLANTIC

OCEAN

SCOTLAND

IRELAND

ENGLAND

London

North

Sea

NORWAY

Christiania

SWEDEN

Stockholm

(FINLAND)

Baltic Sea

ESTONIA

LIVONIA

Novgorod

Moscow

R U S S I A

DENMARK

Königsberg
PRUSSIA

LITHUANIA

POLAND

Warsaw

UNITED
NETHERLANDS
Amsterdam
SPAN.
NETH.
Antwerp
Cologne

BRANDENBURG
Berlin

SAXONY

BOHEMIA

Paris

FRANCHE
COMTE

SWITZERLAND

AUSTRIA

Vienna

HUNGARY

Buda
Pest

TRANSYLVANIA

MOLDAVIA

CRIMEA

FRANCE

BAVARIA

SAVOY
MILAN
PIEDMONT
GENOA
REP.
OF
VENICE

WALLACHIA

Black

Sea

Avignon

TUSCANY

BOSNIA

SERBIA

Madrid

CORSICA

PAPAL
STATES
Rome

NAPLES

ALBANIA

OTTOMAN

EMPIRE

Constantinople

Lisbon

PORTUGAL

SPAIN

(under Bourbon control)

SARDINIA

Mediterranean

SICILY

Sea

CYPRUS

CRETE

KEY

Spanish Hapsburgs

Austrian Hapsburgs

Boundary of Holy Roman Empire

Europe About 1648

Emperor and the Catholic Church could never
be realized under these conditions.

3. Two republics, the United Netherlands
and Switzerland, were recognized as independent of the Holy Roman Empire.

4. The Thirty Years' War marked the further
decline of Spain and the rise of France in European affairs. For over a century Hapsburg
Austria and Hapsburg Spain had encircled
France, at times threatening her very independence. Following the Thirty Years' War, this
threat disappeared. In the last part of the seventeenth century the growing power of France
made her the leading state in Europe.

CHECK-UP

1. Why did the rise of nation-states lead to
rivalries and wars?

2. What were the sources of Charles V's immense power? Why did France feel threatened
by him? What prevented Charles V from unifying
his lands? What were the results?

3. Why did Philip II enforce religious conformity
in Spain? What actions did he pursue in foreign
policy? What were the results?

4. Why did Spain decline in power?

5. What caused the Thirty Years' War? What
lasting impact did it have on Europe?

Henry IV strives for a peaceful and prosperous nation. The prolonged struggle between French Huguenots and French Catholics in the second half of the sixteenth century, marked by fanaticism and massacres on both sides, led to years of chaos and destruction. Rival groups of nobles, struggling for power and prestige, seized the opportunity to weaken further the authority of the French king. For a while it appeared that France would again be dominated by powerful nobles. Eventually Henry of Navarre, leader of the Huguenots and a member of the Bourbon family, succeeded to the French throne as Henry IV. Henry IV was intelligent, brave, and a born leader of men. But since Catholic France would not accept a Huguenot king, Henry converted to Catholicism to gain the support of the French people.

Henry IV was one of the greatest and best-loved monarchs in French history. He gave France order after decades of civil war and brought a large measure of prosperity to his kingdom. To protect the Huguenots and eliminate religious conflicts, Henry issued the Edict of Nantes (*nahnt,* 1598). It granted the Huguenots liberty of worship (except in Paris and the surrounding region), equal treatment under the law, and equal opportunity to hold positions in the government. The freedom of religion ensured by the Edict of Nantes was unusual for its time. It was a major advance in the struggle for liberty.

Henry's talented superintendent of finances, the Duc de Sully, increased the amount of money raised for the royal treasury, reduced waste and graft in the government by reforming the tax system, and encouraged trade by having roads and canals built and port facilities improved. He also made sure that the king's laws were enforced.

Richelieu and Mazarin increase the power of the king. Following Henry's murder by a religious fanatic, however, France entered another period of struggle among great nobles. Not only the power of the French monarch but the unity of the French state was endangered by the ambitions of French nobles.

Louis (*l'wee*) XIII, the young son of the assassinated Henry IV, was unable to provide effective leadership. But when Cardinal Armand de Richelieu (ar-*mahn'* deh rish-eh-*lyoo'*), became the king's leading minister, the power of the French monarch was restored. Richelieu was determined to humble the great nobles, give France greater unity by strengthening royal authority, and increase France's international power and prestige. Cool-headed, clear-sighted, realistic, and ruthless—particularly in dealing with the arrogant nobility—Richelieu largely achieved his goals. He is therefore regarded as one of the great statesmen in French history.

Richelieu died in 1642 and Louis XIII the following year. The new king, Louis XIV, was only five years old. He was guided by the new chief minister, Cardinal Mazarin (mah-zuh-*ran'*), who had been trained by Richelieu. The great nobles, eager to take advantage of a young king and an unpopular minister, seized the opportunity to regain the powers they had lost. But the rebellious nobles were unable to agree with each other and failed to win the support of the rising middle class. Their rebellion was crushed. This uprising convinced Louis XIV that only the unchallenged power of the king could prevent civil war and the destruction of the French state.

Under Louis XIV French absolutism reaches its height. Believing that kings "are born to possess all and command all," Louis claimed unlimited power by *divine right*—that is, the ruler is chosen by God to rule. A French bishop expressed this theory:

It is God Who establishes kings....

Princes thus act as ministers of God and [are] His lieutenants on earth. It is through them that He rules. . . . That is why . . . the royal throne is not the throne of a man but the throne of God Himself. . . .

It appears from this that the person of kings is sacred, and to move against them is sacrilege. . . .

There is something religious in the respect which one renders the prince. Service of God and respect for kings are things united. . . .

God . . . gave His power to kings only to ensure the public welfare and to . . . [aid] the people. . . . Thus princes should understand that their true glory is not for themselves [but for the achievement of the public good]. . . .

The prince may correct himself when he knows that he has done evil, but against his authority there is no remedy other than his own authority.

But Louis recognized that power also meant responsibility. He worked tirelessly and carefully to perform his kingly duties. "In addition to peace and security and good order, I wish to contribute by my efforts to the return of wealth and abundance and happiness of my people."*

When Mazarin died, Louis did away with the office of a first minister. He told his chief officials:

. . . up to this moment I have been pleased to entrust the government of my affairs to the late Cardinal. It is now time that I govern them myself. You will assist me with your counsels [advice] when I ask for them. . . . [Sirs], my secretaries of state, I order you not to sign anything, not even a passport, . . . without my command, to render account to me personally each day, and to favor no one.*

Louis XIV listened to the advice of the capable ministers he had chosen, but he ruled France alone. No minister, however capable and loyal, determined policy for the king. The triumph of absolutism in France under Louis XIV was the fulfillment of developments begun in the Middle Ages.

Louis' court at Versailles becomes the model for Europe. Louis gave France greater unity and a stronger central government than it had ever had. To prevent the nobility from challenging royal power, he chose many of his chief ministers as well as provincial administrators from the middle class. The great nobles, "princes of the blood," enjoyed great social prestige but exercised no real power in the government. Louis XIV encouraged princes of the blood and nobles to live in the magnificent palace he had had built at Versailles (vair-*sigh'*). This was a clever move, for at court they could be watched. Separated from their estates in the provinces, performing no significant military or governmental duties, and caught up in the gay social life at court, the nobles lost their independence and much of their power.

As the symbol of France, and the greatest ruler in Europe, Louis XIV insisted that the social life at Versailles provide an appropriate setting for his exalted person. Virtually every action of the king was accompanied by elaborate ceremonies. American historian John B. Wolf describes the dazzling world of Versailles:*

It became important who "gave the king his shirt," who "held his candle at night," the service of his table. . . . There was a crowd in his chamber when his chaplain led him through his prayers, sometimes a noisy mob that had to be warned to silence. There was a crowd when he ate; a crowd followed his strolls through the garden, his expeditions of the hunt, his attendance at the theater. Since it was the king who could give offices in the church, in the army, in the households, in the civil [service], pensions, and *gratifications* from the treasury—all of these people were on the alert to be noticed and anxious to please. . . .

* Selections from *Louis XIV* by John B. Wolf are reprinted with the permission of the publisher, W. W. Norton & Company, Inc., New York, N.Y. Copyright © 1968 by W. W. Norton & Company, Inc. Reprinted also with the permission of Victor Gollancz Ltd.

* Selections from *Louis XIV* by John B. Wolf are reprinted with the permission of the publisher, W. W. Norton & Company, Inc., New York, N.Y. Copyright © 1968 by W. W. Norton & Company, Inc. Reprinted also with the permission of Victor Gollancz Ltd.

. . . life at court was indeed delightful: hunting parties during the days, at night boating trips on the moats and ponds, or strolls through the gardens or forest paths . . . [to the music of] violins. It was a life spiced with gallantry, with young men and young women eager for each other's favors. . . . For entertainment . . . [there were] ballets, balls, horse shows, pageants, and contests of skill of all sorts. The king and his brother . . . thought it proper to take a role in the ballet, a part in the pageant, or even a try at amateur dramatics. Figure dancing was great fun; dogs and horses were good companions in field and forest; entertainers provided music and comedies, and in the background there was plenty of food and drink to spice the hours of pleasure.

Louis XIV was king of France for 72 years. During his incredibly long reign architecture, art, and literature flourished in France. France set the style for Europe. The splendor of Versailles was the talk of Europe, and other monarchs sought to copy the fashions and manners of Louis' court. Louis XIV was recognized as the supreme example of the divine-right ruler and the absolute king.

Louis XIV's prestige was enhanced by Jean Baptiste Colbert (*zhahn'* bah-*teest'* kohl-*bair'*), his minister of finance. Colbert did much to strengthen the French economy. By improving methods of tax collecting, Colbert increased the king's revenue. He also supported shipbuilding and improvements in agriculture, and had canals and roads built. He encouraged new industries by inviting foreign craftsmen to teach their skills to Frenchmen. As a result of Colbert's efforts France developed prosperous silk, tapestry, and furniture industries. But the prosperity resulting from Colbert's policies unfortunately did not last. The spending of the revenue gained was controlled by the king and not limited by a national legislative body. Louis' policy of religious persecution and a long series of ruinous wars greatly damaged the French economy.

Louis XIV seeks religious conformity. Today we take freedom of religion for granted. In the sixteenth and seventeenth centuries, however, few people believed in freedom of religion. It was generally accepted that the ruler had the right to determine the religion of his subjects. The Edict of Nantes was unusual for its time, and was not acceptable to Louis XIV. He was convinced that a nation with a large religious minority always faced the danger of civil war. Moreover, like Philip II of Spain, he believed that the Catholic faith not only welded his people together, but that the Church in France strengthened royal power. He dreamed of a France with "one king, one law, and one God" and therefore opposed religious freedom for the Huguenots. Huguenots had served France well in the armed forces and as government officials. They had demonstrated their loyalty to the king during the rebellion of the nobles and played an important role in the nation's business and industry. Nevertheless, Louis XIV demanded that the Huguenots embrace Catholicism. When persuasion failed, he turned to persecution. Finally he simply repealed the Edict of Nantes in 1685. Huguenots were forbidden to practice their religion. As persecution increased, tens of thousands of Huguenots fled to Protestant lands—England, Holland, Switzerland, and later North America. Their flight deprived France of many of her ablest businessmen and skilled craftsmen.

Louis XIV wages war to establish French supremacy. Most seventeenth-century monarchs sought to expand their domains and waged war to that end. Louis XIV was no exception. His foreign-policy goals were as grandiose as his court. (1) He sought territorial expansion to the north and east of France, with the ultimate hope of gaining a border that was easier to defend. (2) He planned to extend French power by placing a Bourbon prince on the throne of Spain. This would enable France to control Spain and her huge overseas empire.

During the sixteenth century European states had become concerned with preventing any one power from dominating Europe. In order to maintain a balance of power, nations formed alliances. When one state threatened to grow too strong, other states joined forces to resist it.

Louis XIV dominated his age. As the planets orbit the sun, so social life in France revolved around Louis, the "Sun King," whose dress and surroundings reflected his splendor. A major source of entertainment at Louis' court was the theater, which had the king's patronage. In the picture below a play by Molière is being presented in the Hall of Mirrors at Versailles. A brilliant satirist of contemporary manners, Molière is seen at the far left, acting with his troupe. After his death, the troupe became the nucleus of the Comédie Française, France's national repertory theater.

ATLANTIC
OCEAN

KINGDOM
OF
SWEDEN

(NORWAY)

Christiania

Stockholm

St. Petersburg

ESTONIA

LIVONIA

Moscow

Riga

RUSSIAN

EMPIRE

North
Sea

IRELAND

GREAT BRITAIN

Baltic Sea

LITHUANIA

Königsberg
EAST
PRUSSIA

POLAND

Warsaw

London

UNITED
NETHERLANDS
Amsterdam

HANOVER

PRUSSIA

Berlin

SAXONY

SILESIA

Antwerp

AUSTRIAN
NETHERLANDS

Cologne

Paris

LORRAINE

BOHEMIA

AUSTRIA

BAVARIA

Vienna

MOLDAVIA

BESSARABIA

CRIMEA

F R A N C E

SWITZERLAND

TYROL

Buda Pest

H U N G A R Y

Black
Sea

SAVOY

MILAN

REP.
OF
VENICE

BOSNIA

Avignon

PIEDMONT

GENOA

TUSCANY

PAPAL
STATES

SERBIA

BULGARIA

MONTENEGRO

Constantinople

PORTUGAL

Madrid

CORSICA

Rome

Lisbon

S P A I N

MINORCA
(Br.)

SARDINIA

KINGDOM
OF
NAPLES

O T T O M A N

E M P I R E

Gibraltar
(to Britain 1713)

M e d i t e r r a n e a n

SICILY

S e a

KEY

Bourbon control

Boundary of Holy Roman Empire

Europe About 1721

During the Thirty Years' War, France and other countries had fought to foil Hapsburg plans that threatened the balance of power. Now the situation was reversed. It was France that threatened European peace and stability by seeking to dominate the continent. To foil French ambitions, other European states formed alliances and waged war. From 1667 to 1714 four wars were fought to curb Louis XIV. Writes one twentieth-century historian critical of the Grand Monarch:

Louis XIV . . . so constantly menaced the independence of his neighbors and the security of Europe by capricious use of armies, the largest and most highly organized ever known, that he must

be regarded as an inaugurator of that era of European history when peace is no more than an [insecure] interval between great wars.

The most destructive of Louis XIV's wars was the final one, the War of the Spanish Succession (1701–1714). This war is often referred to as the first of the world wars because most of the European countries were involved.

The reigning Hapsburg king of Spain was the last of his line. To prevent the division of the Spanish possessions upon his death, King Charles II named as his successor Philip of

Anjou (ahn-*zhoo'*), grandson of Louis XIV. This naming of a Bourbon to the Spanish throne was a great diplomatic victory for France, but unacceptable to the other European powers. Clearly a Bourbon Spain would be closely linked to Bourbon France, which would hopelessly upset the balance of power in Europe. England, Hapsburg Austria, the Dutch Netherlands, and the German state of Brandenburg-Prussia formed an alliance opposed to Louis. They proposed that Archduke Charles of Hapsburg Austria be named to the throne of Spain. Nevertheless, Louis XIV not only accepted the bequest in behalf of his grandson but struck the first blows himself by seizing some border fortresses in the Spanish Netherlands. Although the war went badly for France, Louis XIV refused to accept the harsh peace terms offered. Then, in 1711, Archduke Charles suddenly found himself heir to the Austrian throne and most likely the next Holy Roman Emperor. If he were to gain the throne of Spain as well, the Hapsburgs would once again control much of Europe. To England and Holland the prospect of such a concentration of power was quite as dangerous as overwhelming Bourbon power. This caused disagreements among the allies and led to a compromise peace.

According to the peace treaty, Philip of Anjou retained the Spanish throne on condition that the same king would never rule both Spain and France. The Hapsburgs of Austria received the former Spanish Netherlands (Belgium) and land in Italy, while England retained Gibraltar, captured during the war, and took over some French colonies in Canada. The peace treaty attempted to maintain a balance of power in Europe. The France of Louis XIV, as had Hapsburg Austria and Hapsburg Spain before it, had failed in its attempt to dominate Europe.

Louis XIV's long wars and expensive palaces and buildings emptied the royal treasury and left the country in debt. Nothing was done to improve the system of taxation, which provided for heavy taxes on peasants and many exemptions for clergy and nobility. Despite Colbert's efforts to improve the economy, by the time Louis XIV died in 1715 France faced financial disaster. Under Louis XIV royal power had been greatly strengthened at the expense of the nobility. During the eighteenth century his successors saw their power weakened by a resurgent nobility. The failures of absolutism and the attempt of the nobility to strike back at the throne, as we shall see, helped bring on the French Revolution at the end of the eighteenth century (see Chapter 19).

European history reflects certain trends. The following trends could be seen in European political history during the sixteenth and seventeenth centuries.

1. During the period European states sought to maintain a balance of power on the continent. When one state threatened to dominate Europe, other states joined forces and resisted. Up until the Thirty Years' War (1618–1648), the balance of power was threatened by Hapsburg Austria and Hapsburg Spain. Largely because of French resistance, the Hapsburgs failed to become masters of Europe. In the last part of the seventeenth century, it was Bourbon France that sought to dominate Europe. But the plans of Louis XIV were thwarted by an alliance of European states.

2. By the middle of the sixteenth century Spain, enriched by her vast overseas empire and possessing the finest army in Europe, had achieved national greatness. But constant warfare and a fundamentally unsound economy led to Spain's downfall. Even before the Thirty Years' War, Spain was slipping into the ranks of a second-rate power.

3. Despite the efforts of Hapsburg Austria, Germany failed to achieve unity. When Germany was eventually unified late in the nineteenth century, the lead was taken not by Austria but by the German state of Prussia. Under the rule of the resourceful Hohenzollern family, Prussian power grew in the decades after the Thirty Years' War. During the eighteenth century Prussia built an excellent army, main-

tained a well-stocked treasury, expanded her territory at the expense of Austria and Poland, and survived wars against Austria that threatened her very existence. In the following century Prussia would extend her power over the other German states.

4. In the last part of the sixteenth century French nobles sought to undermine the authority of the French king. This led to decades of civil and religious warfare. In the seventeenth century French kings tried to strengthen royal power at the expense of the nobles. During the long reign of Louis XIV, French absolutism reached its height as nobles lost much of their independence and power. Never before had a French king wielded such power. But absolutism left France with many problems. During the eighteenth century, France was moving toward a social and political upheaval—the great French Revolution.

CHECK-UP

1. Why is Henry IV considered one of the greatest French monarchs? What was the Edict of Nantes?

2. What did Richelieu contribute to making France a strong nation-state?

3. How did Louis XIV justify his unlimited power? Why can his reign be said to be the fulfillment of a trend that began in the Middle Ages?

4. How did Louis XIV prevent the nobility from challenging royal power? How was the French economy strengthened? Why did Louis enforce religious conformity? What were the results?

5. What were Louis XIV's foreign policy goals? Why were they opposed by other countries? What was the result?

6. What was the condition of France at the end of Louis XIV's reign? Why?

The Triumph of Limited Monarchy in England

As absolutism and divine right were triumphing in seventeenth-century France, across the English Channel Parliament was successfully challenging and reducing the power of the English king.

The Tudors strengthen royal power. From 1485 to 1602 the Tudor family ruled England. Many of them were strong rulers who increased the authority of the crown. During the reign of Henry VIII (1509–1547) the Protestant Reformation reached England and the Church of England, with the king as its head, was established. Eventually the English (now Anglican) Church broke with the Pope, rejected a number of Catholic beliefs and practices, and joined the Protestant ranks.

The greatest of the Tudor rulers was Queen Elizabeth I, who reigned from 1558 to 1603, a period during which many European countries were torn by destructive civil and religious wars. Elizabeth succeeded in keeping England out of

war during most of her reign, although she did encourage English efforts to diminish Spanish power, especially in the Netherlands and the New World.

Elizabeth exercised considerable power but used it wisely. She showed good sense in respecting English traditions and managed to get approval from Parliament for her policies. Under Elizabeth, England was a strong, united, and prosperous kingdom.

During the last years of Elizabeth's reign, however, Parliament became increasingly independent and aware of its strength. It began to balk at the strong rule of the queen. The storm clouds that gathered in those years hinted that Elizabeth's successors might run into difficulty.

Stuart kings quarrel with Parliament. During the seventeenth century Parliament and the Stuart kings engaged in a contest for supremacy which was to have important consequences. The struggle began in 1603 when James I of the

With Elizabeth, shown above dancing La Volta, England embarked on the course which was to make her mistress of the seas and ruler of an empire which spanned the globe. Elizabeth was a shrewd ruler interested in increasing England's power. During her reign, England gained its first trading post in India, the Spanish Armada was defeated, and London (top, left) became a thriving commercial center. Few English rulers have so stamped their personality upon a period. Elizabethan England, influenced by both the Renaissance and the Reformation, was dynamic culturally as well as politically and economically. The English courtier, skilled in warfare and a writer of lyric poems and sonnets, expressed the humanist ideal of the versatile man. The Reformation was reflected in the rise of those who wished to simplify ceremonies in the Church of England. The artistic rebirth on the continent was paralleled in England by a literary flowering. The down-to-earth language of Chaucer (page 173) became more polished. Outstanding among Elizabethan authors was William Shakespeare, generally considered the greatest writer in the English language. No playwright, except for the ancient Greek dramatists, has had so enduring an impact. Historical plays, tragedies, comedies, lyric poems, sonnets— whatever he wrote, the master was unsurpassed. His plays, as applicable to man's problems today as is Greek drama, continue to be performed to capacity audiences. The scene at left is from a production in modern dress of the historical play Henry V.

Stuart family of Scotland succeeded to the throne. Since James I believed that kings ruled by divine right, clashes with Parliament were inevitable. That body was scarcely likely to concede that the king had absolute powers. Members of Parliament, eager to play an increasingly important role in governing England, were angered when James I stated:

The state of monarchy is the supremest thing upon earth: for kings are not only God's lieutenants upon earth and sit upon God's throne, but even by God Himself they are called gods. . . . In the Scriptures kings are called gods, and so their power [is] compared to the Divine power. . . .

I conclude . . . that, as to dispute what God may do is blasphemy, . . . so is it [treason] in subjects to dispute what a king may do in the height of his power. I will not be content that my power be disputed upon; but I shall ever be willing to make the reason . . . of all my doings [clear], and [to arrange] my actions according to my laws.

Tensions between Parliament and the king intensified during the reign of Charles I, the son of the first Stuart king. The conflict between Charles and Parliament centered around two issues, taxes and religion.

1. Because of extravagant spending and foreign wars, both James I and Charles I were constantly short of funds. When Charles I had to ask Parliament for more money, Parliament refused unless the king agreed to abide by the provisions of the Petition of Right (1628). Like the Magna Carta, the Petition of Right is one of the foundations of English liberty. It limited the power of the king in some important respects: (a) The king could not collect taxes without Parliament's consent; (b) soldiers could not be fed and sheltered in private houses; (c) military officers could not impose martial law in time of peace; (d) no person could be imprisoned except upon a specific charge.

Although Charles agreed to the Petition of Right, he continued to levy taxes in a manner that Parliament considered illegal. When Parliament protested, Charles dismissed it and arrested some of its leaders. For the next eleven years (1629–1640) the king ruled without Parliament. During these years the methods used by Charles I in raising money aroused increasingly bitter opposition.

2. Charles' religious policies also aroused bitter opposition. Anglican ritual was distasteful to English Puritans, who wished to purify the Church of England of what they termed Catholic ways. They criticized the rich robes of the clergy, ornamentation in the churches, the impressive ritual, and kneeling at communion. Many powerful members of Parliament were Puritans. But urged on by the Anglican archbishop, William Laud, Charles imprisoned, fined, and persecuted dissenters.

When the king and Laud in 1637 tried to impose Anglican forms of worship in Scotland, the Lowland Scots, most of whom were Presbyterians, rose in revolt. Lacking the funds to put down the rebellion, Charles was forced to call Parliament back into session in 1640. The hostility of the new Parliament caused Charles to dissolve it immediately. It is thus known as the Short Parliament.

Still in need of money, Charles called for new elections to Parliament. This time Parliament would be in session for many years, hence the name *Long Parliament.*

Most members of the Long Parliament were determined to put an end to absolute rule once and for all. Among the reforms enacted by the Long Parliament were: (1) the provision for regular meetings of that body, (2) the abolition of extralegal courts and commissions used by the king in trying those who opposed him, and (3) the prohibition of taxation by the king without the consent of Parliament. The laws passed by the Long Parliament considerably reduced the powers of the king. They represent another landmark in the growth of liberty and limited monarchy in England.

Supporters of the Stuarts fight a civil war against supporters of Parliament. Whereas the members of Parliament had been substantially united on the points listed, the Puritan majority wished to make more drastic changes in the direction of reducing further the power of the king and of the Anglican Church. They urged abolition of the existing organization of the Anglican Church and its ritual and the granting to Parliament of control over the army and over the king and his ministers. Parliament now faced a split in its ranks; Puritans and all-out supporters of Parliamentary supremacy were opposed by Anglicans and supporters of the king. Encouraged by this split, Charles I boldly attempted to arrest opposition leaders in Parliament. Though this attempt failed, it roused the anger of the House of Commons, which began to raise an army. A revolution had been born.

The supporters of the king—Anglicans and Catholics, most members of the House of Lords, and royalist members of the House of Commons —were called Cavaliers. Those who sided with Parliament were known as Roundheads because of the Puritan practice of closely cropping the hair.

Cromwell rules without king or Parliament. The Roundhead army of fervent Puritans was well-disciplined; its outstanding general was Oliver Cromwell, a gifted commander. The Parliamentary forces defeated those of Charles I in the first stage of the English Civil War. But then the revolution took an unexpected turn. A quarrel broke out between Parliament and Cromwell's New Model Army. Cromwell won, expelled his opponents from Parliament, and abolished the House of Lords. As the nation's new leader, Cromwell had Charles I tried and executed. This action shocked the English people. Although many Englishmen objected to the policies of Charles I, they did not want to execute their king, nor did they favor an end to monarchy in England.

Cromwell is a most difficult figure to understand. Both contemporary observers and later historians have conflicting views of him. To some, Cromwell was a tyrant and a murderer; to others, he seemed a man of intelligence and a defender of liberty. He refused to become king after Charles I was executed, taking the title Lord Protector instead. Cromwell's goals were (1) an end to the fighting that had caused so much distress in England, (2) greater freedom of religion, and (3) a written constitution defining the powers of each branch of government. However, unable to establish a smoothly working government that had the support of the English people, Cromwell assumed more and more power for himself. During the nine years of Cromwell's military rule, England prospered at home and was respected abroad, but uprisings in Ireland and Scotland were harshly put down, leaving bitter memories, especially among the Irish.

The Stuart restoration leads to further conflict between king and Parliament. After Cromwell died in 1658, his son Richard ruled briefly. His inability to control Parliament, which continued to meet after he had ordered it dissolved, led to Richard's resignation in 1660. Parliament then invited Charles II, son of the executed king, to assume the throne, a restoration which was welcomed by most Englishmen.

Once again a Stuart king sat on the throne of England, but conditions had greatly changed since the days of James I. The legislation enacted by the Long Parliament had by now become the law of the land, and the king's power was limited by law.

Following the death of Charles II, the crown passed to his Catholic brother, James II. Parliament again had reason to believe that a Stuart might be seeking to restore absolute rule. Parliament also feared that James would give Catholics greater power in England. After a son was born to James, his Protestant daughter Mary was unlikely to succeed to the throne. Parliament therefore offered the crown jointly to Mary and her husband, William of Orange, the Staatholder (head) of the Dutch Republic. This solution to the tyranny that seemed to threaten England was greeted with acclaim by the English people.

The Glorious Revolution establishes the supremacy of Parliament. In deposing James II in this "Glorious Revolution" (1688–1689) Parliament had clearly asserted its supremacy over the English monarch. The Bill of Rights nailed down Parliament's victory. The monarch was forbidden to suspend laws, to tax without the consent of Parliament, or to raise a standing army during peacetime without Parliament's approval. Nor could he interfere with the freedom of speech and debate within Parliament.

The English revolutions of the seventeenth century had a great impact on England and the western world. By the end of the seventeenth century parliamentary government, the rule of law, limited monarchy, and the protection of individual liberty were firmly established in England, completing a trend that started in the Middle Ages. The Glorious Revolution brought England centuries of stable government. England never again experienced a political revolution. In the words of nineteenth-century British historian Thomas B. Macaulay, "The highest eulogy [praise] which can be pronounced on the revolution of 1688 is this, that it was our last revolution."

In the almost 300 years since the Glorious Revolution many states have experienced violent civil wars and revolution, long periods of disorder, and ineffective government. But in England the orderly process of parliamentary government has met every political crisis. The fact that the English form of government became the model for many European states and more recently for new nations in Africa and Asia proves that the English parliamentary system is one of the most successful forms of government developed by a national state.

CHECK-UP

1. What were the characteristics of Tudor rule?
2. Why did James I clash with Parliament? What was the Petition of Right? What policies of Charles I aroused opposition?
3. What reforms were enacted by the Long Parliament? What led to civil war in England? What was the outcome?
4. How did Cromwell rule England? What were his goals?
5. Why were the Stuarts restored to the throne of England? How had the role of the king changed? Why did Parliament depose James II? What is the significance of the Glorious Revolution? Of the English Bill of Rights?

The Rise of Russia

To round off this chapter, one must take a brief look at Eastern Europe. What kind of states emerged there? How did they compare with France, Spain, or England?

There is no true nation-state in Eastern Europe. At the time of England's Glorious Revolution, Eastern Europe was divided among several states. A traveler going east from Brandenburg-Prussia (the up-and-coming state in northeastern Germany) would enter the kingdom of Poland, a large and proud state stretching from the Baltic coast almost to the Black Sea. Journeying still farther east, he would cross into Russia, the lands of the Grand Prince of Mos-

cow. Russia was a vast state reaching from the Arctic Ocean to the Caspian Sea, and eastward across the endless tundra of Siberia to the Pacific Ocean. Another traveler riding southeast from Germany along the Danube River would, after passing through the lands of the Hapsburg monarchy, find himself in the domains of the Ottoman Turks. Their sultan ruled over all the peoples of the Balkan Peninsula and the northern approaches to the Black Sea as well (not counting his lands in Asia Minor and beyond).

Unlike England or France, none of these eastern states was a nation-state in the making. The subjects of Louis XIV or of William and Mary spoke a common language and subscribed, for the most part, to a common religion. The eastern states, by contrast, were inhabited by a variety of peoples, each speaking its own language and often following its own creed. They also lacked clear-cut geographic boundaries such as the mountains or oceans that offered a measure of protection to the Western European states. Northeastern Europe, for the most part, is a vast, wide open plain stretching from northern Germany into Asia without natural obstacles. Great waterways and their interlacing tributaries had for centuries served as highways for commerce and migration, from the Baltic to the Black Sea and even to the Pacific Ocean.

In Southeastern Europe the Hungarian plain is a continuation of the vast stretch of grasslands which reach all the way to Mongolia and serve as a superb highway for armed horsemen bent on plunder and conquest. Of the invaders coming out of Asia only the Magyars (Hungarians) created a state that has survived to the present. All others were absorbed by local populations or survived in small groups under alien rule. To this day the Balkan Peninsula contains hundreds of separate ethnic groups too small to set themselves up as nations.

North of the Carpathian (kar-*pey'*thih-un) Mountains the ethnic variety is less. Yet even here the map shows a bewildering multitude of peoples. South and east of the Baltic coast, for instance, one finds Germans, Swedes, Poles, Masurians, Lithuanians, Estonians, Latvians, Finns, Jews, and Russians (White- or Bielo-Russians, Great Russians, and Little Russians or Ukrainians). The states that emerged in Eastern Europe were, in short, multi-national states that had not achieved the uniformity of citizenship that had come to prevail in Western Europe.

The Slavs are the major ethnic group in Eastern Europe. One common feature, however, prevails in Eastern and Southeastern Europe: the ethnic and linguistic similarity of the Slavs. The Slavs probably originated somewhere between the Carpathian Mountains and the Baltic Sea.

From this center some migrated westward. Among these "western" Slavs are the Poles and Czechs, who fell under the influence of the Roman Catholic Church and wrote their language in Latin script. Other Slavs moved south and are known as the Yugoslavs (or South Slavs). Some, such as the Croats (*kroh'*ats), were converted to Catholicism and became part of Western European culture. Serbs or Bulgarians, on the other hand, fell under the sway of the Byzantine Empire, used the Cyrillic alphabet,[1] and belonged to the Eastern Orthodox Church. The eastern Slavs lived in what is now called Russia and were also converted to the Orthodox creed. Thus the Slavs were split into two groups. Those who looked toward Rome and Western Europe quarreled with those who looked toward the Orthodox Church and Constantinople.

Russia has its beginnings in Kiev. Of all the Slavs only the Russians managed to create a great state comparable to France or England. During the reign of Peter the Great (1689–1725) Russia became an empire and a power to be reckoned with in Europe. What were the origins of the Russian state? How did it expand to become a multi-national empire?

There is an ancient story that in the age of the roving Norsemen the Slavic tribes on the Dnieper (*nee'*per) River sent a delegation to Scandinavia with the plea: "Our whole land is great and rich, but there is no order in it. Come and rule and reign over us." Accepting this invitation, a leader named Rurik and his followers, called "Russes," in 882 founded the first Russian state centered on the city of Kiev (*kee'*-yehf). This story has vexed patriotic Russians who in recent times have stressed the contribution of the Slavic tribes. But there is no doubt that the Norsemen, who plundered the coasts of France, conquered Sicily and England,

---

[1] The Cyrillic (sih-*ril'*ik) alphabet was adapted from the Greek alphabet by St. Cyril and St. Methodius, missionaries sent to convert the Slavs to Orthodox Christianity.

and probed into the North American continent, also roamed the waterways linking the Baltic with the Black Sea. Their expeditions, combined with the example of the Byzantine Empire, stimulated the formation of some kind of local government wherever geographic conditions were favorable. The most secure spot along the lower Dnieper was a high bluff on the west bank, not far from where the forests of the north gave way to the grassy steppe and above the rapids that blocked river traffic to the south. From this stronghold the successors of Rurik subdued neighboring Slavic tribes and created, by the year 1000, a resplendent outpost of Constantinople. This state was more than equal to the Frankish empire in Western Europe.

At its height, in the reign of Iaroslav (yah-ruh-*slahv'*) the Wise (died 1054), Kiev was a city renowned for its culture and religion. An earlier ruler, St. Vladimir (vluh-*dyee'*myihr), had been converted to Orthodox Christianity in

988. Less than 50 years later the great Cathedral of St. Sophia, to this day the founding symbol of the Russian Orthodox Church, was consecrated in Kiev. By the middle of the eleventh century Kiev had extended its rule along the inland trade routes from the Baltic to the Black Sea and from Central Europe into the Asian heartland. Its power was limited only in the steppe lands of the south where nomadic tribes constantly attacked the Kievan domains. Under the sway of Kiev a number of lesser cities sprang up.

The rulers of Kiev, called Grand Princes, were merchant warriors who, with their retinue of lesser warriors (called *boiars*, boh-*yahrs'*) collected tribute from their subjects and established a far-flung network of trade that linked Constantinople with the Baltic. Greek, Roman, and Arabic coins are still being dug up in the lands they ruled. The Grand Princes also drew on the products of a well-developed agriculture. Their government was simple. The rulers of Kiev governed more by persuasion than by force. Before deciding on policies, they conferred with important boiars and the people of Kiev; the princes ruling lesser cities did likewise. Landownership counted less than the control of trade; feudalism as practiced in Western Europe was unknown. This made government more flexible and at the same time more unstable.

The successive rulers of Kiev spent much time warring against rulers of the lesser towns and the nomads on the steppes. Yet they also found time to promote law and learning, and a distinct Kievan civilization developed. It owed much to Byzantine, Slavic, Muslim, and other cultures. The continuing campaigns against the nomads gave rise to a folk literature dealing with the heroic exploits of Kievan warriors. Images of Christ and the saints, called *ikons* (*eye'*konz), were painted in the manner of Byzantine art yet in a distinctly Russian style. Written chronicles, as in the West, recorded events of significance in the Kievan state. Visitors from as far away as Western Europe

KEY

Kievan Russia, 1237

Muscovy, 1462

Russia, 1533

Temporary Acquisitions, 1533–1598

Acquired to 1598

Acquired to c. 1700

admired the splendors of Kiev. While the city of Kiev was destroyed early in the thirteenth century, its glories—and the very term "Russia"—remained a living memory out of which the Russian state was eventually born.

Towns are founded in the northeast. To escape the frequent wars and gain greater security, many of the harassed people from Kiev and its vicinity began to migrate into the forests of the northeast. While Kiev declined and Kievan Russia fell apart, the northern and northeastern towns, each one with churches like Kiev's and walled fortifications called *kremlins,* rose in prominence.

Chief among them was Novgorod (*noff′*guh-rut), like Kiev a great center of commerce and

often endangered by invasions of Swedes and Teutonic Knights from the West. At the end of the Crusades the Teutonic Knights had moved to the Baltic area to win new lands for the Roman Catholic Church. In the ensuing wars, a prince of Novgorod named Alexander Nevsky not only repelled the Swedes but defeated the Teutonic Knights in 1242. His victory has been celebrated as an early triumph of the Slavs over German invaders. Yet the glory of Alexander Nevsky was shortlived. A far more dangerous enemy, the Mongol hordes from Central Asia (page 126), soon subjected his lands to foreign rule.

The Mongols take over Russia. The Mongol period of Russian history begins with the destruction of Kiev in 1240. From Kiev the Mongols penetrated deep into the forests of the north. The great Mongol strongholds on the lower Volga were not conquered until the 1500's. In the Crimean (kry-*me'*un) Peninsula, which juts out into the Black Sea, Mongol rule survived until the 1770's.

Mongol occupation marked a period of stagnation in the Russian lands. Russian wealth was drained away to the Mongol court by a ruthless tribute paid in money and men. Russian princes were skillfully set one against the other, each competing for the favor of the Mongol khan. The khan awarded the traditional title of Grand Prince only to those princes who served him unconditionally. In addition, the princes in small principalities weakened their strength by dividing their lands among their heirs.

The Mongols made no lasting contribution to the rise of the Russian state; indeed, they delayed its development and gave it a tragic twist. The peoples of Western and Central Europe, safe from the Mongol invasion, pursued their cultural advance without disruption. The peoples of Russia meanwhile made little progress. Their only consolation was the continued ascendancy of the Orthodox Church, which the conquerors left undisturbed. Yet the Russian church was unlike the Church of Rome. The latter was heir to the learning of the ancient world and the culture of the Roman Empire. Its monks promoted skills and techniques for improving agriculture and industry; its teachers laid the groundwork for subsequent improvements in the arts and sciences. The Russian Orthodox Church was cut off from this rich heritage. Its language was Church Slavonic; its literature was devotional, aimed not at improving man's lot in this world but at saving his soul through simple, self-denying piety and faith. The monks sent north and northeast from Kiev created many new monasteries, but none of these became centers of cultural progress. The development of the Russian state and society continued to suffer from the fact that, in the first centuries after the introduction of Christianity, the Orthodox believers were cut off from the civilization of the Roman Empire and from the subsequent development of civilization in Western Europe.

Muscovy emerges as an important principality. Yet Russian development did not stop altogether under the Mongols. Out of the interminable wrangling among the princes there emerged in the thirteenth century one promising center, the town of Moscow. Advantageously located near the headwaters of four rivers, sufficiently distant from both the steppes and the Baltic, it became the center of the state of Muscovy. It had the additional advantage of able leaders who did not divide their lands. The princes of Moscow were clever men, miserly (one of them was called Ivan Moneybag), and greedy for more land. They were not above flattering the Mongol khan to get the better of their neighbors; they were also ready to betray him when the chance of success seemed good. Thus they built a reputation as national leaders, soon winning the support of the Orthodox Church. By the fifteenth century they had built a principality that was stronger than its rivals and even surpassed "the great lord Novgorod."

The first tsars strengthen Muscovite power. Thus began the expansion of Moscow called the "gathering of the Russian lands," which eventually was to include extensive non-Russian lands as well. At the time when French kings created a nation-state following the Hundred Years' War and the Tudors ascended to the throne in England, two great rulers of Moscow, Ivan III (sometimes called the Great) and his son Basil or (Vassily) III laid the foundation for a national state in Russia. Ivan III (1462–1505) repudiated the Mongol overlordship and forced Novgorod and lesser rivals to submit to Moscow. By the title of *autocrat* he stressed his claim to all Russian lands and asserted his independence from the Mongols. He also stepped forward as the heir to the emperor of Constantinople, which had just fallen to the Turks. Having married the niece of the last Byzantine emperor, Ivan III adopted the title of *tsar* (from caesar). The new tsar furthermore adopted the symbols of Byzantine rule and claimed for Moscow the leading role in all Christianity. In Moscow, so his spokesmen asserted, history would fulfill itself with the second coming of Christ. (The kings of France and Spain, incidentally, claimed similar distinctions for their countries.)

As the symbol of the power of Moscow, the first two tsars built a great fortress, the Moscow Kremlin, in the center of their city. A triangle of massive red brick walls at the meeting place of two rivers, the Kremlin towered impressively above the dwellings of the common people. Within the walls were the chief offices of the government and the church, the palace of the tsar, the houses of the leading boiars, a monastery and a nunnery, and the arsenals. Painters of ikons, jewelers, and other craftsmen were employed to match the best work of Western Europe. The chief pride of the Kremlin, however, was its churches. Though Russian in appearance, the Kremlin contained many architectural elements borrowed from Renaissance Europe.

Yet there was one difference. In Western and Central Europe there were many cities, each enjoying considerable rights of self-government and a rich civic life. In the Russian lands Moscow was unique. It was the sole center of government, dominated by a tsar who was less restrained by church, feudal lords, or municipal privilege than any Western European king. The "gathering of the Russian lands" had exacted a staggering price from both rulers and ruled. By cunning and ruthlessness the grand princes of Moscow had swept aside all challenges, forced conquered lands into unconditional surrender, and wiped out the institutions of self-government that existed in Novgorod and other towns. They were constantly trying to reduce the boiars who served them to greater subservience. They allowed no feudal contract, no Magna Carta, no local custom to check their will. To be sure, a council of boiars was supposed to advise the tsar, but it possessed no firm authority. Since they recognized no equals, the tsars were in danger of abusing their power.

Autocracy becomes more rigid. Like their counterparts in Western Europe, the tsars were constantly at work strengthening central authority. But they were hampered by the poverty of their lands. They rewarded supporters and agents for their services by giving them landed estates, which were often obtained by robbing established landowners and princes in the conquered lands. Then, in order to provide their supporters with a living, the tsars increasingly compelled peasants to stay on the estates no matter how burdensome the obligations. At the same time serfdom was on its way out in Western Europe, it was being introduced into Russia. The Russian state could survive, in short, only by forcing subjects into compulsory service to the tsar.

The tsars had little other choice if they wished to provide the security needed for civilized life. In the west they were threatened by Lithuania, a temporary creation of the Lithuanian princes that, at its height in the fifteenth century, inherited many lands of the old Kievan state. In the north the Swedes were rising as a major European power. To the east and the southeast the Mongol hordes with their swift plundering expeditions were a constant threat. How could the tsars, ruling a sedentary, agricultural population, safeguard the open steppe frontier? One answer was to build a chain of fortifications as a protective screen for the capital. Another was to permit the establishment of irregular troops, part peasant, part soldier, part freebooter, from among the adventurers along the open frontier. Thus the Cossacks, who obeyed only their own elected leaders, came into existence. Defenders of the faith against the Muslims, the Cossacks were excellent though unruly fighters, fiercely jealous of their freedom.

Red Square, named for the red bricks of the original buildings, has long been the center of commercial and social activities in Moscow. The seventeenth-century view below shows the Cathedral of St. Basil and, to the right, the Spassky Gate, the main entrance to the Kremlin. From the treasury of the Romanovs come the magnificent works in gold which symbolized the splendor of the tsar.

Ivan IV expands Russia's boundaries and terrorizes his subjects. In the long reign of Ivan IV ("The Terrible"), the "gathering of the Russian lands" entered a new phase. It began to include some non-Russian lands. The abuses inherent in autocracy also began to show. Ivan IV had grown up amidst court intrigues that caused him to become an unstable and morbidly suspicious man. Yet he was also an able and energetic ruler who continued the work of his predecessors. He waged war both to the east and the west, though he failed to win access to the Baltic Sea, which he realized was vital for Russian communications with Western Europe. Fortunately, however, English merchant adventurers opened a route to Russia through the Arctic Sea, thus establishing direct trade between Russia and England. In the east Ivan was gloriously successful in conquering the Mongol strongholds on the Volga, thus making possible expansion into Siberia and Central Asia. In honor of his victory, he built a many-towered, onion-domed church on the square outside the Kremlin walls, the famous church of the Blessed Basil (included in every picture of Red Square). When the Mongol lands were annexed, many leading Mongol families entered the tsar's service. Thus Muscovy became a Eurasian state, linking Europe and Asia. Cossack explorers, pushing eastward, reached the Pacific Ocean in 1637.

Ivan IV also forced the boiars in his service into further dependence. He increasingly disregarded the council of boiars and razed Novgorod to the ground. Eventually the wrangling undermined his sanity. In the winter of 1564, Ivan suddenly abandoned Moscow, accusing his subjects of having betrayed him. Subsequently, he organized a special corps of avengers, a state within the state. His black-clad knights riding black horses were unleashed upon all traitors and evil-doers. Thus terror descended upon the boiars and the common people. At the end of his life Ivan even killed one of his sons in a towering rage.

The Times of Troubles follow Ivan's death.
After Ivan's death the country reaped the whirlwind of his wars and terrorism. The killing off of thousands of princes and landowners left Russia with few trained government officials. Peasants were overburdened with forced service; newly conquered peoples wanted to regain their freedom. The great unrest came to a climax in the Times of Troubles at the beginning of the seventeenth century, the most calamitous era in Russian history between the Mongol occupation and the civil war that started in 1918. For a time all government broke down; the ruling family, which traced its origins to Rurik, was left without an heir. There were several pretenders to the throne, among them one backed by a Polish army. Moscow was in danger of becoming part of the kingdom of Poland, as had recently happened to Lithuania. A Swedish army was also invading the country from the northwest. Within the country civil war raged; all those who had suffered under Ivan IV were bent on revenge. Yet at this moment of supreme peril, a popular assembly representing all classes of the population gathered in Moscow and raised Michael Romanov (roh-*mah'*nuff) to the throne of the tsars. The Romanov family continued to rule over Russia until 1917. It transformed Muscovite Russia into the Russian Empire.

Peter the Great builds up the autocracy of the tsar.
The tsar who added the title "emperor" was Peter I, the Great (1689–1725). Among the proud monarchs of that age he stood out as a giant. Nearly seven feet tall, he was endowed with immense physical strength and vitality. He possessed a boundless curiosity in all fields of learning and statecraft, never satisfied until he himself had mastered the necessary knowledge and skill. He himself pulled the teeth of his lieutenants, or built boats and navigated them, dispensing with all royal pomp and ceremony. He was a dynamo of incessant and hasty innovation, always working, body and soul, to strengthen Russia, impatiently trying to make her catch up with the nation-states of Western Europe. During Peter's reign Russia was hardly ever at peace; all his reforms were designed to strengthen his army and navy. By comparison with the more orderly governments of Western Europe, Peter's rule was characterized by improvisation; failure and corruption dogged his efforts at every turn. Above all, he was a brutally demanding tsar, drawing all his subjects, whether high or low, into obligatory

and exhausting service to the state. In this reckless fashion he raised Muscovy into an empire respected throughout Europe.

Peter the Great's reign was a culmination of trends long visible in the past. He brought the wars with Sweden to a victorious end, acquiring the eastern coastlands of the Baltic Sea with their non-Russian populations. He also strengthened the borders of Russia against Poland. A rebuilt Kiev became a center of western learning in Russia. To the south Peter battled with the Turks, losing as much as he gained. In the distant east, Russia had concluded a border treaty with China in 1689. This signified the arrival of Russia in the Far East. Peter himself pushed the exploration of eastern Siberia.

He also continued to build up the autocracy of the tsar. He put an end to the council of boiars and never called the popular assemblies that earlier Romanovs had occasionally summoned. The landowners lost their independence and became servants of the state. Nobility henceforth depended on state service, which was carefully regulated by rules that opened careers to talent. The Orthodox Church, suspected of undue devotion to the past, in effect became a department of the government. Merchants and townspeople likewise were closely tied to the state. Like most monarchs of the time, Peter believed that the government had a responsibility for the good conduct of its subjects: "The police," so one of his edicts announced, "is the soul of citizenship and of all good order, the fundamental support of civil security and propriety." In the use of the police—as of all his autocratic powers—he was far less restrained than even Louis XIV at the height of French absolutism.

The peasants fared worst of all under Peter's rule. They were tied to the land where they were born. On their shoulders rested the burden of supporting the nobility as well as the state. Russian serfdom, which differed little from slavery, reached its climax in the time of Peter, but it continued to the middle of the nineteenth century. The rage of the Russian serfs exploded from time to time in mass uprisings. Peasant rebellions had already flared up in the seventeenth century; there were more of them in Peter's reign. Having to pay the price for the glories of autocracy and the Russian Empire, the peasants never forgave the tsars or the noble landlords.

Peter tries to westernize Russia. Yet the chief victim of Peter's reforms, one might say, was not the peasants, but the Muscovite way of life. Peter was the greatest "westernizer" in Russian history. Bringing to a culmination a process that started in the late sixteenth century, he abolished the external forms of Muscovite custom—dress, beards, calendar, script, and the exclusion of women from social life—and tried to replace them with western customs. He also tried to create an elite, a special segment of the population educated in the Western European manner. If the Russian Empire were to endure, he argued, it had to conform to the ways of its rivals in Western Europe. Thus a profound cultural and social cleavage arose between the westernized elite, composed of the Russian nobility, and the bulk of the population.

As a symbol of Russia's western orientation, Peter founded a new capital, St. Petersburg, on the bleak marshes near the Baltic coast. The new city was far removed, geographically and spiritually, from the old capital in Moscow; it accentuated the rift within the Russian people. St. Petersburg was Russia's window to the West. Its fortifications, palaces, and government buildings had a trim and alien look of efficiency. From St. Petersburg the tsar-emperor ruled over his reluctant and rebellious subjects with a doubly cruel hand, as autocrat and as promoter of foreign ways.

Autocracy ensures political stability in a country that lacks unity. At the time of Peter I the peoples in the nation-states of Western Europe had achieved a fair sense of unity. Soon the rise of the concept of "the nation" was to testify to their ability to work together even in the absence of absolute monarchy. Imperial Russia never attained such unity. It remained divided ethnically, socially, and culturally. Under these conditions the concentration of power in the hands of the autocrat was the sole guarantee of political stability and security. The proof for this assertion may be seen in the fate of the kingdom of Poland.

More advanced than Russia because of its close ties to Western Europe, Poland had absorbed the Lithuanian kingdom at the time of the Counter Reformation. Poland was a powerful state, reaching from the Baltic to the Black Sea, and even threatening for a time to absorb Moscow. It also boasted of being a free state in which the authority of the king was severely limited by the many rights of the landowning nobility. Their privileges were the envy of noblemen throughout Europe. But the weakness of the king in time proved to be the undoing of the Polish state. At the time of Peter the Great, outside powers (including Russia) interfered in its internal affairs, and by the end of the eighteenth century Poland had been divided among its neighbors. Thus state-building in Western and Eastern Europe proceeded differently.

CHECK-UP

1. Why did nation-states develop later in Eastern Europe than in Western Europe? How are eastern and western Slavs alike? Different?

2. Why did Kiev become important? Why were towns founded to the northeast of Kiev?

3. Why were the Mongols able to take over Russia? What were the results? Why did Muscovy become the most important principality in Russia?

4. What type of government was established by the tsars? Why? What were the results?

5. What caused the Times of Troubles? How were they brought to an end?

6. What goals were sought by Peter the Great? How did he try to achieve them? To what extent was he successful?

Summing Up

The origins of nation-states go back to the Middle Ages when growing towns began to contribute money to help kings to establish law and order and curb the power of feudal lords. Gradually kings acquired more land, began to collect taxes, and extended the power of royal courts. As the power of kings increased, that of feudal lords and the Church diminished.

Various factors slowed the growth of national unity, among them English-held territory in France, Muslim rule in Spain, and foreign-ruled holdings in both Italy and Germany. France, England, and Spain achieved unity in the Middle Ages; Germany and Italy did not. France moved in the direction of absolutism and divine-right monarchy. England, largely because of the rise of Parliament, moved in the direction of limited monarchy. Efforts to establish divine-right rule in England led to the execution of one king and the dethronement of another. By 1689 representative government was firmly established in England. But in France and other countries kings continued to exercise arbitrary power.

The rise of nation-states greatly reduced feudal warfare but led to national rivalries. Religious strife and the need to maintain a balance of power became the chief causes of wars between nations. First Hapsburg Spain and Hapsburg Austria sought to dominate Europe. They were resisted mainly by France. In the last part of the seventeenth century, France under Louis XIV sought to become master of Europe. An alliance of European states thwarted this ambition.

Nation-states such as England and France did not develop in Eastern Europe during the period discussed in this chapter. The variety of peoples inhabiting the countries of Eastern Europe, their different languages, customs, and even religious beliefs, stood in the way of national unity. In Russia, however, the concentration of power in the hands of the tsar made it possible for Russia to acquire and exercise control over an empire reaching from Eastern Europe to the east coast of Asia.

Chapter Highlights

Can you explain? ────────────────────────────────────

common law   tsar   kremlin   balance of power

autocrat   divine right   precedents   absolute monarchy

principalities   nation-state   limited monarchy

Can you identify? ────────────────────────────────────

Normans	Ivan IV	Cavaliers	Petition of Right
Colbert	Philip II	Ivan III	Edict of Nantes
Kiev	Huguenots	Netherlands	Thirty Years' War
Tudors	Richelieu	Cromwell	Glorious Revolution
Mazarin	Ferdinand	Roundheads	Spanish Armada
Charles V	Gregory VII	Parliament	Long Parliament
Muscovy	Hapsburg	Isabella	Hundred Years' War
Henry IV	Versailles	Joan of Arc	Gustavus Adolphus
Moriscos	Papal States	*Domesday Book*	William the Conqueror
Romanov	Magna Carta	Peter the Great	War of the Spanish
Stuarts	Switzerland	Ottoman Turks	Succession
Louis XIV	Reconquista	Holy Roman Empire	

What do you think? ────────────────────────────────────

1. Have all codes of law evolved in the same way as the English common law? Why?

2. Why was Muslim Spain more liberal than Spain after the Reconquista?

3. Why did rulers of the Holy Roman Empire clash with the Pope?

4. Why did France become a more powerful nation-state than Spain?

5. Why did most nations have a state church or an official religion?

6. What is meant by balance of power? What usually happens when it is threatened?

7. What explanations can be given for the rise and continuation of autocracy in Russia?

8. Why did kings claim to rule by divine right? Why was this view challenged? What was the outcome?

9. Did Peter the Great westernize Russia? Explain.

10. How did each of the following contribute to the growth of liberty and the development of limited monarchy in England: (a) Magna Carta, (b) common law, (c) rise of Parliament, (d) Petition of Right, (e) Bill of Rights?

Revolution and the Rise of Nationalism

Unit Five————

428

The Enlightenment

During the Enlightenment artists came to realize that the everyday activities of the common man were worthy subjects of serious art. Reflecting this trend away from the exclusive concentration on the upper classes is Chardin's painting of a peasant woman peeling turnips (above, left). The acceptance of commonplace subjects in art was also reflected in the belief that man should live a simple life close to nature. This led to an interest in the countryside, reflected in landscape painting. In this Dutch painting (left) Solomon van Ruisdael captured the effect of the sun on clouds and hillside. Accompanying the interest in nature was curiosity about the Amerind, who was romanticized as the "Noble Savage" (above), an uncorrupted child of nature.

CHAPTER FOCUS

Leading Thinkers of the Enlightenment
Trends of Thought During the Enlightenment

The eighteenth century has been called the Age of Reason or the Enlightenment. The thinkers of this period, who called themselves *philosophes* (fihl-oh-*zuhfs'*), believed that man should learn to look at life through the eyes of reason. In many ways the Age of Enlightenment was an outgrowth of the Scientific Revolution. The philosophes admired Newton because he had used reason to make sense out of the physical universe. The philosophes now urged applying reason to all aspects of social and political life—government, religion, economic systems, law. If accepted ways of doing things did not make sense, they should be revised or discarded.

Many of the philosophes were French. Before the Age of Enlightenment most Frenchmen held these views: (1) They believed that the King of France ruled by divine right (page 406); (2) they accepted the teachings of the Church without question; and (3) they did not question the right of the nobility to enjoy special privileges. Few Frenchmen found it unusual that royalty, nobility, and clergy led society. By the end of the eighteenth century all this was changed. Largely due to the efforts of the philosophes, many Frenchmen and other Europeans challenged the traditional view of the social order.

The philosophes found much that was wrong with eighteenth-century society. Everywhere there were signs of tyranny, ignorance, prejudice, superstition, and injustice. The philosophes were social reformers who believed that, by using reason, man could discover a better way of doing things. Man had the ability to improve himself and the conditions under which he lived. "Ignorance and [tyranny] . . . make men wicked and unhappy," said a French philosophe. "Knowledge, reason, and liberty can alone reform them and make them happier. . . . Men will be good when they are well [educated and] well governed, and when they are punished or despised for the evil [they do], and justly rewarded for the good." This was the creed of the Enlightenment.

Leading Thinkers of the Enlightenment

Locke develops the theory of natural rights. John Locke, an English philosopher, is one of the key figures of the Enlightenment. Locke defended the Glorious Revolution in which the English Parliament had ousted a tyrannical king and limited the powers of successors to the throne. Developing the theory of *natural rights,* Locke said that all men are born free and equal, with a right to life, liberty, and the ownership of property. He maintained that it is the duty of government to protect these natural rights of its citizens. But what if a government fails to meet its responsibility? What if government officials imprison citizens unfairly, unjustly seize their property, and deny them freedom of speech? Then, said Locke, the leaders of the government have "put themselves into a state of war with the people," and the people have the right to overthrow the government and establish a better one.

Locke's theory of government is of immense importance. By setting limits to the power of government and recognizing the right to revolt when those limits are not respected, he advanced the cause of liberty. First, Locke stated, rulers are not free to act as they please. They must respect the natural rights of men. Second, rulers do not receive their power from God, but from the people. The principle that government derives its power from the consent of those governed is the foundation of democracy. Third, men have the right to overthrow tyrants. Since the purpose of government is "the good of mankind," people do not have a duty to put up with cruel and unjust rulers.

Locke's words inspired many democratic revolutions. Our own Declaration of Independence echoed Locke's theory of natural rights:

We hold these truths to be self-evident, that all men are created equal, that they are endowed by their Creator with certain inalienable Rights, that among these are life, liberty, and the pursuit of happiness. That to secure these rights, governments are instituted among men, deriving their just powers from the consent of the governed. That whenever any form of government becomes destructive of these ends, it is the right of the people to alter or abolish it.

Locke believes that man's character is formed by society. In addition to political theory, Locke made another major contribution to the thought of the Enlightenment. He said that man is not born good or evil, wise or ignorant. Rather, man's character and knowledge are shaped by his experience. We enter the world with minds as blank as a slate on which nothing is written. Our later ideas are the result of the impressions made upon our minds by our sense experience of the world. Under the right conditions, then, poor children can learn as well as children of the wealthy. Men are indeed created equal in that all are born with the capacity to learn and to develop into reasoning, moral, and happy citizens. Locke's view of human nature was therefore eagerly accepted by reformers. Evil exists not because of human nature but because of society. It is thus society, not man, which needs reforming. If ignorance, superstition, prejudice, and tyranny are eliminated, man can become good.

Montesquieu advocates separation of powers in government. Baron de Montesquieu (bah-*rohn'* deh mohn-tehs-*kyew'*) was a French aristocrat who opposed all forms of tyranny and cruelty. He criticized the French absolute monarchs for limiting the power of the nobility. He wanted the aristocrats restored to the position of power that they had enjoyed in an earlier day. To Montesquieu, an absolute king is a poor ruler because he crushes liberty. Montesquieu admired the government of England. He praised the English for having limited the power of the king and for introducing a large measure of freedom of speech, press, and religion. Montesquieu insisted that "liberty does not consist in an unlimited freedom." Liberty is undermined when people feel free to disobey the law. For Montesquieu, "liberty is a right of doing whatever the laws permit."

In his *Spirit of the Laws* Montesquieu advocated a government in which power was not concentrated in the hands of one man or a small group. He wanted authority to be distributed among three branches of government. One branch, the *legislature,* would make the laws. A second branch, the *executive,* would see that the laws were carried out. The third branch, the *judiciary,* would interpret the laws, judge and punish lawbreakers, and handle disputes between individuals. By thus separating the powers of government, no individual or group could gain absolute control. In this way the liberty of the people would be safeguarded. This principle of *separation of powers* was adopted by the men who drew up the Constitution of the United States.

The Enlightenment

1690	Publication of Locke's *Two Treatises on Government*
1748	Publication of Montesquieu's *Spirit of the Laws*
1751–1772	Compilation of Diderot's *Encyclopedia*
1762	Publication of Rousseau's *Émile*
1764	Publication of Voltaire's *Philosophical Dictionary*
1795	Publication of Condorcet's *Historical Picture of the Progress of the Human Mind*

In addition to attacking absolute monarchy, Montesquieu condemned slavery, religious persecution, and censorship. He criticized the use of torture, insisted that a man is innocent until proven guilty, and denounced militarism:

A new disease has spread over Europe and has attacked our princes. It induces them to keep on foot an absurd number of troops. It goes on increasing, and is of course contagious, for as soon as one state increases its army the other states increase theirs, so that nothing is gained but the common ruin.

Voltaire opposes religious persecution. The leading spokesman of the Enlightenment was François Marie Arouet (frahn-*swah'* mah-*ree'* ah-*rweh'*), better known as Voltaire. Few of the philosophes had a better mind and none had a sharper wit. Voltaire was an outspoken opponent of ignorance, superstition, torture, religious persecution, and other evils of eighteenth-century France. He particularly condemned religious persecution. For centuries non-Christians had been persecuted throughout Christian Europe. The split in the Church into Protestantism and Catholicism increased religious persecution. In countries that were strongly Catholic, Catholics persecuted Protestants. In countries with largely Protestant populations, Protestants persecuted Catholics.

Voltaire considered it an act of great injustice and stupidity to harm a man because of his religious beliefs. "It is clear that every individual who persecutes a man . . . because he does not share his opinion is a monster." And again: "I shall not cease . . . to preach tolerance from the rooftops as long as persecution does not cease."

A deist, Voltaire criticizes organized religion. Like most philosophes, Voltaire rejected many of the teachings and practices of religion. He considered most religious doctrines to be superstitions that no intelligent man should accept. While critical of Christianity, Voltaire was not an *atheist* (*ey'*the-ihst)—one who does not believe in God—but rather a *deist*. He maintained that we must believe only those ideas about God which are arrived at by reason. If God created us as rational beings, we ought to respect the power of reason He gave us.

It seemed reasonable to Voltaire to believe that our orderly universe was created by God, but that once God set it in motion and established its laws, He did not interfere with its running. To Voltaire, God was the great Watchmaker or Master Architect of the universe and not the miracle-performing Father of Christianity.

To deists the essence of "rational" religion was morality. A rational, moral individual serves God by treating his fellow men fairly and justly. "What is a true deist?" asked Voltaire. "One who says to God I adore and love you, one who says to a Turk, a Chinaman, an Indian, and a Russian, I love you." Deists insisted that ceremonies and religious myths did nothing to help men be better, and were therefore unnecessary. If anything, the dogmas and ceremonies of the various churches prevented men from behaving justly toward each other.

Because he had little use for the narrowmindedness of organized religion, Voltaire often criticized the clergy. Clergymen, said Voltaire, cared more about strengthening the power of the Church than about making men good. They forced men to obey teachings that were contrary to reason and common sense. Because churchmen were certain that they were right, that they were doing God's work, Voltaire argued, they often became fanatics (page 154). They killed Christians and non-Christians whose beliefs differed from theirs. Voltaire claimed that over the centuries Christian fanatics had killed over nine million people. He strongly condemned these crimes which were committed in the name of God.

Voltaire finds more to admire in England than in France. Because Voltaire loved liberty, he admired England. In England, said Voltaire, freedom of religion was an accepted fact. "An Englishman, like a free man, goes to heaven by the road that pleases him."* In comparing France and England, Voltaire's native land came out second best. In England the nobility are useful and productive people, said Voltaire. They contribute to the prosperity of the country by engaging in business. In France, however, the nobility look down upon the businessman's way of life. They live idly, and are interested only in gossip and winning the favor of the king. They consider it important to know exactly at what time the king awakes or goes to bed. No wonder they contribute little to French society! Always an admirer of intelligence and the advancement of knowledge, Voltaire gave high praise to British men of science. A scientist such as Newton, who helps man to understand nature, is a far better person than a conqueror who reduces "mankind to a state of slavery by brutish force and downright violence." Voltaire also praised English law:

* From George R. Havens, *The Age of Ideas,* copyright by Holt, Rinehart & Winston, Inc., 1955. Courtesy Holt, Rinehart & Winston, Inc.

Houdon's bust of Voltaire (left) captures the philosophe's keen sense of irony, of belittling by pretended compliment. One of Voltaire's main targets was fanaticism which led to events such as the St. Bartholomew's Day Massacre (detail, below) in which Huguenots were attacked by French Catholics.

. . . English law . . . has restored each man to all the rights of nature of which he has been deprived in most monarchies. These rights are: full liberty of his person [and] of his goods; freedom to speak to the nation by the pen; freedom not to be tried under any criminal charge except by a jury formed of independent men; freedom not to be tried in any case except according to the precise terms of the law; freedom to profess peacefully any religion he wishes. . . . [In England you are] sure on going to bed that you will awake the next morning with the same fortune you possessed the evening before; that you will not be torn from the arms of your wife or your children in the middle of the night, to be lodged in a dungeon or exiled to a desert; that, on opening your eyes from sleep, you have the right to publish all you think; that, if you are accused, either of acting or speaking or writing ill, you will be judged only according to law. This [right] extends to everyone landing in England. A foreigner there enjoys the same liberty of property or person, and, if he is accused, can require that half of his jurors shall be foreigners.*

Voltaire advocates reforms in France. Voltaire wanted to change French society. He wanted to eliminate the privileges of the nobility, reduce the power of the clergy, and reform the system of taxation. He called for freedom of speech, press, and religion, and for equality before the law. Yet Voltaire was not in favor of democracy. He believed that the common people were incapable of governing themselves. "Once the [common people] begin to reason," Voltaire wrote, "then everything is lost. I [hate] the idea of government by the masses."* He considered the common people "silly and barbarous," in need of wise supervision. The best form of government was a monarchy led by an enlightened king—a wise man familiar with the teachings of such philosophes as Voltaire. Such a king would introduce needed reforms. In a society ruled by an enlightened king the hardworking, reliable, and sensible middle class would play a major role.

* From George R. Havens, *The Age of Ideas,* copyright by Holt, Rinehart & Winston, Inc., 1955. Courtesy Holt, Rinehart & Winston, Inc.

Diderot's Encyclopedia *expresses the views of the philosophes.* Denis Diderot (deh-*nee'* dee-droh') was chiefly responsible for the preparation of the *Encyclopedia,* whose purpose, said Diderot, was "to collect all the knowledge scattered over the face of the earth . . . so that the work of the past centuries may be useful to the following centuries, that our children, by becoming more educated, may at the same time become more virtuous and happier."

The *Encyclopedia* contained many articles that expressed the views of the philosophes. Few things aroused their anger more than religious fanaticism. How contrary to reason it was to torture and to kill people for their religious views! In the *Encyclopedia* fanaticism was defined as a "blind and passionate zeal born of superstitious opinions, causing people to commit ridiculous, unjust, and cruel actions, not only without any shame or remorse but even with a kind of joy and comfort. *Fanaticism* therefore is only superstition put into practice."

Diderot saw the Crusades, the Inquisition, the persecution of the Jews, and the religious wars between Catholics and Protestants as examples of fanaticism. Like Voltaire, he could not condemn religious fanaticism strongly enough.

In addition to attacking religious fanaticism and persecution, the *Encyclopedia* spoke out against other evils of eighteenth-century society. It called war "violent sickness," that results in "devastated fields and . . . cities reduced to ashes." If men would act according to reason, they would never "surrender themselves to the fury of war." The *Encyclopedia* denounced tyranny. "No man has received from nature the right to command others," said Diderot. "Liberty is a gift from heaven, and each individual . . . has the right to enjoy it." Slavery was also condemned in the *Encyclopedia.* Freedom is a natural right of man. It is part of our birthright. No man can deprive another man of his freedom. "Men and their liberty are not objects of commerce; they can be neither sold nor bought nor paid for at any price. . . . There is not, therefore, a single one of these unfortunate peo-

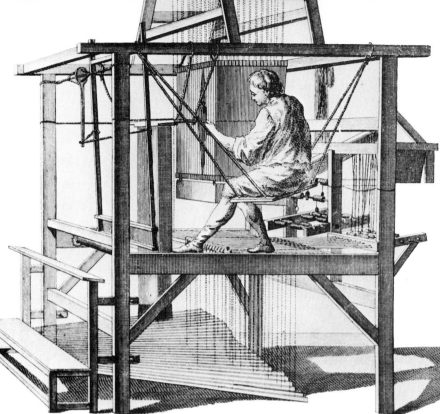

Diderot's Encyclopedia, *as well as communicating the Enlightenment's views of man and society, was a source of factual information. Published from 1751 to 1772, it included eleven volumes. Many of the accompanying engravings were devoted to France's key industries. Although the precise explanations of many skilled crafts helped raise the dignity of the workingman, they also revealed trade secrets. In the engraving below, a worker operates a giant loom.*

ple regarded only as slaves who does not have the right to be declared free."

Rousseau questions the benefits of civilization. Perhaps the most severe critic of eighteenth-century society was Jean Jacques Rousseau (*zhan′ zhahk′* roo-*soh′*). It is unjust, said Rousseau, for some men to have great wealth while others know only the misery of poverty. It is unjust for aristocrats to receive special favors. It is absurd to place governments in the hands of child-kings, stupid kings, or tyrants.

Whereas his fellow philosophes were great admirers of progress in the arts and science, Rousseau had his doubts. These advances in civilization, said Rousseau, have not made man a better person. Civilized man is unhappy, insecure, and selfish. Primitive man living simply in the forest was a better and happier person than a civilized Frenchman. Since he was not greedy for possessions, Rousseau stated, he was less likely to mistreat his fellow human beings.

"Man is born free and everywhere is in chains!" cried Rousseau. Man, who is born good, must be saved from a society that is turning him into a monster. For man to become a better and happier person, society must be changed. Rousseau knew that it was impossible to return to the simple life of primitive man. What he wanted were social and political reforms, a reorganization of society, so that the civilized individual could realize his natural goodness.

Rousseau urges improved education and government by the people. One way of making man a better person, said Rousseau, is to improve the education of children. Rousseau criticized fathers and teachers who made life miserable for youngsters and took all the pleasure out of childhood. How can children enjoy the magic of youth, asked Rousseau, when they are constantly being ordered about by their fathers and teachers? Rousseau felt that a child under twelve should not be stuffed with book learning. "Reading is the curse of childhood," he said. Instead of chaining a child to a desk, "give his body constant exercise, make it strong and healthy in order to make him good and wise; let him work, let him do things, let him run and shout, let him be always on the go; make a man of him in strength, and he will soon be a man in reason." But you must be careful not to make him into a person with no mind of his own. "If you are always giving him directions, always saying come here, go there, stop, do this, don't do that, . . . his own mind will become useless." Encourage him to be self-reliant and independent so that he is able to carry out "his own ideas, not those of other people." Above all, be kind to children, for childhood is brief and the child too soon acquires the problems of the adult.

But Rousseau knew that changing education would not alone reform society. The system of government also had to be changed. Unlike most of the philosophes, Rousseau had faith in democracy. He believed it would bring great benefits to man. He wanted to put an end to laws that favored one class over another. Law, said Rousseau, must consider the good of the community as a whole.

Rousseau had much greater faith in the common man than did Voltaire. Only by putting the power of government into the hands of the people, said Rousseau, could men regain the freedom that was once theirs. Rousseau felt that people, acting together, were capable of making wise decisions. He disagreed with the view that the traditional rulers of Europe—kings, nobles, and clergy—had a special gift for governing men. Because Rousseau believed that people should govern themselves, he is a leading figure in the history of democracy.

CHECK-UP

1. What criticisms of eighteenth-century society were made by the philosophes? By what means did they think men could improve life?

2. What is John Locke's theory of natural rights? What action did Locke recommend if governments ignore these rights? What is the significance of this theory of government?

3. Explain Montesquieu's plan for the separation of powers in government. What was its purpose? Why did Montesquieu praise the English system of government?

4. Why can Voltaire be called a critic of his time? What were his religious views? Did he believe in democracy? Explain.

5. Why did Diderot prepare the *Encyclopedia*? What attitude toward religious fanaticism was expressed in the *Encyclopedia*? What social evils did it denounce?

6. What did Rousseau mean when he said, "Man is born free and everywhere is in chains"? How could man find fulfillment in society? What were Rousseau's views on education?

Trends of Thought During the Enlightenment

Not all thinkers of the Enlightenment held the same views. Nevertheless, there are certain principles which are representative of their thinking.

The philosophes stress reason and science. The philosophes had confidence in human intelligence and in man's ability to improve conditions in society by approaching life with reason. They gave their support to the new attitudes developed during the Scientific Revolution. They attacked ignorance and encouraged investigation and freedom of thought which would help man to widen his knowledge of nature and society. Diderot expressed this scientific spirit when he urged man not to believe something to be true merely because someone famous said it was so. Avoid prejudice, criticize everything, and search for new ideas—that was his advice. To the philosophes the methods of science were the surest and most reliable way of gaining knowledge. They believed that science could speak with greater authority than could religion because it was based on sound inquiry.

Secularism is characteristic of both the Renaissance and the Enlightenment. The views and values of people in Western Europe had changed greatly since the Middle Ages. Medieval man lived in an Age of Faith, and his thoughts and actions were greatly influenced by his religious beliefs. His chief interest was to prepare himself for heaven. The Renaissance, with its emphasis on humanism (page 323), gave impetus to a different outlook on life. It stressed living a well-rounded life in this world. There was a moving away from a society dominated by the Church and religion and a growing concern with life on earth. The eighteenth-century philosophes reinforced this *secular* or nonreligious trend. They expressed belief in God as the Creator of the universe, but generally rejected many other religious beliefs and ceremonies. They were interested not only in expanding knowledge through science, but in using reason to improve society.

The philosophes condemn injustice and persecution. The philosophes wanted to improve social conditions. They protested against long jail sentences for minor crimes, the torture of prisoners, and the foul conditions characteristic of prisons. They condemned slavery as a violation of man's natural right to liberty and regarded war as a madness unworthy of civilized man. Because they cried out against injustice, the philosophes are called *humanitarians.*

A key idea in the program of social reform was freedom of conscience. The philosophes denounced religious persecution, insisting that every man should be free to worship God in his own way. Nor did the philosophes think that a man should be punished if he did not believe in God. They insisted that a man's religious beliefs were his own business. In America, Thomas Jefferson maintained that "it does me no injury for my neighbor to say there are twenty gods, or no god. It neither picks my pocket nor breaks my leg." The great English thinker John Locke summed up the views of the philosophes: "The care of each man's soul, and of the things of heaven, . . . is left entirely to every man's self."

The philosophes seek political freedom. The Enlightenment led to important advances in political reform. Locke's theory of natural rights, Montesquieu's principle of separation of powers, Voltaire's praise for English institutions, and Rousseau's stress on democracy were all attempts to safeguard man's liberty. The philosophes convinced men there was a better form of government than absolute monarchy or tyranny. "Every age has its dominant idea," wrote Diderot; "that of our age seems to be Liberty."

The idea of liberty led the philosophes to oppose all restrictions on freedom of thought. During the eighteenth century, it was common practice for church and state to *censor* speeches and publications and to suppress those that they considered dangerous. Men who criticized the privileged position of church and aristocrats, found fault with government policies, or stirred up unrest were forbidden to speak to groups and often were imprisoned. There was constant control by government and church over the printed and spoken word. The philosophes demanded the right to speak and write without restriction. They felt that society could be improved only if the minds of men were open to new ideas and men were made aware of injustices. "The motto of the Enlightenment," said a German thinker, is "Dare to Know! Have the courage to use your own intelligence!"

The philosophes support progress in education. The Enlightenment led to important advances in education. In the eighteenth century there were few public schools, and poor parents could not afford to send their children to private schools. Moreover, most people believed that only the rich and well-born could be educated. Some of the philosophes, however, insisted that if proper conditions were provided, all children could learn, poor as well as wealthy, commoners as well as aristocrats. They hoped that one day even the common man would learn how to read and write, that he too would develop his mind and his ability to reason. In the years to come, theories such as these led to the establishment of public education for all.

The philosophes have faith in the future of man. Lastly, believing in man's ability to improve himself, the men of the Enlightenment were generally optimistic about the future of society. Some philosophes believed that advances in science and the spread of liberty would usher in a golden age of continuous progress. In a sketch for his *Historical Picture of the Progress of the Human Mind,* the Marquis de Condorcet (mahr-*kee'* deh kon-dor-*sey'*) presented a magnificent picture of the future of mankind. Condorcet's vision was shared in part by other philosophes.

The time will therefore come when the sun will shine only on free men who know no other master but their reason; . . . when we shall . . . learn how to recognize, and so to destroy, by force of reason, the first seeds of tyranny and superstition, should they ever dare to reappear among us. . . .

When at last the nations come to agree on the principles of politics and morality, . . . then all the causes that . . . poison national relations will disappear one by one; and nothing will remain to encourage or even to arouse the fury of war.

But the philosophes were not starry-eyed dreamers. They knew that progress was painful and slow. "Let us weep and wail over the lot of philosophy," said Diderot. "We preach wisdom to the deaf, and we are still far indeed from the Age of Reason."

CHECK-UP

1. Why did the philosophes have great faith in reason and the scientific spirit? Why were they considered humanitarians?
2. How did the Enlightenment affect education? Government?

Legacy of the Enlightenment

Some two centuries have elapsed since the Enlightenment. Today we retain many of the attitudes expressed by the eighteenth-century philosophes. We too favor freedom of speech, of the press, and of religion, and we want governments to protect these freedoms. For the same reasons that the philosophes opposed tyrant kings, we are opposed to dictatorial or oppressive regimes. We too criticize war, torture, injustice, and human suffering. We also place reliance on the methods of science and foster education to expand knowledge. We too try to fight prejudice, ignorance, and superstition. Many of our values we owe to the philosophes of the Age of Enlightenment.

But unfortunately the promise of the Enlightenment—that man was about to enter a golden age—has not been fulfilled. Condorcet's vision of a perfect future has not been achieved. We are still burdened with evil and injustice. More education for more people has not eliminated ignorance and superstition or violence and war. Says Peter Gay:

The world has not turned out the way the philosophes wished and half-expected that it would. . . . Problems of race, of class, of nationalism, of boredom and despair in the midst of plenty, have emerged almost in defiance of the philosophe's philosophy. We have known horrors, and may know horrors, that the men of the Enlightenment did not see in their nightmares.

The Enlightenment raised fundamental questions about the nature of man. Is evil the result of a grossly imperfect environment—of wicked leaders, bad institutions, and ignorance—or does it reside in man himself? The philosophes had confidence in man's intelligence. They thought that, given a chance, man was capable of creating a better world. But perhaps the true enemy to progress is man himself—his greed, his cruelty, the fascination he feels for violence. Perhaps man would rather harm his neighbor than love him. Perhaps man is ruled not by reason but by emotion. If such is the case, it is difficult to share the optimism of Condorcet and of other philosophes. We have confidence that man can send spaceships to the moon, but we are less certain that he will do away with war, religious and racial hatred, poverty, and other evils. We are no longer certain that man is able to create the society of which Condorcet dreamed.

It is no doubt true that we are still far from an age of reason. Nevertheless, the humanitarian spirit of the philosophes, their love of freedom, their stress upon cultivating intelligence, and their rejection of fanaticism and superstition continue to provide man with hope. These are still the means by which man battles the forces of evil that darken his present and threaten to destroy his future.

Chapter Highlights

Can you explain?

atheist	secularism	executive	humanitarians
rational	deist	judiciary	scientific attitude
censorship	philosophes	fanaticism	separation of powers
natural rights	Enlightenment	legislature	

Can you identify?

Condorcet	Rousseau	Diderot	*Spirit of the Laws*
Voltaire	*Encyclopedia*	Locke	Montesquieu

What do you think?

1. What are the basic ideas of the Enlightenment? Which of these ideas are still accepted?

2. How have Locke's theories been used to justify democratic revolutions?

3. How did Voltaire look upon the common man? Compare this with Rousseau's views.

4. How are the ideas of Montesquieu and Locke reflected in the government of the United States?

5. Why has the Enlightenment also been called the Age of Reason?

6. What did the Renaissance and the Enlightenment have in common? In what ways were the two different?

7. How did Condorcet picture the future of mankind? Why has man failed to achieve this golden age?

The French Revolution

On January 21, 1793, a heavily guarded coach rumbled slowly through the streets of Paris. Inside the coach King Louis (*l'wee*) XVI, who had lost his throne four months earlier, sat in silence. Drummers marched in front of the horses. Citizens armed with pikes and guns lined the streets. The doomed king climbed down from the coach and mounted the steps to the platform holding the guillotine. Drums rolled as he spoke, "I die innocent of all the crimes of which I have been accused. I pardon those who have caused my death." Seconds later the blade of the guillotine descended, beheading the king. The crowds burst into cheers, shouting, *"Vive la République!"*[1]

The people of France had set in motion a great revolution, executed their king, and changed the course of history. Why? What were the causes of the French Revolution?

[1] *Vive la République* (*veev'* lah ray-poo-*bleek'*): Long live the Republic.

Every year French citizens celebrate July 14th as their national holiday. On that date in 1789 the Bastille was captured, an act symbolizing the end of the Old Regime. The contemporary engraving (left) shows the defenders flying the white flag of surrender after being surrounded by Parisians and the National Guard. Claude Monet's painting (above) of the celebration of Bastille Day a hundred years later captures the patriotism which is aroused by this historic event. The Paris streets are alive with red, white, and blue—the colors of the French flag.

The French Revolution had roots deep in eighteenth-century French society. The time before the French Revolution is called the *Old Regime*. Under the Old Regime, France was a nation with a large population, a powerful army, and a glamorous court. Paris, the capital, was a center of culture. Educated people in all Europe spoke French, read French literature, and copied French customs. France seemed to be the leading nation in a glorious age. Everyone wanted to be like the French. But beneath the surface France suffered from many serious problems that had been ignored for too long.

PRIVILEGES OF THE FIRST TWO ESTATES

The French people were divided into three *Estates*. The *First Estate* was made up of the clergy, and the *Second Estate* of the nobility. Together the First and Second Estates accounted for only about two per cent of the French people. Everyone else in France belonged to the *Third Estate*. The laws and customs of France favored the first two Estates.

The First Estate has many privileges. The Church owned perhaps ten per cent of the land. It provided not only religious services but operated schools and gave relief to the poor. French citizens paid a tax (tithe, *tieth*) to the Church. Instead of paying taxes on its property, the Church made a "free gift" to the government. The clergy determined the amount, and the free gift was usually a smaller sum than if the Church land had been taxed.

The First Estate was divided into two groups: *upper clergy* and *lower clergy*. In the former were the highest officers of the Church —archbishops, bishops, and abbots. By the eighteenth century only men of noble birth, the *aristocrats,* were named to these honored positions. The upper clergy usually lived in luxury, spending huge sums on hunting dogs, horses, carriages, entertainment, fine furniture, and servants. This emphasis on aristocratic ways often led the upper clergy to neglect their religious duties.

The lower clergy was made up of parish priests who came from middle-class families in the towns and cities and from the country peasantry. Unlike the upper clergy, few priests neglected their religious duties. In poverty themselves, many parish priests were concerned with the problems of the poor people of France.

Members of the Second Estate hold high offices and live well. Like the clergy, the nobility was a privileged order in eighteenth-century France. Besides filling the highest offices of the Church, aristocrats held the highest positions in the government and army. They served as ambassadors and advised the king on foreign affairs. Many of them received gifts and pensions from the king. Though they owned large estates, they paid almost no taxes to the government. And from the peasants on their estates they received manorial dues in the form of produce, labor, and money.

Like the clergy, not all nobles were wealthy or powerful. Although the nobles as a class owned fifteen to twenty per cent of the land in France, not all were rich. Many lived simple lives on run-down country estates which they could barely afford to maintain. Some lords felt a sense of responsibility, tried to treat their peasants fairly, and were often well liked by the people. These country nobles had no share in the brilliant life led by the nobles who thronged to the court at Versailles.

The court nobles lived an idle life of luxury. They dressed in extravagant fashions and attended elaborate banquets. Men as well as women wore wigs which were powdered and curled. Ladies of the court went to fantastic extremes in their hair styles. They pictured in their hair different scenes: birds pecking at fruit, nurses tending children, ships riding on

Once acclaimed for her beauty and grace, Marie Antoinette became a hated symbol of the extravagance of the French court and its indifference to the needs of the people. Accused of treason for her efforts to gain Austrian help to preserve the monarchy, the queen was executed in 1793, several months after Louis XVI had died on the scaffold.

waves. These hair styles grew so great that the ladies could barely walk through doorways.

French nobility compares unfavorably with the English upper class. Unlike the English aristocrats, who were increasing their wealth and importance to the state by the efficient management and improvement of their lands, most French court nobles contributed little to France. They believed that most work was beneath their dignity. Many nobles looked with contempt on earning a living through commerce or industry. They hired agents to squeeze more income from their already overburdened peasants or tried to get pensions or soft jobs from the king. Most of them had a mansion in Paris as well as a country estate which they visited briefly in the summer. Their chief interest in country living was hunting and collecting income from the estate. Among the court nobility there were some reformers, such as the Marquis de Lafayette (mar-*kee′* deh lah-fuh-*yet′*), a hero of the American Revolution, who recognized the faults of French society. These liberal nobles were attracted to the reforming ideas of the philosophes and looked to England's limited monarchy or even the American Revolution as a model for change.

PROBLEMS OF THE THIRD ESTATE

Three groups made up the Third Estate—peasants, city workers, and the middle class. Members of the Third Estate had many complaints. Above all, they resented the special privileges of the nobility.

Peasants have a hard life. By 1789 the 21 million French peasants were better off than the peasants in most European countries. In Prussia, Austria, Russia, and Poland most peasants were still serfs who could not leave the land without the lord's permission. All but about one million French peasants were freemen. Nevertheless, the French peasant had many complaints. Although some French peasants were prosperous farmers who lived in neat homes and ate well, most were poor and miserable. They worked from sunrise to dark and lived in small stone or mud huts which were often shared with their animals. Bread and soup were their daily fare; meat was a rare luxury. Most peasants owned only one shabby outfit of clothes and wore it year round. In 1772 a French priest, describing conditions in his country village, said, "In my parish there are 2200 souls, of whom at least 1800 beg for bread which they cannot find, and most of them live on the boiled stalks of cabbage or . . . on grass." Sixteen years later, Arthur Young, an English expert on farming, wrote of the poverty in the French countryside. In one region he met a French peasant woman who "might have been taken for 60 or 70, her figure was so bent and her face so [wrinkled] and hardened by labor—but she said she was only 28."

Why are the peasants poor? The poverty of the peasants was due to four things: (1) insufficient land, (2) heavy taxes, (3) manorial obligations, and (4) inefficient methods of farming.

1. Insufficient land. The twenty million free peasants owned nearly half of the land in France. But since this land was divided up among many peasants, the farms were usually small. The crops grown on a farm often could hardly support the peasant family. Moreover, there were still many free peasants who owned no land at all. Some were farm laborers. Others were renters who usually had to turn over half of their produce to their landlords. It is not surprising that the peasants looked with resentment on the nobles, who paid practically no taxes. Why should the nobles, who did not work, live in luxury, while the hard-working peasants had little to show for their labor?

2. Heavy taxes. Peasants paid burdensome taxes to king, Church, and feudal lord. In some regions, taxes took almost 60 per cent of the peasants' income. Every time the state needed more money, the peasants' taxes were increased. No consideration was given to their ability to pay these tax increases. An army of government tax collectors terrorized peasants into paying by threatening them with the loss of their homes, imprisonment, whipping, or forced labor in the galleys—ships rowed by groups of prisoners.

3. Manorial obligations. Although serfdom had ended in most parts of France, the nobles continued to demand many privileges that they had enjoyed during the Middle Ages. Lords still had the right to decide local cases in their manorial courts. Peasants were still required

to grind their corn in the lord's mill, bake their bread in his oven, and press their grapes in his winepress—and to give the lord a part of their produce in payment. Although peasants owned their own land, they were still required to make a number of burdensome tax payments to the lord of the manor. One peasant woman complained to Arthur Young that although she, her husband, and seven children had "but a morsel of land, one cow, and a poor little horse," they had to give 42 pounds of wheat and three chickens to their lord each year. And still he demanded more.

Moreover, only the nobles could hunt the wild animals that roamed the countryside and often destroyed the peasants' crops. Instead of food crops for their own use, peasants were forced to plant crops that would provide good feed for these animals. A peasant who killed one of these wild animals would be arrested and sent to row in the galleys. Furthermore, peasants had to repair roads and bridges on the lord's estate—free of charge.

4. Inefficient methods of farming. Agriculturally, France lagged far behind England, where an agricultural revolution was causing significant improvements in farming methods. In France—as in the rest of Europe—farming methods were little changed from those used in the Middle Ages. These inefficient methods yielded small crops, often of poor quality. Farm animals had been little improved over the centuries. Peasant holdings usually consisted of a number of small plots which were scattered over the countryside. This made good management difficult.

The peasants have many demands. By 1789 French peasants were in an angry mood. Renters and farm laborers wished to own land. Peasants who owned land were not satisfied with their small plots. The peasants felt ill treated. They were tired of paying the bulk of the taxes and of being treated as "beasts of burden" who existed for the benefit of the nobles. They wanted a more just tax system and an end to *all* manorial obligations. Poor

A painting of a family gathered at home for a meal allows an artist to reveal much about their life style. Boucher's picture of a middle-class family at lunch (left) shows the comforts available to the bourgeoisie and the parents' new interest in spending time with their children rather than leaving them in the care of servants. In contrast, Van Gogh's somber painting of a Dutch peasant family at dinner (above) shows both the harshness of their world and the compassion the artist felt for them.

harvests in 1787–1789 added to the distress of the peasants.

City workers are also ill treated. Although there were few industries in France in 1789, a class of city workers had developed. Some townspeople did manufacturing, such as spinning, in their homes. A few—less than two per cent of the population—worked in factories. Most city workers provided the labor for the menial tasks that are part of city life—cleaning, carrying loads, moving freight, serving in the homes of the wealthy. Like the peasants, these city workers had serious complaints. They were forced to work hard under poor conditions for low wages. The bad harvests of 1787–1789 forced up food prices, causing hunger and unrest in the towns.

The bourgeoisie have many complaints. The *bourgeoisie* (boor-zhwah-*zee'*, middle class) was made up of lawyers, merchants, bankers, doctors, and professors. The most important group in the Third Estate, the bourgeoisie had money, education, talent, and ambition. They owned as much of the land as did the nobles. All that they lacked was noble blood. Since the 1600's wealthy bourgeoisie had been able to purchase titles of nobility. These titles enabled them to hold important offices in the state. But their chances for advancement were limited. In the eighteenth century the best positions in the government, army, and Church were monopolized by the aristocrats. To the bourgeoisie, it appeared that noble birth counted more than talent, that despite their education and ambition, the road was blocked in every direction.

445

But this was not all. Noblemen looked upon the bourgeoisie as members of a lower social class. If a bourgeois challenged an aristocrat to a duel, the aristocrat would refuse. He would not cross swords with a commoner. The bourgeoisie would never forget these insults. Their hatred of the nobility grew.

The bourgeoisie have many demands. The bourgeoisie felt that their talent and education were not appreciated. They wanted a chance to carry out their ideas for improving France. They wanted to limit the king's power, and to prevent him from wasting the nation's money on gifts and pensions for favorite nobles. They demanded a written constitution and freedom of speech and the press. They wanted to remove restrictions on trade, such as tolls and tariffs paid on goods going from one region of France to another. The end of government interference with business and the introduction of free trade would contribute to the prosperity of bourgeois merchants. Above all, the bourgeoisie wanted equality. They wanted all positions in government, Church, and army to be open to men of talent, regardless of birth. They demanded that nobles and the Church pay a fair share of taxes. Remove the privileges of the First and Second Estates, said the bourgeoisie, and all France would benefit.

SHORTCOMINGS OF THE GOVERNMENT

In addition to inequalities resulting from the social system, France was burdened with other serious problems. (1) The government was nearly bankrupt. (2) The administration of France was inefficient. (3) The system of justice was unfair. (4) Liberty was limited. (5) The king was a poor ruler.

The government is nearly bankrupt. France's greatest problem was money. France was not a poor country. But the unfair and inefficient tax system made it impossible for the government to raise enough money to cover its expenses. It

had borrowed money that it could not pay back —the interest alone amounted to half of the annual income raised by taxes. Its many wars during the 1700's and its aid to the United States during the American Revolution had drained the treasury. The king's gifts and pensions to favorite nobles and the extravagances of court life wasted money. Few wealthy Frenchmen—including the bourgeoisie—paid their fair share of taxes. The burden of taxes therefore fell most heavily on the peasants. Because tax income came chiefly from the part of the population with the least income, it was bound to be inadequate. The king recognized the need for tax reforms but his efforts were resisted by the nobles, who refused to surrender their privileges. As we shall see, it was the inability of the king to reform the tax system that led directly to the revolution.

The administration of France is inefficient. The government of eighteenth-century France was poorly organized and marked by confusion. Officials bought their positions from the king and could not be dismissed unless the king returned the money paid. This practice, introduced as a means of raising money, resulted in many incompetent office-holders. Moreover, French kings had not succeeded in eliminating many practices and laws that prevented the effective exercise of royal power throughout France. In some provinces the nobility had more power than did the king, and many towns and regions enjoyed long-standing privileges that the king dared not take away. Conflicting local laws, tariffs on goods shipped from one province to another, and differing systems of weights and measures were not only barriers to trade and travel but also hindered the development of a strong central government.

The system of justice is unfair. There were many abuses in the law courts of France. The common people were often denied fair treatment. The king could protect a nobleman who had done wrong, and he could imprison an enemy without investigation or trial. Once a person was in prison, he might remain there for years. Penalties were often severe, and sometimes people were sentenced to death for minor crimes. There were 300 different law codes in France, making it difficult for the poor man to understand the law and get justice. Commoners received harsher punishments than did nobles.

Liberty is limited. In Great Britain, Parliament had limited the king's power. In France, the parliament (the States-General) had not met for one hundred and seventy-five years, since 1614. In Great Britain, people enjoyed considerable freedom of speech and the press. In France, censorship was common and critics of the government and the Church faced arrest. By 1789, many Frenchmen wanted to follow Britain's lead in limiting the king's power. They wanted an effective parliament which would pass laws to reform French society and draw up a written constitution which would define and guarantee the rights of Frenchmen.

The king is a poor ruler; the queen, extravagant. Louis XVI inherited the throne of France when he was twenty years old. He had studied several languages, enjoyed eating, hunting, and drinking, loved to tinker with clocks, and was a skilled swordsman. Although well intentioned, he was dull, indecisive, and knew little about ruling a great nation. Nevertheless, like the previous French kings, he believed that God had selected him to rule. Though his ability was limited, he claimed unlimited power.

Timid, awkward, and unsure of himself, Louis XVI lacked the strength of character needed to lead France. He turned to his advisors, favored nobles, and his wife for guidance. They often misled him.

Marie Antoinette (muh-*ree'* an-twah-*net'*), Queen of France and daughter of the Empress of Austria, was a glamorous spendthrift. Unlike her awkward husband, Marie Antoinette looked like royalty. Her foster brother wrote: "Nature . . . [had] formed Marie Antoinette to occupy a throne. A royal [appearance], a noble beauty, a manner of holding her head . . . inspired respect."

At first the people of France loved Marie Antoinette. She was the "idol of the nation" who set the style in dress and manners for French nobility. But eventually Marie Antoinette lost favor with the people. They felt that "that Austrian" was wasting France's money on luxuries a nation in debt could ill afford.

Besides a weak king and an extravagant queen, France had a corrupt and inefficient government. There was a crying need for reform. The king realized that France was in serious trouble, but he lacked the ability to act decisively. Moreover, when his ministers tried to introduce reforms, they were resisted by aristocrats who feared the loss of their privileges. Louis XVI insisted that he was absolute ruler, chosen by God. In reality, however, he could not overcome the opposition of the nobles who clung tenaciously to their ancient privileges.

CHECK-UP

1. Who made up each Estate in France? What special privileges did members of the First and Second Estates enjoy?

2. How did the outlook of the French nobility differ from that of the English upper class?

3. Why were French peasants poor? What were their demands? What were the problems of city workers? Of the bourgeoisie?

4. Why was the government nearly bankrupt? Why was the system of taxation inefficient as well as unfair?

5. What were the major shortcomings of the French government? Of the system of justice? What made Louis XVI and Marie Antoinette poor rulers?

The Bourgeoisie Gain Control of France

France under the Old Regime seemed incapable of reforming herself by peaceful means. There was too much hostility between bourgeoisie and aristocracy; there were too many points of conflict between lord and peasant. There was too much resistance to reform on the part of aristocrats. By 1789 France was in grave danger.

But bad conditions alone do not usually lead to revolution. For centuries the untouchables of India and the peasants of Egypt lived under the most wretched conditions. Yet they bore their misery without raising a voice in protest. In the eighteenth century the people of Eastern Europe, Italy, and Spain were far worse off than was the average Frenchman. Yet it was in France that the great revolution occurred. It is clear that something more than poverty is needed to touch off a revolution. One reason why revolution broke out in France is that the bourgeoisie as well as the poor were discontented. It was the relatively prosperous bourgeoisie who provided the drive and the leadership for revolution.

Some historians say that the philosophes provided the inspiration for revolution. By attacking all the evils of the Old Regime, the philosophes awakened the French people to the injustices of their society. The philosophes convinced many Frenchmen, particularly the bourgeoisie, that these abuses could be corrected by sensible reforms. The philosophes led Frenchmen to challenge the centuries' old notion that Church and nobility were the natural leaders of society. The ideas of the philosophes were eagerly received by the bourgeoisie, who had the education to understand them and the wealth and ambition to do something about them. Although the philosophes did not call for revolution, their writings helped to set the revolution in motion. They demonstrated that ideas are powerful weapons which may arouse people to anger and to action.

The middle class seeks a place in the sun. To a great extent the French Revolution was a struggle between an ancient aristocracy and a rising bourgeoisie. For centuries French nobility had enjoyed special privileges. The bourgeoisie, on the other hand, had become increasingly important. The merchants and shipowners of thriving Atlantic ports controlled a rich trade in slaves and sugar with Africa and the West Indies. France's overseas trade had enjoyed a fivefold increase during the eighteenth century and seriously rivaled Great Britain's commerce. By 1789 the bourgeoisie controlled the business life of France and were prominent in French intellectual life. But the bourgeoisie were not satisfied with economic and intellectual power. They wanted to hold the most honored positions in France, positions traditionally reserved for the nobility. But in every way the nobility stood in the way of the bourgeoisie. "The feeling against the nobility is so strong that I fear its destruction," wrote the American ambassador to France in 1789. He was right. The day of the aristocracy was nearing its end.

The nobility hopes to turn back the clock. The aristocrats, however, did not consider themselves a dying class. Their privileges gave them a feeling of pride in their ancestry. They were determined to hold on to these privileges, which they felt were being threatened by the ambitions of the bourgeoisie and by the king's desire to introduce tax reforms. Aristocrats wanted to return France to the days when lords were stronger than kings. They deliberately tried to weaken the king's power. In doing so, they helped to bring on the revolution which destroyed them.

BOURGEOISIE GAIN POWER

The States-General is called. In 1789 France was in serious financial trouble. Throughout the eighteenth century French kings had wasted the nation's money. To meet the expenses of maintaining a large army and waging war, they were forced to borrow money. When the government found it difficult to pay even the interest on money loaned it, businessmen and bankers would not extend further loans. France was in the peculiar position of being a prosperous nation with an empty treasury. The problem could have been solved had the nobility, the clergy, and the wealthy bourgeoisie paid their fair share of taxes. Faced with national bankruptcy, Louis XVI appealed to the First and Second Estates to give up some of their tax privileges. When they refused, he called a meeting of the States-General.

The nobility applauded the king's move. They wanted the States-General to meet regularly as the permanent lawmaking body of France. The nobility expected to use the States-General to protect their privileges and to strengthen their power at the expense of the king.

The nobility react. The nobility were willing to surrender some of their tax privileges if this would give them a chance to govern France. The conflict between their aims and those of the king triggered the French Revolution. For centuries French kings had tried to unite the nation under strong royal rule. To achieve this goal of centralization and absolutism, French kings had to overcome the resistance of nobles who sought to hold fast to their feudal power and privileges. Under Louis XIV the power of the nobility had been greatly weakened. But the weak and ineffective rule of his successors (Louis XV and Louis XVI) encouraged the nobles to challenge royal power. "It is customary to characterize the eighteenth century as the age of the rise of the bourgeoisie . . . but the century also witnessed the last offensive of the aristocracy," writes French historian Georges Lefebvre (leh-*fay*′vr′).

Hoping to dominate the States-General, the nobility insisted that the three Estates follow

The French Revolution

May 5, 1789	Opening session of States-General
June 17, 1789	Formation of National Assembly
July 14, 1789	Fall of the Bastille
August 4, 1789	Abolition of feudal privileges of nobles
August 27, 1789	*Declaration of the Rights of Man* drafted
June 20–25, 1791	Flight of Louis XVI
September 14, 1791	Louis XVI accepts constitution
October 1, 1791	Formation of Legislative Assembly
April 20, 1792	France declares war on Austria
September 21, 1792	Formation of National Convention
January 21, 1793	Execution of Louis XVI
April, 1793	Formation of Committee of Public Safety
1793–1794	Reign of Terror
1795	Directory set up to govern France

the traditional practice of meeting and voting separately. Under this system each Estate, not each delegate, had one vote. For a reform to pass, two of the three Estates would have to approve it. Since the nobility and clergy were likely to vote alike, the Third Estate would always be outvoted two to one.

But the Third Estate would not agree to this proposal. Most of the delegates of the Third Estate were educated bourgeoisie who had plans of their own. They felt the time had come to put an end to special privileges. To carry out its plans for reform, the Third Estate thus wanted the three Estates to meet together as one body with each delegate having one vote. There were some 610 delegates from the Third Estate. The nobility and the clergy together had about the same number. If the three Estates met as a single body, with each delegate having one vote, the nobility and clergy could not outvote the Third Estate. Because many delegates from the lower clergy and some liberal nobles were as reform-minded as the bourgeoisie, they were likely to support the Third Estate.

The Third Estate forms the National Assembly. The delegates of the Third Estate invited the clergy and nobles to join them in a combined assembly. When this invitation went unheeded, the Third Estate simply assumed the right to organize all delegates in a single body. On June 17, 1789, the delegates of the Third Estate declared themselves the National Assembly. Claiming that it represented the entire nation, the National Assembly stated it would enact needed reforms whether or not the other two Estates cooperated.

When the delegates of the Third Estate came to their meeting hall on June 20, they found the door locked. Not at all discouraged, the delegates went to a nearby covered tennis court. There they took an oath "never to separate" until they had given France a constitution. A day or two later the majority of the clergy, mainly parish priests,[2] joined the National Assembly. Almost all of the nobles refused. They were determined to break up the National Assembly.

Louis XVI was angered by the action of the commoners. On June 23 he ordered the National Assembly to "separate immediately." He realized that the Third Estate was now a much greater threat to his power than were the nobles who had tried to weaken royal authority by forcing the king to call the States-General. Would the Third Estate retreat? Would it break up the National Assembly as the king and nobility wanted? The Third Estate would not give in. One delegate shouted, "We are here by the will of the people and . . . we will go only if we are driven [out] by the point of a bayonet."

The king backs down. How would Louis XVI react to this challenge to his authority? Each day more members of the clergy joined the National Assembly; some nobles also were taking seats in the Assembly. Seeing that his efforts to break up the National Assembly were ignored, the king yielded. He requested the remaining clergy and nobles to join the National Assembly. Thus, ten days after the Third Estate had formed the National Assembly, the States-General came to an end. The bourgeois leaders of the Third Estate had successfully resisted the king.

But the victory of the bourgeoisie was not complete. Though Louis XVI had ordered the first two Estates to join the National Assembly, he and his aristocratic advisors continued to oppose it. The nobility realized that their strug-

---

[2] About two thirds of the delegates from the First Estate were parish priests.

gle with the king must end if they were to withstand the Third Estate's threat to their privileges. They turned to Louis XVI as the only one who could hold back the Third Estate. Urged on by the nobility, Louis decided to use force to crush the Assembly. At the end of June he ordered special foreign regiments to be brought together on the outskirts of Paris.

What had started out as a struggle for power between the aristocracy and the king had developed into something much more significant. It had become a struggle between the bourgeoisie and the privileged Estates. As the most powerful group in the Third Estate, the bourgeoisie had the upper hand in the National Assembly. Could they overcome the determined resistance of the nobles and the king to enact the reforms that France needed?

COMMON PEOPLE IN PARIS AND THE COUNTRYSIDE REACT

At this point the common people of Paris and the peasants in the countryside came to the aid of the bourgeoisie. Their support ensured the success of the Revolution. Let us see how this happened.

The people of Paris were fearful of the king's troops on the outskirts of the city. Anxious to protect the National Assembly and fearing attack by the royal troops, the Parisians searched Paris for weapons.

The Bastille falls to the Paris crowd. On the morning of July 14, 1789, the Parisians raided the Invalides[3] and obtained some 30,000 muskets. Later that day a crowd gathered outside the Bastille (bas-*teel'*), a fortress long used as a prison. The people hated the Bastille, for, as American historian Leo Gershoy writes:

Many horrifying stories were told about it, tales of vaults and dungeons deep in the earth, of prisoners doomed for years to maddening darkness, of cruel tortures and agonizing deaths. The stories were largely false, but the Parisians believed

[3] Originally a hospital, the Invalides (an-vah-*leed'*) later became an arms museum.

them; and in the eyes of all liberty-loving people in Europe the Bastille was the hateful symbol of despotism and oppression.

The Parisians gathered that day not only to free the handful of prisoners in the Bastille, but to obtain gunpowder and to remove the cannon that threatened a heavily populated area of the city. A delegation of Parisians met with the Marquis de Launay (loh-*nay'*), Governor of the Bastille. Outside, the crowds, increasing with every moment, shouted, "Attack the Bastille!" Soon the mob, growing more daring, charged into the courtyard. When the Marquis de Launay ordered his troops to fire, nearly a hundred Parisians were killed.

At that moment the French Guard, troops who sided with the Parisians, arrived on the scene. When they threatened to bombard the Bastille, de Launay surrendered. He was promised that no harm would come to him or his men. The angry crowd rushed into the fortress to free any prisoners. An eyewitness tells what followed: "Several of these soldiers, whose lives had been promised them, were assassinated; others were dragged like slaves through the streets of Paris. . . . De Launay, torn from the arms of those who wished to save him, had his head cut off."

The next day the frightened king told the Assembly that he would withdraw the troops stationed outside Paris. Leading nobles who had urged the king to break up the National Assembly fled the country. The National Assembly had been saved by the people of Paris.

The peasants panic. After the fall of the Bastille, panic spread across the French countryside. Rumors spread that the nobles were organizing armed bands to kill the peasants. Desperate with fear, the peasants let loose centuries of stored-up hatred against the nobles. They plundered the estates and destroyed the records of feudal dues. Without these records, the lords could not demand that the peasants meet their obligations. This period of peasant upheaval is known as the Great Fear. The peasant uprisings, like the storming of the Bastille, worked to the advantage of the bourgeoisie dominating the National Assembly. Popular support strengthened their determination to strike at the privileges of the aristocracy.

Feudalism is ended. Frightened by the loss of life and property, the National Assembly moved to put an end to the peasant uprisings by abolishing feudalism. Even the aristocrats realized that they could not protect their privileges any longer. One noble after another rose in the National Assembly to give up his special privileges—exclusive hunting rights, tax exemptions, monopolization of highest offices in the government, and the right to demand labor services from peasants and to try peasants in their own feudal courts. "During that long night of August 4," states Gershoy, "France of the

Like Marie Antoinette, Louis XVI began his reign as a popular monarch, yet was deposed and executed. In the formal portrait (right) Louis wears an ermine-trimmed robe embroidered with gold fleurs de lis, the symbol of the Bourbon dynasty. (Compare his portrait with that of Louis XIV, page 409.) The contemporary print below reveals that by June, 1791, much had changed in France: the royal family, having attempted to flee Paris, was captured by revolutionary troops and forced to return to the capital under arrest.

Old Regime came to an end, and a New France was born with the dawn. Henceforth, all Frenchmen would be citizens, subject to one law, paying the same taxes, and eligible to all offices." The National Assembly announced the end of feudalism in France.

The king, however, was cool to these changes. He kept postponing his approval of the decree abolishing feudalism. He also refused to approve the *Declaration of the Rights of Man and Citizen* (see page 454)—a statement of human rights also drawn up by the Assembly in August, 1789. He did not foresee the events which would force him to agree to reforms.

Hunger causes unrest. While the peasants were attacking the manor houses on the estates, Paris remained comparatively calm. After the storming of the Bastille, there were few outbreaks of violence. But by early September the people of Paris were again in an angry mood. Thousands of unemployed workers roamed the streets. There was little bread to eat, and food prices were soaring. Hungry mobs began to raid bakeries.

At eight in the morning of October 5, a crowd of women and men disguised as women gathered in the streets to demand bread. Soon the cry was raised "To Versailles (vair-*sigh'*)!" Both the king and the National Assembly were at Versailles, twelve miles from Paris. On the march to Versailles the original protesters were joined by more angry men and women and by companies of the National Guard, organized to maintain order in Paris.

At Versailles the crowd rushed into the Assembly to protest the lack of bread. An eyewitness described the scene: "the women . . . appeared to be drunk. . . . Some of them showed a piece of black and moldy bread and added, 'We will make the Austrian [Marie Antoinette] swallow it and we will cut her throat.'"

The mob compels Louis XVI to move to Paris. The next morning some of the marchers found a way into the palace at Versailles. Before the National Guard could come to the rescue, two members of the king's bodyguard were killed. The people called out, "We want the king in Paris—the king in Paris." In the rain, mud, and falling darkness, surrounded by the cheering and swearing crowd, the coach carrying the royal family moved slowly toward Paris. Two days later the National Assembly also moved to Paris.

Once again the common people of Paris had strengthened the hand of the bourgeoisie who dominated the National Assembly. Before the October riots, Louis XVI had refused to accept the reforms approved by the National Assembly —the *Declaration of the Rights of Man* and the August decrees abolishing feudalism. Moreover, some members of the National Assembly had allied themselves with the king and were trying to keep further reforms from being passed. There was still the ever present fear that the king, supported by the nobility, would use force against the Assembly. But the October Days changed all this. Many nobles hostile to the Revolution fled the country. Louis XVI, aware that he no longer could control the people of Paris and fearful of further violence, now approved the reforms passed by the National Assembly.

REFORMS OF THE NATIONAL ASSEMBLY

Sweeping reforms end the Old Regime. The reform-minded bourgeoisie, aided by liberal nobles, were clearly in control of the National Assembly. They had won out over aristocrats and the king. The alliance of bourgeoisie, Parisian workers, and peasants had destroyed the Old Regime. Having gained control of the National Assembly, the bourgeoisie continued the work of reform begun in the summer of 1789. What were the reforms of the National Assembly?

1. Abolition of special privileges. On the night of August 4, 1789, as we have seen, the National Assembly did away with the special privileges of the nobility. The nobles no longer could administer justice on their estates or collect taxes from the peasants. They lost their hunting rights as well. The National Assembly declared that all offices in Church, government, and army were open to all citizens regardless of birth. The bourgeoisie had obtained the equality they had demanded.

2. Rights of man. The National Assembly issued the *Declaration of the Rights of Man and Citizen.* Calling for a society based upon liberty and equality, the Declaration expressed the ideas of the philosophes and the hopes of the bourgeoisie. One French historian appropriately called it the "death certificate of the Old Regime." Like the British Bill of Rights and the American Declaration of Independence, the French *Declaration of the Rights of Man,* excerpts of which follow,* is a landmark in the history of liberty.

Men are born and remain free and equal in rights. . . .

The aim of every [government] is the preservation of the natural . . . rights of man. These rights are liberty, property, security, and resistance to oppression.

The source of all sovereignty [authority] is essentially in the nation [people]. . . .

Liberty consists in the power to do anything that does not injure others. . . .

The law has the right to forbid only such actions as are injurious to society. Nothing can be forbidden that is not [prohibited] by the law, and no one can be [compelled] to do that which it does not order.

Law is the expression of the general will [of tne people]. All citizens have the right to take part personally, or by their representatives, in its formation. It must be the same for all, whether it protects or punishes. All citizens, being equal in its eyes, are equally eligible to all public dignities, places, and employments, according to their capacities, and without other distinction than that of their [character] and their talents.

* From *The Constitutions and Other Select Documents Illustrative of the History of France 1789–1907,* edited by Frank Maloy Anderson (Minneapolis, Minn.: The H. W. Wilson Company, 1908). Reprinted by permission of Dr. Gaylord W. Anderson.

No man can be accused, arrested, or detained, except in the cases determined by the law and according to the forms that it has prescribed. . . .

Every man [is] presumed innocent until he has been pronounced guilty. . . .

The free communication of ideas and opinions is one of the most precious of the rights of man; every citizen, then, can freely speak, write, and print, subject to responsibility for the abuse of this freedom in the cases determined by law.

Property being a sacred and inviolable right, no one can be deprived of it, unless a legally established public necessity evidently demands it, under the condition of a just and prior [payment].

3. State control of clergy. The National Assembly also weakened the power of the clergy. In August the Church had lost its right to collect taxes. A few months later, as the financial situation grew worse, the National Assembly confiscated the lands held by the Church and put them up for sale. The clergy were placed under state control. Clergymen were paid salaries by the state and given pensions when they retired. Monastic orders were suppressed. Under the Civil Constitution of the Clergy, bishops were to be elected by popular vote in which non-Catholics would participate.

4. Constitution. In 1791 the National Assembly achieved the goal for which it had been aiming since June, 1789. It drew up a constitution limiting the power of the king and guaranteeing all Frenchmen the right to equal treatment under the law. But the constitution did not turn France into a democracy. About half the adult population was denied the right to vote because it owned too little property or did not pay sufficient taxes. Clearly the bourgeoisie were not eager to share power with the common people.

5. Business aided. The National Assembly aided businessmen by abolishing duties on goods transported within France and by passing laws prohibiting strikes and labor unions.

By these reforms the National Assembly sought to give power to the bourgeoisie. This could only be achieved by ending absolute monarchy, eliminating the privileges of the nobility, and preventing the mass of people from gaining any control over the government. With one arm the National Assembly broke the power of aristocrats and king; with the other it held back the common people. French historian Jacques Godechot concludes: "The essential goal of the National Constituent Assembly was to construct a new regime which would guarantee to the bourgeoisie the peaceful exercise of power and eliminate the possibility of either a return to absolute monarchy, or rule of the aristocracy, or rule of the mass of the people."

What are the effects of the reforms? The reforms made France a different nation. Absolutism and feudal privileges had disappeared. The Church had been weakened. The liberties and rights of Frenchmen were guaranteed by the *Declaration of the Rights of Man*. Most Frenchmen were pleased with the reforms. Some were not. Who were the dissatisfied?

Churchmen felt that they had suffered the most. The Church had lost its land, its right to tax, and much of its power. The Pope could not accept legislation that substituted state control over the Church for papal control. Priests who swore allegiance to the French government were excommunicated (page 147). Many priests and bishops refused to take the oath. This cost them their offices, and many high churchmen fled the country.

Most nobles opposed the Revolution. They felt it had gone too far. They resented their loss of feudal privileges, and the coming to power of the bourgeoisie. Disappointed by the turn of events, some nobles fled the country. Once outside France, many urged foreign rulers to overthrow the Revolution. Many of the nobles who remained in France engaged in counterrevolutionary acts.

CHECK-UP

1. How did the philosophes contribute to the outbreak of the French Revolution?

2. In what sense was the French Revolution a struggle between the middle class and the aristocracy?

3. Why did Louis XVI call a meeting of the States-General? Why did this suit the nobles? What were the plans of the Third Estate? What was the outcome?

4. What is the significance of the fall of the Bastille? How did this save the National Assembly?

5. Why did the peasants panic? Turn on the nobles? How did this affect the National Assembly?

6. What were the October Days? How did they affect the position of the king? Of the bourgeoisie?

7. What were the major reforms of the National Assembly? What effect did they have on the common man? On churchmen? On nobles?

Reactionaries, Radicals, and Moderates Compete for Power

Reactionaries want to restore the Old Regime. Those who were opposed to the reforms of the Revolution wanted to bring back the Old Regime. Because the aristocrats and many clergymen wanted to set the clock back to the days before the Revolution, they are called *reactionaries*. But it was too late for aristocrats, clergy, and the king to regain their power.

Once started, revolutions—like landslides halfway down a mountain—cannot easily be stopped. The Old Regime had been shattered beyond repair.

Radicals feel that the Revolution has not gone far enough. Frenchmen who demanded more drastic changes were called *radicals*. Radicals wanted France to have no king, not even one with limited powers. Instead, they desired France to become a *republic*—a nation governed by the people through a parliament. Supporting the radicals were the wage earners and shopkeepers of Paris, the so-called *sans-culottes* (*san'*-koo-*lut'*). Though they had played a significant role in the Revolution, they had gained little, for the reforms passed by the National Assembly largely benefited the bourgeoisie. The people of Paris wanted more than an end to the privileges of nobles and clergy. They wanted a greater voice in the government. They wanted the government to raise wages, lower food prices, and put an end to food shortages. "Often rough men without education, their souls inflamed by poverty," they wanted the government to imprison or execute food hoarders and limit the profits of wealthy businessmen. To them free trade was not a sound economic principle but a way for food speculators and profiteers to grow rich at the expense of the city poor. Their ideal was a nation of small shopkeepers and no millionaires. "Let no one have more than one workshop, more than one store" read a sans-culotte petition. There can be no equality, said a spokesman for the sans-culottes, "when the rich . . . exercise the right of life and death over their fellow men." In 1789 the bourgeoisie had demanded equality with the aristocrats—the right to hold the most honored positions in the government and an end to the special privileges of the aristocracy. But the bourgeoisie did not regard the sans-culottes as equals. The Constitution of 1791, drawn up by the bourgeoisie, had denied many of the sans-culottes the right to vote. Now the sans-culottes were demanding equality with the bourgeoisie and a government that favored the common man.

Most of the bourgeoisie are satisfied. The bourgeoisie had obtained what they wanted—an end to special privileges of the aristocracy, a king with limited powers, and a parliament which they dominated. Most of them thought it time the Revolution came to an end. They were particularly fearful of the radical demands of the sans-culottes, which they felt threatened bourgeois property rights and bourgeois control of the government. Few realized that the violence they had seen was mild compared to what was to come. By 1792 leadership of the Revolution had passed out of the hands of the moderate bourgeoisie and into radical hands. How did this come about?

The royal family tries to escape. By the end of 1790, Louis XVI was a prisoner in his own palace. Greatly upset by his loss of power, the king made plans to escape. Plans were made to concentrate foreign regiments loyal to the king near the frontier with the Austrian Netherlands (Belgium). After reaching them, Louis XVI would seek the support of other European monarchs in overthrowing the Revolution.

On the night of June 20, 1791, the royal family slipped out of the palace in disguise and headed toward the frontier in a coach. But the alarm was sounded when the king was recognized by a villager. The royal family was arrested and sent back to Paris. When their coach reached Paris on June 25, it was greeted by stony silence. Parisians refused to remove their hats and soldiers refused to salute the king.

France moves toward war. The king's flight had two important consequences. First, it turned the people of France against their king. There were demonstrations calling for his abdication and the establishment of a republic. Such demands helped to make the Revolution more radical. Secondly, the flight of the king increased tensions between France and other countries of Europe.

His power gone and the respect of the people lost, Louis looked for help outside France. His advisors, especially the queen and the nobles and churchmen who had fled France, hoped to force a restoration of the old order. Kings of other European countries were angered and frightened by Louis XVI's arrest, for a France ruled by revolutionaries threatened their power as well.

The increased tension between France and the kings of Europe was revealed in the meeting of the Legislative Assembly—the lawmaking body which replaced the National Assembly in October, 1791. In its first session it became clear that some members of the Legislative Assembly also favored war. One group, the *Girondins* (zhee-ron-*dan'*), had ties with powerful shipowners and merchants who thought that war would be good for business. Moreover, the Girondins believed that a successful war would unite all patriotic Frenchmen under their leadership. The Girondins also regarded themselves as crusaders in the struggle of liberty against tyranny. They wanted to spread the French Revolution to other lands and to liberate Europe from tyrant kings: "Let us say to them that ten million Frenchmen, kindled by the fire of liberty, armed with the sword, with reason, with eloquence, would be able, if incensed, to change the face of the world and make the tyrants tremble on their thrones."

Some military leaders also wanted war, but for different reasons from those of the Girondins. They believed that a war would strengthen the army and enable it to save the king and keep the radicals in line.

THE SECOND FRENCH REVOLUTION

The Revolution enters a radical stage. On April 20, 1792, the Legislative Assembly declared France at war with Austria. Soon after Prussia hurried to the support of Austria, France was invaded. At first, the war went badly for France. Then the Duke of Brunswick, Commander-in-Chief of the invading army, demanded that the French restore Louis XVI's power and threatened Paris with destruction if the king were harmed. Enraged by this threat, on August 10, 1792, the Parisians took their anger out on Louis XVI. They attacked the king's palace in Paris and killed hundreds of his palace troops and servants. Six weeks later the king lost his throne and France became a republic. Accused of encouraging foreign troops to invade France, Louis XVI was executed as a traitor on January 21, 1793. The attack upon the king's palace in August, the massacre of supporters of the king and others by a Parisian mob in September, the establishment of a republic, and the execution of the king were signs that the Revolution had moved from a moderate into a radical stage. Some historians refer to this period as the Second French Revolution.

European kings fear the French Revolution. European kings and aristocrats were alarmed by developments in France. If the king of France could be killed by his subjects, no ruler was safe. What would happen if the ideas of the French Revolution spread to their own countries? Republican France's power was increasing steadily. Already her army had forced the invading Austrians and Prussians to retreat and had conquered the Austrian Netherlands. Moreover, the Republican government was offering to assist other peoples in overthrowing absolutism and ending the special privileges of the nobility and clergy. The kings of Europe responded to this challenge to their thrones and lives by joining forces. Britain, Holland, Spain, Sardinia, and the German states joined Austria and Prussia in the war against the French revolutionaries.

Enemies at home and abroad seek to destroy the Republic. In 1793 the infant French Republic was threatened on all sides. A leading general had deserted to the enemy, and many officers had turned out to be poor leaders in battle. Troops short of arms, food, and clothing suffered several defeats by the combined enemy forces.

In France itself conditions were becoming desperate. The value of the money issued by the government dropped as food prices soared. Widespread hunger caused the desperate people of Paris to riot and loot food stores. The National Convention, which had replaced the Legislative Assembly, was torn by disputes. Moreover, not all Frenchmen supported the Republic. Deeply religious peasants objected to the restrictions the Civil Constitution of the

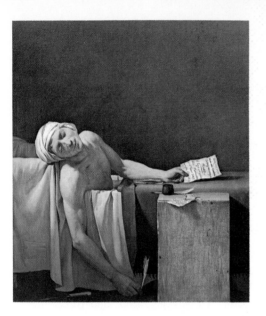

Horrified by the excesses of the Terror, Charlotte Corday assassinated Jacobin leader Jean Paul Marat. Many artists have re-interpreted this act. Jacques-Louis David, Marat's contemporary, presented a classical version (left), while the recent play Marat-Sade *(above) gives a different view.*

Clergy placed on the Church. Peasants hated the new laws that forced all unmarried men to serve in the army. Few were interested in spreading revolutionary reforms to all Europe. Backed by aristocrats plotting to overthrow the government, peasants took up arms against the Republic. The Republican forces were thus caught between invading armies and revolts by people hostile to the Republic.

Radical leaders take over. Radical leaders came forward to rescue the tottering Republic. By June, 1793, the *Jacobins* had replaced the Girondins as the dominant group in the Convention. Whereas the less radical Girondins had considerable support in the provinces, the Jacobins had the backing of the people of Paris. The Girondins favored a government in which the different provinces would have considerable control over their own affairs, while the Jacobins wanted a strong central government with Paris as the center of power. Whereas the Girondins opposed government interference with business, the Jacobins were willing to support temporary government controls to deal with the economic crisis. This last point was crucial; it won the Jacobins the support of the sans-culottes.

Both the Girondins and the Jacobins came from the bourgeoisie, but the Jacobins were more willing to listen to the economic and political demands of the poor people of Paris. While the Girondins distrusted the common people and sought to further the interests of wealthy shipowners, bankers, and merchants, the Jacobins hoped to rally the common people to defend the Revolution against foreign and domestic enemies. The Jacobins had a further advantage in that they were tightly organized, well disciplined, completely devoted to the ideals of the Revolution, and convinced that only they could save the Republic from being overrun by its enemies. On June 2, 1793, some 80,000 armed sans-culottes surrounded the Convention and demanded the arrest of a number of Girondin delegates. The act enabled the Jacobins to gain control of the Convention.

The Parisians' faith in the Jacobins was not misplaced. The Jacobins not only passed laws controlling the price and supply of bread and other essential goods. They also tried to make it easier for the common people to buy the confiscated Church lands. The Jacobins drew up "the first genuinely democratic constitution proclaimed by a modern state." It gave all men the right to vote and the right to work. It maintained that the purpose of government was to protect the welfare and rights of all men. This constitution of 1793–1794 was never put into effect. The Jacobins also outlawed slavery in the French colonies, though this decree could not be enforced.

The aroused French defeat their foreign enemies. To ensure greater unity in the government, the Jacobins established the Committee of Public Safety. It sent deputies with wide powers to the provinces to oversee the organization for defense. The Committee of Public Safety united the French into a people with a single purpose—to drive out the foreign invaders. The whole nation was called to serve. Young men went to battle. Women worked in hospitals and children collected clothing. The elderly were expected to give speeches that would arouse the courage of the troops and further the unity of the Republic. Love for France replaced personal ambitions. Each citizen felt he played a part in France's undertaking. This organization of all the resources of the nation toward a common end resulted in a loyal and highly effective army. Soldiers marched off to war singing the thundering words of the "Marseillaise" (mar-seh-*yayz'*), the anthem of the Revolution:

> Arise, sons of the motherland,
> The day of glory has arrived! . . .
> To arms, citizens! . . .
> March on, march on!

It was an army in which officers were chosen on the basis of merit, not birth, and everyone was addressed as citizen. Inspired by love for France and by the ideas of "liberty, equality, and fraternity," the soldiers of the Republic threw back the enemy.[4]

THE REIGN OF TERROR

Robespierre calls for a new society. At the same time that the Jacobins were forging a

[4] Since Prussia and Austria had long been enemies, their effort to join forces against France was only half-hearted.

revolutionary army to resist the foreign invaders, French society was undergoing violent upheavals. The outstanding figure during this period was Maximilien de Robespierre (mak-see-me-*lyun'* deh roh-behs-*pyair'*), a leading Jacobin and the most prominent member of the Committee of Public Safety. Robespierre did not look like a leader. He was short, thin, and had a weak voice. But he did have complete confidence in himself and was certain that everything he did was right and for the good of France.

Robespierre hated the Old Regime and sympathized with those who had suffered under it. He wanted to create a new and better society based on reason and good citizenship. In this society all men would be free, equal, and educated. There would be no luxury, greed, or vice. The poor would be aided by social reforms.

Every law which violates the inalienable rights of man is essentially unjust and tyrannical; it is not a law at all. . . .

The right of property is limited, as are all other rights, by the obligation to respect the rights of others. . . .

Society . . . must place education within reach of all citizens. . . .

. . . the most important of [man's] duties are: to detest bad faith and despotism, to punish tyrants and traitors, to assist the unfortunate, to respect the weak, to defend the oppressed, to do all the good one can to one's neighbor, and to behave with justice towards all men.

Robespierre pursued his ideal society with the zeal of a religious fanatic. He knew that such a society could not be established while the Republic was threatened with foreign enemies and traitors. "Whoever [may] make war on a people in order to check the progress of liberty and [destroy] the rights of man must be prosecuted by all, not as ordinary enemies, but as rebels, brigands, and assassins."

The radicals introduce a Reign of Terror. Because the radicals believed that the foes of the

Revolution should be executed, they instituted a Reign of Terror. A new criminal court was created to try anyone denounced by a citizen or by the court itself. To be seized for trial indicated guilt in the eyes of the court, and trials were a mockery of justice. Conviction usually brought the accused, many of them innocent of any crime, to the guillotine. Some 20,000 (some say as many as 40,000) men, women, and children were killed in this terrible bloodbath. In the cities and in the countryside radicals used mass executions to destroy real or imagined enemies. Although Robespierre opposed mass executions in the provinces, he was powerless to stop them.

The Reign of Terror was a period of mass madness. Every day carts arrived at the prisons to carry victims to the guillotine. These carts, loaded with the condemned and guarded by soldiers, rolled through the streets to the square where the guillotine was set up. A twentieth-century historian describes what followed:

On one side of the scaffold were a large number of carts bearing huge baskets painted red, these being . . . for the heads and bodies. The condemned mounted the scaffold and were strapped to a . . . plank. . . . The blade [of the guillotine] fell; two men tossed the body into a basket, while another performed the same service for the head. If, however, the [head] had happened to belong to a person of note, [the executioners] held it up . . . [and the] spectators would cry *"Vive la République!"*. . . The remains were then taken away to the cemetery . . . and cast into deep graves.

Huge crowds watched these executions, shouting insults at the victims. When a famous person was to be guillotined, men and women took a holiday to be among those present. People were gripped by a lust for blood. Some women wore silver and gold guillotines as pins and combs, and children played with toy guillotines.

As a leading and powerful Jacobin, Robespierre had become the most feared man in France. To most people, he *was* the Reign of Terror. Robespierre did not approve executions because he was bloodthirsty or power-

mad. In fact, as a member of the National Assembly, he had opposed capital punishment. Doubtless he sincerely believed that the executions were necessary to protect France and save the Revolution. His love of France and liberty and his desire to benefit mankind turned him into an executioner.

In time even the radicals came to realize they had gone too far. Not even Robespierre's fellow leaders were safe from suspicion, trial, and death. Moreover, victory on the battlefield had reduced the need for the Terror. Feeling the cold chill of the guillotine blade at their throats, Robespierre's associates ordered his execution and that of about a hundred of his supporters in the Jacobin Club. The sans-culottes, who had originally supported Robespierre in hopes that he would relieve their poverty, made no attempt to save his life. Apparently they felt that he had not done enough to aid the poor.

Was the Terror necessary? Why, it has been asked, did the Jacobins resort to a policy of crushing political opponents and executing those whom they thought to be enemies of the Republic? Some historians regard the Terror as a way of dealing with the serious problems confronting the Republic. In order to save the Revolution, the Jacobins felt compelled to use the extreme methods of the Terror. Therefore, say some historians, the Jacobins were not bloodthirsty fanatics but responsible leaders forced by difficult circumstances to use harsh measures.

Though the Reign of Terror was cruel, it did save the Revolution. Aristocrats who plotted to restore the Old Regime were guillotined. The peasant uprisings were crushed. No longer faced with rebellion, the French were able to throw back the invading foreigners. British historian E. J. Hobsbaum sums up the achievements of the Jacobin Republic:

In June, 1793, sixty out of the eighty departments of France were in revolt against Paris; the armies of the German princes were invading France from

In revolutionary France, execution was a public event attended by jeering crowds. After the condemned were beheaded, their heads were displayed and the bodies were carted away. This print shows the execution of Robespierre and his fellow partisans.

the north and east; the British attacked from the south and west; the country was helpless and bankrupt. Fourteen months later all France was under firm control, the invaders had been expelled, the French armies in turn occupied Belgium and were about to enter on twenty years of almost unbroken and effortless military triumph. Yet by March, 1794, an army three times as large as before was run at half the cost of March, 1793, and the value of the French currency . . . was kept approximately stable, in marked contrast to both past and future.

Nevertheless, many consider the Reign of Terror the low point of the French Revolution. They feel that its accomplishments were far outweighed by the suffering and loss of lives. They regard Robespierre as a fanatic who killed people in the name of a "just cause," as a means of improving society. Like all fanatics, Robespierre was convinced that he knew the right way, that the new society he wanted to create would benefit humanity, and that those who disagreed with him were traitors and sinners who had to be crushed for the good of the people.

MODERATES REGAIN CONTROL

Moderates return to power. By 1795 the moderate bourgeoisie were back in power. They wanted no more of the Jacobins or of Robespierre's society. They had good reasons for their feelings. (1) Robespierre's new society would have given the common people a considerable voice in the government. (2) Robespierre had believed that the government should try to improve the living conditions of the common people. (3) Included among the victims of the Terror had been not only reactionary nobles and rebellious peasants but moderate bourgeoisie.

The moderate bourgeoisie had never intended to establish a democracy in France. In 1789 they had wanted to end the absolute rule of the king and the feudal privileges of the aristocracy. They had wanted a constitutional government in which they could play a major role, but did not object to a king with limited powers. Just as the aristocracy looked down upon the bourgeoisie, so did the bourgeoisie scorn the common people. They believed that the masses had to be kept in line and were unfit to govern.

461

The Directory is inefficient. From 1795 to 1799 France was governed by a committee of five men called the *Directory*. The directors were weak, inefficient, and dishonest. France was still at war and even deeper in debt. Industry and trade were suffering. There was suffering and unrest among the poor people of Paris. Aristocrats who wanted to have a king again tried to overthrow the bourgeois republic. The rebellion was crushed with the assistance of a young army officer named Napoleon Bonaparte. As the government grew weaker, power began to pass into the hands of the generals. In November, 1799, one of the generals, Napoleon Bonaparte, overthrew the government he had earlier saved. In the new government Napoleon had most of the power. France had returned to absolute rule.

CHECK-UP

1. By 1791, what groups thought the Revolution had gone too far? Not far enough? Just far enough? Why?
2. Why did the royal family attempt to escape from Paris? What was the result? Why was Louis XVI willing to see foreign powers invade France?
3. Who were the Girondins? Why did they want war?
4. Why did the Revolution move from a moderate to a radical stage? Why did the rulers of other countries fear the French Revolution? What was the result?
5. How did the Jacobins come to power? Why did they institute the Reign of Terror? How did Robespierre justify it?
6. Why did the moderates oppose the Jacobins? What kind of government did they establish?

Results of the French Revolution

The French Revolution destroyed the Old Regime in France. Its influence was felt throughout Europe and the world. What were the results of the French Revolution?

1. The French Revolution furthered the cause of liberty. The French Revolution advanced the cause of liberty. The people of France gained a written constitution guaranteeing the peoples' right to freedom of speech, press, and religion. A fairer system of justice was established and local government was made more efficient. Although civil rights were often denied, the fact that they were put in writing marked a great advance in the struggle for liberty. In time, all peoples in Europe and in other continents were to demand the same rights.

2. The Church was weakened. The power of the Church declined. It had lost the right to tax the people. Much of its land was taken over by the state and sold to farmers. Since the Roman Catholic Church no longer was the only church approved by the state, other religious groups gained more freedom.

3. Aristocrats lost their privileges. The aristocrats lost the special privileges they had enjoyed under the Old Regime. They no longer could collect feudal dues from peasants. They had to pay taxes like everyone else. Most of their estates had been seized by the state and the land sold to the richer peasants and the middle class.

4. Absolute monarchy declined. The execution of Louis XVI marked the end of absolute monarchy in France. It eventually served to reduce the power of other European rulers. The peoples of Europe now realized that kings could be overthrown. Throughout Europe, reformers wanted to replace absolute rulers with more representative government and written constitutions. In time they succeeded.

5. The bourgeoisie became the new leaders of France. The bourgeoisie had become the most important class in France. They had wealth and education. The most honored positions in government and the army were now open to them. Talent and ambition—two traits with which the bourgeoisie were well endowed—counted more than noble birth. The equality demanded by the bourgeoisie before the Revolution had been achieved.

6. The French Revolution introduced modern warfare. The French Revolution introduced warfare on a large scale. Wars no longer were fought by hired soldiers but by the whole population of a country—the "nation in arms." They were starting to become life-and-death struggles in which all the people of the nation took part.

7. *The French Revolution gave birth to modern nationalism.* The French Revolution marks the beginning of modern nationalism (deep love of one's country). Frenchmen fought not for a king but for their nation. Defending France became a Frenchman's highest duty; conquering other lands for her became a noble mission. In time this intense love of one's nation spread throughout Europe and to other continents.

Chapter Highlights

Can you explain?

aristocrats	radicals	"nation-in-arms"	reactionaries
bourgeoisie	Estates	moderates	*sans-culottes*

Can you identify?

Bastille	October Days	National Convention	Civil Constitution of the Clergy
Directory	Legislative Assembly	Reign of Terror	Committee of Public Safety
Girondins	Marie Antoinette	States-General	
Jacobins	National Assembly	*Declaration of the Rights of Man*	Great Fear
Louis XVI	Old Regime		

What do you think?

1. One of the major abuses of the Old Regime was special privileges. Why? Are there privileged classes today? Explain.

2. Were there differences within each Estate? Explain.

3. Why was there deep and long-standing hostility between the bourgeoisie and the aristocracy?

4. Why is July 14 the French national holiday?

5. Could the Old Regime have been changed by peaceful reforms instead of violent revolution?

6. Why did the French become involved in a foreign war in 1792?

7. Why can the French Revolution be called a power struggle on many levels?

8. Why has the *Declaration of the Rights of Man* been called the "death certificate of the Old Regime"? Are the ideals of this document still cherished?

9. Did the reforms of the National Assembly eliminate the abuses of the Old Regime? Explain.

10. What were the causes of the Reign of Terror? In what sense did it save the Revolution? Do you think it was justified? Why?

11. How did the Revolution change traditional relationships between Church and state?

12. The end of the French Revolution not only brought about a new France but also vastly affected the rest of the world. How?

BONAPARTE

ANNIBAL

KAROLVS MAGNVS

The Enlightenment interest in reason led French artists to turn to ancient Greece and particularly Rome for inspiration. Jacques Louis David, a leader in the Neoclassic movement, dramatically portrayed Napoleon (left) in the Roman tradition of honoring military leaders. The French occupation of Egypt led decorators to combine Egyptian themes, such as the sphinx above, with Neoclassic designs.

The Napoleonic Era

In November, 1799, Napoleon Bonaparte, a young and popular general, overthrew the government and became ruler of France. During the next fifteen years Napoleon was the most important man in France and perhaps the world. He inspired hundreds of thousands of soldiers to fight for France—and thousands died for him. He won great battles and conquered a good part of Europe. Most Frenchmen saw Napoleon as a great leader who brought glory to France.

What kind of man was Napoleon? How did he rise to power? How did he make history?

Young Napoleon prepares for leadership. Born on the island of Corsica on August 15, 1769, Napoleon Bonaparte showed an independent spirit and strong will from an early age. Of his childhood, he said: "Nothing [frightened] me; I feared no one. I struck one, I scratched another. I was a terror to everybody." After finishing military school in France, Napoleon became an artillery officer and in the early wars of the French Revolution proved himself a good soldier. A fellow officer said that Bonaparte had "plenty of talent, an unusual [amount] of courage, [and] tireless" energy. In battle, "I always find him at his post. If he needed a moment's rest, he took it on the ground wrapped in his cloak." Because of his skill as an artillery officer, Bonaparte was noticed by the leaders of the Revolution and was promoted to the rank of general when he was only 25 years old.

Napoleon was brave, intelligent, ambitious— but little known. He needed a chance to make a name for himself. He did not have to wait long. In October, 1795, Napoleon was in command of the troops who broke up a rebellion led by aristocrats who wanted to overthrow the Republic and restore a king to France. A few months later the ambitious young general was given command of the French army that was to invade Italy. His star was rising.

General Bonaparte wins battles. In Italy Napoleon showed great talent for military planning and leadership. He aroused the fighting spirit of the soldiers under his command by praising their courage and promising them "honor, glory, and riches." By fighting alongside his men and sharing their difficulties, he won their loyalty and respect. He knew how to inspire his troops:

You have won battles without cannon, crossed rivers without bridges, made forced marches without shoes, camped . . . often without bread. . . . Soldiers, . . . you have our thanks!

. . . you still have battles to fight, cities to capture, rivers to cross. Is there one among you whose courage is [weak]? . . . No . . . All of you are [filled] with a desire to extend the glory of the French people; . . . all of you wish to be able to say with pride as you return to your villages, "I was with the victorious Army of Italy!"

Napoleon becomes a popular hero. Napoleon won great victories in Italy. This made him the most popular general in France. Shopkeepers displayed his picture in their windows. Proud Frenchmen compared him with Julius Caesar and Alexander the Great. He was the man of the hour. Most men would have been satisfied to have won such fame.

But Napoleon was no ordinary man. He sensed that he was headed for greatness: "[In Italy] I realized I was a superior being and conceived the ambition of performing great things." Napoleon was not content to be a general; he wished to rule France. The opportunity soon came for him to fulfill his dreams.

France needs a leader. After his victories in Italy, Napoleon was given command of a French army that was preparing to invade England. Realizing that he had insufficient forces for such a major compaign, Napoleon suggested instead an attack upon Egypt. If France could gain a foothold in the Near East, she might be in a position to threaten India, Britain's most valuable possession.

For a while Napoleon was as successful in Egypt as he had been in Italy. Elsewhere, however, things were not going well for France. Ten years of revolution and war had exhausted the

French people. Roads and bridges needed repair. The government was known to be corrupt and was opposed by many reactionaries as well as radicals. Britain and Russia were organizing a new alliance to attack France. Patriotic Frenchmen cried out for a leader to save the country. Napoleon saw his opportunity. Sailing across the Mediterranean, he landed in France on October 8, 1799. He told the French people that he had come to save the nation.

Napoleon hoped that France's leaders would turn to him as the only man who could rescue the country from misfortune. After all, he had a reputation as a brilliant general and his popularity with the French people was undeniable. But it immediately became clear that power would not be handed over to him willingly. Napoleon therefore prepared to seize it by force. At this point a group of influential politicians who also sought to overthrow the government approached Napoleon and invited him to join them. As soon as he accepted, the conspirators prepared for a *coup d'état* (koo-day-tah′)—a quick seizure of power.

The Directory is overthrown. To hasten the end of the government, on November 10 Napoleon appeared before the two lawmaking bodies of France, the Council of Elders and the Council of Five Hundred. The lawmakers, however, were hostile to Napoleon, fearing that he aimed for absolute rule. The great general who had been able to inspire courage in his soldiers could make no impression on the members of the Council of Elders. Before he could address the Council of Five Hundred, deputies climbed onto their seats shouting, "Down with the tyrant! Down with the dictator! Outlaw him." Some deputies rushed at the general and tried to strike him. White with rage, his pride wounded, Napoleon had to be helped from the room by a squad of soldiers.

Once outside, Napoleon mounted his horse and asked his troops to help him oust the lawmakers. "Kill anyone who resists!" shouted Napoleon. "Follow me! I am the god of bat-

The Napoleonic Era

1769	Birth of Napoleon
1799	Napoleon becomes First Consul
1801	Napoleon makes Concordat with Pope
1804	Napoleon becomes Emperor of the French
1805–1812	Napoleon gains control of much of Europe
1806	Continental System established
1808	French troops invade Spain
1812	Grand Army invades Russia
1813	Allied troops defeat Napoleon's forces at Leipzig
1814	Napoleon exiled to Elba; Bourbon dynasty restored in France
1815	Napoleon returns, is defeated at Battle of Waterloo, and is exiled to St. Helena
1821	Death of Napoleon

tles." The soldiers hesitated. Napoleon's brother Lucien (luh-*syun′*) then made a dramatic move. Seizing a sword, he pointed it at Napoleon's heart and cried: "I swear that I will run my brother through should he . . . threaten the liberties of France." With bayonets fixed, the soldiers marched into the council hall, and the deputies fled. The Directory, which had governed France since late 1795, was overthrown.

CHECK-UP

1. What qualities did Napoleon have that marked him for leadership? That won him the loyalty and respect of his soldiers?

2. What conditions in France made it possible for Napoleon to come to power?

The men who had overthrown the Directory established a *provisional* (temporary) government. By the end of the year it was replaced by the Consulate. Napoleon was First Consul, the official title for the head of the French government. Two other consuls were to aid him as advisors. But Napoleon kept the real power for himself. "I . . . love power," he once said. "I love it as a musician loves his violin."

Napoleon becomes Emperor of the French. The pretense of divided rule through the Consulate did not last long. In 1802 the French people voted overwhelmingly in favor of making Napoleon consul for life. They also voted him the right to name his successor. Thus what had been a dictatorship became in effect a monarchy. On December 2, 1804, a magnificent ceremony took place in the cathedral of Notre Dame in Paris. While the organ played, the splendidly robed Napoleon led his wife Josephine to the altar. He approached the Pope, who sat holding the crown of France. The congregation, consisting of high dignitaries, waited for Napoleon to kneel before the head of the Church. As the Pope raised his hands to place the crown on Napoleon's head, Napoleon took it and crowned himself Emperor of the French. This showed all the world that he, Napoleon, was a self-made emperor. General, First Consul, and now Emperor—it was a breathless climb to the heights of power!

Napoleon brings about important reforms. Napoleon wanted to win the respect and support of the French people. To do this, he knew that the reforms introduced during the French Revolution must be preserved and that the problems facing France must be solved. As First Consul and as Emperor he introduced some effective reforms.

1. The Code Napoléon. During the early years of the Revolution, a committee had been set up to draw up a code of laws for all France. Napoleon appointed a staff of lawyers to complete the task. The finished code, still in use in France today, carries his name. The Civil Code, the *Code Napoléon* (nuh-poh-lay-*ohn'*), reflected many of the ideals of the philosophes and the French Revolution. For example, it guaranteed *equality:* no matter what their wealth or birth, the law regarded all Frenchmen as equals. The Code ensured certain *freedoms:* it allowed Frenchmen to practice the religion of their choice, and it protected property rights, including the small holdings of peasants. The Code also contained some harsh provisions. It greatly increased the power of the father, and treated women as inferior to men and workers as inferior to employers.

2. Agreement with the Church. Napoleon was not a religious man, but he knew that religion could be used to increase his power. Many Frenchmen were devout Catholics. To keep them loyal to the government, Napoleon realized he must show them that the government respected the Catholic Church and was on good terms with it. During the Revolution the French government had dealt harshly with the Catholic Church (see page 454). To end the quarrel between the government and the Church, in 1801 Napoleon reached an agreement with the Pope. While the government continued to pay clergymen's salaries and to appoint members of the clergy, the Pope had the right to confirm or refuse these appointments. For its part, the Church gave up its claims to the land seized from it during the French Revolution. While this pact did not restore the Church's earlier power, it did improve relations between the Church and the French government.

3. University of France. Napoleon well knew the importance of education. France needed trained officers to lead her armies and capable officials to carry out her laws. To educate citizens to serve the needs of the state, Napoleon established the University of France in 1808. In time this university became something like a board of education for the entire nation. It established a course of study for all French school children and supervised schools and colleges.

4. Napoleon tries to please all Frenchmen. Napoleon tried to satisfy all classes of the people. To please the peasants, he allowed them to keep the land that they had gained during the Revolution. To please businessmen, he promoted trade and industry, established tariffs which protected French businesses from foreign competition, and founded the Bank of France. He also favored businessmen by forbidding workers to strike. On the other hand, Napoleon's encouragement of trade gave workers more sources of employment in jobs repairing roads, clearing harbors, draining swamps, and building canals. Fearing a revolution "based on lack of bread," Napoleon made food available at low prices. Napoleon's policies won him the support of all the French people. Except for the diehards, even the aristocrats, whose old privileges were not restored under Napoleon, tended to find places in the Empire.

Napoleon allows no opposition. Napoleon lived in an age of revolution. He had seen governments overthrown and heads of state executed. He had seen the people turn against leaders they had once applauded. To prevent this happening to him, Napoleon kept a close watch on events and tried to control public opinion. His agents spied on suspected persons and brought him reports of what people thought, said, and did. Newspapers, books, and plays were censored.

Napoleon used the schools to strengthen his power. The government decided what books students would read. Napoleon expected teachers to teach their students state-approved ideas. Children were taught to honor the Emperor Napoleon. Just as their parents and grandparents had been taught to honor the Bourbon kings, children of Napoleon's time were ex-

David was court painter to Louis XVI and to Napoleon. The grandeur he portrayed in painting Napoleon's coronation would have pleased a Roman emperor.

pected to memorize the following questions and answers:*

Q. What are the duties of Christians with respect to the princes who govern them, and what in particular are our duties towards Napoleon I, our Emperor?

* From *The Constitutions and Other Select Documents Illustrative of the History of France 1879–1907,* edited by Frank Maloy Anderson (Minneapolis, Minn.: The H. W. Wilson Company, 1908). Reprinted by permission of Dr. Gaylord W. Anderson.

A. Christians owe to the princes who govern them, and we owe in particular to Napoleon I, our Emperor, *love, respect, obedience, [loyalty], military service;* . . . we also owe to him . . . prayers for his safety. . . .

Q. Why are we bound to all these duties towards our Emperor?

A. First of all, because God, who creates empires and distributes them according to his will, in loading our Emperor with gifts, both in peace and in war, has established him as our [ruler]. . . . *To honor and to serve our Emperor is then to honor and to serve God himself.* . . .

Q. What . . . of those who may be lacking in their duty towards our Emperor?

A. . . . they would be resisting the order [set] by God himself and would make themselves *worthy of eternal damnation.*

CHECK-UP

1. How did France move from the Consulate to an empire? Why did Napoleon crown himself?

2. Why did Napoleon introduce a new code of laws? Make peace with the Church? Strengthen education?

3. What steps taken by Napoleon won the support of the peasants? Businessmen? Workers?

4. How did Napoleon control public information and opinion? Why? How did he use the schools to strengthen his power? Why?

The Overthrow of Napoleon

Napoleon is overthrown. Napoleon's victories, which had brought glory to France, made him popular. But he was wise enough to realize that military defeat could well turn the French people against him. "Conquest has made me what I am and conquest alone can maintain me [in power]," he said. He wanted to control all of Europe. He almost succeeded.

Between 1805 and 1807, Napoleon won stunning victories over the armies of Austria, Prussia, and Russia. By 1812 he was master of most of the European continent west of Russia. His battle-tested, loyal soldiers, the best in Europe, would die for him. He had won brilliant victories and had driven rulers from their thrones. To reward relatives and able generals, he had made them rulers of kingdoms. People began to call Napoleon the greatest conqueror in history. All Europe trembled before his might.

But although Napoleon seemed invincible, he was nearing the end of his glorious adventure. By 1815, he had lost great battles and had seen thousands of troops destroyed. His empire was gone, and Napoleon himself was a prisoner of the British. What were the reasons for his downfall?

1. Unlimited ambition: Napoleon reaches too far. Perhaps the most important reason for Napoleon's downfall was his *limitless ambition.* He wanted to be a greater general than Alexander, to rule an empire greater than the Roman Empire. But France had neither the men nor the resources to carry out his dreams.

2. The Continental System: Napoleon hopes to bankrupt England. Napoleon had led his armies to victory on the continent. But he could not gain complete control of Europe without defeating Great Britain. The British regarded any nation which controlled the Netherlands as a threat to their security. Since Republican France's conquest of the Austrian Netherlands in 1793, Britain had tried to undermine France's power. She spent great amounts of money to keep the armies of her continental allies in the field. British warships seized French merchant vessels and kept neutral ships from reaching French ports.

An angered Napoleon decided to crush this island nation which caused him so much

KEY

French Empire

States under Napoleon's control

States allied with Napoleon

Independent States

Napoleon's Empire at its Height (1812)

trouble. But how? To land troops in England, he first would have to defeat the British navy. In 1805, at the Battle of Trafalgar (truh-*fal'*-ger) off the southern coast of Spain, the British fleet, commanded by Lord Nelson, had defeated the combined French and Spanish fleets. Though half of Napoleon's ships were destroyed, not one British ship was lost. After Trafalgar, not even Napoleon questioned Britain's mastery of the seas.

Napoleon decided to defeat Britain without invading England. He planned to prevent Brit-

ain from selling goods of any kind in Europe. Therefore he ordered all countries under France's control not to import British products. Napoleon hoped that this *Continental System* would ruin Britain. A ruined Britain would be unable to carry on the struggle against France. It seemed a shrewd plan.

But the Continental System turned out to be a great blunder. The people of Europe needed British goods. Moreover, the System

The Spanish painter Francisco Goya captured the agonies of war for all time in paintings and etchings inspired by the French invasion of his country and the patriotic resistance of the Spanish people to aggression. Goya made no attempt to romanticize war. His work reveals the terrible brutality of which man can be capable. Above, French troops execute Spanish rebels.

failed to destroy British trade. British merchants increased their exports to the New World and smuggled goods into Europe. The Continental System not only failed to crush Britain, but it made more enemies for Napoleon. It hurt European businessmen, including Frenchmen, more than it hurt the British.

3. Nationalism: conquered people rise up against Napoleon. When Napoleon's armies first marched through Europe, they were often greeted with enthusiasm. Most people looked upon Napoleon as a liberator. They believed that he had come to carry out the slogan of the French Revolution—"liberty, equality, and fraternity." They hoped French conquest would free them from selfish rulers and unjust laws. Napoleon himself tried to strengthen this belief.

As early as 1796, when he was still a general commanding the Army of Italy, Napoleon had told the Italians:

Peoples of Italy, the French army comes to break your chains; the French people is the friend of all peoples; approach it with confidence; your property, your religion, and your customs will be respected.

We are waging war as generous enemies, and we wish to crush the tyrants who enslave you.

But, although Napoleon talked about liberty, his rule of conquered peoples denied his words. His policy of "France First" soon made Napoleon the most hated man in Europe. The treasure of conquered lands was seized and sent to France. Nations controlled by Napoleon had to supply men and money for the emperor's army. They were ordered to send raw materials to France to build up her industries. Napoleon's opponents were executed. Moreover, the French occupation brought a spirit of nationalism as well as a desire for liberty to peoples Napoleon conquered. They had no desire to be ruled by France.

In 1808 Spain was invaded by 100,000 French troops. The incompetent king was forced to abdicate and Napoleon put his brother Joseph on the Spanish throne. Immediately the Spanish people showed their resentment of the invaders. Small groups of Spaniards began to carry on a hit-and-run war against the French. The French troops, trained for normal warfare and hampered by the rugged Spanish terrain, did not know how to cope with this *guerrilla* warfare. The patriotic guerrillas were encouraged by a Spanish clergy enraged at Napoleonic reforms that weakened the Church. They were also greatly aided by British troops commanded by the Duke of Wellington. Though it took five years of seesaw battles, their combined forces finally succeeded in driving the French out of Spain.

Anti-French feeling also broke out in the German states. Some German university professors, writers, and Prussian officials called for an uprising of the German people against the French occupation. They urged the creation of a unified Germany. Other than this handful of intellectuals, however, few Germans were aroused by a desire for unification. Nor did there occur anything like the general uprising that took place in Spain. Though German nationalism was born during the Napoleonic Wars, it was still in its infancy. Nevertheless, the Napoleonic Wars mark the first faint stirrings of German nationalism.

In the German state of Prussia reformers strengthened the army in preparation for a future war against the French invaders. Cruel punishments that weakened the morale of soldiers were abolished. Men who showed ability were allowed to become officers even if they were not of noble birth. Soldiers were urged to fight not for pay or because their officers forced them but because it was their patriotic duty. Prussia had learned from the French experience. She too would become a nation in arms by arousing deep feelings of patriotism. In 1813 an influential group of Prussian patriots forced the king of Prussia to declare war on France. The Prussian people showed a far greater patriotism than they had in 1806 when Napoelon had inflicted a humiliating defeat on Prussia at the Battle of Jena (*yay'*nah). At the Battle of Leipzig (*liep'*sihg) in 1813 the combined armies of Austria, Russia, and Prussia defeated Napoleon. Most of Germany was liberated from French domination. The spirit of nationalism that was born in the French Revolution had spread to other countries and helped bring about Napoleon's downfall.

4. The Moscow Campaign: Napoleon marches to disaster. Relations between France and Russia in 1812 were strained. Tsar Alexander I ignored the Continental System and Napoleon feared Russia would make an alliance with Britain. Napoleon therefore decided to bring Russia into line. Although he was aware of the huge size of Russia, the harsh climate, and the determination of the Russian people, Napoleon thought that an invasion of overwhelming force would compel Russia to surrender. In the spring of 1812 he ordered his Grand Army of nearly half a million men to march on Russia. Though Napoleon realized the difficulty of keeping his troops supplied, he thought he would have the aid of the Poles ruled by Russia. This would give him a source of supplies closer to the front line. But the Poles showed little eagerness for French rule. The problem of supplying the Grand Army was thus acute before Napoleon even entered Russia.

After crossing into Russia, the Grand Army fought and won bloody battles. When it reached the outskirts of Moscow in September, Napoleon was overjoyed. "March on, let us open the gates of Moscow!" he shouted. He expected to be greeted by some of the Russian officials. But the troops marched into a silent, nearly deserted city. What had happened? The Russians had abandoned Moscow. Late that night a great fire spread throughout the city. It raged for five days. The Russians were deliberately destroying their city! Napoleon's capture of a burned-out and nearly deserted city was an empty victory.

October came. Food became increasingly scarce. Realizing that his army could not survive a Russian winter, Napoleon ordered a retreat. Of the original Grand Army only about 100,000 soldiers remained. On October 19, 1812, they began the long march westward.

The retreat turned into a disaster. There was little food, and not enough warm clothing. No order was maintained among the troops. Russian peasants and Cossacks, skilled horsemen from Russia's southern frontier plains, attacked stragglers. The temperature fell to 30° below zero. "The road is littered with men frozen to death," wrote one of Napoleon's generals. "The soldiers throw away their guns because they cannot hold them; both officers and soldiers think only of protecting themselves from the terrible cold." Fewer than 40,000 soldiers survived this retreat.

The emperor had lost his army. Now he would lose his throne.

Napoleon loses his throne. After the Russian disaster, nearly all the nations of Europe joined forces to crush Napoleon. In October, 1813, the French armies suffered a great defeat at Leipzig, Germany. Six months later, the victorious allies were in Paris. Napoleon lost his throne. Louis XVIII, younger brother of the executed Louis XVI, was crowned King of France.[1] Napoleon was exiled to the small island of Elba, which lies off the coast of Italy. He was only 44 years old.

Napoleon returns. Napoleon did not believe he was meant to die on this tiny island. He longed for the excitement of battle, the cheers of his soldiers, and the glory of victory. "All France . . . wants me," he said.

On March 1, 1815, Napoleon landed on the French coast with a thousand soldiers. King Louis XVIII ordered his troops to stop Napoleon's advance. When Napoleon's small force

[1] Prince Louis, son of the executed Louis XVI, never lived to reign as Louis XVII. Imprisoned during the Revolution, he died at age ten from neglect and abuse.

approached the King's troops, Napoleon walked up to the soldiers who blocked the road. "If there is one soldier among you who wishes to kill his Emperor, here I am." It was a brilliant move by a man who thoroughly understood the French soldier. The King's troops shouted, "Long live the Emperor!" and joined Napoleon. On March 20, 1815, Napoleon entered Paris to a hero's welcome. Although he had lost his throne, to the French people he remained their emperor.

Napoleon's return led France back into war. Though Napoleon had been defeated once, the memory of his past victories kept the nations of Europe fearful. A second time they united against the French armies. In June, 1815, the opposing forces met at Waterloo in Belgium. Napoleon's soldiers were decisively defeated by troops led by the Duke of Wellington of Britain and Field Marshal Gebhard von Blucher (*bloo'*ker) of Prussia. This time the European allies took no chances. They sent Napoleon to St. Helena, a lonely island in the South Atlantic a thousand miles off the coast of South Africa. On this gloomy and rugged rock, Napoleon Bonaparte, Emperor of the French and would-be conqueror of Europe, spent the last six years of his life.

CHECK-UP

1. What goals did Napoleon seek through conquest?

2. What was the purpose of the Continental System? Why did it turn out to be a serious blunder?

3. Why did people in conquered countries greet Napoleon as a liberator? Why was this image short-lived?

4. What was the result of the French occupation in Spain?

5. Why did Napoleon invade Russia? Why was this campaign a disaster?

6. What government was established when Napoleon was overthrown? Why did Napoleon return from Elba? What was the outcome?

Assessment of Napoleon

The life of Napoleon continues to fascinate students of history. The great emperor is both criticized and admired.

Critics call Napoleon a selfish, ruthless man who lived only for power and conquest. They state that he harmed rather than helped mankind. From Madrid to Moscow his driving ambition brought suffering and death to hundreds of thousands. He claimed to be a child of the French Revolution—one who believed in liberty. But, say the critics, all his policies aimed at increasing his own power. He betrayed the Revolution by crushing liberty. These critics agree that Napoleon had great ability, but they maintain that he used it unwisely.

Many historians, on the other hand, praise Napoleon's keen mind, his energy, and his determination to succeed. They regard him as a general without equal, a reformer who carried out the ideals of the French Revolution. Had Napoleon not been defeated, say his admirers, he would have united all the peoples of the continent into a United States of Europe. Having established a nineteenth-century state even greater than the Roman Empire, Napoleon would have spread the reforms of the French Revolution to the peoples of Europe and put an end to wars between nations.

The debate continues today. While historians differ in their judgments of Napoleon, they agree that his was a remarkable life. One statesman said of the great adventurer: "His genius was unbelievable. It is the most astonishing career that has been witnessed for the last thousand years. He was certainly the most extraordinary man I ever saw."

Chapter Highlights

Can you explain?

provisional
censorship

coup d'état

indoctrinate

guerrilla war

Can you identify?

Elba
Waterloo
Leipsig

St. Helena
Consulate

Wellington
Trafalgar

Code Napoléon
Continental System

What do you think?

1. To what do you attribute Napoleon's great achievements?

2. Was Napoleon more popular in France than the Bourbon kings? Why?

3. Which of Napoleon's reforms and policies prove that he was a skillful politician? Explain.

4. How was unlimited ambition a major cause of Napoleon's downfall?

5. Nationalism helped bring Napoleon to power and it contributed to his overthrow. Explain this statement.

6. Were Napoleon's policies and outlook true to the ideals of the French Revolution? Why?

7. Which of Napoleon's qualities and achievements do you find admirable? Why has he been bitterly criticized?

The Metternich Era: Reaction and Revolution

CHAPTER FOCUS

Reaction, Liberalism, Nationalism
Congress of Vienna
An Era of Revolution

One of the most stirring national anthems ever written, the "Marseillaise" was composed during the turmoil of the French Revolution. The sculpture (left) suggests the spirit aroused by this call to arms. During the period 1815–1848 the forces of reaction were led by Metternich. The painting above reveals the Austrian statesman's unshakeable confidence in the rightness of the reactionary cause.

In 1815, after 25 years of revolution, terror, and war, Europe was finally at peace. The armies of France no longer marched across the continent. Preachers of revolution, for the time being, were silenced. Napoleon, who had dreamed of conquering Europe, was a prisoner on a far-off island. Kings, aristocrats, and churchmen, looking back on the disorder of the past 25 years, were determined to restore the conditions that had existed before 1789.

Reactionaries seek to restore conditions that existed before the French Revolution. To the ruling classes of Europe, the French Revolution was a great disaster, a crime against civilization. It challenged the authority of kings and took away the property and privileges of the nobility and the Church. It led to the Reign of Terror, in which thousands of aristocrats were put to death. It turned the people of Paris into a violent mob, said the aristocrats, and put power into the hands of the wicked, the ignorant, and the lowborn. It produced Napoleon, who conquered nations, overthrew kings, and kept Europe at war for fifteen years.

People who wanted a return to the ways of life before the French Revolution were called *reactionaries.* Reactionaries hated the ideals and reforms of the French Revolution. They wished to restore the powers of kings, aristocrats, and churchmen. Reactionaries also were determined to crush future revolutions and threats of revolution. To them, revolutionary leaders were wild-eyed fanatics seeking to destroy all established authority. Reactionaries feared that the civilization developed over the centuries would be destroyed by the madness and violence of short-sighted revolutionaries. If only the ideas which had led to the French Revolution could be stamped out, they felt that Europe would be safe from disorder and war. From 1815 to 1848 most of the leaders in Europe were reactionaries.

But ideas do not die easily. Two ideas that grew out of the French Revolution continued to excite people and to serve as causes of revolutions. These ideas were *liberalism* and *nationalism.* They were opposed by reactionaries.

Liberals demand reforms. The French Revolution called for an end to the absolute rule of kings and to the special privileges of the nobility and clergy. Its leaders demanded voting rights, a written constitution, a parliament, equality, and freedom of speech, press, and religion. These liberal goals were expressed in the American Bill of Rights and the French *Declaration of the Rights of Man and Citizen.* Liberalism appealed mainly to the middle class —university students, professors, lawyers, journalists, and businessmen. Bourgeois liberals wished to take political power away from kings and nobles and to eliminate Church interference with man's right to write and to pray as he pleased. Taking the French Revolution as their model, these bourgeois liberals planned to overthrow the reactionaries and finish what the Revolution had started. They hoped to reform society and government.

Not all liberals thought alike, however. *Moderate liberals* mistrusted the common people, who far outnumbered them. They opposed voting rights for the poor and labor unions for the workers. Moderate liberals did not want to give the common people too much power. They favored a limited monarchy controlled by wealthy businessmen. Like churchmen and aristocrats, these moderate liberals trembled at the memory of Robespierre and the Jacobin Republic. *Radical liberals,* on the other hand, believed in full democracy. They wanted to establish a republic in which all citizens, rich and poor, could vote and hold office.

Nationalism becomes a powerful force. Nationalism is a feeling shared by people speaking the same language, belonging to the same religion, and having similar traditions and a similar history. It makes one group of people feel different from every other group. Nationalists have a feeling of belonging together. They believe that their people are special, favored by God or fate. Nationalists insist that it is the obligation of every person in a nation to work towards that nation's greatness. In the nineteenth century nationalism was identified with liberty. There can be no liberty, said nationalists, if a people is not free to rule itself in its own land. As we shall see, nationalism awoke powerful emotions in men's hearts, driving men to commit acts of great courage and of great evil. It led to wars of liberation, wars of unification, and wars of expansion.

The history of modern nationalism began with the French Revolution. When foreign invaders threatened to conquer France and overthrow the Revolution, Frenchmen—young and old, men and women—united to defend their homeland. There had never before been such an army in Europe's history. The soldiers of the Revolution fought not for money or for a king, but for *la patrie* (lah pah-*tree'*), the nation. "When *la Patrie* calls us for her defense," wrote a young French soldier to his mother, "we should rush to her. . . . Our life, our goods, and our talents do not belong to us. It is to the nation, to *la Patrie*, . . . [that] everything belongs." For many French nationalists the glory and greatness of France became the most important thing in their lives, more important than family, friends, God, or life itself.

"The citizen is born, lives, and dies for the fatherland." These words were written in public places for all citizens to read and ponder. The "Marseillaise," the hymn of the Revolution, echoed across France. In schools, in newspapers, in speeches, in poems, at meetings of patriotic clubs, Frenchmen were told of the glory won by the sons of France on the battlefield.

Although not himself a nationalist, Napoleon thoroughly understood the power of nationalism. He knew that it united people and made them fight harder. He tried to keep alive the spirit of devotion to France born during the Revolution. "I want to raise the glory of the French name so high that it becomes the envy of all nations," he told the French people.

Nationalism soon spread to other parts of the world. In many parts of Europe nationalities did not live in a united country. For example,

The Metternich Era

1814–1815	Congress of Vienna
1820	Rebellion breaks out in Spain
1821	Greeks rise in revolt against Ottoman Turks
1824	Charles X succeeds to throne of France
1830	Charles X ousted by revolution, succeeded by Louis Philippe Belgium proclaims independence from Holland
1848	Liberal and nationalist revolutions sweep across Europe Louis Philippe ousted, Louis Napoleon becomes President of France
1852	Louis Napoleon becomes Napoleon III, Emperor of the French

millions of Poles in Eastern Europe had no country of their own. Some were governed by Austria, some by Russia, and some by Prussia. Polish nationalists longed to see a united and independent Poland and dedicated their lives to this end. "Poland is not yet lost, . . . so long as we live," they sang. This same spirit of nationalism spread throughout Latin America. As in Europe, patriots secretly planned revolutions to throw out their Spanish or Portuguese rulers and to unite their people into one nation. (See Chapter 36.)

CHECK-UP

1. What is a reactionary? Why did reactionaries view the French Revolution as a great disaster?

2. What were the liberal ideals of the French Revolution? What were the goals of liberals after 1815? How did moderate and radical liberals differ?

3. What is nationalism? Why was it such a powerful force?

Reaction, liberalism, and nationalism—these were the forces that shaped European history from 1814 to 1848. The period opened with a meeting of diplomats and kings, most of them reactionaries, at Vienna, the capital of Austria. The purpose of the *Congress of Vienna* was to work out a peace settlement after the defeat of Napoleon. The period ended in 1848 when a wave of violent revolutions swept across Europe.

Statesmen meet at Vienna to work out a peace settlement. In 1814 the eyes of all Europe were on Vienna. In all of Vienna's history there had been nothing like this gathering of the rich, the famous, and the high-born. Emperors and empresses, kings and queens, dukes and duchesses with their horse-drawn carriages and servants could be seen everywhere. Every day there were dances, concerts, operas, or hunting parties. The wealthy visitors drank the most expensive wines and ate the finest food. They spied, flirted, and gossiped. Not everything, however, was party and pleasure. Europe's leading statesmen spent long hours at the serious business of planning a lasting peace.

Metternich opposes reform. The major figure at the Congress of Vienna was Prince Metternich (*meht'*er-nik), a handsome, intelligent, and polished Austrian aristocrat. A typical reactionary, Metternich hated the ideas of liberty and equality proclaimed by the French Revolution. He looked upon the common people as "fools" and "nervous women." He saw no reason why they should have a voice in the government. To Metternich, the natural leaders of society were kings, aristocrats, and the Church. Only they could provide order and preserve the ways of civilized life. Metternich regarded middle-class revolutionaries as the most dangerous of men, for he saw as destructive and misguided their belief that society could be reshaped according to the ideals of liberty, equality, and fraternity. To Metternich, the ideals of the French Revolution led not to a better society but to unending revolutions, executions, and wars.

Metternich also considered nationalism dangerous, for he realized that it could wreck the Austrian Empire. If the many different peoples under Austrian rule—Italians, Hungarians, Poles, and Czechs—were aroused by the spirit of nationalism, they might seek to create their own nations. This would mean the end of the Austrian Empire.

The Congress of Vienna is a conservative settlement. After months of discussions, quarrels, threats, and secret deals, the delegates finished their work. What did the Congress of Vienna accomplish?

1. In most cases the Congress of Vienna returned to power the princes and kings who had lost their lands and their thrones during the Napoleonic Wars. The Bourbon family was restored to the throne of France in the person of Louis XVIII, brother of Louis XVI.

2. The Congress rewarded with territory the nations which had fought and defeated Napoleon (see map).

3. The Congress of Vienna tried to strengthen the countries on the borders of France in order to guard against future French expansion.

4. The Congress did not severely punish France. It was careful not to hurt French pride. The statesmen at Vienna feared that harsh treatment might cause the French people to seek revenge. This might lead to new Napoleons and new wars. Moreover, with the flames of Jacobinism no longer raging, with Napoleon a prisoner and a Bourbon king once more on the throne, France seemed far less of a threat than she had in the past 25 years. Although she had to pay an indemnity (compensation) to the victorious nations, France was treated fairly.

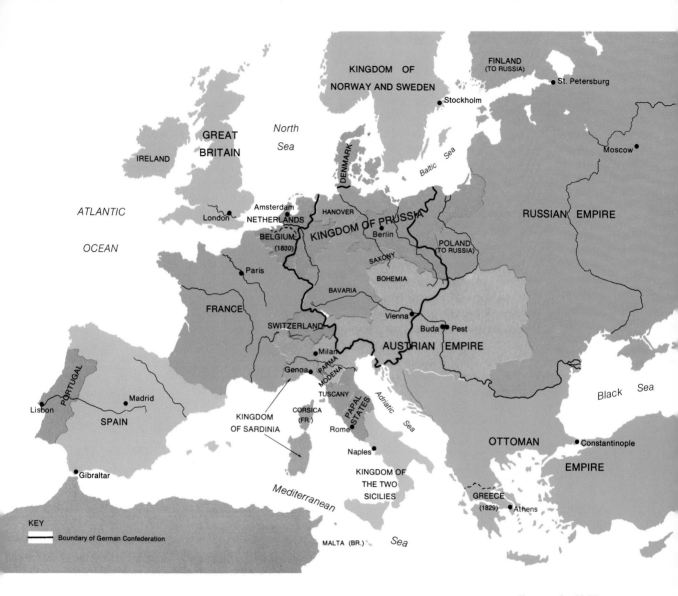

KEY
—— Boundary of German Confederation

She lost the lands conquered by Napoleon but kept her 1792 boundaries. Metternich had a good reason for preventing France from being severely weakened. He counted on using France to offset the growing power of Russia and Prussia.

5. The Congress tried to prevent any one nation from becoming too powerful. Napoleonic France had swallowed up other countries and had become master of Europe. With Napoleon gone, France was no longer a threat. But Metternich saw a new and greater danger in Russia.

The Russian tsar was trying to bring all Poles under his rule. If Russia succeeded in acquiring the Polish lands held by Austria and Prussia, she would be in a position to threaten all of Europe, and Tsar Alexander might even succeed where Napoleon had failed. To prevent a Russian take-over of all Polish lands, France, Britain, and Austria threatened Russia with war. This threat forced the tsar to back down, and Russia acquired much less Polish territory than she had sought. Metternich also limited Prussian expansion in Germany.

6. To maintain the Vienna Settlement, and peace as well, Austria, Russia, Prussia, and Britain agreed to continue their wartime alliance. They agreed to confer whenever a crisis threatened and to act together to maintain peace. After this *Quadruple Alliance* accepted Bourbon France as a member in 1818, the alliance was called the *Concert of Europe*.

Did the Congress of Vienna arrange a wise peace settlement? It has been customary to criticize the delegates of the Congress of Vienna for ignoring the wishes of the common people. By opposing nationalism and liberalism, the delegates left Europe open to revolution. Belgian nationalists did not want to be united with Holland. Italian nationalists resented the fact that Italy was broken up into many states. German patriots wanted to unite the 39 German states into one nation. The Poles still dreamed of a country of their own. Throughout Europe, liberals who had cheered the reforms of the Napoleonic period were saddened by the return of reactionaries to power. They felt that the

Vienna peace settlement was a drastic step backward.

Yet historians point out that many wise decisions were made at Vienna. France was not punished severely. Russia was prevented from moving deeper into Central Europe. And, most important of all, the Great Powers—Britain, France, Prussia, Russia, and Austria—reached an understanding that another war involving all the Great Powers must be prevented at all costs. The delegates at Vienna accomplished what they had set out to do. They preserved the peace of Europe. For the next 100 years, there was no major war involving all the Great Powers of Europe. This in itself was a remarkable achievement.

CHECK-UP

1. How did Metternich view nationalism? Why?
2. What was the purpose of the Congress of Vienna? What did it accomplish?
3. What was the purpose of the Concert of Europe?

An Era of Revolution

The spirit of revolution lives on. Even though reactionaries were back in power, the spirit of revolution was not dead. It was kept alive by liberals and nationalists who organized secret societies, printed revolutionary newspapers, collected weapons, and planned revolutions. Between 1820 and 1848, Metternich and his fellow reactionaries crushed many revolutionary outbreaks. Their secret police and spies were everywhere, imprisoning liberal and nationalist leaders, warning students and professors not to spread dangerous ideas, and censoring books and newspapers.

When revolutions did break out, the Concert of Europe crushed them by force. France aided King Ferdinand VII of Spain to crush an uprising of army officers who had forced the king to reinstate the liberal constitution drawn up during the Napoleonic era. Ferdinand took savage revenge against the revolutionaries when they were defeated three years later. Their leader was put in a basket, dragged through the streets by a donkey, and hanged in a public square. His body was then cut into five parts and placed on exhibition in different Spanish towns—a warning to all liberals who still

Romanticism, born as a reaction to the overdetailed and formal arts of the Old Regime, appealed to men's emotions and reflected a fascination with the exotic. Living during the Napoleonic and Metternich eras, Romanticists reflected the turbulent feelings of their times in paintings, music, and literature. The Romantic spirit influenced the life as well as the poetry of Englishman George Gordon, Lord Byron (right), who died while helping the Greeks win their independence from Turkey. Inspired by Byron's poem The Giaour (Infidel), *French artist Ferdinand Delacroix painted the* Venetian Giaour *(above, left) about to slay the Turkish pasha responsible for the death of the girl he loved.*

dreamed of revolution. Metternich's Austrian troops put down revolts in Italy. An attempt by army officers to set up a liberal government in Russia failed. Leaders of the revolt were executed, imprisoned, or exiled to Siberia. When Polish nationalists revolted against Russian rule, the tsar's soldiers crushed the uprising and had hundreds of Polish patriots executed. German revolutionaries failed to achieve their aim of a united and liberal Germany.

But cracks were beginning to appear in Metternich's system. Not all revolutions ended in failure. Greece succeeded in breaking away from the Ottoman Empire (Turkey, page 127). Belgium gained her independence from Holland. Spain and Portugal lost all their colonies (except Cuba and Puerto Rico) in Latin America.

Louis XVIII makes necessary compromises. The spirit of liberalism and the readiness to revolt also lived on in France. When Louis XVIII became King of France, he realized that he could not erase all the reforms of the French Revolution and Napoleon. If he did, there might be another revolution. Therefore, he granted France a charter that guaranteed freedom of speech, press, and religion, and equality before the law. All Frenchmen, regardless of birth, could hold positions in the government, and a parliament was established. Nor did Louis XVIII try to restore to the nobility or the Church the lands lost during the Revolution. He wisely understood that France could not return to the conditions of the Old Regime.

Charles X's reactionary policies cause revolt.
When Louis died in 1824, he was succeeded by his brother Charles (*sharl*) X. The French Revolution had taught Charles nothing. He was determined to bring back absolute rule and special privileges for the nobility and the Church. When Charles censored the newspapers and reduced the number of Frenchmen eligible to vote, the people rose in revolt. In Paris workers and students stormed into the streets, made barricades out of paving stones, furniture, tree trunks, and wagons, and raised the flag of revolution. Behind these barricades, guns in hand, they defiantly sang the "Marseillaise." This time the revolt of the people of Paris lasted only three days. When Charles ordered his troops to crush the revolutionaries, the people stood firm. The frightened king gave up his throne and fled to England.

The Parisians who had ousted Charles X hoped to establish a republic, which they believed would do more for the common man. But the republicans were disappointed. Although they had done the fighting, their goals were not realized. The Revolution of 1830 was a victory for moderate liberals. The well-organized, wealthy, and influential upper middle class took control of the revolution and named Louis Philippe (fee-*leep′*) King of the French.

Louis Philippe's government ignores the poor.
The government of Louis Philippe favored the businessmen and bankers who helped put him in power. It limited the right to vote to those who owned property. The poor had little say in the government. When they protested, Louis Philippe's chief minister said: "Get rich, then you can vote." By 1846 only some 2.8 per cent of the adult male population could vote.

Louis Philippe was not a bad ruler, but many people in France were dissatisfied with the "businessman king." Frenchmen who remembered the glorious days of Napoleon complained that the pear-shaped king, who dressed like a businessman and disliked war, was not fit to rule a nation of warriors. Some Frenchmen still dreamed of making France a republic. The most serious complaints, however, came from the growing working class living in the Paris slums. Prevented by law from striking, unable to meet the property requirements for voting, often suffering from unemployment, and poorly paid when able to find work, these workers were in an angry mood. One wise Frenchman who understood the workers warned: "I believe that we are at this moment sleeping on a volcano." He was right.

One revolution results in a republic, a second in class warfare.
Two revolutions broke out in 1848. In February Louis Philippe was forced to flee, and a republic was established. But the workers of Paris were not satisfied with the February revolution. They felt it had not gone far enough. It had done nothing to end their poverty. Workers called for a *social revolution* which would take away the power and property of the rich, place some industries such as railroads and insurance companies under government ownership, put an end to poverty and unemployment, and treat all people fairly. To create this new *socialist* society, the workers of Paris prepared to fight.

In June they set up barricades in the streets of Paris. There had been many revolutions in France, but none like this one. It was a revolt against the French social and economic system. The first socialist revolution, it foreshadowed the great social revolutions of the twentieth century. The workers' revolt of June, 1848, split France in two—the have-nots against the haves, the property owners against the propertyless and impoverished working class. One observer compared it to a slave revolt.

The rest of France—wealthy people with large estates, businessmen, and even peasants—was frightened by the uprising of the Parisian workers. "The fear that gripped [them]," writes present-day American historian Priscilla Robertson, "was like that in Rome at the invasion of the barbarians." If the workers succeeded, no one's property would be safe. From many parts of France men rushed to Paris to help the army crush the workers' revolt.

The workers found themselves alone. But though they had no leaders, they showed remarkable courage. Women and children fought alongside men behind the barricades. After

Propaganda played an important role in the revolutions of 1848. A popular form of political commentary was satire—works intended to arouse people to correct injustices by presenting material in a witty but critical manner. Below, a French cartoonist satirizes Louis Philippe's appearance. Open rebellion was expressed by workers and students who built barricades in the streets (bottom).

three days of violent street fighting, in which over 1500 people were killed, the revolution of the workers was crushed. Thousands of working-class revolutionaries were thrown into dungeons. One of these prisons was described by Flaubert (floh-*bair'*), a famous French writer:

Nine hundred men were there, crowded together in filth, . . . black with [gun]powder and clotted blood, shivering in fever, and shouting in frenzy. Those who died were left to lie with the others. Now and then, at the sudden noise of a gun, they thought they were all on the point of being shot, and they flung themselves against the walls, afterwards falling back into their former places. They were so stupefied with suffering that they seemed to be living in a nightmare.

The workers' revolution left deep scars in French society. Workers resented the fact that the rest of France had united against them. The rest of France, on the other hand, feared that the workers might revolt again.

Another Napoleon comes to power. The determination to prevent another battle between the classes led the French to elect Louis Napoleon as President of France. Nephew of the great general whose deeds still inspired Frenchmen, Louis Napoleon promised France strong rule, order, and an end to violence. In 1852, with the overwhelming approval of the French people, he became emperor. The republic born in 1848 had lasted only four years. Once again France was ruled by an emperor.

Revolution spreads through Europe in 1848. "When France sneezes, all Europe catches cold," Metternich had said. Like an epidemic the fever of revolution raced across the continent. Not even Metternich could stop it. News of the events in France was eagerly received by European liberals and nationalists. They saw a splendid chance to win independence, unity, and reforms. Carl Schurz (*shoorts*), a young German university student, felt that "now had arrived . . . the day for the establishment of German unity." The Germans should be granted "civil rights and liberties, free speech, free press, the right of free assembly, equality before the law, a freely elected [parliament]. . . . The word democracy was soon on all tongues."

All through Europe dramatic scenes took place. In Berlin, the capital of Prussia, revolutionaries held a weird parade. They carried their dead comrades, covered with blood and flowers, into the palace courtyard. There they demanded that the Prussian king come to the window to look at the bodies of revolutionaries killed by his soldiers. Frederick William removed his hat; the queen fainted. On that day "we all crawled on our stomachs," the king declared afterwards.

In Vienna students and workingmen armed with shovels, axes, and stones clashed with government troops. Later they obtained weapons and gained control of the city. The emperor of Austria was forced to grant a constitution giving the people more freedom. When a man carried a banner through the streets with the word "Constitution" written on it, writes Priscilla Robertson, "women kissed his clothes, mothers held their children up so that they would always remember the sight." For the student revolutionaries, these were unforgettable days. They were fighting for liberty; they were making history. "Just to have lived through those days is enough for one lifetime," recalled one student years later.

News of revolutionary successes in Austria spread quickly to Italy. Church bells rang, flags flew, and the people shouted "Italia! Italia!" The hopes of Italian nationalists and liberals soared. Now was the time to shake off Austrian rule, unite Italy, and speed democratic reforms. Revolts broke out in many places. In the northern Italian city of Milan the people erected barricades made of anything in sight. An eyewitness described these strongholds:

As soon as they could get hold of a couple of tons of soil, they erected a barricade. . . . In the rich quarters they used carriages, luxurious furniture, harpsichords, beds, looking-glasses; in the business quarters barrels, bales of goods, packing cases, chairs from the cafes; in the poor quarters [mattresses], . . . benches; near the churches, seats, pulpits . . . ; near schools, armchairs and benches; near the theaters, machinery, . . . statues. . . . Whenever possible, trees or shrubs were felled across the openings; then [the barricade] was completed with . . . doors, paving-stones, . . . bottles, and dirt.

Behind these barricades the citizens of Milan stood ready to fight the Austrian oppressor. "The moment has arrived when we can be rid of him forever. *Viva l'Italia!*"

When Austrian soldiers moved down the streets towards the barricades, they were fired upon from nearby windows. From the rooftops Italians hurled stones and boiling water. After "Five Glorious Days" of street fighting, the Austrians withdrew, leaving the people of Milan in power. Similar scenes took place in other parts of Italy.

At first, the revolutions appeared successful. The emperor of Austria and the king of Prussia were forced to grant liberal constitutions. Reactionary princes were driven from some Italian and German states. Italians weakened Austrian rule; for a few months Hungarians won independence from Austria. German liberals and nationalists were meeting to work out plans for a united and democratic Germany. Convinced that it was "not in the power of men" to check these revolutions, Metternich, now an old man, escaped to England.

Why did the Revolutions of 1848 fail? Despite their early successes, revolutionaries were unable to hold their gains. The following are underlying reasons for the failure of the Revolutions of 1848.

1. The leaders were often better at debating than at organizing. They had difficulty putting their plans for reform into effect. In Germany, says twentieth-century German historian Veit Valentin, "the revolution had practically talked itself to death." The revolutionaries were filled with ideas enough to last for generations but "there was no strong man whose personality could have held the thing together. . . . Ideas are splendid but men are better."

2. Moreover, the revolutionaries quarreled amongst themselves. Middle-class liberals, favoring moderate goals, grew fearful of the radical working class. The middle class wanted a constitution granting a parliament and basic freedoms. The workers wanted more than a constitution. They demanded bread, jobs, and a new society which favored the workingman. To the bourgeoisie, the workers were an uneducated mob which threatened middle-class property. The middle class quickly deserted the cause of revolution and opposed the working class.

3. The revolutionaries were divided in still another way. It soon became evident that nationalism was an overwhelming force. Peoples of different nationalities were not anxious to work together to achieve the liberty of all. In many cases they hated each other more than they did their reactionary rulers. German revolutionaries quarreled with Polish patriots. Hungarian revolutionaries were not interested in freedom for Slavs and Italians.

The reactionary rulers of Europe regained confidence, and their armies moved to crush the revolutions. The courage of the revolutionaries was no match for these armies. Thousands of liberals and nationalists were killed or imprisoned. Many more fled to America.

American historian Peter Gay summarizes the reasons for the failure of the revolutions of 1848:

[The bourgeois liberals] were rich in ideas but not arms—and in the dangerous arena of politics ideas are weapons only if they are backed by physical power. [Liberals] soon found that the old society was too strong for them. The landholders, supported by the peasants, were against them. So were the Church, the military, and, in most cases, the [government officials]. Worse, the liberals, strongly imbued with the [sacredness] of property rights, considered the working class too dangerous to make it an ally. Wherever workers claimed the fruits of the revolution, . . . they were massacred in the streets by the very [bourgeois liberals] who had proclaimed the end of tyranny and corruption.

What were the results of the Revolutions of 1848? Some of the reforms won by the revolutionaries were retained. All French males gained the right to vote. Serfdom was abolished in Austria, and a parliament was established in Prussia. Yet the hopes of liberals and nationalists were not realized. Germany and Italy had not achieved unity. Hungary returned to Austrian rule. Many of the freedoms demanded by liberals were still denied. One disappointed revolutionary summed up the failure of 1848: "We have been beaten and humiliated. We have all been scattered, imprisoned, disarmed, and gagged. The fate of European democracy has slipped . . . from the hands of the people."

1848 was an eventful year in European history. *Liberal* revolutionaries had fought for democratic reforms—for a constitution guaranteeing basic freedoms, for the right of all men to vote and to hold government office. *Nationalist* revolutionaries tried to win independence from foreign rule or to unite their people under one flag. *Socialist* revolutionaries, driven by extreme poverty, took up arms to get bread and work. They hoped to establish a new society in which there would no longer be rich and poor. In the decades following 1848 these three forces—liberalism, nationalism, and socialism —shaped the history of Europe. We shall speak of them again.

CHECK-UP

1. How did reactionaries cope with revolutionary unrest between 1820 and 1848?

2. What liberal concessions were made by Louis XVIII? Why? What were the policies of Charles X? What was the result?

3. Why were many Frenchmen dissatisfied with the government of Louis Philippe?

4. Why did the workers' revolt of June, 1848, divide the French people? Why was it different from earlier revolutions? Why did it arouse fear in the rest of Europe?

5. Where did revolutions break out in 1848? Why were they suppressed? What gains were made?

Summing Up

Following the overthrow of Napoleon, the Congress of Vienna sought to restore conditions as they were before the French Revolution. But in the long run reactionary statesmen were to find it impossible to contain two ideas that grew out of that Revolution—liberalism and nationalism.

In general, the Vienna settlement (1) restored rulers who had lost their thrones during the Napoleonic Wars, (2) rewarded with territory nations that had helped overthrow Napoleon, (3) strengthened countries bordering France to prevent future French expansion, and (4) provided for the continuation of the wartime alliance, which became the Concert of Europe with the admission of Bourbon France. This settlement disappointed liberals but did prevent a general war in Europe for a hundred years.

Revolutions (1820–1848) inspired by nationalists and liberals broke out in Spain, Poland, and Italy, only to be crushed by the intervention of the Great Powers. In France the ousting of reactionary Charles X brought Louis Philippe to the throne but ensured no gains for the working class. This contributed to a worker's revolution in 1848, an uprising which was crushed by the property owners of France. A second republic was established, but it fell under the rule of Louis Napoleon who reigned as Emperor Napoleon III.

In 1848 there were also liberal revolts in Germany, Austria, and Austrian-held lands. Despite early successes, liberals made few gains because (1) they were not efficiently organized, (2) bourgeois revolutionaries opposed the goals of working-class revolutionaries, and (3) revolutionaries were unable to overcome nationalist bias and unite against reactionary rulers.

Chapter Highlights

Can you explain? ————————————————————————————

reactionaries   nationalism   moderate liberals   radical liberals

la patrie   socialist

Can you identify? ————————————————————————————

Congress of Vienna   Quadruple Alliance   Concert of Europe   Revolutions of 1848

Metternich   Louis XVIII   Great Powers   Louis Napoleon

Charles X   Louis Philippe

What do you think? ————————————————————————————

1. How does a sense of nationalism develop?

2. How did reaction, liberalism, and nationalism shape European history after the French Revolution?

3. Why was France treated generously at the Congress of Vienna? Did this policy work?

4. Considering the turmoil that had swept Europe between 1789 and 1814, was the Vienna peace settlement harsh and reactionary? Explain.

5. "When France sneezes, all Europe catches cold." What did Metternich mean by this statement? Give examples.

6. Nationalism was an inspiration for the Revolutions of 1848, yet it was nationalism that helped destroy them. Why?

7. What is the difference between a nationalist revolution and a socialist revolution? Give examples of each.

The Unification of Italy and Germany

The painting at left suggests the contrasting personalities of Garibaldi (left) and King Victor Emmanuel II. The king has the appearance of a statesman who works through diplomatic channels. Garibaldi is the gallant and reckless military leader who shares his troops' triumphs and defeats. The photograph of Bismarck (above) reflects the grim determination which earned the Prussian statesman the name "Iron Chancellor."

CHAPTER FOCUS

Unification of Italy
Unification of Germany
Nationalism: Blessing or Curse?

The dreams of Italian and German nationalists were not realized in the Revolutions of 1848. Large parts of Italy remained under foreign rule. Germany was still divided into many states. Revolutionaries were hunted down, imprisoned, and in some cases executed. Many nationalists began to doubt that they would live to see a nation unified under one flag, with one national anthem and one government. Yet by 1871 nationalism had triumphed in Italy and Germany. Both had become unified states. How did this happen?

Many rulers oppose Italian unity. During the first half of the 1800's, Italian patriots tried a number of times to unite their country. Each attempt ended in failure because the enemies of Italian unity were too powerful to be defeated by small groups of brave Italians. Who were the opponents of a unified Italy?

1. Austria, which governed the Lombardo-Venetian kingdom in northern Italy, was the chief foe of Italian unity. Austria was determined to hold on to her Italian possessions. Her

Unification of Italy

1832	Mazzini founds Young Italy
1848	Revolutions sweep across Europe
1849–1878	Victor Emmanuel II ruler of Sardinia (King of Italy, 1861–1878)
1852–1861	Cavour Premier of Sardinia
1852–1870	Napoleon III rules France
1855	Sardinia enters Crimean War
1858	Napoleon III agrees to help free Italy from Austrian rule
1859	Austro-Sardinian War
1860	Parma, Modena, Tuscany, and Romagna vote for union with Sardinia; France receives Nice and Savoy Naples and Sicily, liberated from Bourbon rule by Garibaldi, vote to join Sardinia Umbria and the Marches vote for union with Sardinia
1861	Victor Emmanuel named king of a united Italy
1866	Alliance with Prussia against Austria results in return of Venetia to Italy
1870	Rome incorporated into the Italian state; Italian unity achieved

secret police spied on Italian nationalists, and when uprisings took place anywhere in the Italian Peninsula, Austrian troops went into action.

2. The small Italian states of Parma, Modena (moh-*day'*nah), and Tuscany were ruled by princes friendly to Austria. These rulers realized that they would be ousted if Italy became united.

3. The Pope ruled the Papal States in central Italy. He feared that unification of Italy would end his control of these states.

4. Finally, the Bourbon ruler of the Kingdom of the Two Sicilies (Sicily and the south of Italy) also opposed unification because it would cost him his throne.

That Italy finally became united was due mainly to the efforts of three Italians—Giuseppe Mazzini, Count Camillo di Cavour, Giuseppe Garibaldi—and of Napoleon III, Emperor of the French.

Mazzini appeals to Italian patriotism. Throughout his life Giuseppe Mazzini (joo-*zep'*pay maht-*tsee'*nee) was driven by one desire—to liberate Italy from foreign rule and to unite his people into one nation. To further this end, Mazzini reminded the Italians of the past glories of their land. The ancient Romans had ruled the greatest empire of the ancient world! In the Middle Ages the Church of Rome had carried the message of Christ to all Western Europe. And during the Renaissance Italian artists, craftsmen, and writers were the envy of all Europe. But "all is now changed," said Mazzini, the soul of Italy is filled with sadness. "We have no flag of our own, . . . no voice among the nations of Europe. . . . We are broken up into eight states that are independent of one another. . . . And all these states that divide us are . . . governed [by tyrants] without participation of any sort by the people [in the government]. One of these states, containing almost a quarter of the population of Italy, belongs to a foreign power, Austria. The others, either owing to family bonds or to their own weaknesses, never oppose Austria's will."

Mazzini hoped to restore Italy to her former greatness. With words that reached the hearts of his countrymen, he cried out for unity and independence: "We demand to exist. We demand a name. We desire to make our country powerful and respected, free and happy. . . . In other words, we demand independence, unity, and liberty, for ourselves and for our fellow-countrymen." To throw out the hated Austrians and the lesser princes, said Mazzini, the people must unite, take up arms, and shed their blood. He did not expect an easy victory. "If one attempt fails, the third or fourth will be successful. And if failure is repeated, what matter? The people . . . must learn how to rise and be defeated and rise again a thousand times, without becoming discouraged."

To wage the struggle for independence and unity, in 1832 Mazzini formed Young Italy, an organization of dedicated revolutionaries. Its members, many of them students, shared the patriotism and determination of their leader. They took the following oath:

I give my name to Young Italy . . . and swear: To dedicate myself wholly and forever to the endeavor . . . to [make] Italy one free, independent, republican nation.

Cavour seeks allies in uniting Italy. Mazzini was the soul of the nationalist movement in Italy. His words kept alive the dream of a united Italy. But the Revolutions of 1848, in which Mazzini participated, showed that fiery words, noble thoughts, and brave patriots were not enough. To drive out the Austrians and the tyrant princes, trained soldiers and powerful allies were also needed. The man who understood this better than anyone else was Count Camillo di Cavour (kah-*meel*'loh dee kah-

Unification of Italy

voor'), Prime Minister of the Kingdom of Sardinia in northwestern Italy.

Cavour differed from Mazzini in both personality and policy. Unlike the excitable Mazzini, Cavour was neither a dreamer nor a speechmaker. "I cannot make a speech, but I can make Italy," he is supposed to have said. Mazzini hoped to establish a democratic republic. Cavour, mistrusting the common people, preferred a limited monarchy. Mazzini called for a mass uprising of the Italian people against Austria. Cavour, always cautious and practical, realized that brave students behind barricades were no match for the well-trained Austrian troops. He wanted the Kingdom of Sardinia to take the lead in defeating Austria and uniting northern Italy and perhaps eventually all Italy. But how could this be done? Austria was a Great Power; Sardinia, a comparatively small state. Slowly and carefully Cavour made his plans.

1. First he modernized the economy of Sardinia and increased its army. He built railroads, improved agriculture, developed industry, and strengthened the state's finances.

2. Next Cavour looked for allies to support Sardinia in a war against Austria. In 1855 Sardinia became an ally of Britain and France in the Crimean War against Russia.[1] Cavour had no quarrel with Russia, but he wanted the friendship of Britain and France. The two western powers might prove useful friends in Italy's drive for unification. Moreover, the prestige of Sardinia would be increased if she fought alongside the Great Powers and participated in the peacemaking. At the peace conference in 1856 Cavour urged the Great Powers to support Italian unity.

3. In 1858 Cavour reached an understanding with Napoleon III, Emperor of the French. If Austria threatened Sardinia, France would help to free Italy from "the Alps to the Adriatic." In return for such help Sardinia would cede to France two small border territories, Nice (*nees*) and Savoy. Unfortunately the ultimate goals of each partner to this deal conflicted. Cavour hoped to unite Italy; Napoleon wished to establish an Italian Confederation under French influence.

4. Once Cavour had France as an ally he stirred up trouble with Austria. When the Austrians moved against Sardinia in 1859, Napoleon kept his promise. The large French army won two quick victories, and it seemed that the Austrians might be driven from all of northern Italy. But to Cavour's surprise, the

[1] The Crimean (kry-*me'*un) War broke out when France and Russia disagreed over which nation should have custody of the holy places in Palestine. Russia also claimed the right to establish a protectorate over the Christians in the Ottoman Empire.

French emperor signed a truce with Austria. Sardinia acquired Lombardy but not Venetia.

Napoleon breaks his promise to Cavour. Why did Napoleon fail to keep his promise to Cavour? The French emperor had good reasons for making peace. First, he realized that a united Italy might prove a threat to southern France. Furthermore, a united Italy would include the Papal States. Napoleon III had agreed to protect lands ruled by the Pope. Almost certainly French Catholics would blame their emperor for any territory the Pope might lose. Perhaps most important, Prussia, fearful lest the war might lead to an increase in French power, had readied her forces on the borders of France.

Outraged by Napoleon's action, Cavour demanded that Sardinia continue the war until all northern Italy was liberated. But King Victor Emmanuel accepted the Austrian peace terms. Developments proved the wisdom of this decision. The aroused people of Parma, Modena, and Tuscany ousted their rulers and voted for union with Sardinia. Romagna (roh-*mah'*-nyah), one of the Papal States, also voted to join Sardinia. Despite his promise to protect the Pope's lands, Napoleon III offered to approve this substantial enlargement of Sardinia. In return, he claimed and received Nice and Savoy.

Garibaldi strikes a blow for liberty. While northern Italy was making progress toward unification under the guidance of Cavour, important developments were taking place in the south. In the spring of 1860, some 1000 red-shirted Italian patriots sailed from Genoa to invade the island of Sicily. They were determined to liberate the Kingdom of the Two Sicilies from its Bourbon king. Their leader was Giuseppe Garibaldi (gah-ree-*bahl'*dee), a man whose bravery, patriotism, and love of liberty would make him a hero to all Italy.

In 1833, after joining Mazzini's Young Italy, Garibaldi became involved in its revolutionary

activities. Captured and sentenced to death, he managed to escape to South America. There he helped the people in southern Brazil (now Uruguay) fight for freedom from Brazil. In Brazil Garibaldi learned the skills of the revolutionary's trade. "Shipwrecked, ambushed, shot through the neck, captured, imprisoned, strung up by his wrists for attempting to escape and refusing to say who helped him, marching exhausted for days on end through the jungle with nothing to eat but the roots of plants, and riding at night over the cold sierra [*syey′rah*, mountain range]," Garibaldi toughened his body and his will for the great struggle that lay ahead. He returned to Italy just in time to fight in the Revolution of 1848.

Garibaldi was a born leader of men. A young Italian artist who fought beside Garibaldi in 1848 said of his commander: "I shall never forget that day when I first saw him on his beautiful white horse. He reminded us of . . . our Savior; . . . everyone said the same. I could not resist him. I went after him; thousands did likewise. He only had to show himself. We all worshiped him. We could not help it."

In 1860 Garibaldi led a small force against the Kingdom of the Two Sicilies. Soon after the invasion, thousands of local patriots joined his army. They were inspired by his deeds and his words:

Italians! The Sicilians are fighting against the enemies of Italy, and for Italy. To help them with money, arms, and especially men, is the duty of every Italian. . . .

To arms, then! Let us by one blow put an end to our [constant] misfortunes. Let us show the world that this is truly the land once trodden by the great Roman race.

In a little more than two months, Garibaldi's Red Shirts, aided by local patriots, liberated Sicily. They then crossed to the Italian mainland to liberate the rest of the Kingdom of the Two Sicilies. Early in September, 1860, Garibaldi occupied Naples without a fight. The Bourbon king fled, and the overjoyed people of Naples welcomed the "Red Man," as they affectionately called Garibaldi. For him the final step was an advance on Rome, the center of Italy.

Garibaldi's plans alarm Cavour. Cavour feared that an attack on Rome would compel Napoleon III to keep his pledge to defend the Pope's lands. Cavour realized that war between France and Italy would be fatal for Italy. Moreover, Cavour considered Garibaldi too emotional, rash, and stubborn, too attracted to democratic ideas, and too much of a hero to the common people to be entrusted with leadership in the unification of Italy. That goal was to be achieved under Sardinian leadership.

Napoleon III was equally disturbed by Garibaldi's plans. It was not difficult, then, for Cavour to persuade the French emperor to permit Victor Emmanuel to lead a Sardinian army across the Papal States to head off Garibaldi. A papal force offered only token resistance, and the Papal States of Umbria and the Marches soon voted for union with Sardinia. In October, 1860, Victor Emmanuel took command of the troops in the Kingdom of the Two Sicilies. The Bourbon army held out until early in 1861. But meanwhile the people in Naples and Sicily voted to join the lands ruled by Victor Emmanuel, who was proclaimed King of Italy on March 17, 1861. Worn out by the tensions of the past twelve years, Cavour, the architect of Italian unification, died June 6, 1861.

Italian unity is soon achieved. Two important regions remained outside Italian control. (1) The Pope, protected by French troops, still ruled the city of Rome and adjacent territory. (2) In northern Italy, Venetia remained in Austrian hands. Italy did not have to wait long to annex these lands.

In 1866 Austria and Prussia were at war. By becoming Prussia's ally, Italy received Venetia when Austria was defeated. Four years later, when Prussia and France were at war, the

French garrison was pulled out of Rome. Italian troops then marched into the city, and the citizens voted by a great majority to become part of a united Italy.[2] Thus nine years after Cavour's death the goal of Italian unification was achieved.

[2] The loss of papal territory left an open wound between the Pope and the Italian nation, a wound that was not healed until 1929.

CHECK-UP

1. What forces opposed Italian unification? Why?
2. What contributions to Italian unification were made by Mazzini? Cavour? Napoleon III? Garibaldi?
3. What progress toward Italian unification was made by war in 1859? 1866? 1870?

Unification of Germany

The Revolutions of 1848 had aroused great hopes among German nationalists. They had seen an opportunity to unite the 39 separate German states into one nation. Many of these nationalists were liberal professors, lawyers, and students who wanted the new united Germany to have a constitution guaranteeing basic liberties. But a united and free Germany was not born in 1848. When the flames of revolution had died out, Germany remained a loose union of separate states ruled by kings and princes with nearly absolute power.

Bismarck and Prussia create a united Germany. It was unfortunate that liberal nationalists were unable to unite Germany. Perhaps they could have given Germany liberty as well as unity. As it turned out, Germany was united by Otto von Bismarck (fon *bis'*mark) a man who supported absolute power for the Hohenzollern (hoh-en-*tsohl'*ern) king of Prussia and mistrusted parliaments. Bismarck became the chancellor (prime minister) of Prussia in 1862.

Bismarck was a Junker (*yoong'*ker)—an aristocratic Prussian landowner. Whereas liberals wanted to transfer power from the king to parliament, Bismarck sought to strengthen the position of the king, whom he considered the symbol of autocratic and military rule in Prussia. "I believe that I am obeying God when I serve the king," he said. When Bismarck talked of a united Germany, he really meant that Prussia, under its Hohenzollern king, should dominate the other German states.

Shrewd and practical, Bismarck insisted that Germany could be united only by the sword. "Not through speeches and majority decisions are the questions of the day decided," he said, "but through iron and blood."

At the end of the Napoleonic Wars, the German states had been reduced from more than 300 to 39, a step towards unity. But the remaining German princes were very jealous of their own independence and therefore opposed any attempt to unify Germany. The rivalry between Austria and Prussia, the two leading German-speaking states, was a further obstacle to unification. Neither Prussia nor Austria would allow a Germany dominated by the other. Austria, in particular, feared that a Germany united by Prussia might prove to be a threatening neighbor. Because of all these forces opposed to unification, the 39 states were linked in a loosely organized German Confederation in which Austria had the dominant influence.

Determined to increase the power of Prussia, Bismarck planned to expel Austria from the German Confederation and to subject the other German states to Prussian rule. But the Prussian army was not strong enough to conquer, occupy, and control all the other German states. Bismarck therefore shrewdly took advantage of German nationalist feelings to give the impression that he was uniting Germany rather than conquering territory for Prussia. How Bismarck achieved his goal of a united Germany led by Prussia is a story of three wars: (1) with Denmark, (2) with Austria, and (3) with France.

Prussia and Austria defeat Denmark and quarrel over their gains. The coastal provinces of Schleswig (*shlays'*vihk) and Holstein (*hohl'*-styne) had largely German populations but were ruled by the king of Denmark. That ruler clearly was seeking a way to incorporate Schleswig in his kingdom. Bismarck convinced Austria that this move must be stopped. In 1864 the united forces of Prussia and Austria overran the two provinces in the name of the German Confederation. Once Austria and Prussia had occupied Schleswig and Holstein, however, they violently disagreed over what should be done with them. Austria wished to refer the issue to the Diet (parliament) of the German Confederation, where she was sure of support. Bismarck preferred to settle the question through war. He was confident that Prussia could defeat Austria.

Most military "experts" believed that Austria would win the conflict. Austria not only was larger than Prussia but had nearly double the population as well as the backing of most of the other German states. But the "Seven Weeks' War" of 1866 proved the importance of expert Prussian planning, efficient railway transportation, and superior weapons. Sweeping aside the forces of Austria's German allies, Prussia crushed the Austrian army. But instead of advancing on Vienna, Bismarck wisely urged King Wilhelm (*vil'*helm) I to make peace with Austria. Through the peace settlement, (1) Austria ceded Venetia to Italy, Prussia's ally; (2) the German Confederation was dissolved; and (3) Prussia annexed Schleswig and Holstein.

Bismarck increases Prussia's power and gains popular support. With Austria excluded from German affairs, the unification of Germany

Unification of Germany

1815	Formation of German Confederation
1861–1888	Wilhelm I King of Prussia (German Kaiser, 1871–1888)
1862–1890	Bismarck Chancellor of Prussia
1864	Prussia and Austria defeat Denmark in war over Schleswig-Holstein
1866	Seven Weeks' War between Prussia and Austria
1867	Formation of North German Confederation
1870–1871	Franco-Prussian War; Germany gains Alsace and Lorraine
1871	German Empire is proclaimed with Wilhelm I as kaiser

could proceed. Prussia first annexed about 30,000 square miles of German territory in the north. Bismarck then invited the 21 North German states to join Prussia in a new union, called the North German Confederation. Prussia's supremacy in the new confederation was assured. Although the people of the German states were represented in the legislature, the king of Prussia served as its permanent president. Prussia also had 17 of the 43 members of the upper house of the legislature, as well as control of the armed forces and foreign affairs. Thus Prussia was much more powerful in the new union than Austria had been in the old. In establishing the North German Confederation, Bismarck had strengthened the position of the Prussian king and the Junkers.

It seemed that everything was going right for Prussia. By winning two wars, Prussia had increased the territory under her control and become master of the North German Confederation. Bismarck had become a national hero. When he first took office, German liberals had strongly opposed him. Bismarck had collected taxes without parliament's approval, and had strengthened the king's power at the expense of parliament. But two successful wars changed the liberals' views.

KEY

German Confederation, 1815

German Empire, 1871–1918

North German Confederation

CONSISTING OF

Kingdom of Prussia

Other members

South German States

Unification of Germany

If Bismarck had weakened parliamentary government, he had given the German people something more important—power. "If Germany is faced with the choice between *Einheit* [ine′hite, unity] or *Freiheit* [fry′hite, freedom], it must . . . unconditionally choose the former," wrote a liberal newspaper. In late nineteenth-century Europe, many liberals placed the glorification of the nation ahead of the strengthening of democracy. They were nationalists first and liberals second. Bismarck, therefore, could count on the support of the people, even the liberals, as he carried forward plans for German unity.

Bismarck's plans for German unity lead to war with France. Only the four South German states remained outside Prussia's control. The overwhelmingly Catholic population of South Germany had no desire to be dominated by Protestant Prussia. This split between north and south naturally pleased French statesmen, who considered a united Germany a threat to France. Some Frenchmen regretted that France had not sided with Austria in the Seven Weeks' War. Having lost that opportunity, France must seek ways to keep Prussia from absorbing South Germany.

Bismarck realized that the surest way to bring the South German states into a united Germany was to arouse a spirit of nationalism so strong that it would overcome separatist tendencies. War with France would serve this purpose, and quite unexpectedly a cause for conflict developed.

In 1868 a revolution had driven the Spanish king from his throne. Two years later the throne of Spain was offered to a German prince of the Hohenzollern family. The thought of Hohenzollern Prussia to the east and a Hohenzollern king of Spain to the south alarmed the French. Surely the two countries would become allies! The French government, therefore, protested. Tension eased when the prince declined the honor extended him. Unfortunately for France, Napoleon III's advisors persuaded him to demand assurance from King Wilhelm I of Prussia that if Spain renewed the offer, it would again be rejected. Since this was an insulting demand, it was not surprising that the Prussian king would have no part of it.

When he sent a telegram reporting the incident to Bismarck, the chancellor was quick to take advantage of the situation. He shortened the telegram and released it to the press. When the French read this release, they got the impression that their ambassador had been humiliated. To the Prussians, it seemed that their beloved king had been insulted. Soon the people in both countries were demanding war.

Expecting victory, the French suffer a crushing defeat. The French believed that their armies would sweep across Germany as had those of the great Napoleon. "On to Berlin!" shouted French patriots. But France needed more than the memory of Napoleon to defeat Prussia. Outnumbered, poorly prepared, led by incompetent officers, and armed with inferior weapons, the French were no match for Prussia's powerful military machine. Moreover, the South Germans, as Bismarck had anticipated, came to the aid of Prussia.

The Franco-Prussian War began on July 19, 1870. In six weeks the French armies were defeated, and the one commanded by Napoleon III himself had surrendered. Paris was under siege by the Germans. Hoping for a miracle, France refused to surrender. But no miracle occurred; French heroism could not break the siege. As the food supply dwindled, Parisians ate roots, animals from the zoo, and even rats. Finally, late in January, 1871, Paris surrendered. A month later negotiations to conclude peace began at Versailles.

The peace terms compelled France to pay a large indemnity to Germany. France also had to surrender two border provinces, Alsace and Lorraine. French nationalists swore that one day they would regain their lost provinces. Meanwhile, on January 18, 1871, in the palace built by Louis XIV at Versailles, German princes offered the title of "German Kaiser" (*ky′*zer, emperor) to Wilhelm I. After three wars, Bismarck had united Germany and created a German Empire. The constitution of the new German Empire was based on the constitution of the North German Confederation. Despite the existence of a democratically elected national parliament and of political parties, the real power rested largely with the Prussian king and the Junkers. Bismarck had taught the German people to respect power more than liberty. He had convinced them that the sword provided an effective answer to Germany's problems. These were lessons the German people would long remember.

United Germany becomes a great power. The Franco-Prussian War resulted in the unification of Germany. A powerful nation had risen in Central Europe. Her people were educated,

Nationalism was often reflected in music. Drawing upon myths and medieval literature, German composer Richard Wagner created complex and brilliant operas glorifying German traditions. At right the hero Siegfried reforges the magic sword Nothung. Lohengrin (above) deals with Christian German knights.

hard working, and efficient; her industry and commerce were rapidly expanding; her army was the first in Europe. Vigorous and confident, the new German Empire was eager to play an important role in world affairs. Strongly nationalistic, she wanted to become not only the foremost power in Europe but to acquire a colonial empire as well. No nation in Europe was a match for the new Germany. The unification of Germany helped to create fears, tensions, and rivalries that would lead to world war.

CHECK-UP

1. What progress toward German unification had been made before 1862? Why did Bismarck wish to expel Austria from the German Confederation? How was this goal achieved?

2. What was Prussia's role in the North German Confederation? Why did relations between France and Prussia become strained? Why did both sides come to want war?

3. What was the outcome of the Franco-Prussian War? How was German unity finally achieved?

Nationalism: Blessing or Curse?

Many view nationalism as desirable. The dreams of Italian and German nationalists had been realized. In the struggle for unification patriotic poets had inspired their countrymen with stirring words. Young soldiers had marched into battle certain that they were fighting for a just cause. Italians were thrilled by the deeds of Garibaldi. Germans were proud of their victories over Austria and France and of the creation of the German Empire. In Germany and Italy, love of the Fatherland became man's great duty. And so it was throughout Europe, for the spirit of nationalism spread to many lands and to many peoples.

In 1871, as in the Metternich era, many people looked upon nationalism as a great good. It was considered desirable for a people with a common history, common language, and similar traditions to be independent of foreign rule, to be united in one nation instead of being broken up into many separate states. Many people identified nationalism with liberty. They agreed with Mazzini that when nations gained unity and independence, their citizens would enjoy greater freedom. Having fought to gain their own rights, new nations would respect the rights of all nations and all peoples. United in brotherhood, these nations, said Mazzini, would seek to make "things better for all men. . . . Man will greet man, from whatever land he comes, with the name brother."

Few thought that nationalism might also lead to great evil. But how could nationalism result in evil? Shouldn't citizens love their country? Shouldn't a man be proud of his country's achievements? Is it wrong to celebrate national holidays, sing the national anthem, salute the flag, honor the nation's war dead, praise its great men, rejoice in its victories, suffer in its defeats, and defend one's homeland against attack? Have not patriots throughout the ages fought to preserve their nation's liberty? Does not a sense of national pride contribute to a nation's cultural accomplishments?

Nationalism can be carried to extremes. Few men would deny that national pride is expected of a good citizen. But, as we shall see, in the period after 1871 nationalism was often carried to an extreme. Large numbers of people in many lands became *chauvinists* (*shoh'*vin-ists)—extreme nationalists or super-patriots. Chauvinism often flourished in countries that suffered from insecurity. In some cases chauvinists claimed that the nation was threatened by foreign enemies; in other cases they insisted that the nation was endangered by ineffective government or strife between political parties. In still other cases chauvinists expressed envy of countries that were stronger, wealthier, or owned more colonies. Chauvinists urged war in order to overcome past humiliations or to enable their nation to obtain the land, prestige, and power in world affairs that they felt it deserved.

Chauvinists may be racists. Chauvinists searched for common bonds to hold their people together. Often they developed racist theories. Rejecting and distorting scientific evidence, they claimed that some groups belonged to inferior races and that their own people represented a noble, "master" race with a superior biological inheritance. To maintain this superiority and preserve the purity of the race, they opposed intermarriage with "inferior peoples." (They conveniently overlooked the fact that no national group is all of one racial stock, but represents a mingling of different peoples. Who can say that he is "pure" French or "pure" German or "pure" Italian?) As a superior race they had a right to conquer and rule other peoples. The absurd end to which chauvinists carry their racist thinking can be seen in the theories of nazism (see Chapter 29).

Chauvinists may support militarism and dictatorship. Chauvinists often glorified war, claiming that it brought out the finest qualities in man. They agreed with the German general who said: "Everlasting peace is a dream and an ugly one." To chauvinists, the nations of the world were engaged in a struggle for existence in which only the strong would survive. Hence they supported large expenditures for the army and navy and greater power in the government for generals.

Convinced that national greatness was more important than individual liberty and welfare, many ardent nationalists advocated dictatorship as the best form of government. They felt that centralized authority was needed to meet the crises that threatened their country. Experience indicated that democracy often failed to provide a government capable of coping with the problems of the times. To chauvinists, world power was far more important than individual freedom.

Chauvinism appeals to men's emotions. Rejecting appeals to reason, chauvinists tried to arouse people's emotions through rallies, parades, and stirring speeches and music. Such appeals to emotion tend to make people *irrational*—unreasoning and excitable. Human decency, love of one's fellow man, the rights of other people, the ethical teachings of religion have little meaning for men caught in the spell of irrational chauvinism. Swayed by emotional appeals, the masses follow their leader without question and place the fatherland above everything. When nationalism is pushed to an extreme, wrote a German philosopher in 1902, "just and unjust, good and bad, true and false lose their meaning; what men condemn as disgraceful and inhuman when done by others, they recommend in the same breath to their own people as something to be done to a foreign country." So great has been the power of chauvinism over men's minds and emotions that some historians regard it as the greatest evil of the twentieth century.

Many historians maintain that nationalism failed to unite men in brotherhood and liberty as Mazzini had hoped. Instead, it soon became apparent that love of nation was a stronger emotion than love of one's fellow man, or love of liberty. To build a nation's power and prestige seemed a greater goal than liberty and brotherhood.

In the twentieth century, nationalism became as much a "curse" as a "blessing." Chauvinists sought lands to conquer and foreign peoples to dominate. In time the flames of nationalism spread throughout Europe. The entire continent, and other continents as well, became engulfed in wars of conquest and wars of revenge.

CHECK-UP

1. Why is nationalism desirable?

2. What are causes of extreme nationalism (chauvinism)?

3. What are some of the unfortunate results of chauvinism?

Summing Up

The major obstacle to Italian unification was the political fragmentation of the peninsula. Yet the efforts of four men were to overcome political separatism and unite Italy.

Mazzini lit the fire of Italian patriotism. Cavour modernized Sardinia, gained the goodwill of Britain and France, and enlisted the support of Napoleon III in war against Austria. This war gained Lombardy and aroused people in the duchies to oust their rulers and join Sardinia. Meanwhile Garibaldi undertook an amazingly successful expedition in southern Italy and overthrew the Bourbon king of the Two Sicilies, whose people voted to join Sardinia. In 1861 Victor Emmanuel became king of Italy. By siding with Prussia in a war against Austria, Italy obtained Venetia in 1866. Four years later Rome became part of a united Italy.

German unification was largely brought about by Bismarck, a Prussian Junker who became chancellor of Prussia in 1862. He recognized that war would provide the quickest route to the unification of the 39-state German Confederation, which was dominated by Austria. Prussia allied with Austria to seize two German states ruled by the king of Denmark. A quarrel over their administration led to war between Prussia and Austria. Victory enabled Prussia to annex Schleswig and Holstein, take over territory from North German states that had sided with Austria, and eliminate Austria from playing any role in German affairs. Prus-

sia then created a North German Confederation, in which she controlled foreign affairs and the armed forces.

The four South German states outside Prussia's control became part of a united Germany when a quarrel over the succession to the Spanish throne led to the Franco-Prussian War. Again Prussia was victorious. The King of Prussia was named kaiser of the new German Empire, which became one of the leading states in Europe.

Chapter Highlights

Can you explain?

chauvinists   chancellor   racist theories   kaiser
nationalism   Junker

Can you identify?

Mazzini   Napoleon III   Victor Emmanuel   German Confederation
Bismarck   Garibaldi   Alsace-Lorraine   North German Confederation
Prussia   Papal States   Schleswig-Holstein   Lombardo-Venetian
Cavour   Young Italy   Seven Weeks' War   Kingdom
Crimean War   Sardinia   Kingdom of the Two Sicilies

What do you think?

1. Why did Italian and German unification come so much later than the unification of other European countries?

2. How did Mazzini, Cavour, and Garibaldi differ in their approach to Italian unification? Which leader saw most clearly how to unify Italy? Why?

3. Austria and Prussia had been allies in overthrowing Napoleon and maintaining the peace settlement of 1815. Why did they become rivals after 1850?

4. Did France make a mistake in becoming the ally of Sardinia in 1859? In not siding with Austria in 1866? Explain.

5. What were the crucial decisions made by Bismarck in unifying Germany?

6. Why did the South German states go their own way in 1866 only to become part of the German Empire in 1871?

7. What parallels were there in the process of unification in Italy and in Germany? How did it differ?

8. What role did nationalism play in the French Revolution? In the Napoleonic Wars? In the unification of Italy and Germany?

9. Is nationalism a blessing or a curse? Explain.

The Era of the Industrial Revolution

CHAPTER FOCUS

Impact of the Industrial Revolution on England

Reforms Resulting from Industrialization

Germany and France During the Industrial Revolution

Legacy of the Industrial Revolution

As the Industrial Revolution progressed, men became aware of the way it had transformed their lives and the opportunities it could offer for the future. The pace of industrialization was speeded by the building of new railroads, and smokestacks became a town's most visible landmarks (left). The wonder and optimism Britain felt in 1851 were expressed in the Great Exhibition of the Works of Industry of All Nations. British supremacy in industry was clearly demonstrated in the section devoted to steam powered machines (above). In the forefront is a lathe which produced railroad wheels.

During the summer of 1851 millions of visitors flocked to London to visit the Great Exhibition, the first modern world's fair. Housed in Hyde Park in a gigantic glass structure known as the Crystal Palace, the Exhibition was designed as "a true test and living picture of the point of development at which the whole of mankind has arrived . . . and a new starting point, from which all nations will be able to direct their further exertions." Historian Thomas Babington Macaulay described the opening of the Exhibition as follows:

I should think that there must have been near 300,000 people in Hyde Park at once. The sight among the green boughs was delightful. The boats and little frigates darting across the lake; the flags;

the music; the guns; everything was exhilarating. . . . I made my way into the building: a most gorgeous sight; vast; graceful; beyond the dreams of the Arabian romances. I cannot think that the Caesars ever exhibited a more splendid spectacle.

The Crystal Palace featured more than thirteen thousand exhibits. They were "wonderfully ugly," according to one fascinated visitor, who was impressed by the number of new inventions. Among the machines on display were an electric telegraph, a locomotive, and a sewing machine. Perhaps of greatest interest was a machine that made over fifty million medals per week. The Exhibition of 1851 was a striking symbol of the industrial gains that Europe had achieved during the preceding century.

Impact of the Industrial Revolution on England

The Industrial Revolution, which began in England in the middle of the eighteenth century, profoundly influenced the course of modern history. Europe's economy was transformed from a rural to an urban one. Large cities sprang up and population increased. The variety of agricultural and industrial goods brought about noticeable improvements in the standard of living.

But the Industrial Revolution also brought with it numerous problems. The growing towns were often overcrowded and unsanitary. Housing, education, and other social services were inadequate. Work in the factories was dull and uncreative. And for many persons—particularly the poor, many of them just off the farms—the mental adjustment to the demands of city life and factory work was extremely difficult.

How did the Industrial Revolution, a development without precedent in history, begin? And why did it occur first in England? The answers to these questions are complex. To provide an explanation we must analyze several important developments in England.

FACTORS LEADING TO THE INDUSTRIAL REVOLUTION

The population of Britain increases steadily after 1700. In 1730 the population of England was approximately six million. By 1851, when the first complete census (population count) was taken, the number of inhabitants had surpassed twenty-one million. This spectacular increase was an important cause of the Industrial Revolution.

For hundreds of years prior to the mid-eighteenth century the population of England was relatively stable. Greater technical knowledge allowed marked improvement of the physical conditions of life after 1700. Soap became commonly available, diets became better balanced as new foods poured in from America, and towns began to make some provision for sanitation. The bubonic plague, which had killed millions of persons in England and Western Europe over several centuries, disappeared. (The black rat whose fleas carried the disease was slowly destroyed as better housing and methods of sanitation were introduced.) With these improvements people could expect to live longer. Not only did more and more adults have a longer life expectancy, but infant mortality (death rate) declined. A child born in 1700 had only half the chance to live to the age of five as one born ninety years later. Moreover, people began to marry at an earlier age and to produce more children who survived to become adults.

This population explosion in England, a country no larger in size than the State of New York, created a tremendous demand for food and for manufactured goods. Since producers had a greater chance for earning profits, investment and economic growth were stimulated.

Perhaps most important, the population increase meant a larger and more mobile work force. Growing numbers of laborers, many of them women and children, were now available for employment in the new factories. Others were prepared to work in agricultural areas, which were also undergoing fundamental changes.

Population growth was a necessary precondition to industrialization, for it provided a labor supply and a home market for manufactured goods. But in itself it does not account for the Industrial Revolution. For example, the population of Ireland, a small country lacking in natural wealth, increased as fast as that of England during the eighteenth century. But Ireland did not experience an industrial revolution. Consequently, its standard of living declined.

England becomes a leading commercial nation. Another factor which aided England's industrial growth was her leadership in world trade. During the seventeenth century she had begun to build up a sizeable overseas empire. By defeating France and the Netherlands in a series of naval and colonial wars, England in the eighteenth century gained unchallenged control of the seas and developed an extensive trading network. The key centers of Britain's overseas trade were West Africa, the West Indies, India, and the American Colonies. (When the Thirteen Colonies gained their independence and became the United States, England continued her profitable trade with them.)

These commercial gains were a distinct advantage. England's imports and exports increased sixfold during the eighteenth century, resulting in greater wealth for many of her inhabitants. This increased prosperity, much of it derived from the profitable but inhumane slave trade, raised the demand for goods. It also made available large amounts of capital for investment in industry.

But the growth of commerce had even wider ramifications. London became the central market of the world, replacing the Dutch city of Amsterdam. London had Europe's best credit and insurance facilities and many capable businessmen. And due to her command of the seas England was far better equipped than other countries to draw upon overseas territories for raw materials. The most notable example of this was cotton, a fiber imported in huge quantities from the southern part of the United States and, to a lesser extent, from India. The reverse process was no less important. This involved the sale of English manufactured goods, including cotton cloth, to the United States and to other overseas markets.

England's position as the greatest trading country in the world helped prepare the way for the Industrial Revolution in three ways: (1) The capital obtained from trade was invested in young industries. (2) Raw materials important for industry but unavailable at home were obtained from overseas. (3) Trade gave England established overseas markets to which she could sell the goods produced by her developing industries.

Canals improve transportation and reduce costs. Another important cause of the Industrial Revolution was the availability of cheap, efficient transportation. Only with adequate transportation can goods be purchased and marketed on a national scale. The movement of money and of men willing to take financial risks in order to make large profits is also dependent upon sound transport.

Railroads have provided the major source of transportation for most countries that have become industrialized. But the first English railroad, connecting the cities of Liverpool and Manchester, was not in operation until 1830. Railroads subsequently covered the entire country, causing the poet Wordsworth to complain: "Is there no nook of English ground secure from rash assaults?" However, transportation in England in the early stages of the Industrial Revolution depended largely on canals rather than on transportation by rail.

England's geography favored the building of canals. No section of the country is more than ninety miles from the sea and many navigable rivers—notably the Mersey and the Tyne in the north, the Thames (*temz*) in the south, and the Clyde in Scotland—crisscross it. Beginning in the 1750's canals were constructed which effectively linked all the major rivers. By 1790 it was possible to travel to any part of England solely by water.

These canals, often given added value by the improvement of adjoining roads, were not built by the government. Instead, they were financed entirely by private persons. The profits were often astonishing. The Oxford Canal, for example, gave a 30 per cent annual return to its investors for more than thirty years.

The "canal revolution" reduced significantly the prices of raw materials and finished goods because it reduced the costs of transportation. Coal could be transported by water from mines to factories for half the cost of transportation by road. The economic gains brought by the canals may be illustrated in a more abstract way. Whereas one packhorse could pull a load weighing 1000 pounds by road, an equivalent amount of labor could pull 100,000 pounds of goods on the canals.

Banks provide cheaper credit. T. S. Ashton, a leading authority on the Industrial Revolution, has stated: "If we seek . . . for a single reason why the pace of economic development quickened about the middle of the eighteenth century, it is to [the lowering of the rate of interest that] we must look." Because of the low interest rate (rate charged on loans), investors were encouraged to borrow money with which to build factories and machinery. Adequate credit facilities are vital to industry in order that sufficient funds may be made available for investment. And it was in this area that England possessed perhaps her most decided advantage. Between 1700 and 1757 the interest rate on most loans dropped from 10 per cent to about 3 per cent. This speeded up investment in both long- and short-term business ventures, that is, in the construction of canals and roads as well

as in the production of goods for immediate sale.

There are other reasons why the Industrial Revolution began in England. The availability of coal and iron and of other natural resources greatly aided industrialization. By not interfering with businessmen, the British government also contributed to industrialization. Most political leaders, regardless of their social background, were sympathetic to the needs of industry. Finally, England had a number of capable inventors and resourceful businessmen. Their combined efforts made possible the application of power machinery to industry and the rise of the factory system of production.

THE REVOLUTION IN AGRICULTURE

The economic revolution that took place in England after 1750 had far-reaching consequences for agriculture. Since some of the agricultural changes preceded those of industry, it is possible to describe them as a cause of the Industrial Revolution. But in a larger sense the "agrarian revolution" can be said to have paralleled that in industry. There was both an Agricultural Revolution and an Industrial Revolution.

The transformations in agriculture were of two basic types: (1) application of technology and (2) consolidation of land.

Technological developments are applied to agriculture. During the eighteenth century there were improvements in farm equipment. Better plows, threshing machines, and other implements aided English agriculture, though not in all sections of the country. But of greater importance was the development of more efficient methods for using the soil. The older system of crop rotation, by which one-third of the land lay fallow each year, was abandoned. Instead, turnips and seed grasses were sown. These new crops served a double purpose: they restored the fertility of the soil, and also served to feed livestock during the winter months.

In the latter half of the eighteenth century many associations were formed to popularize these new agricultural discoveries. Prominent individuals actively circulated information about improvements in agriculture, and in 1793 the government established the Board of Agriculture. Involved were great landowners and even the king, George III, who prided himself on his nickname, "Farmer George."

The consolidation of land leads to more efficient farming. The extent to which the land is divided often affects a nation's economic growth. Small landowners, for example, find it difficult to use machinery on their property because the machinery is usually too expensive. Owners of large estates are far better able to take advantage of advances in farm equipment. During the eighteenth century the number of small farmers in England rapidly declined, mainly due to the *enclosure movement.*

Initiated either by Parliament or by private persons, enclosure brought about the forcible consolidation of land. Whereas in earlier times the land had been divided into narrow strips, it was now combined into larger fields. Most villages possessed a *commons,* which belonged equally to all inhabitants. This communal land, used by the poor for grazing cattle and chopping wood, was now enclosed—absorbed into large private estates. Between 1760 and 1880 several million acres of English land, most of them quite good, were enclosed and sold to owners of large estates by commissioners who were appointed by Parliament. The *economic advantages* of enclosure are obvious. The owners of large tracts of land purchased the new machines and took advantage of the growing demand for food. They also introduced other agricultural improvements and sometimes invested in manufacturing or mining enterprises. Thus, in several ways enclosure aided the expansion of industry.

But the *social disadvantages* of enclosure are equally clear. Oliver Goldsmith, an English poet, graphically described these disadvantages in a famous poem entitled "The Deserted Village."

> Ill fares the land, to hastening ills a prey,
> Where wealth accumulates, and men decay:
> Princes and lords may flourish, or may fade;
> A breath can make them, as a breath has made;
> But a bold peasantry, their country's pride,
> When once destroyed, can never be supplied.

Conditions were not everywhere as bad as those depicted by Goldsmith. There is no doubt, however, that the poor suffered considerably. With the village commons gone, many poor persons had no land on which to build cottages and graze their animals. The independent English peasant, who had tilled his own land for centuries and taken pride in his work, now found himself landless. Rather than leave the land, most farmers went to work on the new, large estates. But the low daily wages drove a growing number to seek work elsewhere. By the thousands they drifted into the bleak, uninviting towns of the north to work in the new cotton mills.

THE REVOLUTION IN INDUSTRY

By 1850 England was producing much of the coal mined in Europe and was manufacturing more than half of that continent's cotton cloth. Her iron, woolen cloth, and machine industries were of the first rank. Manchester, Birmingham, and Liverpool, with populations in excess of 100,000, were among the leading cities of Europe. England was rightly coming to be known as the "workshop of the world."

Several key industrial developments shaped England's history from 1750 on. Among the most important were (1) the spectacular growth of the cotton industry, (2) expanded coal and iron industries, (3) the application of the steam engine, and (4) the rise of the factory system.

The cotton industry experiences spectacular growth. "No other industry could compare in importance with cotton in the first phase of

British industrialization, writes historian E. J. Hobsbaum. So significant was the growth of the cotton industry that the phrases "Industrial Revolution" and "cotton manufacture" are almost synonymous. The factory system, child labor, and the emergence of trade unions are all closely linked to cotton.

The cotton industry grew spectacularly because there was a rapidly rising demand for a clothing material cheaper and lighter than wool.

The human costs of England's industrialization were great. The overcrowded town below, shrouded in factory smoke, might be Dickens' Coketown. The loss of privacy and lack of fresh air troubled the many workers who had moved in from the country. Conditions on the job were as bleak as those in the worker's home. Mining (right) was especially dangerous, requiring backbreaking labor under conditions which could permanently ruin a worker's health. Even children toiled long hours at heavy labor. Although working conditions have improved, the problems of poverty, urban slums, and pollution remain with us.

England was able to import raw cotton easily from America and India. Favored by a damp climate that facilitated the spinning of thread and by an abundance of coal, she manufactured and marketed the cotton. In so doing, England created the first great industry based entirely upon the needs of ordinary consumers.

Machines were invented to speed up cotton production. The water frame, developed by Richard Arkwright in 1769, revolutionized the *spinning* of cotton. In 1785 the power loom, created by Edmund Cartwright, speeded up the *weaving* of cotton yarn into cloth. By the end of the century, therefore, all aspects of cotton manufacture were performed in factories. Domestic or cottage manufacture, important for several centuries but necessarily inefficient, began to disappear. The new factories were located near the coal mines in the north, and close to the port of Liverpool, to which American cotton was shipped. Manchester, a city less than forty miles from Liverpool, became the world's center for cotton manufacture.

Large coal deposits make possible an expanded iron industry. Next in importance to cotton were the coal and iron industries. The construction of industrial machinery and the rise of the factory system depended upon iron, a basic metal, and upon coal, an inexpensive fuel. England was fortunate in having large supplies of both. However, until the late eighteenth century it was not feasible to use the two minerals together in smelting iron. Coal (or coke) caused impurities in the iron, and charcoal (obtained by burning timber) was the preferred fuel. But most of the large forests had been destroyed earlier and adequate supplies of wood were thus no longer available in England.

As early as 1709 attempts had been made to employ coke in smelting iron. However, it was not until 1784 that the *puddling* process was invented by a man named Henry Cort. This process made it possible for coal to be used as a fuel in the iron industry, thus launching England into the age of heavy industry. The iron industry, previously located in country areas near supplies of timber, now shifted to the region of coal and iron mines. Large new factory districts appeared. With manufactured iron available at low prices, the construction of more and better machines and of improved transportation became possible.

The steam engine provides inexpensive power. The steam engine was the invention which had implications for all the major industries. With the use of steam power it no longer was necessary to rely upon mills powered by wind or water to move machinery. Steam provided more power at less expense, and it was more easily harnessed. Since industries were now chiefly dependent only upon adequate supplies of coal and of labor, they could be located almost anywhere. In T. S. Ashton's opinion, the steam engine was "the pivot on which industry swung into the modern age."

Steam engines first came into use for mining operations early in the eighteenth century. But the invention of a rotary engine in the 1770's by James Watt, a Scottish instrument-maker, gave the machine wider applicability. Watt also introduced improvements such as the invention of a separate condenser to save energy. With the growing use of steam engines after 1785, industry became fully mechanized. All of England was changed as a result.

The factory system creates problems for workers. Before 1750 most work had been done either in the home or in small workshops. But the machines of the Industrial Revolution were too large and too expensive for this "cottage-type" industry. Large, impersonal factories became the centers of work. At first these were located near fast-running streams which could be harnessed to operate the machines. After the steam engine came into use, factories were built closer to the supplies of coal and iron. They grew rapidly in size, some of them coming to employ several thousand workers at once. For the hundreds of thousands of laborers who were faced with the prospect of factory work for the first time, this meant many hardships. A working day of 12–14 hours was not uncommon, and since most factory "hands" did not own watches or clocks, they were often forced to report for work earlier than necessary.

Conditions in the factories ranged from inadequate to poor. Contagious diseases such as the mysterious "factory fever" took many lives. Serious accidents, sometimes involving the loss of an arm or leg, were common. These were mostly the result of inadequate protective devices on the machines. And a harsh discipline, different from the easier relations of cottage industry, was continually imposed. A cotton spinner testified before a Parliamentary committee in 1833 why he beat child workers:

I have frequently had complaints against myself by the parents of children for beating them. I used to beat them. I am sure that no man can do without it who works long hours; I am sure he cannot. I told them I was very sorry after I had done it, but I was forced to do it. The master expected me to do my work, and I could not do mine unless they did theirs. I used to joke with them to keep up their spirits.

In the early stages of the Industrial Revolution a majority of factory workers were women or young children. Though child labor had existed for hundreds of years without arousing any criticism, the labor of children in factories, by its very nature, directly threatened the health of the child and the stability of family life. A commission investigated child labor in mines in 1842 and concluded: "Chained, belted, harnessed like dogs in a go-cart, black, saturated with wet, and more than half-naked—crawling upon their hands and feet, and dragging their heavy loads behind them—they present an appearance disgusting and unnatural." Reformers denounced the evils of "infant slavery," and during the nineteenth century a series of factory acts was passed which eliminated child labor.

Industrialization contributes to the rapid growth of cities. In 1750 about 15 per cent of the English population lived in towns. A century later, due to the growth and concentration of factories, the figure had risen to more than 50 per cent. Industrial cities such as Manchester (cotton manufacturing), Leeds (woolen cloth), and Sheffield (cutlery) sprang up. But only slowly did adequate facilities develop, and in these cities first appeared the kinds of social problems that still exist today. Poor housing, inadequate education, crime, poor sanitation, and lack of leisure-time activities were of concern then as they are today. To a people accustomed to rural life, the stresses of urban life produced frustrations and tensions. At their best the new cities offered greater possibilities for cultural and social stimulation. At their worst (and more often than not they were at their worst) they resembled Coketown, the fictional city that Charles Dickens satirized in his novel *Hard Times*:

It was a town of red brick, or of brick that would have been red if the smoke and ashes had allowed it. . . . It had a black canal in it, and a river that ran purple with ill-smelling dye, and vast piles of building full of windows where there was a rattling and a trembling all day long. . . . It contained several large streets all very like one another, . . . inhabited by people equally like one another, who all went in and out at the same hours, with the same sound upon the same pavements, to do the same work, and to whom every day was the same as yesterday and tomorrow, and every year the counterpart of the last and the next.

Historians debate the effects of the Industrial Revolution. Most historians have been critical of the social effects of the Industrial Revolution in England. They emphasize the problems of urban life, and argue that the factory workers were grossly underpaid. They describe the appalling conditions of work that existed in the factories. Most of all they assert that the *quality* of life deteriorated because of the process of rapid change. In an influential book entitled *The Town Labourer*, J. L. Hammond writes: "Their towns were as ugly as their industries, with an ugliness in both cases that was a symptom of work and life in which men and women could find no happiness or self-expression; the brand of a race disinherited of its share in the arts and beauty of the world."

But recently a number of economic historians, led by T. S. Ashton, have challenged this interpretation. These historians are sometimes called "optimists" because of their more positive conclusions. They maintain that factory workers enjoyed a higher standard of living than other groups of workers and that they were able to purchase goods that were not available in country districts, including inexpensive clothing and household items. Furthermore, they point out that factory workers labored fewer hours *on an average* than other workers and that their wages were higher. And they stress that, although equal opportunities did not exist for the very poor, those who lived in cities had greater possibilities for developing their lives than those residing in rural areas.

CHECK-UP

1. How did the Industrial Revolution transform Europe? What problems accompanied it?

2. What factors led to the Industrial Revolution in England?

3. What caused the revolution in agriculture? What was the enclosure movement? What were its effects?

4. What inventions revolutionized the cotton industry?

5. What changes took place in the English iron industry during the 1700's? How did the steam engine revolutionize industrial production?

6. Why did the factory system replace cottage industry? What problems did the factory system create?

7. Why did industrialization contribute to urban growth? What problems developed in the industrial cities? What were the benefits of urban life?

Reforms Resulting from Industrialization

Between the end of the eighteenth century and the beginning of World War I, Britain experienced significant changes. The Industrial Revolution led to reforms in her political system and modification in her social and economic policies. By 1914 Britain had developed a parliamentary government that was uniquely stable and a social welfare system that was as advanced as any in Europe.

Britain does not have a written constitution. Over the centuries its system of government has been shaped by customs, by decisions of judges, by acts of Parliament, and by historical events. Some important developments in the shaping of the political structure of Britain by the end of the seventeenth century have already been discussed: common law, Magna Carta, the rise of Parliament, the jury system, the Petition of Right, decisions of the Long Parliament, the Glorious Revolution, and the Bill of Rights. Taken together, these developments served to weaken the king's power and to give the British a large measure of liberty under the law.

The power of the monarchy declines. In the century following the Glorious Revolution of 1688, British kings slowly continued to lose power to Parliament. Unlike eighteenth-century French monarchs, no British king after 1689 claimed that he had been selected by God to rule. The British monarch was still in theory the head of the political system. He had the power to summon and dissolve Parliament, to appoint ministers, and to approve or disapprove legislation. In addition, he was commander-in-chief of the armed forces and responsible

513

Growth of Reform in Britain

1832	Reform Act gives middle-class males the right to vote
1839	Beginning of Chartist movement
1867, 1884	Extension of male suffrage
1870	Expansion of public education
1872	Secret ballot introduced
1911	Parliament Act reduces power of House of Lords
1918	Women over 30 gain right to vote
1928	Voting age for women lowered to 21

for defense and foreign policy. But during the eighteenth century many of these powers had not been exercised. Since the early 1700's no British monarch has vetoed (rejected) an act of Parliament. Parliament thus continued to gain strength at the expense of the monarch. By the end of the eighteenth century, limited monarchy had been firmly established in Britain. The king was little more than a figurehead; real power in the government rested with Parliament.

The House of Lords is weakened. The British Parliament consists of a House of Lords and a House of Commons. Members of the House of Lords are not elected by the people but inherit their seats from their aristocratic fathers or are appointed. For several hundred years the Lords had been dominant in Parliament, but during the eighteenth century power had clearly shifted to the Commons. Control over financial bills gave the Commons a distinctive advantage. During the nineteenth century the power of the House of Lords continued to decline, and the Parliament Act of 1911 permanently weakened it. By the terms of this act, the Lords could only delay but not prevent an act of the Commons from becoming a law. Money bills could be held up for only one month, non-money bills for no longer than two years. (In 1949 this was reduced to one year.) A basic reason why Britain is considered a democracy is that the true power

in the government rests, not with the hereditary House of Lords or the king, but with the House of Commons whose members are elected by the people.

The prime minister heads the British government. The prime minister is usually the leader of the political party that commands a majority of votes in the House of Commons. In the United States the president *cannot* be a member of Congress; in Britain the prime minister *must* be a member of Parliament before he can be considered for the highest office in the government. The prime minister is assisted by a *cabinet,* a small inner council drawn from members of Parliament. The prime minister and his cabinet formulate programs and policies which they submit to Parliament for approval. If the Commons rejects their leadership, the prime minister and members of the cabinet resign and new elections are usually held. Theoretically, the prime minister is elected for a five-year term, but his term of office may be cut short at any time if he loses the support of the majority in the House of Commons.

By 1800 the prime minister had clearly surpassed the monarch in political power. After 1800 the office was more fully defined by such outstanding politicians and statesmen as William Pitt (1783–1801), Robert Peel (1841–1846), William E. Gladstone (1868–1874, 1880–1885), and Benjamin Disraeli (diz-*ray'*lih, 1874–1880).

Political parties develop. The modern party system is the cement which holds the British political system together. A large number of local party associations are brought together on the national level. Members of the House of Commons are subject to discipline from these party associations and almost always support their party in Parliament. There is considerably less independence in voting situations in Parliament than in the United States Congress.

The modern party system dates from the late eighteenth century. The French Revolution, with its violence and social radicalism, divided public opinion in Britain. On one side stood the *Whigs,* a group of large landowners and businessmen who sympathized with the need for reform. Opposed to them were the *Tories,* who attacked the French Revolution and everything it represented. The Tories were committed to preserving a stable, landed society, and to maintaining a significant role for the Church of England. During the 1830's the Tories, under the moderate leadership of Peel, became known as the Conservatives. The Whigs evolved into the Liberal Party several decades later when they chose Gladstone, a brilliant politician, as their leader. A two-party system has prevailed since the late nineteenth century, although occasionally third parties have had some success. After 1900 the Labour Party, committed to improving the position of the working classes, largely replaced the Liberals as a major political force in Britain.

More of the British obtain the right to vote. The Industrial Revolution forced significant political changes upon Britain. By concentrating large numbers of workers in overcrowded and unsanitary cities, it unleashed powerful demands for reform. Successive governments made meaningful responses to these demands. This moderation perhaps explains why Britain was able to avoid revolution during the nineteenth century. But unrest became widespread in the first half of the century, and urban and rural laborers sometimes rioted on behalf of political reform.

The major debate concerned the *franchise,* or right to vote. Under the system which prevailed prior to 1832 the franchise differed from area to area. Ownership of property was usually required for a person to qualify for voting. Thus the poor and many in the rising middle class were unable to participate in politics. And representation in the Commons was not based upon districts of equal population. For example, Portsmouth, an important port, had a population of 33,000 inhabitants, only 110 of whom could vote. Old Sarum, a once flourishing town, by the early nineteenth century was an unin-

habited estate. The Earl of Caledon, who owned the property, chose two men to represent him in the House of Commons.

In 1832, after two years of agitation, the Reform Bill was passed. A landmark in the history of modern Britain, the Reform Bill extended the right to vote to many more of the people. Previously, one adult male in nine could vote; after 1832 the proportion was one in five. The Reform Bill also reorganized the electoral districts so that the newer industrial areas had a fairer representation in the House of Commons. It gave the middle class a strong and perhaps decisive role in shaping British politics.

The Reform Bill of 1832 gave the vote only to the middle class. During the 1840's the Chartist Movement, representing a large segment of the working class, urged further political reform. The Chartists presented petitions to Parliament demanding universal manhood suffrage, a secret ballot, abolition of property requirements for serving in Parliament, pay for members of Parliament, and annual elections. By the standard of the day, the Chartist demands were considered revolutionary. Therefore Parliament at first rejected their demands. But the Reform Bill of 1832 had opened the floodgate of reform. In the years to come all the Chartist demands, except that of annual elections for members of Parliament, were eventually realized. In 1867 under Disraeli and in 1884 under Gladstone, the right to vote was extended to virtually all adult males. An act initiated by Gladstone in 1872 provided for the secret ballot, an important stepping-stone to democracy. In 1911 members of Parliament received payment, enabling the poor to hold office. And finally, in 1918 and 1928 democracy became a reality with the extension of voting rights to women, a previously excluded group.

Social reforms improve living conditions. Political reform was paralleled by legislation in other areas. As the nation became more receptive to growing pressures from the poor, demands for social reform increased. In the last half of the nineteenth century it slowly came to be accepted that government would have to intervene directly in the complex problems of modern society. The modern welfare state, in which government makes direct provisions for its citizens, was emerging.

Laws dealing with factory conditions, education, and public health were passed during the nineteenth century. These increasingly thrust the central government closer to the needs of its citizens. Hours of work were regulated in factories and mines, conditions of work were improved, and cities and counties were encouraged to tackle the problems of sanitation and housing.

Under Gladstone and Disraeli, who together dominated British government during the second half of the nineteenth century, striking reforms were instituted. Gladstone was responsible for the establishment of a system of state education in 1870. This was made voluntary at the outset and a small fee was charged pupils. The present system of compulsory, free education for all stems from this act. Disraeli was equally committed to reform. More of a pioneer than Gladstone in social legislation, he sought to unite the interests of the landed classes and the poor. To create a society based upon social justice, he freed trade unions from existing

One of man's most vital senses is that of sight. A significant advance in the nineteenth century was the development of photography, then both a practical art and a hobby for the affluent. Photographs of news events and the people who made them happen gave the public the feeling that it was participating in history. The portrait above shows Queen Victoria holding a photograph of her husband, Prince Albert. Robert Fenton, one of the earliest war correspondents, had the first portable darkroom (above, right). Trick photography intrigued many; the photograph at right shows French artist Toulouse-Lautrec sketching himself.

516

restrictions, expanded public-health and factory measures, and began the first slum-clearance program in Britain.

Between 1900 and 1914 the framework of the modern welfare state was established by the Liberal Party. In response to labor unrest and growing discontent in Ireland, and spurred on by social reforms in Germany, many important laws were passed. David Lloyd George, a future prime minister, and Winston Churchill, who was to become one of Britain's most renowned statesmen, were the major advocates of this social program. They helped to establish a system of minimum wages, flexibly adapted to differing industries; an unemployment-insurance system, the first in the world; and a number of social welfare services, including free medical treatment for injured workers. By 1914 Britain was well on the road toward solving many of the problems which had beset her during the previous century. Perhaps most important of all, she had demonstrated that the British political system was capable of resolving problems of great political and social importance without recourse to violence. In coping with the problems created by the Industrial Revolution, Britain chose the path of peaceful reform rather than violent revolution. This is high tribute to the quality of the British system of government.

CHECK-UP

1. What developments weakened the power of the British monarch? Of the House of Lords?

2. What is the structure of the British Parliament? What are the powers and responsibilities of the Prime Minister?

3. How did political parties develop and grow in Britain?

4. What were the important stages in the expansion of the right to vote?

5. What major reforms did the British government introduce to improve living conditions?

Germany and France During the Industrial Revolution

In the last part of the nineteenth century Europe underwent vast changes, many of them due to the spread of the Industrial Revolution. The factory system, the railroad and canal system, and the shift of population from farm to city created an industrial civilization. In this new age the traditional rulers of Europe—kings, aristocrats, and churchmen—were losing power to middle-class bankers, industrialists, and merchants. Under the influence of liberal ideas and the British experience in government, most European states acquired parliaments and constitutions. Under the influence of democratic ideas, the common man was gaining the right to vote. The growing importance and power of the working class could be seen in the rise of labor unions and socialist political parties, the extension of schooling for the masses (mainly in Western and Northern Europe), and the emergence of newspapers that catered to the common man. Considerable class conflict marked the political history of Europe during this period. Landowners, merchants, bankers, and shopkeepers feared the increased power of the workers. A united and powerful working class might one day gain control of the government. With the government under its control it could pass laws that would hurt the pocketbooks of businessmen and farmers or, even worse, seize their property.

GERMANY

The German government is more autocratic than democratic. In Chapter 22 we saw how Prussia under the leadership of Otto von Bismarck had created a unified Germany by waging successful wars against Denmark, Austria, and France. After the Franco-Prussian war of 1870–1871, the German Empire or *Reich* (*rike*) came into existence. Like the United States, the German Reich was a federation consisting of several state governments and a central government. The various state governments were ruled largely by kings, princes, or dukes, and power remained in the hands of the wealthy upper class. The rulers of the states were hostile to democracy.

Nor was the central government democratic. While the Reich did have a parliamentary form of government, the parliament had little power. Members of the *Reichstag* (*rikes'*tahk), the lower house of parliament, represented the people and were elected by adult male citizens. The heads of the different states appointed members of the *Bundesrat* (*bun'*des-raht), the upper house. The Bundesrat had more power than the Reichstag. Members of the Bundesrat were generally conservatives who resisted attempts to make Germany more democratic. Describing the limited power of the Reichstag, one German observer wrote, "The people call the Reichstag a talk-shop, because they know that German policy is not made there but in a quite different place."

If power did not rest with the popularly elected Reichstag, who then made policy in Germany? The Reich was a creation of the Prussian army and the Prussian chancellor, Bismarck; Prussia therefore dominated the nation. The king of Prussia was the Kaiser of the Reich and its chancellor was the Prussian prime minister. Through the chancellor, whom he appointed and dismissed at his discretion, the German kaiser, unlike the British monarch, exercised considerable power over lawmaking. The kaiser also had authority over the army and navy, and in time of war the armies of the different German states came under the command of the Prussian army. Prussian delegates, by dominating the Bundesrat, prevented a change in the constitutional framework of the nation. Through his chancellor the kaiser also controlled foreign affairs. The kaiser was thus independent of parliamentary control. Real power in Germany rested with the kaiser, the chancellor, the Prussian generals, the Junkers (page 496), and a growing number of wealthy bankers and industrialists.

Thus despite the parliamentary system, Germany was largely an autocratic state. While France, Britain, the United States, and other western nations were becoming more democratic, the rulers of Germany steadfastly opposed democratic ideas and a western-style parliamentary government. The failure of democratic attitudes and procedures to take root in Germany was to have dangerous consequences for the future.

Germany becomes a leading industrial power. The Industrial Revolution reached Germany in the late 1800's and transformed the newly united nation from a basically agricultural nation into one of the world's great industrialized states. During this period German cities grew rapidly as the population increased from about 41 million to 68 million. Coal, iron, and steel production increased at an extraordinary rate. Between 1871 and 1910, for example, pig-iron production increased nearly tenfold, and by the turn of the century Germany was producing more steel than Britain. Aided by the skill of her scientists and inventors, Germany became a leader in the chemical and electrical industries. She built an extensive and efficient network of railroads, a merchant marine that rivaled Britain's, and an armaments industry second to none. A tremendous increase in foreign trade accompanied this industrial expansion.

Bismarck institutes reforms to aid the working class. The rapid industrialization of Germany created typical problems for the working class. To fight for its interests, a socialist party arose which attacked capitalism. German socialists declared that "the means of production must be transformed into common property of society." They also called for greater democracy, free compulsory education, a progressive income tax, and abolition of a standing army.

Chancellor Bismarck saw the socialist party as a threat to property rights and the security of the state. Blaming two attempts on the emperor's life on the socialists, Bismarck launched a violent attack against them. In 1878 he pressured the Reichstag into passing the Anti-Socialist Law. This gave the government power to suppress socialist publications, break up working-class organizations, prevent socialists from holding meetings, and imprison or exile socialist leaders. For a time the socialist party controlled fewer votes. But soon socialist representation in the Reichstag increased, and the Anti-Socialist Law was not renewed in 1890. Bismarck's attempts to crush socialism in Germany had failed.

At the same time Bismarck bore down on the socialists, he was also trying to win the support of the working class by inaugurating a program of social welfare. Workers were provided with sickness, accident, and old-age benefits. By showing that the state would help the worker, Bismarck hoped to weaken the attraction that socialism held for the working class. In time additional laws were passed to eliminate unsafe working conditions and to prevent children from laboring in factories and mines. Before World War I, Germany had taken the lead in social legislation in Europe.

Nationalism and imperialism grow stronger. As Germany was becoming a major industrial power there was a trend toward extreme nationalism or *chauvinism* (see pages 501–502). German chauvinists, seeking to increase the power of Germany, expressed hostility to democratic, liberal, and humanitarian ideals. Their aim was to increase German prestige, symbolized by the authoritarian Prussian king and the might of the Prussian army; for this reason the chauvinists also urged imperialist policies. Some talked of adding to Germany areas in Europe inhabited by German-speaking peoples. Others spoke vaguely of Germany's destiny to dominate the continent, even though it might be necessary to wage war in order to achieve this goal.

Within a short period of time Germany had become a powerful industrialized nation ready and eager to play an important role in world affairs. Her growing industrial and military might, along with her chauvinism, alarmed other nations. This combination of Germany vitality, aggressiveness, and the fears of her rivals helped lead to World War I (see Chapter 27).

FRANCE

The Franco-Prussian War leads to the formation of the Third French Republic. The Franco-Prussian War that brought about the unification of Germany also had important consequences for France. It ended the rule of Louis Napoleon and led to the creation of the Third French Republic. Louis Napoleon had been elected president of France in 1848—the year that France experienced two revolutions (see pages 484–486). Many Frenchmen voted for Louis Napoleon because they expected him to restore the greatness that his uncle, Napoleon Bonaparte, had given the nation. Peasants, artisans, shopkeepers, and businessmen saw in Louis Napoleon a strong man who would protect property owners from radical workers. Remembering the June Days of 1848, when a working-class revolt was crushed only after three days of vicious street fighting, French property owners were determined to keep the workers in line. In 1852 the people of France supported Louis Napoleon's desire to follow in Napoleon's footsteps and he became Emperor of the French. Once again a French republic had been followed by an empire.

Napoleon III gave France a typically authoritarian government which permitted no opposition, censored the press, and allowed parliament little power. But in 1860 Napoleon III's policies shifted drastically. Liberal reforms were introduced. Napoleon III pardoned political prisoners, removed press censorship, allowed workers the right to form unions, and gave parliament greater power. These reforms have perplexed historians. Was Napoleon III, after all, a sincere believer in liberal ideals who waited until his power was firmly established before trying to put his ideals into practice? Or did he introduce reforms only because he feared unrest?

Captured by the Prussians during the Franco-Prussian War, Napoleon III could do nothing to prevent republicans from taking over the leadership of France. The new republic tried in vain to arouse the fighting spirit of the French people in order to drive back the German invaders. But there was no stopping the Prussian war machine, and the peace settlement forced France to surrender to Prussia the province of Alsace and most of the province of Lorraine. It also called for a large indemnity. This was a terrible blow to French patriots.

The Third Republic establishes itself amidst opposition. During the spring of 1871 the new French Republic was faced with the problem of crushing an uprising by radical elements in Paris. Angered by defeat in war and by the terrible economic conditions, and dissatisfied with the policies of the conservative leaders of the Third French Republic, Paris radicals and revolutionaries formed a government called the *Commune.* The government troops finally crushed the uprising after bloody street fighting. With the leaders of the Commune dead, jailed, or exiled, it was clear that the Republic would be led by moderates rather than radicals.

Even after crushing the Paris Commune, the Third French Republic still faced opposition. Monarchists came very close to restoring a king to the throne of France. Between 1885 and 1900 the Republic was threatened by aristocrats, nationalists, churchmen, and army leaders who wanted to establish a strong authoritarian government. The most serious of these threats sprang from the Dreyfus Affair.

Alfred Dreyfus, a Jewish army captain, was accused of spying for Germany. Found guilty, Dreyfus was sentenced to life imprisonment in the French penal colony at Devil's Island off the coast of South America. When new evidence was uncovered indicating that Dreyfus was innocent and that he had been framed, France became a nation divided. Opponents of Dreyfus —army leaders, nationalists, churchmen, and anti-Jewish groups—insisted that Dreyfus was guilty and that to reopen the case would cast doubt on the honor of the army.

The defenders of Dreyfus insisted that justice must be served regardless of the consequences; if Dreyfus were proved innocent, he must be freed no matter whom it embarrassed. (A number of years passed before Dreyfus was declared innocent and his commission restored.) By replacing anti-Republic army leaders with officers loyal to the Republic, the Republic survived this threat to its existence.

The Third French Republic suffered from a basic political weakness. Unlike Britain and the United States, France had many political parties. With the vote split among a number of parties, no one party had sufficient support within parliament to provide strong leadership. Prime ministers were unable to win sufficient support within parliament and resigned in rapid succession. France gave the appearance of a government without direction. Nevertheless, the Third Republic did overcome threats from within and did endure. Not until the Nazis conquered France in 1940 was it destroyed.

France makes economc gains. Despite political instability the French economy made substantial gains between 1871 and 1914, though the rate of growth lagged behind that of Britain, the United States, and Germany. France's population grew only 3.5 million in the same period that the German population grew by about 27 million. By 1910 Germany was producing more than four times as much steel as France and almost seven times as much coal and lignite. (One reason for this was that Alsace and Lorraine, the provinces Prussia had taken from France in the Franco-Prussian War, were rich in coal and iron ore.) The statistics reveal that France was no longer the great power that she had been under Napoleon Bonaparte. In the new industrial age, in which national power was measured by size of population, coal and steel production, volume of trade, and railway mileage, France had fallen behind Germany. By herself, France was no match for Germany.

In the late nineteenth century a new school of art, *Impressionism, reached public attention. Centered in Paris, it reflected an attempt to communicate the illusion of natural light and color, rather than to concentrate on reproducing the details of a subject. Since Impressionism was also dedicated to expressing the artist's personality, each Impressionist soon developed his own style of painting. Each continued, however, to rely on color and light for effect, a trend which continues in contemporary art. The Impressionists, most of them living in Paris, captured the variety of the city and the French countryside. The detail of Georges Seurat's* La Grande Jatte *(left) conveys the quiet pleasure of a park on a Sunday afternoon. Seurat's dots of color blend in the viewer's vision and add vitality to the scene. In the detail of Vincent Van Gogh's* Cafe Terrace at Night *(above, left) short brush strokes convey an energy which adds to the vibrancy of the yellow background. Many leading artists also did commercial art such as "Le Divan Japonais" (1892) above, designed for a Paris music hall by Henri de Toulouse-Lautrec. The use of sharply outlined areas of strong color reveals a new influence on European art: the traditional woodblock prints of Japan.*

This, we shall see, is important for an understanding of the causes of World War I and World War II.

Living conditions for workers improve slowly.
As in other industrializing states, a labor movement emerged in France in the nineteenth century. Not until after World War I, however, was it generally successful in winning benefits for the French worker. For a number of reasons the French worker remained at the bottom of society. Only about one million of some six million industrial workers belonged to unions. Fear of the workers and of increased taxes caused small shopkeepers and peasants—the majority of the population—to resist demands for reform. The French Socialist Party and the French labor unions disagreed over aims and methods and failed to present a united front. The Socialist Party sought to increase working-class representation in parliament. It hoped that a strong Socialist Party would be joined by sympathizers in other parties, enabling it to command the votes needed to enact legislation favorable to the working man. The labor unions, on the other hand, wanted no part of parliament or politics. Their more militant leaders called for violent strikes, hoping thus to weaken and eventually destroy the capitalist system.

CHECK-UP

1. What was the structure of the government of the German Reich? Who had most of the political power? Why?

2. How did the Industrial Revolution transform Germany? What welfare legislation was enacted? Why?

3. How did growing industrial might affect Germany's relations with her neighbors?

4. What problems troubled the Third Republic? What was the Dreyfus Affair? What effect did it have?

5. Compare industrialization and its results in France with that in Germany and Britain.

Legacy of the Industrial Revolution

By 1914 a largely industrial civilization had been created in Western Europe. Cities had grown in population and size. Despite the existence of great inequalities in wealth, the standard of living had risen enormously. Factories produced a wide variety of goods that the average man could afford to buy. Labor unions grew more powerful and governments introduced reforms to deal with some of the problems created by industrialization. The common man received the right to vote and in many cases his children attended school. Western Europe appeared on the verge of a new era. In most areas an urban society, capable of creating vast opportunities for human development, had replaced an older, more stable agricultural pattern of life. From the standpoint of *material* gains, predictions for the future were understandably bright.

But the problems posed by industrialization have not yet been solved. Some of the most dazzling hopes of the nineteenth century were to be shattered during the twentieth.

Because it meant the destruction of customary social relationships, industrialization carried with it tensions and stresses. Large cities, often unmanageable due to their very size, came to dominate the landscape. As problems of government became increasingly complex, hundreds of thousands of civil servants were brought into existence in order to solve them. In the midst of these changes the ordinary person came to feel more and more helpless. He felt himself challenged, perhaps overwhelmed, by the growing impersonality of life.

The spread of industrialization also raised the problem of preserving quality in a mass society. Newspapers and periodicals, and in the twentieth century radio and television, came to serve the needs of a large majority. These forms of communication helped to create a mass culture. Some critics believe that a mass culture will lower the quality of intellectual and artistic life. To these critics, the literature, art, music, newspapers, movies, and television programs preferred by the masses are often lacking in artistic merit. As pressures to conform to the tastes of the majority increase, it becomes more difficult to retain levels of cultural quality. It is not clear even today whether western society will be able to combine high quality with the demands of mass culture.

Finally, and perhaps most significantly, industrial advances posed the basic question of human purpose. Science and technology can improve the conditions of life for much of humanity but they also can create weapons of mass destruction and pollute and plunder our natural environment. Will man be able to use science and industry in order to improve the quality of human life? Will he become the master of technology rather than its slave? The answers to these questions will hopefully become clear in the final decades of the twentieth century.

Chapter Highlights

Can you explain?

commons   social welfare   factory system   authoritarianism
franchise   prime minister   cottage industry   enclosure movement

Can you identify?

Arkwright   Tories   Dreyfus   Agricultural Revolution
Watt   Bismarck   Liberal Party   Reform Bill
Disraeli   Reichstag   Third French Republic   Industrial Revolution
Whigs   Bundesrat   Labour Party   Chartist movement
Gladstone   Napoleon III   Paris Commune   Parliament

What do you think?

1. How did the enclosure movement change the pattern of life for many people in England?

2. Was a working-class family better off under cottage industry or the factory system?

3. How did industrialization and rapid change affect the quality of life in England?

4. How does the role of the British prime minister and his cabinet differ from that of the American president and his cabinet?

5. Why was nineteenth-century Britain able to avoid the revolutions that plagued France?

6. Why might a conservative statesman, such as Bismarck, sponsor liberal reforms?

7. How did the role of the British monarch differ from that of the Prussian kaiser?

8. Why was the Third French Republic unstable?

9. What were the advantages and disadvantages of industrialization? Should we continue to make advances in technology? Why?

10. Do you believe that the demands of mass culture have lowered the quality of art, music, and literature? Why?

*The pressure of life in an industrialized society
has provoked many responses. Such dedicated anarchists as the editors of* La Révolte *(left) urged
the destruction of a society they despaired of reforming. A personal response to overwhelming pressure is captured by Edvard Munch's painting* The
Scream *(above). No specific cause of the outburst
is given or is needed; the reaction is provoked by
the totality of modern life. The red of the sunset
sky suggests the color of emotion and of revolution.
In widening waves the individual's reaction to social
stress spreads out through the world around him.*

Patterns of Thought and Protest

CHAPTER FOCUS

Liberal Responses to Industrialization
Socialist Responses to Industrialization
Changing Intellectual Outlooks

The Industrial Revolution transformed English
society and eventually all of Europe. The rise
of the factory system, the growth in population,
and the movement of people to cities created
serious problems: slums, unemployment, children and women laboring in factories, dangerous working conditions, long hours, low wages.
How could these problems be solved? What
role should the government play? Let us examine the approaches various thinkers suggested
as a means of dealing with the problems created
by the Industrial Revolution.

525

Liberal Responses to Industrialization

Liberalism emerged in England in the seventeenth century during the struggle between Parliament and king. By the end of the eighteenth century British liberalism stood for religious toleration, parliamentary government and the rule of law, freedom of the press, natural right of the individual to life, liberty, and property, and the right to resist arbitrary and tyrannical government seeking to interfere with these natural rights. British liberals had confidence in human intelligence, supported science, and attacked superstition. In the seventeenth and eighteenth centuries British liberals had been mainly concerned with protecting the rights of the individual against the dangers of oppressive government. But by the beginning of the nineteenth century a new set of problems had arisen in Britain. These problems focused around the plight of the working class and the impact of industrialization.

Thought and Protest

1776	Publication of Adam Smith's *The Wealth of Nations*
1798	Publication of Malthus' *Essay on the Principle of Population*
1813	Publication of Owen's *A New View of Society*
1848	Publication of the *Communist Manifesto* by Marx and Engels
1859	Publication of Darwin's *Origin of Species*
1867, 1894	Publication of Marx's *Capital*
1883–1888	Publication of Nietzsche's major works
1900	Publication of Freud's *Interpretation of Dreams*
1905	Publication of Einstein's theory of relativity

British liberals advocate a laissez-faire policy. British liberals had come to support the doctrine of *laissez faire* (leh-sey *fair'*)—the notion that government should not interfere with business. They based their thinking largely on the writings of Adam Smith. In *The Wealth of Nations,* published in 1776, Smith stated the following: (1) Only when a man is free to operate his business in the way that brings him the most profit can a healthy economy be achieved. (2) By acting in his own self-interest—by trying to achieve a maximum of profit—the businessman benefits the entire community, for his actions lead to increased production, distribution, and consumption of goods. (3) The government harms business and the community when it interferes with the activities of businessmen. (4) The duty of government is to maintain peace and order within the community and not to meddle with the affairs of business.

The supporters of laissez faire insisted that poverty is natural. Since some are meant to be wealthy and some poor, government can do nothing about poverty. Any governmental reforms might hurt business and make things worse.

Malthus blames poverty on overpopulation. Another English thinker who helped shape the liberal attitude in the early days of the Industrial Revolution was T. R. Malthus. In his *Essay on the Principle of Population* (1798), Malthus declared that the population always increases faster than the food supply. As a result mankind is always threatened with starvation. The real cause of poverty, according to Malthus, is overpopulation. Until the poor learn to keep down the size of their families, poverty will never be eliminated. Malthus concludes:

When the wages of labor are hardly sufficient to maintain two children, a man marries and has five or six. He of course finds himself miserably distressed. . . . He accuses the [greed] of the rich. . . . He accuses the [prejudiced] and unjust institutions of society. . . . The last person that he would think of accusing is himself.

Malthus also argued that as the population increases, the supply of workers becomes greater than the demand. This leads to unemployment, low wages, and perpetual poverty. For Malthus, lowering the birth rate was the only effective way to combat poverty.

In effect Malthus was saying that, since the misery of the worker is his own doing, no laws passed by the state can eliminate poverty. Factory owners were delighted with Malthus' views. It soothed their consciences to be told that they were not responsible for the sufferings of workers.

Democratic liberals propose reform legislation. The problems of the working class persisted. Convinced that a laissez-faire policy was not acceptable, a growing number of liberals in England and elsewhere urged the government to introduce reforms to aid the working man. They wanted legislation that would improve conditions of work in the factory, allow the growth of labor unions, eliminate property requirements for voting, and increase educational opportunities for the poor. Whereas the older liberals insisted that government did not have the right to interfere with a man's business or property, democratic liberals came to recognize that the Industrial Revolution had created problems that could be solved only by governmental actions.

CHECK-UP

1. What are the basic ideas in *The Wealth of Nations?* How did British liberals react to them?
2. How did the ideas of Malthus help shape the liberal attitude? Why did factory owners applaud his views?
3. What kind of reforms did democratic liberals propose?

Socialist Responses to Industrialization

Other thinkers, called *socialists,* went much further than the democratic liberals. They wanted the government to take possession of factories, mines, railroads, insurance companies, banks, and the like. They believed that only government management of these means of production and distribution would aid the poor. The most important socialist thinker of the nineteenth century was Karl Marx.

Before turning to Marx, let us examine the views of two other socialist thinkers who lived in the early nineteenth century. These socialist thinkers, Charles Fourier and Robert Owen, are called *Utopian Socialists.* They believed that putting their theories into practice would enable man to achieve an ideal society, or Utopia.

UTOPIAN SOCIALISM

Fourier describes an ideal community. A clerk and traveling salesman, Charles Fourier (fooryey') saw at first hand the vicious competition and the mistreatment of workers in the silk factories at Lyons, France. Fourier drew up elaborate plans for a new society that would enable humanity to find happiness. He wanted to form small communities called *phalanxes,* each consisting of about 1000 human beings and 400 acres of land. Measures would be taken to prevent the wealthy from growing too rich. There would be no poverty because the people of the community would all have a share in the property and in everything produced by the phalanx. The poorer members would thus share in the general prosperity of the community. But Fourier did not advocate an equal distribution of money and goods. People with special skills and responsibilities would be rewarded.

Fourier's phalanx was based on the principle that man should engage in activities that bring him pleasure. To avoid the monotony of always doing the same work, men would learn a variety of trades and would escape boredom by changing jobs during the day. Fourier realized that no community could entirely eliminate disagreeable work, but he believed that he had found an answer to the question of who would do the dirty work. The children, of course. Because they loved to play with dirt, they would actually find pleasure in picking up garbage, working in slaughterhouses, and spreading manure on fields.

In accordance with Fourier's principle of pleasure, five sumptuous meals a day would be served in the community dining room. All members would wear good clothes and enjoy fine entertainment. Fourier believed that both men and women would be happier without the responsibilities of marriage. Because married women had to devote all their time and strength to housework and children, they had no time or energy left to enjoy life. Married life also made the man selfish, caring only about his own family. Fourier hoped that eventually the family would disappear and the care of children would become the responsibility of the entire community. But Fourier's grandiose plans found little support. Though a number of phalanxes were established after his death, they all failed.

Owen's socialist communities seek to improve conditions for workers. By the time he was nineteen, Robert Owen was managing a cotton mill in Manchester, England. Some years later he became manager and part owner of the large New Lanark mills in Scotland. Distressed by the poverty of the working class, Owen sought to turn New Lanark into a model town. Since virtually everything in the town—including stores and homes—belonged to the owners of the factory, Owen could experiment with his ideas. Whereas most factory owners regarded the workers only as labor to bring them profits, Owen felt that he had a responsibility towards his employees. He raised wages, improved working conditions, reduced hours of work, and refused to employ children under the age of ten (other factories were hiring six-year-olds). Owen provided his workers with neat homes and food and clothing at reasonable prices. The children of New Lanark attended school. Owen also sought to control drinking and reduce crime.

Owen believed that the cause of evil was not human nature but a bad social environment. The poor were not to blame for their uncleanliness, ignorance, drinking, and crime. If they lived in a better society, they would have become good citizens. It was poverty that made them evil. Bad conditions turned men into criminals. By improving the conditions under which men worked and lived, said Owen, men would realize the good that is within them. They would be kind to their families and neighbors and would live satisfying lives. If children were properly educated and not made miserable by poverty, they would become fine adults.

Eventually Owen urged the formation of socialist communities to eliminate capitalist competition for profit. In 1825 he set up such a community in the United States, at New Harmony, Indiana. Here men would not seek gain for themselves but would cooperate with each other for the good of all the members of the community. But the experiment ended in failure. Owen returned to England to become a leader in the emerging British trade-union movement.

THEORIES OF KARL MARX

To Marx, the Utopian Socialists were only misguided dreamers. Unlike the Utopians, said Marx, his theories were not based upon hopes or dreams, but upon a scientific and therefore correct analysis of history. German-born Karl Marx was the most influential socialist of the nineteenth century. His works, written in association with Friedrich (*free'*drik) Engels, provide the foundation from which modern communism evolved.

Marx believes that economic forces shape history. Marx believed that, just as the world of nature is governed by scientific law, so is the history of mankind. This law shapes history into a pattern and makes understandable major events of the past and present. It also determines the essential outlines of the future. To understand the inner meaning of history, said Marx, one must realize a basic truth about man. His first concern has always been to obtain food and possessions. Since man's foremost goals are economic, by concentrating on economic forces one can make sense out of history. This is the law of history that Marx claimed to uncover. The struggle for food, the way goods are produced, the conditions that determine who is rich and who is poor—these are the forces that shape history. And historians must study these economic forces if they want to understand the past, the present, and the direction of the future.

Marx argues that there is a class struggle between capitalists and the proletariat. Throughout history, said Marx, there have been two basic classes in society—the "haves" who control the production of goods and gain the lion's share of wealth, and the "have nots" whose labor is *exploited* (taken advantage of) to enrich the upper class. The "have nots" do all the backbreaking work and know nothing but poverty and hunger. The exploitation of the "have nots" by the "haves" results in a continuous class struggle. In the ancient world, the struggle was between master and slave; in the Middle Ages the lord and serf represented the two conflicting classes. In the modern industrial world the struggle is between the *bourgeois* (boor-*zhwah'*) *capitalists* who own the factories, mines, banks, and transportation systems, and the exploited wage earners or *proletariat*.

Marx maintained that the class that holds economic power also controls the government.

Capitalists use the government to their own advantage. Lawmakers pass laws to help capitalists increase their profits; the army fights wars to further capitalist business interests; the police keep the workers in line. People who threaten the property of capitalists are imprisoned or executed. Children are educated to believe in the capitalist way of life. Engels expressed this relationship between economic and political power thus:

. . . the state [is controlled by] the most powerful, economically dominant class which by virtue thereof becomes also the dominant class politically, and thus acquires new means of holding down and exploiting the oppressed class. Thus the ancient state was above all the slaveowners' state for holding down the slaves, as a feudal state was the organ of the nobles for holding down the . . . serfs, and the modern . . . state is the instrument of the exploitation of wage-labor by capital.

But, said Marx—and this is the heart of his doctrine—capitalist control of the economy and the government will not endure forever. Slaveowners and feudal lords have disappeared as important sectors of society. According to this historical pattern, the bourgeoisie and the capitalist system will also perish. Like feudalism before it, capitalism is doomed. History operates according to scientific law, and this law demands that a new social structure, socialism, will be built on the ruins of capitalism. History will then have entered a new stage.

Marx holds capitalism responsible for poverty of the body and spirit. Marx maintained that it was desirable for man to move from an agricultural-feudal society to an industrial, capitalist economy. The machinery and technical skills developed under capitalism give man tremendous potential to improve his standard of living. Nevertheless, continued Marx, the great majority knows only poverty because capitalism does not use the means of production (factories and machines) effectively. It fails to distribute its benefits to the great mass of people. Private ownership of factories, mines, railroads, banks, and so on fails to provide a decent standard of living for the masses. The potential is there, but it remains unfulfilled. Factories should produce enough to provide full employment and a decent standard of living for all. No one should be hungry or poor or unemployed. But such is not the case. The conditions observed by Marx and Engels in nineteenth-century England fell far short of this ideal. Wrote Engels:

It is not at all uncommon . . . to find fourteen to twenty children huddled together in a small room, . . . employed for fifteen hours out of the twenty-four, at work that . . . is exhausting. . . .

Children of nine or ten years are dragged from their squalid beds at two, three, or four o'clock in the morning and compelled to work for a bare subsistence until ten, eleven, or twelve at night, their limbs wearing away, their frames dwindling, their faces whitening, and their humanity sinking into a stone-like torpor, utterly horrible to contemplate.

Such conditions will continue to exist, said Marx, because the capitalists care only about increasing their own wealth. While the worker slaves in the factory under miserable working conditions and receives low wages, the capitalists reap large profits. Capitalism has brought wealth only to a few; for the great masses there is only poverty. When capitalism is destroyed, said Marx, the wealth derived from the sale of factory goods will not fall into the hands of capitalists but will be distributed fairly to the workers who are responsible for its production.

Capitalism produces another kind of poverty, said Marx, poverty of the human spirit. Unlike a carpenter in his small shop, the factory worker finds no pleasure in his work. He works only to feed his family, not because it brings him satisfaction. This is no way for a human being to live, declared Marx. Capitalism degrades man because his character and worth are judged in terms of how much money he makes. This is a peculiar way to measure character. One cannot build worthy human relationships under capitalism, continued Marx. The boss and the foreman care nothing for the worker as a human

being; they are concerned only with his efficiency. Moreover, said Marx, once he is no longer needed, the worker is fired. Capitalists are unmoved by the misery a worker or his family may suffer. This system that exploits man's labor and cripples his personality will cease under socialism, Marx claimed. No longer treated as an instrument for increasing the capitalists' wealth, man can become fully human. He can learn to love his fellow man, to enjoy his work, and to develop the talent and goodness that are within him.

The class struggle will overthrow capitalism. Marx predicted the destruction of capitalism and how it would come about. Frequent and periodic unemployment would drive workers deeper into poverty, increasing their misery and intensifying their hatred of capitalists. Small businessmen and shopkeepers (the lower middle class, between the proletariat and the capitalists), unable to compete with capitalists, would sink into the ranks of the proletariat. Soon there would be only a few very rich and the great proletarian masses. Made desperate by their poverty and aroused by communist intellectuals, the workers would revolt, seize control of the government, take over the means of production, and destroy the capitalist system and the capitalist exploiters. Marx saw violent revolution as "necessary—not only because the *ruling* class cannot be overthrown in any other way, but also because the class *overthrowing* it can only in a revolution succeed in ridding itself of all the muck of ages and become fitted to found society anew."

The *Communist Manifesto,* written by Marx and Engels, ends with a resounding call for a working-class revolution:

The Communists . . . openly declare that their ends can be attained only by the forcible overthrow of all existing social conditions. Let the ruling classes tremble at a communistic revolution. The proletarians have nothing to lose but their chains. They have a world to win.

Workingmen of all countries, unite!

The great differences between the lives of the capitalist and the worker aroused Karl Marx, shown above with his wife. Typical of the working class is the mining family (left). Poorly fed and clothed, they have been locked out of the mines. This method was used by mine owners to "starve" workers until they would abandon demands for higher wages and improved living conditions. In sharp contrast are the comfort and security reflected in the painting of the American capitalist family (above, left).

With the destruction of capitalism the class struggle at long last comes to an end. A classless society emerges in which there no longer are capitalists and proletariat, exploiters and exploited, "haves" and "have nots." All will share fairly in the wealth produced by the industrial system. Since there are no more exploiters, there will be no need for a state which is merely an instrument for maintaining and protecting the privileges of the exploiting class. Therefore the state will eventually disappear. No longer factory slaves, workers will at last become full men—healthy, sensitive, loving, kind, and intelligent.

Marxism has a worldwide impact. More than a century has passed since Marx called upon the working class to unite and to prepare for the coming revolution against capitalism. During that time Marxism has exerted an extraordinary impact upon world history.

1. The revolutionary heirs of Marx. Leading revolutionaries of the twentieth century—Lenin in Russia, Mao Tse-tung in China, Castro in Cuba, Ho Chi Minh in North Vietnam—in one way or another have considered themselves the heirs of Marx.

2. The "evolutionary" socialist parties. In many European countries Marxian socialist parties have formed since the last part of the nineteenth century. They have worked for laws that aided the working man. Many of them rejected the doctrine of inevitable revolution in favor of social evolution. They advocate using constitutional channels to bring about a democratic, socialist society. Socialist parties play an important political role in many countries today.

3. Interpretation of history. Marxist emphasis on economics has caused historians to pay more attention to the historical role of economic forces in understanding social change. They have thus gained greater insight into the causes for the fall of the Roman Empire, the decline of seventeenth-century Spain, the French Revolution, the American Revolution, and the American Civil War. "It is virtually impossible to write history today without some attention at least to the relation of economic forces and conflicts to political, military, and international issues," concludes Professor William Ebenstein.

4. Psychological effects of factory work. Marx was one of the first thinkers to consider the effect of factory work upon the personality of the worker. Marx pointed out that, unlike the skilled craftsman in his shop, the factory worker dislikes his work and gets no satisfaction from the finished product produced by machine. Will not such a man, asked Marx, end up hating himself? Today psychologists and sociologists (those who study man in society) are much concerned with the attitudes of workers towards their work. Virtually all large corporations try to make work more pleasant. They recognize the value of vacations, coffee breaks, piped-in music, company-sponsored socials, and athletic contests in building the morale of employees.

5. Influence of economic interests upon ideas, values, and beliefs. In still another way sociologists are indebted to Marx. Marx pointed out that there is a close connection between man's views and his economic interests. A man will accept an idea as true, desirable, and good for society because he derives economic benefits from it. For example, the slave owner insisted that slavery was good for the slave, that some men were born to be slaves, or that God approved slavery. While the slave owner may have believed that he arrived at this opinion through careful thinking, in reality his views were based solely on a desire to preserve the practice of slavery from which he drew his wealth. The slave owner viewed slavery as beneficial to all society only because he himself benefited from it economically. Today sociologists are aware that man, often without even realizing it, is likely to cover up his selfish economic aims and activities with noble-sounding arguments. Social scientists owe this valuable insight into human behavior to Marx and his writings.

Historians point out weaknesses of Marxism.
While historians recognize Marx's valuable contributions to an understanding of history and human behavior, they also point out weaknesses of Marxism. Many of Marx's theories no longer seem valid; many of the events Marx predicted have failed to occur. "To acknowledge that in Marx's account of history there is an element of truth is one thing; to elevate it into the whole truth is another." Among the criticisms that historians and others direct at Marxism are the following:

1. Capitalism has not developed as Marx predicted. Marx did not foresee that capitalism would undergo enormous changes. He predicted that the worker would sink deeper into poverty and that the lower middle class would be destroyed, its members falling into the ranks of the impoverished proletariat. The exact opposite has occurred in the western nations.

Marx did not foresee the enormous power labor unions would wield in the interests of the working class. Labor unions have won for workers higher wages, shorter hours, and better working conditions. Instead of the oppressed and impoverished worker that Marx had described a century or more ago, there is a growing number of workers who own substantial material goods such as cars and homes and who do not feel or behave at all like the oppressed proletariat, the "wage slaves" that Marx had described. They have become members of the middle class and accept bourgeois values.

In the capitalist countries the standard of living has steadily increased. The tens of millions of skilled craftsmen, office workers, government employees, lawyers, accountants, teachers, engineers, scientists, small businessmen, and shopkeepers in industrialized western nations are all members of a large, growing, and prosperous middle class.

2. Governments initiate reforms. According to Marx, the state, controlled by the capitalists, is used to preserve and enhance capitalist power. But in the western world the state represents workers and businessmen alike. Social reforms on a large scale show that capitalism is capable of reforming itself. Measures such as social security, unemployment insurance, minimum wages, factory inspection, welfare payments, progressive income taxes, and corporate income taxes indicate that the capitalist society described by Marx has undergone considerable reform. Western democratic lands have eliminated many of the worst abuses of capitalism while preserving some of its chief benefits.

3. Economic factors are not the only forces shaping history. While no one would deny the importance of economic factors in shaping history, Marx greatly underestimated the role of noneconomic forces. The historian who seeks only economic explanations is closing his eyes to other important causes which sometimes are more valid explanations for events. In addition to economic influences, there are political, religious, geographical, and psychological forces which have helped shape the history of mankind.

4. Revolutions have not broken out in the great industrialized nations. Marx predicted that working class revolutions would break out in the industrialized western nations. These revolutions never occurred. It was in the underdeveloped regions of the world, in nations that were predominantly agricultural, that communist revolutions took place against a privileged minority that exploited the masses. This fact seems to contradict Marx's notion that history moves according to scientific laws.

5. Socialism has failed to produce an ideal society. Marx saw capitalism primarily as a system of exploitation. He could not foresee the enormous benefits that could be derived from a capitalist system modified by government regulation and responsive to the power of labor unions. Private ownership of the means of industrial production and distribution has led in western nations to the highest standard of living ever achieved in human history. There is little evidence to support the view that government ownership necessarily leads to increased efficiency, greater inventiveness, and better products at lower costs to the consumer.

By the end of the nineteenth century the followers of Marx had split into two main camps: (1) *Orthodox Marxists* who regarded the basic principles of the master as unquestionably true, and (2) *Revisionists* who made major modifications in Marx's theories. Orthodox Marxists attacked the revisionists as traitors to the Marxist cause. They insisted that all the energies of the working class should be directed towards the great day when the oppressed proletariat would rise up against their capitalist exploiters, seize control of the state, destroy the capitalist system, and proceed to build a classless society.

Revisionists seek reform through legislation. The revisionists saw that the worker's standard of living was improving rather than falling, that the middle class was growing instead of declining, that governments were introducing major reforms. As Marxists, the revisionists still wanted the workers to gain control over the government, but they hoped to accomplish this through ballots rather than bullets. They felt that by extending the right to vote and by raising the worker's standard of living by giving him better wages, better housing, old-age pensions, unemployment insurance, and compulsory education swifter progress would be made toward an ideal society. To revisionists, such reforms represented progress along the road to democratic socialism; to orthodox Marxists, reforms were only crumbs granted by capitalists to weaken the revolutionary ardor of workers.

Anarchists advocate a stateless society. A radical form of revolution was advocated by *anarchists.* Insisting that governments served only to crush individual freedom, anarchists sought the immediate and complete destruction of the state. They believed that only in a stateless society could workers and other oppressed people become free. One of the leading nineteenth-century anarchists was Mikhail Bakunin (myih-kuh-*eel'* buh-*koo'*nyin). "So long as states exist," he said, "there will be no peace." Man, who is born free and good, cannot live in freedom or demonstrate his inner goodness so long as the state orders him about.

The state, however [democratic] it be . . . in form, will always be an institution of domination and exploitation, and it will therefore ever remain a permanent source of slavery and misery. Consequently there is no other means of emancipating the people economically and politically, or [of] providing them with well-being and freedom, but to abolish the state, all states, and once and for all do away with that which until now has been called *politics.*

Like Marx, Bakunin believed in the class struggle between capitalists and workers. Also like Marx, he believed that the capitalists use the state to control and exploit the workers. But Marx said that after the proletariat gained control of the state, it would use the machinery of the state (parliament, police, government officials) to destroy the remnants of capitalism. To strike at the enemies of socialism and lay the foundations of the socialist state, the leaders of the proletariat must assume great powers. There must therefore be a *dictatorship of the proletariat.* In some distant time—once the triumph of socialism was guaranteed—there no longer would be any need for the state and it would "wither away."

Bakunin objected to the dictatorship of the proletariat. He believed that it would lead to a new form of domination of a powerful few (the leaders of the proletariat) over the great mass of workers. Though it had been waged in the name of the working class, the revolution, said Bakunin, would benefit only the handful of men who led the proletariat. He feared that the dictatorship of the proletariat would become permanent as its leaders sought to preserve and to increase their own power. They will, said Bakunin, become a "privileged minority . . . of *ex-workers,* who, once they become rulers or representatives of the people, cease to be workers and begin to look down upon the toiling people. From that time on they

[will] represent not the people but themselves and their own claims to govern the people." Bakunin therefore insisted that "once the proletariat captures the state, it should immediately proceed with its destruction as the everlasting prison for the toiling masses."

CHECK-UP

1. What were the goals of socialists? How did these goals differ from those of democratic liberals?

2. What was Fourier's ideal community?

3. Why was New Lanark a model town? How did Owen think environment influenced behavior?

4. What did Marx consider the most important factor in history? What conclusions did he draw?

5. What is the class struggle? How did Marx think it influenced history?

6. Why did Marx blame the capitalist system for poverty? How would capitalism be destroyed according to Marx? What would be the result?

7. How have Marx's views influenced present-day thinking and practices?

8. What are the weaknesses in Marxism?

9. How do the orthodox Marxists and revisionists differ? How did the revisionists hope to bring about a better society for workers?

10. What are the basic ideas of the anarchists? Why did Bakunin reject Marx's concept of the dictatorship of the proletariat?

Changing Intellectual Outlooks

In the last part of the nineteenth and early twentieth centuries a number of important changes took place in European intellectual life. Among the most important movements of thought that emerged during this period were (1) Darwinism, (2) anti-rationalism or irrationalism, and (3) modern physics.

DARWINISM

In the *Origin of Species* and *The Descent of Man,* two of the most important works in the history of science, Charles Darwin provided evidence in support of his theory of evolution. (For an explanation of Darwin's scientific views, see pages 5–6.) Darwin's theory of evolution greatly increased man's understanding of himself and nature. It had such a wide impact upon religious, social, and economic thinking that historians speak of a Darwinian Revolution.

Fundamentalists attack the theory of evolution. The theory of evolution touched off a great religious controversy. Some religious leaders considered Darwin's views in conflict with the Bible. *Fundamentalists*—those who insisted upon literal interpretation of the Bible—held that Darwinism challenged the account of creation as presented in Genesis, the first book of the Bible. Fundamentalists insisted that God had created the world some 4000 years before Jesus was born. Darwin's theory of evolution, on the other hand, suggested that organisms had been evolving for millions of years. If this theory were accepted, the world was much older than a literal interpretation of the Bible would allow. Fundamentalists also held that God had created a fixed number of species, each distinct from the other. But Darwin's theory of evolution suggested that species evolved from older species, that new species are constantly emerging. Fundamentalists held further that man was specially created by God. Darwin's theory of evolution, on the other hand, taught that man had evolved from earlier forms of life. Today the controversy between religion and

The lonely shores of the Galápagos Islands (left), 600 miles from the coast of Ecuador, serve as a laboratory of nature. Volcanic in origin, the islands have many unique life forms such as giant tortoises and iguana-like lizards. The several species of finches Darwin (above) found on the islands gave support to his theories of natural selection and evolution.

evolution has largely subsided. Few religious leaders see evolution as a threat to their beliefs. After all, say most of them, whether the world is a few thousand or a few billion years old, evolution proceeds according to God's plan.

Social Darwinism supports laissez-faire capitalism. Darwin's theories also had an impact upon social and economic thought. Those who applied Darwin's scientific theory to social and economic issues are called *Social Darwinists*. Social Darwinists used the notion of survival of the fittest to defend laissez-faire capitalism. They stated that the successful businessman had demonstrated his fitness to succeed in the struggle of life. Financial success was society's way of rewarding the most fit. The poor lost out because they were lazy, stupid, weak, or in other ways unfit to compete successfully with other members of society. Hunger, sickness,

poverty, and early death were the price paid by the poor of the species for their lack of fitness. According to the Social Darwinists, the law of survival of the fittest operated in the world of social relations just as it did in nature.

Social Darwinism sometimes leads to racism. Some Social Darwinists also supported racist theories. In strikingly unscientific manner, they claimed that within the human species some races were brighter, stronger, healthier, more advanced—in short, superior to other races. In defending Britain's claim to rule over Ireland one British historian wrote, in the language of Social Darwinism: "The superior part has a natural right to govern; the inferior part has a right to be governed." And an American writer predicted that when there is not sufficient living space or food for the world's population, then will the world enter upon a new stage of history—*the final competition of races for which the Anglo-Saxon is being schooled.* If I do not read amiss, this powerful race will move down upon Mexico, down upon Central and South America, out upon the islands of the sea, over upon Africa and beyond. And can anyone doubt that the result of this competition of races also will be the "survival of the fittest"?

Racist notions also were used to justify claims of superiority of whites over blacks, Northern Europeans over Southern Europeans, Britons over Asians, Germans over Jews, Greeks over Turks, Germans over Slavs, and Slavs over Germans. Social Darwinists glorified wars between nations and peoples, holding that such wars benefited civilization by killing off inferior peoples and giving more land and power to superior races. These ideas gained popularity among chauvinists, militarists, and imperialists.

IRRATIONALISM

Nineteenth-century thinkers continue the tradition of the Enlightenment. In many ways nineteenth-century thinkers continued to accept the views of the philosophes of the eighteenth-century Age of Enlightenment (see Chapter 18). The philosophes had had confidence in man's ability to solve the evils of society by eliminating ignorance, prejudice, superstition, and poor government. Believing that man was essentially good, many of the philosophes were optimistic about the future.

Developments in the nineteenth century seemed to bear out these hopes. Advances in science, expanding industrialization, education for the masses, greater political liberty, and decades of comparative peace all seemed to indicate that western civilization had made tremendous strides.

Theories of irrationalism challenge the assumptions of the philosophes. By 1900, however, doubts about the basic assumptions of the philosophes began to be voiced. Some thinkers stressed the nonrational or *irrational* side of man's nature. They said that man's behavior was influenced far more by his feelings, impulses, and drives than by his mind. John Locke, one of the leading early Enlightenment thinkers, had claimed that a man's character reflected his environment—his rearing and education. These conclusions were disputed by those who emphasized man's irrational nature. They said that the newborn infant already possessed powerful emotions which have far greater influence on human behavior than does the mind. These inner forces cannot be shaped at will by parents and teachers. Whereas the philosophes thought man was born good and were hopeful about his future, those who stressed irrationalism called attention to the hidden fears and desires in man's nature.

Nietzsche's superman expresses an irrational will to power. An important thinker who stressed the power of the irrational was the German philosopher Friedrich Nietzsche (*nee'-chee*). Man, said Nietzsche, searches for scientific knowledge, draws up what he considers sensible and rational rules of proper conduct, and plans systems of government. By so doing he overestimates the importance of his mind. Reliance on intellect causes man to neglect a more important part of his nature—his instincts, those drives that lurk below the surface. Man's inner yearnings, those forces of life which are the true essence of man, must be heard. The truly great man, said Nietzsche, is the *superman,* a man who listens to no other voice but the one surging within him. The superman makes his own rules. Because he is not like ordinary men, ordinary definitions of good or evil have no meaning for him. The superman is not afraid of what society calls evil thoughts or evil deeds. He cares nothing about middle-class morality or the teachings of Christianity. When society tells him, "Thou shalt not," the superman replies, "I shall if I want to!" He is not a follower but a leader. He is, said Nietzsche, a Julius Caesar, a Napoleon, a man of restless energy who enjoys living dangerously and has only contempt for the weak, the meek, the humble:

What is good?—All that enhances the feeling of power, the Will to Power, and power itself in man. What is bad?—All that proceeds from weakness. What is happiness?—The feeling that power is increasing—that resistance has been overcome.

Not contentment, but more power; not peace at any price, but war. . . . The weak and the botched shall perish. . . . And they ought even to be helped to perish.

For Nietzsche the superman is no Christian preaching the blessings of peace and the duty of caring for one's neighbor; he is no democrat asserting the equality of man; he is no shop-keeper seeking comfort and security. Nietzsche sensed that the core of man's being is a will to achieve power—power entirely for its own sake, for the pleasure it brings.

This single impulse dominates the behavior of man and the history of peoples and states, insisted Nietzsche. Men are either climbing higher or falling behind; peoples are either winning or losing the struggle for survival; nations are either conquering or being conquered. Compared to the will to power that burns within us, our thinking mind is puny indeed, said Nietzsche. Whereas Christianity urged man to control his inner drive for power and domination, Nietzsche said that the superman was free of all restrictions, rules, and codes of behavior set by society. He bursts upon the world propelled by that something within that urges us to want and take, strike, create or destroy, struggle, seek, dominate!

Nietzsche had emphasized the nonrational side of man's nature. A number of other thinkers showed how these nonrational (or irrational) forces entered into political life.

Weber stresses the importance of the charismatic leader. A German sociologist, Max Weber (*vey′*ber), showed that in times of distress and confusion people choose for their leader someone with a certain dash or flair, a forcefulness that makes him stand out from other men. This leader has *charisma* (kah-*rihz′*-mah)—an extraordinary quality of personality that generates excitement and attracts admirers and followers. People cannot resist the attraction of such a leader's charisma. They cannot resist his claim that he has been selected by God, fate, or history to perform a special mission for his people. Clearly the appeal of the charismatic leader is nonrational. He gains supporters not by appealing to their minds but by arousing and capturing their feelings.

Wallas stresses the role of emotions in elections. Similarly, Graham Wallas, a British social scientist, stressed the significance of emotions in elections. Today the role emotions play in elections is common knowledge. We know very well that people often ignore the issues and vote for a candidate on the basis of his looks, personality, war record, religion, and a variety of other emotional factors. As a result, election campaigns tend to resemble advertising campaigns. Instead of trying to win votes by presenting voters with logical arguments, the politician plays on their emotions. Wallas was the first to draw these conclusions after studying voting patterns in an election.

Freud emphasizes the importance of the unconscious. Nietzsche and a number of other thinkers had focused on the irrational elements of human behavior. But the most important thinker who developed a theory of the irrational —the instincts and feelings that make up our *unconscious* mind—was Sigmund Freud (*froyd*), a Jewish doctor who spent most of his adult life in Vienna, Austria.

Nietzsche had experienced firsthand the power of those feelings that inhabit our unconscious mind. Tormented by migraine headaches, humiliated by critics with inferior intelligence, and brooding about suicide, he was eventually driven insane. Freud sought to penetrate this world of the unconscious in a scientific manner. While treating patients suffering from mental disorders, Freud concluded that "the interpretation of dreams is the royal road to a knowledge of the unconscious activities of the mind." One's dreams express even the desires and feelings which our conscious, waking mind *represses* (controls or censors). Expressed in dreams are even the most primitive and infantile desires that one would not dare think when awake because they would arouse uneasiness, guilt, and even disgust or horror.

Freud's work with the unconscious mind led him to draw some disturbing conclusions about man and the future of civilization. Freud concluded that man is ultimately ruled by his instincts, not by reason; by his emotions, not by his intellect; by his unconscious, not his conscious, mind. Man's intellect, said Freud, is feeble, a mere plaything in comparison to the impulses and emotions that rage within him. Among the most powerful of man's instinctual drives is a desire for *aggression*. Freud concluded that "men are not gentle, friendly creatures . . . but that a powerful measure of desire for aggression has to be reckoned as part of their instinctual endowment." As a result of these aggressive feelings the first inclination of man is not to love his neighbor as himself but "to seize his possessions, to humiliate him, to cause him pain, to torture and to kill him." The fulfillment of this unconscious drive gives us deep pleasure. Freud saw aggression as an inborn urge that is apparent in newly born infants and shows itself more clearly with the young child. The bully who hurts other children, the youngster who torments animals— each is expressing his aggressive feelings. "If we are to be judged by the wishes in our unconscious," said Freud, "we are, like primitive man, simply a gang of murderers."

"Our unconscious," said Freud, "will murder even for trifles." Society imposes laws, rules, customs, and religious teachings to guard itself from this dangerous instinct for aggression, to prevent man from doing what his deepest feelings may urge him to do. A civilized man is one who can control his aggressiveness— something that is most difficult to accomplish. During wartime, murder becomes legitimate, and the aggressive drive that men had kept under control is released. With relief we cast off the heavy burden of civilization and lay bare our true nature. Thus for many men the violence of warfare is a source of great pleasure.

Freud believes that man's instinct for aggression threatens civilization. Man's instinct for aggression, said Freud, menaces civilization and darkens man's future. How can we stop wars, violence, and religious and racial persecution when men find it extremely difficult to repress their aggressive feelings, when mistreating our fellow man often brings us pleasure?

In many ways Freud was a child of the Enlightenment. Like the philosophes, he wanted man to be reasonable and good. He too favored scientific progress, denounced superstition, and wanted intelligent and civilized leaders to direct the affairs of nations. But he did not share the basic optimism of the philosophes. "I have found little that is 'good' about human beings on the whole. In my experience most of them are trash." Freud did not feel that the overwhelming majority of men were capable of controlling their aggressive drives. This put civilization in constant danger of being destroyed. Since it is so difficult for man to be rational and in control of himself, civilization is fighting a losing battle with human nature. If such is the case, how can mankind look forward to a bright future?

By the beginning of the twentieth century a revolution had taken place in man's intellectual outlook. Darwin's theory of evolution altered man's conception of his biological past; theories of the irrational changed his view of human nature. Both Darwinism and irrationalism raised doubts about human rationality, human goodness, and progress toward social justice at the very time when industrialization was forging powerful new instruments of destruction. Both contributed to the feelings of insecurity and anxiety that characterize the twentieth century. Such feelings were heightened by developments in a totally different area of thought, the world of physics.

Beginning in the last part of the nineteenth century a revolution occurred in man's understanding of the universe. The emergence of a "new physics" forced scientists to question, modify, and in some cases abandon accepted notions of matter, motion, light, space, time, cause and effect, and the meaning of scientific truth. Because of their complexity and seeming defiance of common sense, these new theories remain a mystery to most men.

Classical physics sees the universe as precise and predictable. According to traditional or classical physics, which is based largely on the theories of Isaac Newton (pages 353–354) the universe is a giant machine whose parts all function in perfect harmony and regularity. Just as the pressure from a gas expanding will repeatedly and unerringly move a piston, so too do all physical objects behave in accordance with strict laws of cause and effect. If we were to drop a bowling ball down a 500-foot airless shaft, it would always take the same number of seconds to reach the ground.

In accordance with this mechanical view of nature, classical physics assumes that it is possible to know both the exact position of a particle at a single instant and its exact speed at that same instant. With the speed and position of a particle known, we can accurately compute its future path. Classical physics, then, assumes (1) that the universe operates with the precision and regularity of a machine, (2) that for a specific cause there is a predictable effect, and (3) that the scientist can speak with certainty about the operations of nature.

Probability replaces certainty in modern physics. Modern physics has forced man to rethink these views. German scientist Werner Heisenberg (*ver'*ner *high'*zen-berk) showed that the nature of electrons makes it impossible to determine at one and the same time both their position and their speed. If we calculate the exact speed of an electron we cannot at the same time locate precisely its exact position; if we can pin down its exact position, we cannot at the same time calculate its speed. Explains science writer Dr. Alan E. Nourse:*

[Heisenberg showed] that physicists never *would* come close to pinning down an electron in minute detail. . . . The very best one could ever do would be to discover the *probability* (within certain limits) that an electron would be one place doing one thing at a given instant of time rather than some other place doing something else, and that the very act of attempting to examine that electron any more closely in order to be *more certain* of where it was and what it was doing at a given instant *would itself alter where the electron was and what it was doing at the instant in question.* Heisenberg, in effect, was saying that in dealing with the behavior of electrons and other elementary particles the laws of cause and effect do not and cannot apply, that all we can do is make predictions about them on the basis of probability and not a very high degree of probability at that. . . . But in the last cold analysis probability is *not* certainty. The more we try to reduce the limits of probability—that is, the more certain we try to become about a given electron's *position* at a given instant, the wider the limits of probability we must accept with regard to what its *momentum* [speed] is at the same time, and vice versa. The more closely either one property of the electron or the other is examined, the more closely we approach certainty with regard to one property or the other, the more wildly uncertain the other property becomes. And since an electron can really only be fully described in terms of *both* its position and its momentum at any given instant, *it becomes utterly impossible to describe an electron at all* in terms of absolute certainties. We can describe it only in terms of uncertainties or probabilities.

It is a basic proposition of modern physics that the law of cause and effect does not operate in the interior of the atom. In the small-scale world of electrons, an *individual* electron does not behave according to strict laws. Concludes British scientist Sir James Jeans: "The concept

* From *Universe, Earth and Atom: The Story of Physics* by Alan E. Nourse (New York: Harper & Row, Publishers, Inc., 1969). Reprinted by permission.

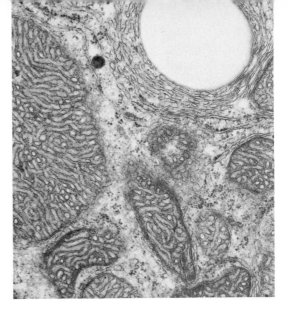

of strict causation finds no place in the picture of the universe which the new physics represents to us." As a result, scientists have to speak of *probability* rather than certainty.

The inability to apply the law of cause and effect to the micro-universe of electrons is further illustrated in the case of radioactive atoms. We know that over a period of 1620 years half the atoms of the element radium will have decayed and transformed themselves into atoms of another element. Now there are billions of atoms in a small lump of elemental radium. But it is impossible to predict when a particular atom in a lump of radium will decay and change itself into something else. Here, too, certainty is not in the nature of things.

Einstein's theory of relativity shatters traditional concepts of the universe. Besides upsetting accepted views of cause and effect, modern physics also forced a modification of other theories of classical physics. Perhaps no other thinker was more instrumental in creating modern physics than was Albert Einstein, the brilliant German-born Jewish scientist.

(1) Classical physics rests on the assumption that Newton's laws of motion are *universal,* that they apply throughout the universe under all circumstances. But according to Einstein's *theory of relativity,* Newton's laws must be modified when studying objects that move at speeds approaching the speed of light.

(2) Einstein forced man to alter accepted notions of matter and energy. He asserted that matter and energy are not separate categories but two differing expressions of the same physical entity. The source of energy is contained within matter; and the source of matter is within energy. The research brought about by this aspect of Einstein's work has enabled man to transform tiny quantities of matter into staggering amounts of energy. The result of this transformation is, of course, the atomic bomb.

(3) Einstein also altered man's conceptions of space and motion. The theory of relativity maintains that the only way we can describe the motion of a body is to compare it with

another moving body. This means that *there is no motionless, absolute fixed frame of reference anywhere in the universe.* All motion must be treated as *relative* to some other moving body. To the average person, this statement had little meaning; to the physicist it came as a shock, for it shattered traditional assumptions. To illustrate this notion of relativity of motion, let us turn to an example given by science writer Isaac Asimov.

Suppose we on the earth were to observe a strange planet ("Planet X"), exactly like our own in size and mass, go whizzing past us at 163,000 miles per second relative to ourselves. If we could measure its dimensions as it shot past, we would find that it was foreshortened by 50 per cent in the direction of its motion. It would be an ellipsoid rather than a sphere and would, on further measurement, seem to have twice the mass of the earth.

Yet to an inhabitant of Planet X, it would seem that he himself and his own planet were motionless. The earth would seem to be moving past him at 163,000 miles per second, and it would appear to have an ellipsoidal shape and twice the mass of *his* planet.

One is tempted to ask which planet would *really* be foreshortened and doubled in mass, but the only possible answer is: that depends on the frame of reference.

(4) Einstein's theory of relativity also altered man's idea of time. Like space, mass, and motion, time is also relative. It is not a fixed and rigid measurement but is different for two observers traveling at different speeds. Time does not exist apart from man; rather, we ourselves determine what time is. Surely the following example based upon Einstein's theory defies all common-sense experience. Imagine twin brothers involved in space exploration, one as an astronaut, the other as a rocket designer who never leaves earth. The astronaut takes off in the most advanced spaceship yet built, one that can maintain a speed close to that of the speed of light. After several months

of space travel, the astronaut reaches his destination and returns home. According to the calendar in the spaceship the whole trip took a little more than a year. But when the astronaut lands on earth, he finds totally changed conditions. While he has aged about a year, his brother has been dead for almost 500 years! To the people living on earth, the returning astronaut would be a stranger from outer space, for according to earth's calendars, 500 years have elapsed since his rocket ship set out on its journey.

We have not yet felt the full impact of modern physics, but there is no doubt that it has caused and continues to cause a revolution in man's thinking. Classical physics regards nature as something outside of man. The universe is a giant machine that operates according to universal laws. Man was confident that with increased knowledge he would gain a complete understanding of the laws of his machine-like universe. Now science no longer views nature as an objective reality that exists independently of man. Rather, modern physics teaches us that our position in space and time determines what we mean by reality and how we view it. Our very presence affects what reality is. When we observe a particle with our measuring instruments, we are interfering with it, knocking it off its course; we are participating in reality, disturbing it and altering it. There are no rules that apply everywhere under all circumstances. Nothing seems certain anymore—except, says modern physics, that it is impossible to exceed the speed of light. And if nature cannot be fully comprehensible to man, how much less certain must man be about his theories of human nature, government, history, and morality? If scientists must be cautious in formulating theories about nature, how much more cautious and tentative must we be in framing conclusions about man and society?

Darwinism, irrationalism, and modern physics alter man's outlooks. Darwinism, irrationalism, and modern physics altered man's view of his origins, human nature, and the laws of nature. In a sense the intellectual revolution which began in the last part of the nineteenth century was related to the Copernican revolution of the sixteenth century. Copernicus' heliocentric theory (page 348) had upset the centuries-old notion that Earth was the center of the universe. Once man realized that Earth is merely a tiny ball spinning about in an infinity of space and an eternity of time, he felt less important and less certain that the universe had been created just for him.

Darwin's theory of evolution contributed further to man's discomfort. The theory of evolution caused some thinkers to cast doubts on the existence of God and heaven. If man has descended from lower animals after millions of years of evolution, they argue, perhaps he is not a special creation of God but a mere accident of nature and of time. These doubts contributed to man's distress. And what of man's ability to reason, which has enabled him to create civilization? To Freud and to various social thinkers, man's mental powers are feeble in comparison to the irrational and selfish drives lurking in his unconscious, often exploding into hostile and aggressive acts that threaten civilization.

The discoveries of modern physics transformed the commonsense world of classical physics. Man has come to recognize that, in the small-scale world of electrons and the large-scale world of space, accepted concepts have to be modified. Complete certainty is not to be found even in physical science. Far from being a machine whose operations are fully knowable to man, the universe contains elements of uncertainty and mystery.

CHECK-UP

1. Why did Fundamentalists attack Darwin's theory of evolution? How did Social Darwinists misuse the idea of survival of the fittest?
2. How do the theories of irrationalism conflict with the basic assumptions held by the philosophes?
3. What were the basic ideas expressed by Nietzsche? Weber? Wallas?
4. What did Freud mean by the unconscious mind? Why did he think that man is ruled by instinct and emotion rather than reason and intellect?
5. What were the basic assumptions of classical physics? How were these challenged by modern physics?
6. What did Einstein contribute to modern physics? What are the implications of his work?

Summing Up

Despite the plight of the working class under the impact of industrialization, liberals at first endorsed the laissez-faire theory. But gradually democratic liberals demanded government legislation to aid workers and their families.

Socialists went much further, urging government ownership and management of the means of production and distribution. Early nineteenth-century socialists were preoccupied with the establishment of ideal communities (Utopias). Marx criticized the Utopians for not understanding the laws of history. Marx saw history as a series of struggles between the "haves" and the "have-nots." In the industrial world he believed the capitalists were doomed and urged the proletariat to overthrow them by violent revolution. That achieved, the class struggle would come to an end and a classless society would emerge.

In the last part of the nineteenth century and the early twentieth century a number of important changes took place in European intellectual life. Among the most important movements of thought that emerged during this period were (1) Darwinism, (2) irrationalism, and (3) modern physics. These changing outlooks altered man's view of his origins, human nature, and the laws of nature. They contributed to the sense of insecurity that characterizes the twentieth century.

Chapter Highlights

Can you explain?

aggression	bourgeoisie	charisma	socialism
unconscious	probability	repression	laissez faire
anarchists	capitalists	evolution	class struggle
relativity	proletariat	irrationalism	

Can you identify?

Bakunin	Fourier	revisionists	Darwinian Revolution
Malthus	Engels	Fundamentalists	means of production
Einstein	Owen	modern physics	and distribution
Adam Smith	Marx	*Communist Manifesto*	Social Darwinism
Heisenberg	Freud	dictatorship of	
Nietzsche	phalanxes	the proletariat	

What do you think?

1. Do you agree with the assumptions of laissez faire? Why?

2. Why did the communities established by the Utopian Socialists fail?

3. Do you think Marx overemphasized the role of economics in shaping history? Why?

4. Why did Marx insist that the revolution must be a *violent* one? Why did he reject the possibility of social reform through legislation?

5. How did the intellectual outlook of the nineteenth century parallel that of the Enlightenment? How does the twentieth-century outlook challenge the basic assumptions of both those eras?

6. Nietzsche sensed that the core of man's being is a will to achieve power—for its own sake. Has history proved Nietzsche right? Explain.

7. Do irrational forces influence man's political decisions? How?

8. Do you agree with Freud that man's intellect is a mere plaything compared to his impulses and emotions? Why?

9. Why did modern physics compel scientists to rethink and modify accepted scientific knowledge?

10. How did Darwinism, irrationalism, and modern physics shake the foundations of man's views of his origin, his own nature, and the laws of nature?

11. In the years since Marx, has socialism produced the ideal society that he predicted? Has capitalism proved to be the failure he predicted? Why?

The Age of Imperialism

Unit Six —————

European Imperialism in Africa

Imperialism and Modernization in Asia

European Imperialism in Africa

CHAPTER FOCUS

Europe and Africa Before the "Scramble"
Theories of the New Imperialism
The "Scramble for Africa"
European Administration of the Colonies
The Legacy of Imperialism in Africa

On a November day in 1871, a young Englishman with many days' travel behind him reached the town of Ujiji (oo-*jee'*jeh), which lies to the west of Lake Tanganyika (tan-gan-*yee'*-kuh). There he met, sitting on the verandah of a thatched-roofed, mud-walled hut, the aging man he had come so far to find:

As I advanced slowly towards him I noticed he was pale, looked wearied, wore a bluish cap with a faded gold band, had on a red-sleeved waistcoat, and a pair of grey tweed trousers. . . . I walked deliberately to him, took off my hat, and said, "Dr. Livingstone, I presume?" "Yes," he said with a kind smile, lifting his cap slightly. "I thank God, Doctor, I have been permitted to see you." He answered, "I feel thankful I am here to welcome you."

And so H. M. Stanley, explorer, adventurer, and reporter, pinpointed attention in Western Europe on what an unknowing public saw as an obscure village in the darkest jungles of that

As leader of the movement to end the slave trade, Britain sent ships such as the Pickle (*bottom left*) to seize slave ships and free their cargo. The abolition of the slave trade encouraged explorers, missionaries, and traders to move into Africa. The photo of a bush cart (*above left*) indicates the relationships between whites and blacks. Some Europeans, fascinated by the contrasts of the land and its many different peoples, made drawings of what they saw. The Africans were equally intrigued with the white man. The above impression of a European was done by a woodcarver from Yoruba, Nigeria.

547

great unknown and savage continent, Africa. The Dr. Livingstone he had found was already well-known in England. A medical doctor, an explorer in his own right, an author, and a missionary, Livingstone had for years been traveling through southern Africa, coming home from time to time to relate his findings and to ask for help in ending the slave trade.

The publicity of Stanley finding the "lost" doctor and Stanley's continued and much publicized explorations of the African interior awakened the European public's interest in Africa. Stanley's adventures were a prelude to what historians call the *New Imperialism*—the frantic effort of European states to gain control over vast areas of the world after 1880. The effects of the New Imperialism were worldwide and are still in evidence today.

This chapter describes one aspect of the New Imperialism—the "scramble for Africa" —which by 1914 led to European domination of virtually the entire African continent.

Myths and half-truths abound in discussions of imperialism in Africa. Some arise because Europeans, at the time and since, have not understood the African continent and its peoples. Some arise because of efforts to explain in too simple terms the attempt of Europeans to rule much of the world. Some arise because the events of the late nineteenth century are often not seen in relation to earlier European connections with Africa, and therefore seem so sudden. To understand imperialism in Africa, then, it is necessary to examine European relations with Africa before the era of the New Imperialism.

Europe and Africa Before the "Scramble"

THE SLAVE TRADE AND ITS ABOLITION

At the end of the eighteenth century relations between Europeans and Africans grew largely from the slave trade. A few individuals, especially in England, had begun to view the continent in other terms, but in their planning even they had to take account of the "iniquitous traffick," as the slave trade was called. Although European countries as yet had almost no real colonies in Africa, many of them had trading posts and, in some places, forts to protect those posts. Along the west coast were the French, the English, the Dutch, the Danes, and—maintaining their contact of over four centuries— the Portuguese. Virtually all this European activity was in trade, and most of that trade was in slaves.

England abolishes the slave trade. Early in the nineteenth century, however, changes came about in the relations between Europeans and Africans. These changes must be understood chiefly in terms of England's role. As leader in

the Industrial Revolution (see Chapter 23), as the chief sea power of Europe, and as the foremost empire-builder of the day, Britain had the greatest "outside" effect on Africa in these years.

In 1807 the British took a step that was to change radically the earlier relationships based on slave trading. In that year Parliament made it illegal for British subjects to trade in slaves.[1]

[1] The British anti-slavery movement combined many interests. One was genuine humanitarian feeling, expressed in the belief that enslaving men was evil and un-Christian. Especially important in getting slavery abolished in British colonies in 1833 was the belief that slave-grown sugar was becoming less and less profitable, and only causing Englishmen to pay higher prices than necessary for sugar. What finally made the abolition of slavery possible in 1833 was passage of the Reform Bill of 1832 (page 515). Through this act the English absentee owners of West Indian sugar plantations lost the seats they had bought or otherwise controlled in the House of Commons. They could no longer block measures which interfered with either their sugar monopoly or the slave labor force of their plantations.

To enforce this ruling, the British charged part of their fleet with the task of intercepting slave ships and taking them where their captains could be tried and their cargoes released. Finally, Britain took over as a colony Sierra Leone (sih-*ehr'*uh lih-*ohn'*), a settlement on the West African coast, founded by Englishmen more than a decade earlier as a refuge for freed slaves.

Despite Parliament's ruling, the slave trade did not end completely for many years. It took decades to get other countries to agree to having their vessels searched by the British. Nor could the Preventive Squadron, as it was called, intercept all slavers that tried to slip past it. Indeed, despite the patrols, the number of slaves exported from Africa actually increased for a time.

Europeans seek to learn about the interior of West Africa. But the fact that Britain abolished the slave trade in 1807, and in 1833 abolished slavery in all her possessions, had important consequences for contacts between Europeans and Africans. One was that Europeans soon concluded that the best way to end the trade in men was to replace it with a more profitable trade in something else. That idea had consequences of its own.

1. It encouraged groups in England with scientific interests in exploration to send out men to learn about the African interior, and to seek resources useful to their country's economy.

2. It encouraged various religious denominations, which had already formed missionary societies to work among the "heathen" (non-Christians), to act on a new call to spread knowledge of "the Bible and the plow." They believed that the presence in Africa of Europeans would serve several useful ends. Missionaries would teach Christianity and promote literacy. Furthermore, the converted Africans could be taught to raise export crops, useful to the mother country, to replace trade in slaves. Advocates of this view hoped to carry out such

Imperialism in Africa Before 1880

1787	British charter Sierra Leone Company
c. **1795**	European explorations of African interior begin
1807	British abolish slave trade
1808	Sierra Leone becomes British colony for freed slaves
1814	Dutch cede Cape Colony to British
1822–1847	Republic of Liberia established
1830	French colonization of Algeria begins
1843	British take over forts on Gold Coast British establish colony of Natal
1861	British establish colony at Lagos (later, Nigerian capital)
1867	Diamonds discovered in southern Africa
1869	Suez Canal opened
1870's	Christian missionaries active in Central and Eastern Africa

plans in many parts of Africa, using Sierra Leone as their starting point.

3. A third consequence of replacing the trade in men was that it encouraged the British government, reluctant to take on the expenses of acquiring and administering new colonies, to join missionaries and explorers in trying to penetrate the African interior.

Malaria and opposition of Africans block direct European trade with the interior. All saw the Niger (*nie'*jer) River as a great "highway" for opening up trade and extending British influence. There were two Niger Expeditions—1841 and 1857—and both proved disastrous from the point of view of the mother country. It is important to understand why they failed, because the reasons apply to nearly all of the early European attempts to move inland in

Africa. The first baffling problem was disease, particularly malaria. The causes of malaria were then unknown but its consequences were not. Many of the deaths of Europeans in West Africa were from malaria. In the 1850's the famous traveler and writer, Richard F. Burton, described the British consulate at Lagos (*lay'-gohs*)—now the capital of Nigeria—as "a corrugated iron coffin containing one dead consul every year." But already Europeans had learned to take quinine to make the disease less severe —a fact that clearly changed the prospects for Europeans in the tropics.

The second obstacle for Europeans wishing to trade directly with the interior was opposition from Africans living along the coast. Organized into states (see Chapter 10), these peoples of West Africa traditionally served as middlemen between European traders visiting the coast and the people of the interior, who provided what was traded, whether slaves or goods. The coastal states wished to retain a position that was both economically and politically profitable. Not until the Europeans began to bring military and technological power to bear on these coastal states could they begin a deep and lasting penetration of the interior.

What, then, was the position of European countries in Africa before the "scramble" began in the early 1880's? In West Africa, the Europeans remained on the coast (map, page 552). The whole southwestern coast, except for a French enclave at Libreville (in Gabon, *guh-bohn'*) and the territory long claimed by the Portuguese in Angola, was untouched by Europeans.

Abolition of the slave trade in East Africa has important results. In East Africa both the presence of Europeans and their impact were far less than in West Africa. Except for a persistent, if weak, Portuguese claim in Mozambique (*moh-zam-beek'*), there was no official European penetration of the East and Central African interior before the 1880's. But the same events and interests that were bringing Europeans to West Africa affected the other

side of the continent, too. Again, the key was the abolition of the slave trade. In the Indian Ocean trade Arabs, not Europeans, were the major slave dealers; indeed, except for Portuguese trade from Mozambique to Brazil, few European ships had even tried to bring East Africans to the New World as slaves.

By the middle of the nineteenth century some English reformers were beginning to urge an end to the East African slave trade, whether by persuasion or force. Their activities brought what European presence there was in East Africa by 1880.

As on the west coast the Europeans who first came to East Africa were of three kinds—explorers, missionaries, and consuls. But in East Africa they were fewer and they came in a different order. Explorers, to be sure, came first, searching especially for the source of the Nile River. Then came the consuls, one at a time, who tried to influence the sultan of Zanzibar to abolish the trade in men and substitute another trade. They urged any other trade except that in ivory, which worked hand in hand with slaving, since slaves often had to carry the tusks to the coast. The missionaries came last, encouraged by explorers' accounts.

By 1880 the explorers had found the source of the Nile (the White Nile flowed out of what would be called Lake Victoria), and were charting much of the interior of East Africa. By then the British consuls had been working for some thirty years with the sultans of Zanzibar, under an agreement which, in theory at least, ended the slave trade. And by then the missionaries were working in parts of the interior to spread Christianity. They hoped to commit Christianized rulers to end slave trading. In the process these missionaries became entangled in both African and European politics.

EUROPEAN SETTLERS

Tensions arise between Boers and Bantu in southern Africa. In South Africa the European presence before the 1880's was unlike that elsewhere on the continent, except in Algeria (see page 553). Few of the missionaries, explorers, or consuls had any intention of remaining permanently in East, Central, or West Africa. But at the extremities of the continent Europeans had come as settlers, to take over African lands and make them their homes. In South Africa the first settlers, the Dutch, arrived in the mid-seventeenth century. Later they were joined by French Protestants called Huguenots. The British took over the Cape Colony from Holland in 1806 as a by-product of victories in the Napoleonic Wars.

Tensions already existed between the Boers (as the Dutch settlers came to be called) and the Bantu-speaking peoples (see page 251). Their meeting represented a clash of radically different cultures. To the Africans, the Boers were another expanding tribe with whom they had to compete for land. To the Boers, the Africans were savage heathens, an inferior people meant, by strict Biblical interpretation, only to serve as "hewers of wood and drawers of water." In the eyes of the Boers the worst fault of Africans was that they did not acknowledge their "proper place." Unable or unwilling to understand each other's customs, and competing for similar economic resources, especially land, Boers and Bantu fought each other for decades along shifting frontiers.

Britain extends its control in southern Africa.

The British government came onto this difficult scene with its own view of empire. Britain had taken the Cape on the assumption that a way station on the sea route to India (and, in a sense, control of that route) should be in British hands. By the early nineteenth century Britons had doubts about the benefits to be gained from their overseas empire. Though the British were not ready to abandon the empire, or even to make drastic changes in governing it, they revered the concept of empire less than they once had. Some recognized that colonies could create problems for the mother country as well as benefit her. Colonies could be expensive to administer, and if they revolted, as had the

American Colonies, they could involve Britain in burdensome wars. Indeed, sometimes the problems seemed to outweigh the benefits. The opponents of imperial expansion wanted to eliminate the need to control colonies and, more important, the need to be responsible for them and their problems. Therefore they urged that no more colonies be acquired and no more boundaries extended, and supported demands for self-government in regions of white settlement. By the 1850's this view was dominant in Britain.

British missionaries who moved into the interior to work with Hottentots (page 249) and Bantu groups put pressure on policymakers in London to protect Africans and their interests from land-hungry Boers. This led to increased British control over more and more land in southern Africa. To be secure, the Cape had to have stable boundaries that were not threatened by any other power. The only way to protect the Bantu from Boer aggression was to control the land on which both were living and fighting each other, and to impose order and peace.

Leaving aside the question of whether either the Boers or the British had any right to African lands, those who did not want to extend the empire challenged this policy of tighter British control. Realizing that colonies with white settlers were likely to demand greater control of their own affairs and might even take up arms in pursuit of this goal, those opposing further expansion urged that such colonies be granted self-rule. This would also make colonies responsible for their own financial affairs, thus relieving Britain of an expensive burden.

The expense of fighting frontier wars to protect Africans from the Boers and the decreased influence of missionaries led Britain to reduce her responsibilities in southern Africa during the 1850's and 1860's. She gave the white settlers in the Cape a greater voice in their own government and instructed her other territories in southern Africa not to extend their boundaries. And, to avoid a conflict with the Boers, Britain allowed them to go their own way, uncontrolled by British authority.

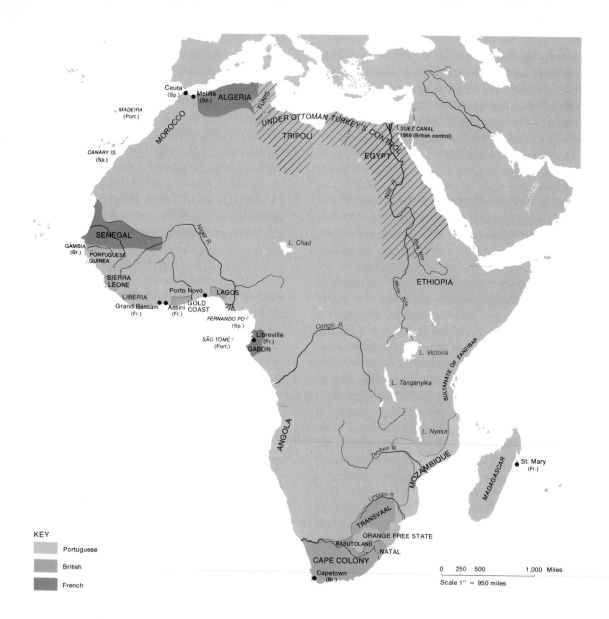

KEY

Portuguese

British

French

Ceuta (Sp.)
Melilla (Sp.)
ALGERIA
TUNIS
MADEIRA (Port.)
MOROCCO
UNDER OTTOMAN TURKEY'S CONTROL
TRIPOLI
SUEZ CANAL 1869 (British control)
EGYPT
CANARY IS. (Sp.)
Nile R.
SENEGAL
GAMBIA (Br.)
PORTUGUESE GUINEA
Niger R.
L. Chad
Blue Nile
ETHIOPIA
SIERRA LEONE
LIBERIA
Grand Bassam (Fr.)
Assini (Fr.)
Porto Novo
GOLD COAST
LAGOS
FERNANDO PO (Sp.)
SÃO TOMÉ (Port.)
Libreville (Fr.)
GABON
Congo R.
White Nile
L. Victoria
SULTANATE OF ZANZIBAR
L. Tanganyika
ANGOLA
L. Nyasa
Zambezi R.
MOZAMBIQUE
MADAGASCAR
St. Mary (Fr.)
Limpopo R.
TRANSVAAL
ORANGE FREE STATE
BASUTOLAND
NATAL
CAPE COLONY
Capetown (Br.)

0   250   500   1,000 Miles
Scale 1″ = 950 miles

European Imperialism in Africa, 1880

Officials at the Colonial Office in London wrestled with the problem of how to make the South African colonies self-supporting. For the South African territory was thought to be poor. Although diamonds were found in the late 1860's, only a few saw great promise in them. No one dreamed of the still undiscovered wealth in gold. Few Englishmen worried about the treatment of Africans, except to the extent that their clashes with the Boers were making a dif-

ficult frontier problem even more difficult. The Boers were more and more determined to make South Africa *their* homeland. British colonists were also beginning to commit themselves more and more seriously to permanent settlement there. The seeds of future conflict had been planted.

France takes over Algeria. In the years before the "scramble" there was a similar white settler presence in the North African land of Algeria (whose population had been largely Arab since the Muslim invasions from the seventh to eleventh centuries). The French invaded Algeria in 1830. In the words of one historian of the African continent, this was "one of the most unprincipled and ill-considered acts of policy in the whole of the nineteenth century. It was undertaken for no positive reason at all, but for the purely negative one of diverting the attention of the French people . . . from their resentment of the misgovernment of the kings Louis XVIII and Charles X." Actually the French people were not so easily diverted, for Charles X was overthrown in that same year. But the French government remained in Algeria.

The French were no more able than other colonizers to avoid being drawn into the interior by local politics. Their policy became one of conquest; their rule was maintained by military force. The government brought in colonists, most of them French wine-growers whose vines had been ruined by blight. In the coastal region of Algeria they planted new vineyards. But most newcomers to the Algerian towns came from Spain, the Italian states, and the Mediterranean island of Malta. They migrated to Algeria to escape poverty and overcrowding, to find jobs, or to carry on small-scale trade. Because there was continuing danger of attack from Algerians, most settlers lived in the cities and kept in touch with their Mediterranean homelands. Some companies and wealthy individuals eventually developed large and prosperous estates on the rural lands cleared for European settlers, who abandoned them because of fear of attack. Living mostly in the cities, few of these settlers had much interest in the welfare of the indigenous (local, non-European) population. Their ties were elsewhere. When their aims conflicted with those of the Algerians, the European settlers, then and later, were motivated by self-interest.

CHECK-UP

1. Who were Stanley and Livingstone? How did they help awaken European interest in Africa?

2. Which European countries traded with West Africa in the late 1700's? What was the nature of this trade?

3. How did Britain's abolition of the slave trade affect other European nations? How was Africa affected?

4. What factors blocked direct European trade with the African interior? How far had Europeans penetrated into Africa by the 1880's?

5. What brought the first Europeans to the coast of East Africa? How did the situation in East Africa differ from that in West Africa?

6. Why were there tensions between the Boers and Bantu in South Africa? What led to British involvement?

7. Why did Britain decide to reduce her responsibilities in South Africa during the 1850's and 1860's? What were the results?

8. Why did the French take over Algeria? What types of Europeans settled in Algeria?

Theories of the New Imperialism

Now that we have discussed the European presence in Africa before 1880, let us examine the European "scramble for Africa" in the era of the New Imperialism, from the early 1880's to 1914.

The New Imperialism develops in the 1880's. Imperialism is a term that arouses great controversy and, often, strong emotions. Since the late nineteenth century, few defenders or critics of imperialism, or even scholars who have written about it, have been able to discuss it objectively. It is even hard to get agreement as to what imperialism really *was*. For even if imperialism is seen simply as the extension of political control by Western European countries over other parts of the world, it was a very complex series of complex events.

The late nineteenth century in Europe was a time of increasing nationalism, accelerating industrialization, changes in the balance of power, and growing participation of the common man in politics. It was a time when greater opportunities for education and a new popular press expanded the views of more people, enabling them to put more pressure on their governments. It was a time when countries found themselves locked in fierce rivalry. Under such circumstances, imperialism could—and did—easily gain momentum.

But how can one explain why the imperialism of the late nineteenth century started—and why it started when it did? Answers can be grouped into several kinds of interpretation, according to the factor considered most important in starting the New Imperialism. Various authorities have tended to stress (1) economics, (2) international politics, or (3) emotional or irrational human drives.

Some see industrialization as the cause of the New Imperialism.

Those who stress economics as the vital (if not the only) force behind imperialism connect European expansion with the capitalist system. They therefore see imperialism as an outgrowth of the Industrial Revolution. Within this context economic interpretations emphasize either trade or investment, both seen in terms of the effects and demands of the Industrial Revolution.

Some writers have argued that industrialization caused the Western European countries, especially England, to need more raw materials for factories and more markets for manufactured goods. Others, especially those influenced by the writings of Karl Marx, believe that the economies of the imperialist countries had reached a point where capitalists could no longer invest their profits at home in order to make still greater profits. They therefore demanded that their governments seize control of lands overseas to ensure new opportunities for investment. The home governments, dominated by the capitalist class, complied. This Marxist view, particularly as expanded by Lenin, had great influence in shaping both popular and scholarly opinion.

Others believe that imperialism arises from European rivalries.

One political interpretation of imperialism argues that the "scramble for Africa" was an extension of rivalries on the European continent itself. European countries in the late nineteenth century were jockeying for power. But, according to this view, either because they were wary of starting wars that might lead to a general conflict, or because they feared defeat at the hands of neighbors, they shifted the competition away from Europe to far-off lands. This kind of analysis often ascribes the start of imperialist ventures to policies pursued by the Germans or the French. The Germans, to divert the French from seeking revenge for their defeat in the Franco-Prussian War (page 519), encouraged France to compete for colonies; the French believed that they could assert their strength and importance, despite their defeat by the Germans, through building a colonial empire.

Another interpretation based on European diplomacy looks at imperialism from the point of view of the world role already played by European countries. Those who hold this view focus on Britain, with her desire to preserve a dominant position in world trade. They argue that the building of the Suez Canal in 1869 forced the British to take steps to preserve this new lifeline of the empire—the much shorter route to the all-important British colony of India (see pages 576–583). To protect the Suez Canal, the British first bought controlling shares in the Canal and in 1882 intervened in Egyptian affairs. British intervention in Egypt aroused the desire of other European powers for colonies as symbols of power and national importance or as protected markets or places for investment. Failure to compete successfully for colonies meant that a nation was falling behind her rivals.

The argument that France, Germany, or even Belgium's King Leopold II wanted colonies to increase national strength and prestige relative to Britain's fits this view. A noted French economist and advocate of French imperialism wrote in 1882 that colonization was "for France a question of life and death; either France will become a great African power, or in a century or two she will be no more than a secondary European power; she will count for about as much in the world as Greece and Romania in Europe."

Some attribute imperialism to emotional factors. Some historians stress the importance of powerful human emotions as the driving force of imperialism. Some nineteenth-century Europeans affirmed that the racial and cultural superiority which they themselves took for granted gave them a duty to spread western civilization among peoples they regarded as "backward." Rudyard Kipling, the well-known British writer who lived for many years in India, described this mission as the "White Man's Burden." In the words of one leading British statesman and advocate of imperial expansion, England had a responsibility to "carry civilization, British justice, British law, . . . and Christianity to millions and millions, to people who until our [coming] had lived in ignorance, in bitter conflict, and whose territories have fallen to us to develop. That is our duty." Such a statement reveals the Europeans' great ignorance of Africans and other nonwestern peoples. The Frenchman Louis Binger (ban-*zhey'*), who worked in the late 1880's to establish his country firmly on the Ivory Coast and its hinterland, wrote:*

* From *West Africa Under Colonial Rule* by Michael Crowder (Evanston, Ill.: Northwestern University Press, 1968). Reprinted by permission of Northwestern University Press and Hutchinson Publishing Group Ltd.

I feel that a white man traveling in this country, whoever he may be, should not prostrate himself before a black king, however powerful he may be. It is necessary that a white man should inspire respect and consideration wherever he goes; for if the Europeans should ever come here, they should come as masters, as the superior class of the society, and not have to bow their heads before indigenous chiefs to whom they are definitely superior in all respects.

Imperialism often appealed to nationalist sentiments that had been aroused in the last part of the nineteenth century. Feeding national vanity, the newspapers provided—on a scale impossible earlier—a steady flow of highly colored and detailed accounts that stimulated mass enthusiasm for colonial ventures. These were the days of the first popular press, sometimes called the "jingoist" press after a much-recited English rhyme of the day:

> We don't want to fight
> But, by jingo, if we do
> We've got the ships,
> We've got the men,
> We've got the money too.

Such sentiments stirred vast numbers of people to believe that the glory and even the very existence of their nations depended upon the acquisition of overseas territories at the expense of other European countries.

Imperialism doubtless results from several factors. None of these theories of imperialism has gone unchallenged; none of them has been able to stand by itself as the cause of imperialism. Critics of the purely economic explanations raise some challenging points. Industrialization certainly brought the need for expanding markets. But statistics reveal that industrialized countries, especially England whose need was greatest, carried on far more trade with other industrializing countries of Europe and with the United States than with tropical countries recently "opened up" by Europeans. Trade with the older colonies—India, and those of white settlement such as Canada and Australia—far surpassed trade with the new tropical possessions.

Similarly, European investment overseas was primarily in either independent countries (ranging from the United States and Russia to the countries of Latin America), or in colonial territories of long standing (such as Canada or India). Most investors believed that their money would be safer in these lands than in the more unstable and less developed African colonies. However, none of these arguments should conceal the fact that *some* European traders and investors expected to profit from protected colonial markets and fields for investment. And some individual European traders and investors did profit handsomely under the New Imperialism. But there is no doubt that economic explanations cannot be accepted as the sole factor. Similarly, convincing objections have been raised to explanations based solely on political considerations or on irrational factors.

As with other important developments in history, it is often impossible, if not mistaken, to propose a single theory that explains everything. Imperialism was a complex movement; it cannot be adequately explained by a single, simple, all-embracing theory. The historian must look at specific cases of imperialism, and in each one determine the relative importance of particular European motives.

European adventurers stake out claims for their countries. Also important was the role played by "men-on-the-spot"—the individual Englishmen, Frenchmen, Germans, and others who, for as many reasons as there are human motives, planted the flags of European nations overseas. Pushing outward what they hoped would be borders, they acquired land for their countries. In some cases, then, it was not the deliberate policies of a European nation but the individual efforts of adventurers and other "men-on-the-spot" that led to the acquisition of empire.

But even unraveling all the European motives will not give the whole picture of imperialism. Europeans were seeking to take over much of the world; within each continent they touched, they found vast differences, and those differences affected what happened. Disregarding these differences is part of an outdated assumption that non-Europeans (Africans, Indians, Chinese, or whoever) sat passively by as the Europeans swept over them. The fact that non-Europeans did play a role helps to account for differences both in the processes and the outcomes of episodes in the story of imperialism.

These last two factors—the African setting and the initiatives of the individual "men-on-the-spot"—lead us to look closely now at events in Africa itself.

CHECK-UP

1. What is imperialism? What were major causes of the New Imperialism? How did European industrialization contribute to the New Imperialism?

2. What was the Marxist view of imperialism?

3. How did European rivalries contribute to imperialism? Why did some historians believe that Germany and France started imperialist ventures? How did Britain contribute to the growth of imperialism?

4. How can human emotions be considered a driving force behind imperialism? What did Kipling mean by the "White Man's Burden"? What role did the "men-on-the-spot" play in the growth of imperialism?

The "Scramble for Africa"

Except in South Africa and Algeria, in 1880 European claims in Africa were limited to points along the coast. Individual explorers, traders, and missionaries had tried to persuade their governments to extend those claims, but with no success. Livingstone, for example, wanted Britain to expand in East and Central Africa to force the end of slave trading. In West Africa governors of the coastal settlements had long advocated extending European control into the interior; they wanted to put an end to what they considered unrest there and to increase their trade and influence so that their colonies would be both easier to administer and self-supporting. But the governments of Britain and France were not interested in the plans of these officials, or of individuals with their own visions of empire. In the words of the British Foreign Minister, Lord Salisbury (*solz'*ber-ih), "When I left the Foreign Office in 1880, nobody thought about Africa. When I returned to it in 1885, the nations of Europe were almost quarreling with each other as to the various portions of Africa which they could obtain."

THE DIVIDING UP OF AFRICA

Trading posts evolve into colonies. In almost all cases the scramble to acquire African land started from points, usually small trading posts, where European countries had had marginal interests for decades. The locations of the early nineteenth-century trading posts were to have great influence on the boundaries European powers were ultimately to draw upon the map of Africa. The specific definition of borders was the work of decades. Boundaries reflected both the dramatic adventures of a few men and negotiations in which European governments bargained with each other over lands they themselves knew not at all. The more treaties one European country signed and the more territory it claimed, the more frantically did other European nations seek to stake their own claims and to assert their own glory. It was a game that many played: Britain, France, Germany, Portugal, and Italy, and, on his own behalf, King Leopold II of the Belgians. It was a game in

The "New Imperialism"

c. 1880–c. 1914	Era of the "New Imperialism": the "Scramble for Africa"
1884	German colonization in Africa begins
1884–1885	Berlin Conference: division of Africa into European spheres of influence
1885–1908	Leopold of Belgium controls Independent Congo State
1886	Major gold strikes in Transvaal
1886–1889	British charter Royal Niger Company, British South Africa Company, and Imperial British East Africa Company
1895	French consolidate West African territories
1898	Fashoda Crisis
1899–1902	Anglo-Boer War
1900–1914	British, French, and German governments take full control of African colonies
1908	Belgian parliament takes over administration of Congo
1910	Union of South Africa established as independent state

which the African peoples received little consideration, if any at all.

Britain and France race to acquire territory on the Niger River. To gain an idea of the frenzy which accompanied the scramble, and the key role of individual men-on-the-spot, let us look at the race between Britain and France to secure the upper reaches of the great Niger River. One French newspaper called it "a veritable steeplechase in which France, England, and Germany are engaged." Frederick (later Lord) Lugard, one of England's greatest empire-builders, was Britain's major contestant in this venture. A man with years of experience—starting with service in the Indian Army and moving through diplomatic missions for the Imperial British East Africa Company in Uganda (yoo-*gan'*duh)—Lugard was working for the Royal Niger Company. Like other trading companies it served as the advance agent of official imperialism, at a time when governments were still reluctant to take on the expense of administering colonies but unwilling to concede the spoils to rivals.

Lugard sailed for the West African coast from England on July 28, 1894. Four days earlier the French agent had sailed from France, his destination the same as Lugard's—a place called Nikki, known to them only by hearsay. There they expected to find the ruler of a key region which they sought to control. The Germans, as the French press rightly reported, had also launched a similar expedition.

Lugard's route was far longer than that of his French counterpart, who could simply head north from the French posts in coastal Dahomey. Lugard had to travel up the Niger River for over 500 miles, and then head an unknown distance overland. The French were sure they would reach Nikki first.

Lugard's party of over 200 men set off overland in late September, during the rainy season. An excerpt from Lugard's diary reveals some of the difficulties that plagued the venture:

Sept. 29: Steady rain all evening—the ammunition, put up in temporary boxes not tin-lined and hardly closed, is wet. . . . The bales and *everything* are wet, [in] spite of my *incessant* efforts. My orders are not to lose a single day—and cost what it may, I will never be accused of unnecessary delay, but the task is superhuman. The donkeys are completely tucked up, the goods are getting damaged, Mottram [his assistant] is down [with malaria], and we shall have a daily increasing number of sick.

His view of Africans helps to explain why his relations with them were often poor:

Joseph is only fit to be an interpreter. Though a full-blooded Negro, [he] is treated to a personal valet, a horse and [groom], a private cook, three porters, and European provisions! Robinson [the other African with some authority] would like to

have the same! Both have no weight or personal dignity. They are Negroes and nothing more—and I never yet saw the Negro who had the dignity and command of men, the self-respect that the straight-haired races of Africa have—the Arabs, Bedouins, Somalis, and so on.

On November 10 Lugard and his expedition reached their destination and started back with the signature of someone they called the "King of Nikki." In this treaty the African ruler agreed to come under the control of the Royal Niger Company as "a government" representing "Her Majesty the Queen of Great Britain and Ireland." The agent of the French government did not reach Nikki until sixteen days after Lugard left. France had lost that race for territory.

British and French imperialism clash in Egypt. There were other such "races" in the history of the scramble. The most famous was one that took place in 1898, ending at Fashoda in the southern part of the country called Sudan. It led to a confrontation between British and French forces in which the latter eventually backed down. The reason for it all was Egypt, so important to England in particular that some historians see it as the key to the whole scramble. Egypt's importance was strategic. After the Suez Canal was opened in 1869, it became, in the words of British Conservative leader Benjamin Disraeli, "a highway to our Indian Empire." The new route had to be protected. Just as the Cape of Good Hope had been thought vital (and continued to be important as a secondary route), Egypt, its stability, and its friendliness were seen as essential to British interests. Egypt's strategic location on the Mediterranean Sea and its connection with the Ottoman Empire increased its importance.

The British and French were quite satisfied with the informal "dual" control they had exercised in Egypt since the mid-1870's. But to exert their influence, they had to interfere internally in Egypt. They had to prop up the politically and economically weak regime of the ruler of Egypt. Among Egyptians themselves, displeasure with both Turkish and European influence led to a nationalist reaction starting in 1882. There were riots in cities and battles in the countryside; everywhere rose shouts of "Egypt for the Egyptians." This nationalist reaction was but one of many instances of the resistance of Africans or Asians to the European advance.

France refused to aid Britain in holding together the Egyptian government in the face of this uprising, and joint Anglo-French influence in Egypt came to an end. When a religious revolt broke out in the Sudan, the defeats suffered by Egyptian armies made their government more dependent than ever on Britain.

Even British statesmen who were reluctant to lead their nation into imperialist ventures felt compelled to intervene more and more in Egypt. They were increasingly concerned that some other European power would move into Egypt from the south and be in a position to control the flow of the all-important Nile. Fear of such a threat led an Anglo-Egyptian army to invade the Sudan, held by revolutionaries, in the late 1890's.

As the British reconquered the Sudan, the French, pushing eastward from Lake Chad, raised the French flag over Fashoda, a town on the White Nile in southeastern Sudan. News of this event reached Kitchener, the British commander of the Anglo-Egyptian force, soon after the conclusion of a victorious campaign. At stake was control of the region bordering the upper Nile. One historian of imperialism has commented:

At first sight there is a certain absurdity about the struggle for Fashoda. The massive advance of Kitchener's army took two and a half years, and it ended by browbeating a few [French]men by the side of the Nile. There was a strange disproportion between ends and means. . . . The greatest absurdity of all might seem to be that for two months two Great Powers stood at the brink of war for the ownership of the *sudd* [masses of vegetation that choke the White Nile] and desert of the upper Nile.

A historian, writing with the perspective of time, can use the term "absurdity" in describing the Fashoda incident. But the reaction of statesmen and indeed of Britons and Frenchmen generally was deadly serious. Not only land but national prestige was at stake. Quarrels over colonies heightened international tensions.

Statesmen meet in Berlin to consider conflicting claims. The formal carving up of the African continent was done in European capitals by men who had never even seen Africa. These statesmen, making use of claims and signed treaties provided by the men-on-the-spot, divided up Africa for their own reasons without considering the African peoples.

The most important of the conferences held to divide up Africa was at Berlin in 1884–1885. Called by Bismarck (page 496), who wished to make it clear that German strength was not to be overlooked in Europe or overseas, the Congress of Berlin did not start the scramble for Africa. But it did recognize certain results of the "scrambling" that had already taken place. There were long-established British, French, and Portuguese interests in West Africa. Claims were also being advanced by two newcomers—Germany itself and Leopold II, King of the Belgians.

Leopold's aims in Africa in the 1860's had been to enhance his personal fame and wealth and the prestige of his small country by acquiring territory there. To these aims were later added commercial and financial goals. The man who gave Leopold the chance to achieve his aims was Stanley. After charting the course of the Congo River in 1874–1877, Stanley had proposed a scheme for opening up the Congo basin to British trade and control. When the British government rejected his plans, Stanley turned to Leopold. The Belgian king eagerly hired the explorer to make treaties which would give Leopold complete control of the Congo trade.

Soon French claims to land along the northern bank of the Congo River were to conflict with Leopold's plans. To settle this conflict, as well as differences over British and French claims in West Africa and long-standing Portuguese claims to the south and east, the European powers met at Berlin. Besides dealing with the problems of the present, they intended to establish rules for the future.

But the Berlin Conference actually accomplished few of its goals. Though it provided for free trade on both the Niger and Congo Rivers, in each case one small group came to control commerce. The conference wanted the center of Africa "internationalized," but it became the private property not just of one country but of one ruler, Leopold II (see page 565). Statements of high humanitarian principles had little to do with the future reality. In the words of

European Imperialism in Africa, 1891

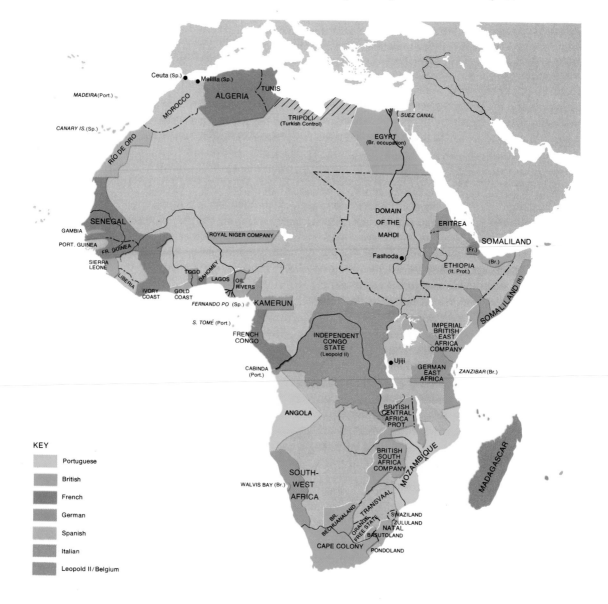

KEY

- Portuguese
- British
- French
- German
- Spanish
- Italian
- Leopold II/Belgium

one historian, "the basin of the Congo, if not the Niger, became . . . the scene of some of the worst brutalities in colonial history."

By 1900 Africa is divided up—on paper. The participants agreed that claims must be supported by "effective occupation." In other words, if a European nation claimed territory, it must occupy that territory. The reality of "effective occupation" took many years, and in practice, the statement that it had taken place was enough to make a claim hold. But the idea that the more actually effective the occupation, the stronger would be the claim intensified the competition among the nations of Europe; it led to frantic races to gain territory. This did not help make the division of Africa orderly.

Later conferences were often meetings between two European powers and dealt mainly with drawing boundaries in specific regions. In 1885 the British and Germans agreed to recognize each other's "spheres of influence" in East Africa; five years later they drew specific boundaries there, allotting Zanzibar, Kenya, and Uganda to Britain, thus securing for her the source of the White Nile. Germany received Ruanda-Urundi (ruh-*wahn′*duh oo-*ruhn′*dee), Tanganyika, and the North Sea island base of Heligoland. Sneered some Germans, "We have exchanged two kingdoms for a bathtub." They did not know, any more than did the British, that this unimpressive island would be a key German base for submarines some twenty-five years later. Through these and other agreements Africa had by 1900 been divided up among the countries of Europe —but only on paper. Making good those claims was another matter.

AFRICAN RESISTANCE TO EUROPEAN
ADVANCES

Europeans disagreed on how to bring about "effective occupation" of their African possessions. All stated a preference for peaceful methods, but many were willing to use force if necessary. Joseph Chamberlain, despite the high-sounding claims he made as to the benefits of imperialism, put his case clearly: "You cannot have omelettes without breaking eggs. You cannot destroy the practices of barbarism, of slavery, of superstition, which for centuries have desolated the interior of Africa, without using force."

Africans respond to European force with force. African resistance to European claims ranged from skirmishes to full-scale wars. Where conflict failed to take place it was usually because, for "reasons of state," African rulers were trying to use Europeans as counters in African diplomacy. From an African ruler's point of view, why could he not use a European force against his African enemies? Only through time and experience did Africans learn that European governments were now determined to seize African land. That determination backed by technological advantages would ultimately overcome all such African maneuvers. Some Africans, reached by later waves of Europe's forces, knew already of others' experiences with empire-builders; they realized the futility of resisting Europeans who had superior weapons and would use them. But some military resistance to the Europeans occurred even before the 1880's.

The Ashanti offer determined resistance to British rule. On the Gold Coast the British first clashed with the Ashanti (uh-*shahn′*tee) in 1806, when the Ashanti confederacy was trying to expand to the sea. The Ashanti saw the British alliance with the Fante on the coast as a force to be opposed, for it stood in the way of Ashanti goals. There was sporadic fighting between British and Ashanti for decades. The first British defeat of the Ashanti, in 1874, made it clear to the Asantehene (ruler) that the Europeans were a greater threat than any African foes. In 1888 the Asantehene wrote the British Governor of the Gold Coast Colony:*

The suggestion that Ashanti should come and enjoy the protection of Her Majesty the Queen and Empress of India I may say . . . is a matter of a very serious consideration and . . . I am happy to say that we have arrived at this conclusion, that my kingdom of Ashanti will never commit itself to any such policy; Ashanti must remain independent as of old, at the same time to be friendly with all white men.

Despite being confronted by European technology, the Ashanti continued to fight the British until they were finally subdued in 1902.

The Matabele try to check British expansion.
In what became Southern Rhodesia, the Matabele faced all the resources and the determination of the great British empire-builder, Cecil Rhodes. Rhodes had gone to South Africa for his health in 1870 and by the age of nineteen had made his fortune in diamonds. But more important to him than personal wealth were his dreams for England and her empire. The British, he declared, "are the finest race in the world, and . . . the more of the world we inhabit, the better it is for the human race." Patriotism became an obsession with him: "For four months I walked between . . . earth and sky and when I looked down I said this should be English and when I looked up I said the English should rule the earth."

Rhodes' dream of British control from the Cape to Cairo met a major obstacle in the Matabele. To realize his commercial and political goals, Rhodes had established the British South Africa Company. This company served as the agent of the British government, which preferred to leave the expense and responsibility of "effective occupation" in private hands. Lobengula (loh-beng-goo′luh), the king of the Matabele, understood fully what Rhodes' company was after. In 1888, when the company's agents were starting to move into his lands, he asked a missionary:

Did you ever see a chameleon [lizard] catch a fly? The chameleon gets behind the fly and remains motionless for some time, then he advances very slowly and gently, first putting forward one leg and then another. At last, when well within reach, he darts his tongue and the fly disappears. England is the chameleon and I am that fly.

Rhodes' agents set about getting mineral wealth for the company by making a treaty with Lobengula. With the advice of missionaries, Lobengula wrote Queen Victoria:

Some time ago a party of men came into my country. . . . They asked me for a place to dig gold and said they would give me certain things for the right to do so. I told them to bring what they would and I would show them what I would give. A document was written and presented to me for signature. I asked what it contained and was told that in it were my words and the words of those men. I put my hand to [signed] it. About three months afterwards I heard from other sources that I had given by that document the right to all the minerals of my country.

Lobengula had foreseen what would happen. Queen Victoria made no move to intervene, and company troops marched into Matabeleland. With "a dart of the tongue" Lobengula's kingdom became part of Southern Rhodesia. Almost 450,000 square miles had been added to the British Empire by the efforts of Rhodes' agents. Lobengula's people and their neighbors were powerless to oppose their guns.

Africans in the western Sudan and the forest resist the French.
African opposition to the French was no different. The organization and sense of commitment that the Islamic revolution (pages 236–237) brought to the western Sudan during the nineteenth century strengthened African resistance there. Strongly religious Muslim Africans, equipped by their leaders with western weapons, fought to preserve their

* From *West Africa Under Colonial Rule* by Michael Crowder (Evanston, Ill.: Northwestern University Press, 1968). Reprinted by permission of Northwestern University Press and Hutchinson Publishing Group Ltd.

newly formed states from European domination. It took the French military, who played a crucial role in building France's West African empire, years to defeat them.

The French encountered difficulties in the forest regions, too. The kingdom of Dahomey (dah-hoh-*may'*, page 240), for example, used diplomatic means to resist French penetration for decades. When the French decided to move in by force in 1892, the king of Dahomey wrote:*

I have just been informed that the French government has declared war on Dahomey. . . . I warn you that you may start a war . . . if you wish and that I myself will do the same. . . . I would like to know how many independent villages of France have been destroyed by me, King of Dahomey. Be good enough to remain quiet, carry on your commerce at Porto Novo [on the coast], and [in that way] we will remain at peace with each other as before. If you wish war, I am ready. I will not end it even if it lasts a hundred years and kills 20,000 of my men.

Not discouraged by this letter, the French moved in. In the words of one historian, it

* From *West Africa Under Colonial Rule* by Michael Crowder (Evanston, Ill.: Northwestern University Press, 1968). Reprinted by permission of Northwestern University Press and Hutchinson Publishing Group Ltd.

"took [them] nearly five months to subject Dahomey, whose cannon . . . were so efficient that the French . . . believed they were operated by Germans—unwilling to concede such skill to Negroes."* But the French did defeat the Dahomeans and deported the king to France's island of Martinique (mar-t'n-*eek'*) in the West Indies.

The Anglo-Boer War leads to the Union of South Africa. One example of resistance to Europe's expansion was unique: the Anglo-Boer War in South Africa did not involve conflict between Europeans and Africans. It was an expression of a local opposition to control from Britain, but it was a war of Europeans against Europeans, and neither side was much concerned for the well-being of the Africans.

By the late 1800's South Africa—or rather its component parts, for it was not yet a single country—had become more than just a difficult frontier problem for the British. The Cape and Natal (nuh-*tal'*) were British colonies, and the Cape remained strategically important as a way station on the alternate route to India. But in South Africa there were also two independent Boer Republics—Transvaal (trans-

* From Crowder, *West Africa Under Colonial Rule*, *ibid*.

Angered by Britain's concern for the Africans and seeking more land for their herds, the Boers started the Great Trek. The reenactment (below) of their journey resembles pictures of pioneers in the United States.

vahl') and Orange Free State. Founded in the early 1800's by Boers who had trekked inland to escape British control, these republics had suddenly become of great commercial importance. In 1886 gold in vast quantities was discovered in Transvaal. Instead of being the poorest area in South Africa, Transvaal gave promise of being the richest. This new importance might enable the Boer Republic to replace the Cape as a focus for unifying South Africa. The result might well be a nation controlled by the Boers, unfriendly to England and a potential ally of Germany, a country which had shown an interest in the Boer Republics. Even if the statesmen in London had been willing to accept such a development, Cecil Rhodes could not. He insisted on nothing less than an uninterrupted stretch of British territory running from the Cape to Cairo.

At the end of 1895 an agent of Rhodes named Jameson led a band of armed Englishmen into the Transvaal and was decisively defeated. Tensions between Boers and British increased, and in 1899 the Anglo-Boer War broke out. Most Europeans and Americans saw the conflict as one between "imperialist" Britain and the greatly outnumbered but "brave, hardy, individualistic" Boers, fighting for "their independence." It took the British three years to defeat the Boers in a war that introduced the terms "commandos" and "concentration camps" (where the British *concentrated* or brought together Boer civilians).

There was irony in Britain's 1902 victory. True, the British increased their empire. But such guilt did the world make them feel for being the great power attacking the small that they were willing to make almost any concession to the Boers. In 1910 the former Boer Republics and the two British colonies were joined as the independent Union of South Africa. But, once again, no one consulted the Africans; no one listened to their objections and their fears of the Boers who treated Africans as inferiors. Clearly, whatever the apparent outcome of the Anglo-Boer War, the real losers were the Africans.

"EFFECTIVE OCCUPATION"

African resistance to the European scramble for territory came up against superior technology and weaponry. This military superiority sooner or later brought defeat to the Africans. But if the European powers had drawn virtually all the lines on the map by 1900, it still took over a decade for them to make their occupation truly effective. In the lands north of the delta of the Niger River, the Ibo (*ee'-boh*) part of what would be called Nigeria, the British had to fight from village to village, taking one at a time, trying to gain acknowledgment of their authority. Not until the First World War (1914–1918) were all outbursts of African resistance subdued.

European administrators try to make colonies pay for themselves. The colonial powers, concentrating their interest and energies on increasing tensions in Europe, had to face the difficult problem of administering millions of people in lands about which they still knew little. Most of their attention was focused on the worsening situation in Europe. They could spare neither the money nor the men to run their new colonies. Yet Africa could be developed only if huge sums of money were spent to build roads and railroads, and later install telephone, telegraph, and postal services, modernize agriculture, and establish industry.

European countries had never planned to supply the necessary funds; they would have to come from taxes and exports. Colonial administrators found a way to recruit labor while collecting taxes. They simply demanded that taxes be paid in cash. To earn the money needed to pay these taxes, Africans were forced to hire themselves out as laborers. The colonial economy thus was sure of a supply of workers and revenue to run the government as well.

In addition, another kind of tax was introduced—forced labor. Colonial administrators demanded that chiefs provide men from their villages to complete needed public works projects. Whether they liked it or not, Africans had to help build their countries according to European plans. Systems of forced labor, in some cases only a step removed from slavery, existed in all colonies in the early years. But the harshness of conditions varied. By far the worst were found in the Independent Congo State.

Leopold II ruthlessly exploits the Congo. The Independent Congo State was often called, ironically, the Congo Free State. Under the agreements signed at Berlin in 1885, the state had been assigned to the personal control of Leopold II of Belgium. But the Berlin agreement also had insisted that Congolese trade be open to all and therefore "free." As Leopold wrote in 1906:

The Congo has been, and could have been, nothing but a personal undertaking. There is no more legitimate or respectable right than that of an author over his own work, the fruit of his labor. . . . My rights over the Congo are to be shared with none; they are the fruit of my own struggles and expenditure.

In the early years of his rule Leopold insisted that he and his officials wanted only "to carry on the work of civilization in . . . Africa," a statement scarcely true in practice. Less than any other colonial ruler, including the Portuguese, did Leopold show concern for the welfare of the Africans. There was no question of providing schooling, or even medical care. Leopold's only concern was the profit to be gained from exploiting the Congo's spectacular resources, especially rubber and ivory. To gain maximum profits at a minimum of expense, Leopold's administrators made use of the forced labor of the Congolese. This was not a government that, with some restraint, levied taxes and demanded labor in payment, but rather administration by private companies. Leopold gave these companies, in which he was part owner and whose vast profits he shared, the right to exploit the Africans by demanding forced labor.

After 1900 public opinion, especially in Britain and the United States, denounced Leopold and called attention to atrocities in the Congo. Writers told how Africans were beaten, mutilated, crippled, and killed for not gathering enough rubber. Soldiers led by white officers burned villages and took women and children as hostages, while the men were sent out to bring in rubber. An Englishman who sought to expose these cruelties published the following testimony of Africans:

It used to take ten days to get the twenty baskets of rubber—we were always in the forest, . . . [looking for] the rubber vines, [going] without food, and our women had to give up cultivating the fields and gardens. Then we starved. . . . The leopards killed some of us when we were working . . . in the forest and others got lost or died from exposure and starvation, and we begged the white men to leave us alone, saying we could get no more rubber, but the white men and their soldiers said: "Go. You are only beasts yourselves. . . ." We tried always going farther into the forest, and when . . . our rubber was short, the soldiers came to our towns and killed us. Many were shot, some had their ears cut off; others were tied with rope . . . and taken away. The white men . . . at the post [sometimes] did not know [what] . . . the soldiers did to us, but it was the white men . . . who sent the soldiers to punish us for not bringing in enough rubber.

Thanks to the efforts of such publicists, in 1908 the Congo was taken out of the brutal hands of Leopold II and his companies and became a Belgian responsibility.

Fertile lands attract white settlers. Even under colonial rule, most of West Africa remained unsettled by whites. Realizing in later years how much added difficulty they had escaped because of that fact, some West Africans suggested, at the time of their independence, that the mosquito might make an appropriate national emblem. Malaria carried by the mosquito had caused West Africa to be called the "White Man's Grave."

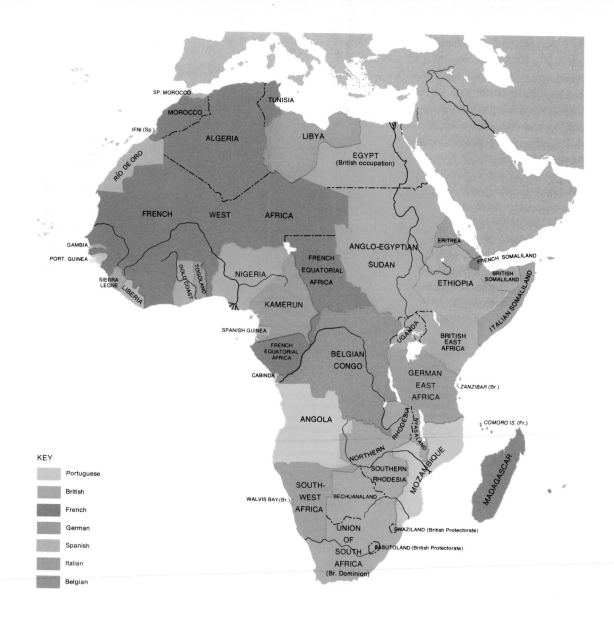

KEY

- Portuguese
- British
- French
- German
- Spanish
- Italian
- Belgian

European Imperialism in Africa, 1914

But in Central and East Africa, as earlier in South Africa and Algeria, beautiful and productive land, good climate, and rich natural resources attracted European settlers. These colonists took the best land for themselves and settled down to stay. In the Congo and the Rhodesias, white men came to run and profit from the mines, especially copper. In East Africa, particularly in Kenya and Tanganyika, the fertile soil encouraged white settlers to develop large estates. Whether on plantations or in mines, in all instances the hard work was done by the Africans. The Africans were forced to stand by helplessly, though not always silently, as outsiders profited from the land and enjoyed a standard of living denied to blacks.

CHECK-UP

1. How did trading posts evolve into colonies?

2. Why did Britain and France race to establish claims on the Niger River? Describe the hardships that Lugard encountered in his race to the Niger. What was his attitude toward Africans? Why was this evaluation significant?

3. Why was Egypt important to the British? How did the Egyptians react to European influence? What was the nature of the Fashoda incident?

4. What was the purpose of the Berlin Conference of 1884–1885? What did it accomplish? What is meant by "effective occupation"?

5. Who was Cecil Rhodes? What were his plans for Africa? How did he achieve his goals? What was the African reaction?

6. How did Africans seek to resist European claims? With what success?

7. Why was the Anglo-Boer War a unique reaction to European expansion in Africa? What factors led to the Anglo-Boer War? What was the outcome?

8. Why were colonial powers eager to make colonies pay for themselves? What methods did they use?

9. How did Leopold exploit the Congo? Why was administration of the Congo reassigned to Belgium?

10. What attracted white settlers to Central and East Africa? What were the results?

European Administration of the Colonies

European colonial administrators face several problems. To set up colonial administrations—that is, impose effective outside control over millions of people in millions of square miles—Europeans faced fundamental problems.

1. Law. The first problem, after setting up a skeletal administration itself, was legal: what system of laws should prevail? Of first importance, how should questions of land and its ownership be handled? Should Europeans be allowed to take land away from Africans?

2. Education. The second problem was education: how could the colonial rulers train whatever African manpower they needed? What should the relation be between education and religion? Should missionaries run the schools?

3. Economy. The third problem was economic: how could change come about most rapidly and efficiently? How, that is, could African economies be (depending on one's point of view) "developed" or "exploited?" Especially urgent were systems of communications and transportation, particularly railroads.

4. Political participation. The fourth problem, least thought about at first, was political: could Africans participate in the new governments at any level? If so, how much, and when?

The various European countries had different theories about how to rule their African colonies. On one point, however, they were in agreement: they regarded themselves as superior to the Africans, whom they saw as "primitive" and inferior on racial grounds.

The French adopt a policy of assimilation. The French, through their revolutionary tradition, stressed the doctrine of the equality of man. Men could be regarded either as equal *now,* or as *potentially* equal. The second interpretation was applied to the colonized peoples; it could, without contradiction, be combined with the notion of European superiority. European, and especially French, civilization could be seen as superior, but if it were transferable—that is, if non-Frenchmen could become culturally French

The wealth Europe drew from Africa was gained only at tremendous human costs. Most people in Europe seemed indifferent to this, perhaps because imperialist propaganda was so strong. The poster for a popular operetta (below) gives a romanticized view of British defeating the Zulu. Taking an anti-imperialist stance is the cartoon (below left) of a Congolese being choked by Belgian rubber interests represented by Leopold II, whose head the snake bears. The picture (left) of a diamond mine in southern Africa reflects the continuing exploitation of Africans through forced labor and the use of physical punishment by overseers.

—then men were clearly equal. Thus the French accepted potential African human equality while completely dismissing the possible value in African culture or the existence of an important African past.

Within the terms, then, of their "civilizing mission," the French formulated a policy called *assimilation*. The goal of assimilation was the eventual cultural and political integration of colonial peoples. It was to be carried out by *direct rule* of French administrators. What this policy meant was that no concessions would be made to African ways: education would be in French and students would study the same subjects as were studied in France; laws and legal procedures would be as in France; administration would run along strictly French lines, and local African political power would be broken. As Africans became sufficiently French, they would gradually participate in politics, but the politics would be those of metropolitan France.

The British follow a policy of indirect rule. The British worked on a different assumption. By the early twentieth century they maintained that Africans (and other non-Europeans) could not and should not become Englishmen. This difference did not come from a British refusal to accept ideas of human equality. Like the French, they shared in the Enlightenment's ideals of freedom and equality. But they had over a century's experience in running an empire in the wake of the influence of such ideas. They had tried a kind of policy of assimilation in India and what it got them, some thought, was a rebellion in 1857 (pages 577–578). They had paid a price for encouraging the English-educated Indians and ignoring traditional Indian leadership. Britain's experience in Africa also contributed to her changing views of governing non-Europeans. Though the British encouraged western education and Christianization from the founding of their African colony of Sierra Leone, they had seen that some westernized and Christian Africans began to challenge British rule. Indeed, in the Gold Coast and Lagos, the western-educated Africans had been talking about self-government since the 1880's. Therefore, reasoned the British, simple exposure to our culture will not create black Englishmen. There were two further strands to the argument: in line with racist assumptions of the day, many Englishmen doubted whether Africans were truly capable of learning English ways and becoming black Englishmen. Secondly, other Englishmen began to recognize that cultures of different peoples were and possibly should be different. A series of conclusions followed: an African *cannot* become an Englishman; an African *should not* become an Englishman; an African *should not want* to become an Englishman. These ideas supported the British administrative policy called *indirect rule*. It could be advocated both by those who believed in the racial inferiority of non-Europeans and by those who came to believe that there were particular, even unique, and always valuable, characteristics of different cultures, and that they should be preserved.

In theory indirect rule was almost the opposite policy from the assimilation of the French. According to the theory of indirect rule, the traditional structure and working of African society would be preserved; a European administrator would be installed only as the final authority at the top. And this system had advantages more important to the English than the preservation of African culture: it required very little European manpower when little was available. It would keep down unrest because there would be little disruption in the Africans' way of life. The legal systems of the Africans would go on as usual, political authority of African rulers would appear to be maintained, and ideas of western education would not be disturbing. For the moment there would be no new African political role, though eventually, far in the future, colonies would become self-governing. The British, after all, had experienced the American Revolution and seen virtual independence established in Canada, Australia, New

Zealand, and South Africa. They were able to visualize that other colonies, even with non-European populations, would someday achieve self-government.

In practice, British and French administrations differ less than in theory. Although the French theory of assimilation and the British theory of indirect rule differed, in practice Britain and France often ran their colonies in similar ways. Certainly educational systems differed: the French reached fewer Africans and taught them French subjects in French; the British reached more Africans, taught them courses slightly modified to be less rigidly English, and used local African languages in the early grades. But in administration the French, for want of man-power, often worked through local institutions, especially where they encountered a strong and manageable chief. And where the traditional African system was not adaptable to new law codes and did not have a structure that lent itself to easy administration, the British changed it in ways that destroyed it effectively or used methods that differed little from direct rule.

Economic policies showed even less difference. All colonial powers sought to introduce cash economies and encourage agriculture, trade, and eventually industry along European lines. Most Africans accepted these changes and the technology accompanying them—not always without resistance, but with less opposition than they met change in other aspects of their lives.

Belgian rule is paternalistic. For the two other major colonial powers in Africa—Portugal and Belgium—the story was somewhat different. While France and Britain were Great Powers, Portugal and Belgium were small and relatively weak European states. Portugal had acquired some of her African territories in the fifteenth and sixteenth centuries during the Age of Exploration. She had the longest unbroken tradition of overseas empire.

The Congo was Belgium's only colony. The personal possession of King Leopold II from 1885 to 1908, the Congo came under the administration of the Belgian government after the disclosure of terrible mistreatment of its peoples. In reaction to the horrors of King Leopold's Congo, the Belgians vowed to make that country a "model colony." To be sure, wrongs would be righted, and the Belgians would make amends. But there was no suggestion, then or for many decades, that the Africans would be given any role to play in their own country; even in theory, they were not to look forward to participating in the decisions that ruled their lives. All colonial attitudes were in some measure *paternalistic*. But Belgian policy was complete paternalism: the "father" country (Belgium) would make all decisions in the best interests of the "childlike" Congolese. Like the British and French, the Belgians assumed African inferiority, but unlike the other two European nations, they did not raise any questions about the political future of their colony.

Working through the tightly centralized administration inherited from Leopold's rule, the Belgians governed the Congo by direct rule with no commitment to preserving African traditions. The Catholic Church played a large role in education, controlling it until the 1950's; after that, schooling in the French language came to be widespread—in the lowest grades more widespread than elsewhere in Africa, though few were allowed to go to secondary school and almost none to universities. Some of the wealth of copper-rich Katanga province went into the running of the country, though most made its way into the hands of the European investors who owned the mines. Commented one authority on the Congo, "The Belgian view was that what the African needed was work, money in his pocket, food in his belly, education, religion, welfare, and health services, peasant agricultural reforms, and technical training." The Belgian administration directed its efforts toward achieving these goals—all within moderate limits—and was to some extent successful. But in no case were Africans in the Congo, or for that matter white settlers, permitted to participate in planning and carrying out Belgian policy. All the decisions were made by the Belgian government.

Portuguese colonial policy is negative.

The Portuguese administration of African colonies shared several characteristics with that of Belgium: paternalism, failure to plan for the future, refusal to consider political participation by black Africans or white settlers. But there were differences: Portuguese paternalism was almost wholly negative. It involved less doing things for the Africans than knowing best what the Africans should not do. Education, law, and economic development were neglected except insofar as the colonies could be made to serve Portugal. Colonies and mother-country were seen from the start as an indivisible unit. Although some slogans of assimilation appeared, especially after World War II, the Portuguese imposed so many rules and restrictions that very few Africans could hope to qualify as black Portuguese. While all the colonial governments used forced labor between the world wars, Portugal's practices were harshest. When other countries stopped using forced labor, Portugal continued. Political prohibitions in Portuguese colonies were the more rigid because Portugal itself had been a dictatorship since 1926. For her rulers, any loosening of strict control for anyone in the "colonies" or "provinces" was a threat to their existence.

Whites dominate the African majority in South Africa.

White settlers affected policy towards Africans no matter what the colonial power, but in colonial situations the "mother country" had the last word. However, in the Union of South Africa, which had gained virtual independence from Britain in 1910, the white population was largely free to order the lives of the Africans (and other non-Europeans, such as the Indians) for the benefit of whites. As time went on, those most determined to keep power and opportunity from Africans took control over the government of South Africa.

South Africa became a model which whites elsewhere in Africa wished to duplicate. Why, asked settlers in the Rhodesias and Kenya, shouldn't we have control over "our own" government? Canada, Australia, New Zealand, South Africa—all have gained political concessions which have even led to self-government; why not follow their example? Though in most cases the home government held out under such pressures, it is clear that where white settlers lived, African opportunities of all kinds were restricted, and the road to self-government for nonwhites was a much harder one. Where there were whites, *they* could have representation in the government; *they* could demand (and vote themselves) funds for education; *they* could control taxes and the labor supply for their own economic benefit. And, on the other side, they could place limits on opportunities for Africans.

Africans resist European rule.

European domination did not mean an end to African resistance. Opposition to foreign rule merely changed from military to political tactics. It was also a shift from traditional methods to European-influenced ones, designed to oppose the European rulers in terms they would understand. The earlier a European country seized control, and the more western education Africans had obtained, the sooner it encountered such movements. In West Africa, especially Lagos (Nigeria) and the Gold Coast, western-educated Africans started asking for representation in the colonial governments as early as the 1870's. By the 1880's they had started newspapers, demanding in their editorials political participation on the grounds that "the present order of things will not last forever. A time will come when the British colonies . . . will be left to regulate their own affairs. How far, or how near the time, it is impossible to say." These western-educated Africans came out strongly against "taxation without representation."

It was partly because of this kind of pressure, which was to some extent successful in West Africa even before 1914, that the British administrators preferred to deal with traditional rulers rather than with western-educated Africans. The French had a different experience. At least at first, Africans in coastal Senegal were as much attracted by the idea of assimilation as were the French. Because of long contact with France a special status was given these Senegalese.

Where the European powers had been for a shorter time, political resistance to their rule developed later. In all cases it depended on contact with European ways, which Africans had to know both to use themselves and to oppose their rulers. Where western education was denied Africans, the task was harder; where white settlement was a factor, it was harder yet, whether education had been offered the Africans or not—for in those cases the interests opposing African exercise of political rights were both on the scene and powerful.

CHECK-UP

1. What fundamental problems did Europeans face in administering their African colonies? What racial outlook was basic to their thinking?

2. What was the French policy of assimilation? How was it to be carried out?

3. How did British policy differ from French? Why did Britain reject the idea of creating black Englishmen?

4. Why was the policy of indirect rule advantageous for the British?

5. How different were British and French policies in practice?

6. Why were the Belgians determined to make a model colony out of the Congo? Why was their rule paternalistic? Give examples of Belgian practices in the Congo.

7. What was Portuguese colonial policy? Why has it been called negative and neglectful?

8. What advantages did the establishment of the Union of South Africa give white settlers?

9. How did the form of African opposition to European rule change? What demands were made by Africans?

The Legacy of Imperialism in Africa

European control of the African continent was no longer effectively challenged by the time World War I broke out. The new rulers brought certain benefits. As one African nationalist has put it, "the advent of European powers . . . not only saw slavery come to an end, but also the terrible tribal wars." Over the decades came western education and medicine, improved transportation, and the multitude of changes made possible by modern technology. Colonial governments created a setting in which more Africans from more places met each other and talked together about what mattered to them.

Some Africans, through higher education abroad, came into increasing contact with the peoples of Europe who ruled them, and with others from all parts of the world. They met Asians, Africans from different parts of the continent, West Indians, and Latin Americans who, though different from themselves, were experiencing too the consequences of the outward thrust of the West. Africans, like the others, started thinking of themselves in a global setting, sharing the impact of changes affecting more and more of the world, changes especially in communications and technology, with their political and economic as well as cultural consequences for everyone.

But the Africans could never forget that they were ruled in their own land. Whatever was done by white men there was done *to* Africans or *for* them, without consideration of their desires. What Africans wanted, as do all peoples, was to deal with their problems and challenges themselves.

Resistance to European rule was to grow into full-blown nationalist movements in the years following World War II. As we shall see, these nationalist movements brought independence to most of Africa by the early 1960's.

Chapter Highlights

What do you think?

1. How was European penetration in East Africa different from that in West Africa? Why?

2. Why did early nineteenth-century Britain have second thoughts about acquiring a large overseas empire? Why did this thinking change?

3. Why did the United States not become interested in the "scramble for Africa"? Did she reject the New Imperialism?

4. Did Kipling correctly interpret Britain's mission? The needs of Africans? Why?

5. Which of the major causes of the New Imperialism seems most important to you? Why?

6. Why was the Congo better administered by Belgium than by Leopold II?

7. Why did the Boers clash with the Bantu? With the British? Why was the establishment of the Union of South Africa acceptable to both Boers and British?

8. What is your reaction to the transactions that transformed the Matabele kingdom into part of Southern Rhodesia?

9. How do you explain the deep-rooted hostility with which Africans viewed a European colonial administration?

10. If you were an African living in a French colony, how would you react to assimilation? How did the French defend this policy?

11. How was a belief in the racial inferiority of Africans fundamental to both direct and indirect rule?

12. In what respect was the administration of Belgian and Portuguese colonies similar? Different?

Imperialism and Modernization in Asia

CHAPTER FOCUS

India
China
Japan

During the Age of Imperialism the degree of modernization in Asia was reflected in the receptivity of Asians to western influences. China feared foreign influence and limited traders in Canton to warehouses on the waterfront (left), outside the city walls. Japan, in contrast, welcomed western ideas and adapted them to her own culture. Reflecting this blend is the kabuki actor (above, left), who wears a western officer's uniform. India, too, made adaptations: the railways introduced by the British were quickly accepted (above), but in other ways the Indians tended to retain the customs of centuries.

As the world entered modern times, the western nations began to outstrip all others in the development of military power and weapons, industry, and scientific knowledge. As a result of this technological, scientific, and military superiority, western nations eventually came to dominate Asian and African lands. In the last chapter we saw how Europe gained control over the African continent. In this chapter we shall examine western expansion in Asia.

The political expansion of the West in modern times had an extraordinary impact upon Asia's traditional, agrarian societies. In the process Asian societies underwent a prolonged period of shock as absorption of western ideas and ways caused great upheavals in the traditional ways of life. The actual process of westernization or *modernization* varied from one Asian country to another. This chapter will trace the modernizing process in the three leading countries of Asia—India, China, and Japan.

575

The Mughal Empire (see pages 209–210), which had dominated India in the mid-sixteenth century, declined steadily. The power vacuum left by its decline and the breakup of India into many small states ruled by princes was soon filled by new foreigners—the Europeans. Western interest in Asia had greatly increased when the Portuguese discovered the sea route to the East at the end of the fifteenth century (pages 366–367). This all-water route enabled the Portuguese to trade directly with Asia rather than having to buy Asian goods from Muslim merchants. The prospect of buying goods at their source, cheaper transportation costs, and therefore greater profits had a powerful appeal to European commercial interests.

European nations establish trading posts in India. In the sixteenth century the Portuguese established trading posts on the west coast of India, and they were followed in the seventeenth century by Dutch, English, and French traders. Each of these Northern European powers organized its own "India Company," granting it monopolistic trade. The Dutch company had its chief trading post in the Spice Islands, and the English and French established themselves along the Indian coast. Each European power sought and gained exclusive trading privileges from local rulers, mainly by helping these rulers to defeat their rivals. The partnership between foreign trader and native ruler thus seemed to be to the advantage of both, and trade and politics became intertwined. Gradually the competition between England and France grew fiercer. The two nations were competing not only for trading rights in India but for supremacy in Europe and North America as well.

The English East India Company becomes a political power in India. Britain was represented in India by the English East India Company,
which had received its charter in 1600. Thirteen years later the Mughal Emperor Jahangir (jah-*hahn'*geer) granted the East Indian Company the right to a trading post at Surat. From this small beginning Britain was to acquire the brightest jewel in its empire.

Organized to make money, by the late 1600's the East India Company had also gained the right to acquire territory, negotiate treaties, and wage war. To keep its trade profitable, it soon found it necessary to interfere in Indian politics. When Robert Clive, a very able but unscrupulous official of the East India Company, defeated the French and their Indian allies at Plassey in 1757, he obtained control of the large state of Bengal. The company had become a territorial power in India. This was the turning point for British policies in the Indian subcontinent. France, having been decisively defeated on land and sea by 1763, no longer could block British expansion.

To watch over Britain's growing interests in India, Parliament appointed a governor-general and an advisory council. Corruption became a growing problem with the East India Company; its officials often sought personal gain. This led Parliament to try to supervise the East India Company's activities. At the same time it appointed Lord Cornwallis, the general who had surrendered his army to the Americans in 1781, as governor-general. As did most British officials, Cornwallis believed that British civilization was indisputably superior to Indian civilization. Cornwallis improved administration in the British-held territory. His attempt to reform the tax system was not an unqualified success, but his establishment of the Indian civil service was to have great importance for India.

Britain gains control of a divided India. During the next century Britain gained complete political control of India; the Punjab, the last area to resist, fell in 1849. Why did Britain encounter so little resistance in taking over an area many times her size? This achievement was not the result of a carefully planned long-range policy; it "just happened." Indeed, much of Britain's success can be explained in terms of India's weakness. The English East India Company did have a series of very capable and ambitious governors and an efficient administrative staff. Its private army, which included both British and Indian troops, was better disciplined and armed than the forces of the Indian princes. Moreover, it was held together and inspired by the desire to make money. India, in contrast, was politically divided. Most of its princes were weak and often at odds with each other. Their governments were inefficient, poorly financed, and often oppressive, and their armies lacked discipline and were poorly armed. Also, British expansion aroused little opposition among the Indian masses.

The East India Company exploits India. Exploitation characterized the rule of the East India Company, which was, after all, a corporation committed to making money for its shareholders. Many of its officials missed no opportunity to acquire fortunes of their own. Money drained into British pockets through company profits and through pensions paid retired officials who returned to England to live. Taxes were squeezed from the peasants, and when revolts occurred, heavy fines were levied against those involved. Sometimes land and wealth were seized outright.

By the last part of the eighteenth century graft on the part of high officials and the East India Company's heavy-handed exploitation of the Indian people aroused increasing criticism in England. Members of Parliament demanded that the East India Company be more closely controlled by the British government and that reforms be introduced. Finally, in 1813, Parliament revised the company's monopolistic charter and ordered the East India Company to spend a part of its profits for social and educational reforms in India.

India

1600	English East India Company chartered
1613	British win trading post at Surat
1757	Clive defeats French at Plassey
1784	English East India Company put under crown control
1853	Civil service opened to Indian applicants
1857–1858	Sepoy Rebellion
1858	British government takes over control of India
1885	First meeting of Indian Nationalist Congress
1905	Muslim League founded
1919	Amritsar massacre
1920	Gandhi becomes head of Indian Nationalist movement, advocates civil disobedience

Gradually extensive transportation and communication systems were developed in the subcontinent. In the first part of the nineteenth century the British launched a limited program of social reform against those Indian customs which the white men considered to be wrong. But the reforms were unsuccessful because these traditional customs still meant a great deal to the Indians. In addition, some western-style schools were established; and the universities of Calcutta, Bombay, and Madras were founded in the mid-nineteenth century. This was tardy concern for the welfare of India and its people, and the reforms reflected a British rather than an Indian orientation. For example, when the civil service was finally opened to Indian applicants in 1853, the examinations emphasized knowledge of the English language and of western history. It is not surprising that few Indians qualified for civil-service posts.

Resentment of British rule leads to the Sepoy Rebellion. The growing Indian resentment of British rule was starkly revealed in the Sepoy

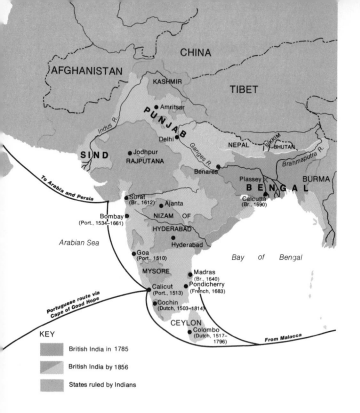

European Rule on the Indian Subcontinent

KEY

British India in 1785

British India by 1856

States ruled by Indians

Rebellion. The *sepoys,* Indian soldiers under the command of British officers, made up five-sixths of the British army in India. In 1857 many of these troops mutinied because certain military practices offended the religious beliefs of both Hindus and Muslims. Cartridges which had to have the tips bitten off were rumored to be greased with animal fat. Hindu soldiers were offended because they believed the fat came from cows, which are sacred to Hindus. Muslims were outraged, believing the fat came from pigs, which they are forbidden to eat. Behind the incidents which set off the explosion was long-smoldering unrest stemming from British attitudes of superiority, their scorn for Indian customs and traditions, and their continued economic exploitation of the subcontinent.

In their spontaneous rebellion against British rule, the mutinous soldiers were soon joined by other elements of the Indian population—native landlords, Indian princes, anti-foreign traditionalists. Declared one nationalist proclamation:

[The English] will destroy religion, property, and even the life of everyone. . . . The people should . . . strive in unity to destroy the infidels. . . . [We] must [all] . . . exert ourselves for the protection of our lives, property, and religion, and root out the English from this country.

But the great majority of the population, including the small western-educated segment, took no part in the uprising. Some of the sepoy regiments also refused to revolt and indeed helped to suppress the rebellion. Severe repressive measures were used to stamp out the revolt.

The Sepoy Rebellion has important results. The Sepoy Rebellion marked the beginning of anti-western nationalism in India. At first this nationalism primarily stressed traditional customs and religious beliefs. Nationalists urged Indians to be proud of their customs and their long history and to remain faithful to their religious beliefs. Conversion to Christianity and the adoption of western dress were discouraged. Gradually, however, nationalist sentiments led to demands for political independence.

The Sepoy Rebellion also had important immediate results. It caused Parliament to abolish the East India Company. The secretary of state for India, a member of the British cabinet, had the final say in Indian affairs. A viceroy replaced the governor-general, and he was advised by an appointed council of British and Indian notables. India thus became an integral part of the British Empire, a relationship that continued for nearly a century.

British administration of India varies. The British system of law and justice extended throughout India. All Indians, regardless of caste or religion, were entitled to equal treatment before the law. About three-fifths of India came under direct British rule (see map). The rest, some 562 states ranging from the size of France to that of a town, continued to be ruled by Indian

The British brought order to India by eliminating local wars, but often found it necessary to use force to maintain control. The brutal public execution of the leaders of the Sepoy Rebellion (above) warned Indians that armed rebellion was futile. One successful reform made by the British was the ending of thuggee: the offering of human sacrifices to the Hindu goddess Kali (right). Followers of Kali made travel hazardous, for their victims were often unwary travelers.

princes. However, these princes were under British authority and often were provided with British advisors and technical experts. As long as the Indian princes remained loyal to the British crown and kept the peace, their rule was not threatened.

British India was divided into a number of provinces, each headed by an appointed British governor. To staff the government, Britain depended on a reformed civil service that made it possible for more Indians to achieve responsible positions. (By the last year of British rule, nearly half the civil servants were Indians.) But the top posts continued to be held by British officials. Moreover, there was considerable pressure on Indian civil servants to conform to British policies. The civil service was efficient but it was clearly no instrument for reform. Because reforms had to be initiated by the British, they were but slowly introduced. And since reforms were often enacted to meet specific crises, there was little long-range planning. But the civil service did give Indians practical training in administration. When independence came, this civil service proved invaluable. It gave India trained and experienced administrators, an advantage not possessed by some other newly independent nations.

British rule leads to some modernization. Under British rule, India experienced the beginnings of *modernization,* the introduction of western methods of science, technology, and administration. The British built an extensive railway system, the best in Asia, to facilitate the movement of goods. A class of Indian businessmen emerged and, along with British capitalists, invested in textile and jute factories and tea and indigo plantations. In these industries western technical and administrative skills were used. These developments in industry and commerce led to the growth of large industrial centers to which increasing numbers of Indian peasants migrated to escape rural poverty.

A British historian who served with the Indian civil service describes Britain's impact upon urban life in India:

There were, of course, many large towns in Mughal India, but most of them grew up round the court of the emperor or of a great noble and all their activities were directed to satisfying the needs of that court. There was in them no class comparable to the men of commerce, the industrialists, the bankers, the lawyers, the doctors, and the other professional men who constitute the upper class of Calcutta and Bombay today.

Cities became centers of modernization. There Indians could read western-style newspapers and magazines and attend schools and colleges established by the British. Gradually a small number of Indians became educated in western ways and in such western ideas as nationalism, democracy, and socialism.

While Britain did launch India on the path of industrial modernization, the pace was slow. Concludes Barbara Ward, a respected British commentator on world affairs:

Roads remained inadequate and in large parts of the country quite primitive. There was no large development of electric power. Coal production, having risen from a million tons to 20 million tons a year between 1880 and the First World War, rose little further. Technical and scientific education . . . expanded hardly at all. At independence, the number of students graduating in engineering and technology was still only about 3000 a year.

In 1939, after a hundred years of British investment, peace, order, and modern commercial law, after nearly a century of modern railways, ports, and export industries, after eighty years of Indian enterprise in a vast internal market of 300 million souls, India still had an industrial establishment of only two million workers, a steel output of less than a million tons, and a population which still depended for as much as 80 per cent of its livelihood on a static, overcrowded, agrarian economy. Not by any stretch of the imagination can this be called a record of dynamic growth.

British rule also affects Indian agriculture. The clearing of forest lands and the building of irrigation works led to increased agricultural production in India. But this growth was not nearly sufficient to feed India's rapidly expanding population, which increased by 250 million between 1850 and 1945. This larger population meant that farms had to be subdivided. To pay for a wedding, to buy a buffalo, or to survive after a poor harvest, Indian peasants were forced to borrow from moneylenders at exorbitant interest rates. Traditionally, the moneylender could not claim the land of a peasant unable to pay back his loan. But under British law he was permitted to seize the land of peasants unable to repay loans. This added to rural poverty. The persistence of inefficient methods of production, the system of moneylending, the expanding population, and the unwillingness of Britain to introduce a policy of land reform—all tended to limit progress in Indian agriculture. British rule thus led to little improvement in rural India. The caste system and village communities continued much as they had for centuries.

Modernization intensifies the spirit of nationalism. The process of modernization, of course, also made the urban people increasingly sensitive to the differences that existed between themselves and the British. British rule aroused opposition, particularly among western-educated Indians. They were angered that top positions in the government were reserved for the British, that schools emphasized European history rather than Indian, that many industries and large-scale businesses were owned and run by the British. They blamed the severe poverty in India upon British exploitation:

. . . those parts of India which have been longest under British rule are the poorest today. . . . Nearly all our major problems today have grown up during British rule and as a direct result of British policy: . . . the lack of industry and the neglect of agriculture, the extreme backwardness in the social services, and, above all, the tragic poverty of the people.

They accused the British of racism:

In Bombay there is a well-known club which . . . does not allow an Indian (except as a servant) even in its visitors' room, even though he might be a . . . prince or a captain of industry. . . . Every European . . . is automatically a member of the ruling race. Railway carriages, station retiring rooms, benches in parks are marked "For Europeans Only" . . . To have to put up with it in one's own country is a humiliating and exasperating reminder of our enslaved condition.

Moreover, westernized Indians were torn between traditional Indian ways and those of the West, and many felt that they belonged to neither world. Modernization thus bred discontent. From this discontent among western-educated Indians emerged a growing nationalist sentiment. Indian nationalism reflected the aspiration, shared by other non-western peoples, to imitate the economic and technical achievements of western nations, even though Indians resented western pressures.

The vehicle of Indian nationalism was the Indian Nationalist Congress, founded in 1885 by a small group of western-educated Indians. Its initial purpose was to promote social and political reform in India, to give Indians more representation in the government and more opportunities for better jobs. At first Englishmen as well as Indians were members of the Congress. By the beginning of the twentieth century, however, Indian nationalist leaders had become increasingly dissatisfied with the vague promises of their British rulers and the slow pace of reform. Moderates wished to continue the agitation for reform, whereas radicals began

to demand total self-government for India. The Congress Party was torn between these two groups. It was also weakened by religious differences. Muslims feared their interests would be neglected by the Hindu-controlled Congress Party. As elsewhere in the developing world, colonial rulers wished to go slow, whereas nationalist leaders wished to move rapidly toward self-government. To gain Indian support during the First World War, the British promised some form of self-rule for India. Yet in 1919, when there was a mass meeting in Amritsar (um-*rit'*ser) in northwest India to protest against British policies, some 400 Indians were massacred by British troops.

Gandhi advocates nonviolent opposition to British rule. In this difficult situation there emerged Mahatma ("Great Soul") Gandhi (*gahn'*dee), whose teachings and leadership brought inspiration to millions. Gandhi (1869–1948) was a middle-caste Hindu who had left his caste and gone to England to be educated as a lawyer. For a time he practiced law both in India and South Africa. In South Africa he worked among the immigrant Indian minority, whose civil rights were impaired by Boer policies and legislation. Then this able and well-educated man, thoroughly familiar with western society, decided to devote his life to the achievement of self-government (*swaraj,* swah-*rahj'*) for India. When he returned to India in 1915, Gandhi had worked out his nationalist program. The basic weapon against British rule was to be nonviolent disobedience.

One method Gandhi advocated was nonviolent resistance carried out on a nationwide basis. He called for peaceful protest marches and deliberate non-cooperation, such as refusing to pay taxes. For example, as a protest against the tax on salt, Gandhi led hundreds of Indians on a march to the coast, where they made their own salt by evaporating seawater.

Many Indians, however, found nonviolent disobedience too gradual a method of attaining self-rule. Peaceful demonstrations sometimes ended in bloody riots. Although he continued to

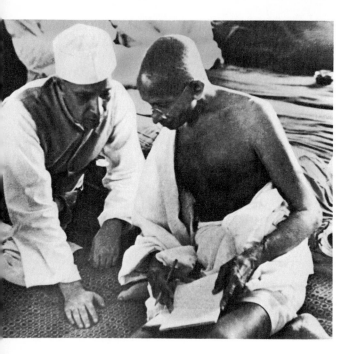

Mahatma Gandhi, who opposed all killing, found a special irony in Britain's campaign to save Europe from Hitler in the name of freedom while the British continued to deny freedom to India. Here Gandhi (right) confers with Nehru on ways to oppose the war.

urge nonviolence, Gandhi sorrowfully admitted that the people were not ready for civil disobedience.

Though Gandhi was born a Hindu, he struck at the very foundations of Hinduism by condemning the caste system and asserting that all men, including the despised outcastes (page 203), had the same rights. Gandhi's efforts in behalf of rights for women aroused opposition among both Hindus and Muslims. On the other hand, the concept of nonviolence had as much of a basis in the Hindu tradition as it did in the teachings of Jesus. Perhaps most important, Gandhi urged social service as a religious duty. He believed that aid to the oppressed, the poor, and the needy was the obligation of every person who professed to have religious beliefs.

Gandhi's program was based on the beliefs expressed in the following words:

I hold myself to be incapable of hating any being on earth. . . . I hate the system of government that the British people set up in India. I hate the ruthless exploitation of India even as I hate . . . the hideous system of untouchability for which millions of Hindus have made themselves responsible. But I do not hate the domineering Englishmen, as I refuse to hate the domineering Hindus. I seek to reform them in all the loving ways that are open to me.

. . . things of fundamental importance to the people are not secured by reason alone but have to be purchased with their suffering. Suffering is the law of human beings; war is the law of the jungle. But suffering is infinitely more powerful than the law of the jungle for converting the opponent and opening his ears, which are otherwise shut. . . . The appeal of reason is more to the head but the penetration of the heart comes from suffering. It opens up the inner understanding in man.

In my opinion nonviolence is not passivity in any shape or form. Nonviolence, as I understand it, is the most active force in the world.

Gandhi becomes the leader of the Indian nationalist movement. Gandhi's program was a way out of the deadlock between moderates and radicals in the Indian Nationalist Congress. And in 1920 the Congress adopted his program for *hind swaraj*—Indian self-rule. Thereafter Gandhi was the leader of the Indian nationalist movement until his death by assassination in 1948. Gandhi was enormously popular with the Indian people. The simplicity of his personal life—symbolized by his change from the western business suit to the Indian loincloth—captured the imagination of the masses. He was able to control the more militant radical leaders who urged immediate and complete independence for India. Among these militants was Jawaharlal Nehru (jah-*wah'*har-lal *nay'*roo), the future prime minister of an independent India. While Gandhi urged a return to the simple life of the peasant, Nehru—the son of a Brahmin (page 203)—wanted to bring the peasant into the mainstream of a modern India.

Nehru urged a speeding up of the pace of modernization. He wanted more Indians to be trained in the professions, and he urged the construction of more railways, roads, and hospitals. Until the 1930's, however, Gandhi's views prevailed, for Nehru did not become prominent in Indian politics until then.

Indian nationalists and Britain reach an impasse. In the period between the two world wars, Gandhi led dozens of nonviolent demonstrations against British laws and policies. Again and again he and his followers were arrested by the British authorities. But each time Gandhi emerged from prison more popular than before. The Indian nationalist movement grew despite all British attempts to contain it, for the British were unable to cope effectively with millions of people practicing passive civil disobedience. Piecemeal reform would no longer satisfy the Indian nationalists; on the other hand, Britain remained reluctant to grant self-rule to India. The impasse between the Indian nationalists and Britain continued until after World War II when the Indian subcontinent finally gained its independence (see Chapter 33).

CHECK-UP

1. Why did Holland, England, and France each establish an East India Company? What rights did such a company have?

2. How did the English East India Company increase its power in India? Why did Parliament seek greater control over the company?

3. How did the East India Company exploit the Indian people? What restraints were imposed by Parliament? What did the company contribute to India?

4. What were the causes of the Sepoy Rebellion? The results?

5. How was India administered by the British?

6. In what ways and to what extent was India modernized? Why were the cities most affected? Why was progress in agriculture disappointing?

7. Why did modernization intensify Indian nationalism? What was the role of the Indian Nationalist Congress? What divisions were there in that body?

8. How did Gandhi become a leader of the nationalist movement? What methods did he advocate? What reforms did he urge? What was the British reaction?

China

Ch'ing rule declines in effectiveness as problems multiply. During the early seventeenth century semi-nomadic Manchus from the northeast invaded China and overthrew the Ming dynasty (page 221). The Ch'ing dynasty set up by the Manchus lasted until 1911, almost three centuries. While Manchu culture was quite different from Chinese, the Manchu rulers wisely entered into a close partnership with the Confucian-educated, landowning mandarins (see pages 218–219). This led to stable, effective government until the mid-1700's. At the height of its prosperity the Ch'ing was a most powerful empire, extending well into Central Asia.

By the second half of the eighteenth century, however, the empire was undergoing a steady internal decline. The long period of peace and security had led to neglect of the army. Costly border wars and rebellions took place in the late eighteenth century. The government became less effective as the mandarin officials grew increasingly corrupt. The emperor took more and more power into his own hands. This concentration of power worked well only when the emperor was a capable ruler.

To make matters worse, between 1700 and 1850 the population of China probably doubled. Despite the introduction of new foods from the Americas and better public health standards, the standard of living declined. Forests had been cut down, land was eroding, fishing was already developed to its utmost, and resources such as coal and iron were exploited only on a local scale. China was self-sufficient, but the population was growing so fast the economy could not keep up with it. The gentry, who held most of the land, bribed officials to keep their taxes low. Thus the burden of taxes fell, as it had for centuries, upon the peasant farmers. Corrupt officials often added so many charges to taxes that peasants ended up paying as much as ten times the official tax. By the nineteenth century the discontent of the peasants was expressed in an increasing number of revolts. Secret societies, aimed at overthrowing the Ch'ing, became more numerous.

Europeans establish trade with China. China's traditional society also faced a new threat—the trading rights demanded by European merchants. Portuguese merchants had arrived on China's coast in the sixteenth century. Dutch, English, and French traders followed. In 1699 England established a trading post at the largest of the southern ports, Canton, which was connected to the Chinese interior by land routes. This foreign presence was to have an unforeseen impact on China's development.

Officially, the Chinese government scorned trade and restricted the Europeans to the port of Canton. This policy reflected an attitude centuries old—that business dealings were unworthy of the Confucian scholar. In practice, however, port officials largely ignored this official policy, for trade with the West promised them private wealth. Eventually a guild of Chinese merchants, the *Cohong,* was formed to control trade with the West.

The opium trade poses a threat to China's economy. The foreign trade initially was to China's advantage. There was great demand in Europe for Chinese porcelain, silk, and especially tea; China, on the other hand, had little interest in European goods. The western traders therefore had to pay cash, usually silver, for Chinese goods. This situation changed after 1800, however, because of the increased use of opium in China. First the Dutch, then the English East India Company brought opium from India to China, where the drug was exchanged for Chinese goods. The Ch'ing government, realizing the demoralizing effect of opium addiction, had made the use or sale of opium illegal by 1800. But the trade was so profitable that bribed officials found ways to get around the law. By 1825 so much opium was being imported that China, lacking enough goods to exchange for it, had to pay silver to make up the difference.

Europeans resent Chinese trade restrictions. The limited trade through Canton satisfied neither the Chinese government nor the British merchants. The Chinese traditionally believed their land to be the center of the civilized world; they regarded all other nations as barbarians. Foreign contacts were at best unwelcome.

In 1793, the Emperor Ch'ien-lung (chee-*en' loong'*), replying to a British request for less restricted trade, wrote King George III a scornful letter:

I have [carefully read] your [letter]; the earnest terms in which it is [written] reveal a respectful humility on your part, which is highly praiseworthy. . . .

As to your entreaty to send one of your nationals to be accredited to my Celestial Court and to be in control of your country's trade with China, the request is contrary to [our practice]. . . .

Swaying the wide world, I have but one aim in view; namely, to maintain a perfect [government]. . . . Strange and costly objects do not interest me. If I have commanded that the tribute [gifts] . . . sent by you, O King, are to be accepted, this was solely in consideration for the spirit which prompted you to dispatch them from afar. Our Dynasty's [achievements have] . . . penetrated into every country, . . . and kings of all nations have offered their costly tribute. . . . As your ambassador can see for himself, we possess all things. I set no value on objects strange or ingenious, and have no use for your country's manufactures. . . .

Consider . . . that England is not the only barbarian land which wishes to establish . . . trade with our Empire: supposing that other nations were all to imitate your evil example and beseech me to present them each and all with a site for trading purposes, how could I possibly comply? . . .

The distinction between Chinese and barbarian is most strict, and your ambassador's request that barbarians shall be given full liberty to disseminate [spread] their religion is utterly unreasonable.

The Ch'ing government furthermore recognized that the trade with Britain was corrupting its officials. For their part, the British merchants resented all the obstacles and restrictions imposed on trade by the Ch'ing. Foreign merchants could not bring their wives to China, had to remain outside the city gates, and could trade only with the Cohong merchants, who demanded fees, duty payments, and "presents." In addition, they were subject to Chinese criminal law which had fewer safeguards against imprisonment and torture than did western criminal law. The British resented being regarded as inferiors. Moreover, they wanted all of China, not just Canton, opened to trade.

Westerners gain unequal trading privileges. In 1841 the Opium War broke out between the British and the Chinese. Opium was only a side issue in the war; the real conflict was over restriction of trade. China was disastrously defeated and the weakness of the Ch'ing government became apparent to the world. The western powers were prompt to act on this knowledge. Within the next twenty years, Britain and other western nations compelled China to grant them "extraterritorial" privileges. Foreign trade and residence were permitted in a number of Chinese coastal cities, known as *treaty ports* (map, page 588). Foreigners living on Chinese soil were subject to the laws of their own countries instead of Chinese law; they could not be tried in Chinese courts. The Cohong monopoly of trade was abolished and tariffs regarded as fair by the westerners were established. The interior of China was opened to merchants and missionaries. Moreover, whatever rights one foreign nation received from China had to be granted to all other foreign powers in China. The Ch'ing government was powerless to resist this nibbling away of its territory, resources, and rights. This quotation reflects Chinese resentment of the unequal treaties:

The westerners frequently take advantage of the differences in language and in law to profit themselves at the cost of others, and [they] do as they please. . . . When a foreign stagecoach hurts a Chinese, the latter is . . . charged with not knowing how to yield the right of way. . . . Even if the [foreign] driver is taken to court, he only pays a small fine. Furthermore, Chinese employed by

Changing western attitudes toward China are reflected in these two pictures. Left, late in the nineteenth century the Ch'ing emperor still commanded the respect of foreign envoys to his court. In 1900, however, an American cartoonist depicted the Middle Kingdom as a fallen dragon about to be carved up by foreign powers (above).

foreign companies or as sailors on foreign ships frequently have their wages cut on some pretext. . . . When a Chinese merchant owes money to a foreign merchant, . . . his property is [seized]; . . . whereas when a westerner is in debt to a Chinese, even though he has abundant private savings, by following the regulations for declaring bankruptcy, he is entirely free from obligation.

Mounting discontent leads to the Taiping Rebellion. While the western powers were gaining increasing influence in China, poverty and resentment of corrupt mandarin officials led to a series of uprisings. The most serious for the Ch'ing dynasty was the Taiping (*tie′*ping) Rebellion (1850–1864), stemming from the widespread discontent among peasants. The revolt broke out in southern China in 1850. The rebels aimed for a new order, *Taiping* ("Great

Peace"). Their aims reflected a strange mixture of Chinese and western ideals: equal distribution of land to the peasants, the Christian ideal of the brotherhood of all men, equality of sexes, filial piety (page 220), and Confucian principles of proper conduct. The movement spread rapidly and at its height the Taiping rebels controlled most of South and Central China and proclaimed their own dynasty.

The Ch'ing dynasty, already under pressure from the western powers, was unable to quell the rebellion. However, the Taiping program proved too radical for the Confucian mandarins. Instead of joining the rebels, they rallied around the Manchu rulers. Some able mandarins began to organize their own provincial and regional armies. The provincial armies, supported by local taxes and loyal to the mandarins, used western weapons and military techniques. In 1864 they succeeded in crushing the Taiping rebels, but not before perhaps 20 million Chinese had perished.

Though the Ch'ing dynasty had survived the Taiping Rebellion, it never again was able to wield effective rule over all of China. Instead, various parts of the empire came increasingly under the control of regional mandarin leaders who had armies of their own. The Manchu rulers still had the loyalty of these leaders, but the dynasty depended increasingly on them and therefore had to cater to their wishes. Moreover, the revolt had caused widespread destruction and severely strained the government's financial resources.

Modernization and westernization affect traditional Chinese outlooks. Despite the political turmoil, at the end of the nineteenth century China had made some progress toward modernization. The new customs service, headed by a Briton, succeeded in stamping out much of the opium trade (partly because the Chinese were growing more opium), charted the coast of China, and installed aids to navigation such as lighthouses. Western-owned banks, businesses, and light industries operated with the help of Chinese personnel. Gradually a Chinese business class became familiar enough with western ways to compete with foreign merchants. Although Chinese industry began to manufacture western-style weapons and ships, Chinese attempts to industrialize were generally ineffective. Excessive red tape on the part of the government, lack of planning and of business experience, and favoritism slowed down China's efforts at industrialization.

Much more significant than the effort to industrialize was the emergence of a westernized segment of Chinese society. In the treaty ports the Chinese urban population became increasingly familiar with the outside world. Western dress, stores, streetcars, post offices, and newspapers were copied. The Chinese government followed the lead of foreign missionaries in promoting education modeled on that of the West. Western ideas also had an impact on young Chinese students. Some were sent abroad for advanced studies. The westernized segment of Chinese society thus became a mediator between rural, traditional China and the outside world.

The Ch'ing government clings to traditional ways. The government, however, remained tied to traditional ways. Living conditions in the countryside remained largely unchanged. The peasants continued their customary ways quite unaffected by modernization. The economy also suffered because India took over the tea market and European nations bought silk from Japan or developed their own silk industries. Moreover, the tradition-oriented attitude of the Ch'ing dynasty and its officials hampered industrial development. During this period there were severe floods and drought in different parts of China. Some poverty-stricken peasants began to migrate to the cities in hopes of finding a living. Terrorist activities by secret societies, persecution of Christian missionaries and especially of Chinese converts to Christianity, and growing numbers of bandits led to increased disorder and riots in China.

Both conservatives and radicals find fault with the Ch'ing. In 1894 war broke out between

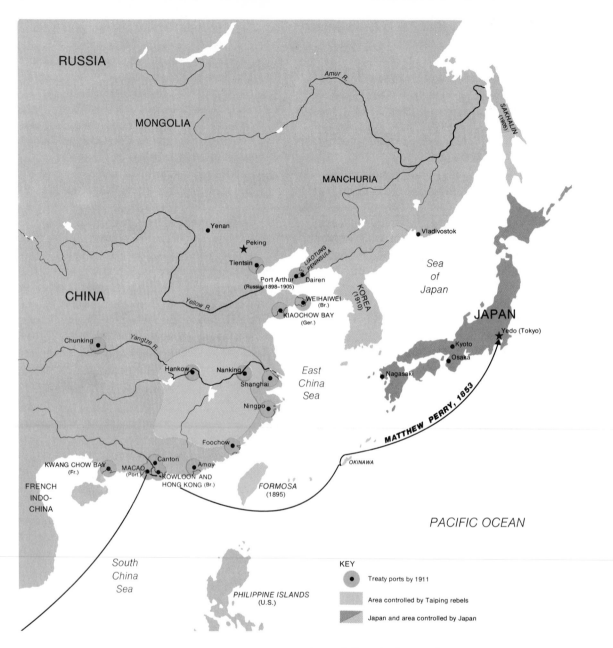

China and Japan over the control of Korea
(page 597). Decisively defeated, China lost
more land, had to pay a stiff indemnity, and was
forced to open still more ports to foreign powers. Even the conservative mandarins realized
that China must undertake reforms to survive
the increasing foreign pressures and mounting

Imperialism in East Asia

*Treaty ports shown in capital letters were like city-
states, virtually independent of China's government.*

domestic unrest. Radicals advocated a government patterned on the western parliamentary
model. Moderates proposed educational reform

and industrialization but, fearing to lose their privileges, showed no interest in political reform. The government played an indecisive role, on the one hand catering to western demands, on the other working with secret societies to drive out the western powers. The Ch'ing could not accept the fact that China, a world power in the seventeenth century, had become little more than a pawn in western politics. Attempts made to drive the foreigners out of China by force—for example, the Boxer Rebellion in 1900—resulted in further loss of Chinese rights. The western nations carved out areas known as *spheres of influence.* Within each sphere of influence, the controlling European power could station troops, control police, and monopolize mining rights and railway building.

To cope with the growing unrest, the Ch'ing finally revised education and abolished the examination system, established western-style military academies, and modernized the army. For leadership in these moves the dynasty looked to Japan, which had rapidly and successfully adopted western ways. But it was too late. New curricula were useless without funds for teachers and schools, and the imperial armies could not cope with the provincial armies which already had been westernized.

Modern nationalism becomes a growing force. But even as China was crumbling apart, there began to arise a spirit of modern nationalism. Instead of trying to preserve China by isolating her from the outside world, the new nationalists demanded that the Middle Kingdom (page 214) become a part of the world by imitating the methods which had proved so successful among western nations. The advocates of the new nationalism were those who were the most deeply aware of the differences between China and the West—the westernized Chinese.

Foremost among them was Sun Yat-sen (*suhn′ yaht′ sen′*). Of peasant origin, Sun came from South China, the region that had had the longest exposure to the West. The Taiping Rebellion was also part of his heritage and in-

spired in him anti-Manchu feelings. Educated in Honolulu and Hong Kong, by the time he was thirty, Sun had won recognition as the leading Chinese revolutionary. Sun gained support not only from bands of rebels and secret societies, who were traditionally anti-Manchu, but also from young westernized patriots and from Chinese living in other lands. Although popular, Sun's movement was poorly organized and several attempts to overthrow the Ch'ing dynasty failed. When the nationalist movement finally achieved a measure of success in 1911, Sun was not even in China.

China becomes a republic in name only. The revolution of 1911 was more nearly a collapse of the ineffective Ch'ing dynasty than a great nationalist victory. Sun and his followers lacked the backing needed to unify China, and their efforts were hampered by powerful regional leaders, the *warlords,* who were in actual control of much of the country. Sun's nationalist movement was unable to overcome the warlords and was plagued with disunity.

China after 1911 was a republic in name only. At the head of the new government was Yüan Shih-k'ai (yoo-*ahn′ shir′ kie′*), the strongest of the warlords. The man who had reorganized the imperial army, using the German army as his model, Yüan had been a key man in the Ch'ing's desperate attempts to stay in power. When the Ch'ing rulers ousted him in 1909, they made a lasting enemy. To the nationalists, Yüan was their only hope, the one man strong enough to unite China and to end the struggle for power among the warlords. Yüan proved to be a stronger man than the nationalists had expected; he was interested not in building a unified republic but in obtaining personal power. The newly established parliament named him president of the republic. But he wasted no time in disbanding parliament and attempting to establish his own dynasty. This brought immediate opposition from the generals and provincial governors. The same people who had helped him gain power thus proved Yüan's undoing, and he died a failure in 1916.

Chinese radicals launch the May Fourth Movement. The failure of the republic greatly disillusioned the young westernized Chinese. Many turned to radical ideas and demanded drastic changes. World War I increased their resentment. The Chinese government had joined the Allies in 1917, hoping to recover the spheres of influence Germany had acquired in China. Actually, this territory had been taken over by Japan early in the war, and the Chinese government had secretly conceded Japan's claims. When the Versailles Treaty of 1919 confirmed Japan's rights to the former German spheres of influence, students at Peking University felt that China had been betrayed by her own government. Angered by western imperialism and inspired by the Russian Revolution of 1917 (see Chapter 28), they started demonstrations which came to be called the *May Fourth Movement.*

The radical May Fourth Movement transformed the outlook of important groups in Chinese society. It quickly spread from Peking to other leading cities and won the support of merchants, businessmen, trade unions, and workers. This union of major sectors of urban society testified to the intense public demand for change. It was a turning point in the growth of Chinese nationalism and radicalism. New ideas and new literature from the West became even more influential than before.

Sun Yat-sen organizes the Kuomintang. Against this background, Sun finally was able to organize his movement into the Nationalist Party, the *Kuomintang* (*gwoh'min'dahng'*). In addition, he systematized his own teaching into the Three Principles of the People:

1. Nationalism. Sun advocated the need for the Chinese to be proud of themselves as a new people, a new nation.

2. Democracy. Sun advocated a modern republican, constitutional type of government, which would retain the traditional Chinese features of the examination system and the government inspectors.

3. Social welfare. Sun hoped to improve conditions for the peasants by reforming methods of taxation. He proposed equalization of land rights by adoption of a single rate of taxation.

Chinese Communists collaborate with the Nationalists. In the 1920's the Kuomintang was in competition with other, more radical intellectuals, who had formed the Chinese Communist Party in 1921. At first small and inexperienced, the Communist Party gained ground very slowly. Most of its members were urban, western-educated radicals; the party lacked popular support. For that reason, the Comintern (Communist International), an organization developed to promote communism throughout the world, urged the Chinese Communists to support the Chinese Nationalists until the warlords were defeated and China reunified. Sun himself welcomed financial and military aid from the Soviet Union, which acted as the directing force behind the Comintern. The disunity that had plagued China since the overthrow of the Ch'ing had disrupted trade, damaged the transportation system, ruined farms and public works, and caused untold misery for China's poor, overtaxed peasants. The Nationalists could not do the job of reunifying the country alone.

Chiang Kai-shek breaks with the Communists. In 1925 Sun Yat-sen died and the head of the Nationalist Army, Chiang Kai-shek (jeh-*ahng' kie'shek'*), took over leadership of the Kuomintang. A military man, Chiang was more conservative than Sun. But he realized that, to unify China and abolish the special privileges of the western powers, he would need all the support he could get. He therefore continued the alliance with the Communists, and their combined forces embarked upon an expedition to reunify the country.

Chiang, however, was suspicious of communist aims and soon undertook a purge of the Communists in China. There were arrests of labor leaders and communist leaders. Following the break with the Communists, the Nationalist Party became less revolutionary and more attractive to conservative Chinese. In 1928 the Nationalists set up their government in Nanking, thus gaining effective control of the east-central part of China. Much of the rest of the country continued under the rule of the warlords. Soon the Nationalists were fighting the Communists and coming to terms with the warlords.

Mao Tse-tung plans a peasant-based revolution.

Among the Chinese Communists was Mao Tse-tung (*mah'oh dzuh'duhng'*). Of peasant background, Mao understood the grounds for widespread peasant discontent and the importance of gaining peasant support through rural reforms. Following the teachings of Marx, Mao urged revolution in China. But unlike most other Communists, who dreamed of a Chinese revolution led by urban workers, Mao realized that in a predominantly rural economy the allegiance of the peasantry was of crucial importance. Mao foresaw that peasant discontent could be harnessed into a powerful force for revolution:

Within a short time, hundreds of millions of peasants will rise in Central, South, and North China, with the fury of a hurricane; no power, however strong, can restrain them. They will break all the shackles that bind them and rush towards the road of liberation. All imperialists, warlords, corrupt officials, and bad gentry will meet their doom at the hands of the peasants.

Mao creates a Red Army.

Mao tried to attract peasants to the communist cause by introducing reforms which made their lives easier. But, in addition, he organized a rural-based Red Army. It was apparent from the first that the small forces of the Red Army could not defeat the Nationalists in a traditional war. Mao therefore urged guerrilla warfare (page 473) away from urban centers.

Guerrilla attacks on Nationalists in South China went badly for the Communists, and in 1934 Mao led his followers northward on the Long March. Constantly harried by Nationalist forces, the Communists marched some 5000 miles over mountains, plains, deserts, and swamps. In 1935 about a third of the original forces established themselves in the rocky cave fortress of Yenan (*yeh'nahn'*) in North China. This became Mao's new communist base.

Internal disorder and foreign invasion threaten China.

Divided among warlords and the nationalist and communist forces, China by the late 1930's was in trouble. Population increases had resulted in a growing number of landless peasants and the rural standard of living had declined as prices and rents spiraled upward. Traditional family ties were weakened by the stresses of urban living and factory work. A small western-educated middle class was emerging but it was powerless to arrest the steadily worsening conditions.

To make matters worse, the Japanese began a large-scale invasion of China in 1937. This outside threat acted as a unifying element on the warring factions within China. With the coming of the war, the Chinese Communists initially set aside their differences with the Nationalists. Even the warlords joined in an all-out effort to save China from foreign conquest (see pages 597–598). But the struggle for power between Nationalists and Communists resumed even while World War II was going on.

CHECK-UP

1. What were the causes of increased weakness in China after about 1750?

2. What was China's official position with respect to foreign trade? Why? What was the Cohong? How did the British react to restrictions on trade?

3. What was the effect of the opium trade on China? What were the causes of the Opium War? The results?

4. What factors led to the Taiping Rebellion? Why did it fail? What were the results of the rebellion?

5. What changes took place in China during the 1800's? What criticisms were made of the Ch'ing government? What efforts at reform were made?

Japan

The early sixteenth century was a period of constant warfare among the various feudal domains in Japan. With the arrival of the Portuguese in the middle of the century, foreign and domestic trade expanded. Improved weapons and stronger fortifications gave the more powerful feudal lords a great advantage over the lesser ones. Toward the end of the sixteenth century Hideyoshi (*he-deh-yoh-shee*), a samurai (page 224) general who had risen from a humble origin by his military ability, succeeded in overcoming many of the other feudal lords.

Tokugawa shoguns establish a powerful feudal state. Hideyoshi was succeeded in the early seventeenth century by another powerful feudal lord, Tokugawa Ieyasu (*toh-koo-gah-wah ee-eh-yah-soo*), who established his supremacy over all other feudal lords, or *daimyo* (*die-myoh*). In 1603 he got the emperor to appoint him hereditary military commander-in-chief, or *shogun*. Though the emperor continued a shadowy existence as a symbol of Japanese sensitivity to tradition, the real ruler of Japan was the Tokugawa shogun. The Tokugawa shogunate, with headquarters at Yedo (*yeh-doh*, present-day Tokyo), lasted for more than 250 years. It was a peculiar compromise between feudalism and centralization. Whereas the development of centralized governments in Europe led to the end of feudalism, in Japan the central government was built upon the feudal system. The country continued to be divided among 200–300 daimyo. Though these lords pledged allegiance to the Tokugawa shoguns, the shogunate never succeeded in completely controlling them or in unifying Japan.

To create a stable state, the Tokugawa shoguns initiated policies designed to preserve their military ascendancy. They redistributed the landholdings of the daimyo, so that the lands of the more loyal lords bordered on the Tokugawa holdings in central Japan. Daimyo of questionable loyalty were assigned land in outlying regions, and important families were bound to the Tokugawa by marriage. In addition, all feudal lords were required to spend part of each year at Yedo; when they returned to their own domains, members of their families remained at Yedo as hostages. Thus the daimyo were under constant surveillance by the shogunate. The Tokugawa shoguns also established rigid class lines, prohibiting members of one class from marrying or otherwise moving into another class. At the top was the samurai class of warriors and daimyo leaders, then the peasants, followed by the artisans, with the merchants at the bottom of society. This social hierarchy reflected the feudal-agrarian outlook of the Tokugawa leaders.

The Tokugawa adopt a policy of isolation. Some European merchants and missionaries had reached Japan in the sixteenth century. And the Japanese, true to their tradition, were quite receptive to these outside contacts and influences. However, because the Tokugawa wished to maintain things as they were, they expelled the missionaries and merchants. In that way Japan was isolated from the rest of the world except for some very limited trade with the Dutch, who had a post at Nagasaki (*nah-*

gah-sah-kee). This isolation policy, so contrary to traditional Japanese receptivity to foreign influences, continued until the mid-nineteenth century.

Urbanization leads to cultural advances. No matter how hard the shogunate tried to preserve the established type of society, it could not prevent change in the Japanese economic and social order. Agriculture, which was the foundation of the economy, made great advances. Land reclamation, technological advances, increased use of fertilizers, and improved seeds made it possible for agriculture to support a much larger population. Instead of growing a variety of crops, many farmers came to specialize in one or two, thus encouraging trade and village industries.

Even more important, the trend toward urbanization continued. Between the end of the sixteenth century and the eighteenth century Yedo grew from a fishing village to a bustling city of nearly a million. Landless farmers and younger sons migrated to towns and cities in search of work. To take advantage of the growing market, large-scale wholesale firms were established to set prices, fix interest rates on loans, and control trade. As the urban standard of living rose, the demand for luxury goods made work for artisans and increased the profits of merchants.

Gradually the cultural life in towns and cities became more varied. The samurai class preserved the traditional tea ceremony, flower arrangement, and Noh drama. But under the Tokugawa, popular forms of amusement developed. Both the puppet theater and kabuki (*kah-boo-kee*) theater made use of themes from everyday life as well as historical events. Literature also emphasized town life. Increasing literacy and the development of printing brought popular novels to a wide audience. Haiku (*hie-koo*), a type of poetry still associated with the Japanese, developed at this time.

Japan

1603	Tokugawa Shogunate established; isolationist policy adopted
1853	Arrival of Perry ends Japanese isolation
1854	Two ports opened to trade with United States
1868	Tokugawa shogun relinquishes office to Satsuma-Choshu leaders; Meiji Restoration
1876	Japan negotiates treaty which recognizes Korea as independent of China and open to Japanese trade
1889	Western-style constitution adopted in Japan
1894–1895	Sino-Japanese War
1904–1905	Russo-Japanese War
1910	Korea annexed
1914	Japan declares war on Germany
1919	Versailles Treaty upholds Japan's claims to German spheres of influence in Pacific
1931	Mukden incident in Manchuria
1937	Invasion of China

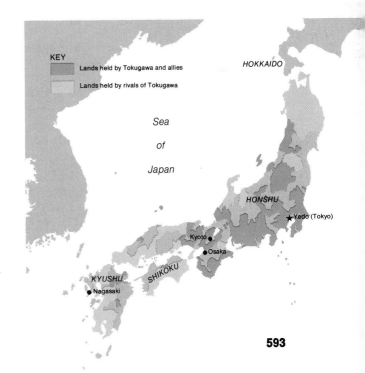

KEY
Lands held by Tokugawa and allies
Lands held by rivals of Tokugawa

HOKKAIDO

Sea
of
Japan

HONSHU

Yedo (Tokyo)

Kyoto
Osaka

KYUSHU   SHIKOKU

Nagasaki

Tokugawa Japan

Traditionally, only men perform in kabuki theater. These actors, playing the roles of a geisha and a samurai, wear costumes typical of the feudal period.

Though simple in form, poets used it to express a surprising range of emotions. One of the most remarkable artistic achievements of the Tokugawa era was the development of woodblock prints depicting landscapes, famous performers in the theater, and daily life, both urban and rural.

The samurai class becomes impoverished.
Artisans and merchants benefited most from the rise of an urban-centered way of life. The daimyo and samurai, preservers of Japanese military traditions, were unable to keep up with the urban world. Their income was dependent on the rice produced on their domains, and rice production and prices failed to keep pace with the spiraling costs of manufactured goods. To maintain their accustomed standard of living, daimyo and samurai had to spend more money than they collected. They obtained needed funds by borrowing from artisans and merchants.

By the eighteenth century certain contradictions characterized Japanese society. Officially, the samurai class was supposed to be at the top of the social pyramid, the artisans and merchants at the bottom. Actually, the daimyo and samurai were becoming impoverished, while merchants and artisans were growing wealthier and acquiring influence.

The Tokugawa try in vain to resist change.
As the samurai class became poorer and more discontented, the Tokugawa shogunate grew weaker and less effective. Revolts by peasants burdened by heavy taxes and often suffering from famine became increasingly common.

The Dutch trading post at Nagasaki served to spread western learning. At the same time, however, there was a revival of the Shinto religion (page 223), with its emphasis on the emperor as the symbol of national glory. As this patriotic sentiment increased, some leaders began to question the right of the shogun to rule in place of the emperor.

By the middle of the nineteenth century, therefore, many powerful forces were at work in Japan:

1. A steadily growing population led to the rise of bustling urban centers.

2. An expanding economy, aided by a long tradition of saving and investment, made possible a rising urban standard of living.

3. As the importance of the samurai class declined and the rigid class structure broke down under the impact of economic realities, the able and industrious sought increased opportunities for advancement.

4. The Tokugawa shoguns tried to prevent change by ruling that people must stay within their own class.

5. The increasing opposition to ineffective Tokugawa rule focused upon a movement which urged giving back power to the emperor.

Although Japanese society was clearly ready for fundamental changes, the Tokugawa shogunate was not. It took pressure from the outside world to bring about revolutionary changes in the island kingdom.

Japan is opened to foreign trade. In 1853 Commodore Matthew Perry of the United States Navy arrived in the harbor of Uraga (*oo-rah-gah*), across the bay from Yedo. He demanded an end to Japan's isolation and the opening of the country to outside trade and contact. The Tokugawa shogun, hoping for nationwide support, made an unprecedented move. He asked the advice of the imperial court and of all the daimyo—not just the men who usually advised him. This move made it clear that the supremacy of the Tokugawa shogunate was at an end. At long last the critics of the shogunate dared to express their views. While most daimyo opposed contacts and trade with the West, a few realized that concessions must be made to fend off western military pressure.

In 1854 Japan opened two ports to the United States, and soon the British, Russians, and Dutch had also gained concessions. As in China, whatever rights one nation gained were to be enjoyed by all. By 1858, besides opening more ports to trade, the Tokugawa allowed foreign residents in Yedo and Osaka, permitted the foreign powers to set tariff rates, and granted extraterritorial privileges. Unlike China, however, Japan was not forced to cede land to the foreign powers.

The new Satsuma-Choshu leaders institute reforms. The shogunate was blamed for these unequal treaties, highly unpopular with most Japanese. The shogun was facing an economic crisis. An unfavorable balance of trade (importing more goods than are exported) caused gold to flow out of the country, and the importation of cheap manufactured goods from abroad was ruining Japan's domestic industries. The tradition-minded samurai, deeply resenting the presence of foreigners in Japan, attacked foreign merchants and had to pay large sums as

recompense. Moreover, to head off the possibility that foreign powers might seek a foothold on Japanese soil, the shogunate began costly defense preparations. But confidence in the Tokugawa was not restored.

A small group of able samurai from the feudal domains of Satsuma (*sahts'-mah*) and Choshu (*choh-shoo*) in southwestern Japan began to agitate for the end of the shogunate and the restoration of power to the emperor. In 1868, after much intrigue and some fighting, the last Tokugawa shogun relinquished his office to the Satsuma-Choshu forces. Mutsuhito (*moo-tsoo-hee-toh*), better known as the Emperor Meiji (*may-jee,* 1868–1912), in theory picked up the reins of authority. Actually, throughout the period known as the *Meiji* (Enlightened Rule) *Restoration,* the emperor continued to be a figurehead. Real power was in the hands of the small group of Satsuma-Choshu samurai leaders.

The Satsuma-Choshu leaders were a remarkable group of young and capable individuals. Their samurai background had given them a tremendous sense of discipline and patriotism. Well aware that Japan had to modernize to survive in the modern world, they, like earlier Japanese reformers, accepted the need for selective borrowing from the outside world. For the first time Japan was unified and the government centralized and modernized. In 1889 a western-style constitution and a two-house legislature were adopted. However, power remained in the hands of the Satsuma-Choshu leaders, who continued to hold the top government posts. And within the government, they led the army and navy, which remained independent of civilian control. To carry out military policies, only the approval of the emperor was needed. This meant that there was no effective check upon army and navy leaders.

Class restrictions and feudal domains and privileges were abolished. Careers were opened to men of talent, though there continued to be social distinctions between the samurai class and the rest of Japanese society. Farmers, given title to the land they had tilled, now paid taxes

As part of a campaign to arouse people's patriotism and confidence, Japanese artists of the Meiji period depicted events that reflected Japan's rising power. The woodblock print shown here presents the 1895 victory over China in stirring colors.

directly to the government. Instead of paying taxes with a percentage of their crops, farmers paid a money tax based on the value of the land. When peasants were unable to meet tax payments, they became tenant farmers. A national army was established, and construction was started on a navy modeled on Britain's. All men, not just samurai, were required to serve in the armed forces. Both the tax reform and the draft caused outrage among the peasants; the samurai, in turn, resented the inclusion of common people in the armed forces. But revolts by dissatisfied elements were easily put down.

Industrialization and westernization bring about changes in Japan. Most remarkable was the rapid industrialization of Japan during the late nineteenth and early twentieth centuries. Having a military background, the Satsuma-Choshu leaders wanted Japan to become a military power. They therefore placed emphasis on those industries directly related to military needs—iron and steel, munitions and shipyards,

railway and maritime transportation. At first the government built and operated some factories; other projects received financial support. Some of the wealthy merchant families soon became involved in Japan's industrial expansion. Commercial expansion was encouraged by the ending of western extraterritorial rights and control of tariffs.

Meanwhile, Japanese society was being westernized, especially in the cities. The new factories, schools, banks, and government offices taught people western techniques and business methods. In certain social circles there was, for a time, a craze for western customs, dress, hairstyles, and manufactured goods. Yet modernization did not erase tradition in Japan. Instead, it resulted in an unusual combination of Japanese tradition and western modernity. A good example of this blend was the national education system. The new schools provided for compulsory education and the study of western science and technology. More important were Asian—Chinese as well as Japanese—literature and history. Special emphasis was placed on traditional and moral values:

. . . be filial to your parents, affectionate to your brothers and sisters; as husbands and wives be harmonious, as friends true; bear yourselves in modesty and moderation; extend your benevolence to all; pursue learning and cultivate arts, and thereby develop intellectual faculties and perfect moral powers; furthermore, advance public good and promote common interests; always respect the constitution and observe the laws; should emergency arise, offer yourselves courageously to the state.

Japan becomes an imperialist power. By the early twentieth century Japan was a rising power that had won the respect of the western nations. Japan began to imitate western imperialism, a new venture for the old samurai military outlook. In 1876 Japan had forced the opening of Korea to trade. This peninsula, which juts out from the Asian mainland, had traditionally been considered under China's protection. But as the major route over which Chinese goods and ideas had reached Japan, Korea was strategically important to the Japanese. In 1894–1895 Japan took over Korea from the tottering Chinese empire, but ten years later tsarist Russia, slowly expanding eastward, threatened Japan's claims. Japan's crushing defeat of Russian army and naval forces in the war of 1904–1905 came as a surprise to the West. It was an eloquent testimony to the effectiveness of Japanese modernization. This made other Asian nationalists look to Japan for inspiration.

Soon Japan was competing with the western powers for concessions and privileges in China. When World War I broke out in 1914, Japan, allied with Britain since 1902, joined the Allies. Taking advantage of the western powers' preoccupation with the war in Europe, Japan compelled the weak Chinese government to agree to the expansion of Japanese rights and influence in China. Japan also took over Germany's holdings in China. These claims were confirmed at the Versailles peace conference in 1919, a conference in which Japan took part as one of the Great Powers.

Modernization creates problems. Following World War I, Japan's interests in expansion abated for a time. Her economic growth slowed down, though the population continued to in-

crease, nearly doubling between 1900 and 1940. The country's rapid modernization had created problems. The gap between rural and urban living standards grew wider; dissatisfaction and unrest increased among both tenant farmers and factory workers. Japan's booming industries needed more and more raw materials, which always seemed in short supply, and agricultural production leveled off.

Nearly all of the old Satsuma-Choshu leaders had died, and their successors were unable to reach agreement on many vital issues. An attempt was made to develop a government representing the views of opposition parties. Japan seemed to be edging toward more democratic government. But in the early 1930's there was a worldwide depression, and it shook the Japanese economy. Though the economy recovered in three years, the depression had further weakened the government's power.

Japan clashes with China. In the early 1920's western powers such as the United States and Britain, alarmed by Japan's military might and expansion, had pressed for a limit of her naval build-up in the Pacific. But by the 1930's the army and navy leaders as well as extreme nationalist groups became increasingly dissatisfied and outspoken. They argued that it was Japan's destiny to replace the western nations as leader in East Asia. They saw the new Chinese nationalism as a threat to Japanese economic interests in Manchuria. In addition they argued that military expansion not only would solve Japan's population problem but provide needed raw materials and markets for the country's economy. Gradually the militarists converted the nation to a war economy and set Japan upon a course of aggressive expansion.

In 1931 the army leaders engineered an incident which served as an excuse to take over Manchuria and set up a puppet government under Japanese control. This provided the Japanese army with a territorial base on the Asian mainland, making the army even more independent of control by the Japanese government. The Japanese army next began a steady infiltration into northern China. In 1937 Chinese and Japanese troops on maneuvers near Peking accidentally clashed. Japanese military leaders seized the opportunity to "blow up" this minor incident to justify a full-scale invasion of China.

Japan was vastly more powerful militarily than China, and initially the war went well for the island kingdom. Within the first year of the war, Japan occupied all of China's important coastal cities and expected that the Chinese would soon sue for peace. The Chinese, however, refused to give up. There was a tremendous surge of anti-Japanese nationalism that for a time united Chinese Nationalists, Communists, and warlords in a struggle against the Japanese invaders. At a terrific cost in human lives, the Chinese bravely fought on as the government and some industries were moved far into the interior. Instead of a quick victory for Japan, the war degenerated into a prolonged struggle from which Japan could not free herself.

CHECK-UP

1. How were the Tokugawa able to establish a powerful feudal state in Japan? Why did they adopt a policy of isolation?

2. What changes had taken place in Japan by about 1850? What forces were contributing to further change?

3. How did Japan's isolation come to an end?

4. Why was the shogunate overthrown? What reforms did the Satsuma-Choshu leaders introduce?

5. What changes resulted from industrialization? Westernization? What traditions persisted?

6. Why did Japan take over Korea? Come to blows with Russia? Enter World War I? What was the result of each action?

7. What problems resulted from modernization?

8. What were the aspirations of Japanese nationalists in the 1930's? Why were they interested in Manchuria? In attacking China? How successful was the invasion of China?

Summing Up

In this chapter we have seen how three Asian nations—India, China, and Japan—reacted to the pressures of western imperialism. While all three had societies closely bound to tradition, each society was distinct and responded in a different way to contact with the West. In India, a single western power (Britain) was in control. This meant that a foreign power had the authority to dictate policy to Indian rulers. In the process Britain brought some unity to a land broken up into many states. The Ch'ing dynasty of China regarded the westerners as inferior, but the dynasty was too weak to offer much resistance to western expansion and was forced to make huge concessions to foreign demands. Japan moved from a policy of almost complete isolation to one of acceptance of and successful adaptation to western ways.

Western control brought some urban, industrial progress to India. Expanded trade and industry were coupled with improved systems of transportation and communication. Nevertheless, modernization introduced by Britain affected only a small number of Indians. The traditions of Hindu society continued to dominate the lives of most Indians; caste was a stronger force than change.

China retained her dynastic government until just before World War I. But it was weak and had to yield to the demands of various foreign nations. Western domination led to the beginnings of modernization in China, but the pace was slow, for both the Ch'ing dynasty and the Confucian-educated mandarins resisted change. The Nationalist program was not very effective. As for the peasants, who made up the overwhelming majority of the population, most had no contact with the western powers and little desire for change.

Both China and India had changed by the end of World War I. However, since both lands were steeped in tradition, the degree of modernization that each achieved was totally inadequate to ensure needed economic growth.

Japan was the only one of the Asian nations which was able to use westernization to become militarily and economically strong. With a long tradition of borrowing from foreign cultures and a people who were eager to get the most out of their way of life, Japan accepted the most adaptable features of modernization and at the same time preserved intact many of her traditions. By the 1930's, when China was beset by turmoil and disunity and India by indifference, Japan had become a major military power capable of pursuing imperialist policies in East Asia. In each case the total cultural heritage of each nation—not just isolated events—led to a distinct response to western contact.

Chapter Highlights

Can you explain?

samurai	opium trade	hind swaraj	guerrilla warfare
modernization	shogun	passive resistance	spheres of influence
daimyo	treaty ports	extraterritorial privileges	monopolistic trade

Can you identify?

Clive	Yedo	Chiang Kai-shek	Sun Yat-sen
Tokugawa	Canton	English East India Company	Meiji Restoration
Cornwallis	Nehru	Commodore Perry	Yüan Shih-k'ai
Kuomintang	Manchuria	Indian Nationalist Congress	Satsuma-Choshu leaders
Gandhi	Red Army	May Fourth Movement	Mao Tse-tung
warlords	Hideyoshi	Taiping Rebellion	Chinese Nationalists
Cohong	Yenan	Sepoy Rebellion	

What do you think?

1. From the point of view of the Indians, what were the long-range advantages and disadvantages of the British presence in the subcontinent?

2. According to Gandhi, "nonviolence . . . is the most active force in the world." Do you agree or disagree? How have Gandhi's methods been used in the United States?

3. Barbara Ward concludes that the rate of progress in British-ruled India was slow. Do you agree? Why?

4. Why did the Chinese regard the westerners as barbarians?

5. Why was the May Fourth Movement a turning point in the growth of nationalism in China?

6. Why was it relatively easy for the Communists to gain a foothold in China?

7. Why did traditional Chinese government break down under the pressures of modernization?

8. Why did Japan's fantastic economic growth help lead her towards imperialism?

9. Why had Japan become a great power by World War I? Why had not China or India?

10. Briefly sum up how India, China, and Japan reacted to the pressures of western imperialism. How did the cultural heritage of each nation determine its response to contact with the West?

The Twentieth Century

With the twentieth century we reach a crucial turning point in the history of the world. The age of imperialism extended western control over many non-western cultures and brought the world under western leadership. Ever since, mankind has truly lived in "One World." This new unity was made manifest in World War I. Starting in Europe, the war rapidly engulfed most of the world. Less than thirty years later, the Second World War demonstrated even more forcibly the interdependence of all continents. Most people today are vaguely and uncomfortably aware of a sense of global community.

There are other forms of interdependence besides politics. A man's livelihood and prosperity depend not only on his own labor but on that of people in other lands. All over the world men are in immediate communication with each other through the daily press, the radio, and television. As a result, people have come to share many common aspirations. They want peace and freedom, food and housing, some material things that make life easier, perhaps an opportunity to travel. Yet because people speak different languages and follow their own ways of life, they remain strangers. Meanwhile, the problems arising out of their interdependence continue to grow.

First, there is the rate of population growth, resulting largely from the worldwide use of western medical skills. Of all the millions of people who ever inhabited the earth, fully one quarter are living today. For the most part they still follow ways of life that have not changed for centuries. Then there is the rapid rate of change itself, much of it caused by western technology. Even in American society many things learned in school will be outmoded in 25 years. How can people reared in civilizations that pride themselves on their traditions adjust to such rapid innovations?

A further source of uncertainty and bitter strife has developed out of the ideal that all men are equal and should take part in their own government. Politics in the 1900's has become "mass politics," propelling people who had lived quietly for centuries into frenzied activity to achieve their vision of a better society. Throughout the world the masses have begun to assert themselves. This has led to seemingly unending political crises, internal violence, unstable governments, revolutions, and foreign wars.

During the twentieth century nationalism, an outgrowth of many centuries of separate development of cultures and states, became more extreme and more widespread. At the same time that our planet has been knit more closely by increased trade, advances in communications and transportation, and the spread of western civilization, men's insistence on their separate political or cultural identity has served as a divisive force, keeping alive old hatreds and creating new ones.

Twentieth-century man, driven by fear, fanaticism, and the complexities of a fast-changing world, has developed monstrous weapons such as hydrogen bombs, monstrous governments such as totalitarian dictatorships, and monstrous ways of forcing people to do the bidding of the state.

Never before has man been forced to live in a world so crowded, so fast changing, and so inescapably interdependent. We have not been able to adjust to this rapidly changing world order. Our social development—our ability to solve problems of war, poverty, unemployment, racism, overpopulation, violence—has not kept pace with our technological advances. The staggering complexities of our century have frightened men more than they have ever been frightened before. What solutions will man find for the tensions and problems that plague his planet in the twentieth century? Will people throughout the world adjust to swiftly changing customs, beliefs, and conditions of life? Will reason, understanding, and above all charity prevail over ignorance, fanaticism, and hatred?

World Wars and Totalitarianism

Unit Seven————

601

Es gilt die letzten Schläge, den Sieg zu vollenden!

World War I

CHAPTER FOCUS

Underlying Causes of World War I
Darkness Falls: Europe Stumbles into War
War Rages on Many Fronts
The Peace That Failed
Results of World War I

On Sunday, June 28, 1914, flags flew in the city of Sarajevo (*sah′rah-yeh-voh*), the capital of Bosnia in the southern Austro-Hungarian Empire. The portrait of Archduke Francis Ferdinand, heir to the throne of Austria-Hungary, was displayed in many windows. Citizens thronged the streets to see the visiting archduke. In the back of an open car sat Francis Ferdinand, wearing a full-dress uniform with all his decorations. His wife, dressed in a white gown and a large hat, sat beside him. Unaware of the fate that awaited them, the party of official visitors headed for the town hall.

Although Austria and Hungary had separate constitutions and legislative bodies, they had the same ruler and joint ministries for foreign affairs and war. Under Austro-Hungarian control were people of many nationalities, about

Men on both sides marched off to the Great War seeking glory. Both sides tried to make soldiers see themselves as modern saviors of the nation, walking in the footsteps of legendary folk heroes. The German poster (above, left) shows the Teutonic warrior Siegfried about to slay the British lion. Above, the patron saint of England, St. George, spears the German dragon. The reality of modern war was far different—a bitter and monotonous struggle that ended in a grim death (left).

half of whom were Slavs.[1] The spirit of nationalism that had brought unification to Italy and Germany was equally strong among the different Slavic nationalities. In some cases Slav nationalists wanted their people to break away from the Austro-Hungarian Empire and form their own independent country. In other cases they wanted to join up with already independent Slav nations. This was particularly true of the South Slavs, who hoped to establish a Yugoslav (South Slav) kingdom by uniting with Serbia and Montenegro (mon-teh-*nee′*groh), two small but independent Slav states.

Serbian nationalists wanted a Greater Serbia which would include Bosnia and Herzegovina (her-tseh-goh-*vee′*nuh)—provinces Austria had annexed in 1908—as well as other Austrian lands inhabited by South Slavs. If Serbia did not annex the South Slavs living in the Austrian Empire, she would continue to be a small weak nation. She would always feel in danger of conquest by the powerful Austro-Hungarian Empire. Serbian nationalists therefore formed secret societies whose aim was the creation of a Greater Serbia. Most active of the secret societies was that known as *Union or Death,* or the *Black Hand.* The Black Hand used terrorism and revolt to further its aims. Francis Ferdinand's visit to neighboring Bosnia gave these Serbian nationalists the opportunity for which they waited. Killing the archduke would be a dramatic way to show their hatred for Austria-Hungary. One of the leaders of the society wrote: "We would kill him to bring once more to the boiling point the fighting spirit of the revolutionaries and pave the way for revolt."

A bomb hurled at Francis Ferdinand's car as it approached a bridge on its way to the town hall wounded spectators and an officer in the car behind the archduke's. Francis Ferdinand arrived at the town hall in a rage. Interrupting the mayor's welcoming speech, he shouted, "I make you a visit, and you receive me with bombs!" After the ceremony of welcome, the archduke insisted upon visiting the military hospital where the wounded officer had been taken. To guard against a second attack, the scheduled route was changed. But the driver of the lead car made an error. He turned off the main avenue into narrow Franz Josef Street. The archduke's driver, unfamiliar with the city, followed. An Austrian general riding with the archduke shouted: "That's the wrong way!" The driver put on the brakes and started to back up. At the corner Gavrilo Princip,[2] a sickly young conspirator, stepped forward and fired two shots. The first struck Francis Ferdinand in the neck. The archduke's wife threw herself across the archduke in an attempt to protect him. The second shot hit her in the stomach. Within fifteen minutes both were dead. Five weeks later World War I began.

Underlying Causes of World War I

The assassination of Francis Ferdinand was the immediate cause of the war. It was the spark that set Europe ablaze. But there were more basic reasons why the nations of Europe were thrust into war. There were four underlying causes of World War I: (1) alliances, (2) militarism, (3) imperialism, and (4) nationalism.

Rival alliance systems come into being. Before World War I, Europe was divided into two rival armed camps of powerful nations. Each of the Great Powers had allies to help it in case of

[1] The Slavs, who live in Eastern Europe, include Czechs, Slovaks, Poles, Serbs, Bulgars, Macedonians, Croatians, and Russians.

[2] Gavrilo Princip (*gah′*vree·loh *preen′*tseep) was born in Bosnia. Because he was too young to receive the death penalty, he was imprisoned in an Austrian fortress, where he died in 1918. The Yugoslavs regard him as a national hero.

war. Why did the Great Powers feel they needed allies?

When Germany won the Franco-Prussian War (1870–1871), she seized the French provinces of Alsace and Lorraine. German statesmen hoped to protect what the German army had won in war by forming alliances. By allying herself with Austria and Russia, Germany would have only the frontier with France to worry about. Italy, long a foe of Austria-Hungary, came into conflict with France over North Africa. Deciding that her interests would best be served by joining France's rival, in 1882 Italy joined Germany and Austria-Hungary in the Triple Alliance. There was one major weakness in Germany's alliance system. Austria and Russia had conflicting interests in the Balkans (southeastern Europe). If Germany drew closer to Austria, her relations with Russia would suffer. Feeling that Austria was more reliable, Germany allowed her pact with Russia to lapse in 1890.

In the Franco-Prussian War Germany had quickly and devastatingly defeated France. It was clear that France by herself was no match for Germany, now the strongest power in Europe. Bitter over the loss of Alsace-Lorraine, French patriots demanded revenge. To the French government, the regaining of Alsace-Lorraine was secondary to its concern over Germany's increasing military strength, expanding industries, growing population, and alliances. France feared another German invasion and another French defeat. Therefore, gaining allies was for France a matter of survival. When Germany broke with Russia, France was quick to take advantage of the situation by becoming Russia's ally. Soon after, she sought Britain's friendship. Fearful of Germany's growing industrial and military strength, particularly her expanding navy, Britain entered into an agreement with France. Russia's defeat by the Japanese in 1905 (page 597) convinced Britain that Germany posed more of a threat to her security than did Russia. In 1907, therefore, Britain became linked with Russia and France in the Triple Entente (on-*tahnt'*).

Events Leading to World War I

1870–1871	Franco-Prussian War; Germany takes Alsace-Lorraine from France
1882	Germany, Italy, and Austria-Hungary form Triple Alliance
1893–1894	Franco-Russian alliance
1904	British-French entente
1904–1905	Russo-Japanese War
1907	France, Britain, and Russia form Triple Entente
1908	Austria annexes Bosnia and Herzegovina

Rival alliances arouse suspicion and fear.
France and Britain viewed Germany as a war-like and aggressive nation that was planning to dominate Europe. France could not forgive Germany for seizing Alsace-Lorraine. Great Britain, mistress of the seas and ruler of a mighty empire, resented Germany's growing naval power and her desire to gain colonies. Germany's expanding military and economic strength gave France and Britain cause to worry. They felt that a confident and powerful Germany would try to gain more land in Europe. This would enable her to dominate the continent. Germany, on the other hand, regarded the Triple Entente as a hostile alliance that threatened the country from two sides. Russia feared German penetration of the Balkans and the Middle East. She was worried that Austria-Hungary, Russia's chief enemy, had the support of so powerful a country as Germany. Austria-Hungary, in turn, feared that Russia was scheming to extend her influence in the Balkans, which threatened Austria's vital interests. She felt threatened by Russian nationalists who called for the liberation of the Slavs from Austrian rule and their union with Russia, "Mother of the Slavs." While the Russian government did not necessarily support the dreams of chauvinists who wanted Russia to rule all the Slavs, Austria-Hungary, ruling over millions of dissatisfied Slavs, could not take the

The Balkans in 1913

gether in a [horse-drawn] carriage. They watch each other and when one of them puts his hand into his pocket, his neighbor gets ready his own revolver in order to be able to fire the first shot."

Militarism sounds a call to arms. In 1914 some people looked forward to war. They agreed with the Austrian historian who wrote that quarrels between nations "must be settled not at the [conference] table, but on the battlefield; not with the pen, but with the sword; not with ink, but with blood." To such persons war seemed exciting and noble. School children were taught that victory in war was a nation's greatest glory and dying in battle a soldier's noblest deed.

For some years the Great Powers of Europe had engaged in an armaments race. Each nation spent huge sums for armaments and (except for Britain, which placed chief reliance on her navy) maintained a large army during peacetime. During the years before 1914, generals worked out detailed plans for attacking their neighbors. Because they wanted to get the jump on a would-be enemy, generals were more likely to urge an immediate attack than to seek negotiation or compromise. In times of crisis it was difficult for a nation's civilian leaders to resist the demands of the military for war. In the fateful days before the outbreak of war, it appeared that in Germany the army, not the civilian leadership, was making the final decision of war or peace. This eagerness and readiness to fight is called *militarism*. Nations feared each other's military might. If one country increased the size of its army or built new and mightier battleships, other countries were frightened into building up their own armies and navies. There seemed no end to the arms race.

The race for colonies creates enemies. As we have seen, European nations competed with each other in an effort to gain colonies, new markets, and new sources of raw materials. This race for overseas possessions led to bitter rivalries among the Great Powers. Quite often more

statements of Russian nationalists lightly. Anyone who encouraged Slav nationalism had to be regarded as an enemy of Austria-Hungary.

Because they knew they had the backing of strong allies, nations were more likely to pursue warlike policies. "If Italy, Germany, and Austria openly and sincerely join hands," said a German general in 1913, "we can calmly face a world of enemies." At any time a quarrel could erupt into war. Such a war would involve all the Great Powers because the warring nations would call upon their allies for help.

Before World War I an armed and uneasy peace existed in Europe. What Bismarck said in 1879 was just as true in 1914: "The Great Powers of our time are like travelers, unknown to one another, whom chance has brought to-than one country was pushing into the same territory. More than once before 1914 colonial rivalry in Asia and Africa almost led to a major war. Ambitious and proud nations such as Germany and Italy, who were late in entering the race for colonies, sought to catch up with others. Disputes over colonies caused the nations of Europe to fear and hate each other.

Nationalists dream of conquest. Nationalism (pages 501–502) was one of the chief causes of World War I. French nationalists, made bitter by defeat in the Franco-Prussian War and by the loss of Alsace-Lorraine, wanted revenge. "I could not see any reason for existing," said a French statesman, "unless it were for the hope of recovering our lost provinces." German nationalists wished to expand both in Europe and overseas. Russian chauvinists were convinced that Russia had a holy mission to expand into the Balkans and to rule over the peoples in Eastern Europe who spoke Slavic languages. By 1914 the peace of Europe was threatened by nationalism which caused people of one nation to believe that they were better than their neighbors. It aroused powerful emotions—love for the fatherland and hatred or contempt for other countries.

National minorities pose a problem. Many areas which had once been independent nations had fallen under outside rule. In many cases their people had been divided among other nations. People who had similar languages and traditions were separated from each other by international boundaries. Poles, for example, were divided among Russia, Germany, and Austria. These peoples resented their foreign rulers and yearned to form their own nations. The problem of national minorities was most severe in Eastern Europe because of the multinational character of the Austro-Hungarian Empire.

Under the spell of extreme nationalism, people were quick to anger and slow to reason. It was difficult for nations aroused by nationalist feelings to settle disputes peacefully. They were all too ready to take up the sword. It was his commitment to the nationalist goal of a Greater Serbia that led young Princip to fire the fatal shot at Sarajevo. And it was the fear of increasing nationalism among the different peoples who made up her empire that led Austria-Hungary to try to put an end to the Serbian threat once and for all.

CHECK-UP

1. Why were the Slavs a source of unrest in the Austro-Hungarian Empire? What were the goals of the Black Hand?

2. What did Serbian nationalists hope to accomplish by assassinating Francis Ferdinand?

3. What were the different alliances in Europe? Why were they formed? Why did they arouse suspicion and fear? Encourage nations to act boldly in their international dealings?

4. What new attitude toward war developed in 1914? Why did the arms race make the outbreak of war more likely?

5. Why did the race for colonies create tensions among the nations of Europe?

6. Why was nationalism an important cause of World War I? What is a national minority? What problems did such minorities present?

Darkness Falls: Europe Stumbles into War

In the summer of 1914 Europe stood on the brink of disaster. Emotions ran high. Armies were preparing to strike; generals were confident and eager for battle. The nations of Europe were moving towards war and the diplomats seemed unable or unwilling to head it off. Moreover, there was no international organization to ease tensions and strive for peace. The murder of Archduke Francis Ferdinand had set Europe afire.

Austria determines to crush Serbia. Feeling that Austria's prestige and standing as a Great Power were at stake, key officials and military men were determined to use the issue of the assassination in order to crush Serbia. American historian Laurence Lafore describes the mood in Austria:

These people wanted to make war on Serbia; they had wanted to do so for a long time, and they knew that with every delay [Austria] would grow weaker, its prestige would sink, its enemies, notably Russia, would grow bolder and stronger. . . . The reaction of the war party to the news from Sarajevo had been instant and unequivocal. "The hour has struck for [Austria]."

But war with Serbia would require the support of Austria's ally Germany. What would Germany do?

German statesmen insisted that Germany must at all costs back Austria. Germany considered Austria her only reliable ally. A threat to Austria was also a threat to Germany, for one day Germany might need Austria's help against the Triple Entente. Kaiser Wilhelm (*vil'*helm) II therefore promised Austria the "wholehearted support" of Germany, hoping that any conflict would be limited to Austria-Hungary and Serbia. Germany did not urge Austria to settle the dispute with Serbia peacefully. Instead, Germany encouraged her ally to take up arms against Serbia. Germany believed that Austria must take decisive action against Serbia in order to preserve Austria's position as a Great Power. Both Germany and Austria wanted a quick strike and a fast war that would be over before other countries could come to the aid of Serbia. But events did not turn out that way.

Confident of German backing, on July 23, 1914, Austria sent Serbia an *ultimatum* (ul-tih-*may'*tum)—a list of demands that country must accept. Serbia was given 48 hours to reply. If Serbia refused to accept the ultimatum, Austria would declare war. Some of Austria's demands were so harsh that it would be next to impossible for Serbia to accept them. This was Austria's intention. She sought a military rather than a diplomatic solution to the problem. Austrian leaders believed that the dream of Serbian nationalists for a Greater Serbia would mean the destruction of Austria. They felt that the survival of their country depended upon the liquidation of Serbia. Austrian statesmen were determined to use the assassination as an excuse to end the Serbian threat once and for all. The ultimatum alarmed Russia. She had long considered herself the protector of the Slavs in the Balkans. Moreover, she feared that an attack on Serbia would be just the first step in an Austro-German plan to gain control of the Balkans. An extension of German and Austrian power so close to Russia was unthinkable. "Austria is seeking [an excuse] to gobble up Serbia; but in that case Russia will make war on Austria," said the Russian foreign minister. Europe was teetering on the brink of general war.

Austria-Hungary insists upon war. To many people's surprise, the Serbs accepted all but one of Austria's demands. Kaiser Wilhelm was relieved by the Serbian response. "A great . . . success for [Austria]," he said. "With it every reason for war drops away." But Austria had already decided that there could not be a peaceful settlement with Serbia. And despite Kaiser Wilhelm's feelings, leading German statesmen and generals still wanted Austria to crush Serbia. Austria insisted that Serbia's failure to accept one provision of the ultimatum meant that Serbia had rejected the entire ultimatum.

A small war escalates into a major conflict. Serbia mobilized for war, and Russia indicated that she would support the Balkan nation. This was a crucial moment for Germany. Would she continue to support Austria, knowing that an Austrian attack on Serbia might bring Russia into the conflict? Determined not to desert Austria, German generals urged war. Some German statesmen urged negotiations with Russia, but others believed that a showdown between Russia and Germany was inevitable. They agreed with the German generals who said better to fight Russia now than to wait till the tsar's empire might be stronger. Confident that their army was the best in the world, they believed Germany could defeat not only Russia but France as well. As for Britain, the third member of the Triple Entente, her army was too small to make much difference in a land war. Most German leaders believed Britain would remain neutral. While Germany would have preferred a limited war involving only Austria and Serbia, she was not dismayed by the idea of a general European war. Indeed, victory over Russia and France would enable Germany to increase the territory of her empire. This would make the German Empire the greatest power not only in Europe but in the world.

Having mobilized its army, on July 28 Austria declared war on Serbia. Reassured of French support, Russia continued the mobilization she had begun three days earlier. On August 1, after Russia had refused a German warning to halt mobilization, Germany declared war on Russia. Two days later she also declared war on France. Germany had no quarrel with France but she knew that France would be likely to support her Russian ally. Moreover, Germany's long-range military plans, worked out years before, called for a war with both Russia and France. A war between Russia and Germany automatically meant a German attack on France. Germany therefore requested Belgium's permission to march through Belgian lands to attack France. Belgium's refusal led to a German invasion, which brought Britain into the war. Britain was pledged to guarantee Belgium's neutrality.[3] She had promised France that the British fleet would protect Northern Europe, for Britain had long felt that any invasion of Northern Europe threatened her security. If Germany defeated France as quickly as she had done in 1870–1871, Germany would be master of Western Europe. A century before,

Britain had fought Napoleon to prevent France from doing this very thing. Britain could never feel secure if one country had control over Western Europe. Moreover, by defeating France, Germany might acquire French colonies. She might build an overseas empire that would rival the British Empire.

Thus Austria's decision to crush Serbia led not to a local war, as Austria and Germany hoped, but to a general European war. Because of the system of alliances and unalterable military plans, the nations of Europe became caught in a chain reaction from which they could not escape.

Patriots cheer the outbreak of war. Once war was certain, politicians, the press, and the clergy urged the people to fight for their homeland. But pleas for patriotism were unnecessary. The people were already aroused. Crowds gathered in the capitals of Europe to express their loyalty to the homeland and their readiness to fight. It seemed as if men wanted violence for its own sake. It was as if war offered them an escape from the dull routine of classroom, job, and daily life, from "a world grown old and cold and weary," as Rupert Brooke, a young British poet, expressed it.

In Paris men marched down the main avenues singing the stirring words of the "Marseillaise." Cheering women showered the young soldiers with flowers. Recalls one eyewitness: "Young and old, civilians and military men burned with the same excitement. . . . Beginning the next day, thousands of men eager to fight would jostle one another outside recruiting offices, waiting to join up. . . . The word 'duty' had a meaning for them, and the word 'country' had regained its splendor." In Berlin people sang the national anthem "Deutschland Über Alles" (doytch'land oo'bear ah'lehs, "Germany Above All"), with deep feeling. "It is a joy to be alive," wrote a German newspaper. "We wished so much for this hour. . . . The sword which has been forced into our hand will not be [put aside] until our . . . territory [is] extended."

[3] Since 1839 Britain, France, Austria, Russia, and Prussia had been pledged to respect Belgian neutrality.

Soldiers bound for battle acted as if they were going off on a great adventure. "My dear ones, be proud that you live in such a time and in such a nation and that you . . . have the privilege of sending those you love into so glorious a battle," wrote a young German law student to his family. Filled with dreams of excitement and glory, few thought of the horrors of war. They expected to return home in a few months— "before the leaves fall," the German kaiser had said. Eager to prove their bravery and patriotism, these foolhardy young warriors did not realize that they were marching to their death. For World War I was the most terrible war that man had yet waged. There were prophets who realized that Europe was stumbling into darkness, but their gloomy words were drowned out by the cheers of patriots and fools. "The lamps are going out all over Europe," said British Foreign Secretary Edward Grey. "We shall not see them lit again in our lifetime."

Was any one country to blame for the war?
Some historians blame Austria-Hungary for wishing to crush Serbia after the assassination of Francis Ferdinand and for failing to seek a negotiated settlement. Others argue that Germany's ambitions to dominate Europe were the underlying causes of the war. They say that Germany's encouragement of Austria's desires to strike at Serbia made Germany as guilty as Austria-Hungary. Austria-Hungary knew an attack on Serbia could mean war with Russia. If German support had not been certain, Austria-Hungary most likely would have held back from starting such a war. Writes German historian Fritz Fischer: "As Germany willed and [desired] the Austro-Serbian war and, in her confidence in her military superiority, deliberately faced the risk of a conflict with Russia and France, her leaders must bear a substantial share of . . . responsibility for the outbreak of general war in 1914."

Russia and France also come in for their share of the blame. It was the mobilization of Russian troops that turned a limited war between Austria-Hungary and Serbia into a world war. By mobilizing her troops Russia forced Germany to act. France is criticized for backing Russia's decision to mobilize. Nor has Britain escaped blame. Throughout the July crisis, Britain failed to make clear the conditions under which she would support her ally France. But would Britain have entered the war if Germany had not invaded Belgium? Had Germany seen clearly that Britain might become involved, then perhaps Germany would have been less confident about victory, less eager to fight, and more anxious to prevent war. "If only someone had told me beforehand that England would take up arms against us," moaned the kaiser after it was too late.

Many historians, however, believe that all nations shared the guilt. The antagonisms arising from the combination of the system of alliances, militarism, imperialism, and nationalism made war inevitable.

One final point needs to be emphasized. The generals and statesmen, some of whom welcomed war or did not try hard enough to prevent it, expected a short war which would benefit their nations. Virtually no one had in mind what the First World War turned out to be— four years of bloodletting, destruction, and barbarism.

CHECK-UP

1. What action did Austria-Hungary take after the archduke was assassinated? Why was she determined to crush Serbia? How did Germany react? What was Russia's reaction? Why?

2. What chain reaction took place in Europe after Austria declared war on Serbia? Why? Which nations became involved? Why did Britain enter the war?

3. How did the press, the public, and politicians react to the outbreak of war?

4. What blame can be assigned to each country for the outbreak of war?

Germany strikes at France and Russia. On August 4, 1914, the German army invaded Belgium. "We have entered the struggle that will decide the course of history for the next one hundred years," said General Helmuth von Moltke (*hel'*moot fon *mohlt'*keh), German Chief of Staff. German war plans called for a comparatively small army to hold off the slow-moving Russians in the east, while the bulk of the German army would swing through Belgium into France. After Paris was captured and France defeated, German railroads would rush the victorious troops to the Eastern Front. The German General Staff felt sure that the spirit and skill of the German army would ensure victory over the much larger Russian army. Everything depended upon speed. Paris must be taken before Russia could build up her army sufficiently to invade Germany. General von Moltke counted on defeating France in six weeks.

The German General Staff thought they had properly assessed the forces Germany would have to beat. But their carefully laid plans failed. The Russians moved faster than expected. Their invasion of East Prussia forced von Moltke to withdraw several divisions of troops from the Western Front in France and rush them east. Unexpectedly stiff Belgian resistance cost the Germans four days. And when they did drive to within thirty miles of Paris, a French counterattack, on September 6, drove a wedge between the advancing German armies. After four days of furious fighting, combined French and British troops forced the Germans to halt. Instead of a quick victory, Germany found herself faced with a long, drawn-out struggle on two fronts.

THE WESTERN FRONT

Opposing armies settle down to trench warfare. After the German advance ground to a halt, the Allies and Germany dug in for a long war on the Western Front. For hundreds of miles across Western Europe, from northern France to Switzerland, a vast network of trenches was dug. In these trenches, protected by barbed wire to slow down an enemy advance and backed up by machine guns and heavy artillery, the soldiers of both sides ate, slept, fought, and died. Between the opposing armies lay No Man's Land, a wasteland of mud, shattered trees, torn earth, and broken bodies. Trench warfare was a battle of nerves, waged to the constant thunder of heavy artillery.

Opposing armies sought to capture each other's trenches, using artillery barrages and machine-gun fire to cover the bayonet charges of the advancing infantry. Soon both sides also used poison gas. But despite the frightful loss of life, little land changed hands. In 1915, for example, France launched numerous attacks against the German lines but never gained more than three miles in any one place. Yet these small gains cost France alone 1,430,000 casualties. Scenes such as the following made up the agony of trench warfare:*

[On July 1, 1916] fourteen divisions of British troops, along a front of eighteen miles, went over the top, many of them for the first time. The vast majority of them had been civilians two years previously. . . .

The Germans sent down an enormous flail of concentrated machine-gun fire. It hummed and whirred through the air around the lines of steadily advancing troops. It thudded home into their sweating bodies, through equipment straps and khaki cloth. In a few minutes the first waves were annihilated [wiped out]. But wave upon wave came pouring out of the trenches to take the place of

---

* From *The Big Push* by Brian Gardner (London: Cassell & Co. Ltd., 1961; copyright 1961 by Brian Gardner). Reprinted by permission of Cassell and Company Ltd. and William Morrow and Company, Inc.

the fallen. They surged over the broken ground at a steady walking pace, loaded with sixty-six pounds of equipment. . . .

Over the roar and crash of battle, cheering could be heard from some of the battalions. Others broke before the murderous hail of machine-gun bullets and began to stumble back. A few got as far as the German wire; as they got entangled in it the Germans used rifle fire to kill them off one by one. Wounded soldiers inextricably caught up in the wire, which had barbs two inches long, vainly screamed for help. . . . Most, however, never got as far as the wire. They lay in No Man's Land as shells exploded among them, and bullets scythed through the deadly air above their heads.

Nostrils sickened by the scent of explosive fumes, ears numbed with noise, senses bewildered and insulted, brains half paralyzed with shock, thousands of men lay there in the grass, among their groaning comrades. Around them lay another twenty thousand British soldiers, all dead. Fathers, sons, brothers, loved-ones . . . had gone to the slaughterhouse because they were told to do so; because they genuinely felt a need to get to grips with the Hun [Germans]; because everyone else did; because they were scared not to; because they did not know what was waiting for them.

Neither side makes a decisive breakthrough.
The stalemated war lasted through 1915. In February, 1916, Germany began a major offensive directed at the French fortress of Verdun (vair-*doon'*). For five months the Germans kept up a continuous attack which cost them about 250,000 men. Although they gained some 100 square miles, the Germans never managed to capture the fortress. The diaries and letters of the soldiers involved reveal the drama of Verdun. In a letter to his mother a French captain described the shelling which made the ground look like the surface of the moon:

I have returned from the toughest trial that I have ever seen—four days and four nights—ninety-six hours—the last two days soaked in icy mud—under terrible bombardment, without any shelter other than the narrowness of the trench, which even seemed to be too wide; not a hole, not a dugout, nothing, nothing. The Boche [*bohsh,* German] did not attack, naturally; it would have been too stupid. It was much more convenient to carry out a fine firing exercise on our backs. . . . Result: I arrived there with 175 men, I returned with 34, several half mad.

There was always the danger of being killed by your own artillery:

Modern war provided little opportunity for the heroic action envisioned by young volunteers. A man might spend weeks in the same trench, awaiting the order to attack the enemy (top). To the danger of machine-gun and artillery fire was added gas, a deadly new weapon which could blind men and burn out their lungs (above).

I told [the company commander] I had brought up some grenades and barbed wire [and] . . . asked where I was to put them. He replied: "Wherever you wish. For two hours our own guns have been bombarding us, and if it goes on I shall take my company and bombard the gunner with these grenades!"

Today a visitor to Verdun might notice a small plaque placed on the outside wall of Fort Vaux (*voh*) by an unknown mother: "To my son: Since your eyes were closed, mine have never ceased to cry."

Throughout 1916–1917 the Allies and Germany were locked in a stalemate. Neither side could make a really significant advance. While gains and losses of land were measured in yards, the lives of Europe's youth were squandered by the hundreds of thousands. Soldiers in the trenches were becoming war-weary. Would the slaughter never end?

THE EASTERN FRONT

Russia suffers heavy losses. On the Eastern Front the Russians had mobilized more rapidly than Germany had anticipated. In early August, 1914, while the main thrust of the German attack was directed at France, the Russians managed to penetrate eastern Germany and Austrian Poland. However, by the end of the month the Germans had decisively defeated the invading Russians. With 90,000 men taken prisoner, the Russians were forced to withdraw from German soil. The Russians suffered further defeats in Austrian Poland, when an Austro-German offensive resulted in a million Russian prisoners. Russia never recovered from these frightful losses of men and supplies. She was also cut off from her allies. Before the end of 1915 Serbia was overrun; Austro-German armies dominated the Balkans; Turkey controlled the straits leading to the Black Sea; and the German fleet prevented Allied aid from reaching Russia by sea.

Revolution takes Russia out of the war. Late in 1916 the Russian war effort was near collapse. The poorly trained, inadequately equipped, and incompetently led Russian army had suffered staggering casualties. Everywhere demoralized soldiers were deserting.

In March, 1917, the accumulated discontent of the peoples of Russia, aggravated by the misfortunes of the war, led to a revolution which overthrew the tsarist regime. Its successor, the Provisional Government, tried vainly to cope with the growing anarchy. In November radical Marxists called Bolsheviks seized power in Russia. They were determined to end the war—an aim supported by the overwhelming majority of the Russian people. In March, 1918, they signed the Treaty of Brest-Litovsk (*brest'* lih-*tohfsk'*) with Germany. This peace treaty took Russia out of the war, but it also forced her to turn over to Germany a quarter of her prewar territory in Europe, 34 per cent of her population, 54 per cent of her industry, and 89 per cent of her coal mines. Russia was also required to pay Germany a huge sum of money. (In the following chapter Russia will be discussed in detail.) The German armies had thus proved victorious in Eastern Europe.

There is fighting on other fronts. Whereas the major campaigns of World War I were fought on the Western and Eastern Fronts, there were still other areas which were involved in the fighting.

1. Italy. A member of the Triple Alliance, Italy decided to remain neutral when the war broke out. In 1915, however, Italy made a secret agreement with Britain and France and entered the war on the side of the Allies. For her support she was promised Austrian territory after the Allied victory. While fighting took place along the Austro-Italian frontier during 1915 and 1916, there were no decisive victories. But combined German and Austrian forces finally broke through the Italian lines in the fall of 1917 at Caporetto. The Italian army was compelled to retreat in disorder, leaving behind huge quantities of food and weapons. Germany and Austria took some 275,000 prisoners. The catastrophe at Caporetto might have been even greater had not France and Britain rushed aid to their Italian ally. Moreover, Germany and Austria found it extremely difficult to supply their troops in Italy.

2. Asia and the Pacific. Japan took over Chinese ports held by the Germans and, with Australia and New Zealand, took possession of German-owned islands in the Pacific.

3. Turkey. Some of the hardest fighting of the war took place on the coast of Turkey. When Ottoman Turkey joined the war against the Allies in 1914, she had placed mines in the strait of the Dardanelles leading to the Sea of Marmara. The Dardanelles and the Bosporus, the strait which connects the Sea of Marmara with the Black Sea, were protected by heavy artillery posted on the shore. These fortifications served two purposes: they prevented Allied aid from reaching Russia and they also kept the Russian fleet bottled up in the Black Sea. A combined force of British, French, New Zealand, and Australian troops tried to open the straits and thus enable the Allies to send much-needed supplies to Russia. Had they been successful, perhaps the Bolshevik Revolution might not have taken place. Allied hopes were dashed

KEY

▨	Central Powers
☐	Allied Nations
▨	Neutral Nations
☒	Battles
▭	Limit of German Advance on Eastern Front (1918)
-----	Western Front

on the cliffs and beaches of the Turkish coast where the Allies suffered some 250,000 casualties and in the end had to withdraw. Wrote one survivor:*

Let the reader imagine himself to be facing three miles of any very rough broken sloping ground known to him. . . . Let him say to himself that he

* Abridged and adapted from *Gallipoli* by John Masefield. Copyright 1916 by John Masefield, renewed 1944 by John Masefield. Reprinted by permission of The Macmillan Company, Inc., and of the Society of Authors, for the Estate of John Masefield.

World War I Divides Europe

and an army of his friends are about to advance up the slope towards the top. . . . Let him imagine himself to be more weary than he has ever been in his life before, and dirtier than he has ever believed it possible to be, and parched with thirst, nervous, wild-eyed, and rather lousy. Let him think that he has not slept for more than a few minutes together for eleven days and nights, and that in all his waking hours he has been fighting for his life, often hand to hand in the dark with a fierce enemy, and that after each fight he has had to dig

World War I carried warfare to the home front. Enemy aircraft bombarded cities; sea blockades caused food and fuel shortages. Certain days were set aside as "wheatless," "meatless," or "heatless." Civilian enthusiasm was mobilized for the war effort by posters (right) and by bond rallies conducted by well-known entertainers. These appeals to patriotism met with considerable success in the early days of the war. But as the war dragged on, enthusiasm was replaced by a general questioning of the meaning of the war and its sacrifices. Many artists turned from themes glorifying war to portray its effects in haunting portraits such as The Survivors (above).

BLOOD or BREAD
Others are giving their blood
You will shorten the war—
save life if you eat only what
you need and waste nothing
UNITED STATES FOOD ADMINISTRATION

himself a hole in the ground, often with his hands, and then walk three or four roadless miles to bring up heavy boxes under fire. Let him think, too, that in all those eleven days he has never for an instant been out of the thunder of cannon, that waking or sleeping their devastating crash has been blasting the air across within a mile or two. . . . Let him think too . . . that hourly in all that time he has seen his friends blown to pieces at his side, or dismembered, or drowned, or driven mad, or stabbed, or sniped [at] by some unseen stalker, or bombed in the dark . . . with a handful of dynamite in a beef-tin, till their blood is caked upon

his clothes and thick upon his face, and that he knows, as he stares at the hill, that in a few moments . . . he himself . . . may be blasted dead, or lying bleeding in the scrub, with perhaps his face gone and a leg and an arm broken, unable to move but still alive, unable to drive away the flies or screen the ever dropping rain, in a place where none will find him or be able to help him, a place where he will die and rot and shrivel, till nothing is left of him but a few rags and a few remnants and a little identification-disc flapping on his bones in the wind. Then . . . let him pull himself together with his friends and . . . go forward against an invisible enemy, safe in some unseen trench expecting him.

4. The Middle East and Africa. In the Arab countries of the Middle East and in Africa, World War I was largely a series of raids on towns and supply lines. There was little direct confrontation between opposing armies.

The Arabs of the Middle East had been ruled by the Turkish Ottoman Empire for over four centuries. Eager to end a rule they had long hated, the Arabs began to support the British forces which were protecting Britain's interests in the Middle East. Driven out of one area after another by Britain and her Arab allies, the Turks finally withdrew from the war at the end of October, 1918.

In Africa, Britain and France seized German colonies on the west coast at the outbreak of the war. By 1915 troops from the Union of South Africa had defeated the Germans in South-West Africa. But in East Africa it was a different story. The British officially took possession of German East Africa soon after the war broke out. A small German force, however, refused to surrender. They learned to live off the country and to use Africans in their attacks on British supply lines and towns, avoiding a direct clash with the British troops who far outnumbered them. British troops spent the war chasing this German force through steaming swamps, forests, and mountains where fever, hunger, and wild animals claimed far more lives than the enemy. Although the Germans were in constant retreat, they were never decisively defeated. Not until they received news of the war's end did they surrender.

The United States enters the war. When the First World War broke out, the United States announced a policy of neutrality. President Woodrow Wilson wished to keep the United States from becoming involved in the conflict. But by 1917 the United States found it impossible to remain neutral, and entered the war on the side of the Allies in April. What was behind this move?

1. Both Britain and Germany interfered with American shipping. To keep war supplies from reaching Germany, Britain stopped American ships and seized goods. Since the German fleet was bottled up in the North Sea, the Germans turned to submarines to cut off American supplies bound for Britain. These submarines attacked without warning, sinking American ships and causing many deaths. While the British were taking American property, the Germans were killing American citizens. Mounting anger over the loss of life and determination to protect her ships led the United States closer to war.

2. During the war American businessmen had loaned one and a half billion dollars to Allied governments. Much of this money was used to buy needed supplies from the United States. The outcome of the war might well affect these loans. If the Allies lost, American bankers and manufacturers would probably lose their money.

3. Most Americans sympathized with Britain and France because they were democratic countries. A German victory would have seemed a triumph for authoritarianism. Moreover, most war news came to the United States from Britain. British propaganda pictured the Germans as militaristic, arrogant, cruel, and evil.

4. Germany tried to persuade Mexico to join her against the United States if the United States entered the war. In return, Germany promised to help Mexico recover Texas and the southwestern part of the United States which Mexico had been forced to give up in 1848. Mexico remained neutral, but news of this offer further aroused American opinion against Germany.

The United States declared war on Germany in April, 1917. It became clear to Germany that she must win the war before large numbers of American troops could be prepared for combat and landed in France. In the spring of 1918, the signing of the Treaty of Brest-Litovsk released German troops from the Eastern Front. These troops were rushed to reinforce Germany's forces on the Western Front. The Ger-

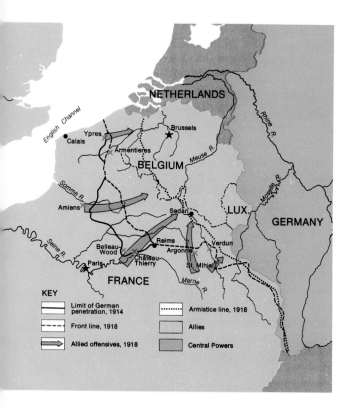

The Western Front

KEY

⟶ Limit of German penetration, 1914	⋯⋯ Armistice line, 1918
--- Front line, 1918	☐ Allies
⟹ Allied offensives, 1918	▨ Central Powers

mans then launched a great offensive. The British and French lines reeled before the German advance. For a while it looked as if the Germans could not be halted before they reached Paris. But, aided by newly arrived American troops, the British and French prevented a German breakthrough.

The Central Powers collapse. Germany had thrown everything she had into this drive. She now found herself in mortal danger. Shortages of food, medicine, oil, and munitions had become acute. Allied British, French, and American troops swept forward in a massive counterattack on every front. Austria and Turkey could give no aid to their ally. Revolts by the peoples they ruled had led to the collapse of the Austro-Hungarian and Ottoman Empires and their withdrawal from the war. Deserted by her allies and threatened by revolts in the army and navy,

Germany was unable to hold back the forces of Britain, France, and the United States. It was clear to the German generals that Germany had lost the war. Anxious to prevent the destruction of their army, the German generals urged the government to ask for an *armistice*—a halt to the fighting.

On November 11, 1918, a sound "like the noise of a light wind" ran along the Western Front as soldiers of both sides rose from the trenches to cheer themselves hoarse. The armistice ending four years of the most destructive war of all time had been signed. Enemies embraced in the midst of No Man's Land, rejoicing that they had been rescued from death. A newspaper correspondent with the British army in France wrote: "Last night for the first time since August in the first year of the war, there was no light of gunfire in the sky, no sudden stabs of flame through darkness, no spreading glow above black trees where for four years of nights human beings were smashed to death. The fires of hell had been put out."

CHECK-UP

1. How did Germany hope to achieve a quick victory? Why did this fail to happen?

2. What is trench warfare? What weapons were used? Why was war on the Western Front stalemated?

3. Why was the Russian war effort near collapse by 1916? What took Russia out of the war? What were the terms of the Treaty of Brest-Litovsk?

4. What part did Italy play in World War I? Why did the Allies attack the Dardanelles? Why did the Arabs side with the British against the Turks? How did the war in East Africa differ from the war in Europe?

5. Why did the United States find it increasingly difficult to remain neutral? Why did most Americans sympathize with the Allies?

6. How did the German military strategy change early in 1918? Why?

7. Why were the Germans finally forced to ask for an armistice?

Wilson envisions a new world. In December, 1918, President Woodrow Wilson crossed the Atlantic to represent the United States at the Paris Peace Conference. To the conference he brought a conception of a better world, in which "the very foundations of this war are swept away." Wilson's program called for:

1. Self-determination. None of Wilson's principles seemed more just than the idea of self-determination—the right of a people to choose their own government free of foreign control. This meant that Austrian lands inhabited by Italians should belong to Italy. France should regain territory taken from her in the Franco-Prussian War. The Slavs in the Austro-Hungarian Empire should be free to form their own nations. The Poles should be free to form a united and independent Poland.

2. "A peace without victory." Insisting that it should be "a peace without victory," Wilson urged fair treatment for Germany. He believed that if Germany were harshly punished, she might well seek revenge. Wilson hoped that a just settlement would encourage the defeated nations to work with the victorious Allies toward a new and better world.

3. Disarmament. Wilson believed that there could be no hope for peace until militarism had been eliminated. He wanted the nations of the world to disarm so that no country would fear or seek to invade its neighbors.

4. Fair treatment of colonial peoples. Wilson was critical of imperialism. He called for "a free, open-minded, and absolutely impartial adjustment of all colonial claims." He hoped that some day the principle of self-determination would apply to colonies and he urged colonial powers to take into consideration "the interests of the populations concerned."

5. Protection of human rights. Wilson felt that World War I had been fought to "make the world safe for democracy." He viewed it as a war by the people against absolutism. In his vision of a new world, people as well as nations should have certain basic rights. The fair treatment of all peoples and the protection of their rights would cause democracy and freedom to spread throughout the world and eliminate the need for war.

6. League of Nations. To preserve peace, Wilson urged the formation of a League of Nations—an international organization to help nations settle their quarrels and discourage aggressors from taking up arms.

At the conference table Wilson fought hard to have his views written into the Treaty of Versailles. But he was only partially successful.

Wilson's idealism clashes with Old World realism. The victorious European Allies were not interested in "a peace without victory" which would leave them little better off than the nations they had defeated. They followed an old concept of peacemaking—reward the victorious and punish the defeated. What other obstacles prevented a peace based on the principles of Wilson?

1. French demands for security and revenge. Wilson's idealism clashed head on with French demands. France was represented at the conference table by "The Tiger," Premier Georges Clemenceau (*zhohrzh′* kley-mahn-*soh′*). He was determined to obtain a peace settlement which would give France security and revenge. France had suffered greatly during the war. Nearly all the war on the Western Front had been fought on French territory. The people of France wanted security from the threat of future wars. They wanted assurance that the events of 1870–1871 and 1914–1918 would never be repeated. French statesmen insisted that Germany be severely punished and her capacity to wage war destroyed. Only then would France be safe. Furthermore, the French had no desire to give Germany a light punishment. They wanted revenge for the industries and farms that had been ruined, the hundreds of thousands of Frenchmen who had been killed. Still bitter over her

619

Major Provisions of Versailles Treaty

1. League of Nations formed.

2. Germany accepts sole responsibility for causing World War I.

3. German territorial losses: In Europe, Germany lost about 25,000 square miles with some six million inhabitants (see map, page 621). She lost all her Pacific islands and all her spheres of influence and colonies in Asia and Africa.

4. Military clauses affecting Germany:

The Rhineland (area west of the Rhine River) was demilitarized, and the Allies, under the terms of the armistice, held the towns of Mainz, Coblenz, and Cologne east of the river.
German army reduced to 100,000 men.
Navy restricted to 36 vessels of various defensive types; submarines forbidden.
Air force prohibited; all planes destroyed.
German General Staff abolished.
Conscription abolished.
Large guns prohibited and small guns limited. Restrictions placed on the production of armaments, and their export and import prohibited.

5. Germany had to pay huge reparations to the Allies, mainly in kind, for property destroyed in occupied lands: ships for ships destroyed, railway stock, automotive equipment, farm machinery, livestock, etc.

6. Germany was forced to repeal the treaties of Brest-Litovsk and Bucharest.

7. Danube River and major German rivers made international waterways.

8. Free zones set up in German ports of Hamburg and Stettin to give Czechoslovakia access to the sea. Danzig was made a free city to provide Poland with a port on the Baltic Sea, and Memel was assigned to the Lithuanian Republic.

9. The Saar Basin was placed under the administration of the League of Nations for fifteen years, with its coal going to France.

10. International Labor Organization (ILO) formed.

humiliating defeat in 1870–1871, France felt it was now her turn to get back at Germany. To many Frenchmen, the Germans were "savages, vandals, assassins." Only when we throw him down and "beat his head on the pavement" will the German realize that he lost the war.

What did Frenchmen think of Wilson's ideas? "Let us try out the new order," said a French editorial, "but so long as we are not assured of its absolute success . . . let us maintain, . . . unsatisfactory though they be, the pillars of the old order, . . . which will seek to maintain peace by the aid of military, political, and economic guarantees [agreements]."

2. The intermingling of nationalities. The populations of the nations and regions of Europe were composed of people of many origins and cultures. Because each European nation had such a mixture of national groups, it was impossible to carry out the principle of self-determination to everyone's satisfaction. No matter how the peacemakers juggled boundary lines, they could not create a Europe free of minority problems. And there were other factors to be taken into consideration. For example, the principle of self-determination called for an independent Poland. But in order to develop a sound economy, Poland would need access to the sea. Between the new Poland and the sea lay lands inhabited predominantly by Germans. Giving this land to Poland would violate German self-determination. Denying it to Poland would mean that the new country had little chance of developing a sound economy. No matter what the decision, one country would regard it as unjust.

3. Secret treaties. During the war the Allies had drawn up secret treaties in which they reached agreement on how to share the spoils of war. These secret treaties did not square with the principle of self-determination. Italy, for example, hoped to acquire Austrian lands inhabited by Italians. But in these lands Slavs and Austrians lived side-by-side with Italians. If the land were taken over by Italy, there would be no self-determination for Slavs and Austrians. In the Middle East, Arab lands freed from

NORWAY

SWEDEN

FINLAND

North
Sea

ESTONIA

LATVIA

Baltic
Sea

Memel

LITHUANIA

DENMARK

GREAT
BRITAIN

NETHERLANDS

Danzig

EAST
PRUSSIA

POLISH
CORRIDOR

POLAND

SOVIET
UNION

BELG.

GERMANY

LUX.

ALSACE-
LORRAINE

CZECHOSLOVAKIA

FRANCE

SWITZ.

AUSTRIA

HUNGARY

ROMANIA

Black
Sea

YUGOSLAVIA

ITALY

BULGARIA

ALBANIA

GREECE

TURKEY

AFRICA

SYRIA AND
LEBANON
(Fr.)

PALESTINE, IRAQ,
TRANSJORDAN (Br.)

TOGOLAND
(Fr./Br.)

CAMEROONS
(Fr./Br.)

RUANDA-
URUNDI
(Belg.)

TANGANYIKA
(Br.)

S.W.
AFRICA
(S. Af.)

KEY

Former Turkish
territory

Former German
territory

JAPAN

PACIFIC OCEAN

MARIANA IS.
(Jap.)

PALAU IS.
(Jap.)

CAROLINE IS.
(Jap.)

MARSHALL IS.
(Jap.)

NEW GUINEA
(Aust.)

SAMOA
(N.Z.)

AUSTRALIA

NEW
ZEALAND

KEY

Former German territory

KEY

- - - - - Nations created by peace settlements

Occupied Rhineland

Former German territory

Former Bulgarian territory

Former Russian territory

Former Austro-Hungarian territory

the Ottoman Empire had been promised independence. But secret treaties placed these regions under French and British control.

4. Bitter hatreds left over from the war. The war had aroused great bitterness. These hatreds did not die when the guns were silenced. In an atmosphere of postwar enmity one could not expect the spirit of compromise and moderation to overcome the desire for the spoils of war and punishment of enemies.

Although the peacemakers included some of Wilson's ideas in drafting the Treaty of Ver-

Territorial Changes After World War I

sailles, certainly no new world had been created. Twenty years later Europe was again at war. Perhaps it was too much to expect that Wilson's ideals could be put into practice. Perhaps it was too much to hope that those nations that allowed themselves to stumble into war had the wisdom to create a lasting peace. Or perhaps Wilson's program was not what the world really needed. Noble thoughts may yield fine-sounding words, but putting ideals into practice so that they solve the vital problems of nations is another matter. Some historians suggest that a close postwar alliance of Britain, the United States, and France against Germany would have given Europe a better chance at peace than all of Wilson's idealism.

Did the Treaty of Versailles offer a just peace?

Was the Treaty of Versailles (see box) unfair to Germany? Did the peacemakers draw up a treaty that reflected a spirit of revenge rather than justice? This has been hotly debated.

Critics of the Versailles Treaty point out that the officials responsible for Germany's entering the war had been replaced by a new government by the time of the peace conference. The new German leaders favored democracy, social reform, and disarmament. Critics of the Treaty of Versailles feel that the peacemakers imposed harsh terms on the young German democracy. They claim that the hand of friendship and cooperation the democratic leaders of Germany offered the victorious Allies was refused. By punishing and humiliating Germany, say the critics, the peacemakers weakened the foundations of democracy in Germany, kept alive old hatreds, and planted the seeds of future conflict.

At the time of the Versailles Treaty many liberals voiced opposition to its terms. Harold Nicolson, who served with the British delegation, expressed this disappointment: "We came to Paris confident that the new order was about to be established; we left it convinced that the new order had merely [worsened] the old. . . . We arrived determined that a peace of justice and wisdom should be negotiated; we left, . . . conscious that the treaties imposed upon our enemies were neither just nor wise."

Defenders of the Versailles Treaty, on the other hand, argue that Germany was not treated too harshly. They point out that, less than ten years after the war ended, German iron, steel, and coal production was considerably higher than before the war, proving that the German economy was not hard hit by the Versailles Treaty. Moreover, say the defenders of the Versailles Treaty, had Germany won the war, she would have imposed harsher terms on the Allies. To prove this point, they call attention to the Treaty of Brest-Litovsk as an example of German peacemaking. Furthermore, defenders of the Versailles Treaty stress that the real mistake was not the treaty itself but the failure of the Allies to enforce its provisions. Had they done so, they might have prevented Germany from dragging Europe into World War II.

CHECK-UP

1. What did Wilson mean by self-determination? "Peace without victory"? Disarmament? Making the world "safe for democracy"? A League of Nations? Which would be difficult to achieve? Why?

2. Why did Wilson's idealism clash with Old World realism? Give specific examples.

3. Why did wartime hatreds and bitterness persist after the war?

4. Why did critics think the Treaty of Versailles unfair and unwise? Why did some defend it?

Results of World War I

World War I was a crucial period in history. The effects of the war are still felt today. What were the results of the Great War?

The war takes a devastating toll of manpower.

Some ten million soldiers had died in the war and 21 million more had been wounded. Europe had become a vast graveyard. Young warriors who had marched to the front singing lay buried in the fields of France and the plains of Eastern Europe. Thousands who returned home were permanently crippled in body or mind.

World War I revolutionizes warfare. World War I brought about many changes in warfare. Sabers and rifles were replaced by rapid-firing machine guns, and long-range artillery was widely used. Tanks, submarines, aircraft, and poison gas were introduced into combat for the first time. World War I also marked the opening of the age of total warfare. American historian Gordon Craig states:*

The war of 1914 was the first total war in history, in the sense that very few people living in the [warring] countries were permitted to remain unaffected by it during its course. This had not been true in the past. Even during the great wars against Napoleon many people could go on living as if the world were at peace. . . . When dirigibles began to drop bombs over London and submarines began to sink merchant ships, war had invaded the civilian sphere and the battle line was everywhere. . . .

Even when the dirigibles did not come, the civilian was caught up in the war and all of his activities were geared to its requirements. Once it had been discovered, in the winter of 1914, . . . that it was not going to be a short war, . . . and that it was not going to be won by military means alone but by the effective mobilization of the total resources of the nation, . . . every mature citizen became an active participant in the war effort. He was subjected to disciplines and deprivations similar to those binding on the soldiers at the front. . . . The energy and morale of the civilian now became just as important a resource as the spirit and determination of the man in the trenches—which, of course, is why the enemy tried to drop bombs on him or starve him into compliance. . . .

Frontline soldiers could feel sympathy for fighting men on the other side who had to put up with the same dangers and miseries that they bore themselves. . . . The civilian, [however], . . . could not look the enemy in the face and recognize him as another man; he knew only that it was "the

* From "The Revolution in War and Diplomacy" by Gordon A. Craig, in *World War I: A Turning Point in Modern History* by Jack J. Roth, Gordon A. Craig, Carl J. Friedrich, *et al.* (New York: Alfred A. Knopf, Inc., 1967; © 1967 by Roosevelt University). Reprinted by permission.

Tanks, planes, and submarines introduced modern warfare. Submarines (right), attacking unseen, could not discriminate between troops and civilians. The early airplane (above) was a fragile machine of war.

enemy," an impersonal, generalized concept, that was depriving him of the pleasures of peace. As his own discomfort grew, his irritation hardened into a hatred that was often encouraged by government propagandists who believed that this was the best way of maintaining civilian morale. Before long, therefore, the enemy was considered to be capable of any enormity and . . . any idea of compromise with him became intolerable. The foe must be beaten to his knees, no matter what this might cost in effort and blood; he must be made to surrender unconditionally; he must be punished with peace terms that would keep him in permanent subjection.

There are great changes in the map of Europe. New nations emerged out of the wreckage caused by the disintegration of the Ottoman and Austro-Hungarian Empires, the collapse of tsarism in Russia, and the defeat of Germany. The creation of Yugoslavia, Czechoslovakia, Poland, Latvia, Lithuania, and Estonia, Finland's independence from Russia, and the separation of Hungary from Austria transformed the map of East and Central Europe. Besides creating new nations, the peace treaties shifted the boundaries of existing European nations, with some nations gaining territory at the expense of their neighbors. While the breakup of the Ottoman Empire had little effect on Europe, its impact on the Middle East was considerable. Only Turkey remained of the once mighty empire. The province of Hejaz (heh-*jaz'*) in Arabia gained its independence. Syria (including Lebanon) became a mandate under French administration; Palestine (including Jordan) and Mesopotamia (Iraq) became British mandates.

These changes in the map of Europe and the Middle East were to have far-reaching effects in years to come. The new nations were relatively small and weak and were no match for a Great Power seeking to expand. In the decade from 1938 to 1948 most of the new nations of Eastern Europe fell first to German and then to Russian aggression. In the mandates the desire for independence, frustrated by the peace treaties of World War I, created a potentially explosive situation.

The German people are embittered by the Versailles Treaty.

To a man, the Germans denounced the Treaty of Versailles as a victor's vengeance. They accused the Allies of trying to drain the lifeblood of Germany by saddling her with reparations and taking away territory containing vital coal and iron deposits needed for the German economy. They called the war-guilt clause, which blamed the war on "the aggression of Germany and her allies," an insult to German honor since all the Great Powers, not just Germany, were responsible for the war. They demanded that the victorious nations, as well as Germany, should demilitarize. They vowed to put an end to the Polish Corridor—that strip of German land given to Poland—that cut through German territory. While many Germans hoped that revision of the Versailles Treaty would be achieved peacefully, militarists and chauvinists looked forward to another war in which Germany would tear up the Versailles Treaty and establish German domination of Europe. World War I had not ended Germany's desire to increase her power and to extend her territory. It had not ended Europe's fear of German ambitions and intentions.

Dictators rise to power.

The destruction caused by the war and the uncertainty it created in the minds of people everywhere led to unrest and disorder. People lost their faith in the world as it had been before the war and turned to authoritarian systems in hopes that they would solve the problems of mankind. Leaders promising to create a new order of society rose to power in Russia, Germany, Italy, and other lands. The personalities and goals of these dictators became the dominant force in international affairs.

The United States returns to a policy of isolation.

When the United States entered the war, the American people were told that they were fighting to save democracy and freedom and to prevent future wars. Soon after the war Americans began to feel that American soldiers had died in vain. It would have been better if we had never gotten involved in the war, thought many Americans. Let those foreigners fight their own wars. They don't deserve our help. In the period after World War I the United States returned to her historic policy of *isolationism*—avoiding involvement in foreign affairs. In this way she hoped to stay out of future wars. An example of this isolationist attitude was the refusal of the United States Senate to approve the Treaty of Versailles. While there were many reasons why the Senate voted against the Versailles Treaty, one of them was the belief that membership in the League of Nations would drag the United States into more wars.

Suspicion, envy, and hatred characterize postwar Europe. It was hoped that from the ruins of World War I would emerge a new world of cooperation, freedom, and peace. This never happened. After World War I hatreds ran deeper as nationalism became more intense and desires for revenge grew more powerful. The older nations of Europe continued to eye each other with suspicion and envy. German nationalists swore to scrap the hated Treaty of Versailles and to regain the territory Germany had lost. Frenchmen continued to fear German ambitions and power. Italy felt she had been cheated at the peace conference. The new nations carved out of the shambles of the Austro-Hungarian and Ottoman Empires were not all satisfied with their borders. Moreover, the problems with minority groups within each nation were often as great as any that had beset Austria-Hungary and Turkey. Difficulties involving treatment of minorities and quarrels among the newly created nations of Central and Eastern Europe prevented these nations from building strong, stable governments and sound economies.

Violence lives on in the postwar world. World War I produced a generation of young people who had reached their maturity in combat. Violence had become a way of life for millions of soldiers who had experienced it and for millions of civilians who had been aroused by four years of battle stories, patriotic speeches, and striving together against a common enemy. This fascination for violence lived on in the period after the war.

Many returned veterans hated to put away their uniforms and weapons. Still yearning for the excitement of battle and the stimulation of avoiding death, and resenting the poverty and unemployment that they faced at home, these ex-soldiers joined extremist parties that preached militarism and political violence. Before World War I most people condemned cruelty and bloodshed. Acts of violence were considered steps backward that would be eliminated with the advance of civilization. World War I changed all that. In the period after the war violence became a common and even acceptable way of dealing with political opponents. How the war had brutalized man is seen in the following statement by a German soldier for whom the war had never ended:

People told us that the War was over. That made us laugh. We ourselves are the War. Its flame burns strongly within us. It envelops our whole being and fascinates us with the enticing urge to destroy. We . . . marched onto the battlefields of the postwar world just as we had gone into battle on the Western Front: singing, reckless, and filled with the joy of adventure as we marched to the attack; silent, deadly, remorseless in battle.

No doubt many people throughout the world, horrified by the rivers of blood that had flowed during World War I, now hoped for an end to war. They sought peaceful reforms to solve social problems; they encouraged negotiations and understanding in dealing with international disputes. But the lovers of violence and the preachers of war and hate were not silent. They became leaders and supporters of extremist political parties.

Optimism gives way to a mood of despair. Before World War I there was considerable optimism in Europe about the future. It was felt that man was making great progress in all fields. In science one advance after another seemed to be leading mankind toward a wondrous golden age. Schooling for the common people would eliminate prejudice, superstition, and ignorance. Before the era of the Great War it was believed that man had become too civilized to engage in a long destructive war. Echoing the philosophes of the Age of Reason were those who believed that man was basically good, rational, and willing to cooperate with his fellowmen for a better world. French scientist Louis Pasteur (pahs-*toor'*) spoke for most men when he stated: "I am utterly convinced that science and peace will triumph over ignorance and war, that nations will eventually unite not to destroy but to [build and improve], and that the future will belong to those who have done the most for the sake of suffering humanity."

All this optimism seemed to collapse with the agony ushered in by World War I. A new age—the Age of Conflict—was born. Was man driven by violent and aggressive instincts too powerful to control? If so, then mankind's prayers, dreams, and plans for peace had little meaning. The Viennese psychoanalyst Sigmund Freud said of the Great War:

It tramples in blind fury on all that comes in its way, as though there were to be no future and no goodwill among men after it has passed. It [tears apart] all bonds of fellowship between the [warring] peoples, and threatens to leave such a legacy of embitterment as will make any renewal of such bonds impossible for a long time to come.

The war left many men with the uncomfortable feeling that there was no escape from violence, that destruction and death would haunt man's future as they had marred his past. The war caused philosophers and poets to have grave doubts about the future of civilization. Man's progress seemed less durable, his future less promising, than had been believed. It seemed that civilization was fragile and perishable, that man was never more than a step or two away from barbarism. To this day man is troubled with anxiety about the future. He knows that all the achievements that have distinguished civilization, all the literature and science created by man's mind, all the beauty that flows from his art and music may be destroyed in a few days of madness.

World War I left an ugly scar upon civilization. Why had the young died? For what great cause had they been fed to the guns? Why were tens of thousands wasting away in veterans' hospitals, hating to look at their crippled and mutilated bodies? The cruel truth sank into men's minds soon after the war ended. To many it seemed that World War I had not been a war of good versus evil. These men felt that there had been no righteous cause for which millions had squandered their lives. To them, World War I "had meant nothing, solved nothing, and proved nothing." It was a disaster for civilization. Surely, it was thought, any civilization that could allow such a senseless slaughter to last

for four years could look forward to only the darkest of futures. Shortly before he was killed in action, a young French soldier expressed the mood of disillusionment and despair that would grip the post-World War I generation:

Humanity is mad! It must be mad to do what it is doing. What a massacre! What scenes of horror and carnage! I cannot find words to translate my impressions. Hell cannot be so terrible. Men are mad!

CHECK-UP

1. How did World War I revolutionize warfare?
2. What were the major changes in the map of Europe? Of the Middle East?
3. How did the German people react to the Treaty of Versailles? Why?
4. How did the unrest and disorder of the postwar period contribute to the rise to power of dictators?
5. Why were the American people inclined to favor a policy of isolation after the war?
6. What was the mood of Europe during the postwar period? Why did some philosophers despair about the future of civilization?

Summing Up

Rival alliance systems, militarism, imperialism, and nationalism were the underlying causes of World War I. Blundering by rulers and statesmen precipitated the world conflict which none of the Great Powers wanted. After the initial rapid advance of Germany on the Western Front, the war settled down into trench warfare. At first the Central Powers seemed to have the advantage, especially on the Eastern Front after the tsarist regime was overthrown in 1917. But when the United States entered the war, a tightened blockade made possible by superior seapower and greatly increased industrial production contributed heavily to an Allied victory.

President Wilson's plan for peace was based on such principles as self-determination for subject peoples, "peace without victory," disarmament, an "impartial adjustment of all colonial claims" to safeguard the interests of colonial peoples, and the establishment of a League of Nations. Because Wilson's idealism clashed with European realism, the peace settlement fell far short of his goals.

World War I involved frightful losses of manpower and destruction of property. It introduced new weapons—aircraft, submarines, tanks, and poison gas. The peace settlement brought about great changes in the maps of Europe, Asia, and Africa. The embittered Germans termed the peace a victor's vengeance on the vanquished. Economic distress resulting from the war led to the rise of dictators. Discouraged by the outcome of the "great crusade," the United States returned to a policy of isolation. Suspicion, envy, and hatred bred by both the war and the Versailles Treaty were the fertile soil from which grew later conflicts.

Chapter Highlights

Can you explain?

alliance	militarism	isolationism	national minorities
offensive	front	reparations	trench warfare
armaments	mobilization	fortifications	secret treaties
escalate	armistice	self-determination	

Can you identify?

Sarajevo	Dardanelles	Central Powers	Alsace-Lorraine
Allies	Balkans	No Man's Land	Treaty of Brest-Litovsk
Wilson	Clemenceau	Triple Entente	League of Nations
Serbia	Black Hand	Kaiser Wilhelm II	Polish Corridor
Verdun	Great Powers	Francis Ferdinand	war-guilt clause
Slavs	Caporetto	Triple Alliance	Treaty of Versailles

What do you think?

1. Which country was most responsible for the outbreak of World War I? Why do you think so?

2. Had there been an international organization such as the United Nations in 1914, could it have prevented the outbreak of war? Why?

3. Why was trench warfare more characteristic of the Western Front than of the Eastern Front?

4. Wilson urged a "peace without victory." What did this mean? Why was it difficult to achieve?

5. Why was the postwar minority problem difficult to solve?

6. Was the Versailles peace settlement just or unjust? Why do you think so?

7. Should the United States have entered the war before April, 1917?

8. Did the provisions of secret treaties make a wise peace settlement impossible? Explain your answer.

9. Why did the United States become isolationist after victory in World War I?

10. Why can we say that World War I left a lasting scar?

Upheaval in Russia: Tsarist Autocracy to Communist Dictatorship

In 1904 and in 1914 Russian troops marched to war for the tsar, expecting victory but instead suffering humiliating defeats. Above left, Nicholas II blesses his departing troops with an ikon (page 418). By spring of 1917, the tsar had abdicated and the country was in chaos. Lenin's arrival in Russia in April is commemorated by this painting (left). An example of socialist realism—portraying reality in socialist terms—it depicts Lenin as a heroic and dedicated man upon whom the people gaze in awe. During the Stalin era all the arts—literature, painting, sculpture, and even ballet—were used to convey an idealized picture of life in the Soviet Union. By arousing national pride and by dignifying the life of the worker, socialist realism hopefully would inspire workers to strive harder to achieve the goals of the socialist state.

In the late autumn of 1917, as the First World War entered its fourth year, the inhabitants of the Russian Empire had reached the limits of their endurance. The tsarist autocracy, their government for over 300 years, had collapsed the previous March under the double strain of defeat and internal disorganization. The tsarist regime was replaced by a temporary regime called the Provisional Government, which tried to introduce a parliamentary constitution. Because it also pledged to continue the war, the new government failed to win the confidence of the war-weary, land-hungry Russian masses. In the months following March the discontent of centuries, made worse by the suffering of the

629

war years, led to the disintegration of civic order. In this climate of unrest, unhappiness, and disorder a small group of Marxist revolutionaries who called themselves *Bolsheviks* prepared to seize power in Petrograd (pyih-troo-graht'), the capital.

On November 7 (October 25 by the calendar then in use in Russia), Bolshevik detachments seized key points in the city and arrested the discouraged government leaders who remained at their posts. The same day a congress of *soviets* (councils) of soldiers, workers, and peasants from all over Russia met in the capital. By the evening of November 8 the take-over of power had been completed. The new Bolshevik government, already endorsed by the congress, made its first appearance before the delegates. A thundering wave of cheers arose from the closely packed, rough-looking men dressed in unwashed uniforms and workclothes and choking from the dense cloud of tobacco smoke that hung over their heads. They craned their necks to catch a glimpse of a short, stocky man with a massive bald head and determined, slightly slanted eyes—the great Lenin (*lyey'*neen), leader of the Bolsheviks. There was an ovation when he rose to speak.

Lenin went straight to the first item of business: peace. Not only did he make clear his determination to proceed at once with negotiations to end the war. Peace, the first act of the Bolshevik regime, was linked with world revolution and with "the cause of liberation of the exploited working masses from all slavery and all exploitation." The great goal, said Lenin, was the achievement of happiness for *all* humanity. When the vote for peace had been taken, all jumped to their feet and, with tears in their eyes, sang the "Internationale": "Arise, ye workers of starvation." For these men and the few women present the war was over and a more glorious era in the social evolution of man had dawned.

Fifty years later, when thoughtful men in the western world took stock of their times, many agreed that the Bolshevik Revolution was indeed the most important event of the century. It had led, by the end of the Second World War, to the rise of Soviet Russia as a super power, second only to the United States. By promoting world revolution the Soviet Union had helped to create a world order greatly different from that prevailing in 1917. A startling transformation of this magnitude calls for careful explanations, not only of developments in Russia but of the impact of the Russian Revolution on the world at large. Let us first survey the history of Russia during the century preceding the Bolshevik Revolution. What conditions helped the Bolsheviks make themselves masters of the Russian Empire? Why did they proclaim world revolution?

Barriers to an Understanding of Russia

To understand what has happened in Russia since 1917, Americans must observe the Russian people in their century of crisis. Most American visitors to Russia, whether in the 1800's or now, cannot understand a word of Russian. When they find that they cannot read signs, newspapers, or books, they begin to realize that language is a profound barrier to extending human understanding across political boundaries. This barrier is strengthened by the fact that the same word may have quite different meanings in Russia and the United States.

GOVERNMENT IN TSARIST RUSSIA

Tsarist government is autocratic. A key word such as "government" has different meanings in Russia and the United States. An American using that term thinks of state and federal officials, democratically elected and responsive to public opinion. To a Russian before 1917, on the other hand, "government" meant first of all the *tsar,* who claimed to be the sole ruler of all the peoples in the Russian Empire, of whom there were over 130 million by 1900. Less than half of them were Russians proper; together with the White Russians, Ukrainians, and Poles they made up the dominant Slavic element. In addition there was a great variety of non-Slavic peoples—Latvians, Estonians, Lithuanians, Finns, Germans, Jews, Bashkirs, Tatars, Turkmen, Mordvinians, and scores more.

As master of the vast territories lying between Germany and the Pacific Ocean, between the Arctic ice and the high mountain ranges of Central Asia, the tsar was an *autocrat.* He recognized no limits to his powers. There was no public agency or political organization that he had not created himself.

The pillars of tsarism are orthodoxy, autocracy, and nationality. Tsar Nicholas I (1825–1855), in addition to maintaining a large army and bureaucracy (government officials), adopted the three slogans that characterized tsarism up to 1917: *orthodoxy, autocracy,* and *nationality. Orthodoxy* signified a common spiritual base —belief in the Russian Orthodox Church— which was firmly controlled by the state, yet dedicated, like the tsar himself, to the Christian tradition. *Autocracy* signified the single will of the tsar that held the country together. Finally, *nationality* stood for the ethnic and cultural leadership of the Russian population in a country that included many other nationalities. Nationality led to a policy of compulsory Russification—making non-Russians into Russians by forcing them to speak the Russian language and adopt Russian customs.

The tsars rely on the police to enforce their policies. Unlimited power and awesome splendor brought the tsars no happiness. They were isolated and overworked men who had not only to make basic decisions on domestic and foreign policy but also to oversee the horde of bureaucrats who carried out their orders. These

Tsarist Russia

1801	Alexander I becomes tsar
1812	Napoleon invades Russia
1825	Decembrist uprising; Nicholas I becomes tsar and promotes orthodoxy, autocracy, and nationalism
1855	Alexander II (the "tsar liberator") succeeds to throne
1861	Emancipation of serfs
1876	Founding of the secret society "Land and Liberty"
1890's	Witte's policies encourage industrialization
1894	Nicholas II becomes tsar
1904–1905	Russo-Japanese War
1905	Revolution leads to creation of Imperial Duma
1907	Stolypin drafts agrarian reforms; Triple Entente
1912–1913	The Balkan Wars create tensions between Russia and other powers
1914	Germany declares war on Russia
1917	In March, strikes, riots, and mutiny of troops lead to establishment of Provisional Government; Nicholas II abdicates; Bolsheviks take over power in November
1918	Murder of Nicholas II and family

bureaucrats, often minor autocrats themselves, were ill paid, lacking in initiative, and generally unsympathetic to the lot of the people. Among these officials the police stood out. The tsars had always relied on the police to ensure obedience to throne and church. When large-scale resistance was encountered, as frequently happened, the Cossacks (a mounted police force) or even the imperial troops were used to restore order. It was therefore no wonder that subjects and even government officials never thought of the tsar without trembling with terror. Strange as it may seem, the tsars, in turn, were afraid of their officials and subjects who, in a moment of rebellion, might murder them.

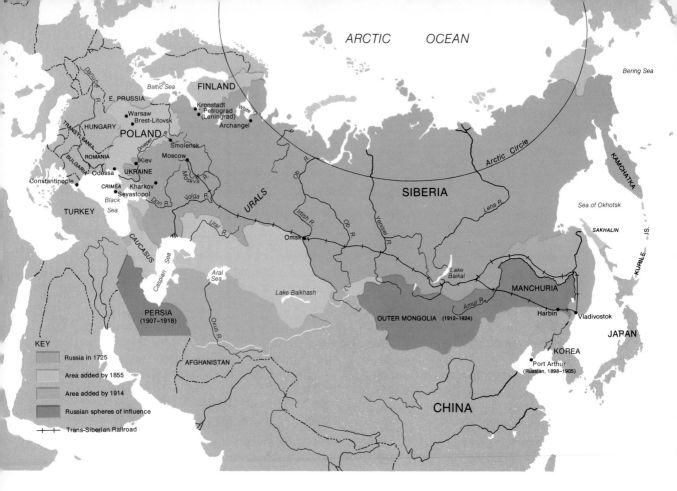

Russia: 1725–1914

The great mission of the tsars is to build a united Russia. Despite the fear, tension, and distress that beset the rulers of Russia, the tsars would never surrender their autocratic power. They felt that Russia needed their absolute rule to hold together the different nationalities and religions that made up the empire. Said Tsar Nicholas I:

Russia is still forced to fight for her existence and the realization of her destiny. She does not yet stand as a monolith [uniform whole], and the elements composing her are not yet harmonized. Only autocracy unites them into a whole. Take away the limitless, all-powerful will of the monarch, and at the least shock [Russia] will crumble.

Despite her outward splendor, Russia was far weaker than the great nations of Western Europe. Unlike France, Britain, or even Germany, Russia's far-flung territories and many nationalities had not been fused into a single nation. Because of this disunity, a parliament was a luxury Russia could not afford. A free Russia might go the way of Poland, breaking up from within and then being divided among its powerful neighbors. In Russia, therefore, the tsar himself had to create the necessary cement of unity. In forging bonds of unity and in seeking to impose their will upon their subjects, the tsars frequently resorted to force and terror.

SOCIETY IN TSARIST RUSSIA

Varied peoples, religions, and cultures stand in the way of Russian unity. Still another concept may prove misleading in a study of Russia —the word "society." When Americans speak of "society," they think of the many groups and

632

associations which work together in relative freedom in the United States. Despite regional and social differences, the United States has considerable uniformity of outlook, language, and social habits. The Russian Empire, by contrast, possessed no such unifying concept of society. Ethnic differences persisted despite the tsar's policy of Russification. Minorities thought of themselves as Latvians, Tatars, Poles, rather than as Russians. They clung to their own traditions in spite of pressures to adopt Russian culture. The great variety of religious beliefs and organizations within the Empire also contributed to disunity. Christians, Jews, and Muslims were represented by various sects and rituals. Equally troublesome were the great differences in cultural standards, which ranged from the Europeanized urban culture of the capital to the primitive backwardness of nomadic Siberian tribes.

Attempts at westernization increase disunity.

This disunity was increased in the late seventeenth century when Tsar Peter the Great turned to Western Europe for inspiration in "modernizing" his backward country. As a result, the Russian population was split into two conflicting parts: on the one side, a large mass of common people, mainly peasants, who remained essentially untouched by European influences, and on the other, a small Europeanized elite, the landed nobility. On this elite, privileged by its education, property, and access to the throne, the tsars relied for Russia's power. The masses, mainly serfs tied to the soil and often mistreated by the nobles, were voiceless and unnoticed. Serfdom, as a system, degraded millions of powerless and abused serfs; it also degraded the nobles, who looked upon their serfs as less than human.

There is also legal, educational, and racial inequality.

There were still other sources of disunity, such as separate legal categories for different subjects. The Jews and the nomads of Central Asia, for instance, were treated as foreigners. Official regulations assigned a distinct status to each group: peasants, townspeople, merchants, intellectuals, priests, landowners, and bureaucrats each formed a distinct class under the law and were treated differently by the law and by the tsar. Education entitled a man to special consideration, although the landed nobility remained the most privileged group as long as autocracy lasted. To be sure, Russia never experienced racial conflict between black and white—no stark contrasts of skin color exist to this day within its boundaries. Yet antagonism between different ethnic, religious, and racial groups was always brutal. Feeling against the Jews, for instance, was fiercer in Russia than anywhere else, leading in the late nineteenth and early twentieth centuries to murderous *pogroms,* mob attacks on Jews and their property.

The exploited peasant lives in a communal world.

Nowhere in American society can one find the like of the Russian peasant. Emancipated from serfdom in 1861, long after serfdom had disappeared in Western and even Central Europe, the Russian peasant remained a stranger to the concept of private property until well into the twentieth century. Households, not individuals, owned what they needed for survival. Groups of households, combined in *communes,* controlled the land used by peasants. This land was usually redistributed periodically as households grew or decreased in size. The bulk of the Russian population thus never learned the sense of individual worth that follows from individual responsibility for the care of property. Most peasants were accustomed to functioning as members of a collective unit—the household and the village commune or *mir (meer).* They continued to settle their affairs by custom rather than formal law. Western observers commented on their poverty, their helplessness in the face of famine, their illiteracy and brutishness, their superstitions, and the tenacity with which they clung to their ancient ways. The tsars, too, were painfully aware of peasant mistrust of all change. What could the tsars do, for instance, when the peasants killed the doctors sent to save them from cholera?

Peasant discontent is often expressed in revolt. Peasants were taken for granted, regarded as submissive and defenseless beasts of burden —except when their pent-up resentment broke out in rebellion. Peasant revolts always had the same goal: full control over all the useful land of Russia (much of which they worked for the benefit of others) and no meddling in their affairs by outsiders. From the tsar's point of view, the peasants were anarchists wishing to destroy all forms of government. Peasant revolts failed because of two basic weaknesses: the peasants could never match the superior organization, intelligence, and force of the government, and they believed that happiness and security lay in clinging to age-old traditions rather than in seeking change.

Russians have no experience in working together as a nation. The greatest difference between Russian and American society, and the chief source of weakness in the former, was that in building Russian power the autocratic tsars never allowed their subjects the freedom of working together for a common cause. Only the government could bring together individuals and groups for the public good. As a result people distrusted each other, quarreled, and took a narrow, selfish view of human relations. Even worse, they distrusted themselves, since in all matters of importance the state rather than their own conscience dictated their actions and even their thoughts.

Movements which transformed Western Europe fail to reach Russia. Russia had never enjoyed the benefits of the great movements that had helped to shape the outlook of Western Europeans. The Russian people had not experienced the individualism and humanism of the Renaissance, the revolt against authority of the Reformation, the questioning attitude of the Scientific Revolution, or the liberal ideas of the Enlightenment. Western man had developed confidence in man's ability to reason; he believed that man was born with natural rights and had a duty to resist tyrant kings. Russians, on the other hand, believed that the teachings of the Orthodox Church and the rule of the tsar should be accepted without question, that their only rights were those privileges granted by the tsar. Russia and the West were thus centuries apart in their political and intellectual development.

THE RUSSIAN CONCEPT OF FREEDOM

Americans are free to work together in the public interest. One further term is of crucial importance in understanding differences between Russia and the United States: freedom. For Americans, liberty has meant that the government does not attempt to control every phase of their lives. American citizens work for the common good through a variety of voluntary associations—political parties, business firms, civic and charitable organizations, churches, schools, and a host of other institutions over which the United States government exercises little control. These organizations have enabled Americans to develop a sense of responsibility, initiative, and independence. Similarly, by serving on juries and on boards of education and by holding offices in thousands of town governments throughout the nation, Americans have —however imperfectly—learned the skills and attitudes of good citizenship.

Freedom may prove dangerous in a land that has never experienced it. By contrast, in Russia the tsar ruled autocratically. The Russian people developed no civic sense. They had no experience in participating in their government or in working together through organizations dedicated to the good of all members of society. In Russia, therefore, freedom could only be gained by smashing the tsar's regime and breaking the chains of all the laws and regulations that he imposed upon the people. But tearing down all social and political restraints leads to chaos, and even the peasants could not survive without some form of order and justice. To prevent revolt and anarchy, the tsars were forced to tighten controls. This reinforced the people's yearning for an explosive freedom, for the chaos of anarchy. Could there have been a more tragic quandary? The tighter the controls, the more the people yearned to destroy them; the more the people sought to end tsarist autocracy, the more rigid became the tsar's rule.

CHECK-UP

1. How is language a barrier to American understanding of Russia? How is the American concept of society a barrier? The American concept of freedom?

2. What was the nature of the tsar's rule? What is meant by orthodoxy, autocracy, and nationality?

3. In what ways were Russian peasants exploited? Why did their revolts always fail?

4. Which movements that transformed Western Europe failed to reach Russia? How did this affect Russia?

5. Why did the Russian desire for freedom lead to a cycle of repression and revolt?

Reasons for the Backwardness of Tsarist Russia

Americans have long lived in spectacularly isolated security. The fear of hostile invasion or internal collapse has not entered deeply into their thought or temperament. They have stood out, moreover, by their influence in the world (already considerable by 1900), by their achievements in technology and in the arts of government, and by their high standard of living. How limited, by contrast, was Russia's achievement under the tsars!

Tsarist Russia is underdeveloped—socially, politically, and economically. The splendor of the Russian court, the power of the tsars, and even the great insight of Russian literature did little for Russia as a whole. Russian subjects were exceedingly poor and ill-equipped for the tasks of building a great country. Compared to Western Europe, the Russian Empire was backward. Whatever advances that were made were initiated by the tsars. They realized that Russia could not become a great world power unless she caught up with the accomplishments of the western states. The tsars therefore tried to bring about improvements in education, transportation, and the treatment of the serfs.

The tsars force reforms upon the Russian people. In trying to make Russia more like Western European states, the autocratic tsars also heightened the contrast between Russia and the West. Reforms were not accompanied by the liberal spirit characteristic of Western Europe; nor did the Russian people gain the experience of participating in their government. Nowhere else in Europe was change for the better so harshly rammed down the throats of the common people.

The intelligentsia wishes to improve conditions in Russia. Russia's weakness and backwardness disturbed not only the tsars but also their educated subjects, who were in a position to compare Russia with Western Europe. From that privileged minority of the educated emerged a Russian phenomenon, the *intelligentsia*. (A similar educated minority is found today in many developing countries.) Recruited originally from the landed gentry, the intelligentsia came to include men and women from other groups as well—minor government officials, university students, and even educated peasants. The intelligentsia was the product of the European influence spreading through Russian high schools and universities and, for a lucky few, through foreign study and travel. Members of the intelligentsia had little use for autocracy, which they blamed for the poverty and brutality

635

Russia's intellectuals were severe critics of tsarist repression. Leo Tolstoy (at left, above) wrote the world-renowned War and Peace *and* Anna Karenina. *Although a large landowner, Tolstoy opposed serfdom and was critical of modern civilization, urging the simple communal life. His philosophy of non-resistance to evil influenced Gandhi. Regarded as the father of socialist realism was Maxim Gorky (at right, above). Gorky's realistic works about the plight of the urban poor, such as* The Lower Depths *(above, left), won widespread acclaim in Soviet Russia. Along with themes with a socialist meaning, the Russians have kept alive their national traditions. In the theater many productions are based on folk tales (left).*

of Russian life. Inspired by the democratic ideals of freedom and the welfare of the people, the intelligentsia took the part of *all* the victims of autocracy. Their own suffering prompted them to cultivate a deep compassion for all suffering mankind, for the victims of injustice, the exploited, the weak everywhere.

Members of the intelligentsia advance conflicting views. Members of the intelligentsia disagreed on how to overcome their country's internal divisions and to make Russia as respected and powerful as the great nations of Western Europe. Their attempts resulted in an outlook which was neither Russian nor European. The "westernizers" looked to the West to provide inspiration for advances in Russia. Russia must have more contact with Europe, they said. Wrote one admirer of western ways, "Isolated from the world, we [Russians] have given or taught nothing to the world. We have added no thoughts to the sum of human ideas, we have in no way collaborated in the progress of reason." The "Slavophiles," on the other hand, glorified the traditions of Russia, particularly as embodied in the Orthodox Church and the peasant village. Yet the distinction between westernizer and Slavophile was never clear-cut. One man might harbor a profound admiration for the West in some matters and fiercely support Slavic culture in others.

The tsars promote technical advances but repress liberal ideas. Among students, hostility toward tsarist autocracy steadily increased. The tsars, understandably distressed by this hostility, wanted students to acquire the technical knowledge of Western Europe but not the social and political ideas that were associated with it; they wanted steam engines but not parliaments, constitutions, or bills of rights. In other words, they wanted "light without fire, or fire that would not burn." Was it any wonder that the growing unrest and disloyalty led the tsars to distrust all higher learning and to try, by censorship and in other ways, to create an "iron curtain" that would isolate Russia from western ideas?

Both tsars and the intelligentsia believe that Russia has a great mission. Though the tsars and the intelligentsia might disagree on the methods by which Russia would become a modern nation, they agreed that Russia was a superior state. In their eyes Russia was the heir of the ancient Roman Empire; like Rome, Russia was an empire headed by an absolute ruler with the title of caesar (tsar). Tsars and intelligentsia alike believed that Russia had a mission, under the banners of the Orthodox Church, to lead the world toward a greater achievement than it had yet known. Both the tsars and the intelligentsia hoped that such a mission would bind the Russian people together.

There was one fly in the soothing ointment of this vision. In the nineteenth century Russia was backward in many ways. The bulk of its population was illiterate, its rulers incompetent, its economy inefficient, if not primitive compared to that of western nations. Unlike America, which made great progress during the century before 1917, Russia experienced a series of failures. Despite the brilliance of her intellectuals, Russia was in no position to fulfill the mission of world leadership.

CHECK-UP

1. In what ways was tsarist Russia underdeveloped? How did the tsars try to improve conditions? Why did their methods lead to failure?
2. Who were the intelligentsia? What were their views of life under the tsars? What opposing points of view developed on how to improve conditions? What did tsars and intelligentsia see as Russia's great mission?
3. What changes did the tsars wish to make in Russia? What did they wish to repress? Why did they fail?

Tsarist Policies of Repression and Reform

Russian history in the nineteenth century began with a disastrous defeat and a redeeming victory. In 1812 Napoleon occupied Moscow. But just two years later Russian troops triumphantly entered Paris at the head of the alliance that defeated Napoleon. In the decades that followed, the sequence of defeat followed by victory was gradually reversed.

Exposure to liberal ideas leads to revolt in Russia. An ominous explosion occurred soon after the close of the Napoleonic Wars. On returning to Russia, some of the young Russian officers who had seen Western Europe began to ask why their motherland should not enjoy some of the blessings of the French Revolution —a written constitution, voting rights, and parliamentary government. Secret societies arose in the army, and from among them was born a conspiracy to overthrow the government. It came to a head in December, 1825, just as Nicholas I ascended the throne. Though the "Decembrist" revolt was easily suppressed, the attempt at revolution cast a shadow over the reign of the new tsar.

Nicholas I plans to build a great state without weakening autocracy.

Nicholas I was determined to make the Russian Empire the stronghold of absolute monarchy in Europe. In Asia, Russia's boundaries were extended; at home the tsar sought to build the monolithic unity for which he envied the western powers. A drillmaster at heart, Nicholas I desired all Russia to move at his command. In the pursuit of unity and power Nicholas I created and personally supervised a secret police to watch over public order, promote loyalty, and stamp out dangerous ideas.

Nicholas I was aware of many flaws in his empire. He deplored the persistence of serfdom, recognizing that serfs made poor soldiers because they could not think in terms of defending *their* country. Their resistance to change made the serfs inefficient farmers; their desire for their own land made them always ready to take up arms against landlords and government officials. (During the reign of Nicholas I there were 712 peasant uprisings.) Despite his conviction of the need to improve the lot of the serfs, Nicholas I dared not end the unconditional servitude of the peasant to his master. Faced with the opposition of the landowning nobility, the autocrat was powerless to ease the burden of the serfs.

Russia fails in her bid for power.

The major aim of Nicholas I was to make Russia as great as the western powers. But in following a policy of increasing Russian influence in the Middle East, Nicholas came into conflict with Britain and France in the Crimean (kry-*me'*un) War (1853–1856). The fighting was on Russian soil under conditions favorable to the tsar's armies. Yet the outcome was a humiliating defeat for Russia. Nicholas I died a broken-hearted man before peace was concluded. Russia had not stood the test. She had failed to hold her own with two of the Great Powers of Europe.

Alexander II seeks to catch up with Western Europe.

Nicholas was succeeded on the throne by Alexander II (1855–1881), whose autocratic rule, plagued with indecision, set the pattern Russia followed until 1917. Defeat in the Crimean War had taught Alexander an important lesson. For the sake of preventing future defeats Russia had to copy as best she could what had made the western countries successful—the creative freedom of the citizen, public participation in the government, private enterprise, and the use of modern techniques in business, industry, and administration. For a time the gates to the West were opened wide, permitting Russians to catch up with the progress made in Western Europe during the years Nicholas I had kept his country isolated. Under Alexander II Russia entered the era of the "Great Reforms."

Serfdom is abolished.

The chief reform was the abolition of serfdom (1861). It liberated the peasants from the landowners, but at the same time denied them full individual freedom. No peasant could move about without the permission of his household or the village commune, which now also acted as an agent of the government. The emancipated Russian serf did receive some land on which to live, but he had to pay dearly for it. Many peasant households were burdened with debt and few had enough land to support themselves. This was due partly to official design. The land left to the landowners—the better plots in many cases—had to be worked by peasants in return for wages. Thus the peasant continued to work the best lands for the benefit of the landlords. But he never gave up his moral claim that he should control that land himself. Occasionally he even tried to take it by force.

Economic, political, and social reforms improve conditions somewhat. Other reforms of the 1860's gave new opportunity to Russian businessmen as well as to foreigners doing business in Russia. A major accomplishment was the construction of railroads to link together the vast spaces of European Russia, thus facilitating the export of Russian grain and the development of the country's natural resources. The promotion of private enterprise called in turn for new laws and law courts, which led to judicial reform. As a side product, law became a profession in Russia centuries after this had happened in Western Europe.

A further set of reforms created a new institution called *zemstvo* (*zyem'*stfuh) to take charge—under government supervision—of schools, roads, health, and agricultural development. While all elements of the population of each district were represented in the district zemstvo, the landowners were put in control. An institution parallel to the zemstvo, the town *duma* (*doo'*mah), was set up in each major city. Controlled by the wealthiest and most conservative citizens and under the dubious supervision of the tsar, the town duma took charge of municipal development. Zemstvos and town dumas were created only in areas where the government expected little opposition. In other areas it was afraid that they might turn into parliamentary institutions seeking to limit the autocratic rule of the tsar.

Still other reforms were made during the reign of Alexander II. The number of elementary schools was increased, and secondary schools were opened to lower-class children. Finally, sweeping changes were made in the army. Every male citizen, regardless of his station, was drafted into military service. The punishment of soldiers by whipping was eliminated. Instead of being treated as serfs, soldiers henceforth were to be treated as citizens. Most of them, however, continued to come from the peasantry and were abused as such.

The desire for modernization conflicts with the desire to maintain autocracy. In all these reforms there was one basic flaw: modernization challenged autocracy. Modernization demanded private initiative, personal freedom, and political participation. Such developments would threaten the tsar's hold over the country. Determined to remain autocrats, the tsars would not allow their subjects greater freedom. The Russian people remained subjects of the tsar, not citizens of a relatively free country. The tsar could not have it both ways. He could not modernize his country without causing his subjects to demand greater freedom. To give in to demands for freedom would mean the end of autocracy, something that the tsars would never willingly allow.

What, for instance, was Alexander II to do about the rising tide of disloyalty among his educated subjects? Opening the gates to the West had justified the worst fears of Nicholas I. Tsar Alexander's subjects were aroused by visions of individual freedom, constitutional government, and even a socialist order. Fires were set in the capital, and pamphlets urging revolt were distributed. The Poles rose in revolt against Russian rule. In the face of such developments did the tsar have any choice other than repression? His first cautious attempts to put down disorder merely strengthened the determination of his opponents. In 1866 a student tried to shoot him. Thereafter the police tightened its grip, and the "tsar liberator" became an unwilling and ineffectual reactionary (page 478).

Radicals seek to overthrow the tsar. When Alexander II's police drove the opposition underground, secret revolutionary circles sprang up, attracting both fanatics and young idealists. Revolutionary creeds were formulated and programs of action tried out. Among the revolutionary heroes was the anarchist Mikhail Bakunin (see pages 534–535), who urged not only violent revolution but the destruction of all government. "A people freed of its chains is gifted with the spirit of destruction; . . . before building, one must destroy," Bakunin wrote in 1874.

In the late 1870's there sprang from the revolutionary society "Land and Liberty" a terrorist organization called "the Will of the People." If the tsar used police terror to suppress the stirrings of freedom, what recourse did would-be liberators have but counter-terror? Thus the brutality of both the police and the revolutionaries escalated. In this struggle many educated Russians sympathized with the revolutionaries. Their tacit approval made possible a wave of assassinations (sometimes announced in advance) that took the lives of many prominent officials and finally of Tsar Alexander II himself.

The conflicting policies of Alexander III hamper progress.
Alexander III (1881–1894), son of the assassinated ruler, was the last tsar who could act the part of the autocrat. His policies, however, lacked direction. On the one hand he redoubled attempts to create a monolithic, unified state and to suppress subversion. Censorship was tightened, the power of the police increased, and revolutionary organizations were strictly banned. On the other hand, the tsar found it necessary to promote modernization modeled on western achievements. Under his prodding, the great trans-Siberian railroad was started and a policy of deliberate industrialization begun. After living with the burden of conflicting aims for thirteen years, Alexander III died of despair, leaving to his son the task of preparing imperial Russia for the brutal struggles of the twentieth century. This gentle, uncertain, and weak-willed—though by no means unintelligent—young heir was Nicholas II, the last of the tsars.

Nicholas II fails to understand the forces of the twentieth century.
The Russians could hardly have asked for a more dutiful and well-intentioned ruler. Nicholas II was a devoted family man in a court notorious for moral laxity. Behind the outward splendor of the court he led a simple, pious life. Viewing Russia and the world from the gilded cage of the imperial court, Nicholas II unfortunately had only

the dimmest idea of the changes taking place in his country and in the world at large. He might have become a good constitutional monarch had he not considered it his highest duty to pass autocracy to his heir unimpaired. Though he pretended to lead the empire, Nicholas II was swept to his doom by forces beyond his grasp.

Autocracy cannot be reconciled with government by consent of the people.
Great changes had taken place in Russia and in the world since the time of Nicholas I, who ruled from 1825 to 1855. Under Nicholas I, Russia might have claimed to be the equal of the other Great Powers of Europe. At the beginning of the twentieth century, however, she was patently backward in several respects. In Western Europe (with the partial exception of Germany) liberal democracy had triumphed as a way of life. Whatever role Western European countries played in the world was founded on the willing consent of their citizens; they combined freedom for their people with power. Although some differences existed among the European states, the trend of the times was unmistakable. The age of the common man participating in politics had begun. How could tsarist autocracy be reconciled to that trend?

Witte urges rapid industrialization.
Aware of Russia's weakness compared to the industrialized nations of Europe and America, Sergei Witte (syihr-*gay′ vyet′*tyeh), Nicholas II's most farsighted minister, urged a program of industrialization. Like the tsar and the intelligentsia, Witte wanted Russia to rank as a Great Power. Yet unlike them he realized that a drastic reorganization of the country's economy was absolutely necessary. Since industrialization has come to play a dominant part in recent Russian history, Witte's warning to the tsar deserves to be quoted in full. Observing that "in comparison with foreign countries Russian industry [was] . . . still very backward," he continued:

At present the political strength of the Great Powers which are called to fulfill great historical tasks in the world is created not only by the spiritual valor [loyalty and courage] of their peoples but also by their economic organization. Even the military preparedness of a country is determined not only by the perfection of its military machine but by the degree of its industrial development. Russia with her vast multinational population, her complex historical tasks in international relations, and her many-sided internal interests needs perhaps more than any other country a proper economic foundation for her national policy and her culture.

At the end was a warning: "Our economic backwardness may lead to political and cultural backwardness as well."

Nicholas II sees industrialization as a threat to autocracy.

But if Russia industrialized to build up her economic strength, the very traditions which the tsar and most of his subjects wished to uphold would have to be sacrificed. You could not preserve the green village and build factories in it, nor continue the slow-moving simple life and also enjoy the glamor of cities. Rapid industrialization called for an economic and social revolution carried out largely against the wishes of the people. It would also strike at autocracy by speeding up widespread participation in politics. Concentration on industrialization, moreover, might limit Russia's military might. If Russia's income went into economic development, there would be less money for armaments. Was it any wonder that after ten years of austerity and unwanted modernization both Nicholas II and his subjects turned their backs on rapid industrialization? The ways of old Russia would not die easily.

Russia lacks the economic base to compete with the western powers.

How, moreover, could Russia participate effectively in the rivalry for power that characterized the age of imperialism? The world was being divided among the great nations of Western Europe. To be sure, Russia too was an imperialist state. During the nineteenth century, the tsars had taken over many scattered peoples at the fringes of the country's natural boundaries. Parts of the Chinese Em-

pire were annexed as well. But the relatively civilized order of European politics was about to give way to a global struggle for the survival of the fittest—with fitness determined by the standards of the most advanced states of Western Europe and North America. Russia could not meet those standards.

Under the circumstances, the lack of monolithic unity in Russia that had haunted Nicholas I posed an even greater threat to Nicholas II. Could Nicholas II repress the growing agitation among his subjects for political rights? If he did not, tsarism would be threatened. Could he, at the same time, build the railroads and schools needed for the development of the country? If he failed to do so, Russia would fall further behind the more developed nations. Could Nicholas II stop the unrest among the land-hungry peasants and the non-Russian nationalities who resented Russification? Could he win over to autocracy the new class of industrial workers, who were increasingly dissatisfied because the tsar did nothing to improve their wretched working and living conditions? Failure to do so would cause Russia to be torn by civil war between nationalities and by class war between capitalists and workers.

CHECK-UP

1. Why were there revolts in Russia following the Napoleonic Wars? What was the outcome?

2. What did Nicholas I see as the role of Russia? What flaws did he see in his empire? Why was he unable to correct them?

3. What did Alexander II learn from Nicholas' rule? Why did the abolition of serfdom fail to satisfy the peasants? What other reforms did Alexander II introduce? What were the results?

4. Why did modernization conflict with autocracy? How did it affect the growth of radical groups? The policies of Alexander III?

5. What great problems confronted Nicholas II? What was Count Witte's plan for Russia? How did Nicholas II react? Why?

Defeat by Japan leads to revolt in Russia. The story of the breakup of tsarist autocracy under Nicholas II and of the empire after his overthrow can be told briefly. The first revolution, hardly deserving that name, occurred in 1905. Its causes lay in the economic and social changes brought about by Witte's policies. Workers and peasants now traveled in large numbers on the new railroads; they became uprooted. The new mobility intensified conflicts between workers, employers, and the government; it spread the knowledge of western democracy and freedom among the discontented elements in the population of Russia; it promoted workers' organizations and agitation for reform.

The tsar had hoped to stem the tide of rising discontent by repression and by fighting a "victorious little war" with Japan (1904–1905). The crushing defeat of the tsar's armies and fleets in the Far East set off a series of uncoordinated uprisings of peasants, workers, non-Russian nationalities, and members of the intelligentsia.

The tsar is forced to grant some reforms. At the height of the rebellion, a council (soviet) of striking workers threatened to take over the government. To prevent the overthrow of autocracy, the tsar granted the establishment of a legislature called the *Imperial Duma.* The first parliament in Russia's history, the Duma was to represent all elements of the population and guarantee their basic civil liberties—freedom of speech, the right to vote for members of the Duma, the right to organize labor unions. But with the return of the troops the uprisings were put down and Nicholas II took away many of the concessions that he had been forced to make. Between 1907 and 1914 there was a slight increase in public participation in the government and in the range of individual opportunity in public affairs. These slight gains only served to accentuate how limited was freedom in Russia and how determined was the tsar to preserve autocracy.

Stolypin attempts to reform agriculture. The most hopeful development in that period was the attempt at agrarian reform made by Peter Stolypin (stuh-*lih'*pyihn). Stolypin, Nicholas II's only outstanding minister besides Witte, was determined to end the collective tradition in peasant agriculture that kept Russia backward. He sought to create a class of conservative peasant landowners by encouraging the *kulaks* (koo-*lahks'*)—"fists," as the hard-headed, tight-fisted, and successful peasants were called. But basic reforms of the type Stolypin urged require time to catch hold, and relatively little progress had been made by the time war broke out in 1914.

Russia is unprepared for war. Both on the home front and militarily, Russia was utterly unprepared for war. The Russian armies found themselves in almost constant retreat before the disciplined and well-armed German troops. There was no question about the bravery of the Russian soldier, but he often lacked weapons and ammunition. The generals were unprepared to cope with the German war machine; the organization of the state, despite its vast powers, was too clumsy for total war; the underdeveloped Russian economy could not cope with the strains of war production and transportation as well as civilian consumption. Something might have been salvaged had there been effective leadership, but by 1915 tsarist autocracy was rotten to the core.

Rasputin, a "Holy Devil," wields power. In the summer of 1915 Tsar Nicholas II, deciding to join his troops at the front, left the conduct of government in the hands of his wife Alexandra. In terms of meeting the requirements of governing a state in the twentieth century, the tsarina was an even more tragically incompetent figure than her husband.

Alexandra started well enough, trying to bolster her husband's weak will and encouraging him to be a strong autocrat. But as the years passed she learned the sorrows of an empress who for a long time bore no heir to the throne. When after four daughters she at last produced a son, he was found to suffer from hemophilia (a disease that prevents blood from clotting). In her misery she sought the comfort of religion, and soon fell under the spell of a monk who had the power of healing and an air of saintliness. This man, named Rasputin (rus-*poo'*-tyihn) could even stop her son's bleeding. What Alexandra did not know—and forever refused to admit—was that Rasputin was truly a "Holy Devil." Scandal soon surrounded her idol, to the alarm of her husband's most devoted advisors. When they told the tsar the truth, she prevailed upon him to dismiss them one by one. When the direction of government affairs fell into Alexandra's hands in 1915, Rasputin, who had the mind of a shrewd but illiterate peasant, in effect appointed the chief officials. By late 1916 corruption was so flagrant as to border on treason. In their despair loyal supporters of autocracy considered setting aside the tsar and tsarina; in the end they merely murdered Rasputin.

Autocracy is overthrown by the March Revolution. The overthrow of autocracy was accomplished by the enraged masses in the revolution of March, 1917 (February by the old Russian calendar). A strike of workers gave way to food riots, food riots to open rebellion. At the crucial moment the soldiers, ordered to shoot the rioters, shot their officers instead. After two and a half years of a disastrous war, the soldiers had little love for either their officers or their tsar. The March Revolution, like the one in 1905, had not been planned; autocracy simply crumbled from weakness within. Its failure resulted in the cruel murder of the unlucky tsar and his entire family in July, 1918.

Incredible confusion follows the overthrow of autocracy. The March Revolution was merely the beginning of even greater calamities. The new freedom in Russia had the results that the tsars had always dreaded. The differing groups were soon in frenzied competition with each other. Disunity was apparent at the very center of the new order. On one side stood the Provisional Government—provisional because its decisions were to be ratified eventually by a constitutional convention; on the other, the Petrograd Soviet.

The Provisional Government spoke for the educated, Europeanized minority; it was dominated by liberal-democratic members of the Imperial Duma led by Alexander Kerensky (kih-*ryehn'*skih). The Provisional Government desired reforms that would protect the rights of the individual and establish a western-style parliamentary government. It also wanted to continue the war.

The Petrograd Soviet had sprung up in the capital from among the peasant masses, mainly soldiers and workers. Hundreds like it cropped up throughout the country during the months following March. This was the groundswell of popular revenge for centuries of serfdom, of denying land to the peasants, and of exploiting urban workers.

The Petrograd Soviet favored a policy of social reform that would aid oppressed workers and peasants. It did not urge Russia's immediate withdrawal from the war but it did call for an early peace. It thought that this could be accomplished by urging workers and peasants in other warring nations to revolt against their capitalist leaders. Disorder and unrest in their countries would compel the warring governments to call a halt to the fighting. Not trusting its own capacity for leadership, the Soviet reluctantly tolerated the Provisional Government.

Angry at hunger and disorder, impatient with the postponement of crucial decisions such as the redistribution of land and the granting of self-determination to national minorities, and above all wanting to end the war, many people gradually lost confidence in the Provisional

The period between March and November, 1917, was marked by violence as the Provisional Government and the Bolsheviks struggled for power. Armed Bolshevik patrols (right) cruised the streets. Workers' demonstrations protesting government policies were organized by the Bolsheviks. Above, the police under Kerensky's orders fire on demonstrating workers.

Government and turned to the radical left for leadership. It was becoming very apparent that the Provisional Government rested on shaky foundations, that Russia might be engulfed in another revolution—one more radical than the March Revolution that had ushered in the Provisional Government.

Meanwhile, the German armies continued their advance. German generals and statesmen were busily making plans for carving up the Russian Empire. German agents encouraged the discord and war-weariness in Russia and even gave financial aid to the Bolsheviks.

The Bolsheviks succeed after democracy and military dictatorship fail. By midsummer of 1917, in this time of supreme crisis, three forms of government were being offered to the bewildered people of Russia. The first was a parliamentary government, dedicated to the hope of uniting the divided country through the ideal of liberal democracy. This was the goal of the Provisional Government. By September this possibility was ruled out. The hard fact was that there existed no common patriotism sufficient to unite the newly liberated population; freedom destroyed rather than created agreement.

The second possibility was a military dictatorship which, headed by a popular general, would hold the country together by force. This course, attempted by General Lavr Kornilov (*lah′*ver kur-*nyee′*luhf) in August, failed. Even his most loyal troops melted away under the propaganda of the Soviet. The third choice was an original and daring combination of a government based on rule by the Soviet under the control of a small, tightly organized, and determined revolutionary party. This was the Bolshevik solution. It succeeded. Who were the Bolsheviks? How did they succeed in gaining control over Russia?

The professional revolutionary emerges. For an explanation of the Bolshevik success we must look back at the age of Alexander II. Out of the escalation of police repression and revolutionary terror emerged the Russian professional revolutionary. He was a fanatic idealist who did not hesitate to use any means whatever to overthrow autocracy and give land to the peasants. The weakness of that first generation of revolutionaries was that it lacked mass support. It counted on angry peasants to increase its power, but found that they would not trust the intellectuals. The next generation of revolutionaries had learned new tricks. It discovered Karl Marx (page 528) and the Russian industrial *proletariat* (workers), the product of industrialization. Marx contributed a great deal to his Russian disciples: a theory of society that claimed to be based on science, an all-embracing creed that advocated an end to exploitation and suffering, and a philosophy of history that predicted the victory of socialism. If history was on their side, who could withstand the revolutionaries? Devoted to the Marxist cause, this second generation of revolutionaries began to agitate among the workers. Yet failure still dogged them. How could Marxist revolutionaries elude the increasingly efficient police and find the opportunity to mobilize the masses? The answer was given by Lenin: only a tight-knit secret organization of professional revolutionaries could destroy autocracy and capitalism. A third generation of Russian revo-

lutionaries, schooled in the teachings of Lenin, succeeded where the others had failed.

To gain his goals, Lenin combines force with promises. Why should an able, well-educated young man named Vladimir Ilich Ulianov (vluh-*dyee′*mihr ihl-*yeech′* uhl-*yah′*nuhf), born in a successful family loyal to the tsar, turn revolutionary, ruin his career as a lawyer, go to jail and Siberian exile, change his name to Lenin, and spend many years in political exile? His answer was that of many other young Russians. Out of a deep sense of patriotism and human service, he would gladly sacrifice all he had to overthrow tsarist autocracy and bourgeois capitalism. The bourgeois era of world history, Lenin believed, was coming to an end. A new and better age, the age of socialism, was beginning. During the period of transition, violence was inevitable, particularly in Russia where autocracy repressed all stirrings of freedom.

As an idealist Lenin deplored violence; as a practical revolutionary he merely adjusted to existing conditions. In Britain and the United States—countries with a long history of political liberty—political differences might be settled by ballots. In Russia—a nation with a long history of repressive autocracy—it was bullets that counted, bullets plus organization.

Lenin's authoritarian views reflect distrust of the masses. Not all Russian Marxists agreed with Lenin. A group called the Mensheviks still hoped that a revolutionary party could achieve its goals through peaceful means. But they had no reply to Lenin's argument that in the fight against autocracy a revolutionary party could not afford to follow western procedures. Because the Bolsheviks had to be as secret and violent as the tsarist police, they could not help being authoritarian. Lenin himself dominated his followers, and his party tended to dominate the masses.

As an authoritarian, Lenin thus absorbed another trait from the regime he hated: distrust of the masses, the very people for whom he was fighting. In his eyes they were incapable of understanding the events of the past and the needs of the present. Only the revolutionary intelligentsia, the Bolshevik leaders, could do that. Only they could give direction to the revolutionary forces at work in the contemporary world.

Lenin sets goals for the Bolsheviks to attain.

When tsarism crashed, Lenin was ready with a sweeping program for the Bolsheviks: overthrow the Provisional Government with the help of the Soviet and take over power during the period of confusion which followed. In the first stage of the revolution, the bourgeoisie took power; in the second stage, power will be seized by the proletariat and the poorest peasants.

Specifically, Lenin demanded the "abolition of the police, . . . confiscation of all private lands and the nationalization of all lands in the country, . . . immediate merger of all the banks in the country into one general national bank, . . . the immediate placing of the Soviet of Workers' Deputies in control of all social production and distribution of goods."

Lenin promises the Russians "peace, land, and bread."

After the March Revolution, Lenin possessed what no rival politician could claim: a party of professional revolutionaries—by August about 200,000 strong—disciplined and obedient despite the growing anarchism in the country. He adopted the crude demands of the masses as his own: peace, land, bread, and the transfer of power to the Soviet. To the peasants, desperate to increase the size of their meager holdings, he promised the *land* of the rich landlords. To the near-starving factory workers, he promised *bread*, provided by a government that takes surplus products from the parasites and gives them to the hungry, that . . . moves the homeless into the dwellings of the rich, that . . . forces the rich to pay for milk, but does not give them a drop of it until the children of *all* the poor families have received adequate supplies.

And to the soldiers and their families back home he promised *peace*. In 1917 no word could be sweeter to the Russian people. With his slogan of "peace, land, and bread," Lenin gained wide popular support. Many of those who were not ready to accept his leadership were even more unwilling to oppose him. Thus he was helped by the neutrality of large numbers of people.

Why are the Bolsheviks able to take over power in Russia?

But how could the Bolsheviks, who numbered about 200,000 by August, 1917, seize power in a nation of almost 150,000,000 people? The secret lay in organization, discipline, and strategy. In 1902 Lenin had written: "Give us an organization of revolutionaries and we shall overturn the whole of Russia." By the fall of 1917, he had built such an organization.

The Bolsheviks prevailed over their rivals because Russia had not yet achieved the monolithic solidarity of a true nation capable of holding itself together under the stress of a terrible war. The grant of political freedom by the Provisional Government, combined with the sacrifices of the war, magnified the disunity within Russia. Anarchy appeared in the government, the army, the economy, and in the relations between Russian and non-Russian peoples in the empire. It destroyed the weak bonds of confidence between the peasant masses (to which most workers and soldiers belonged) and the Europeanized educated elite on whom the tsars had relied. Under these circumstances only a tight-knit dictatorship, stressing discipline and obedience and identifying itself with the masses, had any chance of forming an effective government. As Lenin held the center of the stage on the night of November 8, he saw himself as both the heir of the nation-building tsars and the herald of the Russian intelligentsia that hoped for a modern, strong, united, and socialistic Russia to rise from the shambles of autocracy.

CHECK-UP

1. How did the Russian people react to the defeat by Japan? Why? Why did the establishment of the Imperial Duma cause further unrest?

2. In what respects was Russia unprepared for war in 1914? How did the war increase Russia's difficulties?

3. How was the tsar's government overthrown? What was the result?

4. What were the goals of the Provisional Government? Of the Petrograd Soviet? Why did the Provisional Government lose support?

5. How did the professional revolutionary develop?

6. Who were the Bolsheviks? How did they gain power in Russia?

7. What were Lenin's views? What goals did he set for the Bolsheviks?

8. Why did Lenin's slogan of "peace, land, and bread" win wide support?

Lenin's Foundations for a Strong Soviet State

Russia faces disintegration. There was a monstrous gap between the extravagant Bolshevik hopes for the future and the grim realities of the situation following the coup (*koo,* overthrow) in November. The Bolshevik Revolution hastened the breakdown of all established order in Russia; the miseries that had discredited the Provisional Government—hunger, cold, fear, civic chaos—multiplied. Russia was torn by a vicious civil war between the Bolsheviks (Reds) and their opponents (Whites). Political terror was soon added to this beastly and unrelenting civil war. The cities lost much of their population as people sought shelter in the country, only to be cut down there, too, by war or famine. The different nationalities that comprised Russia threatened to form their own national states. There was no army, no industry, no railway transportation.

In the winter of 1917–1918 Russia lay prostrate before the German invaders. When the Bolshevik peace negotiators met with the Germans in the town of Brest-Litovsk, they had to accept peace on the terms Germany dictated. Unwilling to endanger his regime by permitting a continued German advance, Lenin signed the harsh peace treaty in early March, 1918. Never had Russian fortunes fallen so low. Gone were the Polish lands, the Baltic provinces, and Finland. Lost was most of southern Russia west of the Caspian Sea, the richest and most productive region of the empire. If British and French troops, increasingly bolstered by American

manpower and equipment, had not kept German armies occupied on the Western Front, Russia might have been wiped off the political map. The subsequent defeat of Germany, to be sure, canceled the Treaty of Brest-Litovsk and restored the Ukraine to Russia. But it did not relieve Russia's basic weakness. The lesson of Brest-Litovsk was obvious: The price of national weakness, backwardness, and discord was national humiliation or, even worse, disintegration. Russia had to become strong. No sacrifice would be too great to achieve this end.

In the twenty years between the First and Second World Wars the Bolsheviks—who after their revolution called themselves *Communists* —managed to overcome staggering problems and to make Russia into a super power. How the communist leaders managed this remarkable achievement will be explained in the remainder of the chapter.

Lenin takes positive steps to reduce chaos in Russia. The first years of communist rule were marked by considerable confusion. While the civil war still raged, the Bolsheviks moved to take control of the economic life of the country. Industry, banks, and foreign trade were put under state control. Everyone over sixteen and under fifty was required by law to work, and strikes were forbidden. So much paper money had been issued that it became worthless, and peasants refused to sell their produce. To provide the cities and the army with food, the government had the army seize crops and distribute them. These emergency measures, called *war communism,* strengthened Bolshevik control but did not improve the Russian economy. Agricultural and industrial production fell drastically, and hundreds of thousands of Russians died from hunger, cold, and disease.

During the period of war communism Lenin realized that he could not prevent the peasants from satisfying their hunger for land. He therefore approved the distribution to the peasants of all land owned by nobles, churches, and monasteries. Large portions of the extensive uncultivated lands once held by the tsar and the tsarist state were also included. Yet the number of peasants was large and the land hitherto held by other groups rather limited. The individual peasant household hardly increased its holdings.

During its first three years the communist dictatorship lived from hand to mouth. It began uncertainly in Petrograd, Moscow, and other industrial and military centers of the Russian heartland, reaching but slowly out into the countryside. Russia's southern and eastern borderlands were absorbed only by conquest. Unable to establish a firm grip on the country, the dictatorship considered its revolutionary decrees as good propaganda even if they could not always be carried out. In this manner it made the workers into the privileged class of Soviet Russia, promising them unprecedented social security and enjoyment of all its political and cultural opportunities. It also guaranteed full legal equality to women, caught up with western practice by separating church and state, simplified the alphabet, and adopted the Gregorian calendar. More significantly, the communist dictatorship created a new secret police (successively called Cheka, GPU, and N.K.V.D.) and, under the leadership of Leon Trotsky (*trohts'*kih), the new Red Army. Discipline in the Red Army was as strict as that of the tsarist army; its "proletarian" morale, hopefully, even higher.

The Soviet Union is threatened by civil war and invasion. With the help of the Red Army the Communists collected food from the peasants, got the railways running, and reduced the anarchy of freedom to civil order. After savage fighting during the civil war which broke out between the Red Army and the anti-Soviet forces, the enemies of the regime were beaten back and dispelled. The Communists also repelled the intervention of Germany, Britain, France, Japan, and the United States, which for various reasons had occupied bits of Russia's borderlands. Lenin himself had been partly responsible for such foreign interference. He had created such fear of revolution in the "capitalist" countries that these powers felt compelled to lessen the danger of world revolution by invading Russia, the very source of communist power.

The New Economic Policy marks a retreat from war communism. When at last all resistance had been overcome, the communist dictatorship seemed excessively restrictive even to some of its most ardent supporters. In March, 1921, the sailors at the Kronstadt (krun-*shtaht'*) naval base near Petrograd rose against the Communists. Although Lenin was able to suppress their revolt, he realized that, to consolidate his regime, there must be a retreat from the terror of war communism. In 1921, therefore, Soviet Russia, utterly exhausted by bloodshed and famine, entered the period of the *New Eco-nomic Policy* (NEP), which lasted from 1921 to 1928.

Under NEP life gradually returned to a semblance of normalcy. In order to strengthen the economy and to heal the wounds of war, revolution, and famine, Lenin temporarily put aside the socialist goal of complete nationalization of industry and agriculture. He allowed a return to limited private ownership; small-scale manufacturing, domestic trade, and agriculture were placed again in private hands. By 1927

Trotsky's Red Army combined revolutionary education with military discipline. The poster contrasts the socialist goal of freedom with the tsarist goals of exploitation and imperialism. Below, an armored train heads for the battle zone.

Russia had regained and in some areas surpassed levels of production reached before World War I. Kulaks and small businessmen became relatively prosperous. The government retained control of the major industries and transportation but for the time being did not push the plan to build a socialist society. Indeed, in the last years of his life, Lenin became noticeably soft as he began to realize the inhuman price of his revolutionary impatience. Weakened by a series of strokes, he died in January, 1924. Lenin's command of the Communist Party, however, had come to an end many months earlier.

Marxism-Leninism defines communist policies.

During their first years as rulers of Russia the Bolsheviks were fashioning a set of power tools with which to master the turmoil in their country and to survive in a hostile world. Some of these instruments of power came from the pre-revolutionary period. During these years of preparation the Bolsheviks had created a well-organized and ably led party, which put into practice the theories of revolution known as Marxism-Leninism (or Leninism). These theories, geared to a world in revolutionary change, were essentially the work of Lenin. From quarters in the Kremlin, an old palace-fortress in the city of Moscow, where the capital had been moved in the spring of 1918, Lenin directed the Communist Party. Like the tsars and like many present-day statesmen in the developing countries, Lenin was concerned with nation-building.

The Politburo provides an elite leadership.

The key to success, Lenin argued, lay in achieving a monolithic unity of the Russian people—a people divided by nationality, religion, language, and culture. This was to be accomplished through the Communist Party, an institution far superior to the ineffective and corrupt tsarist bureaucracy. The party was a dynamic elite, geared to effective political action under adverse conditions. Its top leadership consisted of a small number of able and energetic men associated with Lenin in the party's *Politburo*

(Political Bureau). Each of these men had risen to power the hard way, through apprenticeship in the practical work of revolution. Each had become a master at handling the masses and in a crisis was capable of wrenching victory from defeat. Because these men knew that the survival of the party depended on their comradely unity, they took drastic steps to prevent discord. They knew that the party could be effective only if its members were in agreement on all basic issues. Those who disagreed were thrown out of the party.

Members of the Communist Party are expected to serve the party without question.

The Politburo leaders had at their disposal some half-million Communist Party members, loyal to the party and trained to strict obedience. Crucial to the preservation of monolithic unity in the Communist Party was the recruitment process. Candidates were drawn from a rather narrow social group, the industrial working class. Because they came from one group, party members shared a common upbringing and a common outlook on life. Peasants found it difficult to be admitted to the party; members of the former ruling classes and their descendants were virtually excluded.

Once admitted, a party member faced constant scrutiny of his conduct in the "cell," the primary unit in the party organization. He was also required to evaluate himself by constant self-criticism. If the party member abused his powers or shirked his duty, he would be dismissed. Purges of opportunists and slackers were routine practice, very necessary in the period of rapid growth following the November Revolution. (In 1921–1922 party membership thus fell from 730,000 to 515,000.) The chief requirement for a Communist was selfless, energetic devotion to the party. He was a political soldier whose obligation was constantly to improve his capacity for serving the party.

The party member could not claim a will of his own. In theory, he could help shape the decisions of the party by electing delegates to the party congresses which in turn elected the members of the Central Committee. On that committee sat the most important Communist Party officials, eventually numbering over a hundred. They acted as the party's watchdog over party congresses. They also helped choose the members of the Politburo, the real center of political power in Soviet Russia. Ideally, the party was guided by the principle of "democratic centralism," a process of constant give and take of advice up and down the ladder of party organization. In reality, however, the "democratic" and representative facets of the party constitution meant little. As under autocracy the crucial decisions were made at the top. In this manner Lenin and his followers forged from a traditionally quarrelsome and undisciplined population a remarkable instrument of power—the tightly knit, thoroughly disciplined, carefully supervised, and fanatically devoted Communist Party.

The Russian Revolution results in a population dependent upon the state. In his efforts to give Russia the unity and sense of common purpose of which Nicholas I had dreamed, Lenin was aided by the social consequences of the Bolshevik Revolution. Dictatorship by the Communist Party had wiped out the propertied, educated, and Europeanized minority through which the tsars had ruled the peasant masses. Thus it had greatly simplified the social structure of Russia by abolishing all privilege and privacy. It also reduced the possibility of resistance. Over the years the Communist Party succeeded in transforming all Russian subjects into "toilers" who had to earn a living in enterprises controlled by the state. Thus it took away their independence. By abolishing or severely limiting income-producing private property, the Communists created a population heavily dependent on the state. The peasants, however, were an exception; for the time being they were allowed to continue in their traditional ways.

Another target of the Bolshevik Revolution was the Orthodox Church, and indeed all other organized religions. Being otherworldly, traditionalist, and indifferent to the demands of citizenship in a communist state, the Church

During the anti-religious campaigns after the Bolshevik Revolution, many places of worship in Russia were closed. Above, workers store grain in an abandoned church.

clearly was an obstacle to the monolithic unity sought by the Communists. By eliminating the old upper class, by turning everyone into a worker for the state, and by destroying the Church's privileges, the Communists tightened their grip over the nation. There was a lesson in this for other nation-builders. Clearly Soviet-style socialism created a social order that is more easily controlled than that which evolved under the political, economic, and spiritual ideals of western-style democracy.

The soviets provide a system of government for Russia. The new society of "toilers" was directed at every turn by the Communist Party. Lenin transformed the soviets of workers and peasants into regular organs of government. Under the party's guidance local soviets, locally elected, discharged the functions of local government and elected delegates to district soviets. The latter, in turn, took charge of the government in the districts and elected delegates to the provincial soviets. The all-Russian Soviet, elected from its subordinate soviets, represented the highest government authority in the country, a sort of national parliament. Its Council of Peoples Commissars (the communist name for the cabinet customary in a western government) formed the executive branch of the government. It was staffed with experienced and loyal party members.

Through the local soviets the Russian masses, under the close and constant supervision of the Communist Party, were encouraged to take an interest in local government. In like manner the party controlled other public organizations —trade unions, cooperatives, communist youth groups, and professional and cultural organizations—wheedling and needling (and if necessary compelling) to achieve conformity to its directives. These agencies, said Lenin's successor Stalin, were "conveyor belts" carrying the will of the party down to the grassroots. Of these public bodies the organs of the Soviet government were the most important. As their responsibilities grew, they began to rival the party in shaping the policies of Soviet Russia.

The people are indoctrinated with Marxist-Leninist teachings.
The Communist Party regarded Marxist-Leninist ideology as the cement for a new "proletarian" unity. By their natural mode of thinking and feeling—their "spontaneity," as Lenin put it—the Russian masses traditionally had disagreed and quarreled. But given a unifying force, a common set of beliefs, the much divided peoples of Russia might be welded together. Lenin hoped to unite the Russian masses, something the tsars had never succeeded in accomplishing, by indoctrinating them in the teachings of Marxism-Leninism, the same set of principles that guided the party.

Lenin tries to eliminate national barriers.
To further unity, Lenin also introduced basic changes in the treatment of the country's many ethnic minorities. He taught that party stood above nationality, that the class solidarity of the "toilers" was capable of overcoming divisions caused by language or culture. He demanded that the different ethnic groups obey the dictates of the Communist Party. Not wishing to arouse unnecessarily the hostility of these groups, Lenin did allow them to keep many of their cultural traditions and the use of their own languages. There would be no compulsory Russification under communist control—though there would be a powerful drift toward the use of the Russian language as the most advantageous for all concerned.

Lenin advocates state control of the economy.
State ownership of industrial enterprises and state planning for the economy of all Soviet Russia served as a further guarantee of unity. Marxism had long denounced the "capitalist" system for its chaotic booms and busts—periods of prosperity and periods of depression. Soviet socialism, by contrast, was to proceed rationally, by plan. Effective planning, however, required complete control over all factors involved in production and distribution, a condition that the Communist Party could not achieve for many years. Yet it made a cautious beginning in 1921 when it introduced the State Planning Agency (Gosplan). What terrifying implications loomed ahead! Lenin called for "iron discipline at work" and promised to take whatever steps were necessary to enforce it. Modernization was to be achieved in Soviet Russia through planned and coordinated compulsion.

Lenin promotes communism at the international level.
Hoping to unleash a world revolution, Lenin issued a ringing appeal to those who blamed their power-mad governments for the death and destruction caused by the world war, or their "capitalist" employers for poverty and suffering, or their imperialist colonial masters for oppression and exploitation. Who among the millions of bewildered and angry victims of a world undergoing great change would not rise to fight for a vision of peace, freedom, and plenty for all? In the aftermath of the First World War, communist parties sprang

up in many western countries, as well as in India, China, Egypt, and Turkey.

Soon Lenin was busy yoking these ragged revolutionary forces together as an instrument of Soviet foreign policy. In 1919 he formed a new Socialist International, designed to bring the communist parties of the world under the control of the Soviet Union. Foreign Communists thus became an effective substitute for Russian armies. They could operate on enemy territory and through agitation or threat of revolution prevent hostile action against the Soviet Union. In countries without a proletariat, Soviet influence was extended by "national liberation movements" encouraged by Lenin's anti-imperialist ideology and Soviet financial assistance. In their fear of revolution western governments magnified the communist threat out of all proportion. Nothing could have served Lenin better than the power which this fear conferred on him. As it turned out, both Lenin and his adversaries were wrong. The western (or "capitalist") system endured, and Lenin's dream of world revolution faded.

Lenin tries to give the Russian people a sense of mission. In his drive for monolithic unity Lenin devised several improvements over tsarism. He proclaimed the superiority of the Soviet socialist system over "capitalism" in order to foster self-confidence among the Russian peoples. If they did not automatically accept the superiority of the "higher" system of socialism, he would teach them by indoctrination. Lenin realized that no people can achieve great things without a sense of conviction, a feeling of mission, a belief in their own worth. And, lest the inadequacies of Russia be discovered through direct comparisons with western countries, Lenin deepened the isolation which had cut off Russia from the outside world since 1914. He sought to prevent the rise of a new intelligentsia that might challenge communist ideas or criticize communist methods. By isolating the Russian people from the West, by indoctrinating them with Marxist-Leninist ideas, by bringing them under the close supervision of the Com-

munist Party, Lenin was more successful than any tsar in creating a monolithic Russia. It was he who laid the foundations of Soviet Russia as a super power.

At the time of Lenin's death many instruments of communist power had been fashioned. These included: (1) the creation of a powerful, tightly organized party dedicated to Marxist-Leninist ideals; (2) the elimination of the pre-revolutionary upper class and the transforming of the Russian people into workers for the state; (3) the establishment of organs of government directed by the Communist Party; (4) the indoctrination of the people with Marxist-Leninist teachings; (5) the introduction of a large measure of state control over the economy; and (6) the promotion of communism on an international level. To enforce their policies, the Communists resorted more and more to force and terror. The history of Soviet Russia from 1917 to 1939 shows an almost continuous perfection of these methods of the police state.

CHECK-UP

1. What was the situation in Russia following the Bolshevik take-over? What was the effect of the Treaty of Brest-Litovsk? What lesson did it teach?

2. Why did Lenin institute war communism? How successful was it? How did NEP mark a change in policy?

3. What was the Politburo?

4. What was the political role of the Communist Party? What gave the party its power?

5. Why did the Bolshevik Revolution make the people dependent upon the state?

6. What political role did the soviets play?

7. In what ways did Lenin attempt to increase national unity?

8. What innovations did Lenin make in Russian foreign policy?

9. How successful was Lenin in creating a monolithic Russia? What instruments of communist power had been fashioned by the time of his death?

Among the men associated with Lenin two stood out, Trotsky and Stalin. Leon Trotsky came from a background unusual in Russia, a successful Jewish farm. A rebel since his youth, he had become a well-traveled journalist, a forceful orator, and a man of brilliant ideas. He excelled as an organizer—it was Trotsky who had engineered the Bolshevik take-over in November, 1917. Josef Stalin was of a different mold. The son of a cobbler from what is today the republic of Georgia in the Caucasus Mountains, he turned rebel while a scholarship student at the best school in the area. Subsequently Stalin became one of the toughest Bolshevik revolutionaries. His strong point was durability —being on the job at all times; though not a key man, he proved indispensable, with an infinite capacity for organization and detail.

Stalin becomes head of the Soviet Union. In 1922 Stalin was appointed Secretary-General— a position that gave him tremendous influence over the Communist Party machinery. It was Stalin who translated Lenin's ideal of the monolithic state into hard reality, building up a network of obedient party secretaries at all levels of the party hierarchy. This assured him of a reliable majority at the party congresses as well. Stalin's methods were efficient though occasionally rough. By the time of Lenin's death, Stalin's power in the party was so well established that not even Trotsky could successfully challenge it. Any opposition to him was regarded as a threat to party unity and therefore to be condemned. The Communist Party, as represented at its congresses by majority vote, which Stalin controlled, could never be wrong.

The struggle over leadership of the party lasted from 1923 to 1927. In 1929, on his fiftieth birthday, Stalin was formally hailed as Lenin's successor and the "great wise father" and leader of the peoples of Russia. This marked the beginning of the "cult of personality," as

the almost mystical veneration of Stalin came to be called after his death. Stalin was no longer regarded as an ordinary mortal but rather as the head of a "Church embodying the Truth." Those who faltered in their allegiance were sinners; those who disagreed were heretics. Under such conditions Stalin's rivals either had to submit unconditionally or be eliminated. Yet Stalin would never come to feel as secure in his position as would a western leader whose office is sanctioned by tradition. Like Lenin, Stalin had seized power and maintained his position solely by his personal appeal and by his successes. But far more than Lenin, Stalin showed the strains of that burden.

Stalin attempts to build confidence in Russia's future. Stalin's rise to power was based on solid achievement and on physical endurance. His chief rival, Trotsky, was often sick or indisposed. The new head of the Communist Party further demonstrated leadership in his ability to cope with the doubts which the strategic retreat represented by NEP had cast over the future of communist rule. He was confronted with a number of problems: When would the party resume the advance toward socialism, not to mention communism, which Marxists consider the highest stage of human development? How could the party overcome Russia's profound backwardness without help from the more advanced West? Was the party to be satisfied with the snail's pace set by the peasants and small businessmen under NEP? This last course was supported by some communist leaders (among them the dying Lenin) whom Stalin called the "right deviation"—those who had turned aside from revolutionary communism to pursue more conservative measures. Or, as the "left deviation" urged, was the party to forge ahead to achieve the glorious vision of the younger, more militant Lenin? Yet rapid industrialization, the key to super-power status, would require untold sacrifices from the population. How could a regime dedicated to the welfare of the "toilers" deliberately lower their standard of living, already much too low by comparison with living conditions in "capitalist" countries?

In the face of these difficult alternatives Stalin stepped forward with the reassuring message that Soviet Russia could march forward to socialism and rapid industrialization by relying on her own resources; she need not depend on socialist revolutions elsewhere. Stalin's terse slogan, "socialism in one country," expressed that self-assurance and breathed confidence into the party; it appealed to the yearning for national self-assertion. Trotsky, by contrast, held out no such hope. In 1927 Stalin, having overcome the opposition and expelled Trotsky from the party, was ready to implement his promise with deeds, to raise Soviet Russia by its own bootstraps. Thus began the grim and terrifying era of Stalinism.

In his endeavor to save Soviet Russia from backwardness Stalin saw himself as a mighty prophet of a superior world order, a lonely mortal with superhuman responsibility. "We are fifty or a hundred years behind the advanced countries," he said. "We must make good this distance in ten years or they will crush us." It was Stalin's historic mandate to whip his people to the utmost exertions so that Russia would overtake and surpass the capitalist pacesetters of the world. No one was to be spared in this awesome task.

Stalin turns to forced industrialization as the key to Soviet development. The key to Soviet Russia's development was to be the deliberate, forced growth of industry through a series of Five-Year Plans. The first and most drastic began in 1928. Imagine the immense difficulties of drafting a plan establishing production goals in steel, coal, oil, transportation, and hydroelectric power, as well as consumer goods, and of making sure that all the necessary supplies and raw materials would be available where and when they were needed. Imagine

further the immense difficulty of holding men and machines to specific production and distribution schedules. The planners were ambitious indeed, setting down in percentages the increase of output for each branch of industry, and even of the productivity of labor itself.

With the first Five-Year Plan all private business came to an end; the corner store, the basement cobbler, the florist, the plumber, and a host of others ceased to exist. All economic activity (with the important exception of agriculture) fell under state management: the state was responsible for producing all goods in the economy, buying and selling, hiring and firing of workers, and even training them for their jobs. For consumers, that meant waiting in line, delays, red tape, and poor service. Planning could never achieve the sensitivity to consumer demand characteristic of private enterprise. But what did the demands of consumers matter when the plan was designed to strengthen the state?

Needless to say, economic reorganization on so immense a scale created incredible inefficiency that made a mockery of planning. In addition, the emphasis upon output at any price led to the production of shoddy or even unusable goods. For these reasons the first Five-Year Plan was scrapped ahead of schedule; subsequent plans were somewhat more detailed and realistic and placed greater stress on quality. Throughout, however, the mood was one of heroic sacrifice, much as in wartime. Against their will, large numbers of men and women were drawn into factories and workshops. Paid low wages based on piecework, they were housed in dismal, overcrowded quarters and poorly fed; their thoughts and bodies were regimented in obedience to "the single will of the leaders of the labor process," as Lenin had said in 1918. The Communist Party tried to create a fighting morale by rewarding workers who outproduced their comrades and by holding victory celebrations when production goals were achieved. Young people were encouraged to believe that they were building a beautiful new world.

Even literature and the arts were mobilized for industrialization. Novelists described the joys of working for the socialist state; in a simple, direct style painters portrayed people at work on farms and in factories. The purpose of this *socialist realism* in the arts was to inspire the workers to devote all their energies to building the socialist state.

Forced collectivization of agriculture causes bitterness and famine.

The years of rapid industrial expansion were exceedingly harsh and bitter for the Russian people. They were made doubly grim by the revolution that took place after 1929 in agriculture. Stalin discovered that a mighty advance in industry required state control over the peasants also. He immediately called for the most fundamental and brutal of all communist attacks on Russian tradition.

Though he had given the Russian peasant a free hand in 1917, Lenin had never abandoned hope that some day his regime would introduce the same rational control over agriculture that prevailed in industry. Stalin was confronted with the necessity of putting agriculture under state control when he discovered that the peasants would not voluntarily produce the crops required under the first Five-Year Plan. Why should they? With shops emptied of goods, there was no incentive for peasants to prolong their labors in the field. Were the peasants to foil the party's great plan? Was the communist future to be made dependent on the snail's pace of peasant progress? The communist answer was, of course, Never! Stalin decided on the forcible collectivization of agriculture.

On paper, the form of *collective farming* which he envisioned was not extreme. It called for the pooling of land, livestock, tools, and buildings, but permitted the peasant to retain his hut and to engage in backyard farming for private profit. The innovation and the hardship

To control agricultural production, Stalin (above) forced the collectivization of Soviet farms. Though this policy imposed great hardships on Russian peasants, it helped modernize Russian agriculture by making the use of heavy machinery (left) profitable.

lay in the surrender of hitherto privately owned property. It made possible the consolidation into one collective of the small, scattered, and inefficient plots of individual farmers. Collectivization permitted the use of machinery and the introduction of scientific methods of farming. Seen in this light, collectivization was indispensable for any progress in Russian agriculture and essential for providing the growing industrial population with food. Yet collectivization ran counter to the deepest instincts of peasants who had a long memory of serfdom and its abuses.

Despite peasant opposition, in the winter of 1929–1930 Stalin proceeded to collectivize the farms by armed force. This disregard for peasant attitudes resulted in two years of warfare in the countryside. Rather than turn over horses, cows, and pigs to the collective, the peasants slaughtered their animals in an orgy of defiance. The losses in livestock were appalling. There were to be frightful consequences for decades to come in terms of diet, loss of horsepower in agriculture and transportation, lack of animal fertilizer, and shortage of leather goods. The fields were also neglected, causing famine in many sections of the country at a time when Stalin had planned to sell unusually large amounts of foodstuffs abroad in order to buy urgently needed industrial equipment.

Stalin felt no concern for the starving peasant rebels and never considered abandoning the plan. In his attack on peasant conservatism and traditions Stalin determined to "liquidate the kulaks as a class." Thus he wiped out the most efficient private producers in agriculture, broke up their families, and scattered the most resourceful agricultural manpower among forced-labor camps and industrial construction projects.

By the mid-1930's the agitation among the peasants had died down. Collective farms, each composed of several scores of households, were now the rule. In theory these farms managed their own affairs, but they were also subject to the indirect control of another product of the collectivization drive, the *Motor Tractor Stations* where mechanized equipment and scientific know-how were concentrated. The collective farms also had to comply with the current Five-Year Plan, which set up rigid delivery schedules for specified crops. Looking back on collectivization a full generation later, it is still too early to tell whether Soviet Russia gained more by imposing strict controls on stubborn, backward, and independent peasants or lost more by the frightful destruction wrought in the wake of collectivization. Collective farmers, sullen and suspicious of the regime, continue to prefer to work on their private plots. To this day about half—and certainly the more toothsome half—of the food on Russian dinner tables comes from the private plots.

Opposition arises to Stalin's forced revolutionizing of society. In the early 1930's the modest rise in living standards achieved under NEP was wiped out. Food and housing were rationed. Men and women were exhausted by long hours of bleak work, their minds bewildered by the constant repetition of the slogans of Marxism-Leninism. Industrialization and collectivization brought a new Iron Age to the peoples of Russia. Stalin claimed that they had been raised to a superior stage of human development. In 1935 he officially declared that "socialism" had been achieved; in 1936 he issued a new constitution suitable to that "higher" form of social existence.

Yet the ideological gloss could not hide the deep tensions of a society revolutionized against its will. High-tempo nation-building by force and terror—the essence of Stalinism—creates a silent tide of resistance that breaks forth whenever controls are relaxed. In Stalin's Russia it made the party's role more difficult and it threatened the power of the Secretary-General. Stalin had to accept responsibility for the sacrifice of the millions of lives lost in the wild plunge into industrialization and collectivization. The reproaches even reached into his family, for his wife was driven to commit

The Soviet Union in 1939

The Soviet Union is made up of fifteen republics, each named for the major nationality which inhabits it.

KEY

Annexed in 1939 under terms of Nazi-Soviet Pact

Annexed in 1940

suicide in 1932. There was grumbling in the Communist Party as well, clearly expressed at the Party Congress of 1934. Stalin, it was said, had gone too far. Was he going to step down now in favor of the Leningrad Party Secretary, Sergei Kirov (*kee'*ruhf), an able and moderate Communist whom the Central Committee of the party seemed to be grooming for the succession? The mere thought of losing power drove Stalin to insane fury.

Stalin turns to purges to create a monolithic state. Refusing to resign, Stalin struck back with stark, relentless terror. Terror had been part of communist rule since 1917. During the first Five-Year Plan it had been used in public trials of "saboteurs and wreckers" to intimidate those who deplored the inefficiencies of hasty planning. Now Stalin employed terror in self-defense. In December, 1934, he plotted the murder of Kirov, whom he subsequently glorified as the victim of a conspiracy involving all Stalin's enemies among the right and left deviation. Thereafter, with fiendish vengeance Stalin pursued his enemies and would-be enemies in the party and among the population at large in a purge of mass proportions. This purge, lasting from 1935 into 1939, claimed the lives of several million Russians. Whenever a new wave of arrests was imminent, the streets of Moscow and other cities would empty as men and women sat tight in their rooms awaiting the midnight call of the secret police, the N.K.V.D. After their arrest they were subjected to days of unending interrogation without being allowed to sleep. After 1937, they were subject to bodily torture as well. The interrogation continued until the prisoners signed their "confessions." Fictitious accounts of the most incredible crimes against Stalin and the Soviet state, these confessions implicated not only Trotsky and the "right deviation" but even the closest friends of those who "confessed."

For some of the most prominent Bolsheviks, public "show trials" were staged in 1936, 1937, and 1938, designed to build up public confidence in and awe of Stalin. The world was stunned by the spectacle of hardened Communists denouncing and demeaning themselves like mindless puppets. Many of the accused were shot without delay, some praising Stalin as they died. Others were sent to forced-labor camps, where most of them perished after enduring unspeakable hardships. In this fashion Stalin "purged" 70 per cent of the members of the Central Committee that had tried to promote Kirov. He killed off practically all the "old Bolsheviks" who had joined the Communist Party before 1917; in 1940 he even contrived the murder of Trotsky, in exile in Mexico. Those who survived the purges were marked as docile organization men who would never dream of challenging Stalin or the party. By striking terror into every potential source of opposition, Stalin created an abject docility in the party, which had grown to about 1.5 million members. The same brutality was used to intimidate the entire population by striking at the leaders or potential spokesmen of non-Russian nationalist movements, intellectuals, workers, collective farmers, men, women, youth—indeed, all those who disliked the innovations Stalin had introduced. The terror killed more non-party people than Communists, many of them innocent of even the thought of the crimes to which they "confessed."

In a famous speech made in 1956, Khrushchev (kroosh-*tchohf'*), Stalin's successor, made much of Stalin's "distrustful, sickly suspicious nature." Stalin, he said, would look at a man and say: "Why are your eyes so shifty today?" or "Why are you turning so much today and avoid[ing] looking me directly into the eye?" Under Stalin's glance even his closest advisors never knew whether they were to live or die. There can be no question but that Stalin's sanity was undermined by the incredible responsibilities that he carried. Yet in looking at the huge organization required for the conduct of the purges, one cannot but be impressed by their thoroughness. Whatever Stalin's personal vengeance, the fact remains that the peoples of Russia would hardly have accepted so quickly the revolutionary upheavals of industrialization and collectivization without the threat of such bloody punishment. Stalin wiped out much of Soviet Russia's creative spontaneity, but he also created, for generations to come, that monolithic uniformity for which Russia's rulers had yearned for centuries.

CHECK-UP

1. How did Stalin establish himself as the unquestioned head of the Soviet Union? What was the "cult of personality"?

2. Why did Stalin see industrialization as crucial to Soviet development? Why did he decide on forced industrial growth?

3. How did the Five-Year Plans affect consumers? Private businessmen? Workers?

4. What were Stalin's plans for agriculture? What were the advantages of collective farms? How did peasants react to forced collectivization?

5. Why did the Russian people resist Stalin's forced revolutionizing of society?

6. What were the purges? What do they reveal about Stalin's character? What was their effect?

Soviet Communism as a Continuation of Tsarist Autocracy

In the century after the reign of Nicholas I, Russia had fallen to great depths. Yet under Soviet rule it reasserted itself and impressed the world. To this day Soviet Communists insist that the revival of Russian power was the work of the Communist Party. To those who look more deeply, realizing that the Soviet Union has roots in tsarist Russia, it will be apparent that Leninism and Stalinism were a continuation of major aspects of tsarist autocracy. Lenin and Stalin adapted the traditional form of Russian government to the conditions of the twentieth century—mass politics, industrialism, and, above all, the murderous pace of international competition among world powers. Key elements of the old regime were visible in the institutions of the new:

1. Whether under the Orthodox Church or Marxist doctrine, there was concentration of political leadership in one man and the tendency to endow this man with a superior authority.

2. The Communists, as did the tsars, insisted on ideological orthodoxy as a major guarantee of monolithic unity.

3. Like the tsars, the Communists sought to unify state and society for the single purpose of making Russia great and respected in the world.

4. There was a sense of world mission, with Russian leaders of all types advertising the Russian form of government and society as the best for all mankind.

5. In the pursuit of this goal there continued to be a readiness to sacrifice human life on a large scale.

6. The Communists, as did the tsars, showed a marked impatience with the unenlightened ways of the common people and a determination to modernize the masses against their will.

7. Under both tsars and Communists, there was heavy reliance on the police—a secret police at that—for enforcing the leader's will and for creating obedience among the people.

To these traditional elements the Communists added new insights. They recognized that the assertion of Russian power in the world required the fullest use of modern industry and technology. Willingly or not, all of Soviet society had to be trained to have a modern, industrial outlook. Secondly, communist leaders were aware that effective government must be close to the people; it must speak their language and recognize their needs. The Communists never would let the attitudes of the masses stand in the way of their policies; these leaders would not be led by the will of the majority. More than the tsars, they used terror to soften the people's will and make them ready for change. Yet they never relented in their efforts to win the people's good will. They insisted that they were building a workers' state—a society without classes, without exploitation, and without poverty. The Communists, furthermore, realized that building up Russia's international power called for extensive agitation and propaganda throughout the world. Lenin had taught them how to make use of the widespread unrest created by the spread of industrialism and democracy in an unprepared world. Stalin continued the policy of drawing discontented elements into service in the cause of communism.

Above all, to the traditional ambition of the tsars the Communists added a radical fierceness. In their attempts to deliver Russia from backwardness and humiliation they would let no obstacle stand in their way—neither vested interests, nor tradition, nor "sentimental" respect for human life and dignity. In this refusal to let anything stand in the way of their goals lay the secret of their success in making Russia not only a world power, but a super power. That their achievements were accomplished by methods alien and repulsive to Western Europeans and Americans mattered little to the communist leaders. Measured in terms of Russia's adverse conditions, of her backwardness and poverty, the communist leaders made a giant step forward.

Chapter Highlights

autocracy	bureaucracy	repression	Russification
soviets	orthodoxy	purge	indoctrinated
tsar	communes	nationality	monolithic
mir	anarchists	subversion	duma
kulaks	war communism	socialist realism	
zemstvo	Five-Year Plan	collective farming	

Can you identify?

Lenin	Rasputin	Nicholas I	Bolshevik Revolution
Witte	Kerensky	Imperial Duma	Russian Orthodox Church
Trotsky	Stolypin	Red Army	Decembrist revolt
Stalin	Communists	Khrushchev	Provisional Government
Alexander III	Soviet Union	intelligentsia	March Revolution
Slavophiles	Politburo	Nicholas II	Peter the Great
Alexander II	Crimean War	New Economic Policy	

What do you think?

1. Why was unity more difficult to achieve in tsarist Russia than in a Western European nation?

2. Why might an American find it more difficult to understand the Russian than the British way of life?

3. Why did Russia lag behind Western Europe in 1815?

4. In the 1800's, what did Russians see as the great mission of their country? How capable was Russia of realizing this mission?

5. Why might the abolition of serfdom in Russia be termed "too little and too late"?

6. Why did Nicholas II regard modernization and industrialization as a threat to autocracy? Do you agree? Why?

7. Why were the Bolsheviks able to take over Russia?

8. Why did Lenin follow a more conciliatory policy than Stalin?

9. Why did Lenin encourage international communism?

10. Why did Russian farmers resist collectivization? Do you think their attitude has changed since Stalin's day?

11. How does communist dictatorship resemble tsarist autocracy? Differ? Why were the Communists more successful than the tsars?

12. Is the Soviet government democratic in theory? In practice? Explain.

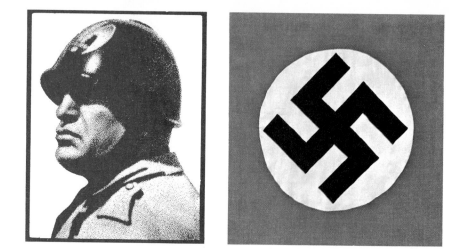

Fascist dictators stirred their people by recalling past glories and promising to restore this greatness. Mussolini (top left) used symbols drawn from the Roman Empire and marched his young fascists past the Forum (below left). Hitler reached back to ancient times for his emblem, the swastika, which he associated with the Aryans. The colors of the Nazi banner (left) are also symbolic: red for socialism and white for nationalism, the original goals of the party.

Fascist Dictatorships

On June 30, 1934, loyal followers of Adolf Hitler went into action to crush a possible revolt in the ranks of the Nazi Storm Troops. Under the orders of Chancellor Hitler, they shot hundreds of victims at home, in offices, in prison, or in the streets. "Like a panther on a dark night so I spring on my enemy and destroy him," said Hitler. In the years to come, millions of people would perish because of the policies of this man.

World War I was supposed to have made the world "safe for democracy." This did not happen. Instead, in many countries ruthless dictators rose to power and established totalitarian states. In Russia, Stalin ruled under the banner of communism (see Chapter 28). In Italy under Benito Mussolini and in Germany under Adolf

Hitler, *fascist* (*fash'*ist) dictatorships were established. Fascist movements developed in Hungary, Romania, Spain, Belgium, France, Britain, and other European countries. So widespread was fascism after World War I that some historians call the period 1919–1945 "the era of fascism." To understand fascism we must first look at conditions that burdened postwar Europe and at the men who took advantage of these conditions to rise to power.

Factors Underlying the Rise of Fascism

In the months immediately following World War I unemployment, low wages, and hunger caused great suffering in Europe. Strikes for higher wages and shorter hours often turned into bloody battles. Inspired by the success of the Bolsheviks in Russia, communist revolutionaries in other lands tried to overthrow existing governments and establish socialist republics. Capitalists, landowners, government officials, army leaders, professional people, and shopkeepers grew increasingly fearful of the working class. The growing strength of labor unions and of socialist parties in politics, and the terrorist activities of communist revolutionaries, worried these men. If the working class is not checked, they said, then what happened in Russia may also happen here. We, too, will lose our property and maybe our lives if the workers gain control of the state. To resist this fear of communism and socialism, fascist parties sprang up throughout Europe. *One factor, therefore, that contributed to the rise of fascism was the fear of communism, especially among members of the middle class.*

Hundreds of thousands of veterans returning from the war added to the unrest in postwar Europe. The years of fighting had hardened many of these men. Veterans who could not get the war out of their blood longed for the excitement of battle and the fellowship they had shared with their comrades in the trenches. Moreover, these men returned home to unemployment and poverty. They felt as if no one cared about their sacrifices at the front. Angry and discouraged, veterans gathered on street corners and in cafes to complain about postwar conditions, to relive their wartime experiences, and to wait for something to happen. They made ideal recruits for fascist movements that preached violence and formed their own private armies. *A second factor contributing to the rise of fascism was the disillusionment of war veterans and the mood of violence bred by the war.*

In the years following World War I, European lands experienced periods of disorder, unrest, and violence. During these crises governments seemed helpless to introduce effective reforms. Many people lost faith in political parties, the process of parliamentary government, and the ideals of democracy. Fascists

Fascist Dictatorships

October, 1922	Fascist "March on Rome," Mussolini becomes prime minister
November, 1923	Attempted overthrow of the government of Bavaria fails; Hitler imprisoned
January, 1933	Hitler becomes Chancellor of Germany
March, 1935	Hitler repudiates disarmament clauses of Versailles Treaty
October, 1935	Italy invades Ethiopia
July, 1936	Outbreak of Spanish Civil War
October, 1936	Berlin-Rome axis formed. Franco appointed Chief of the Spanish State, establishes a fascist-type dictatorship

offered a new system of government. Instead of a number of political parties with differing aims, there would be only one party, the fascist party, with one goal. Instead of endless discussions in parliament, which seemed to get nowhere, the fascists promised one all-powerful leader to enact and enforce meaningful laws. Instead of trying to meet the conflicting wishes of individuals and to protect their rights, the fascists would concentrate on building a powerful and respected state. Fascist promises proved particularly attractive in countries where democracy had a short and unsuccessful history. In these countries many people, feeling that democracy was a failure, were eager to experiment with what seemed a more promising system of government. *A third factor contributing to the rise of fascism was the apparent inability of democratic parliamentary governments to cope with the many pressing problems that burdened postwar Europe.*

In a sense, fascism was the fulfillment of the aggressive nationalism that arose in many European countries in the last part of the nineteenth century. Fascist leaders promised to gain new lands for their nations or to win back lands lost as a result of World War I. By stressing nationalism, fascism could appeal to all men, both rich and poor, who felt that nothing was more important than the glory of their country. *A fourth factor contributing to the rise of fascism was its appeal to nationalists who longed to expand the frontiers of their fatherland and to avenge defeats.*

World War I caused men to challenge the traditional values of western civilization. Many men lost faith in Christianity. They lost confidence in the power of reason (rationalism) to solve men's problems. Liberal doctrines stressing individual freedom seemed outdated. Confidence in man's ability to progress was replaced by insecurity and lack of faith in the future. Many men, particularly the young, sought new beliefs and values. To them, fascism seemed a dynamic and noble cause. *A fifth factor contributing to the rise of fascism was the insecurity which caused men to lose confidence in traditional values and to seek a new faith and new values.*

Economic insecurity, fear of communism, disenchantment with democracy, a growing stress on violence, an intensified nationalism, and the yearning for new causes were among the postwar conditions that contributed to the rise of fascism. How did fascist leaders take advantage of these conditions to gain power in Italy and Germany?

CHECK-UP

1. Why was there a growing fear of communism in Europe immediately following World War I? How did war veterans contribute to postwar unrest?

2. Why did people lose faith in parliamentary government in the postwar period? What promises were held out by fascism? How did fascism appeal to nationalists?

Fascist Italy

Mussolini craves power. Fascism achieved its first successes in Italy under the guiding hand of Benito Mussolini (bay-*nee'*toh moos-soh-*lee'*nee). Mussolini was born on July 29, 1883, in a small Italian village. His father was a blacksmith, his mother a schoolteacher. Mussolini's character was shaped by his home life. Taught by his father to hate the government and the Church, Mussolini grew up a rebel against authority. His teachers found the young Mussolini difficult to control. His school record contained the following evaluation:

His character is passionate and unruly; and he cannot adapt himself to the life of the school, where, he is convinced, he has been sent as a punishment. . . . He places himself in opposition to every rule and discipline of the school. . . . One personal motive guides him; . . . he wishes to [avenge] every injury inflicted [on him]. . . . He rebels against every punishment and correction.

But the troublemaker was also intelligent. In his final examinations he ranked first in four subjects.

After graduation Mussolini became a schoolteacher. Hungering for a life of action, he found the classroom boring. He wanted the excitement of being a leader of men. Mussolini soon found an outlet for his ambitions. He became a socialist revolutionary, hoping to lead the working class in a life-and-death struggle to overthrow capitalism. His talents were quickly recognized and rewarded. In 1912, at the age of 29, he was made editor of *Avanti!*, the Italian Socialist Party newspaper. However, during the early days of World War I, Mussolini was expelled from the Socialist Party for urging that Italy enter the conflict. (Italian socialists strongly opposed Italy's entry into World War I.) When Italy went to war in 1915, Mussolini enlisted in the armed forces.

After the war, Mussolini saw himself as a man destined for greatness, a second Caesar or Napoleon. Organizing his own political movement, the Fascist Party, Mussolini made plans to gain control of the government. But first he had to win popular support and, even more important, the backing of Italian industrialists, military leaders, and high government officials. How did Mussolini appeal to the Italian people?

Postwar conditions foster unrest in Italy. In the years following World War I Italy experienced hard times and disorder. Food shortages, rising prices, and lack of jobs made people restless and dissatisfied. Many businesses went bankrupt. Land-hungry peasants were seeking to break up the estates of the large landowners. A wave of violent strikes swept across the nation as workers demanded more pay and shorter hours. Italian businessmen feared that these strikes were the beginning of a working-class revolution. The return of hundreds of thousands of war veterans added to the unrest. Though Italy had been on the winning side of the war, she had the appearance of a defeated state.

Italian nationalists were disappointed with the peace settlement. They had expected Italy to gain more land from the former Austro-Hungarian Empire. They also expected to receive some of Germany's former colonies. When Italy got less than expected, nationalists protested that their country had been cheated and humiliated at the peace conferences. Despite her 500,000 dead and one million wounded, Italy had been robbed of the fruits of victory, said these nationalists. The nationalists were ready to welcome the leadership of anyone who would lead Italy to greatness and gain lands denied her in the peace settlement.

Worsening economic conditions had led to the outbreak of violence in many areas. Strong leadership and a reform program might have solved Italy's problems. But the government was weak, and the Italian parliament, paralyzed by party disputes, seemed unable to cope with the crisis. The feeling grew throughout Italy that new leaders and a different system of government were needed.

Mussolini tries to appeal to all levels of society. The widespread unrest gave Mussolini an opportunity to appeal to the various dissatisfied groups.

1. He promised big business and the large landowners that the fascists would save Italy from communism. Although there was really little danger of a communist takeover in Italy, most capitalists were badly scared. They saw what was happening in Russia, and realized that if communists seized power, capitalists would lose their property and perhaps their lives. Big business and wealthy landowners therefore contributed large sums of money to the Fascist Party.

2. Fascism proved particularly attractive to the middle class. Joining the ranks of the fascists were university students eager for adventure and shopkeepers and professional people who feared the growing power of the working class. The Italian middle class considered itself better than the working class. It regarded labor unions and the Socialist Party as threats to private property and feared the rise of a working-class state. To counter the growing strength of the working class, fascist gangs engaged in acts of terrorism against workers' organizations.

3. At the same time Mussolini was wooing capitalists and the middle class, he also tried to convince the working man that fascism would improve his living and working conditions. He promised workers an eight-hour day, workmen's compensation, old-age insurance, and worker participation in the management of certain industries. Impressed with Mussolini's promises, thousands of workers deserted the Socialist Party to join the ranks of the fascists. Nevertheless, it was the middle class rather than the workers that gave Mussolini his chief support.

4. Nationalists applauded Mussolini's demands for a greater and more powerful Italy. He was the leader they were looking for.

5. Thousands of veterans became active members of the Fascist Party. Fascism offered men hardened by war an escape from the boredom of civilian life. The fascists, organized along military lines, wore uniforms, carried weapons, and paraded in the streets. They also fought bloody battles with their socialist and labor-union opponents. Fascism made the veteran feel important.

6. Many army officers wanted a strong government that would put an end to the strikes and disturbances that plagued Italy. They also dreamed of an Italian empire. These army officers gave Mussolini encouragement and support.

Mussolini concentrates power in his own hands. By 1922 the fascists had gained sufficient strength to convince Mussolini that he should make a bid for power. Speaking at a giant rally of his followers in late October, Mussolini said, "Either they will give us the government or we shall take it by descending on Rome. It is now a matter of days, perhaps of hours." A few days later thousands of fascists began a march on Rome. Leaders in the Italian parliament demanded that the army be used to defend the government. It would have been a simple matter for the army to crush the fascist columns, but King Victor Emmanuel III refused to act. The King's advisors, some of them generals who supported fascism, exaggerated the strength of the fascists. The weak king, thinking that he was saving Italy from violence, appointed Mussolini prime minister. Fascism had triumphed because few people felt that the government in power was worth fighting for, and because key officials in the government, the army, and the police sided with the fascists.

Once Mussolini was in power, he gradually established a totalitarian state in which all activities of the Italian people were controlled by the fascist government. "Nothing, human or spiritual, . . ." said Mussolini, "has value outside the State." In time Mussolini crushed all other political parties, created a secret police to spy on possible enemies, and imprisoned or deported anyone who threatened his power. Since the government controlled the radio, press, and movies, the Italian people were told only what Mussolini wanted them to know. In the schools youngsters were taught to admire *Il Duce* (eel *doo'*chay, The Leader) and to accept his teaching without question, for "Mussolini is always right." Professors in the universities were required to swear an oath of loyalty to the fascist state. Fascist propaganda stressed obedience to *Il Duce* ("Believe! Obey! Fight!"), devotion to the fatherland, the greatness of fascism, the glory of war ("A minute on the battlefield is worth a lifetime of peace"), and the duty of fascists to conquer new lands for Italy.

The fascists hoped to build a great and powerful Italy by regulating social and economic life. To ensure a steady supply of soldiers, Mussolini made it difficult for Italians to leave the country and encouraged Italian families to have more children. Heads of large families received cash bonuses and government jobs. The fascist state tried to make Italy self-sufficient—independent of other nations for agricultural and industrial goods. To win the "battle of wheat," marshes were drained and Italian farmers were encouraged to adopt improved methods of cultivation. Industries were ordered to increase output, particularly of products meeting military needs. If important raw materials were in short supply, scientists were ordered to find synthetics. Although production did increase, fascist Italy never came close to being self-sufficient.

Mussolini puts an end to industrial strife. Mussolini was particularly concerned about labor disputes which led to violent and wasteful strikes. Pointing out that such strife weakened the nation, the fascists abolished labor unions and outlawed strikes. Instead, associations were formed that included both workers and employers in the various industries. These associations were actually controlled by the state and in general favored employers. Although in theory worker and employer representatives in a given association were supposed to cooperate in solving problems, labor had little voice in economic matters. Fascist officials, in cooperation with businessmen, actually determined wage rates and hours of employment. Although courts established to settle labor disputes at times ruled in favor of the workers, the most important cases were settled to the advantage of employers. "As long as I am in power," said Mussolini, "the employers have nothing to fear from the Labor Courts."

Mussolini claimed that farmers and factory workers were better off under fascism than ever before. Actually, whereas the big industrialists and the large landowners reaped huge profits, the standard of living for the common people declined after Mussolini came to power. Writes American historian S. William Halperin:

The condition of millions of agricultural laborers was especially wretched; their working day was lengthened without a corresponding increase in pay; their right to unemployment insurance was disregarded; and their purchasing power, like that of the urban proletariat, fell consistently. Despite the [many] official pronouncements about the importance of developing an independent, healthy, and prosperous peasantry, Mussolini bestowed his favors not on the [peasants] but on his allies, the big landowners.

Mussolini proclaimed that Italy was the heir of ancient Rome. He promised to restore Italy to her former greatness and to found a second Roman Empire. Italians would once again control the Mediterranean as had their Roman ancestors. Mussolini enjoyed playing the role of a Roman emperor. He gloried in the wild cheers of his followers: *"Duce! Duce! Duce!* We are yours to the end." But modern Italy lacked the military might, industrial resources, and technical skills to build a great empire. The Italian people, basically peace-loving, had no desire to become a nation of warriors. Mussolini might be cheered by crowds but few who cheered were willing to die for him.

CHECK-UP

1. Who was Benito Mussolini? What were his hopes and interests as a young man? How did his views change during World War I?

2. What were conditions like in postwar Italy? Why were Italian nationalists disappointed with the peace settlement? Why was the Italian government unable to solve Italy's problems?

3. How did Mussolini's program appeal to big business and landowners? The middle class? The working man? Nationalists and veterans? Army officers?

4. How did Mussolini come to power? What kind of state did he create? How did he regulate social and economic life? What was his approach to settling industrial strife?

5. Which groups in Italian society benefited from Mussolini's rule? How? Which groups suffered? Why?

6. Why was it unlikely that Fascist Italy could achieve the greatness of ancient Rome?

If Fascist Italy lacked the power to pose a serious threat to world peace, the case of Germany was different. It was in Germany under Adolf Hitler that fascism became a most dangerous and destructive force.

Both Mussolini and Hitler sought power, glorified the military, and stressed the importance of the party leader. But there was a basic difference between Italian fascism and German nazism. Mussolini sought power for its own sake, and had no clearly defined program. "It is not programs that are wanting for the salvation of Italy," said Mussolini, "but men and will power." Hitler, on the other hand, wanted power in order to impose his strongly held beliefs upon Germany and upon the rest of Europe.

Hitler's early life influences his outlook. Hitler was born April 20, 1889, in a small town in Austria. A mediocre student, Hitler left school at sixteen without receiving a diploma. Hoping to become an artist, he set out for Vienna, and applied for admission to the Academy of Fine Arts. He was rejected for lack of talent.

In Vienna, Hitler was a loner. Though always short of cash, he never cared about holding a steady job. From 1909 to 1914 he made a meager living designing postcards and posters, and spent hours reading books on history and politics. These years in Vienna, said Hitler, were the "saddest period of my life."

When World War I broke out, Hitler was overjoyed. "I fell down on my knees and thanked heaven from an overflowing heart for granting me the good fortune of being permitted to live at this time." Hitler was eager for combat. Up to now he had been a failure. Perhaps the war would change all that. Rejected by the Austrian army as "too weak for military service," Hitler volunteered to serve in the German army.

He proved to be a good soldier, and twice was decorated for bravery. When the war ended, Corporal Hitler was in the hospital recovering from being gassed, which had temporarily blinded him. The years as a drifter in Vienna and as a soldier at the front had hardened Hitler. Filled with violent hatreds, he was without any feelings of pity for those who opposed him. Possessing great confidence in himself, he was determined never again to be a "nobody." To satisfy his overwhelming desire for power, he decided to enter politics.

The German Empire collapses. In the last days of World War I and just afterwards, life in Germany was marked by confusion, unrest, and strife. Almost to the end of the war the German people had been convinced that their army would be victorious. Defeat left them in a state of shock. Early in November war-weary soldiers, sailors, and workers seized control of cities in northern and western Germany and raised republican flags. The revolt soon spread to other parts of the country, and the German state of Bavaria established an independent Bavarian Republic under socialist leadership. On November 10, Kaiser Wilhelm II fled to Holland, and the following day German delegates accepted the armistice terms dictated by the Allies.

The Weimar Republic faces opposition on all sides. An elected national assembly meeting in Weimar (*vye'*mahr) adopted a republican constitution in February, 1919. The socialist majority elected Friedrich Ebert (*free'*drihk *ey'*bert) President of the new German Republic, often referred to as the Weimar Republic. The leaders of the Weimar Republic were eager for democracy to succeed. But many Germans, used to authoritarian rule, had no confidence in parliamentary democracy. Not surprisingly, the

669

Weimar Republic faced attacks from both the left and the right.

On the left, communists felt that the revolution which overthrew the kaiser had not gone far enough. Communists wanted to establish a workers' state patterned after the Soviet Union. In January, 1919, the communists actually had staged a bloody uprising in Berlin which was crushed by the army aided by organizations of ex-servicemen. In the months that followed, other communist uprisings broke out in German cities, including Berlin and Munich, and in neighboring Austria and Hungary, but all ended in failure. These uprisings and the violent changes introduced in Russia by the Bolsheviks terrified the German people.

On the right, the Weimar Republic was attacked by nationalists, militarists, the great industrialists, large landowners, and all other people who favored the old imperial regime. The leading political party under the Weimar Republic was the Social Democratic Party. The Social Democrats supported democracy and wanted to introduce moderate social reforms in order to improve conditions for the working class. To the great industrialists and the large landowners, the Social Democrats seemed little better than communists. Men of wealth feared that the Social Democrats might decide to break up large estates and to nationalize industry (put it under government control).

When a great nation passes through a shocking and bitter experience, there is a tendency for people to seek a *scapegoat* on which to heap the blame. This is what happened to the leaders of the Weimar Republic. Militarists and nationalists spread the myth that the German soldiers had not been defeated in battle but had been "stabbed in the back" by the socialists, communists, and peace lovers who launched a revolution at home. Somehow the liberal Weimar Republic came to be blamed for things for which it was not responsible: the defeat in World War I and the Versailles Treaty. In reality it had been the German generals who had urged the government to sue for peace. The men who took power in November, 1918, had no

choice but to agree to a cease-fire and to sign the Treaty of Versailles. The German army had been defeated and was in no condition to continue the fighting. Nevertheless, the leaders of the Weimar Republic were blamed for Germany's defeat, for the humiliating peace terms, and for the postwar misery in Germany.

In time, militarists and chauvinists, and doubtless many who were neither, came to favor a policy of replacing the Weimar Republic. They wanted a government that would rebuild the German army, revise the Treaty of Versailles, and restore Germany to a position of power in world affairs. The demand for revision of the Versailles Treaty was widespread both among the traditionally nationalistic middle class and the peasantry. Hitler later was to draw considerable support from these groups. Among the rightist foes of the Weimar Republic, none looked forward to its destruction more eagerly than did Adolf Hitler.

Hitler sets down his views in Mein Kampf. Hitler began his political career in the south German city of Munich. There he joined an insignificant political party which had few members and no money. Displaying extraordinary talent as a public speaker, Hitler soon gained control of the party, which was named the National Socialist Workers' (Nazi) Party. With Hitler as its leader, the party began to grow. In 1923, following an attempt to overthrow the government of Bavaria, Hitler was sentenced to five years in jail. Although he served less than nine months of this sentence, his imprisonment was of great importance. It gave him the opportunity to write down his political views in a book entitled *Mein Kampf* ("My Struggle"). What did Hitler and National Socialism stand for?

1. An extreme nationalist, Hitler demands expansion. Above all, Hitler advocated German nationalism. He appealed to nationalist sentiments by denouncing the Treaty of Versailles. He said its terms were unjust and degrading to all true Germans. Germany should refuse to pay reparations; she should rearm and prepare to regain her "rightful lands"—lands taken away from her after World War I. Hitler talked of uniting all the Germans in Europe under one flag and declared that someday Germans would expand eastward in Europe:

... we National Socialists ... aim ... to secure for the German people the land and soil to which they are entitled on this earth. ... Only the might of a victorious sword ... will win soil for us. ... We ... primarily have in mind ... Russia and her ... border states.

2. Success depends on leadership. To avenge Germany's defeat in World War I and build a mighty German empire, it was necessary, said Hitler, to destroy the Weimar Republic. Democracy enabled cowardly, weak, and stupid men to rise to high positions. The quarrels of politicians and political parties kept a nation weak and divided. Germany could become strong only if there were but one party, one policy, and one leader to guide her. Hitler was certain that he was *Der Führer* (fyoo′rer, The Leader) who could rescue Germany from defeat and despair.

3. Great goals call for aggressive action. From the outset, Hitler urged violence and war. He wanted to replace Christian teachings of brotherly love with the law of the jungle—survival of the fittest. He stated it plainly:

The whole of nature is a continuous struggle between strength and weakness, an eternal victory of the strong over the weak. ...

Struggle is the father of all things. ... As it is with the individual so it is in the destiny of nations. Only by struggle are the strong able to raise themselves above the weak. And every people that loses out in this eternally shifting struggle has, according to the laws of nature, received its just desert. ...

If men wish to live, then they are forced to kill others. ... One is either the hammer or the anvil. We confess that it is our purpose to prepare the German people for the role of the hammer. ...

We confess further that we will dash anyone to pieces who should dare to hinder us in this undertaking. ... Our rights will be protected only when

the German Reich [state] is again supported by the point of the German dagger.

4. Jews are the enemies of the "master race." Racism was a basic doctrine of National Socialism. Hitler was certain that the Germans were a superior people, descended from the ancient Aryans.[1] "All the human culture, all the results of art, science, and technology that we see before us today," said Hitler, "are almost exclusively the creative products of the Aryan." Other "races," such as Jews, Slavs, and gypsies, were inferior to the Aryan and existed only to serve their German masters. When such inferior "races" intermarried with Germans, said Hitler, they made the Aryan blood impure and weakened the nation. These crude ideas were an outgrowth of racist thinking that had become popular in the last part of the nineteenth century (see pages 536–537).

Nazi racism took its most deadly form in *anti-semitism,* hatred of Jews. For centuries Christians had persecuted Jews for religious reasons—because the Jews had rejected Christ. For Hitler and his fellow Nazis, Christian reasons for persecuting the Jews had little meaning. They hated the Jews for other reasons.

(*a*) *Nationalist reasons.* The Nazis were extreme nationalists who felt every action and thought should be devoted to serving the fatherland. To them, the Jews were a foreign, inferior, and dangerous "race" that threatened Germany. In Nazi minds even Jews whose families had been living in Germany for centuries could not be considered Germans. For Germany to attain its rightful place as the greatest nation on earth, these foreign elements must be destroyed. "Death to the Jews," became a Nazi slogan. Instead of quarreling among themselves, the Germans could direct their anger at the Jews.

[1] The Aryans were an ancient people, one branch of which conquered India (page 200). Another branch invaded Europe, and most European languages are derived from their language. Since the Aryans long ago merged with the peoples they conquered, it is incorrect to speak of an "Aryan race," as did Hitler. Germans, Jews, Slavs—all are ethnic groups, not races.

Hatred of the Jews became a convenient way of uniting the German people.

(*b*) *Economic and social reasons.* Out of Germany's total population of 60 million there were only some 550,000 Jews. But this small percentage of Jews had achieved success in many fields—10.9 per cent of the doctors, 10.7 per cent of the dentists and dental technicians, and 3.6 per cent of the druggists were Jews. The Jews accounted for 5.1 per cent of the editors and authors, 16.3 per cent of the lawyers, and 2 per cent of the musicians. Jews were active in the retail trades and many department stores were owned by Jews. Jews played an important though declining role in small- and medium-sized banking. (The largest banks were controlled by corporations in which Jews had virtually no influence.) While the Jews had achieved great social and economic success, in reality they had little power in Germany. In the most important segments of German society—the army, heavy industry, large landownership, big banking, and the highest levels of the civil service—the Jews played no role. Nevertheless, many Germans resented the Jews for their achievements, particularly in cultural life and in the professions, and believed that they had too great a part in German life.

(*c*) *Political reasons.* In general, European Jews were strong supporters of liberalism and social reform. Most of them favored parliamentary government, help for the needy, respect for individual rights, the equality of man, international cooperation, and peace—everything that the Nazis rejected. The Nazis felt that "Jewish liberalism" and "Jewish Marxism" threatened the German people. The true character of Germany, said the Nazis, was based on the peasants' love for the soil, the closely knit German family, respect for the army, devotion

Hitler (above) rose to power through a combination of careful planning and charismatic oratory. His use of military pageantry helped generate a collective loyalty in the audiences he addressed. Swastikas, the Nazi symbol, predominate in this view of Hitler's most spectacular rally (right), held in Nuremberg in 1938.

to the fatherland, and obedience to the ruler. Capitalism and Marxism, the Nazis insisted, were foreign ideas, part of a Jewish conspiracy to kill the German spirit and enslave the nation. The German people, who had been united as brothers, said Hitler, were being torn apart by class warfare, capitalist exploitation, and Marxist revolutionaries. The Jews, insisted Hitler, were plotting to force communism on Germany. This must be stopped.

(*d*) *Psychological reasons.* Ultimately there may be no rational explanation for Hitler's hatred of the Jews. Hitler had convinced himself that the Jews were an evil people engaged in a mortal racial struggle with the Germans. In this he revealed a deeply warped personality, one given to rage, fanaticism, and obsession. It seems absurd to believe that 550,000 Jews could threaten a nation of 60 million people. In reality the Jews were a weak minority, proud of their German citizenship and their many contributions to German culture. Alan Bullock, British historian and author of an excellent biography of Hitler, describes the irrationality of *Der Führer's* anti-semitism:

In all the pages which Hitler devotes to the Jews in *Mein Kampf* he does not bring forward a single fact to support his wild assertions [claims]. This was entirely right, for Hitler's anti-semitism bore no relation to facts; it was pure fantasy. . . . The Jew is no longer a human being, he has become . . . a . . . devil. . . . The Jew is everywhere responsible for everything . . . Hitler disliked.

Searching for simple explanations for Germany's misfortunes and convinced that *Der Führer* always knew what was best, Hitler's followers embraced the anti-semitism of their leader. Hated because they were considered different, resented for their prominence and achievements, powerless to fight back, the Jews were convenient scapegoats. The Nazis told the German people: You are out of work because of the Jews. Germany lost the war because of the Jews. Jewish capitalists have impoverished Germany. The Jews are spreading communism in Germany. Hitler and his henchmen screamed:

"We know the enemy, we have called him by name for the last twenty years: He is the World Jew. And we know that the Jew must die."

5. *Mass support is essential.* Before the French and Industrial Revolutions, most governments were controlled either by a king or a small group of aristocrats and upper-class businessmen. Throughout Europe the political changes resulting from the Industrial Revolution gave the common people a greater voice in the government. Having won the right to vote, the masses became an important force in politics; their vote could decide elections. Better than any politician of his time, Hitler understood the importance of the masses in the modern state. "To be a leader means to be able to move masses," he wrote. The man who could arouse, organize, and control the common people would be invincible. Such a man could become master of Germany.

Hitler knew how to win the support of the masses. Repeat over and over again what you want them to believe. Give them enemies to hate and a leader to obey. Do not confuse them with complicated ideas. Arouse their emotions with rallies, parades, and speeches. Use violence to impress them with the power of your movement. Tell the people what they want to hear. Never compromise or show any other signs of weakness.

Hitler's ideas were not new. Notions of extreme nationalism, violence, militarism, racism, dictatorship, and appealing to the masses had been circulating around Europe since the last part of the nineteenth century. But Hitler also had the political genius and the charismatic personality (page 538) to organize and lead a political party that could gain control over a modern state.

Hitler capitalizes on hard times and the fear of communism. When Hitler was released from prison, one might have thought that his political career was at an end. His plot to seize power had failed. In the election of 1928 the Nazi Party won only 12 of the 472 seats in the *Reichstag* (*rikes'*tahk), the German parliament. But Hitler's confidence in his destiny was unshaken. He continued to build for the future.

Movements like nazism thrive when times are hard, when there is unrest and disorder, when men are poor, hungry, insecure, and unhappy. For the first five years of its existence the Weimar Republic had faced one crisis after another. Between 1924 and 1929, when conditions in Germany were relatively good, the Nazi Party gained little support. But in the fall of 1929 the world was hit by the Great Depression.

The Depression caused great suffering throughout the world: trade declined, banks collapsed, factories closed down, prices of stocks and bonds fell drastically, businesses in large numbers went bankrupt, and unemployment soared. The Depression hit Germany particularly hard, and by 1932 there were over six million unemployed. Throughout the nation there was great misery.

Hitler welcomed the Depression. He knew that misery breeds unrest. From the ranks of the unemployed Hitler gained many followers. Made desperate by the hard times, people turned to Hitler, who promised an immediate solution to Germany's problems. When the Nazis come to power, you shall have work and no one shall go hungry, Hitler told them. We shall end corruption in government and exploitation in business.

The Nazi Party helped the unemployed to regain their pride. States Professor William Ebenstein:

The worst feature of unemployment is . . . the feeling of being useless, unwanted, outside of the respectable ranks of society. . . . By putting an unemployed person into uniform, a fascist movement makes him feel that he "belongs," and by telling him that he is a member of a superior race or nation, such a movement restores some of his self-respect.

Young men without work joined the Storm Troopers, Hitler's private army. They were given food, shelter, and uniforms and a chance to do something. The Nazi Party made their lives exciting and meaningful. "For us National Socialism is an idea, a faith, a religion," wrote one of Hitler's Storm Troopers at this time.

Bands of Storm Troopers broke up meetings of politicians hostile to National Socialism, attacked Jews, and engaged in street fights with communists. Violence in the streets was leading to the disintegration of the Weimar Republic.

Hitler also capitalized on the German people's fear of communism. Between 1928 and 1932 the communist party had almost doubled its representation in the Reichstag. While there was little chance that the communists would gain control of the government, many Germans regarded communism as a great threat to the fatherland. They saw Hitler as the man who could save Germany from communism. Looking back on these days, one German stated:

The Nazi slogan in 1932 was, "If you want your country to go Bolshevik, vote Communist; if you want to remain free Germans, vote Nazi!" . . . Bolshevism looked like slavery and the death of the soul. It didn't matter [whether] you were in agreement with Nazism. Nazism looked like the only defense.

The National Socialists gain strength. By the end of 1932 the National Socialists had become the strongest political party in Germany, though they were still far from having a majority in the Reichstag. A small group of influential industrialists, large landowners, bankers, politicians, and some generals wanted Hitler to be appointed chancellor. Although they disliked Hitler's extreme views and were unhappy because he came from the lower class, they counted on him to save Germany from communism. They also believed that he would reduce the power of the labor unions and the socialists, put an end to the political quarrels that weakened the government, and restore the profitable armaments industry. Although army leaders regarded Hitler as a troublemaker who whipped up the emotions of the masses, they did nothing to prevent the Nazi take-over. They regarded the Weimar Republic as inefficient and weak, and they expected Hitler to rebuild the German army and to destroy the hated Treaty of Versailles. Hostile to the Weimar Republic from its birth, many influential Germans gave their support to the man who was the sworn enemy of democracy. They urged the elderly President of the Republic, Paul von Hindenburg, to appoint Hitler chancellor. Both the capitalists and the generals believed that they could control Hitler. They were mistaken; Hitler took orders from no one.

CHECK-UP

1. Why did Hitler welcome the outbreak of World War I? How did it shape his life?

2. What were conditions like in Germany after World War I? What groups opposed the Weimar Republic? Why? How did the Weimar Republic become a scapegoat for Germany's defeat and postwar problems?

3. What views did Hitler express in *Mein Kampf?* Why did he advocate aggressive action to achieve nationalist goals?

4. What did Hitler mean by the "master race"?

5. Why were Jews singled out as the enemies of the "master race"? Consider nationalist reasons, economic and social reasons, political reasons, and psychological reasons.

6. How did Hitler obtain widespread acceptance of his views?

7. How was the Nazi movement affected by the threat of communism? The Great Depression? Why did a growing number of Germans turn to Hitler for leadership? Why did German army officers support the Nazi movement?

Germany Under the Nazis

From a nobody in Vienna, Hitler had climbed to the heights of power. Now he had an opportunity to put the theories of National Socialism into practice. What was life like in Hitler's *Third Reich?*[2]

The Third Reich becomes a dictatorship. Soon after taking office Hitler made himself an absolute dictator and turned Germany into a totalitarian state. He banned all political parties except his own, dissolved the trade unions, gained control over the army, and had real and imaginary enemies killed. Many innocent people were sent to concentration camps where they were degraded, beaten, and tortured. Later, during World War II, certain concentration camps became murder factories in which mil-

[2] Reich (*rike*) is the German word for empire. The First Reich was the Holy Roman Empire that began in the Middle Ages; the Second Reich was created in 1871 after the Franco-Prussian War.

lions of people from all over Europe, particularly Jews, were systematically and brutally exterminated. The secret police and the Nazi-controlled law courts made certain that everyone obeyed *Der Führer:* "Whosoever in the future raises a hand against a representative of the Nazi movement or state must know that he will lose his life without delay. It will [be enough] to show that he even nursed the intention of committing such an act." The rights of the individual counted for nothing. All that mattered was obedience to the Leader and the State.

As Hitler's grip over Germany tightened, many Germans were unaware that something unusual was taking place in their country. Nazi terror struck swiftly and silently; Nazi consolidation of power occurred in stages, often unnoticeably. Few Germans were touched by the terror. To the man concerned with little else but his family, his job, and his friends—and this includes most men in any country—life in the first few years of the Nazi regime seemed quite normal. The average German did not feel persecuted by the new system. Indeed, he felt that the Nazi government was trying to solve Germany's problems in a vigorous and sensible manner. The Nazis skillfully established their totalitarian state without upsetting the daily life of the great majority of the population. To many people the Nazis appeared as the legal government, not as the gangsters they really were. Moreover, the Nazis found jobs for the unemployed. This won Hitler the support of the great majority of Germans.

The state regulates cultural life. Hitler understood the value of propaganda in converting people to the cause of National Socialism. Propaganda had helped bring Hitler to power. Once the Nazis were in control, it was used to strengthen their hold on the German nation.

All cultural life was regulated by the state. The radio, the press, films, books, art, and the schoolroom—all were used to impress Nazi beliefs on the German people. The Nazis burned books which praised democracy or advocated peace. History was rewritten and taught to fit Nazi views. In German universities, students spent hours studying "race science." Loudspeakers were provided in factories and all work stopped for important propaganda broadcasts. Over and over again Germans were told that they were a superior race of brave warriors, that the Jews were their enemies, that they must obey the teachings of National Socialism, and that Hitler was the greatest leader in German history. In the schools students learned a peculiar kind of science:

The Nordic [German] does not speak much. . . . The people of other races talk a lot, and what they say is superficial, devoid of judgment, and untrue. . . .

To "talk with hands and feet" is typical of the non-Nordic, whereas the Nordic stands quiet when speaking. He may even put his hands into his pockets.

The Nordic possesses a feeling for internal and external cleanliness, while the non-Nordic always lives in dirt when he is among his own people. Many of the animals even stand high above him so far as cleanliness is concerned. . . .

. . . all the better developed characteristics are typical of the Nordic body and the Nordic soul. . . . Non-Nordics are more or less equal to the animals or they form a . . . link to them. *The non-Nordic . . . ranks next to the man-apes.* He is therefore . . . a . . . "sub-man." . . .

Nordic man is . . . the creator of all culture and civilization.

Hitler held that "propaganda must appeal to the feelings of the public rather than to their reasoning power." To arouse people's emotions, the Nazis made clever use of flags, songs, salutes, posters, speeches, rallies, and torchlight parades. The most impressive propaganda spectacles were the giant rallies staged in the city of Nuremberg. The Nuremberg rallies, like the other Nazi propaganda drives, were designed to turn the German people into National Socialists. At these rallies thousands of Germans gathered to witness a spectacle that had tremendous emotional impact and to pledge loyalty to Hitler. Everything was done to impress Germany and the world with the irresistible power, determination, and unity of the Nazi movement. Hundreds of thousands of youths waving flags, Storm Troopers bearing weapons, and workers shouldering long-handled spades paraded past Hitler, who stood at attention, his arm extended in the Nazi salute. The endless columns of marching men, the stirring marches played by huge bands, the chanting and cheering of the spectators, the burning torches and beaming spotlights, and always *Der Führer* looking on like a mighty Nordic chieftain—all combined to cast a magic spell over the people. Aroused to a frenzy of patriotism, they were ready to surrender body and soul to their *Führer* and their fatherland. "Wherever Hitler leads, we follow," thundered thousands of Germans in a giant chorus. Nazi propaganda had done its job well.

Nazi economic policies help business and end unemployment. When Hitler became chancellor in January of 1933, there were some six million unemployed in Germany. In 1937, after four years of Nazi rule, unemployment had fallen to less than one million. By aiding business, starting a program of public works, and by launching a large-scale armaments program, the Third Reich provided work for its citizens. By ending unemployment, Hitler won the enthusiastic support of the common people. Nazi economic policy benefited big business. The elimination of strikes and the expansion of production, especially in armaments, meant increased profits. However, business, like all other aspects of life in the Third Reich, was closely supervised by the state. Like the Italian Fascists, the Nazis sought to make Germany self-sufficient.

Jews are persecuted. The Jews, many of whom were prominent in the intellectual and cultural life of pre-Nazi Germany, lost their citizenship. They were forbidden to hold government jobs or to work as journalists, teachers, lawyers, doctors, actors, stockbrokers, or farmers. Places of business owned by non-Jews would not sell Jews goods or rent rooms to them. Signs reading, "Jews strictly forbidden in this town" or "Jews enter this place at their own risk" were posted in many places. On November 10, 1938, in retaliation for the assassination of a German diplomat in Paris by a young Jew, gangs of Nazis set fire to synagogues, looted Jewish stores, and killed or wounded scores of Jews. Thousands of male Jews were arrested. Many Jews who could fled the country, leaving behind most of their property. For the Jews of Europe this was just the beginning.

National Socialism conflicts with Christianity. The principles of National Socialism conflicted with the teachings of Christianity. Hitler preached the glory of war, racism, and disregard for human rights. Christianity, on the other hand, stresses the blessings of peace, the equality and brotherhood of man, and respect for the individual. To Hitler, Christianity was a Jewish

German caricaturist George Grosz depicted postwar conditions with biting sarcasm. The pessimism characteristic of the postwar period is reflected in this painting of a frenzied demonstration.

invention that turned warriors into sheep. "The heaviest blow that ever struck humanity was the coming of Christianity," said Hitler.

In 1933 Nazi Germany and the Pope reached an agreement that the Nazis would not interfere with the Catholic religion and clergy within Germany as long as Catholics refrained from political activity. This agreement was soon broken by the Nazis. Protestant ministers also came into conflict with the Nazi state. Some pastors joined the underground resistance movement aimed at overthrowing Hitler. One brave clergyman attacked the Nazi regime in these words:

The question at stake is whether there is an authority that stands above all earthly power, the authority of God, Whose commandments are valid independent of space and time, country and race. The question at stake is whether individual man possesses personal rights that no community

677

and no state may take from him; whether man in the final analysis is and should be free, or whether the free exercise of his conscience may be prevented and forbidden by the state.

Over the years many German clergymen, Protestant and Catholic alike, were thrown into concentration camps. Nevertheless, most German clergymen—frightened into silence like their fellow Germans—did not openly protest against Nazi views or policies. As members of a state church, most Protestant ministers were expected to take an oath of loyalty to Hitler. Some clergymen, both Catholic and Protestant, even spoke out in favor of the Nazi state.

Hitler's chief lieutenants impose the policies of the Third Reich. While Hitler was the all-powerful leader, he had devoted lieutenants who also wielded considerable power. Three of the most important were Joseph Goebbels, Hermann Göring, and Heinrich Himmler.

Joseph Goebbels became a supporter of Hitler while the Nazi Party was still struggling to gain power. Goebbels considered Hitler "the only captain with whom one can conquer the world." As Minister of Popular Enlightenment and Propaganda, Goebbels used any and all means to whip up support for nazism. He was a master in the art of propaganda. A German who suffered under nazism said of Goebbels:

The masses are his puppets; he makes them feel, believe, laugh, and cry, as his fancy strikes him. . . . He lies in everything and admires himself for it, and he mocks the masses who fall for him.

The number-two man in the Third Reich was Hermann Göring, a World War I flyer who became head of the German air force. Fat and vain, a one-time drug addict, a lover of art and luxury, Göring used his power in the Third Reich to acquire great wealth. He dressed in fancy uniforms and played the part of a great lord on his country estate. Yet the pleasure-loving Göring could be as ruthless as any other Nazi. During World War II he played a major role in plundering the countries conquered by

Germany. He told the German governors of these lands:

. . . you were not sent out here to work for the welfare of the people in your charge but to squeeze the utmost out of them so that German people may live. . . . This everlasting concern about foreign people must cease once and for all. . . . It makes no difference to me if you say that your people are collapsing from hunger. Let them do so as long as no German collapses.

Heinrich Himmler headed the dread Gestapo—the secret police that came to terrorize much of Europe. Himmler was a fanatic believer in Nazi racial theories. During the war he instructed his S.S. officers (who made up Hitler's most trusted guard) how to treat conquered peoples:

What the nations can offer in the way of good blood of our [German] type, we will take, if necessary by kidnapping their children and raising them here with us. Whether nations live in prosperity or starve to death like cattle interests me only insofar as we need them as slaves.

A man of orderly and disciplined habits, Himmler supervised the murder of Europe's Jews. He carried out his grisly project with the thoroughness of an efficiency expert and the singlemindedness of a fanatic.

National Socialism achieves popular support. Six years after Hitler had come to power the German people saw many things in the new Germany that pleased them. True, they knew of the secret police and concentration camps, and even witnessed the persecution of the Jews. But many Germans, not being directly involved in these things, found it easy to close their eyes to such unpleasantness. Germans admired the new vitality of the fatherland. Businessmen had their profits, workers their jobs. Hitler had rebuilt the German armed forces and showed a spectacular disregard for the Versailles Treaty (see page 620). He had made the world take note of the new Germany. National Socialism, said his admirers, had succeeded where the Weimar Republic had failed. The German people had regained confidence in themselves and pride in the fatherland. Only a few Germans realized that their nation had passed into a long night of barbarism.

What are the reasons for the German acceptance of National Socialism? "Will one ever fully understand the monstrous experience which fell to our lot in the twelve years of the Third Reich?" asks Friedrich Meinecke (*mine'-eh-keh*), a distinguished German historian. "Who is able to explain completely . . . [the] deeper causes?" How could Hitler come to power in a modern European state? How could Nazi doctrines win widespread support among the German people? Why were millions of Germans devoted to *Der Führer?* Historians have suggested a number of reasons for the triumph of National Socialism and its popularity with the German people.

1. Failure of the multi-party system. A major reason for the triumph of National Socialism was the weakness of the multi-party system of the Weimar Republic. Unlike the two-party system in the United States, the Weimar Republic had a number of political parties competing for leadership. No one party was able to control enough votes to get a program through the Reichstag. The government was paralyzed by bitter party disputes which prevented the solution of Germany's problems. During the critical months before Hitler was named chancellor, the leading political parties were in such conflict with each other that they were unable to unite against the Nazis. The failure of the multi-party system soured Germans on parliamentary government. Convinced that democracy was not practical for Germany, many Germans welcomed the strong leadership that Hitler promised them.

2. German tradition. Some historians believe that nazism was a continuation of earlier trends in German history. William L. Shirer, author of *The Rise and Fall of the Third Reich,* states: "The mind and the passion of Hitler . . . had roots that lay deep in German experience and thought. Nazism and the Third Reich, in fact, were but a logical continuation of German history." Extreme nationalism, racism, anti-semitism, and authoritarianism were not invented by Hitler. These ideas had won considerable support before the Nazi era. National Socialism, writes British historian A. J. P. Taylor, "represented the deepest wishes of the German people. . . . The generals, the judges, the civil servants, the professional classes, wanted what only Hitler could offer—German mastery of Europe." This view that nazism was the product of German history and German traditions has been challenged by historians. In the history of many European countries, they say, there could be found extreme nationalism, racism, anti-semitism, authoritarianism, and hatred of democracy. The Germans were not especially wicked; their traditions need not have culminated in nazism. These historians say that it was not German tradition but the conditions that existed in Germany, particularly during the Great Depression of the 1930's, that led to the triumph of nazism.

3. A capitalist plot. Some historians blame capitalism for the triumph of National Socialism. Wealthy industrialists and landowners, hostile to labor unions, social reform, and democracy, contributed large sums to nazism. They were pleased when National Socialism weakened labor unions, preserved and protected the estates of large landowners, crushed communism, ended democracy, and launched a great rearmament program. Big business prospered under the Nazi regime.

4. Failure of the generals. The German officer corps has been criticized for helping Hitler rise to power. Many officers supported Hitler because they expected him to rearm Germany and do away with the humiliating Versailles Treaty. Young officers, in particular, were impressed with Hitler's strong nationalism. Believing that they could control him, the generals were not concerned about Hitler's appointment as chancellor. Nor did they oppose Hitler when as a dictator he began to carry out his ruthless policies.[3] The army officers, states Professor Gordon A. Craig, "followed their master to the bitter end, and in doing so inevitably assumed a large share of the responsibility for the crimes of his regime."

5. *Appeal to the lower middle class.* While National Socialism drew support from all classes of society, historians stress its particular appeal to the lower middle class—shopkeepers, small farmers, office workers, teachers, artisans. The lower middle class believed in traditional values of close family ties and loyalty to the fatherland. They felt threatened both by big business and by organized labor. They believed that Hitler would save Germany both from the big capitalists and from those planning to turn Germany into a communist state.

6. *The role of the masses.* Another group of historians sees in National Socialism the dangers resulting from the involvement of the common people of Germany in politics. Politically immature and excitable, the masses demanded quick solutions to very complex problems. Often unwilling to reason or compromise and attracted to simple explanations, they believed many of Hitler's promises. Hitler knew how to play on their fears and arouse their hopes. Whereas absolute kings had based their right to rule on the will of God, Hitler claimed he had the support of the common people. He was right, for his road to power was paved with the cheers and the votes of the masses. "No totalitarian dictatorship has been so willingly accepted by so many people as Hitler's was in Germany," writes American historian George H. Stein. *Der Führer,* a man of the people himself, could only have succeeded in an age when the masses had become a force in politics.

7. *Psychological explanations.* Historians suggest that psychology can help us to understand the Nazi movement. National Socialism appealed to lovers of violence, to men filled with despair, bitterness, and frustration because of their low position in society. George F. Kennan, American diplomat and historian, reminds us that totalitarian movements attract "the ghouls of human society, [who in difficult times come] slinking out of the shadows, ready to take over, ready to flog, to intimidate, to torture, to do all those things in the company of armed men, and preferably against unarmed ones, that help to give them the illusion of success and security." Nazi thugs delighted in humiliating, degrading, and torturing human beings. For centuries civilization has sought to teach man to control his savage and brutal desires. Hitler appealed to and used the evil that is within man.

Besides appealing to what is lowest in man, National Socialism also gave its followers a feeling of fellowship and a cause in which to believe—the greatness of Germany and the unity of the German people. The dedicated Nazi felt he had a mission for which to live; he felt heroic, important, and needed. A young girl described her feelings when Hitler took power:

. . . Hitler wanted to bring greatness, happiness, and well-being to this Fatherland; he wanted to see to it that everyone had work and bread; he would not rest or relax until every single German was an independent, free, and happy man in his Fatherland. We found this good, and in whatever might come to pass we were determined to help to the best of our ability. But there was yet one more thing that attracted us with a mysterious force and pulled us along—namely, the compact columns of marching youths with waving flags, eyes looking straight ahead, and the beat of drums and singing. Was it not overwhelming, this fellowship? Thus it was no wonder that all of us . . . joined the Hitler youth.

Many Germans welcomed rule by a strong man. Hitler relieved them of the uncertainties of life. Many people find it painful to make their own decisions. By following *Der Führer,* the Germans traded their freedom for security.

[3] In July, 1944, a small group of German officers tried to kill Hitler. But as Professor Gordon A. Craig indicates, "the most significant aspect of the officers' revolt was that it failed, and it did so because the great majority of the army's leaders refused to participate in it."

Foreshadowing the horrors of the war that would break out in Europe in 1939 was the Spanish Civil War (1936–1939). It reflected a buildup of hate against oppressive government, crushing poverty, a powerful and intolerant Church, and great social inequalities. Not only the Spanish population, but foreign governments and foreign volunteers became involved in the brutal struggle between right-wing and left-wing factions. In the picture of a woman fleeing her village (right) the photographer has captured a timeless expression of human suffering. Pablo Picasso's Guernica (above), painted in 1937, symbolizes the artist's anguish at the bombing of the small Spanish village by German planes aiding the Falangist forces of Francisco Franco. In this universal protest against the horrors of war, Spain is symbolized by the surviving bull, the dead warrior, and the dying horse. Franco's victory brought the war to an end and established a fascist-style government, but three decades of his rule failed to erase the scars of the war.

8. *The man and the times.* While historians may quarrel with some of the above interpretations, they all agree that the victory of National Socialism was due in large measure to the extraordinary talents of Adolf Hitler and the conditions that existed in Germany after World War I. This evil genius used to his advantage all the grievances of the German people—the frustration of losing World War I, the humilia-tion of the Versailles Treaty, the fear of communism, dissatisfaction with the Weimar Republic, the anguish of unemployment, the misery of the Great Depression, the mistrust of big business, the lack of strong leadership. Eyes burning and voice vibrating with the intensity of his emotion, Hitler persuaded the German people that he had solutions to all their problems. Few Germans were able to resist the spell

of his voice or the magnetism of his personality. In nazism many Germans found a new religion. The swastika replaced the cross, *Mein Kampf* the Bible, and Hitler the Savior. Hitler had an extraordinary ability to win the hearts and minds of men. An early follower of Hitler described his feelings when he first heard *Der Führer* address a mass meeting:

I do not know how to describe the emotions that swept over me as I heard this man. . . . When he spoke of the disgrace of [Germany's defeat in World War I and of the Versailles Treaty], I felt ready to spring on any enemy. . . . Glancing round, I saw that his magnetism was holding these thousands as one. . . . I was a man of thirty-two, . . . a wanderer seeking a cause, a patriot without a channel for his patriotism, a yearner after the heroic without a hero. The intense will of the man, the passion of his sincerity, seemed to flow from him into me. I experienced an exaltation that could be likened only to religious conversion. . . . I felt sure that no one who had heard Hitler that afternoon could doubt that he was the man of destiny, the vitalizing force in the future of Germany. . . . I had found myself, my leader, and my cause. . . . I had given him my soul.

Having captured the soul of a nation, Hitler led Germany down a path of madness and shame, dragged the world into the most destructive war in history, and pushed civilization to the edge of disaster.

CHECK-UP

1. How did daily life change under Hitler's dictatorship? Why did the average German not object to Hitler's new system?

2. In what ways did the state seek to influence the thinking of Germans? What uses did the Nazis make of propaganda? Of dramatic spectacles?

3. How did Hitler end unemployment? Help business?

4. What restrictions were placed on Jews? What seemed to be the purpose of this persecution? How did Nazi principles conflict with Christianity? What were the results?

5. Who were Hitler's chief lieutenants? What powers did each exercise?

6. After six years of Hitler and National Socialism, what was the reaction of the German people to the new Germany? Why?

7. What reasons are given for the triumph of nazism? Why did it depend in large part on the extraordinary talents of Adolf Hitler?

Summing Up

Among the factors contributing to the rise of fascism after World War I were economic insecurity, fear of communism, the shortcomings of parliamentary governments, the disillusionment of war veterans, and the resurgence of militant nationalism. In Italy, Mussolini promised to make the nation a second Rome. He rose to power because the king refused to act. Mussolini's Fascist Party offered a program that appealed to all dissatisfied groups. But it did more for the large landowners and the big industrialists than for the common people and workers.

In Germany the postwar Weimar Republic came under attack from both the right and the left. It was made the scapegoat for everything that went wrong—signing the Versailles Treaty, German humiliation, and hard times. Both communists and rightists wished to overthrow the Republic, and many of those in the middle were only lukewarm in their loyalty. The situation was favorable for the rise to power of a strong leader who would promise to regain lost lands, unite all Germans, restore prosperity, and create an enduring and powerful empire.

Hitler capitalized on the hard times caused by the Depression and the resultant fear of communism; he made the Jews scapegoats for all that had gone wrong in Germany. Having become chancellor, he instituted a public works program, rearmed the nation, and persecuted the Jews. Propaganda, great rallies, and a sense of economic security generated widespread support for Hitler's Nazi Party, while the secret police, concentration camps, and terrorism stifled opposition.

Chapter Highlights

Can you explain?

chancellor	scapegoat	nationalize	totalitarian
fascism	dictatorship	persecution	propaganda
veterans	"master race"	anti-semitism	National Socialism

Can you identify?

Ebert	Göring	*Der Führer*	Great Depression
Aryans	Third Reich	*Mein Kampf*	concentration camps
Il Duce	Mussolini	Himmler	Weimar Republic
Nazi	Reichstag	Social Democrats	National Socialist
Gestapo	Goebbels	Storm Troopers	Workers' Party
Hitler			

What do you think?

1. Can Mussolini be called a product of his times? Why?

2. Why did some people see fascism as the "wave of the future"?

3. What would be the advantages of associations including both employers and workers? The disadvantages?

4. Why was the Weimar Republic blamed for Germany's defeat in World War I? For postwar problems? Was either charge justified?

5. How did Hitler use the Treaty of Versailles to gain popular support?

6. Why did Hitler adopt a policy of anti-semitism? Why was there not more opposition to this policy in Germany? Outside Germany?

7. Was Hitler's totalitarian state more successful than Mussolini's? Why?

8. What special powers and privileges did the title "Der Führer" confer on Hitler?

9. Which reason given by historians seems to you the most valid explanation for Hitler's rise to power?

10. "No totalitarian dictatorship has been so willingly accepted by so many people as Hitler's was in Germany." Do you agree? Why?

War correspondents and photographers who covered the home front and accompanied the troops into battle left a graphic record of World War II. On the home front they depicted civilian contributions to the war effort—the women who took over men's jobs, civil defense, rationing, and courage in the face of frequent bombing raids. In Bill Brandt's photo (top left) St. Paul's Cathedral in London looms unscathed above a bombed site. On the battlefields of the war, correspondents and photographers went with the troops to the front. Robert Capa's photograph of the D-Day landing at Omaha Beach (left) reflects the excitement of a man who had only seconds to capture history in the making. When Russian troops reached Berlin in the closing days of the war in Europe, an anonymous photographer captured the moment of triumph when the invaders raised the Soviet flag over the Reichstag (above). This act marked the attainment of a long-sought goal. But, in the years following World War II, the Soviet presence in Berlin would raise more problems than it solved.

World War II

On September 1, 1939, Hitler's troops invaded Poland. Ten days before the invasion, Hitler had fixed a date for war. Soon Germany will wage a war, he told his generals, in which "the destruction of Poland shall be the primary objective." Hitler promised to "give a propagandist cause for starting the war—never mind whether it is plausible [logical] or not. In starting and making a war . . . what matters [is] Victory." Fifty hours after Germany attacked Poland, Britain and France declared war upon Germany. Thus, just 21 years after the end of World War I, "the war to end all wars," the world was tormented by a second and even more destructive conflict. What events led to World War II? What were the underlying causes of the most disastrous war in man's history?

Hitler's plans lead to World War II. Hitler had become master of Germany by 1933; all German society was dominated by the Nazi Party. Now that Hitler had given the nation one-man rule, he would secure for Germany its destined place in the world. He would undo the Treaty of Versailles (page 620), regain Germany's lost lands, and conquer "living space" for the German people. He would build the greatest empire in Germany's history. Hitler did not shrink from the idea that this could be accomplished only through war. War would offer him new opportunities to demonstrate his genius for leadership. War was also the surest way of demonstrating the superiority of the German people and of avenging Germany's bitter defeat in World War I. Historians may debate which nation was most to blame for World War I, but few would deny that World War II was Hitler's war. British historian H. R. Trevor-Roper states: "The Second World War was Hitler's personal war in many senses. He intended it, he prepared for it, he chose the moment for the launching of it; and for three years, in the main, he planned its course."

Germany's defeat in World War I and the Versailles Treaty create conditions leading to conflict. Although Nazi ideas and Hitler's policies brought on World War II, the conflict grew out of problems left over from World War I. The treaty ending the war had disarmed Germany and taken away her conquests, colonies, and even border lands long part of the German nation. But despite defeat Germany remained a Great Power. She had a population of 60 million, compared to 40 million for France, and far greater industrial strength than France. Germany had made clear her intention to undo the provisions of the Versailles Treaty.

Before Hitler came to power, the German government had followed a policy of gradual and peaceful revision of the treaty. Hitler, however, wanted immediate and dramatic successes in foreign affairs and was willing both to threaten and to use force. How could he be stopped? Both Britain and France seemed dedicated to a policy of "peace at any price." In both nations the destruction and death caused by the Great War had created strong anti-war feeling. Neither country felt strong enough to resist Hitler. Consequently, neither Britain nor France was willing to take a firm stand against Hitler until it was too late to head off another major war. As for the United States, the refusal to ratify the Versailles Treaty and the sharp reduction in military spending reflected the isolationist mood of the American people. With the onset of the Great Depression, Americans had enough problems at home without getting involved in European affairs.

Given these conditions, a clear pattern developed in the 1930's. (1) Germany sought to revoke the restrictions imposed by the Versailles Treaty. (2) Britain, unprepared for war and inclined to believe that the Versailles Treaty should be revised, was unwilling to resort to force when Germany violated the treaty. (3) France, invaded by Germany in 1870 and 1914, recognized the German danger and took steps to resist another invasion. But the French hoped to preserve the peace and did not feel strong enough to take up arms alone to enforce the Versailles Treaty. French reluctance became unwillingness once her British ally refused to take military action against Germany. (4) With each violation of the treaty, Germany grew stronger, and the likelihood of containing her without a major war grew slimmer.

German rearmament violates the Versailles Treaty. Before Hitler could achieve his foreign-policy goals, Germany had to be rearmed. The Versailles Treaty denied Germany submarines and an air force, restricted the navy to a few defensive vessels, and limited the army to 100,000 men, lightly armed. Under the Weimar Republic, Germany had begun to rearm secretly on a modest scale. But in 1935 Hitler openly declared that Germany would build a peacetime army of 550,000 men, a clear violation of the Versailles Treaty. When Britain and France denounced Germany's move but took no action, the future pattern was set.

Italy invades Ethiopia. In 1935 Fascist Italy invaded Ethiopia, an independent kingdom since ancient times. When the East African nation appealed to the League of Nations for assistance, the League condemned Italy for committing an act of aggression. Member nations were urged not to sell Italy arms or strategic raw materials. But only some nations cooperated. More serious, imports (such as gasoline) that were essential to Italy's war effort were not included. It had been hoped that successful economic action against Italy would discourage future aggression on the part of Nazi Germany as well as Fascist Italy. These hopes were dashed to pieces. The failure of Britain and France to pursue a hard line against Italy made possible Mussolini's conquest of Ethiopia. Hitler was strengthened in his conviction that Britain and France lacked the will to resist aggression.

Germany marches into the Rhineland. In March, 1936, German troops marched into the Rhineland, the demilitarized German region bordering France. The Versailles Treaty forbade Germany to build fortifications or to station troops in the Rhineland. German generals had warned Hitler that this move was dangerous because the German army was too weak to resist a French countermove. Hitler later said: "If the French had then marched into the Rhineland, we would have had to withdraw with our tails between our legs, for the military resources at our disposal would have been wholly inadequate for even a moderate re-

Events Leading to World War II

September, 1931	Japan invades Manchuria
March, 1935	Hitler announces German re-armament
October, 1935	Italy invades Ethiopia
March, 1936	Germany reoccupies the Rhineland
October, 1936	Berlin-Rome axis formed
November, 1936	German-Japanese anti-communist pact concluded
July, 1937	Japan invades China
March, 1938	Austria's union with Germany proclaimed
September, 1938	Munich Conference: Britain and France approve Germany's annexation of Sudetenland
March, 1939	Germany takes over Czechoslovakia
April, 1939	Italy invades Albania
August, 1939	Hitler and Stalin conclude pact
September, 1939	German invasion of Poland leads to World War II

sistance." But he also felt certain that neither Britain nor France would fight. He was right, for French and British leaders would do almost anything to avoid another war.

The Spanish Civil War is a victory for fascism. The Spanish Civil War, lasting from 1936 to 1939, was yet another victory for fascism. It is unlikely that General Francisco Franco could have overthrown Spain's republican government and have established a fascist-type state without massive help from Germany and Italy —more than 100,000 troops, as well as artillery, military planes, and other supplies. Soviet Russian support to the Spanish Republicans prolonged the conflict. But the failure of Britain and France to come to its aid doomed the Spanish Republic. It was becoming increasingly clear that fascist nations would fight to spread fascism whereas the great European democracies, Britain and France, were reluctant to take up arms. To many observers, fascism seemed dynamic, irresistible, the wave of the future; democracy appeared tired, unready to fight for its principles, lacking in leadership, and ready to be swept into the dustbin of history.

Germany annexes Austria. In 1938 Hitler made another dramatic move by annexing Austria. With the breakup of the Austro-Hungarian Empire at the close of World War I, Austria began a difficult existence as a small independent state. (See map, page 621.) German-speaking Austria might have sought union with Germany, but this was prohibited by the peace treaties of 1919. It is not surprising that Austrian-born Hitler seized on the principle of self-determination to justify the "redemption" of German minorities and their incorporation in the Reich. In March, 1938, pro-German demonstrations in Austria were followed by an invasion by German armored units. Six million Austrians became German citizens and Austria became a province in the Reich. Again the Versailles Treaty had been violated. Again Hitler had triumphed by a show of force, while France and Britain made only weak protests.

Germany demands the Sudetenland. With a population of over three million Germans, and a common border with Germany to the north, west, and south, Czechoslovakia became Hitler's next target. The Czechs had many reasons to be proud of their young nation, which had emerged from the breakup of the Austro-Hungarian Empire. Following World War I, Czechoslovakia alone among the nations of Central Europe preserved a democratic way of life. The Czech leaders were committed to the liberal, humanitarian ideals of western civilization. The country had alliances with France and Russia, a large armaments industry, a network of border defenses, and a population willing to fight to preserve the nation. Nevertheless, Czechoslovakia was doomed.

In the Sudetenland (zoo-*day*'t'n-land), the western region of the Czech republic, lived most of the German minority. Hostility between Sudetenland Germans and Czechs had existed for centuries, and the Czech government was unable to solve the problem of its German minority. Matters were worsened by Nazi propaganda and funds provided the Sudetenland Germans by the Nazis. When Sudetenland Nazis accused Czechoslovakia of oppressing its German minority, Hitler began to threaten the Czech Republic. To meet this crisis, the British prime minister, Neville Chamberlain, made two vain attempts to reason with Hitler. Seeking to prevent war, Franklin D. Roosevelt, President of the United States, as well as Chamberlain and Edouard Daladier (ey-*dwar*' dah-lah-*dyey*'), the Premier of France, urged Hitler to do nothing until a diplomatic conference might have a chance to work out a settlement. Hitler agreed to a conference involving Britain, France, Italy, and Germany. Czechoslovakia was not represented, and Russia was ignored.

The Munich policy of appeasement dooms Czechoslovakia. At the Munich Conference on September 29, 1938, Prime Minister Chamberlain of Britain and Premier Daladier of France agreed that German troops should occupy the Sudetenland. Britain did not feel Czechoslovakia was worth a war. France would not risk war unless sure of British support. The four powers also promised to guarantee the new Czech boundaries. Deserted by her western allies, Czechoslovakia surrendered the Sudetenland without a fight. "Silent, mournful, abandoned, broken, Czechoslovakia recedes into the darkness," said Churchill. "She has suffered in every respect by her association with the western democracies."

Chamberlain and Daladier have been harshly criticized for their role at the Munich Conference. They abandoned Czechoslovakia, a democratic nation willing to fight to preserve her independence. Although they yielded to Hitler's demands in order to buy peace, a year later they had to fight anyway. Had Britain and

ATLANTIC OCEAN

NORWAY
SWEDEN
FINLAND
ESTONIA
LATVIA
LITHUANIA
Moscow

North Sea
DENMARK
Baltic Sea
Memel

IRELAND
GREAT BRITAIN
London
NETH.
BELGIUM
LUX.
Paris
Maginot Line
RHINELAND 1936
Rhine R.
GERMANY
Weimar
Nuremberg
Berlin
Danzig
POLISH CORRIDOR
EAST PRUSSIA
Warsaw
POLAND
SOVIET UNION

Prague
CZECHOSLOVAKIA 1939
Vienna
Munich
SWITZ.
AUSTRIA 1938
HUNGARY
ROMANIA

FRANCE
ITALY
Adriatic Sea
YUGOSLAVIA
BULGARIA
Black Sea

PORTUGAL
Madrid
Barcelona
SPAIN
(Civil War — 1936–1939)
Rome
ALBANIA 1939
GREECE
TURKEY

Mediterranean Sea

LIBYA
AFRICA
ERITREA
ETHIOPIA 1935–1936
IT. SOMALILAND

KEY

▓	Germany and Italy
▒	Italian possessions in Africa before 1935
░	Axis territorial aggressions, 1935–1939

German and Italian Aggressions to April, 1939

France backed Czechoslovakia, say these critics, the Soviet Union would also have come to Czechoslovakia's aid. The combined might of Britain, France, Czechoslovakia, and Russia probably would have persuaded Hitler not to risk an invasion of Czechoslovakia. Had Germany attacked, this formidable alliance would have defeated her quickly. Or perhaps angry and fearful German generals who opposed an invasion of Czechoslovakia would have overthrown Hitler. Thus the long and bloody war which began a year after Munich could have been avoided. But other historians point out that Britain was not prepared for war in 1938. In the

689

year after Munich, Britain strengthened her air force and developed radar to protect her cities from German bombers. Chamberlain's policy bought Britain the time needed to prepare for war. Moreover, it was not certain that Russia would have defended Czechoslovakia.

Germany dismembers Czechoslovakia. In March, 1939, six months after the surrender of the Sudetenland, Czechoslovakia lost her independence. The Slovaks—one of the two major Slavic peoples making up Czechoslovakia (the other being the Czechs)—were encouraged by Germany to establish their own state. Hitler also gave his approval for Poland and Hungary to take over adjacent parts of Czechoslovakia. The final blow came on March 15 when German troops occupied Prague, the Czech capital. Czechoslovakia had ceased to exist.

Britain was disturbed and angered by Germany's destruction of Czechoslovakia and the annexation of territory inhabited by Czechs. When Hitler had taken over Austria and the Sudetenland, Britain had offered no military resistance. Both these territories were inhabited by Germans, and Britain was sympathetic to peaceful revisions of those terms of the Versailles Treaty that clearly ignored the principle of self-determination. But the occupation of Prague and the seizure of Czech territory were a different matter. For the first time Hitler had taken territory not inhabited by Germans. Moreover, he had broken his promise made at Munich not to demand additional territory. Now that he had destroyed the Czech nation and enormously increased German power, Hitler was viewed as a serious threat by Britain and France. It was becoming clear to many observers that Hitler's real goal was to dominate Europe and that his promises meant nothing.

The Hitler-Stalin Pact dooms Poland. After destroying Czechoslovakia, Hitler turned to Poland. He demanded that the port of Danzig and the Polish Corridor be restored to Germany. The Versailles Treaty had created the Corridor, which separated East Prussia from the rest of Germany, to ensure Poland an outlet to the Baltic Sea. Danzig, an old German port, was nominally a free city but economically tied to Poland by a common tariff system. Realizing that loss of the Polish Corridor would threaten their economy and military security, the Poles rejected Hitler's demand.

Convinced at last that there was no end to Hitler's demands, Britain and France declared their intention to assist Poland. During the first half of 1939 British and French statesmen tried to persuade Russia to join their countries in a triple alliance to contain Germany. These efforts came to nothing for various reasons. Poland, fearing Russia even more than Germany, refused to have Russian troops within her borders. After being excluded from the Munich Conference, Russia had no confidence in the western nations. Indeed, she believed that Britain and France were trying to drive Germany into a war with Russia. Even more important, Nazi Germany was making Russia counteroffers involving economic concessions and a nonaggression treaty. Germany would permit Russia to gain spheres of influence in the Baltic republics of Lithuania, Latvia, and Estonia. And the two partners would divide Poland. Late in August, 1939, the world was stunned by the announcement of the Hitler-Stalin Pact of friendship and nonaggression.

The pact spelled the doom of Poland. Although Britain and France renewed their pledges of aid in case of an attack on Poland, these meant little. Were Poland attacked from both sides by Germany and Russia, the western powers could not possibly provide massive aid soon enough to affect the outcome. From the point of view of Stalin and Hitler, the pact made sense. Russia was getting a buffer zone and time to increase its armaments against the day when Hitler would move farther eastward. Moreover, Russia had long-range goals of expanding westward to regain land and influence lost during World War I. Hitler could do what he wished to Poland without having to worry about Russian intervention. And should Britain and France go to war to help Poland, which

Hitler rather doubted, Germany would be spared the problems of a two-front war as in World War I.

Appeasement and isolation encourage aggression. During the years before the outbreak of World War II the western powers had developed no effective machinery for cooperation in checking aggression. Indeed, their willingness to stand by while small countries were taken over by aggressors served only to whet the appetites of the dictators. Why did Britain and France follow a policy of *appeasement,* of giving in to Hitler's demands in hopes of preventing a large-scale war? Why didn't they stop Hitler before Germany became powerful?

1. The horrors of World War I had created a strong anti-war feeling in Britain and France. Both countries hoped that by appeasing Hitler they could avoid another disastrous world conflict. Moreover, neither was prepared to fight. Britain had drastically reduced spending for armaments. While France had a large army, she was prepared only to fight a defensive war. She devoted her full energy to building an elaborate network of border fortifications—the Maginot (*mazh'*ih-noh) Line. Furthermore, there was a defeatist attitude at all levels of French society. The French people felt that their nation was no match for dynamic Nazi Germany.

2. The United States, a powerful ally in World War I, had returned to a policy of isolation. The overwhelming sentiment among the American people was clear: let the Europeans fight their own battles.

3. With the United States unwilling to resist Hitler, why didn't Britain and France turn to Russia, their ally in World War I? Surely a strong alliance between the western nations and Russia would have forced Hitler to back down. In the years before the Munich Conference Russia had urged the two western powers to join with her in just such an alliance. But Britain and France distrusted the Soviet Union. They doubted whether Russia was serious about such an alliance. Moreover, they feared that Russia wanted to spread communism throughout Europe. After the Munich Conference, Russia suspected that Britain and France were allowing Germany to grow stronger so that she would attack Russia. This was one of the reasons why Stalin made a deal with Hitler.

4. Feelings of guilt about the Versailles Treaty contributed to the policy of appeasement. The feeling grew in Britain that the Versailles Treaty was unjust and should be changed. When Hitler's troops marched into the Rhineland, British newspapers asked what harm is there for German troops to move into German territory? When Nazi troops marched into Austria, British public opinion was not greatly disturbed. After all, the Austrians were German-speaking. Had not President Wilson said that self-determination was a just principle? What was wrong if these two German-speaking peoples united? The same reasoning was applied to the Sudetenland Germans. But after Germany took over the rest of Czechoslovakia, this feeling changed. It had become obvious that Hitler intended to take over lands inhabited by non-Germans.

5. Western statesmen misjudged Hitler's character and his intentions. Many sincerely believed that Hitler was a responsible statesman seeking to gain for Germany its rightful place in the world. "If I may judge from my personal knowledge of Herr Hitler," wrote one British appeaser, "peace and justice are the key words of his policy." At the Munich Conference, when Hitler told Chamberlain that the Sudetenland was his last demand, Chamberlain believed him. He hoped that Hitler would be satisfied with just a few boundary changes. He did not suspect that Hitler had unlimited ambitions.

6. Lastly, the quality of leadership in Britain and France between the two wars left much to be desired. British historian A. L. Rowse characterized Britain's leaders of the 1930's thus:

One way or another they had none of the old eighteenth-century aristocracy's guts—they were middle-class men with pacifist backgrounds and no knowledge of Europe, its history or its languages, or of diplomacy—let alone of strategy or war. . . . Churchill has a verbal comment: "Grovel, grovel, grovel!" . . . The plain truth is that their deepest instinct was defeatist, their highest wisdom surrender.

CHECK-UP

1. What were Hitler's goals?

2. How did Germany's defeat in World War I and the Versailles Treaty pave the way for World War II? Why did neither Britain nor France take a firm stand against Germany's violation of that treaty? How did the United States react?

3. Why did Mussolini invade Ethiopia? What was the reaction of the League? Britain? France?

4. Why did Hitler reoccupy the Rhineland? What was the British and French reaction? Why?

5. What role did Italy and Germany play in the Spanish Civil War? Why?

6. How did Hitler justify his seizure of Austria? His demands in Czechoslovakia? How did France and Britain react?

7. What nations took part in the Munich Conference? What did each want? How did the conference doom Czechoslovakia?

8. What demands did Hitler make in Poland? Why did Britain and France pledge their assistance to Poland?

9. Why did Hitler and Stalin sign a nonaggression pact? Why did this agreement doom Poland?

10. Why did Britain and France follow a policy of appeasement?

Axis Victories in Europe, 1939–1941

THE EUROPEAN THEATER OF WAR

Poland falls before the German blitzkrieg. On September 1, 1939, Germany began an all-out attack on Poland. Two days later Britain and France declared war on Germany when Hitler ignored their demands that German armies cease their advance. Fast-moving German tanks, armored cars, and other mechanized units, supported by fighter planes and dive bombers, struck at Poland. These motorized divisions quickly penetrated deeply into Polish territory, encircling large units of Polish troops. They raced across Poland and surrounded Warsaw, the capital. The German blitzkrieg (*blits*′kreek), or lightning war, was a total success. On September 17th Soviet troops invaded Poland from the east to occupy the territories promised Russia in the Hitler-Stalin Pact. Ten days later, battered by German guns and short of food and ammunition, Warsaw surrendered. Poland had fallen before Britain or France could begin to provide effective aid.

Northern Europe falls to the Germans. The pace of the war slowed after Germany's stunning victory in Poland. The French remained behind their Maginot Line and the Germans behind their newly built West Wall. Meanwhile, the British were frantically trying to speed arms production and to establish a blockade that would help bring Germany to her knees as in World War I. But this so-called "phony war" came to a sudden end when Germany struck with lightning speed at Denmark and Norway in early April of 1940. Using both ships and airplanes in their invasion of Norway, the Germans soon compelled the withdrawal of Anglo-French forces rushed in to hold some of the country's northern ports. With little delay the Germans began the construction of air bases and submarine "pens" along the coast of the two conquered Scandinavian nations. Fortunately for the Allies, most of the large Norwegian merchant fleet escaped the Nazis. These ships put in at British ports and came to play an important part in the Allied effort.

One month after the strike at Denmark and Norway, the Nazi blitzkrieg struck at Belgium, the Netherlands, and Luxembourg. German paratroopers seized transportation and communications centers. Ruthless bombing terrorized the population and leveled the center of the Dutch city of Rotterdam, killing 40,000 people. Although some British and French troops were rushed to Belgium's aid, the Belgian defense could not cope with the Nazi blitzkrieg, and in little more than two weeks Belgium, too, had fallen.

The speed of the Nazi attacks bewildered the French. They had hoped to fight a defensive war that would cost the German army dearly as it sought to pierce the Maginot Line. But the Nazi invasion of Belgium made possible an "end run" around the Maginot Line. Swift-moving tanks and motorized infantry burst through French fortifications near Sedan (seh-*dahn'*). Racing along the Somme River to reach the English Channel, the Germans met no effective opposition.

Although the French had as many tanks as the Germans, many of them superior in quality, they did not properly deploy them. Nor did they make proper use of their aircraft. Wrote a former commander-in-chief of the French army after the war: "Why, out of 2000 modern fighters on hand at the beginning of May, 1940, were fewer than 500 used on the Northeast Front? . . . What is behind this mystery about our planes? . . . I humbly confess to you that I don't know." France met with disaster largely because her military leaders, unlike the German command, had not mastered the techniques of motorized warfare. Explains American historian William L. Shirer:

The whole German Army . . . [was] geared to a tempo made possible by the speed of gasoline-engined machines: tanks to make a breakthrough, motor vehicles to transport infantry and artillery to hold and enlarge it, . . . and planes to disrupt the enemy's reinforcing movements in the rear and to paralyze his positions at the front in the moment of assault. . . . The French Command . . . still stuck to the tempo of the 1914–1918 war. . . . Too

World War II

1939

September	Poland invaded by Germany from the west and Russia from the east
November	Russia invades Finland

1940

April	Germany occupies Denmark and invades Norway
May	Germany invades Netherlands, Belgium, Luxembourg; British and French forces evacuated from Dunkirk
June	Fall of France
August	Battle of Britain begins
September	Japan begins conquest of Southeast Asia

1941

June	Germany invades Russia
December	Japan attacks Pearl Harbor; United States declares war on Japan

1942	Turning point of the war: Stalingrad (Russia), El Alamein (North Africa), Midway (Pacific)
1943	Allied invasion leads to Italy's surrender
1944	D-Day: Allied forces land in France on June 6, begin major offensive

1945

January	Russians advance into Germany
March	Allies invade Germany
May	Germany surrenders
August	United States drops atomic bomb on Hiroshima; Soviet Union invades Manchuria; Japan surrenders

much of the French Army and too many minds in its command were geared to the three-mile-an-hour pace of the foot soldier.

Britain rescues Allied forces trapped at Dunkirk. The surrender of the Belgian army and the German wedge separating Anglo-French

693

forces north of the Somme from Paris endangered an Allied army. Some 330,000 British and French troops fell back on Dunkirk, a port on the English Channel. Their only hope was evacuation. Under bombardment from German planes, these men were taken aboard destroyers, merchant ships, motorboats, fishing boats, tugboats, private yachts—on anything that could cross from Britain to Dunkirk and back. In the great rescue operation called the "miracle of Dunkirk," the British brought back the soldiers, but artillery, tanks, trucks, and supplies had to be left on the beach. Though a defeat, Dunkirk inspired and united the British. On the last day of the evacuation, Winston Churchill, the new British prime minister, spoke for the entire nation when he said:

We shall not flag or fail. We shall go on to the end. We shall fight in France, we shall fight on the seas and oceans, we shall fight with growing confidence and growing strength in the air. We shall defend our island, whatever the cost may be. We shall fight on the beaches, we shall fight on the landing-grounds, we shall fight in the fields and in the streets, we shall fight in the hills. We shall never surrender; and even if, which I do not for a moment believe, this island or a large part of it were subjugated and starving, then our Empire beyond the seas, armed and guarded by the British Fleet, would carry on the struggle, until, in God's good time, the New World, with all its power and might, steps forth to the rescue and liberation of the Old.

France falls. Meanwhile, in France all was confusion; the country was near collapse. The French army could not cope with the Nazi blitzkrieg, and in many places French forces just disintegrated. Tens of thousands of French refugees fleeing the advancing Nazis clogged the roads, interfering with army movements. A proud nation—the nation of Louis XIV and Napoleon, the nation that had gallantly defended its soil for four years in World War I —fought without spirit because it lacked confidence in its leaders. Writes one angry Frenchman who served his country in 1940:

Apparently the hour for courage had not struck. France had forgotten the word. . . . I can find only one reason for our defeat: stupidity and cowardice. The generals were stupid, the men did not want to be killed. These two things often go together. Troops know that an idiot has no right to ask them to get themselves killed.

On June 10, 1940, Mussolini took advantage of hard-pressed France when he launched an invasion from the south. Four days later the Germans marched into Paris and on June 17 the French requested a cease-fire. The surrender document was signed in the same railway car in which the Germans had agreed to the armistice ending World War I. The Germans gloried in their revenge; the French wept in their humiliation. The British gathered their courage, for now they stood alone.

The Battle of Britain begins. Hitler had hoped that Britain, recognizing the hopelessness of continued resistance, would make peace. But Britain rejected Hitler's peace offers, realizing there could be no security or comfort in a Europe dominated by Hitler's Germany. No one expressed these sentiments better than Churchill:

The Battle of Britain is about to begin. Upon this battle depends the survival of Christian civilization. Upon it depends our own British life and the long continuity of our institutions and our Empire. The whole fury and might of the enemy must very soon be turned upon us. Hitler knows that he will have to break us in this island or lose the war. If we can stand up to him, all Europe may be [freed], and the life of the world may move forward into broad sunlit uplands. But if we fail, then the whole world, including the United States, including all that we have known and cared for, will sink into the abyss of a new Dark Age made more sinister and perhaps more prolonged by the lights of a perverted science.

His peace offers rejected, Hitler made plans to invade Britain. To demoralize and weaken his island foe, Hitler ordered large-scale bombing of British factories, ports, and centers of population. He also hoped to destroy the British air force before attempting an invasion of Britain. Accordingly, on August 8, 1940, hundreds of German bombers escorted by fighter planes attacked Britain fom the sky. They were met by the British Royal Air Force (R.A.F.); the Battle of Britain had begun. Bombing raids were carried out by day until the loss of bombers and fighters discouraged the Nazis. Then they shifted to nighttime raids on the large cities and prime industrial targets.

Despite the furious bombing of London, people in the British capital remained calm and resolute. Unlike France, Britain was not weakened by a defeatist attitude. The air war over Britain continued until June, 1941, but by the middle of September, 1940, Hitler had abandoned plans for an invasion. The development of radar by British scientists and its use in detecting enemy planes, the skill and courage of the British fighter pilots, the inability of the Germans to replace very heavy losses in aircraft, and control of the English Channel by the British navy saved Britain in this grim struggle for survival.

Germany invades Russia. In the course of 1940 Hitler turned his attention eastward. The Soviet Union, with whom Hitler had signed a nonaggression pact the year before, was frantically rearming and building up its industry. By invading Russia, Germany would acquire the "living space" which Hitler had long promised. The Reich would take over Russia's rich grain fields and mineral wealth, particularly oil, coal, and iron ore. Moreover, the Russian plains provided an ideal terrain for mechanized warfare. Once Russia was defeated, there would be opportunities for further conquests—perhaps Britain, North Africa, Asia Minor, or even India.

In December, 1940, Hitler gave his generals five months to complete plans for the invasion of Russia. To prepare the way for this invasion, early in 1941 Hitler's forces occupied Bulgaria without resistance, overran Greece, and attacked Yugoslavia, where they met stiff resistance from guerrilla forces. By June Germany

German troops advancing into Russia in 1941 encountered the same scorched-earth tactics that had defeated Napoleon. By destroying everything that might prove useful to the Germans, the retreating Russians greatly hampered the Nazi drive.

had massed on the Russian border some four million soldiers, 3300 tanks, and 5000 planes.

Leningrad holds out against a long German siege. In June, 1941, Nazi armies swept into Russia along a front that extended from the Black Sea to the Baltic. Could the Germans keep their army supplied in the light of Russia's vastness and cruel winter? Could they break the will of a people renowned for their ability to endure hardship and their devotion to the motherland? The early German offensive was successful. In little more than three months 3.5 million Russian soldiers had been killed, wounded, or captured; 14,000 tanks had been lost, and the Soviet air force was virtually wiped out. By the first week in October, 1941, German troops were 50 miles from Moscow, and a large Russian army was trapped in the city of Leningrad, which was under constant bombardment by artillery and from the air. During the 900 days and nights of this dreadful

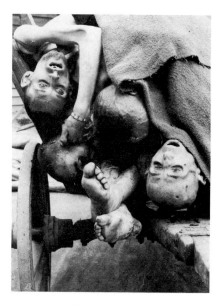

The Nazi policy of exterminating the Jews resulted in unimaginable horrors. In Nazi-occupied lands, as well as in Germany, Jews were rounded up like cattle (above) and taken to concentration camps where they met death in gas chambers, through forced labor, or from starvation (right).

ordeal the citizens of Leningrad held out despite famine, disease, and nearly one million dead. *New York Times* editor Harrison Salisbury called the siege of Leningrad "the greatest and longest siege ever endured by a modern city, a time of trial, suffering, and heroism that reached peaks of tragedy and bravery almost beyond our power to comprehend."

The German invasion of Russia is stymied. Despite enormous losses, Russia was not defeated. Fresh troops arrived from Russia's eastern regions. Winter was setting in, and the snow, mud, and severe cold of the Russian winter had been major factors in the defeat of other invading armies. Nor had the Russian people lost heart. The atrocities committed by the invaders only strengthened the Russians' determination to defend their soil. Many Russians who hated Stalin the Communist rallied behind Stalin the Nationalist when he said: "The German invaders want a war of extermination against the peoples of the Soviet Union. Very well then! If they want a war of extermination they shall have it. Our task now . . . will be to destroy every German . . . come to occupy our country. . . . Death to the German invaders!"

On December 5–6 the Russians launched a counterattack which drove back the German forces on the outskirts of Moscow. The German soldiers, still in their summer uniforms, froze as the temperature dropped to thirty degrees below zero, and without anti-freeze German tanks would not start. Hitler had failed to bring Russia to her knees, but in the following spring he would try again.

HITLER'S NEW ORDER

The Germans had had an almost unbroken run of victories in Europe. By the spring of 1942 German power was unchallenged from the arctic region of Norway to the Mediterranean, from the Atlantic coast to deep within Russia. Over this vast empire Hitler sought to impose a New Order. Europe would be reorganized in the interest of the "master race." What were the goals of Hitler's New Order? How were these aims carried out?

Hitler plans a program of resettlement and Germanization. The Polish population of regions of Poland annexed to Germany was expelled to make room for German settlers. Hitler spoke of settling ten to twenty million Germans on choice lands in Russia, but this had to await a final Russian defeat. Norwegians, Danes, Luxembourgers, Alsatians, Dutch, and Estonians—regarded as racial "cousins" of the Germans—were to receive favored treatment. After undergoing a process of Germanization—re-education to make them think and act as Germans—it was expected that they would become valuable citizens of the Greater Germany. Ukrainian, Polish, and Czech children who "looked German" would be taken from their parents and sent to Germany. It was hoped that these stolen children, brought up by German parents and trained in German schools, would be absorbed into the Greater Germany.

The New Order calls for exploitation of German conquests. The New Order called for the exploitation of the economic wealth of conquered Europe to meet the needs of the German war effort. "The real profiteers of this war are ourselves," said Hitler, "and out of it we shall come bursting with fat! We will give back nothing and will take everything we can make use of."* Vast amounts of property were confiscated and shipped to Germany. German soldiers were fed with food harvested in occupied France and Russia. German soldiers fought with weapons produced in Czech factories. German tanks ran on oil delivered by Romania, Germany's satellite. Trainloads of vital war materials rolled to Germany from Belgium, Holland, and other occupied lands. "Whenever you come across anything that may be needed by the German people, you must be after it like a bloodhound," ordered Göring. "It must be . . . brought to Germany."

The Nazis also exploited the conquered peoples as slave labor. Some seven million foreign workers, many of them prisoners of war or recruited by force, were sent to Germany as slave laborers to work in German factories and on German farms. Many never lived to see the

* From *The Ordeal of Total War, 1939–45* by Gordon Wright (New York: Harper and Row Publishers, Inc., 1968; copyright 1968 by Gordon Wright). Reprinted by permission.

end of the war. They died of disease, hunger, and exhaustion.

The New Order is characterized by terror and extermination. The victorious Nazis imposed a rule of terror on the conquered peoples of Europe. The prison cell, the concentration camp, the torture room, and the firing squad discouraged resistance to Nazi rule. For every German soldier killed by a resistance fighter, the Gestapo would execute many civilian hostages. Hitler ordered the execution of high Russian government officials, and three million Russian prisoners of war died in German prison camps.

No one suffered more under Nazi rule than did the Jews of Europe. A policy of *genocide* (the murder of an entire people) was termed by the Nazis the "final solution of the Jewish problem." As the German army advanced into Russia, special squads executed hundreds of thousands of Jewish men, women, and children.

Nazi policy seeks the extermination of Europe's Jews. To speed up the "final solution," Jews were transported to concentration camps outfitted with gas chambers and crematoria. From all over Europe Jews were rounded up, loaded in sealed cattle cars, and shipped to the death camps. When they arrived at Auschwitz (*oush'-vits*), the most notorious of the murder factories, the prisoners were examined by two S.S. doctors. Rudolf Hoess, the commandant of the camp, who was executed after the war for crimes against humanity, described what followed:

[I] estimate that at least 2,500,000 victims were executed and exterminated [at Auschwitz] by gassing and burning, and at least another half million succumbed to starvation and disease, making a total dead of about 3,000,000. This figure represents about 70 per cent or 80 per cent of all persons sent to Auschwitz as prisoners, the remainder having been selected and used for slave labor in the concentration camp industries. . . .

The "final solution" of the Jewish question meant the complete extermination of all Jews in Europe. I was ordered to establish extermination facilities at Auschwitz in June, 1941. . . . It took from three to fifteen minutes to kill the people in the death chamber, depending upon climatic conditions. We knew when the people were dead because their screaming stopped. We usually waited about one-half hour before we opened the doors and removed the bodies. After the bodies were removed our special commandos took off the rings and extracted the gold from the teeth of the corpses. . . .

The way we selected our victims was as follows: . . . Those who were fit for work were sent into the camp. Others were sent immediately to the extermination plants. Children of tender years were invariably exterminated since by reason of their youth they were unable to work. . . . We endeavored to fool the victims into thinking that they were to go through a delousing process. Of course, frequently they realized our true intentions, and we sometimes had riots and difficulties due to that fact. Very frequently women would hide their children under [their] clothes, but of course when we found them we would send the children in to be exterminated.

Concentration camp inmates who were not exterminated in the gas chambers toiled until they dropped in their tracks. Sadistic guards beat, starved, and tortured them to death, and sometimes they were used for cruel medical experiments.

Of all Hitler's war aims, the one that he came closest to achieving was the extermination of European Jewry. In all, almost six million Jews were slaughtered by the Nazis. Some 1.5 million of the murdered were children. Tens of thousands of entire families were wiped out without a trace. Centuries-old Jewish community life vanished, never to be restored. Burned into the soul of the Jewish people was a wound that would never entirely heal.

The systematic extermination of European Jewry was the terrible fulfillment of Nazi racial theories that regarded Germans as a master race and Jews as subhuman. Nazi executioners convinced themselves that they were cleansing Europe of a lower and dangerous form of humanity that threatened the German Fatherland. If they had any second thoughts about their evil work, they convinced themselves that they

bore no personal responsibility for these deeds, that they were only following orders, doing their duty like good soldiers. By utilizing the technology and bureaucracy of a modern state and by relying on the dedicated service of thousands of "little men" who rounded up the victims, transported them to the death camps, served as concentration camp guards, and kept careful records of those destined for execution, the Nazis committed the greatest crime in human history.

Resistance fighters undermine Nazi rule. In each Nazi-occupied country there emerged a resistance movement opposed to Nazi rule. Resistance fighters engaged in sabotage—blowing up bridges, railways, power stations, and factories. They ambushed German patrols. Over hidden radios they relayed important information to the Allies. They printed an underground newspaper to keep alive the hopes of their people. They hid from the Nazis escaped prisoners and men picked for slave labor in Germany.

The French resistance kept crews that had been forced to bail out of Allied aircraft from falling into the hands of the Nazis and aided the Allies when they invaded France in 1944. The resistance in Denmark smuggled into neutral Sweden almost all of Denmark's 8000 Jews, thus preventing the Nazis from sending them to concentration camps and certain death. Russian and Yugoslav resistance fighters called partisans waged guerrilla war against the Germans. The Polish resistance numbered 300,000 at its height. In 1944, counting on cooperation from the Russian army which was across the river from Warsaw, the Poles rose in a desperate effort to free the city from the Nazis. After two months of vicious street fighting, the Polish underground army was destroyed and Warsaw was left in ruins. The Russians had made no effort to help the Poles.

Even Italy and Germany had their resistance movements. After the Allies landed in Italy, bands of Italian partisans helped the British and Americans liberate Italy from fascism and German occupation. In July, 1944, German opponents of Hitler, many of them army officers, tried to kill *Der Führer* by planting a bomb in his conference room. The bomb exploded, but Hitler escaped serious injury. Some 5000 suspected anti-Nazis were tortured and executed in typical Nazi fashion.

The Pacific Theater, 1941–Mid-1942

The German invasion of Russia in 1941 brought Britain and Russia closer together. They would soon be joined by a third Great Power, for on December 7, 1941, Japan's attack on Pearl Harbor brought the United States into the war.

The Japanese attack Pearl Harbor. Early in the morning of December 7, 1941, Japanese planes took off from aircraft carriers to attack Pearl Harbor, the United States naval base in Hawaii. Two American army privates manning a radar station saw what seemed to be a large force of planes moving towards Hawaii. Shortly after 7 A.M., their observations were relayed to the military information center. The lieutenant who received the message thought these planes were from an American aircraft carrier or perhaps aircraft expected from California. No alert was sounded. Shortly after 8 A.M. Japanese torpedo planes and dive bombers roared out of the sky. The Americans were caught by surprise. The warships in the harbor and the planes standing in neat rows on the air fields were easy targets for the low-flying Japanese planes.

What reasons motivate the attack on Pearl Harbor? The Japanese attack on Pearl Harbor was another step in the policy of imperial expansion that began with Japan's take-over of the Chinese province of Manchuria in 1931–1932. In 1937 war broke out between Japan and China. Japan's military superiority soon gave her control over China's coastal region (see page 598). By 1940 Japan was looking greedily at the riches of Southeast Asia—French Indo-China, British Malaya, the Dutch East Indies, and the American Philippines. These countries had such resources as oil, rubber, and tin, vitally needed by Japanese industries. Moreover, the region's rice fields would help to feed Japan's expanding population. Embattled Britain and Nazi-occupied Holland and France were in no position to check Japanese expansion. Only the United States could stop Japan from dominating and exploiting Southeast Asia. Japan decided upon war, hoping that a quick strike against American bases in the Pacific would prevent the United States from interfering with Japan's conquests in Asia. Once this was accomplished, Japan would seek to negotiate peace with the United States. But despite the heavy damage inflicted by Japan on the American fleet and despite her lack of military preparedness, the United States declared war on Japan immediately after the attack on Pearl Harbor.

Shortly after, Germany and Italy declared war on the United States, which then joined Britain and Russia in their struggle against Nazi Germany and Fascist Italy.

Japan makes many conquests in the Pacific and in Southeast Asia. The attack upon Pearl Harbor was followed by many Japanese victories. By May, 1942, the Japanese empire included French Indo-China, Thailand (*tie'*-land), Burma, Malaya, the Dutch East Indies, the coast of China, Hong Kong, the Philippines, and other islands in the Pacific.

At first the Japanese conquerors won the support of many Southeast Asian nationalist leaders, who welcomed the defeat and departure of the western nations. But it soon became apparent that Japanese imperialism was no better and in many ways considerably worse than western imperialism. The Japanese failure to win the loyalty of the Southeast Asian peoples they had conquered, says American historian Willard H. Elsbree,

can be illustrated by the contrast between the welcome accorded their arrival in Southeast Asia and the conditions under which they departed. In the Philippines they were beset by guerrillas everywhere, in Burma they were under attack by a Burmese army, officered and manned by their recent collaborators, in Indo-China and Indonesia they found safety only in numbers. Even if there was a noticeable lack of enthusiasm for the white man's return, scarcely a hand was lifted in support of the Japanese.

The conquered lands of Southeast Asia turned against the Japanese for a number of reasons. First, the Japanese often mistreated the people under their control, using them for forced labor. For example, Asian laborers and Dutch, Australian, and British prisoners of war were forced to build a railway from Thailand to Burma. Working without engineering equipment in difficult mountain and jungle country, poorly fed, and driven mercilessly by their Japanese guards, over 40,000 prisoners and laborers died.

Secondly, Japanese exploitation and the dislocations caused by the war created severe economic hardships in the lands occupied by Japan. Japan claimed that she had liberated Asian lands from European rule, that she was creating an Asia for the Asians. In reality, Japan controlled and exploited a huge empire of some 450 million people. From these conquered lands Japan obtained vital rubber, tin, and oil resources. They also served as markets for Japanese products. In Manchuria, Japanese firms built factories and opened mines. Manchuria also provided overpopulated Japan with food. One Burmese nationalist expressed the feelings of many Asians who experienced both British and Japanese rule: "We often told you the British were sucking the blood out of you. Well, the Japanese are here to suck the marrow out of your bones."

Thirdly, regarding the Asian peoples they had conquered as inferior, the Japanese had no intentions of sharing authority. To win local support, they granted Southeast Asian nationalist leaders some limited power, but never gave them enough authority to undermine Japanese rule. The nationalist leaders quickly saw through this, and used every means in their power to harass the invaders.

CHECK-UP

1. What conquests did Japan make in the Pacific and Southeast Asia?

2. How did conquered peoples react to Japanese rule?

KEY

Japanese empire, 1931

Japanese empire, 1942

- - - - Extent of Japanese expansion

Allied advances

World War II in Asia and the Pacific

701

The year 1942 opened with the Axis powers holding the upper hand; by its end the Allies were almost certain of victory. Three battles in the second half of 1942 reversed the course of the war. These decisive Allied victories were Midway, Stalingrad, and El Alamein.

At Midway the United States turns back the Japanese thrust. The island of Midway is located 1135 miles to the northwest of Pearl Harbor. If Japan could seize it, land-based airplanes would be within striking distance of the Hawaiian Islands. The Japanese did not want Midway just for strategic reasons; they hoped to draw the crippled American navy into an all-out battle. The destruction of the American fleet might well put an end to the war. Unfortunately for the Japanese, Admiral Chester Nimitz, using naval intelligence reports, correctly analyzed Japanese plans. The United States fleet, although badly outnumbered, was prepared to meet the enemy.

The battle of Midway (June, 1942), was a strange naval battle since the ships on neither side fired their big guns. The first step to victory was the suicidal attempt made by American carrier-based torpedo and dive bombers to penetrate the Japanese defense of its aircraft carriers. American torpedo planes from the aircraft carriers *Hornet, Enterprise,* and *Yorktown,* in what one historian calls "an epic of raw courage unsurpassed in American war history," dove low at their targets despite the concentrated fire from Japanese planes and antiaircraft guns. Thirty-five of forty-one American torpedo planes were shot down; not one torpedo struck a Japanese ship. But the attack of the torpedo squadrons forced the Japanese pilots in swift Zeros to fly low over the water, enabling high-flying American dive bombers to move unopposed within striking distance of the Japanese carriers. Moments after the American torpedo pilots sacrificed themselves in a flaming death,

the dive bombers roared down out of the sky on the Japanese carriers. The Japanese fighter planes, writes a Japanese historian, "which had engaged the preceding wave of torpedo planes, . . . had not yet had time to regain altitude. Consequently it may be said that the American dive bombers' success was made possible by the earlier martyrdom of their torpedo planes."

When the battle ended, four large Japanese aircraft carriers had been sunk, and the United States had regained naval superiority in the Pacific. The tide of battle was turning.

Germany suffers disaster at Stalingrad. Although stymied by the Russian counteroffensive in December, 1941, by the summer of 1942 the Germans had resumed their advance in Russia. Hitler directed the main thrust of the German attack at the Russian city of Stalingrad (now called Volgograd), located on the Volga River in the southern part of European Russia. Stalingrad was a symbol of Russian resistance to the German forces. The country that held it would also be able to control transportation on the Volga, the major route for north-south traffic.

Der Führer had ordered that Stalingrad be captured by August 25. Three days before the deadline German troops reached the Volga. Six hundred German planes bombarded the city, enveloping it in flames and killing 40,000 civilians. Soon Germans and Russians were battling amidst the ruins of the city's outskirts. Russian civilians and soldiers, in the words of a Soviet general, fought "for every brick and stone, for every yard of Stalingrad earth." The battle dragged on into fall. One German officer wrote in his diary:

Stalingrad is no longer a town. By day it is an enormous cloud of burning, blinding smoke. It is a vast furnace lit by the reflection of the flames. And when night arrives . . . the dogs plunge into the Volga and swim desperately to gain the other bank. The nights of Stalingrad are a terror for them. Animals flee this hell; the hardest stones cannot bear it for long; only men endure.

In November the Russians brought up fresh troops and caught the Germans in a trap. Exhausted and short of food, medical supplies, weapons, and ammunition, the commander of the German Sixth Army urged Hitler to order a withdrawal before the Russians closed the ring. *Der Führer* refused: "The Sixth Army will stay where it is. . . . I am not leaving the Volga." After suffering tens of thousands of additional casualties, their position hopeless, the remnants of the German Sixth Army surrendered early in 1943. Some 260,000 German soldiers had perished in the Battle of Stalingrad; over 110,000 were taken prisoner. The Russian victory marked the turning point in the war on the Eastern Front. With the Germans on the defensive, the Russians began to launch attacks that would eventually bring them to Berlin.

El Alamein marks the turning point of the war in North Africa. In the autumn of 1940 Italy expanded the war to North Africa in an effort to gain control of the Suez Canal. British resistance pushed back the Italians and compelled Germany to come to their aid. In 1941 General Erwin Rommel, the commander of the German Afrika Corps, launched a drive toward the Egyptian city of Alexandria. Beyond Alexandria lay the Suez Canal, vital for Allied trade, and beyond the Canal lay the rich oil fields of the Middle East. The British Eighth Army, commanded by General Montgomery, stood between Rommel and his goal. Confident and tough, an inspiration to his troops, "Monty" was a match for Rommel, the "Desert Fox." In 1942 at El Alamein (al-ah-*main'*) to the west of Alexandria, the two armies clashed.

Commanding the air, the British R.A.F. blasted German positions and prevented supplies from reaching Rommel's troops. On October 23, British tanks and troops attacked in force after hours of heavy bombardment of the German positions. Outgunned, short of tanks, the Germans and their Italian allies turned in full retreat. The Axis powers were driven out of Egypt.

While the British Eighth Army rolled to victory at El Alamein, an armada of British and American ships was carrying almost 200,000 men to ports in French Morocco and Algeria. Because of the effective work of Allied sympathizers in North Africa, these troops, led by General Dwight D. Eisenhower, encountered little opposition. Six months later, in May, 1943, the German and Italian forces in North Africa were caught between Montgomery's Eighth Army and American, British, and Free French troops (French troops who had refused to surrender when France fell). The Axis troops were forced to surrender.

Allied forces invade Italy. The defeat of the Axis in North Africa paved the way for an Allied invasion of Italy. In July, 1943, British and American troops landed on the island of Sicily. That same month Mussolini was overthrown. The Italian king told the crushed Mussolini: "Italy has gone to bits. Army morale is at rock bottom. The soldiers don't want to fight any more. At this moment you are the most hated man in Italy." A new Italian government sought peace with the Allies and on September 8 surrendered unconditionally.

Meanwhile, Allied troops landed on the Italian mainland and moved northward over difficult terrain and against stiff German resistance. The campaign to drive the Germans out of Italy was a long one, and the fighting did not end until the German troops laid down their arms in May, 1945.

The Allies plan a great invasion of France. After many months of planning, training, and preparations, a huge Allied invasion force, that included over 12,000 planes and 5000 ships, crossed the English Channel from English ports to make landings in Nazi-occupied France. General Dwight D. Eisenhower, Supreme Commander, told the troops: "You are about to embark on a great crusade. . . . You will bring about the destruction of the German war ma-

GREAT
BRITAIN

North Sea

Berlin ★

NETH.
Antwerp
Rotterdam
BELGIUM   GERMANY
Dunkirk
Somme R.   Battle of the Bulge
                (Dec., 1944)
                Bastogne
Paris ★   LUX.

FRANCE   Rhine R.

                                SWITZ.

FINLAND

NORWAY   Leningrad
SWEDEN   Volga R.
        Baltic
        Sea   Moscow ★

DENMARK   SOVIET UNION

North
Sea

IRELAND

GREAT
BRITAIN   NETH.
    London   Rotterdam Berlin ★
ATLANTIC   Dunkirk BELG. GERMANY   Warsaw   Stalingrad
                English   POLAND
OCEAN   Channel
                NORMANDY   Rhine R.
                        Sedan   CZECHOSLOVAKIA
                Paris ★
                FRANCE SWITZ. AUSTRIA   HUNGARY   ROMANIA
                                                            Yalta
                        ITALY   YUGOSLAVIA BULGARIA
                PORTUGAL   Black   Sea
                                Rome   TURKEY
                SPAIN   Anzio   ALBANIA
                                         GREECE   SYRIA

                                                                  LEBANON
                            Algiers   SICILY   PALESTINE TRANSJORDAN
                Casablanca   Tunis   Suez
                                          Mediterranean   Sea   Canal
                                                    CRETE   Alexandria
MOROCCO   TUNISIA   El Alamein Cairo ★

KEY
    Axis nations
    Axis-controlled areas, 1942
    Allies   ALGERIA   EGYPT
    Neutral nations   LIBYA   Red
    Allied advances   Sea

World War II in Europe and Africa

704

chine, elimination of Nazi tyranny over the oppressed peoples of Europe, and security for ourselves in a free world. . . . We will accept nothing less than full Victory."

The success of D-Day depended upon what happened during the first few hours. Should the Allies fail to secure beachheads, should German guns and tanks stop efforts to push inland, the operation would end in disaster.

After bitter fighting, the Allies expand their beachhead. On June 6, 1944, the assault forces landed on five beaches along a 60-mile line. On some beaches the soldiers struggled ashore in the face of heavy enemy fire. At Omaha Beach the Americans almost failed to make it:*

Through waves that were four to five feet high the assault craft surged forward. . . . The first boats were barely 400 yards from the shore when the German guns . . . opened up. . . .

. . . weighed down by their equipment, unable to run in the deep water, and without cover of any kind, men were caught in crisscrossing machine-gun and small-arms fire. . . .

Men fell all along the water's edge. Some were killed instantly, other called pitifully for the medics as the incoming tide slowly engulfed them. . . .

The second wave of troops arrived. . . . Landing craft joined the ever growing graveyard of wrecked, blazing hulks. Each wave of boats gave up its own bloody contribution to the incoming tide, and all along the crescent-shaped strip of beach dead Americans gently nudged each other in the water. . . .

Men lay shoulder to shoulder on the sands, stones, and shale. They crouched down behind obstacles; they sheltered among the bodies of the dead. Pinned down by the enemy fire, . . . confused by their landings in the wrong sectors, . . . and shocked by the devastation and death all around them, the men froze on the beaches. They seemed in the grip of a strange paralysis. . . .

* From *The Longest Day* by Cornelius Ryan. Copyright © 1959 by Cornelius Ryan. Reprinted by permission of Simon & Schuster, Inc., and Victor Gollancz Ltd.

. . . Sergeant Philip Streczyk had had his fill of being pinned down. . . . Some soldiers remember that Streczyk almost booted men off the beach and up the mined headlands, where he breached the enemy barbed wire. . . .

Everywhere intrepid leaders, privates and generals alike, were showing the way, getting the men off the beach. Once started, the troops did not stop again.

Having established beachheads, the Allies rushed more men and supplies into battle. An important factor in the success of D-Day was the Allied control of the air. Allied planes supported the assault troops by bombing enemy positions and supply lines. A second factor contributing to the success of the Allies was that the Germans were caught by surprise. Although expecting an Allied invasion, the Germans did not know where the landing would take place. And they had dismissed June 6 as a possible date because weather conditions were unfavorable.

Allied forces advance on Germany from west and east. Less than a month after D-Day a million Allied soldiers were in France. By the end of August Paris was liberated, and the Allies were pushing towards Germany. By autumn the German cause seemed hopeless. Russian armies were invading Germany from the east; in the west American and British forces already had crossed the German frontier. Allied bombers were striking at German factories and military installations, and mass bombing attacks on cities were turning loose a rain of terror and death on German civilians.

Hitler launches a desperate counteroffensive. The frantic Hitler made one last gamble. In mid-December, 1944, the Germans launched an offensive in the west to split the Allied forces and recapture the Belgian port of Antwerp, vital to Germany. Hitler hoped that a German counteroffensive in the west, together with German production of new jet planes and huge rockets that could strike targets in Britain, might compel the western powers to seek peace.

To carry out this desperate plan, Hitler threw in all available men and material. On December 16, 1944, when the weather kept Allied planes on the ground, 250,000 German soldiers and hundreds of tanks attacked the Allied lines in the Belgium-Luxembourg sector. Some 50,000 Americans were caught by surprise and the Germans broke through the line. But they failed to keep up their drive. What stopped the German offensive in the Battle of the Bulge, writes American historian Kenneth S. Davis, was "the courageous tenacity of handfuls of American soldiers, fighting against overwhelming odds." In no place did the courage of the Americans reveal itself more clearly than in the town of Bastogne (bahs-*tohn'*), which commanded a network of key roads of vital importance to the German advance. The Germans surrounded the town. The American defenders were outnumbered, short of food and ammunition, and sub-

The white trails of ships and the smoke of exploding shells lend an impressionistic tone to the Allied invasion of Iwo Jima (below), giving little hint of the savage fighting to come.

jected to a terrific pounding from German artillery. Yet they refused to surrender. Unable to crush American resistance and short of gasoline, the German offensive ground to a halt. At the beginning of January the Allies launched a counteroffensive that in two weeks wiped out the German gains.

Hitler commits suicide and Germany surrenders. The Battle of the Bulge was Hitler's last desperate effort, and for Hitler's Germany the end was near. By April, 1945, British, United States, and Russian troops were advancing into Germany from the west and the east. From his underground bunker near the chancellery in Berlin a bitter Hitler, physically exhausted, engaged in wild fantasies about new German armies and new victories. Finally, on April 30, 1945, with the Russians only blocks away, *Der Führer* took his own life. His gasoline-soaked body was then burned and buried to prevent it from falling into the hands of the Russians. (Twenty-three years later the Soviet government revealed that Russian soldiers had found Hitler's badly burned corpse soon after its burial.) On May 7, 1945, a demoralized and devastated Germany surrendered unconditionally. The long and horrible war in Europe had ended. But the war with Japan continued.

The Pacific war moves steadily closer to Japan's home islands. After the victory at Midway in June, 1942, the United States took the offensive against Japan. The plan was to seize only those Japanese-held islands which occupied strategic positions. These islands would be used as bases for American bomber attacks on Japanese-held islands and on Japan itself. Two months after the fall of Midway, American marines and soldiers attacked Guadalcanal. In six months of jungle fighting they demonstrated that they could overcome the Japanese soldier in jungle warfare, a type of fighting in which the Japanese were supposedly invincible.

From Guadalcanal the fighting moved from island to island, ever closer to Japan. After naval and aerial bombardment United States troops would dash ashore onto beaches covered by Japanese mines and artillery fire. Often the Japanese had fortified the islands with steel and concrete pillboxes and blockhouses. The Japanese attitude to war made Allied conquest doubly difficult. Centuries of the samurai tradition (page 226) had imbued the Japanese with the feeling that it was an honor to be a warrior. The greatest disgrace for the Japanese soldier was surrender. Thus, even when it became clear that Japan's defeat was only a matter of time, the Japanese soldier would not give up. At Iwo Jima (ee'woh jee'muh), for example, American planes and ships pounded the island for two and a half months before marines were sent ashore. Nevertheless, it took the marines three days to gain only 700 yards, and the casualties were enormous. In nearly a month of fighting, almost 5000 Americans were killed and another 15,000 were wounded. More than 21,000 Japanese soldiers lost their lives, for virtually none surrendered. Another 100,000 perished on Okinawa in June, 1945.

The atomic bomb is dropped on Japan. Plans had been made to turn Okinawa into a jumping-off base for an American invasion of Japan. This invasion never materialized, for on August 6, 1945, an atomic bomb—the equivalent of 20,000 tons of TNT—was dropped on the Japanese city of Hiroshima (hee-rosh-mah). President Truman ordered the atomic attack in order to avoid an American invasion of Japan that would have cost hundreds of thousands of casualties. Two Japanese doctors described the horrible effects of that first atomic bomb:

"It was a horrible sight," said Dr. Tabuchi [tah-boo-chee]. "Hundreds of injured people who were trying to escape to the hills passed our house. The sight of them was almost unbearable. Their faces and hands were burned and swollen, and great sheets of skin had peeled away . . . to hang down like rags on a scarecrow." . . .

Mr. Katsutani [kahts-tah-nee] . . . went on: . . . "There must have been hundreds and thousands who fled to the river to escape the fire and then drowned.

"The sight of the soldiers, though, was more dreadful than the dead people floating down the river. I came onto I don't know how many, burned from the hips up; and where the skin had peeled, their flesh was wet and mushy. They must have been wearing their military caps because the black hair on top of their heads was not burned. It made them look like they were wearing black lacquer bowls.

"And they had no faces! Their eyes, noses, and mouths had been burned away, and it looked like their ears had melted off."

The world had never seen so destructive a weapon. This single atomic bomb completely demolished about 60 per cent of the city of Hiroshima. For a radius of four miles virtually no buildings were left standing. More than 78,000 people were instantly killed; 10,000 more disappeared without a trace. Thirty-seven thousand Japanese suffered severe injuries, and thousands of others later developed agonizing and often fatal diseases from having been exposed to the deadly gamma rays released by the explosion.

Japan's surrender ends World War II. The end of the war was in sight for Japan. On August 8 Russia entered the Pacific conflict by invading Japanese-held Manchuria. The next day, when the Japanese had made no reply to an American demand for unconditional surrender, a second atomic bomb was dropped on Nagasaki, an important shipbuilding city. Shortly afterwards Japan asked for peace. On September 2, 1945, representatives of the Japanese government signed a document of surrender aboard the United States battleship *Missouri,* anchored in Tokyo Bay. On that occasion, General Douglas MacArthur expressed the hopes of a war-weary world:

It is my earnest hope and indeed the hope of all mankind that from this solemn occasion a better world shall emerge out of the blood and carnage of the past—a world dedicated to the dignity of man and the fulfillment of his most cherished wish —for freedom, tolerance, and justice.

1. Why was Midway a crucial battle?

2. Why were the Germans determined to capture Stalingrad in 1942? Why did the attack fail? Why was Stalingrad a major disaster for the Germans?

3. Why was El Alamein the turning point in the war in North Africa?

4. Why did the Allies invade Italy? What was the situation in Italy by 1943?

5. How did the Allies plan to invade France? Why was their invasion successful? What was Hitler's response? What was the result?

6. How did the United States bring the war closer to Japan?

7. Why did the Japanese attitude toward war make the fighting even more difficult?

8. What brought the Pacific war to a close?

Results of World War II

World War II is tremendously destructive. World War II was the most destructive war in human history. More than 30,000,000 soldiers and civilians perished. Destruction was frightful. American historian Gordon Wright describes the shattered condition of Europe at the war's end.*

The destruction of physical property was . . . unprecedented. . . . In the Soviet Union, 1700 cities and towns and 70,000 villages had been devastated; so were 70 per cent of the industrial installations and 60 per cent of the transportation facilities in the invaded areas. In Berlin, 75 per cent of the houses were destroyed or severely damaged; someone estimated that to clear the city's rubble would require the use of ten fifty-car freight trains per day for sixteen years. In some cities (for example, Dusseldorf), 95 per cent of the homes were uninhabitable. In France and the Low Countries as well as in Germany, most waterways and harbors were blocked, most bridges destroyed, much of the railway system temporarily unusable. In England, whole sections of central London and of other industrial cities had been laid waste by incendiary bombs. Almost everywhere on the continent, industrial and agricultural production was down by more than half; food, clothing, and consumer necessities were in desperately short supply; circuits of trade had been almost totally disrupted. Except for a few oases like [neutral] Sweden and Switzerland, Europe seemed destined to be, at least for some years, a vast dilapidated slum and poorhouse.

The Allies occupy Germany and Japan. The war resulted in Allied occupation of both Japan and Germany. In Japan virtually all the occupation troops were American, but Germany was divided into separate American, British, French, and Russian occupation zones. Because relations between Russia and the western Allies became strained after the war, no peace treaty was ever signed with Germany. Today Germany is still a divided nation—a communist East Germany and a democratic West Germany that includes the former American, British, and French zones.

Nationalism declines in Western Europe. World War II led to a decline of nationalism in Western Europe. The disastrous Hitler years convinced West Europeans of the dangers of extreme nationalism, and fear of Russia and a desire to strengthen their economies contributed

* From *The Ordeal of Total War, 1939–45* by Gordon Wright (New York: Harper and Row Publishers, Inc., 1968; copyright 1968 by Gordon Wright). Reprinted by permission.

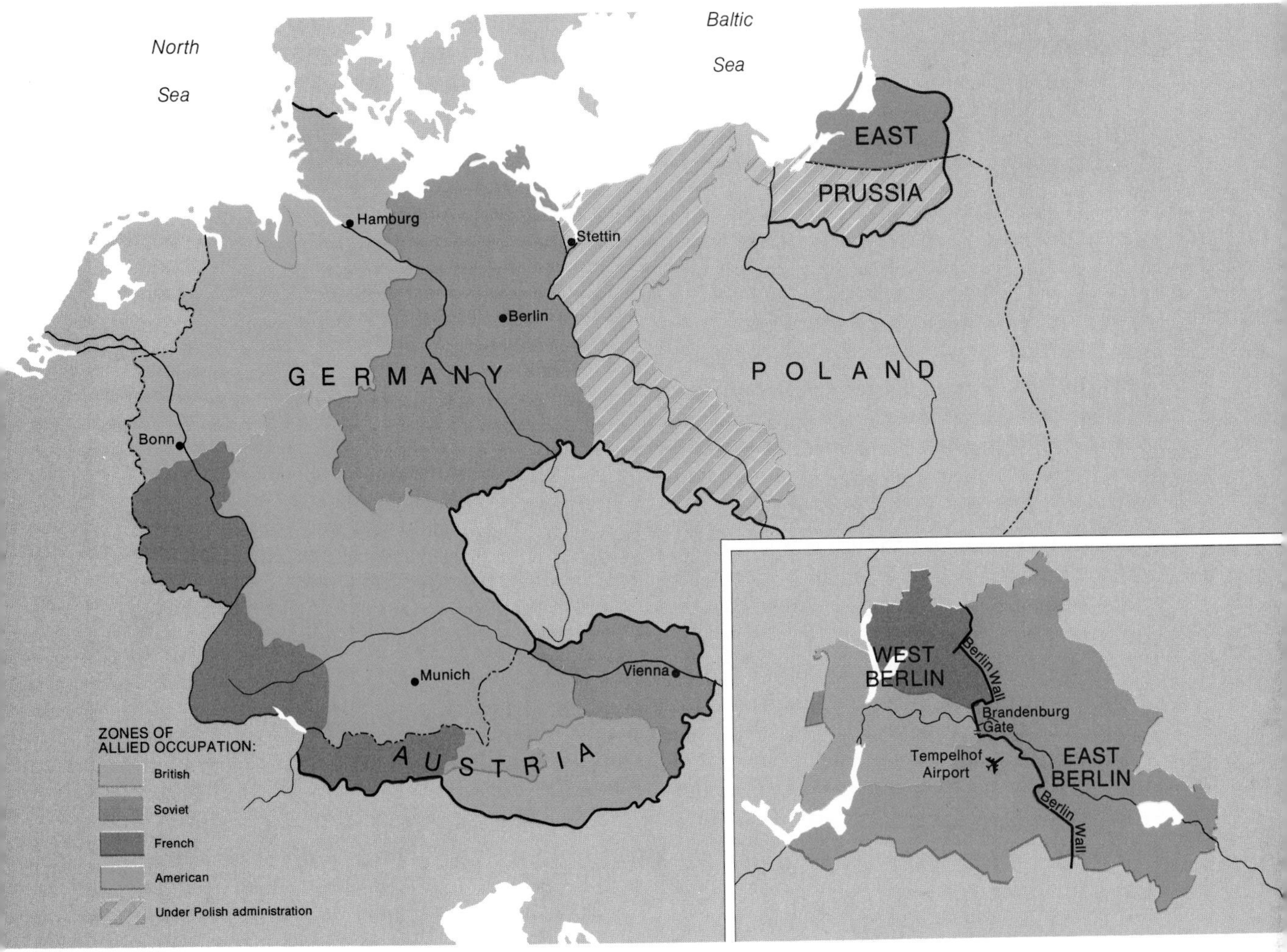
North
Sea
Baltic
Sea
EAST
PRUSSIA
Hamburg
Stettin
Berlin
GERMANY
POLAND
Bonn
Munich
Vienna
AUSTRIA
ZONES OF
ALLIED OCCUPATION:
British
Soviet
French
American
Under Polish administration
WEST
BERLIN
Berlin Wall
Brandenburg
Gate
Tempelhof
Airport
EAST
BERLIN
Berlin Wall

The Occupation of Germany and Austria

to various forms of international cooperation. The romantic nationalism that helped to usher Hitler into power was discredited in Germany, and those who talked of wars of conquest and wars of revenge had lost their audience.

The United Nations is founded. In the fall of 1944, when Germany's defeat seemed certain, representatives of the United States, Britain, China, and Russia met at Dumbarton Oaks in Washington, D.C., to make plans for a world organization. In the spring of 1945 representatives of 50 nations drafted the Charter of the United Nations (UN). The UN was established to prevent disputes between nations from turning into wars. It would also help the nations of the world combat poverty, disease, hunger, and injustice.

World War II speeds independence for colonies. World War II speeded the disintegration of the overseas empires of European nations. Weakened by the long war, the colonial powers were in no position to resist the demands of Africans and Asians for an end to imperial rule. In some cases independence was achieved peacefully; in other cases, the mother country fought long and bloody wars to retain a valuable part of its empire, only to lose its colonies in the end.

Eastern Europe comes under Soviet domination. In the last stages of the war, as the Red Army moved west towards Germany, the Russians installed Communists in the governments of the East European nations. Soviet troops remained in occupation of these lands. By 1948, backed by the Red Army, the Communists were in control of the Eastern European governments. Thus virtually all of Eastern Europe, in one way or another, had come under the control of the Soviet Union.

The United States and the Soviet Union emerge as Super Powers. The United States and Russia emerged from the war as the two most powerful nations in the world, not just Great Powers but Super Powers. The United States had the atomic bomb, and her economy, stimulated by the production of war materials, was booming. Despite enormous losses, Russia had the largest army in the world, and she was tightening her grip on the nations of Eastern Europe and threatening to extend her influence westward. The cooperation that had marked American-Russian relations during the war came to an end with the defeat of the common enemy.

Western Europe loses its pre-eminence in world affairs. The weakened condition of Western Europe immediately after the war, the emergence of the United States and the Soviet Union as Super Powers, the loss of overseas empires—all indicated that Western Europe had lost its dominant position in world affairs. In the decades after World War II many of the most important happenings and developments did not take place in Europe and did not directly involve the chief nations of Western Europe. The non-European world was growing increasingly more important.

The Atomic Age begins. World War II ushered in the Atomic Age. In 1945 only the United States had the atomic bomb, but during the years that followed, other nations acquired the bomb or the know-how to build one. The United States, the Soviet Union, and still other nations learned how to build increasingly larger and more destructive bombs. And they developed ever larger rockets to deliver them. Today one frightening truth stands out above all others —that man has stored enough powerful weapons to destroy himself and his civilization. This is the ever present, ever terrifying, and ultimately most significant legacy of World War II.

CHECK-UP

1. What estimates can be made of the destructiveness of World War II in Europe? What did the victorious powers do about Germany and Japan after the war?

2. How did World War II affect the spirit of nationalism in Western Europe? Colonial empires? International organizations?

3. How did World War II affect Eastern Europe? What were its effects on the status of the United States and the Soviet Union?

Summing Up

Hitler's policy of ignoring restrictions placed on Germany by the Versailles Treaty and of including all Germans in an expanded Reich met with no effective resistance from Britain and France. Nor did Mussolini's imperialist attack on Ethiopia. Having dismembered Czechoslovakia, in 1939 Hitler concluded a nonaggression pact with Stalin that doomed Poland. Although they could provide no effective aid to Poland, Britain and France at last abandoned their policy of appeasement.

Having overrun Poland, Hitler struck at Denmark and Norway, and then launched a blitzkrieg against Belgium, the Netherlands, and France. All three were crushed, and only her navy and air force enabled Britain to hold out against Nazi attacks. In 1941 Hitler suddenly launched a massive strike at Russia, hoping to find there the natural resources and "living space" promised the Germans. Despite terrible losses, the Russians managed to hold Leningrad,

Moscow, and Stalingrad on the Volga. Meanwhile, under Hitler's New Order the Germans were ruthlessly exploiting all resources of the overrun countries and using their peoples as slave labor. The New Order also called for the extermination of all Jews.

Japan's determination to exploit the resources of Southeast Asia led her to attack Pearl Harbor in the Hawaiian Islands. This attack late in 1941 brought the United States into the war against both Japan and Germany. Both Britain and the Soviet Union encouraged resistance movements in countries occupied by the Axis powers. Gradually the Russians began to drive the Germans westward. Britain and the United States freed North Africa and slowly pushed back the Japanese attack in the Pacific.

Allied invasions of the European mainland pushed the Germans back in Western Europe, while the Russians were rolling the Nazis back in the East. On May 7, 1945, Germany surrendered unconditionally. In the Pacific war the United States dropped two atomic bombs on Japanese cities to hasten Japan's surrender. By September, 1945, the most destructive war in history had come to an end. The Soviet Union and the United States emerged as Super Powers from a conflict that ushered in the Atomic Age. World War II led to an agreement to establish the United Nations and to the breakup of colonial empires. But Soviet imperialism, which established firm control over Eastern Europe, would contribute to the postwar feeling of international tension and insecurity.

Chapter Highlights

Can you explain?

aggression	appeasement	annex	self-determination
underground	evacuation	demilitarized	rearmament
blitzkrieg	redemption	"living space"	cease-fire
sabotage	genocide	satellite	concentration camps

Can you identify?

Axis	Midway	Stalingrad	Churchill
R.A.F.	Iwo Jima	Guadalcanal	MacArthur
Hitler	Rommel	Montgomery	Munich Conference
Warsaw	Ethiopia	Rhineland	United Nations
Franco	Leningrad	Mussolini	Hitler-Stalin Pact
Stalin	Daladier	Sudetenland	Maginot Line
Dunkirk	Auschwitz	Chamberlain	Czechoslovakia
D-Day	Hiroshima	Pearl Harbor	
Gestapo	Eisenhower	Baltic republics	

1. Could cooperation among the Soviet Union, France, and Britain have prevented World War II? Why was such a policy not adopted?

2. Why was fascism regarded by many as the irresistible wave of the future?

3. Chamberlain and Daladier have been harshly criticized for their role at Munich. Why? Why have some historians been less critical?

4. How was it possible for Hitler and Stalin to make a deal? Are dictators more free to make political deals than statesmen in democratic countries? Why?

5. Does appeasement ever make sense?

6. How was it possible for the Nazis to plan and carry out a program to exterminate Jews?

7. Why was Britain able to hold out against Nazi attacks?

8. Stalin believed that the western powers could and should have invaded France long before D-Day. Do you agree? Why?

9. The Russians believe they made the greatest contribution to the defeat of Germany in World War II. Why? What was the contribution of the western allies?

10. Was the use of the atomic bomb justified? Why?

11. Did American isolationism after World War I contribute to the rise of dictatorships and World War II? Why?

12. Why was the resistance movement important?

13. Why did the extremes of nationalism in the 1930's give way to a desire for international cooperation by 1945?

14. Why did the United States and the Soviet Union emerge as the Super Powers after World War II?

15. World War II ushered in the Atomic Age. Why is this the most significant legacy of World War II?

The World in Change

Unit Eight———

Shaping of the Postwar World

Relations between the Super Powers have varied from near war to peaceful coexistence. The tension aroused by Stalinist policies is symbolized by the barbed wire blocking access to the Brandenburg Gate (left), one of the entry points into East Berlin. In the space race, the United States took a clear lead when her astronauts walked on the moon (top, above). De-Stalinization policies led to cultural exchange; American and Russian artists such as the Bolshoi Ballet (above) visited each other's countries.

The Second World War ended in the summer of 1945. Less than two years later, in April, 1947, Bernard Baruch (buh-*rook′*), one of the most distinguished elder statesmen in the United States, remarked: "Let us not be deceived— today we are in the midst of a cold war." The phrase *cold war* stuck in the mind of a public frightened and dismayed by the mounting tensions between the United States and the Soviet Union. Added to people's uneasiness was the recent invention of nuclear weapons that could unleash the destructiveness of the terrifying energies stored in the basic building block of nature, the atom.

The cold war heralded an altogether new age in world history. The Europe-centered world order—from which we are still drawing our main concepts about politics, society, and the world at large—disappeared. By 1950 a global order had taken shape. It was an order so revolutionary that even now men are barely beginning to grasp its essentials. The crises of the cold war have no doubt shaped much of current events. Yet we cannot understand such basic turning points in human destiny without taking a long, sweeping view, as if looking from a satellite circling the earth. From these lofty heights this chapter introduces the present.

The Era of Monoculture and Overkill

Viewing the present world order from a lofty perspective, we might see it as the product of three basic developments: (1) the outpouring of the European (or western) way of life over the entire world; (2) the changeover from a Europe-centered framework of power politics to a global framework; and (3) the development of weapons that have the capacity to obliterate all mankind. Let us explain these massive changes one by one.

OUTPOURING OF WESTERN CIVILIZATION

The outpouring of the European—or, as it is often expressed, the "western"—way of life over the entire globe is one of the most remarkable events in the history of the human race. Never before has one civilization dominated all others in the world, undermining and often destroying them altogether while trying to substitute its own achievements. Never before has one civilization created an inescapable single world order, endowed with a common awareness of unity and interdependence. Never before, indeed, has one civilization assumed a global significance and convinced all mankind that its ways alone are "modern." This breathtaking expansion of western civilization has resulted in a cultural earthquake in lands that have sought to imitate western ways.

Western civilization is characterized by four ideals. There has developed over thousands of years a great variety of civilizations throughout the world, each endowed with unique attitudes towards life, with a religion or philosophy and a language of its own. Western civilization is only one of many in the world. But it developed differently and differed considerably from the civilizations of Hindu India, Confucian China, the Islamic Middle East, and tribal Africa. As we have seen, western civilization grew up in Western and Southern Europe, out of a blend of the moral and monotheistic beliefs of the ancient Hebrews and the secular and rational interests of the Greeks. In the Middle Ages the unity of western civilization was embodied in the Catholic Church and the memory of the Roman Empire. Even though Western Europe became divided into national states, it preserved a sense of unity and common identity. In the past two centuries western leadership has been rooted in Western Europe, especially Britain and France, with the United States recently assuming an informal command.

By the first decade of the twentieth century western civilization was characterized by the following ideals: (1) *democracy*—respect for the rights of the individual and confidence in parliamentary government and the rule of law as the most effective safeguards against abuses of power; (2) *rationalism*—confidence in man's ability to solve his problems through reason; (3) *the capitalist ethic*—the notion that work is man's duty and that success in business is a desirable aim in life; and (4) *progress*—faith in human progress through science, technology, and education. These western ideals, despite much resistance, have become dominant in a large part of the world.

European expansion exposes the world to western ways. Let us recognize that the desire for power and more territory and the belief that one is the bearer of a superior civilization is by no means peculiar to western civilization. Practically all civilizations have tried to enlarge their territory and have assumed that they are superior to all other civilizations. None has expressed that presumption more strongly than the Chinese. What is peculiar to western civilization is its ability to carry its ways to all points of the globe. The process of western expansion began, as we have seen, in the Age of Exploration in the fifteenth century. Some societies resisted westernization and clung to their past. But after the middle of the nineteenth century the superior power of European civilization, in terms of weapons and organization, became obvious. As a matter of course western civilization discredited or overthrew Chinese emperors, Ottoman sultans, Indian princes, and the chiefs of great African tribes.

Outright political control of nonwestern nations was accompanied, or prompted, by economic penetration. European and American businessmen exploited the natural riches of Asia, Africa, and Latin America and carried western goods to all parts of the globe. They thereby harnessed the resources of the entire world to the Euro-American economy. They imposed their currencies, their banking and accounting systems, their systems of weights and measures, their calendars, their technology, and above all, their impatient pace of economic progress, upon people quite unprepared for these innovations. Was it surprising that men all over the world complained of being exploited?

The western masters did even more: They implanted in the minds of men the idea that they must take western civilization as the model for their own development. Native traditions provided no defense against western penetration and were obviously "backward." As Kemal Atatürk (keh-*mahl'* ah-tah-*turk'*), the father of modern Turkey, expressed it: The Turkish nation "has now accepted the principle that the only means for the survival of nations in the international struggle for existence lies in the acceptance of contemporary western civilization."

The imitation of western ways centered around three principal goals. The first was democracy as the best form of government. Had not the success of western civilization shown the universal benefits of democracy? It encouraged the participation of all men and women in the running of their government, under laws regulated by a constitution; it also guaranteed individual freedom. Secondly, men looked to industrial technology and science as the key to the improvement of their social and economic conditions. "Industrialize!" became their rallying cry. They believed industrialization would make their nations internationally powerful and bring their people individual prosperity.

Finally—and most important—the political power of the West impressed the rest of the world. Those who lived under western domination agitated for self-determination and statehood. And they dreamed of imitating their model by also becoming world powers. Thus the competitiveness of power politics, an inevitable by-product of westernization, was extended over the entire globe.

The loss of traditional values in nonwestern nations leads to humiliation. To statesmen, philosophers, chieftains, or elders in countries which were dominated by the West, the western influence was ruinous to native culture. It undermined inherited values and traditions. Styles of life that had developed over centuries were altered and replaced with innovations that humiliated nonwesterners. Men grew dispirited and insecure and society became deeply divided. But continuing the old ways, no matter how glorious they once had been, merely deepened the current humiliation of the nonwestern world. Traditional values seemed hopelessly ineffective, backward, and inefficient in comparison to western technology, business, and governmental organization. To this day nonwestern societies are torn between westernization and the restoration of ancient traditions.

Throughout the world nonwestern societies seek to modernize. After World War II, western imperialism declined. Intensified nationalism among Asians and Africans and the weakened condition of the European powers forced the withdrawal of the colonial powers from Asia and Africa. The British, French, Dutch, and Belgians were in no position to resist the trend, and the United States would not stand in the way of self-government for colonial peoples as long as the government was not in the hands of Communists.

Within two decades Asia and Africa, proud of their liberation from western rule, were crowded with new states patterned closely after the western nations. Each tried to "modernize" itself in order to be considered a worthy member of the emerging global community. Yet each was wracked by many-faceted internal discord: modernizers who wanted to adopt western techniques battled with traditionalists who wanted to preserve ancient ways, advocates of "capitalism" with those favoring "communism," centralizers who sought to create a unified national state with spokesmen for local and regional interests. Leaders of these emerging nations sought to apply western technology, business practices, and forms of government in order to adjust to the modern world. But it was most difficult to introduce the institutions and procedures of democracy in societies that had little or no democratic traditions. Some were profoundly impressed by the Soviet experience, which seemed to provide a good example of how a nation could be unified, industrialized, and strengthened in a short period of time.

In the new nations freedom and democracy often led to disunity, chaos, and eventually the establishment of one-party governments or military rule. Instead of becoming democracies, many new nations began to resemble dictatorships. And each was burdened by the need for armies, industries, schools, and prestige in a world that scorned poverty, helplessness, and backwardness. Forced to submit to the worldwide domination of western standards of efficiency and human well-being, the peoples of the nonwestern world were bound to express their resentment over their continued humiliation. This expression of resentment heightened the tensions of the cold war. The frightful difficulties of westernizing nonwestern societies have hardly been understood, let alone solved, and the cultural earthquake has by no means ended.

POLITICS ON A GLOBAL SCALE

Now let us turn to the second of the basic factors which seem to shape the present: the changeover from a Europe-centered framework for world politics to a global framework.

Until 1945 world politics are Europe-centered. By 1914 the European nations had come to dominate the affairs of the entire world. Parts of Asia and most of Africa had been seized by European states. The affairs of nonwestern lands were settled in European capitals. Even the United States (not to mention the rest of the western hemisphere) was tied, politically, economically, and culturally, to the great centers of Europe. Europe spoke for all mankind, and when Europe went to war in 1914, nearly the entire world population became involved in one way or another.

The United States and Soviet Russia emerge as Super Powers. At the end of the Second World War the Great Powers of old—Britain, France, Italy, Germany—were eclipsed. Above them towered two political giants from outside the European neighborhood, the United States and the Soviet Union, the "Super Powers." The United States had not only emerged victorious in Western Europe and the Pacific, but had also grown so prosperous during the war that it could afterwards rebuild the shattered economies of its allies and even of its enemies. It even extended its protection into those parts of the world from which the former colonial powers were forced to withdraw. Thanks to the heroic self-sacrifice of its soldiers and civilians and no doubt thanks to the forced industrialization carried out by Stalin, Russia had contributed vastly more of its substance to the defeat of

Hitler than had the United States. As Hitler's armies withdrew, the Red Army occupied Eastern and Central Europe while the American, British, and French troops were held back by continued German resistance. The might of the Soviet Union at the end of the war was, as we shall see, more apparent than real. Yet, except for the United States, Russia had no rival in the world.

The greater number of sovereign states has led to power struggles everywhere. It was with the prompting and assistance of the two Super Powers that many new states in Asia and Africa obtained their independence. With their rise to independence the complexity of international relations increased greatly. Whereas twenty-odd states had participated in the wrangles in the European neighborhood before World War II, now well over 130 states of all sizes crowd the global framework. These states represent a far greater variety of cultures, living standards, and political systems than was ever found in Europe. Many of them are troubled by greater political and economic instability than ever beset even the weakest members of the old European community. Their internal divisions aggravate tensions between the Soviet Union and the United States. The weakness of many of these states invites aggression, and former powers as well as new nations have spent huge sums for arms and have engaged in wars of aggression against their neighbors. For the sake of its own security, each nation tries to dominate its neighbors. The tensions and conflicts familiar from European history are thus re-enacted, but on a vastly wider stage. People in the new states are mainly poor, illiterate, and consumed with the daily struggle for survival. Most of them are eager to avenge their loss of dignity and glory. This has made the world situation more explosive. The power struggle penetrates all corners of the world and affords no shelter of neutrality.

There is also growing evidence of unity and cooperation. The new states, despite different cultural traditions, are brought closer to each other by the uniformity imposed upon the world by the outpouring of western ways. No state can escape the fact that its external security is a matter of concern to all others. Its foreign policy is set into a global network of alliances and power rivalries. No one can deny, furthermore, that power in global politics is measured by the same weapons, whether atomic bombs and jet planes, or automatic rifles and mortars. Raw courage alone avails nothing; machines do most of the killing. Moreover, all states—large and small—are tied together by a common economic network of trade, finance, currencies, and interrelated schemes for economic development centered in the United States, Western Europe, Soviet Russia, and increasingly Japan as well. Whether willingly or not, all people share the need to follow the western standards of economic development, prosperity, and health. No people, for instance, has yet been able to resist the lure of electricity, labor-saving machinery, piped running water, or life-saving medicine.

So it is with a thousand necessities of life. As we look at pictures of cities in all parts of the world, we see a striking uniformity. The mass-produced automobile, an American invention, dominates the paved streets. High-rise apartment buildings and skyscrapers show a common architectural inspiration and technical skill. The same office routines prevail, aided by telephones, typewriters, and computers. Managers or secretaries, all dressed in western clothes, conduct themselves with the same air of efficiency. Even those who increasingly protest the tyranny of the organization, of the "Establishment," show an international uniformity in their slogans, dress, and attitudes.

The appearance of world unity is deceptive. It is easy for Americans to spot familiar sights as they survey the world. Yet the appearance of world unity is deceptive. Although contact with western civilization has weakened, threatened, and altered traditional non-European cultures, many of them are far from dead. As long

Founded to preserve peace, the United Nations (above) has had mixed results in achieving its goal. In general, it has functioned best in situations not involving the Super Powers, which have tended to settle matters by direct diplomacy. The UN includes six principal organs and a number of dependent organs and related agencies. The main body of the UN is the General Assembly in which every member state is represented and casts one vote. The General Assembly deliberates issues and makes recommendations to its members and to the Security Council. The Council holds the primary responsibility for preserving peace. Fifteen nations, five of them permanent members with veto power, make up the Security Council. All of the "Big Five" (the United States, the Soviet Union, the United Kingdom, France, and Communist China) must agree on serious issues. On many occasions the Soviet Union has used its right to veto major issues, thereby blocking action desired by other members of the Security Council.

Other major organs of the UN are the Trusteeship Council, which supervises territories not yet ready for independence; the International Court of Justice, which is the chief judicial arm of the UN; the Economic and Social Council, which coordinates the work of many specialized agencies; and the Secretariat, which handles all administrative work. Head of the Secretariat is the Secretary-General, who presides over the General Assembly and may refer matters to the Security Council.

Among the many specialized agencies which deal with world problems are the Children's Fund (UNICEF); the Educational, Scientific, and Cultural Organization (UNESCO); the World Health Organization; the World Bank; the Food and Agricultural Organization; and the Commission on Refugees. Work done by the agencies includes resettling refugees (top left), the production of inexpensive foods (center left), literacy programs and technological training (bottom left), improving agricultural techniques, providing loans to needy nations, improving health conditions, and sponsoring cultural exchange.

as they retain their native language, they will continue the struggle to survive. The Chinese aspire to a restoration of their former greatness. The Arabs fiercely defend their Muslim culture. The Jews are creating a new territorial base in Israel, their ancient homeland. Africans south of the Sahara are searching for the creation of an "African personality" and for a suitable political expression of it. Sometimes this fight to preserve the ways of the past takes the form of an embittered anti-Americanism or anti-westernism. In Latin America, for example, the tide against "Yankee" influence is running strong, as it is in Western Europe. The leaders of the Soviet Union are determined to assist in the doom of "capitalism," which is their way of saying that American and Western European influence in the world must give way to their own. Wherever we look, we see the evidence of deep antagonisms, heightened by the continued arms race.

THE NUCLEAR THREAT

Nuclear weapons have not intimidated the smaller nations. The third development that made the end of the Second World War a crucial turning point in human destiny was the invention of weapons capable of destroying much or all of the human race. At the push of a button, these weapons have the power to destroy whole cities and communications centers at one stroke. The deadly effects of protracted radiation are added to the instant physical destruction. The only protection which men have so far devised against such a threat has been the mounting of a counter-threat or deterrent, the buildup of weapons to make it suicidal for one country to fire its bombs at another. What are the political consequences? In their vain competition for security, since 1953 the Super Powers have assembled so huge a stockpile of atomic warheads that they can wipe out ("overkill") each other several times.

The complex technology required for the perfection and accurate delivery of these weapons is—and will continue to be—the property of only the most highly industrialized

and resourceful countries. It accentuates the inequality of power found in the world. The smaller countries, who find these weapons beyond their means, will be much less able than before to compete with the global leaders. This means, of course, that it is to their interest that the bomb not be used as an instrument of power politics. As long as it is ruled out, guerrilla forces under favorable conditions can hold out against a vastly superior force, as has been shown in the Vietnam War.

More than ever before, international conflicts need to be settled by compromise. For the entire global community and foremost for those nations which possess nuclear weapons, all international relations are now fraught with the ever present and acute choice of life or death for mankind. Before the French Revolution, war affected primarily the soldiers, men trained to fight. In the two world wars, the civilian populations were also involved in that they suffered regimentation, hunger, and bombardment. The huge air raids of the Second World War at one blow destroyed whole sections of cities. Atomic war threatens to carry war to its extreme—the annihilation of entire cities and even countries. Will international conflicts be allowed to build up to the bitterness that might lead to the use of the bomb, or can they be settled by compromise? Will nations choose to make compromises to escape the nuclear holocaust, or will they prefer death to sacrificing self-interest? Never before have the foreign relations of a country cut so demandingly into both the life of every individual and the fate of his society.

What impact does the new world order have on the United States? Looking from our detached perspective, we first see that, although the United States stands out as a pacesetter in almost all achievements that give unity to a westernized world, it too is being subverted by the new order. United States ascendancy as a Super Power, for instance, has given rise to a large defense industry. This "military-industrial complex," as President Eisenhower called it, has no precedent in American history. The founding fathers and their descendants, until the First World War, never had to contend with so powerful a pressure group, whose business is war or potential war on a huge scale.

Secondly, Americans today are burdened with the necessity of thinking about the problems of the entire world—at a time when their own affairs need close attention. Poverty in the cities and in certain rural areas and racial discrimination—to mention but two outstanding issues—are greatly aggravated by international developments. The emergence of black Africa —indeed, of the world's colored majority— has given a militant edge to the drive for racial equality and recognition among Afro-Americans and other minority groups. The problems of some of the developing lands (such as the war in Vietnam) have diverted scarce resources from America's poor. Where indeed is the greater need, at home or abroad? Thus foreign and domestic policy intertwine as never before. Meanwhile, Americans, more affluent than ever, groan over high taxes and the upward spiraling cost of living. The demands made on American society have led to growing social and political disunity, accompanied by a mounting sense of failure and frustration. In the past, Americans have managed to keep their house in relatively good order. But can the United States cope with the problems of this new era of power politics?

CHECK-UP

1. What three basic developments shaped our present world order?

2. What ideals characterize western civilization?

3. Why did the nonwestern nations feel they had to imitate the West? What did they imitate? Why did this lead to humiliation for nonwesterners?

4. In what ways did modernization based on the Western model speed up after World War II? What conflicts took place within each country as a result?

5. What changes took place in world politics between 1914 and 1945?

6. In what ways is there a power struggle on the international level? How has cooperation among nations increased? Why is world unity far from a reality?

7. Why did the invention of nuclear weapons mark a turning point in human destiny? How have they affected world politics?

8. What impact has the new world order had on the United States?

The Super Powers Compete

In 1947 when Bernard Baruch tried to make sense of world events by setting them into the framework of a cold war, he stated two obvious facts of political life in the contempory world: (1) global politics were now shaped by the worldwide competition between the United States and the Soviet Union; (2) this competition was softened by the determination of both countries to prevent the escalation or buildup of their conflicts into a shooting war. A hot war inevitably would lead to—or even start with—the launching of atomic warheads, with predictably disastrous consequences. "Brinkmanship," the carrying of each dispute to the edge of a hot war while making sure of not falling into the thermonuclear abyss, became the essence of diplomatic relations between the two Super Powers.

There is a long history of hostility between the Super Powers. The relationship between the United States and the Soviet Union was burdened by a history of mutual hostility. Long before the Bolshevik Revolution there was ideological conflict between American democracy and tsarist autocracy. After World War I the global appeal of western democracy was pitted against that of Soviet socialism. Longer than any other major power the United States withheld diplomatic recognition from the Soviet Union. Americans cheered when the League of Nations expelled the Soviet government in 1940 after it attacked helpless Finland. Hitler's invasion of Russia in 1941 somewhat reversed the trend, forcing Stalin to accept the support of Britain and later the United States. But the relationship between the Allies was always difficult. Despite President Franklin D. Roosevelt's manifest goodwill, Stalin would never abandon the Leninist hatred of "capitalism." He would not let his country suddenly be thrown open to American influence. American help during the war was therefore carefully disguised on Stalin's orders.

In addition, major conflicts of policy arose. In the last stages of World War II, Russian troops overran much of Eastern Europe. British and American statesmen wanted to preserve the freedom and independence of the countries lying between Germany and Russia. While Stalin paid lip service to the ideal of self-determination (and even had Russia join the United Nations as a charter member), he had his way in lands occupied by his armies.

The unprecedented expansion of Soviet power into Eastern Europe raised profound fears in western nations. Had it not always been the ambition of revolutionary Russia to dominate the world in the name of Soviet socialism? Stalin, in turn, knowing how narrowly Soviet Russia had escaped defeat, was in no mood to surrender his dearly bought gains. He watched the growing hostility of his wartime partners with deep suspicion, feeling that the "capitalists" had always schemed to destroy Soviet socialism. Thus the stage was set for the cold war, a struggle fed by thwarted ambition and, even more, by blind mutual fear.

How did the United States become a Super Power? Let us briefly sketch the condition and character of the two champions in this relentless conflict. The United States had not moved into the foreground of world events by a deliberate ambition for global domination. Nothing could have been further from the American mind in 1939. With many misgivings the United States arrived at its Super Power status when it resolved to prevent Nazi domination of the peoples of Western Europe. The fact that the United States increasingly stood out as a global model of the good life for all of mankind, imitated even when it was denounced and hated, was a welcome by-product of America's internal development, not a conscious political aim. For about a decade America's new global power failed to penetrate the mind of the average citizen. Even now, few Americans realize their overwhelming superiority of resources.

In 1945 the United States was a large and rich country, untouched by the ravages of war, with ample, highly trained, and intelligent manpower long conditioned to combine individual initiative with large-scale government action. It possessed the most advanced industries in the world and the knowledge for their further development. Despite repeated shifting of economic gears during the cold war, there was no major economic slump after World War II. The soundness of American prosperity became the envy of the world; it disproved all communist prophecies of a "capitalist" collapse. The United States furthermore could boast of a loyal population—men and women who were willing to work together under a government that ruled by majority vote, and who were confident of their capacity to achieve success in the future.

Yet in 1945 there was an obvious weakness in the American position. Most Americans wanted to bring the troops home and be rid of war for good. Roosevelt himself, who died shortly before the end of the war in Europe, was convinced of the rise of a new isolationism; he even told Stalin about it. Yet there was one factor that offset the immediate demobilization of the armed forces: the Americans possessed the atomic bomb; the Russians did not.

How did the Soviet Union become a Super Power? At Potsdam in 1945 Churchill and Truman, who succeeded Roosevelt as President of the United States, were impressed by the might of Soviet Russia. Soviet Russia possessed the largest army in the world, hardened in nearly four years of combat with Hitler's legions. It occupied vast territories stretching from the Pacific Ocean to the center of Europe; it held sway over many peoples. It was ruled, furthermore, by a ruthless dictatorship which, in peace and war, had not hesitated to sacrifice millions of lives for the sake of political survival. Stalinism, as Stalin pointed out at the victory banquets, had been vindicated; it had made Soviet Russia a Super Power.

Soviet Russia could boast of an impressive achievement. Stalinism had turned a backward nation into a modern industrialized state; Russia had survived crushing defeats in the early stages of World War II to emerge victorious. These Soviet accomplishments impressed intellectuals who sought to develop their nations' resources and end their industrial backwardness. Soviet socialism appealed particularly to the non-European world that was just awakening to political awareness. Some African and Asian intellectuals insisted that imitation of American capitalism would not lessen the tremendous gap between rich and poor. To develop their nations, they needed not private enterprise but a state-directed economy, such as Soviet-style socialism, to point the way. They also needed self-confidence in their capacity to "modernize." Furthermore, the Marxist view of history guaranteed the inevitable victory of "socialism" (see pages 528–532).

The United States overestimates Soviet power. The Soviet ambition was to outdo the United States in terms of what the latter could do best—technology, industrial productivity, and standard of living. The fact that Soviet communism itself had not yet succeeded in its much publicized ambition proved a source of weakness. Russia still lagged behind the United States, and its achievements were stained by ter-

ror. But in 1945 who could be sure of the continued vitality of western "capitalism"? Clearly France, Holland, Belgium, and even Great Britain were in no condition to resume their former positions of power in the world. Who would fill the political vacuum created by their decline, the United States representing the West or the Soviet Union, which claimed to speak for the nonwesterners? Looking back, it would appear that in 1945 Truman and Churchill were perhaps unduly frightened of Soviet power, for at the height of its triumph Stalin's empire was far from strong. The war had taken the cream of its manhood and reduced much of the population to near starvation. Its richest and most productive regions had been destroyed by the scorched-earth policy. In some areas every house was burned, every tree cut down, every stretch of railroad torn up, every mineshaft flooded and dynamited, every factory demolished. Years of hard, selfless labor from all citizens would be needed to overcome these ravages.

Equally important, the political morale of the population had been undermined. During the fighting the Stalinist authority of terror, regimentation, and indoctrination had been put aside; there was even talk of freedom. Worse, many soldiers, having seen for themselves a different way of life in Germany and Czechoslovakia, recognized the falseness of Soviet propaganda. The tales they told upon their return spread doubt. In fact, many Russians refused to return, escaping to freedom in the West. Worse yet, in Stalin's expanded empire were millions of subjects who fiercely hated Russian rule. The Poles had been a pawn between Russia and Germany too long not to hate both. The peoples of the Baltic had seen their nations disappear under the foot of the Russian bear. In the Balkans centuries of thwarted nationalist feelings were not alleviated by having to submit to new masters. These peoples hardly constituted reliable supporters in the struggle with the United States. Thus, with respect to popular loyalty, Soviet Russia could hardly compete with the United States. Nor could it do so, as

Stalin was aware, in terms of technical know-how or in the development of its natural resources. Russia had always been a poor country; after the ravages of the long war, she was doubly poor. Under these conditions how could the Soviet Union match the other Super Power?

Stalin had the answers. They were no more pleasant in western eyes than those supplied by Lenin under somewhat similar circumstances after the First World War. Lenin's prescription for the Russian condition had been simple: If you lack the solid strength of your opponents, try harassment, diversion, and petty aggression by any means that are handy; revolutionary offense is the best defense. Unfortunately, it also provokes a counteroffensive.

Distrust and competition characterize the cold war.

Thus began the cold war, which came to be characterized by constant escalation of hostility and armed pressure. Ignorant of the true state of affairs on the other side and profoundly unsympathetic toward each other's history and goals, each Super Power tended to assume the worst. Each kept a constant watch on the other through espionage, intelligence agencies, electronic devices, high-altitude airplane flights, and eventually spacecraft. Each tried to undermine the loyalty of the other's population by means of radio, newspapers, propaganda agencies, and organized subversion. Each kept a finger on the trigger of all-out war, ready to pull it on split-second notice. No expenditure seemed too extravagant when it came to providing for security against the other.

The area of confrontation and competition shifted from Central Europe to the European periphery, to Asia, to the Middle East and Africa, to Latin America, even to space, and back and forth between all these places. The armed threats changed from the conventional weapons used in World War II to nuclear bombs and weapons. The race for prestige had many facets—economic growth rates, medical advances, supersonic transports, space exploration, the measure of creative freedom allowed the individual. If the Americans came up with a novelty, sooner or later the Soviets would boast of an improvement, or *vice versa*. The Soviets launched *Sputnik;* the Americans landed the first man on the moon. The power competition, in short, was total; it touched all aspects of life. But let us take a closer look at the major political and military maneuvers of the cold war.

Stalin's aggressive actions boomerang.

It would appear that Stalin, then at the height of his power, took the initiative. In June, 1945, he suggested to the Turkish government, a bystander during the war, that Russia share in the control of the straits leading from the Black Sea to the Mediterranean. This was clearly a bid for added power, at a time when Churchill and Truman were upset over Soviet expansion in Central Europe. They already had quarreled with Stalin over the joint occupation of Germany and the reorganization of Eastern Europe. Another shock followed when the western statesmen learned in November, 1945, that a soviet republic was being organized in northern Iran. After March, 1946, the Communists incited civil war in Greece, a country Churchill had always been anxious to save from Soviet influence. In March, 1946, speaking as a private citizen, Britain's wartime leader poured out his forebodings to the American public in a famous speech at Fulton, Missouri:

A shadow has fallen upon the scenes so lately lighted by the Allied victory. Nobody knows what Soviet Russia and its communist international organization intend to do in the immediate future, or what are the limits, if any, to their expansive and proselytizing [seeking converts] tendencies. . . . From Stettin in the Baltic, to Trieste in the Adriatic, an iron curtain has descended across the continent. Behind that line lie all the capitals of the ancient states of Central and Eastern Europe— Warsaw, Berlin, Prague, Vienna, Budapest, Belgrade, Bucharest, and Sofia [soh'-fih-uh]. All these famous cities, and the populations around them, lie in the Soviet sphere, and all are subject in one form or another, not only to Soviet influence, but to a very high and increasing measure of control from Moscow. . . . Whatever conclusions may be drawn from these facts—and facts they are—this is certainly not the liberated Europe we fought to build up. Nor is it one which contains the essentials of permanent peace.

In their alarm the British and American governments took a counterstep in Germany that was bound to offend Stalin. In May, 1946, they stopped all reparation (payment for war damage) deliveries from their zones of occupation to the Soviet zone. Up to that time the Russians not only had taken industrial equipment, whole factories, and even skilled manpower from their own zone but had also drawn on the resources of other zones. The United States and Britain were unwilling to continue this subsidy. Their move hurt Russia's recovery, for it deprived her of goods and equipment from West Germany and caused Stalin to adopt a still more threatening policy.

Stalin refuses to compromise on control of bombs. Stalin therefore was in no mood to cooperate with the United States for the control of the atomic bomb. In 1946 the United States, then the sole possessor of the bomb, had submitted a proposal (the Baruch Plan) to the United Nations for the future control of that super weapon. The Americans called for free inspection of all sites where such weapons might be produced. To the ever suspicious Stalin such control spelled "capitalist" espionage in his country. He wanted that weapon himself, on his own terms, with no outside supervision. Stalin therefore vetoed the Baruch Plan.

United States aid speeds the economic recovery of Europe. Early in the following year, the American public was shocked into awareness of the cold war when the British government gave notice that it could not carry its share of responsibility for stemming the communist tide. The previous year Britain had helped, by a show of force, to drive the Soviets out of northern Iran. Now the British could no longer support the Turks and the Greeks against Soviet pressure. Britain was on the verge of economic collapse—as, in fact, was much of Western Europe. The only ones likely to benefit from economic disaster would be the communist parties, which were especially strong in France and Italy. It seemed as if all of Europe might suddenly fall under communist rule. A thoroughly aroused American government began to stir.

In March, 1947, President Truman asked Congress to send military and economic aid to Greece and Turkey. Thus the United States stepped in when Britain was forced to withdraw. At the same time Truman laid down basic American policy for the cold war:

Our way of life is based on the will of the majority, and is distinguished by free institutions, representative government, free elections. . . . The second [Soviet] way of life is based upon the will of a minority forcibly imposed upon the majority. It relies upon terror and oppression. . . . The free peoples of the world look to us for support in maintaining their freedom. . . . If we falter in our leadership, we may endanger the peace of the world—and we shall surely endanger the welfare of our nation.

A few months later, American diplomat George Kennan formulated the philosophy of the Truman Doctrine even more clearly. He pleaded for a policy of "containment," of preventing Soviet Russia's expansion until its leaders recognized the futility of communist revolutionary goals. The climax of the American response to Stalin's challenge came in June, 1947, when the American Secretary of State, George Marshall, announced the Marshall Plan for the economic recovery of Europe.

Thus began a new era of prosperity for Britain, France, Italy, and the other countries of Western Europe, including eventually—and most spectacularly—West Germany. On Stalin's orders, Eastern Europe was forbidden to participate in the Marshall Plan.

Stalin imposes strict party discipline. The mobilization of the immense resources of the United States for the recovery of Western Europe was a defeat for Stalin. Since his policy of threats had weakened rather than strengthened his position, he was forced to devise counter-measures which inevitably led to a further escalation of tension. The year 1947 was an exceedingly lean one in the Soviet Union. Food was scarce, as were all other necessities of life. Discontent was rife; the people lacked the common purpose that had sustained their spirits during the war. The sacrifices of war seemed to have led to nothing better than a return to Stalinism, and the people of Russia were once again in the throes of another series of Five-Year Plans. Moreover, the party line again became a stiff one.

In 1947 Andrei Zhdanov (*zhdah'*nohf), one of Stalin's closest advisors, pressed a new ideological drive to restore discipline in the Communist Party and among the people. All dissenters were purged. Leading writers disappeared, and the forced-labor camps became crowded with persons suspected of disloyalty. With the peoples of the Soviet Union reduced to terrified obedience, Stalin turned his attention to the peoples of Eastern Europe, whom he had "liberated" from the Nazis. The states of Eastern Europe became helpless satellites of Soviet Russia.

Stalin's instrument for carrying out his will was the Communist Information Bureau (Cominform). Set up in October, 1947, it directed the work of the communist parties of Eastern Europe, and also maintained ties with communist parties in France and Italy. With customary ruthlessness the Cominform crushed any trace of nationalism that had crept into the communist ranks in Eastern Europe and prohibited all links with Western Europe. This prevented membership in the Marshall Plan, however desirable. By way of compensation, in 1949 Stalin created a Council for Mutual Economic Assistance (COMECON) within the Soviet bloc. It had but a feeble effect.

The Communist take-over in Czechoslovakia leads to western defense pacts. The greatest single act of Stalinization in Eastern Europe

The Cold War

1946 Soviet Union suggests joint Russo-Turkish control of straits leading to Black Sea; Communists wage civil war in Greece; Stalin vetoes plan for control of atomic bomb

1947 Truman doctrine ensures aid to Greece, Turkey, and other countries threatened by communist aggression; Marshall Plan furthers recovery of Western Europe; Cominform created to strengthen Soviet control of Eastern Europe

1948 Communist coup in Czechoslovakia; Western European states sign mutual defense treaty; Yugoslavia breaks with Soviet Union; Stalin's blockade of Berlin leads to airlift

1949 North Atlantic Treaty signed; division of Germany formalized; Soviet Union explodes an atomic bomb; Communists gain control of China

1950 Outbreak of Korean War

1954 Geneva Conference results in temporary division of Vietnam; formation of SEATO

1955 Baghdad Pact (later CENTO) for mutual defense in the Middle East; Warsaw Pact unites communist nations in Eastern Europe

1956 Khrushchev denounces Stalin and announces policy of peaceful coexistence; riots in Poland lead to liberalization; rebellion in Hungary crushed by Soviet Union; Suez crisis

1957 Common Market formed; *Sputnik* launched

1959 Castro gains control in Cuba

1960 Cuba becomes a communist state

1961 Berlin wall erected

1962 Cuban missile crisis

came in February, 1948. The world watched in horror as the Stalinized Communist Party of Czechoslovakia overthrew the parliamentary regime in Prague and crushed the western-oriented democratic tradition established when

Czechoslovakia had attained independence in 1918. Stalin could afford to take no chances. To uphold the Soviet empire in the mounting competition with the United States, he needed monolithic unity (see page 632), no matter how achieved. To that end he also tried to bolster communist strength in Western Europe. Many observers in Western Europe and the United States were prepared for the worst. When it was claimed that communist spies had penetrated into the inner circles of the United States government, the alarm bordered on panic. Militant anti-communism—a further response to the Stalinist challenge—was on the rise.

In 1948 the revival of Western Europe proceeded from economic to military mobilization, again with American help. The communist take-over in Czechoslovakia had made a profound impression. However repulsive were the memories of war, in the face of the Russian danger there seemed to be no alternative to rearming. While Marshall Plan aid was extended to West Germany, the major states of Western Europe—Britain, France, and the Benelux countries (Belgium, the Netherlands, and Luxembourg)—signed a mutual-defense pact (the Brussels Treaty), with obvious American approval. This treaty signified that Stalin had lost another round in the cold war. Three months later, he suffered an even greater defeat when Yugoslavia defected from the Cominform.

Yugoslavia breaks with Moscow. Yugoslavia was the only nation among the Soviet satellites that during the war had maintained a vigorous resistance movement, communist in orientation but also patriotic. It was also the only satellite to have a location that ensured easy access to western support. When Stalin began to purge the nationalists in Eastern European communist parties in 1947, the leader of the Yugoslav Communist Party, Marshal Tito (*tee′toh*), faced a difficult choice. Was he to surrender the independence that he and his men had won during the war, or should he profess his own form of Marxism, communist but independent of

Stalin? In June, 1948, he took the latter road, thereby destroying the myth of the unity of world communism. With western assurance he defied the mighty dictator who had boasted that he could bring Tito to heel by merely wagging his little finger.

Stalin attempts to drive the western powers out of Berlin. That same month, however, Stalin was looking forward to a resounding victory in Berlin. Germany's former capital, Berlin was the outpost of western power in Central Europe. Two million people were crowded into its western sectors. The eastern sector had been taken over by the Soviet regime. Three land routes linked West Berlin to the western zones of Germany, but access through East Germany was based on Soviet permission. Without warning, Stalin suddenly closed these supply lines, expecting to starve West Berlin into submission and to block the establishment of the independent West German government being planned as part of the West's policy of containment. Yet Stalin had failed to reckon with American determination and resourcefulness. By an incredible feat of organization, an airlift was established that supplied the West Berliners with food and fuel through a bitter winter and well into the following spring. West Berlin not only held out and remained free but eventually became prosperous—a bone in the Soviet throat, as Stalin's successor Khrushchev (khrooshtchohf′) put it in later years.

The western nations unite in NATO. In April, 1949, Stalin suffered yet another crushing setback. The military buildup in Western Europe had grown into an anti-communist alliance, the North Atlantic Treaty Organization (NATO). It included Norway, Denmark, Iceland, Britain, France, the Benelux countries, Portugal, Italy, and, in the western hemisphere, the United States and Canada. The partners agreed "that an armed attack against one or more of them in Europe or North America shall be considered an attack against them all." The treaty sanctioned the presence in Western Europe of American troops and planes loaded with nuclear weapons. Even West Germany was thereby protected from Soviet attack. In the face of such unprecedented buildup of power, Stalin adopted a policy of retrenchment (backing off). He called off the blockade of West Berlin and halted Soviet pressure on Greece and Turkey. He then stepped forward as the champion of peace and disarmament, for even pacifism had become a tool of power politics. Stalin's only consolation in the year 1949 was that the Soviet Union also possessed an atomic bomb. News of its existence greatly alarmed the American government and its European allies and led to further escalation in the cold war.

China becomes communist. Meanwhile, the center of the cold war was shifting from Europe to the Far East. In 1949 Chinese communist forces under Mao Tse-tung drove out the Kuomintang and Mao became master of all China (except for the island of Taiwan). This brought over 600 million Chinese into the communist fold. It is doubtful that this achievement pleased Stalin, for he feared all mass movements which he did not control himself, and the Chinese revolution was decidedly the work of Comrade Mao. Yet it seemed to demonstrate the inevitability of the victory of "socialism" and was interpreted, by Stalin and world opinion, as a communist triumph. This communist victory in China was followed in 1950 by a flagrant act of aggression in Korea. The cold war had broken out into a small hot war.

Communists attempt to take over South Korea. In 1945 the Korean Peninsula had been divided between the American and Russian forces along the 38th parallel of latitude. Each power set up its own kind of government—communist in the north, pro-American in the south. In early 1950, feeling the pinch of the cold war in Europe, American policy makers decided to withdraw the American troops stationed in South Korea. They thereby unwittingly invited a North Korean bid for reunification of the peninsula. In June, 1950, the North Korean army, no doubt with Stalin's blessing, crossed the border and swept south, anticipating an easy victory. But the North Koreans had neither reckoned with President Truman's determination to resist aggression nor had they considered world opinion. Soon American troops landed to stem the communist advance. The withdrawal of the Soviet representative at the United Nations when the case came before the Security Council allowed a unanimous vote for the defense of South Korea. The allied forces soon drove back the North Korean army to the Chinese border, and for a brief moment Korean unification under American patronage seemed likely.

Mao Tse-tung acted quickly, for he could not afford to have the Americans at the doorstep of Communist China. A surprise attack by Chinese "volunteers" rolled back the UN troops until the old border was restored in 1951. The decision to settle for the 38th parallel was a hard one for Washington, though the compromise was in keeping with American cold war strategy. The armistice negotiations dragged on until July, 1953. The status established after the Second World War was restored in Korea. The cold war, however, continued and entered a new phase.

CHECK-UP

1. What is brinkmanship? Why can it be called the essence of diplomatic relations between the United States and the Soviet Union during the cold war?

2. Trace the history of hostility that existed between the two Super Powers. What were the major conflicts of policy?

3. How did the United States become a Super Power? The Soviet Union?

4. Why was the power of Soviet Russia after World War II "more apparent than real"?

5. What was the nature of the cold war?

6. What aggressive actions did the Communists take starting in 1945? How did Britain and the United States respond? What was the Baruch Plan? Why did Stalin veto it?

7. What was the Truman Doctrine? The Marshall Plan? What role did the Cominform play in the cold war?

8. What became of Czechoslovakia in 1948? Of Yugoslavia? Why were events in Yugoslavia a bitter blow for Stalin? What move did Stalin make in Berlin? Why did it fail?

9. What was the purpose of NATO? Who were its members? How did Stalin react to it?

10. Why did war break out in South Korea? How did it become a contest between Truman's determination to resist aggression and Mao Tsetung's determination to unite Korea under communism?

The Super Powers Encounter Obstacles

Khrushchev relaxes controls in the Soviet Union. In March, 1953, Stalin died. His successors, taking stock of their position in the cold war, had cause for dismay. Stalin's policies had diminished rather than enhanced Soviet prestige and security. They had led to a mighty United States counteroffensive. The situation in Russia, though better than in 1947, gave little hope of matching "capitalist" levels of economic development. Stalinist techniques of economic planning were outdated and often acted as obstacles to increased production. A faster pace could be ensured only by granting more creative freedom, in carefully controlled doses, to the peoples of Soviet Russia. Above all, it was urgently necessary to do away with the central features of Stalinism, terror and the "cult of personality" (page 654). Thus Khrushchev began a policy of de-Stalinization which culminated in his famous denunciation of Stalin at the Twentieth Party Congress in February, 1956.

. . . Stalin showed in a whole series of cases his intolerance, his brutality, and his abuse of power. . . . Here we see no wisdom but only a demonstration of . . . brutal force. . . .

This terror was actually directed not at the remnants of the defeated exploiting classes but against the honest workers of the Party and of the Soviet state; against them were made lying, slanderous, and absurd accusations. . . .

Confessions of guilt . . . were gained with the help of cruel and inhuman tortures.

Abroad, the picture was equally dark for the Soviet leadership in 1953. In the Far East, the military superiority of the United States had been demonstrated in Korea. Communist China, while drawing heavily on Soviet aid, was not easily guided by Moscow. Soviet prospects in Europe were even worse. Not only did Tito continue to defy Moscow, but all of Western Europe was up in arms against Soviet power. Under the shock of the Korean War NATO had become a military reality. Moreover, Western Europe, with its skilled manpower and advanced technology, was on the way to economic and possibly even political unification. Worst of all, German power was again on the rise even though the division of Germany had become a fact in 1949. The German Federal Republic under Konrad Adenauer (ah-deh-*now*'er) now confronted the German Democratic Republic under Walter Ulbricht (*vahl*'ter *ool*'brikht). Bigger and more prosperous than Communist East Germany, West Germany attracted vital manpower from East Germany, and its successes damaged the Ulbricht regime. The Federal Republic gained sovereignty in 1954, and as a member of NATO it began to train an army after 1955. Nothing could have alarmed the Russians more.

Russia encounters problems in the satellite countries. Even among its satellites in Eastern Europe, Moscow was to encounter opposition. To be sure, the Soviet Union had little difficulty in creating a counterweight to NATO—the Warsaw Pact. Under the terms of the Warsaw Pact—which remains the military mainstay of Soviet power in Eastern Europe—the satellite countries reached agreement with Moscow on a common plan of defense. Poland and Czechoslovakia especially welcomed the added protection against German rearmament. But in other respects the trend in Eastern Europe was toward decentralization. If Stalinism was on the way out in Soviet Russia, it must go elsewhere, too. In 1956 the relaxation of controls resulted in rioting in Poland and Hungary. In Poland the appointment of Gomulka (goh-*mool'*kuh) as head of the Communist Party led to a peaceful transition to greater freedom from Soviet interference. In Hungary, on the other hand, opposition to Soviet control became outright. In October, 1956, Imre Nagy (*im'*reh *noj'*), newly appointed head of the Hungarian Communist Party, promised free elections and an end to one-party government, withdrew his country from the Warsaw Pact, and requested western help. To Moscow this was treason. Within hours Soviet tanks and troops rolled into Budapest, the capital. After some days of bitter street fighting, the Soviets crushed the insurgents. There were cries of deep outrage in the West, but no military aid was sent to Hungary. Why had not the United States answered the plea for help and liberated Hungary from Soviet tyranny? An effort to pull Hungary out of the Soviet bloc could very likely have started World War III. The West was also caught between two fires as Britain and France, in support of Israel's invasion of Egypt, bombed the Suez Canal which Egypt had nationalized earlier that year.

Communism has little success in the developing nations. In the world at large as well, Stalin's heirs faced new challenges. Stalin had bungled his opportunities to win over Asia and Africa. His propaganda, for instance, had called Gandhi an "agent of British imperialism." Denouncing popular nationalists was not the way to win friends among the new states struggling for self-respect. There was ample evidence, too, of the inability of communism to lead the national liberation movements in the new states. Communist parties failed to thrive in India, Pakistan, Burma, Indonesia, Egypt, the Sudan, or sub-Saharan Africa. Indeed, these countries declared their aloofness from the cold war by calling themselves the "Third World." In 1955 there was a conference of Asian and African leaders at Bandung, Indonesia, to which no Europeans (including Russians) were invited. The honor of representing communism at Bandung fell to the Chinese.

In terms of their world mission, in short, Stalin's heirs had to catch up to changing world conditions. To compete with American and European aid to the developing countries, they would have to help new nations to help themselves, putting less stress on communism and more on national liberation. Among the developing peoples, the urgent demand was for economic and technological know-how. Being poor, the Soviet Union and its European satellites never gave as much aid as the United States, Western Europe, or Israel. Yet they distributed their aid shrewdly so as to appear more generous. Although the Soviets raised striking monuments to their technical capabilities by building a steel mill in India or the Aswan Dam in Egypt, they made few converts to communism. People in the developing nations cheerfully accepted Soviet aid and remained neutral. They showed little liking for Soviet communism, although they welcomed Soviet support in any dispute with the United States or a Western European country.

The Soviet Union takes the lead in the space race. Stalin's heirs also had to come to grips with the nuclear arms race. Stalin had helped to lay the foundations for the Soviet achievements in rocketry and space exploration that would astound the world in the next decade. At the time of Stalin's death, Soviet Russia had acquired the latest weapon, the hydrogen bomb. Equality in the arms race had a sobering effect upon Soviet leaders. As Khrushchev kept emphasizing: for the time being, the main fact of global politics was the peaceful coexistence of "socialism" and "capitalism"; nothing was to be gained by a nuclear war. The cold war had to be fought by the peaceful weapons of propaganda and threat. This, however, did not mean an end to the nuclear arms race. The Soviet government, like its American counterpart, labored strenuously to perfect its atomic arsenal. The competition shifted to rocket delivery systems. The world gasped when the Soviets took a clear lead in the space race by lifting *Sputnik* into orbit around the earth in October, 1957. This event raised extravagant hopes throughout the communist camp, and Mao Tse-tung predicted that henceforth the communist east wind would out-blast the capitalist west wind.

Secretary of State Dulles acts to contain communism. Meanwhile, the Americans had not been idle. In the assessment of world conditions that followed the election of Dwight D. Eisenhower to the presidency in 1952, United States Secretary of State John Foster Dulles drew some drastic conclusions. Mindful of a rising opinion against communism, he added to the containment policy a touch of boldness. Said he in early 1956: "The ability to get to the verge without getting into . . . war is the necessary art [of foreign policy]. If you cannot master it, you inevitably get into war. If you try to run away from it, if you are scared to go to the brink, you are lost." The crux of his brinkmanship was the threat that if communist powers engaged in new acts of aggression anywhere in the world, the United States would unleash "massive retaliation" at the Soviet Union, considered the "source of all evil." No American statesman had yet spoken so forthrightly. Dulles thus moved atomic weapons into the center of the cold war.

He also tried to make clear where he drew the line that communism was not to cross. In

Europe there could be no question. NATO, with Greece and Turkey added in 1952, stood ready to defend Berlin or any other Western European boundary. In the Far East, the United States was committed to the defense of Japan, and Dulles added a similar commitment to Nationalist China, established on the island of Taiwan. Uncertainty, however, prevailed with respect to Indo-China (the Southeast Asian lands between India and China), especially Vietnam. A national liberation movement under Ho Chi Minh defeated the French at Dienbienphu (*dyen'byen'foo'*) in May, 1954. When it seemed as though all of Indo-China might fall under communist domination, a conference was called at Geneva. Among the delegates were the representatives of the three Indo-Chinese states—Laos, Cambodia, Vietnam—and also Soviet Russia, Communist China, France, Britain, and the United States. The Geneva Conference tried to put the affairs of Vietnam in order. It provided for a temporary division of Vietnam until elections could be held. It also guaranteed the territorial integrity of the three states in Indo-China. Distrustful of so shaky an agreement, in September, 1954, Dulles announced the establishment of the Southeast Asia Treaty Organization (SEATO). SEATO included the United States, Britain, France, Thailand, Pakistan, Australia, and New Zealand and was intended to hold the line against communist aggression in Southeast Asia. In addition, the United States took the place of the French, who had pulled out of Southeast Asia.

Dulles created a similar protective alliance against communism for the countries of the Middle East. With his encouragement Turkey, Iraq, and Britain signed the Baghdad Pact in 1955, and were joined a few months later by Iran and Pakistan. The alliance maintained close military and political relations with the United States. When Iraq withdrew in 1959, the alliance was renamed the Central Treaty Organization (CENTO). Thus the communist bloc was hemmed in by alliance systems, each ready to safeguard its own area, and all under

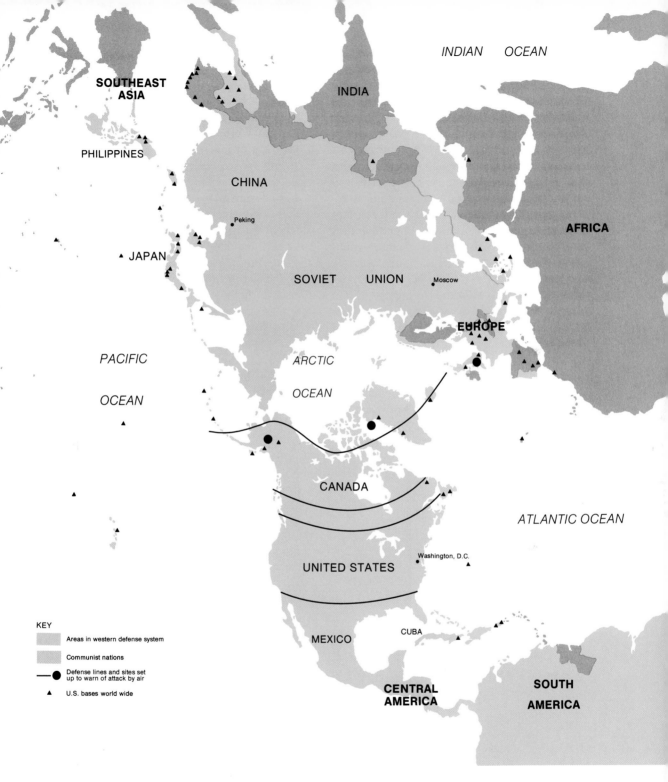

INDIAN OCEAN

SOUTHEAST ASIA

INDIA

PHILIPPINES

CHINA

• Peking

AFRICA

JAPAN

SOVIET UNION

• Moscow

EUROPE

PACIFIC

OCEAN

ARCTIC

OCEAN

CANADA

ATLANTIC OCEAN

UNITED STATES

• Washington, D.C.

KEY

Areas in western defense system

Communist nations

Defense lines and sites set up to warn of attack by air

U.S. bases world wide

MEXICO

CUBA

CENTRAL AMERICA

SOUTH AMERICA

The Cold War Divides East and West

the ultimate protection of American "massive retaliation." This containment of communism was an impressive achievement of American policy—at least on paper.

The reality never lived up to the promise. Not all members of the alliance systems proved reliable, and many had unstable governments which could be easy prey for pro-communist groups. Where along the perimeter of Soviet power, except in Europe, was government reliably stable and pro-American? Only constant alertness and manipulation of—if not interference in—the internal affairs of member countries could keep these alliances intact.

The cold war is stabilized. During the Eisenhower administration the various fronts of the cold war became stabilized, but there were a few crises. In the Far East the Chinese Communists twice bombarded the small offshore islands held by the Nationalists, thus threatening invasion. In the Middle East, Moscow stepped forward as the champion of the Arab cause in conflicts between Israel and Egypt. The main

concern of the Soviet Union, now firmly led by Khrushchev, was German rearmament and European unification. Under the Treaty of Rome (1957) the European Economic Community was formed, uniting the key countries of continental Western Europe in a common market with a growing prosperity and a guarantee of lasting peace. West Germany, which had achieved a phenomenal economic recovery, was a rising star in Western European unity. Khrushchev fought the trend as best he could. He relied on the nationalist pride of General Charles de Gaulle (*sharl'* deh *gohl'*), President of the Fifth French Republic after the summer of 1958, to keep West Germany in check and also to limit American influence in Europe. Several times Khrushchev also threatened to seize West Berlin, if West German rearmament were not stopped.

West Berlin, indeed, continued to be a problem for the Communists. It enabled East Germans freely to run away from communism, causing a serious loss of skilled manpower. Unable to interfere with the freedom of West Berlin, in a surprise move the Ulbricht regime closed the escape routes from East Berlin. In August, 1961, after secret preparation, the Communists erected a concrete wall through the city, cutting off East Berlin from West Berlin. The wall inflicted hardships upon the Berliners —and on all Germany as well—but it helped to stabilize the division of Germany. From now on Ulbricht could breathe more easily. The economic development of East Germany was reassured. Its standard of living, while much below that of West Germany, still was higher than that of any other communist country, Soviet Russia included.

Although peaceful coexistence remained Khrushchev's policy toward the West, his relations with the United States varied from year to year. An informal visit in 1959 and the scheduling of a summit conference with President Eisenhower raised hopes of improved relations. By 1960 ties were strained again with new grievances on each side. At left, Khrushchev displays some of the Iowa corn he inspected and praised during his 1959 visit.

Khrushchev's predictions fail to materialize, and problems multiply. Thwarted in his political moves, Khrushchev pressed for Soviet successes in other fields. He predicted that within a dozen years or so from the launching of *Sputnik* the Soviet Union would overtake the United States in the production of key items of consumption. Communism, stated Khrushchev, seemed within reach. The Soviet leaders believed it would bring about a society of plenty that could satisfy the needs of men and women regardless of their individual earning capacity. Khrushchev maintained that soon the Soviet Union would emerge as the supreme model of human happiness in the world. Khrushchev's optimism was reflected even in Britain where a Labour Party ideologist, echoing Chairman Mao, maintained that the West was bound to be defeated in any kind of peaceful competition with the East.

Yet Khrushchev was racing against time. Several "capitalist" countries, Japan foremost, boasted of more rapid economic growth than Soviet Russia. In other respects, too, Khrushchev was bucking the tide. The unity of the world communist movement, already endangered by the defection of Tito (whom Khrushchev had been unable to persuade to return to the Soviet fold), was further threatened by the open rebellion of the Chinese Communist Party. When at the 22nd Party Congress in 1961 Khrushchev attacked the Albanian communist leader Hoxha for his disloyalty to Moscow, Chou En-lai (*joh' en-lie'*), the Chinese delegate, walked out—with all the world watching. To preserve the traditional ascendancy of the Communist Party of the Soviet Union, Khrushchev felt that he had to stage a spectacular success.

Soviet armaments aid to Cuba leads to a world crisis. Soon an opportunity presented itself. Fidel Castro (fee-*del' kahs'*troh), whose guerrilla forces had succeeded in 1959 in ousting Cuban dictator Fulgencio Batista (fool-*hain'*-syoh bah-*tees'*tah) soon declared himself a follower of Marx and Lenin. By 1961 Castro had lost United States economic aid and was distrusted by many Latin American governments. During the first months of the Kennedy administration in 1961 a group of Cuban exiles, with official American support, attempted an invasion of Cuba. Although the attempt ended in disaster, an alarmed Castro begged for Soviet protection. Besides granting economic aid, Khrushchev promised to place on Cuban soil Soviet intermediate-range nuclear missiles aimed at United States cities. By this attempt at brinkmanship at the very doorstep of the United States he hoped to blackmail Washington into submission.

When in October, 1962, President Kennedy had definite proof of the presence of Soviet missiles in Cuba, he was thoroughly alarmed. There was no choice: should Khrushchev persist in his mad threat, Cuba had to be invaded, though this would mean a direct confrontation of the United States and the Soviet Union. Since the dispute was over nuclear missiles, "massive retaliation" might have to be used. The world hung on the edge of a thermonuclear war for several days, before Khrushchev, spared an outright humiliation on President Kennedy's insistence, decided to withdraw the Soviet missiles. This withdrawal in the western hemisphere was a major defeat for him and the Soviet Union.

The Cuban missile crisis was the climax of the cold war. Never before had the Super Powers faced each other at such close quarters; never before had the nuclear holocaust seemed so imminent. Yet at the same time the Cuban missile crisis marked the end of an era. In 1962 the Super Powers no longer monopolized the world stage. Their exclusive right to regulate the affairs of the world was being disputed by a number of newcomers. Decentralization, or *polycentrism,* as international analysts called the new situation, was becoming the rule, even in world communism.

Russia and China split. Belgrade under Tito may never have mattered much as an independent center of communism. But Peking under

To feed the world's people adequately, the productivity of all lands, especially in the Third World, must be increased. Built with Soviet aid, the Aswan Dam (above) has given Egypt more reliable irrigation, but its benefits have already been outstripped by Egypt's population growth. Aid to developing nations has featured in the competition between the Super Powers. Among Third World nations, only Japan and Israel are sufficiently developed to set up aid programs. At right, an Israeli instructs an African farmer in improved agricultural methods.

Chairman Mao, controlling Communist China with its 700 million inhabitants, was something else. Chinese and Russians had quarreled for centuries over border territories. Though Stalin had returned Soviet-occupied Manchuria to the Chinese after World War II, Russia kept other lands which the tsars had plucked from China. Moreover, there had been antagonism between Soviet and Chinese Communists almost from the first. In 1961 this became an open rift when Chou En-lai walked out of the 22nd Party Congress. The reasons for the Sino-Soviet split are complex. Chief among them is nationalism. The biggest appeal of Leninism in China (and elsewhere) was to national pride, for it promised to help all those who wanted to resist western penetration. Mao was Chinese before he turned communist, and he shared the traditional sentiment of Chinese superiority. He therefore gave Marxism-Leninism a peculiarly Chinese twist. By the same token he endowed Chinese communism with a global mission of its own—"hoisting the banner of Mao Tse-tung over the entire globe" and competing with Soviet Communists for the leadership of the anti-imperialist world revolution. This could not be reconciled to the Soviet Union's position as the leader of world communism. No effort on the part of

Khrushchev's successors has been able to heal the breach.

National communism takes precedence over world communism.
The Sino-Soviet split indicated the eventual breakup of the worldwide communist movement. Communist parties would act under Moscow's orders only as long as they failed in their primary goal of seizing power in their own countries. Once they had succeeded, they asserted their sovereignty as vigorously as had their predecessors. The only exceptions to the rule were the European satellites, which lived under the "protection" of the Soviet Red Army. But even greater disillusionment loomed ahead for Soviet Russia. The appeal of communism in any form was waning. Not that the cry for revolution was dying out in the great cultural earthquake of the present age. On the contrary, more revolutionary movements were springing up. But their formulas for action bore little resemblance to the tightly disciplined Soviet model.

Rising nationalism tends to reduce the influence of the Super Powers.
While the tides ran against Soviet ambition in the world at large, the goals of communism at home also proved beyond Khrushchev's grasp. Having aroused many expectations which did not materialize, he was unceremoniously deposed in 1964. His successors pursued a sounder and more cautious course. They recognized that they could not simultaneously raise the standard of living at home, keep up with the nuclear arms race, and maintain leadership in space exploration. Although they continued to play the game of global power politics to the best of their abilities, their zest for world revolution cooled.

A somewhat similar fate befell their chief rival. Rising nationalism also lessened the influence of the United States. Despite the United States' contribution to the economic recovery of Western Europe, American statesmen in the 1960's became aware of a strong anti-American undercurrent. It was most strongly represented by French President de Gaulle, guardian of France's glory, who tried to mobilize European opinion against the great "outsider." He even withdrew France from the military organization of NATO and concentrated on building France's own nuclear power. Who could be sure in this age of nationalism, he asked, whether the American people would sacrifice their cities to Soviet missiles over an issue of European security? Besides, as the Soviet threat receded, what was the need for NATO's expensive armaments? Wherever Americans looked in the 1960's, they found less enthusiasm for their policy of containing communism. No longer did it seem to fit the needs of the times.

The greatest source of weakness for the United States was its growing and increasingly frustrating involvement in Vietnam. In the eyes of the world this intervention in Vietnamese affairs dimmed the luster of American achievement. While the war in Vietnam raged, moreover, Americans became increasingly preoccupied with internal problems such as race relations, poverty amidst great affluence, the need for urban renewal, the need to combat water and air pollution. Worst of all was the growing disaffection of American youth, who asked, What justification was there for a world order seemingly unconcerned about human welfare? Thus Americanism, like Soviet communism, has found its rating for global stardom slipping. The cold war has become submerged in the growing complexities of the global state system. The cold war champions, though still much in evidence on the global stage, have joined a host of lesser states that are engulfed in their own crises and wars, many of them trying to involve the Super Powers in their own ambitions.

CHECK-UP

1. What was Khrushchev's de-Stalinization policy? What problems faced Khrushchev in Germany? In Eastern Europe?

2. Why did communism have little success in the developing nations?

3. What was Secretary of State Dulles' policy of containment? What problems did Vietnam present to this policy?

4. What was the purpose of SEATO and CENTO? Why were they achievements only on paper?

5. Why was West Berlin a continuing problem for the Soviet Union? What steps were taken to solve the problem?

6. What problems was Khrushchev unable to solve?

7. How did Soviet military aid to Cuba lead to a world crisis? Why was this a major defeat for Khrushchev and Russia?

8. Why are relations poor between Soviet Russia and Communist China?

9. How has rising nationalism tended to reduce the influence of the two Super Powers?

Summing Up

Three basic developments have shaped the present world order: (1) the outpouring of the western way of life over the entire world, (2) the shift from a Europe-centered framework of power politics to one that is world-centered, and (3) the production of weapons that can wipe out mankind.

After World War II, the United States and the Soviet Union emerged as Super Powers. In the Soviet Union the patriotic desire to surpass the scientific, industrial, and military potential of the great western powers led to the adoption of totalitarian means. Through "socialism" the Soviet leadership promised the common man an equal share in the benefits flowing from a modern industrial civilization. Soviet Russia also claimed leadership of a worldwide liberation movement whose goal was to ensure self-determination to all peoples chafing under western domination. Many of the new Asian and African states achieved independence with prompting and assistance from one or both of the Super Powers.

Before World War II there were a few major powers and many small powers and colonies. Today there is a global community of over a hundred states of all sizes, many troubled by economic and political instability. Their weakness has invited aggression, encouraged spending for armaments, and led to wars. The developing nations seeking to modernize as rapidly as possible feel that western technology is the key to their goals. But worldwide acceptance of western science and technology has not created a united world.

The development and use of the atomic bomb in World War II led to a nuclear arms race between the United States and the Soviet Union. So far, the only protection against nuclear attack has been the certainty of retaliation and mutual destruction. There is thus a growing necessity to settle international conflicts through negotiation and compromise.

Political life in the contemporary world is shaped by the worldwide competition between the United States and the Soviet Union. Soviet determination to retain lands acquired through the Hitler-Stalin Pact, to dominate Eastern Europe, and to extend Russian power into Germany conflicted with the views of western leaders. Since neither western statesmen nor western peoples generally understood how serious were Russian losses during World War II or the low morale of the Soviet peoples, there was a tendency to overreact in responding to Soviet pressures.

To stem the communist tide, the United States put into effect the Truman Doctrine and the Marshall Plan, and western nations signed mutual defense pacts. The United States developed a policy of containment and tried to draw a line that communism must not cross.

During the last two decades rising nationalism has tended to reduce the influence of both Super Powers and to weaken rival alliance systems. Yugoslavia's refusal to follow docilely in Russia's footsteps and the growing split between Russia and Communist China were indications that world communism was an illusion. On the other side, the growing involvement of the United States in Vietnam caused international disapproval and domestic tension.

Chapter Highlights

containment	capitalist ethic	defection	national liberation
modernization	subversion	escalation	iron curtain
airlift	deterrent	cold war	developing nation
retrenchment	annihilation	satellites	massive retaliation
anti-westernism	polycentrism	overkill	military-industrial complex
brinkmanship			

Can you identify?

Tito	Marshall Plan	CENTO	German Federal Republic
Truman Doctrine	Adenauer	Berlin wall	de-Stalinization
Baruch Plan	Ulbricht	Super Powers	German Democratic Republic
Warsaw Pact	NATO	Castro	Cuban missile crisis
Cominform	Third World	*Sputnik*	Sino-Soviet split
Nagy	SEATO	Ho Chi Minh	

What do you think?

1. How does a nation become a Super Power? Can a nation resign from the club?

2. Why have freedom and democracy often led to disunity, chaos, and military rule in newly independent nations?

3. Have developing nations profited from the rivalry between the Super Powers? Explain.

4. Was Stalin a great leader for the Soviet Union? Why?

5. Why can one say that the cold war was kept alive by thwarted ambition and by blind mutual fear?

6. Why did Stalin want Eastern and Central Europe under Soviet control? Should the United States have opposed Stalin's plans?

7. How do you evaluate the importance of the Marshall Plan?

8. Why was NATO organized? Has it lived up to expectations? Why?

9. Is the communist world as monolithic as Americans feared at the close of World War II? Why?

10. Why was the Hungarian uprising a tragedy? Why did the United States not respond to the Hungarian plea for help?

11. Why did the Cuban missile crisis develop? Who gained or lost from it?

12. Is it possible to modernize one aspect of a society without affecting the entire society? Explain.

Europe and the Soviet Union Since 1945

CHAPTER FOCUS

Western Europe Since 1945
The Stalinist Period
The Era of Peaceful Coexistence
Life in the Soviet Union Today

Appalling destruction and a sense of despair characterized Western Europe at the end of World War II. Most of Germany's major industrial cities lay in ruins. To the east, Warsaw and Stalingrad were heaps of rubble. The fertile plains and fields of Europe had been torn apart, denuded of their plant cover and their topsoil. Livestock had been slaughtered by the thousands; farm equipment destroyed. The task of reconstruction was so great that it was difficult to know where to begin.

The political situation was scarcely more cheering. Eastern-Central Europe lay under the "protecting" arm of the Soviet Red Army, and communist parties were gaining strength daily. Germany was divided into occupation zones;

The nations of Western Europe have begun to work together for common goals. The Common Market encourages economic prosperity among member states, which exchange agricultural and industrial goods such as wine from French vineyards and West German automobiles (left). In Soviet Russia the majority of the people have never lived under any government but that of communism. Government control of education ensures the training of students (above) for careers most essential to the growth of the Russian economy.

Russian expansion had pushed Poland's boundaries westward. Governments in Western Europe were beset by inflation and instability and the growing strength of communist parties. Western Europe had lost its leadership in international affairs.

Nevertheless, Western Europe made a rapid and extraordinary recovery. The Soviet Union became a Super Power rivaling the United States and controlling the affairs of Eastern-Central Europe. How did these changes come about?

Western Europe Since 1945

Before examining the important changes that have taken place in Western Europe since 1945, the extent of wartime damage must be discussed.

The costs of World War II are staggering. The human costs of World War II are almost beyond belief. Approximately thirty million persons—both civilians and soldiers—were killed. The three largest Western European countries (Germany, Britain, and France) alone lost almost seven million persons. Millions of Europeans suffered permanent wounds, psychological as well as physical. Many had been uprooted from their homes, in some cases after seeing their families murdered. The refugee problem was overwhelming. Throughout Europe untold numbers of persons were homeless and starving.

Billions of dollars' worth of property had been destroyed in Western Europe. Railroads, bridges, and canals lay in ruins and systems of communications had been destroyed. Stocks of goods were low, and thousands of factories and mines had been severely damaged. Nearly everywhere production was well below the 1939 level.

Moreover, it had cost billions of dollars to finance the war; funds had been raised partly through increased taxation but mostly by heavy borrowing. The accumulation of debts was enormous, and credit was desperately short.

Profound psychological damage also resulted from the war. A feeling of pessimism was generated by the immense destruction, which had contributed to Western Europe's loss of status as the center of world power. Temporarily at least, Western Europe had lost the ability to shape its own destiny. This diminished power was passively accepted by many Western Europeans. It was possible, though difficult, to achieve material regeneration fairly quickly, but it was far more difficult to regain the hope and optimism that had characterized centuries of European history.

The United States aids European recovery. On June 5, 1947, the United States Secretary of State, George C. Marshall, delivered a commencement address at Harvard University which was to have momentous consequences. After speaking of the dislocation of the European economy and the enormous economic needs of Europe, Marshall pledged a program of massive economic assistance:

It is logical that the United States should do whatever it is able to do to assist in the return of normal economic health in the world, without which there can be no political stability and no assured peace.

Our policy is directed not against any country or doctrine but against hunger, poverty, desperation, and chaos. Its purpose should be the revival of a working economy in the world so as to permit the emergence of political and social conditions in which free institutions can exist.

Three months earlier President Truman had announced a program of military and economic assistance to Greece and Turkey, both threatened by Soviet expansion. The Marshall Plan, officially called the European Recovery Program, was as much an extension of this concern with communism as it was a program of economic assistance to Europe. Despite its political context, the Marshall Plan was enormously significant for the economic revival of Western Europe. (Stalin did not permit Eastern Europe to take part.) It made the recovery of Britain, France, and especially West Germany far more rapid than would otherwise have been the case.

Between 1948 and 1952 more than sixteen billion dollars in United States aid was extended to sixteen European countries, most of it in the form of direct grants and in accordance with plans worked out by each participating nation. Marshall Plan countries were enabled to purchase food and natural resources, machinery, and equipment. The results were striking. By 1952 the industrial levels of these countries had surpassed prewar figures. The worst effects of inflation and depression had been overcome.

WEST GERMANY

Many problems confront postwar Germany. The postwar situation in Germany was more critical than elsewhere. Millions of homes had been destroyed and, in the words of one observer, "whole cities were reduced to heaps of rubble and tangled iron." In the urban areas where bombing attacks had been concentrated, the majority of all types of buildings had been destroyed.

To govern Germany right after the war, four zones of military occupation—British, French, American, and Russian—were set up. The occupation zones of the western powers soon were merged, but Russian-occupied Germany remained separated from the rest of the nation. By 1949 what had been the German nation was divided in two: communist East Germany and democratic West Germany.

The political and administrative burdens which confronted the occupying powers were immense. Governmental institutions had to be restored to permit the making of basic economic decisions. Policies had to be developed for military demobilization, taxation and social services, and food rationing. Perhaps the greatest need was to re-establish the international standing of the country, for the majority of the inhabitants had supported Hitler.

Through denazification the occupying Allies try to change German attitudes. There were three major domestic problems facing Germany after 1945: (1) denazification, (2) economic revival, and (3) political stability. Probably the least successful steps were taken in the area of denazification. At the close of the war millions of Germans stood morally convicted of having accepted the Nazi program. Large numbers had belonged to Nazi organizations and some had directly participated in atrocities against anti-Nazis, Jews, and conquered peoples. In an attempt to root out the scars of nazism, the Allied powers initiated a policy of "denazification." Twenty-two Nazi leaders were tried at Nuremberg and sentenced for "crimes against humanity." This trial of "war criminals" by an international tribunal was without precedent and aroused much controversy. The trial, conducted with fairness, raised many important questions, including that of personal responsibility for crimes committed when acting under orders. In the three zones of Germany occupied by the western powers thousands of Germans were tried for complicity in Nazi programs; some were convicted, but many were freed and gradually were permitted to assume positions of importance in the West German government.

Denazification was also a policy in the system of education. Nazi ideology had shaped the attitudes of a generation of German young people. In postwar Germany textbooks presenting the truth about nazism were introduced, and Nazi-oriented teachers and school officials were replaced. Similar policies were introduced into other areas, such as the civil service. But since 1947 the policy of denazification has not been pursued with vigor, and many observers have seen little value in it. Despite continuing attempts by the West German government to

ICELAND

ATLANTIC

OCEAN

SWEDEN

NORWAY

FINLAND

Helsinki ★

SOVIET

Oslo ★

Stockholm ★

Baltic
Sea

ESTONIA

Moscow ★

UNION

GREAT

North Sea

LATVIA

Copenhagen ★

LITHUANIA

DENMARK

From Germany
to Poland

EAST
PRUSSIA

IRELAND

BRITAIN

Lubeck •

Stettin •

Oder-
Neisse
Line

• Poznan

From Poland
to Russia

NETH.

Amsterdam ★

Berlin •

1945

★ Warsaw

London ★

Brussels •

WEST

EAST
GERMANY

Potsdam •

POLAND

1939

BELG. •

Bonn •

• Prague

LUX.

GERMANY

CZECHOSLOVAKIA

Paris ★

Vienna ★

★ Budapest

FRANCE

Bern •

AUSTRIA

HUNGARY

ROMANIA

Geneva •

SWITZ.

Trieste •

Bucharest ★

Black Sea

Belgrade ★

YUGOSLAVIA

BULGARIA

ITALY

Adriatic Sea

★ Sofia

Istanbul •

PORTUGAL

Madrid ★

Rome ★

Tirana ★

Ankara ★

Lisbon •

SPAIN

ALBANIA

TURKEY

GREECE

Athens ★

M e d i t e r r a n e a n

KEY

◼ Soviet Union

▨ Soviet territorial gains since 1939

◻ Other Communist countries

◻ NATO (also U.S. and Canada)

- - - Prewar boundary

Sea

Europe Today

punish war criminals, there have been few indications of a serious rethinking by individual
Germans of the meaning of the Hitler era. For
many German leaders it has become more im-

portant to establish Western Germany as a
firm ally of the West against the communist
nations than to continue to root out Nazi sympathizers of minor importance. By 1970 the
Nazi past had largely been forgotten in the enjoyment of a profitable present.

West Germany becomes an economic power.

West Germany's economic recovery, one of the most spectacular developments of the postwar period, was partly a function of the country's human and material resources. She possessed the advantages of a large, skilled population and considerable natural resources, including coal and iron. Unless a conscious, deliberate effort were made to keep her down, Germany was bound to achieve rapid economic recovery.

Some statesmen urged that Germany's industrial base should be permanently destroyed to guard against future aggression. While this proposal was rejected, key industries such as steel and chemicals were closely regulated by the occupying powers. Goods were transferred from Germany to twenty countries, notably France and the Soviet Union, to pay reparations. West German industry was decentralized in order to eliminate the great prewar trusts, and attempts were made to seize the property of large industrialists. But Germany's size and resources enabled her to rise above these restrictive policies. The merging of the three western zones in 1949 was followed by the dismantling of most of the controls introduced by the occupying powers.

In 1948 the almost worthless reichsmark was replaced by stable currency, a reform that permitted economic recovery to get under way. At the same time rapid recovery was assured by the decision to extend Marshall Plan assistance to Germany. Foreign capital also began to flow into West Germany. In one sense the heavy wartime destruction contributed to the amazing recovery that followed. So much had been destroyed that it was relatively easy (as it was not in Britain, for example) to rebuild the entire economy. Within a few years overall production had climbed past 1939 levels. Wages rose and profits increased. By the 1960's West Germany had outdistanced her nearest European competitors and had established her claim as a first-class economic power.

West Germany becomes a stable republic.

Political recovery was slow because of the division of Germany into four military zones in 1945. Berlin, the former German capital, was located inside the Soviet zone. It also was divided into four zones, but was administered separately from the rest of Germany. Military occupation in the western zones of Germany was of short duration. By 1947 local and state assemblies had been reintroduced, and trade unions and political parties had been permitted to resume their normal activities. A substantial degree of self-government was permitted within the three western zones. In 1949 increased tension between the United States and the Soviet Union led to the formation of a semi-independent West German government. The Allies retained authority in such fields as disarmament, reparations, international affairs, and foreign trade. Known as the German Federal Republic, this nation has been completely independent since 1954, when all restrictions were permanently removed.

West German politics since 1949 has been dominated by the Christian Democratic Union (CDU), a party that was formed after the war. The Social Democrats (SDU), a moderate socialist party with a history dating back to the Bismarck era, have provided the major opposition. The Christian Democrats monopolized political office until 1969, when the Social Democrats under Willy Brandt took office. Third parties, such as the Free Democrats, have functioned with some effectiveness, but German political life has been overwhelmingly dominated by the two major parties. The communists were banned from legal participation in 1956, and smaller neo-Nazi organizations have had only small success.

Adenauer helps restore German prestige.

"Tough and autocratic, stiffened with the self-confidence of vigorous old age," so one historian has described Konrad Adenauer (ah-deh-*now*'er), first Chancellor (1949–1963) of the German Federal Republic. Without question, Adenauer was the overpowering personality in postwar German politics, as well as one of the towering figures in European politics as a whole. From 1949 until his death in 1967 Adenauer stamped his conservative, fatherly image upon Germany. Authoritarian by temperament, yet democratic and moderate by conviction, Adenauer rose rapidly to a position of leadership after the war. Until 1933 he had been Mayor of Cologne (koh-*lohn'*), with a reputation as an anti-Nazi. This record placed him in a strong position after the war.

Adenauer's policies were more notable in foreign than in domestic affairs. The Federal Republic took on an important international role, becoming concerned in the formation of the Common Market (page 751), the strengthening of NATO, and the resistance to Soviet policy in Eastern-Central Europe. Adenauer worked hard to solidify friendships with the United States and France. At the same time, he refused to make any concessions to communist East Germany. His greatest achievement in foreign affairs was to restore Germany's voice to the highest councils of western policymaking.

Internally, Adenauer emphasized economic growth by offering tax privileges to companies that would reinvest their profits. Government controls were reduced to a minimum. Because industry boomed, labor was greatly in demand. Workers from other European countries flocked to West Germany. Unemployment insurance and pension programs were introduced along with other governmental benefits. However, trade unions continued to be weak, and the social orientation of government remained conservative.

Today West Germany is a prosperous, democratic country. It has not been permanently scarred by the Nazi experience, although the possibility of a resurgence of nazism cannot be totally excluded. West Germany's major problems are similar to those of other European countries and the United States: cultural dissatisfaction, student unrest over the shortcomings of contemporary society, concern for social and economic equality, economic bargaining with other countries, and relations with the communist bloc (particularly acute in West Germany because of the existence of a communist East Germany).

GREAT BRITAIN

Postwar Britain seeks social reform. The war caused less direct damage in Great Britain than elsewhere in Europe. London and other important ports, which had suffered heavy damage from German bombing raids and rocket attacks, underwent a vast program of rebuilding. In other areas wartime damage was not heavy. In the same way the political system was little damaged by war. During World War II it functioned smoothly under the brilliant leadership of its prime minister, Winston Churchill, with the able support of the Labour Party under Clement Attlee. A coalition government, formed in 1940, continued in office until the end of the war. For these reasons, despite severe economic and social problems created by the war, the emphasis in postwar Britain was more upon social reform than recovery. In the area of welfare legislation, in particular, notable advances were made in the postwar period.

The general election of 1945 was to have a decisive impact upon Britain's development. The war against Japan had not yet ended when British voters went to the polls in July, 1945. At stake in this first parliamentary election since 1935 was control of the country's postwar policies. Few observers doubted that Churchill, who had led Britain capably through the war years, would win.

The outcome was just the reverse. The Labour Party won an overwhelming victory, and Clement Attlee became the new prime minister. Though lacking the dynamic image of his predecessor, Attlee brought to the office a keen intelligence and a strong sympathy for the poor and the underprivileged. This outlook, together with Churchill's failure to take a consistent stand on domestic issues, probably explains the outcome of the election. There was a growing national demand for social reform and it was felt that the Labour Party could best bring this about.

The Labour Party introduces a policy of austerity. Times were hard after 1945. Though Britain was victorious in the war, the British people tasted few of the fruits of victory. Fuels remained in short supply; meat, sugar, and other consumer goods were severely rationed. The importation and distribution of raw materials, such as cotton, and of many luxury items were strictly controlled. Price and wage controls were extended into the peacetime period. In some cases taxes on goods were so high that the retail price was doubled. Shortages of materials and rising costs hampered the construction of new housing.

Austerity is the word that best describes the financial and economic policies of the postwar Labour government. Nearly all of Britain's credit had been wiped out during the war. Extensive loans, mostly from the United States, had to be repaid. Industry had to be converted to peacetime production, and consumer demand, long held in check by wartime needs, had to be satisfied. Finally, if Britain were to continue to play an important economic role in the world, her currency had to be stabilized.

Some of these problems were easier to solve than others, but even in such cases hardships continued for several years. Such was the case with the scarcity of consumer goods and the shortage of adequate housing. But solving the problems related to Britain's continuing decline as a world power was far more difficult.

Tied in with Britain's economic decline (and with her political decline) was the loss of her empire. In response to growing national movements abroad and in accordance with prewar promises, Britain began to give her overseas colonies their independence in the years after 1945. Among the important areas from which Britain severed her control were India, Pakistan, Malaya, Burma, and Singapore in Asia; Ghana, Nigeria, and Kenya in Africa; Iraq, Jordan, and Cyprus in the Middle East; and Jamaica and Guyana in the western hemisphere. Some of these countries have continued to maintain good relations with their ex-mother country through the loosely knit Commonwealth of Nations. Nevertheless, as the newly independent nations have sought to extend their contacts beyond Britain, Britain's economic position has been gravely weakened.

The Labour Party lost much of its popularity by its policy of austerity, though a restrictive economic policy doubtless was necessary in order to check inflation and place the economy on a solid footing again. This meant that wage and price increases had to be held back, which produced many hardships. Austerity could never be completely successful, but the British economy had recovered to a considerable extent by the 1950's and the country had begun to experience unprecedented prosperity.

Labour creates a model welfare state. Outside the economic area the record of the Attlee government was more striking. The Labour election platform had called for a sweeping program of social reform. In putting this program into effect with speed and energy, Labour created a model "welfare state."

One aspect of the welfare state—perhaps the least effective—was *nationalization:* the take-over by the government of many industries. This was an extension of the role government had played in business during the Second World War. As well as control over most industries, railroads and other forms of transport, mining, and all essential services were placed directly under the control of the state. Public acceptance of this wartime policy enabled the postwar Labour government to put into action a gradual peacetime nationalization. In 1946 it nationalized the coal industry and the Bank of England; the following year all types of public transport, including railroads and docks, were taken over, and the gas, electric, and steel industries followed. These measures were angrily described by Churchill as "not a plan to help our patient struggling people, but a burglar's jimmy to crack the capitalist crib." They revolutionized British life in the sense of drawing the government into every aspect of it. But nationalization did not always produce greater efficiency or more social justice.

In 1942 Sir William Beveridge of the London School of Economics issued a report which profoundly affected Britain's postwar history. Beveridge asserted that every person was entitled *by right* to receive support from the state and that this aid should extend from "the cradle to the grave." In exchange for a fixed percentage of his income, every citizen should receive unemployment insurance, disability payments, old age pensions, and other forms of social assistance as these were needed.

The Beveridge Report became the basis for a welfare system unequaled among the leading western powers. Between 1946 and 1950 several pioneering laws were passed. The National Insurance Act of 1946 made available to individuals a variety of welfare payments in return for a weekly sum paid to the state. In addition to the more obvious forms of relief, maternity and funeral benefits and direct subsidies in needy cases were introduced. The National Health Service Act (1946) provided essentially free medical treatment for all persons. Although those who can afford it may consult physicians in private practice, more than 90 per cent of the British people avail themselves of the National Health Service. In the words of Professor R. K. Webb, "probably no single action of the Labour government contributed more to the well-being of the country or has had more complete acceptance."

Some of Britain's problems remain unsolved. Since the early 1950's Britain has experienced considerable prosperity. Like the United States, Britain has become consumer-oriented to a large degree. Her people are better fed and clothed than ever before. Most families own television sets and cars, and many are able to purchase their own homes. Health and medical statistics are impressive, partly as a result of the National Health Service.

But there are serious problems as well. Racial tensions have begun to emerge in recent years as immigrants from India, Pakistan, and the West Indies have reached Britain in large numbers. The economy is less than sound in certain areas, for although the standard of living has continued to rise, the nation as a whole is living beyond its means. Unable to raise enough food to feed her population, Britain imports more goods than she can afford. High production costs limit the amount of exports. Britain's sources of good, easily mined coal are nearing exhaustion, and she is increasingly dependent on foreign supplies of oil. The empire "upon which the sun never set" is gone, and with it much of British affluence. Even the pound sterling—with the dollar and the Swiss franc the symbol of stable currency—has decreased in value. Britain finds it difficult to accept her loss of status as a world power. To many, the unconquerable spirit that led Britain through the war seems far less in evidence today.

FRANCE

The key themes of French history following 1945 have been economic revival, political instability, and the rule of an extraordinary man, Charles de Gaulle, between 1958 and 1969. Since 1945 France has *seemed* to play a more important role in world affairs than has actually been the case. Like Britain, she has been unwilling to face up to her diminished international status.

France recovers economically but faces political chaos. France made a rapid recovery from World War II despite the heavy damage she had suffered and the economic problems which plagued her before 1939. Even before the war her economic position was not encouraging, for she had never fully industrialized, relying heavily upon high tariffs to protect French industry. Yet, through German reparations and Marshall Plan aid, France was enabled to make remarkable economic advances. Official governmental policy played a major role in France's revival. Key industries were nationalized and incentives to investors were provided. Despite their traditional conservatism, French businessmen responded enthusiastically to this policy for furthering industrial expansion. By 1950, in spite of a weak currency, French productivity had easily surpassed 1939 levels.

But political instability, mainly a result of her multi-party system, continued to haunt France during the Fourth Republic (1946–1958). One government official followed another in what seemed an unending game of musical chairs. This was a period of instability encouraged by a constitution which provided for a weak executive and a strong Assembly. Many political parties competed for power, and for a time the communists were the largest party in the Assembly. Few governments remained long in office. It became clear that only strong leadership could rescue France from the political chaos which plagued her.

De Gaulle restores the spirit of France. To Frenchmen who could still be moved by the deeds of Napoleon, only one man seemed capable of doing this job. They urged their wartime hero, General Charles de Gaulle, to take over the reins of government in 1958. De Gaulle seemed to be above party rivalries and hatreds. Political strains over a worsening situation in Algeria were threatening to produce a civil war in France. De Gaulle took firm and immediate action. Since 1954 supporters of Algerian independence had engaged in acts of terrorism both in Algeria and France. De Gaulle, brought to power by forces wishing to keep Algeria in French hands, instead announced his support of Algerian independence. This led to a bitter civil war in Algeria, which lasted until that country became independent in 1962.

During the eleven years of his rule President de Gaulle introduced his own form of government and politics. He strengthened the power of the presidency to such a degree that his opponents called him a dictator. He also reduced the influence of the National Assembly and of political parties. De Gaulle had enormous charisma (page 538), and seemed to many Frenchmen to be restoring France to a position of grandeur. Like other strong leaders, de Gaulle took orders from no one. Despite the protests of his western allies, he opened diplomatic relations and later carried on trade with Communist China. At the height of the cold war he maintained cordial relations with Moscow. He startled the other colonial powers when he gave the French colonies in Africa the choice of in-

Late in the 1960's student concern with national and international conditions often turned into demonstrations or even riots against established authority. Some of the most severe unrest occurred in France, where workers joined students to protest government policies. Nevertheless, support for de Gaulle, France's savior in many past crises, remained firm and was reflected in rallies (below).

749

dependence or a continuance of colonial status (only one French possession did not choose independence). At a time when Soviet Russia and the United States were becoming increasingly concerned with the threat of nuclear war, de Gaulle began building up France as a nuclear power. He refused to allow Britain to join the European Common Market, even though many statesmen regarded Britain's membership as essential. Finally, he upset his western allies by withdrawing French troops from NATO and demanding that NATO bases in France be closed.

For the most part, these moves added to his popularity in France. De Gaulle had made his nation a force with which to reckon; he would not allow France to be pushed around. Within France, however, the picture was not so bright. Rising inflation threatened the economy and there was growing social unrest among students and workers throughout the nation. Nevertheless, de Gaulle won a rousing victory in the 1968 elections. It seemed to him that any program he proposed would be overwhelmingly accepted. But when he proposed constitutional reforms in 1969, his program was defeated. De Gaulle immediately resigned. Nevertheless, de Gaulle's rule of France had raised the spirit of the nation and had enabled her once again to play a positive role in the world. When he died late in 1970, all France mourned the passing of the man who had restored the nation's pride.

OTHER NATIONS OF WESTERN EUROPE

Italy makes promising gains. Postwar Italy suffered from considerable war damage, political instability, and inflation. There also were glaring inequalities of wealth, the south traditionally being far poorer and less developed than the north. Failure to industrialize sufficiently left Italy economically weak, and after 1945 the communists made rapid gains and became the largest political party. In the early postwar years the value of the lira dropped steadily and brought severe inflation. But Italy, too, experi-

enced an "economic miracle." During the 1950's and 1960's production rose at one of the highest rates in the world and the export trade made great gains. A start was made in coping with the problems of social inequality and widespread illiteracy. Italy never achieved the heights of which Mussolini had dreamed, but by the end of the 1960's she had regained the respect of other nations and her future seemed promising.

Other European nations prosper. The Low Countries (Belgium and the Netherlands) have prospered since World War II despite war damage. Belgium has become an industrialized nation whose population enjoys one of the highest living standards in the world. Her loss in 1960 of the Congo, a source of rich resources, has not significantly affected Belgium's development. The Netherlands, earlier geared more to trade and agriculture than industry, has broadened its economic base with the aid of American investments. Withdrawal from Indonesia in 1949 after a bitter four-year struggle was a considerable blow, since Dutch overseas interests were concentrated in that country. But closer relationships with Western European countries, particularly Britain, have since been forged, and Dutch influence has once again begun to increase.

The Scandinavian countries (Denmark, Norway, and Sweden) have continued to prosper and have created advanced social welfare systems. Spain, burdened by the dictatorial rule of Franco, has only just begun to introduce economic and political reforms. Portugal has pursued an even more discouraging course than Spain. Burdened by an outmoded economic system and by a political dictatorship, she has refused to give up her remaining interests in Africa. This has brought her into increasing conflict with African nationalist movements.

Of the other major countries of Western Europe, Austria and prosperous Switzerland have followed independent, neutral policies, giving support to neither of the Super Powers. Turkey and Greece, on the other hand, have supported NATO and together form an important extension of American power in the eastern Mediterranean. But their quarrels over the fate of Cyprus have more than once threatened world peace, and neither nation approaches the economic well-being enjoyed by the countries of Northern Europe.

Will Western Europe unite? With the emergence of the Super Powers came the realization that only through unification could the nations of Western Europe hope to achieve equality with the Soviet Union and the United States. This drive toward common Western European economic, political, and cultural institutions is one of the critical themes of European history since 1945.

The Marshall Plan and NATO gave stimulus to this drive for continental unity. But it was in 1957 that a major step towards unity was taken with the formation of the European Economic Community, better known as the Common Market. The immediate goal of the Common Market was to merge the economies of its members. This would permit each country to specialize and to concentrate on supplying what it could most efficiently produce. Within the Common Market, member nations would be able to buy needed goods from each other at reduced rates. Common tariffs on goods from non-member nations would protect the prices of Common Market goods and enable them to compete favorably with products from non-member countries. Eventually there would develop uniform monetary systems throughout the Common Market area. The elimination of customs barriers is also planned to permit a free flow of workers and capital and the ending of all trade restrictions among member nations. Some even hope that the Common Market will eventually create common political institutions such as a single parliament, a United States of Europe.

As of the end of the 1960's, Western Europe's future seemed unusually bright. Economic prosperity was widespread. Millions of Europeans were able to visit other parts of the world. At the same time, their governments were in a position to extend loans and credits to weaker nations. Despite the enormous impact of decolonization (felt decisively in Britain, where an entire empire was lost) and the emergence of the two Super Powers, Western Europe again was playing a solid and important role in international affairs. The conflict between generations and other stresses that have produced violence seemed to be problems that most prosperous, advanced societies were experiencing.

CHECK-UP

1. What was the effect of World War II on Western Europe? How was European recovery accomplished?

2. Why was the postwar situation in Germany especially difficult? What was denazification? How was it carried out?

3. What enabled West Germany to make a speedy economic recovery? What slowed political recovery?

4. What were Adenauer's foreign policies? Domestic policies?

5. Why did the Labour Party win the 1945 election in Britain? Why did it institute a policy of austerity?

6. What were the important aspects of the welfare state? Which were successful? Which unsuccessful?

7. What serious problems remain unsolved in Britain?

8. How did France recover economically from World War II? Why did political instability persist?

9. What policies did de Gaulle carry forward in France? In France's colonies? In foreign affairs?

10. What European countries have made rapid advances since World War II? Done less well? Why?

11. What is the outlook for greater unity in Western Europe?

After Soviet Russia's victory in World War II had been celebrated amidst fireworks and public rejoicing, Stalin met with Churchill and Truman at Potsdam, near the city of Berlin. The Potsdam Conference was the last of the war's great summit meetings in which the fate of much of mankind was settled by three heads of state. Among them Stalin, though younger than Churchill, was the senior statesman. For over two decades he had exercised power over nearly 200 million Soviet citizens. Now that his armies had conquered all of Eastern Europe and half of Germany, he ruled over an additional ninety-odd million people. As he had his picture taken with Churchill and Truman, the Russian leader looked hale and confident.

EASTERN-CENTRAL EUROPE

Eastern and Central Europe fall into Russian hands. Stalin had cause to be pleased. His blunders at the outset of the war were now forgotten. What counted was that under his leadership Russian power reached unprecedented heights. The boundaries of Soviet Russia ran from a point just east of the German town of Lübeck on the Baltic Sea in an almost straight line to the city of Trieste on the Adriatic. In the north Russia virtually controlled the destiny of Finland. To the south, only Greece lay outside Stalin's reach (and even there, as we have seen, Communists sought control). The advance of the Red Army, in short, had drawn a brand-new political map for Europe. West of the line lay the old "capitalist" Europe, most of it just starting to recover from German occupation. In Stalin's realistic estimate, whatever strength remained in Western Europe came from distant America. Everything east of that line belonged to the "socialist bloc." Determined to make the most of his opportunity, Stalin brought about a new age for the many peoples of Eastern and Central Europe.

Many obstacles have to be overcome in establishing Soviet rule. Many of the peoples of Eastern-Central Europe were hostile to the Soviet Union. Fiercely nationalistic, they resented foreign domination. The bulk of the population consisted of stubborn and conservative peasants opposed to collectivization. The people in this area, so used to feuding and quarreling, had never been easy to govern. Moreover, throughout Eastern and Central Europe there was little communist strength. Only Yugoslavia boasted a native communist movement (page 755). Finally, Soviet economic exploitation of these lands won Stalin no friends.

Stalin lays the foundations for Soviet rule of Eastern-Central Europe. Stalin knew that, left to their own fate, the peoples of Eastern-Central Europe would turn against the Soviet Union. To them freedom meant, above all, liberation from Russian domination. Stalin could not tolerate this prospect. Russia had paid too dearly for the insecurity of her western borders and had lost millions of lives in two world wars. Soviet Russia would take no more chances; she would suppress all political freedom in Eastern-Central Europe.

Stalin began to lay the foundation of Soviet rule even as the Red Army was driving the Germans out of Eastern Europe. He incorporated the former Baltic states—Lithuania, Estonia, and Latvia—into the Soviet Union as new Soviet Socialist Republics; they had, after all, been part of the Russian Empire for centuries. He also took a large slice of eastern Prussia under direct Soviet control, and turned over the rest to Poland, whose boundaries were pushed several hundred miles westward (see map, page 709). The loss of regions long colonized by Germans was a great blow to German nationalism. The fact that the Oder-Neisse (*oh'*der *nigh'*seh) line is still an unresolved issue in European politics has some advantages for Soviet Russia. In the face of continued German hostility, the Poles must seek Soviet support, no matter how distasteful. Another major boundary change involved the transfer from Hungary to Romania of Transylvania, long a bone of contention between these countries.

More significant, perhaps, than these boundary changes was the vast migration and uprooting of peoples following the war. Here Stalin merely let developments take their natural course. Eastern-Central Europe was a patchwork quilt of ethnic groups often scattered helter-skelter among each other. In the aftermath of the German withdrawal, old scores were settled with vengeful thoroughness. The chief victims were the many scattered German groups in Eastern Europe. By the hundreds of thousands, Germans had their land taken over and were driven from Poland, Czechoslovakia, Romania, and Yugoslavia. Brutal as was the great uprooting of minorities, it led to a considerable simplification of the ethnic map, largely in favor of the Slavic peoples.

Coalition governments appear. The biggest change, of course, occurred in the governments of Eastern-Central Europe. Although Stalin was their master by right of military conquest, he was shrewd enough to realize that he could not simply sovietize them. He therefore respected their national independence, at least outwardly, and took into account the special circumstances prevailing in each country. In Finland he merely insisted that no anti-communist party or politician should come to power. In Poland he started out with a puppet government of his own creation but agreed, under British and American pressure, to add representatives of non-communist parties. In Czechoslovakia the Communists emerged as the largest single party in the first postwar elections, thus simplifying Stalin's task. Yugoslavia, ruled in Stalinist style, presented no problem at all. In Romania, on the other hand, Stalin was forced to tolerate the monarchy for two years. Everywhere the policy was coalition government composed of what Stalin called all "democratic" and "anti-

fascist" elements, of which the communists were the most active. This generally excluded the upper and middle classes, which had either been associated with the Germans or had taken part in anti-communist underground movements. Their elimination left the field to parties of workers and peasants. The workers' parties, socialist in orientation, were soon infiltrated and taken over by the small communist parties. The peasant parties, by far the strongest, were gradually undermined by intrigue or terror and their leaders discredited. In the coalition governments, the communists usually claimed control of the police, the armed forces, and the trade union organizations. From these vital posts they gradually expanded their power. Although small in number, the communists soon gained the upper hand in these coalition governments that sprang up under the "protection" of Stalin's soldiers.

In communist eyes the coalition governments were not true soviet socialist republics. They belonged to a special category called "People's Democracies." To Stalin this term signified a halfway station between "bourgeois" (or western) democracy and soviet socialist democracy. The People's Democracies were moving toward soviet socialism, but were still distant from that goal. Stalin made sure that Soviet Russia was kept constantly before the peoples of Eastern Europe as the model they must follow. East Germany, incidentally, was merely a "democratic republic," located on the "bourgeois" side of the People's Democracies.

Stalin adopts a hard line. A realist, Stalin was keenly aware that the regimes he had established after the war might not endure. He had reason to fear that traditional nationalism would revive as the nations recovered economically. Even good Communists trained in the Soviet Union would become infected by economic recovery. If they took their responsibilities seriously, they had to bring prosperity to their peoples; for their own survival they had to make communism popular. The trend was most obvious in Czechoslovakia, where the government even applied for Marshall Plan aid in 1947. In Stalin's eyes this bordered on treason. Having few illusions where the sympathies of the peoples of Eastern-Central Europe lay, Stalin decided to change his policy and to insist on the full Stalinization of the states of Eastern-Central Europe. He also demanded the monolithic consolidation of Soviet rule and established the Communist Information Bureau (Cominform). Thus the People's Democracies became full-fledged satellites of the Soviet Union.

Czechoslovakia falls to the Communists. The new policy brought an era of terror and social revolution to Eastern-Central Europe, which, country by country, was transformed after the Soviet image. The first and most striking blow was dealt in Czechoslovakia, where parliamentary democracy was overthrown in February, 1948. Acting through the police, the trade unions, and newly formed Action Committees, Czech Communists forced a change of government which placed the hard-line Stalinists in command. While still retaining the semblance of a coalition government, the new regime was tightly linked to Moscow. Among the non-communist members who agreed to serve the new regime, Jan Masaryk (*yahn' mah'*suh-rik), the son of the founder of Czechoslovakia, headed the Ministry of Foreign Affairs. Three weeks after the take-over he was found dead below a bathroom window of the Foreign Office building. A few days later the physician who had declared him a suicide was also found dead. In June, President Eduard Benes (*beh'*nesh), who had seen his country through many crises with Hitler, resigned. He was the last representative of parliamentary democracy in Eastern Europe. Soon thereafter he died, a broken man.

Communists take over other governments in Eastern-Central Europe. In other countries of Eastern-Central Europe the changeover was less spectacular but equally effective. The communist parties tightened control over non-communist members of the coalition govern-

ments. At the same time, within the communist parties the Stalinists gained the upper hand. Soon a Stalinist purge was in full swing, with public trials for the chief victims. A number of prominent Communists were executed. All told, the purges eliminated about one in every four Communists in Eastern Europe.

The purges also terrorized the population at large. Any contact with the West, whether by correspondence, newspaper, radio broadcast, or association with foreigners, was prohibited. People ceased to trust their neighbors; speech became cautious or inhibited. Religion, still a powerful force, was under attack; the Catholic Church in particular suffered from persecution. Human spontaneity and warmth, once so conspicuous in Central and Eastern Europe, disappeared and fear ruled in their place.

Satellite economies follow a Soviet pattern. Stalin also insisted on the introduction of other forms of Stalinism. All business and industry in Eastern-Central Europe became nationalized and subject to five-year planning. Private enterprise ceased almost entirely. The emphasis in economic planning, as in the Soviet Union, was on the promotion of heavy industry. Consumer goods were slighted; life became austere and drab. Hardest hit by Stalinization, however, were the peasants. The collectivization of agriculture in the Soviet pattern was extended into Eastern Europe, leading to another tragic clash between peasant conservatism and the need for scientific farming. Herded against their will into collective farms, peasants retaliated by slowing down, being careless, and doing poor work. As a result, agriculture, the mainstay of the economy in Eastern-Central Europe, steadily declined, and young people moved to the towns to work in the factories. Instead of exporting foodstuffs these countries soon required grain imports, a burden upon the Soviet economy.

Stalin permits no cooperation between satellite countries. Another feature of Stalin's control over Eastern-Central Europe was the rigid isolation in which each country was kept. The satellites were not allowed to undertake common projects of economic development or political cooperation. All had to look to Moscow for guidance. The borders of each were as carefully guarded as those of the Soviet Union. Despite numerous treaties of mutual friendship and assistance, the satellite peoples could not visit each other except on official missions. They were deliberately kept in ignorance of each other's affairs.

The "cult of personality" is imposed. The culmination of Stalin's policy, however, was the extension of the "cult of personality" (page 654) into all satellite countries. In each, Stalin set up a dictator after his own image, a man who would rule that country as Stalin ruled Soviet Russia. In this manner Eastern-Central Europe was integrated into the Soviet system. Upon the former diversity of ethnic groups and cultural traditions Stalin foisted a new and repulsive uniformity. A traveler in these countries, looking at the postwar innovations, would never feel far from Moscow. If he had known these countries before the war, he would also marvel at the grave-like order and quiet that had descended upon this traditionally strife-torn part of the world. It had no life of its own; its fate was decided in Moscow.

Yugoslavia is an exception to the rule. Only Yugoslavia escaped Stalin's heavy hand. Josef Broz (*yoh'*sef *brohz'*), who as Marshal Tito had led the Yugoslav partisans against the Nazis, had ruled Yugoslavia since the end of the war. A good Stalinist in his own right, Tito refused to submit to Stalin's dictates. In order to stand up to Stalin's threats, he not only had to purge the pro-Stalin elements from his party, but also to court the goodwill of his subjects. This caused him to give up his plans for collectivizing agriculture and to allow Yugoslav peasants to return to their private plots. In the factories he created workers' councils that allowed the workers to share in industrial management. Bureaucracy was not allowed to stifle

criticism and suggestions from the rank-and-file. Yet communism remained the ruling ideology in Tito's state. Dissidents continued to be silenced, although without unnecessary cruelty. Yugoslav communism was Tito's own brand, a shade closer to the daily needs of the people than Stalin's.

THE SOVIET UNION

Russia faces an enormous task of reconstruction. While the peoples of Eastern-Central Europe were passing through these trials and hardships, the inhabitants of Soviet Russia fared little better. Stalin's chief task at home was healing the wounds of war, rebuilding the destroyed cities, towns, villages, factories, and farms, and moving forward toward the ideal of communist society. The Great Fatherland War, as Russians called the Second World War, had claimed the lives of about eight million soldiers and eleven million civilians; another three million had been crippled. Twenty-five million were rendered homeless. The human tragedies behind these figures defy description. There were drastic economic losses as well. Iron and steel production was down to half or even a quarter of prewar levels; so was production of oil and gasoline. In consumer goods and foodstuffs, near-starvation was the rule. Victory, to be sure, introduced a note of cheer and confidence into the postwar bleakness. The war, Stalin said in 1946, was "the most bitter and arduous of all wars in the history of our Motherland, . . . something like an examination for our Soviet system, for our state, for our government, for our party, . . . not only a curse but also a great school as well." Compared with tsarist Russia's performance in the First World War, Soviet Russia had indeed acquitted herself well. But the security of Russia, let alone the communist era of plenty, remained a distant goal.

Stalin resorts to terror in imposing economic planning and discipline. There was no choice for Stalin but to return to the building of Russian strength by his tried methods—Five-Year Plans, rigid party discipline, and terror. By

1947, all three were again in full operation. There seemed no escape from the old necessity of putting all efforts into heavy industry and defense, now that the development of atomic weapons was added to the burden. Housing and other essential consumer needs were again neglected. After the outbreak of the Korean War (page 729), Stalin concentrated even more on defense industries. Meanwhile, agriculture on the collective farms suffered from lack of equipment and government concern.

Stalin's death marks the end of an era. By 1950 Stalin was getting old and increasingly inflexible. Stalinism was in a rut, but innovation was out of the question. For months the dictator failed to appear at Politburo meetings, and urgent matters were held up indefinitely. Carefully guarded and kept apart from the people, he remained ignorant of the changes taking place in his country and in the world. In his isolation he increasingly fell victim to morbid fears: "You are like blind kittens!" he shouted at the members of the Politburo. "What will happen without me? The country will perish because you don't know how to recognize enemies." Trusting no one, he saw enemies everywhere. Even Lavrenti Beria (luhv-*ryain'*-tee *byeh'*ree-yuh), the infamous chief of the secret police who had abetted so many of Stalin's crimes, fell from favor. Stalin was paying the penalty for the exceptional burden of responsibility he had carried for so long. In the winter of 1952–1953, the Kremlin physicians in charge of his health became the victims of Stalin's wrath. He imagined that they were plotting to kill him and other Soviet leaders. The leading medical specialists of the Soviet Union were arrested and subjected to torture (under which two of them died). Stalin personally gave advice on the use of torture. He even threatened to "shorten by a head" the prosecutor in charge of the public trials, if he could not obtain "confessions" from these eminent men.

At that moment, with all of Russia trembling with fear, death struck Stalin. In the night of March 1–2, 1953, he suffered a stroke and died a few days later. When they heard the news, the peoples of Soviet Russia were stunned. Some men and women wept in public, as did even one of Stalin's principal lieutenants. The others were glum. In sullen silence Stalin was laid to rest in the mausoleum of polished red granite that he had had built for Lenin under the great brick walls of the Kremlin. There he lay, next to Lenin, under a heavy glass case, dressed in his marshal's uniform with many decorations, his moustache gray but still bristling, his hair protruding beneath the visor of his military cap, a symbol of steel-like energy and command. Millions of spectators came to see him, reverently passing through the mysterious twilight in the cool underground chamber of the mausoleum. (In the course of de-Stalinization, Stalin was eventually reburied elsewhere under the walls of the Kremlin.) Lenin, dressed in a simple dark business suit with but one small decoration, now occupies the mausoleum alone.

CHECK-UP

1. Why was the Soviet Union able to dominate Eastern and much of Central Europe after World War II? What were the chief obstacles to Soviet domination?

2. What boundary changes were made in the area? Why? What were the results?

3. What is a coalition government? What steps were followed in "communizing" a country? What countries became Soviet satellites? Why was complete Stalinization sought? What did this imply?

4. What were the results when satellites were forced to adopt the Soviet economic pattern? Why did Stalin discourage cooperation among the satellites?

5. How was Yugoslavia able to escape Stalinization?

6. What major tasks of reconstruction faced Soviet Russia after World War II? What methods were adopted to achieve them?

Stalin's death marked the end of an era for Soviet Russia, Eastern-Central Europe, and world communism as well. Never again would there arise such a towering figure commanding such profound awe. Stalin had made Soviet Russia feared and respected in the world. Yet he had also driven political terror to inhuman heights. What were his heirs to make of the double inheritance? And what should history's judgment be of a man who had risen so far beyond the station in life granted to ordinary mortals?

Stalin's heirs face great problems. To the surprise of foreign observers, no acute crisis developed over the succession to Stalin. His principal lieutenants readily cooperated under the slogan of "collective leadership," which, they said, with pointed reference to Stalin, had always been the true communist tradition. Only Beria, whom all remembered as Stalin's evil spirit, was eliminated at once.

Stalin's lieutenants took up their burden with a heavy heart. They knew that serious weaknesses lay underneath the imposing façade of Stalinism. While no one doubted the continued necessity for collectivization, something obviously had to be done about Soviet agriculture. The problem was how to make it produce more crops. The expanding Soviet industry and the growing urban population both needed a sound agricultural base. The threat of famine still haunted Soviet leaders. In industry, too, the Stalinist prescription of planning had proved inadequate. What had worked reasonably well in the case of iron and steel worked much less well for chemicals, which had become increasingly important. Centralized planning could not possibly cope with the great variety of specialized items needed for the operation of an increasingly complex economy. The growth rate of the Soviet economy, closely watched as an index of socialist efficiency, was too slow. While "capitalist" prosperity grew by leaps and bounds, Soviet productivity lagged.

The remedy for these shortcomings lay, Stalin's heirs realized, in rekindling the spirit of enterprise and innovation among the people at large. Minds had to be released from fear; effort must be rewarded by material gain. A population cowed by terror and deadened by regimentation could never be inspired to build the society of plenty promised by communism. The communist doctrine, furthermore, had grown stale under Stalin. The need now was for greater honesty in public affairs, for more goodwill from the people, for a more lively version of Leninism. The Communist Party still had to prove that it could lead the peoples of Soviet Russia to a better life, one that could stand comparison with "capitalism." It was a huge task and, in one basic respect, an impossible one. How could the party leaders grant greater freedom to their subjects when they knew that freedom endangered the monolithic unity needed for their other goals?

Khrushchev introduces "goulash communism." The boldest and least conventional among Stalin's lieutenants was Nikita S. Khrushchev (nee-*kee'*tuh khroosh-*tchohf'*), a down-to-earth, round-faced man, who spoke in everyday language spiced with proverbs and was unafraid of mixing with crowds. Khrushchev was ever ready to interpret Marxism-Leninism in simple terms of human self-interest, and his brand of communism was jocularly called "goulash communism." If you work hard enough under communist guidance, he told his listeners, you will have chicken in every pot (it was goulash for Hungarians). He was ever ready to try new schemes, often with dubious preparation, such as expanding grain production in the virgin deserts of Kazakhstan, planting corn where experts told him it would not grow, or decentralizing industrial management. Being of a

757

hopeful nature, he assumed that the problems of Soviet Russia could be solved by enthusiasm. Stalin had emphasized determination and will. Khrushchev stressed optimism and self-confidence, particularly after *Sputnik* had been launched in 1957. It was then that Khrushchev boasted of the Soviet Union overtaking the United States in the production of such foodstuffs as meat and milk (of which Soviet shops were notoriously bare), and of surpassing American productivity altogether. In the peaceful competition of the socialist way with the capitalist way, he prophesied, the former would soon prove its superiority. Believing that nothing succeeds like success, Khrushchev assumed that such an upsurge of optimism as occurred after *Sputnik* would be a better cement of unity than Stalin's terror. With that assurance he attacked the biggest problems which Stalin's heirs faced: the cult of personality and the tradition of terror, repression, and deceit.

Khrushchev adopts a policy of de-Stalinization. De-Stalinization began a few months after Stalin's death. His name was mentioned but rarely; his pictures disappeared. The role of the secret police was downgraded. Purge victims who had survived the hardships of forced labor camps began to reappear in Moscow. Some of the more prominent men of those who had perished had their reputations restored. Writers were even allowed to criticize Stalin, although very cautiously indeed. People began to speak more freely, having less dread of being denounced and punished. In this manner began the Thaw, a general loosening up after the rigidity of Stalinism.

Khrushchev himself took the lead in this process in February, 1956, when at the Twentieth Party Congress he unmasked Stalin's crimes in a secret speech. In a well-documented attack on the "cult of personality" he showed for the first time the cruel madness of Stalinism, citing case after case of torture and murder of party members conspicuous for their long service and loyalty. He even hinted that Stalin himself had been responsible for the murder of

Kirov (page 658) and proved that all terror purges down to the doctors' plot had been based on fabricated evidence obtained by the vilest methods. His audience reeled under these unexpected revelations. If everything they had so fervently worshiped during the past decades had been a fraud, what were men to believe? Many party members broke down; some committed suicide.

De-Stalinization leads to unrest. Khrushchev's attack on the "cult of personality" was a necessary moral cleansing of the party. Although he himself had been implicated in many of Stalin's crimes, he realized that for the sake of a better future Communist Russia must be rid of this crushing burden. Yet even the repudiation was marred by falsehood and ambiguity. Khrushchev obviously did not tell the whole truth, and he hedged in his judgment of Stalin. Much of Stalin's achievement, he said, was still sound: industrialization, collectivization, the condemnation of Trotskyism or any deviation from the Communist Party line, and above all, the monolithic party itself. Yet if these foundations were sound, how could one explain the abuses of Stalinism? Was it one man or an entire system that was at fault? In this question lay the seeds of new doubts and disloyalty. Some party members, therefore, soon complained of the foolhardiness of Khrushchev's speech. The official image of Stalin has been a matter of anxiety to the party ever since. And for most contemporaries of the two men in the Soviet Union, the prestige of Stalin far surpasses that of Khrushchev.

The consequences of such vigorous de-Stalinization were not slow in coming to light. In Soviet Russia itself, where the habit of submission was deeply ingrained, the Thaw progressed slowly, under the watchful eye of the Communist Party. In Eastern-Central Europe, however, the new policy produced two explosions. Ever dependent on trends in the Soviet Union, the little Stalins in Eastern Europe had begun to change their course soon after Stalin's death. They now allowed more expression of opinion and insisted on greater recognition of their country's interests. They knew they were sitting on a volcano of discontent. The peasants were restless under collectivization; workers and intellectuals chafed at Soviet domination of the national economy and cultural life. In all layers of the population national sentiment ran strong. The Soviet leaders under Khrushchev, recognizing the trend, began to refer to the socialist bloc as a "socialist commonwealth." Soviet control was toned down: the new line stressed the equality of the satellites with the Soviet Union.

Gomulka makes some gains for Poland. In Poland and Hungary, the two most anti-Russian and nationalist countries, the process of de-Stalinization did not go far enough. Both ran into special trouble after Stalin's death. In Poland widespread dissatisfaction alarmed the party. In late June, 1956, the workers of the city of Poznan staged an uprising that had to be suppressed by the army. The Poznan uprising aroused further unrest throughout Poland. Wladislav Gomulka (vwah-*dee'*swahv goh-*mool'*kuh), deposed as party secretary during the Stalin era, pointed out that if nothing were done to meet the dissatisfaction, the communist regime might be overthrown and the country drowned in a bloodbath by the Red Army. He advised an independent course for Polish communism but, unlike Tito, opposed breaking with Moscow. Poland could not stand alone. But within limits, he would demand recognition for Poland's legitimate self-interest. On these terms Gomulka was reinstated, after a crisis that threatened both a Polish revolution and armed Soviet intervention. On careful investigation in late October, 1956, Khrushchev decided to let Gomulka proceed; the alternative would have been a return to Stalinism. Thus Poland started on a new course in domestic politics. The drive for collectivization was abandoned; Soviet Russia granted immediate relief to the stagnating Polish economy; the Soviet occupation force in the country was reduced. Poland pursued a Polish road to socialism, yet remained loyal to the "socialist commonwealth."

Despite years of repression, Hungarian nationalism was not crushed by Soviet control. In 1956 defiant Hungarians risked their lives to burn Russian books, records, and pictures of Stalin (above).

The Hungarian Revolution is brutally crushed. During the Polish crisis, a catastrophe occurred in Hungary. Here the Stalinist leadership had failed to relax the rule of the secret police, even though forced to admit that convictions in the purges of 1949–1950 had been based on fabricated evidence. In the turmoil following this revelation the Stalinists were dropped from the Hungarian party leadership. Popular unrest, however, did not subside, and the reinstatement of Imre Nagy (*im'*reh *noj'*), a former prime minister and Communist ousted by the Stalinists, was demanded. The agitation was reflected in the press and in protest meetings at the university in Budapest, the capital. Writers and students took the lead in demanding concessions, including the end of compulsory classes in Russian. Soon the workers joined the protest movement. By October, 1956, Hungarians openly demanded the withdrawal of Soviet troops from their land. Words quickly led to deeds. On October 23 a crowd in the center of Budapest toppled the huge statue of Stalin, the symbol of Hungary's oppression. Thereafter events moved rapidly. The insurgents broadcast their demands over the radio; the police opened fire upon them and Soviet tanks rolled into action. For three days the rebellion spread, uniting students, workers, and even Hungarian soldiers in street fighting which succeeded in ousting the Soviet troops and establishing Nagy as head of the government. This was a parliamentary government composed of several parties, not a communist-controlled government. The new Hungary looked west, not east.

The glory of Hungarian freedom, however, was shortlived. The Soviet troops had been withdrawn merely to await reinforcements. On November 1, over 2000 tanks of the Red Army rolled across the Hungarian plain toward Budapest. Meanwhile, Nagy had announced the withdrawal of Hungary from the Warsaw Pact and declared his country's neutrality. In Soviet eyes this was treason. When the Russian troops entered Budapest, bloody fighting raged for several days. But no matter how courageous, poorly armed civilians cannot win against tanks and airplanes. Within a week Hungary was once again in chains, this time under a new communist government headed by Janos Kadar (*yah'*nohsh *kah'*dahr). Yet the uprising had not been entirely in vain. Under Kadar the new regime pursued a course not unlike Gomulka's in Poland.

Khrushchev works toward a "socialist commonwealth." Many Soviet intellectuals were deeply ashamed when they heard that Soviet tanks had mowed down Hungarian workers and students. The Stalinists, on the other hand, gloated: "We told you . . . de-Stalinization would end in disaster." Khrushchev, however, continued to work toward a slightly decentralized "socialist commonwealth." Under the supervision of the Communist Party of the Soviet Union, a variety of national experiments were permitted.

For the European satellites the new course brought some improvement. Individual farms were restored as collectives were broken up. Consumers found shops better supplied, and people could speak more freely. Yet the new freedom did not penetrate all satellites equally. Poland seemed bold in comparison to the Soviet Union, whereas Czechoslovakia remained timid. Yet even in countries where the communist leadership did not change drastically—East Germany, Bulgaria, and Romania—life became easier. The basic dilemma, however, remained: How could satellite regimes gain popular support and yet continue under Soviet domination? How could the Soviet leadership make sure of the loyalty of Eastern-Central Europe without crushing all hope and initiative in satellite countries?

Increasing freedom in Czechoslovakia provokes Soviet repression. These questions came to the fore again in 1968. In that year the reform-minded elements of the Czechoslovak Communist Party, under the leadership of Alexander Dubcek (*doob'*chek), moved boldly toward a relaxation of party controls. Dubcek did not repudiate the Warsaw Pact; indeed, he repeatedly affirmed his loyalty to the Soviet bloc. Yet at the same time he opened his country to broader contact with the West. These reforms rallied popular support for the government as never before. To the Soviet Union this policy smacked too strongly of western democracy; it was a threat to all communist regimes that could never match Dubcek's popularity. Besides, might not the preference of the people push Czechoslovakia still further away from Soviet Russia? As in the case of Hungary twelve years earlier, Soviet leaders saw no alternative to military occupation and repression, even if this step would further discredit communism as a humane ideology.

Are freedom and communism incompatible? The forcible return of Czechoslovakia to Soviet control did not solve the basic problem which confronted communist leaders. How could diversity be tolerated without endangering the unity of the Soviet bloc? Within Soviet Russia itself, how could freedom be tolerated without disrupting the unity of Soviet state and society? A measure of freedom was necessary if Soviet Russia and its European satellites were to make appreciable progress towards the goals of communist ideology. Yet freedom always seemed to degenerate into disloyalty, inefficiency, a slackening of discipline at the factory, the office, or in the army; it tended to become subversive.

In the face of these intolerable alternatives Soviet leaders since the death of Stalin have been beset by uncertainty. They have curtailed the secret police and censorship and have raised the standard of living. Yet they have been forced to limit their concessions because they could not do without a monolithic society. After an auspicious beginning, Khrushchev's experiment of careful liberalization, which he hoped would be matched by growing popular faith in the communist regime, came to a miserable end. In foreign as in domestic affairs none of his experiments paid off. The Cuban missile crisis ended in a Soviet retreat; Communist China broke away from Moscow. At home Khrushchev was discredited by poor harvests and economic stagnation. Such failures led to his sudden removal from power in 1964.

Khrushchev was replaced by a team of two men, Kosygin and Brezhnev. Aleksei Kosygin (uh-lih-*ksey'* koh-*see'*gihn) headed the government administration; Leonid Brezhnev (lyeh-oh-*nyeet'* breh-*zhnyef'*), the Communist Party organization. These men have pursued more cautious and soundly planned policies than Khrushchev, yet they have failed to achieve striking results at home or abroad. Their inability to produce successes to match the promises held forth by communism—or even to suggest a convincing escape from the basic dilemmas of communist rule—has been a major burden to the Soviet leadership as well as to world communism.

CHECK-UP

1. What problems faced Stalin's heirs? What remedies were needed?

2. Who was Nikita Khrushchev? What was his version of communism? What methods did he use?

3. Why was the policy of de-Stalinization adopted? What were the results in Russia? In the satellites?

4. Why was there unrest in Poland in 1956? How did Gomulka cope with it?

5. Why was there a revolution in Hungary? Why did the Soviet Union intervene? What were the results?

6. What was Khrushchev's goal for the satellites?

7. Why did the Soviet Union intervene in Czechoslovakia in 1968?

8. Why was Khrushchev replaced?

Life in the Soviet Union Today

Soviet achievements are impressive. The Soviet regime celebrated its fiftieth anniversary in November, 1967, with fireworks, military parades, and speeches, all praising its achievements. Who could deny that under communist leadership Russia had become a Super Power, second only to the United States? The Soviet Union boasted a fearful array of atomic weapons and had achieved signal successes in space exploration. Its technology was superb where it counted most—in the weapons needed for power politics. Soviet Russia, furthermore, had risen to pre-eminence by its own efforts, borrowing "capitalist" skills on its own terms. It was indebted to no outsider. It had done the seemingly impossible, raising itself by its own bootstraps. The regime had also wrought great changes at home and had proved its mettle in the Second World War. In the great cultural earthquakes of the twentieth century it had proved capable of winning friends and swaying the minds of men throughout the world. If it had lately run into difficulties in achieving its ambitions, it could at least argue that all governments were beset by grave problems; Soviet Russia was not the only nation facing great unrest.

In his anniversary speech Brezhnev called attention to the Communist Party's domestic achievements. Soviet Russia had made great strides in industrialization. More than half of its peoples were now engaged in urban-industrial occupations; less than half worked on the land. By trial and error it had worked out valuable techniques for economic planning on the largest scale. In these great transformations the Soviet Union had worked hard to stay in touch with the common people. The Communist Party had greatly increased in numbers since World War II. It now claimed about fourteen million members, the elite of the country in every field of human endeavor. In its efforts to mobilize the country's resources, the regime had built up a vast machinery for drawing its subjects, body and soul, into the common task of building a greater Soviet Russia.

There are many changes in Soviet society. In the process of building up Russia, the Soviet regime had removed the grossest forms of privilege, making every citizen alike in his dependence on the regime. In this sense it could claim that a classless society had been achieved. Differences, to be sure, still existed in Soviet society. Officially three different yet equal categories of "toilers" were recognized: the workers, the collective farmers, and the intelligentsia. The last-named group was composed of all white-collar workers with higher education and/ or managerial functions—administrators in the party, the government, or the economy, members of the professions, writers, and artists. Since Soviet society has not yet attained the final stage of communism, its leaders claim that inequality is still justified under the slogan: *"From* each according to his ability, *to* each according to his merits." In plain talk this means that every citizen is supposed to contribute to the common welfare as much as he can; in return he will be paid according to the contribution which he actually makes. If there is a scarcity of managers or physicists, managers or physicists will be paid exceedingly well. By contrast unskilled laborers will be paid very little, since there are more than enough of them.

The crux of a good socialist system, as of "capitalism," lies in its ability to open careers to talent. In this respect the Bolshevik Revolution has certainly earned the goodwill of most of its subjects. It did open vast new opportunities to multitudes who felt excluded in tsarist Russia. In recent decades, however, the social mobility of the revolutionary era has slowed down. Even under Stalin observers noted the rise of a new class of privilege, despite the Party's continued vigilance and sensitivity on this matter. Those who held high positions strove to pass them on to their children. But since the newly privileged groups are not independent of the state, they do not constitute a class in the traditional (Marxist) sense. They can claim no guarantee of immunity from government rule, for a purge or strict application of existing laws will quickly dispossess them.

In a similar manner the communist regime has insisted on the equality of the sexes, another matter of pride to the Communist Party. Women are entitled to the same treatment as men, and such professions as teaching and medicine are largely in the hands of women. Women certainly did much of the heavy work in industry and agriculture during the war. Russian customs, however, tend to counteract the official rule of equality. Even in the Communist Party women are decidedly in the minority.

The Soviet Union makes advances in food production, housing, and social welfare. Men and women alike judge the performance of their political system by the material comforts which it allows them. In this respect the Soviet regime could look back over the past fifty years with satisfaction. It had worked hard to provide enough food for its people. After 1965 collective farmers could raise more produce on their private plots and sell the surplus for profit on the open market. Consequently their own standard of living slowly increased. Housing in the cities was still exceedingly scarce (as it still is in many countries), but year after year new blocks of apartment houses were opened on the outskirts of cities, allowing the average family more than the one room customary in the past. If Soviet housing is cheerless by western standards, it is also exceedingly inexpensive by comparison.

In matters of health socialized medicine was one of the many social services introduced by the communist regime almost from the start. The basic needs of Soviet citizens are taken care of by public health authorities. While allowing little attention to individuals, this service at least assures a high standard of public health under rather adverse conditions. Besides health, the state provides such other forms of social security as free maternity care and vacations with pay at health resorts. Most important, it offers every adult a job and a wage. No one need to worry about unemployment or economic insecurity—an effective propaganda item in the days of "capitalist" depressions. Admittedly, the conditions or the nature of the work provided may not meet with the worker's approval, for the Soviet regime is not geared to the high degree of individual welfare to which Americans are accustomed. The greatest merit, perhaps, of the extensive system of Soviet social security is that it has publicly provided for the needs of large numbers of people who used to face the transition from peasant village to urban-industrial employment with fear and trembling. To relieve the emotional insecurity stemming from the transformation of their work, the state provided for all their material wants. The Soviet peoples are deeply grateful to their re-gime for this security. Few want to return to the "capitalist" system, which to them means that men and women have to fend for themselves. Aware of the bewildering complexities that characterize modern life, few Soviet citizens feel ready for "individualism."

Education makes great advances under the Soviet regime. Dedicated to the advancement of the "toiling masses," the Soviet regime also has made praiseworthy strides in public education for every youngster. Under plans already started by the last tsar, the Soviet government has virtually put an end to illiteracy in Russia. Indeed, reading is one of the great pastimes of all Russians. The benefits of continuous education are constantly impressed upon all. In its educational program, however, the regime has avoided excessive emphasis on academic learning. Its goal is polytechnical education that combines intellectual and manual training and instills in pupils a practical outlook on life and work. Concerned about the traditional prejudice against physical labor, the Soviet government fears the emergence of a bookish intelligentsia, always the breeding ground of subversive ideas. Admission to universities and other institutions of higher learning is therefore carefully controlled to ensure that students possess not only superior ability but ideological reliability as well.

Individualism is subordinated to collectivism. Soviet schools allow little opportunity for classroom discussion. Students must master prescribed subjects in a prescribed way, and no member of the class is allowed to fall behind. Less able students are helped by the entire class, as a matter of collective responsibility. Mathematics and science occupy a larger share of the curriculum than in the United States; students have no elective courses. History is taught in order to promote patriotism, and Marxism-Leninism is also important. Indeed, indoctrination for citizenship is the overriding purpose of Soviet education. The schools are the cradle of a new generation of socialists and communists;

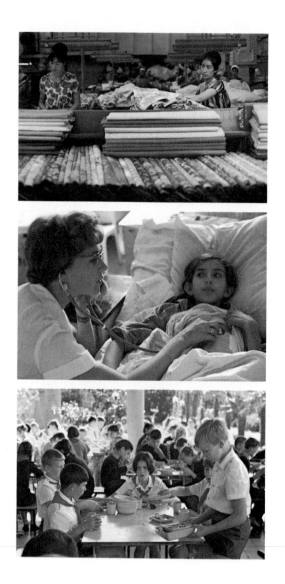

In recent years daily life in the Soviet Union has improved greatly. Replacing the drab materials of Stalinist austerity are colorful textiles (left, top). Although the average family has a standard of living lower than that in the United States, people enjoy many benefits. Above, women relax in a state-sponsored recreation center. Fully equal by law, Soviet women are employed at all levels from factory work to the professions. The majority of doctors are women (left, center). The state reaches out to the young through education and through recreation such as providing free camps for Pioneers (left, bottom).

they serve as one of the key generators of the monolithic society. Yet they also teach the classics of Russian literature, which reflect values that do not fit into Marxist-Leninist ideology and often are contrary to the realities of Soviet life. The schools are assisted in their work of shaping model citizens by the Communist Party's youth organizations—the Pioneers for children up to fourteen and the

Young Communist League (or *Komsomol*) for adolescents. These organizations provide the opportunity and services which in American society are offered by a wide range of private and public organizations. Voluntary organizations whose avowed purpose is to produce good Communists, the Pioneers and the Komsomol have a virtual monopoly on the activities of young people.

In education, as in housing and social services, the regime proudly and constantly emphasizes the need for greater collectivism. The individual, it argues, needs to be integrated more perfectly into the community; he must become a member of the "social team." This implies willing sharing of common facilities in apartment houses or transportation, brotherly responsibility for the proper conduct of one's neighbor. Anti-social behavior is one of the worst crimes of which a Soviet subject can be accused. Those guilty of drunkenness, tardiness, laziness, or other forms of social irresponsibility are publicly shamed into conformity. Soviet collectivism also calls for "cultured" behavior —cleaning one's fingernails, using a napkin at meals, trimming one's hair, avoiding profanity in speech, and being courteous to women. Much of what we consider facets of "individualism" is associated with collectivism in the Soviet Union: civic initiative and responsibility, orderly routine and promptness at work, neat appearance, and good manners.

Disillusionment characterizes the Soviet people. As the Soviet leaders looked beyond the festooned platforms from which they celebrated the half-century mark of the Soviet regime, they found much that merited praise. Yet they were also keenly aware of the high price which Russia had had to pay for these accomplishments. The Soviet Union was still poor by comparison with the leading "capitalist" countries. Whereas the United States could boast of both the highest standard of living for its people and leadership in the atomic arms race and the conquest of space, the Soviet leaders had to make agonizing choices in determining their priorities. Their determination to give first place to whatever directly contributed to Soviet power and prestige in the world meant that consumers were usually slighted, and, as a result, apt to be resentful. For most people the promise of communism remained remote; the Marxist-Leninist ideology was merely empty words.

By 1967 the majority of the Soviet people had lost whatever faith in the official ideology they had ever possessed. They attended the compulsory indoctrination sessions in school, factory, or office with closed ears, painfully aware of the discrepancy between the ideal and the reality of Soviet life. Said one of the leading Soviet authors, Anatoly Kuznetsov (koos-nyee-tsohf'), after running away from Soviet Russia in 1969: "[Marxism-Leninism is] utterly obsolete, rigid, and naive, . . . incapable of resolving the contradictions in society today, . . . leading to frightful social tragedies." How, then, can Marxism-Leninism provide the cement of unity so badly needed in Soviet society; how can it keep together the world communist movement?

The Soviet regime has continued to function only because of its incessant and ever more refined corruption and evasions and its equally perfected controls and compulsions. The system and the secret police ensnare every citizen. At the slightest sign of opposition, his telephone will be tapped, his mail opened, his conversations reported. In order to rehabilitate himself, he might be ordered to spy on friends and associates. Failure to cooperate might result in banishment from his home town or exile to a concentration camp. For minor penalties a citizen might be denied promotion or his vacation, or merely have a critical comment entered in his personnel file, an entry that would count against him later.

The socialist ideal is far from the Soviet reality. Behind the front of official self-congratulation, the realities of Soviet Russia are sordid when judged by the moral standards of the great Russian writers of the past. Truthfulness and sincerity in thought, speech, and conduct do not thrive in Soviet life. Those who practice these virtues soon find themselves ridiculed or branded as public enemies. A note of falsehood pervades all official statements and is echoed in the press, in art, architecture, literature—wherever one looks. Under such conditions, honesty and creativity are driven underground. The works of the best authors circulate secretly or are published abroad—Boris Pasternak's

Doctor Zhivago or Solzhenitsyn's (sohl-zheh-nee'tseenz) *Cancer Ward*. Imagine thinking of your country as a cancer ward, filled with diseased people! When some United States writers shout from the rooftops that American society is sick, many people listen. In Soviet Russia such a protest brands the author as criminal— and not without justification. If his protest were allowed to be heard, the tragic fact is that the entire Soviet regime would be seriously impaired and might even collapse. Its great achievements, its security and power in the world, would be undermined. It is no wonder that politically minded Soviet citizens who are not Communists are faced with a great dilemma. They recognize the desirability—and even the necessity—of power and prestige in the world; they appreciate the generous social security and the economic planning undertaken by their government. They even admit the necessity of a dictatorship. Yet they abhor the methods by which Soviet greatness has been achieved. But what other methods are available that will not diminish Russia's power in the world?

Soviet society has never been able to combine individual freedom and well-being with national power. It is a one-sided society with the welfare of the individual subordinate to international power.

CHECK-UP

1. What are the major achievements of the Soviet Union since World War II? Has a classless society been achieved? Explain.

2. What advances have been made in the field of housing? Health? Social security? Is there equality of opportunity? Equality of the sexes?

3. What advances have been made in the Russian educational system? How does it subordinate individualism to collectivism? Why?

4. What is the mood of the Soviet people today? Why? How has the Soviet regime been able to maintain itself in power?

Summing Up

Europe was faced with an enormous task of reconstruction after World War II. Recognizing the dangers in continued hunger and want, the United States provided economic aid through the Marshall Plan and, through NATO, tried to discourage further Soviet expansion in Europe.

In the nations of Western Europe various paths were taken to achieve reconstruction. The unification of the three western occupation zones and the introduction of a stable currency helped West Germany rebuild a prosperous industrial economy and establish a democratic form of government. The austerity program of the British Labour Party, its establishment of a welfare state, and the granting of independence to most of Britain's colonies changed the British way of life and eventually led to unprecedented prosperity. Despite economic recovery, France continued to be plagued by political instability until de Gaulle came to power in 1958. His rule at times antagonized his allies, but did restore the prestige of France. Italy and especially Northern Europe have prospered since World War II, while recovery in Spain, Portugal, and Greece has been hampered by repressive governments. Membership in the Common Market has proved rewarding for much of Western Europe and some look forward to the development of a Europe united culturally and politically as well as economically.

European reconstruction was hampered by Stalin's determination to establish a buffer zone between the Soviet Union and Western Europe. Willingly or not, the nations of Eastern-Central Europe soon found themselves satellites of the Soviet Union. Only Yugoslavia escaped Stalin's heavy hand. Attempts to lessen Soviet control in Eastern-Central Europe met with little success and sometimes with stern repression.

In the Soviet Union, Stalin's harsh dictatorship drove the Russian peoples to superhuman efforts. Heavy industry, defense, and atomic weapons received priority over the development of consumer industries and agriculture. Stalin's successors realized the need to develop agriculture as well as industry; they turned from Stalin's hard line to a policy of peaceful coexistence. By the 1960's the Soviet Union boasted a technology that rivaled that of the United States. Great progress had been made in housing, social equality, welfare services, and education. Individualism, however, remained subordinate to the collective welfare, and the Soviet reality was still far from the socialist ideal.

Chapter Highlights

Can you explain?

apathy	austerity	war criminals	peaceful coexistence
refugees	socialist bloc	denazification	coalition government
charisma	welfare state	nationalization	cult of personality
satellites	occupation zones	goulash communism	psychological damage

Can you identify?

Cominform	Kosygin	Social Democrats	Federal Republic of Germany
Dubcek	Gomulka	Adenauer	Christian Democrats
Warsaw Pact	Attlee	Jan Masaryk	People's Democracies
Brezhnev	Brandt	de Gaulle	European Common Market
Komsomol	Khrushchev	Oder-Neisse Line	
Beveridge Plan	Labour Party	Pioneers	

What do you think?

1. Both Germany and Japan suffered great damage during World War II, yet today both are among the world's leading nations. Why?

2. What are the implications of the trial of German and Japanese "war criminals" following World War II?

3. What are the advantages and disadvantages of the welfare state that evolved in Britain after World War II?

4. Why did the French welcome the return of de Gaulle to power in 1958? What were his achievements? Limitations?

5. What has prevented most of Southern Europe from achieving economic prosperity?

6. Should Stalin's policy toward Eastern and Central Europe have come as a surprise to statesmen in western countries? Why?

7. How were communist regimes established in the countries of Eastern-Central Europe?

8. Why was Stalin determined to speed the reconstruction of Russia following World War II? Was his policy a success?

9. In what respects were Khrushchev's policies similar to Stalin's? Different?

10. To what extent does Soviet reality conform to the socialist ideal?

11. Are freedom and communism incompatible? Why?

Asia Since World War II

*China, India, and Japan contrast markedly in their out-
look and development. Forward-looking Japan excels
in many modern industries such as the manufacture
of precision instruments (far left) and offers strong
competition to other industrialized nations. Under
communist rule, the face of China has been greatly altered. At left, students recite quotations by Mao Tse-
tung, the man primarily responsible for the changes.
While Communist China is regaining her former
prestige, she has not developed as quickly as her
leaders had hoped. Of the three Asian giants, India has
undergone the least change. Development has
been hampered by traditional outlooks, lack of
capital and trained manpower, and a rapidly growing population. India's conflict with Pakistan has
hindered the development of both countries. Above,
Muslims stream northward toward Pakistan after the
partition of the subcontinent in 1948.*

Asian society has been greatly changed since
the end of the Second World War. Before that
war, the Indian subcontinent and all of Southeast Asia except the kingdom of Thailand were
colonies of the western powers. China was weak
and divided. The only truly powerful and independent Asian country was militarist Japan.
The Second World War weakened the western
hold on Asia and greatly stimulated anti-western
nationalism. These two factors resulted in independence for all of the Asian colonies.

Political independence, however, failed to
provide an automatic solution for the underlying
problems which faced the countries of Asia.
Rapid population growth, combined with a

769

slow rate of economic growth, kept standards of living low. At the same time, people's expectations for a better life continued to rise. The demand for funds to improve agricultural production conflicted with the demand for funds to speed industrialization. In each country government policies, whether conservative or radical, failed to satisfy the expectations of the people.

This chapter discusses developments since 1945 in Japan, China, India, and Pakistan, and makes a brief survey of Southeast Asia.

Japan's Phenomenal Growth

Japan's development was unique in Asia. A major power before World War II, by 1945 Japan had been devastated (page 707). Today, however, Japan is among the leading industrial nations. What made this recovery possible?

With United States assistance Japan brings about basic reforms. Unlike the Allied partition of postwar Germany, the postwar occupation of Japan was completely under the control of the United States. This meant that the United States could carry out policies with little interference from other powers. Though American occupation was resented by the Japanese, United States policies proved beneficial to Japan. Rather than set up a new form of government, the United States decided to work in partnership with the Japanese governmental authority. The first step was to demilitarize Japan. Military leaders were purged, and there were trials for war crimes. Then a series of basic reforms was brought about.

1. Government reform. In 1947 the authoritarian Meiji constitution, a grant from the emperor, was replaced by a democratic constitution which put sovereignty in the hands of the Japanese people. The emperor, for centuries considered sacred, became merely the "symbol of the state." The 1947 constitution established a two-house Diet (legislature) popularly elected by the people, with a cabinet government (as in the British system) responsible to the Diet. Human rights were guaranteed and war was outlawed.

2. Agrarian reform. There was a nationwide land reform. In prewar Japan land had been concentrated in the hands of large landlords. Almost half of the land was cultivated by tenant farmers who paid a high percentage of their produce to the landlords as rent. After World War II the government limited the amount of land each farmer could own, purchased the surplus, and sold it to landless peasants. This was a remarkably successful reform. A class of prosperous, small landowning peasants emerged. With the burden of rents removed, they could invest earnings from the sale of produce in improving their farms.

3. Educational reform. Prewar education in Japan emphasized the virtues of loyalty and obedience. Learning was mainly by memorization. Postwar reforms patterned education after the American system. Textbooks were rewritten to introduce democratic values and concepts and to provide modern methods of learning.

4. Political reform. In prewar Japan the conservative, authoritarian government often dealt harshly with opposition political parties and trade unions. In the postwar period political parties and trade unions were encouraged. The police were charged with safeguarding the constitutional rights of the people, as well as providing security for the government. This enabled both conservative and socialist groups to compete openly in the political arena.

5. Business reform. Large economic trusts, the *zaibatsu* (*zie-baht-soo*), had long been characteristic of prewar Japan. Each zaibatsu was controlled by a wealthy and powerful family and combined financial, industrial, and business operations. For example, a zaibatsu would own railways, shipping, and banks as well as industries. There was a close partnership between government leaders and zaibatsu families. In postwar Japan the United States decided to break the zaibatsu up into smaller units. This policy was soon abandoned, for it threatened to wreck the Japanese economy. The zaibatsu provided the organization necessary for Japan's economic recovery. However, the zaibatsu lost some of the power and the rigid economic control they had exercised before the war.

Japan becomes an American ally. The American occupation lasted for seven years. Its original policy of transforming Japan into a democratic state soon had to give way to the realities of the time. By 1948, with the threat of a communist take-over in China, United States policy in Japan shifted from democratic reform to place major emphasis on political stability. The importance of Japan to the American policy of containment of Communist China became obvious when the Korean War broke out in 1950 (see page 729). Japan became vitally important not only as an American base for military operations in Korea but also as a source of supplies. By this time the United States was beginning to look upon Japan as an ally rather than a defeated enemy, and in 1951 she signed a peace treaty with Japan. This restored Japan's political independence. At the same time a security treaty was signed to permit the United States to keep military bases in Japan. This arrangement was necessary. Except for small defense forces, under the 1947 constitution Japan has neither an army nor a navy.

This has actually been beneficial to Japan, since she does not have large military expenditures. But the continued American presence in Japan has aroused opposition, especially among Japanese pacifist and left-wing groups. It has also caused anti-American sentiments among the younger generations in Japan.

East Asia

1945	United States occupies Japan
1947	New Japanese constitution drafted
1949	Communists gain control of China; Nationalist seat of government moved to Taiwan
1950–1953	Korean War
1951	Japan and Western Allies sign peace treaty
1952	United States and Japan sign Mutual Security Treaty
1953	First Five-Year Plan announced in China
1958	China's Great Leap Forward
1961	Sino-Soviet split
1966	Cultural Revolution in China

Japan moves toward political democracy. A number of small political parties were active in postwar Japan. Gradually these were consolidated into two major parties—the Liberal Democrat on the right and the Socialist on the left—each a combination of various shades of opinion. The Liberal Democrats, advocating free enterprise plus some government planning and directing, have been in power continuously since World War II. They represent government officials and zaibatsu interests, and receive support from most of the rural classes and the conservative urban middle class. The Socialists demand reform rather than revolution as the means of achieving social and economic goals. With support from trade unions, urban workers, and the liberal urban middle class, the Socialists have gradually gained political strength. In foreign affairs the Liberal Democrats adopted a pro-western, anti-communist policy, whereas the Socialists favored neutrality for Japan. Over the years parliamentary government has worked well in Japan, with the Liberal Democrats the party in power.

Japan's economy booms. Much more fundamental than political change has been the postwar social and economic transformation of Japan. Today Japan ranks behind only the United States and the Soviet Union as an industrial power. Before the war only heavy and military industries were modernized in Japan. Light consumer industries for the most part remained at the traditional handicraft, cottage level, and agriculture tended to be underdeveloped. This one-sided modernization, directed by the military-zaibatsu ruling group, prevented the majority of the population from receiving higher wages and achieving better living standards. During the war Japanese factories, shipyards, and transportation systems suffered great damage. But Japan had the human resources and capability which enabled her to make a surprising comeback. The literate, hardworking population was eager to rebuild the economy. There was ample technological and managerial skill for modernizing industry, and the tradition of personal savings and frugality gave Japan a strong base of credit. With American aid the Japanese economy not only recovered, but soon surpassed the prewar level.

For several years Japan's gross national product has averaged an increase of about ten per cent yearly—the most spectacular rate of growth in the world. Remarkable development in metal, machinery, and chemical industries has made Japan a leading producer of heavy electrical machineries, railroad cars and equipment, optical goods, motor vehicles, electronic equip-

The changing outlook of the Japanese is reflected in student attitudes. Students in elementary and secondary schools show the same respect to instructors that Meiji students did (left). University students, however, often protest official policies by staging demonstrations (above).

ment, petrochemicals, and plastics. She leads the world in shipbuilding, is second only to the United States in the production of radio and television sets, third in petroleum refining and in steel production. Before the war much of Japan's trade was with China. Today, her leading trade partner is the United States, despite the geographic separation of the two countries. The United States, for her part, has more trade with Japan than with any other nation except Canada.

The future of Japan appears bright. Unlike the rest of the nonwestern nations, Japan has virtually solved the problem of overpopulation, which in earlier periods caused so much social and economic strain and which threatened to wipe out any economic gains the country might make. Birth-control programs have resulted in a population stabilized at about 100 million—a number the economy can take care of without undue strain. The movement of people to the cities—especially sprawling Tokyo —still causes massive transportation tie-ups and has led to the extension of slum areas. But the rising expectations of the people are being met by Japan's prosperous, growing economy. As more of the national income is paid out in wages and salaries, the standard of living will continue to rise. Japan's present-day affluence compares favorably with that of the leading western nations. This is a far brighter picture than that presented by any other Asian nation. The problems faced by the Japanese are much like those which confront people in affluent western societies.

CHECK-UP

1. What basic reforms were introduced in postwar Japan in government? Agriculture? Education? Business?

2. How did the United States change its Japanese policy? Why?

3. What are the chief political parties in Japan? The goals of each?

4. Why has Japan's economy boomed? What are its chief exports?

5. Why is Japan's future bright?

Communism's Impact on China

Clashes between Communists and Nationalists lead to civil war. The war which broke out between China and Japan in 1937 lasted for eight dreary years. The Chinese played a waiting game rather than trying to attack the militarily superior Japanese. At first the Sino-Japanese War united Chinese Nationalists and Chinese Communists against the common foe. As the war dragged on, however, this unity fell apart. Lacking the money to support the war, the Nationalist government resorted to printing more and more paper money, causing the purchasing power of money to decline. This created special hardships for those with fixed incomes. Faced with growing corruption in the Nationalist government, decreasing incomes, extensive destruction of property, and confiscation of food supplies, the people became demoralized.

The anti-Japanese united front of Nationalists and Communists, led by Chiang Kai-shek (*jeh-ahng' kie' shek'*), fell apart. Even when they had been united in name, Nationalists and Communists continued to maintain independent governments, armies, and currencies. The much more powerful Nationalist government was based in Southwest China, with its capital at Chungking. The communist headquarters was at Yenan (*yeh'nahn'*) in North China. Conflicting goals of each led to mutual suspicion. Soon there was little more than an armed truce between them, and tension often erupted into civil war.

In North China the Communists won popular support by reducing land rents and interest

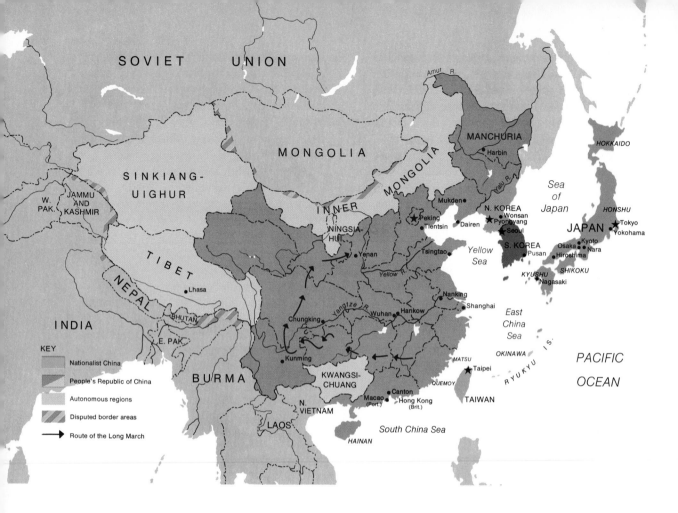

East Asia: China, Korea, and Japan

rates, whereas the Nationalist government was blamed for its corruption. The Communists were also applauded for fighting behind the Japanese lines and for continuing to harass the Japanese army. Mao Tse-tung (*mah'oh dzuh' duhng'*), leader of the Communist government, gradually gained stature. By the war's end he had a loyal and disciplined army of one million men.

When the war finally ended, Chiang and Mao clashed in their moves to take over the parts of northern and eastern China which had been occupied by the Japanese. The United States, following a policy of supporting pro-western governments, helped Chiang by supplying transport

planes to ferry Nationalist soldiers to take over major cities. Meanwhile Mao, in line with his guerrilla tactics, concentrated on occupying the countryside. Hoping to persuade Chiang and Mao to cooperate in the reconstruction of the war-ravaged nation, United States President Harry Truman sent General George C. Marshall to China as mediator. But by 1947 it had become clear that there would be no cooperation between Nationalists and Communists.

The struggle came to a head in Manchuria, whose industries were vitally important in rebuilding the Chinese economy. Nationalist garrisons in Manchurian cities were forced to surrender when their long supply lines were cut by Communist guerrillas. This gave the Red Army military equipment which had been supplied Nationalist forces by the United States, and Chiang lost some of his best troops. The victorious Red Army then took the offensive, and by the spring of 1949 had occupied key Chinese cities—Peiping (*bay'ping'*), Shanghai, Nanking, Hankow, and Canton. On October 1 of that year the Communists proclaimed the establishment of the People's Republic of China. Chiang and the Nationalist forces withdrew to the island of Taiwan (*tie'wahn'*).

There are several reasons for the communist victory. Many factors contributed to the victory of the Chinese Communists in 1949. Most of the Chinese people wanted peace more than anything else. Disillusioned by the inefficiency and corruption which had become common under the Nationalists, they believed the Communists would bring improvements. But the communist victory in China was essentially a military one. The communist troops were disciplined and dedicated. They simply swept aside Chiang's troops. Despite good equipment and greater numbers, the Nationalist soldiers lacked the high morale of the Communists.[1]

NATIONALIST CHINA

When the Chinese Nationalists first took over Taiwan, which had been held by the Japanese, they embarked upon a ruthless policy of repression against the indigenous Taiwanese. But the loss of mainland China had a sobering effect and led to the abandonment of such policies. With the technical advice and financial assistance of the United States, the Chinese Nationalists promoted the industrialization of Taiwan. They

---

[1] There are those who argue that persons in the State Department of the United States contributed to the communist victory by advocating mediation, minimizing the communist danger, and opposing outright military support for the Chinese Nationalists. But an analysis of various factors within Chinese society reveals the hopelessness of the Nationalist cause. The recent experience of the United States in South Vietnam suggests that generous economic aid and massive military intervention serve at best only to prop up a government which lacks popular support.

set up a very effective land-reform program modeled on that in postwar Japan. The standard of living for the people of Taiwan began a steady improvement. However, the government of Taiwan remained in Nationalist hands with basically one-party rule. The aging authoritarian figure of Chiang Kai-shek continued to lead the Nationalists. Nationalist control of the government caused discontent among the Taiwanese majority, who resented the take-over of their land by the Chinese.

COMMUNIST CHINA

Whatever one's views on communism, there can be no doubt about the importance of the victory won by the Chinese Communists in 1949. For the first time since the decline of the Ch'ing dynasty in the late nineteenth century there was an effective central government wielding authority over all of mainland China. Once they achieved unchallenged power, the Chinese Communists embarked upon a revolutionary transformation of Chinese society. This deliberate policy of modernization differs from both the Soviet and the Japanese models.

Mao's China becomes a communist dictatorship. The People's Republic of China in theory is a "new democratic" society in which the lower urban and rural classes dictate government policy. Actually, the Chinese Communist Party rules in the name of the lower classes. The party, in turn, is controlled by its leader. In Communist China, then, the leader controls the party, the party controls the government, and the government controls the people. All newspapers, radio stations, movies, and other means of mass communication are state-owned. The state controls all levels of education as well as admission to various types of schools. Finally, all social groups are indirectly controlled by the state. The Chinese people are subjected to a constant flow of propaganda and agitation. They have to undertake group criticism and self-criticism so that their thoughts can be molded along the line desired by the party leadership.

Everyone has to participate in prescribed activities; opportunities for individual thought and action and for privacy are at a minimum.

Plans are made to industrialize China. During their first years in power the Chinese Communists effectively coped with the problem of inflation, took over control of all industries and most business firms, restored production to prewar levels, and redistributed land among the peasants. These moves put the party leadership in complete control of China's economy. Thereafter, it tried to develop the economy in the desired direction.

Though they realized the importance of agriculture to the economy, the Communists were even more interested in industrializing China. They felt China must be developed industrially to be acknowledged as a world power. The leaders of Communist China therefore planned a rapid industrial development, with emphasis on heavy, strategic, military industries. The needed funds would have to be squeezed out of agriculture. But industrialization was hampered by shortages in trained manpower and investment capital. Moreover, the high rate of increase of China's population tended to offset increased production.

Until about 1957 China received some aid from the Soviet Union in the form of machinery, industrial blueprints, Russian experts and technicians, and limited financial aid. This assistance enabled the Chinese Communists to undertake a five-year plan similar to those followed in the Soviet Union. The First Five-Year Plan (1953–1957) was carried out quite successfully. But the Soviet model of development did not permit rapid enough industrialization to satisfy the hopes of Communist China's leaders. The industrial resources of China were much more limited than those of the Soviet Union, and her economy depended even more on agriculture. Furthermore, the Chinese feared that excessive dependence on Soviet assistance was not in the best interests of the country. By 1958 there was a steadily widening split between the two communist nations.

Agricultural production fails to increase appreciably. The initial redistribution of land in the early 1950's represented an attempt to win the support of the peasant masses. But land redistribution by itself failed to increase agricultural production significantly. Because they also had to develop China industrially, the communist leaders had to limit the technological and financial resources allocated to agricultural development. Since manpower was plentiful, ways had to be found to get the peasantry to put forth greater effort to improve agricultural production.

In the mid-1950's agricultural cooperatives and collective farms were set up. Members of cooperative farms pooled funds to buy expensive machinery which all could use. The collectives merged farm households and cooperatives into large agricultural units. The land was owned by the government and the machinery by the collective. In this way the limited resources in money, machines, and know-how could be more efficiently used. But the increase in production failed to satisfy the party leadership.

Communes and the Great Leap Forward prove a dismal failure. To increase agricultural production further and at the same time develop industry without dependence on Russian assistance, in 1958 the Chinese leaders announced the "Great Leap Forward" and the communization of agriculture. A campaign designed to make maximum use of China's human resources, the Great Leap aimed at the development of many local industries on a small scale, instead of large factories for which China lacked the capital and technical know-how. The communist leaders believed that the country's industrial needs could be met at less expense by developing many small industries.

The plan also called for more efficient development of agriculture. It was decided to organize agricultural workers into *communes.* The communes called for the complete regimentation of all phases of the peasant's life and work. Farm households, collectives, and small commures were merged into giant communes which averaged about 22,500 workers each. Members of a commune woke at the same time, ate together in huge mess halls, marched to and from work in formation, and attended political sessions after the evening meal. Families were often broken up, with men and women housed in separate dormitories and children raised in a group as part of the communal program. Everything was done on schedule by the commune as a whole; each worker was like a cog in a huge machine.

These policies proved too harsh even for the long-suffering Chinese. Commune-style agriculture was poorly suited to the intensive farming practiced in China for centuries. The communes and the Great Leap program meant additional hardships for people who already lived at a low level. Drought, floods, and insect pests damaged crops and caused a decline in farm production. Shoddy manufactured goods proved worthless; industry seemed to be slipping backward instead of leaping forward. Because of the discouragement which swept the nation, commune regimentation and the Great Leap home industries were de-emphasized.

Mao's reliance on the masses leads to the Cultural Revolution. But the Communists continued to make maximum use of China's human resources, an approach which Mao Tse-tung had found effective in the past. In dealing with China's problems Mao relied less on Marxist theory than on his own sense of the realities in China. It was clear to Mao that China's strength lay in her people, that solutions that worked in other nations would not necessarily work in China. The communist victory in 1949 confirmed the effectiveness of his policy of mass mobilization. Maoist policy reflected a belief in the possibility of making the masses an instrument for revolutionary change. In this regard, Mao showed more faith in the people than had either Lenin or Stalin. Despite the failure of the communes and of the Great Leap Forward, Mao once more turned to the masses in 1966–1968.

Chairman Mao and his close followers had come to believe that both the Chinese Communist Party and government had become too bureaucratic, too burdened with red tape. In order to overcome this trend, the Maoists launched the Great Proletarian Cultural Revolution. Youths were organized into Red Guards, who then were sent into the cities and countryside to criticize government and party officials who had become too set in their ways. The Red Guards would agitate for radical, drastic changes. The Cultural Revolution was an attempt by Mao's followers to maintain the momentum of a permanent revolution. The Maoists believed that a revolutionary outlook was most important; it might even overcome economic and material obstacles. And they wanted to make sure that the younger generations in China recognized the importance of this revolutionary outlook.

China plays a major role in Asian politics. China, occupying a vast area on the Asian continent and possessing a huge population (about 800 million), has been and is a major power in the East. In traditional times China dominated her neighbors. From the mid-nineteenth century to the mid-twentieth century, however, internal weaknesses often left her at the mercy of foreign powers. This century of defeat and humiliation made the proud Chinese overly sensitive and extremely chauvinistic (page 501). Since World War II Communist China's leaders have been able to capitalize on this anti-foreign nationalism and have instilled in the people a sense of pride in their country. This has inspired them to do their utmost to restore China's greatness. Despite her low level of industrialization, China has reasserted her place in Asian politics. As her power and prestige grow, Communist China comes more and more to the attention of the United States and the Soviet Union.

China and the United States are at loggerheads. In the Second World War the United States had fought to prevent a Japanese-domi-

China has long disputed border territories with her neighbors. Scene of a Sino-Soviet clash in 1969 is the Ussuri River border in the north, under constant patrol by Chinese and Soviet troops (right). Vital to the People's Republic of China as a source of trade is Hong Kong (above), which today overflows with thousands of Chinese refugees who, since 1949, have fled communist rule in China.

nated Asia. As Japan neared collapse, the United States sought to fill the power vacuum by building up Nationalist China. She continued to aid the Nationalists during the initial stages of the Chinese Civil War. This support of the Nationalists, as well as the fundamental conflict between communism and western democracy, has made the Chinese Communists extremely hostile toward the United States. Communist China regards the United States as the leading imperialist nation of the world. In turn, the United States has refused to recognize the government of Communist China, and has led the fight to prevent that country's admission to the United Nations. Moreover, the United States has maintained a policy of containment, surrounding China with military, naval, and air

bases. The Korean War was one episode in the continued tension between the two nations. The war in Vietnam is yet another.

Finally, in 1971, Communist China was admitted to the United Nations. And, early in 1972, President Nixon paid a personal visit to China. After more than twenty years of tension, both the United States and Communist China appear interested in improved relations. However, there are still basic disagreements between the two nations. Especially troublesome is the issue of Taiwan. The Chinese Communists consider Taiwan to be a part of their country, whereas the United States supports an anti-communist government on Taiwan. It will probably thus be some time before normal relations are established between the two countries.

Relations between Soviet Russia and Communist China become strained. Immediately after the communist victory of 1949 Mao Tse-tung made it clear that China sided with the Soviet Union in the struggle between the socialist and the capitalist nations. In return China received technical and financial assistance from the Soviet Union. By 1958, however, there was evidence of increasing tension between the two communist nations. Unquestionably, Chinese chauvinism finds it difficult and perhaps impossible to be part of a world communist movement dominated by Moscow. The two communist giants disagree about the interpretation of Marxist theory, the use of nuclear weapons, and many other points. The Sino-Soviet conflict is clearly revealed in the different approaches of China and the Soviet Union to world politics. The Russians stress peaceful, competitive coexistence. The Chinese call for establishment of communism through anti-imperialist wars of national liberation. The Chinese Communists believe their experience is more applicable than Russia's to the needs of developing countries. More recently, there have been border clashes between China and Soviet Russia over a boundary dispute dating back to pre-communist days. Since 1958 the split between Communist China and the Soviet Union has seemed to widen. Today, the view held by most Americans following World War II—that world communism is a monolithic movement—is no longer accurate. In fact, in 1972 the increasing rivalry with Soviet Russia led the Chinese Communists to welcome a relaxation of tension between the People's Republic of China and the United States.

CHECK-UP

1. Why did the popularity of the Chinese Nationalists diminish during World War II? Why did the Chinese Communists gain support?

2. How did the Chinese Communists gain control of Manchuria? Oust the Nationalists from mainland China?

3. What policies have the Chinese Nationalists pursued in Taiwan?

4. What kind of state did Mao Tse-tung create in China?

5. Why has Communist China stressed industrialization? With what success?

6. How did the Chinese Communists hope to increase agricultural production? How successful were they?

7. What is the Cultural Revolution? Why did Mao use this approach?

8. Why have the Chinese Communists encouraged an anti-foreign nationalism? How has this affected China's relations with the Soviet Union? With the United States?

South Asia's Slow Rate of Development

Indian society had its foundations in the two major religions of the subcontinent—Hinduism and Islam. To a large extent religious beliefs and practices determined patterns of living. This reliance upon religion meant a separation between the Hindu majority and the Muslim minority. The division of India by religious beliefs remained unchanged throughout the period of British rule. The Indian National Congress, which under the leadership of Gandhi (page 581) agitated for political self-rule, was basically a Hindu movement. To protect Muslim interests in India, in 1905 the Muslim League was founded. In 1934 Mohammed Ali Jinnah (uh-*lih' jin'*nuh, 1876–1948), a British-educated Muslim lawyer, became the leader of the League. Under his guidance the League began to demand that a separate Muslim state be set up in the subcontinent. By World War II there had evolved a triangular relationship: Hindu

779

nationalists agitated against the British for self-rule; Muslim nationalists sought separatism from the Hindus; the British stalled for time by playing one group against the other.

British rule of the Indian subcontinent ends. British defeats suffered in Europe and in East Asia during the early years of the Second World War greatly damaged Britain's prestige in the eyes of her colonial subjects. During the war, the Indian National Congress refused to support the British war effort and continued to agitate for political independence. Relations between Britain and Hindu nationalists continued to deteriorate. The end of the war brought increased agitation by the Congress. In 1947, realizing the futility of further delay, Britain's newly elected Labour government put an end to British rule over the Indian subcontinent. In an attempt to satisfy both Hindus and Muslims, Britain created two independent states—India and Pakistan (see map, page 783)—based on religious lines. Areas which had a majority of Muslims became Pakistan; Hindu areas became the nation of India.

Violence accompanies the separation of India and Pakistan. The sudden withdrawal of the British, who had generally kept the antagonism between Hindus and Muslims to a minimum, had immediate and disastrous results. A series of terrible riots broke out between Hindus and Muslims, as Hindus in Pakistan fled to India and Muslims in India sought safety in Pakistan. Hundreds of thousands were killed, and millions became homeless refugees. A Muslim minority remained in India and a Hindu minority in Pakistan. While the partition was justified because of tensions between the Hindu and Muslim communities, certainly it makes no sense in either economic or geographical terms. Independent India has a population five times that of Pakistan and three and a half times as much territory. Between West and East Pakistan lie over a thousand miles of Indian territory. Instead of solving problems, independence thus created new ones.

India adopts a parliamentary form of government. India is a federal republic headed by a president who exercises only ceremonial duties. In the two-house legislature the real lawmaking body is the lower house. Its members are elected by popular vote. The prime minister, appointed by the president, is leader of the majority party in the lower house and chooses his own cabinet. As in the British system, the Indian prime minister's stay in office depends on how long he can retain the support of a majority of the members of the lower house. Provincial (state) governments are organized in a similar way. The states ruled by princes, which had existed during the period of British rule, were absorbed into the Indian republic.

However, a brief description of a country's constitutional-legal framework sheds little light on the actual workings of state and society. It is necessary to look at some of the social and economic problems which confront India and see how the government has dealt with them.

India faces many social problems. The vast majority of the Indian people are impoverished and illiterate. The new government realized the urgency of improving standards of living and expanding education. The new constitution of India guaranteed civil rights, abolished the caste system (page 203), and promised social equality and equal economic and educational opportunities for all Indians. But the new government lacked the resources to meet all the needs in social welfare and education. Improvements would have to be accomplished gradually. The rising expectations of the masses made them impatient, however. The constitutional abolition of the caste system did not automatically put an end to social inequality and discrimination, for old habits tend to persist regardless of law. In addition, India lacks a national language. Hindi, the official tongue, is spoken by less than a third of the population. There are many other languages, and the people speaking them resent the special status of

Hindi. The result is that Indians often communicate in English, the language of their former rulers.

Raising living standards is proving difficult. The economic problems of India are those faced by any developing society under great pressure to modernize. The foremost problem is that of a rapidly growing population in a land where the amount of cultivable land is limited. Population growth first became a problem during the period of British rule. The introduction of modern medicine led to a sharp decline in the death rate. The birth rate, while lower than in 1900, has not declined greatly. With a population of over 537 million growing at a rate of 2.5 per cent yearly, India has not been able to produce enough food to feed the people adequately despite some advances in agriculture. Living standards for the masses remain low.

Three approaches have been proposed as a means of resolving this urgent problem.

1. Population control. The government hopes to limit population growth by promoting birth control. Experience indicates, however, that widespread acceptance of birth-control programs depends upon improvements in education and living standards. Since better living conditions depend in part on slowing population increase, it is clear that birth-control programs alone cannot solve India's problems.

2. Agricultural reform. India desperately needs improved agricultural productivity to provide for her present population. Many farms are too small to feed even the people who own them. Agricultural reform is needed to combine small farms into larger, economically practical units. Then funds would be needed for farm machinery, better seeds and livestock, and chemical fertilizers. Most of India's small farmers have no money to put into such programs of development. Throughout history, farmers have tended to oppose change unless they have clear evidence that it will be to their advantage.

3. Industrialization. From a long-range viewpoint, surplus rural population can be absorbed

South and Southeast Asia

1946 Philippines become independent

1947 India, Pakistan, and Burma become independent; Nehru becomes prime minister of India

1948 Ceylon becomes a self-governing dominion; Gandhi assassinated

1949 Indonesia becomes independent

1953 Laos gains independence

1954 Geneva Conference divides Vietnam pending elections and grants independence to Cambodia; formation of SEATO

1955 Bandung Conference of Asian and African leaders

1958 Ayub Khan becomes president of Pakistan

1961 United States sends troops into Vietnam

1962 Border crisis between India and China

1966 Indira Gandhi becomes prime minister of India, first woman to hold the highest elected office in a nation

1970 Prince Sihanouk ousted in Cambodia, civil war breaks out.

into an expanding industrial program. But so great an expansion of industries would require time, technology, and capital. Thus it can be seen that the problems of population, agricultural production, and industrialization are interrelated. All need to be solved quickly. But where does a developing nation with limited resources start?

Nehru introduces socialist economic planning. In 1948 Gandhi was assassinated and his place at the head of the National Congress Party was taken by Jawaharlal Nehru (jah-*wah′*har-lal *nay′*roo, 1889–1964). The son of a high caste Brahmin family and educated at Cambridge University in England, Nehru was far more westernized than Gandhi. During the First World War, Nehru joined Gandhi's nonviolent nationalist movement. He was a faithful follower of Gandhi, though the two Indian leaders sometimes differed on specific questions of policy or tactics. Gandhi advocated nonviolent resistance. Both a democrat and a socialist, Nehru tended to urge active resistance. Unlike the leaders of the Soviet Union and Communist China, Nehru believed that it was possible to combine political democracy with massive economic planning by the state. This twofold policy was carried forward by his government. In 1950 a National Planning Commission was established to provide centralized socialist planning for the development of the Indian economy. Several five-year plans were issued by this commission, but the results were not too successful. Agricultural gains have been more than offset by population increase, and the lack of investment capital has caused industrialization to fall far short of the goals set.

The inertia of the National Congress increases.

The Indian National Congress has been the majority party in India since the nation became independent. It has controlled the federal government since 1947. But disagreements over policy within the party have caused the National Congress to lack a clearly defined sense of direction. As the party's leaders—most of them the same men who agitated for independence—have grown older, their policies have reflected growing conservatism. Since the death of Nehru in 1964, the inertia of the Congress Party has increased.

India maintains a neutral position in world affairs.

In foreign affairs independent India has maintained a policy of strict neutrality. With China practically on her doorstep and with the Muslim Middle East separating her from the western nations, India has little choice but neutrality. This policy has irritated some Americans, who would have liked to see India join the anti-communist front led by the United States. But from the Indian point of view, neutrality has been a sound and popular policy. As a newly independent and developing nation,

India must solve her domestic problems before she can play the role of a world power. Being neutral has also benefited India, for she is courted by both sides. This has brought the country badly needed financial and technical assistance. Nevertheless, Indian neutrality suffered a severe setback in 1962 when China and India clashed over a border area. Although the Chinese troops were soon withdrawn from Indian soil, this act of aggression plus the strained relations between India and Pakistan have caused India to worry about the problem of national defense. To provide security, she has felt obligated to spend for defense money badly needed for development.

PAKISTAN

Pakistan was created to meet the demands of the Muslim League for a state independent of India. But can religion alone provide an adequate foundation for the establishment of a modern political state? The partition naturally was bitterly opposed by Indians. Confronted by a hostile and much larger India, Pakistan has had a number of difficult problems to solve in addition to those which usually beset developing nations.

Pakistan has some unique problems.

Pakistan's most pressing problem after independence was the resettlement of more than six million Muslim refugees who had fled from India. The fact that West Pakistan is separated from East Pakistan by more than a thousand miles of Indian territory has caused another problem. East Pakistanis have regional interests which differ from those of West Pakistanis. They bitterly complain that the West Pakistanis discriminate against them. An even more serious concern for Pakistan has been the continuing problem of political instability and corruption. Mohammed Ali Jinnah, who had led the struggle for an independent Pakistan, died in 1948. When no Muslim leader proved able to take his place, a long struggle for power led to political instability.

KEY

░░ Disputed between India and Pakistan

/// Disputed border areas

= River valley projects

Ayub Khan tries to stimulate economic development. Finally, in 1958, the commander-in-chief of the army, General Ayub Khan (*ah'*yoob *kahn'*), took over the government. Though he established a military dictatorship, Ayub Khan had the best interests of Pakistan in mind. He gave his country more than ten years of political stability, and for a time did away with corrup-

tion. Ayub undertook a moderate land reform, breaking up some of the large estates in West Pakistan. He was also quite successful in stimulating increased agricultural production and in developing new industries. But Ayub Khan

Because labor is cheap in India, much of the work of modernization is done by hand, as at the fertilizer plant above, and the pace is therefore slow.

tan continued to deteriorate. In 1971 there was a bitter civil war. With the help of India, East Pakistan drove out West Pakistani troops and set up the independent state of Bangla Desh.

Pakistan's relations with India remain strained.

In foreign affairs Pakistan's major problem has been her relations with India. All her other policies are determined by this central problem. Tension between the two countries has centered on their dispute over Kashmir. At the time of the 1947 partition Kashmir had a Muslim majority, but a Hindu ruler who wished to join neither India nor Pakistan. But when his country was invaded by tribesmen from Pakistan, he requested military aid from India and joined that country. Pakistan insisted that the people—not the ruler—should vote whether to join India or Pakistan. In 1965 the Kashmir question caused armed conflict between India and Pakistan, and it still has not been settled. The fact that Kashmir's rivers supply water for Indus River irrigation projects, vitally important to both India and Pakistan, helps explain why each side continues to press its claim to Kashmir.

CHECK-UP

1. Why did British rule in the Indian subcontinent come to an end in 1947? What two independent states were created? Why? Why did violence break out in each?

2. What kind of government was established in India? How effective has it been in coping with India's problems?

3. What major problems plague India? Why has it proved difficult to raise the standard of living in India?

4. What three approaches have been proposed for solving India's problems? Explain each.

5. What major problems have plagued Pakistan?

6. How did Ayub Khan try to stimulate Pakistan's economic development? With what success?

7. Why have relations remained tense between India and Pakistan?

was working for long-range results. The rate of progress was not fast enough to meet the rising expectations of the Pakistanis, who wanted better conditions immediately. The masses could not see the wisdom of a program of austerity in the present to ensure prosperity in the future. By the late 1960's government policies were meeting increased opposition from students and trade-union workers. Continued public agitation and demonstrations forced Ayub Khan to resign in 1969. Relations between West Pakistan and the much poorer East Pakis-

Southeast Asia covers an arc ranging from Burma on the Asian continent to the Philippine Islands (map, page 786). Blessed by a temperate climate and plentiful rainfall, this area produces an abundance of food, especially rice, for its population. In addition, it is rich in such natural resources as timber, tin, rubber, and oil.

Southeast Asia has a rigid social system. In this vast area dwell more than 270 million people of varied backgrounds. The original population was of Malay ethnic stock. Later, other groups, such as Viets, Thais (*ties*), and Burmans, settled in Southeast Asia and mixed with the Malays to form different nationalities. It can be generally stated that traditional Southeast Asian society was rigidly divided between a small ruling aristocracy and the peasant masses. Aristocratic life, centered at court, was marked by luxury. There was constant struggle and intrigue for political power. The life of the peasants, on the other hand, was tuned to the seasonal cycle of rice cultivation. Religious rituals and festivals marked important events and changes in season. Southeast Asian society failed to produce its own urban middle class. That role was filled by Indian and, to a lesser extent, Chinese merchant-immigrants.

Foreign trade with Southeast Asia has a long history. Since the time of the birth of Christ, Hindu traders have visited Southeast Asia, carrying Hindu culture through the area. Later, Arab and Chinese merchants traded with Southeast Asia. All sought the spices so highly prized in Europe (page 360). The Indian influence on Southeast Asia has remained the strongest, however. From India came the religions of Hinduism, Buddhism, and Islam.

Over the centuries Southeast Asia's riches attracted the adventuresome. The coming of European traders and colonizers was merely another chapter in a long history of contact with foreigners. The Portuguese and the Spaniards, seeking spices, first reached Southeast Asia in the sixteenth century. They were followed by the Dutch, English, and French. Each nation chartered its own East India company which set up trading posts at strategic locations. These were basically ventures of private commercial monopolies (see page 385–387). The fortunes of the various trading companies waxed and waned. The only exception was found in the Philippines, where the Spaniards set up a colonial administration similar to that established in Spanish America.

Europeans establish colonies in Southeast Asia. During the second half of the nineteenth century, however, European nations began to look upon Southeast Asia as something more than a source of trade. Imperialist rivalry caused western nations to compete aggressively with each other for colonies. By the end of the century the British had acquired control of Burma and Malaya; the Dutch East Indies was comprised of the major islands of Sumatra and Java, and the French had moved into Indo-China—consisting of present-day Vietnam, Laos, and Cambodia. As a result of war with Spain in 1898, the United States acquired the Philippines. The only Southeast Asian country that preserved its independence was Thailand. This happened partly because it had able rulers and partly because of rivalry between the British and French.

From the late nineteenth to the mid-twentieth century, colonial society in Southeast Asia was generally divided into three layers. At the top were the colonial administrators and other westerners. Sometimes the local non-European aristocracy, which gradually had become westernized, was included in this top layer of society. At the bottom of society were the indigenous peasant masses, who were generally poor and illiterate. There was a complete sepa-

Southeast Asia Today

ration between the top and the bottom of society. Between rulers and peasants was a small urban middle class, usually made up of the Chinese and Indian minority. This middle class served as a buffer between the colonial rulers and the peasant masses. There was little opportunity for a person to move out of his class and to get ahead in such a society. The colonial rulers did not wish to encourage change. Popular education consisted mainly of basic technical training, and general education was discouraged. Some administrators tried to govern in the best interests of the people; others

exploited the Southeast Asians shamelessly. Generally speaking, colonial administrative policy was unenlightened.

Japanese occupation leads to a growth of nationalism. World War II brought great changes to Southeast Asia. Within a few months after the attack on Pearl Harbor, the Japanese occupied nearly all of the area. This was a severe blow to the prestige of the western powers, a setback from which they never recovered. By its slogan of "Asia for the Asians," wartime Japanese propaganda encouraged the growth of small nationalist movements in the various Southeast Asian countries. The Japanese, of course, hoped to have these nationalists serve them. The nationalists, on the other hand, believed the Japanese had come to free them from western imperialism. They soon discovered that the Japanese had other plans. Many nationalists nevertheless took advantage of the Japanese occupation, using it to advance their own cause. The growth of nationalism was a permanent legacy of Japan's wartime occupation of Southeast Asia.

Southeast Asian nations become independent. At the end of the war the western nations, blindly believing that they could restore colonial rule, were confronted by a rising tide of nationalism in Southeast Asia. Of all the colonial powers, the United States had followed a relatively enlightened policy in governing the Philippines, gradually preparing the Filipinos for self-rule. Filipinos fought bravely against the Japanese and in 1946 gained the independence promised before World War II.

It soon became apparent to the other western powers that they must give up their colonies in Southeast Asia. In 1948 Britain granted independence to Burma and to Malaya (now the Federation of Malaysia). Later Singapore was also granted independence and was for a time part of the Federation of Malaysia. The next year the Dutch gave up the East Indies they had ruled since the seventeenth century, but only with considerable reluctance and after great nationalist pressure from Indonesians.

Vietnam becomes a pawn in the cold war. The case of French Indo-China was complicated and tragic. During World War II the Vietnamese nationalist movement had come under the control of the capable communist leader, Ho Chi Minh. In 1945 Ho proclaimed an independent Democratic Republic of Vietnam in the northern half of the country, while the French tried to restore their own rule in the south. Conditions ranged from pitched battles to armed truces until the French were disastrously defeated at Dienbienphu (*dyen'byen'-foo'*) in 1954. At Geneva, Switzerland, shortly thereafter, France agreed to withdraw her troops from Vietnam. The country was temporarily divided into North Vietnam, under Ho Chi Minh's control, and South Vietnam, which was controlled by conservative landowners and military interests. The Geneva Conference also promised the eventual unification of Vietnam following a popular election.

However, this election was not held and conflict developed between North and South Vietnam. Soon Vietnam became a pawn in the cold war between Communist China and the United States. China provided Ho's government with military and technical aid. To bolster the tottering South following the French withdrawal, the United States provided large-scale financial, technical, and military aid. But even with this aid, South Vietnam was unable to withstand North Vietnam. Finally, in 1961, the United States decided to intervene directly by sending troops to Vietnam.

The war in Vietnam proves costly and indecisive. As United States involvement increased, the war—in terms of casualties and financial outlay—proved costly but indecisive. The United States soon found that conventionally trained troops stood little chance of victory in the jungles of Vietnam. Small groups of enemy soldiers would attack suddenly and melt into the jungle before United States troops could mobilize against them. By the end of the 1960's the war had become a hopeless morass. The communists in South Vietnam (Viet Cong) were absorbed by the National Liberation Front in 1960. Both were controlled by the People's Revolutionary Party, the South Vietnamese branch of the Lao Dong (the Communist Party of North Vietnam). These communist groups received a steady flow of arms and supplies from the Soviet Union and Communist China. The United States provided arms for her own troops as well as those of South Vietnam and other allies. North Vietnam possessed the advantage of a well-disciplined army with high morale, fighting a guerrilla war in familiar terrain. In addition, the North could lay claim to the popular cause of anti-western nationalism. The government of South Vietnam, in Saigon, represented conservative and military interests. Uninterested in reform and change, the Saigon government was not only ineffective but also corrupt. It thus lacked the popular support necessary to wage a victorious war. As long as that held true, no amount of American financial aid and military involvement could offset the advantages held by North Vietnam.

Common problems plague the new nations in Southeast Asia. In general, the newly independent countries of Southeast Asia are confronted by a series of interrelated problems.

1. There is a wide gap between the small ruling class and the rural masses. The ruling body usually represents the conservatives, the owners of large estates, and the military. Their goals and outlooks are quite different from those of the impoverished, illiterate peasant masses. The ruling class wants to retain its social prestige and its control of land and wealth. The people want peace, better living conditions, a fair share of the wealth, and more land. Communist propaganda therefore has a strong appeal for the masses.

2. Southeast Asia's problems cannot be solved overnight. There is need for land reform, industrialization, and popular education. Also needed is a literate middle class capable of bridging the gap between rich and poor.

3. Surging nationalism tends to discriminate against the Chinese minority, the traditional middle class of the society. This discrimination not only creates social tension but hurts the economy.

4. Finally, there is the danger that Southeast Asia may become a battleground between Communist China and the United States.

CHECK-UP

1. Explain the role of the aristocracy in Southeast Asia. What is the role of the peasants? The urban middle class?

2. What foreign countries carried on extensive trade with Southeast Asia? When? Why?

3. What European nations established colonies in Southeast Asia? What colonies did each establish? Why did the Southeast Asians benefit little from this relationship?

4. How did Vietnam become a pawn in the cold war? What was the role of France? Of the United States? Why has North Vietnam been comparatively successful in the long struggle?

5. What interrelated problems plague most of the nations of Southeast Asia?

Summing Up

Since the end of the Second World War, Asia has undergone tremendous transformation. Japan emerged from the ashes of her defeat to become a leading, prosperous industrial democracy. In the civil war in China, 1945–1949, the Communists triumphed over the Nationalists. For the first time in a century, effective unified political authority was established in China. The Second World War also witnessed the collapse of European power and influence in South and Southeast Asia. India and Pakistan gained political independence, as did former colonies in Southeast Asia. However, political independence has not automatically ensured stability, for these nations are confronted with deep-seated social and economic problems.

The nations of Asia (excluding Japan) must cope with problems of overpopulation and low agricultural productivity, resulting in a low standard of living. In addition, they are under pressure to industrialize but lack the necessary financial and technological resources. This is the dilemma of modernization. Whether democratic, communist, or authoritarian, experts increasingly are agreed on the need for some form of planning, so that modernization can be accomplished more rationally and efficiently.

In addition to their economic problems, Asian nations must cope with the social problem of impoverished masses and their rising expectations. Inevitably, for many years to come, most Asian countries will have to deal with unrest and discontent among their peoples. There will be tension between the ruling class and the masses, between the older and the younger generations.

The international situation in Asia has also changed a great deal since the Second World War. Before that war military Japan threatened the imperial interests of the western colonial powers. In postwar Asia there is a direct confrontation between the United States and Communist China, with Soviet Russia standing in the background as a third interested power. Japan, up to now, has been an American ally. As befits a leading industrial power, Japan will gradually reassert her diplomatic autonomy, and resume her position of influence in East Asia.

Chapter Highlights

Can you explain? ───────────────────────────────────

agrarian	zaibatsu	mass mobilization	anti-western nationalism
communes	confiscation	buffer	Cultural Revolution

Can you identify? ───────────────────────────────────

Diet	Ho Chi Minh	Sino-Japanese War	National Liberation Front
Nehru	Pakistan	Muslim League	People's Republic of China
Ayub Khan	Kashmir	Chiang Kai-shek	Mohammed Ali Jinnah
Saigon	Red Guards	Mao Tse-tung	Great Leap Forward
Manchuria	Indo-China	Geneva Convention	Indian National Congress
Hindi	Taiwan	Liberal Democrats	

What do you think? ───────────────────────────────────

1. Why has Japan achieved third place among the world's great industrial nations?

2. Are Japan and the United States in agreement on all questions of foreign policy? Explain.

3. What are Mao's goals for China? How successfully has each been achieved?

4. How did Mao regard the masses? How do his policies reflect this attitude?

5. In what ways are the problems of China and India similar? Different? What approaches has each nation followed in attempting to solve its problems? With what success?

6. What are the conflicts of interest between the United States and China? Can they be reconciled? Why?

7. What problems did the separation of India and Pakistan solve? Create? Was the decision wise? Why?

8. Why are India's problems of population, agricultural production, and industrialization related? What priority would you give each? Why?

9. Why has the United States role in Vietnam been unpopular in many Asian countries? In Europe? In the United States?

The Changing Middle East

Immense contrasts of wealth and poverty prevail in the Middle East. Under the barren wastes of the desert lies the world's greatest reservoir of oil (above, left). The bedouin family at left lives in two worlds: the father left the life of a nomadic herdsman to work for an oil company but he continues to live in a tent. His children will probably go to school; his wife continues to wear the heavy traditional veil. Iran is beginning to find its way into the twentieth century under the guiding hand of its shah, shown above at his coronation. The splendor of his office contrasts markedly with the poverty of most of his people. Nevertheless, it has generally been the shah who has initiated reforms in Iran.

Since World War II the Middle East has been convulsed by persistent tensions. Modernization has proceeded too slowly to relieve the pressures of poverty and overpopulation. The orderly processes of parliamentary government have not taken root in most countries of the Middle East, and many of them suffer from political instability. There is a constant threat of revolution, political assassination, and civil war. The major cause of tension in the Middle East doubtless has been the prolonged and bitter conflict between the Arab states and the Jewish state of Israel. Jews and Arabs have already fought three wars, and peace is not in sight. To understand why the Middle East is in turmoil, we must go back into history.

The Ottoman Empire collapses. In the nineteenth century the Ottoman Empire, which dated back to the fourteenth century, began to crumble. As Turkish power waned in the Middle East, the European nations took over former Ottoman lands. One of the defeated Central Powers in World War I, the Ottoman Empire was stripped of its non-Turkish provinces, including Arabia, Iraq, Syria, and Palestine. Only a strip of territory around Constantinople in Europe and most of Anatolia in Asia Minor remained of the former Ottoman possessions. The straits leading to the Black Sea, the Turkish army, and Turkey's finances were placed under international administration by the victorious Allies.

Turkey becomes a republic. Following the war, Greek forces, with the approval of the Allies, sought further to dismember Turkey. To a nation without allies and short of military supplies, this might have been a crushing blow. Indeed, the Ottoman sultan made no effective move to halt the invasion. But under the leadership of Mustafa Kemal (muhs-tah-*fah′* keh-*mahl′*), a young army officer, the Turks established a provisional government in Ankara. As its president, Kemal organized an army, drove out the Greeks, and abolished the sultanate. In 1923 the Turkish Republic was formally proclaimed.

Kemal became the republic's first president and took the name Atatürk ("Father of the Turks"). It was clear to Atatürk that his nation was hopelessly behind the times; ways of living in Turkey had changed little since the sixteenth century. Atatürk believed Turkey's only hope lay in modernization, and he felt strong authoritarian rule was the way to initiate reform.

Atatürk introduces reforms. Atatürk's first move was to separate the state from the tradition-bound Islamic religion. Religious control of education was replaced by state control; religious courts were replaced by government courts modeled on the western legal system. Although most Turks continued to be Muslims, Islam was no longer given the status of an official religion. A more radical step was the translation of the Koran into Turkish. This horrified the faithful, who believed that the holy book of Islam could only be reproduced in the language of Mohammed. Later the Arabic script used in written Turkish was replaced by Latin characters, which made it much easier for people to learn to read and write. A full-scale attack on illiteracy followed this reform.

Atatürk also introduced social reforms. He outlawed the wearing of the fez, demanding that men adopt western headgear. The loud outcry of protest this occasioned was mild compared to the protest that met changes in the status of women. Polygamy was abolished, and women were encouraged to wear western dress. Women were given equal rights with men, including the right to vote. To a nation where women had for centuries been little more than jealously guarded property, this was a drastic (and to many, unwelcome) reform.

Efforts are made to strengthen the economy. Once the transformation of Turkish society was under way, Atatürk began economic reforms designed to eliminate western control of industry and trade. State banks were established, and agricultural training stations and cooperatives were set up under government supervision. Poor industrial planning and traditional peasant resistance to change hampered Atatürk's economic program, although some advances were made. Change made the most impact in urban areas; in the countryside people continued to cling to Islam and its traditional ways.

Many of Atatürk's reforms were just starting to take hold when the dictator died in 1938.

The Middle East

1919–1926	Ibn Saud gains control of most of Arabia (renamed Saudi Arabia, 1932)	**1946**	Jordan gains independence
1920	Atatürk becomes president of Turkey's provisional government; Britain receives mandate of Transjordan and Palestine; France receives Syria and Lebanon	**1947**	United Nations votes to divide Palestine into Arab and Jewish states
1922	End of British protectorate over Egypt	**1948**	State of Israel proclamed; first Arab-Israeli war; beginning of Arab refugee problem
1923	Formal proclamation of the Turkish Republic	**1952**	Revolt of Egyptian officers ousts king
1927	Independence of Iraq recognized	**1954**	Nasser becomes head of Egyptian government
1941	Syria and Lebanon proclaim independence (not recognized by Britain and France until 1946)	**1956**	Nasser nationalizes Suez Canal; Israeli attack on Egypt supported by Britain and France
		1967	Third Arab-Israeli war (Six Days' War)

In comparison with European nations Turkey still had a long way to go. But judged by her status after World War I and her development in the period between the two world wars, Turkey had made great advances.

CHECK-UP

1. How did the Turkish Republic come into being?

2. What major reforms were introduced by Atatürk? How successful were they?

Creation of Independent Arab States

For hundreds of years the Arab lands of the Middle East had been part of the Ottoman Empire. The winds of nationalism that had swept across Europe in the decades after the French Revolution began to reach the Muslim world at the end of the nineteenth century. Early Arab nationalists stressed as unifying forces the common religion (Islam), language (Arabic), and culture (Muslim). They did not at first seek independence from Ottoman rule, for the Turkish sultan was also the head of Islam. But soon Turkey's repressive measures against non-Turks led Arab nationalists to demand political independence. At this time only a small group, mainly intellectuals, was attracted to Arab nationalism. The vast majority of Arab peasants

and bedouins remained untouched by nationalist feelings.

The Arab lands become mandates. World War I caused many changes in the Arab world. For helping the British fight the Ottoman Empire, Arab nationalists had expected to receive independence. But Britain had no intention of letting oil-rich lands slip from her grasp. In secret treaties the British and French had reached agreements which were respected by the League of Nations in assigning mandates. Iraq and Palestine became British mandates, and newly created Transjordan came under British protection. France received as a mandate what is today Syria and Lebanon. (See map, page 621.)

Arab nationalists felt betrayed. The establishment of these mandates contributed to the bitter anti-western feeling which persists to this day in the Middle East.

Saudi Arabia is created.

One Arab state created between World Wars I and II was Saudi (sah-oo'dih) Arabia. A sense of nationality developed only slowly among the impoverished, illiterate people of Saudi Arabia, most of them bedouins. But with the discovery of vast reserves of oil, Saudi Arabia was abruptly shoved into the twentieth century. Bedouins, whose fathers and grandfathers had been herdsmen, began to drive trucks and to work on oil rigs. But most of the huge income from oil went into the purses of the rulers, the Saud family.

Not until after World War II were reforms initiated. In 1950 Prince Faisal (fy'suhl) began a modernization program by building hospitals, schools, and extensive irrigation projects. These changes were accepted only slowly by the population and by Muslim religious leaders. By 1964, when Faisal became king, Saudi Arabia had modern urban centers in which lived foreigners connected with the oil companies. Most of the nation, however, still had a long way to go before its people became part of the twentieth century.

Egypt achieves independence.

In 1922 the British granted Egypt partial independence, but Britain continued to supervise Egypt's foreign affairs. In 1936 she recognized Egypt's independence and agreed to withdraw her troops from Egypt except for the region around the Suez Canal. But during World War II British interference in Egyptian affairs increased, as did Egyptian resentment of Britain's presence. In 1952 Egyptian army officers took over the government. A leading figure in the revolt was Colonel Gamal Abdel Nasser (juh-mahl' ub-duhl-nah'ser), who wanted not only to end British interference in his country but also to introduce needed social reforms. In 1954 Britain agreed to withdraw her troops from the Canal, a decision joyfully received by the Egyptian people. Nasser was rapidly becoming the most prominent and popular figure in the Arab world. The masses viewed him as an Arab nationalist able to hold his own in dealings with the West, as a strong leader who could restore honor and prestige to the Arab peoples after centuries of foreign rule, economic stagnation, and humiliation.

Iraq is hampered by political instability.

The development of its oil resources allowed the British mandate of Iraq to make considerable economic progress in the years after World War I. Political leadership was provided by a strong and capable prime minister, Nuri Pasha es-Said. Between the world wars Iraq "burst out from the cocoon which four centuries of Ottoman rule had woven around it and burgeoned into a rich and thriving modern community." In 1932, with her admission to the League of Nations, Iraq's independence received official recognition. But the fact that Nuri had close ties with the West, particularly Britain, aroused the hatred of Arab nationalists who regarded him as a tool of western imperialism. In 1958 he and the king were murdered by Iraqi army officers. Since that time, Iraq has been torn by dissension as cliques of army officers and politicians have competed for power. The Kurds, a nomadic people in the north of the country, have contributed to the unrest by demanding self-government. These problems have slowed Iraq's economic and social progress despite her wealth in oil.

Palestinian refugees endanger the stability of Jordan.

After World War II Britain granted independence to Transjordan, which was renamed the Hashemite Kingdom of Jordan. In 1948 Jordan annexed much of western Palestine, bringing under its rule over half a million Palestinian Arabs, refugees from Arab-Israeli warfare in what is now Israel. These Palestinian refugees have organized commando units which launch raids against Israel. The Palestinian refugees threaten to overthrow King Hussein (hoo-syne') and to take control of Jordan.

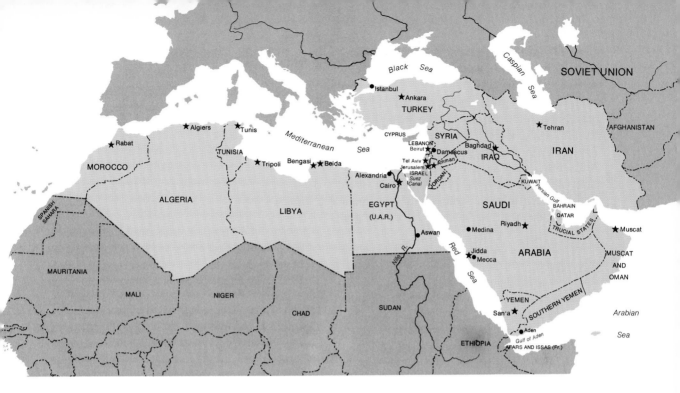

Today Jordan is an impoverished nation with an uncertain future. Whether Hussein's government can survive thrusts from within is questionable.

Syria and Lebanon face many problems. Syria and Lebanon gained their independence from France in 1946. Strongly anti-western, Syria has sought closer ties with the Soviet Union. Syria's hostility to Israel is matched only by Egypt's, and for some years the two nations were joined as the United Arab Republic. But Syria's unwillingness to submit to Egyptian domination ended this experiment in Arab unity. Internal turmoil has caused Syria's leaders to rule with an iron hand. Economically undeveloped and politically unstable, Syria's future does not seem promising.

Lebanon is different from other Arab lands, whose population is overwhelmingly Muslim. Somewhat more than half the population of Lebanon is Christian. To avoid internal strife, the Lebanese government seeks to maintain a delicate balance between Christians and Muslims in parliament and in government offices.

The Middle East Today

North Africa gains independence. North Africa shares the religion, language, and culture of the Middle East. Its cultural ties with the Middle East began with the early expansion of Islam and were strengthened under Ottoman rule. Only Morocco escaped Turkish control. When Ottoman power began to decline in the nineteenth century, countries in Western Europe established colonies in North Africa. There were unsuccessful revolts against European rule, but not until after World War I did nationalism become a strong force.

After the Second World War, demands for independence were followed by a period of repression and terror in French-held Tunisia, Morocco, and Algeria. Tunisia and Morocco gained their independence in 1956, but Algerian independence came only after a long period of agony (page 749). Today the countries of North Africa are trying to modernize. They face economic underdevelopment and political instability. Socialism has considerable appeal to

795

many North African leaders, who view it as a solution to their economic problems.

Pan-Arabism appeals to some Arab nationalists. Some Arab nationalists dream of uniting all the Arab peoples into one great nation. The leader in the struggle for *Pan-Arabism* or Arab unity was Nasser. Nasser expressed the goals of Pan-Arabism as (1) elimination of all European control over Arab affairs, (2) unification of the Arab world, and (3) destruction of Israel.

The drive for Arab unity has encountered considerable resistance. Despite a common language and religion, the memory of the great Muslim empire of the past, and a common hatred of Israel, the Arab world remains disunited. Rulers and the wealthy fear Arab unity might cost them their power, their property, and even their lives. Oil-producing states are not always eager to share their wealth with less fortunate neighbors. Perhaps the greatest obstacle to Pan-Arabism, however, is that the Arab nations fear domination by Egypt. Even Nasser, in his last years, recognized that Arab unification was at best a distant goal. Since his death in 1970, no Arab leader has commanded sufficient power or respect to unite the Arab world. Only on one issue is the Arab world united—hatred and fear of Israel.

CHECK-UP

1. Why did Arab nationalists seek independence? What happened to the various Arab lands after World War I?

2. How did Egypt achieve independence? What goals did Nasser seek for Egypt? How did the Arab world view him?

3. What problems confront Iraq? Jordan? Syria? Lebanon?

4. How did the Muslim states in North Africa achieve independence?

5. What is Pan-Arabism? Its goals? What obstacles does it face?

The Arab-Israeli Dispute

The Arabs view the existence of Israel as an insult to Arab honor and a violation of Arab rights. How did Israel come into being? What has been its impact upon the Middle East?

The Jews have long maintained their identity as a people. The Jews, or Hebrews, are an ancient people who originated in Mestopotamia. They gave to the world the idea of monotheism and set up rules of conduct that are followed today by Christians and Muslims as well as Jews (see pages 34–35). In the fourteenth century B.C. the Hebrews settled in Palestine and a Jewish state developed with its capital in Jerusalem. A revolt against their Roman rulers in the first century A.D. proved disastrous. The victorious Romans destroyed Jerusalem and many Jews were sent into exile, joining other Jews who had settled outside of Palestine in earlier periods. While thousands of Jews continued to live in Palestine, there was no longer a Jewish state.

The exiled Jews, scattered throughout the world, were often the victims of persecution, particularly in Christian lands. Yet despite centuries of torment and terror, the Jews preserved their ancient traditions and rituals, their firm belief in one God, their respect for learning, and the memory of Palestine. Their family life grew stronger and their determination to survive as a people remained unbroken.

In the early nineteenth century, largely as a result of the liberal ideals of the French Revolution, Jews were permitted to leave the crowded ghettoes, where they had been forced to live as social outcasts for centuries. They began to en-

The continued tension between Arabs and Israelis magnifies the possibility of a direct confrontation between the Super Powers. The Egyptian tank above, of Soviet origin, was captured by Israeli forces in the 1967 war. Land taken from Jordan during the war included the Wailing Wall in Jerusalem (right), for centuries a place of pilgrimage and prayer for Hebrews. Most severely affected by the Arab-Israeli conflict are the Arab refugees, some of whom have lived since 1948 in squalid temporary camps (top).

ter the mainstream of European life. Their sense of identity as a people and their capacity for survival in a hostile environment had been excellent preparation for success in the competitive western world. In the following decades Jews rose to prominence in many fields, particularly learning, and contributed greatly to western culture and economic life. Marx, Freud, and Einstein, three giants in the intellectual life of western civilization, were of Jewish ancestry. Many Jews became assimilated into western nations. They adopted European and American ways and gave less attention to their ancient traditions.

The Zionist movement develops. In the last part of the nineteenth century, anti-semitism increased in Europe. The hostility to Jews revealed in the trial of Dreyfus (page 520) and violent persecution in Russia convinced some Jews that their people would never be secure until they had a state of their own. This belief led to the founding of the Zionist movement, whose goal was return to Zion (Palestine). Eighteen hundred years after its conquest by the Romans, the Jews still regarded Palestine as their homeland. For centuries Jews had prayed: "Sound the great horn for our freedom . . . and gather [the exiles] from the four corners of the earth. . . . And to Jerusalem . . . [let us] return in mercy; . . . rebuild it soon in our days as an everlasting building."

The first major success for the Zionists came during World War I when Britain declared that she "viewed with favor the establishment in Palestine of a National Home for the Jewish people." Zionists regarded this statement as an invitation to return to Palestine and make it as "Jewish as England is English."

Hostility develops between Arabs and Jews in Palestine. While Palestine became a British mandate after World War I, Jews did not migrate to Palestine in large numbers. However, after Hitler came to power in Germany and began to persecute the Jews, the Jewish migration to Palestine, particularly from Germany, in-

creased enormously. Resentment of the Jewish population sprang up among the Arabs, who saw the European Jews as foreigners and intruders. Arab opposition sometimes broke out in violent attacks upon Jews. Nevertheless, by 1946 Jews made up over a third of the population of Palestine.

The reaction of Palestinian Arabs to increased Jewish immigration caused Britain to abandon her plans for creating a Jewish state in Palestine. Even if westernized and friendly, an isolated Jewish state could not compensate for the loss of goodwill among the Arab states, whose population totaled 40 million and whose oil resources were vital to Britain's economy.

However, World War II had made the Zionists more determined than ever to build a Jewish state in Palestine. The Nazi period had been a nightmare for the Jews of Europe (pages 697–698). Survivors of the holocaust were scattered in refugee camps throughout Europe. Most wanted to emigrate to Palestine.

The UN divides Palestine. Arab hostility mounted and there were increasing acts of violence by underground Jewish organizations. Unable to settle the differences between Arab and Jew, Britain turned the Palestine problem over to the United Nations in 1947.

In the UN the Jews argued that: (1) Palestine had been their land until the Romans drove out the Jews; (2) the Jews had never given up hope of returning to Palestine; (3) the Jews had suffered persecution for centuries and would not be safe until they had a state of their own; (4) the Arabs had several countries of their own, the Jews none; (5) Jewish pioneers in Palestine had made the desert bloom, built cities, established industries and schools, and introduced modern medicine that had benefited Arabs as well as Jews; and (6) long as the Arabs had lived in Palestine, they had never established a state there.

The Arabs argued that Palestine had been an Arab land for centuries, that its population was predominantly Arab. Why should Zionist imperialists be allowed to take it away from the

Arabs? While they sympathized with Jewish suffering, it was not the Arabs who had persecuted the Jews for centuries. Arab spokesmen said that it would be an act of great injustice to solve the Jewish problem at the expense of the Arabs. A UN committee concluded: "The claims to Palestine of the Arabs and Jews, both possessing validity [worth], are irreconcilable. . . . Among all the solutions advanced, partition [of Palestine] will provide the most realistic and practicable settlement." By a vote of 33 to 13, with 10 nations abstaining, the General Assembly voted to divide Palestine into two states—one Arab, the other Jewish.

The 1948 Arab-Israeli War has important consequences. Although the Jews had hoped to obtain a greater portion of Palestine, they welcomed the UN decision. Protesting that the rights of the Palestinian Arabs had been violated, the Arab nations prepared to prevent by force the establishment of the Jewish state. As the last British troops were leaving Palestine in May, 1948, the creation of the state of Israel was announced. Immediately the armies of six Arab nations attacked Israel. Lack of organization made the Arabs ineffective foes of a people inspired by a long-held dream and determined to hold on to the homeland they had gained. United Nations diplomats arranged a truce between victorious Israel and the Arab states.

The 1948 Arab-Israeli War was only the first round, and it had important results for the future. (1) No Arab state of Palestine came into being. Israel and Jordan took the bulk of the land that had been assigned to the Palestinian Arabs by the United Nations; Egypt occupied the Gaza Strip. (2) No final peace settlement followed the truce, for the Arab states refused to recognize the existence of Israel. They continued to talk of the day when Arab arms would drive the Israelis into the sea and restore Palestine to its rightful Arab owners. (3) The first Arab-Israeli war produced an enormous refugee problem. Hundreds of thousands of Palestinian Arabs fled into Arab states to escape the fighting and Jewish rule.

The problem of the Palestinian Arabs remains unsolved. The problem of the Palestinian Arabs still has not been solved. They remain in squalid refugee camps sponsored by the UN. Few Palestinian Arabs have wavered in their determination to return to their old homes and in their hostility toward Israel. Along with the Arab states, the Palestinian refugees insist that the only solution to their problem is for Israel to take them back. The Israelis strongly oppose such a solution, arguing that there would have been no refugee problem if the Arab states had not invaded Israel. Moreover, to admit more than a million hostile Arabs into Israel, argue

Modern Israel

the Israelis, would mean the eventual destruction of the country as a Jewish state. The Israeli solution to the refugee problem is to resettle the Palestinian Arabs in the neighboring Arab states, from which hundreds of thousands of Jews have fled to live in Israel. Here the matter rests. The refugees, their numbers growing because of a high birth rate, remain without a country. Some have joined Palestinian commando organizations that carry out raids against Israel.

Israel attacks Egypt. In 1956 President Nasser nationalized the Suez Canal, which was then controlled by a company whose shareholders were predominantly French and British. This meant that most of the revenues brought in by the Canal benefited not Egypt but foreign shareholders. Egyptian nationalists naturally regarded foreign ownership of the Canal as a glaring symbol of western imperialism, and applauded Nasser's move. Britain and France, however, decided to oust Nasser from power. They found a willing ally in Israel.

Egyptian purchases of modern weapons from the Soviet Union indicated to Israel that Nasser might soon try to carry out his threat to destroy the Jewish state. Alarmed by increased attacks by Egyptian commandos, in 1956 Israel decided to strike. Quickly and decisively Israeli forces defeated the Egyptian army and overran the Sinai Peninsula, which lies between the Suez Canal and Israel. Britain and France, which had planned this attack with Israel, entered the war in an attempt to overthrow President Nasser, whom they resented for nationalizing the Suez Canal. Under pressure from the United States and the United Nations, and with the Soviet Union threatening intervention, the three countries withdrew their forces from Egyptian territory. A UN Emergency Force (UNEF) was stationed on the Egyptian side of the Israel-Egypt border in an effort to prevent further hostilities.

The Six Days' War is a humiliating defeat for the Arabs. For the next ten years an uneasy peace existed between Israel and Egypt. Then in June, 1967, war broke out again. Egypt had (1) massed its forces in the Sinai, (2) ordered UNEF to leave Egyptian territory, (3) repeatedly threatened to destroy Israel, (4) supported her ally Syria in attacks along Israel's border, (5) entered into a military pact with Jordan, Israel's Arab neighbor to the east, (6) blockaded the mouth of the Gulf of Aqaba which is crossed by ships calling at Israel's vital port of Elath. Interpreting these acts as a threat to her existence, Israel decided to attack. She struck with remarkable speed and power. Within a few hours she destroyed the numerically superior Arab air force, catching hundreds of planes on the ground. Within six days Israeli forces shattered the Egyptian army in the Sinai, destroying and capturing large quantities of Soviet equipment. Israel had conquered the Sinai Peninsula, the Golan heights of Syria, and the west bank of the Jordan River, including the half of Jerusalem controlled by Jordan. Israel has refused to withdraw from the conquered Arab lands unless the Arab states negotiate a peace settlement that recognizes the Jewish state's right to exist, ensures secure borders, and puts an end to Arab acts of hostility. Attempts to get Arabs and Israelis to negotiate have met with many obstacles.

The Arab-Israeli conflict continues unresolved. The quarrel between Israel and the Arab states continues unabated. The Six Days' War brought Israel neither peace nor security. Today the Arab armies are armed with the most modern Soviet weapons. Arab commando raids into Israel have not ended. The Egyptians, supported by their Soviet "advisors," have massed a huge army across the Suez Canal. If anything, Arab hatred of Israel has grown stronger. The Arabs regard the existence of Israel as an affront to Arab honor; they view the plight of the Palestinian refugees as a crime against the Arab people. To have had their armies defeated three times by Israel is an unbearable humiliation. Many Arabs continue to demand the destruction of the Jewish state.

In numbers of men and weapons, the Arab nations are far superior to Israel. (The Jewish population of Israel is 2½ million; Egypt alone has 34 million people.) However, Israel is an efficient and modern state. Unlike the Arab states, she has mastered the techniques of electronic and mechanized warfare. Her military leaders have acted with exceptional daring and skill; her superbly trained pilots and ground crews have enabled Israel to maintain air supremacy in the Middle East.

The chief handicap of the Arab states is that they lack the skills needed to wage modern war. The Arab states, writes an American reporter, resent western science, technology, and administration—the very things in which Israelis excel. The Arabs recall that, during the golden age of Islam, Muslim armies and Arab technology were unsurpassed:

But while the steam engine, the telephone, the airplane, and the heat-seeking air-to-air missile were being developed in the West, the Arab world was in a cocoon. When it emerged again, it was mindful of past glory and resented its eclipse. Part of the Arab nationalist rallying call was to end western influence in the Middle East. So severe was the reaction—and still is—that all things western are viewed with suspicion in the Arab world.

This suspicion of western products and ideas has prevented the Arab states from developing modern armies.

Another reason for Arab military failure against Israel has been the poor quality of Arab officers. Many Egyptian officers, seeking a military career only for the money and social prestige it brings, lack the stomach for combat and the ability for leadership. They have proved ineffective in the field, at times even deserting their men in the midst of battle. Moreover, since the Israelis feel that their very existence is at stake, they fight with a special determination. Before the Six Days' War broke out, Arab propagandists, in highly emotional tones, urged directing "a blow of death and annihilation to Israel and all its presence in our Holy Land. It is a war for which we are waiting and in which we shall triumph." The Israelis, with the memory of the slaughtering of the Jewish people by Hitler's Nazis during World War II still fresh in their minds, do not take lightly these Arab threats.

The tension in the Middle East is aggravated by the power struggle between the Super Powers which, directly or indirectly, have taken sides in the Arab-Israeli dispute. The Soviet Union, for example, supplies Arab nations with weapons, sends them military advisors to train Arab troops and pilots, and supports the Arab cause at the UN. Russian experts operate Egypt's missile defense system, and Russian pilots guard this defense system and Egyptian cities from Israeli air attacks. The Soviet goal is to widen the gulf between the United States and the Arab world, which feels that the United States is siding with Israel. The Soviet Union has used the Arab-Israeli dispute to increase her power and prestige in the Arab world.

Having become a seapower in the Mediterranean, Russia is eager to reopen the Suez Canal, closed since the Six Days' War. She would like to become the paramount power in the region which supplies Western Europe with most of its petroleum and serves as a vital trade artery between Europe and South Asia.

No solution seems in sight. Most Arabs continue to view Israel as an imperialist state that has seized Arab land, caused suffering for the Arab peoples, and offended Arab honor. Arab hardliners, particularly the Palestinian refugees, insist that they will accept nothing less than the dismantling of the Jewish state. Some Arab moderates favor a more realistic approach to the problem of Israel. But popular sentiment against the Israelis is so strong in the Arab states and Arab politics so unstable that few of these moderates dare to voice their views. On the other hand, Israeli leaders have come under criticism for not making enough concessions to the Arabs. The belief that the Arabs respect only Israel's strength has caused Israelis to reply to Arab attacks on the border by striking back at Arab outposts. Emotions have run high for so long on both sides that there seems little hope of peace in the Middle East for a long time to come.

CHECK-UP

1. What is the Zionist movement? Why did the Jews claim the right to settle in Palestine? What was the reaction of the Arabs? Why?
2. What solution to Arab-Jewish hostility was proposed by the United Nations? What were the results?

3. Why did war break out in 1948? With what results?

4. Why did Nasser nationalize the Suez Canal in 1956? Why did this lead to war? What were the results?

5. What were the causes of the Six Days' War? The outcome? Why is the Arab-Israeli conflict unresolved?

Modernization in the Middle East

The Muslim nations face many problems. The Muslim lands of the Middle East suffer from many of the problems that burden much of the nonwestern world: illiteracy, disease, poverty, political instability, inefficiency, and overpopulation. American historian Don Peretz concludes:*

A major problem in the Middle East has been the need to curb soaring populations. . . . [The Arab] nations are engaged in a race to increase economic productivity at least at the same rate as the population. Shortage of tilled land and of water for irrigation continues to block greater food production. Less than ten per cent of all the land in the Middle East is cultivated under present conditions. Even if the great river development projects envisaged for the region are carried out, there still will be insufficient farm land. Since about eight of every ten people in the area live on the land, it will prove difficult to raise their low living standards. Disease, primitive agricultural methods, poor water allocation, crop pests, and the control of property by a small number of large landholders have perpetuated heart-rending poverty in the area. Population pressure worsens the situation. . . .

* From *The Middle East* by Don Peretz (Boston: Houghton Mifflin Company, 1969). Reprinted by permission.

Planners hope to reduce rural overpopulation in the Middle East by attracting surplus farm labor to the towns. Egypt, Turkey, . . . and other countries have been developing new industries. But rapid industrialization raises many problems. Large-scale capital is required to erect great factories. Engineers, factory managers, technicians and skilled workers must be found or trained to run the new plants and mills. Sources of power, whether oil, coal, or hydroelectric, must be provided. An efficient system of distribution of goods to home and foreign markets is needed to dispose of mass-produced industrial products. Most Middle Eastern countries are too small to absorb the materials produced by modern industry; hence they must seek foreign markets. But . . . new markets are hard to find, especially for newly established industries which may not produce goods at competitive prices.

The population explosion hampers Arab attempts to modernize. After Nasser came to power in Egypt, he had to face the enormous task of building a modern nation. One of his first moves was to reform land ownership by breaking up large estates. Today no Egyptian is permitted to own more than 104 acres. Land has been redistributed to peasants, although often the plots are so small that they cannot provide farmers with a living.

Attempts to modernize in the Middle East began well before the twentieth century. Mohammed Ali, whose mosque (above) overlooks Cairo, arrived in Egypt with the Ottoman troops sent to oust Napoleon and founded the dynasty that ruled Egypt until 1952. His attempts to modernize agriculture and develop industry had limited success. Recent Middle Eastern leaders, aided by oil income and foreign loans, have followed in his footsteps. Thus far their greatest success has been within the oil industry, where men such as the Iraqi at right have become skilled technicians adapted to twentieth-century ways.

Along with land reform Nasser initiated a massive program of flood control for the Nile. With Soviet aid the Aswan High Dam was constructed on the Nile River. Other land-reclamation projects involve increasing water for irrigation and finding ways of controlling the desert sands which threaten to engulf cropland. All these projects are expected to increase the amount and productivity of land under cultivation, although recent studies indicate that the increase will not be as great as was hoped.

Other Middle Eastern nations have planned similar projects—though none is so extensive—to increase cultivable land. A number of nations share with Egypt the problem of exploding populations. Epidemics and fatal diseases have been eliminated or are under control. However, as in other parts of the developing world, the birth rate has not decreased. In Egypt, writes a *New York Times* correspondent,

. . . an already burdensome population will double in less than 30 years unless measures are enacted to reduce the birth rate.

At the turn of the century, there were 10 million people in Egypt and the country was self-sufficient in food. Life was not idyllic, but at least it was not crowded. Today there are close to 34 million people and they are living in the same confines of the life-giving Nile Valley. By the end of the century it is feared that the population will be approaching 70 million.

Voluntary programs of birth control have met with little success, particularly in the countryside. Large families are an economic asset on farms, where much of the labor continues to be done by men rather than machines. The population explosion is becoming so critical that the government is considering drawing up legislation that will force Egyptians to limit the size of their families.

The situation is not far different in the rest of the Middle East. All of the Arab nations are trying to modernize their agriculture. It has become clear to many Arabs that industry must also be developed, as in the oil-producing countries, to give the Arab nations balanced economies. Throughout the area, programs of modernization are hampered by overpopulation and resistance to change. Some states lack the necessary income; others have plenty of money (from oil sales), but encounter opposition to modernization. Much of the social reform in Iran and Saudi Arabia, for example, has been initiated by the ruling family and has met with opposition from conservative subjects and religious leaders.

A further obstacle to modernization is the Arab-Israeli conflict. Arab fear of and hostility to Israel has caused money badly needed for economic development to be used for military spending.

Israel has made great progress but also faces problems. Israel's progress stands out from that of the rest of the Middle East. She has flourishing industries and extensive irrigation and land reclamation programs. Lands once desert now produce valuable crops. Israel's standard of living is relatively high. In education and medical care Israel compares favorably with any developed nation. Her scientists, some of them world-famous, have made valuable contributions to the improvement of agriculture and to the de-salting of seawater.

But Israel also has problems. Like the Arab nations, she is burdened with huge expenditures for armaments. Moreover, Israel is not economically self-sufficient. She depends heavily upon aid from abroad: loans from friendly nations and generous contributions from Jews throughout the world. After World War II reparation payments from West Germany for Nazi persecution of Jews provided Israel with the capital needed to build a modern state. The heavy immigration of well-educated European Jews with technological and scientific backgrounds was also a great asset. Since the founding of Israel, however, hundreds of thousands of immigrants have come from the developing Arab lands in North Africa and the Middle East. Many of the new immigrants are uneducated and unskilled and fit poorly into Israel's modernized economy. Sometimes they encounter discrimination from the Jews who have come to Israel from Europe.

CHECK-UP

1. What problems plague Arab lands in the Middle East? Which are most serious? Why?
2. What problems confront Israel?

Summing Up

The lands of the Middle East (including Africa north of the Sahara) became part of the Muslim world during the period of Islam's great expansion. Later most of these lands were part of the Ottoman Empire. With the collapse of the Ottoman Empire in World War I, the Arab states hoped to achieve independence. Instead, they found themselves linked to Britain or France as mandates or protectorates. Not until after World War II did most of them achieve independence.

Under Kemal Atatürk, what remained of Turkey defeated invaders, established a republic, and introduced sweeping reforms in an effort to modernize the nation. Modernization elsewhere in the Middle East proceeded slowly. Arab lands with income from oil have made some progress, but nations lacking such wealth remain desperately poor. Rapid population growth, shortage of water, and insufficient arable land pose major problems for most Arab states. The Arab states are also hampered by internal political instability and by their hatred of Israel, which causes them to maintain large armies and spend huge sums for weapons.

Since 1948 Arabs and Israelis have fought three wars and still peace does not seem in sight. Will the Arab world ever accept a Jewish state in its midst? Will Israel and the Arab states engage in a fourth and even more destructive war? Will intervention in Middle Eastern affairs lead to a direct confrontation of the Super Powers? These questions point up the problems that continue to make the Middle East an area of high tension.

Chapter Highlights

Can you explain?

mandate   partition   refugee camps   commandos

Can you identify?

Atatürk	Nasser	Faisal	Pan-Arabism
Suez Canal	Gulf of Aqaba	Israelis	Palestinian Arabs
Zionism	Hussein	Six Days' War	Aswan High Dam

What do you think?

1. Was Atatürk's modernization of the Turkish Republic a success? Explain.

2. What do the Arab states have in common? Why are they not more closely united?

3. Why have the Jews maintained their identity as a people?

4. Why are the Arab states hostile to Israel?

5. How has Israel been able to survive?

6. Why has no solution been found for the Arab refugee problem?

7. Why are the Super Powers interested in the Middle East?

8. Do you think the United States made the right decision in the 1956 war? Why?

9. Do you think tensions between the Arab nations and Israel can be reduced? Explain.

Sub-Saharan Africa
Since 1945

CHAPTER FOCUS

African Independence
Challenges to Independent Africa
Present-Day Africa

"Seek ye first the political kingdom and all else shall be added unto it." So, in a Biblical paraphrase, said Kwame Nkrumah (*kwah'*mee en-*kroo'*mah), who led the Gold Coast to independence in 1957. In that statement lay a basic truth about the way the European colonies in Africa had to look at their future in the years after World War II. Unless you are in control of your own affairs, your own destiny—unless, that is, you have self-government—no other issues count. This lesson was one European peoples had had to learn in the past; the colonial powers should not have been surprised if those they ruled insisted that it was a lesson for all the world, not just for Europeans and their descendants or agents.

Because Africans saw independence as more and more essential, little in their history from 1945 to the 1960's was not in some way polit-

Africa combines the old and new in many ways. The Togolese women at left show their loyalty to their first president by using material imprinted with his image for their traditionally draped dress. Jomo Kenyatta, one of the most dynamic personalities in the African independence movement, holds the traditional fly whisk of authority as he presides over Kenya's independence day celebration (above). The bank of Ghana (left, below) combines the figures of traditional Ashanti gold weights with modern design.

ical. Politics was the central theme in those years. If the demands for self-government came at different times, were stated in different ways, or were fulfilled through different constitutional arrangements, it was not because the underlying assumption of African leaders—that Africans must run their own affairs—varied. It was because of important historical differences, differences which were more of Europe's making than Africa's.

African Independence

POLITICAL NATIONALISM: SELF-GOVERNMENT

Pressures resulting from World War II encourage African independence. Before looking at those differences, however, we must recognize worldwide changes that, just like the growing demands from inside Africa, pressured the colonial powers from the outside. They all stemmed from World War II. The war showed Africa and the rest of the world that European countries were not all-powerful. The British and the French, especially, called on their colonies to help in the fighting, and the African colonies supported war efforts of the mother countries. Some of the Africans answered the call for aid more voluntarily than others. All the Africans who served overseas—even if they were denied, as they usually were, a combat role—gained new ideas and views from the experience. They met Europeans who were ordinary people, not in elevated positions as were the whites they had known in Africa. They met American soldiers, some black like themselves, in the same uniforms as the white soldiers and carrying arms, and started asking questions about their own role. They came into touch, especially in the Pacific, with Asians, also under colonial rule, who were preparing to fight to escape that domination. They listened to Churchill's and Roosevelt's speeches about freedom, self-determination, and the rights of man, and wondered why these ideals should not be extended to them. Later they were to insist that this must come to pass.

When these Africans returned home from the wars of their colonizers, they wanted not only jobs (often lacking), but their just rewards for their aid. And they insisted that these rewards be granted in the terms Europeans had themselves proclaimed—freedom.

The war had other effects as well. The United States and the Soviet Union had replaced Europe as the center of world power. Neither was a colonial power; indeed, for their own totally different reasons, the Super Powers were opposed to the colonialism of Europe in Africa and Asia. The Soviet Union opposed this colonialism all the time; the United States, for cold war reasons more loyal to her European allies, did at least some of the time. This opposition, clearly expressed on the stage of the United Nations, helped the growing nationalist movements everywhere. The colonial powers, weakened by the war and less powerful than the United States and the Soviet Union, found pressure to disband their empires growing on many sides. And their moral claim to rule much of the world was increasingly questioned.

European imperialist outlooks are not easily discarded. These changes, clear to historians looking back, were not immediately obvious to the countries involved. No Frenchmen or Englishmen or Portuguese and few Belgians remembered a time when they did not have an empire; even those who were starting to think that it might not last forever did not expect the beginning of the end, especially in Africa, for many decades—some even said a hundred years, or two hundred.

Each of the colonial powers continued, then, with its earlier assumptions. The British could foresee eventual political independence for Britain's colonies, but not for some years to come. The French saw increasing integration of colonial resources into France's economic life and more (even if carefully limited) colonial participation in the politics of France itself. The Belgians and Portuguese apparently saw little reason to think about political change at all.

It is not surprising that it was in the British colonies that effective political movements for independence started, nor is it surprising that the nationalist movements had their first successes against the British. In 1947 Britain had yielded to Indian demands for self-government. Moreover, Britain's new economic weakness (page 747) made it nearly impossible for her to resist pressures for independence. The result was a pattern that had started with the American Revolution and had been repeated peacefully with other colonies settled by white Europeans: independence with a political system modeled after Britain's own. India—and Pakistan—would extend that precedent to non-European peoples, and Africa would benefit.

New African leaders intensify demands for independence. It would be wrong, however, to imply that changes outside Africa itself somehow conferred independence upon a waiting continent. As we have seen, Africans resisted European domination from the start, and they continued during the colonial period to make demands. If the way of making them changed because of contact with the rest of the world, that shows simply that Africa did not, in an age of increasing communication, exist in a vacuum. No part of the world did.

The great change in African political demands came after the war. It was a change less in goal than in timing: no longer were African leaders willing to work towards self-government at the very slow pace acceptable to the colonial rulers. It was also a change in method: in British West Africa (especially the Gold

African Independence

1957   Ghana

1958   Guinea

1960   Cameroon, Central African Republic, Chad, Congo (Brazzaville), Congo (Kinshasa), Dahomey, Gabon, Ivory Coast, Malagasy Republic, Mali, Mauritania, Niger, Nigeria, Senegal, Somali Republic, Togo, Upper Volta

1961   Sierra Leone, Tanganyika

1962   Burundi, Rwanda, Uganda

1963   Kenya, Zanzibar

1964   Malawi, Zambia

1965   Gambia

1966   Botswana, Lesotho

1968   Equatorial Guinea, Swaziland

Coast and Nigeria, where the movements first started) came the shift to mass-based political parties. No longer would a few with western education make demands in a gentlemanly manner on behalf of large African populations, with tiny concessions graciously made by Britain.

The young leaders of these mass-based parties came to their leadership role with different experiences from those of the men who had formed the first, less insistent protest groups. The new political figures knew more of the world at large; they had often been overseas for their higher education. Much of their political knowledge was a product of firsthand experience. Two of the major West African nationalist figures, Kwame Nkrumah (the Gold Coast's first Prime Minister) and Nnamdi Azikiwe (en-*nam'*dee ah-*zik'*uh-we, Nigeria's first African Governor-General and later President), had lived and studied in the United States before the war. Both had learned there about organizing large numbers of people politically; both recognized the importance for their own countries of involving the masses in the political struggle for freedom. Back home they, and others, amazed colonial rulers by successfully mobilizing broadly based political organizations.

White settlers hamper independence movements in East and Central Africa.

Africans under British rule in East and Central Africa had a more difficult time than on the West Coast. Both in political organization and in their largely successful, if gradual, move towards self-government, their path was harder and their successes came later. The reason was simple. White settlers were involved. These settlers may have shared with the Africans a wish to be independent of British rule. But they understood independence differently. In Kenya and the Rhodesias especially, their wish was to follow the South African model. They wanted to have power in their own hands and, just as important, to keep it away from the African majorities whom they still saw as inferior. (The Africans' political problem was not made easier by the presence of numbers of Asian settlers, especially Indians, brought in to East and South Africa as laborers early in the twentieth century.) Where there were white settlers who had already obtained some political rights before World War II, the Africans had a different view of the British than did their counterparts in West Africa. In East and Central Africa, Africans came to see the British as buffers between themselves and the white settlers, who hoarded political power and thought of the Africans largely as a labor force.

Africans in French colonies develop a different outlook from those in British colonies.

The education and experience of political leaders in French-speaking Africa were quite different from those of their British counterparts. French stress was on the importance of culture—especially French culture—rather than politics. The French also envisioned Africans as playing a political role in Paris itself rather than in Africa. Thus, it is not surprising that the demands were different. For years, French-speaking Africans concentrated their political efforts on gaining greater representation in France and a greater role in what would be called the French Community, rather than on complete independence for their own lands.

In much of Africa independence comes peacefully.

In 1957 the Gold Coast became independent Ghana; it was the first sub-Saharan state to achieve self-government. French-speaking Africa, like the rest of the continent, would feel the impact. The drive for political freedom was to sweep the continent regardless of colonial boundaries. In West Africa, where each British colony bordered on some part of France's empire, the move towards independence in Ghana, Nigeria, and Sierra Leone (sih-*er'*uh lih-*ohn'*) was bound to have effects on French colonies.

By 1960 the "winds of change," as the British prime minister phrased it, were truly blowing across Africa: some twenty African states, mostly in West Africa, were free. By 1970 the number of independent states in black Africa had risen to over 35. The pattern had not been the same everywhere, although almost everywhere change had come through constitutional means and without violence. Less than ten years before, Europeans were predicting that it would take decades. The more the colonial power had been willing to recognize the rights of Africans to self-government, the more she had yielded to African pressure, the more peaceful had been the transition.

Where colonial rulers had less vision, the consequences were tinged with tragedy, even if the result was still self-government. The Belgians, most of whom had scoffed at a plan courageously advanced in 1955 for Congo independence in 30 years, were to hand over power amid bloodshed in 1960 and the UN would find itself forced to intervene in sub-Saharan Africa for the first time.

White settler resistance to African self-rule was overcome in most of the East and Central African colonies Britain had controlled. It was similarly overcome by the Arab population in

Algeria, after prolonged fighting in Algeria itself and turmoil in France. The exception to these nationalist successes was Southern Rhodesia.[1] There the settlers followed the South African precedent and declared that they, the white minority, could seize independence from Britain on their own terms. In an era of African self-determination the British would not agree to hand over the government to a minority dedicated to keeping the Africans out of power. But unwilling or unable to send troops, Britain could do no more than declare the new regime illegal. The UN imposed economic sanctions against Southern Rhodesia, but these did not bring rapid change. The country came more to resemble its southern neighbors than it did the vast continent to the north.

The Portuguese continued adamantly opposed to any change in status for their colonies, on whom they were more dependent economically than any other European power. Nor did their own political dictatorship permit even discussion of a different policy. And finally the most entrenched white government of all, in South Africa, tightened its hold on the African population, relentlessly cutting back whatever meager political opportunities nonwhites had ever had there.

CULTURAL NATIONALISM: NÉGRITUDE

Demands for cultural recognition accompanied demands for independence. That there were cultural differences between Africa and Europe was obvious to all. That Europeans asserted their own cultural superiority over their colonial subjects, no African could escape knowing. So it is not surprising that Africans, and especially African writers and artists, insisted that they must become "culturally as well as politically independent." Those were the words of Léopold Senghor—poet, statesman, and first president of independent Senegal. This view, called *négritude,* means, roughly, "African-ness" or black cultural values or "soul." Négritude stresses the unique human and creative qualities of the African heritage and insists that only Africans and those of African descent can experience and express those qualities.

Similar ideas had appeared among some black thinkers and writers in the New World, especially in the West Indies, even before World War II. In Africa itself certain writers, largely those who had been under French rather than British colonial rule, proclaimed the African cultural identity. The French doctrine of assimilation (page 569) stressed French culture rather than French political institutions. And so, while English-speaking Africans were demanding the political rights held implicit in the British tradition of government, French-speaking Africans were proclaiming their cultural freedom from the western values imposed on *them.* They continued to place supreme importance on culture, much as the French did; but they insisted that the culture they would value should be fundamentally African. Naturally, French-ruled Africans wanted to be self-governing, too, and Africans under English rule also asserted the value of their own cultures. But the differences in emphasis were, nonetheless, important, not least because they would affect communications and relations across former colonial boundaries, among leaders and peoples of independent African states.

[1] The self-declared white government prefers to call the country Rhodesia, and the African nationalists call it Zimbabwe. But since Britain does not recognize the legality of its independence, the international community continues to call it Southern Rhodesia, its legal colonial name.

CHECK-UP

1. What was the major goal of Africans after World War II? Why?

2. What outside pressures encouraged African independence movements after World War II? Why were these difficult to resist?

3. Why were new African leaders more insistent in demanding speedy independence?
4. What hampered independence movements in East and Central Africa?
5. In what states was independence achieved with little friction? Why? Where was independence opposed? Why?
6. What is négritude? Why did the former French colonies place more emphasis on cultural independence than did the former British colonies?

Challenges to Independent Africa

The independent states of Africa south of the Sahara share many challenges with other developing countries. But the term "developing" points to what many see as the most important challenge: the need for economic growth, with all that it implies in the modern world.

Economic development depends on political stability. For African countries problems of development are closely tied to questions of political unity. Economic development requires stability, but stability in what terms? A country defined by its colonial boundaries? A country made up of several former colonial territories? A country carved out of a one-time colony? These questions cannot be answered by the demands of economic planning. The answers, in many cases not clear in the early years after independence, depend on centuries of African history and culture, on the historical accidents and coincidences of Europe's "scramble for Africa," on twentieth-century trends and ideas and pressures from outside Africa, on the integrity, vision, and skill of African leaders, and on all the factors we can put together and call luck.

Any change from a condition as it exists (the *status quo*) is bound to arouse controversy. Many observers had thought that self-determination might bring large-scale readjusting of colonial boundaries in Africa. It would be a chance to correct the errors Europeans had made out of ignorance or lack of concern. But there has been little redrawing of boundaries, despite some agitation for it. The fact is that pre-European historical and cultural identities in Africa were affected by the decades of rule by separate colonial nations. Nothing in human history remains unchanging, and Africans with the same ethnic background but divided between, say, French and British administrations were bound to find that there were tensions as well as bonds between them. The different educational systems, theories of local government, views of African culture, ideas of African political action—all encouraged contrast rather than unity.

The new nations oppose ethnic separatism. In some newly independent countries the common experience of the colonial period was not enough to overcome traditional differences. Sometimes ethnic rivalries built up into conflicts even under colonial rule. The new African nations feared the breakup of the countries Europe had defined; they resisted any solution that made tribal identity the basis for statehood. To them, the claims of tribal separatism would result in the splintering of Africa into hundreds and hundreds of states. Not the least consequence of this, they argued, would be economic disaster.

Pan-Africanism faces several problems. The opposite answer to the question of size came from those who urged *Pan-Africanism*. Originally an intellectual movement started by blacks in the New World, Pan-Africanism took political root in West Africa after World War II. Starting as support for freedom of individual African countries from colonial rule, the movement came in the 1950's to mean the attempt

KEY

Independent by end of 1960

Independent since 1960

Areas under European rule

Status disputed

to form ever larger states in Africa. Some of its advocates even thought that the whole continent might eventually be a single country. Basic Pan-Africanist beliefs declared the need to make Africa truly independent: economically self-sufficient, politically influential and important on the world scene, with power to protect itself from outside encroachments. Pan-

Sub-Saharan Africa Today

Africanism, particularly popular in English-speaking countries, was partly a political counterpart of négritude.

The problems facing those wanting to create larger political units were many. Not only were

former colonial boundaries in the way; policies and traditions of different European powers created barriers among Africans. Most important of the barriers was communication. The use of different western languages and the different systems of education were hard to overcome. Moreover, the colonial powers had discouraged African contacts across borders: roads often ended some distance from boundaries and railroads were built from the coast inland to bring produce, minerals, and timber to waiting European ships, rather than to link African communities and resources.

In addition, by the time of independence each African country had its own leaders, and many of them did not wish to see their new states subordinated or absorbed. For each independent state, representation in the United Nations was an important symbol of identity on the world scene. Would African influence in the UN diminish if the number of black representatives were reduced because African states merged?

Finally, there were economic problems. In Africa, as everywhere, some nations were richer than others, or at least less poor. Would those

which had valuable mineral or other resources share such sources of income with those who did not? Their own people badly needed the higher standard of living and the greater opportunities that these resources might provide.

The African nations seek political stability. Whatever the size, then, of the political units in Africa—and on the whole they remained in the years after independence the same countries that had won their freedom—these states faced two challenges. One was how to maintain stable governments. The other was how to deal with what came to be called "neo-colonialism"— continuing influence and even control exerted by western countries.

In most newly-independent African nations attempts to gain stability often resulted in one-party states; in numerous instances military rule later replaced that of the single party. Both solutions grew out of many factors. (1) One was a view that inter-party rivalries were a luxury that newly-independent countries could not afford. (2) In many African political traditions, decisions were reached after long discus-

The leaders of independent Africa are concentrating most of their efforts on solving their nations' basic problems: health, nutrition, and education. With the assistance of foreign capital they have acquired modern machinery to speed the construction of much needed roads (far left) and to build dams to provide water for irrigation, control floods, and supply electric power (right). Improved agricultural methods are helping to feed the growing population and to provide cash crops for export. To fully develop their economies, the African nations desperately need educated people. But they cannot yet employ all graduates, even of the primary schools (left), at a level for which they have been educated.

sion, but once made, they were followed by all; the Western European model of parties alternating in power was not part of those traditions. (3) The colonial situation had not encouraged the growth of an opposition—a party not in power but expected to debate policy with a view to gaining power one day. Clearly, there had been no possibility of African parties alternating with European rulers to control a colony. There were those, both inside and outside Africa, who continued to believe that only representative government with repeated opportunity for choice would guarantee freedom of expression, true representation, and flexibility of policies. No more readily than others can Africans find easy answers to the age-old question of authoritarian or representative government.

Neo-colonialism affects African economies.

The challenge of "neo-colonialism" was not unrelated to stability, but it concerned mainly African economics. After the African nations became independent, economic influence and even control exerted by western countries be-

came less formal. But Africans still saw them as posing political and economic threats. Africa's dilemma was that it depended on foreign capital and technicians for economic growth. In the past other developing countries had experienced a similar dependence. Africans were determined to manage their own affairs in their own self-interest. Because they often saw that goal threatened, all African states felt the need to remain alert.

Outside interference in African affairs did exist and was sometimes unscrupulous. But many Africans protested that outside interference did not cause all their problems. After all, they argued, all countries have complex challenges to face, and they face some more successfully than others. And if all frustrations continue to be blamed on outsiders, doesn't this encourage the old racist view that Africans are incapable of dealing with their own affairs? Don't such explanations imply that Europeans call the tune and Africans dance to it? No, they argued, freedom is the right to make your own mistakes as well as achieve your own successes; Africans are as capable of both as anyone.

815

White domination in southern Africa vexes free Africans. The issue most profoundly affecting all free Africans has been the continuing ruthless domination in the southern part of the continent of the black majority population by the white settler minorities. For south of the Zambezi River, whites were determined not to yield any measure of equality—political, economic, social—to the Africans whose lands they claimed for their own. In Portuguese Africa formal colonialism continued; the Portuguese were prepared to fight to prevent any lessening of their control. Possibly even more serious was the situation in independent South Africa and in Southern Rhodesia.

To the rest of the continent, as for the non-European populations in these southern African countries, the situation was intolerable. It was a leading principle of Pan-Africanism that, in Kwame Nkrumah's words, "The independence of Ghana [and the other African nations] will be meaningless unless it is linked up with the total liberation of Africa." On that, virtually all Africans could agree. It was clear, however, that the fight for true African self-determination in the south of the continent would be a long and a hard one. Effective internal resistance was all but impossible against the well-armed, well-organized, and determined white minority, which controlled the police, the armed forces, and the courts. Freedom for the black majority seemed to depend on help from outside, and the free countries of Africa committed themselves to that struggle. But they were hampered by their own lack of resources and the pressing needs within their own borders. For even the new nations most favored by substantial mineral and agricultural resources faced serious problems: high costs of education, the drift of the younger generation from the villages to the cities, growing unemployment, uncertain prices for their exports, and the high costs of imports, especially the machinery which would aid development. Despite these problems, the liberation of southern Africa continues to preoccupy those who shape the foreign policy of the independent African states.

CHECK-UP

1. Why has political instability been a problem in many African states? What solutions have been introduced?

2. What is Pan-Africanism? What have been obstacles to this goal?

3. What is neo-colonialism? Why is it resented by Africans?

4. What is the reaction of independent African states to the policies of South Africa and Southern Rhodesia? Why?

Present-Day Africa

Modern communications and technology have created global influences that affect Africa as they do the rest of the world. More people in more places are in contact with others, are learning other ways of life or other views of the world. But that does not mean that people quickly change their own way of seeing their world. The history of Africa (and Africa is not alone in this) suggests that, despite change, people continue to hold many of their traditional beliefs and to act according to certain life styles that long have been specifically their own. There was never, after all, a single, set, unchanging tradition. Traditions have themselves changed with time, and it is therefore not surprising that they should continue to do so.

But some of the old remains along with the new, and particularly so when people regard their own special ways with pride. Tradition appears to prevail in the countryside, where schools and radios and television are less common; it persists in the cities, too, where people from neighboring villages may live near each other and remain in touch. It persists even among those sometimes called the "westernized elite": college-educated men and women with jobs in government service or as university professors or seasoned diplomats. These men and women often have kept contact with relatives who still live on family lands in the rural parts of the country. Frequently they have owed their own opportunities, especially for study abroad, to the sacrifices of those in their home villages; they cannot, on their return, neglect obligations to their extended families. Often, in spite of formal Christian or Muslim affiliations, they do not neglect to attend ceremonies honoring their ancestors. Most Africans feel that they can maintain both their traditional and modern loyalties—to their peoples and to their countries, to what they value in their past, and to changes that will bring higher standards of living and new opportunities.

This African blending of old and new is present in all aspects of life—as much in the writing, carving, music, and all the arts, as in politics and economics and social relations and even religion. However the African states and their peoples meet the challenges ahead of them —for genuine independence and self-determination for all, for stability, for economic growth, for continuing artistic creativity, for an important and positive role in the world—the continent holds vast wealth in its people, its natural resources, its history, its traditions, and its art. Those resources, brought to bear upon the problems of the continent and beyond, may bring answers not yet dreamed of, Africa's contributions to her own future and that of a world that has too often in the past failed accurately to assess her worth.

Chapter Highlights

Can you explain?

assimilation
négritude

Pan-Africanism

neo-colonialism

cultural independence

Can you identify?

Azikiwe

Senghor

Nkrumah

French Community

What do you think?

1. Was it a mistake for the colonial powers to involve colonial peoples in World War II? Why?

2. What was the attitude of each of the following countries toward independence for its colonies: Britain, France, Belgium, Portugal? How do you account for the differences?

3. What was the tragedy of the independence movement in the Congo? In Southern Rhodesia?

4. What is meant by négritude? How is it expressed in Africa? In the world outside Africa?

5. Why has the quest for political stability in new African nations often resulted in one-party or military rule?

6. Why has self-determination not led to extensive readjustments in "colonial" boundaries?

7. The issue most profoundly affecting all free Africans is the continuing ruthless domination in southern Africa of the black majority by the white minority. Discuss this problem. How does it affect the entire continent?

8. "Freedom is the right to make your own mistakes." Do you agree? Why?

36

Changing Latin America

Latin American artists often act as social commentators. Mexican artist José Clemente Orozco expressed the meaning of the Mexican Revolution as a peasant revolt against foreign exploitation, military intervention in politics, and the greed of landowners and industrialists (left). The problem of land ownership and use is crucial to all of Latin America. Arid, overworked land, cultivated by outmoded methods such as those used by the Peruvian farmer above, cannot produce enough to feed rapidly growing populations.

Latin America is the most commonly used term for the area running from the tip of South America north to the Rio Grande and across the Caribbean Sea. The bulk of the population speaks one of three languages derived from Latin—Spanish, Portuguese, or French. Moreover, the bulk of European immigrants came from the Iberian Peninsula (Spain and Portugal) or Italy. While one can use the terms Ibero-America, Hispanic America, Indo- and Afro-America for certain regions, the dominating element in the overall culture is European; hence we say *Latin* America. Latins in this hemisphere call themselves *americanos,* Americans. (The people of the United States and Canada, the majority of whom speak English, are often called Anglo-Americans to distinguish them from Latin Americans.) Along with Africa and Asia, Latin America is a developing area of the world.

819

The Wars of Independence

At the beginning of the nineteenth century, most of the colonies in Latin America gained their independence from their European rulers. What were the causes of rebellion? How did the revolts affect the future of Latin America?

There are several causes of unrest in colonial Latin America. By the late eighteenth century a number of factors combined to make many Latin Americans feel that they were being exploited by the European mother countries: (1) rising taxes on the poor classes; (2) regulations that prevented the colonies from selling goods to countries other than the mother country; (3) the desire of Britain to open up Latin America to British trade (once the Latin American colonies gained their independence it would be Britain, desiring to protect her growing trade with these lands, that prevented European states from re-establishing colonial rule in Latin America); and (4) the liberal doctrines of the American and French Revolutions.

Starting in 1779, different groups revolted at different times and for different reasons. Resentment was first expressed in a number of servile (peasant and slave) rebellions. Later the white upper class, the creoles, also conspired against the Crown. With time great leaders emerged from the aristocracy, the clergy, and the people. These heroes united armed men from all classes and of all colors in the struggle against the European mother countries. (Only in Brazil was independence declared by a European rather than an American leader.) Plots and massacres, betrayals and revolts, battles and lengthy discussions mark the long and bloody struggle for independence in Latin America.

The downtrodden rise in revolt in Peru. José Gabriel Condorcanqui (hoh-*sey'* gah-*bryel'* kon-dor-*kahn'*kee), also called "Tupac-Amarú" (too-*pahk'* ah-mah-*roo'*), claimed direct de- scent from the last Inca of Peru. In 1779 he ambushed the local Spanish official and after a short trial executed him. This encouraged Amerinds to raise the banner of revolt.

The rebels had little chance against the well-equipped and organized forces of the colonial power, and the rebellion was put down by Spanish officials commanding Amerindian troops. Tupac-Amarú was brutally executed:

[He was] brought into the middle of the square [in Cuzco], and there the executioner cut out his tongue. Then they took off his chains and laid him on the ground. They tied four ropes to his hands and feet and attached the ropes to the girths of four horses, which four mestizos [men of mixed blood] drove in four different directions. Cuzco had never before seen a spectacle of this kind. Either because the horses were not very strong or because the Indian was really made of iron, they simply could not tear him apart, although they tugged at him for a long time, while he dangled in the air like a spider. . . . [So] they cut off his head. . . . Then they laid his body under the gallows and cut off his arms and legs.

Haitian slaves revolt and gain independence. In the French colony of St. Domingue (*san'* doh-*mang'*, Haiti) on the island of Hispaniola occurred the first successful servile rebellion in Latin America. St. Domingue was one of the most profitable of the European colonies in America. Sugar planters exploited the toil of 400,000 slaves, most of whom had been transported from Africa. Segregated from both white and black castes were freemen of color. Mostly of mixed African and European descent, they numbered 22,000—about the same as the whites. In 1791 these free mulattoes responded to the French *Declaration of the Rights of Man and Citizen* (page 454) by demanding full citizenship. The white legislature refused to grant them equality before the law.

Unconcerned with the unrest among French-speaking freemen, voodoo leaders (probably mostly African) drummed out messages that started a full-scale slave rebellion. The mulattoes somewhat reluctantly supported the slaves' bid for liberty. In 1794 emancipation was proclaimed by the Jacobin government in France. It came too late. By then all political order and economic well-being had vanished from the once rich colony of St. Domingue. Under the skillful military leadership of Toussaint L'Ouverture (too-*san'* loo-ver-*tyoor'*), an ex-slave himself, the blacks and mulattoes joined forces and drove out the whites. Toussaint was captured and imprisoned but the rebellion went on. The black revolutionaries defeated the large French force sent to the island by Napoleon and in 1804 declared their island an independent nation. To symbolize their rejection of white Europe, they restored the old Amerindian name, Haiti, to their new republic.

Creoles grow cautious. The successful revolt of the black masses on Hispaniola frightened the white planter class throughout the Americas. It cooled creole enthusiasm for French Revolutionary equality, and left educated whites yearning to effect the conservative solution arrived at in Britain's Thirteen Colonies: independence from the mother country, but no civil rights or social equality for Amerinds and slaves. To change the colonial government without altering the society of separate classes and races, creoles needed a political excuse. Napoleon supplied it in 1808 by putting his own brother on the Spanish throne. Immediately creoles started plotting to gain their independence from Europe, while protesting their loyalty to their former Spanish king.

Servile revolt breaks out in Mexico. In the Viceroyalty of New Spain (Mexico) a creole conspiracy for independence in 1808 led to mass revolt in 1810. Among the conspirators was Miguel Hidalgo (mee-*gehl'* ee-*dahl'*goh), an obscure, idealistic creole priest. When the Spaniards discovered the plot, Hidalgo gave the cry for open revolt. On September 15, 1810, he rang the church bell in the town of Dolores

From Independence to Nation-States

1780–1782	Amerindian revolt led by Tupac-Amarú in Peru
1789	Creole conspiracy led by "Tiradentes" in Brazil
1791–1804	Slave rebellion led by Toussaint L'Ouverture ends with independence of Haiti
1808	Spanish Crown overthrown by Napoleon
1810	Hidalgo incites revolt in New Spain
1823	Monroe Doctrine
1824	Battle of Ayacucho wins independence from Spain
1830–1837	Portales forms nation-state in Chile
1835–1852	Rosas forms nation-state in Argentina
1846–1848	War between Mexico and United States
1857–1860	War of the Reform in Mexico
1863–1867	French intervention in Mexico
1864–1870	Paraguay at war with Brazil, Argentina, and Uruguay
1889	Empire of Brazil becomes a republic
1898–1899	War between United States and Spain results in cession of Puerto Rico and a protectorate in Cuba
1903	Panama proclaims independence from Colombia; grants United States a canal zone

to proclaim Mexican independence. Unexpectedly, Amerindian peons (peasants) and despised *mestizos* (mehs-*tee'*sohs, men of mixed blood) swarmed to his banner. It bore the portrait of the Virgin of Guadalupe (gwah-dah-*loo'*peh), the dark Virgin, regarded by Mexicans as one of them rather than some fair, white figure imported from Europe. Guadalupe became the patron saint of the insurrection. Its rallying cry was: "Long live religion! Long live our most Holy Mother of Guadalupe! Long live America! Down with bad government!"

Hidalgo was carried away with social revolutionary fervor. He abolished slavery and Amerindian tribute. As his followers moved southward, they looted estates and murdered the hated Spaniards and creoles. Peons did not care whether white planters were born in Spain or in New Spain—they were still looked upon as oppressors. Violence had turned into a race war. Before long the raging mob numbered 50,000 and was approaching Mexico City. While Hidalgo hesitated to attack the capital, the horrified creoles turned to the Spanish royalists, who routed Hidalgo's ragged army. Hidalgo was captured, tried, defrocked, and executed in 1811. Today he is regarded as the father of his country. The mestizo priest José María Morelos (moh-*rey'*lohs) carried on Hidalgo's mission, but in 1815 he too was executed. Many priests, however, and all bishops remained loyal to the Crown during the years of bitter fighting in the Viceroyalty of New Spain. Servile insurrection had failed.

Mexican creoles establish a republic. In New Spain most creoles supported the Spanish viceroy until 1820, when conservative Spain itself fell into liberal hands for a short period. The creoles then shifted to the side of the revolutionaries, most of whom were mestizos. In 1824 Mexico was proclaimed a republic. In control were the landowning creoles, who achieved independence without granting the mestizo rebels any of the promises made by Hidalgo in 1810. Amerindian tribute payments and black slavery continued unchanged.

Creole conspiracy fails in Brazil. The Portuguese viceroyalty in Brazil had no trouble in snuffing out a conspiracy of creoles who wanted a republic similar to that in the United States. In 1789 the rebel leader, Tiradentes (tee-rah-*dehn'*tehs, "Tooth-puller"), was caught and executed as brutally as Tupac-Amarú. Like Tupac-Amarú and Hidalgo, he is considered a national martyr.

Venezuelan creoles begin a revolt. In Venezuela the first creole conspirator was Francisco de Miranda (mee-*rahn'*dah), who had fought as a general in the revolutionary French army. In 1806 he organized what proved to be an unsuccessful expedition of creoles and North American adventurers. They gained little support. Four years later, after the Spanish king had been deposed by Napoleon, the creoles of Caracas gave support to his cause, but the old general quarreled with young Simón Bolívar (see-*mohn'* boh-*lee'*bahr). Indeed, throughout Latin America the revolutionary creoles who displaced the Spanish officials often disagreed violently. In Venezuela the creoles did manage to organize an independent state, the Confederation of New Granada, with Camilo Torres (kah-*mee'*loh *toh'*rehs) as president. But the confederation did not last long.

The Confederation put Bolívar in charge of military operations. Bolívar soon found that the great obstacle to independence was not the Spanish army but its Latin American allies, dark, mounted troopers from the swampy *llanos* (*yah'*nos, plains) of interior Venezuela. These llaneros (cowboys) detested white creoles such as Bolívar for being citified rich landowners who looked down on ignorant mestizos. The llaneros were far more interested in looting the coastal lands than in creole-Spanish politics. Unable to defeat them, Bolívar was forced to seek refuge in Haiti. It became clear to him that the creoles alone could not drive out the Spaniards and defeat their formidable mestizo allies. When Bolívar promised to abolish slavery in New Granada, the Haitian president provided him with ships and arms. Unlike many creole leaders, Bolívar kept his word. On his return to the mainland in 1816 he announced the emancipation of the slaves in New Granada.

Political rivalries plague Bolívar's independence movement. Much of the fighting in northern South America amounted to civil war. Under Bolívar's command were creole officers, mestizo horsemen and troops, ex-slaves, mission Amerinds, and (after the Battle of Waterloo) British soldiers of fortune. Except for the latter and perhaps a few African-born freemen, all were *native* Americans. Despite their social differences, these men all adored their leader for his dash and courage; they admired his eloquence and endurance. For fifteen years he led his ragged troops through the humid marshes and frigid mountain passes of the Viceroyalty of New Granada. He had to contend not only with royalist forces, but also with the Colombians and Ecuadoreans. They suspected that his projected Greater Colombian Confederation was actually a plot for Venezuelan control of the Andean region.

San Martín leads the revolt in the south. The same kind of political jealousies, regional rivalries, and social divisions were found in southern South America, in what is today Argentina. In the area of the Río de la Plata (*ree'*oh dey lah *plah'*tah), fighting had begun even before Napoleon overthrew the Spanish king in 1808. When British forces captured Buenos Aires (*bwey'*nohs *eye'*rehs) in 1806, other considerations were set aside in the common creole effort to drive out the British invaders.

From 1808 to 1816 the creoles of Buenos Aires concealed their hopes and plans for independence from Spain behind a mask of loyalty to the deposed Spanish king. Meanwhile, they made careful plans for independence. In 1816 the provinces of the Río de la Plata declared that independence at Tucumán (too-koo-*mahn'*), Argentina. The newly independent land was threatened by Spanish troops in Chile and Peru. Besides the creoles, the Army of the Andes, quietly organized by José de San Martín (mar-*teen'*), included the Pehuenche (pey-*wain'*cheh) Indians, who controlled the eastern slopes of the Andes. San Martín also attracted black slaves by promising them emancipation. A third of his army was black.

San Martín's army and its heavy artillery filed through mountain passes of the Andes and in February of 1817 crushed the Spanish forces in the Central Valley of Chile. This operation matched Hannibal's crossing of the Alps.

Between Santiago and Lima, San Martín's goal, lay the barren Atacama Desert. The impossibility of marching a large army across the desert caused San Martín to turn to the sea. In 1820 a small navy commanded by a dashing Scottish admiral transported San Martín's expeditionary force to Peru.

Bolívar and San Martín meet. Few creoles or even Amerindians in Peru favored independence. Memories of bitter race wars in the 1780's made them fearful. Yet for the first time there was a possibility of joint American action against the Spaniards. At the same time San Martín had been moving north, the forces of Bolívar were moving south.

In 1822 San Martín, called the "Protector of Peru," came to Guayaquil (gwy-ah-*keel'*) in the Land of the Equator (Ecuador) to talk with Bolívar, the "Liberator." Since no one else attended the famous "Interview of Guayaquil," we cannot know for certain why San Martín, the ablest of the Latin American military leaders, withdrew from Peru and went into exile in Europe. The field was Bolívar's.

The final battle for Peru lasted but an hour. In the thin, cold Andean air, near the mile-high village of Ayacucho (eye-ah-*koo'*choh), outnumbered American troops crushed the Spanish-led army. Ayacucho (1824) marked the final triumph of the collective revolutionary forces in South America.

Brazil becomes independent. Brazil achieved its independence through the decision of its ruler. For years colonial Brazil had far more land, people, and resources than the mother country, Portugal. When Napoleon's armies invaded Portugal in 1807, the monarch escaped to Brazil with the help of the British navy. The king immediately ended mercantilism and opened Brazilian ports to British trade. In 1814 he made the colony a kingdom and in 1821 appointed his son Pedro to rule it. A year later, when Pedro declared Brazil an independent empire, the Portuguese offered little resistance. The Brazilian emperor granted little power to the creoles. When growing unrest threatened to lead to civil war, Pedro I abdicated in favor of his creole son, Pedro II. In independent Brazil social structure of the plantation economy remained unchanged. The sugar planters ran things, and slavery lasted until 1888.

In the Caribbean, Puerto Rico and Cuba remained in Spanish hands. The creoles, fearing that an armed strike for independence might lead to a slave revolt such as that in Haiti, preferred colonial status. Not until 1886 was slavery abolished.

There are several important results of the Wars of Independence. The fifteen years of military combat and civil strife in Latin America had several important results.

1. Sixteen independent republics were established.

2. Heroic "men on horseback," local strong men called *caudillos* (kow-*dee'*yohs), became the symbols of national glory. In years to come, military leaders would gain political power in many Latin American countries.

3. The booming economies of the former colonies were shattered by the long and costly wars.

4. Normal channels of trade and communication between one American land and another were broken, isolating the new republics from each other.

5. The Latin American ports were opened to world trade, especially in Chile, Argentina, and Brazil.

6. Caste and race lines, especially between whites and near-whites, became blurred.

7. Because it had not favored breaking away from Spain, the clergy lost its prestige (except among the Amerinds).

The creole rulers of the newly independent American nations scarcely changed things. They merely replaced the Iberian governing officials with American-born officials who did little to alter the social structure of colonial Latin America. A few wealthy and powerful creole landowners continued to live off the toil of peasants and slaves.

CHECK-UP

1. What were the causes of unrest in Latin America in the late 1700's?

2. What is meant by servile revolts? How successful were they in Peru? In Haiti? What was the reaction of the creoles?

3. What role did the creoles play in the movement for Mexican independence?

4. Why did the creole revolt led by Bolívar fail? Why was Bolívar later successful?

5. How did the creoles of Argentina achieve independence? How did San Martín liberate Chile? How were the Spaniards defeated in Peru?

6. How did Brazil become independent? Did independence really change things?

7. What were the major results of the Wars of Independence?

The Building of Nation-States

The new republics face difficult political problems. The creoles had little or no experience in governing. They drew up constitutions that tried to copy some of the political practices of Britain, the United States, and France. But the peoples of Latin America had had virtually no experience with regular elections, parliamentary government, and political compromise. These constitutional, liberal, democratic practices did not take hold in Latin America. Indeed, the Latin American republics still appear to be searching for constitutional forms lying somewhere between electoral democracy and presidential dictatorship. Although the constitutions of the Latin American republics express many liberal ideals, in practice these ideals are often ignored. Since independence the Latin American republics have been characterized by the following political practices:

1. Caudillism. The distant king was replaced by the caudillo, a strong man bearing the official title of President of the Republic and a semi-official one such as Benefactor of the People. He gave the state strong central authority.

2. Personalism. The population was loyal to the man, not to the office he held.

3. Legalism. The law was used for economic ends. For example, lawyers found legalistic ways to dispossess Amerinds and the Church of the lands they had held in colonial times.

4. Bureaucracy. Government offices, many of them unnecessary, were created to pay off creoles friendly to the caudillo.

5. Corruption. There was frequent taking of bribes and misuse of funds at all levels of government, particularly in the highest offices, with the spoils going to relatives and supporters of the caudillo and to army officers.

6. Military intervention. Army officers intervened in politics, making and unmaking presidents. In addition, armed bands often fought for control of the countryside. This situation is common in developing lands.

Caudillism characterizes Latin American politics. Each republic experienced a "time of troubles," a period of unrest in which rival caudillos struggled for power. In the less developed states the "time of troubles" continues to this day. The caudillo tried to muscle his way into the presidential palace. To succeed, he had to have the army behind him. Once he became supreme chief, he could plunder the customs house, for most government revenue comes from taxes on exports and imports. He con-

tinued in power until another caudillo gained enough strength to force him out of office. Most barracks revolts involved little bloodshed. A general or group of officers (*junta, hoon'*tah) would notify the caudillo that his term of office had come to an end. Under the informal rules of the game, the caudillo and his family would probably be permitted to go into exile, taking with them the loot acquired during their occupation of the presidential palace.

The caudillo was often of mixed race. He followed popular custom in speech, dress, and prejudice and called himself "father of the people." A new president might have his lawyers write a new constitution to legalize his hold on the top job. If he was not one already, a new president often became a large landholder, for land conferred both wealth and social prestige on its owner. Thus he became a member of the creole upper class and gradually lost the common touch. This happened to José Páez (*pah'*ehs), a former llanero who became one of Bolívar's ablest commanders and was named first president of Venezuela. Caudillism was a good example of the "career open to talent." A bunk in the barracks might be the first step on the road to the presidential palace. Hence the ambitious but poor young man of mixed race no longer entered the clergy as in colonial times. He became a soldier.

There is disagreement over the role of the Church. Two centuries ago the Jesuits were expelled from Latin America (page 378). Ever since, the Roman Catholic clergy has been declining in power, prestige, and relative numbers. The Wars of Independence divided the clergy. While the priests generally supported the revolutionaries, the upper clergy remained loyal to the mother country. This served to discredit the Church in the eyes of many patriots.

Just what was the proper place of the Church in the republic? Conservatives wanted education, social welfare, marriage, and burial to remain under Church control. Liberals, however, wanted to separate Church and state. They wanted the government to collect the tithes in order to build national schools and hospitals. Although the mass of Latin Americans has remained Catholic in name and conservative in outlook, the Church-state conflict has severely reduced the wealth in land and the spiritual authority of the Roman Catholic Church. Bitter struggles are still taking place between pro-clerical conservatives and anticlerical liberals.

Mexican liberals separate Church and state.

The longest and most savagely fought struggle between Church and state took place in Mexico. In 1855 a liberal government set out to "reform" Mexican society. They intended to strip from both the clergy and the military the right to be tried in their own tribunals instead of in state courts. Church authorities warned that anyone who swore to uphold the reform might be denied the Sacraments (page 144). The president of the republic was Benito Juárez (bey-*nee'*toh *hwah'*rehs), a full-blooded Zapotec (page 305) from the state of Oaxaca (wah-*hah'*kah). Liberals praised Juárez for his honesty and rectitude. To conservatives he seemed merely an ugly, silent, little lawyer of simple tastes and homely virtues, much like his contemporary, President Lincoln. Juárez wrote the liberal reforms into his constitution of 1857. They provided for separation of Church and state, confiscation of Church lands, and the suppression of religious orders. When the Conservatives promised to undo the reform and restore the old regime, Mexico's worst civil war began.

The War of the Reform pitted the army against those who wanted an end to military privileges, the Church against the anticlericals (who were often middle-class lawyers), and the capital against the outlying provinces. The war was marked by atrocities, betrayals, and great loss of life. When President Juárez emerged victorious, reactionaries managed to bring about foreign intervention. In 1863 a well-equipped French army of 30,000 landed at Veracruz. It lost one battle to the mestizo general Porfirio Díaz (por-*fee'*ryoh *dee'*ahs). Mexican patriotic forces, however, had little chance against up-to-date European arms. The victorious French set up a puppet empire under Archduke Maximilian of Hapsburg Austria.

Falsely informed that he had widespread popular support, "Emperor" Maximilian expected a warm welcome. He found instead a backward land brimming with hatred and burdened with debts. In 1866 sentiment turned in favor of Juárez, who had been roving around the countryside rallying support for his legal government. Maximilian's attempt to pacify the country was doomed when Napoleon III withdrew the French army. In 1867 Maximilian fell before a republican firing squad. Juárez was re-elected and served as president of a shattered land until his death in 1872.

The scars of the Mexican Reform remain to this day and Benito Juárez, because he deprived the Church of its privileged position, remains one of the most controversial of Mexican presidents.

Portales makes Chile into a nation-state.

Caudillos helped to bring about the psychological change from former colony to nation. Using force, guile, and eloquence, the caudillo would persuade the heads of powerful landed families and provincial chiefs to accept him as the sole authority in the state.

The first unifying caudillo appeared in Chile. Diego Portales (pohr-*tah'*lehs) was neither a general nor a president. From 1830 to 1837 he operated as the strong man behind the scenes. He ran his import business profitably and the government dictatorially. He used censorship, police arrest, speedy trials, and exile to eliminate opposition. Portales pushed the military out of politics and favored landowning and Church interests over small holders. The constitution he had drawn up in 1833, granting the Chilean president absolute veto over legislative acts, endured for a century. Portales started a war against Bolivia and Peru, but was

Latin America After Independence (About 1830)

Independent states
Spanish colonies
French colonies
British colonies
Dutch colonies

UNITED STATES

MEXICO

Mexico ★
Veracruz ●
Oaxaca ●

BAHAMA ISLANDS

CUBA

JAMAICA
HAITI
SANTO
DOMINGO
PUERTO RICO

BR. HOND.

GUATEMALA
HONDURAS
EL SALVADOR
NICARAGUA

UNITED
PROVINCES
OF
CENTRAL
AMERICA

COSTA
RICA

Caribbean Sea

Coro ●
Caracas ★
TRINIDAD

LLANOS

Boyacá ★
Bogotá ●

GREAT
COLOMBIA

GUIANAS

Quito ★

Guayaquil ●

ANDES

Río   Amazonas

EMPIRE
OF
BRAZIL

Lima ★
Ayacucho ●

PERU

BOLIVIA

ATACAMA
DESERT

PARAGUAY

Tucumán ●

Río de Janeiro ★

CHILE

CENTRAL VALLEY

Santiago ★
Buenos Aires ★

URUGUAY

Río de la Plata

ARGENTINA

**Latin America
About 1800**

Spanish rule
Portuguese rule
French rule
British rule
Dutch rule

VICEROYALTY OF NEW SPAIN

Mexico ★

ATLANTIC
OCEAN

Havana ●

VICEROYALTY OF SANTO DOMINGO

Caribbean Sea

PACIFIC
OCEAN

VICEROYALTY OF
NEW GRANADA
★ Bogotá

GUIANAS

Lima ★

VICEROYALTY
OF
PERU

VICEROYALTY
OF
BRAZIL

Río de Janeiro ★

VICEROYALTY
OF
LA PLATA

Buenos Aires ★

Río
Grande

shot to death before the campaign began. Instead of falling into the usual period of anarchy that followed the loss of a caudillo, Chileans remained united and won the war. Somehow they sensed that Portales had stabilized Chile, which had been in turmoil since 1823 when Bernardo O'Higgins, the father of the country, was forced into exile. The Portales legacy formed the basis of Chile's remarkable political stability, military strength, and economic progress throughout the nineteenth century. He had endowed his people with a sense of national loyalty.

The shortness of Chile's time of troubles, however, was due not only to the remarkable personality of Diego Portales. Also important were (1) geographic unity (the population was concentrated in the Central Valley); (2) a racially homogeneous population, largely of European descent; (3) the absence of either a viceregal tradition or a glittering creole caste with its aristocratic passion for social distinctions; (4) a resident colony of British businessmen who were industrious, forward-looking, and influential. In other nations geography and racial and class differences tended to divide the people.

Rosas' tyranny gives Argentines a sense of nationalism.

In the region of the Río de la Plata, Manuel de Rosas (mah-*nwehl'* dey *roh'*-sahs), governor of Buenos Aires province, defeated dissident caudillos and drove Amerinds from good lands. His tyranny lasted from 1835 to 1852. In the port city of Buenos Aires, wrote a conservative countryman:

Rosas had his court of intriguing women and of men who were worth even less. Through them he won the devotion of the lower class and, dazzling them with the prestige which he treacherously offered, used them to launch a secret police and a vast network of informers without equal in the history of tyranny. His daughter danced with the Africans at the base of the social pyramid; [his wife] intrigued tirelessly, making use of domestic servants who betrayed the secrets of [households] and sold them for the wretched pride which the tyrant's court awakened in their hearts. The upper class was the favorite target of his rage merely because . . . he wished to subdue and completely degrade the class that had the greatest resources of vitality because of education and wealth.

In this account one can see the class bias of the port-dwelling elite. They were not impressed that General Rosas rode horseback better than any gaucho (Argentine cowboy) or Amerind. The creoles hated Rosas because he closed the Río de la Plata to British and French commerce. This anti-European action made men of mixed descent—at that time the bulk of the Argentine population—proud to be citizens of the Argentine Confederation. Rosas, who was one of Latin America's most successful tyrants, failed to do one thing. He was unable to incorporate Uruguay and Paraguay into the nation-state that he created.

Nationalism is disastrous for Paraguay.

Three dictators ruled Paraguay from 1816 to 1870—José Rodríguez Francia (roh-*dree'*gehs *frahn'*-syah) and later Carlos López (*loh'*pehs) and his son Francisco. They shut out all foreigners, especially Argentines and Brazilians. These caudillos identified the Guaraní (gwah-rah-*nee'*, Amerindian) population with the Paraguayan republic. Francisco López was an imperialist dreamer who pitted the male population of Paraguay in a hopeless war against Uruguay, Argentina, and Brazil. He lost his life, the war, and most of his men. While Paraguay survived as a nation-state, it still bears the scars of this disastrous war (1864–1870).

Brazilian nationalism gives the army a leading role.

Pedro II, Emperor of Brazil, was not a caudillo in the sense of illegally "continuing" himself in power. He inherited the crown in 1831 and held it half a century. With great political skill he manipulated the wide powers granted him by the Constitution of 1824. In the caudillo tradition he kept the legislature, the judiciary, and the provinces in their place, subordinate to the chief executive. At great cost to Brazil in life and treasure, he insisted that the empire carry to its bloody finish the war against Paraguay. He hoped to give Brazilian nationalism "a good electric shock." Pedro II lived to repent his decision. Swollen with the pride of victory, the military overthrew the monarchy in 1889. Since then the Brazilian military has taken over the emperor's role of judging whether the duly elected government harmonizes with the "national interest."

CHECK-UP

1. What political problems faced the newly independent Latin American republics?

2. How does a caudillo come to power? Lose it?

3. What was the role of the Church according to conservatives? Liberals? Why was the struggle between Church and state in Mexico particularly bitter? What was the outcome of the War of the Reform?

4. What did Portales do to give Chile stability? How was a sense of nationalism developed in Argentina? Brazil?

Modernization: Some Approaches and Problems

There are several reasons for Latin America's underdevelopment. Latin Americans have long been asking why, despite abundant natural resources, their economy has lagged so far behind those of Western Europe and the United States. Why did the booming colonial economy fail to achieve industrialization after independence? Why are there so many poor? Why hasn't Latin America overcome obstacles to modernization?

Baron Alexander von Humboldt, an astute Prussian scientist, spent five years traveling in Latin America about 1800. He noted that the economy and the culture compared favorably with Europe's. He was impressed with the advanced technology in Mexican silver mining and thought that the conditions under which Amerinds worked in textile factories were no worse than those in Glasgow or Leipzig. Certainly Lima and Mexico City were grander than Philadelphia and New York. Why, then, does the standard of living in Latin America today lag behind that in Western Europe, Russia, and the United States?

1. Geography. The size of Latin America has little to do with the usefulness of the land. The rugged terrain of mountains, the dryness of extensive deserts, and the poor soils of tropical lowlands pose obstacles to farming.

2. Single-product economy. A look at the map will show that North and South America have the same triangular shape. But little of North America lies in the tropical zone, while most of South America lies there. Tropics nearly always mean plantations, and plantations almost always mean one-crop farming, such as sugar, cacao, or coffee. A country which depends on only one or two crops for its income can lapse into economic trouble when prices on the world market drop. Mining also fits into this one-product pattern. Mexican author Carlos Fuentes (*fweyn'*tehs) explains the predicament of one-product countries:

You [Anglo-Americans] are proprietors of Latin American foreign trade. Sixty per cent of our foreign trade is with you, in accordance with the prices you set. American companies manage 75 per cent of our commercial movement. . . . Last year [1962] the Alliance [for Progress] gave 150 million dollars to Colombia; but in that same year Colombia lost 450 million dollars because of the decrease in [world] coffee prices [set in New York].

In other words, the export of Chilean nitrates or Peruvian guano (used as fertilizer), of Bolivian tin or Argentine hides, enriched Europe and the United States and impoverished Latin

829

America. Indeed, this Latin American wealth helped to finance the development of western capitalist economies. Though of no *political* importance to Europe, Latin America was essential to its *economic* well-being.

3. Foreign ownership. Capitalist investors in Latin America were usually foreigners. (Wealthy Latin Americans tended to invest their money in Europe.) When the Iberian businessmen departed in 1825, their place was taken not by creoles but by more industrious foreigners: British, French, Germans, Italians, and Anglo-Americans. They had more cash and more technical know-how than creoles. The creole elite continued to look upon commerce as grubby business beneath the dignity of planters and their sons. Caudillos, meanwhile, were eager to acquire foreign capital. In Venezuela, for example, the ruthless caudillo Juan Vicente Gómez (*hwahn'* bee-*sehn'*teh *goh'-*mehs) lined his pockets with some 30 million dollars gained from granting oil concessions to foreign countries.

Foreigners directed the digging of mines and the construction of railroads from those mines to the ports. Naturally they had no interest in planning a rail network that would benefit the national economy. Again Carlos Fuentes:

Investments? Yes, you have invested 10 billion dollars in Latin America. It is a curious thing: we have always received your investments, and we are still poor. You speak about *your* property in Latin America and call us thieves when we expropriate it [take it over]. But why don't you ask your investors? Between 1950 and 1955, you invested 2 billion dollars, made three and a half billion, and took back to the States one and a half billion. In . . . 1959 you made 775 million, only reinvested 200 million, and sent 575 back to the United States. In the last seven years, Latin America lost, because of these shipments of money, $2,679,000,000. You take out too much, leave too little, and even this little is distributed unfairly.

4. Social stagnation. Foreign capitalists backed caudillos who kept order, for stable politics meant that their business with planters

and miners would run smoothly. To meet growing foreign demands, capitalists expanded their operations. By bribery and legal manipulations they took land from the Amerinds who, to make a living, were forced to work on plantations or in mines. Because debts could legally be inherited, peons were tied by debt to the *patrón* (pah-*trohn'*), the landowner. The Church was too weak to protect them; the state did not care about them as long as they kept working. As the plantation system expanded, more and more people became landless, illiterate, and diseased. For any help or favors, the peons had to turn to the patrón, on whom they depended for everything except spiritual comfort. Such a dependent status can hardly produce the energetic, ambitious, and educated young men and women needed for a modernizing economy.

By 1900 Latin American society consisted —and still does in many regions—of: (1) an apathetic, tradition-bound rural mass living in villages and dominated by (2) an elite of patrons and absentee landlords, whose markets and interests were abroad. (3) Small clusters of the urban middle class accepted the elite as their model for proper behavior and style of living. (4) Military officers, largely recruited from these middle groups, also looked up to the elite and supported them in order to preserve the special rights of the military. As the plantation economy grew in the nineteenth century, so did the exploitation of human beings.

Diaz pacifies and modernizes Mexico. War hero General Porfirio Díaz, like Juárez a native of Oaxaca, assumed power in 1876. Mexico was still one of the most turbulent states in Latin America. Most of its people were sunk in poverty and had little hope of bettering their lot. The few roads were infested with bandits. Díaz made travel safe by recruiting outlaws as rural police. These *rurales* (roo-*rah'*lehs) used brutal methods to pacify the countryside. Everywhere in Mexico the caudillo made liberal use of "bread or the stick" to keep local chiefs

The bold, clean lines of Brasília (top), capital of Brazil, contrast strongly with the rickety favelas (slums, right) of Rio de Janeiro, the old capital. Here the poverty-stricken live on the verge of starvation, without electricity or sanitary facilities, only blocks away from the luxury hotels that line Rio's breathtakingly beautiful harbor. Brazil has one of the most acute population problems in Latin America. A high birth rate, plantation agriculture, and heavy migration to the cities result in a barely adequate diet. Throughout Latin America there is a desperate need to modernize agriculture, as in the wheat fields of Argentina (above), but the use of machines in agriculture is rare, for labor is cheap.

personally loyal to him. Díaz "continued" in power for 35 years. "Porfirian" order attracted foreign capital that financed the construction of railroads connecting outlying provinces with the national capital. The peso became as sound as it had been in colonial days, when it was one of the few coins accepted everywhere on the globe. By 1910, on the 100th anniversary of Hidalgo's "cry of Dolores," Díaz was telling an admiring world that the Mexican nation was ready for free elections.

Like his admirers in Europe and the United States, the dictator may have thought that a quiet countryside, a modern capital city, and a stable peso meant political maturity. But in pacifying, centralizing, and modernizing Mexico, Díaz had allowed his cronies and foreign investors to take over peasant lands and to incorporate them into broad plantations which produced crops for export. This meant that there was less food to feed the growing rural population. At first the silent, oppressed Amerindian peons paid no more attention to the creole election of 1910 than their ancestors had to the creole conspiracy of 1808. After all, Díaz' opponent, a member of a large, rich family from the northern state of Coahuila (koh-ah-we'lah), had no desire to alter either the landholding or the class structure of Mexico. But when the younger generation of leaders began to squabble among themselves over Díaz' political successor, the discontent of the Mexican peasants and miners broke out into violent revolution. The outcome was quite different from the revolt in 1810.

THE MEXICAN REVOLUTION

Popular unrest breaks out. The Mexican Revolution (1910–1940) dwarfs all other revolutions in Latin America for its size, intensity, duration, and results. It was not the product of the ideals of one man or group of men, but the revolt of an entire nation. Frank Tannenbaum, a noted authority on Latin American history, writes:

How different this from the French and Russian Revolutions! There was not a Rousseau, a Voltaire, a Montesquieu, a Diderot in Mexico. There were no important intellectuals on the side of the Revolution. The whole educated class belonged to the [Díaz] dictatorship and its satellites. The gulf between the rich and the poor, between the landowner and his peons, between the officeholder and the common folk, was so profound that the grievances of the common people found no voice. . . . It was not a revolution that was fought by large armies. There were, it was true, some fairly large battles during the Revolution, but over the whole period these represent only incidents in the way of military history. The real battles were fought anonymously by little bands of peasants and soldiers to vindicate [assert] their right to overthrow the government. Small groups of Indians under anonymous leaders were the Revolution.

As revolution engulfed Mexico, peons retaliated for centuries of humiliation and exploitation by murdering patrons and burning their houses. Rival caudillos waged a constant guerrilla warfare. Some sought personal power; some sought social reform. Patrons learned to fear one caudillo, an illiterate mestizo peasant, Emiliano Zapata (ey-mee-*lyah'*noh sah-*pah'*-tah). Zapata's only goal was to get back the lands of the Amerinds, and he would not stop fighting until this was accomplished. He told his devoted peasant followers, "It is better to die on your feet than to live on your knees."

The revolutionary constitution is both socialistic and democratic. In 1917 the revolutionaries drew up a new constitution which was to serve as a blueprint for reforming Mexican society. It provided for (1) agricultural collectives for Amerinds; (2) national ownership of underground resources such as minerals; (3) labor unions and an eight-hour working day; (4) free, compulsory, secular education; (5) a "free" Church forbidden to own property or engage in politics.

While the provisions of the 1917 Constitution were not all realized at once, they provided the basis for a forward-looking, modernized state. As late as 1936 President Lázaro Cárdenas (*lah'*sah-roh *kar'*deh-nahs) redistributed huge tracts of land; two years later he took over foreign oil holdings. Mexicans greeted Cárdenas' revolutionary action of expropriating foreign-held mineral resources with enthusiasm. Cárdenas' stand against powerful foreign nations filled them with national pride. In the last act of the Mexican Revolution, General Cárdenas drove the military out of politics. He subjected the armed forces to the control of Mexico's ruling civilian party.

The Mexican Revolution has lasting results. Today, as a result of her revolution, Mexico enjoys political stability and the highest rate of economic growth in Latin America. She has built huge industrial complexes and an excellent transportation system. Rivers have been harnessed to prevent flooding and to provide electricity and water for irrigation. Agricultural collectives (similar to the style of farming practiced in pre-Spanish times) and improved methods of farming now enable Mexico to feed her population without importing foods. Far-reaching educational programs have made her about 75 per cent literate. A large urban middle class has developed and is fairly prosperous.

Despite these advances, change has only slightly affected Amerindian and mestizo peasants. Most remain poor, receive only minimal schooling, have an inadequate diet, and do not receive proper medical care. Moreover, Mexico's population of 50 million is growing at one of the fastest rates in the world, and the Mexican economy must therefore make yearly gains just to keep conditions from worsening. There is great pride in the revolution and its accomplishments, but educated Mexicans fret under the restraints of a one-party government.

MODERNIZATION AND ITS PROBLEMS

Caudillos try to modernize Brazil and Argentina. The Great Depression of the 1930's caused enormous economic and social distress in Latin

The Twentieth Century

1876–1910	Díaz dictator in Mexico
1910–1940	Mexican Revolution
1930–1954	Vargas promotes economic diversification in Brazil
1933–1945	Good Neighbor Policy
1946–1955	Perón rules Argentina
1948	Creation of Organization of American States
1952	Bolivian Revolution
1959	Cuban Revolution
1960	Castro declares Cuba communist
1961	Alliance for Progress; United States backs an invasion of Cuba
1962	Cuban missile crisis
1965	United States intervenes in Dominican Republic

America. New leaders, seeking ways to cope with the sharp reduction in trade and terrible economic conditions, replaced the old ruling class. Some tried solutions modeled on socialism, others introduced fascist policies. All became intensely nationalistic; hostility to foreign influences stopped the flow of European immigrants. Nationalist sentiments and popular support gave Latin American leaders dictatorial power to (1) start nationalizing the economy, especially railroads and petroleum, (2) promote domestic industries, and (3) create a program of social welfare and education for all citizens. The Second World War helped to push Latin American states further along the path of modernization. They were forced to develop their own industries because of a drastic drop in manufactured goods coming from the United States and Europe. But the war did not allow the Latin American republics to break the shackles that made them victims of price fluctuations in the world market, for their economies remained tied to one or two crops.

Getúlio Vargas (zheh-*too*'lee-oh *vahr*'guhsh) ran Brazil for nearly a quarter of a century (1930–1954). Known as the "Father of the Poor," Vargas left the Brazilian economy somewhat less dependent on the export of coffee. After World War II, with the aid of United States capital, Brazil constructed a steel mill. This allowed President Juscelino Kubitschek (zhoo-seh-*lee*'noh *koo*'bih-chek, 1955–1960) to set up the first automobile plant in Latin America.

Brazil's great rival in military and economic power was Argentina, controlled by Colonel Juan Perón (peh-*rohn*') from 1946 to 1955. Following a personal version of fascist philosophy, Perón tried to improve the lot of industrial workers. But with Europe's postwar recovery, there was a sudden drop in European demand for Argentine wheat and meat. The bottom fell out of the Argentine economy.

The military dominates Argentina and Brazil.
The old ruling class continued reluctant to let the masses have any say in government. Both Vargas and Perón were overthrown by military leaders who mistrusted their popularly supported programs. By the late 1960's both Brazil and Argentina had fallen under the thumb of the armed forces, and in both countries the democratic constitutions were suspended. Citizens could not exercise civil liberties. Like the property-owning elite, these military dictatorships believe that social reform cannot come *before* economic development.

The hard-hitting regimes of Argentina and Brazil are rightist and pro-United States, which provides much of the capital needed for modernization. The United States tends to support dictatorships (though not always openly), rather than constitutionalist regimes which are relatively unstable, because military rule offers a more favorable climate for investment. The Latin American military is strongly anti-communist and tends to blame communism for: (1) student unrest in universities, (2) the opposition of the Church, and (3) workers' strikes for wage increases. Recently the military has been embarrassed by the subversive activities of revolutionary groups who rob banks, kidnap government officials (often those of foreign embassies), and demand huge ransoms for their return. In 1969 the Brazilian generals suffered the indignity of having to release 15 political prisoners in exchange for the kidnapped United States ambassador.

Socialist nationalism develops in Peru.
In Peru and Bolivia military dictatorships are using other methods to achieve modernization. These countries have biracial societies, and Amerinds are segregated and ruled by whites. The generals, unlike those in Argentina or Brazil, have acted on the theory that economic development is brought about *through* sweeping social reform. In 1969 the Peruvian generals astonished both the great landowners and the landless masses by nationalizing oil wells and sugar plantations owned by the elite and by Anglo-Americans. They are distributing land to peasants and starting new industrial enterprises owned by the workers. By these measures they hope to speed up industrialization and modernization. Neither Marxist nor capitalist, the Peruvian approach to modernization may be called socialist nationalism. Openly Marxist, however, is the political philosophy of President Salvador Allende of Chile, the only Marxist-Leninist ever chosen in free elections (1970) in Latin America.

Population growth presents an increasing problem.
Whether rightist or leftist, all Latin American governments must cope with the problem of rapidly rising populations. Both birth and infant-mortality rates remained high until the Second World War. Since 1945 the infant-mortality rate has dropped sharply and life expectancy of adults has lengthened. The birth rate, however, has not declined at all, and Latin America now has the highest rate in the world. Population grows at three per cent a year. (In some Latin American countries it is even higher.) The population explosion has become critical. While per capita production is rising slightly (1.5 per cent per year), it is only

barely able to keep up with population growth. The distribution of goods (consumption) continues to be extremely uneven. Millions live outside the market economy, eking out an existence by subsistence farming and local barter. These peoples are no better off today than they were a decade ago.

Rural overpopulation has plagued some regions of Latin America. It contributed to peasant unrest in Mexico (1910), Cuba (1930), Bolivia (1952), and Brazil (1960). In other areas population pressure has pushed peasants out of the countryside and into already crowded cities. Unlike cities in Europe and Anglo-America, however, Latin American cities offer only limited employment opportunities. Except for São Paulo (*sown' pow'*loo) in Brazil and Monterrey (Mexico), Latin American cities contain few factories or industrial plants where unskilled peasant migrants can find employment. Nevertheless, people continue to pour into the cities, and slum areas continue to expand, while living conditions fail to improve for most of the poor.

Some observers think that urban inability to cope with the exploding population is evidence of too high a birth rate. Others argue that, since the countryside is being depopulated, a continued high birth rate is necessary to fill up the sparsely populated interior wilderness (as in Colombia and Brazil). The population question is complicated by the opposition of the Catholic Church to most forms of family planning. Nationalists argue that the Anglo-American concern over the high birth rate in Latin America stems from Anglo-Saxon fear that the darker Latins will double in number in this hemisphere by the year 2000. Latin America thus might pose a military threat to the "Titan of the North."

Reformers and conservatives disagree on the role of the Church. During the past century the Roman Catholic clergy has consistently lost standing with republican governments and with the Latin American intellectual elite. As clerical prestige declined in the upper class, so did the number of those called to the Church. Today half the clergy in some countries is composed of monks and priests from Europe and Anglo-America. Religious schools and institutions are controlled by foreigners who often look down on the native clergy. Liberal governments have permitted Protestants to open churches. Some priests are leading reform movements; others believe that the Church should continue to concentrate on preaching and teaching. The same division is found among Protestant clergy. In Colombia, a well-born young priest, Camilo Torres, left the clergy to join the guerrillas of the National Liberation Army. His action pointed up the lack of social concern on the part of both Church and state. When Torres met a violent death, some regarded him as a martyr; to others he was a traitor. The question today in the Church is whether the pull of the colonial past is stronger than the push into the twenty-first century.

Modernization is reflected in the arts. Just as political independence from Spain and Portugal failed to bring economic freedom from Europe, Latin American arts and sciences continued to follow European models after the colonial period. The works of creole poets and painters resembled those of French masters. Artists were members of the elite; they were graduated from the national university, traveled in Europe, and returned home to work in a government office. Few could make a living from their art. And because they had to serve the caudillo who was in power, they might be jailed or exiled by his successor.

While living in exile from the tyranny of Rosas, the Argentine journalist Domingo Sarmiento (sar-*myehn'*toh) wrote *Civilization or Barbarism*. His articles described the cunning and brutal ways of a provincial caudillo, which Sarmiento likened to barbarism. Sarmiento himself later became president of the "civilized" Argentine Republic and encouraged a nationwide school system. In Peru the best writing was done by Juan Montalvo. When the conservative clerical caudillo García Moreno (gar-*see'*ah

In much of Latin America, Amerindian peoples follow ways of life which have changed little over the centuries. Bridging the gap between traditional ways and modernization is a major problem for many nations. The market scene from Atitlán, Guatemala (left), is a mirror of the past. The steel worker at right has successfully adapted to the the twentieth century; in the eyes of his fellow Amerinds he has become a ladino. Many nations are proud of their racial blend. The mosaic from Mexico's University City (far right) combines ancient Aztec symbols with a striking modern design. Dominating the design is the mestizo descendant of Amerind and Spaniard, sustained by life-giving corn.

moh-*rey*'noh) was assassinated, Montalvo boasted from exile, "I killed him with my pen." Cuba's greatest writer, José Martí (mar-*tee*'), the "Apostle of Free Cuba," died fighting for his country's independence. Most inspired of all was the poetry of the Nicaraguan Rubén Darío (roo-*behn*' dah-*ree*'oh). He attacked United States imperialism and set a style later Latin American poets followed. The Uruguayan philosopher, José Rodó (roh-*doh*'), struck a similar note in a famous essay entitled *Ariel*, still read by Latin American students. Rodó compared the practical materialism of the "Colossus of the North" with the spiritual ideals of the Latin American elite, and the United States suffered in his comparison. "I admire them," he wrote, "but I do not love them."

Towards the end of the nineteenth century, Latin American artists turned away from Europe and looked more closely at their own people. Celebrating their national revolution, Mexican painters and poets led the way. Today the arts reflect concern for the wretched conditions that plague Latin American society. In music and literature, in painting and architecture, modernism integrates African and especially Amerindian themes with European ones.

Artists throughout Latin America are producing works that are both beautiful and original. Architects have created some of the most striking works of the modern period. The Latin American artist occupies a high place among his countrymen. The state supports the arts by granting cultural commissions and awards. This gives the Latin American artist prestige, but it may also involve him in politics.

Modernization produces new social outlooks.
Today the Latin American artist reflects the growing prestige of racial mixture in twentieth-century Latin America. In colonial times the state, the Church, and the creole elite built a society in which the upper class was Christian and white; they often blamed Latin America's ills on racial mixing. They felt that only white immigrants from Northern Europe could rescue Latin America from dictatorship and poverty. But now, modern Latin America holds so many

million mestizos, mulattoes, and others of mixed descent that racial hatreds have softened. The mestizo has become the national type in most of Latin America. He is regarded as a new kind of man, a Latin American "race." Today it is less racial bias than class prejudice that divides people. How one talks and dresses is socially more important than the color of his skin or the texture of his hair. In biracial Guatemala, for example, an *indio* (*een'*dyoh) becomes a *ladino* (lah-dee'noh, white) simply by replacing his traditional sandals, tortillas, and indigenous language with shoes, bread, and Spanish. Most Latin Americans are proud of the absence of outward forms of religious and racial prejudice in their nations, although discrimination does exist in jobs, promotions, and choice of wife or husband.

REVOLUTION IN CUBA

Since the Cuban Revolution is still under way, it is difficult to compare it with the Mexican Revolution. The causes of both were: (1) large estates and rural overpopulation which contrib-

uted to hunger in the countryside, (2) economic colonialism that resulted in the wealth of the nation being sent abroad to Anglo-America and Europe, (3) corruption in a dictatorial government, and (4) exclusion of dark-skinned citizens from power.

United States interference halts revolt in the 1930's. With the Great Depression of the 1930's Cuban upper-class students and teachers began to agitate for a genuine social revolution. They wanted not just a switching of offices among the elite, but reforms that would aid the poor. In 1933 the workers and the middle class combined in a general strike and an army revolt to oust General Machado from the presidential palace. Cuban historian Federico Gil (fey-dey-ree'koh *heel'*) writes:

[The] refusal of the United States to recognize Grau San Martín [the new president] was an important factor in the fall of his government. Concerned with the dangers inherent in social revolution and its impact on United States [economic] interests on the island, American policy was aimed at preservation of the *status quo*. . . . [The] personal representative of President Roosevelt played a major role in bringing the revolution to a halt. From then the revolution became chiefly political, not social and economic. One cannot help wondering whether or not events in Cuba would have taken a different course if the United States at that time had favored needed social and economic changes in Latin America. . . . It is valid to pose such a question, for in some respects the Cuban phenomenon of the 1950's was simply the reincarnation of the revolutionary process interrupted in the 1930's.

Castro leads a revolt against Cuba's dictator.

There was no question, however, about the growing harshness of the long and very business-minded dictatorship of the mulatto president, Colonel Fulgencio Batista (fool-*hain'*syoh bah-*tees'*tah). In the 1950's students were again assuming the traditional role of opposing a dictatorship of old men. On July 26, 1953, a former student leader, Fidel Castro, led a daring but unsuccessful attack on the army barracks in Santiago de Cuba. His passionate statement, "History will absolve me!" at his trial made him famous throughout Cuba. In 1956 he secretly returned to Cuba from exile in Mexico. In the rugged mountains of the Sierra Maestra (*syey'*rah mah-*eys'*trah) he brought together and directed a guerrilla band that the well-equipped Batista forces could not track down. Castro was following in the footsteps of a master guerrilla leader, Mao Tse-tung of Communist China. His strictly disciplined bearded rebels paid peasants and shopkeepers for supplies. They treated prisoners and women with strict morality and in this way won support among middle- and upper-class elements that had been backing the Batista dictatorship. Moreover, Castro's vague agrarian reform program sounded patriotic. It promised in some way to break up the large sugar plantations that produced nearly half the world's sugar. Since over half the billion dollars invested in Cuban industry was Anglo-American, many Cubans —even property owners—were unhappy about Cuba's status as an "economic colony" of the United States.

A victorious Castro institutes reforms.

The terrorist tactics of Batista's regime finally turned public opinion in the United States against the Cuban dictator. In April, 1958, the Department of State announced the end of arms shipments to Batista. This act of reverse intervention contributed to the collapse of Batista's army. On January 1, 1959, Fidel Castro became the head of a free Cuba.

The personality of Fidel Castro has stamped the first decade of the Cuban Revolution. In his words: "Revolution means the destruction of privilege, the disappearance of exploitation, the creation of a just society." In the first hundred days of his regime Castro nationalized foreign holdings without compensating their owners, replaced the professional army and navy with a voluntary national militia, and launched a successful campaign against illiteracy and racial discrimination. Castro also enforced rigid standards of honesty among government employees and initiated national programs in adult education, health care, and housing. As the next step in the revolution, Castro's Minister of Planning, Ernesto ("Che") Guevara (gey-*bah'*rah) advocated rapid industrialization. This soon gave way to a more realistic concern with developing a varied agriculture, increasing the sugar crop, and stepping up bauxite production.

Castro's policies arouse protest both at home and abroad.

Castro's sweeping reforms raised a storm of protest in Cuba and in the United States. In Cuba, Castro's repression of criticism turned the revolution into political dictatorship. When he not only spurned American economic aid but declared himself a Marxist-Leninist, the United States halted trade with and aid to Cuba. Despite the drab years of economic squeeze that followed, Castro was undismayed.

Latin America Today

UNITED STATES

Gulf
of
Mexico

Monterrey

MEXICO

Mexico

ATLANTIC

OCEAN

BAHAMA ISLANDS

Havana

CUBA

DOMINICAN
REP.

PUERTO RICO (U.S.)

San Juan

HAITI

JAMAICA

VIRGIN IS. (U.S.)

BR. HOND.

GUATEMALA   HONDURAS

EL SALVADOR

NICARAGUA

Caribbean   Sea

BARBADOS

Port-of-Spain

PACIFIC

OCEAN

COSTA RICA

PANAMA

Caracas

TRINIDAD-TOBAGO

VENEZUELA

Bogotá

Rio Orinoco

COLOMBIA

Georgetown

Paramaribo

GUIANA

GUYANA

SURINAM
(Du.)

Cayenne

HIGHLANDS

FRENCH
GUIANA

Equator

Quito

ECUADOR

Rio   Amazonas

ILHA DE
MARAJO

A
N
D
E
S

PERU

Lima

B R A Z I L

Rio   Amazonas

HIGHLANDS

Titicaca

LA PAZ

BOLIVIA

Sucre

MATO

GROSSO

Brasilia

PARAGUAY

Rio Paraná

BRAZILIAN

GRAN
CHACO

Asunción

Rio de Janeiro

São Paulo

A R G E N T I N A

C
H
I
L
E

Santiago

URUGUAY

Buenos Aires

Montevideo

Rio de la Plata

FALKLAND IS. (Br.)

Strait of
Magellan

U.S.

Miami

Nassau

BAHAMA ISLANDS

Gulf of Mexico

Havana

CUBA

ORIENTE
PROVINCE

DOMINICAN
REP.

Bay of Pigs

Santiago

Guantánamo Bay

HAITI

Santo
Domingo

BR. Honduras

Belize

JAMAICA

Kingston

Port-au-Prince

GUATEMALA

Guatemala

HONDURAS

Tegucigalpa

Caribbean   Sea

San Salvador

EL SALVADOR

NICARAGUA

Managua

CANAL ZONE (U.S.)

TRINIDAD-TOBAGO

COSTA
RICA

San José

Panama

VENEZUELA

PANAMA

COLOMBIA

839

He had no use for "yanqui (*yahn'*kee) imperialism." In marathon speeches he denounced the United States, reaffirmed his support of communism, and swore to export his revolution to all of Latin America.

Thousands of professional and propertied Cubans defected to the United States, where they worked to build a landing force to overthrow Castro. In 1961 the United States backed a disastrous invasion attempt by these exiles. President Kennedy had been led to believe that, given tactical troops to lead them, the people of Cuba would rise against the Castro regime. Instead, Castro's revolutionary militia captured the invaders. Few people in Cuba made any move to support the invasion. The flight of nearly half a million Cubans from their native land had permitted Fidel Castro to fill important posts with young men and women zealously loyal to him, the caudillo. These idealistic leaders have helped maintain a pro-revolutionary fervor in the island.

In 1962 Cuba became involved in cold war politics when the United States learned that Soviet missiles were based in Cuba. President Kennedy's demand for their immediate withdrawal (page 735) blocked Moscow's attempt to gain a foothold in the western hemisphere.

The Cuban Revolution makes headway. Castro's attempts to build socialism have been hampered by an economic boycott. Many nations, principally the United States, refuse to have any commercial dealings with Castro's Cuba. While the island is said to be receiving considerable Soviet aid, its government owes no allegiance to Moscow. Castro has skillfully maneuvered to prevent Cuba from becoming a Soviet satellite. The revolution is raising a new generation of idealistic Cubans—Castroist, socialist, and anti-American. Their cry of *"Cuba sí, yanqui no!"* has been taken up by other revolutionary groups. Castro's political power appears to be unchecked by the militia, the police, the party, or rival leaders. He seems to have kept the popular touch and to enjoy the support of the Cuban nation.

CHECK-UP

1. What reasons help explain the underdevelopment of Latin America?

2. What did Díaz do for Mexico? Fail to do? Why did a revolt break out in 1910?

3. What were the chief provisions of Mexico's revolutionary constitution? What have been the lasting results of the Mexican Revolution?

4. How did caudillos attempt to modernize Brazil? Argentina? Why were Vargas and Perón ousted?

5. What are the characteristics of the military dictatorships in Brazil and Argentina? Of socialist nationalism in Peru?

6. What problems stem from rapid population growth in Latin America? From controversy over the role of the Church?

7. What are the trends in Latin American literature? The fine arts? How has modernization changed traditional social outlooks?

8. Why did Batista lose his grip in Cuba? What were Castro's goals?

9. What reforms did Castro inaugurate? Why did these reforms arouse opposition in Cuba? In the United States? What were the results?

Inter-American Relations

Until the Second World War, relations between the United States and Latin America were largely limited to states bordering on the Caribbean Sea. From Washington's point of view the Latin American republics were either sisters (equals) or children (inferiors). Most frequently, the latter view prevailed. This led Latin Americans to ask, is the United States the sister she claims to be or the tough guy carrying a "big stick"?

The Monroe Doctrine is a warning to Europe. Inter-American diplomacy begins with the Monroe Doctrine in 1823, the year before the Battle of Ayacucho. The United States was already forty years old. Without consulting her new sister republics, the United States seemed to tell the Old World powers: Keep your hands off the New World, and we will keep ours off the Old. Because the United States lacked the military strength to prevent European interference in the Americas, it was the British navy which gave the Doctrine teeth. Great Britain did not want to lose her booming trade with the former Iberian colonies. The British navy could prevent Spain, Portugal, or France from transporting troops to reconquer colonies in this hemisphere.

The Mexican War and the war with Spain are examples of United States intervention. The Monroe Doctrine said nothing about the United States itself meddling in the affairs of the American republics. In 1846 Mexico went to war when the United States annexed the former Mexican province of Texas. The Anglo-Americans then carried out what the Mexicans to this day call "the invasion." Mexican leaders bungled the war and Mexico lost half of her territory. At the time Representative Abraham Lincoln said: "The marching of an army into the midst of a peaceful Mexican settlement, frightening the inhabitants away, leaving their growing crops to destruction, to you may appear a perfectly amicable, peaceful, unprovoking procedure, but it does not appear [so] to us." His was a minority view, for most Anglo-Americans regarded the expansion of the United States as their "Manifest Destiny."

The Monroe Doctrine took on new meaning in 1898, when the United States intervened in Cuba, which was at last winning its long and bloody War of Independence. The United States declared war on Spain, blockaded Havana and Santiago, invaded Oriente province, and routed the Spanish troops. On New Year's Day, 1899 (exactly 60 years before the victory of Fidel Castro's revolutionaries), Havana witnessed the ceremony of Spanish surrender. The United States forces, however, denied the Cubans the patriotic satisfaction of seeing their own troops parade through their own capital. The United States did not take outright control of Cuba, but reserved to itself the "right to intervene" in Cuban affairs "for the preservation of Cuban independence and the maintenance of a government adequate for the protection of life, property, and individual liberty." It also built a naval base at Guantánamo (gwahn-*tah'*-nah-moh) Bay. With its great fleet, the "Colossus of the North" could now keep the Caribbean safe for Anglo-America.

United States soldiers and journalists discovered that the standard of living was low in Cuba. Malnutrition and illness from tropical disease were widespread. The African descent of a third of the Cuban population troubled the race-conscious white Americans. Cubans were not brothers after all, but children needing a firm hand to guide them. United States medical science removed yellow fever and malaria from Cuba. Anglo-Americans increased their investments in sugar and tobacco plantations.

"Gunboat diplomacy" is a more subtle form of United States intervention. Uncle Sam's paternalism was not limited to the Caribbean. President Theodore Roosevelt, who believed in the Manifest Destiny of the United States, declared: "Chronic wrongdoing may in America . . . require intervention by some civilized power. . . . The United States [will act as] . . . an international police power." The United States encouraged Panama to revolt from Colombia and in return gained land for the Panama Canal Zone. A weak, newly formed nation, Panama had no choice but to grant the United States a favorable long-term lease placing the Canal Zone under United States control. To ensure stable conditions for investment in Nicaragua, Haiti, and the Dominican Republic,

United States marines seized customs houses and saw to it that foreign debts were paid and the countryside pacified by a caudillo. This practice was called "gunboat diplomacy." Washington hoped that political stability imposed upon "sister" republics would bring about their economic prosperity. President Wilson's order for United States intervention in Veracruz, Mexico, in 1914, however, was not intended to protect United States economic interests but to punish a government it regarded as bad (undemocratic). These acts of intervention, whether or not they served the interests of the Latin American country involved, created great hostility in Latin America and damaged inter-American relations.

The Good Neighbor Policy is introduced.
In 1933 President Franklin Roosevelt introduced the Good Neighbor Policy, aimed at treating the sister republics as equals. A feeling of goodwill began to appear in inter-American politics. When President Cárdenas expropriated the foreign-held oil industry in Mexico in 1938, he was quick to promise the United States ambassador that foreign owners would be compensated, and Washington decided not to intervene. During the Second World War, only distant Argentina held out against the United States anti-fascist policy. Brazil, traditionally a diplomatic friend of the United States, sent an expeditionary force to Italy.

The Organization of American States calls for equal treatment of nations.
In 1948 in Bogotá (boh-goh-*tah'*), the capital of Colombia, the Organization of American States (OAS) was established. For the first time United States diplomats agreed to outlaw intervention in this hemisphere:

Article 15. No state or group of states has the right to intervene directly or indirectly for any reason whatsoever in the internal or external affairs of any other state.

Article 17. The territory of a state is inviolable; it may not be the object, even temporarily, of military occupation or of any other measures of force taken by another state directly or indirectly on any grounds whatsoever.

During the 1950's, as the cold war intensified, the United States feared communist subversion in the Caribbean area. These fears were magnified when Castro gained control of Cuba and declared it a communist nation. Therefore, the United States felt justified in intervening in the internal affairs of Latin American nations. Sometimes intervention had OAS approval, sometimes not. This policy continued into the 1960's, with direct intervention in Communist Cuba (1961) and the Dominican Republic (1965). There were also instances of indirect intervention. In 1964, when a military revolt overthrew the constitutional president in Brazil, the new government received recognition from Washington only a day later. The worldwide commitments of the United States did not permit Washington to take any chances that Brazil might go the way of Cuba.

Castro tries to export his revolution.
Castro had pledged to carry social revolution to all areas in Latin America which suffered from "yanqui imperialism" and exploitation of the poor by rich landowners. *Fidelistas* (fee-dey-*lees'*tahs, followers of Castro) resorted to terrorism and guerrilla attacks in Venezuela, but the national army remained loyal to the elected president. In the Bolivian Highlands, "Che" Guevara failed to stir the Quechua Indians to revolt. Why? Thanks to the Bolivian Revolution of 1952, poor Bolivians believed that their new regime was different from the old white ruling group; it seemed to have their interests at heart. Moreover, it had the backing of the United States, and United States counter-insurgency forces participated in the manhunt for Guevara in Bolivia's mountains. Killed in 1967 under circumstances which are still disputed, "Che" has become a martyr to idealistic students everywhere. Fidel remains a hero to intellectuals throughout Latin America, and the

Cuban Revolution itself is still regarded as a model of social revolution. On the other hand, the United States has shown that it will not tolerate another Cuba, at least in the Caribbean. This is clearly seen in the hard (military) line adopted by President Johnson when United States troops intervened in the Dominican Republic in 1965. This hard line replaced the soft (economic) line introduced by President Kennedy in 1961.

The Alliance for Progress promises much but the results are disappointing.

In 1958 President Juscelino Kubitschek of Brazil suggested a massive economic aid program for Latin America. Excited by the idea, which seemed to him to promise widespread social reform without violence, President Kennedy announced an Alliance for Progress. The Alliance was designed to provide joint United States-Latin American aid to solve socio-economic problems, win over anti-United States intellectuals and engineers, and frighten the elite into granting land and tax reform. This social reform was intended to prevent the outbreak of the Cuban-type revolutions predicted by the communists. Kennedy wanted to foster political stability through economic reform.

As it turned out, however, the Alliance met with small success. Relatively little of the financial aid that was sent filtered through the hands of government officials to reach those who needed it. United States investments took out more money than flowed in through the Alliance. Moreover, investors in both the United States and Latin America hesitated to risk their capital in unstable countries where property might be nationalized. In Latin America professional people were too suspicious of the Yankee dollar to cooperate. The landed elite, fearing that any agrarian reform would start eating away their privileges, also refused to cooperate. The urban elite saw no need to tax themselves, sensing that Washington was so alarmed by Castro's revolution that it would go on pouring money into Latin America whether they cooperated or not. The judgment of the urban elite was close to the mark. The Alliance is quietly being dropped by the Nixon administration. The "soft" line of economic aid did not bring about the desired socio-economic reforms.

The United States intervenes in the Dominican Republic.

In 1930 Rafael Trujillo (troo-*hee'*-yoh) was elected President of the Dominican Republic, made himself dictator, and for years continued to run the country for the benefit of his family and friends. The Dominican caudillo, a creation of "gunboat diplomacy," imposed order and brought about apparent prosperity in his turbulent country. Thirty years of order found favor in Washington. But it deprived the Dominicans of their civil rights and lined Trujillo's pockets with millions of dollars.

In 1961 the bloodthirsty dictator was assassinated, and a wave of terror swept the island. OAS investigators arrived to restore enough order for holding elections. An exiled intellectual was elected, but Trujillo's backers refused to accept the new regime. As the situation deteriorated, the aging generals and landowners applied to the United States for help. They convinced Washington that a Cuban situation was at hand. In April, 1965, President Lyndon Johnson suddenly ordered airborne forces to occupy key positions in the Dominican Republic. Johnson made clear that the United States would never "let the communists set up any government in the western hemisphere." He acted without the knowledge or, later, the consent of the OAS. In other words, the United States had returned to the hard line established by Theodore Roosevelt.

The Latin American members of the OAS were enraged that the United States had intervened. To most, the principle of nonintervention loomed larger than the policy of anti-communism. Thus the misunderstanding between the United States and her sister republics continues. The United States finds it hard to understand why Latin Americans tolerate caudillism and seem unable to develop stable governments. Latin Americans, for their part, cannot be sure whether the United States will treat them as equals (Alliance for Progress) or as inferiors (intervention in Cuba and the Dominican Republic).

Summing Up

In the late eighteenth century rising taxes on the poor, restrictions on trade, French and American revolutionary doctrines, and growing British interest in trade with the Iberian colonies contributed to growing unrest in Latin America. Unrest led to revolts, which eventually overcame class jealousies and racial antagonisms and won the independence of the Spanish colonies in 1824. Brazil became independent of Portugal through the action of its king, Pedro I.

The new ruling class (creoles) had little experience in government and no desire to upset the existing social structure. Caudillism, personalism, legalism, bureaucracy, and corruption came to characterize government in the Latin American republics. Since Latin America's independence from Spain, the Church has lost much of its wealth and prestige, and today conservatives and radicals disagree over the Church's role in society. The separation of Church and state in Mexico in 1857 led to civil war, foreign intervention, and the Porfirian dictatorship that modernized parts of the economy.

Latin America has great potential in human and natural resources, but it has not yet been fully realized. Geography, single-product economies, social stagnation, and economic domination by foreign powers greatly hinder development. Nationalist sentiments and popular support have allowed caudillos to expropriate private (often foreign-owned) property, to promote domestic industries, and to set up social welfare programs. All governments, whether rightist or leftist, are confronted with the problem of a rapidly growing population. Mexico has seen the most sweeping reforms. The Mexican Revolution, which began in 1910 and in some senses continues today, resulted in a constitution providing for agricultural collectives, national ownership of underground resources, labor unions and an eight-hour day, free and compulsory secular education, and prohibition of Church ownership of property and engagement in politics. In one decade, 1959–1969, Cuba appears to have gone beyond Mexico with its socialist revolution; it is still too soon to predict how much of an impact it will have on the rest of Latin America.

In inter-American relations the United States has frequently played a dominant role. Intervention by the United States—both political and economic—in Latin American affairs has caused much bitterness, and only in recent decades has the "Colossus of the North" begun to regard consultation and cooperation as more productive than demands and intervention. Today Latin America's rate of social change may well be the most rapid in the world. The firm control the ruling elite has long exercised over the state, the Church, and the economy is threatened by new outlooks and increasing demands for greater individual well-being and more political rights. Latin American intellectuals continue to deplore neo-colonialism and to dream of complete independence for their nations.

844

Chapter Highlights

Can you explain?

servile	llaneros	patrón	"gunboat diplomacy"
peons	mestizos	mulattoes	single-product economy
creoles	junta	legalism	bureaucracy
rurales	Fidelistas	caudillism	socialist nationalism

Can you identify?

Pedro II	Haiti	Tupac-Amarú	Organization of American States
Vargas	Díaz	Tiradentes	Alliance for Progress
Trujillo	Ayacucho	Bolívar	Monroe Doctrine
"Che" Guevara	Rosas	Batista	War of the Reform
San Martín	Juárez	Portales	Toussaint L'Ouverture
Castro	Perón	Zapata	Good Neighbor Policy
Hidalgo			Wars of Independence

What do you think?

1. Why did early Latin American efforts to achieve independence fail? Why were Bolívar and San Martín eventually successful?

2. Why has caudillism typified much of Latin American politics?

3. Why did Mexican liberals separate Church and state?

4. Why is Latin America underdeveloped?

5. Why have Latin American countries nationalized foreign-owned mining and petroleum industries? What is the reaction of foreign investors?

6. Why are the rural poor flocking to the big cities? Is there a similar movement in the United States?

7. How has the social position of mestizos and mulattoes changed since colonial times? Why?

8. Why was Castro's revolt successful? Which of his policies were unpopular in the United States? Why?

9. Contrast Latin American views on the Monroe Doctrine, "gunboat diplomacy," and intervention with those held in the United States. How do you account for the differences in outlook?

10. Why do most members of the OAS attach greater importance to the principle of nonintervention than to the policy of anti-communism?

11. Has the United States treated the countries of Latin America as sisters (equals) or as children (inferiors)?

Green forests, open meadows, clear lakes, and fresh air have always been a source of inspiration for man (left). But today unwise use of resources and overpopulation threaten the environment and endanger man's well-being. Thousands die of hunger every day (top, above), and millions live in poverty, surrounded by ugliness and congestion (above).

Problems and Perspectives

CHAPTER FOCUS

Underdevelopment and Overpopulation
Science and Technology: A Mixed Blessing
Violence and Alienation

Before the twentieth century has run its course, it has already received various labels—the Age of Violence, the Age of Overkill, the Age of Fear, the Age of Anxiety, the Age of Insecurity, the Age of Alienation. Clearly this has not been a happy age. Despite extraordinary scientific and technological accomplishments, twentieth-century man feels troubled and insecure. The memory of two world wars haunts his past; the fear of nuclear destruction darkens his future. Population experts warn us that we are reaching the point of no return. If we do not starve to death, the soaring population will make civilized living impossible. Ecologists warn us that we may choke to death by breathing air polluted by fumes from cars and factories, damage our body tissues by eating food contaminated by pesticides, and witness the destruction of forests and wildlife needed to maintain the balance in nature without which life on Earth cannot survive. The future of civilized life or even of life itself depends on how mankind copes with the problems of underdevelopment and overpopulation, expanding technology, and violence and alienation.

Underdevelopment and Overpopulation

The developing nations face great problems. In this unit we have seen that enormous challenges confront the developing nations in the "Third World"—Africa, Asia, and Latin America. Their people, burdened by hunger, disease, poor housing, and debt, have an annual per-capita income of less than $150. They can expect to live ten to thirty years less than people in the developed lands. In some developing areas nearly half the children die before reaching school age. Over 65 per cent of the people in the developing nations cannot read or write and thus have little hope of improving their economic status. Surrounded by misery and despair, haunted by the threat of famine, they flock to already overcrowded cities, hoping to find work. Instead, the majority find themselves living in even more unendurable conditions. Writes Charles Abrams:

Lack of privacy, exposure to contagion [disease], and social disintegration are only a few of the by-products of a life with almost no room to breathe, ail, or die. . . .

In Panama, where shelters bulge at the seams with as many as twenty individuals living in a room 15 by 15 feet, sleeping is done in relays. . . .

In a single shophouse in Singapore, I saw families of six to eight people facing life in airless, windowless rooms 7 by 10 feet, with . . . children sleeping on the roach-ridden floor. . . .

. . . more than a billion people in Africa, Asia, and Latin America, or roughly half the population of these continents, are homeless or live in housing that is described by the United Nations as a menace to health and an affront to human dignity. . . . Many families pay so much for the privilege of bedding down on a floor . . . that little is left for the bare essentials of life. And as the surge to the cities goes on, the competition for space will become keener, rents will rise further, squatting and overcrowding will increase, and the effort to carry on some semblance of family life will become less and less hopeful.

For centuries the poor of Asia, Africa, and Latin America had been resigned to poverty. It was the only life they knew. But today movies, television, radio, and the press depict the incomparably better living conditions in developed lands, and the strident words of social reformers have aroused the people to demand immediate improvements in their standard of living. World peace may depend on how successfully the Third World combats poverty. Concludes David Horowitz, Israeli expert on economic development:

In the last twenty years, no shooting war has occurred in the developed world, while the nations of Asia, Africa, and Latin America are seething with disquiet and are tormented by internal and external collisions that threaten mankind with total conflagration [conflict.] Well over a dozen wars and revolutions have exploded during that period in Asia, Africa, and Latin America, . . . the direct consequences of despair and despondency.

The nations of the Third World are trying desperately to raise living standards by adopting western science and technology. But they face staggering obstacles. Most are short of capital, skilled workers and administrators, engineers and scientists. Writing on the world economy, Richard Bailey notes:

The extent of the problem can be seen from the fact that in some African countries the proportion of engineers and scientists is one per 10,000 of the population. Elsewhere among the developing countries the proportion may be as high as one per thousand. In Western Europe by contrast there is one scientist or engineer to every hundred of the population, and the remaining ninety-nine are not, as in the poorer countries, either illiterate or at best educated to primary school standards.

Modernizing agriculture may be the key to improving living conditions. At one time the developing nations thought the solution to their problems lay in immediate industrialization. Today they realize that they must concentrate on improving agriculture first. Before developing industries, they must be able to feed their populations. Modernizing agriculture thus seems the key to improving the standard of living in these nations. Greater production through more efficient methods of farming and the development of diversified crops may go far toward improving the economy.

Some experts believe that agricultural modernization is blocked by farmers' unwillingness to give up traditional ways, but American agricultural expert T. W. Schultz attributes agricultural backwardness to "the lack of economic opportunities that are rewarding to farmers." Because farmers receive low prices for their products—often as a result of government price controls—they are reluctant to produce more. Moreover, farmers pay high prices for fertilizers, insecticides, tools, machinery, and other ingredients of modernization. Third, while governments have put much effort, planning and

capital into industry, agriculture until recently has tended to be neglected. Not enough capital and energy have gone into schooling to raise the level of agricultural skills, to improve communication and transportation facilities in the countryside, and to build irrigation works. Farmers, says Schultz, are shrewd, hardheaded people. "Whenever there is a real payoff, they respond. We should see to it that our projects and programs create opportunities that induce farmers to increase production because it pays them to do so."

While attitudes and traditions that are centuries old do not die easily, there are many examples of nonwesterners adopting improved techniques when they are convinced that benefits will follow. Pressures from government leaders and increased education are also weakening some of the attitudes that hinder modernization.

Many nonwesterners do not want modernization. Despite the growing use of western technology, many nonwesterners still cling to traditional ways. Many peoples in the developing nations are not motivated by a desire to make money and to get ahead. They are convinced that man can do little to improve his lot in life. In fact, they often criticize westerners for being too competitive, too concerned with money and business. Often the most capable nonwesterners turn their backs on business, preferring careers as professors, lawyers, or government officials.

In other words, it should be realized that many nonwesterners do not want to modernize or to become westernized. They honestly prefer traditional ways, which provide them with a feeling of security. Moreover, they believe that western ways can only worsen the quality of life. Conditions in the more advanced nations seem to them far from idyllic. They hear of class antagonisms, race riots, increasing violence, urban slums, a deteriorating environment, and personal insecurity, and wonder if modernization is worth the price. This view is expressed in the following poem written by an African intellectual, Dei Anang of Ghana:

But whither bound,
O Africa
Oh whither bound?

Backward?
To days of drums
And festal dances in the shade
Of sun-kist palms;
Backward?
To untutored days
When maid was ever chaste
And lad abhorred unhallowed ways
For dread of ancient gods:
Backward?
To dark thatched huts
Where kindness reigned
And solace dwelt
Backward to SUPERSTITION?

Or forward?
Forward! To what?
The slums where man is dumped upon man;
Where penury
And misery
Have made their hapless homes,
And all is dark and drear?
Forward! To what?
The factory
To grind hard hours
In an inhuman mill,
In one ceaseless spell?

Forward! To what?
To the reeking round
Of medieval crimes,
Where the greedy hawks
Of *Aryan stock*
Prey with bombs and guns
On men of *lesser breeds?*
Forward to CIVILIZATION!*

One can understand and sympathize with nonwesterners who cling to tradition and who reject the modern ways of the West. But can traditional ways solve the problems of poverty, hunger, and disease—problems made worse by an exploding population?

* "Whither Africa" by Dei Anang in G. McLeod Bryan, *Whither Africa* (Richmond, Va.: John Knox Press, 1961; © M. E. Bratcher 1961). Reprinted by permission.

Spiraling birth rates are causing a population explosion. Despite significant advances in industrialization and agricultural production, the developing nations may never escape from poverty. The spiraling birth rate cancels out virtually all gains in the economy, for the developing lands do not produce enough food to feed their rapidly expanding populations. For example, from 1960 to 1965, food production in Latin America increased by six per cent, a gain offset by a population jump of eleven per cent. Besides being unable to feed their people, the developing nations are unable to provide jobs, schooling, and homes for the added millions.

The world's population explosion, particularly serious in the poor nations, has become one of mankind's most urgent problems. At the time of Christ there were about 250 million people in the world. By 1850 the population had reached one billion. Just 75 years later the population had doubled to two billion. In 1962 it had soared to three billion and should reach four billion before 1980 and more than six billion by the end of the century.

Every day the world population increases by about 180,000 people. The rate of increase since 1850 has been fantastic. Robert McNamara, President of the World Bank, warns:

A child born today, living on into his 70's, would know a world of 15 billion. His grandson would share the planet with 60 billion. In six and a half centuries from now—the same insignificant period of time separating us from the poet Dante—there would be one human being standing on every square foot of land on earth: a fantasy of horror that even [Dante's description of hell] could not match.

In the past famine, disease, and war kept down the world's population. But in the past 150 years, advances in medicine and improvements in sanitation have greatly reduced deaths from disease. Modern methods of communication and transportation have enabled food and

World Population

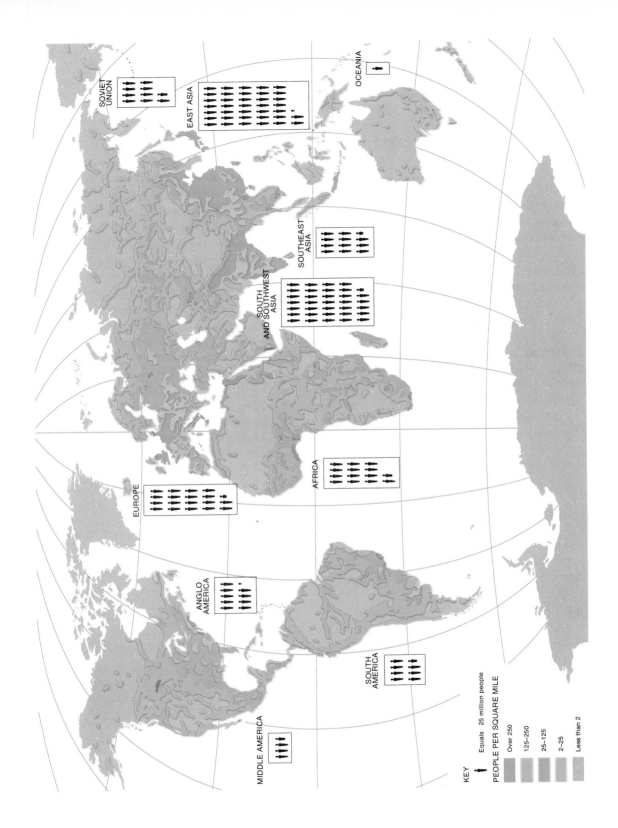

SOVIET UNION

EAST ASIA

OCEANIA

SOUTHEAST ASIA

SOUTH AND SOUTHWEST ASIA

EUROPE

AFRICA

ANGLO AMERICA

SOUTH AMERICA

MIDDLE AMERICA

KEY

Equals 25 million people

PEOPLE PER SQUARE MILE

Over 250

125–250

25–125

2–25

Less than 2

medical supplies to be rushed into areas threatened with famine or epidemics. As a result millions of people who in the past would have perished have survived and reproduced. The number of deaths caused by warfare is not large enough to slow down significantly the rate of population increase. In fact, despite the millions killed during World War II, the world population actually increased between 1939 and 1945.

Overpopulation may cause worldwide famine and exhaustion of resources. Presently some 12,000 people die of hunger every day. Some observers believe that the figure will increase considerably as the population continues to expand. In 1968 British scientist and writer C. P. Snow declared: "We may be moving—perhaps in ten years—into large-scale famine. Many millions of people in the poor countries are going to starve to death before your eyes. We shall see them doing so upon our television sets." Food experts warn of famines of unimaginable horror sweeping across Asia, Africa, and Latin America.

Besides starvation, the pressures of population could have still other distressing consequences for mankind. Our water, mineral, and forest resources are by no means limitless and are already being used up at alarming rates. Moreover, there is no balance in their use; an industrialized nation uses far more of the world's resources than does a developing nation. The United States alone, with only a sixth of the world's population, uses over 50 per cent of the world's resources. As other nations become more industrialized, their needs will increase. Clearly, there is not enough to go around. The demands of an exploding population can deplete our planet of vital resources before the year 2000.

Can anything be done to ward off these disasters? Some experts are hopeful. They base their hopes on scientists who are experimenting with new ways of increasing food production by "farming" the seas, finding ways to irrigate deserts, or developing synthetic foods. Some agricultural experts believe that the race against famine is being won. They talk glowingly of an agricultural revolution resulting from better fertilizers, improved pesticides, and recently developed high-yield cereal grains. Because they often enable the farmer to double his yield per acre, new varieties of rice and wheat are called "miracle grains." The use of high-yield wheat seeds in Pakistan increased wheat production by 67 per cent over a four-year period and enabled Pakistan to become self-sufficient in wheat. Other nations which have converted to the miracle wheat have achieved similar extraordinary gains. What has happened with wheat is also taking place with miracle rice.

Concludes William S. Gaud, administrator of the United States Agency for International Development:

Record yields, harvests of unprecedented size, and crops now in the ground demonstrate that throughout much of the developing world—and particularly in Asia—we are on the verge of an agricultural revolution. I call it the Green Revolution. . . . World agricultral production in 1967 set a new record, and the less-developed countries accounted for most of the increase. Total agricultural output in the developing nations rose by seven to eight per cent over 1966. . . . The world is on the brink of an unprecedented opportunity. The critical food problem of the next twenty years can be solved.

But not all food and population experts are hopeful about averting a catastrophic famine. William and Paul Paddock conclude:

In reviewing all the proposed panaceas [cures] for increasing food production during the next decade, the conclusion is clear: there is no possibility of improving agriculture in the hungry nations soon enough to avert famine.

Thus the amount of food per person will continue to decline in the future as it has in the past few years. No panacea is at hand to increase the productivity of the land, just as no miracle will arrest the population explosion. Those who would turn their hopes to the chemist and his synthesis of food . . . are speaking of another century, not this one.

Science and Technology: A Mixed Blessing

Science has created incredibly destructive weapons. While science and technology hold out immense promises for man, they are also the source of some of his most serious problems, including (1) the creation of weapons of destruction, (2) the upsetting and despoiling of the natural environment, and (3) the threat to freedom and human dignity.

Scientists have created weapons of destruction that stagger the mind. The atomic bomb that devastated Hiroshima and killed more than 78,000 people, leaving thousands of others with horrible skin burns and painful radiation sickness, has been superseded by the far more destructive hydrogen bomb. Nations with nuclear capacity are feverishly piling up nuclear weapons as a deterrent to aggression on the part of other nuclear powers.

Besides stockpiling nuclear weapons, nations are conducting experiments in chemical and biological warfare. Relatively inexpensive and easy to manufacture, chemical and biological weapons have an appeal to nations aspiring to great power status but too poor to afford expensive nuclear weapons. Scientists have developed deadly nerve gases, chemical weapons that cause temporary mental disorders, and plans for germ warfare that would involve introducing deadly bacteria into reservoirs, food-processing plants, and ventilation systems. Millions would die in the resulting epidemics.

Reckless use of technology may destroy our environment. Scientists who study the relationship between forms of life and the natural environment are called *ecologists*. Their message is simple and frightening. If we do not stop overusing and misusing our air, waters, forests, minerals, plants, and wildlife, Earth will become a dying planet.

The demands of an industrial civilization combined with human greed and carelessness are destroying the natural environment. Wildlife, forest, and mineral resources are diminishing at alarming rates. Fumes from motor vehicles and industries pollute the air and increase the danger of respiratory diseases. Industrial and consumer wastes pollute the waters, have already killed off all life in some rivers and lakes, and can contaminate our food. Pesticides carried into streams and rivers and eventually into oceans have had harmful effects upon fish and birds and have found their way into the food we eat.

Modern technology threatens man's freedom and dignity. Modern technology has made possible the totalitarian state in which millions of people can be subjected to the will of the leader and the party. Telephones, teletype, radio, and television enable dictators to manipulate the emotions and control the minds of the masses, to transmit orders instantaneously to obedient bureaucrats, and to regiment all aspects of life. Computers permit the state to keep extensive and revealing files on its subjects; electronic devices so tiny the average person would not notice their existence enable officials to spy on suspected "enemies of the state" without their knowledge.

Even in states that preserve political liberty, technology still may threaten human dignity. To produce goods rapidly and economically, to administer corporations and government agencies efficiently, many jobs—from file clerk to assembly-line worker—have been created. These jobs are usually boring and give employees no sense of pride in or satisfaction from their work. There is the danger that people doing such work may be treated as impersonal objects, without regard for their human feelings and needs.

Used properly, science and technology can significantly reduce world poverty, lengthen man's life span, and provide him with time to improve his mind and talents. Used irresponsibly, science and technology can enslave man's spirit and even destroy his planet.

Soaring violence marks the twentieth century.
The twentieth century has been called the Age of Violence. Two world wars have taken the lives of millions of people. Scores of smaller wars and revolutions have added to the death toll. There is no form of torture that man has not used against his fellow man in our century. Between them, the United States and Soviet Russia have enough nuclear weapons to kill everybody in the world many times over, and developing nations that cannot properly feed their people spend tens of millions for modern weapons. Crimes of violence are commonplace in many nations.

Why is man so violent, so aggressive? Some thinkers believe that aggressiveness is an instinct, a part of man's nature that cannot be erased. British psychologist Anthony Storr writes:

With the exception of certain rodents, no other vertebrate habitually destroys members of his own species. . . . [Man alone] takes positive pleasure in the exercise of cruelty upon another of his own kind. . . . The somber fact is that we are the cruelest and most ruthless species that has ever walked the earth. . . . Although we may recoil in horror when we read in newspapers or history books of the atrocities committed by man upon man, we know in our hearts that each one of us harbors within himself those same savage impulses to murder, to torture, and to war. . . .

Other thinkers argue that conditions within society and man's traditions and values—rather than a destructive inner impulse—encourage violence. Children learn very early that to run from a fight is to be labeled a coward. In school they are taught to respect military commanders and war heroes. They are told they have a duty to fight for the nation. On television and in the movies they are fed a steady diet of violence.

Still other critics point out that man behaves aggressively because he finds himself in unpleasant, frustrating circumstances. The tensions of living in an overcrowded, highly competitive society cause people to react violently. Experiments with rats reveal that, despite an abundant food supply, under conditions of overcrowding mother rats neglect their young and there is constant fighting. It is very likely that human beings crowded together in cities respond in the same way.

Violence is often committed by people who feel alone, hurt, unloved, unimportant, unappreciated, and powerless. Rejected by society, treated as outsiders, and without hope of bettering their condition in life, such people use violence as a form of revenge, as a means of striking back at society.

Dr. Jerome D. Frank reminds us that violence satisfies

. . . certain important psychological needs of men, especially young [men]. The role of warrior, much esteemed in many societies, affords a means of establishing a feeling of manhood as well as an outlet for aggressiveness. Many young men seem to need to stretch themselves to the limit, including risking their lives, to achieve a sense of identity. War affords many opportunities for heroism or the altruism of self-sacrifice for others' welfare. It is a break in the humdrum routine of life, a means of supplying the excitement that everyone craves.

"The main trouble with man," says well-known author Arthur Koestler, "appears to be not that he is an excessively aggressive creature, but an excessively loyal one." He is fanatically loyal to "a person, group, race, flag, or system of beliefs." The vast majority of mankind have a "longing to belong" to a social group, to follow "in blind devotion" a set of beliefs. For his group and his beliefs, man will willingly sacrifice himself and slaughter others.

Modern man feels alienated and insecure. For many present-day thinkers, our modern industrial and technological society has ushered in an Age of Alienation. The alienated person feels that there is no place for him in society, that he is an outsider rejected by the human community. He feels alone and unloved. Wounded by his sense of isolation, the alienated man may withdraw from the activities of society. Often apathetic, bored, and hostile, he is, says Eric Fromm, "a stranger to himself, just as his fellow man is a stranger to him."

Our modern technological society has contributed considerably to the sense of alienation. Our large and complex institutions of government and business, says Anthony Storr, cause man to feel "himself to be an unimportant cog in a very large machine." This deprives him of "a proper pride and dignity" in his life and in his work.

We see examples of alienation everywhere. Millions of people are unhappy with their work, perhaps even with their family and friends and themselves. Soaring rates of divorce, mental illness, and drug use are part of the times. Students complain that their studies are unrelated to their lives, that they do not help them to grow into better human beings or to improve their world. With sadness, with anguish, and often with hatred, blacks protest that centuries of slavery and discrimination have robbed them of their manhood and separated them from their African heritage. Millions of Americans have no confidence in their government, do not participate in elections or civic affairs, feel powerless to change things, and look upon the police as enemies. Newspapers report senseless acts of cruelty and violence. People regard each other as strangers. They close their ears to a cry for help; they close their hearts to a cry of pain. Green forests, open meadows, clear lakes, and fresh air have always been a source of pleasure and inspiration for man. But millions of city dwellers are cut off or alienated from nature. Their days are spent amidst ugliness, congestion, noise, decay, and smog. Feeling that he is driven by forces he cannot control, the alienated man finds political parties, business corporations, labor unions, schools, and churches unrelated to him. He feels ineffective in modern society and his frustrations

The insecurity and alienation of twentieth-century man are reflected in modern art movements. Surrealism, like Freudian psychology, tries to express man's subconscious feelings and his dreams. Spanish painter Salvador Dali, a leader in the Surrealist movement, combines superb technique and treatment of light with fantastic subjects. The impact of the disintegrating and grimacing faces of Perspectives (above) is one of shock. It appeals to the emotions rather than to reason, expressing the agony of modern man, who sees his traditional ways and beliefs disappearing.

may turn to resentment against society. Such a man becomes prone to violence.

Increased knowledge of our universe and our past has contributed to this feeling of insecurity. The very vastness of the universe reduces Earth to an insignificant speck, just one of thousands of billions of other heavenly bodies. In the past man felt certain of a place in heaven if he obeyed the teachings of his religion; in our own day we hear talk that God is dead, that in an age of science there is no place for an almighty Creator, an all-knowing Judge, a merciful Father. Religion gave medieval man a sense of security. Unlike man today, he knew who he was, why he was here. Few medieval thinkers would have called life absurd or meaningless, as do many twentieth-century writers.

Is man powerless to improve conditions?

In the nineteenth and early twentieth centuries every advance in science was considered a sign of progress, as something beneficial to man and civilization. Now we realize that in technology we have also created a monster that can deaden our souls, destroy our bodies, and ruin our environment. Ruined forests, dying wildlife, foul air, polluted oceans, an Earth blanketed everywhere by people—is this the future that we are preparing for our children? In highly industrialized societies many feel that man is becoming dominated by machines; he is a series of statistics which are fed into computers to determine his financial standing, his health, his possibilities for success, even his social preferences and his choice of a marriage partner. Can man retain his essential human qualities if corporations, government agencies, schools, and hospitals all treat him as if he were a punched data card being run through a computer?

Somehow we feel that things have gotten out of hand, that we are powerless to control our lives. We are gripped by loneliness and insecurity; we are prisoners of boredom. We rush about madly but go nowhere. Despite our many possessions and the comforts which surround us, the joy of living eludes us. The feeling that our days are empty, our efforts wasted, and our lives without meaning tears at our insides. What a French poet wrote in the fifteenth century well describes our own Age of Insecurity and Alienation:

Why are the times so dark
Men know each other not at all,
But governments quite clearly change
From bad to worse?

Days dead and gone were more worthwhile,
Now what holds sway? Deep gloom and boredom,
Justice and law nowhere to be found.
I know no more where I belong.*

Some thinkers refuse to give in to despair.

Not all thinkers take such a dark view of these times. These thinkers do not believe that man's journey need end in a nuclear disaster or in a planet plundered of its life-giving resources. Man, they say, has the ability to shape his destiny. With his talent for reason, man can find solutions to those problems that threaten to destroy him. With his capacity for love man can improve the quality of human relationships. Although man is surrounded by forces of darkness, reason and love provide him with a ray of hope.

These thinkers say there is still hope for man if he truly and promptly learns to act with reason and judgment, not for the prestige or welfare of one nation, but for the good of all mankind. Ecologists say the environment can be saved—if everyone puts aside his selfish interests and works for the good of our planet, our spaceship Earth. Political thinkers hope that statesmen, recognizing the uselessness of old hatreds and the futility of war, will search for new solutions to international problems. Economists believe that world poverty can be coped with if the developed nations will become aware of their responsibility and provide capital and know-how for the poorer lands. Scientists are joining humanitarians in urging that technology be directed to serve rather than distort the needs and values of mankind, to enrich rather than cheapen the quality of our lives.

Surrendering to despair and disillusionment brings man no comfort; it only diminishes his ability to reason and to act. A failure of nerve, a loss of will, a listlessness of spirit, a sense of futility will destroy a civilization just as surely as will bombs. This is one of the lessons of history, perhaps the principal one.

*Quoted in *Man Alone,* edited by Eric and Mary Josephson (New York: Dell Publishing Company, Inc., 1962). Reprinted by permission.

Reference Section

857

Bibliography

Starred items indicate titles available in paper.

Unit One The Emergence of Western Civilization

Ancient Egypt, Lionel Casson. From the *Great Ages of Man* series on world cultures, valuable for its picture essays.

*Archaeology, Walter Shepard. A readable explanation of the aims and methods of archaeologists.

Classical Greece, Maurice Bowra. (*Great Ages of Man*)

Cradle of Civilization, Samuel N. Kramer. (*Great Ages of Man*)

*Daily Life in Ancient Rome, Jerome Carcopino. How the Romans worked, ate, played, and lived.

*Everyday Life in Ancient Egypt, John M. White. Discusses all aspects of daily life in ancient Egypt.

Greek Horizons, Helen Hill Miller. A sympathetic treatment of ancient Greece, written by a scholar and journalist.

*The Horizon Book of Lost Worlds, Leonard Cottrell. A stimulating survey of ancient civilizations.

Imperial Rome, Moses Hadas. (*Great Ages of Man*)

The Judaeo-Christian Tradition, Jack H. Hexter. A clearly written presentation of the history, teachings, and importance of Judaism and early Christianity.

Mesopotamia: The Civilization That Rose Out of Clay, Walter A. Fairservis, Jr. A brief survey of the main aspects of civilization in ancient Mesopotamia, written by a professional anthropologist.

Tristes Tropiques, Claude Lévi-Strauss, translated by John Russell. Excellent anthropological study of primitive societies in Brazil.

Unit Two The Middle Ages

Age of Faith, Anne Fremantle. (*Great Ages of Man*)

Barbarian Europe, Gerald Simons. (*Great Ages of Man*)

*The Byzantine Tradition, D. A. Miller. Short, readable account of Byzantine society and culture.

Byzantium, Philip Sherrard. (*Great Ages of Man*)

*The Crusades, Regine Pernoud. Told in the words of the people who lived during the period of the Crusades.

Early Islam, Desmond Stewart. (*Great Ages of Man*)

*French Chivalry: Chivalric Ideas and Practices in Mediaeval France, Sidney Painter.

*Islamic Art, David T. Rice. Covers all ages of Islamic art, with illustrations.

*Islamic Literature, Najib Ullah. An anthology of Muslim literature combined with Islamic history, prepared for western readers.

Life on a Medieval Barony: A Picture of a Typical Feudal Community in the Thirteenth Century, William S. Davis.

The Meaning of the Glorious Koran, Mohammed M. Pickthall, translator. Translation and commentary by an English convert to Islam.

*Medieval Days and Ways, Gertrude Hartman. Simply written, entertaining account of medieval society.

*Medieval People, Eileen Power. Recounts six ordinary lives in the Middle Ages.

*The Middle East, Don Peretz. From the *World Regional Studies* series of companion volumes of general history and selected readings, describing a region from ancient times to the present.

Unit Three The Shaping of Civilizations in Asia, Africa, and the Americas

ASIA

All Men Are Brothers, Pearl Buck, translator. Traditional Chinese novel of bandit heroes and corrupt officials of the Sung dynasty.

*Anthology of Japanese Literature, Donald Keene. Excellent selection of Japanese literature.

The Art of India, Hermann Goetz. A survey of Indian art from ancient times.

The Buddhist Tradition, William T. de Bary, ed. Selections on Buddhism in India, China, and Japan.

China and *India* and *Japan*, Hyman Kublin. (*World Regional Studies*)

Chinese Art, William Willetts. A critical history of China's art from ancient times (2 volumes).

Daily Life in China, Jacques Gernet. City life during the Sung dynasty.

Dream of the Red Chamber, Tsao Hsueh-chin, translated by Wang Chi-chen. A fascinating novel of traditional family relationships in China.

The Enduring Art of Japan, Langdon Warner. A good introduction to Japanese art.

Everyday Life in Early Imperial China, Michael Loewe. Social history of the Han dynasty.

Monkey, Wu Ch'eng-en, translated by Arthur Waley. Excellent translations of traditional tales which help the reader understand Chinese beliefs and customs.

The Pageant of Indian History, Gertrude Sen. Summary of the early history of India.

The Spiritual Heritage of India, Swami Prabhavananda and F. Manchester. A selection of religious and philosophical texts.

The Tale of Genji, Lady Murasaki Shikibu, translated by Arthur Waley. Novel depicting court life in traditional Japan.

Tales of Ancient India, J. A. Van Buitenen, translator. A selection of folktales.

Three Ways of Thought in Ancient China, Arthur Waley. Discusses Confucianism, Taoism, and Legalism in ancient China.

The Way of Zen, Alan Watts. A popular introduction to Zen mysticism.

The Wonder That Was India, A. L. Basham. Carefully written and detailed study of Indian civilization from ancient times to the coming of Islam.

AFRICA

* *Africa*, Fred Burke. (*World Regional Studies*)

African Heritage: An Anthology of Black African Personality and Culture, Jacob Drachler, ed. Stories, poems, and songs illustrative of the African spirit.

Black Mother, Basil Davidson. A well-written treatment of the slave trade and its consequences in Africa.

Chaka, An Historical Romance, Thomas Mofolo. A difficult but fascinating historical novel about the famous Zulu ruler, written by an African.

A Glorious Age in Africa, Daniel Chu and Elliott Skinner. The story of the great Ghana, Mali, and Songhay empires. For beginners.

Great Rulers of the African Past, Lavinia Dobler and William A. Brown. West African rulers before the mid-seventeenth century. For beginners.

Lost Cities of Africa, Basil Davidson. A more advanced treatment of pre-European states in sub-Saharan Africa.

Meroë, P. L. Shinnie. From the *Ancient Peoples and Places* series of studies by archaeologists and anthropologists discussing ancient life in the western and nonwestern world.

Southern Africa, Brian Fagan. (*Ancient Peoples and Places*)

THE AMERICAS

America's First Civilization, Michael D. Coe. A recent and readable study on the Olmec.

The Ancient Maya, Sylvanus G. Morley. Standard in-depth study of the Maya and their way of life.

The Aztecs of Mexico, George C. Vaillant. A standard reference work on the Aztecs.

Indian Art in America; Indian Art in Middle America; Indian Art in South America. Frederick J. Dockstader. Three beautifully illustrated volumes surveying Amerindian arts from Precolumbian times to the present.

Indian Art of Mexico and Central America, Miguel Covarrubias. An excellent study of ancient Mesoamerican peoples and their cultures.

The Indian Heritage of America, Alvin M. Josephy, Jr. An outstanding history of the Amerindian peoples, particularly in North America.

Indians of North America, Harold E. Driver. Studies of Amerindian societies as they had developed by the time of the first European contacts.

The Maya and *Mexico*, Michael D. Coe. Two recent archaeological studies, presenting some interesting theories. (*Ancient People and Places*)

Peru, G. H. S. Bushnell. Recent study of ancient Peruvian cultures and their achievements. (*Ancient People and Places*)

Sons of the Shaking Earth, Eric Wolf. A difficult but highly illuminating anthropological and sociological history of Mesoamerica from Precolumbian times to the colonial era.

Unit Four Transition to Modern Times

WESTERN EUROPE

The Age of Kings, Charles Blitzer. European monarchs of the seventeenth century. (*Great Ages of Man*)

The Age of Louis Fourteenth, Laurence B. Packard. A short account of a critical period in European history.

The Age of Reformation, Harris E. Harbison. A brief account of a controversial age.

England in the Seventeenth Century, 1603–1714, Maurice Ashley. Includes a clearly-written account of the English revolutions of the period. From the *History of England* series, tracing the growth of the English nation from Roman Britain to World War I.

Europe in the Seventeenth Century, David Ogg. Surveys political, economic, and social history of the period.

Here I Stand, Roland H. Bainton. A good biography of Martin Luther.

Horizon Book of the Elizabethan World, Lacey Baldwin Smith. A beautifully illustrated volume.

Imperial Spain, 1469–1716, John H. Elliott. The rise and fall of Spanish power.

Louis Fourteenth, John B. Wolf. Describes the wars during the time of Louis XIV.

The Prince, Niccolò Machiavelli. A translation of Machiavelli's guide to gaining and holding power.

The Reformation, Edith Simon. (*Great Ages of Man*)

The Renaissance, Wallace K. Ferguson. A short account by a leading scholar.

The Renaissance, John R. Hale. (*Great Ages of Man*)

The Renaissance, Edward H. Weatherly, ed. Selections from the writings of Machiavelli, Petrach, Rabelais, and other Renaissance men.

Tudor England, S. T. Bindhoff. (*History of England* series)

The World of Leonardo, Robert Wallace. From the *Library of Art* series of well-illustrated texts on major artists and their times.

The World of Michelango, Robert Coughlan. (*Library of Art*)

AGE OF EXPLORATION

Admiral of the Ocean Sea, Samuel Eliot Morison. An excellent book on Columbus.

The Age of Exploration, John R. Hale. (*Great Ages of Man*)

The Age of Reconnaissance: Discovery, Exploration, and Settlement, 1350–1650 and *The European Reconnaissance,* J. H. Parry. A standard history of the Age of Exploration with a companion volume consisting mainly of eyewitness accounts by men who took part in the voyages of discovery.

The Americas on the Eve of Discovery, Harold E. Driver, ed. Eleven sketches of Amerindian ways of life.

The Atlantic Slave Trade. A Census, Philip D. Curtin. Graphs, charts, and clear text bring together data on the slave trade.

The Broken Spears, The Aztec Account of the Conquest of Mexico, Miguel León-Portilla, ed.; Lysander Kemp, translator. Essential for an understanding of the Conquest.

France and England in North America, Francis Parkman. A readable classic.

Guns, Sails and Empires, Carlo M. Cipolla. Describes the technological innovations and the early phases of European expansion.

History of the Conquest of Mexico and *History of the Conquest of Peru,* William H. Prescott. Narrative history at its very best.

Sons of the Shaking Earth, Eric Wolf. Difficult but illuminating anthropological and sociological history of Middle America from ancient times to the colonial period.

Spain in America, Charles Gibson. A survey of Spanish colonial institutions.

TSARIST RUSSIA

Encyclopedia of Russia and the Soviet Union, Michael Florinsky. A reliable, up-to-date reference book.

A History of Russia, George Vernadsky. A well-organized one-volume overview of Russia's development.

A History of Russian Literature, Daniel Minsky. One of the basic reference works in the field.

The Icon and the Axe, James Billington. A brilliant study of recurring patterns in Russian thought; for advanced readers.

Medieval Russian Epics, Chronicles, and Tales, Sergei Zenkovsky. An anthology of early medieval Russian literature, with an excellent historical introduction.

Readings in Russian Civilization, Thomas Riha. One of the foremost collections of original source materials with commentary, from all periods of Russian history (3 volumes).

Russia, Hyman Kublin. (*World Regional Studies*)

Russian Society, Ronald Hingley. A fully illustrated basic survey.

Unit Five   Revolution and the Rise of Nationalism

The Age of Enlightenment, Peter Gay. (*Great Ages of Man*)

Age of Progress, 1850–1914, Samuel Burchell. (*Great Ages of Man*)

Capital, the Communist Manifesto and Other Writings by Karl Marx, Max Eastman, ed.

The Coming of the French Revolution, Georges Lefebvre. Best introduction to the French Revolution, by a great French historian.

The Encyclopedia, Denis Diderot. Excerpts from the original work.

England in the Eighteenth Century, 1714–1815, J. H. Plumb. (*History of England* series)

England in the Nineteenth Century, 1815–1914, David Thompson. (*History of England* series)

The Enlightenment, Frank E. Manuel. Excerpts from leading philosophes.

Hard Times, Charles Dickens. A difficult but fascinating novel of the effect of the Industrial Revolution on different social classes in England.

A History of Modern France, 1871–1962, Alfred Cobban.

The Horizon Book of the Age of Napoleon, J. Christopher Herold. Beautifully illustrated book which brings the Napoleonic period to life.

The Industrial Revolution: 1760–1830, Thomas S. Ashton. A short but comprehensive and authoritative survey.

Mary Barton, Elizabeth Gaskell. A moving novel about the plight of factory workers during the Industrial Revolution.

Mind of Napoleon, Napoleon Bonaparte, edited by J. Christopher Herold. A selection from Napoleon's writings and speeches.

Nationalism and Realism: Eighteen Fifty-Two to Eighteen Seventy-Nine, Hans Kohn. A short survey by an outstanding authority on the subject.

The Portable Voltaire, François M. de Voltaire, edited by Ben R. Redman. Excerpts from the philosophe's writings.

Queen Victoria: Born to Succeed, Elizabeth Longford. A lively biography of the great queen, illuminating not only her private life but many aspects of life in nineteenth-century England.

Revolutions of 1848: A Social History, Priscilla Robertson. Captures the excitement of the period.

Robespierre, George Rude. Excerpts from the writings and speeches of Robespierre; accounts by his contemporaries and later-day historians.

Romanticism and Revolt, Europe 1815–1848, J. L. Talmon. Explains the main ideas and movements of this critical period.

Set in a Silver Sea, Arthur Bryant. Delightfully recaptures the texture of life in nineteenth-century England.

A Short History of Germany, 1815–1945, Ernest J. Passant. An excellent survey of modern Germany.

Socialist Humanism: An International Symposium, Erich Fromm, ed. Scholars from many nations discuss the meaning and importance of Marxism.

The Town Labourer, John L. and Barbara Hammond. A brilliantly written account of English urban life and of the devastating impact of the Industrial Revolution upon the poor.

Voices of the Industrial Revolution: Selected Readings from the Liberal Economists and Their Critics, John Bowditch and Clement Ramsland, eds. Includes excerpts from Smith, Malthus, Owen, and Marx.

Unit Six   The Age of Imperialism

Africa, Fred Burke. (*World Regional Studies*)

Autobiography, Mohandas K. Gandhi. Autobiography of the Indian nationalist leader.

The Autobiography of Yukichi Fukizawa, E. Kiyooka, translator. An account of the life of a westernized Japanese.

Behind Mud Walls, William and Charlotte Wiser. A study of an Indian village.

China and *India* and *Japan*, Hyman Kublin. (*World Regional Studies*)

China's Gentry, Hsiao-tung Fei. Essays on Chinese landlords and peasants.

Cry, the Beloved Country, Alan Paton. A novel by a white South African liberal which portrays the African characters sympathetically if not always accurately.

Dark Child: The Autobiography of an African Boy, Camara Laye. Autobiography of a boy growing up in the slums of Johannesburg, South Africa.

*The Financial Expert, R. K. Narayan. A modern Indian novel.

The Good Earth, Pearl S. Buck. Sympathetic novel of rural life in China.

Japanese Haiku, K. Yasuda. Explains the art of haiku and gives examples.

Japanese Inn, Oliver Statler. A novel of an inn in Japan.

Kim, Rudyard Kipling. Outstanding novel which captures the flavor of India during the period of British rule.

*The Makioka Sisters, J. Tanizaki. A novel of pre-World War II Japan.

*Modern China, Albert Feuerwerker, ed. A collection of scholarly essays.

*Red Star Over China, Edgar Snow. A report on the rise of communism in China.

*The Story of the White Nile, Alan Moorehead. The story of the discovery of the source of the Nile.

*Suye Mura, a Japanese Village, John F. Embree. A study of a pre-World War II rural community.

*Things Fall Apart, Chinua Achebe. A fine historical novel about the coming of the white man to Nigeria, told from an African point of view.

*The Washing of the Spears, Donald Morris. A detailed and exciting account of the war in 1879 between the Zulu and the British.

Unit Seven   World Wars and Totalitarianism

THE WORLD WARS

*All Quiet on the Western Front, Erich Maria Remarque. A famous novel about World War I, from the viewpoint of a young German soldier.

American Heritage Picture Story of World War Two, C. L. Sulzberger. Illustrates the main action of the war.

*The Battle of Britain, Quentin Reynolds. A readable account of one of Hitler's few failures in the early days of World War II.

*Combat, World War I, Don Congdon. An eyewitness account of battles of World War I.

*Day of Infamy, Walter Lord. A journalist's account of the day Pearl Harbor was bombed.

*Guadalcanal Diary, Richard Tregaskis. A marine's account of the struggle to capture the Pacific island from Japan.

*The Guns of August, Barbara Tuchman. An account of the first days of World War I.

*Hiroshima, John Hersey. A graphic account of the impact of the first atomic bomb on the people of Hiroshima.

*Last Letters from Stalingrad, translated by Franz Schneider and Charles Gullans. The doomed German soldiers at Stalingrad reveal their thoughts and feelings.

*The Long Fuse, An Interpretation of the Origins of World War I, Laurence Lafore. Traces the international developments leading to the war.

*The Longest Day, Cornelius Ryan. A war correspondent's account of D-Day.

*Men Who March Away: Poems of the First World War, Ian M. Parsons, ed. Reveals the thoughts of the young men who went to war.

The Second World War, Winston Churchill and the editors of Life. An illustrated one-volume version of the British prime minister's classic history of the war.

The Two Ocean War, Samuel Eliot Morison. An account of the naval battles of World War II, condensed from a multi-volume work by the navy's official historian.

*World War One: A Turning Point in Modern History, Jack J. Roth, ed. Five scholars discuss the significance of the Great War.

*World War One, The American Heritage History, Samuel L. Marshall. Essays and illustrations on the United States role in the war.

WESTERN EUROPE

*Appeasement, Alfred L. Rowse. An indictment of British statesmen, journalists, and intellectuals who supported the policy of appeasement.

*The Burden of German Guilt: A Short History of Germany 1914–1945, Hannah Vogt, translated by H. Strauss. A short history of Germany written for German secondary-school students, interesting for its treatment of Germany's most controversial period.

The Cypresses Believe in God and One Million Dead, José M. Gironella. Two novels which capture the chaos and agonies of the Spanish Civil War.

A History of Modern France, 1871–1962, Alfred Cobban.

*Hitler, A Study in Tyranny, Alan Bullock. A fascinating biography of Hitler.

*Hitler and Nazi Germany, Robert G. L. Waite. Excerpts from the writings of historians analyzing Hitler's personality and rise to power, and the theory and practice of nazism.

Mein Kampf, Adolf Hitler.

Mussolini and Italian Fascism, William S. Halperin. An excellent short summary with documents.

The Nazi Seizure of Power: The Experience of a Single German Town, 1930–1935, William S. Allen. An absorbing case study of Hitler's methods.

Nuremberg Diary, Gustave M. Gilbert. The account of a prison psychologist who interviewed Nazi war criminals during the Nuremberg trials.

The Theory and Practice of Hell, Eugen Kogon. A remarkable account of Nazi concentration camps by a survivor.

They Thought They Were Free: The Germans 1933–45, Milton Mayer. The life stories of ten ordinary Germans who lived through the Nazi period.

Totalitarianism: Its Changing Theory and Practice, Carl J. Friedrich *et al.* Forty scholars examine the nature of totalitarianism.

Twentieth Century England, David Thompson. (*History of England* series)

RUSSIA

And Quiet Flows the Don and *The Don Flows Home to the Sea*, Mikhail Sholokov, translated by H. C. Stevens. A novel in four volumes about the First World War, the Bolshevik Revolution, and the civil war in Russia, by one of the Soviet Union's foremost writers.

Autobiography, Maxim Gorki. The life of a working-class writer who supported the Bolsheviks.

Collected Works of Lenin, V. I. Lenin. The writings of the Soviet Union's leading revolutionary.

Crime and Punishment, Feodor Dostoevsky, translated by Daniel Magarshack. A psychological novel for advanced readers.

Darkness At Noon, Arthur Koestler. A novel explaining the Great Purge, by an ex-Communist.

Fathers and Sons, Ivan Turgeniev, translated by Rosemary Edmonds. A novel about the clash of generations at the time of the emancipation of serfs.

Mother, Maxim Gorki, translated by Margaret Wettlin. An account of life in a Russian factory during the 1905 revolt.

The Prophet Armed, Trotsky: 1879–1921, and *The Prophet Unarmed, Trotsky: 1921–1929*, Isaac Deutscher. The best biography of Trotsky.

Queen of Spades and Other Stories, Alexander Pushkin, translated by Rosemary Edmonds. Life in Russia in the late eighteenth and early nineteenth centuries.

Rudin, Ivan Turgeniev. Novel illustrating the lives of the nobility and intelligentsia in the first half of the nineteenth century.

Russia, Hyman Kublin. (*World Regional Studies*)

The Russian Revolution, Alan Moorehead. An account of the year 1917, by a skilled writer.

Ten Days That Shook the World, John Reed. A firsthand report of the Bolshevik Revolution, by an American radical.

War and Peace, Leo Tolstoy, translated by Rosemary Edmonds. A long novel about Russian life at the time of the Napoleonic invasion.

Unit Eight   The World in Change

EUROPE AND RUSSIA

Cancer Ward, Alexander Solzhenitsyn. Describes the frustrations of life in the Soviet Union today.

De Gaulle, Alexander Werth. One of the most interesting recent studies of the great French leader.

A History of Modern France, 1871–1962, Alfred Cobban.

The Hungarian Revolution, Melvin Lasky, ed. Documentation of the 1956 revolution, compiled from eyewitness accounts and newspaper and radio reports.

One Day in the Life of Ivan Denisovich, Alexander Solzhenitsyn, translated by Max Hayward and Ronald Hingley. A novel about a Soviet concentration camp.

Russia, Hyman Kublin. (*World Regional Studies*)

Russia and the West Under Lenin and Stalin, George Kennan. An examination of Western-Soviet relations.

Russians As People, William Miller. An informal account of various life styles in modern Russia.

Saturday Night and Sunday Morning, Alan Sillitoe. A searching novel of working-class life in England, suggesting the continuing existence of class barriers.

Selected Poems, Yevgeny Yevtushenko. Works by one of the most gifted young poets in the Soviet Union today.

Twentieth Century England, David Thompson. (*History of England* series)

The Uses of Literacy, Richard Hoggart. A moving discussion of British working-class culture by a sociologist who draws upon his own background for much information.

Why Lenin? Why Stalin? A Reappraisal of the Russian Revolution, Theodore von Laue. An examination of the causes and effects of the 1917 Revolution.

ASIA

Autobiography, Mohandas K. Gandhi. Autobiography of the Indian nationalist leader.

China and *India* and *Japan,* Hyman Kublin. (*World Regional Studies*)

City Life in Japan, R. P. Dore. A study of postwar urban society.

Dragon Seed, Pearl S. Buck. A moving novel of the impact of the Japanese invasion of China.

The Financial Expert, R. K. Narayan. A modern Indian novel.

Hill, Farms and Padi Fields, Robbins Burling. Rural life in Southeast Asia.

Ho Chi Minh, Jean Lacouture. A biography of the Vietnamese nationalist-communist leader.

Home to India, Santha Rama Rau. Experiences of a western-educated Indian girl during the last years of the independence movement.

Homecoming, Jiro Osaragi. A postwar Japanese novel.

India Today, Frank Moraes. A popular general account.

Living Japan, Donald Keene. Photos and essays on present-day Japan.

Mao Tse-Tung, Stuart Schram. A recent biography.

Mao Tse-tung: An Anthology of His Writings, Anne Fremantle, ed. Excerpts from Mao's philosophical, political, and military writings.

Nectar in the Sieve, Kamala Markandaya. A moving novel of the impact of modernization on a rural Indian family.

Peking Diary, Derek Bodde. An account of the Communist take-over during 1949.

Red Star Over China, Edgar Snow. A report on the rise of communism in China.

Report from a Chinese Village, Jan Myrdal. An account of the impact of communism on a small village.

Street Without Joy, Bernard Fall. A report of the war in Vietnam, by a newsman assigned to Saigon.

Thunder Out of China, Theodore White and Annalee Jacoby. China during World War II.

Toward Freedom, Jawaharlal Nehru. The autobiography of Nehru.

MIDDLE EAST AND AFRICA

Africa, Fred Burke. (*World Regional Studies*)

Africa: The Politics of Independence, Immanuel Wallerstein. A largely political analysis of the coming of independence in the countries of sub-Saharan Africa.

The Arab World, Desmond Stewart and the editors of *Life.* An interpretive study which treats unifying and divisive forces; abundantly illustrated.

The Arab World Today, Morroe Berger. Social life in the modern Arab community.

Atatürk: A Biography of Mustafa Kemal, Father of Modern Turkey, Lord Kinross (Patrick Balfour). A difficult but highly illuminating study of Turkey's first president.

Crossroads: Land and Life in Southwest Asia, George B. Cressey. A well-illustrated, comprehensive geography of the area.

The Egyptian Peasant, Henry H. Ayrout. Describes the life of Nile Valley farmers.

Egypt's Liberation, Gamal Abdel Nasser. Background of the revolution, by Egypt's late president.

Ghana, Kwame Nkrumah. The autobiography of the great exponent of Pan-Africanism, including his experiences studying and working in the United States.

The Human Factor in Changing Africa, Melville J. Herskovits. A cultural and political analysis of all aspects of African life at the time of independence; for advanced readers.

The Middle East, Don Peretz. (*World Regional Studies*)

Modern Poetry from Africa, Gerald Moore and Ulli Beier, eds. An anthology which expresses the ideas of *négritude,* with many poems from all parts of Africa.

My People: The Story of the Jews, Abba Eban. The story of the Jews from their ancient beginnings to the 1967 war, told by a leading Israeli statesman.

Political and Social Thought in the Contemporary Middle East, Kemal H. Karpat, ed. Turkish, Arab, and Iranian political writings.

The Six Day War, Randolph S. and Winston S. Churchill. An excellent account of the third Arab-Israeli war.

The Struggle for Mozambique, Eduardo Mondlane. An account of the struggle for independence from Portugal, written by the late leader of the Mozambique liberation movement.

Turkey, Stewart Desmond and the editors of *Life.* An interpretive, well-illustrated study emphasizing culture.

A Village in Anatolia, Mahmut Makal. Experiences of a modern teacher in a tradition-bound Turkish village.

Weep Not, Child, James Ngugi. Historical novel dealing with the tensions of the last years of colonial rule in Kenya, written by an African.

World Ditch; The Making of the Suez Canal, John Marlowe. The role of the canal in international relations.

LATIN AMERICA

Broad and Alien Is the World, Ciro Alegría, translator Harriet de Onís. Moving novel of the customs and way of life of Peruvian Amerinds as well as social commentary on their exploitation.

Child of the Dark, Carolina María de Jesús. Diary of a black ragpicker in São Paulo, documenting the life of the urban poor in Latin America.

Cuba: The Making of a Revolution, Ramón Eduardo Ruiz. A recent, balanced account of the Cuban Revolution.

Doña Barbara, Rómulo Gallegos, translator Malloy. Novel of the Venezuelan llanos and the people who live there.

Five Families, Oscar Lewis. Illuminating tape-recorded conversations with individuals in Mexican families.

The Great Fear in Latin America, John Gerassi. An indictment of United States policy, by Latin American students.

Huasipungo, Jorge Icaza, translator Mervyn Saville. Socio-political novel dealing with the exploitation of Amerinds in Ecuador.

Island in the Crossroads, María M. Brau. A history of Puerto Rico for young readers.

Life in Mexico, Frances Calderón de la Barca. In detailed letters to her family in Scotland the author describes the turbulence of Mexican society in 1840.

Martín Fierro, José Hernández, translator Harriet de Onís. Epic poem of the Argentine gaucho and his way of life.

Rebellion in the Backlands, Euclydes da Cunha, translator Samuel Putnam. Graphically portrays the people and landscape of interior northern Brazil.

Ten Keys to Latin America, Frank Tannenbaum. A brief analysis, first written for United States businessmen.

The Underdogs, Mariano Azuela, translator E. Munguia, Jr. Novel of the Mexican Revolution from the point of view of the people.

U.S. Policy in Latin America, Edwin Lieuwen. A brief historical survey.

The Vortex, José Eustasio Rivera, translator Earle K. James. Novel about rubber exploitation in South America, captures the menace of the jungle and its effect on man.

Zapata and the Mexican Revolution, John Womack, Jr. A superb biography of the popular Amerindian leader.

PROBLEMS AND PERSPECTIVES

The Abolition of Poverty, David Horowitz. An Israeli economist discusses ways of combating poverty in the developing world.

The Environmental Handbook, Garrett De Bell. On the dangers of abusing the environment.

From Empire to Nation, Rupert Emerson. Nationalism among former colonial countries.

Man Against Poverty: World War Three Reader on the World's Most Crucial Issue, Arthur I. Blaustein and Roger Woock, eds. Readings on world poverty.

The Population Bomb, Paul R. Ehrlich. Discusses the dangers of abusing the environment.

The Present in Perspective, Hans W. Gatzke. A straightforward account that places events since 1945 into a meaningful historical framework.

The Rich Nations and the Poor Nations, Barbara Ward. Modernization and the problems it brings to the developing nations.

Unfinished Revolution: America and the Third World, C. L. Sulzberger. Surveys relations between the United States and the developing nations.

The United States in the World Arena, W. W. Rostow. A study of United States foreign policy since 1945.

Acknowledgments for Graphics

Picture Credits

The authors and publisher wish to express their appreciation to persons and organizations listed below for their courtesy in making pictures available for reproduction. The following abbreviations have been used for a few sources from which many illustrations have been obtained: Bettmann—The Bettmann Archive, Inc.; British Museum—Courtesy of the Trustees of the British Museum; EPA—Editorial Photocolor Archives, New York; Historical Pictures—Historical Pictures Service, Chicago; Scala—Scala, New York/Florence; Sellick—Douglas R. G. Sellick, London.

2 and cover   Copyright, Weston Kemp

3   Landesmuseum Johanneum, Graz

4   The University Museum of the University of Pennsylvania

5   Copyright by the California Institute of Technology and Carnegie Institute of Washington/photograph from the Hale Observatories

8   (top left) Michael D. Coe; (bottom left) Dinosaur National Monument

11   (top) Courtesy of French Government Tourist Office, New York; (bottom) Pellegrini/Grimoldi

12   (all photos) Napoleon A. Chagnon

18   Mansell/Sellick

19   Courtesy of the Oriental Institute, University of Chicago

22   (top) Josef Muench; (bottom) Erich Lessing/Magnum

25   (left) Photograph F. L. Kennett, Copyright © George Rainbird Ltd., 1963; (right) EPA; (bottom) The Metropolitan Museum of Art, Museum Excavations, 1928–29, and Rogers Fund, 1930

26   (left) University of Pennsylvania Museum; (center) Ewing Galloway; (right) Directorate General of Antiquities, Ministry of Culture and Information, Republic of Iraq

33   (top right) Giraudon; (center left) Josef Muench; (lower left) American Numismatic Society

34   (top left) Josef Muench; (bottom) Art Reference Bureau

38   Contino/Grimoldi

40   (top) British Museum/Sellick; (bottom) John La Due

41   Courtesy, Museum of Fine Arts, Boston, William Francis Warden Fund

44   (top left) Josef Muench; (bottom left) Josef Muench; (center right) Botts/Grimoldi; (bottom right) Tomsich/Grimoldi

46   (top) The Metropolitan Museum of Art, Fletcher Fund, 1931; (center) British Museum; (bottom) The Metropolitan Museum of Art, Purchase, 1947, Joseph Pulitzer Bequest

47   Scala

56   (right) Douglas Spillane, Stratford, Ontario

59   (top) Scala; (left) Nelson Gallery, Atkins Museum, Kansas City, Missouri (Nelson Fund); (right) Giraudon

62   (top) Pellegrini/Grimoldi; (bottom) Alinari

63   EPA

66   (top) Scala; (right) Pellegrini/Grimoldi

70   British Museum/Sellick

75   (left) Scala; (right) Alinari

80   (top) Josef Muench; (bottom) Photo from Weskemp/Alain Perceval, Paris, Copyright 1965

81   EPA

83   Alinari

87   (top) Josef Muench; (center) Pellegrini/Grimoldi; (bottom) Tomsich/Grimoldi

96   (top left) Catacomb of S. Priscilla; (top right) Brown Brothers; (bottom left) EPA

101   (left) Rapho-Guillumette; (right) Landesmuseum für Vorgeschichte, Halle

108   Alva-Ramphal/EPA

109   Powell/Grimoldi

114   (left) Greek Orthodox Archdiocese of North and South America; (right) EPA

121   (top) Arabian American Oil Company; (left) Josef Muench; (right) Bibliothèque Nationale, Paris

123   The Metropolitan Museum of Art: (left) Rogers Fund, 1913; (right) Bequest of Edward C. Moore, 1891

125   (left) Bruce Humphrey, from the collection of Mr. and Mrs. Christopher D. Reed; (right) Kit Robbins/Rapho-Guillumette

130   (left) Samuel Chamberlain; (lower right) Hans Fischer/EPA

131   Institut Belge d'Information et de documentation

134   (top) Kunstmuseum, Oslo; (bottom) Universitetets Oldsaksamling, Oslo

137   (top) Giraudon; (bottom) British Museum/Sellick

140   Pol de Limbourg: *Très Riches Heures du duc de Berry—Mars*—Chantilly Musée Condé/Giraudon

147   (left) Scala; (right) Trinity College, Cambridge

150   Bibliothèque de l'Arsenal, Paris

151   Ms. 10607, fol. 23, verso/Bibliothèque Royale Albert Ier, Brussels

156 (top) Josef Muench; (bottom) Bibliothèque Nationale, Paris

162 (left) Pellegrini/Grimoldi; (center) The Metropolitan Museum of Art, The Cloisters Collection, 1947; (right) British Museum/Sellick

165 (left) Courtesy of Harvard College Library; (right) Min. 1233/Staatliche Museen Preussischer Kulturbesitz, Kupferstichkabinett, Berlin (West)

172 (left) The Walters Art Gallery; (right) Universitätsbibliothek, Heidelberg

198 (left) Burk Uzzle/Magnum; (right) Nelson Gallery, Atkins Museum, Kansas City, Missouri (Nelson Fund)

199 Y. Ernest Satow/Rapho-Guillumette

205 (top and bottom right) Lynn McLaren; (bottom left) Courtesy, Museum of Fine Arts, Boston

209 Bob and Ira Spring

212 (top) Michael Rougier, *The Cooking of China* © 1968 Time Inc.; (bottom) Seattle Art Museum

220 Courtesy, Museum of Fine Arts, Boston

225 (all) Courtesy, Museum of Fine Arts, Boston: (top) detail from "The Burning of the Sanjo Palace" by Heiji Monogatori, Fenollosa-Weld Collection; (bottom left) "Call of the Cuckoo" by Kitao Masanobu, Spaulding Collection

228 (left) Courtesy of the American Museum of Natural History; (right) EPA

229 Nelson Gallery, Atkins Museum, Kansas City, Missouri (Nelson Fund)

236 Afro Audio-Visual Company

239 Courtesy of the American Museum of Natural History

241 (top) Photo by Else Sackler, courtesy of the American Museum of Natural History; (bottom) Jean Herskovits

245 Radio Times Hulton Picture Library

250 South Africa Museum, Cape Town

258 (top left) Photo by Else Sackler, courtesy of the American Museum of Natural History; (top right) Georg Gerster/Rapho-Guillumette; (bottom left) EPA

262 Afro Audio-Visual Company

263 Collection of T. Holzman, Boston University African Studies Center

270 (left and top right) Lynn McLaren; (bottom right) Afro Audio-Visual Company

273 Courtesy of the American Museum of Natural History

281 (top) Afro Audio-Visual Company; (bottom) B. P. Singer Features

284 B. P. Singer Features

287 Courtesy of the American Museum of Natural History

288 (top, both photos) Afro Audio-Visual Company; (bottom, both photos) Jean Herskovits

292 (top) The Smithsonian Institution; (bottom) Tony Linck

293 Courtesy of the Museum of Primitive Art, New York

301 (left) Private Collection/Clifton V. Rice; (right) Stendahl Galleries, Los Angeles

302 The Brooklyn Museum, lent by Mr. and Mrs. Alastair B. Martin

307 (top) Jane G. Libby; (right) Nelson Gallery, Atkins Museum, Kansas City, Missouri (Nelson Fund)

308 Nelson Gallery, Atkins Museum, Kansas City, Missouri (Nelson Fund)

311 (top) Photo by Else Sackler, courtesy of the American Museum of Natural History; (right) Rubbing and photo by Merle Greene

316 (top and bottom left) Courtesy of the American Museum of Natural History; (bottom right) Courtesy of the Art Institute of Chicago

320 (left) Royal Art Collection, Windsor Castle, all rights reserved; (right) Sistine Chapel/Scala

321 Galleria Palatina/Scala

324 (top) Uffizi Gallery/Scala; (left) Alinari

327 (top left) Pellegrini/Grimoldi; (bottom left) The Metropolitan Museum of Art, New York, Bequest of Benjamin Altman, 1913; (right) Alinari/Grimoldi

329 (left) Louvre/Giraudon; (right) Museo di Palazzo Venesia/Scala

331 Sistine Chapel/Scala

332 Uffizi Gallery/Pineider

334 British Museum/Sellick

335 *Martin Luther* by Lucas Cranach, 1526, Nationalmuseum, Stockholm

338 (top left) Scala; (right) Uffizi Gallery/Scala

340 British Museum

343 Chester Beatty Collection, Dublin

346 Granger Collection

347 Staatliche Museen Preussischer Kulturbesitz, Kupferstichkabinett, Berlin (West)

350 (left) Copyright by the California Institute of Technology and Carnegie Institution of Washington/photograph from the Hale Observatories; (right) Istituto e Museo di Storia della Scienza, Florence

352 N. R. Farbman

355 (left) Bettmann; (right) George B. Griffenhagen

358 Bibliothèque Nationale, Paris

359 André Gamet/Rapho-Guillumette

361 Reproduced in the Bodleian Library color filmstrips

366 (top) Lynn McLaren; (bottom) New York Public Library

373 (top left) Museum of the American Indian, Heye Foundation; (bottom left) Reproduced in the

677 "Homage to Oskar Panizza," by George Grosz, 1918, Staatsgalerie, Stuttgart/reproduced courtesy of the estate of George Grosz, Princeton, N.J.

681 (top) Picasso, "Guernica," 1937, on extended loan to the Museum of Modern Art, New York, from the artist; (right) Robert Capa/Magnum

684 (top) Bill Brandt/Rapho-Guillumette; (bottom) Robert Capa/Magnum

685 Sovfoto

695 Wide World

696 (left) Zionist Archives; (right) U.S. Army

706 Wide World

714 Fritz Henle/Photo Researchers

715 (top) NASA; (bottom) Cornell Capa/Magnum

720 (all photos) United Nations

734 United Press International

736 (top) Arthur Griffin/Photo Researchers; (right) Courtesy of Israel Information Services

740 (top) Marc Riboud/Magnum; (bottom) Fritz Henle/Photo Researchers

741 Marilyn Silverstone/Magnum

749 Bruno Barbey/Magnum

759 Erich Lessing/Magnum

764 (left, all photos) Jacques Jangoux; (right) Elliott Erwitt/Magnum

768 (left) René Burri/Magnum; (right) Eastfoto

769 Acme Photo by Bert Brandt/UPI

772 (left) From *Meiji bunka zenshu, kyōiku-hen,* Vol. 10; (right) Hiroshi Hamaya/Magnum

778 (top) TASS/Sovfoto; (bottom) Clifton V. Rice

784 Marilyn Silverstone/Magnum

790 (both photos) Standard Oil Co. (N.J.)

791 Marilyn Silverstone/Magnum

797 (top) United Nations; (bottom left) EPA; (bottom right) Israel Government Tourist Office

803 (left) Elliott Erwitt/Magnum; (right) United Nations

806 (top) Marc & Evelyn Bernheim/Rapho-Guillumette; (bottom) Jean Herskovits

807 Marc & Evelyn Bernheim/Rapho-Guillumette

814 (both photos) Jacques Jangoux

815 Jacques Jangoux

818 By permission of the Trustees of Dartmouth College

819 Paul S. Conklin

831 (all photos) Paul S. Conklin

836 John Keshishian

837 (left) Paul S. Conklin; (right) T. D. Jones/ Charles Phelps Cushing

846 Erich Hartmann/Magnum

847 (top) Marc Riboud/Magnum; (bottom) Ian Berry/Magnum

855 Kunstmuseum, Basel/Colorphoto Hans Hinz

Map Credits

The authors and publisher wish to express their appreciation to R. R. Donnelly & Company, who prepared the entire map program for the text. Thanks are also extended to the following sources which provided information instrumental in preparing the maps:

Adams, A. E., *An Atlas of Russian and East European History.* Frederick A. Praeger, Publisher, 1966 (1967)

American Heritage Book of Indians and *The American Heritage Pictorial Atlas of United States History.* American Heritage Publishing Co., 1966

Boyd, A., & Rensburg, P., *An Atlas of African Affairs.* Frederick A. Praeger, Publishers, 1962 (1966)

Brown, Joe David, and the Editors of Time-Life Books, *India.* © 1961 Time Inc.

B. S. V., *Grosser Historischer Weltatlas.* Bayerischer Schulbuch Verlag, 1954

Coe, Michael D., *America's First Civilization.* American Heritage Publishing Co., 1968

Covarrubias, Miguel, *The Eagle, the Jaguar, and the Serpent.* Alfred A. Knopf, 1954

Duché, Jean, *Histoire du Monde* (Vol. I). Flammarion, 1958

Dvornik, F., *The Slavs: Their Early History and Civilization.* American Academy of Arts and Sciences, 1956 (1959)

Encyclopedia Britannica. Encyclopedia Britannica, Inc., 1970

Esposito, V. J. (Ed.), *The West Point Atlas of American Wars* (*Vol. II, 1900–1953*). Frederick A. Praeger, Publishers, 1967

Fage, J. D., *An Atlas of African History.* Edward Arnold, Publishers, 1958 (1968)

Fisher, Sydney N., *The Middle East, A History.* Alfred A. Knopf, 1968

Fox, E. W., *Atlas of European History.* Oxford University Press, 1957 (1964)

Gregory, James F., *Russian Land, Soviet People.* Pegasus, 1968

Heibonsha, *Japan: The Pocket Atlas.* Heibonsha, Ltd., Publishers, 1970

Herrmann, A., and Ginsberg, N., *An Historical Atlas of China.* Aldine Publishing Co., 1966

Herrmann, A., *Historical and Commercial Atlas of China.* Harvard-Yenching Institute, 1935 (O. P.)

The International Atlas. Rand McNally and Co., 1969

Lecuona, H. G., y Otros, *Atlas Universal y de México.* Librería Británica and Thomas Nelson and Sons, Ltd., 1966

McEvedy, C., *The Penguin Atlas of Ancient History.* Penguin Books, Inc., 1967 (1968)

Moriya, K., *Teikoku's Complete Atlas of Japan.* Teikoku-Shoin Co., 1968

Morley, Sylvanus G., *The Ancient Maya* (3rd ed.), revised by George W. Brainerd. Stanford University Press, 1956

National Geographic Society, *Archaeological Map of Middle America*. National Geographic Society, 1968

Paddock, John (ed.), *Ancient Oaxaca: Discoveries in Mexican Archeology and History*. Stanford University Press, 1966

Palmer, R. R., *Atlas of World History*. Rand McNally and Co., 1965 (1968)

Pearch, E. E., and Fifield, R. H., *World Political Geography*. Thomas Y. Crowell Co., 1952

Petrov, V. P., *China: Emerging World Power.* Copyright © 1967, by Litton Educational Publishing Inc. by permission of D. Van Nostrand, Inc.

Seltzer, L. E., *The Columbia Lippincott Gazetteer of the World*. Columbia University Press, 1962

Shepherd, W. R., *Historical Atlas (9th Ed.)*. Barnes and Noble, Inc., 1964

Shinnie, Margaret, *Ancient African Kingdoms*. Edward Arnold, Publishers, 1965 (1968)

Starr, C. G., *A History of the Ancient World*. Oxford University Press, 1965

Stavrianos, Lefton S., *A Global History of Man*. Allyn and Bacon, 1966

Steinberg, S. H., and Paxton, J., *The Statesman's Yearbook* (1969–1970). St. Martin's Press, Inc., Macmillan & Co., Ltd., 1970

Strahler, Arthur N., *Physical Geography*. John Wiley and Sons, 1969

Toynbee, A. J., and Myers, E. D., *Historical Atlas and Gazetteer*. Oxford University Press, 1959 (1967)

Treharne, R. F., and Fullard, H., *Muir's Historical Atlas: Ancient, Medieval, and Modern*. George Philip and Son, 1964

Vilnay, Z., *The New Israel Atlas*. McGraw-Hill Book Co., 1969

Webster's Geographical Dictionary. G. and C. Merriam Co., Publishers, 1949 (1969)

Westermann, G. V., *Westermanns Grosser Atlas zur Weltgeschichte*. Georg Westermann Verlag, 1968

Wilgus, A. C., *Historical Atlas of Latin America*. Cooper Square Publishers, 1967

The World Book Encyclopedia. Field Enterprises Educational Corp., 1970

Yalman, A. E., *Turkey in My Time*. University of Oklahoma Press, 1956

This Index contains references not only to the text of the book but also to maps and pictures. These may be identified as follows: *m* refers to a map; *p* refers to a picture.

Britain, *m* 133, *m* 744; and Rome, *m* 72, 76, *m* 84, 85; in southern Africa, 254–255, 551, 563, *p* 568; American colonies of, 380, *m* 381, 382; colonies of, *m* 389; king's power limited in, 447, 513–514; in Napoleonic period, *m* 471, 471–472, 473, 474; in Quadruple Alliance, 482; in Crimean War, 494, 638; Industrial Revolution in, *p* 505, 506–512, *p* 510; political reforms in, 514–515; serves as model for Europe, 517; liberal approaches to problems, 526–527; abolishes slave trade, *p* 547, 548–549; imperialism in Africa of, *m* 552, 554, 557–559, *m* 560, 561–562, 564, *m* 566, 569–570, 572; in India, *p* 575, 576–579, *m* 578, *p* 579, 580–583; imperialism in China, 584, 585, 588; gains trade with Japan, 595; in Triple Entente, 605; and World War I, *p* 603, 605, 617; mandates in Middle East, *m* 621, 624, 793; intervenes in Russia, 648; antiwar sentiment in, 686, 687, 691; declares support of Poland, 690; and World War II, *p* 685, 692, 694–695, *m* 704, 708; occupies Germany, *m* 709; overestimates Soviet power, 724; recovery from World War II in, 726, 746–748; favors establishing state for Jews, 798; supports Israel, 731, 800; regarded as buffer between blacks and whites, 810; in Southeast Asia, 785, 787; blocks Arab nationalism, 793; and Latin America, 820, 823, 824, 841. *See also* England
British Bechuanaland, *m* 560
British Cameroons, *m* 813
British Central Africa, *m* 560
British East Africa, *m* 566
British Guiana, *m* 827
British Honduras, *m* 827, *m* 839
British Isles, *m* 389
Bronze Age, 14
Broz, Josef. *See* Tito
Brussels, *m* 618, *m* 744
Brussels Treaty, 728
Bucharest, *m* 403, *m* 744; treaty of, 609, 620 (box)
Budapest, *m* 159, *m* 405, *m* 744, 759
Buddha: in art, *p* 199; attains enlightenment, 204; worshiped as deity, 207
Buddhism: Greek influence on art of, *p* 59; founded, 204; message of, 206–207; spread of Mahayana, *m* 206, 207, 208; declines in India, 207; Islam conflicts with, 209; influence in China of, 217; impact on Japan of, 224; in Southeast Asia, 785
Buenos Aires, 823, *m* 827, *m* 839

Bulgaria, *m* 606, *m* 621, 695, *m* 744. *See also* Eastern-Central Europe
Burma, *m* 578, 700, *m* 701, 785, *m* 786, 787
Burundi, *m* 813
Business: medieval advances in, 161–162, 173; encouraged by Reformation, 344; expanded by Commercial Revolution, 387; encouraged in France, 454, 469, 484; and *laissez-faire* policy, 526; Soviet Russia ends private, 655; Nazi policies aid German, 677; lower middle class sees as threat, 680; reform of Japanese, 770–771; alienation caused by modern, 856. *See also* Bourgeoisie; Capitalism; Industrial Revolution; Mercantilism; Trade
Byron, Lord: *p* 483
Byzantine Empire: founded, 101–102; survives barbarian invasions, 104, 110; art and architecture of, *p* 109, 114–115; trade of, 110–111, *m* 119; at height, *m* 112; invaders of, *m* 112, 112–113, *m* 155; declines, 113; contributes to civilization, 113–114, 115, 164, 168, 417; Muslims penetrate, 118, *m* 119; contributes to Muslim culture, 120; and Mongol Empire, *m* 127; falls to Ottoman Turks, 127, *m* 128; Italian trade with, 161. *See also* Eastern Orthodox Church
Byzantium, *m* 49, *m* 72, *m* 84; founded, 110. *See also* Constantinople

C

Cabinet (British), 514
Cabot, John: *m* 370, 382
Cabral, Pedro: 366, *m* 370
Caesar, Julius: *p* 75; invades Britain, *m* 72, 76; rise to power of, 76–77; reforms of, 77; assassinated, 78
Cairo, *m* 119, 122, *m* 795, *p* 803
Calais, 394, *m* 618
Calcutta, 577, *m* 578, *m* 783
Calendar: Egyptian solar, 27; Mesopotamian lunar, 31; Muslim, 116; in Mesoamerica, 303, 304, 305, 309–310
Calicut, 362, *m* 578, *m* 783; Portuguese reach, 367, *m* 370
Caliph, 118
Calvin, John: 342, 344
Calvinism, *m* 341, 342, 345
Cambodia, 732, 785, *m* 786. *See also* Southeast Asia
Camel, 230, 233, 363
Cameroon, 809, *m* 813
Cameroons, *m* 621
Canada, *m* 389; French explore and settle, 380; France loses to Britain, 382; British trade with,

555; independence in, 569; in NATO, 728; in western defense system, *m* 733
Canals, 507–508
Canary Islands, *m* 364, 369, *m* 813
Cannae, 70, *m* 71
Canterbury Tales, The: 173–174
Canton, *m* 370, *m* 588, *m* 774; restrictions on Europeans in, *p* 575; becomes trading post, 584; Communists in, 775
Cape Colony, *m* 252; in 1763, *m* 389; British take over, 254, 551, *m* 552, *m* 560; Britain defeats Boers in, 564. *See also* South Africa
Cape Horn, 293, *m* 296
Cape of Good Hope: Dutch found station at, 251; Dias rounds, 366, *m* 370; vital to British interests, 551, 558, 563
Cape Verde Islands, *m* 364, 366
Capetown, *m* 552, *m* 813
Capital, 383, 507
Capitalism: early history of, 383–384, 387; socialists attack, 518, 522; *laissez-faire*, 526, 536; creates gap between classes, 529, *p* 531; fails to provide adequate well-being, 529–530; Marx did not foresee changes in, 533; imperialism connected with, 554; Soviet Union and, 653, 721; blamed for triumph of nazism, 679; ideal of western civilization, 716; in Africa, 718; in Asia, 718; in Latin America, 830. *See also* Class struggle
Capitalists: bourgeois, 529, *p* 531; fear working class, 664; fascism appeals to Italian, 666; fear investment in Latin America, 843
Caporetto, 614, *m* 615
Caracas, *m* 839
Carbon dating, 7
Cárdenas, Lázaro: 842
Caribbean Sea, *m* 370, *m* 839
Carthage, *m* 42, *m* 72; wars with Rome, 69–71, *m* 71; coins of, *p* 70
Cartier, Jacques: *m* 370
Cartwright, Edmund: 511
Casablanca, *m* 704, *m* 813
Caspian Sea, *m* 119, *m* 419, *m* 632
Caste system (Hindu), 203, 580, 582, 780
Castile, *m* 396, 398
Castro, Fidel: heir of Marx, 532; reforms by, 838; maintains popular support, 840; pledges to spread revolution, 842. *See also* Cuba
Cathedral, Gothic: *p* 131, 170, 175
Catholic Reformation. *See* Counter Reformation
Catholicism. *See* Roman Catholic Church

Cattle: in Bantu economy, 250, 266; importance to Boers of, 251

Caucasus Mountains, *m* 419, *m* 632

Caudillos, 824, 825; build nation-states, 826, 828–829; encourage foreign investment, 830, 832; Castro as, 840; Latin Americans tolerate, 843

Caupolican, 375

Cause and effect, law of: 540–541

Cavaliers, 415

Cavour, Count Camillo di: 493–494, 495

Cayenne, *m* 839

Celebes, *m* 389, *m* 786

Cellini, Benvenuto: craft of, *p* 327

Censorship: *philosophes* criticize, 431, 437; enlightened despots and, 432 (box); in France, 447, 469, 519; used by reactionaries, 482, 484; in tsarist Russia, 637, 640; in Soviet Union, 761

Central Africa, *m* 246; slavery affects, 248; trade of, 255–256; impact of Zulu wars on, 256; music of, 276

Central African Republic, *m* 813

Central America, *m* 827. *See also* Latin America

Central Asia, *m* 216; Huns invade Europe from, 102; Turks originate in, 113; and Muslim trade, 120; Mongols originate in, 126; India invaded from, 200, 207, 208; contributions to China of, 213; China invades, 215; Russia expands into, 423

Central Committee, 651, 659

Central Europe. *See* Eastern-Central Europe

Central Treaty Organization, (CENTO), 732

Cervantes Saavedra, Miguel de: 326, 328

Ceuta, 363, *m* 364, *m* 552

Ceylon, *m* 202, *m* 578, *m* 783; trades with Byzantine Empire, 111; religion in, *m* 206

Chad, 809, *m* 813

Chaka. *See* Shaka

Chamberlain, Neville: 688, 691

Champlain, Samuel de: 380

Chardin, Jean Baptiste: depicts common man, *p* 429

Charisma, 538; of Hitler, 673; of de Gaulle, 749

Charlemagne: empire of, 132, *m* 132; school established by, 164

Charles I (King of England), 414–415

Charles I (King of Spain), 401

Charles II (King of England), 415

Charles V (Holy Roman Emperor): 339, 401. *See also* Hapsburgs

Charles X (King of France), 484

Chartist Movement, 515

Chaucer, Geoffrey: 173

Chauvinism, 501–502; in Germany, 519; accepts ideas of Social Darwinism, 537; in Communist China, 777, 779

Chavín de Huantar, 314, *m* 315

Chiang Kai-shek, 590, 773, 774. *See also* Nationalist China

Chichén Itzá, *m* 309

Ch'ien-lung, 585

Child labor, 507, 512, 528, 530

Children: serfdom and, 139, 141; in Hindu society, 201; in traditional China, 219–220; in African society, 266, 269, 271, *p* 270; role in phalanxes of, 528. *See also* Filial piety

Children's Crusade, 156–157

Chile, *m* 839; in Inca Empire, 372; peoples difficult to subdue, 375; emergence of nation-state in, 826, *m* 827, 828; Marxism-Leninism in, 834

Ch'in dynasty, 214, *m* 215. *See also* China

China: early civilization in, *m* 15, 211, trade of early, 85, 111, 120, 161, 208; art in, *p* 199, 217, *p* 220; Buddhism in, *m* 206, 217; agriculture in, 211, *p* 212; culture of traditional, 212–214, 216, 217–220; Ch'in unify, 214, *m* 215; under Han, 214–216, *m* 216; under T'ang and Sung, 217, *m* 218; Mongols in, 126, *m* 127, 221; Japan borrows from, 223–224; and exploration, 362–363; Ch'ing establish dynasty in, 583; restricts European trade, *p* 575, 584–585; peasant discontent in, 584, 586–587; treaty ports in, 585–586, 588, *m* 588; Taiping Rebellion in, 586–587; Japanese aggression in, 588, *p* 596, 597–598, 614; rise of nationalism in, 589; Chinese Communist Party formed, 590; Nationalist-Communist conflict in, 590–591, 773; during World War II, 699, *m* 701. *See also* Communist China; Nationalist China

Chinese Communist Party: formed, 590; and Russia, 736, 779; gains control of China, 729; breaks with Chinese Nationalists, 773; gains popular support, 773–774; controls Chinese society, 775. *See also* Communist China

Ch'ing dynasty, 583–587, *p* 586, 589. *See also* China

Chinggis Khan, 126

Chivalry, 135, 137–138, 175

Chopi musicians, 282

Choshu. *See* Satsuma-Choshu leaders

Chou En-lai, 735, 736

Christianity: Judaic roots of, 35, 93–94; reasons for triumph of,

94–98; art of early, *p* 96; official religion of Rome, 98; barbarians accept, 104; in western civilization, 105, 376; spread of, *m* 111, 115, 132, 146, 377, 383, 395; compared with Islam, 117–118; Muslim tolerance of, 118, 398; monks and friars as models for, 146; in Africa, 238, 247, 569; and slavery, 243, 365; in Ethiopia, *p* 258; guide for way of life, 325; and Reformation, 335–345; factor in Age of Exploration, 362; in Asia, 368, 578, 587; loss of faith in, 665; and National Socialism, 677–678; in Lebanon, 795. *See also* Crusades; Eastern Orthodox Church; Missionaries; Protestantism; Roman Catholic Church

Chungking, *m* 701, 773, *m* 774

Churchill, Winston: urges social reform, 517; inspires and unites British, 694, 746; describes iron curtain, 725–726

Cicero, 78, 90

Circumnavigation of globe, 369, *m* 370

Cities: feature of civilization, 14; man's first, 28; Roman, 84, 92, 100, 104–105; Muslim, 120; decline in West, 132, 158; growth in Middle Ages of, 174–175; in ancient America, 304, 308; culture of, 322; free, 400; result from Industrial Revolution, 506, 512, 522; growth of German, 518; in India, 580; in Japan, 596; uniformity throughout world of, 719; Latin American, 835; overcrowding in, 848, 855

Citizenship: in Greece, 45, 52, 60; benefits of Roman, 69, 83

City-states: Mesopotamian, 28; Greek, 42, 48, 50; Italian, 157, 325; self-governing, 158; East African, 256. *See also* Athens

Civil Constitution of the Clergy, 454; peasants object to, 457

Civil liberties: in Athens, 45; Greek belief in, 60; Roman law protects, 90; medieval contributions to, 175–176; Reformation advances, 344–345; protected in England, 397–398, 416, 434; as natural right, 430; religious, 433; *philosophes* on, 434, 437; furthered by French Revolution, 454, 462; of Code Napoléon, 468; granted by Louis XVIII, 484; Boer policies impair Indian, 581; Imperial Duma and, 642; repressed in Soviet Union, 650, 658–659, 765–766; repressed in southern Africa, 816; in Latin America, 821, 822, 824, 834, 843

Civil service: Chinese, 215–216, 218–219; Indian, 576, 577, 579; West German, 743

Congo Free State. *See* Independent Congo State

Congo River, *m* 232, *m* 246, *m* 364, 559, 560

Congress of Berlin, 559, 560

Congress of Vienna, 480–482

Congress Party. *See* Indian Nationalist Congress

Conquistadores: goals of, 374; conquests of, 374–375; contributions to America of, 376; land granted to, 377

Constantine, 98, 99–100, 110

Constantinople, 102; capital of Byzantine Empire, 102, *m* 112; as trade center, 110–111; Latin Christians capture, 113, *m* 155, 156; falls to Ottomans, 104, 113, 127, *m* 128; Peasant Crusade loots, 153. *See also* Byzantium; Istanbul

Constitution: in ancient Greece, 52; of United States, 431; of French National Assembly, 454; Jacobin, 458–459; Japan adopts western-style, 595; Soviet, 687; in Latin American republics, 825; of Mexican Revolution, 832–833

Consul, 64

Consulate, 467

Containment: United States policy toward communism, 726, *m* 733, 778; brinkmanship added to, 732; loses favor as world policy, 737; Japan important to policy of, 771

Continental System, 471–472, 473

Copenhagen, *m* 396, *m* 744

Copernicus, Nicolaus: heliocentric theory of, *p* 347, 348; criticized, 349; Galileo's work supports, 351; revolutionary aspects of theories of, 543

Copper, 14, 285, 570

Coptic Church, *p* 258

Cordova, *m* 119, 122, *m* 159

Corn: cultivated in ancient North America, 297, 298, 299; Mesoamerica probable source of, 300; importance to world diet of, 388

Corsica: *m* 42, *m* 65, *m* 71; controlled by Carthage, 69; in 1490, *m* 396; about 1560, *m* 403; birthplace of Napoleon, 466; in 1812, *m* 471; in 1815, *m* 481

Cort, Henry: 511

Cortés, Hernán: leads Spanish conquest of Mexico, 374–375; route of, *m* 370

Cos, *m* 49; medical school on, 55

Cossacks: Don, 419; guard Russian frontier, 421; reach Pacific Ocean, 423; attack Napoleon's army, 474; enforce tsarism, 631

Costa Rica, *m* 827, *m* 839; ancient culture in, 314

Cottage industry, 511

Cotton: in British industry, 507, 509–511

Council for Mutual Economic Assistance (COMECON), 727

Council of Trent, 342–343

Counter Reformation, 342–343

Coup d'état, 467

Courts (law): medieval, 135, 138; Church, 144; royal, 394, 396; abuses in French, 446–447; development in Russia of, 639; Nazis control, 675; reform of Turkish, 792; in South Africa, 816. *See also* Inquisition; Law

Craft guild, 160, *p* 162

Crassus, 76

Creoles, 820; exploitation of Amerindian labor by, 377; attack Jesuit missions, 378; and Latin American independence movements, 821, 822, 824; in Argentina, 828; look down on commerce, 830

Crete, *m* 21, *m* 42, *m* 704; Minoan civilization of, *p* 34; in 1490, *m* 306; about 1648, *m* 405

Crimea, *m* 632; Khanate of the, *m* 396, *m* 403; about 1648, *m* 405; under Mongol control, 420

Crimean War, 494, 638

Cromwell, Oliver: 415

Crusades, 120, 152–157, *m* 154, *m* 155, *p* 156

Cuauhtémoc, 375

Cuba, *m* 827, *m* 839; in Age of Exploration, *m* 370; during mercantilist period, *m* 381; missile crisis in, 761, 840; independence movement in, 836; causes of revolution in, 837; Castro's revolution in, 838, 840, 843; United States intervenes in, 841, 842; reform in, 838

"Cult of personality," 654; feature of Stalinism, 730; extended to Soviet satellites, 755; attacked by Khrushchev, 758

Cultural Revolution, 777

Culture: prehistoric, 9–14; modern Neolithic, *p* 12; mass, 522

Cuneiform writing, *p* 26, 28

Cuzco, 315, *m* 315, *m* 370, 372

Cyprus, *m* 27, *m* 799; trades with Greece, 42, *m* 42; in 1490, *m* 396; about 1648, *m* 405; Greece and Turkey quarrel over, 751

Czechoslovakia: creation of, *m* 621, 624; democratic state develops in, 688; German take-over in, *m* 689, 690; in World War II, *m* 704; Communists gain control in, 727–728, 754; as Soviet satellite, 731, *m* 744, 753–754, 760. *See also* Bohemia; Eastern-Central Europe

D

D-Day, *p* 685, 705

Dahomey, *m* 813; kingdom of, *m* 235, 237, 240–242, *p* 241; in slave trade, 242, 244; ruler com-

pared with King of Kongo, 246; children learn adult tasks in, 271; religion of, 272; oral tradition in, 275, 276, 277, 278, 279; appliquéd cloths of, 289; French take over, *m* 560, 563, *m* 566; gains independence, 809

Daimyo, 592, 594

Daladier, Edouard: 688

Dali, Salvador: painting by, *p* 855

Damascus, 118, *m* 119, 122, *m* 795

Dan, *m* 267, 284

Danang, *m* 786

Dance: Hindu, *p* 205; African, *p* 263, 274, *p* 281, 283, *p* 284; Hopi snake, *p* 293

Dante Alighieri: 173, *p* 347, 350

Danube River, 84, *m* 84, 103, *m* 103

Danzig: becomes free city, 620 (box), *m* 621; Hitler demands, *m* 689, 690

Dar es Salaam, *m* 813

Dardanelles, 614, *m* 615

Darío, Rubén: 836

Dark Ages, 132

Darwin, Charles: *p* 536; develops theory of evolution, 5–6; impact of theories of, 535, 542–543

Darwinism: Fundamentalists attack, 535; Social, 536–537; contributes to insecurity, 539

David, Jacques Louis: paintings by, *p* 458, *p* 465, *p* 469

De Gaulle, Charles: nationalism of, 734, 737; popularity of, *p* 749; policies annoy western allies, 749–750

De-Stalinization: leads to cultural exchange, *p* 715; Khrushchev adopts policy of, 730, 758; unrest caused by, 758–760

Dead Sea, *m* 95, *m* 799

Deccan, *m* 202, 208

Decembrist Revolt, 638

Declaration of Independence, 430, 450, 454

Declaration of the Rights of Man and Citizen: Louis XVI refuses to approve, 453; excerpts from, 454; guarantees rights of Frenchmen, 455; expresses liberal goals, 478; Haitian response to, 820

Deist, 432

Delacroix, Ferdinand: painting reflects humanism, *p* 483

Delagoa Bay, *m* 252, 253

Delhi, *m* 210, *m* 578, *m* 783

Delian League, 50

Delphi, *p* 44, *m* 49

Demagogue, 73, 75–76

Demilitarization: of Rhineland, 620 (box); of Japan, 770

Democracy: in ancient Greece, 43–44, 52, 53–54; Rome lacks, 67; government by consent a foundation of, 430; *philosophes* on, 434, 436; limited by National Assembly, 454, 461; chauvinists feel inadequate, 502; German socialist party calls for greater, 518; Sun Yat-sen's version of, 590; disenchantment with, 664–665, 688; ideal of western civilization, 716, 717; in Japan, 771. *See also* Civil liberties

Democratic socialism, 534

Denazification, 743–744

Denmark, *m* 744; about 1520, *m* 337; colonies of, *m* 381; about 1763, *m* 389; about 1490, *m* 396; in Thirty Years' War, 404, *m* 405; about 1721, *m* 410; in 1815, *m* 481; loses Schleswig-Holstein, 497, *m* 498; in World War I, *m* 615; in World War II, 692, 698, *m* 704; joins NATO, 728; postwar prosperity of, 750

Depression. *See* Great Depression

Developing nations: goal of, 718; responsibility to, 722; Soviet Union as model for, 724; cold war reflected in aid to, 731, *p* 736; problems of, 848–849

Diamonds, 552, *p* 568

Dias, Bartholomeu: 366, *m* 370

Díaz, Porfirio: 826, 830, 832

Dickens, Charles: 512

Dictatorship: in Roman Empire, 64, 76, 83; chauvinists advocate, 502; modern, 600 (box); after World War I, 624, 663–664; Soviet, 647–660, 755–756, 761, 765–766; in Portugal and Spain, 750; in Turkey, 792; in Cuba, 838; masses manipulated in, 853. *See also* Authoritarianism; Autocracy

Dictatorship of the proletariat, 534

Diderot, Denis: 434, 436–437

Dienbienphu, 732, *m* 786, 787

Dingiswayo, 253

Diocletian, 99–100, 101–102

Directory, 462, 467

Disarmament, 619

Disraeli, Benjamin: 514, 515, 516–517

Divination, 273, 274

Divine Comedy, 173, *p* 347

Divine right: claimed by French kings, 406–407, 408, 447; Stuart kings claim, 414, 415; widely held view, 429

Djakarta, *m* 786

Dnieper River, *m* 133, 417, *m* 419

Dniester River, *m* 419, *m* 606

Domesday Book, 395

Dominican Republic, *m* 839; United States intervenes in, 842, 843

Don Quixote, 326, 328

Drake, Francis: 386

Drama: Greek, *p* 56, 57; Romans adopt Greek, 86; Shakespearean, *p* 413; in Japan, *p* 575, 593, *p* 594

Dreyfus Affair: 520, 798

Dubcek, Alexander: 760

Dublin, *m* 337

Dulles, John Foster: 732

Duma, 639, 642, 643

Dunkirk, 694, *m* 704

Dürer, Albert: woodcut by, *p* 335

Dutch: trading posts in Africa of, 236; at Cape of Good Hope, 251; explorations of, *m* 370; in America, 380, *m* 381, 383, 386–387, *m* 827; control East Indies, 380, *m* 381, 387, 785; art reflects commercial success of, *p* 384; source of prosperity of, 387–388; peasant family, *p* 445; Indian colonies of, *m* 578; in Japan, 592, 594; grant independence to East Indies, 787. *See also* Boers; Netherlands

Dutch Antilles, 380

Dutch East India Company, 251; success as joint-stock company, 385, 387, 785; opium trade of, 584

Dutch East Indies, *m* 389, 785; in World War II, 700, *m* 701; gain independence, 787

Dutch Guiana, *m* 827. *See also* Surinam

Dutch Republic, *m* 389, 415

Dutch West India Company, 386

E

Early Middle Ages, 131. *See also* Middle Ages

Earth (planet): beginnings of, 3; insignificance in universe of, 4, 348, 349–350, 855; changing concepts of, *p* 347, 348–349, 350, 351; Age of Exploration increases knowledge of, 390; needs balance in nature, 848; science and technology threaten, 853, 856

East Africa, *m* 257; trade of, 120, 217, 221, 231, 256–257; slave trade in, 243, *p* 245, 256, 257, 258, 260, 550; foreign impact on, 259; population movements in, 259–260; Portuguese reach, 366; European influence in, 550; European colonies in, *m* 560, 561, 566, *m* 566; in World War I, 617, *m* 621. *See also* Africa, sub-Saharan

East Asia: imperialism in, *m* 588; population of, *m* 851. *See also* China; Japan; Korea

East China Sea, *m* 588

East Germany, 708, *m* 744; creation of, 730, 743; standard of living in, 734. *See also* Eastern-Central Europe; Germany

East Indies: Indian spice trade with, 208; Portuguese sail to, 259; in Age of Exploration, *m* 370. *See also* Dutch East Indies

East Pakistan, 782, *m* 783

East Prussia, *m* 498; in 1721, *m* 410; Russia invades, 611; after World War I, *m* 621, *m* 689

Eastern-Central Europe, *m* 744; Slavic invaders from, 112, *m* 112; Byzantine influence on, 115; Mongols invade, 126, *m* 127; comes under Ottoman control, 127, *m* 128; obstacles to nation-states in, 416–417; aggression after World War I in, 624; Soviet take-over in, 710, 723, 725–726, 727; and Soviet Union, 731, 737, 752; ethnic groups in, 753; isolation of, 754, 755; effect of de-Stalinization on, 758–760

Eastern Orthodox Church, *p* 109, *p* 114, *m* 341; breaks with Roman Catholic Church, *m* 111, 112, 152; in Russia, 115, 418; Bolsheviks repress, *p* 651

Ecbatana, *m* 37

Ecologists, 848, 853

Economy: 99, 100–101; Byzantine, 110–111; Muslim, 120–122; medieval, 138–139; of southern India, 208; in precolonial Africa, 233, 234, 235, 236, 237, 238, 239, 249, 250, 251, 255–256, 266; of Amerinds, 295, 312; encourages exploration, 360–361; types of, 385; mercantilist, 385–386; development of a world, 388, 390; unsoundness of Spanish, 403–404; English, 506; gains in French, 520; in Europe's African colonies, 567; Chinese, 584; Japanese, 593, 594, 597, 772–773; unsoundness of tsarist Russian, 637, 642; in Soviet Union, 647, 650, 655, *p* 741; Euro-American, 717; capitalist, 735; postwar European, 745, 747, 750; postwar Asian, 770, 772–773, 776, 788; Turkish, 792; in Middle East, 802–804; in sub-Saharan Africa, 812, 815; Latin American, 829–830, 833, 837. *See also* Commercial Revolution

Ecuador, 823, *m* 827, *m* 839

Edict of Nantes, 406

Education: Spartan, 43; in ancient Greece, 43, 52, 54; Greeks influence Byzantine, 111; Muslim, 122; in Middle Ages, 132, 144, 146, *p* 147, 148, 164–165, *p* 165, 174; Confucian, 213, 215, 216, 218–219; in Africa, 269, 567, 569, 570, 571, 814, *p* 815; in Spanish colonies, 377; in Spain, 398; Enlightenment encourages, 431, 435, 437–438; Robespierre urges universal, 459; Napoleon recognizes importance of, 468–469; after Industrial Revolution, 506, 512; British, 516; socialism and, 518, 528; in India, 577, 780; Ch'ing revise Chinese, 589; Japanese, 596, 597, 770, *p* 772; in tsarist Russia, 633, 639; Soviet, *p* 741, 763–764, *p* 764, 765; in West Germany, 743; in Communist

China, 775; in Southeast Asia, 786, 788; reform of Turkish, 792; Jewish respect for, 796; in Latin America, 833, 838; developing nations need, 848

"Effective occupation," 561

Egypt, ancient: *m* 21; civilization arises in, 15, *m* 15, 19–20; importance of Nile to, 20–21, *p* 22; pharaoh as a god-king, 21–23; social classes in, 23; art and architecture reflect religious beliefs, 24, *p* 25, 26; hieroglyphics of, *p* 26, 27; scientific advances in, 27; trade of, 42, *m* 42, *m* 84, 85; Alexander conquers, 51, *m* 51, and Rome, 71, *m* 71, 83–84

Egypt, modern: *m* 795; in Muslim world, 118, *m* 119, 120; French invade, 466; British intervention in, *m* 552, 554–555, 558–559, *m* 560, *m* 566; nationalism in, 559, 800; in World War II, 703, *m* 704; gains independence, 794; republic established in, 793; nationalizes Suez Canal, 731, 800; forms United Arab Republic, 795; Arab nations fear domination by, 796; population growth hampers development in, *p* 736, 801, 803–804, *m* 851; actions provoke war, *m* 799, 800; Soviet aid to, 800, 801, 803; land reform in, 802

Einstein, Albert: *p* 541, 541–542, 798

Eisenhower, Dwight D.: 703, 721, 732

El Alamein, 703, *m* 704

El Salvador, 300, 303, *m* 827, *m* 839

Elath, *m* 799, 800

Elba, *m* 471, 474

Elizabeth I, 412, *p* 413

Enclosure movement, 509

Engels, Friedrich: 526, 529

England, *m* 42; Stone Age remains in, *p* 3; Christianity in, *m* 111, *m* 341; Germanic kingdom established in, 132, *m* 132; Northmen raid, 134, 417; medieval, *m* 159, 173–174; explorations of, *m* 370; American colonies of, *m* 381, 382, 383; grows prosperous through trade, 387–388, *m* 389, 507; as nation-state, 393; William of Normandy conquers, 395, *p* 395, 396; common law develops in, 396, 433; in Hundred Years' War, 394; monarchy limited in, 397, 414, 416; defeats Spanish Armada, 402; Elizabeth increases power of, 412, *p* 413; Civil War in, 415; Glorious Revolution in, 415–416; Voltaire admires, 433–434; upper class in, 443; population explosion in, 506–507; Agricultural Revolution in, 508–509; indus-

trialization in, *p* 505, 509–513, *p* 510; government of, 513, 514, *See also* Britain; Parliament

English Channel, *m* 133, *m* 618, 695, *m* 704

English East India Company, 385; in India, 576–577; abolished, 578; in China, 584

Enlightened despots, 432 (box)

Enlightenment: outgrowth of Scientific Revolution, 429; art of, *p* 429; leading thinkers of, 430–436; stresses reason, 436–437; effects of, 437–439; influences Neoclassic art, *p* 465; continuation of, 537

Environment: affects rise of civilization, 20; Amerinds seek to live in harmony with, 294, 295, 299, 318; science and technology threaten, 523, 853, 856; Owen believes character molded by, 528; in industrialized nations, 849

Epicureanism, 88–89

Equality: under Roman law, 90; Edict of Nantes guarantees, 406; bourgeoisie demand, 446; in United States, 450 (box); bourgeoisie gain, 454, 462; *Code Napoléon* guarantees, 468; French workers demand full, 484; as applied to colonial peoples, 567, 569; concept of, 600 (box); in industrialized nations, 746; in Soviet Union, 762

Equatorial Guinea, 809, *m* 813

Erasmus, Desiderius: 326, *p* 329

Eskimos, 7, 294–295, *m* 296

Estates (French), 442

Estonia: *m* 403, *m* 405, *m* 410; after World War I, *m* 621, 624; Soviet Union and, *m* 658, 724, *m* 744, 752

Ethiopia, 256, *m* 813; Christian tradition of, *p* 258; in Age of Imperialism, *m* 552, *m* 560, *m* 566; Italy invades, 687

Etruscans, 64, *m* 65, *p* 66, 67

Euclid, 55

Euphrates River, *m* 15, 19, 28, *m* 30

Europe, *m* 744; Ottomans feared in, 113; Mongols invade, 126, *m* 127; political disunity of Early Middle Ages in, 132, *m* 132; peoples, *m* 133; religion, *m* 111, 148, 335, 339, *m* 341, 344; Amerinds resist, 298; in 1520, *m* 337; reasons for expansion of, 360–362; changing view toward slavery in, 365; gains control of Asian trade, 367–368; in Age of Exploration, *m* 370; fails to understand Amerindian ways, 376; shift in business centers of, 387; population growth in, 388; controls world economy, 388, 390; rise of nation-states in, 394–425, *m* 396 (1490), *m* 403

(1560), *m* 405 (1648), *m* 410 (1721), *m* 419; attempts to maintain balance of power in, 404, 410–411; fears revolutionary France, 456, 457; Napoleon's conquests in, 467, 470, *m* 471; nationalism in, 472–473, 479, 554, 709; Industrial Revolution transforms, 506, 517; imperialism in Africa of, 548, *m* 552, 553–555, *m* 560, *m* 566; imperialism in India of, *m* 578; imperialism in East Asia of, 585–586, *m* 588; during World War I, 603–627, *m* 615, *m* 618; after Treaty of Versailles, *m* 621, 623–624, 625; fascism in, 663–664; German and Italian aggression in, *m* 689; during World War II, 692–696, 702–706, *m* 704; Hitler's New Order in, 696–698; after World War II, 708, *m* 709, 726, 808; in world affairs, 710, 715–716, 718; westernization of, 717; and Cold War, *m* 733; economic recovery of, 742–743, 751; potential unity of, 751; imperialism in Southeast Asia of, 785; attitude of cultural superiority in, 811; importance of Latin America to, 830; population of, *m* 851. *See also* Eastern-Central Europe; Western Europe; *and individual countries*

European Economic Community. *See* Common Market

European Recovery Program. *See* Marshall Plan

Evolution, theory of: 5–6, 535, 539, 543. *See also* Darwin

Excommunication, 147

Exploitation: of Amerinds, 377; of Africans, 379, 387, 564–565, 566, *p* 568; Marx's view of, 530, 533; by British in India, 577, 581; of conquered peoples by Nazis, 678, 697; Japanese, 700; of nonwestern world, 717; Soviet, 752; in Southeast Asia, 786; in Latin America, *p* 819, 820, 830

Exploration. *See* Age of Exploration

Extended family, 268. *See also* Family

F

Factory system, 511–512

Fair, 161, 505

Faisal, 794

Family: Hindu, 201–203; Chinese, 219–220, 591; Japanese, *p* 225; in Africa, 267–268; among Amerinds, 294–295, 297; Jewish, 796

Fanaticism: religious, 154–155, 432, *p* 433, 434; and Robespierre, 461; and professional revolutionaries, 645; in twentieth century, 600 (box)

Fante, *m* 235; states of, 242; British ally with, 561

Fascism: dictatorships established under, 663–664; factors underlying, 664–665; in Italy, 665–668, *m* 689; appeal of, 666–667, 668; in Spain, *p* 681; Perón's version of, 834

Fashoda, 559, *m* 560

Fertile Crescent, *m* 30, 36

Feudal lords, 131; obligations of, 134; way of life of, 135, 136, 163; treatment of serfs by, 140, 141; appeal of Crusades to, 152–153; power declines, 157, 322, *p* 393, 395, 396; in Germany, 399

Feudalism: rise of, 133–135; decline of, 157, 163; Japanese, 222, 224, *p* 225, 226, 592, 594, 595; in France, 394, 452–453

Fiefs, 134, 399

Filial piety, 220, 587

Finland, *m* 632, *m* 744; relations with Russia of, *m* 621, 624, 752, 753

Fire, 9–10

Firearms: contribute to decline of feudalism, 142, 169; factor in Age of Exploration, 362; *conquistadores* introduce to America, 376

Five-Year Plan, 655; in Soviet Union, 755; in Communist China, 776; in India, 782

Florence, *m* 159, 325, *p* 327, 382, *m* 493

Formosa, *m* 588. *See also* Taiwan

Fossils, 7, *p* 8

Fourier, Charles: 527–528

France, *m* 744; Roman expansion in, 84, *m* 84; law code based on Roman, 90; Christianity in, *m* 111, *m* 341, 429; Normans from, 113; medieval trade with, *m* 159, 161; about 1520, *m* 337; in America, *m* 370, 380, *m* 381, 382–383; religious wars of, 380, 394, 402; colonies of, *m* 389; formation of nation-state in, 394–395, 396; feudal system in, 394, 452; seeks to limit Hapsburg power, 401, *m* 403; in Thirty Years' War, 404, 405, *m* 405; absolutism in, 406–407; serves as cultural model, 407–408; religious persecution in, 408, *p* 433; and balance of power, 408, *m* 410, 410–411; Norsemen raid, 417; causes of revolution in, 442–449; revolutionary, 456, 457–461; Napoleonic, 468–470, *m* 471, and Congress of Vienna, 480–481, *m* 481; joins Quadruple Alliance, 482; Louis XVIII establishes parliament, 483; social revolt in, 484–486; gains Nice and Savoy, 494; defeated in Franco-Prussian

War, *m* 498, 499; Industrial Revolution in, 520, 522; imperialism in Africa of, *m* 552, 553, 554, 557, 558–560, *m* 560, 562–563, *m* 566; adopts policy of assimilation, 569, 570; imperialism in Asia of, *m* 578, *m* 588; in Triple Entente, 605; nationalism in, 607, 625; in World War I, 611–613, *m* 615, 618, *m* 618; effects of World War I on, 619–620, *m* 621; gains mandate over Syria, 624; fascist movement in, 664; anti-war sentiment in, 686, 687, 691; declares support of Poland, 690; World War II in, 692–694, 698, 703, *m* 704, 705, 708; occupies Germany, *m* 709; and NATO, 728, 737, 750; supports Israeli invasion of Egypt, 731, 793, 800; in Southeast Asia, 732, 785, 787; in Common Market, *p* 741; recovery since World War II in, 748–750; colonies gain independence from, 750, 795, 810; intervenes in Mexico, 826; Latin American colonies of, *m* 827, *m* 839. *See also* Enlightenment; French Revolution; Napoleon

Franchise, 478, 484, 488, 515

Francia, José Rodríguez, 828

Francis Ferdinand, 603, 604

Franco, Francisco: 688–689

Franco-Prussian War, 499, 519, 520, 554; factor in World War I, 605, 607

Frankfort, *m* 403, *m* 498

French Community, 810

French East India Company, 360, 765

French Equatorial Africa, *m* 566

French Guiana, *m* 827, *m* 839

French Revolution: causes of, 442–447; bourgeoisie lead, 448–451, 453; events in, 449; common people aid, 451–452; reforms of, 452–455; radicals control, 455–461; results of, 462–463; *Code Napoléon* reflects ideals of, 468; European rulers regard as disaster, 478; birth of modern nationalism in, 479; inspires revolt in Russia, 637–638; promotes better treatment of Jews, 796; influence in Latin America of, 820

French West Africa, *m* 566

Freud, Sigmund: 538–539

Friars, 146

Fujiyama, *m* 223

Fulani, 240, *m* 267

Fulbe, 236–237

Fundamentalists, 535–536

G

Gabon, 550, *m* 552, 809, *m* 813

Galápagos Islands, *p* 536

Galaxy, 4, *p* 5

Galen, 123, 355, 356

Galilei, Galileo: 349, *p* 350, 351–352, 353

Gallipoli, *m* 615, 615–617

Gama, Vasco da: 360, 366, *m* 370

Gambia, *m* 552, *m* 560, *m* 566, 809, *m* 813

Gandhi, Indira: 781

Gandhi, Mahatma: 581–582, *p* 582, 583, 781

Ganges River, 200, *m* 202, *p* 205

Gao, 235, *m* 235

Garibaldi, Giuseppe: *p* 491, 495

Gaucho, 828

Gaul, 64, 132, *m* 132; and Rome, *m* 71, *m* 72, 76, *m* 84, 85. *See also* France

Gautama, Siddhartha. *See* Buddha

General Assembly (UN), *p* 720

Geneva, *m* 159, *m* 341, 342, *m* 744

Geneva Conference, 732, 781, 787

Genoa, *m* 403, *m* 405, *m* 410

Gentry, 217, 219, 221, 584

Geography: Egyptian, 21; Greek, 42, *p* 44; Italian, 64, 67; increase in knowledge of, 121, 390; Indian, 200; Chinese, 211; African, 230–231, *m* 232; Latin American, 829

George III, 585

German Confederation, *m* 481, 496, 497, *m* 498

German Democratic Republic. *See* East Germany

German East Africa, *m* 560, *m* 566, 617, *m* 621

German Federal Republic. *See* West Germany

German states, *m* 341; medieval trade with, *m* 159, 161; criticism of Catholic Church in, 333, 340–342; obstacles to unification of, 399–400, 401, *m* 403; in Thirty Years' War, 404, *m* 405; in 1721, *m* 410; Revolution of 1848 in, 486; reduction in number of, 496, *m* 498; in Franco-Prussian War, 497, 499; unified, *m* 498, 499–500. *See also* German Confederation; Germany; Prussia

Germanic tribes. *See* Barbarians

Germany, *m* 744; Industrial Revolution in, 518–519, 520; nationalism in, 519, 607, 625; imperialism of, 519, 554, 557, 559, *m* 560, 561, *m* 566, *m* 588; 564; patriotism in, *p* 603, 609–610; in Triple Alliance, 605; generals urge war, 608–609; in World War I, 609, 611, 614, *m* 615, 617–618, *m* 618; after World War I, 619, 620 (box), *m* 621, 622, 624, 669, 670, *p* 677; relations with Soviet Union, 644, 648; rise of nazism in, 675–682; aggressions by Nazi, 671, 687–690, *m* 689; resistance movement in, 698–699; in World War II, 702, *m* 704, 705, 706; Allied occupation of, 708, *m*

709; division of, 730, 734; loses territory to Poland, 752. *See also* East Germany; West Germany

Gestapo, 678, 697

Ghana: ancient, 233–234, *m* 235; modern, *p* 807, 809, 810, *m* 813

Ghettoes, 796

Gibraltar, *m* 389, *m* 410, 411

Giotto: painting by, *p* 147

Girondins, 457, 458

Giza, *m* 21, *p* 25

Gladstone, William E.: 514; reforms of, 515, 516

Global order, 600 (box), 716, 718, 816

Glorious Revolution, 415, 416, 430

Goa, *m* 578, *m* 783

Gobi, *m* 215

Goebbels, Joseph: 678

Gogh, Vincent van: paintings by, *p* 445, *p* 521

Gold: in ancient America, 314, 317, *p* 373; Renaissance work with, *p* 327; Portuguese seek African, 363; greed of *conquistadores* for, 374, 375; discovered in Transvaal, 564

Gold Coast, 242, *m* 364; in Age of Imperialism, *m* 552, *m* 560, 561–562, *m* 566; seeks representation in government, 571; gains independence, 807, 809

Golden Horn, *p* 121

Gomulka, Wladislav: 731, 759

Good life: to Egyptians, 27, 32; to Mesopotamians, 31, 32; Socrates' idea of, 52–53; Hebrew concept of, 54, 58; Greek concept of, 54, 58, 60; to Stoics, 89; Christian, 97; of Amerinds, 299; in Renaissance, 323; United States as model for, 723

Good Neighbor Policy, 842

Göring, Hermann: 678, 697

Gorky, Maxim: *p* 636

Gothic cathedral, *p* 131, 170, 175

"Goulash communism," 757–758

Government: as characteristic of civilization, 14; in ancient Egypt, 22–23; in Greece, 42, 43, 45, 52; Roman, 82–83, 90–91, 99–100, 104; Byzantine, 111; Muslim, 118; Ottoman, 127; Aquinas on, 167; idea of limited, 175; in traditional China, 211, 214, 215–216, 217–219; feudal Japanese, 223, 224, 592; in precolonial Africa, 233, 237–238; 239, 241, 246, 249, 256, 264; in ancient America, 298, 299, 313, 316, 372–373; British, 416, 513, 514; of Kiev, 418; protects natural rights, 430; separation of powers in, 431; in France, 446–447, 456, 458–459, 467, 519, 520; by consent of people, 454; role in welfare of, 516, 533; in

German Reich, 518; interference in business opposed, 526; Marx's view of, 529; in African colonies, 567, 569–571; in colonial India, 581; in China, 583, 589, 591; modernization of Japanese, 595, 770, 771; mass politics and, 600 (box); of United States, 630–631; tsar represents Russian, 631; in Soviet Russia, 647, 651–652; weakness of Italian, 666; Nazi German, 675; Spanish, *p* 681; nonwestern nations develop dictatorial, 718; West German, 743, 745; Communist Chinese, 775; in South Vietnam, 787; instability in Middle East of, 791; Africa develops one-party, 814; in Latin America, 825, 833; may cause alienation, 856

Goya, Francisco: painting by, *p* 472

Gracchus, Gaius: 74

Gracchus, Tiberius: 73–74

Gran Chaco, *m* 839

Granada, *m* 159, *m* 396, 398

Great Britain. *See* Britain; England

Great Depression, 597, 674, 833, 837

Great Fish River, 250, *m* 252

Great Leap Forward, 776, 777

Great Trek, *m* 252, 254, *p* 563

Great Wall, 214, *m* 215

Great Zimbabwe, 255, *m* 257

Greece, ancient: *m* 49; contributes to western civilization, 41, 716; art and architecture, *p* 41, *p* 47, 57, *p* 59; colonies of, *m* 42, 64, *m* 65; government in, 42, 43, 45, 52, 53–54; education in, 43, 52, 54; trade of, 42, *m* 42; agriculture in, 42, *p* 44; daily life in, *p* 44, *p* 46, 46–47; defeats Persia, 48–50; civil war in, 50; Alexander spreads culture of, 51; achievements of, 52–58; concept of the good life, 58, 60; Rome conquers, 71, *m* 72, *m* 84; influence of, 64, *p* 81, 85, 86, 88, 89, 110, 111, 120, 122, 123, 124. *See also* Athens; Sparta

Greece, modern: *m* 744, 751; breaks away from Ottoman Empire, 479, *p* 483; in World War I, *m* 615, *m* 621; invades Turkey, 792; in World War II, 695, *m* 704; Communists incite civil war in, 725; United States aids, 726, 743; joins NATO, 732

Greek Orthodox Church. *See* Eastern Orthodox Church

Gregory VII (Pope), 399

Guadalcanal, *m* 701, 706

Guantánamo Bay naval base, *m* 839, 841

Guatemala, *m* 827, *p* 836, 837, *m* 839

Guayaquil, 823, *m* 827

Guerrilla warfare, 698, 721; Spaniards originate, 473; Mao wages, 591, 774; Yugoslav partisans wage, 695, 698; waged against Japanese, 700; success against traditional warfare, 721; in Vietnam, 787; in Mexican Revolution, 832; used by Castro, 838

Guevara, Ernesto ("Che"): 838, 842

Guianas, *m* 381, *m* 827

Guilds, medieval: *p* 131, 160–161, *p* 162

Guinea, 809, *m* 813

Guinea Coast, 230, *m* 232, 237–245, *m* 364, *m* 370

Gulf of Aqaba, *m* 799, 800

Gulf of Mexico, *m* 303, *m* 370, 372

Gunboat diplomacy, 841–842

Gupta period, *p* 199, 208

Gustavus Adolphus, 404

Guyana, *m* 839

H

Hagia Sophia, *p* 109, 114

Haiku, 593–594

Haiti, 821, 822, *m* 827, *m* 839

Hamburg, *m* 159, 620 (box), *m* 709

Hammurabi, 28; empire of, *m* 29; excerpts from Code of, 29, 32

Han dynasty, 214–215, *m* 216. *See also* China

Hannibal, 69–70, *m* 71

Hanoi, *m* 786

Hanover, *m* 410, *m* 481, *m* 498

Hanseatic League, *m* 396

Hapsburgs: empire of, 401; Austrian, 401–402, *m* 403; Spanish, *m* 403, *m* 405; Thirty Years' War causes decline in power of, 404, *m* 405; threaten to destroy balance of power, 411

Harappan culture, 200, 201, *m* 202

Harvey, William: 356

Hausa, *m* 235, 239–240, *m* 267

Havana, *m* 839

Hawaiian Islands, 699, *m* 701

Hebrews: origins of, 33; contributions to civilization of, 34–36, 41, 716, 796. *See also* Jews; Judaism

Heisenberg, Werner: 540

Hejira, 116

Heliocentric theory, *p* 347, 348, 349, 543

Hellespont, 48, *m* 50, 110

Helots, 43

Henry, Prince: 360, 363–368

Henry II (King of England), 396

Henry IV (Holy Roman Emperor), 399

Henry IV (King of France), 380, 402, 406

Henry V (play), *p* 413

Henry VIII (King of England), 412

Heresy, 147, 167, 335, 339, 394, 398

Herodotus, 48, 58

Herzegovina, 604, 605, *m* 606

Hidalgo, Miguel: 821–822

Hideyoshi, 582

Hieroglyphics: Egyptian, *p* 26, 27; Olmec develop, 303–304; Monte Albán uses, 305; Mayan, 308

High Middle Ages, 164. *See also* Middle Ages

Himalayas, 200, *m* 202

Himmler, Heinrich: 678

Hinduism: foundations of, 200; teachings of, 203–204; art illustrates legends of, *p* 205; dominant religion in India, 207, 208; spread of, *m* 206, 208, 785; and Islam, 209, *p* 209, 210; and Sepoy Rebellion, 578, *p* 579; Gandhi opposes, 582

Hippocrates, 55, 123

Hiroshima, *m* 701, 707, *m* 774

History: Greek interest in, 57–58; Muslim interest in, 124; Marxist interpretation of, 532–533

Hitler, Adolf: 669, *p* 672; beliefs, 670–673; rise to power, 674–675; opponents attempt to kill, 680n, 699; and World War II, 686; aggressions of, 688, 690; misjudged, 691; New Order of, 696–698; commits suicide, 706

Hitler-Stalin Pact, 690–691

Hittites, *m* 30, 32

Ho Chi Minh, 532, 732, 787

Ho Chi Minh Trail, *m* 786

Hohenzollerns, 411, 496, 497, 499

Hokkaido, *m* 223, *m* 774

Holland, 161, 326, *m* 337. *See also* Dutch; Netherlands

Holstein, 497, *m* 498

Holy Land, 113. *See also* Palestine

Holy Roman Emperor, 132, 399–400, 401, 404–405

Holy Roman Empire: Christianity spreads to, *m* 111, 339, *m* 341; during Crusades, *m* 154, *m* 155; territory at height, *m* 396, 399; in 1560, *m* 403; in 1648, *m* 405; in 1721, *m* 410

Homer, 55–56

Homo erectus, 6

Homo sapiens, 6, 13

Honduras, *m* 827, *m* 839

Hong Kong, *m* 588, 700, *m* 701, *m* 774, *p* 778

Honshu, *m* 223, *m* 774

Hopi, *p* 293, *m* 296, 300

Horace, 91

Hormuz, 362, *m* 370

Horse: of medieval period, *p* 137; Spaniards introduce to America, 299, 376; in art, *p* 327; Amerinds adopt, *p* 378

Hottentots, 249

House of Commons, 397, 415, 514

House of Lords, 397, 415, 514

Housing: in ancient Greece, 46; Roman, 86; medieval, 136, 141; in industrial areas, 506, 512; in Soviet Union, 763; in developing nations, 848

Hsi (West) River, 211, *m* 215

Hudson, Henry: *m* 370, 380

Hudson Bay, *m* 296, 364, 371

Hué, *m* 786

Huguenots, 251, 402, 406, 408, *p* 433

Humanism, 323; admiration for Graeco-Roman culture of, 323–325; Renaissance art expresses, 330; factor in Reformation, 339; in England, *p* 413

Hundred Years' War, 394, 395

Hungarian Revolution, 731, *p* 759, 759–760

Hungary, *m* 704, *m* 744; Huns settle in, 104; spread of Christianity to, *m* 111, *m* 341; Mongols invade, 126, *m* 127; in 1490, *m* 396; Ottomans move into, 401, *m* 403; in 1648, *m* 405; in 1721, *m* 410; and Austria, 487, 488; separated from Austria, *m* 621, 624; fascism in, 664; communist uprising in, 670; revolt in, 731, *p* 759, 759–760. *See also* Eastern-Central Europe

Huns, 102–103, *m* 103, 104

Hussein, 794–795

I

Iaroslav the Wise, 418

Ibn Batuta, 121

Ibn er-Rushd, 124

Ibn Khaldun, 124, 234

Ibn Saud, 793

Ibn Sina, 124

Ibo, 244, *m* 267, 564

Ice Age, 293, *m* 296

Iceland, *m* 381, 728, *m* 744

Ife, *m* 235; art of, 238, *p* 239, 285, 287, *p* 287

Ikon, *p* 114, 418

Iliad, p 41, 56

Illyria, 64, *m* 65

Imperial Duma, 642

Imperialism: Russian, 423, 424; causes of, 553–556; in Africa, 548–553, *m* 552, 556–566, *m* 560, *m* 566; in India, 576–583, *m* 578; in China, 583–591, *m* 588; in Japan, 592–598; Japanese, *m* 588, 597–598, 700; European competition in, 606–607; Wilson criticizes, 619; Soviet, 710, 725, 752, 753; in Southeast Asia, 700, 785; in North Africa, 795; Suez Canal symbol of western, 800

Impressionism, *p* 521

Incas: culture of, 314–317, *p* 316, *p* 373; empire of, *m* 315, 372–373; Spaniards conquer, 375

Independent Congo State, *m* 560; Leopold II exploits, 565, *p* 568. *See also* Belgian Congo

India, *m* 783; early civilization in, *m* 15, 200–201, *m* 202; invaded, 51, *m* 51, 207–208, 210; art and architecture of, *p* 59, *p* 199, 208, *p* 209, 210; trade of, 85, 111, 161, 215, 217, 221, 507, 511, 785; and Muslims, 118, *m* 119, 120, 208–209; religion in, 200, 203, 204, *p* 205, *m* 206, 208, *p* 579, 582, 779; caste system of, 203, 580, 780; Maurya Empire in, 207–208, *m* 208; Gupta period, 208; Mughal Empire in, 209–210, *m* 210, 576; Portuguese reach, 366–367, *m* 370; British control of, *p* 575, 576–581, *m* 578, *p* 579; agriculture in, 580, 781, *p* 784; nationalist movement in, 581–583; independence, 747, 780, 781; problems of, *p* 769, 780–782; neutrality of, 782; relations with Pakistan, 784

Indian Nationalist Congress, 581, 779, 782

Indian Ocean, *m* 119, 200; trade, 256, 257, 259

Indians, American. *See* Amerinds

Indo-Aryans, 200–201, *m* 202

Indo-China, *m* 701, 732, 785. *See also* Cambodia; Laos; Vietnam

Indonesia, 731, *m* 786

Indulgences, *p* 338, 339, 342–343

Indus River, *m* 15, 200

Industrial Revolution, 509–511; impact of, *p* 505, 506, *p* 510, 511–512; factors leading to, 506–508; Agricultural Revolution accompanies, 508–509; impact on England of, 511–512, 515–517; transforms Germany, 518, 519; legacy of, 522–523

Industrialization: in England, 509–512; attitudes toward, 526–527; socialism and, 527; as factor in New Imperialism, 554, 555–556; in China, 587, 775; in Japan, 596, *p* 769, 772–773; in tsarist Russia, 640; in Soviet Union, 654, 655–656, 756, 757, 762; in Communist China, 776, 777; in India, 580, 781, *p* 784; Southeast Asia needs, 788; problems accompanying, 802

Industry: in third-century Rome, 99; in T'ang China, 217; Muslim, 121–122; medieval, 138; in Spain, 398, 399, 403; in France, 408, 461, 469, 484, 748–749; Sardinian, 494; importance of cotton, 509–511; development of heavy, 511; in Fascist Italy, 668; Nazi German, 677; role of defense, 721; destruction in World War II of, 742; West German, 745, 746; nationaliza-

Kingdom of the Two Sicilies, 492, *m* 493, 495
Kinshasa, *m* 246, 248, 809, *m* 813
Kinship, 251, 264, 267–268
Kirov, Sergei: 658, 758
Kivas, *p* 293, 299
Knights, 135–136, *p* 137, 137–138, 142
Knossos, *m* 30
Komsomol. *See* Young Communist League
Kongo, 244, 246–247, *m* 246
Koran, 116–117, 122, 125, 792
Korea, *m* 206, *m* 774; China becomes model for, *m* 216, 217; Japan annexes, 588, *m* 588, 597; in World War II, *m* 701; Communist Chinese aggression in, 729
Korean War, 729, 756, 771, 778
Kornilov, Lavr: 645
Kosygin, Aleksei: 761
Kraal, 250, 268; of Shaka, 253
Kremlin, 419, 421, *p* 422, 650
Krishna, *p* 205
Kronstadt, *m* 632, 649
Kuala Lumpur, *m* 786
Kuan-yin, *p* 199
Kubitschek, Juscelino: 834, 843
Kulaks, 642, 650, 657
K'ung Fu-tzu. *See* Confucius
Kuomintang, 590–591, 729
Kuwait, *m* 795
Kyoto, *m* 223, 224, *m* 593
Kyushu, *m* 223

L

La Plata, *m* 381, *m* 389, *m* 827
Labor: specialization in Africa of, 265; scarcity in New World of, 376; use in America of African, 379; population explosion increases supply of, 507; impact of industrialization on, *p* 510, 511–512; Europeans exploit African, 564, 565, 566; cheap in Latin America, *p* 831
Labor unions: French, 454, 519; moderate liberals oppose, 478; growing strength of, 522, 664; Marx fails to foresee impact of, 533; in Soviet Russia, 652; middle class feels threatened by, 667, 680; abolished in Fascist Italy, 668; Hitler abolishes, 675; West German, 745; in postwar Japan, 770; in Mexico, 832
Labour Party, 746, 747–748
Labrador, 380, *m* 381
Ladino, *p* 836, 837
Lafayette, Marquis de: 443
Lagos, *m* 364, *m* 552, *m* 560, 571. *See also* Nigeria
Lagos, Portugal: 365
Laissez-faire capitalism, 536
Laissez-faire policy, 526
Lalibela, *p* 258
Land ownership: in Rome, 73–74, 86, in sub-Saharan Africa, 251, 265; Boer concept conflicts with Bantu, 252; in Mesoamerica, 301; in Spanish colonies, 377; in France, 442, 444, 445; affects economic growth, 509; in colonial Africa, 567; in India, 580; in China, 587; in Russia, 634, 638, 646, 648; reform in Japanese, 770; in Communist China, 776; in Southeast Asia, 788; reform in Egypt of, 802; in Latin America, *p* 819, 825, 834, 838
Landowners: fear working class, 485, 664; favored in Fascist Italy, 668; attack Weimar Republic, 670; in Middle East, 802; Mexicans revolt against, *p* 819; fear Alliance for Progress, 843. *See also* Gentry; *Patrón*
Language: Arabic, 125; derivation of, 105; vernacular, 173; development of modern, 175; as barrier to understanding, 630. *See also* Latin
Lao Dong, 787
Lao-tzu, 214
Laos, 732, 785, *m* 786. *See also* Southeast Asia
Las Casas, Bartolomé de: 377
Latifundia, 73
Latin (language): use in Roman Empire of, 85; barbarians adopt, 104; as bond of unity, 105; in medieval learning, *p* 165; languages derived from, 173
Latin America, 819, *m* 827, *m* 839; law code based on Roman, 90; Europe base for culture of, 376, 390; American Revolution influences, 450 (box); art and architecture of, *p* 819, 836, *p* 836; agriculture of, *p* 819, 829–830, *p* 831; Wars of Independence in, 820–824, *m* 827; politics in, 825; Church declines in power in, 825–826, 835; nation-states arise in, 826, 828–829; reasons for underdevelopment in, 829–830; modernization in, *p* 831, 831–832, 833–834; literature of, 835–836; changing social outlooks in, 836–837; relations with United States of, 721, 840–844; Cuban Revolution in, 838, 840; distrust of Castro in, 735; population of, *m* 851. *See also* Amerinds; Mesoamerica; South America
Latin Christendom, 113, 115, 131, *m* 218
Latins, *p* 63, 64
Latvia, *m* 621, 624, *m* 744, 752
Law: in Mesopotamia, 29, 32; Judaic, 35, 93, 94; in Rome, 67, 85, 90, 105; in Middle Ages, 132, 135, 142, 158–159; abuse of power reflected in unjust, 167; in India, 207, 578, 580; in Japan, 224; Calvinist, 342; in America, 376; in England, 433, 434; in France, 454, 468; socialist parties seek reform through, 532; in African colonies, 567, 569; inequalities under Russian, 633
Law of Gravity, 353
Law of Inertia, 353
Laws of Planetary Motion. *See* Planetary Motion
League of Nations, 619, 620 (box), 687, 723
Lebanon, *m* 795; cedars of, *p* 33; mandate, *m* 621, 624, 793; seeks balance between Christians and Muslims, 795
Leeuwenhoek, Anton van: 356
Legalism, 214, 215
Legislative Assembly, 457
Leipzig, *m* 471, 473, 474, *m* 498
Lenin, V. I.: *p* 629; heir of Marx, 532; goals of, 630, 645, 646; institutes war communism, 648; New Economic Policy of, 649; seeks to achieve monolithic unity, 650–652; promotes communism internationally, 652–653
Leningrad, 695–696, *m* 704
Leo X (Pope), *p* 338, 340
Leopold II, *p* 568; and Independent Congo State, 557, 559, 560, *m* 560, 565
Lepanto, 402, *m* 403
Li Po: poetry of, *p* 220
Libby, Willard F.: 7
Liberal Party (British), 515, 517
Liberals, 478; criticize Congress of Vienna, 482; revolts by, 434, 479, 482–483, 484, 486; goals of, 487, 488; Bismarck wins support of German, 497–498; British, 526; advocate social reforms for workers, 527
Liberia, *m* 552, *m* 813
Libya, *m* 566, *m* 689, *m* 704, *m* 795
Life expectancy, 506, 834–835, 848, 850
Light year, 4
Lima, *m* 827, *m* 839
Limited monarchy, 395–398, 412–416, 478, 493. *See also* Monarchy
Lincoln, Abraham: 841
Lisbon, *m* 159, *m* 364, *m* 744
Literature: Greek, 41, 324; Roman, 90–92, 324; Muslim, 125–126; medieval, 171–174; Renaissance, 326, 328–329; in Elizabethan England, *p* 413; Russian, 418, *p* 636, 656, 764; in Romantic period, *p* 483; Latin American, 835–836
Lithuania, *m* 744; in 1490, *m* 396; in 1560, *m* 403; in 1648, *m* 405; in 1721, *m* 410; threatens Mos-

cow, 421; Poland takes over, 423; after World War I, 620, *m* 621, 624; Soviet Union annexes, 752
Livingstone, David: 547, 548, 557
Livy, 70
Locke, John: 430–431, 437
Lombardy, 492, *m* 493, 494
London, *m* 744; and trade, *m* 159, *p* 413, 501, 507; Nazi bombing of, *p* 685
Long March, 580
Long Parliament, 414, 415
Lorraine, *m* 410. *See also* Alsace–Lorraine
Louis XIII, 406
Louis XIV, 406–408, *p* 409, 410
Louis XVI, *p* 452; executed, 441; inefficiency of, 447; calls States-General, 449; authority challenged, 450; opposes National Assembly, 450–451; attempts to flee France, *p* 452, 456; approves abolition of feudalism, 453
Louis XVIII, 474, 483–484
Louis Napoleon, 486. *See also* Napoleon III
Louis Philippe, 484, *p* 485
Louisiana, *m* 381, *m* 389
L'Ouverture, Toussaint: 821
Loyola, Ignatius: 343
Luba, 248, *m* 267
Lugard, Frederick: 557–558
Lunda, *m* 246, 248, *m* 267
Luther, Martin: *p* 335; disagrees with Church teachings, 336–339; attacks system of indulgences, 339. *See also* Reformation
Lutheranism, 341, *m* 341, 401, 404
Luxembourg, *m* 744; in 1490, *m* 396; under Germany, *m* 498; in World War I, *m* 618; Germany invades, 693; Benelux nation, 728
Lydians, *m* 30, 32

M

Macao, 364, *p* 366, *m* 370, *m* 588
Macedonia: conquers ancient Greece, 50–51, *m* 51; Rome and, 64, 71, *m* 72, 85
Machiavelli, Niccolò: 323, 328–329
Machu Picchu, *m* 315, *p* 373
Madagascar, *m* 232, *m* 257; in Age of Imperialism, *m* 552, *m* 560, *m* 566
Madeira, 364, *m* 364
Madrid, *m* 370, *m* 744
Magellan, Ferdinand: 369, *m* 370, 371
Maginot Line, *m* 689, 691, 693
Magna Carta, 175n, 397
Magyars, *m* 133, 134, 417. *See also* Hungary
Malabar Coast, 367, *m* 389
Malagasy Republic, *m* 813
Malawi, 255, 256, *m* 813

Malaya, *m* 206, 699, 700, *m* 701, 785, 787
Malaysia, *m* 786
Mali: part of ancient Ghana, 233; ancient state of, 234–235, *m* 235; modern, *m* 813
Malinche, 374
Malthus, T. R.: 526–527
Man: search for early, 6; Paleolithic, 9–13; Neolithic, 13–14; Egyptians expect great things of, 32; Mesopotamians regard as unimportant, 32; Hebrew idea of duty of, 35; Stoic idea of brotherhood of, 89; Christianity stresses brotherhood of, 97; Renaissance, 323; freedom of, 435; Rousseau on, 436; Enlightenment raises questions on nature of, 438–439; relation to technology of, 523; equality of, 600 (box); alienation of, 855–856, *p* 855; able to shape destiny, 857
Managua, *m* 839
Manchuria, 211, *m* 215, *m* 774; Japan takes over, 597, 699, 700, *m* 701; Soviet Union invades, 707; returned to China, 736; in Chinese civil war, 774
Manchus. *See* Ch'ing dynasty
Mandalay, *m* 786
Mandarins, 218; role in China's government of, 219, 583; organize armies, 587; and reform, 588–589
Mandates, *m* 621, 624, 793
Manila, *m* 701
Manioc, 388
Manor, *p* 131, 132, 138–139
Mansa Musa, 234–235
Mao Tse-tung, *p* 769; heir of Marx, 532; urges revolution in China, 591; forces gain control of China, 729; support grows, 774; Cultural Revolution of, 777
March on Rome, 664
March Revolution, 643
Marches, The: *m* 493, 495
Marco Polo, 221; ships of, *p* 361
Marcus Aurelius, *p* 63, 89
Marie Antoinette, *p* 443, 447
Marius, 74–75, 76
Mark Antony, 81
Market: medieval, *p* 151; in sub-Saharan Africa, 265; in Tenochtitlán, 372; and Industrial Revolution, 507, 511; in modern Latin America, *p* 836
Marne River, 609, *m* 618
Marseilles, *m* 155, 157
Marshall, General George C.: 742
Marshall Plan, 743, 745, 748, 751
Martí, José: 836
Martinique, *m* 389
Marx, Karl: 528, *p* 531, 798; theories of, 529–530, 532, 534; influence of, 554, 645

Marxism: impact of, 532; weaknesses of, 533; offshoots of, 534–535
Marxism-Leninism, 650; in Soviet Union, 652, 757, 763; Communist Chinese interpretation of, 736; Sino-Soviet disagreement on, 779; in Chile, 834; Castro supports, 838
Masai, *m* 267, *p* 270
Masaryk, Jan: 754
Masks: African, *p* 263, *p* 284, 284–285; Amerindian, 295, 298, 305
Mass politics, 600 (box)
Massive retaliation, 732, 733, 735
Masterpiece, 161
Mathematics: Egyptian use of, 27; Greek, 55; Muslims improve, 123; advances in Indian, 208; Mayan, 310; Incas use, 316
Matrilineal family, 268
Matsu, *m* 774
Mauritania, 233, 809, *m* 813
Maurya Empire, 207–208, *m* 208
Maximilian, 826
May Fourth movement, 590
Mayan civilization, 307–310, *p* 308, *m* 309, *p* 311. *See also* Toltec-Mayan culture
Mazarin, Cardinal: 406
Mazzini, Guiseppe: 492–495, 501
Mecca, 116, *m* 119, *m* 795
Medea, *m* 37
Medicine: Egyptian, 27; Mesopotamian, 31–32; Greek, 55; Roman, 89; Muslim, 123–124, *p* 123; medieval advances in, 168–169; advances in Indian, 208; biological advances and, *p* 355; in Africa, 572; and life expectancy, 850
Mediterranean Sea, *m* 65; Greek and Phoenician colonies on, *m* 42; Romans control, *m* 84; Byzantine Empire and, *m* 112; medieval trade around, *m* 159; caravan routes link Sudan and, 233, *m* 235; Venice dominates eastern, 360, *p* 361; Ottoman Turks become power in, 401, 402
Meiji Restoration, 595
Mein Kampf, 670
Mekong River, *m* 786
Memel, 620 (box), *m* 621
Mensheviks, 645
Mercantilism, *m* 381, 385–387
Merchants: ancient Greek, *p* 46; guild of, 160; in Hindu society, 203; among Aztecs, 313, 372; support voyages of exploration, 361; Chinese view of, 363; Inca, 372; Commercial Revolution increases power of, *p* 384, 385; in Japan, 592, 594
Mesoamerica, *m* 15, 300–301; probable contact with North America of, 298, 299; cultures of, 301–313, *m* 303, *m* 306, *m*

p 483; reflects nationalism, *p* 500

Muslim civilization, 109–110, 115–120, 128; science and technology of, 122–124, *p* 123, 801; art and architecture of, 124–125, *p* 125, *p* 236, *p* 803; literature of, 125–126; contributes to Spanish culture, 398; and Arab nationalism, 793. *See also* Islam

Muslim League, 779, 782

Muslim world, 118–119, *m* 119; Seljuks take over much of, 120; economy of, 120–122; conquered by Mongols, 126, *m* 127

Muslims, 116, *m* 133; duties of, 117; trade of, *m* 119, *m* 127, 161, 257, 259, 360; in Mediterranean, 134; and Crusades, *m* 154, 154–156, *m* 155, 157; in India, 208–210, 578, 581, *p* 769; view of slavery by, 365; expelled from Spain, 399. *See also* Almoravids; Islam

Mussolini, Benito: *p* 663; early life of, 665–666; appeals to dissatisfied Italians, 666–667; gains control of government, 667; goals compared with Hitler's, 669; invades France, 694; overthrown, 703

Mutapa, 255, 256, *m* 257

Mutsuhito (Emperor Meiji), 595

Mycenaea, *p* 34

Mystery religions: 97–98

N

Nagasaki, *m* 223, 592, 594; trading post at, 364, 592, *m* 593; atomic bomb destroys, *m* 701, 707

Nagy, Imre: 731, 757, 759

Nairobi, *m* 813

Namib Desert, *m* 232

Nanking, *m* 558, 591

Naples, *m* 159, *m* 493, 495; Kingdom of, *m* 337, *m* 403, *m* 471

Napoleon Bonaparte, *p* 465; rise to power of, 462, 466–467; Emperor of the French, 468, *p* 469; reforms of, 468–469; victories of, 470, *m* 471; reasons for downfall, 470–474; assessment of, 475

Napoleon III, 479, 494, 519–520

Napoleonic Wars, 470, *m* 471; impact of, 473, 637–638

Nara, *m* 223, 223–224, *m* 774

Nasser, Gamal Abdel: popularity in Arab world of, 794; leads Pan-Arabism movement, 796; nationalizes Suez Canal, 800; reforms of, 802

Natal, 252, *m* 252, 254, *m* 552, *m* 560

Nation-states, 322, 347, 393; established, 394–399; Germany and Italy fail to build, 399–400, 411–412; patterns of building, 400;

contention for power among, 401–406; absolutism of French, 406–408, 410–411; limited monarchy in English, 412, 414–416; fail to develop in Eastern Europe, 416; origins of Russian, 417–418, 420; attempts to build unified Russian, 420–425; develop in Latin America, 826, 828, 829

National Assembly: formed, 450; overcomes opposition, 451; abolishes feudalism, 452–453; reforms of, 453–455

National Convention, 457, 458

National liberation, 653, 731, 779

National Liberation Front, 787

National minorities: create unrest in Europe, 607, 617; cause problems after World War I, 620, 625; Lenin tries to solve problem of, 652

National Socialism (nazism): beliefs of, 670–673; grows in power, 674–675; reasons for German support of, 679–682

National Socialist Workers' Party. *See* Nazi Party

Nationalism: French Revolution introduces modern, 463, 479; contributes to Napoleon's downfall, 472; threatens Austrian Empire, 480; Congress of Vienna opposes, 482; as overwhelming force, 487, 498; in German Empire, 500, 519; music reflects, *p* 500; identified with liberty, 501; evils of extreme, 501–502; as factor in New Imperialism, 555; in Egypt, 559; in India, 578, 581, 582–583; in China, 589, 590; in Japan, 597; effect of, 600 (box); among Slavs, 604; contributes to World War I, 607; intensifies after World War I, 625; in Soviet Union, 647; factor in growth of fascism, 665, 679–680; declines in Western Europe, 708–709; increases in colonial countries, 718; Cominform crushes, 727; leads to breakup of worldwide communism, 736, 737; in Eastern-Central Europe, 752, 753, 759, *p* 759; in Southeast Asia, 786–787; in Arab lands, 793; in North Africa, 795; among Jews, 798; cultural, 811; in Latin America, 828–829, 833, 834

Nationalist China, 771, 775; cooperates with Communist Chinese, 590; government of, 591; anti-Japanese attitude in, 598, 773; relations with United States, 732, 774; Communists defeat in China, 773; Communists threaten, 734; in Taiwan, 775

Nationalists: revolutions of, 479; Revolution of 1848 inspires, 486; goals of, 488, 499; Italian, 666,

667; German, 670–671; Southeast Asian, 700

Nationalization: in postwar Britain, 747–748; of French industry, 748; in Eastern-Central Europe, 754; of Suez Canal, 800; in Latin America, 832, 833, 834, 838

Natural law, 352, 353, 354

Natural resources: availability contributes to Industrial Revolution, 508, 511; Japan's need for, 699; West German wealth in, 745; unwise use of, *p* 847, 852

Natural rights, 430

Natural selection, 6

Nature: Greek interest in, 54–55; Muslim interest in, 123; Taoism advocates return to, 214; Amerinds stress harmony with, 295, 299, 318; Scientific Revolution increases knowledge of, 356; unpredictability of, 542. *See also* Environment

Navarre, *m* 396

Nayarit, *m* 303; art of, *p* 301

Nazca, 314, *m* 315, 316

Nazi Party, 670, 673, 676, 678–679

Ndebele, 256, *m* 667

Neanderthal man, 13

Near East, ancient: *m* 30; rise of civilization in, 15–16, 18–37; Persian Empire unifies, 37; legacy of, 38

Négritude, 811, 813

Nehru, Jawaharlal: *p* 582, 582–583, 781–782

Neoclassic art, *p* 465

Neo-colonialism, 814, 815

Neolithic period, *p* 11, 13–14

NEP. *See* New Economic Policy

Nepal, *m* 206, *m* 578, *m* 783

Netherlands: medieval trade with, *m* 159, 161; under Spanish rule, 401, *m* 403; independence of, 402, *m* 405; in 1721, *m* 410; Britain fears French control of, 470; in 1815, *m* 481; in World War II, 693, *m* 704; Benelux nation, 728; postwar prosperity of, 750. *See also* Dutch; United Netherlands

Neutral nations: in World War I, 609, *m* 615; in World War II, *m* 704; today, *m* 744

Neutrality, 617

Nevsky, Alexander: 419

New Amsterdam (New York), *m* 381

New Andalusia (Venezuela), *m* 381

New Castile (Peru), *m* 381

New Economic Policy (NEP), 649–650, 654

New England, *m* 381

New Estremadura (Chile), *m* 381

New France, *m* 381, 382–383

New Granada, *m* 381, 822, *m* 827

New Guinea, *m* 389, *m* 786, *m* 621, *m* 701
New Holland, *m* 389
New Netherlands, *m* 381
New Orleans, *m* 389
New Spain. *See* Mexico
New Sweden, *m* 381
New Testament, 93, 97, 339. *See also* Bible
New World. *See* America
New Zealand, 569–570, 614, *m* 621, 732
Newfoundland, 380, *m* 381
Newton, Sir Isaac: 353–354
Ngodo, 282
Ngoni, 256, 260, *m* 267, 272
Nguni, 253, 256n
Nicaragua, *m* 827, *m* 839, 841
Nice, *m* 493, 494
Nicholas I, 631, 638
Nicholas II, *p* 629, 641, 642, 643
Nietzsche, Friedrich: 537–538
Niger, 809, *m* 813
Niger River: trade on, 231, *m* 232, 549, 560; exploration of, 240, 549, 557
Nigeria, *m* 813; art in, *p* 239, 285, 286–287, *p* 287; resistance to British in, 564, *m* 566; gains independence, 809
Nike of Samothrace, *p* 59
Nile River, *m* 15, *p* 22; importance to development of civilization of, 19–20; importance to Egypt of, 20–21; Europeans seek source of, 550; Aswam Dam on, 803
Ninety-Five Theses, 339
Nineveh, *m* 36
Nirvana, 207
Nixon, Richard M.: 843
Nkrumah, Kwame: 807, 809–810
N.K.V.D., 648, 659
Nobility. *See* Aristocracy
Noh drama, 226, 593
Nok culture, 287
Nonviolence, 581
Normandy, 703, *m* 704
Normans, *m* 133; in Italy, 113; conquer England, 395, *p* 395, 396
Norsemen, 417–418
North Africa, *m* 795; Roman conquest of, 64, 109; Muslim conquests in, 118, *m* 119; Ottoman conquests in, 127, *m* 128; in World War I, *m* 615; in World War II, 703, *m* 704; cultural ties to Middle East of, 795; modernization in, 795–796. *See also* Carthage
North America: Amerinds of ancient, 294–300, *m* 296; in Age of Exploration, *m* 370; French exploration in, 380, 382; European colonies in, *m* 381; in colonial system, *m* 389
North Atlantic Treaty Organization (NATO), *m* 744; development of, 728–729; becomes military reality, 730; Greece and Turkey join, 732; French forces withdrawn from, 737, 750; encourages European cooperation, 751
North German Confederation, 497, *m* 498
North Korea, 729, *m* 774. *See also* Korea
North Sea, *m* 159, 617, *m* 704
North Vietnam, *m* 786, 787–788. *See also* Vietnam
Norway, *m* 744; religion in, *m* 341; in 1490, *m* 396; in 1721, *m* 410; in World War II, 692, *m* 704; postwar prosperity in, 750
Novgorod, *m* 159, 419, *m* 419
Nubia, *m* 21
Nuclear weapons: contribute to insecurity, 715; impact on world politics of, 600 (box), 721; threat of, 732, 853; in Cuba, 735; Soviet possession of, 761; United States leadership in, 765
Nuremberg, *m* 498, *m* 689; and medieval trade, *m* 159; propaganda rallies in, 676; war criminals tried in, 743
Nuri Pasha es-Said, 794
Nyamwezi, *m* 257, 260
Nyasaland, *m* 566

O

OAS. *See* Organization of American States
Oaxaca, 305, 306, *m* 306, *m* 827. *See also* Monte Albán
Ob River, *m* 419
Octavian, 78, 81, 82. *See also* Augustus
Oder River, *m* 498
Odoacer, 104
Oedipus Rex, p 56
Oil: importance in Middle East of, 791, 794, *p* 803; vital to British economy, 798
Okinawa, *m* 588, *m* 701, 707, *m* 774
Old Regime, 442, 453, 455
Old Stone Age. *See* Paleolithic period
Old Testament, 35; Christianity accepts as sacred, 94; Michelangelo illustrates, *p* 331, 332. *See also* Bible
Olmec civilization, *m* 15, *p* 302, 302–304, *m* 303; influences Monte Albán, 305
Olympia, *m* 49
Olympic Games, 47, *p* 47
Oman, 260, *m* 795
Opium, 584, 587
Opium War, 585
Orange Free State, *m* 552; Bantu reach, 250; Boer Republic, *m* 560, 564
Orange River, *m* 232, *m* 252
Orbits (of planets), *p* 347, 352
Organization of American States (OAS), 842, 843
Origin of Species, 535
Orinoco, Río: *m* 839
Orozco, José Clemente: painting commentary on Mexican Revolution, *p* 819
Orthodox Marxists, 534
Orthodoxy, 631
Osaka, *m* 593, *m* 774
Oslo, *m* 744
Ottoman Empire, *m* 128; cultural stagnation of, 128; in 1490, *m* 396; threatens Hapsburg lands, 401, *m* 403; defeated at Lepanto, 402–403; in 1648, *m* 405; lands ruled by, *m* 410, 416; Russia's struggle with, 424; and Napoleonic Wars, *m* 471; North African colonies of, *m* 560; collapse of, 617, 618, 624, 729; strengthens Muslim culture in North Africa, 795
Ottoman Turks, 113, 126–127, *m* 128
Outcastes, 203, 582
Outer Mongolia, *m* 632
Overpopulation: and poverty, 526–527; problem in Middle East, 791; rural Latin American, 835; threatens environment, *p* 847; problems caused by, 852
Ovid, 91–92
Owen, Robert: 528
Oxford, *m* 159, 166, 174
Oxus River, *m* 37, *m* 51
Oyo Empire, *m* 235, 238–239; Fulani take over, 240; undermined by slave trade, 244

P

Pacific Ocean: Magellan crosses, *m* 370, 371; Russia reaches, 418, 423; after World War I, *m* 621; during World War II, *m* 701
Painting. *See* Art
Pakistan, *m* 783; communist failure in, 731; joins SEATO, 732; gains independence, 747, 780, conflict with India of, *p* 769, 784; economic development in, 783; miracle wheat in, 852
Palenque, *m* 309, *p* 311
Paleolithic period, 9–11; Bushman's way of life similar to, 249
Palestine: glazed tile from, *p* 19; Hebrews regard as promised land, *m* 30, 33–34, 93; Holy Land to Christians, 152; Russia and France disagree over, 494n; becomes British mandate, *m* 621, 624, 793; annexations of, 794; Jewish migration to, 796, 798; problem debated in UN, 798–799. *See also* Arab-Israeli conflict; Crusades; Israel
Palestinian Arabs, 794, *p* 797, 799–800

Pan Africanism, 812–813, 816
Pan-Arabism, 796
Panama, *m* 827, *m* 839, 841
Panama Canal Zone, 841
Papal States, *m* 410, 492, *m* 493, 494, 495, 496
Paraguay, 378, *m* 827, 828, *m* 839
Paris, *m* 159, 442, *m* 618, *m* 744
Parliament, *p* 393; limits power of king, 397, 398; establishes supremacy over king, 414–416; gains in power, 513
Parma, 492, *m* 493, 494
Parthenon, *p* 41
Patricians, 64–67, 74
Patriotism: declines in Roman Republic, 74; French, 395, *p* 441, 459; Italian, 492–493; of Cecil Rhodes, 562; Japanese art arouses, *p* 596; in World War I, 609–610, *p* 616; lacking in Russia, 644; Nazis arouse Germans to extreme, 676; important in Soviet education, 763
Patrón, 830
Paul III (Pope), 332
Pax Romana, 83, 84–85, 88
Peaceful coexistence, 732, *p* 734, 779
Pearl Harbor, 699, *m* 701
Peasant Crusade, 153
Peasants, *p* 445; in ancient Egypt, 23; in ancient Greece, 42; in Roman Empire, 73, 74; become serfs, 99, 138; driven into poverty, 101; Chinese, 217, 219, 584, 586, 587, 591; in Japan, 223, 592, 594; Amerindian, 377; Russian, 424, 633, 634, 638, 641, 646, 648, 650, 651, 656; French, 443–445, 451, 457–458, 460, 469, 485; enclosure movement and, 509; in India, 580, 582; in Fascist Italy, 666, 668; Eastern European, 752, 759; lose political control to Communists, 753; Arab, 793; Egyptian, 802; Southeast Asian, 785. *See also* Serfs; Peons
Pedro II, 824, 828–829
Peking, *m* 588, *m* 733, *m* 774, 775
Peloponnesian War, 50, *m* 50, 53
Penance, 144 (box), 339
Peons, 820; provide labor for Spaniards, 377; support Hidalgo, 821; regard creoles as exploiters, 822; tied to landowners by debt, 830; in Mexican Revolution, 832
People's Republic of China. *See* Communist China
Pericles: on Athenian civilization, 45; on art, 57
Perón, Juan: 834
Perry, Commodore Matthew: 595; route of, *m* 588
Persia: influences Muslim culture, 118, 120; Seljuk Turks take over, 120; arts of, *p* 123, 124; falls to

Mongols, 126, *m* 127; literature of, 123, 125–126; carpet from, *p* 359. *See also* Persian Empire
Persian Empire, 36–38, *m* 37, *p* 38; wars with Greece of, 48–50, *m* 50; Alexander conquers, 51, *m* 51, *p* 59; trade of, 85, 111; invades Byzantine Empire, 112; Muslims conquer, 118, *m* 119
Persian Gulf, *m* 21, *m* 119, *m* 795
Persian Wars, 48–50, *m* 50
Peru, *m* 839; ancient cultures of, 314–317, *m* 315, 372–373; Spanish conquest of, 375, *m* 381; agriculture in, *p* 819; revolt of Tupac-Amarú in, 820; resists independence, 823; Viceroyalty of, *m* 827; socialist nationalism in, 834
Peter (Apostle), *p* 96, 145n
Peter I (the Great), 423–424, 633
Petition of Right, 414
Petrarch, Francesco: 326
Petrograd, *m* 615, 630. *See also* Leningrad
Petrograd Soviet, 643
Phaistos, *p* 34, *m* 37
Phalanxes, 527–528
Pharaoh, 21; regarded as a god, 21–22; power and responsibilities of, 22–23; burial of, 24, *p* 25, 26
Philip II, 401, 402–403
Philip Augustus, 394
Philip of Anjou, 411
Philip of Macedon, 50
Philippine Islands, *m* 786; Magellan's fleet reaches, *m* 370, 371; in World War II, 699, 700, *m* 701; United States acquires, 785; gain independence, 787
Philosopher-kings, 54
Philosophes, 429; condemn injustices of society, 430, 434, 437; stress reason and scientific attitude, 436–437; support civil liberties, 437; urge progress in education, 437–438; optimism of, 438; influence of, 448, 468; assumptions doubted, 537
Philosophy, 52; in ancient Greece, 52–54; Rome adopts Greek concepts of, 88–89; similarity of Christianity to Greek, 97; in Muslim world, 124; Chinese, 213–214. *See also* Confucianism
Phoenicia, *m* 30, 32; trade of, *p* 33, 42, *m* 42; founds Carthage, 69
Photography, *p* 516
Physics: Muslim advances in, 123; advances during Scientific Revolution in, 348–354; classical, 540; 541, 542; modern, 540–542, 543
Picasso, Pablo: drawing by, *p* 681
Piedmont, *m* 405, *m* 410
Pilate, Pontius: 94

Pilgrimage: Muslim, 116, 117, *p* 121; Hindu, *p* 205; of Mansa Musa, 234–235
Pizarro, Francisco: *m* 370, 375
Planetary motion, *p* 347, 348; Laws of, 352
Plantations, 364–365, 382, 820; Africans labor on, 364, 365, 379; result in single-product economy, 829; in Latin America, 824, 830, *p* 831, 834, 838
Plassey, 576, *m* 578
Plato, 53; on freedom of speech, 45; criticizes democracy, 53–54; on art, 57
Plebeian Assembly, 66
Plebeians, 64, 65, 66–67
Plow: developed, 14; medieval, 140–141; introduced to America, 376; improved in Agricultural Revolution, 508
Pnompenh, *m* 786
Poetry: Egyptian, 27; Roman, 92; Persian, 123; Muslim, 126; medieval, 173–174; in T'ang China, 217, *p* 220; in sub-Saharan Africa, 277–278; Aztec, 313; Renaissance, 326; Japanese, 593
Pogroms, 633
Poison gas, 611, *p* 613, 623
Poland, *m* 744; Christianity in, *m* 111, *m* 341; Mongols invade, 126, *m* 127; in 1490, *m* 396; in 1520, *m* 337; in 1560, *m* 403; seventeenth-century, *m* 405, 416; in 1721, *m* 410; Prussia takes over land in, 412; relations with Russia, 423, 481, 483, *m* 632, 639, *m* 658, 690, 724, 731, 752, 759; power weakened by weak king, 425; nationalism in, 479, 606; Napoleon takes over, *m* 471; in 1815, *m* 481; after World War I, *m* 621, 624; in World War II, 685, 692, 698, *m* 704; occupies German lands, *m* 709. *See also* Eastern-Central Europe
Police: in tsarist Russia, 424, 631, 640; in Soviet Union, *p* 644, 646, 648, 659, 758, 765; Mussolini creates secret, 667; Nazi use of secret, 675; in Hungary, 759; Communists gain control of, 753; role in Japan of, 770; in South Africa, 816. *See also* Gestapo
Polish Corridor, 624, *m* 689, 690
Politburo, 650, 651
Political parties: British, 515; Japanese, 770; in Africa, 815
Politics: African participation in, 567, 570, 571; participation of common man in, 600 (box), 640; reform in Japanese, 770
Pollution: industrialization leads to, *p* 510, 523; in United States, 737; of environment, 853. *See also* Environment

Polytheism, 30

Pompeii, *p* 87

Pope: Byzantines refuse to accept, 111; takes place of Roman emperor, 143; responsibilities and power of, 143, 144–145, 145n; kings conflict with, 145; Crusades affect power of, 157; criticized for temporal power, 336; Society of Jesus and, 337; Luther refuses to accept, 339; supports Catholic rulers, 343; conflicts with Holy Roman Emperors, 399; rule in Italy of, 400, 495; English break with, 412; refuses to accept reforms of French National Assembly, 455; Napoleon reaches agreement with, 468; opposes Italian unification, 492; Nazi Germany reaches agreement with, 677. *See also* Roman Catholic Church

Population: in Sparta, 43; in Athens, 45; factor in Rome's decline, 100; medieval, 164; Chinese, 217, 583–584, 776, 777; decimation of Amerindian, 376, 388; shift in balance of world, 388; explosion in England of, 506–507; German, 520, 586; rapid growth of Indian, 580; Japanese, 594, 597, 699, 773; problem of growth of, 600 (box), 847–848; Russian, 631; agricultural advances hampered by growth of, *p* 736; increasing Asian, 769; rate of growth of Mexican, 833; in world today, *m* 851. *See also* Overpopulation

Population explosion, 850, 852; in Middle East, 802; in Egypt, 803–804; in Latin America, *p* 831, 834–835

Portugal: early contact with Africa of, 238, *m* 246, 247, 248, 256, *m* 364; leads voyages of exploration, 360–363, *m* 364, *m* 370; establishes fortified trading posts and plantations, 364–365; missionary efforts in Africa, 365–366; finds sea route to India, 366–367, *m* 370; Asian trade of, 368, *m* 578, *m* 588; gains lands by Treaty of Tordesillas, 369, *m* 370; helps lay basis for Latin American culture, 376, 390; uses African slaves in American colonies, 379; colonies of, 380, *m* 381, 388, *m* 389; under Spanish rule, 386, 402, *m* 403; loses American colonies, 483, *m* 827; African colonies of, *m* 552, *m* 560, *m* 566, *m* 813; paternalism in Africa of, 571; joins NATO, 728; dictatorship burdens, 750; opposes independence for colonies, 811, 816

Portuguese Guinea, *m* 552, *m* 560, *m* 566, *m* 813

Portuguese Timor, *m* 786

Potsdam, *m* 744; Conference, 724, 752

Poverty: in Rome, 73–74, 75, 83, 99; industrialization causes, *p* 510; rationalizations for, 526–527; Fourier's plan to end, 527–528; Marx's view of causes of, 530; increases in rural India, 580; in Spain, *p* 681; in United States, 722, 737; in Middle East, 791, 802; in Brazil, *p* 831; in contemporary world, *p* 847; means of coping with, 856. *See also* Sans-culottes; Urban workers

Prague, 174, 396, 690, 725, *m* 744

Praise-songs, 277–278

Prayer rug, *p* 125

Predestination, 342

Prehistory. *See* Neolithic period; Paleolithic period

Priests: in ancient Egypt, 23; in Sumeria, 28; in Middle Ages, 139, 144, 164–165; importance to Indo-Aryan society of, 200; in traditional Japan, 223; in Mesoamerica, 304, 309, 310, 312, 313; parish, 442. *See also* Brahmins

Prince, The: 329

Princip, Gavrilo: 604

Printing, 217, *p* 340, 593

Private plots, 656, 657, 755, 763

Production, means of: and private ownership, 383; public ownership of, 518, 527, 646, 647, 655; liberals urge freedom from government control, 526; capitalism fails to use effectively, 529, 530

Proletariat, 529, *p* 531; Marx's view of, 530; dictatorship of, 534; Russian, 645. *See also* Class struggle

Propaganda: in Revolutions of 1848, *p* 485; imperialist, *p* 568; in World War I, *p* 603, 615, *p* 616; in Fascist Italy, 667; Nazi, 676, 678; Soviet, 724, 731, 763; in cold war, 725; in Communist China, 775–776; Japanese promote nationalist, 786; appeal to Southeast Asia of communist, 788

Property: Roman concept of rights to, 90; European concept introduced to America, 376; as natural right, 430, 454; demands of *sans-culottes* threaten, 456; goals of workers threaten, 484, 485, 487; as requirement for voting rights, 515; and Russian peasant, 633; Soviets eliminate private, 651, 655, 656–657; destruction in World War II of, 708, 741

Protestant Reformation. *See* Reformation

Protestantism: spread of, 339–342,

m 341; Roman Catholic Church tries to check, 342–343; divisions in, 344; Charles V threatens, 401; Philip II eliminates from Spain, 402; in Nazi Germany, 677–678; in Latin America, 835. *See also* Huguenots; Thirty Years' War

Provisional Government (Russian), 614, 629, 643–644

Prussia: religion in, *m* 341; in 1560, *m* 403; in 1648, *m* 405; grows in power, *m* 410, 411–412; Napoleon defeats, 470; *m* 471, 473; Metternich fears growing power of, 481, *m* 481; joins Quadruple Alliance, 482; in Revolution of 1848, 486; parliament established in, 488; in unification of Germany, 495–497, *m* 498, 499; dominates German Reich, 518; Soviet take-over in, 752. *See also* Germany

Ptolemy, 123; earth-centered universe of, *p* 347, 348, 349–350

Puerto Rico, *m* 839; as Spanish colony, 483, 824, *m* 827

Punjab, 576–577, *m* 578, *m* 783

Purges, communist: 650, 658–659, 754, 755

Puritans, 342, 414–415

Pygmies (Congo), 7, *m* 267, 278

Pyramids: Egyptian, 22, *p* 25, 26; Amerindian, 298, 304

Q

Qatar, *m* 795

Quadruple Alliance, 482

Quebec, 380, *m* 381

Quechua, 317, 373

Quemoy, *m* 774

Quetzalcóatl, *p* 293; cult of, 304, 312; Cortés believed messenger of, 374

Quipus, 317

Quito, *m* 827, *m* 839

R

Rabelais, François: 326

Racial prejudice: religious intolerance blends into, 365; in Russia, 633; in United States, 722, 737; in Britain, 748; Castro campaigns against, 838

Racism: in South Africa, 249–250, 254, 571; and chauvinism, 501; Social Darwinism leads to, 536–537; of Europeans in Africa, 567, 569; Indians accuse British of, 581; in Nazi Germany, 671–673, 676, 698

Radar, 690, 695

Radicals, 455; French, 456, 457, 458–459, 460, 484; Chinese, 590; seek to overthrow tsar, 639–640

Railroads: Industrial Revolution and, *p* 505, 507; in India, *p*

II, *m* 704; Stalinist influence in, 753. *See also* Eastern-Central Europe
Romanov, Michael: 423
Romanticism, *p* 483
Rome, city of: *m* 65, *m* 744; origins of, 67; capital of Western Roman Empire, 101; and unification of Italy, 492, *m* 493, 495, 496; Mussolini's march on, 667. *See also* Roman Empire; Roman Republic
Romulus Augustulus, 104
Roosevelt, Franklin D.: 688; Soviet relations, 723; Good Neighbor policy of, 842
Roosevelt, Theodore: 841
Rosas, Manuel de: 820, 828
Rotterdam, 693, *m* 704
Roundheads, 415
Rousseau, Jean Jacques: 435–436
Ruanda-Urundi, 561, *m* 621
Ruisdael, Solomon van: landscape by, *p* 429
Rulers: in Sumer, 28; in Mesopotamia, 31; Persian, 36; have little power, 133; townsmen aid, 142; conflict with Pope of, 145; end disorder, 164; begin to build states, 175; Chinese, 213, 214, 217, 218–219; ancient Japanese, 222; in West Africa, 233, 237–238, 239, 241; in Mesoamerica, 304, 313; in ancient South America, 315, 317; medieval view of, 328; Reformation strengthens, 341–342, 343, 344; Commercial Revolution strengthens, 385–386; limitations of English, 414; autocracy of tsarist, 420, 421, 631; receive power from people, 430; limitations on power of French, 446; nobility oppose power of French, 447, 448, 449; French Revolution limits power of, 454, 462; authority of kaiser, 499; in feudal Japan, 592; military as, 814, 825, 829. *See also* Dictatorship; Nation-states; Pharaoh
Rurik, 417
Russes, 417
Russia (tsarist), *m* 419, *m* 632; Christianity in, *m* 111; trade of, 111, 120, *m* 159; religion in, *p* 114, 115, 417, 418, 420, 632; Byzantine Empire influences, 115; Mongols invade, 126, 420; peoples of, 417; imperialism of, 423, 424, 605, 607, 641; attempts to westernize, 424, 633, 637–639; lacks sense of national unity, 425; Napoleon's defeat in, *m* 471, 473–474; Metternich fears, 481; joins Quadruple Alliance, 482; revolt of army officers crushed in, 483; in Crimean War, 494, 638; defeated by Japan, 597; in Triple Entente, 605; nationalists urge protection

of Slavs by, 607; in World War I, 608–609, 611, 613–614, *m* 615, *m* 618, 620, *m* 621; collapse of order in, 629–630; disunity of, 632–633; inequality and exploitation in, 633; unaffected by movements that shaped western civilization, 634; backwardness of, 635, 637, 640; literature in, *p* 636; Decembrist uprising in, 638; reforms in, 638–639; escalation of terror in, 640; attempts to industrialize, 640–641; western ideas spread in, 642; fall of tsarism in, 629, 642–643. *See also* Autocracy; Bolshevik Revolution; Kiev; Muscovy; Russian Orthodox Church; Soviet Union
Russian Orthodox Church: founded, 418; isolation of, 420; comes under state control, 424; as facet of tsarism, 631; expects unquestioning obedience, 651; privileges destroyed, 651, *p* 651. *See also* Eastern Orthodox Church
Russification, 631, 633, 641
Russo-Japanese War, 597, 605, 642
Rwanda, 809, *m* 813

S

Sacraments, 144 (box), 147, 336
Sagres, 363, *m* 364
Sahara, 230, *m* 232
Saigon, *m* 786
St. Benedict, 145; rule of, 144
St. Domingue, 146, 382, *m* 389, 820–821
St. Francis of Assisi, 146, *p* 147
St. Helena, 474
St. Paul, 95–96, 97; travel of, *m* 95
St. Petersburg, *m* 410, 424
Salamis, 48–50, *m* 50
Samoa, *m* 621
Samurai, 592, 594, *p* 594, 596, 707. *See also* Satsuma-Chosu leaders
San José, *m* 839
San Juan, *m* 839
San Martín, José de: 823
San Salvador, *m* 839
Sans-culottes, 456, 458
Santiago, *m* 839
Santo Domingo, *m* 389, *m* 839; Viceroyalty of, *m* 827
São Paulo, *m* 839
São Tomé, 364, *m* 364, *m* 552, *m* 560
Sarajevo, 603, *m* 606
Sardinia, *m* 42, *m* 65; Carthaginian control in, 69; in 1560, *m* 403; in 1721, *m* 410
Sardinia, Kingdom of: *m* 481, *m* 493, 493–494, 495
Satellite countries. *See* Eastern-Central Europe
Satsuma-Chosu leaders, 595–596
Saudi Arabia, 794, *m* 795, 804

Savanna, 230, *m* 232. *See also* Sudan
Savoy: in 1560, *m* 403; in 1648, *m* 405; in 1721, *m* 410; France gains, *m* 493, 494
Saxony: in 1560, *m* 403; in 1721, *m* 410; in 1815, *m* 481; Kingdom of, *m* 498
Scapegoat, 670, 673
Schleswig, 497, *m* 498
Science: impact on religion of theories of, 5, 535; Romans stress practical, 89; Muslim advances in, 122–123; religion tied to medieval, 168, 348; foundations of modern, 349, 352; stresses scientific attitudes, 356, 357; *philosophes* on, 436–437; British liberals support, 526; advances before World War I, 625; as ideal of western civilization, 716, 717; advantages of proper use o̲f̲, 853; problems created by, 853, 857
Scientific Revolution: ends medieval outlook, 347; in astronomy and physics, 348–354; in medicine and biological science, 354–356; significance of, 356–357; influences Enlightenment, 429, 436–437
Scorched-earth policy, *p* 695, 724
Scotland, *m* 337, *m* 341, 414, 415
Sculpture. *See* Art
Secret ballot, 515
Security: national, 719; freedom sacrificed for, 763; traditional ways bring, 849; religion provided, 856
Security Council (UN), *p* 720
Self-determination: Wilson urges, 619; obstacles to, 620–621; Hitler uses principle of, 688; Britain supports, 690, 691; colonial countries seek, 717; Stalin uses, 723
Self-government: in Rome, 71, 82, 84; tsars end, 421; desired by Africans, 569, 807; Gandhi works for Indian, 582
Seljuk Turks, 113, 120, *m* 127, 152
Senate (Roman): powers of, 64, 82; and Assembly, 65, 66, 76; identifies with interests of Rome, 67; opposes land reform, 74; opposes one-man rule, 75–76
Senegal, *m* 813; part of ancient Ghana, 233, *m* 235; Fulbe originate in, 236; during Age of Imperialism, *m* 552, *m* 560, *m* 566; gains independence, 809
Senghor, Léopold: 811
Seoul, *m* 774
Separation of powers, 431
Sepoy Rebellion, 578, *p* 579
Serbia, 604; in 1560, *m* 403; in 1913, *m* 606; and World War I, 608, 609, 614, *m* 615
Serfdom, 138–142; decline of, 143, 163; in Russia, 421, 424, 633,

m 560, *m* 566; and World War I, 617, *m* 621

Soviet Union, *m* 744; aids Chinese Nationalists, 590; socialist realism in, *p* 629, *p* 636, 656; chaos after revolution in, 647; war communism restores order to, 648; New Economic Policy in, 649–650; peasants in, 650, 651, 656, 763; role of Communist Party in, 650–651; development of monolithic unity in, 650–653, 659; religion in, 651, *p* 651; problems facing, 654, 730–731, 735, 755, 757, 761, 765–766; forced industrialization of, 655–656; collectivization of agriculture in, 656–657, *p* 656; Stalinist purges in, 659, 727, 754, 755, 756; ignored at Munich, 688; Franco-British distrust of, 691; in 1939, *m* 658; expansionist aims of, 690; in World War II, *p* 685, 692, *p* 695, 695–696, 698, 702–703, *m* 704, 707; destructiveness of World War II in, 708, 724; occupation of Germany by, *m* 709; becomes a Super Power, 710, 718–719, 724; gains control of Eastern-Central Europe, 710, 724–726, 727, 752, 753, 754; de-Stalinization in, *p* 715, 730, 758; tensions with United States lead to cold war, 715, 719, 722–723, *m* 733; as model for modernization, 718; in Security Council, *p* 720; seeks to end capitalism, 721; achievements of, 724, 761–763; power overestimated, 724–725; suggests Russo-Turkish control of Black Sea, 725; postwar recovery in, 726, 755–756; satellite relations with, 727–728, 731, 752, 753–754, 758–761, *p* 759; nationalism affects, 728, 737; nuclear weapons of, 729, 732, 854; supports Arab cause in Middle East, 734, 795, *p* 797, 800, 801; aids Cuba, 735, 840; aids Egyptian development, 736, 803; Communist China breaks with, 736, 761, 771, *p* 778, 779; education in, *p* 741, 763–765, *p* 764; French relations with, 749; social welfare in, 763, *p* 764; ideal far from reality in, 765–766; aids Communist China, 776, 779; aids North Vietnam, 787; persecution of Jews in, 798; opposes colonialism, 808. *See also* Cold war; Lenin; Russia (tsarist); Stalin

Soviets: 630, 651–652. *See also* Petrograd Soviet

Space race, *p* 715, 725, 731, 732

Spain, *m* 42, 64, *m* 744; relations with Rome, 64, *m* 72, 72–73, *m* 84, 85; Carthaginian control in, 69; Christianity in, *m* 111, *m* 341; Muslims in, 118, 119, *m* 119, *p* 125, 398; Germanic kingdom established in, 132, *m* 132; and medieval trade, *m* 159; Inquisition in, 148, 343, 402; desires to convert non-Christians, 362; encourages exploration, 369, *m* 370, 371; conquers Aztec and Inca states, 374–375; American colonies of, 376–379, *m* 381; helps lay basis for Latin American culture, 376, 390; exploits Amerinds, 377; expels Jesuits from America, 378; use of African slaves by, 379; economic decline of, 386, 387, 403–404; nation-state develops in, *m* 396, 398–399; Hapsburgs create empire, 401; religious intolerance in, 402; Flemish resist rule by, *p* 404; and Thirty Years' War, 405, *m* 405; Bourbons seek control of, 408, 410–411, *m* 410; Napoleon invades, 457, *m* 471, *p* 472, 473, 477; liberal revolution crushed in, 482–483; loses colonies in Latin America, 483, *m* 827; Hohenzollerns offered crown of, 499; war with United States, 841; in World War I, *m* 615; African colonies of, *m* 560, *m* 566, *m* 813; fascist movement in, 664; civil war in, *p* 681, 687–688; dictatorship burdens contemporary, 750

Spanish Armada, 402, *m* 403

Spanish Civil War, *p* 681, 687–688

Spanish Guinea, *m* 566

Spanish Netherlands, *m* 341, 411

Spanish Sahara, *m* 813

Sparta, 48, *m* 49, 50, *m* 50, 253

Specialization, 13–14

Spheres of influence: in Africa, *m* 560, 561, *m* 566; in Asia, *m* 588, 589; Russian, *m* 632

Spice Islands. *See* East Indies

Spice trade, 111, 785; cultural results of, 208; importance to Europe of, 360; Europeans take over, 367, 368; Dutch gain control of, 380

Sputnik, 725, 732

Stalin: *p* 656; encourages socialist realism, *p* 629; becomes head of Soviet Union, 654; forced modernization by, 655–657, *p* 656; rigid policies affect personality of, 657–658, 659; uses purges to remain in power, 658–659, 727, 755, 756; creates monolithic unity in Russia, 659; makes pact with Hitler, 690, 692; cold war policies of, 725, 726, 728, 754; Khrushchev denounces, 730, 758; policies toward Eastern-Central Europe, 727–728, 753, 755; lays foundations for Soviet successes in space, 731; achieve-

ments of Soviet Union under, 752; rigid rule of Soviet Union by, 755–756

Stalingrad (Volgograd), *m* 658, 702–703, *m* 704

Standard of living: in Rome, 72, 85–86, 100; medieval, 138–142; of Amerinds, 294, 310, 317; in France under Old Regime, 443–445; Industrial Revolution improves, 506, 513, 522; reform movements and, 515–517; French, *p* 521, 522; improves under capitalism, 533; African, 566; in China, 584, 591; in Japan, 594, 597, 773; Soviet, 655, 657, 761, 763, *p* 764; in Fascist Italy, 688; in East Germany, 734; contemporary British, 748; in United States, 765; Asian, 770; in Taiwan, 775; in India, 781–782; in Middle East, 791, 802, 804; Latin American, 829, 833, in developing nations, 848–849

Stanley, Henry M.: 547, 548, 559

State: as characteristic of civilization, 14; totalitarian, 99–100; begins development in Middle Ages, 175; Aztecs set up political, 312; Marx predicts disappearance of, 532; anarchists urge destruction of, 534–535; controls Soviet economy, 652, 655; regulates cultural life in Nazi Germany, 676. *See also* Nation-state

States-General, 447, 449, 450

Stockholm, *m* 159, *m* 744

Stoicism, 88, 89, 97

Stolypin, Peter: 642

Stone Age. *See* Neolithic period; Paleolithic period

Stonehenge, *p* 3

Strip farming, 140

Struggle for existence, 5

Students: in medieval universities, 165–166; unrest of, 746, *p* 749, 750, *p* 772, 834; Communist Chinese, *p* 769. *See also* Education

Sub-Saharan Africa. *See* Africa, sub-Saharan

Sudan, 558–559; states of western, 231–237, *m* 232; Britain and Egypt invade, 559. *See also* Western Sudan

Sudan, Republic of: *m* 813

Sudetenland, 688, *m* 689

Suez Canal, *m* 799; built, *m* 552, 554; importance to Britain of, 558; Axis powers attempt to gain control of, 703; Egypt nationalizes, 731, 800; Soviet Union seeks reopening of, 801

Sully, Duc de: 406

Sumatra, *m* 389, *m* 701, 785, *m* 786

Sumer, 28, *m* 29

Sun Yat-sen, 589, 590
Sung dynasty, 217. *See also* China
Super Powers. *See* Soviet Union; United States
Surinam, 380, *m* 389, *m* 839
Surrealism, *p* 855
Survival of the fittest, 6
Swahili, 259
Swaziland, *m* 560, *m* 566, 809, *m* 813
Sweden, *m* 744; and medieval trade, *m* 159; religion in, *m* 341; American colonies of, *m* 381; Kingdom of, *m* 403; invades Russia, 419, 423; postwar prosperity of, 750
Sweet potato: enriches Asian diet, 388
Swiss Confederation, *m* 337, *m* 396, *m* 403
Switzerland, *m* 744; Calvinism in, *m* 341, 342; becomes independent of Holy Roman Empire, 405, *m* 405; neutral in contemporary affairs, 750
Syria, *m* 21, *m* 795; trade of, 85, *m* 119, 120; mandate, *m* 621, 624, 793; problems facing, 795; in Arab-Israeli conflict, 800

T

Tacitus; on Roman entertainment, 86; on persecution of Christians, 98; on Germanic barbarians, 102
Taika Reforms, 223
Taiping Rebellion, 586–587, *m* 588
Taiwan, *m* 215, *m* 774; independent of Communist China, 729; United States committed to defend, 732; Chinese Nationalists take over, 775
Taj Mahal, *p* 209
T'ang dynasty, 217, *m* 218, *p* 220, 223. *See also* China
Tanganyika, 561, *m* 621, 809. *See also* Tanzania
Tanzania, 254, *p* 270, *m* 813
Taoism, 214, 217
Taxation: in Rome, 72, 99, 100, 101; in Middle Ages, 143, 158, 163; by Church, 144, 340–341; in China, 217, 584, 590; in Japan, 223, 594, 595–596; in England, 397, 414; in France, 411, 442, 444, 446; German socialists demand progressive income, 518; of English East India Company, 577; in Latin America, 820
Technology: impact on modern primitives of, *p* 12; significance to Western Europe of, 169–170, 175, 564, 575; limitation of Amerindian, 305, 371–372; and exploration, 362; impact on America of European, 390; applied to agriculture, 508, 593; problems created by, 523, 853,

856; introduced to Africa, 572; leads to rapid change, 600 (box); as ideal of western civilization, 716, 717; UN sponsors training in, *p* 720; Soviet advances in, 761; contributes to alienation, 856
Tenochtitlán, *m* 309, 312. *See also* Aztecs
Teotihuacán, 304–305, *m* 306
Terracing, *p* 44, *p* 373
Terror: used by Black Hand, 604; in Russia, 640, 745; facet of Stalinism, 658–659, 724, 730, 754, 755; used by fascists, 667; Nazi policy of, 678, 697; in Franco-Algerian relations, 749
Teutonic Knights, *m* 396, 419
Texcoco, *m* 309, 313, 372
Textiles. *See* Weaving
Thailand, 700, *m* 701, 732, 785, *m* 786. *See also* Southeast Asia
Theater: Greek, *p* 56, 56–57; Roman, *p* 80; Louis XIV encourages, *p* 409; Japanese, *p* 575, 593, *p* 594; in Russia, *p* 636, *p* 715
Theodosius I, 98
Thermopylae, 48, *m* 50
Third Estate: problems of, 443–446; calls for voting changes in States-General, 449–450; forms National Assembly, 450. *See also* Bourgeoisie; Peasants; Urban workers
Third Reich, 675n. *See also* Germany, Nazi
Third World, 731, *p* 736, 848. *See also* Developing nations
Thirteen Colonies, 382, *m* 389, 507, 821. *See also* United States
Thirty Years' War, 404–405, *m* 405, 410, 411
Thucydides, 58
Tiahuanaco, 314–315, *m* 315, 316
Tiber River, *m* 65, 67
Tibet, 211, *m* 216, *m* 578, *m* 774
Tigris River: *m* 15, 19–20, *m* 21, 28
Timbuktu, 235, *m* 235, *p* 236, 363, *m* 364
Tito, Marshal: 728. *See also* Yugoslavia
Tlacopán, *m* 309, 313, 372
Tlaxcala, *m* 309, 374
Togo, *m* 560, 809, *m* 813
Togoland, *m* 566, *m* 621
Tokugawa Ieyasu, 592. *See also* Japan
Tokyo (Yedo), 592, *m* 593, *m* 774
Tolstoy, Leo: *p* 636
Toltec-Mayan culture, 312. *See also* Mayan civilization
Tools: hand ax, *p* 4; Paleolithic man learns to make, 9; medieval, 140–141; Amerinds lack metal, 371
Tordesillas, Treaty of: 369, *m* 370
Totalitarian state: Rome turned

into, 99–100; in twentieth century, 600 (box); Mussolini establishes, 667; technology makes possible, 853. *See also* Dictatorship
Toulouse-Lautrec, Henri de: uses trick photography, *p* 516; commercial art of, *p* 521
Towns: decline in Roman Empire, 132; revive in Western Europe, 142; contribute to decline of serfdom, 143; medieval, 158–160; significance of, 163; Harappan, 200; East African, 259. *See also* Cities
Townsmen: help kings grow in power, 142, 393; outlook of, 163; rise of, 321–322. *See also* Middle class
Trade: in present-day Neolithic society, *p* 12; as characteristic of civilization, 14; rivers important to, 19–20; Sumerian, 28; Babylonian, 30; advanced by use of coins, 32; of Minoans, *p* 34; ancient Greek, 42, *m* 42, *p* 44, *p* 46; Etruscan, *p* 66; Carthaginian, 67; Roman, *m* 84, 85, 99; Byzantine, 110–111, 113, 115, *m* 119; Muslim, 120–121, 125, *m* 119, 360; prospers under Mongols, *m* 127, 221; medieval, 157, 158–159, *m* 159; leads to advances in business techniques, 161–162; increases European contacts with East, 164; in ancient India, 200, 208; in traditional China, 215, *m* 216, 217, *m* 218, 362–363; Indian Ocean, 256, 257, 259; importance to West Africa of, 233, 234, 235, *m* 235, 236, 238–239; importance to Central and East Africa of, 246, 255–256, 259; Ethiopian, *p* 258; Amerindian, 298, 303, 304, 308, 312, 317, 372; basis of townsman's life, 322; Portuguese, 360; Venetian-Muslim monopoly on, 360, 363, 367; Dutch success in, 380; French, 382, 406, 448, 462, 469; during Commercial Revolution, 384, 387, *m* 389; Spanish, 386, 398, 399; contributes to English prosperity, *p* 393, 507; extent of Kievan, 418; enlightened despots encourage, 432 (box); and Continental System, 472; industrialization increases German, 518; and New Imperialism, 554, 555–556, 576, *m* 578, 584–585, *m* 588; Japanese, 592, 593, 595; contributes to global order, 600 (box); under state control in Russia, 647; Franco-Chinese, 749; Hong Kong important to Communist Chinese, *p* 778; important to Southeast Asia, 785; Latin America opened to world, 824.

See also Common Market; Mercantilism; Slave trade

Trafalgar, 471, *m* 471

Transjordan, *m* 621, *m* 704, 793. *See also* Jordan

Transportation: Neolithic advances in, 14; Persian achievements in, 36; in Rome, 85, 99; medieval, 142; Olmec overcome obstacles to, 302; in Inca Empire, *m* 315, 317, 372; European technology affects American, 376; Cavour modernizes Sardinian, 494; contributes to Industrial Revolution, *p* 505, 507–508; rail, 507, *p* 575, 639, 640, 833; imperialism improves, 572, 580; in India, *p* 575; contributes to global order, 600 (box); in Russia, 639–640; destruction in World War II of, 742; nationalization in Britain of, 747; in independent Africa, 814, *p* 815; in Mexico, 833; advantages of modern, 850, 852

Transvaal, *m* 552, *m* 560, 563, 564

Treaty ports, 585, *m* 588

Trench warfare, 611–612, *p* 613

Trent, Council of: *m* 341, 342–343

Tribes, 230

Tribunes, 66, 67

Tribute: western Sudan depends on, 233, 234; demanded by Aztecs, 312, *p* 373; Chinese emperor seeks, 362; in Inca Empire, 372; Spain demands Amerinds pay, 377; rulers of Kiev collect, 418; creoles continue in Mexico, 822

Trinidad, *m* 827, *m* 839

Triple Alliance, 605

Triple Entente, 605

Trojan War, *p* 41

Trotsky, Leon: 648, 654, 659

Troubadours, 136, 137, *p* 151, 170–171

Truce of God, 148

Trujillo, Rafael: 843

Truman, Harry S.: reasons for dropping atom bomb, 707; overestimates Soviet strength, 724; determined to halt Soviet expansion, 725; urges aid for Greece and Turkey, 726, 742–743

Tsar: autocracy of, 420, 421, 423, 631, 660; symbols of office of, *p* 422; serves as force uniting Russia, 632; demands unquestioning obedience, 634; responsible for instituting reforms, 635, 637; use of terror by, 640. *See also* Autocracy

Tucumán, 823, *m* 827

Tunisia, *m* 566, *m* 704, *m* 795

Tupac-Amarú, 820, 822

Turkey, *m* 795; after World War I, *m* 621, 624; becomes a republic, 792; reforms of Atatürk in, 717,

792; in World War II, *m* 704; United States aids, 726, 743; joins NATO, 732; contemporary, 750–751. *See also* Ottoman Empire

Tuscany, *m* 481, 492, *m* 493, 494

Tutankhamen, *p* 25; tomb of, 24, 26

Twelve Tables, 67

Twentieth century: overview of, 600 (box); insecurity of, 847; as Age of Violence and Alienation, 854, 856

Tyranny, 167, 434

Tyre, *m* 30, *m* 42, *m* 159

U

Uganda, 259, *m* 813; British in, 558, 561, *m* 566; gains independence, 809

Uji, 222, 224

Ukraine, *m* 419, *m* 632

Ulbricht, Walter: 730

Ulianov, Vladimir Ilich. *See* Lenin

Umayyads, 118

Umbria, 492, *m* 493, 495

Underdevelopment, 829–830, 848–849

Union of South Africa. *See* South Africa

Union of Soviet Socialist Republics (USSR). *See* Soviet Union

United Arab Republic, 795

United Nations, *p* 720; founding of, 709; votes to defend South Korea, 729; decides to divide Palestine, 798–799; nationalistic movements aided by, 807; forced to intervene in Africa, 810; and Southern Rhodesia, 811; African influence in, 814

United Netherlands, 405, *m* 405, *m* 410, 411

United States: racial violence in, 390; English trade with, 507, 511; President compared with British prime minister, 514; relations with Japan, 595, 770–771, 773; in World War I, 617–618; isolationism of, 624, 686, 691; in World War II, 691, 693, 699, 700, *m* 701, 702, 706–707; misunderstanding of Russia in, 630; achievements of, 635; relations with Soviet Union, 648, 715, 719, 772–773; becomes a Super Power, 710, 718, 723; tied to Europe, 718; in Security Council, *p* 720; impact of global order on, 721–722, 737; overestimates Soviet power, 724; lands first man on moon, *p* 715, 725; aids postwar recovery of Europe, 726, 742–743; in NATO, 728; in Korean War, 729; defense commitments of, 732, *m* 733, 734; invasion of Cuba fails, 735; domestic prob-

lems of, 737; in Vietnam War, 737, 781, 787–788; world leadership of, 765; supports Chinese Nationalists, 774, 775n, 778; acquires Philippines, 785; and Arab-Israeli conflict, 800; opposes colonialism, 808; support of dictatorships by, 834; relations with Latin America of, 837–838, 840–844; use of world resources by, 852; overkill capacity of, 855. *See also* Cold war

Universe, 3; origin of, 4; Greek view of, 54; Hebrew view of, 54; changing concepts of, 348, 349, 354, 356, 540, 542; expanding understanding of, 357, 855–856, 857

Universities: Muslims establish, 122, 398; medieval, 148, 164–166, *p* 165; established in India, 577

Untouchables, 203

Upper Volta, 809, *m* 813

Urban II (Pope), 152

Urban centers: as characteristic of civilization, 14; Mesoamerican, 304. *See also* Cities

Urban migration: in Roman Republic, 73; enclosure movement causes, 509; poverty in India causes, 580; poverty in China causes, 587; in Japan, 593, 773; in Eastern Europe, 754; in Latin America, *p* 831, 835

Urban workers: French, 445, 469, 522; demand social reform, 487; and industrialization, *p* 510, 511–512, 513, 517; German, 519; Owen improves conditions for, 528; become members of middle class, 533; in fascist Italy, 668. *See also* Proletariat; Socialism

Urbanization, 593

Uruguay, *m* 827, *m* 839

Ussuri River, *p* 778

Utopian Socialism, 527–528

V

Valley of Mexico: Olmec in, 303, *m* 303; Aztecs in, *m* 309, 312

Vargas, Gétulio: 834

Vassal, 134, 135

Vega, Garcilaso de la: 374

Venetia, 493, *m* 493, 495, 497

Venetian Republic, *m* 337

Venezuela, *m* 827, *m* 839; primitive peoples in, *p* 12; ancient cultures in, 314; creoles begin revolt in, 822; *Fidelista* activity in, 842

Venice, *m* 159, *m* 396, *m* 493; trade enriches, 325, 360, *p* 361; Renaissance in, 325, *p* 327; in Battle of Lepanto, 402

Veracruz, *m* 370, 374

Verdun, 612–613, *m* 618

Vermeer, Jan: painting by, *p* 384
Vernacular, 173
Versailles, 407–408, *p* 409, 453, *m* 471
Versailles, Treaty of (1871): ends Franco-Prussian War, 499
Versailles, Treaty of (1919): Chinese feel betrayed by, 590; Japan gains by, 593, 597; major provisions of, 620 (box); fairness of, 622, 691; Germans denounce, 624, 686; contributes to World War II, 686
Vesalius, Andreas: 354–356; sketch by, *p* 355
Vespucci, Amerigo: *m* 370
Vesuvius. *See* Mount Vesuvius
Victor Emmanuel II, *p* 491, 494, 495
Victor Emmanuel III, 667
Victoria, *p* 516, 562
Vienna, *m* 128, 725, *m* 744; and medieval trade, *m* 159; occupied by Allies, *m* 709. *See also* Congress of Vienna
Vientiane, *m* 786
Viet Cong, 787
Vietnam: French in, 785; provisions of Geneva Conference for, 732; United States involvement in, 737; pawn in cold war, 787. *See also* Southeast Asia
Vietnam War, 721, 778, 787–788
Vikings, 115, *p* 134, 360
Villages: begin in Neolithic period, 13; in ancient America, 294, 295, 297, 301, 314; city-states evolve from, 298; post-conquest Amerindian, 377, 379
Vinci, Leonardo da: 330; sketches by, *p* 321, *p* 332
Violence: heritage of World War I, 625, 626; Lenin's view of, 645; factor in growth of fascism, 664; 674; and nazism, 680; alienation may result in, 854–855, *p* 855
Virgil, 90–91
Visigoths, 103, *m* 103, 104
Volga River, *m* 419, *m* 632; medieval trade and, *m* 159; importance in World War II of, 702, *m* 704
Volgograd. *See* Stalingrad
Volta River, *m* 232
Voltaire, *p* 433; condemns religious persecution, 431–432; admires English society and law, 433–434; advances political freedom, 437
Voting rights. *See* Franchise

W

Wagner, Richard: music expresses nationalism, *p* 500
Wales, *m* 337
Wallas, Graham: 538
Walvis Bay, *m* 560, *m* 566, *m* 813
War criminals, 743

War guilt clause, 620 (box), 624
War of the Reform, 826
War of the Spanish Succession, 410–411
Warfare: relation to hunting of, 10; Sumerians engage in, 28; Spartan stress on, 43; Christians condemn, 98; common among Germanic barbarians, 102; common among bedouins, 115; common among Mongols, 126; medieval, 135, 141; in China, 213, 214; in Japan, 222, 592, 770; Zulu, 252–256, 259; slave trade affects, 244, 365, 390; between Bantu and Boers, 252; among Amerinds, 297, 298, 300, 312; Reformation leads to religious, 343; plays role in rise of nation-states, *p* 393, 394, 395; *philosophes* condemn, 434, 437; French Revolution modernizes, 463; chauvinists glorify, 501–502; World War I revolutionizes, 623; motorized, 692, 693; and population increase, 852; chemical and biological, 853. *See also* Guerrilla warfare; World War I, World War II
Warlords, 589, 591
Wars of Independence (Latin American), 820–824, *m* 827
Warsaw, *m* 337, *m* 704, *m* 744; Grand Duchy of, *m* 471
Warsaw Pact, 731, 760
Waterloo, *m* 471, 474
Watling's Island, 369, *m* 370
Watt, James: 511
Weaving: develops in Neolithic period, 13; medieval, *p* 137; in sub-Saharan Africa, *p* 288, 289; in ancient America, 314, *p* 316; Europeans introduce new techniques to American, 376; industrialized, 511
Weber, Max: 538
Weimar Republic: lacks popular support, 669–670; Hitler demands destruction of, 671; multi-party system fails in, 679
Wellington, Duke of: 473, 474
West: as cultural and political entity, 101; lure of Asia for, 199; views Columbus' voyage as most important, 369; disproportionate fear of communism in, 653, 723; Eastern-Central Europe isolated from, 754. *See also* Imperialism; Western Europe
West Africa, *m* 232; states of, 231–245, *m* 235; Islam in, 234, 236–237; impact of slave trade on, 244–245; music in, 279; cultural unity of pre-Islamic, 287; early European contact with, 366, 507, 549, 550, 557, 559; European imperialism in, 561–563, 565; representation in government sought in, 571
West Berlin, 728, 734

West-Central Africa, *m* 232, 246–248, *m* 246
West Germany, 708, *m* 744; creation of, 730; Allied occupation of, *m* 709, 743; recovery after World War II of, 743–746; rearmament of, 734; joins Common Market and NATO, 734, *p* 741, 746
West Indies, 371, *m* 389; plantations in, 364, 379, 382; Dutch in, 380, 386–387; English trade with, 507; immigration to Britain from, 748
West Pakistan, 783, *m* 783. *See also* Pakistan
Western civilization: foundations of, 41, 131; development in Middle Ages of, 132, 143, 164, 168–174; medieval contribution to, 145–146, 321; family in, 201; ideals characteristic of, 716; becomes model for developing nations, 717, 718, 719
Western Europe: feudalism and serfdom in, 131–143; religion in, *m* 111, 143–148, 335–345, *m* 341; Crusades of, 152–157; growth of towns in, 158–163; cultural development of medieval, 164–174; significance of technological advances in, 169–170, 175; Renaissance, 321–332; Scientific Revolution in, 347–357; Commercial Revolution, 383–388, *m* 389, 390; rise of nation-states in, 393–399, *m* 396, 400; Russia cut off from civilization of, 420; Enlightenment, 429–438; Napoleonic period, 470–474, *m* 471; Congress of Vienna, 480–482, *m* 481; nineteenth-century thought in, 526–543; before World War I, *m* 606; after World War I, *m* 621; advanced in comparison with Russia, 632; before World War II, *m* 689; after World War II, *m* 709, 741–751; loses dominance in world affairs, 710, 742; anti-Americanism in, 721, 737; development of NATO in, 728–729; today, *m* 744. *See also* Age of Exploration; Cold war; Europe; Imperialism; Industrial Revolution; World War I; World War II; *and individual countries*
Western Front, 610–613, *m* 612, 617–618, *m* 618
Western Mexico, 301, *p* 301, 303, *m* 303
Western Roman Empire, *m* 103
Western Sudan: states of, 231–237, *m* 232; trade routes in, *m* 235; impact of Islam in, 234, 236–237
Westernization. *See* Modernization
Wheel: importance to early man of, *p* 3; Neolithic man invents,

14; Amerinds lack, 305, 317, 371
Wheel of Life, 204
White supremacy, 810, 811, 816
Wilhelm I, 497, 499
Wilhelm II, 608, 669
William of Normandy (the Conqueror), 395, 397
William of Orange, 415
Wilson, Woodrow: idealism of, 617; hopes for a better world, 619; orders United States intervention in Mexico, 842
Witte, Sergei: 640–641
Women: have few rights in Athens, 46–47, *p* 46; status in Roman Empire of, 86; Ovid's advice on and to, 91–92; Muslim view of, 117; subservience of medieval, 136–138, *p* 137; subordinate in Hindu society, 202–203; in traditional China, 219, 220; tasks of African, 250, *p* 263, 265, 268; authority of Amerindian, 298, 299; *Code Napoléon* discriminates against, 468; gain franchise in Britain, 515; Fourier sees marriage as hindrance to, 528; Gandhi urges rights for, 582; in Soviet Union, 648, 762, *p* 764; in bedouin life, *p* 791; granted equality in Turkey, 792
Woodblock prints, Japanese: *p* 225, 593, *p* 596; influence European art, *p* 521
Workers: Commercial Revolution causes hardships for, 385; police fire on demonstration of, *p* 644; in Soviet Union, 646, 648, 650, 655; fascism appeals to Italian, 667; revolt of German, 669; communist parties take over parties of, 753. *See also* Urban workers
World Soul, 203, 204, 207
World War I: causes of, 604–607; outbreak of, 608–610; fronts of, 611–617, *m* 618; results of, *m*

621, 622–626, 664, 686, 687, 691; effects on Arab world of, 792, 793. *See also* Versailles (1919), Treaty of
World War II: civil war in China during, 591; World War I contributes to, 622, 624, 686, 691; civilian contribution to, *p* 685; factors leading to, 686–692; Axis victories in, 692–695, *m* 704; German invasion of Russia fails in, 695–696; resistance movement in, 698; Japanese victories in, 700, *m* 701; 1942 marks turning point of, *m* 701, 702–703, *m* 704; D-Day, *p* 685, 703, 705; Allies gain victory in, 705–707; costs of, 707, 708, 755; results of, 708–710, 724, 741; encourages Southeast Asian nationalism, 786–787; contributes to African independence movement, 808; encourages modernization in Latin America, 833; world population increases during, 852. *See also* Hitler, New Order of
Worms, *m* 341
Writing: discovery marks end of prehistory, 14; as characteristic of civilization, 19; value of, 23; Egyptian, *p* 26, 27; Sumerian, 28; Arabic, 124; Chinese, 212; Japanese, 223; Maya combine art with, 308

X

Xerxes, 48, 57
Xhosa, 250, 251, *m* 252, *m* 267

Y

Yalta, *m* 704
Yalu River, *m* 774
Yamato clan, 222
Yangtze River, *m* 215, *m* 774; civilization spreads to, 211

Yanomamö, *p* 12
Yedo (Tokyo), *m* 223, 592, *m* 593
Yellow River: early civilization of, *m* 15, 211–212, *p* 212, *m* 215
Yellow Sea, *m* 215, *m* 774
Yemen, *m* 795
Yenan, *m* 588, 591, 773
Yoruba, 238, 240, *m* 267, 272
Young Communist League (Komsomol), 764
Young Italy, 493, 494
Yuan dynasty, 221. *See also* Mongols
Yüan Shih-k'ai, 589
Yucatan, *m* 303, 312
Yugoslavia, *m* 744; Byzantine art in, *p* 109; creation of, *m* 621, 624; in World War II, 695, 698, *m* 704. *See also* Eastern-Central Europe; Illyria

Z

Zaibatsu, 770–771
Zambezi River, *m* 232, *m* 246, 255, 256
Zambia, 255, 809, *m* 813
Zanzibar, *m* 813; slave trade in, *p* 245; Portuguese settle in, *m* 257, 259; clove plantation in, 260; in Age of Imperialism, *m* 552, *m* 560, 561, *m* 566. *See also* Tanzania
Zapata, Emiliano: 832
Zapotecs, 305, 306–307, *p* 307
Zemstvo, 639
Zen Buddhism: shrine of, *p* 199
Zero, 123, 310
Zhdanov, Andrei: 727
Zimbabwe. *See* Great Zimbabwe
Zionist movement, 798
Zoroastrianism, 37
Zulu, *p* 288; army reformed, 253–254; repercussions of wars of, *m* 252, 254, 255, 256; clash with Boers, 254; British wars with, 254–255, *p* 568. *See also* Bantu
Zuñi, *m* 296, 300